The Two Horizons New Testament Commentary

Joel B. Green, *General Editor*

Two features distinguish The Two Horizons New Testament Commentary series: theological exegesis and theological reflection.

Exegesis since the Reformation era and especially in the past two hundred years emphasized careful attention to philology, grammar, syntax, and concerns of a historical nature. More recently, commentary has expanded to include social-scientific, political, or canonical questions and more.

Without slighting the significance of those sorts of questions, scholars in The Two Horizons New Testament Commentary locate their primary interests on theological readings of texts, past and present. The result is a paragraph-by-paragraph engagement with the text that is deliberately theological in focus.

Theological reflection in The Two Horizons New Testament Commentary takes many forms, including locating each New Testament book in relation to the whole of Scripture—asking what the biblical book contributes to biblical theology—and in conversation with constructive theology of today. How commentators engage in the work of theological reflection will differ from book to book, depending on their particular theological tradition and how they perceive the work of biblical theology and theological hermeneutics. This heterogeneity derives as well from the relative infancy of the project of theological interpretation of Scripture in modern times and from the challenge of grappling with a book's message in Greco-Roman antiquity, in the canon of Scripture and history of interpretation, and for life in the admittedly diverse Western world at the beginning of the twenty-first century.

The Two Horizons New Testament Commentary is written primarily for students, pastors, and other Christian leaders seeking to engage in theological interpretation of Scripture.

Luke

F. Scott Spencer

William B. Eerdmans Publishing Company
Grand Rapids, Michigan

Wm. B. Eerdmans Publishing Co.
4035 Park East Court SE, Grand Rapids, Michigan 49546
www.eerdmans.com

Published 2019
Printed in the United States of America

25 24 23 22 21 20 19   1 2 3 4 5 6 7

ISBN 978-0-8028-2563-6

Library of Congress Cataloging-in-Publication Data

Names: Spencer, F. Scott (Franklin Scott), author.
Title: Luke / F. Scott Spencer.
Description: Grand Rapids, Michigan : William B. Eerdmans Publishing Company, 2019. | Series: Two horizons New Testament commentary | Includes bibliographical references and index.
Identifiers: LCCN 2018035774 | ISBN 9780802825636 (pbk. : alk. paper)
Subjects: LCSH: Bible. Luke—Commentaries.
Classification: LCC BS2595.53 .S73 2019 | DDC 226.4/077—dc23
LC record available at https://lccn.loc.gov/2018035774

To Lauren Michael and Meredith Leigh,

"most excellent" daughters, beloved with all my heart

Contents

Preface

At the 2008 Society of Biblical Literature (SBL) annual meeting in Boston, I ran into Joel Green as we were heading opposite ways in the Prudential Center, foraging for food. We stopped and chatted about this and that, but I made a point of bringing up the Two Horizons series of commentaries that Joel was editing and had recently kicked off with his fine volume on 1 Peter (2007). I expressed keen interest in the series and casually (ahem) mentioned that I would like to help, if I could. He politely acknowledged my offer, said something, I think, about Luke being a possibility, and indicated that he would get back to me. I filed this away in my SBL mental file under "networking." I'm not very good at schmoozing, but I make an effort. And SBL meetings teem with myriads of these types of conversations, talking shop, working deals, angling for better jobs, and such. We're a rather geeky bunch and not slick businesspeople for the most part, but we play the game once a year as best we can. I did my bit with Joel but didn't hold my breath about whether anything would materialize.

I should have known better. Joel is a consummate gentleman and professional—in both scholarship and administration (a rare breed)—and, while a man of good humor, he doesn't waste his time with foolish pursuits. His productivity and efficiency as author, editor, and dean are legendary. He took me seriously and soon officially offered me the THNTC volume on Luke. I had been serious, too, about my desire to contribute, but more on the order of a fishing expedition; at the time I was "seriously" exploring a number of projects. But now it was commitment time, and I don't enter into commitments lightly.

I swallowed hard. I really loved the fresh approach and format of the Two Horizons commentaries, integrating cutting-edge critical, interdisciplinary biblical scholarship and "confessional" theological interpretation of Scripture. But Joel had just started this series with 300 insight-packed pages on the five chapters of 1 Peter! Luke, of course, has twenty-four chapters, and all of them are longer than 1 Peter's (Luke 1 has eighty verses!). Oh, and ten years earlier, Joel himself had written a magisterial 800-page commentary on Luke for NICNT, beautifully sustaining literary, cultural, and theological exposition across the volume. It was hard to imagine myself remotely approximating that achievement, to say nothing of other astute Lukan commentaries, which seem to multiply like rabbits.

Obviously I dealt with my anxiety and got on with the project, encouraged by Joel's faith that I was up to the task. It's been a long journey, but a richly rewarding one intellectually and spiritually; or perhaps, rather, I should say *formatively*, involving mind and heart together, integrally, in what is commonly known these days as *spiritual formation*. Early on in my work on this commentary, I lit on Luke's stated purpose for writing his Gospel—"that you may *know* the truth [assuredly, solidly]" (1:4)—as a guiding star for my trek through the narrative. All written communication, of course, seeks to convey knowledge on some level, but I took Luke's aim in the fullest sense of *knowing God in Christ through the Spirit* in all the interwoven ways we come to know ourselves, other people, and the lives we/they lead, which is to say: experientially, relationally, emotionally as well as meditatively, individually, analytically. As Luke masterfully builds his characters and plots around the main character, Jesus Messiah, readers' knowledge grows along with the characters-in-relation *within the story*. Framing the story of the adolescent Jesus's engagement with temple scholars (found only in Luke among the canonical Gospels) is the assessment of *Jesus's growth* "in wisdom . . . and in divine and human favor" (2:52; cf. 2:40). Luke happily gives student and teacher Jesus an A+, but not gratuitously: Jesus learns his material and earns his grade through conflict and suffering (cf. Heb 5:8–9), with blood, sweat, and tears (Luke 19:41–44; 22:43). Via Luke's narrative, we come to know Jesus as Lord and Christ more fully as *he comes to know and fleshes out (incarnates) his saving identity and mission.*

I make no claim to being a spiritual director (far from it), but I hope this commentary offers some illumination of Luke's narrative tracking of Jesus's and his followers' foundational spiritual pilgrimages. I certify the usual disclaimer that I bear full responsibility for whatever missteps I take and errors I make as Luke's tour guide. Daring to comment on such an iconic text, which better minds than mine have tackled, is a risky venture, to say the least. Perhaps what I appreciate most about Joel Green is that, while nudging me this way and that on key matters—and, of course, providing numerous insights from his own writings—he largely gave me my head to run as I chose. Supportive *freedom* to think and feel afresh through this remarkable gospel, and to explore a wide array of theological, philosophical, and psychological resources for interpretation, is an inestimable gift of grace.

I'm indebted to many others—scholars, colleagues, students, congregants, and friends too numerous to name. For the past decade I've lectured and preached on Luke in a variety of seminary classes and church settings, always benefiting from thoughtful reception and feedback. The staff at Eerdmans has once again proven themselves among the best in the business. I enjoyed working with them on my book about "capable women of purpose and persistence" in Luke (*Salty Wives, Spirited Mothers, and Savvy Widows* [2012]), which I drew on for some of the material in this commentary. This time around, I'm especially grateful for the careful work of copyeditor Craig Noll, which regularly went beyond commas and colons to include a number of perceptive exegetical and theological queries. My interaction with Craig greatly improved the final product.

A couple of bookkeeping matters before my final acknowledgments. First, all Scripture quotations, unless otherwise noted, are from the NRSV. Apart from using standard abbreviations for other versions, I use "AT" (author's translation) for my own renderings. Second, as is standard for THNTC, commentaries are cited in the footnotes by author's name only and page numbers; other sources include short titles. Full bibliographic information appears at the end of the volume.

My wife of forty-four years now (we married young!), Dr. Janet M. Spencer, continues to be the inspiration of my life. We have shared the long journey together at every point and look forward to many more miles to come. Our two "most excellent" daughters, Lauren Michael and Meredith Leigh (to whom Theophilus couldn't light a candle [Luke 1:3]), continue to amaze and challenge us (in good ways!) in their now flourishing lives as adult women. To them I dedicate this book with all due irony: no personal *commentary* I could muster could ever adequately capture how I feel about them.

Abbreviations

AB	The Anchor Bible
ABD	*Anchor Bible Dictionary*
ABQ	*American Baptist Quarterly*
Abraham	*On the Life of Abraham* (Philo)
ABRL	The Anchor Bible Reference Library
Ab urbe cond.	*Ab urbe condita* (Livy)
AcBib	Academia Biblica
ACCS	Ancient Christian Commentary on Scripture
ACNT	Augsburg Commentary on the New Testament
Ag. Ap.	*Against Apion* (Josephus)
AnBib	Analecta Biblica
Ant.	*Jewish Antiquities* (Josephus)
ANTC	Abingdon New Testament Commentaries
Apoc. Ab.	Apocalypse of Abraham
Apoc. Mos.	Apocalypse of Moses
AT	Author's translation
ATR	*Anglican Theological Review*
Aug.	*Divus Augustus* (Suetonius)
AYBC	Anchor Yale Bible Commentaries
b.	Babylonian Talmud
BAR	*Biblical Archaeology Review*
BBR	*Bulletin for Biblical Research*
BDAG	Walter Bauer et al. *A Greek-English Lexicon of the New Testament and Other Early Christian Literature.* 3rd ed. Revised and edited by Frederick William Danker. Chicago: University of Chicago Press, 2000.
BDF	Blass, Friedrich, Albert Debrunner, and Robert F. Funk. *A Greek Grammar of the New Testament and Other Early Christian Literature.* Chicago: University of Chicago Press, 1961.
BECNT	Baker Exegetical Commentary on the New Testament

Ber.	Berakot
BETL	Bibliotheca Ephemeridum Theologicarum Lovaniensium
Bib	*Biblica*
BibInt	*Biblical Interpretation*
Bibl. hist.	*Bibliotheca historica*
BR	*Biblical Research*
BRev	*Bible Review*
BSL	Biblical Studies Library
BTB	*Biblical Theology Bulletin*
BZNW	Beihefte zur Zeitschrift für die neutestamentliche Wissenschaft
CahRB	Cahiers de la Revue biblique
CBQ	*Catholic Biblical Quarterly*
CD	Cairo Genizah copy of the Damascus Document
CEB	Common English Bible
Cels.	*Contra Celsum* (Origen)
CH	*Church History*
CurTM	*Currents in Theology and Mission*
De an.	*De anima* (Aristotle)
De or.	*De oratore* (Cicero)
Decal.	*De decalogo* (Philo)
Di	*Dialog*
Dial.	*Dialogue with Trypho* (Justin Martyr)
Did.	Didache
DJG	*Dictionary of Jesus and the Gospels*. Edited by Joel B. Green, Jeannine K. Brown, and Nicholas Perrin. 2nd ed. Downers Grove, IL: IVP Academic, 2013.
DRev	*Downside Review*
DSE	*Dictionary of Scripture and Ethics*. Edited by Joel B. Green. Grand Rapids: Baker Academic, 2011.
DSS	Dead Sea Scrolls
DTIB	*Dictionary for Theological Interpretation of the Bible*. Edited by Kevin J. Vanhoozer. Grand Rapids: Baker Academic, 2005.
ECL	Early Christianity and Its Literature
En.	Enoch
Epod.	*Epodi* (Horace)
Eth. eud.	*Ethica eudemia* (Aristotle)
Eth. nic.	*Ethica nicomachea* (Aristotle)
ExpT	*Expository Times*
Fam.	*Epistulae ad familiares* (Cicero)
Fast.	*Fasti* (Ovid)
Flor.	*Florilegium* (Stobaeus)
FRLANT	Forschungen zur Religion und Literatur des Alten und Neuen Testaments
Gen. imp.	*De Genesi ad litteram imperfectus liber* (Augustine)
Gen. Rab.	Genesis Rabbah

Geogr.	*Geographica* (Strabo)
Giṭ.	Giṭṭin
Gos. Naz.	Gospel of the Nazarenes
Gos. Thom.	Gospel of Thomas
GOT	God's Time
Haer.	*Heresies* (Irenaeus)
Ḥag.	Ḥagigah
HB	Hebrew Bible
HBT	*Horizons in Biblical Theology*
Helv.	*Ad Helvium* (Seneca)
Hist.	*Historia Romana* (Dio Cassius)
HTR	*Harvard Theological Review*
HTS	Harvard Theological Studies
HvTSt	*Hervormde teologiese studies*
IBT	Interpreting Biblical Texts
Inf. Gos. Thom.	Infancy Gospel of Thomas
Inst.	*Institutio oratoria* (Quntilian)
Int	*Interpretation*
Is. Os.	*De Iside et Osiride* (Plutarch)
JBL	*Journal of Biblical Literature*
JFSR	*Journal of Feminist Studies in Religion*
JGRChJ	*Journal of Greco-Roman Christianity and Judaism*
JJS	*Journal of Jewish Studies*
JSNT	*Journal for the Study of the New Testament*
JSNTSup	Journal for the Study of the New Testament Supplement Series
JSOT	*Journal for the Study of the Old Testament*
JSOTSup	Journal for the Study of the Old Testament Supplement Series
JST	Jewish Standard Time
JTI	*Journal of Theological Interpretation*
JTISup	Journal of Theological Interpretation, Supplements
JTS	*Journal of Theological Studies*
Jub.	Jubilees
J.W.	*Jewish War* (Josephus)
KJV	King James Version
LCL	Loeb Classical Library
Let. Aris.	Letter of Aristeas
LNTS	Library of New Testament Studies
LQ	*Lutheran Quarterly*
LTE	Library of Theological Ethics
LV	Latin Vulgate
LXX	Septuagint
m.	Mishnah
Marc.	*Against Marcion* (Tertullian)

Meg.	Megillah
Mek.	Mekilta
Metam.	*Metamorphoses* (Ovid)
Metaph.	*Metaphysics* (Aristotle)
Mor.	*Moralia* (Plutarch)
Moses	*On the Life of Moses* (Philo)
MT	Masoretic Text
NAB	New American Bible
NASB	New American Standard Bible
Nat.	*Natural History* (Pliny)
NETS	New English Translation of the Septuagint
NIB	*New Interpreter's Bible*
NICNT	New International Commentary on the New Testament
NIGTC	New International Greek Testament Commentary
NIV	New International Version
NJPS	New Jewish Publication Society Version of the Bible (Tanakh)
NovT	*Novum Testamentum*
NRSV	New Revised Standard Version
NT	New Testament
NTL	New Testament Library
NTS	*New Testament Studies*
NVBS	New Voices in Biblical Study
OBT	Overtures to Biblical Theology
ORT	Ordinary Time
OT	Old Testament
OTP	*Old Testament Pseudepigrapha*. Edited by James H. Charlesworth. 2 vols. New York: Doubleday, 1983.
Pan.	*Panarion (Adversus haereses)* (Epiphanius)
PCNT	Paideia Commentaries on the New Testament
Pelag.	*Adversus Pelagianos dialogi III* (Hieronymus)
Pis.	*In Pisonem* (Cicero)
PNTC	Pillar New Testament Commentary
Poet.	*Poetica* (Aristotle)
P.Oxy.	Papyrus Oxyrhynchus
Prot. Jas.	Protevangelium of James
PRSt	*Perspectives in Religious Studies*
Pss. Sol.	Psalms of Solomon
QS	Qumran Scroll
RBS	Resources in Biblical Study
ResQ	*Restoration Quarterly*
RevExp	*Review & Expositor*
Rhet. Her.	*Rhetorica ad Herennium*
RIT	Roman Imperial Time
RSV	Revised Standard Version

Šabb.	Šabbat
Sat.	*Satirae* (Juvenal)
Sat.	*Saturnalia* (Lucian)
SB	The Scholar's Bible
SBL	Society of Biblical Literature
SBLDS	Society of Biblical Literature Dissertation Series
SBLECL	Society of Biblical Literature Early Christianity and Its Literature
SBLMS	Society of Biblical Literature Monograph Series
SBLStBL	Society of Biblical Literature Studies in Biblical Literature
SBLSymS	Society of Biblical Literature Symposium Series
SHBC	Smyth & Helwys Bible Commentary
SHJ	Studying the Historical Jesus
SNTSMS	Society of New Testament Studies Monograph Series
SP	Sacra Pagina
Spec. Laws	*On the Special Laws* (Philo)
ST	*Studia theologica*
STI	Studies in Theological Interpretation
SymS	Symposium Studies
Tg. Ps-J.	Targum Pseudo-Jonathan
THNTC	Two Horizons New Testament Commentary
Tim.	*Timaeus* (Plato)
T. Levi	Testament of Levi
UBS	United Bible Societies Greek New Testament
Virtues	*On the Virtues* (Philo)
Vit. Apoll.	*Vita Apollonii* (Philostratus)
Vit. Caes.	*Vita Caesaris* (Plutarch)
Vulg.	Vulgate
WBC	Word Biblical Commentary
WTJ	*Westminster Theological Journal*
WUNT	Wissenschaftliche Untersuchungen zum Neuen Testament
ZECNT	Zondervan Exegetical Commentary on the New Testament
ZNW	*Zeitschrift für die neutestamentliche Wissenschaft*

Introduction:
Reading Luke Theologically

A Pilgrim's Prospectus

Luke's Gospel opens with a concessive clause acknowledging numerous predecessors: "Since many have undertaken to set down an orderly account of the events" surrounding God's climactic work through Jesus Messiah . . . (1:1). He thus sets up his own contribution to the gospel-writing industry partly, perhaps, to correct and clarify previous deficient treatments ("Here's what a real, true 'carefully investigated' gospel looks like" [see 1:3]), but mostly to complement and certify the dynamic tradition Luke has graciously and faithfully received from "eyewitnesses and servants of the word" (1:2).[1]

I might similarly introduce this study of Luke by tipping my hat to the many commentators who have come before me, but I hesitate to associate myself too closely with Luke himself, who obviously takes priority over anyone who dares to expound his work, or with the cadre of brilliant preceding Lukan scholars. Truth be told—and we all owe Luke that much, since his whole avowed purpose is to reinforce the "truth/solidity" (ἀσφάλεια, *asphaleia* [1:4]) of the gospel—the church today is blessed with several comprehensive, illuminating commentaries on the Third Gospel, which I do not intend (pretend), even if I were able, to replace or outpace. I list a number of these (in English or English translations) in the first section of the bibliography, with which I engage in my commentary; whether explicitly citing them or not, they deeply inform my reflections on Luke's writings over the past three decades of concentrated study. No one expounds an inspired, iconic, canonical Scripture text like Luke in a vacuum. All commentators stand on shoulders broader and sturdier than ours, bearing an incalculable debt of insight we can never repay.

So why bother with another commentary at all, given the current embarrassment of riches? Such questions are better not asked perhaps (repression is

1. See Moessner, "Luke as Tradent."

not always a bad thing), at least not in the presence of publishers and not when I am totting up the years (about ten, I think) I've devoted to researching and writing this volume. But the publisher (God bless Eerdmans), the series editor (God bless Joel Green), and this humble writer would all really like this book to be widely read and discussed. Accordingly, it merits some justification in the "market," some sense of what it brings to the table (a nice Lukan image) that others might not.

Most commentaries these days slot into a larger series. This one forms part of the "Two Horizons New Testament Commentary" (THNTC), which seeks to "bridge the existing gap between biblical studies and systematic theology" via "section-by-section exegesis of the New Testament texts in close conversation with theological concerns." In short, it contributes to the growing interest in "theological interpretation of Scripture."[2]

As recent years have witnessed important ventures in biblical commentary from systematic theologians, church historians, and broader humanities scholars,[3] some biblical commentators have returned the favor and begun to engage more with other religious thinkers, including systematic theologians.[4] I think it is safe to say, however, that the extent of my citing, discussing, and grappling with a range of theologians—including Jürgen Moltmann, John Caputo, Elizabeth Johnson, Elisabeth Moltmann-Wendel, Jonathan Sacks, Paul Tillich, Miroslav Volf, and Nicholas Wolterstorff (and scholars in other disciplines [see below])[5]—within my main commentary on Luke (as well as in a substantial concluding "Integration" section) distinguishes it from most others to date. Indeed, I may well cite these theologians more than I do biblical commentators (I haven't done a formal count), not because I do not appreciate the latter's rigorous work, but because my aim in this volume is different.

I do not seek to provide a compendium of prior research on Luke; truth be told (again), I find it rather tedious in commentaries to read extensive summaries of others' studies (I can read those for myself); I am more interested in

2. Back cover, Green, *1 Peter*. The THNTC series is edited by Joel Green.

3. On Luke, see González in the series "Belief: A Theological Commentary on the Bible," and Jeffrey in the series "Brazos Theological Commentary on the Bible."

4. For example, commentaries on Luke by Baptist scholars Culpepper, Garland, Parsons, and Vinson all have some "theological reflection" components, variously named.

5. I list Moltmann first because I engage with him the most and mostly sympathetically, but not always (this is not a "Moltmannian" commentary, whatever that might be). The other modern theologians I present here in alphabetical order. I also interact with theologians from earlier Christian tradition, especially Cyril of Alexandria, Augustine, and Calvin, though I do not provide anything close to a comprehensive reception history of Lukan commentary. For this, I direct the reader to David Lyle Jeffrey's Brazos commentary and to the very helpful collection of readings edited by Arthur Just.

seeing what the current commentator has to say for himself or herself. Now I hasten to add that I regularly consult journal articles and other essays on specific Lukan passages, as well as studies on Luke's social-historical world, so vital to explicating the biblical text in its own environment. Theological interpretation remains staunchly *contextual* in arcing between ancient and contemporary literary and cultural "horizons."

Speaking of context, I think the section-by-section approach of the THNTC series serves to facilitate a better grasp of the internal literary context—its progressive flow of ideas, building of characters, development of themes and motifs, and sense of the whole argument or picture—than more (potentially) atomistic verse-by-verse analyses. This more holistic "narrative-critical" tack, as it is commonly designated, proves particularly apt for Luke's Gospel, given its explicit identification as a "narrative" or "account" (διήγησις, *diēgēsis* [etymologically, a "leading through"; 1:1]) that unfolds in an "orderly, step-by-step" (καθεξῆς, *kathexēs* [1:3; cf. Acts 11:4]), logically linked plot line. This narrative-literary framework is no less suited to theological reflection than more propositional discourse; indeed, it particularly fits a vivid unveiling of God's work in Christ, a sense of the dynamic, pulsing *story of God's redemptive mission*, a narrative theology not antithetical to a dogmatic one but presented in different form with potentially different effects on the reader.

These readerly effects may be experienced in various ways, but in this commentary I strive toward a rigorously sequential, developmental, mindful interpretive journey that seeks to let the story unfold bit by bit, taking in the sights and sounds as they come, correlating (including questioning, wondering, debating, revising) with what has come before, but avoiding as much as possible any peeking ahead and spoiling the adventure. Now I admit that this is something of a pipe dream, since there's no such thing as a purely naive reading, not least of a well-known canonical text like Luke that has been around for two millennia. We all know Luke's Jesus is going to die and rise at the end of the story; the cross and empty tomb can scarcely be pushed out of our imaginations. But Jesus's closest followers *in the story* do not know that and are not at all happy when it slowly begins to dawn on them; and even Jesus himself struggles with his fate on the night of his arrest (Luke 22:39–46). Just as we pick up new insights every time we thoughtfully reread Scripture with open hearts and minds, even for the umpteenth time, so we benefit from fresh, deliberate, wide-eyed trekking through the text *as if* (as much as possible) engaging it for the first time: moving from *diēgēsis* (reading through) to exegesis (reading out).

Consistent with this "reader-response" approach to narrative criticism, I concentrate on the final form of the Greek text of Luke, as best determined by textual criticism. Redaction criticism, the stock-in-trade of most late-twentieth-century commentaries, giving prime attention to Luke's editorial handling of his Mark and Q sources, receives little play in my volume. I do keep a comparative eye on the other gospels (and Scripture as a whole) but resist concluding that differences between Mark and Luke, for example, constitute significant semantic and thematic changes (redactions) for Luke. They may or may not in light of Luke's overall presentation, but the bare fact of difference does not necessarily make a difference. Moreover, Luke's meaning is conveyed just as much, if not more so, in the large chunks of material shared in common with Mark and other gospels. My goal, in any case, is neither to demarcate Luke from nor to conflate it with the wider gospel tradition, but to let Luke be Luke on Luke's own terms.

I will say more below about my intertextual engagement with the scriptural canon, but a brief word is in order here about this commentary's particular relationship with the book of Acts. I follow the consensus that the same author wrote both Luke and Acts (the common Theophilus addressee and reference to "first book" in Acts 1:1 make this conclusion obvious) with similar language and style and pervasive character and thematic parallels (though different structures). But I am not as convinced as some that the writer had the entire two-volume project mapped out from the start, even less so that "reading backward" from Acts to Luke—in other words, reading the gospel in light of Acts or with a concerted view toward Acts—is the optimal interpretive strategy.[6] Canonically, Luke and Acts have always been separate books (not 1–2 Theophilus), and historically there is scant evidence that they circulated in tandem (no "boxed set").[7] As it happens, I cut my scholarly teeth on the book of Acts with my PhD thesis on the Philip material and subsequent commentary on the entire book,[8] so in fact I come to commenting on Luke *after* years of interpreting Acts. But I remain rather dogged in my commitment to letting Luke's Gospel unfold for itself without overanticipating the Acts sequel. I do not claim that this is the only way to read Luke profitably, but it is the way I have chosen here and found fruitful.

Building on this sketch of my engagement with systematic theology and narrative criticism, I now identify the main planks of my approach to theological interpretation of Luke in this commentary. I present these, with limited supporting examples from Luke at this stage, as a quick orientation to what the reader should be on the lookout for in the commentary—a kind of promotional brochure or pilgrim's prospectus, rather than a detailed travel guide. The proof is in the reading journey.

6. Alexander, "Reading Luke-Acts"; Luke Timothy Johnson, *Writings*, 195–99.

7. See Parsons and Pervo, *Rethinking*.

8. Spencer, *Portrait* and *Journeying*.

"Minifesto" for Theological Interpretation

I riff here on a recent collection of essays edited by Craig Bartholomew and Heath Thomas entitled *A Manifesto for Theological Interpretation*, which aims to crystallize the prime commitments of an avowedly theological hermeneutic of Scripture interpretation that has been building steam over the last two decades.[9] Though I welcome the thoughtful, stimulating contributions to this volume, the whole idea of a manifesto makes me nervous. Chalk it up, perhaps, to my Baptist suspicion of (narrow) dogmatic creeds (many of us prefer to call articles of faith "confessions," "professions," or a "message"),[10] though increasingly some Baptist groups have felt no such qualms and happily jumped on the manifesto bandwagon, including self-styled "Bapto-Catholics," proponents of "Evangelical Baptist Catholicity," and "Reformed Baptists"—groups that intentionally distinguish themselves from each other and other Baptists.[11] It frankly makes my head hurt. As it happens, several contributors to the latest Manifesto collection, including coeditor Thomas, are Southern Baptists; and the preface to this volume readily acknowledges that not everyone involved in the Scripture and Hermeneutics Seminar (2012–14), from which this Manifesto sprang, was fully comfortable with its rigid, procrustean intimation: "The contributors to this volume (and especially the editors) recognize these dangers and affirm that the term 'Manifesto' does not mean the only, first, or final word on theological interpretation."[12] Fair enough, but they still promulgate twelve points in bold print, explicated in twelve chapters.

Nothing wrong with this approach, especially since the authors convey their views in an irenic spirit toward the aim not of scoring points, but of trying "to make public the central tenets that help to orient theological reading of Scripture so as to hear God's address."[13] Moreover, I share many of their interests, though they would not share all of mine, I suspect (not a lot of interaction,

9. For other helpful essay collections and monographs on theological interpretation, see Green and Turner, *Between Two Horizons*; Green, *Seized by Truth* and *Practicing Theological Interpretation*; J. Todd Billings, *Word of God*; Adam et al., *Reading Scripture*; Fowl, *Theological Interpretation*; Treier, *Introducing Theological Interpretation*.

10. "The Baptist Faith and Message" (1963) guided a wide swath of Southern Baptist life in the last half of the twentieth century until its more fundamentalist revision in 2000—particularly emphasizing women's "submissive" roles—unacceptable to more moderate Baptists.

11. On the "Bapto-Catholic" Manifesto, see Freeman et al., "Re-envisioning" (see my discussion in concluding "Integration" section, 682–87); for other contemporary Baptist Manifestos, see Waldron and Barcellos, *Reformed Baptist*; and http://www.centerforbaptistrenewal.com/evangelical-baptist-catholicity-a-manifesto/.

12. Bartholomew and Thomas, *Manifesto*, x.

13. Bartholomew and Thomas, *Manifesto*, x.

for example, in their *Manifesto* with feminist criticisms or theologies, which I find very illuminating and challenging). I also can't shake my manifesto-phobia (except for following scholars of various theological persuasions in dubbing Luke 4:18–19/Isa 61:1–3; 58:6 as Jesus's mission "manifesto") or muster the self-confidence to propound *twelve* planks, good biblical number though that may be. So rather cowardly, and somewhat cheekily, I set forth my *mini*festo for theological interpretation (of Luke) with a measly six points.

Theologically Centered

This plank is an easy one—and an obvious one—but worth presenting first because it has tended to get lost in the thicket of the hardest-core historical criticisms of Luke and the rest of the Bible. On its own terms—its own historically and culturally situated terms—Luke is first and foremost a narrative about *God* (θεός, *theos*) and God's dealings with the people of Israel and the entire world through God's Son Jesus Messiah and God's Spirit in dynamic, interpenetrating, *theological* union (trinitarian, as we would say). Because it tells a story in "real" space and time, Luke's Gospel charts a *history*, but generically it is not a "mere," dispassionate history, if there were such a thing (a congressional record or business meeting transcript comes closest), but a *theological-biographical history* of God-in-Christ in the framework of first-century Palestine.[14]

And it is not an outsider's history by a professional historian, like, say, an American academic or researcher might write a biography of Otto von Bismarck. However little we might know about the author of Luke (we do not even know that his name was "Luke"; I use that moniker only by convention) and however much investigative work he might have done, what comes through loudest and clearest, as with all the gospel writers, is that he writes *within* the Christian tradition in its first few generations as a committed believer in Christ as God's Son and Messiah. He writes from faith for faith (cf. Rom 1:17) and does so for *Theophilus* and all "God-lovers," as the name signals, for all who seek to know God more fully (see commentary on the prologue, Luke 1:1–4).

Historians of religion, classics scholars, and literary critics of all stripes are free to comment on Luke as they will and often provide illuminating insights. But they inevitably miss the boat and the full haul of fish teeming in its depths (to evoke Luke 5:1–11) if they do not engage with this gospel for what it was, is, and always will be: a compelling, complex narrative confession of faith in God. To what degree anyone faithfully joins Luke in that faith journey is up

14. See Burridge, *What Are the Gospels?*, on the βίος (bios) genre.

to them, but any responsible interpreter must at least attend considerately to Luke's theological roadmap.

Philosophically Expanded

The only use of φιλοσοφία (*philosophia*) in the NT has skewed a perfectly good term meaning "love of wisdom": "See to it that no one takes you captive through *philosophy* [φιλοσοφίας, *philosophias*] and empty deceit, according to human tradition, according to the elemental spirits of the universe, and not according to Christ" (Col 2:8). Of course, in ancient Greek life there were various philosophies, various paths of wisdom to follow promulgated by purported sages. In Colossae, one idiosyncratic philosophy, the contours of which remain sketchy in the Colossian letter, struck Paul as antithetical to Christ and Christian virtues. But this one example hardly disqualifies all wisdom (σοφία, *sophia*). Indeed, in the same letter Paul prays that the Colossian congregation "may be filled with the knowledge of God's will in all spiritual wisdom [σοφίᾳ, *sophia*] and understanding, so that you may live lives worthy of the Lord, fully pleasing to him, as you bear fruit in every good work, and as you grow in the knowledge of God" (Col 1:9–10). God is the source of all true wisdom. "Spiritual (πνευματικός, *pneumatikos*) wisdom"—that is, the wisdom of God's Spirit—far from eschewing so-called secular expressions of wisdom that may not acknowledge the name of God or Christ, in fact encompasses all truth under whatever banner. In "Christ himself . . . are hidden *all* the treasures of wisdom and knowledge" (Col 2:2b–3).

Such a "hidden," "mysterious" state (see μυστήριον [*mystērion*] in Col 1:26–27; 2:2; 4:3), however, does not denote a body of secret plans and programs,[15] some gnostic codebook for the privileged few, but the wisdom of God (in Christ through the Spirit) obscured by human sinfulness and short-sidedness, which God desires to disclose fully. God desires deep and wide "knowledge" and "understanding" of God's wise will for the purpose of fruitful, flourishing living pleasing to God (1:9–10; 2:2–3). God longs to *reveal*, to *be known*.[16]

This epistemological and sophialogical thrust also characterizes Luke's Gospel and will be a major focus of the present commentary. I take my first cue from the long prologue sentence, which concludes with the explicit pur-

15. I find misleading the CEB rendering of μυστρήριον (mystērion) in these Colossians texts as "secret plan."

16. In addition to Paul's wisdom discussion in Colossians, see also his balanced views on "spiritual" and "worldly" wisdom in 1 Cor 1–4, especially 1:17–31; 2:1–16; 3:18–20.

pose clause for the entire narrative. My translation, discussed more fully in the opening section, which I entitle "Knowing God the Savior in Solid Assurance through the Story of Jesus" (Luke 1:1–4), runs: "I decided . . . to write . . . to the end that you may *come to know* the solidity of the matters which you have been taught" (1:3–4). It is of critical importance that Luke's Jesus, the protagonist of the entire story, *embodies* or *incarnates* this progressive knowledge of God's will—this faithful growth in wisdom (see 2:40, 52)—as the Son and chief Prophet of divine wisdom (7:34–35; 11:49). Among other portions of the Jewish Bible (see next section, "Canonically Connected"), the wisdom materials in the Writings part of the HB and additional books in the LXX (Sirach, Wisdom of Solomon) also inform Luke's Gospel, as we shall see. And it is well known that this literature, though firmly rooted in theological soil ("The fear of the LORD is the beginning [and end] of knowledge/wisdom" [Prov 1:7; 2:5–6; 3:7; 9:10; Eccl 12:13]), also welcomes creational (natural) and cosmopolitan (international) observations. Nowhere in the Bible do theology and philosophy intersect more than in the wisdom traditions.[17]

Aptly, then, theological interpretation of Luke should track the horizons of both ancient and modern philosophical reflection. Systematic theologians routinely engage philosophy, some more than others (esp. Caputo, Tillich, and Wolterstorff, among those cited above)—and not just philosophy of religion per se. Moreover, in line with philosophy's close alliance with psychology until the early twentieth century (William James was an adept philosopher, psychologist, and physician, resisting specialization silos that have increasingly divided Western academics), the full range of the human sciences provides much food for thought for critical, open-minded theological exegetes. Of course, this interdisciplinary impulse is fraught with obstacles as well as opportunities. It is hard enough to keep up with the flood of Lukan studies these days, let alone the tsunami of knowledge from the natural and social sciences. I make no pretense to being a polymath. But despite my limitations, I try to be a "minimath" (to keep up the "mini" image) and do the best I can. In any case, the reader will find regular references to philosophers, psychologists, anthropologists, and other scholars in various fields not customarily cited in exegetical commentaries.

I find not a little encouragement for my efforts in Plank #5 of the *Manifesto for Theological Interpretation* related to "The Role of Hermeneutics and Philosophy in Theological Interpretation." The opening synopsis of this plank puts it very clearly:

17. See Fiddes (*Seeing the World*) for a rich, recent comparative analysis of HB wisdom traditions and contemporary Continental philosophy.

> Notwithstanding the sometimes uneasy relationship between philosophy and theology, the resources of philosophy—and by extension of all scholarship—remain essential for maintaining a properly life-affirming and integrated intellectual habitat for theological interpretation. For the task of theological interpretation, philosophy is practiced with an awareness of both its limits and its vocation within God's creational ordinances. . . . "Philosophical" insights can . . . be expressed in terms of Christian wisdom. Indeed, the extent to which these philosophical developments owe their inspiration to convictions learned in the language of faith is a moot point. It therefore becomes somewhat artificial to attempt to draw clear lines of division between theology on the one side and philosophy on the other.[18]

Or more succinctly stated: "Theological interpretation must be interdisciplinary, learning to speak with multiple conversation partners."[19] Accordingly, the reader (like the writer) of this commentary does not walk alone; theological interpretation of Scripture is not a silent, solo adventure. Get ready to hear—openly, joyfully, and critically—a lot of voices. As Luke's Jesus put it, "Let anyone with ears to hear listen!" (8:8; 14:35).

Canonically Connected

Because theological interpretation of the Bible is not a solo, straitened intellectual exercise, but rather is deeply informed by ecclesiastical tradition and interdisciplinary wisdom, it challenges somewhat the famed Reformation dictum of *sola Scriptura*. The priority of Scripture, yes, and even its singularity in the sense of a unique, written (scripted) repository of divine revelation; but the exclusivity of Scripture, Scripture *alone* as self-interpreting, as the *only* word one needs to know God—not so much: that notion shrinks the immeasurable horizon of God to a manufactured object, an artifact (bibliolatry is a real and present danger). God does not live in a scroll, a codex, a book (βίβλος, *biblos*) made with human hands (any more than God lives in a temple), however good and holy that book is, however fine a leather binding or gold edging may adorn the tome.

Of course, the Bible, though most commonly produced and purchased in modern times in one volume, is not one book at all, but an anthology of books of varying sizes originally written in Hebrew (with some Aramaic) and Greek

18. Bartholomew and Thomas, *Manifesto*, 10.
19. Bartholomew and Thomas, *Manifesto*, 10.

over a thousand-year period or so, eventually compiled into an authoritative canon of sacred Scripture. Here too, then, the *sola* adjective should be clarified, especially when commenting on *one* biblical book, like the Gospel of Luke. Though I intend, as stated above, to keep my interpretive eye firmly fixed on Luke's narrative to see/hear what Luke has to say on his own terms, I know full well that Luke did not write, and no one has ever read this narrative, in a hermetically sealed chamber; again, the making and consuming of books is never a purely solitary affair. All writing and reading are *intertextual* in large measure. And even without the modern conventions of footnotes and bibliography, Luke makes abundantly clear his debt to other canonical books, to *tota Scriptura*, the "whole purpose [counsel] of God" (Acts 20:27) in Scripture.[20]

At the end of Jesus's earthly journey in Luke, the risen Lord makes explicit what has already been evident across the story, namely, that "everything written about me in the law of Moses, the prophets, and the psalms must be fulfilled" (Luke 24:44; cf. vv. 26–27). This wording covers all three principal sections of the Jewish Scriptures. Throughout the commentary, I will make much of Luke's ongoing conversation with texts and books of the Law/Torah (esp. Genesis and Deuteronomy), the Prophets (esp. "former" prophets Elijah/Elisha in 1–2 Kings and "latter" prophets Isaiah, Jeremiah, and Ezekiel), and the Writings (esp. Psalms). But beyond explicating many patent OT citations and allusions, I also probe thick thematic resonances of major ideas/events—particularly, creation, exodus, exile, and restoration—between Luke's Gospel and the sweeping OT story of God's dealings with Israel and "all families of the earth." It is no exaggeration to say that Luke is thoroughly immersed in biblical narrative theology. Far from simply raiding Scripture as a proof-text grab bag and limiting himself to a hyperliteral, mathematical equivalence of "old" predictive pointers and "new" fulfillment events (OT = NT), Luke engages in the *art* of theological interpretation,[21] a dynamic, creative, Spirit-infused process of thinking through, praying over, wrestling with, and writing out (and no doubt rewriting many times) the complex event(s) of God's coming into the world afresh in Jesus Messiah—but not de novo. The God who comes in Christ is the God of all creation and covenant, the God of the world and Israel, the God of Genesis and Malachi. Luke *picks up* this biblical story and *unpacks it* further in light of Christ. The journey continues.

And just as Luke does not undertake this gospel-writing journey alone, winding up sharing canonical status with Matthew, Mark, and John, he also

20. I owe this felicitous *tota Scriptura* phrase and Acts reference to Bartholomew and Thomas, *Manifesto*, 12–13.

21. See Davis and Hays, *Art*.

walks and writes alongside the apostle Paul (perhaps literally—as well as literately—for a time)[22] and other authors whose letters and apocalypse (John's Revelation) came to compose the NT part of the Christian canon alongside the OT. Leaving aside the vexed question of how closely Luke studied Paul's antecedent letters and how many allusions to these letters we might detect in the book of Acts (where Paul is a major figure),[23] we can certainly justify correlating (comparing and contrasting) the presentation in Luke's Gospel with Pauline thought in a theological commentary like this one. I freely bring in Paul and other NT writers to help elucidate Luke's narrative, with no special claim to strict literary dependence, but with every intention to allow Scripture to interpret Scripture, in toto.

Salvifically Aimed

> You have known the sacred writings that are able to instruct you for salvation through faith in Christ Jesus. All scripture is inspired by God and is useful for teaching, for reproof, for correction, and for training in righteousness, so that everyone who belongs to God may be proficient, equipped for every good work. (2 Tim 3:15–16)
>
> You search the scriptures because you think that in them you have eternal life; and it is they that testify on my behalf. (John 5:39)

The Pauline and Johannine writers firmly link the study and interpretation of Scripture with the practical-theological goal (*telos*) of good, full, flourishing life, presently and eternally—the very life of God-in-Christ thriving in God's people.[24] In a word, used in 2 Tim 3:15 (and 2:10) and repeatedly in Luke and Acts, the goal is *salvation* (σωτηρία, *sōtēria*) (Luke 1:69, 71, 77; 19:9; Acts 4:12; 13:26, 47; 16:17; 27:34).

The Spirit-inspired prophetic hymn placed on the lips of Zechariah the priest early in Luke's Gospel clearly melds this soteriological (salvific) theme

22. The famous "we" sections in Acts 16:11–17; 20:6–15; 21:1–16; and 27:1–28:16 may indicate the author's eyewitness presence in these stages of Paul's journeys, but they may also function as literary devices drawing the narrator and readers more closely into the "we"-circle; see Spencer, *Journeying*, 14–16, and *Gospel of Luke*, 34–36.

23. See the vigorous supporting argument for the deep familiarity of Acts with Paul's collected writings in Pervo, *Dating Acts*.

24. On this telos of theological interpretation, see Manifesto Plank #9 (Bartholomew and Thomas, *Manifesto*, 17–19); and Thomas, "Telos."

with theological, epistemological, scriptural, and ecclesial strains: "[God] has raised up a mighty savior [lit. *horn of salvation*—κέρας σωτηρίας, *keras sōtērias*] for us in the *house of his servant David*, as he spoke through the *mouth of his holy prophets* from of old. . . . The prophet of the *Most High* . . . will go before the *Lord* to prepare his ways, to give *knowledge of salvation* [γνῶσιν σωτηρίας, *gnōsin sōtērias*] to *his people* [*Israel*]" (Luke 1:69–70, 76–77). Luke's narrative seeks to *make known* the continuation and consummation of the scriptural (prophetic) story of God's saving purpose for God's called-out (ecclesial) people as a graced community, not simply a random assortment of individuals, in the person and work of Jesus Messiah.

This "soteriological principle" in Luke, as I've called it elsewhere, accentuates God's preeminent role as *Savior* (σωτήρ, *sōtēr*) of God's creation, including God's human family, personally and corporately.[25] The first confession of faith in Luke's story comes from Mary of Nazareth in the opening hymn (just before Zechariah's), extolling from the start the magnificent work of "God my *Savior*" (1:47). Soon the angel of the Lord chimes in, announcing to a group of nomadic, nocturnal shepherds the birth of Jesus the "*Savior*, who is the Messiah, the Lord" (2:11). As common as this "Savior" title for Jesus (less so for "God") has become in modern Christian hymnody, it is quite rare in the gospel tradition outside of Luke and Acts (Luke 1:47; 2:11; Acts 5:31; 13:23 [otherwise only in John 4:42]).[26] The primary, programmatic position of God (and Christ) as "Savior" in liturgical formulation commends "God *our* Savior" (Mary's "my Savior" quickly extends backward and forward to "all generations" of God's people in her prophetic song [Luke 1:50–55]) as a virtual banner over the entire Lukan narrative.

The dominance of this saving theme throughout Luke's Gospel is further reinforced by some seventeen occurrences of the verb σῴζω (*sōzō*) (plus thirteen more in Acts), signaling God's *saving action* in Christ. Of course, linguistic statistics do not tell the whole tale, but the contexts of these saving events, as the commentary will unpack, evince a rich range of restorative, right-making activity in the lives of human beings and the surroundings of the world. "Saving" in God's terms defies narrow definition, bursting forth into a cosmic, holistic vision of God's re-creational purpose for all creatures and environs. In short, Luke wants his readers to know how the Savior God has acted dynamically in Christ to make their broken lives and world *whole*.

25. See Spencer, "Narrative," 129–30 (and throughout).

26. As it happens, the "Savior" title also appears ten times in the Pastorals (1 Tim 1:1; 2:3; 4:10; 2 Tim 1:10; Tit 1:3, 4; 2:10, 13; 3:4, 6); these references together with the four in Luke and Acts account for over 50 percent of the NT usage (fourteen of twenty-four occurrences).

Ecclesially Located

The communal-ecclesial commitment of theological interpretation is rooted in the nature of (1) *God*, who dwells in perfect, perichoretic (interpenetrating) trinitarian fellowship—Father ↔ Son ↔ Spirit—and creates and calls people made in God's image to share in that communion; (2) *Scripture*, whose canon is forged and affirmed in the community of God's people (the individual authors likely had no clue they were writing Scripture as such, and in any case, their writings would have long gone out of print without faithful reading groups and distribution centers [churches]); and (3) *salvation*, with its holistic concern for the health of the entire body of God's creation.

Jews, Christians, and Muslims are aptly called "*people* of the Book," and however valued private, devotional reading might be, the principal locus of scriptural interpretation remains the local synagogues, churches, and mosques where people gather for worship, prayer, and study. While Luke's Jesus happily talks about Scripture on the Emmaus Road and other "outside" venues, he launches his messianic campaign with the reading and exposition of prophetic Scripture in the Nazareth synagogue, which in fact sets the agenda (manifesto!) for his saving mission on behalf of people within Israel and beyond (Luke 4:16–30; cf. 6:6–11; 13:10–17; Acts 13:13–47). The ecclesial biblical vision is manifestly *ecumenical*, encompassing the entire inhabited world that Rome fancied as its privileged imperial domain in pretentious usurpation of God's realm (see οἰκουμένη [*oikoumenē*] in Luke 2:1; 4:5; 21:26; Acts 11:28; 17:6, 31; 19:27; 24:5).

Of course, not only tyrannical, megalomaniacal Caesars threaten God's salvific, ecumenical vision. Outreaching and in-bringing evangelistic missions that dare to cross ethnic, social, and religious boundaries often breed conflict *within* established communities of faith. Jesus barely makes it out of hometown Nazareth alive after suggesting—via well-known stories from 1–2 Kings—that God might care about Sidonian widows and Syrian lepers as well as fellow Israelites (Luke 4:25–30). He routinely and, at times, hotly debates legal-scribal religious experts about various aspects of table fellowship and border security. The early church in Acts, for all its amazing unity, soon has a major crisis on its hands concerning Greek-speaking widows neglected by the dominant Aramaic-speaking wing of the Jerusalem church (Acts 6:1–7).

Nothing new or shocking here, sadly. Today we know all too well the bitter splits that wound the body of Christ within local churches, denominations, and among Christian communions across the globe, to say nothing of virulent strains that continue to plague interfaith fellowship among Christians, Jews, Muslims, and other religious groups. So what's an ecumenically minded theological interpreter of Scripture to do? Cry a pox on all their houses and claim to be a pristine member of the church universal above the fray? Yeah, right—that works as well as claiming to be a "citizen of the world" (cue Cicero) when my US passport is checked and stamped every time I venture overseas for a short visit, which hardly qualifies me as a concerned participant in that country or culture. Although I lived and studied for four years in England and passed my various language exams for advanced biblical study, I am still a born-and-bred American citizen who sees the world first and most familiarly through my American lenses, which themselves are multifocal. (I could write a book on the differences between my native Texas roots and my current Virginia residence.)

Oh, and back to the matter at hand: I am a lifelong *Baptist*, sort of. It has become fashionable to put the biblical interpreter's autobiographical cards on the table. Honest disclosure about one's social and ideological location is fine as far as it goes; but just as with biblical books, so with commentaries on those books, author profiling can easily overdetermine and skew reading of the *texts* themselves, which remain primary and to some degree independent (see more below under "Author"). Texts are composed by writers but not controlled by them when texts leave their hands; then readers take the reins, readers who indeed need to be as honest as possible about what *they* bring to the interpretive process. So I am not sure what is to be gained about confessing my sixty-year pilgrimage from an independent, fundamentalist Baptist upbringing to a Southern Baptist adolescence and young adulthood, into a moderate Baptist maturity that has included considerable interaction with other faith groups in the church and academy. (I happily maintain an "evangelical" commitment, if I can define it in the vein of Jesus and Luke's evangel/gospel.)

But does this six-decade history affect how I interpret Luke theologically or otherwise? Of course! I can't jump out of my skin to read and study the Bible. *My name is Scott, and I am a biased Bible reader.* Do I resist this background with all its attendant slants and try to be open to challenging perspectives posed by the text of Scripture itself and interpreters from other traditions? You bet. When you get enough history behind you, you acknowledge (hopefully) how much you've *changed* your views through the years, even on some matters you were once most dogmatic about. Have I been successful in this openness to God's Spirit, God's word, God's people? Partly, perhaps, but by no means completely. Am I the best judge of my competence? Absolutely not! Our potential to delude ourselves is very potent indeed.

As a theological interpreter, I freely admit to being *formed* by my ecclesial communities for good and ill (we still live in a fallen, broken world) and by the wider span of ecclesiastical Christian traditions for good and ill (the church fathers are useful, but not infallible, and would have been more useful if they'd talked more with faithful church *mothers*)—all of which deeply *inform* my commentary writing about how I think Luke's narrative aims to *form* "solid," being-saved Christian pilgrims and to *inform* the Christian faith journey in Luke's day and ours. This forming-and-informing happens on an unconscious level more than a conscious one. It is in my bones and marrow. In the commentary, I do not flag very much which "Baptist" points I might be pushing, which would be quite a trick anyway, since Baptists are notorious for disagreeing with one another. (I am not shy, however, about noting, for example, my appreciation for the so-called social gospel of the American Baptist theologian, pastor, and reformer Walter Rauschenbusch [though not without critique], which would not warm the hearts of my erstwhile Independent and Southern Baptist friends.)

I try to engage theologians, exegetes, and philosophers from a wide spectrum, but still with a patent preference for some over others. I am not sure how I would "systematize" these influential thinkers in the commentary, except in their illumination of Luke's unfolding story from my viewpoint. I do, however, following the broad guidelines of this series, endeavor to become more "systematic" in the final "Integration" section, including more particular interaction with Baptist colleagues, though even here I selectively associate with more "moderate" Baptist commentators, as they are commonly classified. In my mind, ecclesial theological interpretation of Scripture inevitably entails a messy, yet necessary and meaningful, dialectic between local and ecumenical expressions of faith.

Emotionally Invested

I present this miniplank last because of its rare discussion in matters of biblical interpretation.[27] Textual analysis and theological synthesis in Western scholarship have typically given pride of place to reason over emotion, *logos* over *pathos*. Emotions (passions, affections, sentiments, by whatever name) have often been viewed as irrational disturbances and therefore not simply negligible, but even deleterious, to moral thought and life. Inflaming one's passions of any sort surely leads to no good.

This long-standing dualistic paradigm, however, pitting sound reason against wild passion, has been systematically collapsing over the past few de-

27. Recent years have seen greater interest in emotions: see Spencer ("Getting a Feel"), introducing a volume of essays on the Bible and emotions (Spencer, *Mixed Feelings*, 2017); Koosed and Moore ("Introduction"), introducing a thematic issue *Affect Theory and the Bible* (*BibInt* 22, nos. 4–5 [2014]); and Mirguet and Kurek-Chomycz ("Emotions"), introducing a thematic issue *Emotions in Ancient Jewish Literature* (*BibInt* 24, nos. 4–5 [2016]). See also, with particular focus on Luke, Kuhn, *Heart*.

cades across a wide range of disciplines in the sciences and humanities, in favor of a more holistic anthropology integrating physical, mental, emotional, social, and environmental aspects of human experience. We think—and feel—on multiple levels; and thus we are. Indeed, feelings entail various thoughts—good, bad, and in between—and vice versa. Emotions involve some degree of cognitive judgment, and judgments inevitably carry some affective valence.

To be sure, biblical characters do not come with full psychological profiles, but they are scarcely automatons void of emotion. Right out of the box, Adam becomes *afraid*, and Cain becomes *angry* (Gen 3:10; 4:5). And while they might feel and think somewhat differently than modern Westerners about their "fear" and "anger"—in other words, the Hebrew terms might not perfectly map on to our modern English labels—we might safely assume, though always paying close attention to contexts, some reasonable overlap. It makes pretty clear sense that Adam would be terrified when he first crossed his Maker and that Cain did not coolly and calmly murder Abel just to see what would happen, but was motivated by some type of bitter feeling against his brother.

Fine, but that doesn't get us to the heart of biblical interpretation, especially to *theological* interpretation focused on God and, from a Christian perspective, on Jesus Messiah, the Son of God and chief protagonist in Luke. Emotional outbursts from flawed human beings are no surprise; indeed, starting with the Adam and Cain examples just cited, emotions might be viewed as telltale signs of humanity's *fallen* nature. These first humans' problems, we might suppose, owed to their marked drift from the core *rational* dimension of the divine image in which they were created, the logical Word (*logos*) that brought all created life into existence and then became holy flesh on earth in Jesus, the incarnate God. God—Father, Son, and Spirit—though dynamic, is thoroughly *impassible*, incapable of volatile passion(s), in classic "orthodox" formulation.

Yet theology, like other fields of thought, especially in conversation with other disciplines, moves on; and some modern theologians have jettisoned an impassible, immutable God in favor of "the passion of the passionate God," as Moltmann puts it.[28] The personal and persevering commitment of the biblical God to God's people and world involves a deep divine dive into the full human condition—passions and all. God allows God's self—indeed, positively embraces the opportunity—to be *fully affected by*, as well as to actively affect, the lives of God's beloved people in all their ups and downs, faithfulness and fickleness. I track this move more fully in the section "Passional Theology" in the concluding "Integration" section. For now, I simply alert the reader to my perspective that Luke's Jesus is emotionally invested with God in the saving

28. Moltmann, *"Crucified God,"* 74 (see 69–73).

mission to God's needy people. Though granting that Luke's emotional profile of Jesus is somewhat less raw and edgy than Mark's, I do not find that Luke has chiseled Jesus into some sort of stoic supermartyr. Luke's Jesus grieves, gets frustrated, even snippy from time to time, and he becomes surprised (confused?), along with displaying remarkable compassion (we have always allowed that emotion, though usually elevating divine "love" to a superhuman level). In other words, the "passion" of the Lukan Jesus is not just a convenient handle we use for the last week of his life. His fully embodied life and ministry is filled with passion, both positive and painful.

Accordingly, the many characters in Luke's Gospel who come to *know the saving Lord* in various ways inevitably do so through *their embodied-impassioned* selves engaged with Jesus's *embodied-impassioned* life. Without mutual emotional investment, the knowledge of God suffers and diminishes. More than most commentaries, this one stays alert to emotional elements provided in the narrative as signals of what matters most to characters (Jesus included), what concerns them most deeply,[29] drives them hardest, and imbues them with purposeful passion.

Introductory Addenda

The reader will have wondered by now when I am going to get to standard matters treated in commentary introductions related to a book's author, date, audience, provenance, style, themes, and such. These introductions can be quite extensive, constructing a detailed profile based on the text, to be sure, but designed to be read *before* delving into a careful, sequential study of the book's contents. That is why it is called an "introduction" and why it is placed before the running commentary on the text itself. Though these introductions are chock full of valuable information, they can be problematic for at least three reasons.

First, after receiving such a thorough introduction to a book, why bother with reading *through* the text and commentary? You can just dip into here or there whatever verses or passages you might be interested in at the time and simply slot them into the framework the introduction has provided. We're all busy people after all. It is not quite like depending on *CliffsNotes* or *SparkNotes*, but it's in the ballpark. Of course, every commentator insists that the introduc-

29. For a carefully argued philosophical theory of emotions as "concern-based construals," see the following studies by Roberts: *Emotions*, 141–51, 320; *Spiritual Emotions*, 11–14, 23; and "Emotions."

tion is no substitute for careful engagement with the biblical text—the whole text. But we commentators have no power of enforcement: as with all texts, when it leaves our hands, readers do with it as they will.

Second, and more critically, profiling a text before working through it can guide the reading (assuming one then goes ahead and does read the text) *too much*. That is, it constructs guardrails that are too rigid along a track that is too narrow for the reader's journey. It tells the reader what he or she will or should find, thus foreclosing elements of surprise and challenge. The reading process becomes a scavenger hunt, which has its own joys, but remains limited in comparison with a closely attentive, step-by-step ("orderly") journey of discovery cued by the reflective previews and reviews provided *within* the narrative (or another biblical genre).[30] The pitfalls of preprofiling a book are analogous, though not as perilous perhaps, as profiling a person before getting to know them (we all do this to some degree; we consciously have to resist snap judgments about people).

Now, to be clear and fair, serious commentators always write their introductions *after* they have plodded through their study of a particular writing. Ideally, then, the introduction simply summarizes and categorizes the results of close engagement with the text and related historical data supporting and illuminating the text. But nothing is ever fully ideal in the writing and reading of texts, including Scripture. And problems of *circularity* routinely raise their heads. Material *in* the text suggests something about something or someone *outside* the text (like the author, audience, or setting), which then lodges in our minds (consciously or not) and influences (controls) what or who we "find" *in* the text and external sources, and so the process keeps swirling. There's no way to escape this circle fully—even by reading linearly!—but we can try to minimize its most egregious traps. Particularly for the less-experienced reader, but sometimes even for seasoned scholars, a certain profile formed mostly outside the text becomes the dominant force shaping interpretation of the text. An extreme case in point related to Luke's Gospel, which has gone out of fashion but once fueled the preaching and teaching tradition, concerns the supposed authorship of this book by a physician. If we accept up front that Dr. Luke wrote the Third Gospel, then we become poised, to one degree or another, to "see" medical touches in the narrative, not least in the numerous healing stories. Such a reading strategy, however, is as imaginatively frivolous as it is historically dubious.[31]

30. On previews/reviews in Luke's narrative, see Tannehill, *Narrative Unity*, 1:20–23, and "Israel," 106–7; Spencer, *Gospel of Luke*, 46–48.

31. Henry Cadbury dealt the fatal critical blow to Dr. Luke, revoking his medical license,

Third, and most patently though oddly downplayed, with most biblical books—and certainly with Luke—we *do not know* with any great assurance who wrote this gospel to whom (other than "Theophilus," whoever he was, *if* he was a historical individual) from where at what point in time. Our earliest manuscripts, the most complete of which stem from the fourth century CE, do not come with book jackets and copyright pages indicating author, date, publisher, and ISBN number. Educated guesses are worth making but not building much interpretation upon.

Anyway, to round out this introduction, here, in brief, are my educated guesses pertaining to Luke, which I am sure influenced my reading in some measure, but I hope did not overly control it. I reference the clues provided in the prologue (Luke 1:1–4), setting the stage for a fuller exposition of this pithy introductory sentence in the commentary.

Author

The elegant single sentence stretching over the first four verses in our versification system suggests an educated, cosmopolitan Greek writer. But he is not an author who needs to showcase his name. He refers to himself (and only here throughout the gospel narrative) only by first-person pronouns "I" and "us" (1:1, 3; cf. Acts 1:1). A masculine participle betrays the author's male identity ("and I, having followed [κἀμοὶ παρηκολουθηκότι, *kamoi parēkolouthēkoti*]" [Luke 1:3]).[32] Though commonly supposed to be the only Gentile writer in the NT, he could just as easily have been a Hellenistic Jew, like Saul of Tarsus, especially given his thorough knowledge of the Jewish Scriptures in Greek (LXX). Whatever his fuller profile, the primary identity of the writer that shines through his narrative is his unabashed devotion to the Jesus the Savior, Jesus the Christ and Lord, Jesus the Son and Revealer of the one true God.[33]

so to speak, and debunking medical-centered readings of Luke's writings; see his *Style*, 39–72, and *Making*, 119, 219, 273, 338, 358. On the problem of circular interpretation of Luke based on a priori introductory claims, see Spencer, "Preparing."

32. Gaventa, *Acts*, 50.

33. Cf. Jennings, *Acts*, 14: "Luke invokes the very reality that he renders historiographically. He writes history, but he is inside the history he writes, and he offers us a picture of Jesus who is alive, reading what Luke wrote, watching over its reading, and ready to speak through its words, his words."

Audience

Here we seem to be on firmer ground, since we have a personal name the author addresses, one Theophilus (1:3; Acts 1:1). Or maybe not. Theophilus may be a discrete individual (an "excellent" Greek/Roman official) or a collective symbol ("God-lover") or both. I discuss this issue in the commentary. In any event, he is surely not the *only* intended reader. (Theophilus may be the main patron of the work and thus due a dedicatory nod in the prologue.) Luke's Gospel is no private communiqué. If characters within the narrative are any indication of the types of people readers might identify with (and such mirror-reading assumptions remain speculative), then the target audience is not very targeted at all. No writings in the NT come close to matching the wide cast of characters from all walks of life that we encounter in Luke and Acts. This breadth probably indicates a provenance for writing and reading outside the confines of first-century Palestine. The oft-suggested Ephesus is as good a guess as any.

Date

Luke's Gospel is at least one generation removed from "eyewitnesses" to the life of the earthly Jesus (Luke 1:2) and at least a few years removed from the first evangelist-writers who provided narrative accounts of the events involving Jesus (1:1). I am happy to follow the still-majority view that touts Mark as the first written gospel and theorizes that Luke knew Mark, as well as some literary traditions shared with Matthew outside of Mark (the so-called Q material). Chronologically, these observations seem to place Luke some time in the last third of the first century CE. We may further surmise a date after the destruction of Jerusalem in 70 CE, given the narrative's interest in Jesus's anticipation of this cataclysmic event (Luke 13:33–35; 19:41–44; 21:20–24). If one assumes the writer's thorough knowledge of Paul's *collected* letters and a *conscious* polemic against Gnosticism of the Marcionite variety, then a date into the early decades of the second century is plausible.[34] But though I both correlate Luke's Gospel with Pauline thought at various points and indicate Luke's sharp divergence from gnostic perspectives, this acknowledgment does not require Luke's literary dependence on Paul's writings or direct engagement with developed Marcionite dogma. If I have to vote, I still opt for a date for Luke around 80–90 CE.

34. Pervo, *Dating Acts*; Tyson, *Marcion*; see Spencer, Review of Pervo and Tyson.

Purpose

In my judgment, it is a fool's errand to try to distill *the* purpose of Luke or Luke-Acts, though many have tried. But a richly textured, complex narrative like Luke's Gospel defies singular intention. I take Luke as a multipurpose, multifaceted, manifold composition. That said, however, I do stress the overarching, broad-vision, *general* purpose announced in the last line of the prologue: "that you may come to know the solidity of the matters that you have been taught" (1:4 AT). I referred to this purposive statement above and develop it in the following commentary on the prologue and throughout my interpretation of Luke's narrative.

Coming to know or growing in knowledge may seem like a rather obvious, banal purpose. But in Luke's case, it teems with pregnant possibilities and abundant opportunities for spiritual insight and formation. Let the pilgrimage proceed!

Interpretation: Theological Commentary on Luke

Knowing God the Savior with Solid Assurance through the Story of Jesus (1:1–4)

The preface to Luke's Gospel—consisting of a single, sophisticated sentence chock full of insights into Luke's composition—aims not primarily to preview *what* will follow (table of contents) but to promote *how* readers should engage the story. I focus in particular on the prologue's final purpose clause, which comes immediately after identifying the first reader (and possible sponsor), Theophilus. *Why* Luke writes to "most excellent Theophilus," thus implying *how* he would like Theophilus and wider audience to experience this narrative, is "to the end that you may come to know the solidity of the matters that you have been taught" (1:3–4 AT).

Luke writes neither a primer for naive novices nor an advanced text for seasoned scholars. He writes for interested parties, like Theophilus, who know a fair bit about gospel "matters" (λόγων [*logōn*], "words, issues, things")—and are favorably disposed to what they know—but need further understanding of such matters and deeper assurance of their validity. The last word in Luke's Greek preface is key: ἀσφάλειαν (*asphaleian*), denoting "security," "certainty," "stability," "solidity"—particularly "security against stumbling/falling."[1] Associated with intellectual knowledge, it tilts toward apologetic and polemical concerns: knowing with "certainty" the truthfulness of a claim or concept. But knowledge is scarcely confined to facts and propositions; it also encompasses intuitions, emotions, experiences, relationships (getting to know someone), and behaviors (knowing how to act and live)—in short, the full range of human being and doing.[2] And with so much of our knowledge filed away in subconscious and

1. BDAG, 147; related to the verb σφάλλω, *sphallō*, which often "refers to the act of making someone fall or trip."

2. While BDAG glosses the meaning of ἀσφάλεια (*asphaleia*) in Luke 1:4 as "stability of idea or statement, *certainty*, *truth*," it broadens the notion with the related adverb ἀσφαλῶς (*asphalōs*)

semiconscious vaults,[3] all of us could use more "certain, secure, solid" understanding of just about everything.

But while Luke's narrative ranges across the rich landscape of human experience, it coheres around a pivotal, preeminent figure. Instead of providing Theophilus and company with an encyclopedic book of knowledge, Luke offers an encomiastic portrait of one person who set the standard for human flourishing and changed the course of history. It is this person above all whom Luke wants his readers to know with all solid assurance. In a strategic text in Luke's second volume, Peter identifies this protagonist: "Therefore, let all the house of Israel know *assuredly* [ἀσφαλῶς, *asphalōs*] that God has made *this Jesus*, whom you crucified, both Lord and Christ" (Acts 2:36). Here the ἀσφαλ- (*asphal-*) term is placed first in Greek for emphasis, stressing the solid-rock position Jesus holds as Lord and Christ at the heart of God's plan for Israel. The firm foundation of "this Jesus" is confirmed through the story of his birth, life, ministry, crucifixion, and resurrection in Luke's Gospel—the "first word/matter [λόγον, *logon*]" Luke crafted for Theophilus concerning "the things Jesus began to do and to teach" (Acts 1:1 AT).

Peter has come to know the solid truth of Jesus's christological status, which he now commends "all Israel" to affirm with him, not simply as intellectual data or theological dogma, but as deeply personal experience and practice. Peter and fellow Israelites had heard, seen, and felt Jesus in Luke's Gospel as "a man attested to you by God with deeds of power, wonders, and signs that God did through him among you, as you yourselves *know*" (Acts 2:22); and now "all of us are witnesses" to the grand finale of God's raising up "this Jesus" from the dead (v. 32; cf. 10:37–42). But as amazing as that story is, it is not the end of the matter. Peter caps his initial sermon in Acts by inviting his hearers to embrace the living Jesus through baptism and communion with other believers (2:37–47). Knowing the Lord Jesus Christ is a lifelong pilgrimage of discipleship (experiential learning).

While the epistemological-christological (getting to know Jesus) thrust of "the events that have been fulfilled among us" (Luke 1:1) seems clear from the ensuing narrative, we must not ignore the overarching *theological horizon* that shapes these events and illumines their meaning. Here I use "theological" in its strictest sense—that is, concerning the person and purpose of *God* the Creator and Savior, in whom "we live and move and have our being" (Acts 17:28). Peter unequivocally attributes Christ's significance to the *work of God*. To repeat parts

---

in Acts 2:36 to encompass "being certain, *assuredly*, *certainly*, of intellectual and emotive aspects" (147 [emphasis original]).

3. See Wilson, *Strangers*; Damasio, *Self*.

of Acts 2:22–26, with emphasis: "Jesus of Nazareth, a man attested to you *by God* with deeds of power . . . that *God did* through him among you. . . . This Jesus *God raised up*. . . . Therefore let the entire house of Israel know with certainty that *God has made him* both Lord and Christ, this Jesus whom you crucified."

The gospel preface is more subtle, but no less theocentric. The use of a passive verb without a designated subject often suggests a divine passive construction, presuming *God* as the actor. While perhaps lost on a general Greek reader, a biblically informed reader, as Luke assumes, would readily pick up the point: "the events which *have been fulfilled* among us" are those events purposed and precipitated *by God*.[4] Luke dares to narrate an account of God's climactic work in Christ "among *us*" (Luke 1:1), including the author, who, while remaining anonymous, does not remain aloof. He writes *inside* the story, *out of* his own faith experience and community, regarding what he has come to know about God. He is no mere chronicler of others' eyewitness accounts (1:2); while committed to certitude and "truth" (1:4), he presents his case, his story, as a fully engaged "subject," not as a putative "objective" reporter. Regarding Luke's "I" claim to "investigating everything carefully from the very first" (1:3), as the NRSV renders it, David Moessner significantly amends this translation in light of his extensive comparative study of the perfect participle + adverb (παρηκολουθηκότι . . . ἀκριβῶς, *parēkolouthēkoti . . . akribōs*) by ancient authors, especially Demosthenes and Josephus. Rather than "investigating carefully" in the more pedestrian sense of a dogged reporter or professional historian, the language connotes "one who has a thoroughly informed familiarity" with all the matters one relates. The resulting narrative is less formally factual (though it presents reliable information) than faithfully familiar—the outgrowth and overflow of "faithful adherence" more than of rigorous research.[5]

Luke writes as one of "us" in the fellowship of Theophilus and like-minded readers. "We" are called to read sympathetically *with* the faithful writer *as* Theophilus-types: not as a Greco-Roman official, if that is what the historical Theophilus was, but as a *God-lover*, as the name "Theophilus" means.[6] The divine passive construction at the beginning of the preface modulates into a divine nominative appellation at the end. Luke aims to expound in narrative form the significance of what *God* has done in Christ for those who love *God*.

4. Johnson, 27; cf. Luke 4:21; 22:37; 24:44; Acts 1:16; 3:18.

5. Moessner, "Luke as Tradent," 293–94; see 291–300.

6. Though names can be overinterpreted, their etymological meanings are often linked with characters' identities in biblical narratives. Numerous names ending in "el" or "jah/ah" signify integral relationships with God or Lord: e.g., Samuel ("God hears"); Elijah ("the Lord is God"), Zechariah ("the Lord has remembered").

More than an invitation, however, for interested God-lovers to hear and read his Gospel, Luke's "theophilic" address also intimates the means and ends of interpretation. Those who seek after and *love God* with all their heart, strength, and mind (10:27) will find God, though God "indeed is not far from each one of us" (Acts 17:27). Luke will not argue or strong-arm anyone into receiving the good news about God's saving work in Christ. He lays out his story for those with an open mind and (pre-)disposition for knowing God better.[7] Love for God, however tenuous and imperfect, begets more love with ever-increasing faithfulness and understanding. Luke presents his Gospel as a labor of love for God in hopes that all who encounter it will grow toward a more mature, stable, "solid" loving knowledge of God. Playing on the original Greek nuance of ἀσφάλεια (*asphaleia*) as surefooted balance and the derivative English term "asphalt," we may envision Luke's narrative-theological purpose as *paving the solid path for progressive knowing, loving, and living for God as faithful followers of Jesus Christ.* Let the journey begin!

7. On the importance of faithful, "yielding" attitudes and dispositions in biblical-theological interpretation, see Green, *Seized by Truth*, 11, 24.

Knowing God the Creating Savior in the Birth and Growth of Jesus (1:5–4:13)

Though not matching the Fourth Gospel's commencement "in the beginning" of God's creation (John 1:1; cf. Gen 1:1), Luke also echoes Genesis and emphasizes God's powerful activity in generating the earthly lives of God's Son Jesus and prophet John and equipping them to blaze the way of renewed life for God's people. The conceptions of both John and Jesus are "impossible" (Luke 1:37) in natural terms. Elderly, postmenopausal women like Elizabeth and young, sexually inactive girls like Mary cannot conceive children apart from divine intervention. And intervene God does via angelic announcement and dynamic operation—quite intimately in Mary's case. As God's Spirit brooded over the chaotic waters at creation (Gen 1:2), so this same Spirit "comes upon" and "overshadows" the amniotic waters destined to permeate Mary's womb and generate the Holy One "called Son of God" (Luke 1:35). Genealogically, Luke tracks Jesus's ancestors back to primordial origins as "son of Adam, son of God" (3:38), thus representing "all flesh" (3:6) via Israel ("son of David . . . son of Abraham" [vv. 31, 34; cf. 1:54–55, 68–73; 2:11]) and realizing God's good purposes for all creation. The temptation scene following the genealogy demonstrates Jesus's commitment to faithful worship and exclusive service of the Lord God (4:8), where Adam and Israel had both tragically failed.

In the face of the world's barren, broken condition, God's creative work in Christ is in fact re-creative and restorative. Nothing less than this complete, cosmic re-creation is envisioned in God's *salvation* extolled in three foundational Christmas carols.

- Mary's *Magnificat* (1:46–55) magnifies "God my Savior [σωτήρ, *sōtēr*]," not only for elevating her "lowly" state, but also for "lifting [other] lowly" persons and feeding the hungry exploited by proud, prosperous elites

(1:46–48, 51–53). Salvation thus redresses social, political, and economic injustices.

- Zechariah's *Benedictus* (1:68–79) extends the scope both outward to international politics, rejoicing in God's appointing Christ as a "horn of *salvation* . . . [through whom] we would *be saved* from our enemies," and inward to spiritual "knowledge of *salvation* . . . by the forgiveness of sins" (1:69–71, 77).
- Simeon's *Nunc Dimittis* sums up the theological and universal thrust of "your [God's] *salvation*, which you have prepared in the presence of all peoples" (2:29–32).

These holistic salvation themes are echoed in the angel's heralding the newborn Jesus as Savior, Messiah, and Lord "for all the people," yet particularly for nocturnal, nomadic shepherds on the fringes of society (2:8–11). Such "last," lowbrow folk are the first invited to see the Savior-child lying in a *manger*, an apt site for shepherds' attendance instead of a mansion suitable for Caesar Augustus, whose census edict provides the political backdrop for Jesus's birth (2:1–2, 12–16). Subtly, but surely, Luke polarizes the antithetical "Savior (σωτήρ, *sōtēr*) / Lord (κύριος, *kyrios*)" agendas of Caesar and Christ: the former boosting the rich and powerful at the expense of the poor and lowly; the latter dismantling this unjust hierarchy, so that "all flesh shall see the salvation of God" (3:6).

Zechariah's stress not only on God's accomplished activity of salvation, but also on the communicated *knowledge* of that salvation (γνῶσιν σωτηρίας, *gnōsin sōtērias* [1:77]), reinforces the epistemological goal set forth in Luke's preface. Ironically, however, key characters' experiences of knowing remain problematic and incomplete. Zechariah's query to Gabriel, "How will *I know* [γνώσομαι, *gnōsomai*] that this [birth promise] is so?" seems right on target. But instead it is met with sharp angelic rebuff and total tongue-tying for nine months (1:18–20, 64)! And after "not knowing [οὐκ ἔγνωσαν, *ouk egnōsan*]" where twelve-year-old Jesus was, his frantic parents eventually find him with the temple teachers and ask him to explain his aberrant behavior (2:43–48). But rather than politely and clearly enhancing their understanding, Jesus responds somewhat petulantly and cryptically: "Did you *not know* [οὐκ ᾔδειτε, *ouk ēdeite*] that I must be in my Father's house?" The narrator then adds, "They did *not understand* what he said to them" (2:49–50). Knowing God is a complex process in Luke's story, demanding extended time for quiet reflection (Zechariah) and intense rumination (Mary in 1:29; 2:19, 51).

Solid knowledge will come surely, but slowly *for Jesus*, no less, though more fully, than for his family and followers. Framing the temple incident and spanning the crucial "hidden" period of Jesus's life from adolescence at age twelve (2:42) to adulthood at age thirty (3:23) are summary references to Jesus's dynamic "growing," "becoming strong," and "progressing" in *wisdom* concerning the ways of God and humanity (2:40, 52).[1] His precocious performance among the temple scholars promises great things but does not leapfrog the rigorous process of spiritual formation. Even when Jesus appears poised at his baptism to burst on the public scene as God's anointed Son and Messiah (3:21–22), the Spirit dispatches him into the desert for an arduous forty-day boot camp and battle with the devil (4:1–13). Conceived as an embryo by the Spirit in Mary's womb, delivered as a newborn nine months later, and nurtured by his parents as a boy, teenager, and young adult in Nazareth, Jesus continues to *develop* and *expand* his loving knowledge of God in the crucible of human experience.

Birth Announcements and Celebrations (1:5–80)

Following the preface, Luke juxtaposes two characters—an elderly male, married priest from Judea named Zechariah and a young female, betrothed virgin from Galilee named Mary—coming to grips with God's shocking promises of Spirit-filled sons who will bless Israel and the world. Zechariah and Mary each respond to stunning birth announcements from the angel Gabriel, eventually bursting forth in prophetic canticles extolling God's wondrous plan of salvation to be enacted through their special sons. Mary's maternal experience with Jesus, "the Son of the Most High" (1:32), is central to the narrative, bracketed by Zechariah's paternal relationship with John, "the prophet of the Most High" (1:76).

- Angelic Announcement to Zechariah (1:5–23)
  - Angelic Announcement to Mary (1:26–38)
  - Prophetic Announcement of Mary (1:46–55)
- Prophetic Announcement of Zechariah (1:67–80)

This natal drama also features a third character who, though given fewer lines and less stage time than Mary or Zechariah, plays a key triangular role between them. This figure, named Elizabeth, appears as a pious descendant of Aaron (Israel's first high priest; 1:5), Zechariah's longtime "barren" or "sterile"

1. All three verbs in 2:40, 52 describing Jesus's growth—ηὔξανεν (*ēuxanen*, "growing"), ἐκραταιοῦτο (*ekrataiouto*, "becoming strong"), and προέκοπτεν (*proekopten*, "progressing")—are imperfect forms, suggesting progressive action. A similar sense of process is implied with the present participle "being filled [πληρούμενον, *plēroumenon*] with wisdom" (2:40).

(στεῖρα, *steira* [1:7]) wife, and Mary's co-pregnant "relative" (συγγενίς, *syngenis* [1:36]). Elizabeth slots in between the major Zechariah/Mary segments, providing her own incisive "Spirit-filled" (1:41) perspective on events concerning both her husband and kinswoman, but more with the latter. Women lead the way in Luke 1 as creative, perceptive partners with God.[2] Zechariah gets there eventually but lags behind the women's experience.

Angelic Announcement to Zechariah (1:5–23)
Interlude: A Word of Affirmation from Elizabeth (1:24–25)
Angelic Announcement to Mary (1:26–38)
Interlude: A Word of Acclamation from Elizabeth (1:39–45)
Prophetic Announcement of Mary (1:46–55)
Interlude: A Word of Appellation from Elizabeth (1:56–66)
Prophetic Announcement of Zechariah (1:67–80)

Zechariah Ponders God's Promise (1:5–23)

We expect Zechariah to know better. Should he need to ask Gabriel for clarification and confirmation ("How will I know that this is so?" [1:18])? Shouldn't he be leading the way and providing answers for Theophilus and other God-lovers and -seekers, not struggling with them? Consider Zechariah's "blameless" profile: a "righteous," law-abiding man, advanced in years and (presumably) wisdom, a faithful "priest before God"[3] devoted to prayer and service (1:5–8, 13). Yet, a great void haunts his life, the absence of children with "barren" wife Elizabeth—a terrible "disgrace" in the minds of many, including Elizabeth, perhaps even a sign of God's disfavor (1:25). Shouldn't this God-honoring couple be blessed with children? Isn't there something wrong here, perhaps with Zechariah, some skeleton in his closet? Or is something wrong, God forbid, with *God's* faithfulness? These questions are as old as Job but do not seem to vex Zechariah. Infertile Elizabeth, sadly, seems to bear the brunt of shame "among [her] people" (1:25), but Zechariah stays with her long past normal childbearing years, keeps praying, and keeps doing his priestly duty. And you never know: the biblical record shines with wondrous examples of God's blessing barren women with significant sons: Sarah has Isaac, Rachel has Joseph, the wife of

2. See Bauckham, *Gospel Women*, 47–76.

3. This passage repeatedly stresses that events are unfolding *before* (ἔναντι/ἐναντίον, *enanti/enantion*; ἐνώπιον, *enōpion*) *God*, that is, "in the presence, in the judgment/view of" God (1:6, 8, 15, 17, 19). Everything and everyone exist in the realm of God's purview (cf. Acts 17:26–28), in the light of God's presence, for the fulfillment of God's purpose.

Manoah has Samson, and Hannah has Samuel—all enduring testimonies to the indomitable creative power of God (Gen 21:1–7; 30:22–24; Judg 13:1–24; 1 Sam 1:1–20). Surely Zechariah the priest knows these stories well.

Beyond his rich background of knowledge and experience, Zechariah's present moment marks one of the most propitious opportunities in his life. He hits the priestly jackpot, as his "lot" finally comes up to offer incense on the temple altar (Luke 1:8–9). Since the days of Aaron, priests presented "fragrant incense" to God as a daily morning-and-evening ritual of prayer (Exod 30:7–8). As the temple system developed in Jerusalem, this and other offerings were managed by twenty-four priestly divisions (1 Chr 24:1–19), each serving two-week annual terms.[4] In Luke's account, the eighth Abijah division now takes its turn, with Zechariah drawing the incense assignment, perhaps for the only time in his career. This is as good as it gets for a rank-in-file priest (Zechariah is *not* the high priest, as alleged in Prot. Jas. 8:3–9). With the congregation "praying outside" in the temple courts (Luke 1:10), Zechariah does his part in representing the people before God and maintaining their covenantal bond with God.

Though Zechariah can scarcely be faulted for his terror at the sight of Gabriel, known for his dramatic revelations to Daniel (Dan 8:16; 9:21),[5] or even for his initial shock at Gabriel's announcement that "your prayer [for a child] has been heard" and will (finally!) be granted (Luke 1:13)[6] in a son destined to be a "great" reformer of God's people (1:15–17), shouldn't Zechariah's knowledge of God's ways have promptly kicked in to spark joyous, faith-full thanksgiving, instead of the banal, dubious query: "How will I know that this is so? For I am an old man, and my wife is getting on in years" (1:18)? Perhaps, but then again, isn't the question Zechariah raises—"How will *I know*?"—precisely what Luke's Gospel aims to address (1:4)? Does Zechariah, then, in his humble pursuit of fuller knowledge exemplify the disposition of an ideal reader, all the more so because of his maturity? If a model elder, a lifelong servant of God, keeps pursuing greater, more "solid" knowledge of God's ways, how much more should newcomers to the faith (like Theophilus?) follow suit!

But Gabriel is not so impressed with Zechariah's response. Promptly scolding the old priest for not believing the good news he's just received, the mighty angel, who takes none too kindly to being interrogated ("I am Gabriel. I stand in the presence of God" [1:19]), informs poor Zechariah that he will now

4. See Bovon, 1:33; Fitzmyer, 1:322.

5. Zechariah is no Daniel; cf. Brown, *Birth*, 270–71.

6. The use of the aorist simply suggests that Zechariah's prayer "was heard" (εἰσηκούσθη, *eisēkousthē*) at some undefined time in the past, recent or distant. Though the elderly priest might have just prayed again for a child at the temple's altar, more likely Gabriel is indicating that his much earlier prayers, during normal childbearing years, have finally been answered.

"be silent and unable to speak"[7] until the promised child is born (1:19–20). A nine-month mute sentence: so much for wanting to know more about God's plans. Apart from stifling his own knowledge, Zechariah is now throttled in his ability to teach others: when he exits the sanctuary, the waiting crowd "realized/knew [ἐπέγνωσαν, *epegnōsan*] that he had seen a vision," but they remained more befuddled than enlightened about this experience by Zechariah's flailing sign language (1:21–22). This scene does not seem to offer the most encouraging start to Luke's knowledge-enhancing narrative or promote what we might call faith development or spiritual formation. It is more like the "imposition of silence or fifty blows," mandated by the Rule of Columbanus on monks who challenged a point of community doctrine,[8] or like popular bumper-sticker theology that trumpets, "God said it, I believe it, that settles it!" Do not think too hard or ask too many (any) questions—just believe!

However, while Luke stresses Zechariah's need to believe the good news of God's word, this does not short-circuit the process of spiritual probing and progress. Zechariah's imposed silence need not be interpreted as a *punishment sentence* (take that, you doubter!). It does not pack the punch of a righteous-indignant "curse," like that which Peter levies on Simon Magus (threatening death) or Paul on Elymas (inflicting blindness) (Acts 8:20–23; 13:9–11); moreover, both of these punished parties are meddlesome outsiders to the faith, not faithful servants like Zechariah. Furthermore, the biblical parallels adduced above do not support corporal punishment for dubious husbands of "barren" wives. Of course, Zechariah's faith is shaky regarding this unexpected birth notice, but so was the faith of Abraham and Manoah in the face of similar incredulous prospects, and God kept nurturing them (Gen 17:15–22; Judg 13:15–23). At least Zechariah doesn't fall on his face laughing (Abraham) or request a second corroborative angelic visit (Manoah). Still, we might repeat that Zechariah should have known better with the benefit of these scriptural precedents. Fair enough, but does his push for more assurance merit such a harsh penalty?

I suggest we read this strategic opening scene as a sign less of Luke's *retributive* theology and more of his *contemplative* approach in the sense of progressive, thoughtful engagement with the faith rather than mere blind and dumb acceptance.[9] Zechariah's muteness may be viewed as more of a blessing,

7. This redundant expression of Zechariah's mute state drives home Gabriel's verdict: "You will not utter so much as a single word or sound!"

8. See Greenblatt's (*Swerve*) discussion of "the high walls that hedged about the mental life of the monks—the imposition of silence, the prohibition of questioning, the punishing of debate with slaps or blows of the whip" (27–28).

9. Two otherwise fresh and stimulating recent studies of Zechariah still retain traditional "punishment" language. Kuhn (*Heart*, 68–76) refers to Zechariah's silencing as a "punitive sign" of

though a mixed one to be sure, than a curse. Silence, especially in the face of doubt and confusion, provides opportunity for reflection, rumination, and reorientation. Zechariah suddenly has a lot to process, and he is granted the "quiet time"—or "time out," if one wants to retain a disciplinary element—to let his faith catch up with his experience. When this dutiful priest speaks again after John's birth, it will be with the conviction and insight of a Spirit-inspired prophet (Luke 1:67–79). Like his promised son, destined to prepare the Lord's way in "the spirit and power of Elijah" (1:17), Zechariah plays out his own Elijah-style drama. He discovers God not only—and perhaps, not optimally—in the angelic trumpet blast in the temple, but in the "sound of sheer silence" in more isolated quarters ("When his time of service was ended, he went to his home"; cf. 1 Kgs 19:4–13).[10]

Luke is in no hurry to tell his story. He allows his characters (and readers) time and space to grasp his message. The crowd awaiting Zechariah's priestly blessing begins "wonder[ing] at his delay in the sanctuary" (1:21). Accustomed, as worshipers tend to be, to a set ritual schedule, the people expect the order of service to proceed apace. But while authorizing normal temple rhythms, God is not bound by any clock. Some critical events go into overtime; priest and people alike must learn to wait, "wonder," and ponder God's unpredictable ways.

Interlude: A Word of Affirmation from Elizabeth (1:24–25)

The pace of Luke's narrative is further decelerated in a brief interlude, displaying a marked tension between *story time* (how long the events run) and *discourse time* (how long it takes to narrate the events). From an extended, suspenseful account of an event on one momentous day in Zechariah's life, Luke modulates to a *two-verse* (discourse time) report of a *five-month period of seclusion* (story time) in Zechariah's home with his now-pregnant wife, Elizabeth (1:24–25). But this brief summary is enough to introduce Elizabeth's perspective into the story. From her viewpoint, five months of joyous pregnancy after a lifetime of jaded

shame (75). Though his "rhetorical-affective" analysis is well attuned to the cognitive and emotional dynamics of Zechariah's experience, Kuhn does not see the potential for reflection and reprocessing afforded by Zechariah's imposed "quiet time." Brittany E. Wilson (*Unmanly Men*, 79–112) views Zechariah as a "punished male who lacks faith" (83); however, she still appreciates "the full arc of his journey" (111), that is, his coming to greater faith and understanding, particularly in terms of disrupting gender hierarchies and power relations, through his "emasculating" period of muteness.

10. Admittedly, the NRSV's "sound of sheer silence" in 1 Kgs 19:12 is only one possible rendering of a difficult Hebrew phrase. Here I offer a broad theological connection rather than a strictly exegetical observation.

barrenness might have seemed like one great, glorious moment. In any case, her short but substantive statement in 1:25 demonstrates incisive theological and psychological awareness.

Theologically, Elizabeth affirms the Lord's power to create life and concern to ameliorate suffering: "This is what the Lord has done [πεποίηκεν, *pepoiēken*][11] for me when he looked favorably on me." Psychologically, she exclaims release from her chronic experience of social reproach because of her childlessness: "[The Lord] took away the disgrace I have endured among my people." But why, then, in the face of such wonderful liberation, does Elizabeth "remain in seclusion [περιέκρυβεν, *periekryben*]"—"keep private, hide, conceal (entirely)"[12]—well into the second trimester? One would think she would want to announce her good news from the rooftops and have her friends throw her the mother of all baby showers! Instead, her remaining hidden appears to perpetuate her shame of being barren.[13]

So what is the narrative significance of Elizabeth's five-month seclusion? Perhaps, as some have suggested, it marks dramatic time for her and Zechariah to exit completely so as not to upstage Mary's grand entrance in the next scene; or maybe it represents a practical interest on Elizabeth's part not to "go public" with her pregnancy before the riskiest stages for miscarriage had passed; or perhaps it balances the supernatural dimension of Elizabeth's sudden conception with the natural process of fetal gestation over several months. But then again, maybe the long isolation furthers Luke's theological-contemplative emphasis on pondering the great acts of God. There will be plenty of time and opportunity for celebrating the miracle of John's birth with family and friends (1:57–58). But first it is vital that Elizabeth and Zechariah be prepared for their new parental vocation. They are being called to fulfill God's purpose along with their son, and as such they must be turned wholeheartedly both to the Lord and to their child, in anticipation of John's mission: "He will turn many of the people of Israel to the Lord their God. . . . [He will] turn the hearts of parents to their children . . . to make ready a people prepared for the Lord" (1:16–17). A season of concentrated silence and seclusion can aid the "turning"—and tuning—process by blocking out noisy distractions and winding detours.

11. The perfective aspect may be used to "frontground" an especially salient event (cf. Porter, *Idioms*, 20–26). The verb for "do" (ποιέω, *poieō*) also means "make, create," as "in the beginning God made/created [ἐποίησεν, *epoiēsen*] the heaven and the earth" (Gen 1:1 LXX). The double meaning befits Elizabeth's experience: what the Lord "has done" for her is to "make/create" life within her barren womb.

12. BDAG, 802. The imperfect form here stresses an ongoing state of seclusion across the five months.

13. On the hiding-shame connection, see Nussbaum, *Hiding*.

Mary Ponders God's Promise (1:26–38)

We do not expect Mary to know much of anything, and we do not expect anyone of any importance to know Mary or to care one whit what she knows, thinks, or feels. Here we should try to suspend our familiarity with the Christmas story and Marian hagiography and imagine ourselves in the position of Theophilus, not only spiritually, as a neophyte "God-lover," but also socially, as a "most excellent" Greco-Roman sophisticate. Encountering a village girl named Mary—by far the most common Jewish female name in Roman Palestine[14]—from no-account Nazareth in Galilee (cf. John 1:46; 7:52; Acts 2:7; 4:13) would not have instantly impressed Theophilus.[15] Ditto the fact that she is introduced as a virgin engaged to be married, though the mention of fiancé Joseph's lineage from "the house of David" might have piqued some interest (1:26–27). But that is what ordinary Marys (our "plain Janes") would be expected to do: marry as young virgins and have children by their husbands. The cultural script was deeply embedded in Nazareth and throughout Palestine. Why, then, would "the angel Gabriel [be] sent by God" (1:26) to such a girl in such a place with a birth announcement? To a long-married, veteran priest in the Jerusalem temple—that makes sense; to a betrothed girl-next-door some place in Nazareth—that is pointless.

But after a prosaic introduction, matters become anything but ordinary—expectations not merely stretched, but shattered. For Gabriel announces to Mary that she will bear not just any child, but the very "Son of the Most High [God]" and messianic ruler of David's eternal kingdom. And while she will carry and bear this Son by natural means, she will *conceive* him by God's *Holy Spirit* or *Breath* (πνεῦμα, *pneuma* [1:35]) and thereby *remain in a sexually virginal state* (until she conceives Jesus's half-brothers through normal intercourse; cf. 8:19–20; Acts 1:14). Luke (like Matthew) does not suggest some kind of sexual union between God and Mary reminiscent of pagan myths, some implantation of divine seed in Mary's womb. The process retains an air of mystery, emphasizing the agency of inspiration rather than insemination: "The Holy Spirit will come upon [ἐπελεύσεται, *epeleusetai*] you, and the power of the Most High will overshadow [ἐπισκιάσει, *episkiasei*] you" (Luke 1:35)—not invade and violate you. The two *epi*-verbs stress a powerful coming "on, upon, over" Mary in the sense of engulfing, enveloping her in divine presence and potency. She is to be caught up in the Spirit as whirling force (cf. Acts 2:2; 8:39; John 3:8)—no gentle breeze, to be sure, but still a generative rather than destructive exhalation of

14. Ilan, "Notes," 186–200.

15. On Mary's ordinary, lowly social position, see Green, 85–87, and "Social Status."

divine wind power—like that which "swept over [ἐπεφέρετο, *epephereto*] the face of the waters" at creation and invigorated the first human with the "breath of life" (Gen 1:2 LXX; 2:7). Mysteriously, but materially, Mary's entire embodied being, not least her amniotic waters, will be swept up and over in the dynamic crosswinds of trinitarian vitality. Mary is thus incorporated as partner with God in God's climactic and eternal ("there will be no end" [1:33]) self-revelation to God's people.

That is a lot for us to take in after two millennia of theological reflection by the church's best minds, and only arrogant dogmatism would claim that we have plumbed the depths of Christ's incarnation and God's trinitarian life. So what's a poor Galilean girl to make of all this when first hit with this incredible word-event? If Zechariah was thrown for a loop by a lesser, though still amazing, birth announcement, what's Mary to do? What indeed can she do? What "right to choose," to respond, to reflect, does she have in any of this? How could this sudden prospect of God's "overshadowing" her be anything but overwhelming, commandeering her full surrender, which she famously gives, right on cue: "Here I am, the slave [δούλη, *doulē*] of the Lord" (1:38 AT)? But in fact this acquiescence comes at the end of Mary's thoughtful engagement with Gabriel. She *actively*, not apathetically, accepts God's choice of her. She aims to *know* what God's up to and what she's in for.

Mary's exchange with Gabriel unfolds in three stages, each initiated by the angel's speech and followed, first, by the narrator's assessment of Mary's initial deliberation (1:29); second, by her direct interrogation (1:34); and third, by her submissive declaration (1:38).[16]

First Response: Deliberation (1:26–29)

Gabriel greets Mary as one abundantly graced by the Lord's presence (Luke 1:28). From our safe observation point, we might assume Mary's brimming enthusiasm over this angelic visit, but in the heat of the moment, she's not at all sure this is a blessed event. Why on earth should she be singled out? Nazareth's record of heavenly epiphanies is slim to none. Perhaps Gabriel has lost his way, misread his assignment. Even if he has the right place, does he have the right person? It is easy to imagine, as the theologian Serene Jones suggests, that "with women who, through the ages, have not recognized their value, Mary is looking over her shoulder to see who else Gabriel must be

16. Throughout the discussion of Mary in Luke 1–2, I draw on my fuller discussion in Spencer, *Salty Wives*, 55–100.

talking to."[17] She's caught completely off guard. In comparison with Zechariah's "troubled" and "terrified" reaction to "seeing" Gabriel (1:12), Mary becomes "much perplexed" (διαταράσσομαι, *diatarassomai*) and begins to "ponder" (διαλογίζομαι, *dialogizomai*) "the word" (λόγος, *logos*) of Gabriel, not simply the spectacle (1:29).[18] The two *dia*-compounds stress Mary's "feisty and challenging,"[19] affective-cognitive working "through" the implications of this strange visitation.[20] The one term, an intensified form of ταράσσω (*tarassō*), designating Zechariah's roiling distress (1:12; cf. Matt 14:26; Mark 6:50), connotes strong, emotional "upheaval of thought,"[21] "vexation," "consternation,"[22] while the other indicates a more philosophical disputation or argument.[23] Together they resist stereotypical, dismissive caricatures of young women like Mary as hysterical or gullible. She reacts with robust emotional and intellectual engagement. No angel, even the imposing Gabriel, is going to pull one over on Mary. She sets the stage for a cast of deliberative characters in this narrative: "Throughout Luke's Gospel, characters think, consider, ponder, wonder . . . marvel."[24] Yes, indeed—and none more so than Mary.

17. Jones, *Trauma*, 115.

18. The third verb in 1:29—"she was much perplexed by his words and pondered what sort of greeting this *might be* [εἴη, *eiē*]" is an optative form, used only by Luke in the NT in oblique or indirect questions (1:29; 8:9; 18:36; 22:23; Acts 17:11; 21:33; 25:20). In the present case, its indirectness may shave off a slight edge from Mary's response, but it still implies a pointed query. If reported in direct speech, Mary would have asked: "What sort of greeting *is* this?" See Wallace, *Greek Grammar*, 483.

19. Gomes, *Good Book*, 232: "Mary has been so often depicted as weak and submissive, 'the handmaiden of the Lord,' . . . that we forget the feisty and challenging nature of her initial response. . . . Rather than rushing to anticipate her humility or to make an argument about the doctrine of the Virgin Birth, we might do well to pause and ponder her wariness, her caution, indeed her reluctance to being pushed into joy."

20. On the affective-rhetorical dynamics ("cardiography") of Luke 1:5–56, see Kuhn, *Heart*, 63–95.

21. I appropriate the title of Nussbaum's magisterial work on the emotions (*Upheavals of Thought*, which she borrows from Proust). More than mere impulses, strong emotional reactions—like fearing a mighty angel's sudden appearance—remain integrally wrapped up with cognitive reflections. Indeed, emotions like fear routinely evoke strategic appraisals and actions.

22. Garland, 79.

23. Elsewhere in Luke, διαλογίζομαι/διαλογισμοί (*dialogizomai/dialogismoi*) refers to the crowds' deliberations about John's message (3:15), the scribes/Pharisees' arguments with Jesus (5:22; 6:8), and the disciples' wrangling about their social status (9:46). Though the latter examples reflect misguided disputes, they still entail engaged thinking rather than knee-jerk responses.

24. Dinkler, "Thoughts," 376; cf. 376n14: "The narrator typically mentions *that* a character is thinking (without citing the thoughts), as when Mary ponders 'in her heart' (2:19)" (emphasis original).

Second Response: Interrogation (1:30–37)

After a perfunctory word of assurance ("Do not be afraid, Mary"), Gabriel ratchets up the tension with a stunning announcement: "And now, you will conceive in your womb and bear a son, and you will call his name Jesus" (1:31). Like any betrothed young woman in this culture, Mary had no doubt thought a great deal about childbearing; it did not take an angel to jumpstart her maternal aspirations. But here he is, the Lord's mighty messenger, coming on rather strong about this birthing business: calling Mary to attention ("Now look here!" [ἰδού, *idou*] AT), claiming control over her womb (γαστήρ, *gastēr*), and dictating her baby's name. Her body, her life, her plans are not her own. But isn't this still good news in Mary's context, this golden promise of her producing a firstborn son, the "great Son of the Most High" no less, destined to rule in perpetuity on David's throne (1:32–33; cf. 2 Sam 7:16)? Good news, indeed—but maybe too good to be true, and in any case, not easy for Mary to accept.

Unlike legendary depictions of Mary's pious childhood, where she is groomed for sacred service by parents and priests in her little nursery shrine at home and then in the temple until the onset of menses at age twelve (Prot. Jas. 6–9),[25] Luke offers no trace of Mary's preparation for messianic motherhood. There was little consensus at this time regarding how the messianic age would be established, and no common, starry-eyed dream among first-century Jewish girls to nab some nice Judahite man in hopes of bearing him the once and future king of Israel.[26] Mary's shock over Gabriel's announcement is mounting by the minute—leading her, however, not to crumble in a helpless heap, but to ask for clarification. She does not immediately give herself over to the angel's plan, however much he claims divine authorization. This is her body, and she would like to know how it is going to be used.

Sensing the urgency of Gabriel's proposal in advance of her marriage to Joseph, Mary asks the logical question: "How will this be, since a male [ἄνδρα, *andra*] *I do not know* [οὐ γινώσκω, *ou ginōskō*] [and do not intend to know sexually until my wedding night]?" (Luke 1:34 AT). We tense up as readers at this point, because we know from Zechariah's story that Gabriel does not take questions well or deal patiently with what (or whom) one *does not know*. Although Mary's query is qualitatively different from Zechariah's, focusing more on process than on proof and leaving more room for faith than doubt, she still displays remarkable moxie and agency in challenging Gabriel. Even more remarkably, however, Gabriel respects Mary's personal role in God's plan by

25. See Hock, *Infancy Gospels*, 41–49.
26. See Collins and Collins, *King*.

elucidating what will happen to her body rather than stifling her vocal cords. Perhaps if Zechariah had been more concerned about Elizabeth's involvement than his own uncertainty—it was *her* body, after all, that would be most affected—he would have merited a more sympathetic response.

Juxtaposing his prior forecast of John's fetal filling with the Holy Spirit in Elizabeth's womb (1:15–17), Gabriel predicts Mary's enveloping by the same divine power, as we have seen, with double *epi*-verbs describing the Spirit in forceful coming "upon/over" Mary and counterpointing the two *dia*-verbs stressing her careful thinking "through" the situation. Does *epi* now trump *dia*, coercively overwhelming and undercutting Mary's agency? Question all you want, but if God comes upon and over you, forget it: your fate is sealed. True enough, but must this divine overpowering be viewed as brute, imperious, patriarchal force?

Here we confront the thorny problem of *divine providence*, especially "personal" or "particular" providence affecting individual lives. In a stimulating study, Kalbryn McLean grasps the nettle of the "personal politics of providence" in dialogue with John Calvin, who seeks "to preserve God's utter freedom of action, God's agency," with the corollary that "nothing and no one exercise their own power except insofar as God wills them to do so." Though Calvin does not eliminate human free will—including the pursuit of selfish interests against God's will—God's sovereignty always wins the day, as "God's plan 'absorbs' the resulting human behavior into the divine goodness without nullifying creaturely impetus." Affirming Calvin's "pastoral intentions" and acknowledging that "there is something theologically sound and empowering about holding fast to the idea that God is directly involved in our lives," McLean hastens to imagine "the possibility that God, or particular providence, works through persons *who invite God to do so*," who demonstrate "hospitality toward God."[27]

Moreover, for women's sake, McLean urges picturing this guest-God less as dictatorial Father-Patriarch ruling the household (Calvin's main image), less as dominical Son-Lord micromanaging the Father's interests, and more as dynamic Holy Spirit, the "wild child of the divine family"—"one who does not stand over us in a controlling position but instead swirls around us, ever present and shape shifting, ready to infuse us with energy when our bodies grow weary, ready to sharpen our vision when our eyes become heavy, ready to give us tongues of fire when we need to denounce injustice and still sing God's praise." Such "agency-empowering" vision resonates with Mary's conception of divine-human life by the Spirit in operation.[28] The prospect of Mary's dizzying dance with God's "wild" Spirit, which mightily blows where it wills but always

27. McLean, "Calvin," 109, 110, 115, 121 (emphasis added).

28. McLean, "Calvin," 123; cf. 122–24.

in the interest of creating and nurturing "new birth" (cf. John 3:3–8), allows for Mary's full cooperation *as she is*. The Holy Spirit's reproductive work makes Jesus a holy son within Mary's body ("the child to be born will be holy" [Luke 1:35]),[29] not Mary a holy mother fit for Jesus. Mary's purity, sexual or otherwise, is not at issue. She's been a virgin all her life, like scores of other girls in her society. She doesn't need to be "made holy" or "made over" in any sense to become a vessel of God's Son. The whole point of her being "favored/graced" is that God chooses her in her "humble state" (cf. 1:48 NIV)—an ordinary human female, not some unique paragon.[30] Moreover, since God's life-giving Spirit will come over/upon Mary (see above), not *within* her, Father-God will not "know" Mary in the sexual sense her question assumed. She thus retains freedom *within herself* to receive and respond to the Spirit's creative initiative.

Third Response: Declaration (1:38)

Mary's final response may be rendered: "Look, the slave of the Lord; if at all possible, let it be to me according to your word" (1:38 AT). Though obscured in the NRSV, Mary's reaction here matches the beginning of Gabriel's report: as he exhorted Mary to "look" (ἰδού, *idou*) and carefully consider his birth announcement, she now implores the angel to "look" (ἰδού, *idou*) at her as a willing participant in God's plan. Ironically, however, she freely gives herself over to the Lord as his *slave* (δούλη, *doulē*), totally surrendering her autonomy, it seems. She then offers her embodied self as the tablet on which God's angel-mediated "word" may be inscribed. Nevertheless, this is no impulsive, clueless decision she makes. It is also not formulaic or robotic, the expected dutiful acquiescence to the divine will. The use of the optative mood for "let it be [γένοιτο, *genoito*]" carries, vis-à-vis the imperative and subjunctive, "slightly remoter, vaguer, less assured, or more contingent" connotations,[31] which I've tried to capture with "*if*

29. "Therefore" (διό/, *dio*) in 1:35 indicates a direct causal connection between the Spirit in coming over Mary and working within her womb to produce a holy child.

30. See Schüssler Fiorenza's sharp critique of "the ideal-typical ecclesiological approach" to Mary (*Jesus*, 164–72); cf. Gaventa, *Mary*, 73: "Certainly Luke gives no indication that he regards Mary as a type or symbol confined to women. Indeed, if Mary is a symbol at all, she symbolizes God's gift of grace to all humankind" (cf. 54–55).

31. Porter, *Idioms*, 59. Mary employs a "volitive" type of optative in Luke 1:38 typical of *prayerful petitions*. Wallace (*Greek Grammar*) suggests this usage "is largely a carry-over from Attic [Greek]" in contexts where "prayers offered to the semi-gods of ancient Athens could expect to be haggled over, rebuffed, and left unanswered." But he hastens to add that such contingency or doubt is mitigated, though not entirely eliminated, in NT petitions to the one true and gracious God: "Although the *form* of much prayer language in the NT has the tinge of remote possibility . . . its

at all possible, let it be." In the present situation, according to van den Hengel, it "expresses Mary's intense desire . . . [and] longing [that] was not blind to the obvious difficulties she also foresaw."[32]

As her prophetic song will soon make clear, Mary longs not for personal acclaim but for the salvation of her beleaguered people (1:46–55). If her bearing God's messianic Son will catalyze such liberation, then so be it. But she knows it will not be easy, not least because of the "impossible" (1:37) scenario of virginal conception sketched by Gabriel. Elizabeth's geriatric pregnancy by husband Zechariah is one thing; conceiving as a virgin by the Holy Spirit is quite another. The former at least has some biblical precedent; the latter doesn't, except by a novel interpretation of Isa 7:14 in Matt 1:22–23, which Luke does not advance. So Mary wants to believe Gabriel's decree that "nothing is impossible with God" (1:37), but she's not entirely sure. *If at all possible*—and she hopes against hope that it is—let this miracle happen within her for the sake of God's redemptive rule.

While I try not to peek too far ahead in Luke's narrative, as I track its "orderly" plot, I can't resist commenting on a notable resemblance between Mary's present decision and the crisis that her son will face at the end of his life. In one of the most famous scenes in the Gospel tradition, Jesus petitions his heavenly Father for a reprieve from imminent crucifixion, "If you are willing," but then quickly adds: "Yet not my will but yours be done" (22:42). Though using a stronger imperative expression, "let it be done [γινέσθω, *ginesthō*]," Jesus, like his mother, struggles as a human agent with life-and-death decisions and needs, no less than she, an "angel from heaven . . . [to give] him strength" (22:43).[33] The overarching divine will orchestrates the drama of salvation throughout Luke's Gospel *in concert with* key players, like Mary and Jesus, functioning as voluntary cooperative agents.

In sum, as an ordinary young woman, Mary accepts God's claim upon her life as a willing follower—the "first disciple" in Luke and "model disciple" for others, male and female[34]—though not without doubts, desires, and demurrals appropriate to a free-thinking agent. Using McLean's language, we might say that, with eyes wide open, Mary deliberately accepts the divine invitation to welcome the Spirit and co-host the birthing of God's Son.

---

meaning often moves into the realm of expectation. If uncertainty is part of the package, it is not due to questions of God's ability, but simply to the petitioner's humility before the transcendent one" (481 [emphasis original]).

32. Van den Hengel, "Miriam," 144.

33. Barbara E. Reid, *Choosing?*, 69–70.

34. See Gaventa, *Mary*, 51–59, 72–75, and "All Generations," 126–29.

Interlude: A Word of Acclamation from Elizabeth (1:39–45)

From Mary's acceptance of her messianic maternal mission, the action shifts to her heading south "with haste" to a town in the Judean hills (1:39). Thus begins the journey motif that propels much of Luke's narrative. This first trek takes us by surprise: no discreet seclusion in Mary's own home, but rather a mad dash *out of town* and *on her own* fifty miles through rough terrain to Elizabeth's house. Luke does not dwell on the scandal from Joseph or anyone else's perspective (cf. Matt 1:18–25), but the picture is clear enough of a *lone runaway, unwed, pregnant teenager* seeking refuge outside her hometown. No one in the gossipy hamlet of Nazareth is likely to appreciate her predicament, less so with some fantastic report of her visitation by Gabriel and virginal conception by the Holy Spirit. This won't be the last time Nazareth has a hard time supporting Mary and her son Jesus (cf. Luke 4:16–30), and it is hard to blame them, since these events are truly hard to swallow. As we have noted, Mary herself struggles with all that is happening, both spiritually (what God is doing in and through her) and physically (what her reproductive organs and hormones are doing).

Understandably, though at some risk, Mary seeks to work out these issues in the safe company of her relative Elizabeth in Judea. Technically, Mary goes to "the house of Zechariah," the family head (1:40), but this patriarch remains in reflective "time out," with little to offer in his mute state. In any event, Mary ignores him and "greets Elizabeth" (1:40). This is women's business anyway, certainly on the gynecological front: the older, pregnant Elizabeth, further along than Mary, is poised to provide the adolescent girl with counsel and comfort. But that is not Luke's emphasis. More important, the women take the lead in *spiritual discernment*. Elizabeth opens with a perceptive prelude, setting the stage for Mary's magnificent prophecy in 1:46–55.

Actually, baby John kicks things off—literally!—"leaping" in Elizabeth's womb in jubilant recognition of Mary's arrival with cousin Jesus in her womb. Note the double emphasis on this kick-off, first, by the omniscient narrator (1:41) and then focused through Elizabeth's testimony (1:44). It is as if John already begins his vocation of heralding the joyous news of the Messiah's coming (cf. 1:17, 76–79; 3:4–6, 15–18). Of course, though already "filled with the Holy Spirit" in utero (1:15), John cannot yet articulate his message, any more than his father Zechariah can. That leaves Elizabeth to speak for both of them—and for herself—which she does with great force ("a loud cry" [1:42]) and prescience. But how does she *know* what to say, and how to interpret her baby's kick as anything more than restless movement or indigestion from a spicy dinner? She voices, as both Zechariah and Mary before her, a plea for explanation in her perplexed state: "How/why [πόθεν, *pothen*] has this happened to me?" (1:43).

Who can answer her? To belabor the point, Zechariah is in no position to answer; moreover, Mary has just walked through the door with a bare salutation. With no time yet for deliberative contemplation, Elizabeth must receive *direct inspiration* from the Holy Spirit. As Mary was enveloped by the Holy Spirit, Elizabeth is now said to be "filled with the Holy Spirit" (1:41). Though Mary also pondered the significance of Gabriel's "greeting" (1:29), Elizabeth responds to Mary's "greeting" (1:40) with immediate Spirit-sparked exclamation. Luke thus promotes a dialogic means to solid knowledge of the saving God through the intercommunication of divine Spirit and human heart-and-mind. Epistemology intertwines with pneumatology and psychology.

Inspired by the Spirit, Elizabeth registers two benedictory acclamations of Mary with significant theological corollaries. First, she blesses Mary's honored position "among women" (not apart from them) as bearer of one whom Elizabeth extols, without hesitation, as "my Lord" (1:42–43). To this point, "Lord" (κύριος, *kyrios*) has been used by the narrator (1:6, 9, 11), Gabriel (1:15–17, 32), Elizabeth (1:25), and Mary (1:38) as the traditional biblical designation for the God of Israel (cf. Deut 6:4), that is, the true "Lord God [κύριος ὁ θεός, *kyrios ho theos*]" (Luke 1:16, 38). With her trumpeting of Mary as "the mother of my Lord," Elizabeth becomes the first character in Luke to identify Jesus expressly in *divine* and *relational* ("*my* Lord") terms.[35] As "Son of God" (cf. 1:32, 35), Jesus is distinct from, though intimately related to God; as "Lord," Jesus is coequal and continuous with God. We again confront that mysterious trinitarian swirl of Sovereign Creator, Incarnate Son, and Holy Spirit—now with Elizabeth caught up in this dynamic divine fellowship alongside Mary. The Triune God is not a gated community. The Lord's incarnation in Mary's womb opens the way for intimate human congress with divine being. Elizabeth's announcement "that the mother of my Lord comes to me" effectively marks Mary's role as "mother of God," as well as Elizabeth's participation in the family of *her* Lord God, who reaches out *to her*.

Second, Elizabeth blesses not only Mary's fruitful relationship with God and God's Son, but also her faithful response to "what was spoken to her by the Lord" (1:45). Here Elizabeth evokes the Creator God, who spoke the cosmos into existence through the Spirit and has now conceived divine life in Mary by the same Spirit. God has done God's work: blessed be the name of the Lord. But blessed also be Mary, who has cooperated with God by "believing

35. See the thorough and carefully nuanced discussion of Elizabeth's "mother of my Lord" statement in Rowe, *Early Narrative Christology*, 34–49. For example: "Such an introduction should profoundly shape the way we conceive of Lukan Christology . . . for it is in fact as κύριον that Luke first brings Jesus into the human realm" (43).

[πιστεύσασα, *pisteusasa*] that there would be a fulfillment" of God's creative word within her (1:45). Faith in God's potent "fulfilling" word is a fundamental human disposition toward God demanded in Luke (cf. 4:21; 24:44). But Luke also grants time and space for faith to grow. Though Zechariah initially "did not believe [ἐπίστευσας, *episteusas*] [God's] words, which will be fulfilled in their time" (1:20), he will get there over the course of Elizabeth's pregnancy, which will prove as developmental for him as his son. And though Mary's faith sprouts sooner, as Elizabeth confirms, it does not burst forth full-grown but is cultivated in the soil of investigation and rumination.

Mary Proclaims God's Mercy (1:46–55)

In antiphonal response to Elizabeth's benediction, Mary breaks out in soaring prophetic song also inspired by God's Spirit, though she expresses the joyous attunement of *her body, mind, and spirit* with the saving Lord God (1:46–47).[36] Mary's personal spiritual engagement with God's Spirit continues. Her Magnificat, so called after the first Latin word in the Vulgate (the Greek verb is μεγαλύνω [*megalynō*], "magnify, make great, enlarge, extend"), starts the soundtrack for Luke's nativity story. Luke's theology is first communicated in lyrical song as much as rhetorical prose, tapping into primal yearnings for shared poetic-aesthetic experience.[37] No songs are truly solo: we are meant to sing along. Mary sings not only to and for God and Elizabeth, but *with* them (and us),[38] implicitly inviting them (and us) to join in the chorus, raise the volume, enhance the timbre, and add their (our) own flourishes.

Here we engage with Mary's song on four levels or tenors: theological, emotional, temporal and social.

36. In the traditional rendering, "My soul [ψυχή, *psychē*] magnifies the Lord, and my spirit [πνεῦμα, *pneuma*] rejoices" (NRSV, KJV, NIV, NAB, NASB), "soul" and "spirit" appear in poetic, synonymous parallelism. Both terms, in Greek and English, have unfortunately been heavily freighted with a dualistic opposition to "body" and "flesh" (good "soul/spirit" vs. evil "body/flesh") beyond what is warranted by both ancient biblical anthropology and modern cognitive science. My use of "body, mind, and spirit" attempts to capture the *embodied* and *unified* totality of Mary's experience. She by no means praises God in some disembodied spiritual "tongue"; rather, she glorifies God with her entire being, or "whole heart" (cf. Ps 138:1), if we understand "heart" in broad terms reflecting her (embodied) thought, will, feeling, and intention. The CEB represents a marked improvement: "With *all my heart* I glorify the Lord! In *the depths of who I am* I rejoice" (Luke 1:46–47). For a superb appraisal of biblical anthropology, see Green, *Body*.

37. Cf. Mithen, *Singing Neanderthals*.

38. The ἐπί (*epi*) + dative construction here could be rendered "My spirit rejoices *with* God [επὶ τῷ θεῷ, *epi tō theō*] my Savior."

Theological Tenor: Salvation and Mercy (1:46–50, 54)

Thus far God has been identified as "Lord" and as "the Most High," both titles denoting divine authority, majesty, and potency. Mary echoes these names in her opening lines: "My soul [self] magnifies *the Lord* . . . for *the Mighty One* has done great things for me" (1:46, 49).[39] But between these statements she also introduces a striking new divine title: "My spirit rejoices in *God my Savior* [σωτήρ, *sōtēr*]" (1:47). This in fact marks the *only* time God is so designated in Luke and Acts,[40] but its unique usage in such a prominent place, beginning the first hymn, commends "God Our Savior" as a virtual banner over the whole Gospel, borne out by the pervasive development of "save/salvation" language and themes. Moreover, the idea of God as personal (my/our) Savior picks up key strains from the Jewish Scriptures, particularly Psalms and Isaiah (favorite Lukan sources), and Judith too. For example:

> O come, let us rejoice in the Lord; let us make a joyful noise to God our savior [σωτήρ, *sōtēr*]! (Ps 94 [95]:1 NETS)
>
> Behold, the Lord is my God, my savior [σωτήρ, *sōtēr*]; I will trust in him and will not be afraid, because the Lord is my glory and my praise, and he has become my salvation [σωτηρία, *sōtēria*]. (Isa 12:2 NETS)
>
> For your strength is not in numbers, nor is your dominance in those who are fit, but you are a God of the lowly; you are the helper of the inferior, the supporter of the weak, the shelterer of the desperate, the savior [σωτήρ, *sōtēr*] of the hopeless. (Jdt 9:11 NETS)

The poetic-prophetic setting of joyful praise in Psalms and Isaiah resonates with Mary's hymn, as does the prayerful affirmation of Judith on behalf of her "lowly and weak" people, as discussed below. But for now, we simply note the beneficent shape that "Savior" gives to "Lord" and "Most High/Mighty One," assuring God's people that God's supreme power will be used for salutary purposes.

While Mary does not repeat "saving" language in her song, she explicates salvation themes, notably in double reference to God's *mercy* (ἔλεος, *eleos* [Luke

39. Lauding God as "the Mighty/Powerful One [ὁ δυνατός, *ho dynatos*]" is closely associated with ascribing to God the plenipotentiary "power of the Most High [δύναμις ὑψίστου, *dynamis hypsistou*]" (1:35).

40. The "Savior" title is not common in the NT. Interestingly, the only other references to God as "Savior" appear in Jude 25 and the Pastoral Epistles: 1 Tim 1:1; 2:3; 4:10; Tit 1:3; 2:10; 3:4. Luke applies the title to Christ three times: Luke 2:11; Acts 5:31; 13:23.

1:50, 54]). God's saving nature is expressed through acts of mercy. BDAG defines ἔλεος (*eleos*) as "kindness or concern expressed for someone in need, mercy, compassion, pity, clemency."[41] But the nuances of these various English terms do not necessarily apply in every case. "Compassion" and "pity" suggest an empathetic element that may or may not motivate mercy. While this song pulses with emotion (see below), the main "mercy" accent falls not on God's tender feelings but on the mega-acts (μεγάλα, *megala*) of mercy God "has done" (1:49) in "helping" or "coming to the aid of" (ἀντιλαμβάνομαι, *antilambanomai* [1:54; cf. Acts 20:35])[42] God's long-suffering people. Mercy is what God *does* for needy people or, in turn, what people *do* for one another (see 10:37). As liberation theologian Jon Sobrino unpacks this "principle of mercy": "It suggests a sense of compassion. The danger is that it may seem to denote a sheer sentiment, without a praxis to accompany it. . . . We call this activity of love, thus structured, mercy. And we find that we must say of this mercy that first it is an *action*, or more precisely a *reaction* to someone else's suffering, now interiorized within oneself—a reaction that has come to penetrate one's own entrails and heart (in this case, the suffering of an entire people, inflicted upon them unjustly and at the basic levels of their existence)."[43]

Back to Israel's hymnbook. Nowhere is God's mercy extolled more profoundly than in Psalm 136, which Walter Brueggemann describes as "the credo recital of [the Lord's] mighty deeds . . . provid[ing] the fullest evidence for the concrete, specific, nameable content of *hesed* [steadfast love] and *'emeth* [faithfulness]."[44] The former Hebrew term predominates in this psalm, resounding in the refrain ending each of the twenty-six verses: "For his *steadfast love* endures forever." Here, as elsewhere, the LXX renders חסד (*ḥesed*) with ἔλεος (*eleos*), understanding God's "mercy" along the lines of "steadfast, enduring love," specifically evidenced in God's *mighty acts* throughout the history of Israel and the world. Following a threefold thanksgiving introit, verse 4 presents what Brueggemann suggests is "a thesis statement for the entire psalm": "[The Lord] who alone is doing great wonders [ποιοῦντι θαυμάσια μεγάλα, *poiounti thaumasia megala*]—because his mercy [ἔλεος, *eleos*] endures forever" (Ps 135 [136]:4 NETS).[45] The remaining verses trace these merciful deeds through the epochs of creation (5–9), exodus (10–15), wilderness journey (16), and land conquest (17–22), capped by grateful memories of the Lord's general rescuing and feeding work (23–26).

41. BDAG, 316.

42. BDAG, 89.

43. Sobrino, *Principle*, 16 (emphasis original).

44. Brueggemann, *Israel's Praise*, 79.

45. Brueggemann, *Theology*, 213.

Though Mary of Nazareth's psalm may more personally echo Miriam's (Exod 15:20–21) and Hannah's (1 Sam 2:1–10) biblical songs, as many have noted,[46] and focuses historically on God's covenant with Abraham (and descendants) (1:55), it otherwise resonates strongly with the dominant "mercy" key of Psalm 136 [135].

Mary's Song in Luke	**Psalm 136 [135] NETS**
God has looked with favor on the lowliness [ταπείνωσιν, *tapeinōsin*] of his servant (1:48). He has . . . lifted up the lowly [ταπεινούς, *tapeinous*] (1:52).	In our humiliation [ταπεινώσει, *tapeinōsei*] the Lord remembered us (135:23).
He has shown strength with his arm [κράτος ἐν βραχίονι, *kratos en brachioni*] (1:51).	With a strong [κραταιᾷ, *krataia*] hand and a raised [ὑψηλῷ, *hypsēlō*] arm [βραχίονι, *brachioni*] (135:12).
He has brought down the powerful from their thrones, and lifted up [ὕψωσεν, *hypsōsen*] the lowly (1:52).	Who struck down great kings (135:17; cf. vv. 18–20).
He has filled the hungry with good things (1:53).	Who gives nourishment to all flesh (135:25).
He has helped his servant Israel, in remembrance of his mercy [μνησθῆναι ἐλέους, *mnēsthēnai eleous*], according to the promise he made . . . to Abraham and to his descendants forever [εἰς τὸν αἰῶνα, *eis ton aiōna*] (1:54–55).	A heritage to Israel his slave. . . . The Lord remembered [ἐμνήσθη, *emnēsthē*] us—because his mercy [ἔλεος, *eleos*] is forever [εἰς τὸν αἰῶνα, *eis ton aiōna*] (135:22–23).

"Mercy" strains of God's (1) lifting the lowly, (2) plummeting the powerful, (3) feeding the famished with his (4) strong arm, and (5) remaining faithful to the forgotten (6) forever echo in close harmony between these two psalms, while also introducing major themes reverberating across Luke's Gospel.

To clarify further Mary's understanding of God's mercy, her song offers no trace of *legal* aspects of pardoning misconduct or reducing punishment common in discussions of mercy in Greco-Roman moral philosophy[47] and

46. For example, O'Day, "Singing."

47. See the discussion in Nussbaum, *Therapy*, 426–29, 480–83, and *Upheavals*, 364–68, 397–98; Konstan, *Pity*. Different terms with various nuances associated with "mercy, compassion, pity, kindness" complicate the picture. In Greek, for example, along with ἔλεος (*eleos*) are ἐπιείκεια (*epieikeia*) and οἰκτιρμός (*oiktirmos*); and in Latin, *misericordia* and *clementia*.

modern jurisprudence (throwing oneself on the mercy of the court). To be sure, God's mercy toward Israel could include forgiving sin as *part* of its work (e.g., Exod 34:6–7), but not the whole. It certainly does not fit Mary's situation: she's done nothing wrong for which she receives "mercy," and the lowly and hungry beneficiaries of God's mercy are scarcely blamed for their conditions. They merit God's mercy purely on the basis of their need and suffering. If any sin is in view in Mary's song, it is the *structural sin* of ruling powers who squeeze the poor, neglect the needy, and thus fail to "do judgment and to love mercy [ἔλεον, *eleon*] and . . . to walk with the Lord your God" (Mic 6:8 NETS).

Emotional Tenor: Joy and Fear (1:46–47, 50)

The only way to capture the range of emotion in Mary's Magnificat is to read it aloud—better yet, to hear it set to music, as often done in Anglican Evensong services. At the risk of diminishing the full impact, I briefly highlight two emotions that Mary explicitly mentions—joy and fear—typically regarded as discordant.

To this point Mary's emotional state has been characterized as "much perplexed" (1:29), likely laced with anxiety and dread. Gabriel's "do not be afraid" rejoinder to Zechariah and to Mary (1:13, 30) presumes a fearful response, though only Zechariah is actually reported as hyperphobic ("he was terrified; and fear overwhelmed him" [1:12]). The good news that he "will have joy and gladness, and many will rejoice at [John's] birth" (1:14) has not sunk in yet. Confusion and tension prevail for both Zechariah and Mary until John "leaps for joy" in Elizabeth's womb, and the pregnant Mary starts to "rejoice in God my Savior" (1:44, 47). Now the beat has accelerated to reflect the joyous expectation of blessed new lives. The birthdays of the prophet John and the Messiah Jesus will be high happy occasions (cf. 1:58; 2:10, 14, 20)—for centuries and millennia to come in Jesus's case ("Joy to the world, the Lord has come!"). The emotion of joy is a particularly apt response to that most intimate and intense embodied experience of (re)producing another human being with his or her own potential for growth and fruitfulness. As the neuroscientist Antonio Damasio observes, "Joyous states signify optimal physiological coordination and smooth running of the operations of life. They not only are conducive to survival but to survival with well-being. The states of joy also are defined by a greater ease in the capacity to act."[48] Or as the theologian Jürgen Moltmann, with special reference to Christianity as a "unique *religion of joy*," puts it: "*Joy* is strength for living, the

48. Damasio, *Looking for Spinoza*, 137.

empowerment to love, the delight in a creative beginning. It wakes us up, and makes alive from within."[49]

But for all the ebullient enthusiasm surrounding the conceptions and births of John and Jesus, the parents' fear never fully dissipates. No surprise here. Parents from all backgrounds and generations remain anxious. What have we gotten ourselves into? Are we up to the daunting demands of nurturing a human life from cradle to maturity? And upping the ante in Mary's unique case, how in the world could she fathom bearing and raising the Son of the Most High God? Her excitement predictably soars with a queasy mix of joy and fear—all the more, since God is intimately involved, and human response to God inevitably entails *fear*. As Mary exclaims: "[God's] mercy is for *those who fear him* [τοῖς φοβουμένοις αὐτόν, *tois phoboumenois auton*] from generation to generation" (1:50). Fearing is fundamental to knowing God, as the biblical wisdom tradition attests: "The fear of the LORD is the beginning of knowledge" (Prov 1:7); "then you will understand the fear of the LORD and find the knowledge of God" (2:5). While godly fear is often glossed as "respect" or "reverence," such notions blunt the force of healthy trepidation over God's utter otherness, including God's fiery power and volatility.[50] The "arm" of God in Mary's hymn signifies not only the tender outreach of God's uplifting support but also the mighty thrust of God's scattering and toppling oppressive forces (1:50–52; cf. Ps 135 [136]:12–15). To know God is to fear God, to participate in dynamic, risky relationship with the Source of all being, and to cling for dear life to God's outstretched arm.

Temporal Tenor: Generation to Generation (1:48–50, 54–55)

The temporal horizon of Mary's Magnificat spans "all generations. . . . from generation to generation": from the covenant God sealed with Abraham in the distant past and "from now on" throughout the ages "forever" (Luke 1:48, 50, 54–55). Although firmly rooted in the historical moment, Luke's story sets each event within a cosmic arc. Mary marvels that the God of Israel has favored her in all her "lowliness" at this (pregnant) moment and given her an honored place in her people's sweeping history. "God our help in ages past, our hope for years to come"[51] has "done great things" for Mary (1:49) and, through her, has certified the covenantal promise for all generations.

49. Moltmann, *Living God*, 88, 90 (emphasis original); cf. 87–101.

50. See the commentary on 12:1–34 for a fuller discussion on fearing God.

51. From the classic hymn "O God Our Help in Ages Past," by Isaac Watts (1719), based on Psalm 90.

Social Tenor: Low and Lofty (1:51–53)

As Mary extends the temporal-horizontal axis from antiquity to eternity, she also stretches the social-vertical axis from lowborn to highbrow. In fact, she stretches the hierarchy to the breaking point, not simply redistributing resources among lowly servants (like herself) and lofty elites, but *reversing* their positions. The humble and hungry will be lifted high and fed full, while the prominent and prosperous will be brought down and left destitute (1:51–53). As Justo González remarks, with special reference to Mary's song: "Luke's unfinished history includes a *grand reversal* as a sign of the reign of God, and invites us to consider the reversals that we encounter in our day as possible signs of that reign."[52]

Four lines set in chiastic structure punctuate the radical reversal (1:52–53):

A He has brought down the powerful from their thrones [θρόνων, *thronōn*],
  B and lifted the lowly [ταπεινούς, *tapeinous*];
  B′ he has filled the hungry with good things [ἀγαθῶν, *agathōn*],
A′ and sent the rich away empty [κενούς, *kenous*].

The "grand reversal" is evident in the placement of the lowly/hungry at center stage, with the powerful/rich pushed to the margins.

Moreover, the end-stress rhyme scheme in Greek further accents the contrast.

A . . . θρόνων, *thronōn* (thrones)
  B . . . ταπεινούς, *tapeinous* (lowly)
  A′ . . . ἀγαθῶν, *agathōn* (good things)
B′ . . . κενούς, *kenous* (empty)

The *-ōn* (A/A′) and *-nous* (B/B′) rhyming pairs trade on the logical coupling—the powerful sitting on *thrones* (*thronōn*) normally enjoy *good things* (*agathōn*) in life, while the *lowly* (*tapeinous*) struggle to run on *empty* (*kenous*) tanks—only to dash the logic and disrupt the pattern: the mighty, merciful God breaks in with divine free verse to fill up *the lowly with good things* they have long lacked and to divest *the enthroned* of their power and riches, leaving them *empty*.[53] Equations of lowly/good and enthroned/empty do not compute in

52. González, 6 (emphasis added; cf. 5–9). See also Verhey, *Great Reversal*, 93–97.

53. Carroll (51n14) also notes the linguistically consonant-assonant pairing of the socially

standard economics. Patron-client systems fall apart, and "trickle down" theories wash away. Such radical reversal might well have shaken up wealthier Christian readers (Theophilus?). Can the faithful serve God and money at the same time? Though Luke's Jesus will eventually answer that question with a blanket negative (16:13), it remains to be seen how rich and powerful characters respond to Jesus and to what extent their wealth and position help or hinder their knowledge of God.

For now, Mary puts the upper crust on notice and gives rich hope to the lower classes. Overall, true to her opening word of "magnification" (enlargement, extension, expansion), she boldly plumbs the boundary-stretching height, depth, and "wideness in God's mercy," to borrow from the classic nineteenth-century hymn by Frederick William Faber. Note not only the "mercy" echo in stanza 1, but also the resonances with "mighty" and "magnify" from less familiar stanzas 10–11.

> There's a wideness in God's mercy,
> Like the wideness of the sea;
> There's a kindness in his justice,
> Which is more than liberty. (stanza 1)
>
> It is God: His love looks mighty;
> But is *mightier* than it seems.
> 'Tis our Father: and His fondness
> Goes far out beyond our dreams. (stanza 10)
>
> But we make His love too narrow
> By false limits of our own;
> And we *magnify* His strictness
> With a zeal He will not own. (stanza 11)

Interlude: A Word of Appellation from Elizabeth (1:56–66)

The transitional note gets Mary offstage and back to Nazareth, but not before reinforcing her solidarity with Elizabeth: "And Mary remained *with her* about three months and then returned to her home" (1:56). This monthly tracking of Mary and Elizabeth's pregnancies (three months, five [1:24], six [1:26])

---

dissonant "hungry" (πεινῶντας, *peinōntas*) and "rich" (πλουτοῦντας, *ploutountas*) in 1:53. We might approximate the effect with "penurious" and "prosperous."

continues to link the two women within "ordinary time" (ORT).[54] However miraculous their conceptions are, pregnancies and deliveries follow a natural course—which brings us now to month 9 (6 + 3): "the time [χρόνος, *chronos*] . . . for Elizabeth to give birth" (1:57).[55]

As "neighbors and relatives [συγγενεῖς, *syngeneis*]" celebrate the birth of Elizabeth's son, familiar tones again resound around themes of magnification, mercy, and joy. They begin "rejoicing together [συνέχαιρον, *synechairon*]" in the Lord's magnanimous mercy toward Elizabeth, or more literally, because "the Lord had magnified [ἐμεγάλυνεν, *emegalynen*] his mercy [ἔλεος, *eleos*]" on God-fearing Elizabeth's behalf (1:58). God's life-giving mercy has overcome Elizabeth's unbearable shame; grace has trumped disgrace (cf. 1:25). God's "magnificent" mercy remains rooted in the lowly, ordinary embodiment of women's wombs, young and old, and of promising, yet precarious, infant life.

The birth celebration includes naming and circumcising baby John on the eighth day (1:59), enacting the sign of the Abrahamic covenant (Gen 17:9–14; cf. Luke 1:55). But the naming process hits a snag. The gathered community assumes the boy will be called "Zechariah, after his father" (1:59), but Elizabeth stoutly objects, insisting that he be named John, as Gabriel mandated to Zechariah (1:13), though Elizabeth does not mention that datum. In fact, we're not told how Elizabeth came to know her baby's divinely appointed name: either Zechariah somehow managed to communicate it, or the Spirit revealed it to her. At any rate, *her word* does not settle the matter. The community counters that "none of your relatives has this name," and then solicits Zechariah's input, which he provides by *writing* "His name is John" on a wooden notepad.[56] That does settle the issue, as the assembly responds with "amazement" and acceptance of Zechariah's word (1:61–63).

However Elizabeth herself came to know John's name, this snippet reveals three important aspects regarding *community knowledge of God's will*, a major concern in this commentary. First, a *woman's word* is challenged in favor of patriarchal authority. Such resistance appears surprising in a narrative featuring Elizabeth and Mary's vocal inspiration in contrast with Zechariah's muted in-

54. Luke's narrative is set within various overlapping "time zones," which I designate ordinary time (ORT), Jewish Standard Time (JST), Roman Imperial Time (RIT), and God's Time (GOT). For a different discussion of the various temporal perspectives in Luke 1, see Kahl, "Reading Luke," 76–83.

55. In the NT, χρόνος (*chronos*) tends to denote the durational/chronological passage of time, in distinction from καιρός (*kairos*), which signifies the more occasional/situational moment, as in Luke 1:20: "my words, which will be fulfilled in their [appointed] time [καιρόν, *kairon*]."

56. See BDAG on the diminutive form πινακίδιον (*pinakidion*) in Luke 1:63: "little (wooden) tablet esp. of a writing-tablet for notes" (814).

put. Elizabeth knows what her son must be named and says so in no uncertain terms; but her knowledge is questioned until confirmed by the paterfamilias. A gendered tension, rooted in vocal power, thus emerges in Luke's story.[57] We will remain alert to how this conflict plays out across the narrative.[58] In the present case, we should note that it was not unusual for Israelite women to take the lead in naming sons (see Ruth 4:13–17). With the famous biblical barren women—Sarah, Rachel, the wife of Manoah, and Hannah—finally blessed with a child, all but Sarah name their famous sons: Isaac (Gen 21:3; here Abraham has the honors), Joseph (Gen 30:24), Samson (Judg 13:24), and Samuel (1 Sam 1:20), respectively.

Second, we begin to confront a more expansive sense of *kinship ties*. Just because a name—or a person, group, value, or practice—comes from outside one's natural family circle is no reason to reject it. "The Lord is gracious" (the root meaning of John's Hebrew name) and merciful to all people, beyond boundaries of clan, race, and nation. The native, biological family of John and Jesus—including their esteemed mothers—will be subsumed under the fictive, spiritual household of all those "who hear the word of God and do it" (8:21), including Mary (1:38), but by no means exclusive to her and her relatives (cf. 8:19–21; 11:27–28).

Third, the name game is ultimately decided by the *written word*. To be sure, Zechariah's writing (γράφω, *graphō*) John's name on a little tablet is no great scribal feat and simply confirms Gabriel's and Elizabeth's mandates. But it does mark a key moment of Zechariah's affirmation and the community's recognition. Moreover, "immediately" following his inscriptional message, "his mouth was opened and his tongue freed, and he began to speak, praising God" (1:64). Written word sparks oral witness to God's saving acts. Luke thus drops a subtle hint of the revelatory significance of the authoritative Jewish Scriptures (γραφή, *graphē*; cf. 4:21; 24:27, 32, 45; Acts 8:32, 35; 17:2, 11; 18:24, 28). God's Word, first inscribed on stone tablets in the case of Torah (Exod 24:12; 31:18; 34:1; Deut 4:13; 9:9–11), provides rock solid knowledge of God's will.

But of course no writings, sacred or otherwise, are self-interpreting. They prompt responses, debates, questions—from men and women, insiders and outsiders—seeking truth and greater understanding. In the present situation, Elizabeth's oral and Zechariah's written revelations of John's name trigger fear (emotion), buzz (discussion), and amazement (reflection), this time among "all their neighbors" (Luke 1:63–65). Fear again pushes beyond proper respect

57. On the connection between voice, knowledge, and power in gender relations, see Spencer, "Feminist Criticism."

58. Cf. Spencer, *Dancing Girls*, 144–65.

for God. Excitement, nervousness, and uncertainty bubble up over what the mighty "hand of the Lord" will do with newborn John. So much to talk about throughout the region (1:65), so much "to weigh and ponder in their hearts [ἔθεντο . . . ἐν τῇ καρδίᾳ αὐτῶν, *ethento . . . en tē kardia autōn*]" (1:66 AT). The audience asks the key question propelling the narrative forward: "What then will this child become?" (1:66). Though Gabriel has charted a promising course—confirmed by John's joyous birth, Zechariah's restored speech, and Elizabeth and Zechariah's agreement on John's name—there remains much we do not know, much to unfold regarding God's saving purposes. We read on in faith, hope—and a measure of healthy fear and suspense.

Zechariah Proclaims God's Mercy (1:67–80)

Zechariah puts his renewed speaking facility to good use, overflowing with the Spirit in inspiration into the second hymn, the Benedictus ("Blessed"). Unfortunately, these will also be Zechariah's last words in Luke. But far from being an old priest's swan song capping off an "old" era of God's work and yielding to a "new deal," Zechariah's canticle, like Mary's, stresses the *progressive continuity* of God's covenantal faithfulness. Though the Benedictus flips the structure of the Magnificat, proceeding from a national-historical focus (1:68–75) to a more personal-contemporary horizon (1:76–79), both songs propound similar themes surrounding salvation, "looking with favor," mercy, fear, and ancestor Abraham, albeit in distinctive keys. We will concentrate on Zechariah's adaptations.

Soteriology (1:68–71, 74, 79)

Zechariah places heavier stress on God's saving Israel from violent forces through God's Davidic ruler. Whereas Mary exulted in "God *my* Savior," who also topples the powers that be and aids the lowly among God's "servant/child [παιδός, *paidos*] Israel" (1:54),[59] Zechariah blesses God, who "raised up a mighty savior [lit. 'horn of salvation'] *for us* in the house of his servant/child [παιδός, *paidos*] *David*," in order that God's people "would be saved from our enemies and from the hand of all who hate us" (1:69–71). Whereas Mary echoes Ps 136,

59. Distinct from διάκονος (*diakonos*) and δοῦλος (*doulos*), common terms in Luke's writings for "servant, slave," παῖς (*pais*) can denote not only "servant" but also "child." In light of Israel's and Jesus's roles as God's servant and (firstborn) son, Mary and Zechariah's nativity carols likely play on both "servant" and "child" meanings (cf. Acts 3:13, 26; 4:27, 30).

Zechariah especially recalls Ps 18 (= 2 Sam 22 LXX), set in the historical context of David's reign. The LXX heading reads "Pertaining to Dauid, the servant [παιδί, *paidi*] of the Lord, what he said to the Lord . . . in the day in which the Lord rescued him from the hand of all his enemies, and from the hand of Saoul" (Ps 17 [18]:1 NETS). The psalm then develops these themes in language that Zechariah picks up, particularly "horn of salvation [κέρας σωτηρίας, *keras sōtērias*]" (Luke 1:69) and "salvation from enemies [ἐχθρῶν, *echthrōn* (twice)]" (1:71, 74).

> The Lord is my firmness and my refuge and my rescuer;
> my God is my helper, and I will hope in him,
> my protector and *horn of my deliverance* [κέρας σωτηρίας, *keras sōtērias*], my supporter.
> When I praise I will call upon the Lord,
> and from my *enemies* [ἐχθρῶν, *echthrōn*] I shall be saved.
> (Ps 17:3–4 [18:2–3] NETS)

Salvation by God's mighty "horn"—as in the head thrust of a fighting ram or bull, not a trumpet or shofar blast—trades on military imagery, building on David's final battles with the Philistines and reinforced within his victory song in 2 Samuel: "The Strong One [God] . . . training my hands for war and breaking a bronze bow with my arm. And you gave me protection for my salvation. . . . And you will strengthen me with power for battle; you will make those who rise up against me bow down under me" (2 Sam 22:33–36, 40 NETS; cf. 21:15–22; Ps 17:33–37 [18:32–39]). In Zechariah's song, the martial tone is more defensive and liberating than aggressive and colonizing: assaulted by malevolent forces, God's people need to be "redeemed" (Luke 1:68) and "rescued from the hands of our enemies" (1:74). And they shall walk in the "way of peace" (1:79)—but only after a fierce freedom fight.

Neither David's nor Zechariah's hymn is a pacifist manifesto. If we didn't know better, we might think that the Davidic Messiah Jesus advanced by Zechariah's son John was destined to lead a David-style thrashing of Roman legions on the battlefield. We might expect, along with some first-century Jews, that the Messiah would wield God's mighty arm of deliverance by taking up military arms against Israel's conquerors.[60] Of course, Jesus's execution on a Roman cross and Jerusalem's destruction by a Roman army would have shaken these

60. Though messianic expectations varied in early Judaism, one strain longed for a Davidic warrior-king who would strike Israel's foes with his mighty "horn" (Pss 89:17; 132:17; Sir 47:5, 7, 11) and dash them with an "iron rod" (Ps 2:1–9; Pss. Sol. 17:1–4, 21–25).

messianic hopes to the core. Luke writes his Gospel in the throes of these insecurities—but also in the hope of resurrection (cf. 24:21, 25–35). Knowing the truth of Jesus's liberating work is no easy proposition; solidity of faith in shaky times is hard to muster. But it may be bolstered by bold songs, like Zechariah's (and Mary's), trumpeting God's ultimate salvation in the midst of crisis.

Emotional Tenor (1:74–75)

While matching Elizabeth and Mary's joyous tone, Zechariah's note about *fear* counterpoints both Mary's positive endorsement of fearing God and his own experience of cringing terror at the temple altar. Now Zechariah trumpets the prospect "that we, being rescued from the hands of our enemies, might serve [God] *without fear* [ἀφόβως, *aphobōs*]" (1:74). This lack of fear, while colored by rescue from enemy hands, also connects with fear*less* religious observance,[61] specifically, liturgical or cultic practices through which a priest like Zechariah "serves" (λατρεύω, *latreuō*) God (1:74).[62] He now realizes that, even in the face of God's fearsome power, he can approach God fearlessly—not so much because he needn't worry about attacks from human enemies at the altar, but because he has been delivered from hostile forces *in order to* freely serve and love the saving, welcoming, covenant-keeping God. To fear God or not to fear God?[63] That is the question, with no answer but paradox: we must do both, leaving us in a taut emotional-spiritual state ripe for anxiety and rich in possibility.

Epistemology (1:76–79)

The concluding section of the Benedictus, in which Zechariah confirms Gabriel's commission directly to his infant son ("And you, child, will be called prophet of the Most High" [1:76a]), focuses on John's preparing the Lord's way and "giving *knowledge* [γνῶσιν, *gnōsin*] of salvation to his people" (1:76b–77). John's mission will serve an illuminating, educative purpose, as he lights the way and guides the feet of pilgrims through shadowy, snaky paths of danger and death (1:79). Such saving knowledge will come through two specific means: "*by*

61. The adverb ἀφόβως (*aphobōs*, "without fear"), placed first for emphasis in the Greek clause, modifies the verb λατρεύω (*latreuō*, "serve").

62. On the meaning of λατρεύω (*latreuō*), see BDAG, 587: "'work for pay, be in servitude, render cultic service' . . . in our lit[erature] only of the carrying out of religious duties, esp. of a cultic nature, by human beings."

63. Again, see an extensive discussion of this key question below on 12:1–34.

the forgiveness of their sins" and "*by* the tender mercy of our God" (1:77–78). The latter emphasis on mercy (cf. 1:72) echoes Mary's song, though with some distinctive touches. Here the NRSV describes God's mercy as "tender" (also KJV, NIV, NAB, NASB). While a nice sentiment, "tender" does not, however, adequately capture the ancient image of "bowels/innards of mercy [σπλάγχνα ἐλέους, *splanchna eleous*] (1:78). The CEB comes closer with "deep compassion." But I suggest something more robust like "gut-level/gushing mercy."[64] At any rate, God's merciful dispositions, affections, and actions do not only attend to human social and material needs, as vital as these are; they also provide a nurturing environment in which people come to know fully the saving God. It is hard to learn anything when you're starving or besieged on every side. God's overflowing compassion elicits deep trust and understanding.

While Mary's notion of God's mercy, as argued above, does not appear to entail juridical pardon, Zechariah now closely links mercy with forgiveness in the process of knowing God's salvation. As prophet and priest, John will "prepare" people to know God's Messiah by "turning" them to the Lord's ways (1:16–17) and granting them "forgiveness of their sins" (1:77; cf. 3:3). But again, the stress on forgiveness in Zechariah's song falls not on avoiding punishment from God but on attaining knowledge of God. Sin inevitably veils divine knowledge and vitiates human flourishing. Forgiveness frees sinners to see the "light" of God that will "dawn from on high" and to walk with God in "the way of peace" (1:78–79). The image of "dawn" (ἀνατολή, *anatolē*) naturally reflects the "rising" (ἀνατέλλω, *anatellō*) of the sun and scripturally evokes the coming of God in the Messiah, as in a climactic text from Malachi: "And for you who fear my name a sun of justice shall rise [ἀνατελεῖ, *anatelei*], and healing is in its wings" (Mal 4:2 NETS).[65] Expounding on this key verse, Moltmann writes

64. σπλάγχνα (*splanchna*), always in the plural in the NT, designates "inner parts of the body, especially the intestines" (Louw and Nida, *Greek-English Lexicon*, 1:101) or "the viscera . . . entrails" (BDAG, 938). BDAG further notes: "As often in the ancient world, inner body parts served as referents for psychological aspects: of the seat of emotions" (938), like "gut feeling" or "heartfelt" in modern English (see, however, the vivid use of the image applied literally and negatively to Judas's death in Acts 1:18: "he burst open in the middle and all his bowels [σπλάγχνα, *splanchna*] gushed out"). The verb form σπλαγχνίζομαι (*splanchnizomai*) occurs three times in Luke at strategic points of emphasis (Luke 7:13; 10:33; 15:20). Through meticulous word counting, Menken ("Position") pinpoints the noun as the "central word" in the second segment of Zechariah's hymn (1:76–79) and the verb as marking the focal "turning point" of the resuscitation story (7:11–17) and parables (10:25–37; 15:11–32). Whether or not one buys Menken's numerical scheme, "deep compassion" stirs at the heart of divine activity in these passages. See further discussion of Luke's "Passional Theology" in the concluding "Integration" section.

65. Cf. Num 24:17; Jer 23:5–6; Zech 3:8; 6:12; Matt 2:9; and the helpful discussion in Carroll, 61–62.

that "Israel's God is . . . taking over the functions of the life-giving, healing, saving, and justice-bringing righteousness" of various sun-related deities (like Shamash) in antiquity.[66]

Finally, while Zechariah forecasts his son's destiny as an authoritative guide to God's saving knowledge, John himself must first be schooled and strengthened in such knowledge, as the narrator concludes: "The child grew and became strong in spirit, and he was in the wilderness until the day he appeared publicly to Israel" (1:80). This summary of John's spiritual growth and empowerment fits Gabriel's promise that John will be "filled with the Holy Spirit" from the womb, preparing him "to turn many . . . to the Lord their God," doing so "with the spirit and power of Elijah" (1:15–17). But again, though Spirit-imbued from conception, John will not spring from Elizabeth fully formed and ready to reform Israel. He must grow into his Spirit-anointed vocation through rigorous Nazirite discipline requiring, among other abstinences, "never drink[ing] wine or strong drink" (1:15), reminiscent of Samson and Samuel, also born to longtime barren mothers (Judg 13:4; 1 Sam 1:11; cf. Num 6:1–21). Spirit-dynamism and self-discipline go hand in hand in advancing the knowledge of God.

In John's case the discipline factor also sets the ascetic curriculum in a *wilderness* environment. This datum is more puzzling than revealing at this stage. Are we supposed to imagine young John thrown out into the wilderness to fend for himself (à la Hagar and Ishmael [Gen 16:7–14; 21:14–21]) or farmed out to some wilderness sect, like that at Qumran on the Dead Sea shore?[67] Hannah dutifully gave up young Samuel to priestly service in the sanctuary (1 Sam 1:22–28), but Gabriel demanded no such vow from John's parents, and they certainly do not volunteer to let someone else raise their son. Moreover, sectarian wilderness training and cultic sanctuary apprenticeship are quite different courses.[68] No doubt John's early wilderness experience previews his later base of operations (Luke 3:2–4 [see below]). But at this stage, it also keeps us from reducing Luke's story of John's nativity and childhood to a sentimental birthday card. Yes, John's life brings great joy to his aging parents and longing people. But

66. Moltmann, *Sun*, 128,

67. See the balanced discussion of 1:80 and the location of John's early life and ministry in Joan E. Taylor, *Immerser*, 42–48.

68. Joan E. Taylor (*Immerser*, 29–31) successfully refutes the suggestion that John's wilderness orientation marks a rejection of the temple system and/or its current corrupt leadership, like that promoted in the DSS. While the rank-in-file priest Zechariah struggles at first to accept God's word, he remains "righteous before God" (1:6) and scarcely represents a wicked (high) priesthood. Moreover, as we will see, Jesus's infancy and childhood are marked by positive, Torah-faithful experiences in the temple.

these remain perilous times, with much to learn and sort out in the wilderness before reaching the promised land.

Jesus's Birth and Childhood (2:1–52)

Luke continues to shift between scenes featuring the auspicious children, John and Jesus, and their respective parents. From John's birth (1:57), growth (1:80), and future mission sketched by father Zechariah (1:76–79), the spotlight moves to Jesus's birth and childhood and the continuing role of mother Mary. Joseph also comes on stage as Mary's husband and Jesus's stepfather, though he stays in the background with no lead part, as he has in Matt 1:18–25 and 2:13–23.

This section comprises three scenes: the first set in a Bethlehem residence, the last two in the Jerusalem temple. All three involve southward trips from hometown Nazareth in Galilee. From the start, Jesus assumes the life of a journeyer and exile within his own homeland, now colonized by Rome. The specter of Roman rule and the standard of Roman Imperial Time (RIT) loom large over the birth of Jesus. These are "the days of Emperor Augustus," who reigns over "all the world" in general and decrees a census in particular that forces Joseph and Mary to Bethlehem, with no consideration for Mary's advanced pregnancy (2:3–5). But Rome does not control everything, certainly not the glorious God of highest heaven, who blesses "all the people" of Israel with Lord Jesus Messiah (2:9–14). Moreover, within Roman-ruled Israel or Palestine (as Rome dubbed it), God's faithful ones, like Mary and Joseph, persevere in honoring God through rituals and festivals of faith (circumcision, purification, presentation, and Passover) set to Jewish Standard Time (JST):

> After eight days had passed, it was time to circumcise the child; and he was called Jesus. (2:21)

> When the time came for their purification according to the law of Moses, they brought him up to Jerusalem to present him to the Lord. (2:22)

> Now every year his parents went to Jerusalem for the festival of the Passover. And when he was twelve years old, they went up as usual for the festival. (2:41–42)

These were times of celebration, but also, given the present regime, times of potential conflict.

The seminal events surrounding Jesus's birth and childhood reveal much about the saving God to a number of characters. Parents Mary and Joseph, a band of nomadic shepherds, elderly prophets Simeon and Anna, temple teachers, and wider Judean audiences receive various signs (σημεῖον, *sēmeion* [2:12, 34]) disclosing God's messianic agenda. Signs are not sermons or seminars, however. They flash key messages but leave much to ponder, both pleasant and painful. Again Mary takes the contemplative lead, continuing to grow in wisdom, along with her special son (2:40, 52). But all is not meditative bliss. Mary mulls over the stunning signs she encounters with a range of roiling emotions, from soaring joy to searing anxiety (2:18–20, 34–35, 48–51).

Born and Blessed (2:1–20)

Mary's Magnificat boldly announced God's scattering the proud, upending the powerful, and divesting the rich in the interest of succoring the weak, uplifting the lowly, and aiding the poor. That is the grand messianic hope of reversal. But for now, political reality tilts in favor of mighty Emperor Augustus and cohorts. This Augustus scatters his subjects and asserts his authority for his own economic ends. Because of his census order, Joseph must travel at the worst possible time to register with his very pregnant fiancée in his ancestral Bethlehem hometown, a seventy-mile trek from Nazareth through hilly terrain.[69] It is hard to imagine a more "penetrating symbol of Roman overlordship"[70] than a census. Make no mistake: this head count has nothing to do with determining proper distribution of social services and civic projects; it is all about *taxation* rolls to stock imperial coffers, to make the rich richer—*not* send them empty away. Mary seems to have skidded back to the "lowest" rung on the socioeconomic ladder under the domination of lordly, "kyriarchal" rule,[71] literally reducing her to a registration number, if she counts at all.[72]

69. Cf. Bovon, 1:85: "The shocking character of the pregnant bride-to-be who travels with her fiancé should not be smoothed over; it is provoked by Luke."

70. Green, 122.

71. Derived from κύριος (*kyrios*)—designating "lord, master, owner"—"kyriarchal" was coined by leading feminist NT scholar Elisabeth Schüssler Fiorenza "to mean a social-political system of domination and subordination that is based on the power and rule of the lord/master/father" (*In Memory*, xix, and *But She Said*, 8–12, 121–25). The term has been widely adopted by feminist biblical scholars.

72. "He went to be registered *with Mary*" (2:5) may imply her individual enrollment in the census, as well as her accompaniment of Joseph. Though leaving the matter open, Brown (*Birth*) notes that Mary's registration "is not an impossibility in Roman practice" (396–97).

Davidic King and Shepherd (2:1–5, 8–11, 15–16)

But all is not as it seems in the Roman imperial "world [order]" (οἰκουμένη, *oikoumenē* [2:1]), as an alternative and superlative system breaks into view: the divine-royal "economy" of Israel's God operative through God's appointed "Son" from the Davidic line (cf. 2 Sam 7:13–14; Ps 2:6–7). The historical King David reigned with august power comparable to Caesar's centuries later, and when David functioned as God's faithful son, a "man after God's own heart" (1 Sam 13:14; Acts 13:22), he also ruled, unlike foreign despots, as the benevolent servant of God's people. Unwittingly, Augustus plays right into the Davidic drama by dispatching Joseph and Mary on their taxing journey to Bethlehem, where Mary will give birth to God's preeminent ruling Son. For Bethlehem is the quintessential "city of David" (Luke 2:4, 11), where David was born, raised, and anointed as king (1 Sam 16:1–13). The glory days of David thus seem poised for revival through the Bethlehem-born Jesus.

But note well: Luke's Jesus will reign as David did *when he truly followed God's heart*, which, as anyone familiar with OT history knows, was not all the time. There came a time, in fact, when David (and son Solomon) more mirrored than challenged rulers of Augustus's ilk: amassing wealth, expanding borders, flexing military muscle, building a name for oneself, and most evocative of current events in Luke, ordering a nationwide *census* to consolidate his own power and portfolio—which greatly displeased God (2 Sam 24; cf. 1 Chr 21)! The new son of David, who is also Son of the Most High God, is born on the low rather than lordly side of the census. The Lord Jesus Christ is first counted *among* the people, an essential qualification for merciful, empathetic rule.

The original David started out in similar humble circumstances, preparing him for kingly duty in God's eyes, against popular conceptions. Even Samuel was initially preoccupied with royal stereotypes focused on tall stature and handsome appearance. But reminded of the premium the Lord places on inward character, Samuel anoints the *shepherd boy* David to replace the self-serving Saul as Israel's king (1 Sam 16:1–13). Whether felling the Philistine hulk Goliath with bold trust in God and combative skills honed in protecting helpless sheep (1 Sam 17:34–37, 49–51) or fleeing the maniacal Saul with a ragtag band of "everyone who was in distress, and . . . in debt, and . . . discontented" (1 Sam 22:1–2), David proved his virtuous mettle on behalf of the vulnerable. This is the man after God's own heart, who at the highest point of his reign, proclaimed (in the hymn echoed by Zechariah): "You deliver a humble people, but your eyes are upon the haughty to bring them down" (2 Sam 22:28).

It is *this David* Luke evokes as a prototype for Jesus Messiah, not only in his Bethlehem birthplace, but also in the birth announcement to David-like "*shepherds*, living in the fields, keeping watch over their flock by night" (Luke 2:8). As dramatically as Gabriel appeared to Zechariah and Mary, "an angel of the Lord" shines in the darkness (cf. 1:79) and proclaims to these nocturnal shepherds: "*To you* [ὑμῖν, *hymin*] is born this day in the city of David a Savior, who is the Messiah [Christ], the Lord" (2:11). Jesus is first and foremost *their* Savior, Messiah and Lord. We see again how matter-of-factly Luke identifies Jesus with the same "Lord" (κύριος, *kyrios*) title owned by God, and also note the correlation with God the "Savior" (σωτήρ, *sōtēr*) extolled by Mary (1:47). As it happens, Augustus and other emperors regarded themselves as Savior and Lord, promoting these divine titles throughout the realm on coins, monuments, statues, civic centers, and all other manner of social media.[73] The point would not have been lost among roving Judean shepherds, some of whom had been displaced from their lands and recruited into rebel bands against Roman and Herodian overlords.[74] Many shepherds were seeking a true Savior and Lord who would support their interests—and lo and behold, God now provides them one in the city of Israel's most renowned revolutionary shepherd.

But as was asked of the newborn John, "What then will this child become?" (1:66), we inquire of the infant Jesus: "What kind of Savior and Lord will this child become?" The shepherds no doubt have their preferred programs, but the angel stakes a clear signpost: "This will be a sign *for you* [ὑμῖν, *hymin*]: you will find a child wrapped in bands of cloth and lying in a manger" (2:12). This sign is no mere directional device to get them to the right baby, but rather a *sign*ificant indicator of the messianic rule Jesus will establish. This is a Messiah comfortable in wearing ordinary cloth strips and hanging out at animal feed troughs. Mary deliberately sets up Jesus's nursery this way (2:7), which is exactly how the shepherds see him (2:16). Swaddling strips and manger crib are *defining signs* of this Messiah. So what do they mean?

73. See Crossan, *God*, 7–29, 104–10; Carey, "Book of Revelation," 161–64. Note, however, Galinsky's observation ("Cult") that "Savior" was "anything but unique to the imperial cult. *Sōtēr* had been a cult appellation for centuries—Zeus Soter, Artemis Soteira, and so forth. . . . They were civic cults and so was the imperial cult. The degree of effusiveness of the blessings attributed to the emperor would vary from individual cult to individual cult" (6).

74. Josephus reports a violent rebel-bandit movement against Rome in the first century led by the shepherd Athronges and his four brothers (*Ant.* 17.278–85; *J.W.* 2.60–65); cf. Shaw, "Bandits," 31: "The equation 'shepherd equals bandit' comes close to being one that is true for all antiquity"; Shaw, "Tyrants," 179–80.

Natal Clothes and Manger (2:6–7, 12, 15–18, 20)

Beyond their utilitarian functions of providing snuggly warmth and a place to sleep, the clothes and manger suggest God's visiting the world in the humblest, most common creaturely, of circumstances. The Davidic son figure in Wisdom of Solomon, for all his royal power and privilege, reflects on his earthy roots:

> I also am mortal, like everyone else,
> a descendant of the first-formed child of earth;
> and in the womb of a mother I was molded into flesh,
> within the period of ten months, compacted with blood,
> from the seed of man and the pleasure of marriage.
> And when I was born, I began to breathe the common air,
> and fell upon the kindred earth;
> my first sound was a cry, as is true of all.
> *I was nursed with care in swaddling cloths.*
> For no king has had a different beginning of existence;
> there is for all one entrance into life, and one way out.
>
> (Wis 7:1–6)

The origins of the Solomonic king from normal sexual intercourse ("the seed of man and the pleasure of marriage") do not apply to Jesus's supernatural conception. But otherwise, his fetal gestation over nine/ten months,[75] natural birth, *and swaddled care* follow common human procedure for princes and paupers, though we might imagine royal infants wrapped in softer, silkier cloths (cf. Luke 7:25). Thomas Phillips has suggested that Luke taps into Greek mythology surrounding the origins of gods like Ion and Hermes, appealing to their postnatal swaddling as proof of *divinity*: "Swaddling clothes take on important symbolic significance as a divine son establishes his identity as a true son of god."[76] But while Luke affirms Jesus's identity as God's Son and would welcome evidence supporting the idea that a swaddled infancy does not *disqualify* Jesus's deity, Davidic filial and royal images predominate in the Bethlehem story, thus commending the stronger Hellenistic-Jewish parallel from Wisdom of Solomon (Solomon = David's

75. A common view in antiquity tracked a normal pregnancy over ten lunar months (Winston, *Wisdom*, 162–64; Winston and Tobin, "Wisdom," 1357), though the six + three-month schedule in Luke 1:26, 56 still suggests a nine-month term.

76. Phillips, "Why Did Mary Wrap?, 37; cf. 29–42.

son and successor), emphasizing the king's affinity with *humanity*: "I also am mortal/human [ἄνθρωπος, *anthrōpos*], like everyone else. . . . nursed with care in swaddling cloths" (Wis 7:1, 5).

Common cloths are one thing for a royal infant; makeshift cribs are quite another. Mangers were scarcely preferred furniture in prime birthing suites; they were feed bins for draft animals, not fancy bassinettes for baby kings. While the manger where Jesus is laid might well be in the main room of a small residence where animals also slept and ate on cold nights (the story has no stable or inn), the atmosphere remains lower class and less than ideal. Mangers did not typically double as newborns' layettes; Mary lays Jesus in a manger only because "there was no [other] place [τόπος, *topos*] in the lodging-house [κατάλυμα, *katalyma*]" (Luke 2:7 AT).[77] A certain double dislocation or exile characterizes Jesus's beginnings: no hometown birth in Nazareth, and no household bedroom in Bethlehem.

At the beginning of Isaiah, one of Luke's favorite OT books,[78] the exilic element of the manger sign is reconfigured in relation to Israel's experience of *knowing God*—or rather, *not* knowing and remaining faithful to God:

> The ox knows [ἔγνω, *egnō*] its owner,
> and the donkey its master's crib [lord's manger: φάτνην τοῦ κυρίου, *phatnēn tou kyriou*];
> but Israel has *not* known me [ἔγνω, *egnō*],
> and the people have *not* understood me.
>
> (Isa 1:3 NETS)

Jesus's manger-birth not only signals his alienation from Roman rule in solidarity with his colonized people. It also serves as a prophetic sign of his people's alienation *from God's rule* because of *their waywardness*, from which God's Messiah seeks to restore them, *if* they will turn back to God as any ox

77. Cf. "no space in the lodgings" (Brown, *Birth*, 399–401, 670–71); "no space in their place to stay" (Carlson, "Accommodations," 326, 331–36). The only other NT use of κατάλυμα (*katalyma*) is in Mark 14:14//Luke 22:11, designating the "guest room" where Jesus and disciples have their last Passover meal. Bailey (*Jesus*, 25–37) supports this same meaning in Luke 2:7, imagining a typical two-room peasant home; accordingly, since the "guest room" is full with relatives registering for the census, Mary must give birth in the crowded "family room," where the animals also sleep and feed at night. Alternatively, Carlson ("Accommodations," 326, 336–42) suggests that the small guest space first served as a bridal chamber for the betrothed couple, which, however, proved too limited and isolated as a birthing room.

78. See Evans and Sanders, *Luke*; Pao, *Acts*. On Isa 1:3 and Wis 7:4–5 as texts informing Luke's manger/swaddling clothes "sign," see Byrne, *Hospitality*, 32n3.

or donkey knows to return to its "master's crib." Israel continues to suffer in Luke's day as much from its own transgression as from the aggression of foreign powers; indeed, in prophetic-theological terms it loses its national independence, at least in part, *because* it asserts its arrogant independence from God the true King.

A key question thus arises, which will persist throughout Luke's narrative: Will exiled Israel see the sign of the manger, understand what it means, and know to return to God who meets them anew in Jesus Messiah? A Galilean village girl sees the prophetic sign in Bethlehem; indeed, she enacts it! (Luke 2:7).[79] Likewise, a band of roving shepherds working the graveyard shift see the sign, as the angel exhorts ("see/look!" [ἰδού, *idou*; 2:10]), and they head "with haste" to their Savior's crib (2:15–16). But will others follow their lead, not least Israel's religious and political leaders, more likely to ignore or harass lowly shepherds than heed their counsel? The shepherds do not keep the saving good news to themselves but make it known throughout the region (2:17, 20). Everyone who hears their report becomes "amazed" (2:18), but amazement does not guarantee *true saving knowledge*.[80] This emotion-laden response (astonishment, wonder, surprise) recognizes an extraordinary, but not necessarily salutary, occurrence. The unusual can spark as much fear as joy. Jesus's birth clearly elicits "great joy" (2:10), certainly among the shepherds, who continue "glorifying and praising God for all they had heard and seen" (2:20). But it remains to be seen how the wider audience's amazement will develop.

In any case, we must not miss the crucial epistemological point that God provides clues or signs as *means of knowing God and God's salvation*. But God posts revelatory signs on God's terms, rather than on human whims; signs are to be seen and perceived rather than sought or proposed (cf. 11:16, 29; 23:8). God marks the trail home for God's own, and notably, the main Lukan signs guiding God's people to the Messiah's first "home" are material and mundane—the stuff of *this embodied life and world*—more than heavenly phenomena. Yes, plenty of angelic fireworks supercharge Luke's Birth Narra-

79. Mary is the subject of all verb actions: "She *gave birth* to her firstborn son . . . *wrapped* him in bands of cloth . . . *laid* him in a manger." Like many OT prophets, she enacts a symbolic-theological drama. The angel simply gives stage directions for the shepherds to see what Mary has set up.

80. Cf. Danker, 61: "Their listeners 'wondered' (*thaumazō*), a normal response to description of divine actions (cf. Luke 1:21, 63) but not necessarily indicative of faith (cf. Acts 3:12). Wonderment can even be associated with unbelief (Luke 24:41). The contrast with Mary's response (v. 19) suggests that the person of Jesus will be subject to misunderstanding (cf. 4:22–24; 8:25; 9:43–45; 11:14–16)."

tive, but these are more background special effects than bedrock significant events. *The* sign of God's salvation, the main event to see and know, is that of a flesh-and-blood infant boy swathed in cloth strips made from plant fibers and lying in a wooden feedbox for working animals. We cannot know God fully unless we know God *there*.

Mary's Thoughts and Feelings (2:19)

Mary has come to know a lot about God through her placental nurture of God's Son, whom she then delivers into the world, wraps in cloth, and places in a manger. No one is more closely connected with God's signs than Mary. How does she interpret them? We're not sure, because she's not sure. We're simply told after the shepherds' remarkable visit that "Mary treasured [συνετήρει, *synetērei*] all these words and pondered [συμβάλλουσα, *symballousa*] them in her heart" (2:19).

Reminiscent of her double *dia*-response of "thinking *through*" Gabriel's announcement (1:29), Mary now exhibits a double *sym/syn*-response reflecting her determined striving to "pull/get it all *together*," to "toss them *together* in her heart," to integrate all the new words and events she's encountered in Bethlehem into a coherent whole.[81] More specifically, the first verb (συντηρέω, *syntēreō*) connotes "keeping with concern"[82] or "receiving and retaining the event, as much the deed that one sees as the words one hears."[83] It implies a deep cognitive-affective engagement with matters beyond what the mushy "treasuring in her heart" connotes.[84] Mary is not gushing with sentimental maternal pride or basking in a tender moment she will cherish forever. Far from feeling warm fuzzies about the shepherds' revelations about Jesus, Mary grapples with them like a wrestler, probing them, mulling them, struggling to wrench solid meaning from them.

She functions as a dedicated sage, like that described (of males) in Sirach, poring over wisdom traditions:

81. See Danker, 61 ("trying to get it all together"); Fitzmyer, 1:413 ("tossing them together in her heart"); Carroll, 71 ("turning them over and over in her heart"); and the discussion in Spencer, *Salty Wives*, 83–88, and "Woman's Touch."

82. Brown, *Birth*, 406.

83. Bovon, 1:92.

84. Note Gaventa's ("All Generations") objection to the "treasure" reading (NRSV, NIV, NASV) "suggesting that Mary was simply storing up sweet memories. But the evangelists are not usually sentimental, and what Mary does is not so much to 'treasure' as to 'ponder', to 'reflect', to 'worry'" (127).

> He will seek out the wisdom of all the ancients, and he will be preoccupied with prophecies.
> He will preserve [συντηρήσει, *syntērēsei*] the narrative [διήγησιν, *diēgēsin*] of famous men and he will penetrate into the twists of illustrations [parables (παραβαλῶν, *parabalōn*)].
>
> (Sir 39:1–2 NETS)

The parallel structure links "preserving" information with "penetrating"[85] its subtle significance—more specifically, preserving "the narrative of famous men" with penetrating the nuances of "parables." As it happens, Luke's opening verse identifies the entire Gospel as a "narrative" (διήγησις, *diēgēsis* [1:1]), which, as it unfolds, focuses on the singular hero Jesus and his revelation of God's wisdom through numerous challenging, and sometimes obscure, parables (cf. 8:9–10). Interpreting Luke thus requires patient, penetrating sifting of its dense message—like that exemplified by Mary.

The second verb (συμβάλλω, *symballō*) describing Mary's response carries similar overtones of deep, delving analysis. Moreover, as van Unnik observes, in Hellenistic literature the term relates to seeking "the correct meaning" (*die rechte Bedeutung*) of some divine sign in the face of ambiguous interpretive options.[86] This is no mere meditative exercise but rather a determined act of problem-solving and discerning the significance of God's dealings with the world. Far from daydreaming or musing about curious events, Mary engages her mind and "heart" (the center of will/purpose, along with thought and emotion) to ascertain the solid truth.

As her investigation of complex divine words/acts aligns Mary with *sages* like Ben Sira, it also associates her with *seers* like Daniel and *priests* like Levi and Josephus.[87]

- *Daniel.* In the wake of his tumultuous kingdom visions, culminating in the coming of "a son of man," Daniel reports: "My thoughts were greatly troubling me, and my appearance was changed, and I kept [συνετήρησα, *synetērēsa*] the matter in my heart" (Dan 7:28 [Theodotion] NETS). Such mental and physical upheaval pushes considerably beyond quiet reflection.
- *Levi.* After an angel unveils the enthroned "Holy Most High" and provides a sword and shield to "perform vengeance on Shechem for the sake of

85. Συνεισέρχομαι (*syneiserchomai*): another *syn*-verb + *eis* = lit. "coming/going in together."
86. Van Unnik, "Die Rechte Bedeutung," 75–91.
87. Van Unnik, "Die Rechte Bedeutung," 84–90; Danker, 61.

Dinah, your sister," the priestly patriarch Levi remarks: "And I guarded [συνετήρουν, *syneterōun*] these words in my heart" (T. Lev. 5:1–6:2 OTP). Straightaway, Levi puts "these words" into action by slaying Shechem, demonstrating a tight nexus between heart and hand.

- *Josephus*. Hunted by Roman forces during the Jewish War, the priest and military commander Josephus recalls repeated dreams in which God predicted his people's defeat. With his back against the wall, Josephus acts as an "interpreter [συμβάλειν, *symbalein*] of dreams . . . in divining the meaning of ambiguous utterances of the Deity" (*J.W.* 3.352 [trans. Thackeray, LCL]; cf. 3.340–54). Clearly, the situation calls for more than "throwing together" a few ideas. This is a crucial time for correct decision and action, for clarifying ambiguities to determine what God means and aims for Josephus to do.

The last two examples shade beyond cognitive reminiscence toward active obedience, toward "keeping God's commandments in one's heart."[88] The intent of such Torah-keeping is always productive rather than simply preservative, not just hearing but *heeding* God's word. Later, Luke's Jesus will stress this point, interestingly enough, in juxtaposition with an anonymous woman's adulation of Mary: "A woman in the crowd raised her voice and said to him, 'Blessed is the womb that bore you and the breasts that nursed you!' But he said, 'Blessed rather are those who hear the word of God and obey it'" (11:27–28).

Circumcised and Dedicated (2:21–38)

Knowing God in Luke comes not only through faithful obedience to God's word, but also through ritual observance of God's sacraments. Put another way, faith is experienced and expressed both in everyday practice and in established practices. Following Jesus's birth, his parents carry out two pairs of practices "written in the law of the Lord" (2:23) concerning firstborn sons. Although not designated as such, these practices effectively function as additional *signs* (signifiers) of truth about God and God's creative purpose.

88. This usage of συντηρέω (*syntēreō*) in the context of law- or commandment-keeping is prominent in Sirach (2:15; 6:26; 13:12; 15:15; 35:1; 37:12; 44:20).

Circumcising and Naming (2:21)

The first pair of rituals—circumcising and naming the infant Jesus on the eighth day (2:21)—matches those recently performed on baby John (1:59) and for past generations, beginning with Abraham and Sarah's son, Isaac. From the start, circumcision marked the fundamental "sign of the covenant"—the "everlasting covenant"—between God and God's people (Gen 17:9–14; 21:3–4). Fleshed out more fully, circumcision represented (1) a badge of ethnic-religious identity, (2) an act of gratitude for God's producing life in "barren" places, and (3) a pledge of trust in God's faithful sustenance. As God's anointed restorer of the covenantal promise to Abraham (Luke 1:55, 72–73; Acts 7:8), the blessed son of Mary must be circumcised on the eighth day, the first day of the "new" week. And what more apt name to give him than *Jesus* (Joshua in Hebrew), meaning "Savior" or "Deliverer," which defines his God-appointed vocation (Luke 2:11; cf. Matt 1:21). "Salvation" in biblical thought encompasses the fullness of God's covenantal love, steadfast mercy, and whole-making shalom. As Jesus lives up to his name in Luke's narrative, we witness God's salvation fully embodied in human experience and dynamically engaged in world-mending activity.

Purifying and Presenting (2:22–24)

The other two practices—purifying postpartum Mary and presenting firstborn Jesus—are performed about a month later in the Jerusalem temple. Though plausibly carried out during the same temple visit, these birth-related rites were not as closely linked as Luke suggests. He oddly refers to "*their* purification" for which "*they* offered a sacrifice" of two turtledoves or pigeons (2:22, 24). However, "purification" or "ritual cleansing" (καθαρισμός, *katharismos*) was not a family affair or group project, but rather the exclusive duty of the mother who first supplied and then shed her blood, at considerable risk to her own life, to bring forth the child into the world. Only she needed "cleansing"—not the baby and certainly not the father, biological or adoptive. Some scribal variants substitute "her" or even "his" (curiously) for "their" purification, but the manuscript evidence favors the plural reading. Perhaps Luke is a tad muddled about fine points of Jewish ritual observance.[89] Perhaps he simply aims to show family solidarity: these are devout, traditional parents, intent on raising their

89. See the careful discussion of the legal issues in Brown, *Birth*, 436, 447–51, 682–84; Bovon, 1:98–99.

child Jesus according to Jewish law. But still, *they* by no means bear the burden of purification equally, any more than the labor of parturition.

So what does ritual purification *signify* for Mary? Much misunderstanding persists in Christian circles about ancient Jewish purity laws. At base within early Judaism, ritual impurity or pollution did *not* entail sinfulness or dirtiness from which one must be forgiven or scrubbed clean.[90] Rather, it constituted a boundary state of apartness from the pure, holy God, reminding people not to take God's approachability for granted. They must come to God on God's terms, fit for God's presence. But such fitness did not demand incessant wholeness or perfection; humans, though created in God's image, could never attain full divinity. But God made clear provision for restored fellowship through various waiting periods and sacrificial offerings. In the course of daily living, most of God's people were impure in some way most of the time. But this was not normally an "evil" condition or deadly contagion. The "impure" could be easily "cleansed" and restored access to God in the temple, where holiness boundaries were most strictly enforced, through due ritual process. Even the priests who superintended the cult and submitted to the highest purity standards became "properly" impure after sexual emissions into their wives (that is how they got little priests)[91] and burial actions for deceased parents (that is how they honored dead loved ones [cf. Lev 21:1–3]). They did not then cease to be priests: like everyone else, they waited the required time, performed the required ritual, and got back to work—all the while mindful of their holy, set-apart service to God.

In Mary's case, the law required a forty-day period of "blood purification" after birthing a son, followed by priestly mediated sacrifices of a lamb plus a pigeon or turtledove, or alternatively for poorer folks who couldn't afford a lamb, two pigeons or turtledoves (notice the concern for bringing people from all social strata to God, not keeping them away; Lev 12:1–8). The lowly mother from Nazareth goes with the cheaper, but no less effective, avian option (Luke 2:24). Yet, this forty-day process from birthing to bird-offering marks something critical for Mary and all mothers: their numinous and ominous proximity with sacred borders of life and death.[92] The bleeding, birthing woman shares God's

90. See the positive and corrective discussion of Jewish biblical purity tradition in Levine, "Bearing," 501–4, and *Misunderstood*, 144–49, 172–77; and Knight and Levine, *Meaning*, 181–85.

91. I owe this witty insight to a panel presentation by Amy-Jill Levine at the annual SBL meeting, San Francisco, 2011.

92. Forty days = the seven-day period after giving birth + the thirty-three-day "time of blood purification" after birthing a male child (Lev 12:2–4). The forty days recall other momentous experiences in "thin places" between life/death, divine/human, heavenly/earthy, and sacred/ordinary realms associated with Noah (Gen 7:17–24), Moses (Exod 24:15–28; 34:27–28), Elijah (1 Kgs 19:8–12), and Luke's Jesus (Luke 4:1–2; Acts 1:1–3).

creative work in the most intimate way possible for a human being. Accordingly, such a glorious—and precarious—physical-and-spiritual state demands ritual representation, symbolizing the mother's set-apartness from and reconstitution of "normal" relations with God and God's community.

The baby Jesus needs no purification. As the "firstborn," literally, "the one who opened/ broke through the womb [διανοῖγον μήτραν, *dianoigon mētran*]," his dedication to God must simply be confessed ("every firstborn male *will be called* [κληθήσεται, *klēthēsetai*] holy to the Lord" [2:23 AT; cf. 1:35; Exod 13:2, 12–15]), rather than reconstituted with an offering. So Jesus is "presented," not "purified." Here set-apartness does not signify a *separation from* God to be reconciled but a *consecration to* God to be recognized and enacted throughout Jesus's life. As for Joseph, he's had nothing to do with Jesus's conception or birth and thus requires no purification or any other act (the same would be true of natural fathers). He's merely along for the rite, though his supporting role in accompanying Mary and the infant Jesus merits honorable mention.

Falling and Rising (2:25–38)

The temple dedication ritual is personalized by presenting Jesus before two venerable prophets, Simeon and Anna, who reflect by their different *genders* the inclusive community of God's people and by their advanced *ages* the long-awaited "consolation of Israel" and "redemption of Jerusalem" from centuries of foreign domination (Luke 2:25, 38; cf. Acts 2:17–18). They both praise God for finally setting in motion the wheels of liberation and allowing them to see God's liberating salvation embodied in the infant Christ. This saving knowledge is solid enough now for the elderly Simeon to "go in peace" (CEB) from this world, as he announces at the beginning of his Spirit-inspired song (the Nunc Dimittis [Luke 2:29]). From his perspective, the volatile border between life and death has been peacefully transcended by the Creator-Redeemer God through Jesus Messiah, making little difference which side he (Simeon) occupies. The world to come has gloriously intersected this world, not just for God's chosen prophets and people, but "in the presence of all peoples" (2:31).

Though shorter than Mary's and Zechariah's songs, Simeon's traces the widest scope of God's salvation. Mary's general rejoicing in God's "mercy from generation to generation" and Zechariah's proclamation of God's "light to those . . . in the shadow of death" explode into Simeon's crescendo, in the shadow of his own death, concerning God's life-giving "light for revelation to the Gentiles, and for glory to your people Israel" (2:32). Simeon strongly echoes Isaiah, but with a slight twist. God's saving plan of bringing "light to the nations" through

Israel reprises Isa 49:6: "I have made you a light of nations, that you may be for salvation to the end of the earth" (NETS; cf. 42:6; 51:4; 60:1–3). But Simeon's stress on the "revelation" or "unveiling" (ἀποκάλυψις, *apokalypsis*) of this liberating light for Gentiles (Luke 2:32) *counterpoints* Isaiah's shadow strain of God's "revealed" enforcement of *capital judgment* on foreign enemies in order to secure Israel's salvation: "And the Lord shall reveal [ἀποκάλυψει, *apokalypsei*] his holy arm before all the nations, and all the ends of the earth shall see the salvation that comes from God" (Isa 52:10 NETS).[93] Of course, the mighty hammer of God's arm to defeat Israel's enemies also resounds in Mary's and Zechariah's songs (Luke 1:51–52, 71–74). But Simeon opts to major on more universal salvation themes, uncomplicated by judgment.

This does not mean, however, that Simeon has turned soft and mushy in his old age. On the heels of his praise song, punctuated by a benediction of Jesus's parents (2:34a), he abruptly gives Mary another sign to ponder, more ominous than the swaddling clothes and manger. Simeon warns as much as he blesses:

> A Look, this child is destined for the falling and rising of many [πολλῶν, *pollōn*] in Israel, and to be a sign that will be opposed.
>
> B And for you, too, a sword will pierce your own life,
>
> A′ so that the thoughts of many hearts [πολλῶν καρδιῶν, *pollōn kardiōn*] will be revealed. (2:34b-35 AT)

Mary should not be relegated to a parenthesis (KJV, RSV) or addendum (NRSV, NIV) to Simeon's prophecy: she stands as its centerpiece in the Greek text, her destiny wrapped up with that of Jesus and the *hoi polloi* in Israel.[94] Though spotlighted, however, she is not ensconced on some unique pedestal. Her "blessedness" continues among, rather than apart from, the people, but still as an individual with her own "life" (ψυχήν, *psychēn*)," not as an iconic, representative figure.[95] She remains integral to God's plan *as* Mary of Nazareth, not as some idealized model of womankind or nationhood.

93. Isa 52:1–12 reinforces images of holy warfare against "unclean" enemy nations who threaten the comfort and salvation of Jerusalem. The wider section in Isa 40–66, however, holds in tension both redemptive and retributive plans for the "nations."

94. The NRSV completely obscures Mary's central position by reversing the second and third components in the Greek text and thus ignoring Luke's A-B-A envelope structure. Instead of placing Mary's destiny at the hub of Simeon's prophecy, the NRSV tacks it as an afterthought at the end, following a dash.

95. See Brown, *Birth*, 465: "Mary is not personifying Israel because most of Israel will fall; rather Mary here is part of Israel, to be tested like the rest" (cf. 687–88).

Moreover, it now becomes shockingly clear that Mary's "blessed" state will include conflict and suffering. Far from being protected in some blissful cocoon, Mary will feel sharp pangs like a sword ripping through her inner being. Yet, these painful experiences still suit God's blessed purpose. How so? The flanking points of Simeon's oracle fill out the picture.

First, he announces that Mary's child will represent an objectionable "sign" (σημεῖον, *sēmeion*) that unsettles many. This is the flip side of the shepherds' sign. Jesus Messiah bears a sandwich board, as it were, proclaiming, on one side, the gospel of salvation for lowly shepherd-types, signified by the swaddling clothes and manger (2:12); on the other side, the verdict of judgment and reversal, imaged by an up-and-down, fall-and-rise seesaw. Where the first sign inspired "great joy" (2:10), the second strikes a woeful chord for those who will stumble and "fall" over God's saving plan they refuse to embrace. And Mary will feel the piercing pain of their demise because of her deep awareness of the piston-like mechanics of God's work, not to mention her maternal heartbreak over the opposition that will be mounted against him.[96] She has already affirmed God's intent to bring down the powerful and lift up the lowly (1:52); while such scrambling of hierarchies ultimately promotes peace and justice, it is far from a smooth and painless process. Tidings of "great joy" and "peace on earth" do not tell the whole story (see discussion on 12:51). Mary exhibits an intellectual and emotional range wide enough to grapple with the complex whole of God's saving project.

Finally, Simeon connects Mary's soul-searching and soul-stabbing experience with the climactic "revealing" (ἀποκαλύπτω, *apokalyptō*) of many people's "inner thoughts [διαλογισμοί, *dialogismoi*]." The precise causal link ("so that" [ὅπως, *hopōs*]) remains ambiguous, but it suggests that Mary's psychic turmoil expresses and/or exposes others' internal disputations in some fashion. Some scholars, however, opt to dissociate Mary altogether from dubious "inner thoughts" (διαλογισμοί, *dialogismoi*), since elsewhere in Luke this term designates the machinations of resistant scribes and Pharisees (5:22; 6:8) or misguided disciples (9:46–47; 24:38) in contrast to the positive perceptions of Mary.[97] But the matter is not so cut and dried. We have already seen that Mary thought

96. Although Luke does not place Mary at the cross (as in John 19:25–27), that does not deny her natural maternal angst (*mater dolorosa*) over Jesus's sufferings. Cf. Gaventa, *Mary*, 66: "The piercing of Mary at least *includes* the pain involved in the death of Jesus. . . . Mary's absence at the crucifixion does not mean that it does not concern her or that Luke is unaware of its implications for her" (emphasis original).

97. For example, Brown (*Birth*) interprets "'inmost thoughts' entirely as thoughts hostile to Jesus, unbelieving thoughts, doubting thoughts," and thus ill fitting "Luke's general respect for Mary" (441. 465–66). Accordingly, Brown treats the Mary reference in Simeon's oracle as a "parenthetical" aside rather than, as I take it, integral and central to Simeon's message.

through Gabriel's perplexing announcement "dialogically" (διαλογίζομαι, *dialogizomai* [1:29]), posing hard questions and pondering strange answers in her quest for solid spiritual knowledge. Bland, airheaded acceptance of untested claims is no better than blind, pigheaded resistance to expounded truths. Young Mary sets a standard of "dialogic"[98] growth, challenging scribes, Pharisees, and disciples alike toward her model of progressive learning (discipleship). Perhaps her pressing through where they bog down is how she "reveals" the deficiencies of their inner thoughts. In any case, we should note that apocalyptic "revelation," which Simeon previously applied to Gentiles' salvation (2:30–32), now assumes a judgmental edge for those "in Israel" who "oppose" God and Mary's messianic son (2:34–35). Knowing God is a double-edged sword, cutting to the hearts of many for good and ill, for "rising and falling."

Lost and Found (2:39–52)

Having lingered over the year or so of chronological time involving the conceptions, births, and dedications of John and Jesus, Luke's narrative fast-forwards to a single episode in Jesus's childhood at age twelve (2:39–52) and then zips from there to the adult vocations of John and Jesus almost two decades later (3:1, 23). Luke offers nothing close to a comprehensive biography of Jesus's life. So we are left with gaps in Jesus's career, none more tantalizing than the so-called hidden years of his childhood and adolescence. The apocryphal Infancy Gospel of Thomas steps into the breach with a number of fantastic Superboy tales of the budding Messiah, but the canonical Gospels refrain from such legendary license—except in Luke's singular showcase of the precocious twelve-year-old Jesus in the temple (2:41–52; cf. Inf. Gos. Thom. 19).

However, while Luke's sole snapshot from Jesus's youth features an "amazing," genius-style Wunderkind (2:47–48), he is careful to frame this special picture within a normal pattern of intellectual, spiritual, and social development in Nazareth before and after his temple display.

> They returned to Galilee, to their own town of Nazareth. The child grew and became strong, filled with wisdom; and the favor of God was upon him. (2:39–40)

98. See Bakhtin, *Dialogic*: "The dialogic orientation of discourse is . . . the natural orientation of any living discourse. On all its various routes toward the object, in all its directions, the word encounters an alien word and cannot help encountering it in a living, tension-filled interaction" (279). Consequently, "a passive understanding of linguistic meaning is no understanding at all" (281). As we have seen, Luke's Mary is no passive receptor of divine revelation.

> Then he went down with them and came to Nazareth, and was obedient to them. . . . And Jesus increased in wisdom and in years, and in divine and human favor. (2:51–52)

In short, Jesus's extended "home schooling" under his parents in Nazareth proves as formative, if not more so, for Jesus's maturation as a human being and divine agent as his intensive three-day seminar with the temple scholars in Jerusalem. While Jesus receives special insight from his heavenly Father that his earthly parents do not understand (2:49–50), his *full knowledge* of God, self, and others requires both divine and human nurture across the developmental stages of life. Only Luke provides the chronological note, "Jesus was about *thirty years old* when he began his work" (3:23)—in other words, another *eighteen years* after the temple incident. Jesus *grows in wisdom* over three decades before he's ready to begin his messianic work.

Given that bigger picture, we should not minimize the importance of this one incident from Jesus's childhood, particularly what it contributes to the pilgrimage of knowing God. The story unfolds in four short scenes.[99]

Scene 1: Searching for Jesus (2:42–45)

As Mary and Joseph had Jesus circumcised on the eighth day and consecrated in the temple "according to the law of Moses," so they journey to Jerusalem "every year" to celebrate Passover (2:41–42), presumably with their son in tow, given this festival's popularity as a family affair, befitting its commemoration of Israel's communal identity as God's "firstborn son" (see Exod 4:22). With the family's twelfth Passover, everything proceeds "as usual" (2:42) until Jesus's parents discover he is not among the travel party returning home. While readers know that Jesus purposefully "stayed behind in Jerusalem," Mary and Joseph "did not know it" for a whole day! (2:43). Although this ignorance might raise questions about the parents' attentiveness—how could they *not* know their son was missing for so long—in their tight-knit communal structure, it could easily be assumed that Jesus was "among the group of travelers" comprising "relatives and friends (lit. 'known ones' [γνωστοῖς, *gnōstois*])" from Nazareth (2:44). In a small-village network of trusted neighbors, parents didn't need to know where their children were every minute of the day. At any rate, the narrative doesn't blame Mary and Joseph for losing Jesus or leaving him behind: he chooses to stay in the temple without letting his parents know.[100]

99. I draw on Spencer (*Salty Wives*, 95–100) throughout my comments on this incident.
100. On this point and others in this incident, see Spencer, *What Did Jesus Do?*, 32–36.

Once they become aware of Jesus's absence, however, his parents diligently "search for" (ἀναζητέω, *anazēteō*) him, first among the caravan, and then back in Jerusalem for three days until they find him (2:44–46). Festival traffic would still be heavy in and around the city, making it difficult to find a lost boy, especially one who doesn't seem concerned about being found. But Mary and Joseph press on until they locate their son. This seek-and-find quest for Jesus, diligently handling his divine Father's "business" (2:49 KJV), hints at the critical pursuit to know God in the OT and Luke's writings. Examples abound in the three books closest to Luke's heart: Deuteronomy, Psalms, and Isaiah. To cite one passage each, all featuring "seeking/searching" (ζητέω, *zēteō*):

> And there you will seek [ζητήσετε, *zētēsete*] the Lord your God, and you will find when you seek him out [ἐκζητήσετε, *ekzētēsete*] with your whole heart and with your whole soul. (Deut 4:29 NETS)

> Let the heart of people who seek [ζητούντων, *zētountōn*] the Lord be glad. Seek [ζητήσατε, *zētēsate*] the Lord and be strengthened; seek [ζητήσατε, *zētēsate*] his face continually. (Ps 105 [106]:3–4 NETS)

> Seek [ζητήσατε, *zētēsate*] God, and when you find him, call upon him. (Isa 55:6 NETS)

This strain is echoed in Acts within the context of the Greek agora, challenging Athenian skeptics regarding the "unknown God" to "search [ζητεῖν, *zētein*] for God and perhaps grope for him and find him—though indeed he is not far from each one of us" (Acts 17:27).

On the flip side, God-in-Christ appears in Luke not only as one to be known and found by investigators, but also as initiating Searcher and Rescuer, driven "to seek out [ζητῆσαι, zētēsai] and to save the lost" (Luke 19:10; cf. 15:1–32).[101] No passive waiting around for the ignorant and wayward to find their way on their own, but an urgent outreach compelling the lost to seek-and-find the seeking-and-finding God. Ironically, in the present case, the young Jesus plays the role of the "lost son" his parents must find, and when they do find him, he seems less than sympathetic to their efforts: "Why were you searching [ἐζητεῖτε, ezēteite] for me?" he quips (2:49). Is this one of those matters he needs to grow into, or is the limited knowledge all on Mary and Joseph's side?

101. See the third main unit of this commentary: "Knowing God the Seeking Savior in the Travels and Parables of Jesus" (Luke 9:51–19:44).

Scene 2: Finding Jesus (2:46–47)

Mary and Joseph find Jesus not wandering the streets in a panic, but rather sitting comfortably "among the teachers" in the temple precincts. Most remarkably, he's sitting not at the scholars' feet but "among" or "in the middle of" (ἐν μέσῳ, *en mesō*) them (2:46), "amazing" them and the surrounding audience with "his understanding [συνέσει, *synesei*] and his answers" (2:47). At age twelve, Jesus holds his own with learned elders. Such precociousness confirms the grand promises regarding Jesus's birth and signals even greater things to come. Accounts of exceptional acumen in the childhoods of heroic national figures, like David and Augustus, were the stock-in-trade of Jewish and Greco-Roman biographers.[102] Epic heroes did not emerge out of the blue: they were born and bred for greatness. Even the apostle Paul could not resist an autobiographical reference to his "earlier life" of having "advanced in Judaism beyond many among my people of the same age" (Gal 1:13–14; cf. Acts 22:3; 26:4–5), though he confesses an overzealous application of his expertise in his younger years, incongruous with his divine calling "before I was born" (Gal 1:15).

So a story about Jesus's prodigious "advancement in Judaism" is scarcely surprising. It is more surprising that we have only one such incident in the canonical Gospels and that it is comparatively restrained, as such stories go. Luke's twelve-year-old Jesus demonstrates no brute superpowers, as does the lion-striking and Goliath-slaying young David (1 Sam 17:34–51) or the miraculous foot-healing, grain-multiplying, plank-lengthening, viper-vanquishing apocryphal child Jesus (Inf. Gos. Thom. 10:1–4; 12:1–4; 13:1–4; 16:1–2). Luke parades only Jesus's prescient intellectual and spiritual skills; and while these talents emerge at a youthful age, a twelve-year-old stood on the threshold of early manhood in this society. Luke's portrait thus differs sharply from the Infancy Gospel of Thomas's showcase of little Jesus's fantastic exploits from ages five through eight! Moreover, Luke's Jesus delivers no stunning oration in the temple episode, as nine-year-old Augustus purportedly did before a large crowd, drawing applause from respected elders (Nicolaus of Damascus, *Vit. Caes.* 3), or later, at age twelve, in eulogizing his deceased grandmother (Suetonius, *Aug.* 8).[103] Luke simply reports that Jesus listened to the teachers and

102. See Bradly S. Billings, "At the Age of Twelve," 73–75; Krückemeier, "Der zwölfjährige Jesus."

103. Bradly S. Billings, "At the Age of Twelve," 74–75. Overall, Billings's article provides a thoughtful comparative analysis between Luke's portrait of the adolescent Jesus and Augustus's auspicious youth. I do not agree, however, that Luke 2:40–52 stands out as an independent unit—"Neither in terms of style nor narrative sequence is it integral to what has preceded, nor to that which follows" (71; cf. Fitzmyer, 1:435)—or that Luke's primary audience comprises Gentile

engaged in Socratic dialogue, "asking them questions" and providing perceptive "answers." This is not to minimize Jesus's prowess or his interlocutors' and hearers' wonder (Luke 2:46–47). But he doesn't grandstand or speechify with rhetorical flourish. Rather, he first attends to the teachers' instruction and then lodges his own questions and answers. And Luke gives no hint of Jesus's insolent derision of his teachers, as we find repeatedly in the Infancy Gospel of Thomas, including his inquisitorial "interrogation" of the temple scholars in the parallel scene (Inf. Gos. Thom. 19:5; cf. chs. 6–7, 14–15).[104] Though Luke does not report that Jesus received any extensive rabbinic training, as Paul had under Gamaliel in Jerusalem (Acts 22:3), Jesus's brief tutorial with temple teachers demonstrates his willingness to learn from elders and to "grow in wisdom," along with receiving direct insight from "my Father" (Luke 2:49) and the Spirit of wisdom (cf. Wis 7:22–27). This temple incident thus provides our earliest snapshot of Jesus's developing knowledge of God.

Scene 3: Challenging Jesus (2:48–50)

Though the sages and wider audience respond to Jesus's conduct with "amazement"—which, remember, may or may not involve approbation—when his parents arrive, the scene clearly shifts to a sharper emotional tone. While an idyllic family tale might portray Mary and Joseph as, first, relieved to find their missing son and, then, bursting with pride at his brilliant temple display (that's our boy!), in Luke's more realistic story, they react with considerable paternal angst, appropriate to the family values of the day. They are more "astonished" (ἐκπλήσσομαι, *ekplēssomai*) than "amazed" at Jesus's behavior, the former term tilting more toward "dumbfounded,"[105] "shocked" (CEB), or even *ashamed* at their son's behavior. A displaced son was a disgraced son, who brought shame

Christians with little interest in Jewish matters (including a destroyed Jerusalem temple). Throughout this commentary I stress literary-narrative connections (amid tensions) and Jewish (as well as Roman) religious-political contexts.

104. "All eyes were on him, and everyone was astounded that he, a mere child, could interrogate the elders and teachers of the people and explain the main points of the law and the parables of the prophets" (Inf. Gos. Thom. 19:5 [trans. Hock, *Infancy Gospels*, 141]). Hock opts for the verb ἀποστοματίζει (*apostomatizei*) in the Greek-Slav and Greek C MSS, meaning "interrogate," over ἀποστομίζει (*apostomizei*) in Tischendorf A, meaning "put to silence." In the NT, the first verb appears only in Luke 11:53–54, where "the scribes and Pharisees began to be very hostile toward [Jesus] and to cross-examine [ἀποστοματίζειν, *apostomatizein*] him about many things, lying in wait for him, to catch him in something he might say." In 2:40–52, however, Luke gives no hint of the teachers' grilling the twelve-year-old Jesus with intent to trip him up.

105. BDAG, 308.

on his family. Independence represented insolence, rather than go-getting initiative Westerners admire today. Better that Jesus is "lost" in the temple with scholars than in a "far country" with pigs (cf. 15:11–16), but not as much better as we might think.

Mary minces no words about her frustration with Jesus: "Child [τέκνον, *teknon* (she reminds him of his place)], why have you treated us like this? Look [here] [ἰδού, *idou* (she demands his attention)], your father and I have been searching for you in great anxiety" (2:48). She engages Jesus on multiple levels: *intellectually*, asking him for a rational explanation; *actively*, reporting her extended search for Jesus; and *emotionally*, expressing her "great anxiety." The last component is particularly poignant: elsewhere in Luke's writings, the verb for experiencing "great anxiety" (ὀδυνάομαι, *odynaomai*) describes the rich man's being "in agony" in the flames of Hades (16:24–25) and the Ephesian elders' deep "grieving" over the departing Paul, whom they thought they would never see again (Acts 20:38). We may thus capture Mary's intense distress with the paraphrase: "Child, why have you put us through hell? We feared you were lost for good!" This is not some hysterical response on Mary's part. Any parent, ancient or modern, Eastern or Western, can sympathize (whether you lose a child in a temple compound, a bustling bazaar, or a shopping mall, the same panic buttons go off). Mary continues to respond as a full-blooded thinking, feeling, and acting subject. The fact that she vigorously engages Jesus as he begins to manifest his christological potential confirms a dynamic, dialogic dimension to her understanding of God's will.

However much we might appreciate Mary's angst regarding her lost-and-found son, Jesus is not so congenial in return. He coolly counters his mother's question with two of his own: "Why were you searching for me? Did you *not know* [οὐκ ᾔδειτε, *ouk ēdeite*] that I *must be* [δεῖ, *dei*] about my Father's interests?" (2:49).[106] This retort represents the first words Jesus utters in Luke. On one level, it reflects a typical adolescent chafing against parental authority; but on another level, it introduces Jesus's self-conscious loyalty to a higher power and wider family: that of his Father God. This initial use of "must" in Luke stresses the inexorable divine mandate on Jesus's life,[107] and the reference to "my Father" and "his interests" all but erases stepfather Joseph and puts mother Mary in a subordinate place under Jesus's heavenly Patriarch. Moreover, the

106. Following the alternative NRSV reading. The Greek literally and vaguely reads, "I must be in/about the things/matters of my Father [ἐν τοῖς τοῦ πατρός μου, *en tois tou patros mou*]." There is no reference to "house." Some scholars prefer a translation that includes both vocation and location: "I must be concerned with my Father's business in the temple"; cf. Hock, *Infancy Gospels*, 143n; Sylva, "Cryptic Clause."

107. See Cosgrove, "Divine *Dei*."

heretofore perceptive Mary seems to be no longer as "in the know" as she should be, reinforced by the narrator's comment that Mary (and Joseph) "did not understand [συνῆκαν, *synēkan*] what [Jesus] said to them" (2:50). So far in this episode, only Jesus displays true "understanding" (σύνεσις, *synesis* [2:47]). He begins to take his place as authoritative teacher of divine knowledge and doesn't seem to take kindly to any challenges to this vocation. At least in Luke it doesn't come to violence, as in the Infancy Gospel of Thomas, where on one occasion a teacher strikes little smart-mouthed Jesus on the head, prompting him to curse the instructor and render him comatose! (14:3–5).

Scene 4: Training Jesus (2:51)

While we might expect the "amazing," self-assertive Jesus to launch out now on his messianic campaign, he surprisingly returns home with his "unknowing" and "misunderstanding" parents and, even more strangely, submits himself to them as a dutiful, "obedient" son. For all his advanced knowledge and dawning awareness of his Father's business, he is not yet a fully formed paragon of wisdom. At age twelve he still must grow into his demanding roles as sage, prophet, Messiah, Savior, and Lord—all of which require an abundant measure of divine and human wisdom. As he must heed the word of his Father and the teaching of established scholars, he must also continue to learn from flawed parents whose ignorance about some things doesn't mean they know nothing. The biblical wisdom tradition exhorts all would-be "children" of wisdom (Luke 7:35) to honor and heed their mothers and fathers' instruction (Prov 1:8–9; 4:1–9; 6:20–22; 15:20; 23:22–25; 31:1–9, 26; Sir 3:1–16; 22:3–6).

In the case of Luke's Jesus, he surely has more to learn from mother Mary, who, from about the same age he is now and, indeed, from the moment of his conception in her womb, has been wrestling with God's saving work through her and her divine-incarnate son. As we have traced Mary's development, she has been *increasing in knowledge* by asking probing questions and contemplating mysterious events. There remains much she doesn't know, as the temple incident has just exposed, but she persists in her journey of "faith seeking understanding."[108] Yet again, she "treasured [διετήρει, *dietērei*][109] all these things in her heart" (2:51b). And yet again, the NRSV's "treasure" is off the mark in its implication of precious, misty-eyed memories. Simeon's prediction of sharp growing pains for Mary begins to be fulfilled in her anxious search for Jesus,

108. Anselm, preface to *Proslogium*; cf. Migliore, *Faith*, 2–7.

109. From διατηρέω (*diatēreō*), closely related to συντηρέω (*syntēreō*) in 2:19.

complicated by his enigmatic and dismissive response when found. Mary has a lot more now to search for and sift through in order to discern rightly the significance of all she's heard and seen. And Jesus, too, continues to have much to think and work through *with his mother* over the next eighteen years.

But beyond Jesus's attaining more information (he's already way ahead of the curve) is his learning *obedience* to parental authority (2:51a).[110] Jewish social and religious values were rooted in the parental home as the prime laboratory for faithful loyalty and obedience to Israel's heavenly Father (cf. Exod 4:22–23; 20:12; Deut 5:16; Hos 11:1; Mark 7:9–12). The adult Jesus will offer some nettling challenges to these values (Luke 8:19–21; 11:27–28; 12:49–53; 14:26–27), as he just did in the temple as a youth, but overall he obediently submits to Mary and Joseph as preparation for faithful obedience to his divine Father. Such abiding submission to God is not a foregone conclusion in Luke (cf. 4:1–13). Prodigious power, even in the service of God, remains susceptible to pride; hence, Jesus must learn and prove obedience. Tempering its lofty Christology, the writer of Hebrews offers this stunning assessment of Jesus's life: "Although he was a Son, he *learned obedience* through what he suffered, and having been made perfect [or mature], he became the source of eternal salvation for all who obey him" (Heb 5:8). While Jesus's prayerful struggle on Mount Olivet in the face of impending death seems most in view (Heb 5:7; cf. Luke 22:39–46), Luke pushes back Jesus's rigorous curriculum to include the "hidden" years from twelve to thirty.

Even for Luke's Jesus, knowing God does not stem from theological reflection or spiritual inspiration alone, as important as these are, but also from practical action sparked by a disposition of obedience to God and God's delegates. In narrative form, Luke concurs with the pastoral, pedestrian injunction of 1 John: "Now by this we may be sure that we know him, if we obey his commandments. Whoever says, 'I have come to know him,' but does not obey his commandments, is a liar, and in such a person the truth does not exist; but whoever obeys his word, truly in this person the love of God has reached perfection. By this we may be sure that we are in him: whoever says, 'I abide in him,' ought to walk just as he walked" (1 John 2:3–6). Luke's story of Jesus's youth ends with his walking back from his dazzling performance on the Jerusalem temple stage to backwater Nazareth with Mary and Joseph to live in quiet obscurity and diligent obedience to his earthly parents.

110. The verb is the passive form of ὑποτάσσω (*hypotassō*), meaning "be subject/submissive to, placed under the authority of," commonly used in household codes (Eph 5:21, 24; Col 3:18; Tit 2:5, 9; 1 Pet 2:18; 3:1, 5).

Jesus's Baptism and Temptation (3:1–4:13)

With the childhoods of John and Jesus marked by their "becoming strong in spirit" (1:80) and "increasing in wisdom" (2:40, 52), they appear poised to commence their God-ordained public missions as adults. But even around age thirty, "when he began his work" (3:23), Jesus undergoes further preparation and training. This section focuses on two major events, baptism (3:1–22) and temptation (4:1–13), spliced rather oddly by a genealogy (3:23–38). Along with the Father and the Holy Spirit, John the Baptizer (Baptist), as he now operates (3:2–17), and even the devil (4:1–13) all contribute to Jesus's final preparations. Moreover, a wider audience enters the story and starts to investigate God's saving work through John and Jesus. Crowds of people, including tax collectors and soldiers, become "filled with expectation and . . . questioning in their hearts," particularly about the identity of the Messiah (3:15). As authoritative angels and prophets have already revealed that Jesus is God's consummate Messiah (2:11, 26–38), so God, the Spirit, John, and the devil will all now confirm this fact. But questions persist among the people, not least, "What should we do" with this dawning knowledge of God's Anointed One?—a pivotal question asked three times of John by different groups (3:10, 12, 14). Knowledge of God continues to be certified and clarified by obedient action.

This section blazes a four-lane pathway to knowing God. First, the path leads to *conflict* with power brokers opposed to God's interests. Following the birth-story setting of "the days of King Herod of Judea" (1:5) and the census order of Emperor Augustus while "Quirinius was governor of Syria" (2:1–2), the cast of potential antagonists to God's rule extends in 3:1–2 to:

- Emperor Tiberius;
- Pontius Pilate, the Roman military governor of Judea;
- Herod Antipas, the Roman client-ruler and tetrarch of Galilee;
- Herod Philip, Antipas's brother and tetrarch of areas surrounding Galilee;
- Annas and Caiaphas, the Jewish priestly hierarchs; and
- various political and economic agents (soldiers, tax collectors) of these authorities (3:12–14).

This coalition of Roman, Herodian, and Jewish powers threaten God's saving work of lifting the lowly, feeding the hungry, and freeing the enslaved. In the present context, this opposition is typified by the "evil" Herod Antipas, who was "shutting up John in prison" for denouncing his illicit marriage to his brother Philip's wife (note the fraternal Herodian frame to John's mission in 3:1–2, 19–20). All of these worldly rulers come under the cosmic authority of the devil, who makes his debut in Luke by trying to lure Jesus into the tyrannical system as his viceroy (4:5–7). In the process of John's preaching and Jesus's testing, we learn much about God's right-ordering rule in Christ.

Second, the rocky path to knowing God runs through the *wilderness* or *desert* (ἔρημος, *erēmos*), the setting for both John's prophetic call (3:3–4) and Jesus's temptation crisis (4:1). From the days of Moses and Elisha at Sinai/Horeb (Exod 3; 1 Kgs 19) to the Desert Fathers in Egypt, the wilderness has served as an optimal site for divine encounter and spiritual growth. Sojourns off the beaten path and away from seats of power (Rome, Jerusalem, Tiberias, Caesarea) afford stark opportunities for gaining clearer visions of God's purpose for all creation.

Third, the wilderness path leads to the dramatic experience of *baptism* in water (a precarious resource in the desert) and Spirit (3:16, 21–22), closely linked to repentance, renewal, and immersion in God's saving realm (3:3, 8). In advance of discussing the sacramental significance of baptism below, we simply note now its central place in John's evangelical mission, as part of his "proclaim[ing] the good news [εὐηγγελίζετο, *euēngelizeto*] to the people" (3:18). While Gabriel and Zechariah forecast John's restorative vocation (1:16–17, 76–79), neither mentioned baptism as his chief mode of operation. Hence John's "Baptist" identity stands out as a new development, which will now define him throughout Luke's two volumes (7:28–30; 20:1–7; Acts 1:5; 13:23–25; 18:25; 19:3–4). More striking, however, is that along with "all the people," Jesus himself submits to John's baptism as a banner moment of divine fellowship and empowerment (Luke 3:21–22).

Finally, the desert path refreshed by baptism is illumined by *Scripture*, the written word of God. While we have tracked allusions to the Jewish Scriptures from the start of Luke's story, we now encounter the first "it is written" (γέγραπται, *gegraptai*) citations, charting, from Isaiah, John's wilderness-clearing way for God's salvation (Luke 3:4–6/Isa 40:3–5), and from Deuteronomy, Jesus's trek through testing terrain in undeterred (and undetoured) loyalty to God (Luke 4:4, 8, 12/Deut 8:3; 6:13, 16). Whether formally quoted or allusively intimated, the Scriptures represent for Luke the primary "script" for knowing the saving God. But when cited with the perfective "it is/has been written" introit, they assume a particular solemnity and solidity.

John Prepares the Way (3:1–20)

We left John as a growing boy in the wilderness setting (1:80), without knowing what happened there. We still wonder, "What then will this child become?" (1:66). Though we dismissed the suggestion of John's early rearing by a wilderness sect, it is quite possible that he took off on his own in his young-adult years to explore various religious paths, including desert spirituality. Josephus offers a suggestive parallel in his autobiography. Born into a priestly family (like John), Josephus distinguished himself around age fourteen as a precocious student of Torah (like Jesus) whom the temple leaders consulted on interpretive matters (*Life* 9). Then, from sixteen to nineteen, Josephus investigated three principal Jewish "sects" or "philosophies" —the Pharisees, Sadducees, and Essenes—and lived for an extended period in the desert with an ascetic guru named Bannus, known for his austere garb, diet, and habit of twice-daily bathing in cold water (*Life* 11). Ultimately, Josephus cast his lot with the Pharisees, but without disparaging the other groups. The parallel with John is tantalizing, suggesting that he, too, might have begun developing his desert-based, baptizing strategy with a Bannus-type mentor or some wilderness (Essene?) movement.

Whatever the precise background influencing John's ministry, it crystallized, according to Luke, when "the word of the Lord came to John . . . in the wilderness" (3:2), echoing the classic calls of Israel's biblical prophets, especially Elijah (1 Kgs 19:4, 9). The distinctive program of John's mission emerges: "He went into all the region around the Jordan, proclaiming a baptism of repentance for the forgiveness of sins" (Luke 3:3). The general wilderness setting is now pinpointed in proximity to the *Jordan River* (which flows into the Dead Sea), and John's action is consumed with itinerant preaching focused on repentance and forgiveness surrounding a rite of baptism. John becomes no Bannus-style hermit obsessed with his own purity baths; rather, he catalyzes a social and spiritual reform movement in Israel of Jordan-dipped recruits. To interpret this Baptist movement, we access three guiding biblical scripts, one from Isaiah concerning wilderness preparation, and two involving Joshua and Elijah/Elisha, respectively, in Jordan rites of passage.

Biblical Scripts (3:3–9)

First, Luke describes John's proclamation via *Isaiah* as "the voice of one crying in the *wilderness*," exhorting God's people to prepare "straight" and "smooth" pathways for the Lord who brings salvation to "all flesh" (3:4–6/Isa 40:3–5). Isaiah offers "comfort" to God's people in their "penalty term" of Babylonian exile served "for all [their] sins" (Isa 40:1–2). But now their sentence is finished, their sins forgiven, and a superhighway forged through rough desert terrain over which "our God" will lead the people back home (40:3–5). Later, in exile *within* the land ruled by Rome, the desert sect of Qumran Covenanters prepared for the irruption of God's kingdom on the basis of Isa 40:3: "Members of the Community in Israel . . . shall separate from the habitation of unjust men and shall go into the wilderness to prepare there the way of Him; as it is written [in Isa 40:3]. . . . This [path] is the study of the Law which he commanded by the hand of Moses . . . and as the Prophets have revealed by His Holy Spirit" (1QS 8:13–16).[111] This appropriation of Isaiah tracks a dead-end wilderness road—ending at the Dead Sea—where the faithful quarantine themselves *away from* "unjust" society and await God's final judgment on the wicked (cf. 1QS 9:18–21).

By contrast, John the Baptist employs Isaiah's script to call all Israel into the wilderness to "flee from the wrath to come [and] bear fruits worthy of repentance" (Luke 3:7–8), preparing them to turn around in their renewed state and march *back through the wilderness* to advance God's just and merciful ways *within* society. We will detail below what John requires of his baptismal candidates, but here we simply note that John has no interest in establishing a cloistered desert enclave, shielded from worldly affairs. While he has plenty to say about God's fiery judgment (3:8–9, 16–17), his apocalyptic message ultimately heralds the "good news" of God's salvation for "all flesh" and all creation. Raising every valley and razing every mountain to provide a level playing field for all (Isa 40:4–5/Luke 3:5–6) recalls the reversal program of Mary's Magnificat ("he has brought down the powerful . . . and lifted up the lowly"[1:52–53]) and "the falling and the rising of many" in Simeon's prophecy to Mary (2:34)—a great upheaval, to be sure, a veritable shaking of the unjust world order—but for the final end of restoration (not obliteration), of realizing God's full "salvation . . . prepared in the presence of all peoples" (2:30–31; cf. 1:76–77).

Second, an implicit script featuring *Joshua*, the first "prophet like Moses" (Deut 18:15–22; Acts 3:22–23; 7:37), also informs John's baptismal campaign at the *Jordan River*. Though the Qumran community had its spate of washing rituals, these were performed in carefully constructed and monitored stone pools. Moreover, archaeological evidence attests to many similar structures (*miqva'oth*) for ritual purification throughout Galilee and Judea.[112] Why, then, does John baptize in the common muddy waters of the Jordan? Part of the answer probably relates to Israel's historic fording of the Jordan under Joshua's leadership, capping off the people's exodus from Egypt and forty-year trek through the wilderness (Josh 3–4). Divinely engineered water-partings form the boundaries of this classic journey: first, across the Red Sea out of the alien land of bondage; and finally, across the Jordan River into the homeland of promise.

111. Trans. Vermes, *Dead Sea Scrolls*, 81. On the significance of Isa 40:3 in the Qumran community, see Joan E. Taylor, *Immerser*, 25–29.

112. E. P. Sanders, *Judaism*, 220–29; Crossan and Reed, *Excavating Jesus*, 168–72; Craig Evans, *Jesus*, 24–26.

This original trans-Jordan "conquest" of the land continued to carry symbolic power in John the Baptist's era. For example, Josephus reports that, while Fadus was governor of Judea (44–46 CE), a popular prophet named Theudas mobilized a throng at the Jordan River, promising to divide the waters at his command and lead the people safely across. Such a crusade had scant chance to succeed, for Theudas had no special water powers or military arsenal. But Fadus still sniffed the spirit of rebellion and dispatched a security squad that killed a number of Theudas's followers and captured the ringleader, cut off his head, and paraded it through Jerusalem (*Ant.* 20.97–99; cf. Acts 5:36). Fadus felt compelled to send a strong message to would-be dissidents; but what, pray tell, was the threat of a crazy, riverside rabble rouser? Theudas probably trumpeted a Joshua-style plan, backed by divine power, to dispossess Rome from the Judean homeland, to direct something of a "reverse conquest, a retreat into the wilderness in order to be purified and prepare the way of the Lord" or perhaps a "combination of exodus and conquest."[113]

John seems to enact his own theopolitical drama at the Jordan, leading the people to reenter and reclaim their ancestral land across the river. However, the crossing that John spearheads involves a process of individual submerging in and emerging out of the waters, signifying moral repentance and character reform, rather than miraculous transport through a dry riverbed.[114] Like Theudas, John poses no direct military threat to Rome. He exhorts the soldiers who seek him out to be content with their wages and not to extort the populace; he does *not* tell them to renounce Caesar, lay down their arms, and join John's brigade (Luke 3:14). But also like Theudas, John still loses his head for stirring up the people and fomenting revolution (3:18–20; cf. 9:7–9).[115]

Third, the *Jordan* symbolism is further enriched by associations with *Elijah and Elisha*. Among the historical narratives furthering the agenda of Deuteronomy (Deuteronomic History), the Elijah/Elisha segment in 1 Kgs 17–2 Kgs 9 proves to be fertile ground for Luke's reflection.[116] Prefiguring John's mission,

113. Horsley and Hanson, *Bandits*, 166 (cf. 164–67).

114. Typological connections are broad and suggestive, rather than precise and definitive. The patterns do not have to match up at every point. Other watershed biblical typologies may be seen in 1 Cor 10:1–2, where Paul compares Christians' baptism with "our ancestors [who] were all under the cloud, and all passed through the sea, and all were baptized into Moses in the cloud and in the sea"; and in 1 Pet 3:20–21, which envisions Noah's riding out the flood in the ark as "prefiguring" baptism and being "saved through water."

115. Josephus reports that Herod Antipas imprisoned and executed John the Baptist because of John's mounting popularity and potential to lead a mass rebellion (*Ant.* 18.118–19).

116. See Brodie, *Crucial Bridge*; Craig Evans, "Function"; Kloppenborg and Verheyden, *Elijah-Elisha*.

Elijah receives his final assignment: "The LORD has sent me to the Jordan" (2 Kgs 2:6). Standing on the riverbank with his protégé Elisha, Elijah parts the water with a strike of his rolled-up mantle, allowing the two prophets to cross on dry ground (2:6–8). This transition culminates in Elijah's chariot-chartered ascension to heaven and Elisha's succession as God's chief mediator. Elisha promptly wields his mentor's mantle (which had dropped off during flight) to divide and cross back over the Jordan, where a waiting band of prophets exclaims: "The spirit of Elijah rests on Elisha" (2:15). This statement closely resonates with Gabriel's announcement that John would prepare Israel for the Lord's coming "with the spirit and power of Elijah" (Luke 1:17). It is no surprise, then, that John picks up Elijah's mantle, as it were, at the Jordan and leads seekers through its baptismal waters to renewed life, even as Elisha restored health to a foreign leper (Naaman) by prescribing seven "cleansing" dips in the Jordan (2 Kgs 5:1–19; cf. Luke 4:27). John effects no miraculous physical cures, but he does precipitate changes of moral and spiritual character through his "baptism of repentance for the forgiveness of sins" (3:3).

Baptismal Requirements (3:10–17)

The purpose of John's baptism is *not ethnic-religious*. That is, he does not primarily target Gentiles for "proselyte baptism."[117] If some non-Jews, like the soldiers perhaps, approach John and meet his conditions for baptism, he welcomes them.[118] But he mounts no special campaign to make new converts. John focuses on reform *within* Judaism among fellow children of Abraham, whose covenant with God, John sharply reminds his audience, is fundamentally determined not by ethnic identity but by divine sovereignty ("God is able from these stones to raise up children to Abraham" [3:8]).

Furthermore, John's baptism is *not a cultic-legal* ritual. Though he has a priestly background, John operates as a prophet challenging the whole people of Israel ("crowds"), not the priestly leaders in particular.[119] He does not rail against the temple establishment or suggest that his baptisms should replace temple practices. He coordinates repentance and forgiveness with baptism but

117. See Joan E. Taylor (*Immerser*, 49–100) for a thorough contextual study of John's baptism in light of early Jewish ablution practices.

118. Luke leaves open in 3:10–14, 21 whether the tax collectors and soldiers who ask John for guidance actually follow through with baptism. Though 7:29 confirms that tax collectors were in fact baptized by John, soldiers are not explicitly mentioned; cf. Brink, *Soldiers*, 98–102, 169–70.

119. Contrast Matt 3:7–10, where John addresses "many Pharisees and Sadducees coming for baptism" (3:7). The Sadducees comprised the main party of priestly officials.

does not stipulate baptism as a *means* of sin-cleansing atonement. John's baptism functions more like a purity ritual, signifying separation *from* breaches of sacred life-and-death borders *for* renewed service to God.[120] Perhaps John envisaged his immersion act as a death-and-life, burial-and-resurrection performance, similar to Paul's image in Rom 6 (though Paul stressed dying-and-rising *with Christ*). But this goes beyond Luke's account.

What Luke does stress more than any Gospel is the *economic-ethical* thrust of John's baptism. People must turn or set themselves apart *from* life-diminishing practices of stinginess, greediness, and exploitation before baptism and commit themselves *to* life-supporting practices of generosity, fairness, and compassion after baptism. John gets down to the economic nitty-gritty with three groups, delineating exactly what they should—and should not—do (3:10–14):

> *Crowds:* Share extra coat with the naked and food with the hungry. (*Do not hoard and neglect.*)
> *Tax collectors:* Collect fair amount and no more. (*Do not cheat and bilk.*)
> *Soldiers*: Be content with adequate wages and provisions. (*Do not extort and harass.*)

We will meet each of these groups again in Luke, allowing us to monitor their compliance with John's economic plan, which not by accident, reflects basic Deuteronomic ethics (e.g., Deut 5:19; 15:7–11; 23:19–20; 24:6, 10–22) and what Richard Horsley has aptly dubbed biblical "covenant economics."[121] If God's people are to thrive in the land they "reenter," they must faithfully follow all of God's commandments promoting justice and mercy (cf. Deut 6:1–3).

John the first-century Judean "Baptist" vigorously advances a "social gospel" picked up by the nineteenth/twentieth-century American Baptist Walter Rauschenbusch and associates. Rauschenbusch rightly discerns that John's baptism, as Luke presents it, "was not a ritual act of individual salvation but an act of dedication to a religious and social movement."[122] However, John also packs a strong apocalyptic "fire-and-brimstone" punch largely eschewed by Rauschenbusch and company. John does not believe that God's just and peaceable kingdom will come *simply* by the efforts of God's faithful people. As important as an active turn toward social justice is in preparing for, even participating in, God's right-making rule, God must ultimately come to establish God's kingdom; and

120. Cf. above regarding Mary's purification in Luke 2:22–24.

121. Horsley, *Covenant Economics*.

122. Rauschenbusch, *Theology*, 197–98; see my much fuller discussion of "Social Theology" in the concluding "Integration" section.

given the diabolical entrenchment of antijustice forces, God must come with a blazing iron hand to smash the "crooked" and "high"-handed oppressors, "straighten" things out, and lift the lowly from their downtrodden "valleys" (Luke 3:4–6). Or God must come in God's mighty messianic agent, infinitely "more powerful" than John or any earthly authority. John serves merely as the advance man for this Messiah, who will surge beyond John's preparatory mission to baptize with torrential "Holy Spirit and fire" and gather a refined people into God's storehouse (3:15–17).

Jesus Prays and Is Baptized (3:21–22)

With John's firm disavowal of speculation concerning his own messianic candidacy, together with his declaration of the true Messiah's coming (3:15–16), we expect Jesus, whom we know to be God's Messiah-elect, to appear at any moment and get on with his work. Appear he does, but not yet in a grand launch of his liberating campaign. The only splash he makes now is a literal one in water, when he is baptized with "all the people" (3:21). As familiar as this incident has become over the centuries, we must not miss how problematic it was for the earliest Christians. If John is not the Messiah and his baptism of repentance prepares people to follow the Messiah Jesus on his "straight" path, why in the world is Jesus first baptized by John along with the repentant masses? This would seem to fuel rather than douse interest in *John's* primacy.

The Gospels address this conundrum in various ways. Matthew, for example, has John himself question Jesus's personal desire for baptism: "I [John] need to be baptized by you [Jesus], and do you come to me?" John thus clearly knows his place in the arrangement. Jesus then eases John's mind by announcing that his (Jesus's) baptism fits into a "proper" pattern "to fulfill all righteousness," though without detailing how baptism does so (Matt 3:14–15). The apocryphal Gospel of the Ebionites takes a similar tack, though registering John's discomfort after he sees the dramatic signs attending Jesus's baptism: "Then John, falling down before Jesus, said, 'I beseech you, Lord baptize me!' But Jesus forbade John, saying, 'Let it be so; for thus it is fitting that all things be fulfilled.'"[123] Focusing more on elements of repentance and forgiveness, the Gospel according to the Hebrews has Jesus respond to his mother and brothers' attraction to John's mission: "In what way have I sinned that I should go and be baptized by him? Unless, perhaps, what I have just said is a sin of ignorance."[124]

123. Cited from Epiphanius, *Pan.* 30.13.7–8, in Throckmorton, *Gospel Parallels*, 14.
124. Cited from Jerome, *Pelag.* 3.2, in Throckmorton, *Gospel Parallels*, 14.

Luke deals with the matter more subtly through narrative structure rather than direct statement by Jesus. Just *before* reporting Jesus's baptism, Luke wraps up John's story and even previews his imprisonment by Herod. As John is shut up in jail (3:20), he is effectively shut out from Jesus's baptism, which is reported in the passive tense *without* a designated baptizer ("when Jesus also had been baptized [βαπτισθέντος, *baptisthentos*]" [3:21]). While the focal setting remains John's baptismal mission, John himself has exited the stage. Luke's Jesus could thus be seen as undertaking self-baptism (like most ritual ablutions in early Judaism) in communion with the Heavenly Father, whose voice affirms Jesus as Beloved Son, and the Holy Spirit. Luke uniquely stresses that Jesus is "praying" (προσευχομένου, *proseuchomenou*)[125] during this event, thus reinforcing the dynamics of divine trinitarian fellowship.

The other special element in Luke's account—the Spirit's descent "in bodily form [σωματικῷ εἴδει, *sōmatikō eidei*]" upon Jesus—further solidifies and incarnates this divine activity (3:22). The Spirit is not embodied as essentially (ontologically) as is Jesus, the full-fledged, flesh-and-blood human being; the Spirit has an embodied "form/appearance *as* [ὡς, *hōs*] a dove" (3:22). Yet, as throughout the Bible, Luke is happy to correlate closely the Creator and creature, Maker and matter, spirituality and embodiment.[126] As the theologian Elizabeth Johnson observes, the Syriac tradition of early Christianity has long envisioned the Spirit in maternal avian images representing God's "brooding" care over her children and their environment, as the divine Spirit-Breath hovered over the watery depths at creation (Gen 1:2).[127] Augustine reinforced this interpretation, comparing the Creator Spirit in Genesis to an egg-producing-and-hatching hen, "where that warmth of the mother's body in some way also supports the forming of the chicks through a kind of influence of her own kind of love" (*Gen. imp.* 1.36).[128] Viewed in this maternal-creational light, Jesus's baptism is less self-administered than Spirit-generated, just like his conception in Mary's womb. In effect, Jesus is baptized by the Holy Spirit (not by John), who engulfs, fuels, and indeed "forms" (as Augustine suggests) him for his Spirit-driven ministry, which will include, as John proclaims, Jesus's baptizing others with this very Spirit who baptizes him (3:16; cf. Acts 1:2, 5, 8).

As much as Luke spotlights the distinct, intimate fellowship Jesus the Son enjoys at his baptism with God the Father and the Holy Spirit, this is not to denigrate the prophet John or to demarcate Jesus sharply from John or the

125. Present participle, suggesting durative action.

126. Cf. Mark S. Smith, *How Human Is God?*, 3–24.

127. Elizabeth A. Johnson, *Ask the Beasts*, 139–40.

128. Cited in Elizabeth A. Johnson, *Ask the Beasts*, 140.

people. John has his significant, yet subordinate, place in the unique work of Jesus Messiah, whose sandal strap John readily admits he is "not worthy to untie" (Luke 3:16). John prepares the way and the people *for* Lord Jesus, not Lord Jesus for his mission. Jesus is not John's star disciple who eventually surpasses his master; in other words, John does not mentor Jesus in Luke, however plausible such tutelage might be historically.[129] Not unlike the adolescent incident in the temple, Jesus's adult baptism in the Jordan asserts his prime filial devotion to and dependence upon his *heavenly Father*, who speaks directly to him and to whom he is directly responsible: "You are my Son, the Beloved; with you I am well pleased." Above all, Jesus answers to his Father, who "pleases to choose" (εὐδόκησα, *eudokēsa*) the Son for special service, as Michael Peppard understands the language in 3:22.[130] But just as the twelve-year-old Jesus continued to learn from his earthly parents, so the more mature Jesus can continue to learn from John (cf. Luke 7:24–35; 16:16; 20:1–8) and to grow in solidarity with, rather than isolation from, "sinful" people seeking baptism. However negligible John's role as baptizing agent might be, the *communal fellowship* with other baptized persons is crucial. Luke in fact subsumes Jesus's particular baptism under the general baptism of the people, not the other way around: "Now [1] when *all the people were baptized*, and [2] when Jesus also had been baptized" (3:21). Moreover, as Richard Vinson notes, Luke's report of the Spirit as "bodily" descent on Jesus suggests a public, visible event witnessed by the original crowd and paradigmatic for subsequent embodied experiences of baptism in water-and-Spirit.[131] The trinitarian "communion of the Holy Spirit" nurtured by "the grace of the Lord Jesus Christ" and "the love of God" is an *open, communitarian* fellowship embracing all of God's people through baptism (cf. 2 Cor 13:13).

Jesus Relates to Adam (3:23–38)

Reinforcing this interplay of human and divine communities, Luke tracks Jesus's family line from Joseph back to "son of Adam, son of God" (3:38). At first blush, this genealogy appears to mark a glaring glitch in Luke's otherwise "orderly" arrangement (cf. 1:1, 3). Surely Matthew has the better idea: present

129. See the extensive discussion of John's role as Jesus's "mentor" in Meier, *Marginal Jew*, 2:17–233.

130. Peppard (*Son of God*, 106–12) makes a strong case that εὐδοκέω (*eudokeō*) in the LXX and NT has a strong *elective* connotation: not simply "pleasing," but "pleasing *to choose*" (often by God) for some purpose, such as special leadership (cf. Isa 42:1; Ps 151:4–5 LXX; 1 Macc 14:41–47; Gal 1:15; Col 1:19). Cf. Shrenk, "εὐδοκέω."

131. Vinson, 104.

Jesus's family tree at the beginning before unfolding the story (Matt 1:1–17). So, too, the Chronicler (1 Chr 1–9), but *not* in fact the book of Genesis, which splices ancestries of Adam and Noah at key points within the narrative (Gen 5, 10). We may be confident, then, that Luke has an "orderly" purpose in slotting Jesus's genealogy between his baptism and his temptation.

The baptism link turns on Jesus's identity as "Son." Having reported God's out-loud affirmation of Jesus as Beloved Son (3:22), Luke now certifies that this filial bond is not a momentary "adoptive" status but a permanent relationship from the beginning of creation, extending back to "son of Adam, son of God" (3:38). Moreover, Luke clarifies this primordial lineage through two introductory features. First, the opening statement literally reads: "Jesus *himself was beginning* [αὐτὸς ἦν Ἰησοῦς ἀρχόμενος, *autos ēn Iēsous archomenos*] around thirty years of age" (3:23). Though not in the Greek, adding "his work" (NRSV) or "his ministry" (NIV) to "beginning" is a logical gloss. How could Jesus "begin" at age thirty, especially since Luke has narrated Jesus's nativity and childhood at some length? But Jesus's unmodified "beginning" here may still suggest either/both (1) a new beginning for Jesus, a beginning again, supercharged by the fresh anointing of God and the Spirit at his baptism; or/and (2) a tight nexus between Jesus's earthly ministry and God's creative work "from the beginning"[132] through Adam and his descendants traced in the genealogy. Reflecting on the sweeping arc of God's involvement in human history through Christ and the Spirit, Moltmann uncovers what we might call an "archtheology"—a theology of beginnings—befitting Luke's portrait of Jesus: "I discovered that in every end a new beginning lies hidden. It will find you if you look for it. Do not lose heart!"[133]

Second, while Matthew tracks Jesus's lineage forward from Abraham to Joseph and Mary, Luke moves backward from Joseph (no mention of Mary) to Adam and God; and from the start Luke specifies that Joseph's paternity was only "thought" or "supposed" (ἐνομίζετο, *enomizeto* [3:23]), not actual or natural. Though perhaps seeming to undermine the whole genealogical claim, in fact Jesus's adoptive relationship to Joseph's ancestry clarifies and expands the picture. Legally, adoption does not entail second-class status: adoptees enjoy full rights and privileges of family membership (cf. Rom 8:14–17; Gal 4:5–7).[134] Moreover, adoption effectively extends the kinship pool beyond direct genetic relations. In Jesus's case, the adoptive Joseph link not only incorporates him into the line of Israel's major covenantal figures, David (3:31) and Abraham

132. See ἀπ᾿ ἀρχῆς (*ap' archēs*) in Luke's prologue (1:2), situating Jesus's story within the panoramic sweep of history "from the beginning" of God's creative word; cf. J. A. Sanders, "Isaiah in Luke," 19.

133. Moltmann, *In the End*, 35 (see throughout).

134. See the helpful discussion in Peppard, *Son of God*, 50–85.

(3:34); it also opens familial access to Jesus Messiah for all people regardless of bloodlines, for all "children of Abraham"—whom God is able to raise up "from stones," if need be (3:8)—for all "sons of Adam, sons of God," which is *everyone*.[135]

The Lukan Jesus's universal genealogical connection with Everyman (Everyone) resonates with the philosopher John Rawls's influential theory of justice. Rawls grounds his theory in an ideal social contract presuming every citizen's common "original position." This position proposes "an imagined situation of primordial equality, when the parties involved have no knowledge of their personal identities, or their respective vested interests, within the group as a whole."[136] To maximize the goal of achieving "justice as fairness," Rawls clarifies the "original position" with two concepts: (1) the "veil of ignorance," behind which no one knows what place or identity they will have in society in terms of class, ethnicity, gender, religion, politics, or any other marker: in other words, since they could be *anyone*, they must think about justice for *everyone*; and (2) the "difference principle," by which conditions of social justice "must be to the greatest benefit of the least advantaged members of society" in order to guarantee "fair equality of opportunity" for all.[137] The feminist philosopher Susan Moller Okin helpfully explicates these points:

> The veil of ignorance is such a demanding stipulation that it converts what would, without it, be self-interest into equal concern for others, including others who are very different from ourselves. Those in the original position cannot think from the position of *nobody*, as is suggested by those critics who then conclude that Rawls's theory depends upon a "disembodied" concept of the self. They must, rather, think from the perspective of *everybody*, in the sense of *each in turn*. To do this requires, at the very least, both strong empathy and a preparedness to listen carefully to the very different points of view of others.[138]

I suggest that Luke's genealogy of Jesus back to Adam establishes Jesus's integral connection with all humanity in the "original position" and thus his capacity for realizing social justice for all persons, not least the least of these.

135. What about women? Mothers and daughters were subsumed, but rarely specified, in typical Jewish patrilineal genealogies. Luke follows the pattern, unlike Matthew, who boldly singles out four Gentile foremothers of Jesus along with Mary (Matt 1:3–6, 16).

136. An apt summation of Rawls's viewpoint by Sen, *Idea of Justice*, 54. Rawls's major works expounding the "original position" include *Theory of Justice*; *Political Liberalism*; and *Justice as Fairness*.

137. Rawls, *Political Liberalism*, 291.

138. Okin, *Justice*, 100–101 (emphasis original).

We are poised to see how Jesus plays out this "position" in his ministry. But I also detect a critical theological difference from Rawls's political theory. Rather than assuming a "veil of ignorance," Luke's Jesus operates from a stronger standpoint of what we might call a *vein of cognizance*. As both Son of God and son of Adam, as one imbued by the Holy Spirit as much as embodied in flesh and blood, Jesus *knows* what humanity created in God's image and enlivened by God's breath needs to thrive; or better put in progressive terms, Jesus is steadily *getting to know* the full dimensions of divine-human fellowship (cf. 2:52).

The trajectory propels toward cognizance that overwhelms ignorance in the interest of God's saving justice for all. John's Gospel advances the point earlier and without qualification: "Jesus . . . knew all people and needed no one to testify about anyone; for he himself knew what was in everyone" (John 2:24–25). Hebrews comes closer to Luke's developmental view, though in a context of Jesus's high-priestly calling not supported by Luke (John, but not Jesus, has priestly lineage): "For it is clear that [Jesus] did not come to help angels, but the descendants of Abraham. Therefore he had to become *like his brothers and sisters in every respect*, so that he might be a merciful and faithful high priest in the service of God. . . . Because he himself was tested by what he suffered, he is able to help those who are being tested" (Heb 2:16–18). It is to such empathetic testing that the Spirit now leads Jesus in Luke.

Jesus Resists the Devil (4:1–13)

If we were ready for Jesus to launch his messianic campaign after John's stirring press release announcing Jesus's powerful coming (3:16), we are near bursting with anticipation after his fresh infusion with the Spirit at his baptism (3:21–22) and full inclusion in the line of all humanity created by God (3:23–38). "Full of the Holy Spirit" (4:1), surely Jesus is now ready to launch his saving mission. But still—not yet. For this same Spirit first directs him not into a place of ministry, but deeper into the desert for an intense forty-day boot camp under the devil's charge. Whatever independence he might have gained from his parents and John the Baptist, Jesus continues "being led" more than leading: he "*was led* by the Spirit in the wilderness" (4:1); "the devil *led* him up" (4:5); "the devil *led* him to Jerusalem" (4:9 NIV)—all forms of ἄγω (*agō*, "lead, bring") or its cognate ἀνάγω (*anagō* ["lead, bring up"]). The Spirit permits, yea directs, Jesus to undergo testing by the devil himself to see how Jesus will hold up under fire, but more than that, to see how Jesus will *use his Spirit-power*: to serve selfish interests or those of Father God and God's needy children? It is one thing to say at age twelve (or thirty): "I must be about my Father's business" (2:49 KJV). It is another to see how Jesus actually manages God's business in the face of power's potential to corrupt great men greatly. A "son of" adulterer-murderer *David* (Luke 3:31) who betrayed his vocation as God's appointed shepherd-king (2 Sam 11:1–12:15), of heel-grabber *Jacob* (Luke 3:34) whom God had to slow down and shape up into the eponymous Israel (Gen 32:22–32), and of food-grasper *Adam* (Luke 3:38) whose flouting of God's authority epitomizes overweening human pride (Gen 3:6–7) cannot be too vigilant in resisting the corrosive temptations of power.

The connection between Jesus's genealogy and temptation becomes clear: is Jesus the divine-human "son of Adam, son of God" up to the task of redeeming his human ancestors, of succeeding where they failed in being a faithful steward of God's powerful gifts? Shrewdly, the devil plays up Jesus's divine nature—"If you are the Son of God" (Luke 4:3, 9)—trying to get him to spurn his obedient relationship to his Father and to mark out his own realm, his own turf, which will not only distance him from serving God but also from saving fellow humankind. In short, the devil aims to wreck Jesus's redemptive mission from the start by preoccupying him with his own status and privilege.

But Jesus will not bite. He unequivocally rejects all three of the devil's deals.

- First, though "famished" after his extended wilderness fast, Jesus refuses to zap stones into bread (4:1–4). While he will later mediate the creative power of the Spirit to feed hungry crowds (9:10–17), he refuses to work a culinary miracle for his own benefit. God will provide for his needs in God's way; in the meantime, Jesus will not manipulate divine power for his own ends. It is a slippery slope—today a loaf of bread, tomorrow a fancy suit of clothes, the next a winter palace (cf. 7:25)—all at the expense of the hungry, naked, and homeless in need of God's loving care.
- Second, though entitled to sit on "the throne of his ancestor David" and "reign over the house of Jacob forever" (1:32–33) and enticed by the devil's hypnotic flash "in an instant [ἐν στιγμῇ χρόνου, *en stigmē chronou*] [of] all the kingdoms of the world" (4:5),[139] Jesus will receive his kingdom from God according to God's ways, means, and timetable, not the devil's machinations.[140] And most critically, on the throne as much as on the way to it, Jesus will remain the loyal servant of the one Lord God of Israel and the world (4:5–8).

139. Cf. Garland, 182–83: "The kingdoms flash across the screen, as it were, like a commercial trying to entice his interest with a dashing display of their glory and allures."

140. Following the Davidic pattern: though David had multiple opportunities to slay the pursuing Saul and take the kingdom (which was rightly his by divine choice) for himself, he patiently waited for God to deal with Saul and establish David's reign.

- Third, though Luke's Jesus will face severe threats from hostile forces—demonic, military, judicial, and religious—ultimately leading to his execution, he will not call upon divine power to "save himself" (cf. 23:35, 37, 39). God will protect him until the time appointed for his death, and beyond that, resurrect him on the third day. But Jesus will not force God's hand, certainly not in some daredevil leap off the temple pinnacle presuming a safe landing under the escort of an angelic parachute squad. Such a stunt might titillate the crowds, but it will do nothing to liberate them. It is a blatant travesty of God's saving care for those who really need it: "Do not put the Lord your God to the test" (4:12).

In this triad of critical issues concerning (1) personal provision, (2) political priority, and (3) physical protection, Jesus proves himself faithful to God where both Adam in the garden and Israel in the wilderness had failed, as the following chart sketches. In other words, Jesus proves himself to be the right-making redeemer of Israel and all humanity.

Setting	Issue	Devil's temptation	Deuteronomy's principle	Israel's experience	Adam's experience
Judean wilderness	Personal provision	Magically turn stones into bread for personal food	"One does not live by bread alone" (Deut. 8:3)	Complaining about food; receiving manna from heaven	Consuming the only food God did *not* provide for him
Top of the world	Political priority	Worship the devil in exchange for worldly rule	"Fear the Lord your God, serve him only" (Deut 6:13 NIV)	Worshiping golden calf while Moses met with God on mountain	Grasping to be more "like God" and serving the creature more than Creator
Temple pinnacle	Physical protection	Jump off in expectation of miraculous rescue	"Do not put the Lord your God to the test" (Deut 6:16)	Testing God "ten times" in the wilderness (Num 14:22; cf. Deut 8:3)	Presuming—against God's clear directive—the tempter's claim, "You will not die" (Gen 2:17; 3:4)

While Adam and Israel both remain in view (as in the genealogy), Luke primarily shapes the temptation narrative in light of Israel's wilderness trek and temple worship. The wilderness strains particularly resound in the forty-day period of testing (analogous to Israel's forty-year ordeal) and Jesus's threefold citation from Deuteronomy, the critical bridge text between the Moses-led journey from Egypt and the Joshua-led entry into the Promise Land (Luke 4:2, 4, 8, 12).[141] Jesus's main mission relates to his own people. He embodies Israel's corporate vocation as God's "firstborn son" redeemed from slavery (Exod 4:22; cf. Hos 11:1) in faithful obedience to God's way outlined in Deuteronomy. While John prepared the way for a Joshua-style "reentry" into the land, Jesus will propel the way into God's realm, consummating the restorative mission of his namesake Joshua (see above).

Though Luke interprets Jesus's identity and ministry in close conversation with the biblical-theological story of God's dealings with Israel, he also, as we have seen, confronts the imperial-theological claims of the Roman Caesars. Though Jesus currently clashes with the devil, not the emperor, the devil's authority over "all the kingdoms of the world [οἰκουμένης, *oikoumenēs*]"—that is, the world-order, -economy, and -empire (Luke 4:5; cf. 2:1)—establishes a tight alliance between diabolical and imperial powers, or "domination systems."[142] Effectively, the devil proposes a managerial change while he retains ownership and control: "I'll give you Caesar's job, Jesus, provided you worship me and run things my way—as Caesar has!"[143]

Kingdom language is inherently political, and by resisting the devil's temptations, Jesus spurns Caesar's way of ruling and lays the groundwork for God's alternative, authoritative realm. We could add another column to the chart above, headed "Caesar's experience," which Jesus repeatedly resists. In the second (central) test, Jesus's stern assertion of exclusive loyalty to God (4:8) strikes at the heart of the imperial cult, which demanded, to various degrees in various places, worshipful service to Caesar as Lord, Savior, and Son of God.[144] Moreover, Rome's penchant for appeasing the exploited people with periodic gluts of "bread and circuses" (Juvenal, *Sat.* 10) fits right in with the first and last

141. On the connection with Israel's wilderness journey, see Stegner, "Temptation."

142. See Wink, *When Powers Fall*, 4.

143. Is the devil's emphatic claim to proprietorship of earthly kingdoms ("to me it has been given [ἐμοὶ παραδέδοται, *emoi paradedotai*]" [4:6]) valid or vacuous? A bit of both. As the sovereign Creator of all things, God remains "Father [and] Lord of heaven and earth" (10:21); hence, the devil has no ultimate right to rule. But in this flawed interim age before the restoration of God's realm, the devil has marshaled immense worldly power through wicked ruler surrogates; indeed, in some sense this power "has been given" to the devil, begrudgingly, *by God* during this evil age. Also, however, we must allow for the devil's overreaching deception, promising more than he can really deliver as a hook for his primary scheme to garner Jesus's worship.

144. On the complex phenomenon of the imperial Roman cult, see the incisive essays in Brodd and Reed, *Rome*.

temptations to produce bread stuffs from rock piles and to perform acrobatic stunts in the temple precincts. Luke's Jesus will feed the hungry (9:10–17; cf. 1:53) and forecast a grand messianic banquet (13:29; 14:15–24; 22:16, 29–30) as part and parcel of his core ministry of salvation, not as calculated measures of mollification. It is, again, a question of the use and abuse of power. As Warren Carter states:

> It is important to understand this concern with food within the context of the Roman imperial system. Food was about power. Its production (based in land), distribution, and consumption reflected elite control. . . . Quality and plentiful food was a marker of status and wealth . . . that divided elites from nonelites. . . . The latter struggled to acquire enough food as well as food of adequate nutritional value. . . . Food, then, displayed the injustice of the empire on a daily basis. The irony of this situation was that Roman propaganda claimed that one of the gifts of the Roman Empire to its inhabitants was fertility and abundance![145]

In the temptation scene, Jesus's commitment to counterimperial values is motivated by a different "rule of law." Instead of exploiting the system of Roman law, stacked in favor of elite patrons, Jesus submits to the law of God, the merciful and gracious Patron-Father, revealed in the Torah (cf. Exod 34:6–7; Num 14:17–19). Again he builds on the foundation of Moses and Joshua: "This book of the law shall not depart out of your mouth; you shall meditate on it day and night, so that you may be careful to act in accordance with all that is written in it" (Josh 1:8). Through Scripture, Jesus knows who God is and what God requires. The only words Jesus utters throughout the temptation are the Deuteronomy mandates. Forty days of desert battle with the devil allow for no rhetorical frills. "Basic training" (to borrow US military lingo) demands grounding in the basics; and nothing is more basic for Luke's Jesus than Scripture—not as a cheap formula for success (quote three Bible verses and victory is yours!)—but as *thoughtful theological and ethical challenges* to the devil's nefarious claims.

The devil also plays the Bible game, quoting a psalm text in the final test that legitimately affirms God's comprehensive protective care (Luke 4:10–11/Ps 91:11–12) but applying it in an illegitimate, frivolous fashion divorced from the psalm's address to "you who live in the shelter of the Most High, who abide in the shadow of the Almighty" (Ps 91:1–2)—*not* you who dive off pinnacles

145. Warren Carter, *Roman Empire*, 109–10.

without a parachute![146] Using Scripture as a pathway to knowing God demands continuing, critical discernment in the face of persisting opposition. The devil loses the first three rounds, but he's not done fighting Jesus; he merely "departs from him until an opportune time [καιροῦ, *kairou*]" (4:13). Along this precarious way, Luke's Jesus must continue to live "not by bread alone," but "by every word that comes from the mouth of God," to complete the thought Jesus affirms from Deut 8:3 (cf. Matt 4:4).

146. Cf. Green, 195–96.

Knowing God the Liberating Savior in the Teachings and Miracles of Jesus (4:14–9:50)

Empowered and examined, anointed and tested, Jesus is finally ready to embark on his public saving mission. He begins this work in hometown Nazareth and remains anchored in "all the surrounding country" of Galilee (4:14), until shifting his sights southward toward Jerusalem (9:51). Not surprisingly, given his early engagement with the temple scholars, Jesus spends much of his time teaching in local synagogues (4:15–16, 31–33, 44; 6:6), homes (5:17–19, 29–30; 7:36), and various outdoor venues, including a boat on a lakeshore! (5:1–3; cf. 6:17–18; 8:4; 9:10–11). Such authoritative instruction (4:32) provides a principal avenue to knowing God and God's will for the crowds and disciples in Luke's narrative, *if* they "pay attention to how [they] listen" (8:18).

We may divide the Galilean phase of Jesus's mission into three units, each beginning with a key block of teaching or proclamation:

- *Proclaiming the Freedom of Jubilee* (4:14–6:16): beginning with Jesus's first sermon in the Nazareth synagogue (4:16–30).
- *Leveling the Field of Opportunity* (6:17–8:3): beginning with Jesus's extended lecture on various topics from a "level place" (6:17–49).
- *Cultivating the Fruit of Salvation* (8:4–9:50): beginning with Jesus's first substantive parable and interpretation, illustrating the significance of hearing, holding, and heeding God's word (8:4–15).

Closely intertwined with Jesus's teaching is his working of miracles to meet people's needs, specifically: healing disease and disability (4:38–40; 5:12–26; 6:6–11; 7:22), raising the dead (7:11–17, 22; 8:49–56), delivering from demonic oppression (4:31–37, 41–42; 8:26–39), calming a perilous storm (8:22–25), and feeding a hungry crowd (9:10–17). Multiple summary statements stress the combination of Jesus's didactic and therapeutic work:

> One day, while he was teaching . . . the power of the Lord was with him to heal. (5:17)

> They had come to hear him and to be healed of their diseases; and those who were troubled with unclean spirits were cured. (6:18)

> Soon afterwards he went on through cities and villages, proclaiming and bringing the good news of the kingdom of God. The twelve were with him, as well as some women who had been cured of evil spirits and infirmities. (8:1–2)

> Then Jesus called the twelve together and gave them power and authority over all demons and to cure diseases, and he sent them out to proclaim the kingdom of God and to heal. (9:1–2)

The nexus between Jesus's teaching and miracle-working highlights (1) the extraordinary authority of Jesus's words and (2) the revelatory function of Jesus's mighty deeds. On the one hand, Jesus's words are effective in the most literal sense: not simply instructive and persuasive, but also invigorating and performative, *effecting* saving ministry. Jesus's dynamic word works! Indeed, his first miracle flows naturally from his teaching in the Capernaum synagogue: the same word "he spoke with authority" to the assembly he uses to "rebuke" a disruptive demon possessing a man in the audience (4:31–35). Jesus thus sparks a buzz among the congregation: "What kind of utterance/word [λόγος, *logos*] is this? For with authority and power he commands the unclean spirits, and out they come!" (4:36). On the other hand, all of Jesus's miracles, whether or not directly generated by Jesus's word, serve as dramatic signs or visual aids of Jesus's teaching about the saving God. A miracle is worth a thousand words, prompting as much reflection by observers as rejoicing by beneficiaries. The response of the disciples after Jesus stills the tempest (with a word!) is typical: "They were afraid and amazed, and said to one another, 'Who then is this, that he commands even the winds and the water, and they obey him?'" (8:25). So together, Jesus's teaching and wonder-working forge a dual track to exploring, probing, and knowing the saving God more fully.

Repeated uses of the verb σώζω (*sōzō*) in various contexts display the multifaceted dimensions of God's salvation mediated through Christ's dynamic speech and actions.[1]

1. See Spencer, "Narrative," 131–33.

- *Healing* a man disabled by a withered hand, in order "to save [σῶσαι, *sōsai*] [his] life" (i.e., he can now resume employment) (6:9–10), and a woman afflicted by a bleeding disorder, so that she might be "made . . . well [σέσωκεν, *sesōken*]" (8:48).
- *Resuscitating* the deceased "only son" of a widow (7:11–17), reminiscent of Elijah's ministry (4:25–26; 1 Kgs 17:17–24), and the corpse of the "only daughter" of a synagogue leader after Jesus announces to despairing mourners: "Do not fear. Only believe, and she will *be saved* [σωθήσεται, *sōthēsetai*]" (Luke 8:50; cf. vv. 49–56).
- *Exorcising* a "Legion" of demons from a tormented man (8:26–39) and a seizure-inducing spirit from the "only child" of a desperate father (9:37–43). In the former case, the Legion horde evokes oppressive Roman forces; in turn, this healed/saved (ἐσώθη, *esōthē* [8:36]) man inspires hope for political-national freedom.
- *Forgiving* the sins of a paralyzed man (and enabling him to walk) (5:17–26) and those of a woman of dubious reputation with "many sins" comparable to a massive debt (7:36–49); ultimately Jesus declares the woman "saved" (σέσωκεν, *sesōken*) and dispatches her in the way of "peace" (7:50).
- *Sowing* the seed of the "word of God" in people's hearts so they might "believe" the message, allow it to take root and bear fruit in their lives, and thereby "be saved" (σωθῶσιν, *sōthōsin* [8:12; cf. vv. 11–15]).

In a synonym, we may identify God's salvation in this section with *liberation*: liberation from disease and disability (*healing*), from death and decay (*resuscitation*), from demonic and foreign oppression (*exorcism*), from sin and debt (*forgiveness*), from immaturity and futility (*fruitfulness*). Luke's Jesus foregrounds this liberating theme in his programmatic citation from Isaiah, stressing the release/freedom (ἄφεσις, *aphesis*) of the captives/oppressed in a New Jubilee Year, starting "today"! (Luke 4:18–21/Isa 61:1–2; 58:6; see discussion below).

Though we might expect widespread enthusiasm over the launch of such a propitious messianic campaign, in fact Jesus's fellow Galileans are not sure what to make of his mission. Wonder and amazement are laced with ignorance, ambivalence, and even antagonism at times. What appears to be a promising start among Jesus's Nazareth friends and relatives ends in shocking rage against him (Luke 4:28–29). Satanic forces know full well the liberating power of God's Son (4:34, 41; 8:28), but this awareness scarcely stops them from trying to undermine his work (8:12; cf. 4:1–13). Moreover, not only Jesus's hometown folk but also pious legal experts (Pharisees and scribes) and even his chosen disciples fail to grasp the significance of his saving words and deeds, even vehemently rejecting them on occasion (5:4–9, 17–26, 30–33; 6:1–11; 7:39–49; 8:22–25; 9:12–17, 32–34, 43–50).

Sensing this persisting communication problem, Jesus assures his disciples, both male and female, and "a great crowd . . . from town after town" (8:4) that, while his "mysterious" (μυστήρια, *mystēria*) teaching about God's realm may initially be missed or misappropriated by many hearers (8:10; cf. Isa 6:9–10), ultimately nothing is "hidden . . . that will not *become known* [γνωσθῇ, *gnōsthē*] and come to light" (Luke 8:17). Still, such knowledge will not come easily and may even be concealed for a time from Jesus's closest associates (9:45). Understandably, the most difficult point for them to accept is Jesus's forecast of betrayal and death on a cross for himself—and his followers—as the paradoxical path to salvation: "If any want to become my followers, let them . . . take up their cross daily and follow me. For those who want *to save* [σῶσαι, *sōsai*] their life will lose it, and those who lose their life for my sake *will save* [σώσει, *sōsei*] it" (9:23–24; cf. 9:21–22, 44–45). God's liberating life somehow pulses through, not simply rescues from, cruciform loss. Comprehending that enigma requires not only considerable divine insight but also concerted human effort: "Pay attention to how you listen," or more literally, "See how you hear [βλέπετε . . . πῶς ἀκούετε, *blepete . . . pōs akouete*]" (8:18). It is going to take all senses on deck to solidify true knowledge of God's saving work in Christ.

Proclaiming the Freedom of Jubilee (4:14–6:16)

Thus far we have heard from Luke's Jesus only in a brief exchange with his parents in the temple (2:48–49) and in a private debate with the devil in the wilderness (4:3–12). As he now launches his ministry in the synagogues of Galilee (4:14–15), he gives his inaugural public speech in hometown Nazareth (4:16–27), setting the agenda for his messianic campaign.[2] Prefacing a full discussion of this landmark speech below, we note a strong freedom theme that Jesus appropriates from Isaiah, trumpeting "the year of the Lord's favor" (4:18–19/Isa 61:1–2), otherwise known as the Year of Jubilee, a semicentennial season of release from debt, slavery, and other impingements on liberty (see Lev 25:8–55).[3] With great urgency, Jesus heralds: "Today this [Isaiah] scripture has been fulfilled in your hearing" (Luke 4:21), which is to say: "Today inaugurates a New Jubilee Year!"

2. Cf. Tannehill, *Narrative Unity*, 1:61, and "Mission," 4.

3. The core theme of "release" or "liberty" (ἄφεσις, *aphesis*) links the foundational Jubilee text in Lev 25:10–13 (LXX) with Isa 61:1–2/Luke 4:18–19; cf. Spencer, "Jubilee," 428.

More than simply signaling, however, that another golden Jubilee anniversary has rolled around on the calendar, Jesus implies that the S/spirit of Jubilee is being "fulfilled" in the climactic way envisioned by Isaiah following Israel's exile. "Today" or "this day" (σήμερον, *sēmeron*) in Luke, starting with the angel's proclamation of the Messiah's birth to the shepherds (2:11), often marks not just the current chronological day, but rather the at-last eschatological day of the Lord, the consummate realization of God's redemptive purpose (4:21; 5:26; 13:32–33; 19:5, 9; 22:34, 61; 23:43; Acts 4:9; 13:33). "Today's" moment is truly momentous. Luke's Jesus has a keen sense of operating within God's eternal, salvific "now." He would happily agree with the apostle Paul, also inspired by Isaiah's hope: "See, now is the acceptable time; see, now is the day of salvation!" (2 Cor 6:2; Isa 49:8).[4]

Jesus has now clearly attained solid knowledge of his central role in advancing God's saving work. In breathtaking fashion, he identifies himself as the Spirit-anointed prophet of liberation announced by Isaiah: "The Spirit of the Lord is upon *me* . . . he has anointed *me*. . . . He has sent *me*" (Luke 4:18). Jesus embraces this dynamic divine mission, revealed in Scripture, as his own. As in his temptation crisis, the Bible functions as Jesus's manifesto: the platform he will execute fully authorized by God and energized by the Spirit. But for all of his confidence (faith) in God's "anointing" ("christening" [ἔχρισεν, *echrisen*; 4:18]), Jesus is also aware that others are not so eager to accept him and that he must faithfully demonstrate his liberating ministry in word and deed. Moreover, though leading the way, Jesus does not pretend to usher in God's restorative rule by himself alone: this will be a team effort, a community project. Three passages in this first segment of Jesus's Galilean mission feature Jesus's calling twelve "disciples" ("learners, students" [μαθηταί, *mathētai*]) or "apostles" ("sent-ones, delegates" [ἀπόστολοι, *apostoloi*]; 5:1–11, 27–32; 6:12–16). At first glance, his choices seem surprising, if not suspect, drawing his first followers from the ranks of fishermen (5:9–11), tax collectors (5:27–29), and Zealots (6:15), hardly elite members of society and particularly known for their associations with "sinners" (5:8, 30–32). However, this profile fits perfectly with Jesus's avowal to bring the gospel of God's salvation to the suffering and sinful:

> I must proclaim the good news of the kingdom of God to the other cities also; for I was sent for this purpose. (4:43)
>
> Those who are well have no need of a physician, but those who are sick; I have come to call not the righteous but sinners to repentance. (5:31–32)

4. The same adjective δεκτός (*dektos*), meaning "favorable" or "acceptable," is used in Luke 4:19 ("year of the Lord's *favor*") and 2 Cor 6:2 ("*acceptable* time").

Not everyone, of course, especially those of the social establishment, is thrilled with such a "sinner"-focused campaign. How Jesus negotiates these tensions is a major theme of this section.

Setting the Liberating Agenda and Alienating the Local Assembly (4:14–30)

"All politics is local," as former US Speaker of the House Thomas ("Tip") O'Neill famously espoused. People's deepest concerns are rooted in their own homes and neighborhoods; if a program doesn't reach people where they live and work, it is unlikely to garner much support. We might also say that "all theology is local": not merely a metaphysical exercise of speculation, but a practical exhibition of God's character in our particular contexts. The typical structure of Paul's letters to local churches provides the template, commencing with *doctrine* (what we believe) and continuing consequentially ("therefore") to *ethics* (how we should behave) (cf. Rom 12:1). Living out faith in community is the constructive goal of theology. Negatively put, "Faith without works is dead" (Jas 2:17, 26).

As with Paul and James, the local theology advocated by Luke's Jesus is no private, sectarian project, but rather a robust localized (contextualized) engagement in *political theology* and *social gospel*.[5] He begins, as we have briefly discussed, in his local home synagogue, where he appropriates prophetic Scripture for his own Spirit-fueled, Jubilee-focused mission. But by the end of the event, Jesus pushes his agenda beyond the local community into international and cross-cultural milieus. And his homefolk, already befuddled by Jesus's initial claims, become downright belligerent over his "liberal" foreign policy.

Unpacking the details of this pivotal incident more fully, we start with its notable time and place signatures: on the *Sabbath* in the Nazareth *synagogue*. Foundational to the rhythm of Jewish life (JST) is the observance of every seventh day, sunset to sunset Friday-Saturday, as a sacred period of rest and worship, anchored in the two most formative events of biblical history, creation and exodus: God's resting on the seventh day from the work of world-making (Gen 2:1–3; Exod 20:8–11) and God's rescuing Israel from the inhumane condition of incessant slave-work (Deut 5:12–15). Accordingly, faithful Jews gather together every Sabbath to worship the Creator-Redeemer God.

5. I particularly have in mind the "political theology" advanced in numerous works by Jürgen Moltmann and the "social gospel" advocated by Walter Rauschenbusch. See the broader discussion in the "Social Theology" section of the concluding "Integration" section.

In Jesus's day such worship centered in the Jerusalem temple. But for most Jews who lived outside the city throughout Roman Palestine and the eastern Mediterranean world, weekly worship took place in local assemblies known as synagogues (συναγωγή, *synagōgē*) or places of prayer (προσευχή, *proseuchē* [Acts 16:13, 16]). The former term literally means "assembly, congregation, gathering"; functionally, such congregating could occur in a large home or a separate, purpose-built structure (cf. Luke 7:4–5). Common features of a synagogue service included prayers and the reading and exposition of Scripture, as we observe in the present scene (4:16–22; cf. Acts 13:13–16).[6] (Animal sacrifices were reserved for the temple altar.) Some synagogues even functioned as lodging centers for traveling Jews, as evidenced in this inscription from first-century Jerusalem: "Theodotus, son of Vettenos, the priest and *archisynagogos* [chief synagogue leader], son of an *archisynagogos* and grandson of an *archisynagogos*, who built the synagogue for purposes of reciting the Law and studying the commandments, and as a hotel with chambers and water installations to provide for the needs of itinerants from abroad, which his fathers, the elders and Simonides founded."[7]

So Luke's Jesus finds his proper place in the synagogue on the Sabbath, "as was his custom" (4:15–16; cf. 6:6). But as rooted as Jesus is in Jewish tradition, it doesn't mean he's a traditional figure supporting the status quo. In dynamic prophetic fashion, he seeks to revitalize his people, to "fulfill" God's saving purposes, to break the bonds of sin and suffering in this "year of the Lord's favor," starting "today" (4:18–21). This ordinary synagogue service in the sleepy hamlet of Nazareth proves to be anything but ordinary when Jesus takes his turn in expounding "today's" lectionary text.

This episode provides a paradigmatic sketch, not only of Jesus's liberating ministry, but also of his pedagogy and theology. While Jesus's few words to this point have affirmed his developing relationship with his divine Father (2:49) and faithfulness to the Torah (Deuteronomy in Luke 4:4, 8, 12), they do not amount to theological exposition. Now, however, he does not simply cite verses, as he did to the devil, but interprets them for himself and his people. As prophet, teacher, and theologian, he unpacks what he has come to know about God's saving work. And he does so with rhetorical flourish designed to persuade and provoke. Jesus wants his neighbors and relatives to know what he knows and be moved by it—which indeed they are, though not in the way Jesus hopes. He does not win the day here; his hearers do not fully grasp what he's disclosing.

6. See Philo, *Spec. Laws* 2.62, and *Moses* 2.216; Josephus, *Ag. Ap.* 2.175; m. Meg. 4:3; VanderKam, *Introduction*, 211–13; Murphy, *Early Judaism*, 276–78; E. P. Sanders, *Judaism*, 195–208; Meyers, "Synagogue."

7. See Meyers, "Synagogue," 252; Murphy, *Early Judaism*, 276–77.

The path to knowledge remains fraught with obstacles and pitfalls—and just about pushes Jesus over the cliff! (4:29–30).

Jesus's inaugural sermon proceeds through a three-stage text-and-commentary sequence based on two prophetic passages and one popular proverb. Audience response modulates from initially ambivalent to ultimately violent.

Jesus's First Prophetic Reference (Isaiah) and Commentary (4:16–22)

Jesus reads a blended text from Isa 61:1–2 and 58:6 announcing the Spirit-anointed vocation of God's prophet-servant. Then, at the poignant moment after he "sat down" in the posture of an authoritative teacher (cf. 2:46), with "the eyes of all in the synagogue . . . fixed on him" (4:20), Jesus brazenly affirms that "this scripture has been fulfilled in your hearing" (4:21). Effectively, Jesus claims that he is the one of whom Isaiah spoke.[8] The "me" on whom the Spirit rests is Jesus himself. He is the "anointed (ἔχρισεν, *echrisen*) one" (4:18), the christened one, the Messiah/Christ. The Spirit of God who engulfed him in the womb (1:35), imbued him at his baptism (3:21–22), and empowered him during his temptation (4:1, 14) now commissions him for messianic service.

Specifically, Jesus's Isaianic campaign enacts a five-point evangelical (εὐαγγελίσασθαι, *euangelisasthai* ["to proclaim good news/gospel"]) plan of salvation to bring:

1. Good news to the poor
2. Release (ἄφεσις, *aphesis*) to the captives
3. Sight to the blind
4. Freedom (ἄφεσις, *aphesis*) for the oppressed
5. Year of the Lord's favor (Jubilee) (4:18–19).

The strong liberation-redemptive thrust of this mission is signaled by the double use of ἄφεσις (*aphesis* ["release, freedom"]) and broad application to those in various states of physical, psychological, social, economic, and political distress: the poor,[9] the blind, the imprisoned—including those bound by overwhelming

8. Cf. Cyril of Alexandria, *Commentary on Luke*, Homily 12: "He expressly set himself before them in these words, as the person spoken of in the prophecy" (cited in Just, 81).

9. The poor *simpliciter* includes those materially impoverished, not only the "poor in spirit" as in Matt 5:3 (cf. Luke 6:20; 7:22). Though appreciating that the "blind" aided by Jesus incorporate the physically sight-impaired as well as the spiritually unenlightened, Eusebius more strictly interprets the "poor" in Luke 4:18 in light of Matthew's beatitude (*Proof of the Gospel* 3.1.88–89; see his comment on the "blind" below).

forces of demonization, debt, and domination. This is the hardcore material and social gospel of Jubilee, rooted in liberation of depleted land and enslaved people for the flourishing of God's entire creation.[10] We should not rush to a "spiritual" interpretation of Jesus's saving mission divorced from material realities.

But neither should we downplay the "spiritual" dimension, certainly not in a passage so patently inspired by the Spirit ("The Spirit of the Lord is upon me" [4:18]) and appropriated by one "filled with the power of the Spirit" (4:14). Common dichotomies in Western thought—secular/spiritual, social/spiritual, body/soul, material/metaphysical—are largely alien projections onto a biblical worldview, not least the NT view rooted in the incarnate Christ. Jesus embraces a mission that liberates the whole person, the whole community, the whole cosmos. His good news addresses the fullness of life in all its material and spiritual, political and religious dimensions.[11] On the more "spiritual" side, ἄφεσις (*aphesis*) applies to freedom and forgiveness from sin-debts, that is, moral shortcomings against God and one another (cf. 7:39–49; 11:4).[12] It is no accident that the ecological-economic Jubilee commences every fiftieth year on the annual *Day of Atonement* (*Yom Kippur*), dedicated to "mak[ing] atonement for the people of Israel once in the year for all their sins" (Lev 16:34; cf. 25:9). Jesus's ministry will encompass a wide range of liberating "services" across the material-spiritual spectrum—curing diseases and disabilities, relieving tortured minds, releasing those bound by evil spirits, and forgiving sins. On occasions, he explicitly treats multiple conditions in the same person, such as restoring the paralytic and forgiving his sin (5:17–26) and restoring a man's "right mind" and delivering him from demonic possession (8:26–39).

As for restoring sight to the blind, specifically referenced in Isa 61:1 LXX/Luke 4:18, Luke's Jesus performs only one ophthalmological miracle (18:35–43), but frequently he aims to open intellectual and spiritual "eyes" to perceive God's will and sharpen self-understanding (6:39–42; 7:24–30, 44–50; 8:16–18; 10:21–24; 11:33–36; 12:1–3; 17:20–24; 19:41–44; 21:34–36; 24:31, 36–45).[13] The early church fathers rightly sensed this combination of spiritual enlightenment and physical sight-adjustment in Jesus's ministry to the blind. For example:

> To the blind he gave sight, giving the power of seeing to those whose bodily vision was destroyed. He showered those in ancient times who were blind

10. See Lev 25:8–55; Kawashima, "Jubilee"; Spencer, "Jubilee"; Yoder, *Politics*, 60–75.

11. Cf. N. T. Wright, *Simply Jesus*, 12: "Our culture has become used to thinking of Jesus as a 'religious' figure rather than a 'political' one. We have seen those two categories as watertight compartments, to be kept strictly separate. But it wasn't like that for Jesus and others of his time."

12. See Spencer, "Forgiveness."

13. Cf. Green, 211; Hamm, "Sight"; Hartsock, *Sight*; Culpepper, "Seeing."

in their minds to the truth with the vision of the light of true religion. (Eusebius, *Proof of the Gospel* 3.1.88–89)

"To preach release to the captives." We were the captives. For many years Satan had bound us and held us captive and subject to himself. Jesus has come "to proclaim release to captives and sight to the blind." By his word and the proclamation of his teaching the blind see. There his "proclamation" should be understood not only of the "captives" but also of the blind. (Origen, *Homilies on the Gospel of Luke* 32.4–5)[14]

The integral meshing of "spiritual" and "social" gospels into a holistic mission derives further support from "let the oppressed go free," a phrase from Isa 58:6 that Luke's Jesus inserts into the main text from Isa 61:1–2. While commentators routinely note this splicing, they rarely discuss its wider context in Isa 58. This chapter begins with a sharp prophetic exposure of the people's "sins" and their pretension "to know [God's] ways *like* a people that practiced righteousness" (Isa 58:1–2 NETS). The people have a *spiritual* problem ("sins") and an *epistemological* blind spot (falsely claiming "to know God's ways") manifest in their *ethical* failure to "practice righteousness." To know God and to be right with God means to act in godly ways of justice and mercy, not (simply) to enact certain religious rites. Observing holy rest (Sabbath) and fast days are valuable *if* they serve to meet others' needs rather than one's self-interests; *if* they promote real justice rather than religious affectation.

I have not chosen such a fast, says the Lord;
rather loose every bond of injustice;
undo the knots of contract made by force,
let the oppressed go free, and tear up every unjust note. . . .
If you turn your foot away from the sabbaths, so as not to do the things
you wish on the holy day.

(58:6, 13 NETS)

Moreover, the prophet is not content with a general call for liberty and justice. He gets down to brass tacks concerning just and merciful acts that God's people should pursue:

Break your bread with the one who is hungry . . .
bring the homeless poor into your house;

14. Citations from Just, 80–81.

> if you see one naked, clothe him . . .
> you shall not neglect any of the relatives of your seed.
> (58:7 NETS; cf. vv. 9–10)

If these liberating acts are faithfully performed in God's name, "*then* your light shall break forth early in the morning, and your healings shall rise quickly . . . *then* your light shall rise in the darkness, and your darkness shall be like the noonday. And your God will be with you continually, and you shall be satisfied exactly as your soul desires, and your bones shall be enriched" (58:8, 10–11 NETS). Full salvation, healing, and knowledge of God will come for God's people only *if* they share in God's redemptive mission to others.

This rich coalescence of spiritual service and social justice in Isa 58 fleshes out the Jubilee that Jesus announces and embraces. Preceding the Nazareth episode, he made clear that his practice of fasting was no mere show of piety (Luke 4:1–4). Fasting in the wilderness, far away from any crowds he might seek to impress, Jesus answered the devil's first challenge with a staunch refusal to cater to his own needs. He would live by God's word, first and foremost, and if fasting had taught him anything, it reminded him of the multitude in his world bound by poverty, bereft of life's necessities. He was called to practice God's righteousness on behalf of the destitute and afflicted, which is to say, following Isa 58:7: feeding the hungry, hosting the homeless, clothing the naked, and not abandoning his own relatives. In the present scene, this last item commands particular attention with respect to *Jesus's Nazareth kinfolk*. By starting with them, Jesus clearly does not neglect them, though by the end they are not at all sure he's on their side!

They initially give Jesus a benefit of the doubt, though not an unequivocal endorsement. The NRSV's "all spoke well [ἐμαρτύρουν, *emartyroun*] of him" (4:22) is a valid reading, but not the only one. At base μαρτυρέω (*martyreō*) denotes "bearing witness" or "giving evidence," which could either support or subvert the object of testimony. Obviously, Jesus's followers will bear positive witness to him (24:44–48; Acts 1:8, 22; 2:32; 3:15; 5:32; 13:31; 23:11; 26:16).[15] But at this early stage he has no followers, and it remains to be seen whether his Nazareth family and neighbors will join him in the new path he's blazing. The most we can say now is that his hometown audience is giving him a fair "hearing" (Luke 4:21) and bearing witness to *his* witness, weighing the merit of *his* testimony.

We also learn that the congregants "were amazed at the gracious words that came from his mouth" (4:22). But again, this response is not necessarily

15. Note the good reputation of various Christian figures "spoken well of" (μαρτυρέω, *martyreō*) in Acts: seven table-servants (6:3), Cornelius (10:22), Timothy (16:2), and Ananias (22:12).

as favorable as it may seem. The verb here, θαυμάζω (*thaumazō*), meaning "be amazed, wonder, marvel," again can reflect a range of attitudes; it is not always a transparent "expression of positive marveling," as Bovon assumes here.[16] Thus far in Luke, it has applied to the people's puzzlement about Zechariah's delay in the temple (1:21), the excitement of the neighbors and relatives over Zechariah's confirming John's name (1:63), the hearers' wonderment over the shepherds' witness concerning the Christ-child (2:18), and Mary and Joseph's astonishment over Simeon's prophecy about the infant Jesus (2:33). While positive elements figure into all of these reactions, they do so to varying degrees mixed with various doubts. Amazement marks a first cognitive-affective step toward enhanced knowledge and may or may not blossom into faith and discipleship.

The Nazareth assembly specifically responds with amazement to "the words of grace [τοῖς λόγοις τῆς χάριτος, *tois logois tēs charitos*]" just uttered by Jesus concerning his fulfillment of Isaiah's evangelical promise (4:22 AT). The NRSV reading— "gracious words"—is too soft, if not sentimental. The audience is not assessing the polite tone or winsome way that Jesus has spoken. Though possibly reflecting on God's "amazing grace" bestowed on the unfortunate poor, blind, and captives, more likely, the Nazareth folk are trying to come to grips with Jesus's sudden claim to be the special "anointed" beneficiary of God's grace or favor (χάρις, *charis*), endowing him to mediate God's saving power.[17] The divine and human grace/favor that increasingly strengthened Jesus through his childhood (2:40, 52) has now come to maturity in the "power of the Spirit" (4:14). Another Lukan reference to "word(s) of grace" confirms the close link between powerful, God-graced speech and signs.[18] Summarizing Paul and Barnabas's mission in Iconium, Acts 14:3–4 reports: "So they remained for a long time, speaking boldly for the Lord, who testified [μαρτυροῦντι, *martyrounti*] to the word of his grace [τῷ λόγῳ τῆς χάριτος αὐτοῦ, *tō logō tēs charitos autou*] by granting signs and wonders to be done through them. But the residents of the city were divided." Notice here it is *the Lord* who bears witness to the missionaries' preaching with corroborative signs and wonders. The word of God's grace is performative as well as declarative. Notice, too, the "divided" response of the Iconians, akin to the Nazarenes' ambivalent first reactions to Jesus.

However much Jesus's giftedness (graced nature) might have been evident among the Nazareth villagers through the years, he had never ventured such an

16. Bovon, 1:155.

17. See Nolland, 1:198–99: "Luke uses χάρις, 'grace,' as a quasi-substantial power, especially as resident in or on people (2:40; Acts 4:33; 6:8; 7:10)"; cf. Nolland, "Luke's Use of χάρις."

18. Bovon, 1:155.

absolute and audacious public claim of divine authorization until now. What does he mean that *he* fulfills the Spirit-inspired hope forecast by Isaiah? Who does he think he is? "Is not this Joseph's son?" (Luke 4:22). He's one of us, from no-account Nazareth, like the rest of us. No prophet or deliverer has ever come *to* this place, much less *from* it. Of course, Mary and Joseph (and we readers) know that Jesus is *not* Joseph's natural son, and while, on the one hand, he is a full-fledged human being, on the other hand, he also holds a special identity as God's uniquely favored and empowered Son. Nevertheless, it is unlikely that Mary or Joseph has tried to communicate this Christology to their compatriots, not least because, as we have seen, they continue to wrestle with Jesus's identity themselves. Moreover, the risk of scandalous misunderstanding (a virginal conception? really now!) is too great (cf. Matt 1:18–20).

"Is not this Joseph's son?" "Of course he is," the people of Nazareth would answer. "We have been rubbing shoulders with him and his family for thirty years. We have been worshiping with him every Sabbath in this synagogue. And he's never spoken and acted like this, all high and mighty, like he's God's gift to Israel and the world. He's been a good boy and young man, even a bit special, our favorite son, perhaps—as good as it gets around here. But 'here' is still lowly Nazareth, and Jesus seems to be getting above his raising. We're not quite sure what to make of his audacious claims today, but they are unsettling. We're not into change around here." The confusion is comparable to that of Jewish pilgrims at Pentecost upon hearing Jesus's Galilean followers "speak in other languages, as the Spirit gave them ability" (Acts 2:4): "Amazed and astonished [ἐθαύμαζον, *ethaumazon*], they asked, 'Are not all these who are speaking Galileans? And how is it that we hear, each of us, in our own native language?'" (2:7–8).[19] "Are not these Galileans? Is this not Joseph's son, from Nazareth in Galilee? We do not expect much from such folk. Even we who live here know our limits and wonder about those who do not seem to know their place."

Jesus has certainly managed to capture his hometown's attention. "The eyes of all in the synagogue were fixed on him" (Luke 4:20), which suggests apprehension ("We have got our eye on you, Jesus") as much as attention; and their ears are fine-tuned to "hearing" (4:21) what else he has to say. This is no casual, complacent synagogue audience. They attend carefully to Jesus's message. But with eyes and ears on high alert, will they truly "see" and "hear" what God is revealing through his Son?

19. Bovon, 1:155.

Jesus's Proverbial Reference and Commentary (4:23–24)

Jesus does not go out of his way to mollify the bewildered congregation buzzing about this upstart "son of Joseph." In fact, he plays to the most negative perceptions of his conduct and leaves little room for negotiation. He puts taunting words in the Nazareth citizens' mouths, which he "doubtless" presumes are burning on their tongue tips, in the form of a common proverb—"Doctor, cure yourself!"—glossed for the present context in no uncertain terms: "Do here also in your hometown the things that we have heard you did at Capernaum" (4:23). Rather than granting that some in the audience might be up for a serious theological discussion based on prophetic Scripture, Jesus reduces their response to a flip "Show us what you've got!" challenge popular in Greco-Roman and Jewish culture. The "heal yourself" jibe was commonly leveled at traveling quacks and hucksters who claimed to offer magical cures (for a modest fee, of course).[20]

Jesus further assumes that, apart from doubting his Spirit-power and limiting its exercise to medical marvels, the Nazareth assembly also questions his hometown loyalty. Apparently they have heard some curious reports about Jesus's adventures beyond Nazareth in the bigger, lakeside city of Capernaum twenty miles northeast, where he's supposedly been helping folks in wondrous ways. But if he's really been doing all that great work there, what about those here, at home? "Too big for us now? Does he really expect our support after abandoning us?"

Admittedly, this is not a common interpretation of this scene. Commentators are quick to note that Luke's Jesus heads to Capernaum after the synagogue incident in Nazareth, not before (4:31–41). Thus, Luke must either have clumsily interpolated a later Capernaum miracle tradition or imagined Jesus's forecasting what the Nazareth community "will say" when he goes to Capernaum.[21] Jesus does use the future verb form ἐρεῖτε (*ereite*), "You will say," but this could mean, "You are just about to say" any moment now rather than at some distant point. Either way, Jesus perceives the suspicion lurking in the hearts of his hometown audience that will be expressed sooner or later. But I suggest that Jesus is more preoccupied with their immediate response to his vocation than with their future evaluation. The narrative flow logically suggests that Jesus is tapping into the Nazarenes' simmering concerns over what they "have [already] heard" about his Capernaum exploits. The summary account in 4:14–15 of mounting

20. For example, Cicero, *Fam.* 4.5.5: "Do not imitate quacks, who claim to have credentials when others are sick but cannot cure themselves," cited in Danker, 109 (see 108–9); Noorda, "Cure Yourself"; Nolland, "Classical and Rabbinic Parallels."

21. For example, Tannehill, "Mission," 8–9; Danker, 109.

reports concerning Jesus's dynamic works in various Galilean synagogues allows for prior activity before Jesus "came [back] to Nazareth" (4:16). Naturally enough, Luke's Jesus chooses the venue of his home synagogue to launch "officially" his messianic campaign and lay out the main planks of his agenda. But there's no narrative (or historical) reason Jesus could not have begun to test his messianic mettle in the region before announcing its "fulfillment" at home.

Indeed, Jesus well knew from scriptural history that God's prophets were more often than not unwelcome in their hometowns. Better perhaps, then, to find one's prophetic feet elsewhere before confronting the homefolk. And when one does return home: best not to expect a red-carpet reception. Jesus says as much to relatives and neighbors: "Truly I tell you, no prophet is accepted/favored [δεκτός, *dektos*] in the prophet's hometown" (4:24). Jesus may be the harbinger of the Jubilee "year of the Lord's favor [δεκτόν, *dekton*]" (4:19), but it is most improbable that his hometown will favor him! Robert Tannehill captures well the challenging, unpopular, independent thrust of God's prophetic agents: "A prophet is not going to be pleasing to his hometown, for a prophet is not governed by in-group loyalties. Jesus, who takes the role of prophet during his ministry, is governed by the purpose of God and the precedent of scriptural prophets."[22] So what is Jesus hoping to achieve here? Is he simply rubbing his compatriots' faces in their recalcitrance? Is he bucking for a fight? Does he have some sort of martyr complex? Or is he still hoping, against the odds, to win over his kinfolk and get them on board with his Jubilee mission? Remember, he has come back home with "words of grace" as well as judgment (in fact, his reading of Isa 61:1–2a cuts off right before the announcement of God's "vengeance" in 61:2b). And he has one final point to make, which catalyzes the synagogue's ultimate reaction.

Jesus's Final Prophetic Reference (Kings) and Commentary (4:25–30)

Following his comment about prophets' home-field disadvantage, Jesus bridges back to Scripture and the experiences of two wonder-working prophets, Elijah and Elisha. On the surface, this move might seem designed to promote more positive feelings among the assembly, given the popularity of the Elijah/Elisha stories and the vibrant hope of Elijah's return in advance of God's restored kingdom. But the cases that Jesus selects are not the most congenial to local

22. Tannehill, 93–94; on in/out-group dynamics in the Mediterranean world of Jesus and Luke, see several studies by Malina: *Christian Origins*, 28–97; "Early Christian Groups"; *New Testament World*, 58–80; and *Windows*, 47–70.

interests. Speaking with pointed gravitas "in truth [ἐπ᾽ ἀληθείας, *ep' alētheias*]," Jesus spotlights the two most inclusive, furthest outreaching incidents—Elijah's feeding the destitute Sidonian widow (Luke 4:25–26/1 Kgs 17:1–16) and Elisha's healing the skin-diseased Syrian general Naaman (Luke 4:27/2 Kgs 5:1–14)—cutting across boundaries of gender (female/male), class (poor/powerful), and ethnicity (Sidonian/Syrian). Jesus underscores the ethnic contrast to his own people. However different they may be from each other, Sidonians and Syrians were *Gentiles*, non-Jews; and God's prophets ministered to a hungry widow and leprous official among these foreigners, knowing full well there were many similar needy persons at home "*in Israel*" (Luke 4:25, 27). Jesus pushes the unpatriotic point by stressing that, on these occasions, Elijah and Elisha helped "none" (οὐδεμία/οὐδείς, *oudemia*/*oudeis* [4:26, 27]) of their fellow Israelites. Of course, they did minister to their own people at other times, but Jesus ignores those cases in his present message.

Again, Jesus does little to smooth his homefolk's ruffled feathers. To the contrary, he pushes their parochial buttons, incites their ethnocentric prejudices, and all but shakes their dust from his feet (cf. 9:5; 10:11) before going himself to help lepers and widows beyond Nazareth (5:12–16; 7:11–17). And they are ready to help Jesus on his way—with a swift boot out of town! At the end of the day, they scarcely prove to be a hospitable synagogue to one of their own, much less to "itinerants from abroad" (see Theodotus inscription above). But in turn, Jesus is not exactly proving to be a loyal and grateful native son; in fact, foreign visitors would normally speak more "graciously" than he has. But Jesus is a prophet, not a politician, and on this climactic Day of Jubilee, some tough things need to be said, some bad attitudes need to be corrected, some deficits need to be redressed. The God of heaven and earth aims to liberate all people everywhere, not just a chosen few. And if the citizens at Nazareth remain unwilling to accept this truth, they will find themselves fighting God, and losing (cf. Acts 5:38–39; 11:17).

However, while the strain of prophetic judgment cannot be denied here, it is not the whole score. It is too convenient for Western, mostly Gentile, Christians to say, "Let them have it, Jesus! Burst their cozy, clannish bubble. How narrow-minded of them!" By such bellowing we signal retreat into our own cliquish corners and reinforce the same rigid "us vs. them" mentality we supposedly condemn in "them." More broadly, we should appreciate that it is quite natural—and moral—to care for one's own first and foremost, to begin charity at home with those we know and love most, including ourselves. Such an orientation does not inherently entail hatred, suspicion, and dismissal of distant "others" and their needs. Indeed, it may be argued that proper care for self and those closest to us provides the best framework for genuine care of all persons.

Contemporary proponents of an ethics of care stress the primary rootedness of effective care-giving in the *personal* and *particular*, in nurturing individuals with whom we share a close "relational history."[23] Such intimacies inspire respectful empathy toward the cared-for party and resist paternalistic and tokenistic practices of "foreign aid." Abstract promotions of "justice for all" are well and good, but they are all too often hollow and hypocritical, undermined by neglect of widows, the infirm, and other needy folk on our doorsteps.[24] The fact is: as in Elijah and Elisha's era, there still *are* "many widows" and "many lepers" in Nazareth, in Galilee, in Israel, crying out for care. These are God's suffering people whom God actively and wholeheartedly loves and our suffering neighbors whom God commands we love *as ourselves* (Lev 19:18; Luke 10:27–28). Then, as resources allow, loving care toward one's own spills over social and political borders to "all the families of the earth" (Gen 12:1–3; Acts 3:25).

As we will see, for all his hometown agitating, Jesus's liberating ministry still primarily remains close to home. He will work an Elijah-like miracle on behalf of a bereft *Jewish* widow in the Galilean village of Nain less than ten miles from Nazareth (Luke 7:11–17); he will aid some diseased and demon-possessed persons who *come to him in Galilee* from Tyre and Sidon (6:17); he will cure a leper, but again, one residing "in one of the cities" of Galilee (5:12), not a foreigner;[25] and he will heal the servant of a Roman centurion who had merited the respect of *Jewish leaders* for "loving our people" and building a synagogue in Galilean Capernaum (7:1–10). In short, Jesus by no means ministers to outsiders at the expense of his own people.

So why does Jesus provoke his Nazareth kinfolk and neighbors so sharply? And why do they respond so vehemently? Jesus's prophetic challenge, however pointed, does not amount to rejecting his hometown relatives and friends. He keeps the door open to them, even though right now they are inclined to shut it. But when his mother and brothers come to see him later in another Galilean locale, though he doesn't give them special access, he does include them (potentially) among his extended "spiritual" family of "those who hear the word of God and do it" (8:19–21; cf. 11:27–28; Acts 1:14). Jesus doesn't overturn the policy of "charity begins at home," but he does redefine the boundaries of "home" to

23. Engster, "Rethinking Care Theory," 66: "We have a primary duty to care for our children, parents, spouses, partners, friends, and other intimate relations because we usually are best suited to provide care for them and have a relational history with them that allows us to anticipate and understand their needs"; cf. Held, *Ethics*, 9–15, 119–20, 129–31, 156–59; Noddings, *Caring*, 3–6, 19–21, 32–33; Gilligan, *Joining*, 164–80; Haidt, *Righteous Mind*, 130–34.

24. On the integration of justice and care, see Held, *Ethics*, 15–17, 68–72, 90–103, 158.

25. Later, however, Jesus cures a Samaritan leper, whom he calls a "foreigner" (17:18), along with nine (apparently) Jewish lepers on the Galilee-Samaria border (17:11–19)

encompass every member of God's household. Even so, he trumpets not some amorphous "love all God's children" platitude, but rather a *personal* and *particular* embrace of all "family" members who heed God's word as "my mother and my brothers" (8:21). He endorses God's mandate to "love your neighbor as yourself," even as he limns "neighbor" to include not only kinfolk and fellow Israelites, but also any human being in need of God's merciful care, be they Sidonian, Syrian, Samaritan, or anyone else (Luke 10:25–37; cf. Lev 19:17–18, 34). The ethics of care starts at home but doesn't end there. The ray of God's love radiates to the ends of the earth to restore all creation (cf. Acts 1:8; 3:21; 14:15–16; 17:26–31).

So Luke's Jesus seeks to expand the care horizon of his home village, and he does so through admittedly incendiary rhetoric: sometimes it takes shocking language to shake people up. But he does not question God's abiding love for Israel or call down judgment on their heads. So while we expect some pushback from the Nazareth assembly, their extreme reaction takes us by surprise. Why does their raging anger boil to the point that they drive Jesus to the cliff edge of town with intent to execute him, foiled only by his mysterious escape (4:28–30)?[26] Such a hilltop crisis eerily previews his crucifixion at Skull Hill on the outskirts of Jerusalem (Luke 23:33). In due course, we will explore why the Roman and Jewish authorities want Jesus dead. Now we try to ascertain why his native community aims to murder him before his ministry gets off the ground.

Note how Cyril of Alexandria appraises the Nazareth synagogue's reaction: "Their violence was irrational and their envy untamed."[27] "Irrational" seems on target in light of the extremity of the Nazarenes' reaction. But in ancient analyses of emotion, "irrational" doesn't necessarily mean "thoughtless" or simply "impulsive," like some rabid hysteria that overtakes them. Thoughts, intuitions, convictions, and feelings swirl together toward both positive and negative effects. Good, "rational" emotions are based on true beliefs, while bad, "irrational" emotions flow from unchecked false beliefs.[28] In the Nazarenes' case, Cyril connects their unbridled rage against Jesus with "untamed envy," both of which stem from false judgments about Jesus's message and God's aims.

26. The text is vague regarding the mechanics of Jesus's great escape. Such a gap allows for the possibility of "miraculous intervention," as Bruce Longenecker (*Hearing the Silence*) argues, particularly in light of Luke's narrative worldview that "is shot through with insuperable divine involvement" (43–44); cf. the supernatural prison breaks in Acts 5:19–21; 12:6–11; 16:25–27.

27. Cyril of Alexander, *Commentary on Luke,* Homily 12; cf. Ambrose, *Exposition of the Gospel of Luke* 4.47: "So, you see what measure of evil envy brings. His country is found unworthy because of envy" (cited in Just, 82).

28. See Graver, *Stoicism*; Sorabji, *Emotion*; Nussbaum, *Upheavals*, 19–88; Konstan, *Emotions*, 27–40.

We may correlate emotional responses of *anger* with perceptions of personal injury or harm and those of *envy* with perceptions of personal disadvantage or neglect.[29] In some fashion, Jesus's Nazareth family and neighbors *think and feel* that they are being shortchanged in Jesus's implied distribution of messianic benefits; that they are being traded in, so to speak, as God's covenant people for a "foreign" model. These are indeed *false beliefs*, inconsistent with God's steadfast love mediated by Jesus, and they should be resisted. But that is easier said than done. Their misguided perceptions, while theologically false, are not silly or crazed. Under a century of domination by Rome, preceded by many more centuries of foreign subjection (under Assyria, Babylon, Persia, and Greece), first-century Nazarenes and other Israelites, like their exilic ancestors, no doubt confronted some serious crises of faith (theodicy). The more it *looks as if* God doesn't care about us anymore, or isn't powerful enough to protect us, or just wants to play the international field a bit more, the harder it is to *believe* the contrary. Moral foundations of care, fairness, loyalty, and liberty begin to crack, sparking fear, rage, envy, and other "irrational" responses.[30]

Jesus's prophetic rhetoric of God's concern to feed and heal foreigners may well have touched too raw a nerve—a hungry, diseased, and oppressed nerve—for the Nazarenes to control. Moreover, their evil-eyed envy (following Cyril) is doubtless exacerbated by daily experiences in a "limited goods" economic system, where those who "have" benefit at the expense of those who "have not." It seems like a zero sum, win-lose game.[31] So if a Sidonian widow and Syrian leper win, then our widows and lepers must lose: they are taking food from our tables and health from our bodies. Of course, God's economy does not work on that scale. The Divine Creator, Patron, and Lover of the world has an inexhaustible supply of resources, the fullness of heaven and earth (Ps 24:1), plenty for everyone to share. But in times of famine and suffering—like the days of Elijah and Jesus—God's bounty doesn't always *seem or feel* that bountiful. It takes bold faith to overcome false belief and "irrational" emotion. Along the way, such faith is bolstered by significant acts of grace: like Jesus's multiplying a few loaves and fishes to distribute among the multitude until "all . . . were filled" (Luke 9:17); or the new mixed Gentile-Jewish congregation in Syrian Antioch sharing their food and funds with the destitute Jewish community in Jerusalem during a season of famine (Acts 11:27–30). In

29. On anger in ancient Greek thought, see William V. Harris, *Restraining Rage*; Nussbaum, *Therapy*, 89–96, 239–79, 402–83; Konstan, *Emotions*, 41–76 (cf. 111–28 on envy).

30. On "moral foundations theory," especially related to politics, see Haidt, *Righteous Mind*, 123–54.

31. On a "limited good society," see Moxnes, *Economy*, 76–79 (drawing on Foster, "Peasant Society").

this latter case, concerned Syrian believers support needy Israelites, thus giving the lie to ethnocentric fears and cutting the nerve of envy.[32] But these lessons in the mutuality of all God's people do not come naturally in an oppressive world. Jesus and followers must show as well as tell the inclusive, liberating gospel of Jubilee in convincing fashion.

Removing a Loud Demon and Relieving a High Fever (4:31–44)

Having somehow "passed through the midst" of a hometown mob, Jesus proceeds "on his way" (4:30) to continue fleshing out his Spirit-anointed Jubilee campaign. He returns to the fishing center of Capernaum on the northwest shore of the Sea of Galilee (or Lake Gennesaret [5:1]), where he had already performed some wondrous saving works, as 4:23 alludes to but doesn't describe (see above). Now, as Jesus revisits Capernaum, Luke details particular examples of miraculous release from demonic possession and disease. Before investigating these cases, however, I sketch a broad conceptual framework guiding our approach to Jesus's mighty acts of liberation and restoration.

Frameworks for Interpreting Jesus's Miracles

Consider five perspectives: theological, historical, anthropological, epistemological, and narratological.

Theological. The ministry of Luke's Jesus reveals the core nature of God as Healer. Theology and therapy coalesce.[33] In the first incident following ancient Israel's emancipation from slavery across the Red Sea, the Lord transforms (through Moses) a bitter, undrinkable spring into sweet, potable water and thus demonstrates a foundational principle: "If you will listen carefully to the voice of the LORD your God . . . and keep all his statutes, I will not bring upon you any of the diseases that I brought upon the Egyptians; for *I am the LORD who heals you* (Exod 15:26).[34] As surely as the Lord created all life from chaotic waters (Gen 1:1–2) and redeemed the Israelites from genocidal drowning and enslavement (see Exod 1:8–22) via a divinely engineered water-crossing (14:15–31), so the Lord sustains their health amid scarce, acrid waters in the

32. On the narrative interplay between Elijah's feeding the famished Syrian widow (Luke 4:25–26) and the famine relief extended to Jerusalem by the Syrian Antioch church (Acts 11:27–30), see Crockett, "Luke 4:25–27," 177–81; Spencer, *Salty Wives*, 218–20.

33. See Spencer, "To Fear."

34. Cf. 2 Kgs 5:7; Job 5:17–18; Isa 57:19; Ezek 34:16.

wilderness. The challenge to obedience and reminder of the terrible plagues the Lord had inflicted on the Egyptians warn the people not to presume cavalierly on divine healing. But within a faithful-covenantal context, they have every reason to trust in the Lord's saving, healing, and freeing power. Accordingly, as the Lord God's Son, anointed by God's Spirit after passing through baptismal waters and authenticated through wilderness testing, Luke's Jesus is poised to serve as the Lord's dynamic healing-saving agent.

Historical. Discussions of Jesus's miracles invariably raise the modern scientific question of whether such events could actually happen in the "real" world, seemingly defying natural laws of physics and physiology. Are they empirically verifiable? In terms of Luke's prologue: Can we know that Jesus's miracles represent "solid" truth? The answer largely depends on how we define knowledge and truth. In a pithy excursus "Miracles" in his theological commentary on Luke, Justo González tracks three stages in the history of thought:[35]

- *Antiquity*, from the biblical era up to the Enlightenment, accepting the control of earthly events by mysterious spiritual forces, both good and evil, and expecting supernatural interventions;
- *Modernity*, from the Enlightenment to present times, focusing on the universe as a closed system of natural causes and effects and ruling out miraculous phenomena a priori (what seems miraculous is simply an unusual phenomenon with no *yet* known explanation); and
- *Postmodernity*, an emergent worldview stimulated by unprecedented global awareness and technological advances, confronting new complexities of cosmic proportion and cognitive perception. We thus find ourselves grappling with a more "open reality" not as alien from the biblical perspective as modernity had claimed.[36]

For its part, the biblical view of miracles is not locked into an agonistic-dualistic system, in which a good, external divine force must penetrate (invade, intervene) into an evil, alien material universe. As González more correctly discerns: "A [biblical] miracle is not an interruption of an order, but rather the irruption of the true order—the order of the creator God—into the demonic disorder of the present world. It is a sign of God's victory over the powers of evil. It is an announcement that the new order is at hand, that

35. González, 82–84.

36. The American biblical scholar Frederick Gaiser (*Healing*) reports his greater openness to God's miraculous work resulting from two teaching tours in Zimbabwe, where worldviews more naturally match the Bible's. He came to realize more fully that "God accomplishes healing in all kinds of venues and in all kinds of ways" (3; cf. 1–3).

ultimately power belongs to the God of creation, of true order, freedom, and justice."[37]

Anthropological. As a therapeutic miracle-worker, Jesus operates within a particular sociocultural context of medical practice and healthcare. He functions as an "alternative" folk healer rather than a "professional" physician.[38] Such a mode of operation would doubtless have boosted Jesus's reputation in Galilean villages and countryside, which remained wary of practitioners of Greek medical science, which often proved ineffectual and expensive.[39] But there was also no shortage of traveling hacks promising some "magical" cure, for a modest fee naturally (see, e.g., Acts 8:9–24; 13:6–11; 19:13–19). Jesus's "free healing,"[40] wrought by genuine divine power, stands in sharp contrast both to physicians and to magicians in his day. On a broader level, medical anthropologists typically categorize health systems in relation to:

- *Disease*, diagnosing physiological (anatomical, neurological, viral) conditions and prescribing biomedical treatments;
- *Illness*, treating the whole person as part of an integrated network of physical, psychological, social, political, and environmental relationships; and
- *Disorder*, extending into the macrocosmic sphere, where beneficent and malignant "spiritual" forces battle for domination over microcosmic "natural" bodies.[41]

Whereas modern Western medicine has largely operated with a hard-scientific disease model (though increasingly pushed toward more multifaceted, interdisciplinary perspectives), Jesus's world was much more tuned in to social (illness) and cosmic (disorder) dimensions. Accordingly, Jesus's healings, including exorcisms, address the whole embodied person embedded in a thick web of sociopolitical relations and embattled by a fierce "legion" of demonic forces (cf. Luke 8:30).

Epistemological. To what extent do Jesus's miracles function as a means of *knowing the truth* of his identity and vocation? John the Baptist, perhaps most distinguished from Jesus by *not* performing any miracles, sends messen-

37. González, 83–84.

38. On Luke's Jesus as "folk healer," see Pilch, "Sickness," 197–200.

39. See the case of the hemorrhaging woman who "spent all she had on physicians" to no avail (8:43) and the mocking of "worthless physicians" in Job 13:4; note further 2 Chr 16:12; Jer 8:22; Green, "Healthcare," 359.

40. Crossan, *Historical Jesus*, xii, 361, 422.

41. This threefold classification derives from Hahn, *Sickness*, 28; see discussion in Green, "Healthcare," 358–59.

gers to Jesus later in his Galilean ministry, asking him whether he truly is "the [messianic] one who is to come." Significantly, having "just then cured many people of diseases, plagues, and evil spirits, and . . . given sight to many who were blind," Jesus responds: "Go and tell John what you have seen and heard: the blind receive their sight, the lame walk, the lepers are cleansed, the deaf hear, the dead are raised, the poor have good news brought to them" (7:22). By Jesus's clear demonstration and admission, his working of curative miracles, closely aligned with the agenda set forth in Nazareth (4:18–19), serve as prima facie signs of God's salvation. To see and hear these miracles is to know (believe and experience) the restorative rule of God the Creator through Christ the Redeemer. As Luke's Jesus will further testify: "If it is by the finger of God that I cast out the demons, then the kingdom of God has come to you" (11:20).

It is vital to underscore the probative value in Luke of *beneficent, liberating* miracles on behalf of sufferers, not of power displays for their own sake or for the vainglory of the wonder-worker. In the temptation scene, Jesus already staked out this God-honoring and other-oriented position, which he reinforces throughout his ministry. He also becomes increasingly resistant to anyone—disciples, crowds, religious teachers, political officials—who press him for more miraculous signs, whether out of self-interest, curiosity, or animosity (see 11:16, 29; 17:20–21; 23:8). And he tempers his wondrous works with predictions and, ultimately, demonstrations of service, self-sacrifice, and personal suffering culminating in crucifixion. To know God's saving work in Christ is to know the "foolish" yet profound paradox of power through weakness, salvation through suffering, liberation through subjugation. Luke's gospel narrative provides a dramatic plot for Paul's poignant doctrinal tenet: "For Jews demand signs and Greeks desire wisdom, but we proclaim Christ crucified, a stumbling block to Jews and foolishness to Gentiles, but to those who are the called, both Jews and Greeks, Christ the power of God and the wisdom of God. For God's foolishness is wiser than human wisdom, and God's weakness is stronger than human strength" (1 Cor 1:22–25).[42]

Narratological. Following his penchant for pairing related incidents and characters (e.g., stories juxtaposing male/female figures),[43] Luke frequently narrates two miracle accounts in succession: an exorcism and a healing (4:31–39), a dermatological and a muscular-skeletal cure (5:12–26), a healing and a resuscitation (7:1–17), a meteorological miracle and an exorcism (8:22–39), a hematological cure and a resuscitation (8:40–56), and a facial transfigura-

42. For a contemporary theological and philosophical exposition—and extension—of Paul's "foolish" theology, see Caputo, *Folly of God.*

43. On this gendered pairing pattern, see Spencer, *Gospel of Luke*, 41–44.

tion and a neurological healing/exorcism (9:28–43). This "orderly" Gospel (1:1, 3) encourages us to take these juxtapositions seriously and to interpret these miracle pairs together as mutually informing cases. Moreover, the wide range of correlated conditions reinforces a comprehensive, interconnected approach to health care. Jesus is no medical specialist, but rather a general practitioner concerned about the well-being of the whole person.

The First Pair of Jesus's Miracles (4:31–39)

The initial miracle duo features the liberation of a demon-possessed man in the Capernaum synagogue (4:31–37), followed by healing a fever-afflicted woman in the home of son-in-law Simon (soon identified in 5:8 as Simon Peter) (4:38–39). The exorcism/healing and male/female dyads are matched by a synagogue/home pairing of venues on the Sabbath (4:31, 38). Although Jesus's Nazareth synagogue turned violently against him, this does not deter him from seeking fellowship in other places. At this time, congregations might gather in larger homes or public facilities, as well as purpose-built synagogues, like the one in Capernaum (see 7:5). In any case, Jesus moves easily between these communal assemblies and familial gatherings in smaller residences, blurring boundaries between so-called public and private spheres, and between natural and spiritual kin. The early church in Acts will continue this broad base of meeting and ministering in multiple settings, including the Jerusalem temple and members' homes (Acts 2:46; 5:42), rented rooms (1:13), local synagogues (6:9; 13:14–47), lecture halls (19:8–10), and riverside places of prayer (16:13, 16).

The ministry Jesus provides in the present pair of cases is rooted in the moral foundation of "Care/Harm," to borrow the category of research psychologist Jonathan Haidt, committed to relieving human suffering, doing no harm, and promoting positive well-being.[44] When Jesus orders the evil spirit to leave the man in the synagogue, it first "throws [him] down with considerable force [ῥῖψαν, *rhipsan*],"[45] indicating the demon's violent, malignant nature; but then, remarkably, it leaves the man "without having done him any harm" (4:35). Also, after Jesus relieves the woman of her high fever, "immediately" she gets up and resumes her household work (4:39), having suffered no further harmful effects from her disease. Another way to describe Jesus's healthcare in these instances is that he restores the man and woman to full capability;

44. Haidt, *Righteous Mind*, 131–34.

45. Translation based on Louw-Nida, *Greek-English Lexicon*, 1:208; cf. Luke 17:2; Acts 22:23; 27:19, 29.

he makes them whole.[46] While obviously operating on the physical "disease" level, Jesus also treats the social "illness"—reincorporating the man into synagogue fellowship and the woman into family life. And the man's case particularly involves combat with cosmic "disorder," a titanic clash of good and evil forces: Jesus "the Holy One of God" filled with God's Holy Spirit vs. "the spirit [πνεῦμα, *pneuma*] of an unclean demon" (4:33).[47]

In terms of epistemology, it is striking that the demon personally and fully *knows* Jesus's antithetical holy purpose and superior divine power from the start: "Let us alone! What have you to do with us, Jesus of Nazareth? Have you come to destroy us? *I know* who you are, the Holy One of God" (4:34; cf. 4:41).[48] The battles lines are sharply drawn in the spirit realm, and the outcome is set. God and God's Son win; Satan and his demons lose. The latter are on their last legs; their "doom is sure," to echo Luther's famous hymn ("Ein feste Burg" / "A Mighty Fortress"). But in the human sphere intersecting the spirit-world, matters are less clear-cut. As a result of Jesus's exorcism, the synagogue audience begins to sense the significance of his vocation, but still in a questioning mode short of assurance: "They were all amazed and kept saying to one another, 'What kind of utterance is this? For with authority and power he commands the unclean spirits, and out they come!'" (4:36). As we have noted before, amazement does not amount to full faith in Christ, though it may lead there.

The critical factor is the level of response to Jesus's "utterance" or "word" (λόγος, *logos*) that both reveals (teaching) and restores (miracle-working) with "authority and power" (4:31–32, 36). "One little word shall fell him [Satan]"—to continue Luther's hymn. Luke's Jesus also relieves the woman's fever with a *word* of rebuke (4:39). What kind of word is this? It is nothing less than the dynamic *word of God* that creates, sustains, and restores life: "In the beginning . . . *God said*" (Gen 1:1–3). "In the beginning was the Word, and the Word was with God, and the Word was God. . . . What has come into being in [the Word] was life, and the life was the light of all people" (John 1:1–4). Luke conveys this divine "logical" truth through stories of Jesus's liberating ministry, thereby confronting narrative audiences with God's transformative word demanding responses of faith and obedience. Put another way, Luke presents Jesus as the *incarnate* medium of God's dynamic word through the *inscribed* words of story that the

46. On the "Capabilities Approach" to human rights and development in today's world, see Nussbaum, *Creating Capabilities*; *Frontiers of Justice*, 155–324.

47. Though using different verbs, both miracles feature a forced exit of disorderly power: the demon "came out" (ἔξελθε, *exelthe* [4:35]), and the fever "left" (ἀφῆκεν, *aphēken* [4:39]). The latter is directly correlated with the liberating ἄφεσις (*aphesis*) emphasis in 4:18.

48. Referencing the demonic in both plural ("us") and singular ("I") terms suggests a self-aware ("I know") *collective* identity and *concerted* purpose (cf. 8:28, 30–31).

church calls Gospel and Holy Scripture. This clarion narrative-theological call demands to be heard, believed, and acted upon above the din of all competing voices. However *loudly* (see 4:33) the demons and other agitators might push their agendas and protest Christ's authority, his word drowns and drives them out of business, even as it brings renewed life and health to those suffering from oppressive "noise pollution."

Let those with ears to hear heed this living word of God published in the person of Christ and pages of Scripture. Such a call throbs at the heart of theological interpretation of Scripture imaged by Kevin Vanhoozer and Todd Billings, among others, as participation in *divine drama* and *sacred journey*:

> God's word is not simply an abstract set of propositions about God. . . . We see how God has acted in creation, in covenant with Israel, and in Jesus Christ, incorporating us into this divine drama by the Spirit's power. As ones who are in Christ and empowered by the Spirit, we become participants in *God's drama* and performers of the script of Scripture.[49]

> We should see our encounters with Scripture texts as a *journey* along a path. . . . Where does this journey lead us? The final end of the path is a transforming "face-to-face" encounter with our triune God, a joyful state of "knowing fully" and being "fully known" as children of God in Christ. . . . On this path we grow in the love of God and neighbor as we grow into our identity in Christ, and we grow in the knowledge of and fellowship with God. . . . The reading of Scripture is part of our *journey*, through the Spirit, to be transformed more and more into the image of Christ.[50]

The Expanding Scope and Clarified Purpose of Jesus's Miraculous Mission (4:40–44)

The two featured miracles in Capernaum on the Sabbath lead to "many" more exorcisms and healings that evening, "as the sun was setting" and a flood of people "with various kinds of diseases" are brought to Jesus (4:40). He appears to minister throughout the night, battling the diabolical powers of darkness with a "hands on" (touch), as well as a "shut up" (word), approach.[51] Then, at

49. Billings, *Word of God*, 8 (emphasis added, drawing on Vanhoozer, "Word"); cf. Vanhoozer, *Drama*, 44–48, and *Faith*, 20–32.

50. Billings, *Word of God*, 9–10 (emphasis added).

51. Confronting chaotic forces and restoring life by *word* and *hand* evoke God's modes of creation in Gen 1 and 2, respectively. Note, further, that Jesus silences the demons "because *they*

morning's light, Jesus retreats to a *third site* to which he will also return—synagogue (συναγωγή, *synagōgē*), house (οἶκος, *oikos*), and now *desert* (ἔρημος, *erēmos* [4:42; cf. 4:1–3; 9:12–17])—perhaps desiring space for private reflection and revitalizing prayer after a draining period of ministry (cf. 6:12; 9:18; Mark 1:35) and/or aiming to confront Satan directly again on his stomping grounds (Luke 4:1–4, 13).

Whatever Jesus's motivation for "departing," it becomes frustrated by the crowds' seeking him out and pressing upon him (4:42). Spatial boundaries prove more porous than airtight in Luke's story. Synagogue, house, and desert all become fertile territory for Jesus's roving teaching and healing mission throughout the region. Though Jesus keeps returning to Capernaum (4:23; 7:1–10), it scarcely functions any more than Nazareth as Jesus's mission headquarters or "capital" of God's kingdom. In fact, for the moment Jesus is done with Capernaum and asserts his intentions in no uncertain terms: "I must [δεῖ, *dei*] proclaim the good news of the kingdom of God to the other cities also; for I was sent for this purpose" (4:43). We then learn that Jesus "continued proclaiming the message in the synagogues of Judea" (4:44). The "Judea" reference is curious, since this (southern) region is often distinguished from (northern) Galilee in first-century Palestine, and Jesus clearly remains in or near Galilee until "setting his face" toward Jerusalem in 9:51. But "all Judea" could include Galilee as predominantly Jewish territory in distinction from Samaria and other "foreign" areas (cf. 17:11, 18; Acts 1:8; 8:1). That seems to be the case in Luke 4:44. Accordingly, by incorporating Galilee within all Jewish/Judean country, Luke further checks Galilean parochialism and proprietary claims to Jesus Messiah.[52] As the chief agent of God's restorative realm, Jesus remains on the move and out of the grasp of any single locale or special interest group. His *itinerant* mode of operation signals the *inclusive* scope of opportunity he "was sent" to provide.

---

knew that he was the Messiah" (4:41). Correct knowledge *about* Jesus's identity does not guarantee faithful commitment *to* Jesus's way; also, all publicity is not necessarily good from Jesus's perspective (see below on 5:14; 8:56; 9:21).

52. Not surprisingly, in light of the principal Galilean context of Jesus's present ministry, some scribal witnesses (A, D) read "the synagogues of *Galilee*" in 4:44. But apart from *Judea* representing the more difficult (and thus more likely original) reading, it also enjoys solid external support (P75, ℵ, B, C). In 5:17 Luke notes that people were coming to Jesus "from every village of Galilee and Judea and from Jerusalem." In this case, Judea is both distinguished from Galilee (rather than encompassing it) and linked with it as part of the entire region of Israel or Roman Palestine. Luke's geographic usage is somewhat flexible.

Calling and Seining with Fishermen and Sinners (5:1–11)

The next scene following Jesus's desert announcement that he must proclaim the gospel in other cities and synagogues depicts him, surprisingly, at none of these places or in anyone's home, but at yet another venue: "beside the lake of Gennesaret" (the Galilean "sea") and then on Simon's boat, first near the shore teaching the crowds, and then "out into the deep water," directing Simon and crew toward a huge fish haul (5:1–4). This fourth major setting—*water* (along with synagogue, home, and desert)—for Jesus's ministry will reemerge in another pair of liberating miracles (stilling a storm and delivering a demoniac [8:22–39]). In the current case, however, the theological emphasis of Jesus's waterworks falls more on creation than on liberation, though ultimately Simon and partners are freed from sin to serve and follow Jesus (5:8–11).

Luke now more explicitly affirms Jesus's revelatory role in speaking "the word of God [τὸν λόγον τοῦ θεοῦ, *ton logon tou theou*]." Indeed, this "word of God" is precisely what the crowds are "pressing in on [Jesus] to hear" (5:1). Again, proof of this divine word relates not simply to its convincing, persuasive rhetoric, but also to its creative, performative power—in the present case, its power to produce abundant fish from a deep, dark watery abyss and to transform the lives of ordinary fishermen.

Catching Peter's (and Partners') Attention (5:1–10a)

Simon and company "worked all night long" in the depths of the lake and "caught nothing" (Luke 5:5), recalling earth's primeval state as "a formless void and darkness covered the face of the deep" (Gen 1:2).[53] Yet, at Jesus's *command* (word) to "put out into the deep water and let down your nets for a catch," the fishermen cast their nets where Jesus directs and drag in a load of fish that fills not only Simon's boat, but also James and John's (Simon's associates) (Luke 5:4–7). It is hard to miss the echo with God's original mandates: "Let the [deep, dark, vacuous] waters bring forth swarms of living creatures. . . . Let [humankind made in God's image] have dominion over the fish of the sea" (Gen 1:20, 26–28). Jesus has come to restore God's "very good" (Gen 1:31) rule over all creation.

53. The "deep" connection is conceptual, with different, though closely related, terms. In Luke 5:4 the word is βάθος (*bathos*), whereas Gen 1:2 LXX has ἄβυσσος (*abyssos*), with a precise echo to the watery "abyss" (associated with the same Galilean lake) as the dark prison of demons in Luke 8:31.

At this stage, the fishermen scarcely fathom the deepest dimensions of Jesus's messianic vocation. Their "amazement" (Luke 5:9) again reflects a teetering response between faith and doubt, understanding and confusion. But Simon at least is making progress: he knows that Jesus is more than a fishing savant or wonder-worker profitable for Simon's business. Though no specific reaction by Simon is reported, presumably he knew something about Jesus's dynamic word, since it had operated to relieve Simon's mother-in-law's fever *in his home* (4:38–39). Now he shows enough faith in Jesus's word to follow its lead, even though it constitutes a "counterintuitive command" against Simon's recent experience and seasoned instincts.[54] And the resulting megadraft of fish more than validates Jesus's power and Simon's trust.

Simon is on his way to becoming Simon *Peter*—as he is first called in 5:8—that is, "Simon, whom [Jesus nick-] named Peter [Πέτρος, *Petros*]," meaning *Rock* or *Rocky* (6:14). But Simon's spiritual knowledge is not yet rock solid on terra firma. His rocking on a boat about to sink under a massive weight of fish-flesh in the middle of a deep lake (5:7) aptly images the fearful fragility of his faith. As the boat's hull dips lower and lower, Simon sinks to his wobbly knees "at Jesus' [sturdy] knees, saying, 'Go away from me, Lord, for I am a sinful man!'" (5:8). Oddly enough, this response reprises that of the demon in the synagogue, pleading with Jesus to leave him alone (cf. 4:34); even in his precarious state, Simon would rather sink and swim, it seems, than face Jesus. Though he doesn't identify Jesus as "the Holy One/Son of God" (4:34, 41), Simon's addressing Jesus as "Lord" amounts to the same thing (cf. 1:31–35, 38, 43–45), recognizing Jesus's set-apart divine status antithetical to Simon's "sinful" condition.[55] Along with matching the demon's reaction in the synagogue, Simon also echoes the prophet Isaiah's response in the temple upon encountering the Holy God: "Woe is me! I am lost, for I am a man of unclean lips . . . yet my eyes have seen the King, the Lord of hosts!" (Isa 6:5).[56] Seeing God is a scary proposition for the "unclean" and "sinful"—whether spirits, prophets, or fishermen—with forebodings of death and destruction ("No one shall see me and live" [Exod 33:20; cf. 3:6]; "Have you come to destroy us?" [Luke 4:34]).

54. Jeffrey, 78. González (74) contrasts fisherman Peter's eventual willingness to follow Jesus's command with the ship's captain and prisoner-transporting centurion in Acts 27:9–11, who disregard Paul's seafaring advice—with disastrous results.

55. Peter progresses from addressing Jesus as "Master" (ἐπιστάτα, *epistata*) in 5:5—a term of limited respect—to bowing before him as "Lord" (κύριος, *kyrios*), which connotes divine authority in Luke, as we have seen; cf. Green, *Conversion*, 90. As I will unpack more fully below on 8:22–25, "Master" in Luke typically comes from the lips of Jesus's disciples in their weak moments, reflecting deficient faith and knowledge.

56. See González, 74–75.

In declaring his sinful state, Simon Peter does not reference some ledger account or rap sheet of transgressions of God's law. He may (or may not) have more "sins" than the next guy, but that is not the point here. Even less germane is the supposedly rough character of fishermen. They were by no means saints or priests and may (or may not) have cursed and caroused more than the average citizen, but so what? Otherwise, they were likely as faithful to the Jewish law as any "common person."[57] Peter's point is that he has woefully "missed the mark" or "fallen short of the glory of God" (Rom 3:23) revealed in Lord Jesus. And he's terrified of the consequences, not so much of legal punishment for sins (he's on a boat, not in court), but of proximity to supercharged, sacred presence. But while wicked spirits have every reason to be terror-stricken, should sinful humans' fear of God be so extreme as to push God away and wish God would leave them alone? In his astute analysis of the Bible's complex theology of sin, Mark Biddle uncovers from the Genesis creation accounts forward a concept of sin as *mistrust* alongside the notion of *missing the mark*, not only as falling short of God's character, but also as underachieving God's good purposes *as humans*: "Sin . . . can be manifest either in overreaching or in falling short of proper humanity. Motivating the human propensity to overreach or underachieve is a basic mistrust of God and God's order of creation. . . . In sum, the Bible sees sin as fundamental mistrust of God's constant benevolence, a mistrust manifest in the effort to exceed human limitations or to shirk the wonder of being fully human."[58]

Jesus has just demonstrated God's abundant grace as well as awe-full power, but Peter downplays the former element, choosing to shirk his noble duty, to shrink away from opportunities for growth that Jesus's net-filling and net-ripping miracle has provided. But Jesus won't let him off the hook.

57. The notion promulgated by Jeremias (*Jerusalem*) that the poor, common folk of ancient Palestine, the "people of the land" (*'amme ha' arets*) were, as a class, "uneducated people . . . from whom it was useless to expect exact observance of the Law" (105) has been exposed in recent decades as a gross mis-stereotype derived from post-first-century Rabbinic polemics. See E. P. Sanders, *Jesus*, 174–211; and the succinct summary in Carey, *Sinners*, 7: "We have no evidence that most Jews of Jesus's day regarded ordinary people as sinners. Instead our best evidence suggests that most people in Galilee and Judea observed the basics of the law as they could. Religious specialists may have looked down on commoners, but they would not have excluded them from the covenant people, nor would they have called them sinners."

58. Biddle, "Sin," 732–73; see also his *Missing the Mark*, 75–98.

Catching People Alive (5:10b–11)

As with Isaiah in the temple, the Lord commissions Peter (and James and John) in the boat to serve God's people, though without any preparatory sin-atoning procedure as Isaiah received (Isa 6:6–8). Further unlike Isaiah's experience, Jesus does not ask Peter to volunteer ("Whom shall I send?" [Isa 6:8]). After offering some comfort, albeit as a command ("Do not be afraid" [Luke 5:10; cf. 1:13, 30]), Jesus flatly gives marching orders to Peter: "From now on you will be catching people" (5:10). No negotiation, no invitation: Jesus displays a stunning audacity, even imperiousness, now commandeering this fisherman's life and future, as he had his boat.[59] And though Jesus pointedly directs his commission to Peter ("you will be" [ἔσῃ, *esē*] in 5:10 is a second person singular form), his "partners" James and John also get caught in Jesus's net,[60] and together the fishermen trio respond with equally stunning obedience without objection: upon returning to shore, "they left everything and followed him" (5:11), period. Thus begins discipleship in terms of wholesale following Jesus. Its unqualified *totality* ("they left everything [πάντα, *panta*]") testifies again to Jesus's unquestioned *authority*. Caesar's audacious claims to power have nothing on Jesus's and are scarcely matched by Jesus's self-emptying benevolence.

The specific commission to be "catching people" represents more than an apt analogy fishermen would appreciate for reaching out to people. In at least two respects it hits home in raw reality. First, the verb Luke's Jesus uses (ζωγρέω, *zōgreō*) literally means "catch/capture alive" (notice the "live" ζάω/ζωή [*zaō*/*zōē*] part of the compound), appropriate for ensnaring fish or other animals—though, of course, typically for the purpose of killing and eating them! It appears mostly, however, in military contexts to denote capturing enemies alive, but again usually for harsh treatments such as imprisonment, servitude, exile, and humiliating execution. In the Israelites' wilderness war against the Midianites, for example, avenging the Midianite women's supposed seductive idolatry at Peor (Num 25), Moses angrily thundered at his conquering soldiers: "Why did you take every female alive [ἐζωγρήσατε,

59. See Spencer, "Follow Me," 142–46.

60. Cf. Green, *Conversion*, 89: "Simon thus serves a paradigmatic role in demonstrating the character of appropriate response to Jesus's mission. That Simon is representative of others is encouraged by the narrator's reference to them along with Simon as his 'partners.'" Luke uses two terms that the NRSV translates "partners": μέτοχοι, *metochoi* in 5:7 (lit. "having with") and κοινωνοί, *koinōnoi* in 5:10 ("sharing in common"). The latter term is cognate with the intimate "fellowship" (κοινωνία, *koinōnia*) of the early Jerusalem church, which held all possessions in "common" (κοινά, *koina*) (Acts 2:42, 44; 4:32).

ezōgrēsate]" (Num 31:15 NETS); he then orders them to "kill every woman" who had been sexually active and to keep alive (ζωγρήσατε, *zōgrēsate*) among "the chattel of the women" only "whoever has not known a male's bed" (31:18 NETS; cf. Philo, *Virtues* 43). The latter "chattel" group was hardly set free, however. Centuries later, the Chronicler reports the brutal slaughter of the Edomites by King Amaziah of Judah: "And the sons of Ioudas took captive [ἐζώγρησαν, *ezōgrēsan*] ten thousand and brought them to the cliff edge and tossed them over the cliff edge, and they were all rent asunder" (2 Chr 25:12 NETS).[61]

A notable exception to this terrible fate of live military capture stands out in Israel's conquest of Jericho, as Rahab and her family were not merely spared from extermination but were truly welcomed into the community: "And Raab the prostitute and all her father's house Iesous kept alive [ἐζώγρησεν, *ezōgrēsen*], and it has dwelled in Israel until this very day. For she hid the spies whom Iesous sent to spy out Jericho" (Josh 6:25 NETS; cf. 2:13). But in this context, the immunity for Rahab's household, though advantageous for them, is a classic case of the proverbial exception that proves the rule: except for this one marginal family, the entire population of Jericho is obliterated; moreover, Rahab escapes this holocaust only by betraying her own people.

On the whole, then, netting people alive appears starkly antithetical to life or liberty and thus an eerily disturbing image for Jesus's saving mission. A deeper dive into common fishing scenarios further complicates the picture. Counterbalancing the Creator God's fish-producing munificence, the OT prophets used fish-catching (along with fowl-snaring) as a metaphor of devastating *divine judgment*, not only against oppressive foreign nations (Ezek 29:2–7), but also against the iniquitous people of God (Jer 16:16–18; Amos 4:1–2; Hab 2:14–17). In more concrete political-economic terms, the fishing industry in Jesus's day represented an imperial monopoly thriving on the backs of heavily taxed fish procurers and processors. Caesar claimed ownership of the whole Mediterranean Sea and everything in it, and his client ruler in Galilee, Herod Antipas—bolstered by his new capital of Tiberias, named after the emperor, on the western shore of Lake Gennesaret, and the booming demand for savory Galilean fish stews throughout the realm—seized the opportunity to make this little lake into his own private "little Mediterranean Sea."[62] Family fishing businesses,

61. Josephus reports an internal conflict between rebel leaders Manahem and Eleazar at the outset of the Jewish War, resulting, first, in Manahem's *live capture* (ζωγρέω, *zōgreō*) by Eleazar's forces, but ultimately, the *torturous murder* of Manahem and his henchmen (*J.W.* 2.448).

62. See the excellent discussion in Sawicki, *Crossing Galilee*, 27–30, 143–47; her reference

like Simon's, were caught in Antipas's conglomerate dragnet, forcing them to purchase licenses and leases, produce a large quota, and pay steep taxes, tolls, and other fees to a bureaucratic juggernaut.[63] In a sense, Simon and associates themselves had been captured alive—with little room to breathe. And this kind of suffocating, ensnaring action is what Jesus seems to be calling these fishermen *to do to other people*!

We must resist taming this rough-and-tumble mission scenario into some whistling, bucolic tale of fishing the local creek on a lazy afternoon. This is war, a struggle for life and death. While Jesus by no means summons Peter and partners to lay down their nets and take up arms against Roman or Herodian overlords, he is establishing the just and redemptive kingdom of God, an alternative-subversive rule to the current corrupt and strangling world order. With creative power and wisdom, Jesus paves a bold new path of lordship over people that leads to their true flourishing, of binding them so they may be loosed, of calling them to forfeit control to attain real freedom: in short, the way of daily cross-bearing and defying worldly gain in order to find authentic, eternal life (9:23–25). Far from surrendering in defeat, Jesus claims victory by a different route, that of the Most High and Holy God. And he is under no illusions that the victory will come easily: the enemy remains strong (11:21), and the cost will be high (cf. 14:25–33). The unholy alliance, as we have seen, extends beyond the immediate political regime to encompass the cosmic sphere of the devil. Notably, the only other use of ζωγρέω (*zōgreō*, "catch/snare alive") in the NT relates to the tug-of-war between God and the devil over human destiny. In 2 Tim 2:25–26 Paul advises the young pastor that he should be "correcting opponents with gentleness" in the hope that "God may perhaps grant that they will repent and come to know the truth, and that they may escape from the snare of the devil, having been held captive [ἐζωγρημένοι, *ezōgrēmenoi*] by him to do his will." The captor ("him/his") at the end is ambiguous: either reinforcing the devil's entrapment of the opponents or God's rescuing them from the devil's snare and *recapturing* them to do God's will. The latter option would fit nicely with Luke's image of Jesus's mission: catching people alive to snatch them from the clutches of evil forces and to *resnag* them for godly purposes of "knowing the truth" and "doing God's will" (cf. Luke 1:4; 6:46–49; 8:21).[64]

---

to "the backdrop of Herod's disneyworld, the Mediterraneanized Kinneret [Sea of Galilee]" (185), provides a suggestive modern image.

63. See Hanson, "Galilean Fishing Economy"; Hanson and Oakman, *Palestine*, 106–10.

64. See 2 Cor 10:4b–5, which makes a similar point with a different "capture" verb: "We destroy arguments and every proud obstacle raised up against the knowledge of God, and take every thought captive [αἰχμαλωτίζοντες, *aichmalōtizontes*] to obey Christ." Applied to theolog-

A second key feature of Jesus's people-catching commission is its directive, not only illustrative, impact on the occupation of Simon, James, and John. In effect, Jesus recruits them to change jobs, to leave their fishing business for his, to give over their lives totally to him and his concerns. Remember, they "left everything and followed him"—including their boats chockfull of fish, which they managed to bring to shore (5:11). They do not cash in on their bonanza or try to enlist Jesus as a "special consultant" for future expeditions. They drop it all to adopt Jesus's business model oriented around different values than economic profit. González sets the score in sharp counterpoint to popular "gospels of prosperity":

> What we often do not realize is that these three leave everything at what would have been the height of their career. Their trust and obedience have led them to an unimaginable catch. The "gospel of prosperity" has come true! Because they believed, they prospered. But such prosperity is short-lived. Because they believe—because their success is sign of God's power—they abandon their prosperity and success. They do not take their prosperity as a sign of divine intervention and leave it at that. Rather, their unexpected prosperity itself is a sign that, as Peter declares, they are sinners, that they need a different life. And when Jesus invites them to such a life their prospering and their success are left behind for a life of wandering and hardship.[65]

Restoring a Disease-Riddled Leper and Raising a Bedridden Paralytic (5:12–26)

Jesus continues to demonstrate the nature of his "people-catching" mission in another pair of miracles (5:12–15, 17–26), with another interlude of retreating into "deserted places" (5:16). The following chart compares several elements in the two incidents. Our analysis will concentrate chiefly on Jesus's character and the moral, theological, and therapeutic implications of his cleansing/forgiving, restoring/raising actions.

---

ical hermeneutics, see Billings, *Word of God*, 62: "A theological approach to the interpretation of Scripture . . . should lead toward a more comprehensive hermeneutic that holds together understanding and explanation, theological and critical studies, in a way that seeks to 'take every thought captive to obey Christ.'"

65. González, 75–76.

	Restoring a leper[1] (5:12–16)	**Raising a paralytic** (5:17–26)
Setting:	Outside in "one of the cities" (5:12), where Jesus has an isolated encounter with a leper	Inside someone's home in the same city (presumably), where Jesus is teaching a large audience
Diagnosis:	"Full" (πλήρης, *plērēs*) of various skin sores, scales, and/or lesions	Serious muscular-skeletal incapacity requiring transport assistance
Approach:	Bowing before Jesus as Lord and begging for help in attitude of humility and faith ("Lord . . . you can make me clean" [5:12])	Lowering through the roof (by friends) in front of Jesus as demonstration of faith (5:19–20)
Treatment:	Touch and word	Word
Jesus's character:	Autonomy: "Lord, if you choose . . . I do choose" (5:12–13)	Authority: "The Son of Man has authority on earth to forgive sins" (5:24)
Moral issue:	Cleansing (καθαρισμός, *katharismos*) from disease, illness, and disorder	Forgiveness (ἄφεσις, *aphesis*) of sins
Therapeutic issue:	Restoration to health (wholeness), community, and divine order	"Resurrection," raising (ἐγείρω, *egeirō* [5:24]) or lifting up from impotent disability
Dispatch:	"Go" and have a priest verify cleansing, as required by Mosaic law (but tell no one else)	"Go" and walk home with bed in hand
Isa 35 link:	"A pure way shall be there, and it shall be called a holy way; and the unclean shall not pass by there, nor shall be there an unclean way" (Isa 35:8 NETS).	"Be strong, you . . . feeble knees! . . . Look, our God. . . himself will come and save us. . . . The lame shall leap like a deer" (Isa 35:3–4, 6 NETS).

1. Terms commonly rendered "leper/leprosy" in English Bibles represent a range of scaly skin ailments, from relatively mild to serious, including some types of baldness (and even mold on clothing and houses), not necessarily full-blown Hansen's disease. See the helpful note on Lev 13–14 by Milgrom, "Leviticus," 169; in any case, the present "leper" in Luke is said to be "full of/covered with" (πλήρης, *plērēs*) his skin problem, thus suggesting a severe condition. Interestingly, Lev 13:12–13 distinguishes cases of total coverage with a skin malady "from head to foot, so far as the priest can see," in which the afflicted hair and skin "has all turned white." Accordingly, the priest shall declare the person "*clean* of the disease"—ritually clean, that is, but hardly physically whole. Kaiser ("Book of Leviticus") offers a possible diagnosis: "If the skin condition covers a person's whole body . . . yet no swellings, sores, lesions, or ulcerations are connected with it—it is probably

something like vitiligo (*acquired leucoderma*), a condition where the skin loses its normal color and becomes white . . . where the skin loses its pigmentation" (1096). Yet, that may not be the end of the matter. Leviticus hastens to sound the warning: "But if raw flesh ever appears on him, he shall be unclean" (13:14–15). Though the precise condition of the disease-"covered" leper in Luke is unknown, Jesus sends him to the priests for (re)examination, indicating he had been in some state of "raw uncleanness." And the man's skin served to map his pervasive impairment and debilitation.

The Character of Jesus the Lord and Son of Humankind (5:12–13, 21–26)

The leper echoes Simon's address of Jesus as Lord and reinforces Luke's portrait of Jesus's autonomous character by stressing his freedom to *choose* how and when he will act in accordance with God's will. Embryonic expressions of such autonomy at age twelve, which both Jesus and his parents must "grow into" (2:40–52), now crystallize simply and clearly: as the skin-diseased man makes no presumptions on Jesus's purpose ("Lord, *if* you choose") even as he fully affirms Jesus's power ("you *can* make me clean"), Jesus responds with taut resolve, conveyed in two Greek words: Θέλω, καθαρίσθητι (*Thelō, katharisthēti*)—"I-do-choose. Be-made-clean" (5:12–13).

This emphasis on Jesus's autonomy goes hand-in-glove with his authority, previously on shining display in the Capernaum synagogue (4:32, 36) and reemerging in the next scene involving a paralyzed man (5:17–26). However, a "strange" (5:26) new dimension of Jesus's authority arises, as he first confers *forgiveness* upon the crippled man precisely in order to (ἵνα, *hina* ["so that"]) convey his "authority on earth to forgive sins" as "the Son of Man" (5:24). He purposefully wants his audience, particularly "the scribes and the Pharisees" (5:21), to "*know* [εἰδῆτε, *eidēte*]" that he has such absolute authority to absolve sins. We will discuss the moral nexus between forgiveness and healing below. Now we concentrate on Jesus's bold self-assertion.

This scene marks Jesus's first explicit encounter with scribes and Pharisees, two groups often lumped together in Luke and best described as "teachers of the law," that is, Jewish law, God's Torah (5:17). We might assume that some Pharisees among the temple scholars were ones Jesus engaged with at age twelve (2:46; cf. Acts 5:34–39; 22:3), but they are not specified until now. They are introduced with no hint of opprobrium, as "pharisaical" (hypocritical, legalistic, etc.) has come to connote. In fact, we first observe that these teachers have come from "every village of Galilee and Judea and from Jerusalem" to "sit" at Jesus's feet and learn from him (5:17), not to inspect and find fault. Points of conflict between Jesus and the Pharisees will surface in due course, but we carefully attend to Luke's nuanced "building" of these complex characters and their relationships.[66] Some tension soon spikes in the present scene, but frankly, it is more provoked by Jesus's audacity than by the Pharisees' obstinacy.

From an orthodox Torah perspective, Jesus's abrupt shift from teaching to pronouncing forgiveness of sins is a very questionable move, bordering on the blasphemous, since "God alone" "can forgive sins" (5:21). God's sole power and prerogative to forgive misdeeds against God constitutes a central tenet of biblical theology (e.g., Exod 34:6–7; Jer 31:31–34; Pss 32:1–5; 51:1–9; 103:1–3, 8–13). While priests *mediate* God's forgiveness through a ritual system, God remains the Forgiver. So for priest—or nonpriest like Jesus—directly to declare someone forgiven is to arrogate divine privilege or to speak "blasphemies" (Luke 5:21). The Pharisees have a point, *unless* Jesus doesn't merely represent God but actually *reflects* God and enjoys intimate filial fellowship with God the Father. That is precisely the portrait of Jesus that Luke has been constructing, but it has not yet been fully fleshed out, and the scribes and Pharisees can hardly be blamed at this stage for not grasping the depths of incarnational Christology.

In some respects, Jesus only complicates matters by reasserting, rather than explaining, his authority to grant forgiveness, with the lone added dimension concerning his apparent identification with the mysterious figure of *the Son of Man*. It is hard to know how the story's audience understands this reference, especially since it is "immediately" followed by the paralytic's uprising, bed-rolling, and rejoicing in God's grace (5:25)—after dropping through a makeshift hole in the ceiling! This all makes for a dizzying episode, prompting the usual ambiguous response of "amazement," plus a swelling of "awe" (NRSV) or, more accurately, "fear" (φόβος, *phobos*) and a hubbub of praise to God mixed with puzzlement: "We have seen strange things today" (5:26). That's for sure, and they have *heard* strange things, too, not least about the Son of Man's authority on earth to forgive sins. The crowd and visiting teachers are caught in the middle: not entirely at odds with Jesus, but not fully on board either.

What could Jesus's peculiar "Son of Man" reference mean? The title, if that is what it is, appears several more times in Luke, *always spoken by Jesus* in this and the other Gospels and mostly with clear reference to himself, though awkwardly in the third person. The Synoptic Jesus says little about himself as the "Son of God," "Messiah/Christ," "Savior" or "Lord" (though see Luke 6:46–49; 10:21–22; 22:70). It is largely left to the Gospel narrators and other characters (and to other NT writers and later church theologians) to fill out these identities of Jesus. But not so with "Son of Man," which appears only in a few places in

66. For a careful, comprehensive portrait of the Pharisees in Luke's narrative, see Gowler, *Host*; on character "building" in Luke's story, see Darr, *On Character*.

the NT outside the Gospels, with sparse detail.[67] The idea scarcely registers on anyone else's radar. When Jesus asks the disciples how people are identifying him, answers range from John the Baptist to Elijah or another prophet to "the Messiah of God" (Peter's response), with not a trace of discussion about the Son of Man (9:18–20).[68] We also receive scant help from later church creeds, confessions, and catechisms, which largely bypass expositions of Jesus as Son of Man.

We are left with a smattering of biblical and extrabiblical sources, which scholars have mined for all they are worth. But the evidence is mixed. An *apocalyptic* strain in Daniel, 1 Enoch, and 4 Ezra features an enigmatic heavenly figure that God will dispatch to earth on a messianic-militant mission to rescue and restore God's people from brutal foreign oppression.[69] However, this figure is identified as one "*like* a son of man" (or "*as it were* a son of man" [Dan 7:13 NETS]), which is not quite "like" Jesus's absolute reference (cf. Rev 1:13; 14:14; 1 En. 46:1). Though Luke's Jesus later alludes to the climactic coming of the Danielic Son of Man (Luke 17:22–30; 21:25–29; 22:66–71), his proclamation of forgiveness to the paralytic does not seem to fit this apocalyptic drama (the end-time Son-of-Man-type ruler comes more to punish than pardon sinners).

More relevant to the present case may be *hymnic* and *prophetic* references to "son of man." Psalm 8 reads:

> What is man [ἄνθρωπος, *anthrōpos*] that you are mindful of him
> or *son of man* [υἱὸς ἀνθρώπου, *huios anthrōpou*] that you attend to him?
> You diminished him in comparison with angels;
> with glory and honor you crowned him.
> And you set him over the works of your hand;
> you subjected all under his feet.
>
> (Ps 8:5–7 NETS)

"Son of man" is clearly parallel here to "man" or humankind as God's special creation, somewhat lower than angels, but still remarkably graced by God with crowning honor and authority over the world. Without a definite article before "son of man," the psalmist rejoices in the dignity and responsibility of

67. The NT references to the Son of Man outside the Gospels come from Stephen (Acts 7:56), the writer of Hebrews (Heb 2:5–9 [via Ps 8:4–6]), and John the seer (Rev 1:13; 14:14 [actually "one *like* the Son of Man"])—all with clear reference to Jesus.

68. Achtemeier, Green, and Thompson, *Introduction*, 233.

69. See discussions in Wink, *Human Being*; Murphy, *Early Judaism*, 157–59, 269–76; Collins and Collins, *King*, 75–100. Cf. Ps 80:18 LXX: "Let your hand be upon the man at your right hand, and upon a son of man, whom you made strong for yourself" (NETS).

all corporate humanity, not any particular person. By adding articles, Jesus's self-reference as "*the* Son of [the] Man" (ὁ υἱὸς τοῦ ἀνθρώπου, *ho huios tou anthrōpou*) may suggest his role as *the* Human One/Being par excellence who represents humankind and executes his God-given "authority on earth" (Luke 5:24).[70] However, the psalmist mentions no particular authority to *forgive sins*. The writer of Hebrews applies this psalm directly to Jesus, with clear atonement implications. But unlike Luke, Hebrews stresses Jesus's role as a "merciful and faithful *high priest*," able to forgive sins because of his full identification with the human condition, "yet without sin," and perfect qualification "to make a sacrifice of atonement for the sins of the people" (Heb 2:5–18; 4:14–16). Hebrews provides a marvelous theological exposition of Ps 8, but too much to pour into the merciful statement of Luke's Jesus to the paralytic.

From the *prophetic* Scriptures, Ezekiel provides valuable material too often given short shrift in Son of Man scholarship.[71] Over ninety times God addresses Ezekiel as "Son of man" (Υἱὲ ἀνθρώπου, *Huie anthrōpou*) before instructing him what to say and do before the exiled people of Israel. As "human" prophet,[72] Ezekiel dramatically digests, declares, and demonstrates God's word (see Ezek 3:1–11), and he does all this after a phantasmagoric vision of the enthroned God as "a likeness just as a form of a human [ἀνθρώπου, *anthrōpou*]" (1:26 NETS; cf. 1:4–28). So Ezekiel's human (son of man) identity and vocation are intimately related to God's human-*like* (anthropomorphic) being, which may be a way of conveying Ezekiel's Godlike nature as a man created in God's image.[73] But the highly impressionistic and mystical language of Ezekiel defies ontological precision. In any case, a broad parallel emerges between Jesus and Ezekiel as fellow prophetic "sons of men" to whom the heavens open and God is revealed in some kind of "bodily form" (Luke 3:21–22) and through whom God's word is proclaimed and displayed.[74]

To be sure, the connection is not perfect. Jesus is not a priest, as Ezekiel was, and Ezekiel's primary message was one of devastating judgment on the

70. A collective/corporate association is already hinted at in Daniel: the "kingship and dominion" given to "one like a human being [son of a human]" (Dan 7:13–14) is soon likewise "given to the people of the holy ones of the Most High" (7:27).

71. See Wink, *Human Being* (19–34, 267–69), drawing on the early work of Abbott (*Son of Man*, 82–107) as a notable exception to the neglect of Ezekiel.

72. The NRSV rendering of "mortal" obscures the "son of human one" meaning.

73. Cf. Wink, *Human Being*, 26–34.

74. Wink (*Human Being*, 268–69), drawing on Abbott (*Son of Man*, 97, 101), notes the link between the prophetic modes of Jesus and Ezekiel as speakers of parables (see Ezek 17:2; 24:3) and enactors of symbolic dramas, particularly aimed at arresting Israel's attention and shaking her complacency.

wickedness of Jerusalem, not forgiveness of sins. But then again, Luke's Jesus will also show a strong judgment side (already hinted in Nazareth), including "setting his face against/toward Jerusalem" in the manner of Ezekiel (Luke 9:51–53; cf. 13:33–35; 19:41–44; 21:20–24; 23:28–30; Ezek 6:1–7; 21:1–7); and Ezekiel also presses through the gloom at times to envision a "new heart/spirit" for God's people "clean from all your uncleannesses" (36:25–26) and a restored corporate body revitalized by God's word and breath (37:1–14). The images in Ezek 36–37 of cleansing pollutants and raising the dead are distinct but not that far afield from Jesus's Spirit-inspired work in forgiving sins and raising the paralyzed man.

While no English rendering is wholly adequate, John Carroll's preference for "Son of *Humanity*" marks an improvement over "Son of Man," as it better conveys Jesus's solidarity with "humanity-in-general" along the lines suggested in Ps 8 and Ezekiel.[75] I opt for the slightly different "Son of *Humankind*" in the rest of this commentary, underscoring Jesus's intimate *kind*red fellowship with all human beings. Admittedly, the universal scope of "humankind" is limited somewhat by retaining "Son" language (contrast "the Human One" in CEB). But I agree with Carroll that, whatever our current sensibilities, it is important to maintain Jesus's filial identity befitting his multifaceted christological and cultural profile in Luke. The special privileges and responsibilities accorded to sons in antiquity contextually inform our understanding of Jesus as Son of God and Son of David, as well as Son of Humankind. Moreover, "Son" retains a particular-individual identity resonant with the eschatological figure expected in Daniel, 1 Enoch, and parts of Luke (17:22–30; 21:25–28; 22:66–71). "Son of Humankind" attempts to hold together individual-collective, distinctive-representative, and earthly-heavenly tensions.[76]

The Ministry of Jesus as Cleanser and Forgiver (5:12–14, 20–24)

The language of "cleansing," associated with the leper's cure and domestic functions of removing dirt, and that of "forgiving," associated with the paralytic's healing and economic matters of remitting debt, may—or may not—also carry *moral* implications for dealing with *sins*.[77] While Jesus pointedly tells the disabled man, "Your sins are forgiven" (5:20)," no reference to iniquity or moral impurity emerges in Jesus's dealings with the diseased man. The Torah reflects

75. Carroll, 13n22.

76. See Spencer, Review of Carroll.

77. See the rich and nuanced discussion in Anderson, *Sin*, 3–26 (passim).

two strands of thought regarding the relationship of various skin ailments to moral pollution and punishment.[78] On the one hand, the *priestly tradition* in Lev 13–14 regards various skin conditions as *ritually*, not morally, defiling, separating the "unclean" diseased person from the holy sanctuary and community "camp" (Lev 13:45–46). Lepers are never branded "sinners," and the infirmity is not assumed to signal divine punishment for wicked behavior. Moreover, when the condition improves or dissipates, full provision is made for ritual cleansing and community reinstatement through a priestly certified process. On the other hand, the *narrative tradition* in Num 12 presents Miriam's sudden affliction with necrotic "flesh-consuming" leprosy as directly inflicted by God's "angry" judgment for a sin (rebelling against Moses's leadership) she "so foolishly committed" (Num 12:11).[79] Miriam is ultimately restored, but only after Moses intercedes with God and she serves a shameful seven-day sentence outside the camp (12:10–15).

The case of the skin-diseased man who approaches Jesus for cleansing fits the Levitical model. We hear nothing about the man's sin or punishment, and after Jesus removes the scales and sores ("the leprosy *left him*" [Luke 5:13]), he insists that the man complete the cleansing process by going to the priest and making the prescribed offering, "as Moses commanded" (5:14). Jesus plays it by the Levitical book. No cleansing from sin is implemented or implied. The main emphasis falls on the man's restoration to the community, first indicated when Jesus "stretched out his hand [and] touched him" (5:13) as a personal sign of fellowship, and finally confirmed by priestly evaluation. Social and ritual factors go hand in hand with the skin-diseased man's healing/cleansing.

We should also consider possible *psychological* elements at play in this incident, though with due caution, given the nonpsychological assessments of Luke or Leviticus. But recent research has demonstrated the near universal *psychology of disgust* operative in human societies, albeit with distinctive cultural expressions, applied to various "unclean" bodily conditions and moral judgments. Paul Rozin and associates have mapped three broad areas of disgust:

- *Core disgust*, regulating what enters the body through the mouth with food laws and other taboos concerning proper or polluting consumption;
- *Sociomoral disgust*, stripping individuals or groups of their human dignity because of some branded deviant status based on race, gender, class, dis-

78. For what follows, see Baden and Moss, "Origin."

79. As brother Aaron admits, he committed this sin with Miriam ("we") against Moses (Num 12:11). But Aaron is not physically punished, perhaps because of his priestly status, to say nothing of his status as eldest male.

ability, and other markers, which may or may not include alleged immoral behavior; and

- *Animal nature disgust*, monitoring an array of bodily functions, especially eruptions and emissions (like bleeding, ejaculating, defecating) that humans share with other animals, confirming to our great discomfort that we, too, are mortal creatures with life forces ebbing away and oozing out of us.[80]

Though the Bible does not typically accentuate emotional responses of disgust toward skin-diseased victims, Miriam's case certainly elicits strong visceral reactions from Aaron ("Do not let her be like one stillborn, whose flesh is half consumed") and God ("If her father had but spit in her face, would she not bear her shame for seven days?") (Num 12:12, 14). And it is no great presumptive leap to imagine that the leper in Luke "covered" with scaly skin ("raw" or "white") and possibly seeping sores would be a disgusting sight evocative of a rotting corpse.[81] Though not explicitly stated in Leviticus, there is little doubt that natural disgust toward death and decay contributed to strict regulation and segregation of "unclean" lepers. Most people, Jew or Gentile, ancient or modern, demarcate various objects of disgust best kept at a distance (see Luke 17:12), safely hidden from view.[82] By reaching out and touching the leper, Jesus crosses a disgust barrier that most people, not only observant Jews, would not cross. Contemporary Christians are hardly lining up to minister to lepers and other "disgusting" types in Kolkata (formerly Calcutta). That is what made Mother Teresa so saintly, an exceptional follower of Jesus, without Jesus's special advantage of neutralizing disgust by miraculously healing those ravaged by skin (and other) diseases. While Jesus's therapeutic treatment of lepers reinforces his unique love and power, his example, though not wholly imitable, urges his followers toward a *moral imperative* to overcome prejudicial boundaries of disgust in his name. Those branded "disgusting" may not be morally deficient, but those who reject and neglect such "unclean" persons are morally culpable.

The moral question is more complicated, however, in the paralytic's case, since Jesus appears to connect his physical healing with forgiveness of sins.

80. Rozin et al., "CAD Triad Hypothesis"; cf. Rozin, Haidt, and McCauley, "Disgust"; Richard Beck, *Unclean*, 13–30.

81. Cf. Balentine, *Leviticus*, 107: "Whether because of 'swelling,' 'eruption,' or 'spotting,' the skin's condition makes the body seem as if it is rotting away. Such an appearance suggests disintegration, which, if left unchecked, results in the person's death. And just as Israel must avoid defilement by contact with unclean carcasses (Lev 11), so must it guard against the disintegration of the *body of the person* and the *body of the society*" (emphasis original).

82. See Nussbaum, *Hiding*.

We may detect eerie echoes of Miriam's leprous punishment for her sin (also inflicted on Gehazi [2 Kgs 5:20–27], Amaziah [2 Kgs 15:5], and Uzziah [2 Chr 26:16–23]) and of Eliphaz, Bildad, and Zophar's diagnosis of Job's bodily (and other) afflictions as divine retribution against underlying iniquity. But in fact Jesus never explicitly links the man's lameness and his sinfulness. He never says, "*Because* you sinned in this or that manner, you've been suffering this malady." Indeed, Jesus suggests a more random association: he aims to announce ("so that you may know" [Luke 5:24]) his authority to forgive sins at this opportune moment before a large crowd, including teachers of the law.[83] The paralytic, then, is more incidental than integral to the forgiveness issue. Whereas enabling this man to walk is specific to his condition, forgiving his sins applies to every human being.

The Gospel of John provides instructive comparative texts. Early in his ministry, John's Jesus heals another paralyzed man ("Take up your mat and walk" [John 5:11]) and then adds: "See, you have been made well! Do not sin any more, so that nothing worse happens to you!" (5:14). This sin reference comes out of the blue and hints that the man's bad behavior had somehow contributed to his paralysis. Later John's Jesus meets a blind man whom the disciples, rather like Job's friends, assume has suffered for either his or his parents' sins (9:1–2). But this time Jesus sharply *severs the sin-suffering nexus* before curing the man's blindness: "Neither this man nor his parents sinned: he was born blind so that God's works might be revealed in him" (9:3). Moral judgments about disabled and diseased persons should be made only with due caution and discernment. The better judgment is to accept moral responsibility to care for such persons, lest *we sin* by failing to love our neighbors as God does.

Interlude: Jesus Retreats to the Desert to Pray (5:14–16)

Having compared the two miracle stories juxtaposed in Luke 5:12–26, we attend finally to the interlude between them, where Jesus attempts to restrict the news of the leper's healing and retreats from public view to "deserted places [ἐρήμοις, *erēmois*]" (5:16). The pattern recalls 4:41–42, where Jesus prohibited the demons from speaking "because they knew that he was the Messiah" and then proceeded to a "deserted place [ἔρημον τόπον, *erēmon topon*]." In the

83. The perfect passive verb ἀφέωνται (*apheōntai*) in 5:20, 23 suggests that Jesus announces a past (completed) and permanent state of forgiveness: "Your sins have been forgiven and stand forgiven" (cf. 7:47–48). This blunts a more immediate, present force with causal implications. Jesus does *not* say: "I forgive you [now] so that you can be healed [now]."

present case, we're not told why Jesus "ordered [the restored man] to *tell* no one" (he must only "*show* [him]self to the priest" [5:14]), but again it likely has to do with Jesus's desire to control his messianic message. The healed leper may not yet be ready to swear definitively that Jesus is Son of God and Messiah, as the demons were, but he certainly senses something of Jesus's salvific vocation. The problem is: whatever he *knows* about Jesus at this stage is bound to be limited and preoccupied with Jesus's miraculous power. Unlike the devil (4:1–13) and his demons, who aimed to use what "they knew" (4:41) about Jesus's divine identity against him, the restored leper would have no intentions of undermining Jesus. But he could still do damage, nonetheless, by calling undue attention to a single dimension of Jesus's mission. As significant as Jesus's mediation of "the [healing] power of the Lord" (5:17) is, it does not exhaust the full potential of Jesus's work. The people must also *know* Jesus's God-anointed authority to forgive sins (5:24) and to call disciples (5:11) to follow the way of saving and sustaining *through serving and suffering*, as will soon become evident.

Much remains to be learned about Jesus's vocation as God's Messiah. Of course, the leper is more interested in exulting in his renewed health than in exploring the theological depths of his healer; and despite Jesus's gag order, word gets out "more than ever," forcing Jesus to withdraw to the desert away from the press of cure-seeking crowds (5:15–16). But as suggested above, Jesus's desert jaunts serve as more than retreating escapes. They also afford him vital opportunities for reflecting on his mission, for owning and growing into his Messiah role. The added dimension in 5:16 that "he would withdraw to deserted places and pray" reinforces this contemplative, knowledge-enhancing experience.[84] Jesus's earlier allusion to Elisha's healing of the leprous Naaman (4:27) portends his ministry to those similarly afflicted with skin ailments. Now he actually provides such service—but not quite as Elisha did. Elisha never met Naaman directly; stationed inside his house, the prophet ordered the Syrian general (waiting outside) to dunk himself in the Jordan River seven times (2 Kgs 5:9–14). By contrast, Luke's Jesus chooses to touch the leper and pronounce him clean without any washing ritual. What other messianic choices must he make? How should he handle the constant clamoring of the infirm for his healing power? He can't cure all of them, can he? There is much to pray about, much to wrestle with, that only God can help him sort out.

84. The periphrastic construction with present participles (ἦν ὑποχωρῶν/προσευχόμενος, *ēn hypochōrōn/proseuchomenos*) stresses Jesus's customary, routine practice of retreating and praying: "he was [habitually] withdrawing to and praying in deserted places" (5:16).

Calling and Eating with Tax Collectors and Sinners (5:27–39)

After a series of miracles from 4:31 to 5:26, Jesus's mission now focuses on discipleship (again) and fellowship, specifically table fellowship. Akin to Jesus's recruitment of Simon Peter, James, and John while they plied their fishing trade, Jesus now summons "a tax collector named Levi, sitting at the tax booth." In Levi's case, however, Jesus simply says, "Follow me," without any accompanying miracle or commentary (5:27). Numerous toll booths were stationed around Lake Gennesaret to collect various taxes, tolls, and tariffs on all fish snagged from and goods shipped across Herod's "little Mediterranean."[85] In all likelihood, Levi knew something about Jesus's exploits in the area, including his dealings with the Capernaum fishermen; and like Simon and company, Levi "got up" from his business post, "left everything, and followed" Jesus (5:28). No more tax collecting for Levi. As well as disrupting personal lives and families, Jesus is putting a dent into Herod's economy.

If Levi is traumatized in any way by leaving everything for Jesus, he doesn't show it. And he displays nothing of Simon's overwhelming sense of sinfulness and desire for Jesus to leave him alone. Quite the contrary, before hitting the road with Jesus, Levi throws "a great banquet for him in his house," along with a bunch of his tax-collector associates and other friends (5:29). This event launches a major thematic emphasis in Luke on table-feasting and table-fellowship, not simply as an expression of joyous camaraderie or gracious hospitality, but also as an opportunity for vital instruction, discussion, and debate.[86] The table was a place for conversation as much as consumption, for serious talks as much as frivolous chats. The dining table doubled as a conference or seminar table for various symposia, formal and informal.[87] For Luke in particular, Jesus's mealtime conduct serves as a key source for knowing Jesus's character and aims as God's servant. Luke would have us pause on these occasions, recline with Jesus and fellow diners, and pay close attention.

The lively banquet conversation in Levi's house is stimulated by some Pharisees and scribes (invitees? interlopers?), who once again ask probing questions about Jesus's behavior (cf. 5:21). Here they raise two issues, both related to dining habits: (1) why do Jesus and his disciples "eat and drink with tax collectors and sinners?" (5:30); and (2) why doesn't Jesus direct his disciples to fast regularly, as John's disciples and the Pharisees do? (5:33). This time Luke

85. See Sawicki, *Crossing Galilee*, 27–30; Hanson and Oakman, *Palestine*, 106–10.

86. See Dennis E. Smith, "Table Fellowship"; Pao, "Family," 186–91; Karris, *Eating Your Way* and *Luke: Artist*, 47–78; Neyrey, "Ceremonies."

87. See Dennis E. Smith, *From Symposium*; Steele, "Luke 11:37–54."

explicitly characterizes their questioning in negative terms as "complaining" or "murmuring" (5:30), using the onomatopoeic term γογγύζω (*gongyzō*), reminiscent of the ancient Israelites' grumbling and mumbling against God and Moses about the meager menu in the wilderness (Exod 16:1–3, 8–12; 17:3; Num 11:1–9).[88] But the Pharisees are less bothered by what Jesus eats (no kosher disputes) than by *whom* he eats with ("sinner"-types) and *how often* he eats (never fasting).

Feasting with Tax Collectors and Sinners (5:27–32)

In the first instance, the Pharisees and scribes challenge Jesus's table-fellowship with two overlapping rather than distinct groups: *tax collectors*, representing a well-known type of *sinners*. Jesus's mission progresses from individual sinners (Simon and the paralytic), from whom he stands apart as creating Lord and forgiving Son of Humankind (5:8, 20–24), to a group of sinners with whom he sits as fellow eater and drinker (5:29–30). Association with a "large crowd" of perceived deviants in an activity as intimate as dining together—that is, reclining around the table, rubbing shoulders, and bumping hands grabbing for food to insert in mouths and pass through throats and beyond (recall core disgust boundaries)—greatly compounds the potential for shameful conduct. But don't the Pharisees overreact here? Aren't they now showing their true pettifogging, party-pooping colors? While a few rowdy tax collectors might drink to excess, does that automatically tag them as despicable "sinners"? Isn't Levi's "great banquet" more like a big neighborhood get-together than a Herodian palace orgy (no one loses his head or sheds any blood in Levi's home [see Mark 6:14–29])?

In assessing this situation, we must clarify two related, yet distinct issues: (1) why the Pharisees regarded tax collectors as sinners, and (2) why they avoided eating with sinners. The tax collectors' moral deficiencies had little to do with culinary habits per se; their profession did not necessarily incline them to ignore kosher laws or to indulge in bacchanalian behavior. Their "sinfulness" was more connected with political, economic, and social factors:

- *Politically*, they betrayed their Jewish compatriots by becoming part of the Roman-Herodian bureaucracy, supporting foreign, exploitative interests.

88. The term also appears in Acts 6:1 in the context of table fellowship. In this case Hellenistic-Jewish believers lodge a legitimate complaint/murmur regarding the neglect of their widows in the church's daily food service. In the interest of inclusive ministry, the problem is swiftly addressed by appointing seven servants to oversee the catering operation.

- *Economically*, they manipulated the corrupt system that easily allowed, if not encouraged, profiteering from overcharges of taxes and tolls beyond required quotas (see Luke 3:12–13).
- *Socially*, since they were routinely despised by the general population, they often associated by default with other morally suspect "sinners" (birds of a feather).[89]

Thus, Luke's Pharisees scarcely promote unreasonable judgments against tax collectors. John the Baptist agreed with the Pharisees (3:12–13), as would most Jews of the day, even if Jesus seems to dissent (though see below).

But does identifying a group's sinful proclivities demand not eating with them? The core disgust boundaries sketched above reinforce patterns of not eating with undesirables, however they may be defined (any school lunchroom confirms this tendency). It is hard to see John the Baptist dining with tax collectors (he hardly ate with anyone [cf. 5:33; 7:33]), just as he refused to baptize them unless they changed their aberrant ways (3:12–13); and frankly, it is hard to see Peter and his fishing cohorts happily sitting down and breaking bread (and fish) with Herodian agents who had overtaxed their business. But the Pharisees press the issue further. As a reform group within Judaism, the Pharisees sought to apply God's law faithfully throughout the land in every corner of society.[90] More specifically, it appears that they aimed to extend the sanctity of the temple into ordinary homes throughout Israel, effectively decentralizing and democratizing the presence of God. As homes became, so to speak, "little temples," tables became "little altars"—not for offering sacrifices, but for reflecting devotion to a holy God. As the temple regulated access to God through bounded spaces (courts), reserving inner sancta for "pure" priests, so the Pharisees—a lay, not priestly, party—restricted impious "sinners" from fellowship at the Lord's Table. It does not follow, however, that the Pharisees (or any other Jewish groups) despised "sinners" or wished them ill. They simply insisted that "sinners" repent and purify themselves according to Jewish law *before* entering into intimate contact with God and God's people. Such a policy is just what we would expect from a sober reform movement and is exactly what John did in refusing to baptize tax collectors or anyone else, *until* they bore "fruits worthy of repentance" (3:8).

89. See Carey, *Sinners*, 23–24.

90. See the critical discussion in Neusner, *From Politics*, 67–86, and *Judaism*, 45–61; Murphy, *Early Judaism*, 233–37; and Dunn, "Pharisees." In his important study, Saldarini (*Pharisees*) affirms the likelihood of the Pharisees as a "reformist" movement in first-century Palestine but is more cautious about sifting later Mishnaic-Rabbinic materials to determine their social-religious practices and attitudes (see esp. 220–37, 277–97). That said, Neusner's foundational work is rigorously historical-critical, with full awareness of the biases of the Gospel and rabbinic sources.

The Pharisees' flap with Jesus is that he welcomes sinners around the table *as they are* without preconditions of repentance. But this judgment by no means signifies that Jesus engages sinners without concern for changing their hearts, minds, and deeds. Quite the contrary, in answering the Pharisees' charge, Jesus again plays the *physician* role, as assumed at Nazareth in a polemical context concerning his restorative miracles: "Doctor [Ἰατρέ, *Iatre*], cure yourself!" (4:23). Now he associates his medical-type therapy with reaching out to sinners and reforming their lives: "Those who are well have no need of a physician [ἰατροῦ, *iatrou*], but those who are sick; I have come to call not the righteous but sinners *to repentance*" (5:31–32).[91] Repentance (μετάνοια, *metanoia*) in Luke's writings tightly entwines with wholesale (holistic) "turning" or "converting," not primarily *from* one religion or one party or "denomination" within a tradition, but *to* a whole new way of life, a new way of thinking, feeling, acting, and relating to God and others.[92] For Israel, it marks a returning from exile, as N. T. Wright has stressed, an eschatological (climactic, "at last") restoring of God's people.[93]

Redaction-critical scholars are quick to note that Luke adds the "repentance" qualifier to Mark 2:17 (cf. Matt 9:13), which reports that Jesus "calls sinners," period, as they are, with no pressure to change. Some commentators further opine that Mark reveals the "real" Jesus who annulled conventional "sinner" categories, variously configured by self-righteous judges, and graciously accepted all into God's realm apart from works ("fruits") of repentance (though Jesus would scarcely object if sinners cleaned up their acts). In this respect, the argument runs, the Markan (historical) Jesus diverges from John the Baptist's stricter, reform-focused "baptism of repentance." Uneasy about such a radically free gospel, Luke polishes Jesus's image with a more conformist—and reformist—emphasis on repentance. Or so one theory goes.[94]

91. On the medical-therapeutic model among Hellenistic philosophers as a conceptual guide for offering sage counsel toward the end of living full, flourishing lives, see Nussbaum, *Therapy*.

92. See Green, *Conversion*, 45–86 (and throughout). Nave (*Role*) especially stresses the ecclesial and ethical aims of repentance in Luke's story: "the relationship between repentance and the social, moral, ethical, financial and religious inequities depicted in the narrative structure of Luke-Acts" (6). In this vein, he argues that Luke is concerned as much, if not more, with the repentance of religious insiders (like the Pharisees and the apostle Peter) toward adopting a more embracive, inclusive acceptance of "outside" sinners as with the repentance of these sinners themselves (see the summary section, 220–24). Moreover, Nave does view the repentance of *Gentiles* in Luke-Acts as involving "a change of religion—a conversion" (224).

93. N. T. Wright, *Jesus*, 246–52.

94. The most prominent proponent of this view is E. P. Sanders, *Historical Jesus*, 226–37, and *Jesus*, 200–11. See the critique of this view in N. T. Wright, *Jesus*, 246–48.

However, as responsible theological interpretation demands careful consideration of each Gospel's integrity, it also resists the impulse to parse every distinction among the Gospels as momentous and inimical to an overarching canonical portrait of the *one* Lord and Savior, Jesus Christ. While Luke accentuates the repentance theme more than the other evangelists, they hardly ignore the point (see, e.g., Matt 3:8, 11; 4:17; 11:20–21; 12:41; Mark 1:4, 15; 6:12; John 1:12; 3:1–7; 5:14–15; 8:11). Thus, Luke's addendum about summoning "sinners *to repentance*" may be taken as elucidating what Mark implies rather than blazing a new path.

In relation to the Pharisees and John the Baptist, Luke's Jesus pursues a similar reformative *aim*, even as he adopts a different *strategy* by seeking out and supping with sinners *as the operative context* for spurring their repentance. While Jesus can issue a sharp "repent or perish" ultimatum when the situation calls for it (cf. 13:1–5), his agenda to receive sinners at his table as a first move toward reorienting their lives reveals a stronger emphasis on attraction and restoration than on aversion and retribution. Like Woman Wisdom, whose ways he's been following since his youth (2:40, 52), Jesus seeks to redirect the waywardness of the "simple" ("sinners," "scoffers') by summoning them to feast at "her house" and instructing them at "her table" (Prov 9:1–6; cf. 1:20–33).[95] Actually, he co-opts Levi's home and converts it, as it were, to Wisdom's abode (Luke's Jesus has no private residence [see 9:58]). Jesus's evangelism through hospitality displays a more open and optimistic, inviting and inclusive attitude toward sinners than more preachy and boundary-setting approaches. It places a higher premium on compassion and hope for change, perhaps naively so, given Jesus's eventual unjust death on a Roman cross between two "lawless" criminals (cf. 22:37). But that is a risk Jesus is willing to take in order to save all types of sinners who have lost their way (cf. 15:1–32; 19:1–10).

95. See Moltmann-Wendel, "Self-Love," 24: "The Jesus who dines with tax collectors, sinners, and prostitutes acts and speaks like Wisdom, and the oldest Christology actually seems to have been Sophialogy. The theology of Wisdom—in contrast to patriarchal images of God—knows no instruments of punishment and threat." While I affirm this Sophialogical link between hospitable Wisdom and Jesus, Moltmann-Wendel overstates the "no punishment and threat" point. As much as Woman Wisdom welcomes sinner-types, she also warns them of serious "calamity" and "disaster" if they do not heed her reproof (Prov 1:20–33). Moreover, Wisdom and Jesus take different approaches: the former invites the "simple" to *her* place and steers young men away from sinners' (loose women's) houses (Prov 5:1–14; 7:24–27; 9:1–6), whereas Jesus goes *to* sinners' homes (5:29–32; 19:5–10).

Fasting (or Not!) with the Pharisees and John's Disciples (5:33–35)

The Pharisees' second culinary question concerns Jesus's laxity regarding the religious practice of fasting. While he himself may occasionally fast (4:1–2), he does not encourage his disciples to follow suit, as the adherents of both John and the Pharisees "frequently" do (5:33).[96] Jesus's followers seem more at home feasting than fasting. Hence, Jesus's motley crew of disciples (fishermen and tax collector thus far) does not seem disciplined at all. Again, the Pharisees pose a reasonable question. While the Jewish Scriptures warn against fasting for wrong, self-serving reasons (Isa 58:3–7; cf. Matt 6:16–18), they consistently endorse fasting for proper ends related to mourning disasters, confessing sins, making critical decisions, concentrating attention on spiritual matters, and giving food to the poor.[97] Why, then, would any God-honoring teacher like Jesus not encourage his students to fast?

Jesus answers with metaphoric flourish, moving swiftly from the medical model to matrimonial, textile, and enological images. His clearest response to the fasting query depicts his vocation as a *bridegroom* celebrating with his (disciple) attendants at a *wedding feast*, which is no occasion for fasting or even moderation. Weddings represent highlife community events, rejoicing in the couple's faithful love and prospects for a fruitful life together. Aptly, marriages and wedding banquets also symbolize God's covenantal bond with God's people and the consummating (eschatological) bounty of God's messianic blessings (cf. Isa 62:1–9; Matt 22:1–14; John 3:29; Eph 5:25–33; Rev 19:6–9). As Bridegroom-Messiah, Jesus has come to kick off God's final kingdom gala with all sorts of "guests," including sinners (cf. Luke 14:15–24). It is Jubilee time for feasting, not fasting. Even the call to repentance, which at other times demanded somber responses of weeping, lamenting, and fasting (e.g., Ezra 8:21–23; 9:5–15; Neh 1:4–11; 9:1–5), Jesus now issues in a spirit of joyous banqueting and hopeful renewal reminiscent of Isaiah:

> Ho, everyone who thirsts,
>   come to the waters;
> and you that have no money,

96. The questioners also mention the practice of *prayer* (along with fasting) by John and the Pharisees' disciples as something Jesus neglects to promote. Here, however, he focuses only on the fasting issue. Jesus's instructing his followers about prayer—which they must regularly do—emerges later in 11:1–13.

97. See Lambert, *How Repentance*, 4–64; Muddiman, "Fast." Muddiman notes that "'fasting like a Jew' had become proverbial in the Roman world of the first century (Suetonius, *Aug.* 76)" (2:774).

> come, buy and eat!
> Come, buy wine and milk
> without money and without price. . . .
> Listen carefully to me, and eat what is good,
> and delight yourselves in rich food.
> Incline your ear, and come to me;
> listen so that you may live.
> I will make with you an everlasting covenant. . . .
> Seek the LORD while he may be found,
> call upon him while he is near;
> let the wicked forsake their way,
> and the unrighteous their thoughts;
> let them return to the LORD, that he may have mercy on them,
> and to our God, for he will abundantly pardon.
>
> (Isa 55:1–7)

Jesus is not opposed to fasting, whether for John (cf. Luke 7:33–35), the Pharisees, or for his own disciples in due time. In fact, Jesus insists that his followers "will fast" when he, their bridegroom, "will be taken away from them" (5:35). Though he doesn't dwell on the point, Jesus puts his own damper on the party by alluding to an unspecified period ("the days will come" [5:35]) when he will depart (die) and leave his disciples behind. They will struggle mightily in those days; a "sword will pierce [their] own soul[s] too" (2:35)—and *then* they must engage in much prayer and fasting in order to survive (see Acts 1:14; 4:23–31; 9:9–18; 13:2–3; 14:23). The gospel of God's kingdom is truly good news, but it is not cheap. Liberation comes at the steep price of Jesus's very life.

Fostering a "New" Approach to "Old" Ways (5:36–39)

Jesus briskly shifts metaphoric gears to a pair of short "parables" illustrating the mis-fit of "new" substances with "old": new fabric ill-suits an old garment (5:36); new wine bursts an old wineskin (5:37–38). Though appearing to drop the immediate feasting/fasting issue, except for the oblique association with wine-drinking, a broad connection persists: Jesus's current feasting, nonfasting habits reflect a "new" dimension of his messianic mission bursting the bounds of "older" manifestations of God's work. The kingdom of God coming afresh through Jesus Christ represents a "new creation" (cf. Isa 43:18–19; 65:17; 2 Cor 5:17; Gal 6:15). But in a vital sense, this newness is part of the same "old" process of God's perpetual re-creating, renewing project in "heaven and earth." The contrast should not be drawn in sharp dualistic lines between the "old covenant" with Israel and "new covenant" in Christ; for Luke's Jesus at this point, the "old" is not obsolete or outmoded, and the "new" is not supersessionist or supremacist. He does not advocate ditching the old garments or wineskins: indeed, in picturing the result of pouring new wine into old wineskins, he laments the skins' damage as much as the wine's spillage (5:37). But more to the point is the biblical-theological fundament of God's *ever-creative* nature from Genesis ("In the beginning God created" [Gen 1:1]) to Revelation ("See I am making all things new" [Rev 21:5]) and everything in between. As God spoke through Isaiah in the middle of the "Old" Testament: "I am the LORD, your Holy One, the Creator of Israel, your King. . . . Do not remember the former things, or consider the things of old. I am about to do a new thing; now it springs forth, do you not perceive it?" (Isa 43:15–19).

Adapting the Protestant dictum of *semper reformanda*, stressing the church's "always reforming" toward increasing faithfulness to God and likeness to Christ, we might argue that God is "always reforming" the people and world God created into God's image. The key, as Isaiah exhorts, is to "perceive" (know) the new thing God is doing at any moment, especially at watershed moments of revelation. For Luke, God's consummate work of "new creation" is generated and guaranteed through Jesus Messiah. "Do we not perceive it?"

No modern theologian has perceived the inexorable (re)creative, (re)generative dynamic of God's openness to the future more passionately than Jürgen Moltmann. He contends that Christian tradition has largely focused on "the finished creation and its preservation through God's providence." As a result, "it has overlooked not only the future of creation still to come but, together with that, God's continuing creative process." The OT, in Moltmann's view, stresses both preservation and renewal aspects of God's creative work, with greater accent on God's renewing "activity in history" than on the grand primordial act "in the beginning." Accordingly, the biblical doctrine of creation "is not a creation out of nothing. It is creation afresh out of what is old, a renewal and intensification, and the giving of new form to what has already been created and is already there."[98]

98. Moltmann, *Ethics*, 122–23; see further the "Creational Theology" section in the concluding "Integration" to this commentary.

Feeding Hungry Disciples and Healing a Disabled Man on the Sabbath (6:1–11)

The Pharisees' concerns about Jesus and his disciples' behavior continue in the next pair of scenes: first, involving further questions about their eating habits (6:1–5); second, raising eyebrows about Jesus's healing practices (6:6–11). By the end, the Pharisees' reaction boils into "fury"-fueled plots of "what they might do to Jesus" (6:11). Such vehement emotion marks a considerable escalation beyond "amazement" (5:26) and "complaining" (5:30). What accounts for this explosion?

Two factors exacerbate the conflict in these incidents: their (1) Sabbath settings and (2) scriptural-legal debates—both recalling the Nazareth episode, which also concluded with the audience's "rage" against Jesus (4:28). As the weekly Holy Day in Jewish life, with deep creation (Gen 2:1–4) and liberation (Exod 20:8–11) roots, the Sabbath carries heavy theological weight. What is done—and not done—on this day matters immensely to basic rhythms of divine and human activity. As we have repeatedly seen, Jesus and his family have been faithfully synchronized with Sabbath and other JST tempos in both temple and synagogue. Jesus infuriated his hometown congregation by what he *said* on the Sabbath, not by what he *did*. His synagogue reading and explicating of Scripture is precisely what one should do on the Sabbath. But now he pushes the envelope not only by provocative speech but also by (allegedly) prohibitive activity on this sacred day of rest and worship. And he justifies his actions, considered unlawful in the eyes of certain Pharisees, by appealing to them on their own terms of scriptural precedent and principle (6:3–4, 9–10).

Jesus Goes against the Grain (6:1–5)

In the first clash, "some [τινες, *tines*]," not all, Pharisees object to the Sabbath activity of Jesus's disciples in plucking, rubbing (threshing), and eating heads of grain from unspecified fields (6:1–2). Again, as in the previous fasting controversy, the issue is not so much Jesus's own dietary behavior but what he sanctions for his disciples. In other words: what kind of Lord and Teacher is Jesus? In the present case, the problem is not the disciples' trespassing on others' land or stealing their crops. No landowners (absent from the story) or Pharisees dispute the disciples' right to avail themselves of free "walk-through" food service, likely because of established gleaning legislation, permitting poor itinerants to pick and eat what they needed from the edges of others' fields (Lev 19:9–10; 23:22; Deut 24:19–22; cf. Ruth 2). Recall that the disciples had "left everything" to follow Jesus (Luke 5:11, 28), including purses and provisions (cf. 9:1–6; 10:3–9). So their take-out fare of grain should probably not be viewed as a little "Sabbath snack,"[99] but more like dinner or maybe all they would eat that day.

While not a snack, it is a *Sabbath* meal, governed by various regulations. That is the real rub with the disciples' conduct: "doing what is not lawful *on the Sabbath*" (6:2). But in what way? The fasting issue does not carry over here. Despite the prejudicial misunderstanding of some outsiders that the Jews oddly eschewed both eating and working one full day every week,[100] the Sabbath was in fact a time of celebrating the Creator's goodness, with some sources even *forbidding* fasting on this holy day (Jdt 8:6; Jub. 50:12).[101] While grateful Sabbath eating, even feasting,[102] was encouraged, working was another matter: a suspension of daily labor, business as usual, supported the Sabbath's main focus on restful worship. The world does not depend on human effort, but on God's grace; anything humans accomplish is a gift from God. The Sabbath inscribes this fundamental, graced principle into everyday, every-weekly life.

However, while the written Torah clearly enjoins suspending work on the Sabbath, it does not provide a detailed list of proscribed activities. This regulative lacuna gave rise to considerable, and at times convoluted, debate about proper Sabbath conduct. As the Mishnah acknowledges: "The rules about the Sabbath . . . are like mountains hanging on a hair, for [teaching of] Scripture [thereon] is scanty and the rules many" (m. Ḥag. 1:8).[103] Scripture does, nonetheless, specifically interdict *plowing* and *reaping* fields, even during harvest season (Exod 34:21). One Mishnaic tractate fills in the gaps by delineating thirty-nine Sabbath work prohibitions (m. Šabb. 7:2), but among these *plowing/reaping* again prove most relevant to the present case (cf. Jub. 2:29; 50:6–13; CD 10.14–11.18). Perhaps, then, some Pharisees subsume Jesus's disciples' gleaning under this broad fieldwork category. But hand plucking and nibbling a few heads of grain hardly compare with cultivating and harvesting a whole crop, normally with the aid of yoked animals.

Another line of scriptural-legal reasoning may focus on the disciples' *procuring* and *preparing* food on the Sabbath. During their wilderness wandering period, the ancient Israelites gathered a double portion of manna on the

99. Jeffrey, 86. Against the "snack" assessment, see Warren Carter, *Matthew*, 264: "This scene concerns not merely a quick snack but fundamental justice issues of access to food resources and alleviating human need"; and Spencer, "Scripture," 2–7 (which I draw on for this section).

100. See Feldman, *Jew*, 161–67.

101. Cohn-Sherbok, "Analysis," 35.

102. For a wide-ranging theological reflection on the "feasting" dimension of Sabbath observance, see Dawn, *Keeping Sabbath*, 149–213; cf. Swartley, "Sabbath," 695.

103. Danby, *Mishnah*, 212.

sixth day, enough to carry over to the Sabbath without additional labor (Exod 16:5, 22–30).[104] Closer to Jesus's time, a group of Essenes applied this biblical precedent to their community: "No man shall eat on the Sabbath day except that which is already prepared. He shall eat nothing lying in the fields" (CD 10.20–21).[105] In Luke's story, Jesus's disciples had evidently not stored up grain the day before, which is scarcely surprising, since they lived from day to day ("Give us each day our daily bread" [Luke 11:3]) and since gleaning allowed for satisfying immediate needs, not stockpiling leftovers.

Whatever particular Sabbath violations the Pharisees have in mind, Jesus grants them their basic charge of illegality. His followers are technically engaged in Torah-breaking behavior on this Sabbath. But there are other texts to consider. Arguing on *common scriptural ground* with the Pharisees ("Have you not read?" [Luke 6:3]), Jesus appeals to historical-narrative precedent from David's life in 1 Sam 21:1–6 (part of the Former Prophets in the HB). Like the Pharisees, Jesus accepted the canonical authority of the Law, Prophets, and Psalms (Writings) (Luke 24:27, 44) and the hermeneutical principle of comparing Scripture with Scripture to discern the whole counsel of God (cf. Acts 20:27). In no way aiming to denigrate or abrogate Sabbath law, Jesus cites an *exceptional* case regarding David and his companions as analogous to the current situation of Jesus and his disciples.

While on "expedition" (1 Sam 21:5), David and his "hungry" soldiers entered the sanctuary at Nob seeking bread from the local priest, Ahimelech. However, the only food available that day was the "holy bread" of the Presence reserved only for priestly consumption. Still, after gaining assurances from David about the men's sexual purity, Ahimelech gave them the sacred fare (21:4–6). The law was relaxed: extraordinary times call for extraordinary measures. Though Jesus doesn't elaborate, the parallels seem clear enough with his itinerant disciples' "unlawful" dining. As with David, so with Jesus (Son of David) and his disciples: as Jesus's "special forces" become hungry while carrying out their kingdom "mission," they merit being fed, if need be, by unconventional means.[106] Jesus mounts no campaign for sweeping reform of Sabbath legislation. He simply addresses a special case, with due attention to situational particularities. Hermeneutically, he models *contextual interpretation* of Scrip-

104. Cf. the short, but shocking, incident in Num 15:32–36, in which a man caught gathering sticks (for a cooking fire?) on the Sabbath is stoned to death, "just as the Lord had commanded Moses."

105. Trans. Vermes, *Dead Sea Scrolls*, 109

106. Jesus says nothing about his disciples' sexual purity, but this state may be assumed, since they had left their wives to follow Jesus, and thus far no women have appeared among Jesus's retinue.

ture, correlating a specific snapshot of human behavior within the panoramic horizon of biblical revelation.

Jesus by no means cavalierly relaxes or sets aside scriptural teaching to suit his immediate interests. If he's going to defend some apparently "unlawful" practice, he better have good *scriptural* rationale for doing do. Jesus's growing knowledge of God's will remains deeply rooted in biblical soil. To be sure, the Pharisees might have wished for a tighter analogy, though they do not challenge Jesus's reading of 1 Samuel. If we pushed a "strict constructionist" line, we might note that Jesus's disciples are in the grain fields, not God's house, eating generic heads of grain, not cultic loaves; and in fact, the David story is not explicitly set on the Sabbath, though that may be reasonably assumed.[107]

Of course, by their nature analogies offer broad comparisons; they do not have to score on every point. In any case, biblical interpretation is not a mechanical-legalistic exercise, following a list of exegetical rules that produces the one true, definitive meaning. It is spiritual art as much as grammatical science, guided by the dynamic wisdom of God's Spirit in conversation with God's people seeking to do God's will.[108] Still, decisions eventually have to be made, debates settled, among conflicting opinions. Where do we look for final authority? Luke continues to make a daring case for a christological hermeneutic, for *Jesus's supreme authority* as declarer and demonstrator of God's purpose. Whatever the Pharisees might think of Jesus's handling of the David holy bread incident, his interpretation rings true because of his God-given authority as Son of Humankind: "The Son of Humankind is Lord of the Sabbath" (Luke 6:5). Since the Sabbath is the Lord God's sacred day, and since Jesus is God's Son, Lord Jesus has full and final right to determine what can and can't be done on this day. Again, it is vital to appreciate that Jesus does not exert this right in independent, arbitrary fashion, but rather *within the constraints of Holy Scripture*. But within that canonical framework, he does assume the position of Scripture's ultimate arbiter. Though Luke doesn't report the Pharisees' immediate reaction to Jesus's "Lord of the Sabbath" pronouncement, we can imagine that their anger, which erupts at the end of the next scene (6:11), already begins to simmer. Adding "Sabbath Lord" on top of "Sin Forgiver" (5:24) to his Son of Humankind profile is audacious in the extreme, which is to say, blasphemous to orthodox ears (cf. 5:21). Debating the meaning of Scripture is one thing; assuming intimate identification with God is another.

107. Lev 24:5–9 stipulates the placement of fresh loaves "every Sabbath day . . . before the Lord," but it does not make clear whether the priests consumed all the bread this day. While some later rabbinic traditions set 1 Sam 21:1–6 on the Sabbath, Luke's Jesus stresses *what* David "unlawfully" ate (priestly fare), not *when* he ate it. See Cohn-Sherbok, "Analysis," 35–36.

108. See the wide-ranging essays in Davis and Hays, *Art*.

Jesus Gives a Helping Hand (6:6–11)

The next scene may take place on "another Sabbath" in the synagogue (6:6), but the tense atmosphere carries over from the conflict in the grain fields. The Pharisees (joined again by scribes) have shifted into high-alert gear, closely monitoring Jesus's Sabbath activity. Their motives have deteriorated from arguing with Jesus about serious theological and ethical issues to advancing fresh charges of misconduct against him. In a curious, if not callous, move on the Pharisees' part, they now stand poised to pounce on Jesus if he opts to heal someone on the Sabbath (6:7). No one objected to his Sabbath exorcism in the Capernaum synagogue (of course the demon was making quite a commotion) (4:31–37). And who in their right religious mind would oppose an act of healing in a place of prayer and fellowship? But in fact, just as the Pharisees should not be tarred as unconcerned about sinners, so they should not be feathered as uncaring about the sick. But in their view, there's a proper *place* (not at table with sinners) and *time* (not on the Sabbath for sick folk) for compassionate activity in God's economy. In the latter case, the Bible does not prohibit medical work on the Sabbath, but some oral interpretive tradition did limit curative labor, within the Sabbath framework of rest, only to emergency, life-threatening situations.[109] A disability, like a withered right hand in the present story (6:6), while unfortunate and worthy of assistance, can easily wait another day for treatment. The disabled man might even be better served by devoting his full attention to God on the Sabbath in preparation for better serving God with a restored, functional hand the rest of his days.

Jesus is astutely aware of these possible perceptions and more: "he *knew* what they were thinking," including their disputations (διαλογισμούς, *dialogismous*) (6:8). His ever-deepening knowledge pertains not only to God but to people (cf. 5:22). The Johannine evangelist puts it more strongly: "Jesus . . . knew all people and needed no one to testify about anyone; for he himself knew what was in everyone" (John 2:24–25). For both Luke and John, Jesus's prescience about people owes not to some spooky telepathic talent but rather to a sensitive empathic connection with others, combined with keen empirical knowledge of human nature (as in Israel's wisdom tradition). How Jesus acts upon, as well as acquires, this knowledge is a major concern throughout this commentary. Here he uses what he knows about the Pharisees' scruples to

109. m. Yoma 8:6 establishes the clear principle that "danger to life supersedes the Sabbath," even allowing medical treatment to begin or continue on the Sabbath if there is concern that the patient might not survive the week; cf. Mek. Šabb. 1 on Exod 31:12–17, cited and discussed in McNamara, *Targum*, 31–34.

expand their knowledge of God's ways in a confrontational fashion. Again he pushes the dramatic envelope to maximum effect.

Locking in on the man with the paralyzed hand, Jesus calls him to "come and stand here," literally, "in the middle [εἰς τὸ μέσον, *eis to meson*]" of the assembly. Luke makes sure we get the picture by reporting: "He got up and stood there" (6:8). Jesus stands center stage with the disabled man and commands full attention with a rapid-fire sequence of comments and movements. First, he questions the legal experts: "I ask you, is it lawful to do good or to do harm on the sabbath, to save life or to destroy it?" (6:9). This time Jesus draws not on a specific narrative precedent, but on a general biblical-legal principle with which the Pharisees would concur.[110] Of course, the Sabbath celebrates the goodness of all creation (Genesis) and the salvation of Israel from life-choking slavery (Exodus). Accordingly, if this man—or anyone's child, donkey, or oxen, as Jesus will later elaborate—had fallen into a well, ditch, or any other lethal snare on the Sabbath, any God-honoring and creation-loving good person would be duty bound to secure the trapped victim's well-being on this day as much as any other (Luke 14:5; cf. Exod 23:5; Deut 22:4; Matt 12:11–12). But the man with the withered hand is currently standing alive and otherwise well in the synagogue, not stuck in a well or a ditch. Naturally, if he were so stuck with *two good hands*, he might well pull himself out to safety! So Jesus's act of healing might be viewed as a type of preventive care. But surely the man will make it through one more Sabbath, and Jesus can restore him tomorrow without disrespecting any Sabbath traditions. We must recall, however, that Jesus's mission is operating in urgent "today" mode: now is the day of salvation; it is the climactic, liberating Year of Jubilee, the Sabbath of Sabbaths (Luke 4:18–21). Every day, every moment is Sabbath time for doing good, saving life, and making whole. Far from flouting the Sabbath, Jesus aims to fulfill (fill out) its holistic creative-redemptive purpose.

Second, Jesus pauses momentarily and is "looking around at all of them," particularly targeting the scribes and Pharisees (6:10). This action involves more than making eye contact to connect with the audience. Jesus takes the measure of the legal experts and effectively invites them to expand their field of vision and see what he sees about God's Sabbath purpose "today." He's not simply scoring points and trying to best his opponents: he wants them to know what he knows.

Accordingly, in his third move, Jesus trains the congregation's vision on the man's manual disability by commanding him, "stretch out your hand

110. Also the broad moral principle of "Care/Harm" designated by Haidt, *Righteous Mind*, 131–34; see above on Luke 4:31–39.

[ἔκτεινον τὴν χεῖρά σου, *ekteinon tēn cheira sou*]." Upon following this instruction, "his hand was restored" (6:10)—a dramatic visual demonstration of Jesus's intent to heal on the Sabbath. But there's more: significantly, unlike when Jesus "stretched out his [own] hand [ἐκτείνας τὴν χεῖρα, *ekteinas tēn cheira*]" to heal the leper (5:13), Jesus this time involves the infirm man in his own healing, as it were, exhorting him to do what he was impotent to do but could now accomplish on the strength of Jesus's restorative word. Elements of the man's obedience and faith percolate within the story. Strengthening results from stretching out to grasp Jesus's creative-liberating word.

Focusing on this salient, hand-reaching factor, Ambrose of Milan stretches the point further in a direction wholly consistent with Luke's theological ethics. "That is the common and universal remedy. You who think you have a healthy hand beware lest it is withered by greed or by sacrilege. Hold it out often. Hold it out to the poor person who begs you. Hold it out to help your neighbor, to give protection to a widow, to snatch from harm one whom you see subjected to unjust insult. Hold it out to God for your sins. The hand is stretched forth; then it is healed."[111]

One early tradition indicates that the man in Luke's story had been a stonemason, for whom hand paralysis would have constituted an especially tragic, impoverishing disability.[112] By calling him to extend this limp hand and restoring its use, Jesus functionally puts the man back to work on the other six days of the week. He restores the man's dignity and ability to provide for himself and his family. But more than that, following Ambrose's incisive line of thought, Jesus restores the man's capability to minister to others in need, to "do good" and "save life" on the Sabbath and every other day. Indeed, the man's willingness to offer his hand in obedience to Christ—whose hand is always outstretched to the poor and afflicted—goes hand in hand with his healing.

Where we might expect acclamation, or at least amazement, regarding Jesus's "good" healing deed, the Pharisees and associates respond only with vehemence. They become "filled with fury [ἀνοίας, *anoias*]" (6:11)—an "anoetic," "unthinking reaction," a "blind fury,"[113] "a state of extreme anger as to suggest an incapacity to use one's mind,"[114] being "out of one's mind"[115] with foolish madness (cf. 2 Tim 3:9). While Jesus knows what God desires and how people

111. Ambrose, *Exposition on Gospel of Luke* 5.40, cited in Just, 100; cf. Jeffrey, 88.

112. Gos. Naz. 10 (cited in Jerome, *Commentary on Matthew* 12:13). Only Luke among the Synoptics indicates that the man's *right* hand was disabled—likely his dominant hand, crucial for manual labor.

113. Bovon, 1:204.

114. Louw and Nida, *Greek-English Lexicon*, 1:762.

115. Jeffrey, 89.

think and behave, the Pharisees at this moment succumb to a deranged state of unknowing. Anger, combined with practical reason—so-called righteous indignation—has its place in religious and political society: a useful tack of prophets and reformers, including Jesus. But in their current mania, the Pharisees have lost the moral high ground.

Why? What accounts for their blind fury? Is it simply because Jesus has taken a different interpretive stance from theirs on scriptural-legal Sabbath traditions? Though battles over the Bible can become quite belligerent, more seems at stake here than right exegesis. Cyril of Alexandria again stresses that resentful envy drives Jesus's opponents: his growing reputation among the people diminishes that of established authorities, like the Pharisees.[116] No doubt the authority issue plays a major role, as Jesus speaks and acts as "Lord of the Sabbath." But I am not sure that envy of Jesus's authority and popularity gets at the heart of the Pharisees' temporary insanity. I do not think they want what Jesus has, especially since they assumed—at least until now—that they were scriptural-legal experts and respected teachers. I suggest that something more on the order of shame (a cousin of envy) is firing their present fury: shame over their loss of face as religious authorities, punctuated by Jesus's withering look at them before restoring the man's withered hand.[117] Jesus has not just advanced a different opinion about Sabbath conduct: he's backed it up with concrete action. The healed man stands as living testimony against their authority; his renewed right hand might as well slap them in the face. Public shame is hard to take in any culture, but perhaps more so in the Middle East, and such shame provides volatile fuel for revenge.[118]

I wonder, too, if guilt, another of shame's cousins, does not also come into play. I think the Pharisees merit the benefit of the doubt in their desire to understand and apply God's word faithfully. Their aims align with Jesus's, which is why they pay him so much attention. But he keeps exposing their blind spots and upsetting their cherished convictions in maddening ways not easily dismissed. He cuts deep to their spiritual cores and makes them uncomfortable. Rather than responding with humble repentance (change of mind), they lash out with hostile resistance (out of mind). But this is scarcely the end of the Pharisees' dealings with Jesus in Luke; opportunity for growth and development remains, as well as for further wrath and entrenchment.

116. Cyril, *Commentary on Luke*, Homily 23: "The man's malady [his withered hand] perhaps might shame them [Pharisees] to dispel the flames of their envy" (cited in Just, 99).

117. Cyril (see previous note) suggests that Jesus seeks to inculcate shame in the Pharisees on account of their envy. I propose that they may already be motivated by a sense of shame as lost public status.

118. On shame in Luke's social and narrative world, see Daube, "Shame Culture"; Malina and Neyrey, "Honor and Shame."

Praying All Night and Choosing Twelve Apostles (6:12–16)

After this intense period of ministry and debate, Jesus again withdraws "to pray" in a remote location (6:12; cf. 4:42; 5:16). Though Luke does not specify Jesus's motivation, we might imagine that escalating tensions with scribes and Pharisees drive to some degree his desire for prayerful solitude, sustenance, and perspective. On this retreat, Jesus stakes out a new time and place, heading up to a *mountain* (not a desert) and spending *all night* (not the morning) in prayer. In biblical topography, mountains rank with deserts as optimal zones off the beaten path for spiritual growth and reflection. Sinai, for example, one of the most significant revelatory sites for Moses and Israel, designates both mountain and desert. By virtue of their height, mountains more often represent meeting places with God, merging points between heaven and earth.[119] Nighttime increases the extraordinary and ominous nature of Jesus's praying. This is a crisis point for Jesus: the wrath of his Nazareth compatriots, while intense, remains localized to his small home village; the fury of some influential Pharisees and scribal leaders, however, poses a more ominous potential threat. Jesus finds himself in a vulnerable state needing the help of God—and, as it happens, the help of more disciples. Jesus does not carry out his mission alone.

Emerging from Jesus's nocturnal vigil is his selection of twelve disciples, "whom he also named *apostles*" (Luke 6:13). The chosen number and apostolic designation are no accidents: *twelve* represents the charter tribes of Israel and fits with Jesus's messianic vocation to liberate and restore God's covenant people (cf. 9:17; 22:28–30); and *apostle* (ἀπόστολος, *apostolos*), meaning "sent one," indicates the active role these associates will play in furthering Jesus's work, not simply following behind him (cf. 9:1–6).

Regarding the roster of Jesus's twelve apostles, consider four observations. First, headlining the list are the three fishermen Jesus previously called: Simon Peter, James, and John (6:14; cf. 5:9–11). Their original charge to "catch people" is folded into their apostolic commission. Jesus now adds to this trio Simon's brother Andrew; so Jesus chooses two pairs of biological brothers (Simon/Andrew; James/John). This kinship connection provides a counterbalance to the family leaving and household-dividing tendencies of Jesus's mission (cf. 5:11, 28; 12:51–53; 14:25–26; 18:28–30).

Second, Simon's "Rocky" (Peter [Πέτρος/*Petros*]) nickname given by Jesus is formally introduced (cf. 5:8), partly to distinguish him from another Simon "called the Zealot" (6:15) and partly to suggest his "rocklike" (πέτρα,

119. The symbolic-theological importance of mountains is more prominent in Matthew (cf. Donaldson, *Jesus*), but not insignificant in Luke.

petra ["rock"]) character and leadership position among the Twelve. However, Peter has not yet been featured beyond his initial encounter with Jesus on Lake Gennesaret (5:1–11). We thus await reports of how he succeeds and/or fails to measure up to his new name.

Third, Luke curiously does not include the tax collector Levi in this select apostolic circle (unlike Matthew's Gospel, which names him "Matthew" and does list him among the Twelve [Matt 9:9–11; 10:3]). But Levi still qualifies as Jesus's disciple, indicating a larger contingent of followers beyond the Twelve. While these dozen men enjoy special positions as symbolic heads of the restored Israel, the contributions of other groups of disciples—the inner three (Peter, James, and John [Luke 9:28–36]), three women (Mary Magdalene, Joanna, and Susanna, along with "many others" [8:2–3]), and the seventy-(two) (10:1–12)—should not be discounted.

Fourth, the final pair of apostles stands out by virtue of their controversial political designations: the second Simon is distinguished as the *Zealot*; and Judas Iscariot is identified as an eventual *traitor*. "Zealot" recalls fiery advocates of Jewish law and identity, willing to use violence in defending their cause, like Phinehas (Num 25:7–15; Sir 45:23), Elijah (1 Kgs 18:36–40; Sir 48:1–3), Mattathias (1 Macc 2:15–28), Saul of Tarsus (Acts 22:3–5; Gal 1:13–14; Phil 3:5–6), and the freedom fighters in the first Jewish Revolt against Rome (66–70 CE). "Iscariot" may play on *sicarii*, the dagger-wielding hit squad of Jewish elites who targeted other Jewish leaders they regarded as Roman-sympathizing quislings.[120] Whether Judas was ever involved with this group, he himself would come to betray Jesus. We wait to see how this treachery will unfold (Luke 22:3–6, 47–53). In any event, Luke hints that Jesus's investment in *these particular* twelve apostles will hardly smooth out all conflicts. Jesus takes a big risk to share his ministry with a ragtag band of fishermen, rebels, and no telling what other sorts.

Leveling the Field of Opportunity (6:17–8:3)

This next section continues to feature Jesus's two-pronged liberating mission of teaching God's word and healing infirmities. Short summaries opening (6:17–19) and closing (8:1–3) the section emphasize dimensions of both teaching and healing, and the miracle accounts continue to demonstrate the power of both word and touch, verbal command and physical contact, though in distinctive ways: now the crowds press in to *touch Jesus*, since "power came out from him

120. Though this *sicarii* connection is possible, available evidence does not allow certainty about this or any other meaning of "Iscariot"; see Paffenroth, *Judas*, 4–6.

and healed all of them" (6:19); in a special case, Jesus speaks a curative word for a terminally ill servant *without ever meeting him or his master* (7:1–10); and in an even more remarkable case, Jesus resuscitates a deceased young man by both *touching* his coffin and *telling* him to rise (7:11–15). The long-distance communication exhibits the transcendent power of the Creator God, while the touching incidents reveal the immanent power of the incarnate God in Jesus.

The scope of Jesus's creative-restorative, teaching-healing work stretches beyond a select few beneficiaries. As noted above, Levi's omission from the apostolic dozen hints at a wider company of Jesus's followers. The two summary reports now make this clear: he ministers to "a great crowd of his disciples" (6:17), and juxtaposing the twelve male itinerant disciples is a cadre of three named and "many other" women supporters (8:1–3). Moreover, the three "kingdom of God" references in this section (6:20; 7:28; 8:1) suggest the inclusive nature of the messianic community Jesus forges: God's realm welcomes and nurtures (1) the poor above the rich (6:20, 24), (2) ordinary folk as well as dynamic prophets (7:28–29), and (3) women as surely as men (8:1–3). And the potential for blessing is universal, as "a great multitude of people from all Judea, Jerusalem, and the coast of Tyre and Sidon . . . had come to hear [Jesus] and to be healed of their diseases" (6:17–18). God's election of Israel serves to draw other nations into the orbit of God's saving work, including Gentiles from Tyre and Sidon, historic enemies of Israel (cf. Isa 23; Ezek 26–28). Jesus may not be sent *to* Sidon, as Elijah was (Luke 4:26), but he happily teaches and heals all Sidonians who come to him.

The socially expansive thrust of Jesus's mission is signaled in the striking *setting* and *posture* of Jesus's major block of teaching that provides the firm foundation (cf. 6:46–49) for this section. Unlike the "sermon" of Matthew's Jesus delivered seated on the mountain (Matt 5:1–2), Luke's Jesus *comes down* from the mountain where he's been praying to a "level place," a flat-footed (πεδινός, *pedinos*) area where he *stands* (ἔστη, *estē*) with the people—on their level (Luke 6:17)—rather than in the more customary seated pedagogical position (2:46; 4:20; 5:3). This plain-terrain, toe-to-toe staging suggests an environment of equal opportunity, a level playing field for all people.[121] But it also intimates considerable social reorientation, an upheaval of the established hierarchical order. As Mary belted out, "God my Savior" implements salvation by "[bringing] down the powerful from their thrones and [lifting] up the lowly" (1:47, 52). Chiming in with Mary and Isaiah, John the Baptist heralded that the way of God's saving outreach to "all flesh" bulldozes through the craggy desert such that "every valley shall be filled, . . . and every hill shall be made low, and

121. See Pokorný, *Theologie*, 182–85; Spencer, *Gospel of Luke*, 143–44.

the crooked shall be made straight, and the rough ways made smooth" (3:5–6). Glorious salvation for "all" on a smooth highway, yes, but with potential for much "road rage" as travelers adjust to new traffic patterns and personnel. The lofty rich, righteous, full, and healthy are not used to walking with the lowly poor, sinners, hungry, and sick on an equal footing, much less giving right of way to them on God's royal boulevard.

This review of John's preparatory role in 3:1–20 leads us to observe his reemergence in 7:18–35 and the importance of his and Jesus's intertwined prophetic vocations (see 7:26–28, 33–35). For the first time in Luke's story, an audience acknowledges Jesus's extraordinary *prophetic* authority. Whereas the congregation in Nazareth rejected his vocation, demonstrating that "no prophet is accepted in the prophet's hometown" (4:24), a "large crowd" at Nain proclaims that "a great prophet has arisen among us" after Jesus raises a local widow's son from the dead (7:11, 16). But the fact that Jesus reiterates the historical pattern of persecuting prophets (6:22–23) and that "fear seized" the citizens of Nain, even as they acknowledge Jesus as a special prophet (7:16), alerts us to prospects of persisting audience angst about Jesus's mission. He has no more guarantee of security than his prophetic cousin John, who remains imprisoned by Herod Antipas (7:18–20; cf. 3:19–20) and opposed by certain legal experts (7:30). Indeed, while dining in Simon the Pharisee's home and receiving the ministrations of a "sinner" woman who has crashed the party, Simon queries "to himself": "If this man [Jesus] were a prophet, he would have known who and what kind of woman this is who is touching him" (7:39). Simon correctly pinpoints a key qualification for authentic prophets: they must be "in the know" about the purpose of God and the nature of people. But Simon erroneously disqualifies Jesus on this occasion. *Knowing* full well what Simon is thinking and who "this woman" truly is, Jesus sharply whips back at his imperceptive host: "Do *you see* this woman?" (7:44). Luke's challenge to see and know what and whom Jesus sees and knows runs throughout this section. Even, yea especially, religious teachers must humbly persist in seeking true knowledge and understanding, lest they devolve into "blind guides of the blind" who lead themselves and those they instruct into a pit (6:39–42, also Matt 15:14).

Moreover, Luke's emphasis on knowing and seeing God's truth embodied in Jesus extends, as always, beyond perceptual insight to practical obedience. As God's prophetic spokesman and, beyond that, as commanding Lord, Jesus demands *responsive action* through his words and ways (6:46–49). Overall, such response involves core inner attitudes/dispositions of *faith* and *love* that prompt coordinate acts/deeds, like that encapsulated in Paul's commendation of the Thessalonians' "*work of faith* and *labor of love*" (1 Thess 1:3; cf. 5:8;

1 Cor 3:13; Gal 5:6; Col 1:4; Jas 2:5, 8–17).[122] However, as foundational as faith and love are to Christian life, they suffer from considerable conceptual variability. The fuzziness of "love" is well-known (I "love" chocolate, the theater, baseball, country music, my cat, my wife, and God), but "faith" can prove just as thin and flimsy.[123] Paul Tillich candidly writes: "There is hardly a word in the religious language, both theological and popular, which is subject to more misunderstandings, distortions and questionable definitions than the word 'faith.' . . . Today the term 'faith' is more productive of disease than health. It confuses, misleads, creates alternately skepticism and fanaticism, intellectual resistance and emotional surrender, rejection of genuine religion and subjection to substitutes."[124]

Elisabeth Moltmann-Wendel comes at the "faith" problem from the other side, suggesting it can too easily become a bland, blinkered notion ill-matched to the majesty and mystery of God: "'Faith' is given too high a place in our culture; it is dogmatically loaded, too one-sidedly mediated through words and rationalized through words. Faith as it is narrated in the New Testament, especially in the Jesus stories, touches other senses than just the ear; smell, feeling, touching are also part of it. . . . To experience again the whole God, we also have to use again all of our organs; we must taste, see, and sense how friendly the Lord is, not only through wine and water."[125]

Among the Jesus stories in this section, Luke provides multisensory narrative models of faith and love in action in two surprising cases: (1) a *Roman military officer* shows atypical love toward the Jewish people by building a synagogue in Capernaum (7:4–5) and uncommon faith in Jesus's therapeutic word (7:9); and (2) an *anonymous yet well-known "sinner woman"* conveys "great love" for Jesus (7:47) in an effusive emotional display that also confirms her saving faith (7:50). The jolt of these two unconventional loving and faithful exemplars becomes all the more shocking in light of Jesus's radical exhortation to "love your enemies, do good to those who hate you, bless those who curse you, pray for those who abuse you" (6:27–28; cf. 6:29–36). Astoundingly, the realm of God advanced by Jesus aims to embrace rather than eliminate aggressive *enemies* of God's people. Through nonviolent, divine-inspired merciful love (6:35–36), Jesus aims to transform the battlefield into a level playing field of opportunity for all.

122. Cf. discussion in Morgan, *Roman Faith*, 224–26.

123. On "thin," broadly positive moral concepts that are "enormously multifarious," see Appiah, *Cosmopolitanism*, 46–47 (e.g., the "unconstrained" notion of "good," as in "good soil, good dog, good argument, good idea, good person"); cf. Walzer, *Thick and Thin*.

124. Tillich, *Dynamics*, xxi.

125. Moltmann-Wendel, "Self-Love," 31.

Reversing Social Locations and Loving Oppressive Enemies (6:17–49)

Jesus's "Sermon on the Plain" in Luke is framed by counterbalancing elements. The setting on "level ground" (6:17), as we have seen, represents the open social space of God's realm, where people from all walks of life find equal footing. But this area should not be viewed as a static, flat-lined arena; rather, it symbolizes both a dynamic highway and terra firma on which a productive life is *built up*. In this dimension the sermon's goal becomes constructing a solid life and society, imaged as a "house" founded on the rock of the Lord's word, which *cannot be leveled* by damaging forces (6:46–49).

From the opening series of four beatitudes, Jesus's teaching establishes the conditions for a "blessed," or "happy," existence that stands firm in the face of hardship and hostility. The four absolute "blessed are" affirmations (6:20–22) set the stage for more conditional exhortations prescribing the way for God's people to flourish *if* they enact God's commands, particularly: "love your enemies . . . give to everyone who begs from you . . . do to others as you would have them do to you . . . be merciful . . . forgive, and you will be forgiven" (6:27–37).

A flood of "happiness" publications has appeared in recent years beyond the popular self-help market to include a range of scientific studies across the fields of philosophy, psychology, neurology, politics, economics, and history.[126] If nothing else, these studies suggest that whatever material and technological booms we may have experienced, they have not guaranteed holistic well-being. Happiness remains as elusive as it is desirable. Theological and biblical scholars have largely steered clear of happiness concerns, perhaps thinking them unworthy of serious attention, especially in the face of persisting evil and suffering.[127] In the opening monologue of William Nicholson's poignant play *Shadowlands*, the C. S. Lewis character, closely based on Lewis's writings, announces: "Here I am going to say something which may come as a bit of a shock. I think that God doesn't necessarily want us to be happy. He wants us to be lovable. Worthy of love. Able to be loved by Him. We do not start off being all that lovable, if we're honest." Lewis goes on to expose our chief unlovable quality as a deep-seated *selfishness* that God lovingly seeks to transform through the "mechanism . . . called suffering. To put it another way, pain is God's megaphone to rouse

126. See, e.g., Seligman, *Authentic Happiness*; Haidt, *Happiness Hypothesis*; Achor, *Happiness Advantage*; Derek Bok, *Politics of Happiness*; Sissela Bok, *Exploring Happiness*; Layard, *Happiness*; Graham, *Pursuit of Happiness*; Seppälä, *Happiness Track*.

127. In sharp contradistinction to popular purveyors of a superficial happiness/prosperity gospel. With respect to biblical scholarship, however, see the recent essay collection *The Bible and the Pursuit of Happiness*, edited by Brent Strawn, including the chapter by Green ("We Had to Celebrate") on happiness in Luke-Acts.

a deaf world." Moreover, God's "gift of suffering" drives our hopes beyond the brokenness and emptiness of "this world" (shadowlands) to the "true good [that] lies in another world."[128]

While this tough-love perspective wary of happiness pursuits resounds throughout Christian tradition, it is not the only strain. The Westminster Catechism unabashedly confesses that humanity's "chief end [is] to glorify God and to enjoy him forever," and people today continue to search as longingly as Augustine did for deep satisfaction and restfulness found only in God. In her book *God and the Art of Happiness* (2010), theologian Ellen Charry has begun to fill the void in thoughtful happiness studies with a sweeping investigation of the subject in the biblical and theological-philosophical tradition, with special attention to Augustine, Boethius, Aquinas, and the Anglican divine Joseph Butler. Charry unpacks a major emphasis she calls *asherist* theology, based on the Hebrew term (אשר, *asher*) for "blessed" or "happy" common in poetic and wisdom beatitudes. Its first biblical usage appears in Gen 30:13, as Jacob's less-favored wife, Leah, rejoices in God's favoring her with another son (this time through her surrogate maid Zilpah): "'Happy am I! For the women will call me happy'; so she named him Asher."[129] As it happens, the prophet Anna follows both the ancestral line of this original "happy man" (Luke 2:36) and the attitudinal line of Leah when she "began to praise God and to speak about the child [Jesus] to all who were looking for the redemption of Israel" (2:38).[130]

Charry places this redemptive theme at the heart of God's *asheristic* purpose for humankind. God graciously saves God's people so they might flourish to the fullest. But Charry also stresses the component of human responsiveness—"God and humanity work as a team, with God leading and humanity following"—following, that is, in faithful obedience to God's benevolent commands. Regarding fundamental biblical and Augustinian concepts of happiness, Charry summarizes: "The biblical foundation of asherism [is] enjoyment of life through dynamic obedience to edifying divine commands that enable us to flourish that God may enjoy us and we enjoy God." Furthermore: "Asherism is inspired by the soteriology of Augustine's moral psychology, which he presents in the second half of his *De Trinitate*. Salvation is the healing of love that one may rest in God. Asherism works out that healing process in a life of reverent obedience to divine commands that shape character and bring moral-psycho-

128. Nicholson, *Shadowlands*, 8–9; cf. Lewis, *Problem of Pain*.

129. Charry, *God*, 157–277, xi.

130. Anna's joy culminates the celebratory spirit in Luke 1–2 focused on the birth of the Christ-child Jesus and his prophetic forerunner John. As Elizabeth proclaims to Mary: "Blessed/Happy are you among women, and blessed/happy is the fruit of your womb" (1:42); see Green, "We Had to Celebrate," 171–76.

logical flourishing and enhance societal well-being. Salvation is an excellent pattern of living that is personally rewarding because it advances God's intention for creation. It is a realizing eschatology."[131]

The emphasis on obedience to God's word as the pathway to blessedness/happiness comports well with the teaching of Luke's Jesus, as we have seen.[132] But what about the present-world experience of happiness within the doctrinal framework of a "realizing eschatology," which Charry repeatedly advocates in contrast to otherworldly (cf. Lewis above) and antiworldly perspectives ever lurking in the Christian tradition?[133] In no way naive about the pervasiveness of suffering and oppression in this life, Charry nonetheless clings to brighter prospects of obeying and enjoying God within this fallen world that God has *already* begun to repair through the crucified and risen Christ.

Luke's Jesus would agree. He opens his address, making particular eye-leveling contact with "his disciples,"[134] with the straightforward benediction: "Blessed are you who are poor, for yours *is* the kingdom of God" (6:20). The reign of God is breaking in now through Jesus's mission (4:43), and the poor are accorded full kingdom membership and benefits in the *here and now*. Jesus's followers will still encounter opposition and ostracism in this world, but even these experiences can be counted as "blessed" opportunities for joyous exultation,[135] "for surely your reward is great in heaven" (6:23). Note well: Jesus does not say, "Your reward *will be* great when you *go to* heaven." Popular notions of heaven as an afterlife destination "up there" far removed from everyday struggles "down here" have a much weaker NT basis than often assumed. "Heaven" is less a separate, distant sphere from "earth" than an immanent, interpenetrating reality. "Heaven" is supremely the realm of God—who knows no temporal or spatial bounds—where God's righteous will is realized. We live more in borderlands than shadowlands, in contested overlapping territory of heaven and earth where we pray less, "Take us to heaven and get us out of this mess," than, "Your kingdom come. Your will be done *on earth as it is in heaven*"

131. Charry, *God*, 173, xi (cf. 48–51).

132. In *God*, Charry focuses her NT analysis on the Gospel of John (230–50). But she acknowledges the foundational "asherist perspective" of the Sermon on the Mount in Matthew (230n1) and directs the reader to her previous treatment of this material in *By the Renewing of Your Minds*, 61–83; on the "happiness" theme in Luke's beatitudes, see Green, "We Had to Celebrate," 181–84.

133. Charry, *God*, xi, 238, 254, 268–70.

134. With crowds in the background (6:17–19), Jesus "looked up" or "raised his eyes" (ἐπάρας τοὺς ὀφθαλμοὺς αὐτοῦ, *eparas tous ophthalmous autou*) to speak more directly, eye-to-eye, to his disciples.

135. "Leaping for joy" recalls the exultant response of John in Elizabeth's womb when Mary, pregnant with Jesus Messiah, came to visit (Luke 1:41, 44; cf. Isa 35:6; Acts 3:8).

(Matt 6:10).[136] Jesus's poor, hungry, mournful, persecuted followers need not defer blessed well-being to the afterlife. They may enjoy their "heavenly reward" in the present experience of God's kingdom. This scarcely means that they have hit the jackpot and landed on easy street. The struggle between God's and worldly realms persists (cf. 4:5–8). There will be delays: those who hunger and grieve "now . . . will be" fed and infused with joy at some future point (6:21), but not one limited to postmortem life. The fruit of God's bounty is ripe for tasting and "realizing" here and now.

The path of happiness through divine benediction and human obedience Jesus lays out in this discourse follows a social-moral track from (1) *leveling and reversing* conventional hierarchies (6:20–26) to (2) *loving and aiding* oppressive enemies (6:27–36) and to (3) *forgiving and correcting* wrongdoers, including flawed community members, in a spirit of self-critical, clear-eyed judgment (6:37–45).

Leveling and Reversing Hierarchies (6:20–26)

Reinforcing his mother's theocratic prophecy of social inversion, lifting the lowly and lowering the lofty (1:52–53), Jesus sketches a fourfold antithetical paradigm in which the preferential benefits (blessings) God showers on the disadvantaged of "this world" are countermatched by the downgrading costs (woes) borne by the privileged.[137]

Blessings (6:20–23)	**Woes (6:24–26)**
1. *Poor* possess the kingdom of God.	1. *Rich* have all they are going to get.
2. *Hungry* will be filled.	2. *Full* will be hungry.
3. *Weepers* will laugh.	3. *Laughers* will mourn and weep.
4. *Despised* (for Christ's sake) have heavenly honor like true prophets of old.	4. *Pleasers* (of everybody) are like false and discredited prophets of old.

This new arrangement does not so much raise the poor to the level of the powerful as flip positions in radical, carnivalesque fashion, except that this is no temporary aberration to poke fun at the system. This is the new "business

136. This full phrase comes from Matthew's version of the Lord's Prayer (Luke only has "Your kingdom come" in 11:2); it nonetheless comports with Luke's worldview. For Matthew, "heaven" functions primarily as a circumlocution for "God" ("kingdom of heaven" = "kingdom of God") rather than as a distant celestial territory.

137. The following chart comes (with slight adaptation) from Spencer, *Gospel of Luke*, 143.

model" of God's kingdom, apparently maintaining hierarchy with an inverted ladder. Good news of liberation indeed for those stamped down by poverty and just deserts for the fat cats who have profited on the backs of the powerless. But as history attests, for all its salutary reforms, social revolution soon confronts the moral danger of corruptive power, where the new rulers, however broad-based, run the risk of more replicating than replacing the deposed regime. A crucial test of revolutionary ethics quickly arises regarding how the liberated treat their former oppressors.

Loving and Aiding Enemies (6:27–36)

In Kent Haruf's poignant novel *Benediction*, Pastor Rob Lyle freely admits to his congregation in a sermon on this Lukan text how hard it is to follow Jesus's nonretaliation ethic: "We know the sweet joy of revenge. How it feels good to get even. Oh, that was a nice idea Jesus had. That was a pretty notion, but you can't love people who do evil. It is neither sensible nor practical. . . . There is no way on earth we can love our enemies. . . . They'll think they can get away with . . . wickedness and evil, because they'll think we're weak and afraid. What would the world come to?" But the preacher continues: "What if Jesus wasn't kidding? What if he wasn't talking about some never-never land? . . . What if he was thoroughly wise to the world and knew firsthand cruelty and wickedness and evil and hate? . . . And what if in spite of all that he knew, he still said love your enemies?"[138]

Clearly, Luke's Jesus wasn't fooling around. Note well the direct move he makes from his fourfold curses on exploitative elites to a set of fourfold commands, introduced by a strong contrastive formula ("But [ἀλλά, *alla*] I say to you that listen" [6:27]), demanding merciful, benevolent treatment of enemies:

1. Love your enemies
2. Do good to those who hate you
3. Bless those who curse you
4. Pray for those who abuse you (6:27–28)

Powerful enemies of the poor and afflicted must be taken down to create space for those they have beaten down to rise and thrive. And so God's redemptive rule must begin with radical reversal. But it grows and flourishes on kindness and mercy toward all, befitting the nature of the Creator-Father

138. Haruf, *Benediction*, 140–41.

who seeks the good (happiness) of all his children, including "the ungrateful and the wicked" (6:35). Accordingly, those most "blessed" in God's kingdom are called to act like their Father by blessing their opponents with good deeds (6:27–30, 35), not rubbing their noses in their demotion. The blessed ones are called to embrace and embody the alternative values of God's realm in contrast to worldly economies. Everyone, "sinners" included, loves those who love them—nothing special about that (6:32–34). But actively loving one's enemies marks a whole new dimension, the very realm of God incarnate in Jesus Messiah. The "golden rule" ("Do to others as you would have them do to you" [6:31]) applies here, as it has in much ethical deliberation in the Greco-Roman world and beyond, though often to limited effect because of its generality.[139] But Jesus concretizes this broad principle of reciprocity with his "extraordinary," absurd insistence on magnanimous love toward enemies that prays for abusers, "offer[s] the other [cheek]," gives the last shirt off one's back, and offers charitable aid, "expecting nothing in return" (6:28–30, 35).[140]

This is no weak, milquetoast capitulation, however, to oppressive forces: quite the contrary, it represents a bold move to stop the spiral of violent vengeance in the power of God's love. In Tillich's terms, it demonstrates a "courage to be" an authentic child of God "in spite of" (*trotz*) the deep-seated anxiety and anger that prevails in a precarious world.[141] In Bonhoeffer's terms, backed up by his unflinching integrity in nonviolent protest against the evils of Nazi rule: "When evil meets no opposition and encounters no obstacle but only patient endurance, its sting is drawn, and at last it meets an opponent which is more than its match. . . . Then evil cannot find its mark, it can breed no further evil, and is left barren. . . . Evil becomes a spent force when we put up no resistance [and refuse] to pay back the enemy in his own coin. . . . Violence stands condemned by its failure to evoke counter-violence."[142]

Forgiving and Correcting Wrongdoers (6:37–42)

If Jesus's charge to treat one's enemies with loving-kindness rather than acrid vengeance weren't radical enough, he presses further by calling his disciples to *forgive* evildoers who have wronged them *and* to help them change their aberrant behavior *after* first reforming one's own life! The self-affirmation and

139. Cf. the critical discussion in Appiah, *Cosmopolitanism*, 60–63.

140. On the "extraordinary," "the peculiar," "the more," the "beyond-all-that" (περισσόν, *perisson*; cf. Matt 5:20) character of Jesus's enemy-loving ethic, see Bonhoeffer, *Cost*, 162–71.

141. Tillich, *Courage*, 4, 32, 43, 66, 84, 89, 151, 161, 168, 172.

142. Bonhoeffer, *Cost*, 158.

reciprocity of the golden rule ("as you would have them do to you") is balanced by the self-examination and humble charity enjoined in Jesus's stunning optic image: "First take the log [shaft, beam] out of your own eye, and then you will see clearly to take the speck [splinter, sliver] out of your neighbor's eye" (6:42). The "neighbor" term (NRSV) is actually "brother" (ἀδελφός, *adelphos*) and seems to shift the focus from external enemies to internal community-family relations. But recall that Father God does not so discriminate, but rather embraces all God's children, faithful and wayward (6:35–36). "Enemies" remain within the "brotherhood" of Christ and orbit of God's loving-saving concern. The world will be renewed when evil persons and elements are redeemed, not annihilated; reconciled, not alienated.

All such teaching makes for great idealistic theologizing, but it strains the bounds of common sense to the breaking point. "Killing" one's enemies with kindness, maybe; but forgiving them in a spirit of self-critique? Forget about it! Perhaps no contemporary theologian has written more profoundly about forgiveness than Miroslav Volf, emerging out of his Croatian experience in the travails of the former communist Yugoslavia. He pulls no punches about the bedrock Christian duty to forgive Christians and non-Christians alike: "The injunction to forgive may seem like just one 'nugget' of Christian wisdom. It is that but also much more. It is the defining stance of Jesus Christ, wisdom personified, and a central pillar of the Christian way of life."[143] And the full force of forgiveness doesn't stop with canceling debt while maintaining distance. It propels the way toward reconciliation, or what Volf aptly calls "embrace."

> Forgiveness is the boundary between exclusion and embrace. It heals the wounds that the power-acts of exclusion have inflicted and breaks down the dividing wall of hostility. Yet it leaves a distance between people . . . that allows them either to go to their separate ways in what is sometimes called "peace" or to fall into each other's arms and restore broken communion. . . . Forgiveness . . . is a passage leading to embrace. The arms of the crucified are open—a sign of space in God's self and an invitation for the enemy to come in.[144]

But with his passionate commitment to follow Christ's alternative way, Volf has no illusions about how hard the "nugget" of forgiveness-and-reconciliation can be to swallow: "But forgiveness is difficult, even painful, and sometimes it feels

143. Volf, *Public Faith*, 114.
144. Volf, *Exclusion*, 125–26.

utterly impossible. Why should we give a gift of forgiveness when every atom of our wounded bodies screams for justice or even revenge?"[145]

Though scarcely neutralizing the shock of Jesus's call to forgive and embrace one's enemies from a clear-eyed viewpoint of self-critique, three qualifications temper the rougher edges of Jesus's challenge. First, by demanding that his disciples deal with their own log-sized faults before judging others, including enemies, Jesus by no means suggests that their faults *justify* being ill-treated by adversaries. Jesus does not blame the victims. But he has little patience with smug hypocrisy, even among those who suffer. Sometimes we can be our own worst enemies and exacerbate the damage from others' attacks through our lack of self-awareness and self-discipline. And we severely impair our function as ministers of reconciliation (cf. 2 Cor 5:18–20) and teachers of God's righteous way by failing to correct our own blind spots.

Second, while Jesus initially associates forgiving with not judging and not condemning (Luke 6:37), his fuller teaching indicates he primarily inhibits spiteful snap judgments in the heat of the moment, with no redemptive aim. Jesus advocates candid self-judgment *as a means to* clear-sighted, corrective judgment of others (6:42). Moreover, as Volf discerns, true forgiveness, far from denying condemnable offense, entails honest recognition of harmful activity worthy of condemnation, yet intentionally overcome by God's merciful love. "To forgive means to forgo a rightful claim against someone who has wronged. . . . There's no way to give the gift of forgiveness without the sting of condemnation. We accuse when we forgive, and in doing that, we affirm the rightful claims of justice."[146] Forgiveness does not let enemies off scot-free; rather, it exposes their malevolence for the cancer that it is, even as it irradiates the malignance with the healing fire of God's love.

Finally, the daunting sense of despair over meeting Jesus's seemingly impossible standard of forgiving one's enemies throws us, not for the first or last time in Luke, on God's gracious power to do for us flawed humans what we cannot do for ourselves. "What is impossible for mortals is possible for God" (18:27; cf. 1:37). In no operation is this truer than in forgiving and loving one's attackers: "Be merciful, just as your Father is merciful" (6:36). Such a pithy statement affirms God not only as the standard of merciful conduct, but also as the strength to carry it out.

145. Volf, *Free of Charge*, 126.
146. Volf, *Free of Charge*, 169.

Growing and Building Solid Lives (6:43–49)

Concluding this discourse, Luke's Jesus shifts from an optical illustration to a related pair of *agricultural* and *architectural* images. Both scenarios challenge the audience to productive behavioral responses to Jesus's teaching. As a grove of "good trees" sprouting from the seed of Jesus's word, his disciples must "bear fruits worthy of repentance" (cf. 3:8), that is, a heart, mind, and life conforming to Jesus's way of choosing, thinking, and behaving (6:43–45). And as a block of sturdy houses constructed on the slab of Jesus's word, his followers must build the superstructure of their lives in compliance with the blueprint sketched by their Master Builder if they want to withstand the storms of life (6:46–49).[147]

Reviving a Centurion's Diseased Slave and Resuscitating a Widow's Deceased Son (7:1–17)

After concluding "all his sayings" (7:1) with an image of a physical house damaged by surging flood waters (6:48), Jesus encounters two social households from different ethnic and economic spheres, yet similarly devastated by terminal illness of a loved one. In the first case, a well-to-do Roman centurion in Capernaum humbly seeks Jesus's aid for a cherished slave on the brink of death (7:1–10).[148] In the second, Jesus happens upon the funeral for a young Jewish man in Nain who was the "only son" of a sobbing widow, emotionally aggrieved by her personal loss, but also, in all likelihood, economically bereft of her primary means of support (7:11–17).[149] However distinct the social identities of the Roman centurion and Jewish widow, they share common human-feeling for beloved household members and helplessness to protect their loved ones from disease and death and themselves from loss and grief.[150]

147. Paul uses similar images, though to somewhat different effect, of the church as "God's field, God's building" in 1 Cor 3:5–17.

148. Roman slaves were regarded as household members, and some enjoyed high standing and close bonding within the family; cf. Eph 6:5–9; Col 3:22–4:1; Philemon; 1 Pet 2:18–25.

149. In this era, Jewish widows could be financially stable by virtue of favorable estate settlements, but most would have struggled to make ends meet without the support of male relatives; and even better-off widows remained vulnerable to exploitative legal practices (20:47–21:4); cf. Spencer, "Neglected Widows."

150. See Sen, *Identity*: "Our shared humanity gets savagely challenged when the manifold divisions in the world are unified into one allegedly dominant system of classification—in terms of religion, or community, or culture, or nation, or civilization" (xiii). "The sense of belonging to a community, while strong enough in many cases, need not obliterate—or overwhelm—other associations and affiliations" (37).

Luke continues to juxtapose the common-yet-distinct experiences of character pairs to whom Jesus ministers, inviting us to attend closely to comparative and contrastive elements.

	Reviving a diseased slave (7:1–10)	**Resuscitating a deceased son (7:11–17)**
Client:	Faithful Roman centurion	Mournful Jewish widow
Patient:	Centurion's highly valued slave "close to death"	Widow's "only son," a "young man" who recently died
Associates:	Jewish elders and centurion's "friends"	"Large crowd" of mourners and a group of pallbearers
Setting:	Approaching the centurion's home in Capernaum where the ill slave was lying	Approaching the city gate in Nain as the widow's dead son was carried out
Jesus's means of restoration:	Speaking word of healing without ever seeing the diseased slave	Touching funeral bier, speaking word of resuscitation to dead son, and "[giving] him to his mother"
Jesus's emotional response:	Amazement at the centurion's faith	Compassion for the widow-mother's loss
Elijah/Elisha link:	Elisha's healing the skin disease of a Syrian general who was urged by his wife's Jewish servant-girl to seek Elisha's aid (2 Kgs 5:1–14)	Elijah's raising up the dead son of the widow at Zarephath (1 Kgs 17:17–24) and Elisha's raising up the dead and only son of the Shunammite woman (2 Kgs 4:18–37)

For fuller examination, we consider three aspects of Jesus's developing identity as (1) gracious patron, (2) passionate healer, and (3) "great prophet" (7:16).

Gracious Patron (7:1–9, 11–16)

In the vertical patron-client networks pervasive in the ancient Mediterranean world, a patron or benefactor at the top of the chain controlling vital resources (honor, power, opportunity, property, wealth) "graciously" distributed these "limited goods" to various clients in exchange for loyalty, gratitude, service, and ascriptions of honor. Clients would typically "pay" for patron benefits not merely with one-time economic transactions, but with enduring social commitments to support patron interests, financial and otherwise. In between patrons at the top and clients at the bottom of the social ladder, various middlemen operated as "brokers" and "friends" between the parties, but again, with primary loyalty to the patron. Social and political power remained concentrated in the hands of the few at the top, in *inverse proportion* to the mass of dependent clients below. The image of a *ladder* skews the picture, not only because of its parallel rails and rungs, but also because of the prospects of social *climbing* it offers. A *pyramid* represents a truer picture of ancient society, both in its narrow apex and broad base and in its concrete stability typifying inhibited social mobility.[151]

In Luke's narrative-theological world, God rules as the supreme, most honorable benefactor or patron, employing all the resources of heaven and earth in a cosmic project of redemption and renewal. God's Son and Messiah Jesus functions as the chief broker or mediator of God's immeasurable grace and power. But Jesus's intimate royal (King) and kyriarchal (Lord) kinship with God also makes Jesus the Divine Patron in his own right, a role he dramatically demonstrates in restoring life to desperate "clients" such as the centurion's dying slave and the widow's dead son. Even so, the Roman system of patronage provides only a partial analogy to Jesus's ministry. Jesus breaks the mold as much as he fits it.

In the second story, Jesus comes into Nain with "his disciples and a large crowd" (7:11)—in other words, a retinue of both committed and curious "clients" befitting his "patron" power. But he is greeted with no fanfare or honor ceremony at the village gate (7:12), as a high-level Roman or Herodian official would receive. That is hardly surprising, however, since Jesus of (nearby) Nazareth has no official standing. The funeral procession for the widow's son does not stop for Jesus or take any notice of him as far as we know. Jesus takes the initiative and stops the funeral carriage, but not with an imperious "Halt!" He simply touches the bier, which the pallbearers take as a signal to pause. Jesus then commands the young man to rise up and restores him to his mother (7:14–15). An extraordinary act of benevolence, to be sure, but one that sparks dramatic responses of fearing such death-defying power, along with honoring this dynamic prophetic agent: "Fear [φόβος] seized all of them; and they glorified [honored] God, saying, 'A great prophet has risen among us!'" (7:16). Yet, Jesus does no muscle-flexing or strutting, and he insists on nothing in return from the widow or her son (no call to "follow me" or any other obligation). Jesus moves on with his mission, and the widow and her son go on with their lives. Luke says nothing more about them.

151. See the pivotal studies by Eisenstadt and Roniger, *Patrons*; and Saller, *Personal Patronage*. For patron-client models applied to NT studies, see Moxnes, "Patron-Client" and *Economy*, 22–98; Hanson and Oakman, *Palestine*, 63–97; deSilva, *Honor*, 95–156; and Winter, *Seek the Welfare*.

We might infer their lifelong gratitude toward Jesus, but not as a result of their enrollment in Jesus's register of "clients," whom he will call to account.

The alternative patronage arrangement of God's kingdom becomes even more evident in Jesus's dealings with the centurion,[152] a Roman military commander of a hundred-soldier regiment with considerable authority in remote imperial outposts like Capernaum.[153] The entire story is structured along established lines of patron-client relations, neatly summed up in the centurion's analysis: "I also am a man set under authority, with soldiers under me; and I say to one, 'Go,' and he goes, and to another, 'Come,' and he comes, and to my slave, 'Do this,' and the slave does it" (7:8). The chain of command may be tracked as follows:

ROMAN CAESAR
↕
Roman centurion
(ἑκατοντάρχης, *hekatontarchēs*)
↕
personal friends
(φίλοι, *philoi*)
↕
Jewish elders
(πρεσβύτεροι, *presbyteroi*)
↕
Jesus the Healer
↕
valued slave
(δοῦλος, *doulos*)
↕
Roman soldiers
(στρατιῶται, *stratiōtai*)

The up-down arrows suggest the flow of benevolence/charity downward and of obedience/loyalty upward. Caesar stood at the apex of the imperial pyramid as lord of all people and property, fancying himself as the great benefactor and savior of the realm and as worthy of all honor (pushing to divine worship in some cases). Brokering Caesar's interests were officers like the centurion, operating under the

152. See Moxnes, "Patron-Client," 252–53.

153. Brink (*Soldiers*, 137) notes that the centurion in Capernaum might have been a Roman auxiliary (rather than legionary) officer employed by Herod Antipas (cf. Josephus, *Ant.* 19.357); but in any case, he was ultimately answerable to Rome.

emperor's supreme command through various regional governors and client-rulers (cf. 2:1–2; 3:1). Though ever conscious of these higher authorities, the centurion functioned in Capernaum as a patron in his own right with brokers and clients below him. In Luke's story, the Roman officer first dispatches Jewish elders and then a group of "friends" (perhaps Herodian administrators or confidants) to broker a deal with Jesus to heal his ailing slave. He no doubt begins with the Jewish leaders because of their compatriot connection with Jesus. Also, they owe a great deal to the centurion for building them a synagogue (7:5), a classic act of civic patronage.

In this normal scheme of things, the centurion's solicitation of Jesus's healing services does not automatically signal the officer's submission to Jesus's patron-authority. The centurion is used to getting what he wants and being served by underlings. As a healer (physician), Jesus lumps in with all sorts of service personnel, free or slave, such as bookkeepers, barbers, cooks, cobblers, and carpenters. But that is not in fact how the centurion treats Jesus. In a stunning inversion of standard hierarchies, the Roman officer assumes the place of a humble client before the Jewish Jesus, the superior patron. To be sure, he uses broker-friends to communicate with Jesus, but *not to command* Jesus's action. Rather, the Jewish elders try to persuade Jesus that the centurion "is worthy" of Jesus's attention, not by virtue of his military status, but because of his support for the Jewish people (7:4); and the "friends" relay the centurion's self-deprecating opinion that he is "*not* worthy" for Jesus to enter his home! Accordingly, Jesus's *commanding word* of healing from a distance will be sufficient to heal the centurion's slave (7:6–8). The centurion still works within a strict patron-client system: the spoken order of a superior officer and powerful patron must be heeded. But he dramatically restructures the organizational chart, as the following figure depicts:

GOD OF ISRAEL
↕
LORD (Κύριε, *Kyrie*) JESUS
↕
Jewish elders
↕
personal friends
↕
Roman centurion
↕
valued slave
↕
Roman soldiers

Little wonder that Jesus responds with amazement at the centurion he never meets: a centurion who defies stereotypes of Roman military brutality with love for his slave and for local Jews, displaces the imperial patron authorities with a Jewish Lord (Jesus), and displays extraordinary faith beyond that typically found in Israel (7:9).

Passionate Healer (7:9–10, 13–15)

While Luke's Jesus frequently sparks others' amazement (θαυμάζω, *thaumazō*), this interaction with the Roman centurion marks the only occasion where Jesus himself becomes amazed at someone else. We have noted the potential ambivalence of "amazing" responses along a positive (wow!)–negative (whoa!) spectrum, but here Jesus seems to approve wholeheartedly the centurion's remarkable faith. Even so, we should not minimize the element of palpable surprise and unsettledness in Jesus's emotional reaction. He does not expect the message that the centurion channels through his "friends." However wise Jesus has become about human thought and behavior, the kind of faith the centurion exhibits stretches the limits of Jesus's present knowledge. At this moment, Jesus learns something new and marvelous about faith from a most unlikely teacher. This centurion undermines stereotypes of Roman authorities and soldiers as invariably vicious oppressors of the Jews and opponents of God. As with the charitable, God-fearing centurion Cornelius in Acts 10–11, the officer in Luke 7 appears not as Israel's enemy, to be loved in spite of his antagonism (cf. Luke 6:27–36), but as sympathetic friend of the Jews to whom reciprocal love is due.[154] But this crack in the imperial stereotype scarcely shatters the template: these *particular* centurions stand out as *exceptions* to the prevailing deleterious drift of Roman rule in Luke's narrative. Jesus's life begins in displacement under an Augustan census and ends in unjust death on a Roman cross. The centurion at the latter scene ultimately affirms Jesus's innocence, but only after enforcing the horrible execution (Luke 23:47).

So we mustn't generalize the Capernaum centurion's positive portrayal. He remains exceptional not only among Roman officials but also among the people of Israel. Jesus's amazement spikes because, "I tell you, not even in Israel have I found such faith" (7:9). This statement should not be taken as a prejudicial slam against Israel: Jesus doesn't expect *anyone* to have this kind of faith. It is more the *nature* of the centurion's faith that takes Jesus by surprise than its

154. On the breaking of stereotypes in the correlated centurion scenes in Luke 7 and Acts 10–11, see Brink, *Soldiers*, 128–64.

source. We noted above how fuzzy the concept of faith can be. Here we have an opportunity, with Jesus, to grasp a key element of *great faith*.[155] This is not a blind faith—given the centurion's choice and reasoning based on his chain-of-command experience[156]—but rather a bold faith venturing belief in the creative power of God's restorative word beyond normal spatiotemporal boundaries.[157] Incarnate in space and time, Jesus has needed thus far to make direct contact, visually or tactilely, with those he ministers to. But now, spurred by the centurion's faith, Jesus expands his sense of the cosmic, transcendent nature of God's dominion permeating the present world, much like in the first creation drama, where God's hovering Spirit and commanding Word generated the world without "coming down" and micromanaging the operation. Lord Jesus does not have to be present in immediate-physical form to fulfill God's (re-)creative purpose. This is amazing news, indeed, not only for the centurion and his slave, but for Luke's readers seeking to live out their faith in Jesus's *interim bodily absence* between his resurrection and his parousia. In this meantime, his healing word remains alive and active.

From amazement over the centurion's faith—and by extension, over God's creative power irradiating the world—Jesus's emotional state shifts in the next scene to *compassion* for the grieving widow. Here Jesus is jerked back to the conspicuous realm of sight and touch: "When the Lord *saw her*, he had *compassion for her* and . . . he came forward and *touched* the bier" (7:13–14). As the power of Jesus's word is amplified beyond healing disease to reversing death, it reverts back to direct, on-site engagement: "Young man, I say to you, rise!" (7:14).

Only here is Luke's Jesus explicitly said to "have compassion" (σπλαγχνίζομαι, *splanchnizomai*) for anyone, that is, to be "moved with pity or sympathy," to "have deep, gut-level feeling" for one's affliction.[158] But two of his parables feature figures who have compassion (σπλαγχνίζομαι, *splanchnizomai*) on destitute persons: the merciful, pity-feeling Samaritan toward the half-dead victim of robbery (10:33) and the loving father of the prodigal son (15:20). Jesus's emotional response to the widow who mourns her deceased only son thus provides an experiential foundation for his teaching. Jesus knows what

155. The NRSV's "such faith" mutes the elevated connotation of the adjective τοσαύτη (*tosautē*), "pertaining to high degree of quality . . . so great/strong, to such extent" (BDAG, 1012).

156. I appropriate here language used by Sen (*Identity*, 162) to describe the rational Islamic faith of the sixteenth-century Indian emperor Akbar.

157. Cf. Tillich, *Dynamics*, 56: "The language of faith is the symbol [that] . . . puts the stories of the gods into the framework of time and space although it belongs to the nature of the ultimate to be beyond time and space." The centurion's language of faith bridges into this "beyond" dimension.

158. See the discussion on 1:78 above related to God's σπλάγχνα (*splanchna*).

compassion feels like and knows the tight motivational connection between emotional capacity and ethical conduct—being *moved to act* upon sympathetic impulses with therapeutic responses.[159]

Philosophical discussions of compassion often begin with Aristotle's treatment of this and other emotions in book 2 of his *Rhetoric*. Although he uses the Greek term ἔλεος (*eleos*), typically rendered in English Bible versions as "mercy,"[160] Aristotle's definition encompasses notions of "pity, compassion, and sympathy," specifically: a feeling of "pain at an apparently destructive or painful event happening to one who does not deserve it and which a person might expect himself or one of his own to suffer, and this when it seems close to hand" (*Rhet.* 2.8.1).[161] This analysis pinpoints four elements of someone's misfortune likely to elicit others' compassion: (1) *intensity*—a notably "destructive or painful" affliction; (2) *unfairness*—an arbitrary misfortune not caused or deserved by the sufferer; (3) *commonality*—a calamity that sparks others' fearful sense of vulnerability to the same experience; and (4) *proximity*—a pressing crisis that others feel could also engulf them soon ("close to hand").[162] The last two elements relate to the sympathizer's personal connection with the unfortunate party and perceived threat to the sympathizer's own happiness and well-being (flourishing), known in ancient Greek philosophy as *eudaimonia*.

Jesus's compassion for the grieving widow fits the first two components: death of an only son rates high on any scale of human tragedy, and a woman who had already lost her husband ranks among the least deserving of another family bereavement. In short, the weeping widow represents a thoroughly sympathetic character. But that doesn't mean that Jesus or anyone else *ought* to indulge feelings of compassion for her. In challenging Aristotelian psychology, the Stoics sought not merely to moderate emotions (passions) but to extirpate them through rational discipline as volatile disturbances to inner tranquility. A good Stoic sage might well reach out and help the suffering widow, but such charitable action would ideally stem from a calm, clear-headed decision, not from an impulsive churning of the "bowels" or burning of the heart. For Jesus's part, however, while acting calmly and decisively to restore the deceased youth to his distressed mother, he does so *within the coursing stream of compassionate feeling* rather than stanching its flow. Emotion moves Jesus to act.

159. On the integral "action readiness" or "action tendencies" of emotions, see Frijda, *Laws of Emotion*, 3–46.

160. See the tight association of σπλάγχνα (*splanchna*) and ἔλεος (*eleos*)—"compassions of mercy"—in Luke 1:78.

161. Aristotle, *On Rhetoric* (trans. Kennedy).

162. See the discussion of Aristotle's view in Nussbaum, *Upheavals*, 306–15; Konstan, *Emotions*, 210–15, and *Pity*, 34–35, 49–51, 128–36.

But does emotion move him to act out of eudaimonistic interests reflected in points 3 and 4 above? Does he minister to the widow and her dead son out of his own sense of anxious vulnerability to death and grief or, adapting Martha Nussbaum's analysis of Aristotle, out of a "*eudaimonistic judgment* [that] this person [the widow] . . . is a significant element in [his] scheme of goals and projects, an end whose good is to be promoted"?[163] We can't be sure at this point. Though Simeon forecast that Jesus's mother would suffer considerable emotional distress over Jesus's traumatic destiny (Luke 2:34–35), we do not know yet how heavily the prospects of his own death weigh on Jesus's mind (the first formal "passion prediction" comes in 9:22). Still, Jesus's identification with rejected and mistreated prophets since his tense homecoming to Nazareth betrays his keen awareness of personal threat. But again, does that self-knowledge necessarily *drive* his sympathy toward the widow?

Nicholas Wolsterstorff remains skeptical about self-referential, eudaimonistic assessments of Christian compassion. He draws heavily on Augustine's teaching, which restored the importance of compassion (and other emotions) to Western thought in contrast to the Stoics, as in this text cited from *City of God*: "The Stoics, indeed, are wont to reproach even compassion. But . . . what is compassion but a kind of fellow-feeling in our hearts for the misery of another which compels us to help him if we can? This impulse is the servant of right reason when compassion is displayed in such a way as to preserve righteousness, as when alms are distributed to the needy or forgiveness extended to the penitent" (9.5).[164] While more in line with Aristotelian (Peripatetic) than Stoic views, Augustine also diverged from the former in sharpening the focus of compassion on *moral-theological* miseries of sin and suffering inhibiting righteousness and salvation, though also appreciating a wider "anx[iety] lest [our friends] be afflicted by famine, war, pestilence, or captivity, fearing that in slavery they may suffer evils beyond what we can conceive" (19.8). Moreover, in Wolterstorff's reading, Augustine squeezes all eudaimonistic self-concern out of compassion by emphasizing that "it is not only for their own sakes that the citizens of the City of God are moved by these feelings. They also feel them on behalf of others" (14.9). Wolterstorff gives much more weight to "on behalf of others" than "not only for their own sakes," so much so that he regards Augustinian motivation for compassion strictly in terms of obedience to Christ's "love your neighbor" command carried out in a Christ-like, self-sacrificing spirit. "Compassion occurs when the object of my sorrow is not what has befallen me

163. Nussbaum, *Upheavals*, 321 (emphasis original).

164. Citations of *City of God* here and below from Wolterstorff, *Justice: Rights*, 197, 204 (cf. discussion, 195–222).

but what has befallen *the other*. Compassion is sorrow *for* and *with* the other. . . . Compassion is an alienation of the self from the self, a forgetfulness of self and an emotional identification with the other. . . . Compassion is *kenotic*, to use a term common in contemporary theology; compassion is self-emptying."[165]

Accepting for the sake of argument that Wolterstorff has accurately interpreted Augustine's position, he presses us to think carefully about what impels Jesus to be moved with compassion toward the weeping widow. In his divine nature, a *kenotic* perspective seems apt: Jesus is not moved by any personal deficiency or vulnerability, but rather opts to empty himself on behalf of suffering humanity (cf. Phil 2:5–8). And in his human identity, his compassionate response may flow simply out of obedience to God's commands to love neighbors and to care for widows, without some attendant empathetic sense of his own neediness. As noted above, we are not yet privy to Jesus's attitudes regarding his human limitations, especially his death (that will come most poignantly in 22:39–46). But we can posit Jesus's increasingly strong sense of social solidarity and psychological fellow-feeling with frail people, if not stemming from self-anxiety, at least based on a "eudaimonistic judgment" that persons in pain—like the grieving widow—are significant others in Jesus's "scheme of goals and projects, an end whose good is to be promoted."[166] At least since proclaiming his mission manifesto in Nazareth, Jesus's total *self*-identity—physically, emotionally, spiritually—has been wrapped up in, not merely directed toward, liberating the poor, the blind, the bound, and the bereft.

Great Prophet (7:16)

The crowd's proclamation of Jesus as a "great prophet" in the wake of his raising the widow's son casts him in the mold of Elijah and Elisha, the only prophets in Israel's history who brought people back to life (1 Kgs 17:17–24; 2 Kgs 4:17–37).[167] Moreover, like Luke's Jesus, both prophets resuscitated women's *only* sons, specifically a *widow's* son in Elijah's case. As always, however, in typological comparisons, *differences* among otherwise similar characters and plots stand out. Whereas Elijah restores a Gentile widow's only son in Sidonian Zarephath, Jesus restores a *Jewish* widow's only son in Galilean Nain. Jesus's prime commitment to blessing his own people persists, even after facing opposition in his hometown and commending both Elijah's outreach beyond Israel's borders (Luke

165. Wolterstorff, *Justice: Rights*, 217 (emphasis original).

166. Reprising the citation two paragraphs above from Nussbaum, *Upheavals*, 321.

167. Cf. Brodie, "Towards Unravelling."

4:25–26) and, more immediately, the centurion's faith beyond that presently demonstrated in Israel (7:9). While Jesus's messianic horizon stretches across Israel and the wider world, his raising the widow's son at Nain accentuates God's "gracious visitation to God's people" (7:16 AT),[168] prefiguring God's climactic restoration of broken and bereft Israel.[169] Though not echoing as strongly as the Elijah/Elisha narratives, Ezekiel's prophecy of Israel's national revival from "dry bones" rattles in the background (Ezek 37:1–14).[170]

Jesus's dealing with a foreign officer recalls Elisha's treatment of Naaman, with the obvious difference that Jesus cures the centurion's ill slave rather than the officer himself (though an Israelite slave-girl of Naaman's wife plays an intermediary role in 2 Kgs 5:2–4). Both Jesus and Elisha accomplish their work via therapeutic words relayed through messengers to the afflicted parties. Jewish prophets and Gentile officers never meet directly. But within this similar scenario, another difference emerges. The proud Syrian general Naaman, even in his desperate leprous condition, became incensed that Elisha refused to "come out" and treat him with the personal attention and deference he thought he deserved (2 Kgs 5:10–12); only after Naaman's servants urged him to reconsider did he give Elisha's Jordan-washing prescription a try (5:13–14). By marked contrast, as we have seen, the Roman centurion inverts the normal hierarchy, declaring, on the one hand, his unworthiness to meet Jesus and, on the other hand, the trustworthiness of Jesus's dynamic, transcendent word. We are back to marveling, with Jesus, at this man's "great faith" in God's "great prophet"—a faith not only atypical among the people of Israel, but also antithetical to the swagger and bluster of foreign conquistadors like Naaman. Given this extraordinary expression of faith, we wonder: having found such faith once, much to his surprise, will Jesus find it again during his earthly mission? Indeed, "when the Son of Humankind comes [again], will he find [such] faith on earth?" (Luke 18:8)—by anyone, anywhere?

168. The verb ἐπισκέπτομαι (*episkeptomai*) suggests the notion of "visiting" ("looking in on"). It framed Zechariah's prophecy of God's redemptive care of Israel ("He has *looked favorably on* his people and redeemed them. . . . /By the tender mercy of our God, the dawn from on high will *break upon* us" [Luke 1:68, 78; cf. Acts 15:14]). In his final approach to Jerusalem, Luke's Jesus uses the related noun ἐπισκοπή (*episkopē*), referring to "the time of your *gracious visit* from God" (Luke 19:44 CEB).

169. Cf. the poignant image of exiled Israel as a bereft widow in Lam 1:1–11 and Isa 54:4–6—with hope, however, of ultimate restoration; cf. Levenson, *Resurrection*, 149–55.

170. See the brilliant expositions of HB/OT "resurrection" accounts in 2 Kgs 4:1–37 and Ezek 37:1–14 in Levenson, *Resurrection*, 127–32, 156–65.

Reviewing and Re-visioning the Prophetic Missions of Jesus and John the Baptist (7:18–35)

After a rocky start in Nazareth, befitting the pattern of hometown rejection of God's prophet, Jesus's mission reaches a high point in Nain, from which the people's acclamation—"A great prophet has risen among us!"—spreads like wildfire "throughout Judea [here including Galilee] and all the surrounding country" (7:16–17). Jesus's soaring prophetic reputation would naturally provoke continuing stir about his association with John the Baptist and the potential identification of both Jesus and John with Elijah and/or the Messiah (cf. 3:15; 9:7–8, 18–20). And so Luke now provides a critical reassessment of Jesus and John's respective prophetic missions.

John's Inquiry about Jesus's Mission (7:18–23)

Since being shut up in Herod's prison (3:19–20), John has remained offstage as Jesus has burst into the public arena. After boldly proclaiming God's word and preparing the way for God's Messiah (3:2–18), the imprisoned John has been silenced—until now. But in his bound state John must rely on his disciples (cf. 5:33) for information and communication. And his confidence has been shaken somewhat. Upon hearing from his followers about Jesus's exploits, John dispatches two deputies to ask Jesus flatly, "Are you the one who is to come, or are we to wait for another?" (7:20). John's earlier implied conviction that Jesus was indeed the expected "more powerful" one imbued with God's Spirit (3:15–22) needs shoring up.[171] Faith and knowledge are fluid, rather than rigid, experiences in search of solidity in Luke.

In response to John's messengers, Jesus certifies his messianic status through a crisp résumé of his ministry in Luke 4–7 (including a fresh flurry of miraculous activity in 7:21): "Go and tell John what you have seen and heard: the blind receive their sight, the lame walk, the lepers are cleansed, the deaf hear, the dead are raised, the poor have good news brought to them" (7:22). More than different social and eating habits (7:33–34), what sets Jesus apart from John and confirms Jesus's status as God's ultimate (eschatological) prophet are his miraculous signs of restoration. John is also a dynamic prophet in his own way (1:17, 68; 7:27–28), but *not* as a miracle-worker, like Jesus.[172] Following his list of

171.Recall that John never *explicitly* identified Jesus as the Messiah and was even separated somewhat in Luke's narrative from Jesus's baptism; see discussion above on 3:15–22.

172. Meier, *Marginal Jew*, 2:124, 699; Stanton, *Gospels*, 188.

powerful liberating signs, Jesus offers a benedictory addendum that also carries an implied warning: "Blessed is anyone who takes no offense [σκανδαλισθῇ, *skandalisthē*] at me," or doesn't stumble and fall away from the messianic path Jesus treads (7:23).[173]

We are not told how John responds to Jesus's answer. John and Jesus never communicate directly in Luke, leaving a gap in understanding. Remarkably, the faithful prophet John who cleared the way for Jesus Messiah has been stumbling in the dark from his prison outpost and remains in danger of falling away. This is not so much a critique of John as a reality check and challenge. Distance poses a real obstacle to faith: John has not been able to witness for himself Jesus's words and deeds. He must depend on others' eyewitness accounts; though we may assume his disciples provide reasonably reliable testimony, it remains secondhand for John. He thus occupies the same position as Luke's writer and readers, dependent on reports of "eyewitnesses and servants of the word" to ascertain the "solid truth" of God's coming in Christ (1:1–4).This Gospel calls readers to embrace this word across the spans of space and time, to dare to show the "great faith" of the Roman centurion. But remember how rare and amazing that faith was in Jesus's view (7:9); apparently, it remains elusive even for a redoubtable "prophet of the Most High" (1:76) such as John.

In Luke's tracking the dialectic process of knowledge spurring faith and faith seeking understanding, Jesus and his followers constitute the primary seekers and graspers of God's truth, exhibiting growth in wisdom (even on Jesus's part) and occasional stumbling and backsliding (on the disciples' part). But Luke also continues to feature two other Jewish reform groups, with their own leaders and learners, interacting with the Jesus movement in various ways: (1) *John and his disciples* are mostly sympathetic, but they can question Jesus's status, as in the present story; (2) the *Pharisees and their disciples* (cf. 5:33) have become increasingly antagonistic, but they will continue to host and examine Jesus as a potential prophet, as in the next scene (7:36–50). Jesus's evaluation of these serious-minded, if sometimes misguided, parties provides key insights into his knowledge and practice of God's will—and into others' struggles with fully comprehending Jesus.

173. Σκανδαλίζω (*skandalizō*) can carry the nuance of "stumbling" or "falling down/away" (cf. Matt 13:21; 18:6–9; Mark 4:17; 9:42–47; 1 Cor 8:13; 2 Cor 11:29).

Jesus's Inventory of John's Mission (7:24–35)

After sending John's disciples back to their mentor, Jesus offers a substantial review of John's ministry. Whereas John may be somewhat doubtful about Jesus at this point, Jesus thoroughly backs John's prophetic authority in counterpoint to regal (palace-dwelling), legal ("Pharisees and lawyers"), and popular ("this generation") entities. On the regal front, Jesus affirms John's consummate prophetic career ("a prophet . . . [indeed] more than a prophet") in contrast to "a reed shaken by the wind" and a pampered royal draped in "soft robes" and coddled in the lap of palatial luxury (7:24–26). The latter image directly targets the tetrarch Herod Antipas, basking in his new palace in Tiberias without further annoyance (he hopes) from the pesky Baptist he locked away in prison. But the former *reed* image also has Herodian implications as the symbol of Tiberias (on the reedy shores of Lake Gennesaret) embossed on one side of local coinage.[174] In Jesus's view, despite appearances, John has it all over Antipas. All of Herod's coins can't buy him hard truth, his soft robes can't soothe his guilty conscience (for illicitly taking his brother's wife [cf. 3:19]), and his palace can't shield him from God's judgment mediated through John's prophecy. Herod's tetrarchy will eventually be swept away by the mighty force of God's Spirit (cf. 3:16–17) overwhelming his wicked, reedy realm rocking in the wind. In classic prophetic form, John speaks truth to power, and despite power's resistance to prophetic challenge, God's truth will win out.

The rough-and-tumble "desert-dwelling prophet" who speaks for economic justice (3:10–14) ranks at the top of God's kingdom, displacing the soft-and-spoiled "palace-dwelling man" who dominates earthly kingdoms.[175] Actually, in the paradoxical, topsy-turvy economy of God's realm, John's high status ("no one is greater than John") equates with the lowest member: "yet the least in the kingdom of God is greater than he" (7:28). Like Jesus and the biblical prophets of old, John speaks for the least—the naked, the hungry, the poor, the overtaxed (3:10–14)—and ushers their way into God's realm.

Sadly, however, while many people "acknowledged the justice of God" promoted in John's preaching and baptizing mission, some legal experts among "the Pharisees and the lawyers" refused to endorse John's agenda (7:29–30). Though sharing practices of prayer and fasting and broad interests in spiritual reform with John and his disciples (cf. 5:33), the Pharisees' stricter segregation from tax collectors and other "sinners" (7:29), whether in John's baptismal

174. The head of Emperor Tiberius was featured on the other side of the coin; cf. Rousseau and Arav, *Jesus*, 58; Spencer, *What Did Jesus Do?*, 59

175. Crossan, *Historical Jesus*, 236; cf. Spencer, *What Did Jesus Do?*, 59

river or at Jesus's fellowship table, set them at odds with more direct evangelical movements of liberating justice. As we have seen, both John and Jesus stress the need for sinners' repentance (3:3, 7–14; 5:31–32), but they prove more willing than the Pharisees in Luke's narrative to meet and speak with such sinful folk and to facilitate their saving transformation. To the extent that the Pharisees wall themselves off from wayward people, Luke warns that they have "rejected God's purpose for themselves" (7:30). Far from an optional frill to God's work, inclusive right-making salvation constitutes the very core of God's βουλή (*boulē*)—God's "purpose, plan, will"[176]—in the prophetic train of Amos and Micah, culminating now in John (and Jesus). "But let justice roll down like waters, and righteousness like an ever-flowing stream" (Amos 5:24): John's baptismal waters flow precisely in this justice stream. "What does the Lord require of you but to do justice, and to love kindness, and to walk humbly with your God?" (Mic 6:8): by identifying with the "least in God's kingdom," John walks precisely in this humble path of merciful justice.

Finally, Jesus evaluates his and John's similar yet distinct missions against the broader canvass of popular opinion evidenced in "this generation" (7:31). Later Jesus refers to "this generation" in sharply polemical terms as "faithless," "evil" opponents, destined for God's condemning judgment (9:41; 11:29–32, 49–51; 17:25; cf. Acts 2:40). But in the present case no pejorative adjective qualifies "this generation"; in fact, Jesus compares the current populace to children at play, which would seem to strike a more convivial tone. However, as Jesus's simile unfolds, the mood becomes more mixed. Children do not always play nice, and here, attitudes of stubbornness and sulkiness prevail. One bunch of musical kids tries to get another gang interested in playing "wedding" and "funeral" games by cuing them to dance with a snappy flute ditty or to weep with a sad dirge; but the music group whines that the other group snubs them. Or alternatively, each group has its own preferred game—happy flautists, on the one side, and melancholy singers, on the other—and tries to get the other group to play its tune, but to no avail: "you did not dance . . . and you did not weep" with us (7:32). Well, that is the way it goes with kids sometimes.

But Jesus's scenario suggests that something more serious is involved than a cranky play session in the park. Rather than have them running around and squealing in the streets or playgrounds in typical child's play, Jesus pictures these youngsters "sitting in the marketplace/public square [ἀγορᾷ, *agora*]" and officially addressing (προσφονέω, *prosphoneō*) one another (7:32). As Wendy Cotter has demonstrated, this posture, setting, and type of speech suit a formal

176. See Tannehill, *Narrative Unity*, 1:20–22; cf. Acts 2:23, 4:28; 5:38; 13:36; 20:27.

forensic situation of accusation and judgment.[177] Accordingly, Jesus seems to imply that, instead of dealing maturely and fairly with one another, "this generation" of adults is acting like petulant children, hurling insults back and forth and pouting when they do not get their way.

Such infantile conduct characterizes petty and false judgments making the rounds against John and Jesus (7:32–34). While many have responded properly to these prophets (7:29), others have misjudged them on ridiculous grounds. John's asceticism, for example ("eating no bread and drinking no wine"), while appealing to more sober types like the dirge-singers in the parable, offends the more upbeat jig-players to the absurd point of slandering John as a demoniac (7:33). Conversely, Jesus's enjoyment of table-fellowship ("the Son of Humankind has come eating and drinking") has sparked the extreme calumny from the dour, tight-laced crowd that he is "a glutton and a drunkard, a friend of tax collectors and sinners" (7:34). The dietary charge of overindulgence is doubtless exaggerated, childish name-calling, though it taps into Jesus's happy participation in occasional banquets. The social charge has more merit—Jesus does "play" with tax collectors and sinners, as did John (7:29)—but his "friendship" with such people, as we have seen, involves tough-love calls to repentance and discipleship, not blithe approval of their aberrant behavior.

Jesus's final statement, delivered as the "Son of Humankind" divinely authorized to make final judgments on the world, neatly wraps up this evaluative unit by appeal to personified Wisdom: "Wisdom is vindicated [ἐδικαιώθη, *edikaiōthē*] by all her children" (7:35). As "all" who embraced John's baptism "vindicated" (ἐδικαίωσαν, *edikaiōsan*) God's just purpose for humanity (7:29), so "all" of Woman Wisdom's offspring "vindicate" her partnership with God in creating the world and "delighting in the human race," getting down on their level and romping with them as a "little child" in God's arena (Prov 8:22–31).[178] A universal, solidarity theme continues to ring out. Wisdom's playground is as wide and welcoming as all creation. There is room in her realm, including pub-

177. Cotter, "Parable of the Children," 296–302. In short, "the accusatory children are described as *sitting* in the market-place (ἀγορά); the immature accusations are communicated by means of formal address, or dignified call. Each of these incongruities juxtaposes immaturity and dignity" (298 [emphasis original]). Except for the parallel to Luke 7:32 in Matt 11:16, all the NT uses of the compound verb προσφονέω (*prosphoneō*), "call to/address," appear in Luke's writings (Luke 6:13; 7:32; 13:12; 23:20; Acts 21:40; 22:2), and "in every case Luke's context is a dignified, formal one" (297); cf. 1 Esd 2:21; 2 Macc 15:15; and Cotter, "Children Sitting."

178. "Then I was beside him like a master worker; and I was daily his delight, rejoicing before him always" (Prov 8:30). The NRSV, however, notes that another reading is "little child" instead of "master worker." On the latter phrase in the verse, see the NAB rendering: "I was his delight day by day, *playing* before him all the while."

lic streets and squares where she works (cf. Prov 1:20–33), for all her children. They thrive best when they heed her sage voice and follow her righteous path, but they needn't have identical habits, interests, and personalities. Where would the fun (delight) be in indistinguishable automatons? Her massive fellowship table can accommodate laughers and criers, fiddlers and blues-singers, finicky eaters and gourmets, friends and enemies of God, holy prophets and wayward sinners (cf. Prov 9:1–6).[179] Indeed, the divine Sophia (Wisdom) "renews all things; in every generation she passes into holy souls and makes them friends of God, and prophets" (Wis 7:27). As the theologian Elizabeth Johnson beautifully interprets Sophia's purpose in this text: "Down through the centuries as Holy Wisdom graces person after person in land after land, situation after situation, they form together a grand company of the friends of God and prophets; a wisdom community of holy people praising God, loving each other, and struggling for justice and peace in this world; a company that stretches backward and forward in time and encircles the globe in space."[180]

As in "every generation" (Wis 7:27), so in "this generation" addressed by Luke's Jesus, Wisdom forges her community of God's friends and prophets. The leading roles played by John and Jesus in this project as Wisdom's sons and envoys (cf. 1:17; 2:40, 52) serve to nurture other "holy souls" as fellow children, friends, and prophets of God. The Wisdom repertoire ranges from uplifting, "friendly" dance tunes to more disturbing "prophetic" laments in forming "all her children" into mature people of God.[181] For their parts, John and Jesus do not interpret the Wisdom score in quite the same ways, but they complement each other in God's symphony and deserve to be heard fairly and sympathetically. In some respects, Jesus seems to stray the farthest from Mother Wisdom's path. His snubbing of his earthly parents in the temple (before returning to Nazareth and submitting to them) does not fit the standard "growing in wis-

179. On the solidarity emphasis of "all her children," see Johnson-DeBaufre, "Bridging the Gap," 228–33. In conclusion, she understands Luke 7:31–35 as "promoting solidarity across differences around the emancipator vision of the basileia of God" (233). Yes, indeed. I do not completely agree, however, with her further argument that the passage (which she reads as reflecting the Q community) focuses primarily on "the judgmental infighting of the people of 'this generation' . . . when they judge each other on the basis of different eating practices" and only secondarily on the "singular identity" of Jesus and John (233). Here, I side with the interpretation of Christopher Tuckett (Q) of the short parable-and-commentary as "a call to the audience to stop behaving like the grumbling children . . . and to become one of Wisdom's children, by responding positively to Wisdom's envoys John and Jesus" (203). The central roles of John and Jesus as key "players" or "team captains" drawing and rallying together all of Wisdom's diverse children should not be minimized.

180. Elizabeth A. Johnson, *Friends of God*, 41.

181. See Elizabeth A. Johnson, *Friends of God*, 40–45.

dom" profile of a dutiful, respectful son (cf. Prov 1:8–10; 3:1, 11–12, 21; 23:22); and though overdrawn, the charges of gluttony/drunkenness and consorting with "sinners" are a little too close for comfort to the cliff edge of Wisdom's righteous way (Prov 1:8–15; 23:20–21).[182] Yet, amid these persisting questions about Jesus's character, his broad-based mission of compassion and restorative justice to poor, blind, lame, leprous, demonized, deaf, and dead persons (7:21–22) ultimately vindicates Wisdom's commitment to the flourishing of "all her children."

Revealing Love and Forgiving Debt between Jesus and a "Sinner" Woman (7:36–50)

Though often subordinated within the history of the church, the vital role of women has been affirmed since creation among all the children, friends, and prophets of Woman Wisdom (Sophia). I draw again on Elizabeth Johnson's inclusive "vision of the wisdom tradition":

> It widens the playing field for discourse about the communion of saints insofar as it allows the praxis of the friends of God and prophets to take place in home and other private spaces, in workplace and other public spaces, as vigorously as in the sanctuary. This tradition makes room for women today, largely excluded from official religious circles, to claim their own friendship with God and call to prophecy experienced in the beauty and struggle of every day and to know that this is religiously important—every bit as significant as what occurs in more explicitly sacred times and places. In this manner, new ways of appreciating holiness are being born, less associated with patriarchal control and more in tune with women's collective wisdom, so often discounted as a source of insight.[183]

In Luke 1–2, Mary of Nazareth, Elizabeth, and Anna stand out as dynamic prophets intimately engaged with the purpose of God. However, since the emergence of the prophetic missions of John the Baptist and Jesus the Christ, women's voices have been muted and their actions limited. Although

182. See the stark discipline enjoined against "rebellious" sons in Deut 21:20–21: "They [the son's parents] shall say to the elders of his town, 'This son of ours is stubborn and rebellious. He will not obey us. He is a glutton and a drunkard.' Then all the men of the town shall stone him to death. So you shall purge the evil from your midst; and all Israel will hear and be afraid." On the tension between this stipulation and Jesus's Gospel portrait, see Spencer, *What Did Jesus Do?*, 101–4; Johnson-Debaufre, "Bridging the Gap," 230n59; Kee, "Jesus: Glutton," 390.

183. Elizabeth A. Johnson, *Friends of God*, 43.

Jesus's sympathetic attention to women's needs has been evident in his healing of Simon's feverish mother-in-law (4:38–39) and restoration of the deceased son to the widow at Nain (7:11–17), these women's roles remain anonymous, entwined with male kin (son-in-law/son), and conventional. No sooner is Simon's mother-in-law back on her feet than she is serving Simon, Jesus, and the household (4:39—who was cooking when she was ill?); and the only thing we hear from the widow is customary weeping (which Jesus stops—"Do not weep" [7:13]). A sharp feminist critique might even wince at Jesus's recent statement that "among those born of women no one is greater than John" (7:28)—as if women's chief function were to bear children, male children in particular, to serve God's greater purposes which women could never fulfill on their own (though see 11:27–28).

Before we go too far down the feminist-critical road, however, we perk up to hear Jesus's vindication of *his* Mother Sophia and "all her [other] children [τέκνων, *teknōn*]"—not just sons (7:35). And more important, we discover in the final two scenes of this section remarkable *daughters* of Wisdom playing active roles in Jesus's life and ministry: a "sinner" woman demonstrating extraordinary love and faith (7:36–50), and "many women" serving as Jesus's disciples alongside the twelve male apostles (8:1–3).

A Strange Guest (7:36–40)

At first glance, the "sinner" woman from "the city" who crashes a dinner party in Simon the Pharisee's home[184] and comes on to Jesus in passionate fashion seems to be anyone but a model of Woman Wisdom or of anyone Wisdom's prophet should be consorting with on any level, much less allowing her to drench his feet with tears, kisses, and perfume (7:37–38).[185] The profile seems more apt for Tramp Folly imaged as a "strange" (foreign) or "loose" woman, adulteress, and prostitute who seduces young men—with her aggressive kisses and abundant ointments, among other things (Prov 7:13, 17)—away from the path of wisdom and righteousness (Prov 7:5–27; cf. 2:16–19; 5:3–14; 6:24–35). Something like this scandalous picture may well be in host Simon's mind as he mumbles "to himself": "If this man were a prophet, he would have known who and what kind of woman this is who is touching him—that she is a sinner" (Luke 7:39).

184. Whereas Simon clearly invited Jesus to his home for dinner (7:36, 39), nothing in the story suggests that the woman was a welcome guest.

185. Cf. my previous writings on this scene in Spencer, *Dancing Girls*, 108–44, and "Woman's Touch," 88–94.

Simon exemplifies the Pharisees' mixed response to Jesus. On the one hand, he cordially invites Jesus to share a meal "at the table" (7:36), a core symbol, as we have seen, of the Pharisees' spiritual and communal values. But on the other hand, he watches Jesus closely and raises critical doubts about his knowledge, character, and legitimacy as Wisdom's prophet. A true prophet-sage must *know* the ways of God and people. Luke has been constructing this portrait of Jesus from his youth: "And Jesus increased in wisdom . . . and in divine and human favor" (2:52; cf. 2:40). Is Jesus now revealing a blind spot when it comes to women, "this woman" in particular, as Simon wonders? Jesus would scarcely be the first or last great man who failed in rightly "knowing" a woman. Furthermore, a truly wise prophet must *act* circumspectly, especially regarding the company he keeps. From the Pharisees' viewpoint, Jesus had already become suspect with his sinful table associates, but at least he aimed to "call [these] sinners to repentance" (5:29–32). In the present situation, however, Simon observes that Jesus simply—and silently—allows this "sinner" woman to "touch" him intimately. Is Jesus enjoying this "touching" salon treatment?[186] In any case, his mute assent does not appear to commend his prophetic wisdom.

So says and thinks Simon the Pharisee *to himself*, remember. Why doesn't he just blurt out his concerns and call Jesus on the carpet for his questionable conduct? Perhaps, as host, Simon doesn't want to disrupt his social affair any more than the woman's intrusion has already done. Perhaps, as a general respecter of Jesus as "Teacher" (7:40), he gives Jesus some benefit of the doubt or some time to justify his actions. At any rate, Jesus answers his host in direct, debate-like fashion: "Simon, I have something to say to you" (7:40).[187] Turns out that Jesus is more "in the know" than Simon had imagined: not only does Jesus know exactly who this woman is; he also knows what Simon had muttered to himself! Jesus is fully aware of everything unfolding around him and seizes the moment to vindicate his and the woman's identities as Wisdom's children and to instruct Simon in Wisdom's loving, forgiving, faithful, and hospitable ways. It is a matter of focused vision, of correctly *seeing, perceiving, and knowing* the truth, as Jesus makes clear in his pointed query to Simon: "Do you see [βλέπεις, *blepeis*] this woman?" (7:44).[188]

186. The verb ἅπτω (*haptō*) in the middle voice can have overtones of intimate, sexual touching, as in 1 Cor 7:1, but such a nuance is by no means required. Its uses in Luke refer to either Jesus's touching the infirm and needy (5:13; 7:14; 18:15; 22:51) or their reaching out and touching him (6:19; 8:44–47).

187. The "I-thou" construction conveys a sense of directness and emphasis: "Simon, I-have to-you [ἔχω σοί, *echō soi*] something to say."

188. See Barbara E. Reid, "Do You See?"

Of course, Simon had seen (ἰδών, *idōn*) her superficially, had glanced her way and made snap judgments about "what kind of woman" she was (7:39). But he had not perceptively, knowingly seen *this* woman in her particular, multifaceted, "intersectional" identity,[189] preferring to tag her with the amorphous deviant label of "sinner" and leave it at that. "What kind of" sinner does Simon think she is? Perhaps the sexual kind—a "loose" woman, as suggested above, in line with her lavish public demonstration of affection to Jesus. But are Simon's judgments based on anything more than rumor or gossip? (If he really "knows" that she's a licentious scarlet, Simon himself may have some explaining to do!). Luke never identifies this woman as a specifically sexual sinner, and not because he's squeamish about "adulterers" or "prostitutes" (cf. 15:30; 16:18). He simply lumps the woman in with other "sinners" (ἁμαρτωλοί, *hamartōloi*), like the fisherman Peter (5:8) and tax collectors (5:30). Maybe she's been a fraudulent businessperson or a notorious thief in the city. We're not told; we have no rap sheet on her. Hence, assumptions that this or any sinner-*woman* must have some sexual taint about her are prejudicial in the extreme, though sadly still all too common (of course, we would never dream of accusing fisherman Peter or tax collector Zacchaeus of being gigolos). In the present case, the woman's effusive, even erotic display of love for Jesus need not be interpreted in pejorative, salacious terms (see more below).

A Forgiven Debtor (7:41–43, 47–50)

What—or better, whom—does Jesus see? He freely grants this woman's "sinful" reputation, even that she had committed many sins (7:47), though he says nothing and evidently cares nothing about the type of transgressions. What matters is Jesus's embracive insight into this woman as a *forgiven debtor*. He first prepares Simon to see this image with a brief parable of "a certain creditor" with two debtors, one owing a substantial amount of 500 denarii, the other a smaller sum of 50 denarii (a denarius = typical daily wage for ordinary laborer) (7:41). The creditor cancels both accounts, prompting both debtors to

189. "Intersectionality" is a concept of third-wave feminism aimed at stressing women's distinct and diverse roles and identities. As Naomi Zack (*Inclusive Feminism*) writes, "The term 'intersectionality' refers to multiple oppressions experienced by nonwhite and poor women in particular, but more generally to all women because differences in sexuality, age, and physical ableness are also sites of oppression" (7). She also cautions that such vital recognition of differences may work against inclusivity and solidarity among women working for common causes of equality. Ideally, however, intersectional and inclusive visions of feminism should work together in creative tension (see 1–2, 7–8, 65–66, 72–73).

"love" him. Obviously, however, as Jesus gets Simon to admit, the debtor with the larger balance loved the benevolent creditor more (7:40–43). Jesus's point is clear in the current context. Remitting financial debt, during Jubilee or any other season, serves in the biblical economy as an apt image of releasing moral debt (sin) incurred by faulty stewards of God's blessings.[190] By the logic of the parable, then, those forgiven of greater sin will tend to respond with greater love toward God, the forgiving "creditor"—which is exactly what this "sinful" woman does. Her copious outpouring of love for Jesus certifies that "her sins, which were many [πολλαί, *pollai*], have been forgiven" (7:47).

The repeated perfect passive verb form ἀφέωνται (*apheōntai*), first to Simon ("her sins *have been forgiven*" [7:47]) and then directly to the woman ("your sins *are forgiven*" [7:48]), suggests a *past condition* that continues into the present.[191] The cause-effect trajectory is thus clarified along the lines of the debtor parable. The indebted/sinful woman's loving gesture toward Jesus does not precipitate (earn) his forgiveness; put another way, Jesus does not forgive *because the woman loves him*. Rather, she loves him *because he had already forgiven her*: Jesus's gracious action was primary and prompted her manifold love. Thus it appears that Jesus indeed *had known* this woman both/either in a prior confessional encounter (not in some illicit dalliance) and/or in the present engagement where he senses—as a prophet!—her sincere, heartfelt love. The woman may be intruding on Simon's event, but she has already been—and continues to be—welcomed by the loving-forgiving Jesus.

Though Jesus targets his comments to Simon and the woman, the banquet table represents a public forum. The other guests, likely Pharisees, no doubt crane their necks to hear Jesus's words, even as they gawk at the woman's gushy treatment of Jesus's feet, which has suddenly become the party's headlining event.[192] But whatever their reaction to the woman's performance, they are es-

190. See the discussion above on Luke 4:18–19 related to sin, debt, and Jubilee; on the present passage in light of Jubilee, see Ringe, *Jesus, Liberation*, 66–71.

191. The NRSV's change to "are forgiven" is not incorrect (= your sins "stand forgiven"), but it does obscure somewhat the past dimension. If Jesus were presently forgiving her sin for the first time, he would most likely use the present tense ("I forgive your sins"). Barbara E. Reid ("Do You See?") also notes that the narrator's use of the imperfect tense in introducing the woman ("she was [ἦν, *ēn*] a sinner" [7:37]) could be rendered in a more customary/habitual sense as "she *used to be* a sinner," that is, "she is no longer the sinner she once was" (41).

192. Kathleen Corley (*Private Women*, 24–79, 121–26) provides ample evidence for the popular presence of prostitutes and various other female consorts and entertainers at Hellenistic banquets. Her claim, however, that the woman in Luke 7 fits this courtesan bill doesn't square with Luke's narrative profile: this silent, sobbing woman provides no witty banter, musical entertainment, or flirtatious divertissements. She unintentionally steals the party spotlight and evokes more shock than excitement from spectators.

pecially stunned by Jesus's claim to remit her sins. Reminiscent of respondents to Jesus's pardoning the paralytic's sins, these guests query "among themselves, 'Who is this who even forgives sins?'" (7:49). In the former case, the question contained its own answer: "Who can forgive sins *but God alone*?" (5:21). That orthodox conviction still holds, though without accompanying charges of blasphemy against Jesus in the present scene. As Forgiver, Jesus assumes divine prerogative. Others might perform bona fide miracles drawing on various sources of power, but *only God can forgive sin*. In no action is Jesus closer to the heart of God than in bringing "peace" and "salvation" to troubled lives beset by sin (7:50; see more below).

A Gracious Host (7:44–46)

The woman's transformed forgiven condition is evident, as Jesus makes clear, in her extraordinary demonstration of love. To limn the dimensions of this love, Jesus pointedly invites Simon to "see *this woman*" as the true host Simon failed to be. By inviting Jesus to his home for dinner, Simon was duty bound to provide not only food and drink, but also cultural amenities such as (1) washing water (for dirty feet), (2) greeting kiss (on the cheek), and (3) refreshing ointment (typically olive oil for the head). However, Simon had offered none of these, thereby snubbing Jesus and also shaming himself as a shabby host. Shockingly and embarrassingly—for Simon!—the uninvited woman steps into the breach created by Simon's slipshod hospitality and exceeds all basic requirements.[193] She supplies (1) abundant water from her flooding tears to bathe Jesus's feet and then wipes them with her hair, (2) a profusion of incessant kisses, and (3) precious perfume from an alabaster jar (7:44–46; cf. v. 37). It doesn't take a prophet to see that this woman has shown up Simon and proven to be the superior host.[194]

193. Bertschmann ("Hosting") marshals evidence that hospitality in the ancient world did not necessarily involve any or all of the gestures Jesus singles out from the woman's behavior (head-anointing, foot-washing, and kiss-greeting). Accordingly, since Simon the Pharisee at least provided Jesus with food and a place at the table, he would not have been automatically viewed as shirking his hosting duties. That may be, but in Jesus's view, the woman clearly outperforms Simon as a host—in his own home!—and thus puts him to shame to some degree (though that is not her primary intent). Bertschmann stresses Jesus's acclamation of the woman's hosting role as "disambiguating" or recalibrating the "cycle of hospitality," in favor of the woman's loving actions over Simon's suspicious thoughts and limited, albeit socially acceptable, actions.

194. See Bertschmann, "Hosting," 45: "It is thus not the guest of honour [Jesus] who has usurped the role of host; he [Jesus] has nominated a new and better host."

It does take some biblical insight, however, but well within Simon the Pharisee's purview, to envision the woman's host role in the context of Wisdom. In Prov 9 Woman Wisdom "sets her table" and "sends out her servant-girls" into the city to invite the "simple" to her home for nourishing instruction in God's ways (Prov 9:1–6). Of course, the woman in Luke 7 knows and treats Jesus as anything but a simpleton, but rather as Wisdom's supreme prophet, commanding her deepest love and highest respect. But she, too, as a "simple" woman from the city who has found her way to embrace Wisdom's prophet at the table proves herself to be "vindicated" as Wisdom's child (Luke 7:35) and "servant-girl." She and Jesus have effectively transformed Simon's residence into Wisdom's house.

But doesn't she overdo her hosting duties? Shouldn't Wisdom's servant show a tad more decorum and act a little less like Tramp Folly? One kiss would do the job, along with a dab of ordinary ointment and modest basin of water. A torrent of wet tears and kisses from her own body mixed with her best perfume decanted from an alabaster jar—not to mention her loosened locks entwined around Jesus's feet, massaged dry with her hands—reflects by any honest measure an intimate, passionate, even erotic display. But by no means must "erotic" entail something pornographic or illicit. It all depends on the nature and purpose of the sensual activity. For her part, Woman Wisdom is no prude; she is just as passionate as her foolish counterpart, but for wise and righteous ends. She walks the city streets and stands on public corners strutting her stuff and crying out for consorts in her Wisdom enterprise (Prov 1:20–33; 8:1–21). She desires that her wisdom partners "hold her fast" (3:18), becoming her "intimate friend" (7:4) "intoxicated with her love" (5:19).[195] The quintessential biblical exposition of godly erotic love, attributed to Wisdom's royal patron Solomon, features an ardent female lover with flowing kisses, tresses, fragrances, and bathed feet (Song 1:1–3, 12–14; 3:6; 4:1, 10–15; 5:2–5, 13; 7:5, 13; 8:1)—more than a little evocative of the woman's loving encounter with Jesus in Simon's home at the banquet table (cf. Song 5:16; 8:2). Wise knowledge of God, Christ, and other people comes through deep, passionate loving relationships that are fully *embodied*—including *sexually* embodied—in accordance with God's created purpose.[196]

195. On the similar sensual descriptions in Prov 1–9 of the means employed by Lady Wisdom and Tramp Folly toward polar opposite aims—the former toward life, the latter toward death—see Yee, "I Have Perfumed" and *Poor Banished Children*, 149–53.

196. On the link between this incident and the Song of Songs, see Spencer, *Song*, 187; Barbara E. Reid, *Choosing*, 119.

A Faithful Doer (7:50)

Notably, Jesus is the only character to speak directly *to* the woman rather than about her (7:48), including the final word in the story (7:50). While it would have been nice if Luke had reported some of the woman's own speech, perhaps he thought her actions spoke loudly enough in this case. Leaving the question about his right to forgive sins dangling in the air (7:49), Luke's Jesus reserves his last comment for the woman: "Your faith has saved you; go in peace" (7:50). This sudden focus on *faith* may seem surprising, given the main emphasis on the woman's *love*. But recall the tight nexus between faith and love in Pauline theology, exemplified in Gal 5:6—"the only thing that counts is *faith working through* [ἐνεργουμένη, *energoumenē*] *love*." Far from being a purely abstract state of thought or assent to a set of propositions, Christian faith *works itself out*, pulses with responsive energy, in embodied acts of love toward Christ and others. Remember also Moltmann-Wendel's challenge to broaden hyper "dogmatically loaded" concepts of faith into more sensually vibrant expressions of "smell, feeling, touching. . . . Fabric, wine, balm are experienced in it. Fear of 'natural theology' has made our senses disintegrate, has eliminated nose, eye, skin. . . . To experience again the whole God, we also have to use again all of our organs; we must taste, see, and sense how friendly the Lord is."[197] The woman who lovingly ministers to Jesus clearly has no fear of "natural/sensual theology." She works out her faith through love intimately conveyed through her tears, lips, hair, and hands engaged with Jesus's feet amid odors of dirt and sweat from Jesus's feet and of food and drink from Simon's table, mingled with her outpoured perfume. And in her "natural" faithful loving in response to Christ's loving forgiveness, she enjoys the gift of God's saving peace.

The woman's faith experience is just as commendable as that of the centurion (7:9)—but also distinctive. Whereas the centurion had *no personal contact* with Jesus, trusting simply in the efficacy of his word on the model of Roman military authority, the woman has *elaborate, intimate contact* with Jesus, more spontaneous than "official," more passionate than "rational," embracing Jesus more as prophet, brother, and friend in Wisdom's family than as superior officer. Luke has thus staked out a rich, variegated field of faith with room for women and men, Jews and Gentiles, sinners and soldiers, emotionalists and rationalists.

197. Moltmann-Wendel, "Self-Love," 31. Cf. the chapter "A Spirituality of the Senses" in Moltmann, *Living God*, 157–75.

Redressing the Gender Gap between Male Apostles and Female Disciples (8:1–3)

Jesus's commendation of the anointing woman's remarkable love and faith—in marked contrast to Simon the Pharisee's inhospitality and suspicion—demonstrates how much Jesus values women's passionate participation in Wisdom's household. But the picture is only partly liberating, since the female character remains totally silent and subordinate at Jesus's feet. To be sure, Jesus ennobles the woman's servant role as that which the *male host* should have undertaken (7:44–46) and sets the stage for his own performance as servant-host at the Last Supper ("I am among you as one who serves" [22:27], which, in turn, serves as a model for all disciples, male and female [22:24–30]). So the forgiven, loving woman qualifies as a faithful follower of Jesus *in this incident.* But then she's gone, dismissed by Jesus "in peace" (7:50), yet still sent on her way rather than called to journey with Jesus. That remains, it seems, the vocation of the twelve chosen male apostles (6:12–16), with others like Levi the tax collector tagging along.

But no sooner do we say good-bye to the faithful woman who served Jesus than we encounter, in a key summary text, "many" women, led by Mary Magdalene, Joanna, and Susanna, accompanying Jesus along *with the Twelve* (8:1–3). While this text does not designate the women as "disciples" or "apostles" per se, neither does it label "the Twelve" as such. But the syntax of the single sprawling Greek sentence in 8:1–3, though still giving prominence to the dozen apostles, suggests the women's cooperative, collaborative partnership with Jesus and his male confidants: "[Jesus] went on . . . proclaiming and bringing the good news . . . *and* [καί, *kai*] *the Twelve* [*were*] *with him, as well as* [καί, *kai*] *some women*" (8:1–2). The double conjunction can be rendered "*both* the Twelve *and* some women [were] with him." The lack of a Greek verb for "were" tightens the shared fellowship of the two gendered groups. Literally, the phrase runs: "both the Twelve *with him* and some women." Jesus stands at the center, with male and female groups clustered immediately around him.

Fortunately, "some women" are not just dropped in as an afterthought. We learn some important things about them, as we did about the twelve apostles in the summary capping off the previous section (6:12–16). Notice the following salient features about Jesus's female disciples.[198]

198. See the fuller treatment in Spencer, *Salty Wives*, 101–44.

Residents of Galilee (8:2–3)

This Mary is "called Magdalene" because she hailed from the town of Magdala on the western shore of Lake Gennesaret. Magdala was a thriving fish-processing center at this time, and it is possible that Mary worked in this industry at a level high enough to provide disposable income (see more below). Joanna is introduced as the wife of Chuza, Herod Antipas's "steward" ("business manager," "foreman" [ἐπίτροπος, *epitropos*]).[199] Her marriage to a chief Herodian administrator likely meant that Joanna lived in style in Tiberias, Antipas's new capital not far down the coast from Magdala. We have no further information about Susanna and the "many other [women]," but we may assume their location in similar Galilean social circles as Mary Magdalene and Joanna.[200] The prospects among Jesus's followers of a woman in the fishing business and a well-positioned insider (informant?) within or defector from the Herodian palace (did Joanna leave her husband?) provide interesting counterparts to Peter and other fishermen-disciples and to Simon the Zealot and other politically minded associates. Moreover, the prospects of these family-detached women and men *travelling together* with Jesus "through cities and villages" of Galilee (8:1) raise issues of propriety, if not outright scandal. It is possible that the women, especially the married Joanna, made only occasional excursions or "daytrips" with the Jesus party.[201] It remains to be seen when, where, and how often these women appear in the ensuing narrative of Jesus's mission (see more below).

Beneficiaries of Healing (8:2)

A key motivation for women's discipleship arises from their personal experience of Jesus's liberation from demons and diseases. The narrative reports that Jesus had freed Mary Magdalene from an oppressive gang of "seven demons" (8:2), though it cites no specific maladies for her or any other woman.[202] As natural

199. BDAG, 385; other meanings of "guardian" or "tutor" are unlikely here.

200. See Sawicki, *Crossing Galilee*, 135–53, 179–84, 191–98, and "Magdalenes and Tiberiennes."

201. See the plausible query of Schaberg, "Luke," 375: "Since the area [Galilee] is small, and since only the male disciples are said to have left their homes to follow Jesus (18:28), did the travel for the women consist of day trips from home bases?"

202. Mary Magdalene is infamously branded here as one "from whom seven demons had gone out." Clearly she suffered from some kind of severe oppressive condition (cf. 11:26). But nothing is specified about the types of demons: there is no explicit connection with the seven deadly

as it would be for those whom Jesus heals to want to follow him, in fact this has not happened heretofore in Jesus's mission: neither the demon-possessed man in the synagogue, nor Simon's feverish mother-in-law, nor the leper, nor the paralytic, nor the man with the withered hand enlists, in any identifiable way, as Jesus's disciple. Peter, James, and John are compelled by Jesus's miraculous haul of fish to drop their nets for good and follow Jesus (5:9–11). But this feat is not as personal as an exorcism or healing that touches one's body. While happy to heal people, Jesus does not do so primarily to attract an adoring entourage; rather, he helps people for their own good, as ends in themselves, "objects" of God's love, care, and justice, no strings attached.[203] But if some beneficiaries of his liberating ministry, like these women, do choose to follow him, he welcomes their fellowship (though see 8:38–39). Still we again wonder how this discipleship will play out in the rest of the story, particularly when the road becomes rougher.

Providers of Support (8:3)

Intriguingly, these women disciples emerge as *benefactors* as well as beneficiaries of Jesus's movement. Like Simon's mother-in-law, who "began to serve" (διηκόνει, *diēkonei*) Jesus and the household "immediately" after Jesus cured her fever (4:39), these healed women "were serving" (διηκόνουν, *diēkonoun*) Jesus and his followers (female and male) (8:3). But unlike Simon's mother-in-law, whose service was conventionally domestic, the "service" of Mary Magdalene and company was primarily economic, flowing "out of their resources/possessions [ἐκ τῶν ὑπαρχόντων, *ek tōn hyparchontōn*]." This comment shows the broad potential scope of "diaconal" ministry, for both men and women: providing food and/or funds, serving at dinner table and/or banker's desk.[204] Again, thus far Luke's Jesus has been offered hospitality,

---

sins or sexual sins in particular. Moreover, identifying Mary Magdalene with the anonymous "sinner" woman in the previous scene, popular in later church tradition, has no basis in Luke's text beyond narrative proximity.

203. Central to Martha Nussbaum's "Capabilities Approach" is a (neo-Kantian) commitment to respect "each person as an end," not least female persons, who too often get subsumed within and subordinated to the agendas of men and of patriarchal institutions. See her statement in *Women*, 69: "To sum up: We want an approach that is respectful of each person's struggle for flourishing, that treats each person as an end and as a source of agency and worth in her own right" (cf. 41–110; Nussbaum, *Creating Capabilities*, 18–45).

204. Though not used in the present text, a common word for "table" (τράπεζα, *trapeza*) applied to either meal or money service appears in both senses elsewhere in Luke's writings: Luke

but *no money* by anyone, even by the taxman Levi or the Roman centurion accustomed to paying and being paid for services rendered. As women of some independent means, Mary Magdalene, Joanna, Susanna, and others take the lead in underwriting Jesus's mission, even as some prominent wives of Pharisees supported various political causes of their choice, with or without their husbands' endorsement.[205]

Models of Faithfulness (8:1–3)

Mary Magdalene, Joanna, Susanna, and their women associates are introduced as grateful and generous disciples of Jesus. To what extent they continue to model faithfulness—in the sense of loyal, loving partnership with Jesus and his other followers—remains to be seen. The faithful, loving woman from the previous scene had her poignant moment in the spotlight but was ultimately dismissed from the narrative "in peace." By contrast, Peter and the male apostles have recurring supporting roles. To peek ahead, Mary Magdalene, Joanna, and other Galilean women disciples reappear, but not until the grand finale connected with Jesus's death, burial, and resurrection (23:49, 55; 24:1–10, 22). Retrospective reports indicate that these women "had followed [Jesus] from Galilee" (23:49, also v. 55) and "remembered his words" from prior teaching (24:8). So in the larger narrative frame, from early summary (8:1–3) to concluding scenes (23:49–24:10), Luke *assumes* the persisting presence of Galilean women disciples.[206] But they remain in the background, too easily ignored, too taken for granted. However, a few promising moments for women continue to emerge. Jesus reaffirms women's capacities for heeding God's word as equal members in God's household (8:20–21; 11:27–28); Martha and (another) Mary host Jesus as Lord (10:38–42); Jesus continues to heal some women, who do not, however, become disciples (8:40–56; 13:10–17); he features women positively in parables and lessons (13:20–21; 15:8–10; 18:1–8; 21:1–4); and in addition to Galilean women, some "daughters of Jerusalem" lament his death (23:27–28). These are encouraging signs of a closing gender gap in Luke, but still with room to spare for greater equality in ministry.

16:21; 22:21, 30; Acts 6:2; 16:34 (eating); Luke 19:23 (banking). The "daily table serving" in Acts 6:1–2 could apply to both feeding and funding needy widows, though the former seems primary.

205. See Josephus, *Ant.* 17.32–51, recounting the financial support of the Pharisees by the wife of Pheroras (Herod the Great's younger brother); she pays the stiff fine Herod had levied against 6,000 Pharisees for challenging his loyalty oath to Caesar; see the discussion in Ilan, *Integrating Women*, 11–42, and "Attraction"; and Bauckham, *Gospel Women*, 161–63.

206. See Karris, "Women," 35–39.

Cultivating the Fruit of Salvation (8:4–9:50)

This section fleshes out the roles and responsibilities of Jesus's disciples. Having answered Jesus's call and received the "seed" of his saving word (8:12), the disciples must now begin to cultivate and grow into their new vocation. As Jesus's teaching makes clear, this time in the form of an explained parable (8:4–15), the fruitful product of God's seed/word sown by Jesus varies widely among hearers/disciples, depending on their levels of attentiveness, commitment, and obedience. God's word carries the potential of abundant "hundredfold" harvest, but only in cooperation with faithful respondents who heed what they hear with perceptive, active intent: "Let anyone with ears to hear listen!" (8:8). Later in this section Jesus demonstrates God's capacity to nourish his people with a bumper "thousandfold" crop in spite of the apostles' persisting incapacity to understand fully and act upon Jesus's word (9:12–17).[207] Their ears continue to need fine-tuning.

Jesus challenges his disciples to sharpen not only their aural skills (cf. 8:21; 9:35, 44) but also their visual acuity (8:16–18) and overall clarity of understanding the ways of God in Christ. Disciples (μαθηταί, *mathētai*) are at root students/learners devoted to integrative intellectual and experiential, cognitive and behavioral, *knowledge* of God's will, in keeping with Luke's prefatory goal: "so that you may know the solidity of the things you've been taught" (1:4 AT). Jesus assures his followers that God desires to reveal all truth; it is not God's ultimate aim to tease people and keep secrets from them, though it may sometimes appear that way to finite minds (8:10). But God's purpose to disclose the divine will through Christ must be matched by disciples' keen mindfulness to "pay attention to how [they] listen" (8:18). Problematically, however, the disciples' hearing/seeing impairments are symptomatic of continuing attention-deficit tendencies inhibiting their knowledge. Peter blurts out a silly proposal for a mountaintop building project—"*not knowing* [μὴ εἰδώς, *mē eidōs*] what he said" in Luke's telling aside (9:33)—and soon thereafter the whole apostolic crew "was *not understanding* [ἠγνόουν, *ēgnooun*]" what Jesus revealed (9:45 AT).[208]

Before we mock their ignorance too strongly, however, we must appreciate what they are now being pressed to grasp about Jesus Messiah, namely, that

207. See the optimistic (but by no means naive) response to this parable from a man named Manuel, one of the *campesino* members of the Soltiname community in Lake Nicaragua, reported in Cardenal, *Gospel*: "As I see it, in this harvest a lot of seed is lost, maybe most of it. But in the end the seeds that produce make up for all that loss. That's what I believe will happen with the harvest of these words. The good people, who now are very few, will be a great society, because one will become a lot" (160).

208. Stressing the continuing force of the imperfect form of ἀγνοέω (*agnoeō*).

he is destined to *die—at the instigation of religious authorities!—and rise again* (9:21–22, 44–45). As familiar as Christians have become with Jesus's crucifixion and resurrection, his first predictions of these events would have struck most first-century Jewish hearers as enigmatic at best, lunatic at worst. Crucifixion and resurrection simply did not compute with typical deliverance-and-redemption hopes for God's Messiah. Jesus's disciples, then, were not so much obtuse as ordinary. And theologically, the matter is made thornier by Luke's explanation that the disciples' misapprehension of Jesus's forecasted tragic end derived from the fact that "its meaning *was concealed* from them, so that they *could not perceive* it" (9:44–45; cf. 8:10). Apparently, then, in tension with the illuminating lamp image in 8:16–18, God does conceal some insight, at least for a while. A possible way out of the dilemma (see more below) might surmise that the disciples are temporarily restrained from hearing/seeing the truth because they are not ready to receive/perceive it in a responsible manner. In this respect, the veiling of knowledge may compare with the silencing of witness about Jesus as Messiah (9:20–21; cf. 5:13; 8:56). Jesus charges his disciples "not to tell anyone" about his messianic identity because they would give a distorted profile void of suffering, rejection, crucifixion, and resurrection, which they cannot yet comprehend. For all of God's revelatory efforts, human knowledge of the ways of God and Christ remains partial and progressive.

Along with focusing on the disciples' response to Jesus's saving word, this section also features their interactions with Jesus's liberating miracles. Whereas earlier miracles stories highlighted the reactions of Pharisees and scribes (5:17–26; 6:6–11), these groups drop out of the narrative for a while (until 11:37). Moreover, the "crowds" recede into the background as the disciples move front and center. The first miracle involves Jesus's saving his disciples from a violent windstorm that suddenly erupts on Lake Gennesaret (8:22–25). Upon reaching the shore in Gerasene country, Jesus and his crew of disciples are immediately met by a raving demoniac whom Jesus "heals/saves" (σῴζω, *sōzō* [8:36]). While this incident sparks intense reactions from the local population (8:34–37), oddly no response of Jesus's associates is reported (perhaps they are still in shock from the stormy ordeal). In the next tightly paired scenes, however, Jesus's saving/healing a hemorrhagic woman and saving/resuscitating Jairus's deceased daughter (σῴζω, *sōzō* [8:48, 50]) again provide profound teachable moments for Jesus's disciples. In the first case, Peter attempts, rather unhelpfully as it happens, to answer Jesus's "Who touched me?" question (8:45); in the second, Jesus restricts the witnesses of his revivifying miracle to mourners already inside the house, the little girl's parents, and the apostolic trio of Peter, James, and John (8:51–56).

The Twelve are being trained not only to understand Jesus's messianic identity but also to undertake their own work of gospel preaching and miracle working as Jesus's delegates. But while their initial missionary campaign meets with good success (9:1–6), they again prove that they still have much to learn. No sooner do they debrief Jesus about "all they had done" (9:10) than they debunk his intention to feed the multitude, given the meager means at hand. Jesus persists, however, in producing a cornucopia from five loaves and two fish that "fills" the whole crowd with food to spare. And it is no accident that Jesus enlists the apostles as waiters and busboys, gathering *twelve* baskets of leftovers (9:12–17)—one for each of them to pack up and to ponder about the nature of servant-ministry and God's gracious provision in Christ.

Not that they ponder very long or learn very much. Soon thereafter, while the big three disciples almost sleep through the greatest seminar of their lives with a transfigured Jesus, Moses, and Elijah (9:28–36), the other nine are miserably failing to help a desperate father and his demon-possessed son (9:37–41). Then the entire group begins to wrangle about which of them is greatest (9:46) and to protest a maverick minister outside their circle daring to cast out demons in Jesus's name (9:49). They appear more concerned about promoting their status and protecting their turf than following Jesus's path. They have a long way to go in letting Jesus's word work its fruitful way in their hearts and lives.

Paying Attention to God's Word in Parables and Putting It into Action (8:4–21)

Jesus develops his introductory lesson in three stages: spinning a parable (8:4–15), painting a picture (8:16–18), and seizing a moment (8:19–21). Each part drives home the salient point of attending to God's word, as the following punch lines demonstrate.

- *Field cultivation*: "Hear [ἀκούσαντες, *akousantes*] the word, hold it fast . . . and bear fruit" (8:15).
- *Lamp illumination*: "Look [βλέπετε, *blepete*] how you listen [ἀκούετε, *akouete*]" (8:18 AT).
- *Family relations*: "My mother and my brothers are those who hear [ἀκούοντες, *akouontes*] the word of God and do it" (8:21).

The final "hear the word and do it" punctuates the link between acoustics and action. Hearing without putting what one hears into practice is a waste of precious time and seed—might as well pretend not to hear at all, or from the teacher's perspective, might as well not plant any seed of thought. Or shifting to the visual image: might as well not turn on the light if eyes (minds) remain shut. The visual element is strongest in the "lamp" segment, but it also appears alongside the dominant aural component in surrounding material. In the brief interlude on the purpose of parabolic pedagogy (8:9–10) between telling (8:4–8) and explaining (8:11–15) the story of the soils, Jesus cites Isaiah's dual looking-listening response to God's word (Luke 8:10/Isa 6:9–10). And in the closing scene, setting up Jesus's inclusive spiritual solidarity with all "mothers and brothers" who hear and do God's word, is his natural mother and brothers' desire "to see [ἰδεῖν, *idein*]" him physically (Luke 8:20).

However, while each segment sets forth promising opportunities for hearing-seeing-knowing God's will through Christ, they also frankly acknowledge stubborn opposition and obstacles to such insight. Knowing God in Luke is no simple once-for-all epiphany or easy three-step process: it remains, as stated above, a precarious and progressive pilgrimage. The present passage underscores key aspects of (1) *mystery revealed*, (2) *secret uncovered*, and (3) *lost one discovered.*

Mystery Revealed (8:4–15)

While Jesus's short illustrations concerning "garments and wineskins" (5:36–39) and "the blind leading the blind" (6:39) are each called a παραβολή (*parabolē*), the soils story represents Jesus's first substantial parable, setting the stage for a large cluster of others, many unique to Luke, in the third main unit of the book (9:51–19:44). In the introduction to that unit, we discuss the parable genre more fully. For now, we follow Luke's focus on the *purpose* of Jesus's parables via the paradigmatic soils tale, "the parable of parables," as some have aptly dubbed it.[209] Why does Luke's Jesus choose the parable medium as a means of knowing God and God's will? A simple view that stories—whether formal parables, verbal illustrations, or personal yarns—grab attention and are easier to grasp than theoretical (or theological!) propositions misses the mark of Jesus's purpose. He tells parables as much to *disguise* the truth as disclose it. They are *mysteries* (μυστήρια, *mysteria*), not in the sense of "whodunnit," but *who gets it*, that is: who really gets Jesus's point concerning God's realm embedded in the parable (8:10).

A parable admits different levels of response from superficial (entertaining) to substantial (engaging), especially since most of the time Jesus does not decode its meaning in Aesop fashion ("the moral of the story is . . ."). The pres-

209. For example, Snodgrass, *Stories*, 145: "*the* parable about parables" (emphasis original); cf. Herzog, "Sowing," 187–88.

ent case marks the chief exception, for Jesus does expound the parable of the soils to his disciples, partly to confirm that to them "it has been given to know the secrets/mysteries of the kingdom of God" (8:9–10), but also, more critically, to emphasize through this foundational parable the vital role that hearers/respondents play with the Sower-Teacher in apprehending, appropriating, and applying God's word. At root this is a parable about what it takes to "get" all the other parables, and indeed what it takes to grasp God's word in all its forms. The seed sown on four types of soil/ground "is the word of God" (8:11) broadcast by Jesus (and other Spirit-inspired prophet-teachers) to four types of hearers, who respond in various ways, three negative and one positive (8:11–15).[210]

Parable		**Meaning**	
Ground	*Seed*	*Hearer*	*Word*
Beaten path	Trampled and eaten by birds	Hardened	Taken away by the devil
Rocky	Sprouts but withers for lack of moisture	Fickle	Sparks initial faith but fails in time of testing
Thorny	Sprouts but choked by thorns	Cluttered	Choked by worries, riches, and pleasures of life
Good soil	Produces hundredfold harvest	Steadfast	Produces "fruitful" character with "patient endurance"

Jesus assumes a perilous environment beset by diabolical forces. They assault the faithful with difficult "testing" (πειρασμός, *peirasmos* [8:13]) in desolate territory (trampled, rocky, thorny), just as Jesus was "tested" (πειράζω/πειρασμός, *peirazō/peirasmos* [4:2, 13]) by the devil in the wilderness. As Jesus overcame this ordeal through commitment to God's Torah (4:4, 8, 12), his disciples must "hold . . . fast" to God's word with "patient endurance" (8:15). The divine word is a precious commodity that must be protected and practiced, lest it be taken away (see 8:12). Unlike Matthew's and Mark's itemizing a three-tier sliding scale of thirty-, sixty- and hundredfold harvest (possibly to balance the three unproductive scenarios [Matt 13:23; Mark 4:20]),[211] Luke proposes only *one*

210. I draw this chart and some of the following discussion from Spencer, *Gospel of Luke*, 144–45.

211. Herzog, "Sowing," 190.

positive outcome, albeit the abundant hundredfold profit (Luke 8:8). Although this bumper crop might outweigh the losses from the other three futile operations, it remains a risky venture (25 percent success rate) in the current hostile environment filled with demonic threats (birds), tests (rocks), and temptations (thorns).

However we calculate the math, Luke stresses that the fruitfulness of God's word in this world depends on vigilant, faithful cultivation of the individual heart "ground" that receives this "sown" word in contested territory, a *battleground* with the devil, no less, littered with casualties (8:12). This is life-and-death world war: in Deuteronomy's terms, a critical choice between "life and prosperity," on the one side, and "death and adversity," on the other, determined by what God's people do with the divine word brought "very near to you . . . in your heart" (Deut 30:14–15; cf. 30:11–20). Isaiah may promise that God's seed-word "shall not return to [God] empty, but it shall accomplish that which I purpose, and succeed in the thing for which I sent it" (Isa 55:11)—but such success will not come without considerable struggle and concerted effort.

Further tension comes into play between divine revelation and human responsiveness. No one can "get" God's word—in parable or otherwise—without being "given" understanding by God. While God's faithful people receive the key to unlocking divine "mysteries," they do not forge some secret gnostic society with only a select inner circle in the know and everyone else in the dark. Consider two points.

First, those given the key of knowledge must use it or lose it (cf. 8:18); they must persistently engage with the word and cultivate it toward fruitful ends. In this root parable, the sower sows ample quality seed with rich potential for growth, but he does not water, weed, fertilize, chase away birds and other pests, or otherwise tend the crop. Here the *soil*—representing the *hearer*—does its own work of nurturing the seed.[212] And the four soils represent different types of *hearing* that anyone may evince rather than discrete categories of hearers.

212. Hazony (*Philosophy*), drawing on Deut 30:11–15 (along with 29:29 and Isa 45:19), stresses that "the Mosaic teaching is supposed to capture that which the human mind, if it is thinking straight, *should* be able to understand. . . . His teaching is *not* of the 'hidden things' . . . *not* 'a wonder to you,' but something that is, on the contrary, manifest and very near, presenting that way which brings 'life and the good'" (62; emphasis original). I affirm this biblical focus on the rational hearing-thinking respondent to God's word. But Hazony sets up too stark a dichotomy between the HB, on the one hand, as philosophical wisdom expounded by God's sages and accessible to God's people, and the NT, on the other hand, as "'revelation' of secrets long kept hidden by God" (61; cf. 55–62). Both testaments—and certainly the teaching of Luke's Jesus in the parable of the soils—emphasize the dialectic of God's revelation of special knowledge (sowing the word) and responsible human engagement in thought and action (cultivating the word).

No one, certainly not any of Jesus's disciples in Luke, hears fruitfully all of the time; all have their hardened, rocky, and thorny moments.

Second, while many do not "get" the message on the first round, that doesn't condemn them to permanent outsider status. Jesus and his emissaries continue to sow the word, providing fresh opportunities for fruitful responses by a wider company of disciples, as we have seen, both male and female, beyond the chosen Twelve.

Secret Uncovered (8:16–18)

Shifting from the agricultural to domestic realm, Jesus now illuminates the delicate process of hearing-seeing-knowing God's word with the image of a *lamp*. Following basic circadian rhythms (ORT), darkness, blindness, or cloudiness is a reality of life for everyone about half the time (cf. John 11:9). We do not naturally see in the dark. Much remains hidden in the shadows, including much truth about God in our sin-darkened hearts and habitats. But God has graciously provided God's word as a "lamp to [our] feet and a light to [our] path" (Ps 119:105). Accordingly, as Jesus certifies, "nothing is hidden [κρυπτόν, *krypton*—and it *is* cryptic unless God exposes it] that will not be disclosed, nor is anything secret [ἀπόκρυφον, *apokryphon*] that will not become known [γνωσθῇ, *gnōsthē*] and come to light" (Luke 8:17).

Again, however, Jesus intertwines assurance of divine revelation with demands for human cooperation. If we foolishly shroud the lamp of God's word under a jar or shove it under a bed, it can scarcely light our way. The jar and bed function as obstacles to enlightenment, just as rocks and thorns impede fruitfulness in the preceding parable. God's word needs a free, open, and mindful ("look how you listen" [8:18]) environment, which we must cultivate in order to thrive. And the level of engagement determines the extent of progress—or regress—in knowing God. In a stark statement of stewardship, Jesus lays out a two-lane highway for opposite-heading travelers: those who "have" insight—having seen, heard, and acted on the "given" word of God—"will be given" more to see, hear, and act upon; conversely, those who neglect or resist what's been sown (seed) or shone (light) will lose all trace of what they "seem to have" (8:18).[213]

While the pattern of progressing in knowledge seems reasonable (the more you know, the more likely you'll be to keep learning), the reverse notion

213. The verb for "have/hold" (ἔχω, *echō*) in 8:18 links back to the related compound "hold fast" (κατέχω, *katechō*) in 8:15 as the ideal response to God's sown/shown word.

of "taking away" (αἴρω, *airō* [8:18]) educative opportunities from slower, or even stubborn, learners appears less congenial. But here Jesus may simply be reinforcing the harsh reality of opposing forces bent on blocking knowledge of God. As birds swoop down to pluck seed from the roadside, the devil lies in wait to "take away" (αἴρω, *airō*) God's word sown in the human heart (8:11). Moreover, those on the lower end of society might detect a chafing allusion to elites who exploit workers for their own ends—in other words, "take away" everything they can from underlings, even what little these servants "seem to have." If peasant-tenant farmers, by virtue of hard work and good fortune, happened to produce a hundredfold harvest, they would sadly wind up handing over most of the proceeds to greedy landlords.[214]

So does some oppressive "hidden transcript" underlie the parables of the harvest and the lamp, exposing the problem of society's "haves" boosting their advantage on the backs of subordinate "have-nots" perching on the precipice of losing what little they do possess?[215] If Jesus's images embed such a cryptic code for a peasant audience, what does Jesus want them to *know*? Two related aims may be at work. First, Jesus hints at the reality of an exploitative economy in order to *support resistance*: the vultures (birds) may peck away at your livelihood, but do not let them get your hearts and lives, where God's saving word grows and glows. Second, Jesus ultimately intends to *supplant the unjust system* with the just economy of God's kingdom, which shares, rather than siphons off, hundredfold bounties in an honest and good-hearted community (see 8:15). In the true order of things—where the light-giving Creator ("Let there be light!") owns and sustains the land and cosmos—flourishing life prevails for all inhabitants.

Lost One Discovered (8:19–21)

While Jesus increasingly discloses God's word to a "great crowd" (8:4) and disciples throughout Galilee, he remains largely hidden and unknown to his natural kinfolk in Nazareth. Though Mary has perceived much about her unique son since conception, even she has experienced frustration and confusion. Recall the agonizing three-day search for the missing twelve-year-old Jesus culminating in a less-than-happy reunion where he chides his parents for not knowing his vocation as God's Son (2:49–50). And then, we can scarcely forget the ter-

214. See Cardenal, *Gospel*, 158–62; Herzog, "Sowing," 192–96.

215. In his seminal work on "hidden transcripts," James C. Scott (*Domination*) unpacks his thesis that "every subordinate group creates, out of its ordeal, a 'hidden transcript' that represents a critique of power spoken behind the back of the dominant" (xii); cf. Herzog, "Sowing," 196.

rible fallout from Jesus's first sermon in his hometown synagogue, from which he barely escapes with his life (4:28–30). Jesus has not returned home since, and we can hardly blame him.

But that does not stop his "mother and brothers" from searching for him—again.[216] They discover his location in another Galilean town and want "to see" him (8:20). Unlike Mark's parallel story, where Jesus's family comes to "restrain" or "seize" their wayward son and brother because people think he's gone crazy (Mark 3:20–21), Luke suggests no such negative motivation. Jesus's mother and brothers sincerely want to reconnect with him. But obstacles persist, not only in the surrounding crowd that blocks their access, but also in Jesus's own response upon learning of their presence "outside" (ἔξω, *exō* [Luke 8:20]). For rather than specifically inviting his mother and brothers inside, Jesus seizes the moment to embrace his true family, his true maternal and fraternal associates, namely, "those who hear the word of God and do it" (8:21). Of course, Jesus's natural kin may be included in this spiritual family—as the word-perceptive Mary certainly is (1:38; cf. Acts 1:14)—but they enjoy no special privilege over other hearer-doers. To the extent that Jesus's own people choose not to heed his word, they remain hampered from "seeing" God and cordoned "outside" the center of God's realm. Familiarity breeds not just contempt toward Jesus, as in the Nazareth fiasco, but also complacency, if Jesus's intimates do not pay close attention to how they "listen" (8:18).

Stilling a Tumultuous Lake and a Tormented Demoniac (8:22–39)

After his extended teaching session, Jesus and his disciples are back on the move. His instruction continues, but in a more demonstrative than discursive fashion, through a series of four miraculous acts presented in two tightly linked pairs (8:22–56). The first pair connects a display of Jesus's power over the natural environment of Lake Gennesaret (8:22–25) with his expulsion of demonic forces (8:26–39). While Jesus has performed these types of miracles before (4:31–37, 41; 5:1–11), the present cases involve a higher level of threat and conflict. Whereas Jesus's first sailing adventure with his disciples produced a

216. Stepfather Joseph completely drops from Luke's narrative after his last appearance (2:48) and mention ("Is not this Joseph's son?" [4:22]). Jesus's filial relationship to God as Father is paramount. This marks the first reference to Jesus's (half-) brothers (cf. Acts 1:14). Historically, his most prominent brother was James, who became a major leader of the Jerusalem church (Acts 12:17; 15:13; 21:18; Gal 2:9). In the present text Luke uses no names, only relational descriptors ("mother and brothers"), probably to emphasize the broad scope of extended spiritual family.

massive haul of fish that "filled" two boats to the brink of sinking, but with no ultimate damage (5:6–7), now, while Jesus sleeps on deck, a terrible storm erupts and "was filling" the disciples' boat with water (8:23), posing a clear and present danger of drowning in the lake until Jesus awakes and averts the disaster. And compared to Jesus's first exorcism, silencing a disruptive demon in the otherwise calm environment of the Capernaum synagogue (4:31–37), now he casts out a destructive regiment of demons in the foreign, tomb-dotted, pig-infested "wilds" (8:29) near Gerasa "opposite Galilee" on the eastern lakeshore.[217] The battle with cosmic chaotic forces in the natural and spiritual realms rages hotter and heavier.

We may juxtapose similar and distinct elements of the two incidents as follows.

	Stilling a storm and saving the disciples (8:22–25)	**Stopping a legion and saving a demoniac (8:26–39)**
Setting:	Jesus and his disciples cross Lake Gennesaret in a boat	Jesus and his disciples disembark in Gerasene territory on the lake's eastern shore
Crisis:	Violent windstorm suddenly endangers the lives of Jesus and his disciples, filling the boat with water and threatening to engulf (entomb) them	Violent demonic horde continually ("for a long time") endangers the life of a "man of the city" forced to dwell among the tombs in "the wilds" (deserted areas)
Chaotic watery vortex:	Cyclonic winds "swept down [κατέβη, *katebē*]" (8:23) and whipped up raging waves, threatening to drown the disciples	Crazed herd of swine, into whom Jesus had transferred demons, "rushed down [κατά, *kata*]" (8:33) the steep lake-bank and drowned in the "abyss"
Desperate plea to Jesus:	Disciples: "Master, Master, we are perishing!"	Demons: "What have you to do with me, Jesus, Son of the Most High God? I beg you, do not torment me"
Jesus's counterquestion:	"Where is your faith?"	"What is your name?"

217. "Opposite" (ἀντιπέρα, *antipera*) represents more than a simple geographic marker "on the other/eastern side" of Galilee; it also signifies a certain sociocultural "opposition" to Galilee, a border crossing into potentially hostile territory. The presence of pigs reinforces this territory as alien Gentile (non-Jewish) space.

	Stilling a storm and saving the disciples (8:22–25)	**Stopping a legion and saving a demoniac (8:26–39)**
Political element:	*Lake*: like all commercial waterways, owned and controlled by Roman emperor and deputies	*Legion*: major Roman military regiment
Jesus's powerful command:	Word of rebuke: "commands [ἐπιτάσσει, *epitassei*]" (8:25) desist order	Word of rebuke: "commanded [παρήγγειλεν, *parēngeilen*]" (8:29) expulsion order
Peaceful, saving result:	Disciples rescued from perishing; storm "ceased, and there was a calm" with Jesus in the boat	Man healed/saved (σῴζω, *sōzō*) from demonic destruction; "sitting at the feet of Jesus, clothed and in his right mind"
Fearful response:	Disciples: "afraid and amazed, and said to one another, 'Who then is this?'"	Gerasenes: "they were afraid. . . . They were seized with great fear" and wanted Jesus to leave their country

More broadly, we may track these elements in three stages: (1) *experience of chaos*, (2) *exchange with Jesus*, and (3) *effects of miracle*.

Experience of Chaos (8:23–24, 27–30)

These incidents suddenly plunge Jesus and his disciples into deep environmental crises. The two creation accounts in Genesis feature God's bringing order and life out of watery devastation (Gen 1:2) and arid wilderness (2:5–6) or, alternatively, out of dead sea and barren desert. These primordial settings find remarkable correlations in Jesus's journey: first, on a turbulent lake roiling with lethal winds and waves; and second, in a desert wasteland (or "wilds" [ἐρήμους, *erēmous*; Luke 8:29]) haunted by demons, dead bones, and the near-dead, naked body of a demented demoniac (8:27–30). Jesus experiences these chaotic situations as "son of Adam, son of God" (cf. 3:38), as God incarnate, fully human and divine. *In the midst of* the storm and *firmly planted on* the wasteland, Jesus identifies more closely with the anthropomorphic, hands-on, garden-walking portrait of God in the second Genesis account (Gen 2:7–25; 3:8), though his powerful presence within the tempest also associates with God's Spirit-Wind that sweeps over the primeval deep (Gen 1:2). But along with demonstrating his divine authority to tame watery/wild chaos, Jesus also participates in God's creative/restorative work: both recalling Adam's deep sleep under God's operative care (Luke 8:23; Gen 2:21–22) and reversing Adam's surrender to evil forces and consequent exile to rougher, wilder lands of thorns and thistles, dust and death (Gen 3:18–19). On the latter point, once again Luke's Jesus, "son of Adam," discomfits the devil in the desert and paves the way to renewed life (see discussion above on 3:38–4:13).

Exchange with Jesus (8:24–25, 27–30)

These tumultuous situations spark an intense verbal exchange with Jesus, initiated in each case by panic-stricken subjects. For his part, Jesus remains calm, first napping in the boat and then stepping out on land (8:23, 27), until set upon by distraught disciples on the lake and a deranged demoniac on the shore. In the noisy swirl of the tempest, the disciples roust the somnolent Jesus with three pointed words in Greek (no time for artful pleas), the first two sounding a desperate double address; the third, extreme duress: "Master, Master, we're dying! [Επιστάτα, ἐπιστάτα, ἀπολλύμεθα, *Epistata, epistata, apollymetha*]" (8:24 AT). Titles for Jesus do not tell the whole christological story, but they do provide some gauge of his perceived authority. Only Luke in the NT uses ἐπιστάτης (*epistatēs*), always in the vocative form addressed to Jesus: six times by his disciples (5:5; 8:24 [twice]; 8:45; 9:33, 49) and once by a group of lepers (17:13). Typically translated "Master," the term denotes a high-ranking official who "stands over" or superintends various subordinates. However, while conveying respectful recognition of authority, it appears more suitable to lower echelons of overseers than to the supreme commander. In classical usage on the battlefield, ἐπιστάτης (*epistatēs*) might designate the general's rearguard officer, in distinction from his προστάτης (*prostatēs*), a front-line officer leading the charge, and παραστάτης (*parastatēs*), his right-hand man.[218] In the LXX ἐπιστάτης (*epistatēs*) designates Pharaoh's cadre of "taskmasters" set over the Israelite slaves (Exod 1:11; 5:14) and Solomon's three thousand plus "supervisors" over the temple building project (1 Kgs 5:16 [5:30 LXX]; 2 Chr 2:2)—but would not have been appropriate for Pharaoh or King Solomon himself. A related authority term, κύριος (*kyrios*, "lord"), which we have encountered several times in Luke, ranges from the pedestrian "sir" to various overseers, landlords, and slave owners to the loftiest Lord of divine status, whether applied to Roman emperors or to the God of Israel and Jesus the Christ. The birth narratives firmly established "Lord" as a title of high theology (God)

218. LSJ, "ἐπιστάτης," s.v.

and Christology (Jesus) (Luke 1:28, 32, 38, 43, 45, 46, 76; 2:11, 15, 23, 26, 39). But ἐπιστάτης (*epistatēs*) never rises to such heights, which raises questions about how fully the disciples have apprehended Jesus's divine leadership.

In his initial encounter with Jesus on the lake, Peter comes to echo Elizabeth's and the angelic host's acclamations of Jesus as "Lord" (5:8; 1:43; 2:11). But he first addresses Jesus in the boat as "Master," reflecting his respectful, yet *doubtful*, appraisal of Jesus's oversight, particularly concerning fishing, which Peter and company know a thing or two about: "Master [Επιστάτα, *Epistata*], we have worked all night long but have caught nothing" (5:5). But after the huge haul of fish, following Jesus's command, Peter promptly promotes Jesus to the rank of "Lord," even as he demotes himself by falling down at Jesus's knees (5:9). From this watershed moment, we expect the disciples' understanding of Jesus's lordship to grow as their journey with Jesus progresses.

But in fact, from this point to the second boating incident, they do not expressly acknowledge Jesus as Lord again. The Capernaum centurion and the imprisoned Baptist both indirectly (through messengers) call Jesus "Lord" (7:6, 18–19), but Jesus's closest followers remain mum on the subject. Moreover, Jesus concludes his lecture on the plain by challenging the disciples' professed commitment to his lordship—"Why do you call me 'Lord, Lord,' and do not do what I tell you?" (6:46)—likening their "undone" state to foolish builders constructing a flimsy house vulnerable to surging floodtides (6:49). Are they up to Jesus's challenge to obey him faithfully as Lord? As it happens, in their first opportunity to vindicate their discipleship—in the midst of an actual storm-swell recalling Jesus's earlier flood warning—they counter Jesus's double κύριε (*kyrie*) placed on their hypocritical lips (6:46) with a *lesser* double ἐπιστάτα (*epistata*) plea (8:24). As they begin to sink into the depths of the lake, the disciples regress to their initial "masterly" assessment of Jesus and lose sight of his "lordly" rule over all creation. Their relational knowledge of Jesus still lacks a solid foundation.

And so Jesus responds, not only by taming the tempest (8:24), but also by disciplining the disciples, answering their desperate cry with a pointed query: "Where is your faith?" (8:25). Having recently commended remarkable demonstrations of faith from unlikely sources (a Roman centurion and a "sinful" woman [7:9, 50]), Jesus is flummoxed by his closest followers' backsliding. The faith they placed in him as Lord after the great fish catch seems to have slipped away: "*Where* is your faith [you once had]?"[219] The winds and waves respond to Jesus's word more faithfully (obediently) than do his disciples! (8:24–25).

219. Whereas Matthew's Jesus queries the disciples' "little faith" (8:26) and Mark's Jesus scolds their absent faith ("no faith" [Mark 4:40]), Luke's Jesus focuses on their misplaced faith: "*Where* [ποῦ, *pou*] [is] your faith?" (Luke 8:25).

And for that matter, so does the wild demonic gang Jesus encounters next. Upon seeing Jesus and hearing his expulsion order, the collective horde blurts out: "What have you to do with me, Jesus, Son of the Most High God? I beg you, do not torment me" (8:28). The demons want Jesus to leave them alone because they know full well his identity and the authority he commands to liberate the Gerasene man from their destructive clutches. Bitter irony emerges in their plea that Jesus not torment them, since that is precisely what they have been doing to the demoniac "for a long time" (8:27). Tragic irony also surfaces in juxtaposition with the disciples' failure to grasp Jesus's purpose and power to *save* them from torrential torment (8:24).

As Jesus first answered his panicky disciples with a question, so he interrogates the demonic band: "What is your name?" (8:30). While Jesus immediately knows he's dealing with evil forces, he pushes, as any wise warrior would do, to clarify the enemy's strength and strategy (see 14:31–32). To know one's name or title in the biblical world was to know one's character and intentions, the core of one's identity. Where the disciples struggled to name-and-know Lord Jesus sufficiently, the demons shout Jesus's august name and title in unequivocal terms, and now, at his behest, disclose their own collective name: "Legion" (Λεγιών, *Legiōn*). On one level, this appellation simply confirms that "*many* demons had entered the man" (8:30). But "Legion" represented much more than a generic mathematical category in Jesus and Luke's world, namely, a vaunted Roman military brigade of six thousand troops through which Caesar had conquered peoples and now controlled his empire. As Lord Caesar claimed to own the seas, lakes, and waterways, so he occupied the shores, lands, and roadways. The Legion-possessed demoniac thus reflects a microcosm of Legion-occupied territory stripped bare by Rome and wreaking terrible havoc on a transnational, macrosocietal scale. The tumultuous incidents on Lake Gennesaret and in the Gerasa region typify theopolitical conflict, dramatically overcome, at least for the moment, by Jesus's superior power.[220]

Effects of Miracle (8:25, 31–39)

Wielding a spoken word of breathtaking authority, Jesus calms the turbulent waters of the "sea," stills the anxious hearts of his disciples, casts out the vicious

220. The language of "command" (παραγγέλλω, *parangellō*) and "under guard" (φυλάσσω, *phylassō*) (8:29) evokes a military environment, as well as a "herd/squad" (ἀγέλη, *agelē*) "rushing/charging" (ὁρμάω, *hormaō*) as into battle (8:33). I was alerted to these nuances in commentaries on the parallel incident in Mark; see Boring, *Mark*, 151; Beavis, *Mark*, 94; cf. Ched Myers, *Binding*, 190–94; Derrett, "Contributions," 5–6.

demons in the "desert," and restores the sanity of the man they'd tormented, now "sitting at the feet of Jesus, clothed and in his right mind" (8:35). For those with ears to hear, the echoes with creation, adumbrated above, ring as loud and clear as did the raging storm and raving demons. Jesus channels the divine word and dynamic Spirit-wind that overshadowed the chaotic deep and ordered the seas into life-supporting environments (cf. Gen 1:1–3, 6–10, 20–21). The Lord of the Sea then steps onto dry, skeletal-decaying, demon-occupied desert to drive out the death-dealing forces and breathe spirit-life into a virtually dead, entombed creature, making him a "living being" capable of flourishing (cf. Gen 2:4–8). Moreover, as God graciously *clothed* the first couple after they overstepped their creaturely bounds and became overwhelmed by their shocking, naked state of vulnerability, alienation, and anxiety (Gen 2:25; 3:10–11, 21), so Jesus effectively *clothes* the "saved" Gerasene demoniac and prepares him to "return home" to rebuild his life (Luke 8:35–36, 39).

But as these incidents portray Jesus in glorious *creation* and *re-creation* mode, they also depict him reenacting the victorious *exodus* and *redemption* script. His command over winds and waves to rescue his disciples and lead them securely to shore recalls God's directing of gale-force winds to part the Red Sea for the Israelites' safe crossing (Exod 14:21–22). Of course, Jesus *stops* a storm while God *steers* one for God's purposes, but the point of salvific control of wind-and-water power holds in both cases. Likewise, Jesus's liberating the Gerasene demoniac from his life-sapping bondage (possession) especially evokes God's delivering of Israel from Pharaoh's enslavement through *drowning* the tyrant and his forces. As God "tossed the Egyptians into the sea," which had "returned to its normal depth" after the Israelites' passage (Exod 14:27), so Jesus transfers the demonic Legion, the spirit-cohort of oppressive Roman imperial power, into a herd of swine that hurtles to their demise in the watery lake "abyss" (Luke 8:31–34).[221] Of course, the politics of this scene remains symbolic: the loss of two thousand pigs hurts the local economy, but it scarcely puts a dent in the Roman juggernaut. Caesar's present rule over land and sea remains intact. Yet, Jesus's exorcism is no mere symbolic gesture, but rather carries the force of divine eschatological purpose to reestablish God's rightful and right-making reign on earth. Rome receives its eviction notice. Its days are

221. Only Luke among the Gospel writers uses the term ἄβυσσος (*abyssos*), and he uses it only in the present story. It refers to the place of the dead and prison of the demonic, the pit of "hell," as it were (see Rom 10:7; Rev 9:2, 11; 17:8; 20:1, 3). It also denotes the dark, deep, chaotic waters in Gen 1:2 LXX. In Luke's account, the Legion-demons plead with Jesus *not* to dispatch them to "the abyss," but rather into the swine herd. Though Jesus technically grants their request, their ultimate plunge into the depths of the lake and drowning their hosts constitute an "abyssmal" end, if not a final, apocalyptic doom.

numbered, its doom is sure, not at the hands of a superior naval force (Israel has no armada), but at the hand of the Supreme Creator-Lord of the sea.

Having stressed the cosmic and political effects of this pair of miracles, we finally consider the *emotional* upheavals that occur, with special attention to *fear*. Significantly, the fearful responses reported by Luke come *after* Jesus's calming miracles, which evidently are not entirely calmative! While the disciples are obviously distressed in the throes of the storm, Luke identifies their fearful mien only at the end of the story: "They were afraid [φοβηθέντες, *phobēthentes*] and amazed, and said to one another, 'Who then is this, that he commands even the winds and the water, and they obey him?'" (8:25). And if the demoniac who promptly "meets" Jesus and company sets off any alarm bells within them—which we would expect, given the man's wild, deranged state—Luke says nothing about it, reserving fear—even "great fear"—for those who witness the *transformed* man and for the local population, including the pig-herders, who compel Jesus to leave their country: "They found the man from whom the demons had gone sitting at the feet of Jesus, clothed and in his right mind. And they were afraid [ἐφοβήθησαν, *ephobēthēsan*]. . . . Then all the people of the surrounding country of the Gerasenes asked Jesus to leave them; for they were seized with great fear [φόβῳ μεγάλῳ, *phobō megalō*]" (8:35–37).

In both cases, the object of "great fear" is *Jesus* (not the storm or the demoniac), and to gloss this emotion as "reverence" or "awe," while more palatable to contemporary sensibilities, does not do full justice to the palpably terrifying reaction Jesus evokes from followers and observers, disciples and crowds, alike.[222] In their "saved" condition out of harm's way, the disciples face the fresh terror of wondering "who this man really is" and what he might dare do next. One minute he's fast asleep in a rocking boat; the next he's rebuking the winds and waves—and they obey him! This is not a man to be trifled with. He is much more than another "master," possessing an extraordinary level of authority and power as unsettling as it is soothing.[223] For the Gerasenes' part, it is all well and good that Jesus has tamed this wild man, but by what means and at what cost? If they couldn't restrain the man "with chains and shackles" (8:29), what kind of ominous force must Jesus command to subdue him? On any account, a squealing horde of rabid animals plunging to their watery grave poses a frightful, disturbing scene for "all" who see and hear it firsthand or hear

222. Cf. Lukan parallels to "great fear" in Acts 5:5, 11, indicating the response of the early Jerusalem church to the sudden deaths of Ananias and Sapphira (see the discussion in Spencer, "Scared to Death"); for more on "fear" in Luke, see commentary below on 12:4–34.

223. On the image of the "unsettling" and "disruptive" God in biblical thought, see Brueggemann, *Unsettling God*, and Skinner, *Intrusive God*, respectively. From Skinner, e.g.: "Prophets have eyes to see God's penchant for acting in astounding and disruptive ways" (13).

about it. And while we (and kosher Jews) might not care that much about losing a sizable pack of swine, the herders take a considerable economic hit, and the habitat suffers an ecological blow. Best to get this volatile Jew Jesus out of our country as soon as possible. Better to take our chances with the odd demoniac than this fearful figure.

Although Luke's diptych of stilling the tumultuous storm and the tormented demoniac predominantly parades Jesus's ministry of restoration and liberation, the counterpoint of Jesus's fearsome disruptive and destructive power should not be ignored. In his classic analysis of fear (and other basic emotions), Aristotle defines fear (φόβος, *phobos*) as "a sort of pain and agitation derived from the imagination of a future destructive or painful evil"—especially when such a dreadful prospect "seems near at hand," suddenly rearing its frightful face before our eyes (*Rhet.* 2.5.1–2 [1382a]).[224] And fear upsets most when confronting not merely an overwhelming stressful situation, but an overbearing *powerful person* with the will and means to do harm: "And [people fear] those [that seem a cause of fear] to others who are stronger than they are; for they could harm them more if they could even harm those who are stronger." Moreover, such a powerful figure becomes more threatening the *calmer* he goes about his dominating business, since one never knows when he might erupt; by contrast, it is easier to steer clear of the "quick-tempered and outspoken," who give blustery notice of their intentions (*Rhet.* 2.5.10 [1382b]).

Though the stilling effects of Jesus's miraculous work run deeply through the narrative, some chilling effects linger as well. As the manifestly "stronger one" acting in a "calm," swift manner to overcome the torrential storm and terrible Legion—destroying two thousand pigs in the process (what had these poor creatures done to deserve this fate?)—Jesus provokes as much fear as faith, as much dread as trust. The question Jesus poses the storm-shaken disciples—"Where is your faith?"—thus assumes the force of a stern exhortation way beyond a cozy invitation to rest in Jesus's tender arms. Faith in Jesus negotiates a fearful-restful tension. Following Aristotle's contention that "fear makes people inclined to deliberation" (*Rhet.* 2.5.14 [1383a]), emotional turbulence or "upheaval" thus raises key issues for cognitive reflection.[225] At base, fear helps us evaluate what is most critical for survival and well-being: which terrifying threats merit flight or fight? The tremulous disciples continue to have much to deliberate about this one they have chosen to follow. Jesus is certainly an

224. Citations in this section are from Aristotle, *On Rhetoric* (trans. Kennedy).

225. For an extensively argued cognitive theory of emotions as "upheavals of thought," see Nussbaum, *Upheavals*, 19–88; for a well-informed treatment of emotion and cognition by a contemporary theologian, see Samuel M. Powell, *Impassioned Life*, 297–339.

extraordinary figure with explosive power to heal and save. But will he always use this power for salutary purposes? A fine line can divide self-proclaimed benevolent despots from corrupt tyrants. How solid and secure can trust be in one so fearsome and potentially volatile? Dare the disciples, to say nothing of the general populace, have the courage to maintain and strengthen their trust in Christ amid twinges of uncertainty concerning what he might do and where he might lead?

Aristotle's philosophy that fear, in proper perspective, prompts careful deliberation leading to virtuous conduct and flourishing life coheres well with interwoven epistemological and ethical strands of biblical Torah and Wisdom:

> I will let them hear my words, so that they may learn to fear me [the Lord] as long as they live on the earth, and may teach their children so. (Deut 4:10)

> If only they had such a mind as this, to fear me and to keep all my commandments always, so that it might go well with them and with their children forever! (Deut 5:29; cf. 6:2, 13, 24; 10:12)

> The fear of the Lord is the beginning of knowledge;
> fools despise wisdom and instruction.
>
> (Prov 1:7)

> If you desire wisdom, keep the commandments,
> and the Lord will lavish her upon you.
> For the fear of the Lord is wisdom and discipline,
> fidelity and humility are his delight.
> Do not disobey the fear of the Lord;
> do not approach him with a divided mind.
>
> (Sir 1:26–28)

Among many things fear might teach us about God, not least it signals that God does not conform to human convenience. To know God is to know God's freedom to act in "wild" and wondrous ways, from our limited viewpoints. God moves within and through, as much as over and against, the volatile "seas" and "wilds" to bring peace and order on God's terms and in God's time (GOT).

Restoring a Bleeding Woman to Health and Resuscitating a Synagogue Leader's Daughter from Death (8:40–56)

Jesus's miraculous activity continues without skipping a beat, even in the face of variable audience reactions. Pushed to leave trans-Galilean Gerasa after emancipating the Legion-infested demoniac, Jesus promptly got back "into the boat and returned" across the lake (8:37). And when he returns, he finds a large welcoming party "waiting for him," including a synagogue ruler named Jairus, who wastes no time begging Jesus to visit his dying daughter (8:40–42). Though some Jewish leaders and people have resisted Jesus's work, overall he remains popular among his compatriots; conversely, despite the fact that a couple of individual Gentiles (Roman centurion and Gerasene demoniac) have responded favorably to Jesus, he has become persona non grata in Gentile territory (8:37).

As Jesus proceeds to Jairus's house, "the crowds pressed in on him" (8:42), connoting a "choking" or "suffocating" (συμπνίγω, *sympnigō*) effect, ironically cognate with the "strangling" or "drowning" (ἀποπνίγω, *apopnigō*) of pigs in the previous scene (8:33). Through this throng a bleeding woman pushes to touch Jesus's clothing and precipitate her immediate healing (8:42–44). The brisk pace of the narrative matches the electric power of the miracles *until* the bleeding woman's action interrupts Jesus's progress, sparking him to ask, "Who touched me?" This interruption complicates the condition of Jairus's daughter: while Jesus deals with the intrusive woman, the daughter dies (!), necessitating Jesus's resuscitation feat (8:49–56).

While we will give primary attention to the interconnections between these new works of healing and resurrection, it is also worth noting their links to the preceding pair of nature and exorcism miracles.

First, Jesus continues to deal with critical, life-threatening cases. As he rescued "perishing" disciples from a violent storm and liberated a tomb-dwelling man from destructive demons, Jesus now heals a long-suffering woman slowly bleeding to death, incapable, assuming a uterine hemorrhage, of bearing new life, and resuscitates a deceased young woman on the brink of puberty and reproductive promise.[226] Nothing minor about these miracles: these are big

226. The description of the woman's (irregular) condition as "the flow of blood" (ἡ ῥύσις τοῦ αἵματος, *hē rhysis tou haimatos* [8:43–44 AT]) matches that of (normal) menstrual bleeding regulated in Lev 15:19–33 (and that of a man's genital emission in 15:2–15, 33). The abnormal, chronic nature of the woman's problem in Luke ("*being* [οὖσα, *ousa*] in [the state] of blood discharge" for twelve years [8:43 AT]) would render her unable to have children and ritually unclean. The barrenness aspect fits with Elizabeth's "disgraceful" condition before her miraculous pregnancy (Luke 1:7, 25); the purity/cleanness issue is not raised at all in the present story (unlike with the

events, as big as all *life*, even life from the dead or almost-dead. Jesus operates on crucial battle lines between life and death.

Second, and reinforcing Jesus's death-defying mission, is the motif of *sleep* bracketing the four-miracle cluster. His atypical sleeping in the storm-tossed boat (8:23; cf. 9:58: "the Son of Humankind has nowhere to lay his head")—demonstrates an extraordinary sense of calm and confidence amid a perilous ordeal, and upon his awakening ("rising" [διεγείρω, *diegeirō*]), he quickly quells the lethal maelstrom (8:24). Correspondingly, Jesus's imaging the little girl's dead state as a mode of sleeping (8:52) signals his intent and power to awaken/raise her (ἐγείρω, *egeirō* [8:54]) from the dead.[227] In turn, these stories foreshadow Jesus's own resurrection from the dead as the "author of life" and pioneer of the ultimate (eschatological) "awakening" God's people (see Acts 3:15–16; 5:30–31; 26:23).

Luke forges an especially tight connection between the present pair of miracles via an intercalated, or sandwich, structure:

- A The story of Jairus's daughter begins with a plea for Jesus's aid (8:40–42).
  - B The episode involving the woman with the irregular flow of blood *interrupts the flow* of the narrative: Jesus stops his march to Jairus's house to deal with this pressing case (8:43–48).
- A′ The story of Jairus's daughter resumes and concludes, but with the added complication that the girl had died while Jesus was treating the bleeding woman (8:49–56).

This ordering device, also used with these stories and multiple other times in Mark, invites careful attention to interconnections and tensions between the paired incidents.

---

leper in 5:12–16) and is of limited consequence in the scene, since the woman would not have been subject to strict quarantine (she was not a leper) and was not seeking access to the temple or anywhere near it.

227. It was common to image death as "sleep" to connote its peaceful state of rest and also the prospect of awakening to new life (e.g., 1 Cor 15:51; 1 Thess 4:13–15; 5:6–11). The verb ἐγείρω (*egeirō*) is often used in resurrection contexts.

	Bleeding woman restored to health	Deceased daughter returned to life
Daughter relationship:	Jesus affirms his "spiritual" daughter	Jairus pleads for his biological daughter
Social status:	Impoverished, lacking family?	Reasonably well off, with loving family
Setting:	Public scene; woman "could not remain hidden"; she is compelled to declare "in the presence of all the people" what had happened	Private scene in Jairus's house with only the girl's parents and Peter, James, and John allowed inside with Jesus
Time span:	12 years of debilitating disease and economic deprivation[1]	At 12 years of age, suddenly beset with fatal disease
Support network:	Few to none; acts alone	Father (Jairus) and mother and synagogue community (mourners)
Element of touch:	Woman takes initiative and touches Jesus's clothing to obtain healing	Jesus takes the dead girl's hand and raises her up to new life
Response of faith:	"Daughter, your faith [πίστις, *pistis*] has made you well [σέσωκεν, *sesōken*]"	"Do not fear. Only believe [πίστευσον, *pisteuson*], and she will be saved [σωθήσεται, *sōthēsetai*]"
Reproduction/ barrenness:	Probable condition of chronic uterine bleeding disabling her reproductive system	Death at typical age of puberty (onset of menses) terminates reproductive potential
Rescue from death:	"Saved" from eventual debilitating bleeding to death and virtual social death as "damaged goods" with severely limited prospects of marriage and childbearing	"Saved" from actual death; enabled to get up and "eat" and resume normal life functions
Emotional impact:	Trembling and tranquility ("go in peace")	Fearing, laughing, weeping, and astonishment
Knowing and not knowing:	Jesus knowing (ἔγνων, *egnōn*) that power had gone from him, but not knowing initially who extracted it ("Who touched me?")	Mourners "knowing [εἰδότες, *eidotes*] that she was dead," but not knowing this was a reversible state
Disciples' involvement:	Peter responds to Jesus's inquiry about who touched him: "Master ['Επιστάτα, *Epistata*], the crowds surround you and press in on you"	Jesus permits Peter, James, and John inside the house to witness the resuscitation of Jairus's daughter

Wider Jesus connections:	Woman's bleeding "previews" Jesus's bleeding on the cross (these are the only two "bleeding" characters in Luke)	The experience of the 12-year-old daughter and her parents "reviews" the 12-year-old Jesus's dealings with his parents[2]

1. Carroll (296, 298) argues that the time stamp more naturally indicates that the woman had suffered "*from* [ἀπό, *apo*] [the age of] twelve," linking her even more closely with Jairus's daughter.

2. On "previews"/"reviews" in Luke's narrative, see Tannehill, *Narrative Unity*, 1:2, 20–23, 61, 277–79; Spencer, *Gospel of Luke*, 46–48.

Among these numerous co-textual links, I concentrate on four topics that have received less attention in commentaries and that serve our driving narrative-theological interest in faith formation and knowledge development.

Faith and Salvation (8:41, 43–56)

Each story features the causative nexus between faith/believing and salvation/healing, though from different viewpoints: Jesus commends the bleeding woman's health-producing faith ("your faith has made you well" [8:48]) *after* her miraculous cure, whereas he both comforts and challenges Jairus, upon receiving news of his sick daughter's death *before* Jesus had reached her, to trust that she can yet be restored ("only believe, and she will [still] be saved" [8:50]). While the Capernaum centurion displayed his faith through *verbal confession* of Jesus's healing ability (7:6–9), the bleeding woman, like the paralytic and friends (5:18–20) and the anointing woman (7:44–46, 50), exhibits her faith through *determined action*, specifically matching the latter character by making *physical contact* with Jesus. But more than the anointing woman, whose act of bathing Jesus's feet expressed loving gratitude for sins *already* forgiven as much as her saving faith (see above), the bleeding woman totally *initiates and triggers* Jesus's flow of healing power by *her* touch. In securing salvation without Jesus's prior invitation or knowledge (see more below), this courageous woman stands alone among Luke's characters.

As for Jairus, he seems to show a degree of faith, closely related to hope, in his begging Jesus to come and heal his dying daughter (8:40–42). But we do not know the precise state of his faith after he's informed of his daughter's death and urged not to "trouble the teacher any longer" (8:49).[228] At least he

228. The verb for "trouble/bother" (σκύλλω, *skyllō*) is only used four times in the NT (Matt 9:36; Mark 5:35; Luke 7:6; 8:49). Its only other Lukan occurrence relates the centurion's insistence

doesn't block Jesus's visit to the house and even allows Jesus to control others' access (8:51); fortunately, Jesus permits Jairus and his wife into their own home (!) to witness their daughter's resuscitation. But after Jesus "wakes up" the girl, her parents respond with astonishment (8:56), suggesting that Jesus has greatly exceeded their expectations. As for the mourners, they just flat "laughed at" Jesus's diagnosis that the daughter was merely mired in a deep sleep and not irrevocably dead (8:52–53). We might recall that the otherwise faithful Abraham and Sarah also had a good mocking laugh at God's promise to bring life out of Sarah's "dead," barren womb (Gen 17:17; 18:9–15). However, neither God in Genesis nor Jesus in Luke is deterred from his life-giving mission by others' snarky jeers or shaky faith. While faithfulness—in the fullest sense encompassing belief, trust, and action—is the optimal response to God's outreach, it is not a prerequisite for God's redemptive work. There is no fixed procedure or "order of salvation" (*ordo salutis*): God's saving mission in Christ proceeds apace with and without human cooperation. The call to faithful participation peals forth, but when and how it is answered remains a variable part of discipleship, except for *Jesus himself*, whose faithful commitment to God's liberating, life-giving power remains unswerving and undiminished.[229]

Fearing and Not Fearing (8:45–50)

Yet again the emotional impact of Jesus's healing work focuses on fear, which he both incites and allays. Ironically, the bleeding woman, who boldly pushes through the crowd to touch Jesus (albeit from behind) and trigger her cure, is gripped with tremulous fear (τρέμουσα, *tremousa*) after Jesus demands to know who siphoned his power (8:46–47). Her "falling down before" him and reporting her experience certainly evidence reverential awe toward Jesus, but her trembling also conveys genuine terror over what he might do now! Aristotle observed that fear especially erupts in anticipation of imminent harm from someone with "enmity and anger" or "outraged virtue" plus "power to

to Jesus *not* to "trouble yourself" with coming to the officer's "unworthy" house, a plea that Jesus respects. In the present case, however, Jesus ignores a similar request and *does* trouble himself to come to Jairus's home in the direst of situations.

229. Reflecting on a biblical theology of faith in light of the paradigmatic Abraham narrative, Levenson (*Inheriting Abraham*) offers an incisive rhetorical question probing the tensive balance between "quietism" and "activism": "Does faith in God and his promises require in the beneficiaries a stance of quietism and passivity, or does it, rather, require the opposite stance of human initiative and activism to help bring about the promised result?" (38). The answer, of course, is Yes.

do something" about it (*Rhet.* 2.5.1–6 [1382a–b]). The woman knows firsthand how powerful Jesus is, but she has no clue how he feels about having his power abruptly drawn from him. His initial words carry little assurance: *not* "Wait, a wonderful woman's just been healed; let her show herself so we can praise God with her," *but* "Who touched me? . . . Someone touched me, for I noticed that power had gone out from me" (8:45–46). This query is not too far from, "Let the thief show him/herself!" (a reaction similar to that of a pickpocket victim upon realizing the hit-and-run operation). The moment the tremulous woman bows down before Jesus and confesses what she's done "in the presence of all the people" is an incredibly tense one, which then serves to highlight the *dramatic relief* of Jesus's tender response: "Daughter, your faith has made you well [lit. 'saved you']; go in peace" (8:48). Far from attacking the woman's aggressive approach, Jesus adopts her into the family of faith.

In the crisis surrounding Jairus's daughter, Jesus's "do not fear" exhortation specifically relates to that most visceral human emotion—fear of death—which has just hit home with the report of the girl's passing (8:49–50). This message confirms Jairus's worst fear about his daughter's fate (she "was dying" when he first approached Jesus) and reminds the wider audience of the fragility of life and possibility of having it cut short in its prime, on the cusp of childbearing potential in the present case, thwarting extension of life in Jairus's family (the girl was his "only daughter" [8:42]).[230] Jesus dares to challenge the fear of death—not from some Lucretian-Epicurean premise that death is a blissful void of nothingness where "nothing can befall us, we who shall no longer be, nor move our senses" after we expire[231]—but from a courageous faith in God's life-restoring, death-reversing will and power. Death does not have the last word or last touch. The Creator Lord, who "neither slumber[s] nor sleep[s]," remains poised to "keep your life" secure and to awaken fresh life from the clutches of death (Ps 121:4, 7).

Knowing and Not Knowing (8:44–47, 52–53)

We have already alluded to the bleeding woman and Jairus's teetering between knowing and not knowing how Jesus might respond to their vulnerable states. Only when he commends the fictive daughter's faith, in the first case, and re-

230. Only Luke among the Synoptics indicates that the girl was Jairus's "*only* daughter," a touch of pathos and sense of profound loss coordinate with the widow's "only son" who had died (7:12) and the father's "only child" who suffered from a seizure disorder (9:38).

231. Lucretius, *Nature* 3.840–41, trans. Stallings (see 3.830–43). On Lucretius's view of death, see Nussbaum, *Therapy*, 192–238; Greenblatt, *Swerve*, 3–5, 75–76, 192–202.

stores the natural daughter's life, in the second, does knowledge of his saving purpose solidify. But these two figures are not the only ones who progress in knowledge. Even *Jesus* seems to move from not knowing to knowing who touched him in such an explosive way. Of course, we might assume that Jesus asks "Who touched me?" less to gain information and more to call the woman out and showcase her as a model of faith. But alongside the "hidden" dynamics (8:47) of the scene in which the woman wedges through the crowd and touches the hem of Jesus's tunic from *behind* (ὄπισθεν, *opisthen* [8:44]), the vagueness of Jesus's language—"someone [τις, *tis*, not even gender specific] touched me" (8:46)—suggests genuine confusion, surprise, and even distress on Jesus's part. Nothing like this has happened to him before. He has been in full control of every other miracle; but here someone else has grabbed his power—without his permission—and gone away. When the woman finally identifies herself and tells her story, Jesus *learns* something new about the power of faith and work of God through him.

This is the not the first time we have tracked Jesus's growth in knowledge as he has matured through human life since age twelve (cf. 2:40, 52). But we need not limit such learning to Jesus's human side, as if that were somehow separable from his divine nature. For, though seldom emphasized, biblical theology from Genesis forward charts *God's learning* in critical situations. As an arresting case in point, Jon Levenson gives full weight to God's dawning realization of the deep devotion to God Abraham proves in his willingness to sacrifice Isaac: "*Now I know* [as I didn't before] that you fear God, since you have not withheld you son, your only son, from me" (Gen 22:12). "That God can learn anything is, of course, antithetical to the Aristotelian notion that the deity must be unchanging . . . . But this is not the only place where the description of the personal, interacting, dynamic, and feeling God of Israel is not easily reconciled with the perfect, static, and perfectly static God of the philosophers. However the formidable conundrum of divine learning is to be understood philosophically (if at all), the end of our narrative leaves no doubt that God has acquired knowledge he did not have at its outset."[232] We must admit that this notion of the unchanging, impassible, all-knowing deity has not been limited to Aristotle, but may be fairly said to dominate the history of Christian thought.[233]

Whatever Luke's Jesus may learn in the present pair of incidents, he remains ahead of his disciples and the larger crowd he continues to teach. Scarcely

232. Levenson, *Inheriting Abraham*, 80. On Christ's "learning obedience," see the remarkable text in Heb 5:7–9.

233. See further discussion under "Passional Theology" in the concluding "Integration" section.

grasping the significance of Jesus's query about who touched him—and even mocking it—Peter blurts out in another less-than-prescient *Epistata* response, "Master, the crowds surround you and press in on you" (Luke 8:45), as if to say, "Everyone wants a piece of you, so why bother with one of them?" Earlier the disciples roused their "master," who appeared not to care about them (8:24); now Peter ridicules his "master" for caring too much about a silly matter. But Jesus keeps working with his feckless followers, even inviting the inner three inside Jairus's home to witness his resurrecting power (8:51).

The mourners in the home also deride Jesus, this time for his absurd claim that the daughter "is not dead, but sleeping." They *know* (εἰδότες, *eidotes*) otherwise—she is dead (presumably no breath or pulse)!—but have no expanded knowledge base to entertain the possibility of reversed death and restored life (8:52–53). In their case, Jesus blocks them from direct witness of God's resurrection power. The closest, "inside" knowledge of God's saving work belongs to those whom Jesus "lets in." But ultimately, the "cloud of unknowing" gives way to the clear light of disclosure to disciples and crowds alike. Nothing is "hidden" that is not revealed (cf. 8:17). Though Jesus continues to urge the witnesses to "tell no one what had happened" (8:56), word cannot help but get out.

Jesus and Women

Apart from restoring two females to health and commending one for her energetic faith, Luke's Jesus has symbolic links with these women in the larger narrative. The story of a twelve-year-old youth who causes parental anxiety recalls Jesus's dealings at the same age with Mary and Joseph (2:40–52). Of course, that encounter took place in the temple, not in the family home, though Jesus did claim to be about his Father's business. But both accounts feature the loss and reunion of a beloved child with distraught parents. These broadly parallel incidents, however, also show Jesus's dramatic development: this one who displayed such precocious wisdom among the temple "teachers [διδασκάλων, *didaskalōn*]" (2:46; see vv. 40, 47, 52) now proves in adulthood to be much more than an incisive teacher offering sage advice in a time of crisis. He continues to prove himself as a dynamic "teacher" [διδάσκαλον, *didaskalon*]" (8:49), in deed as much as word, not only willing to be troubled by the death of a twelve-year-old girl, but also able to bring her back to life.

The story of Jesus's death-defying power also has a shocking twist, however, intimated in the older woman's interlaced experience. For her flow of blood stanched by Jesus's flow of power eerily previews Jesus's outpouring of his own blood to seal a "new covenant" between God and God's people (22:20;

cf. 22:44).[234] Renewed life springs from merging streams of human blood and divine power: first, in Jesus's encounter with the woman in the crowd, but ultimately in his own blood-letting death redeemed by God's life-raising power. Though Luke advances no formal theory of atonement, he does intimate that Jesus's saving mission is realized *through suffering, through bleeding and dying.* It is hardly coincidental that soon after his intimate involvement with women's bleeding/dying and healing/rising, Jesus's thoughts turn more directly to his own impending death and resurrection and the radical therapy in God's realm of "saving" life by "losing" it (see below on 9:21–27, 43b-45).

Sending the Disciples and Feeding the Crowds to Advance God's Kingdom (9:1–17)

The life-sustaining and life-restoring force of God's dynamic kingdom continues, though with less attention to individual cases than to groups: (1) the *twelve disciples* participate with Jesus in God's liberating mission (9:1–6), and (2) the *crowds* experience Jesus's healing and feeding miracles (9:10–17); these incidents frame (3) a brief interlude concerning the minikingdom (tetrarchy) of *Herod Antipas* (9:7–9).

> Then Jesus called the *twelve* together and gave them power and authority over all demons and to cure [θεραπεύειν, *therapeuein*] diseases, and he sent them out to proclaim the kingdom of God [βασιλείαν τοῦ θεοῦ, *basileian tou theou*] and to heal [ἰᾶσθαι, *iasthai*]. (9:1–2)

> Now *Herod the ruler* [τετραάρχης, *tetraarchēs*] heard about all that had taken place. (9:7)

> On their return the *apostles* told Jesus all they had done. He took them with him and withdrew privately to a city called Bethsaida. When the *crowds* found out about it, they followed him; and he welcomed them, and spoke

234. Barbara E. Reid (*Choosing*) correctly notes that Mark's account provides sharper linguistic links between the woman's and Jesus's respective ordeals (see the "suffering" [πάσχω, *paschō*] of the woman in Mark 5:25–26 and of Jesus in 8:31 and 9:12; and the woman's "disease [μάστιγος, *mastigos*]" in 5:29, 34, suggestive of the Gentiles' whipping [μαστιγόω, *mastigoō*] of Jesus, which he predicted in 10:34); but Reid wrongly concludes, in my judgment, that Luke's redacted narrative "circumvents any identification of her suffering with that of Jesus" (142). Though Luke's "blood ties" between the woman and Jesus may be more allusive, they still link the two "bleeding" characters together.

to them about the *kingdom of God* [βασιλείας τοῦ θεοῦ, *basileias tou theou*], and healed [ἰᾶτο, *iato*] those who needed to be cured [θεραπείας, *therapeias*]. (9:10–11; the mass feeding follows in 9:12–17)

Twelve Disciples (9:1–6, 10–17)

Jesus's twelve deputies undergo a major transition in their training. Having been called and commissioned for "catching people" (5:10) and being named "apostles" (ἀπόστολοι, *apostoloi* [6:13]), or "sent ones," the Twelve are now "called . . . together" anew, and Jesus specifically "sent them out [ἀπέστειλεν, *apesteilen*]" on their own mission of kingdom-preaching and miracle-working (exorcising/healing) in the villages of Galilee (9:1–2, 6). Along with imparting his "power and authority" to equip the Twelve for their assignment, Jesus also makes arrangements for their "journey," or "way" (ὁδός, *hodos* [9:3])—the way of discipleship paved by Jesus.[235] But in this practical matter of travel, Jesus provides no equipment at all, but rather orders the Twelve to "*take nothing* . . . no staff, nor bag, nor bread, nor money—not even an extra tunic" (9:3)—which, by all accounts, is how Jesus himself operates (cf. 9:58). They must depend on others' hospitality, not as freeloaders, but in exchange for their ministry, though not as payment per se. They certainly are not to charge for their services, since they have no purse to carry money in! And they are not to push their services or personal needs on anyone. If someone welcomes them, fine; if not, they are simply to move on to another town, though not altogether peacefully: on their way out of an unreceptive village, the apostles must "shake the dust off [their] feet" (9:5) as a gesture of protest and judgment (cf. 10:11–12).[236]

Among their restricted kit, the lack of an "extra tunic," or outer garment (lit. "not having two tunics"), recalls previous instructions by John and Jesus. The Baptist insisted that anyone with "two coats/tunics must share with anyone who has none" (3:11), and Jesus exhorted his disciples that, if some opponent

235. The common word ὁδός (*hodos*), designating a "road, path, way," also functions in Luke's writings and the Bible generally as an image of the "way of life/righteousness" or its antithesis, the "way of death/wickedness." In Luke's second volume, "the Way [of God/the Lord]" becomes shorthand for identifying the community of followers of Jesus Messiah and the "way" he taught and lived (Acts 9:2; 18:25–26; 19:9, 23; 22:4; 24:14, 22).

236. Dust-removal gestures in Luke and Acts express more than a distancing, not-my-problem "washing one's hands" of the matter; they also include elements of defiant protest, variously described as "shaking from" (ἀποτινάσσω, *apotinassō* [Luke 9:5]), "wiping off" (ἀπομάσσομαι, *apomassomai* [10:11]), or "shaking out" (ἐκτινάσσω, *ektinassō* [Acts 13:51]) dust residue on the feet, as well as "throwing/hurling" (βάλλω, *ballō*) dust into the air (Acts 22:23 CEB).

took their overcoat/tunic, say in a lawsuit, they should give them their undershirt as well (6:29). Since Jesus now charges the Twelve to carry no spare suit of clothes, this latter scenario could put them in a very awkward "exposed" situation. Traveling light is an understatement here. The disciples must depend on others' benevolence for any extras.

Apart from their sartorial restrictions, the Twelve's packing neither "bread nor money" sets up a glaring moment of backsliding after they return from their excursion. Their mission is a rousing success, "bringing the good news and curing diseases everywhere" (9:6); and evidently, as they go "through the villages," they find enough gracious hosts to meet their basic needs. But when the crowds interrupt their debriefing session with Jesus and require feeding by day's end, the apostles fail to grasp Jesus's hospitality principle. Jesus himself "welcomes" the throng, even though they disrupt his plans to "withdraw privately" with his confidants; and he proceeds to carry out the same kingdom-heralding and healing ministry he assigned the Twelve (9:10–11; cf. 9:2). As night approaches, however, the apostles urge Jesus to "send the crowd away . . . to lodge and get provisions," given the sparse resources available in the "deserted place [ἐρήμῳ, *erēmō*]" they occupy, to say nothing of the difficulties of accommodating kosher diets, proper seating arrangements, or any other mealtime scruples for such a large crowd in such a liminal place (9:12).[237] Of course, the "open table" policy of Luke's Jesus cares little for such limitations, as we have seen (5:29–32; 7:36–50). So, not surprisingly, he has special dinner plans for the multitude—and for his twelve delegates. These apostles who benefited from others' hospitality must now reciprocate: "*You* [ὑμεῖς, *hymeis*] give them something to eat" (9:13).

Although the Twelve had just reveled in the generous, sharing economy of God's kingdom—and might be expected to remember God's manna-supplying largesse in the "desert" (see more below)—they revert back to the old math and hard economics of worldly kingdoms. The five loaves and two fishes that they manage to scrounge up can scarcely satisfy "five thousand men" (and families); still less can they "go and buy food for all these people" with money they do not have (9:13–14). With such a mind-set, they fail to grasp Jesus's divine-kingly authority to apply "heavenly" resources to "earthly" problems. Yet, Jesus proceeds to multiply the loaves and fishes as "he looked up to heaven," and in the process, he makes a point of involving the disciples in organizing the people, distributing the food, and busing the leftovers (9:14–17). So, with more than a little nudge from Jesus, the Twelve cater the crowd after all. And lest they forget this hospitality lesson, the final tally of *twelve* doggy-baskets after everyone eats their fill

237. Poon, "Superabundant Table," 228–30; Neyrey, "Ceremonies," 366, 380.

conveys not only God's abundant provision for God's "wilderness" people, but also Christ's commission to the twelve disciples to serve God's people "at table" as part and parcel of their evangelical mission (cf. 22:24–30).

Hungry Crowds (9:12–17)

For the first time Luke enumerates the crowd attracted to Jesus along with other statistical features: Jesus bountifully feeds five thousand people, divided into units of fifty, from a starter batch of five loaves and two fishes, ultimately yielding twelve baskets of leftovers. Though the numbers and details do not match perfectly, this scene evokes the administration of the Israelite throng in the wilderness (cf. Exod 16:4–12; 18:21–26; Num 11:16–32; Deut 1:15). More than Moses and the elders, however, who simply mediated and managed God's manna/quail feeding program, Jesus directly channels God's power ("looking up to heaven") and breaks and distributes bread and fish with his own hands (Luke 9:16). Though refusing to create bread for himself (4:1–4), he happily does so for God's hungry people in the desert; and he again provides a miraculous supply of fish, though this time without a net (cf. 5:1–11). Jesus stunningly proves himself to be the munificent Lord of land (grain) and sea (fish) on behalf of his people. Mary's politically charged Magnificat comes to fruition: "he has filled the hungry with good things," not "sent [them] away empty" (1:53)—against the disciples' first wishes!

Besides looking back to Israel's formative exodus-wilderness trek, Jesus's hosting and feeding God's hungry people looks ahead to his Passover-Eucharist with his followers and, beyond that, to the culmination of God's restored kingdom. As he now "blessed and broke" the bread (and fish) and "gave" it to the disciples for distribution (9:16–17), so Jesus will take bread at the Last Supper, give thanks, break it, and give it to his disciples as a sign of his soon-to-be-broken body "for you [all]" (22:19; see vv. 14–15). Moreover, the sign extends beyond immediately impending events to offer a poignant taste of the final messianic feast, where all God's people will joyously gather from the four corners of the world to celebrate the climactic fulfillment of God's reign (see 13:29; 22:18, 30).

Herod the Tetrarch (9:7–9)

The awkward splicing of Herod Antipas's "perplexed" response (9:7–9) between the apostles' mission trip (9:1–6) and their reporting back to Jesus and participating in the feeding of the multitude (9:10–17) accentuates the ill-fitted nature of Herod the tetrarch's Galilean turf (a mere quarter/*tetra*-sphere, not a full kingdom) with God's rightful and righteous realm, encompassing the whole created order, manifest in Jesus and his emissaries. Supplementing the earlier report of Herod's imprisonment of John the Baptist (3:19–20), Luke now recounts, by Herod's own lips, the horrible end of the story: "John I beheaded" (9:9). But Herod also betrays a nagging concern that John's execution did not really end the matter, since John's work seems to be perpetuating through this Jesus fellow. Some were even speculating that Jesus was John redivivus or Elijah or one of the prophets—in any case, a potentially greater menace to Herod's authority and popularity (9:7–9). Having heard these troubling rumblings about Jesus's mission, Herod now "tried to see [ἐζήτει ἰδεῖν, *ezētei idein*] him [Jesus]" for himself (9:9; cf. Zacchaeus's identical response in 19:3). But Herod's desire to see Jesus has sinister ulterior motives (unlike those of Zacchaeus) and will not be realized until Jesus's trial preceding his crucifixion ("Herod . . . had been wanting to see [Jesus] for a long time" [23:8]). Not all quests to know Jesus are positive. Motivation matters.

The flanking accounts of Jesus and his apostles' mission reinforce its patent socioeconomic contrast with Herod's regime. Accustomed to fancy clothing and luxurious living (7:25), Herod and his cronies wouldn't last for a second on Jesus's barebones budget of no money, no purse, and no extra tunic. And his plush palace at Tiberias on the west bank of the Galilean "sea," providing him all the fish and imported foodstuffs he could stomach,[238] couldn't be set in starker relief against the itinerant, desert-landscaped environment of Jesus's movement scrounging for a piddling supply of loaves and fishes. But here's the critical difference: in God's kingdom, out of little to nothing, amazing grace and generosity abound in Jesus to satisfy the hungry masses, whereas in Herod's realm, the burgeoning storehouses serve to satiate the already full and fat elites (cf. 12:13–21) at the expense of the masses struggling to survive.

Previewing Jesus's Death and Preparing His Disciples (I) (9:18–27)

With the crowds in the desert duly taught, healed, and fed, the setting shifts back to a private scene with Jesus and the disciples (cf. 9:10), assessing both the crowds' and the disciples' perceptions of Jesus's identity (9:18). Beyond displaying his purpose and power to nourish the hungry masses, what does the feeding

238. On Herod Antipas and Tiberias, see especially Sawicki, *Crossing Galilee*, 28–30, 92–94, 133–34, 141–48, 172–73; cf. Jonathan L. Reid, *Archaeology*, 93–99, 218–20; Rousseau and Arav, *Jesus*, 316–18.

feat reveal about who Jesus *is* (9:18–20)? Jesus poses this very question to the disciples while he is "praying *alone* (κατὰ μόνας, *kata monas*)" (9:18). Though the disciples are present, they do not yet pray *with* Jesus. They have not yet learned how to pray (11:1–4) and remain more observers than participants in Jesus's prayer life (cf. 22:39–46). They still have much to learn about Jesus, and he uses this occasion to stretch their minds to the breaking point. But Jesus's regular practice of prayer (cf. 3:21; 6:12) also suggests his own persisting quest for greater self-understanding, for a firmer grasp on who he is, or better, who God has called him to be. By probing, "Who do the crowds/you say that I am?" (9:18, 20), Jesus is not merely taking an opinion poll; he is also gauging and solidifying his own identity as God's Son and Messiah.[239]

The query to the disciples about crowd perceptions yields the same information Herod had gleaned: some claim that Jesus is "John the Baptist; but others, Elijah; and still others, that one of the ancient prophets has arisen" (9:7–9, 19). So both internal and external polls agree, and both reflect reasonable assessments from Luke's story thus far. Jesus is repeatedly cast as a dynamic, Spirit-anointed prophet in the train, though not the exact mold, of great prophets, not least Elijah and John. So these are positive associations, antithetical to later accusations that Jesus is somehow in league with Beelzebul (11:14–15). But they still fall short of capturing Jesus's full identity in distinction from other prophets. So Jesus presses further to take the pulse of his closest followers, hoping that they ("You-all" [ὑμεῖς, *hymeis*] in emphatic first position) will prove more prescient. However muddled they may have been in the past, here, through the voice of Peter, the disciples correctly exclaim Jesus to be "the Messiah of God" (9:20).

239. Emphasizing the predominant ancient Mediterranean social psychology of "dyadic" or collectivist personality, where one's identity was inextricably tied to social reputation based on others' evaluation to a much greater degree than obtains in modern Western individualist perspective, Malina and Rohrbaugh (*Social-Science Commentary*) offer an important check on popular interpretation of Jesus's "Who do people say that I am?" query: "Viewed through Western eyes . . . this critical passage is usually assumed to signal . . . that Jesus knows who he is and that he is testing the disciples to see whether or not they know as well. If this passage is viewed from the vantage point of the Mediterranean understanding of personality, however, it is Jesus who does not know who he is, and it is the disciples [and crowds] from whom he must get this information" (341; cf. 342–43; Malina and Neyrey, "First-Century Personality"). Though I think that this "dyadic" reading too sharply demarcates between "ancient" and "modern" people and their perceptions (all but denying any introspective thoughts and emotions by ancient individuals and downplaying ongoing heavy influence of social relations on modern identities), I still take the point that Jesus's sense of messianic vocation is *being formed* by public opinion and disciples' reaction, as well as his own thinking forged in prayerful, Spirit-led fellowship with his divine Father.

The Fate of Jesus Messiah, the Son of Humankind (9:21–22)

We might be tempted to stand up and cheer, as we hear the first confession of Jesus's Messiahship by a human being, echoing that of heavenly beings and evil spirits (2:11; 4:18; 4:41). Oddly, however, Jesus doesn't affirm Peter's response. Quite the contrary, in no uncertain terms he "sternly ordered and commanded" the disciples to say nothing about "this" Messiah business to anyone (9:21). Without skipping a beat, Jesus abruptly shifts to speaking of his role as *Son of Humankind*, specifically, his tragicomic fall-and-rise destiny, but with main emphasis on his violent demise. Complementing the head verb, expressing adamant divine purpose ("must"), are four infinitives (one active and three passive), three describing Jesus's horrible fate before "being raised on the third day":

> The Son of Humankind *must* [δεῖ, *dei*]
> [1] undergo great suffering [παθεῖν, *pathein*], and
> [2] be rejected [ἀποδοκιμασθῆναι, *apodokimasthēnai*] by the elders, chief priests, and scribes, and
> [3] be killed [ἀποκτανθῆναι, *apoktanthēnai*], and
> [4] on the third day be raised [ἐγερθῆναι, *egerthēnai*]. (9:22)

The keynote on "great/much suffering" (πολλὰ παθεῖν, *polla pathein*) unpacked in successive passive verbs, with either God as implicit subject or Jewish religious authorities as explicit actors ("elders, chief priests, scribes"), does not readily fit common messianic or Daniel/Enoch Son of Humankind expectations, which focus in various ways on delivering God's people *from* suffering and oppression, not succumbing to enemy forces. In the present context, Jesus clearly has Daniel/Enoch's eschatological-royal figure in view ("when [the Son of Humankind] comes in his glory" [9:26]) more than Ezekiel's anthropological-prophetic counterpart (see discussion above on 5:24). A combined Davidic Messiah/Danielic Son of Humankind projects a dynamic, divinely authorized, judging-saving ruler *in active control of*, not passive acquiescence to, world events. To be sure, Jesus envisions ultimately being "raised" from the dead, in line with the general resurrection forecast in Dan 12:2–3. But as a heavenly figure sent to rescue God's afflicted people and to reign in "an everlasting kingdom," the "one like a son of humankind" was *not expected to die* in the process (Dan 7:13–14). Jesus's prediction strains under the burden of cognitive dissonance.

We do not know the disciples' precise conceptions of the Messiah or Son of Humankind or their assessments of how Jesus fit these images. But Jesus's mighty displays of provision, healing, and deliverance amply support the most vigorous messianic hopes. Of course, Jesus has done nothing to promote military conquest, but since God has never required an earthly army or conventional weapons to subdue hostile forces, the disciples might still entertain some dreams of General Jesus victorious in battle. In any case, Jesus's stern gag order on Peter's Messiah confession and stark announcement of the Son of Humankind's dire destiny of suffering, rejection, and murder could only have stunned the disciples. After this bombshell forecast, they hardly needed a command to silence: who wants to hear about another failed Messiah? In Luke's account, neither Peter nor anyone else musters enough voice to challenge Jesus's seemingly defeatist attitude (contra Mark 8:32–33). They are speechless.

The Fellowship of the Disciples with Jesus in Death (9:23–27)

But Jesus has more to say, though at first he only amplifies the shock, as he *defines* the death that awaits him and *extends* it to include his disciples! Jesus matches the four infinitive markers of his own fate with four verbal requirements, one infinitive and three imperatives, of discipleship. Assonance at the beginning (ἀ, *a*) and end (θω/τω, *thō*/*tō*) of the imperatives stresses their impact. Moreover, though applied to all would-be disciples, Jesus's use of singular verb forms presses the point of individual responsibility (reflected in my following translation).

> If anyone wants [θέλει, *thelei*]
> [1] to come [ἔρχεσθαι, *erchesthai*] come after me, let him/her
> [2] deny [ἀρνησάσθω, *arnēsasthō*] him/herself and
> [3] take up [ἀράτω, *aratō*] his/her *cross* daily and
> [4] follow [ἀκολουθείτω, *akoloutheitō*] me. (9:23 AT)

The *only* reason to "take up a cross" in Jesus's day was to be *crucified* on it, to undergo a gruesome, torturous form of capital punishment for (alleged) rebellion against the Roman state. A *crucified Messiah* would seem to be the most oxymoronic, horrific end conceivable for Jesus, and he aims to take his followers with him on this death march. It is a wonder that they do not run away immediately from this mad scheme.

But Jesus quickly adds some critical mitigating factors, though in their paradoxical form, they scarcely drain the voltage from his jolting message. First, Jesus has not abandoned his *saving-liberating* mission. But he now balances the obvious, proactive means of accomplishing this work with the more obscure, counterintuitive process of saving life by *losing* it, of profiting by *divesting*

(9:24–25). The dynamics of God's realm run in reverse from worldly operations: true life flows from death, real gain from loss. Conversely, those who obsessively guard their lives and self-interests, rather than surrendering to Jesus's cross-bearing way, sabotage their quests for flourishing by forfeiting God's gifts of salvation. Defying conventional logic, proof of this paradox comes only by taking the risk of faith, by taking up the cross and following the crucified-risen Christ wherever he leads.

Second, an element of hope inheres in Jesus's stress, unique to Luke, on *daily* (καθ' ἡμέραν, *kath' hēmeran*) commitment to cruciform living (9:23). While at first blush this call to iterative, everyday cross-bearing may seem like a protracted form of torture crueler than a once-for-all execution, on closer reflection, it marks a critical modification of the monstrous cross image. Jesus calls his followers to take up the cross as a voluntary act (not imposed punishment) of spirited daily engagement with (not cowering from) the chronic pain and suffering experienced by so many in an oppressive society. The charge to bear the cross *day after day* suggests in fact that the cross does not have the last word, does not represent the final solution, as it so arrogantly claims. To "die every day," as Paul "boasts" (1 Cor 15:31), means that new days for fresh cross-bearing keep dawning. Luke's Jesus dares to believe for himself and his followers that dying, even under the colossal crush of imperial tyranny, gives way to rising in a dynamic circadian cycle of life and death. Or in Paul's words again: "We are afflicted in every way, but not crushed; perplexed, but not driven to despair; persecuted, but not forsaken; struck down, but not destroying; always carrying in the body the death of Jesus, so that the life of Jesus may also be visible in our bodies. For while we live, we are always being given up to death for Jesus's sake so that the life of Jesus may be made visible in our mortal flesh" (2 Cor 4:8–11).

Lest this be taken as some platitudinous pablum that "God never gives us more than we can handle" or applied in some trivial way like "this seasonal hay fever [substitute any other niggling ailment] is just one of those crosses I have to bear," it is vital to appreciate the serious, gut-level way that Jesus's call to take up one's daily cross is appropriated among Christians outside comfortable Western societies. For example, immersion with women among the "crucified peoples" of Latin America prompted Lukan scholar Barbara Reid to rethink her theology of the cross:

> I have met women who are part of the "crucified peoples" of Latin America whose daily lives are marked by the threat of death from poverty generated by unjust social and political structures or from violence within their homes and on their streets. I have found that my initial puzzlement and revulsion toward the bloody, tortured images of the crucified Jesus that are so abun-

> dant in Latin America changed to humble reverence when I could see that, for those who live in situations of utter degradation, the only consolation is that Jesus knows and shares the depths of their suffering. . . . Crucified peoples witness to the gospel in extraordinary ways through their solidarity and cooperation with one another in community, their openness to receive and give love, and their determination to find God at the center of everything.[240]

Such a profound, grassroots theology of the cross has become a staple of Latina-feminist or *mujerista* hermeneutics, firmly anchored in Scripture and day-to-day experience or *lo cotidiano*, where women (and men) "live the multiple relations that constitute our humanity. It is the sphere in which our struggle for life is most immediate, most vigorous, most vibrant. *Lo cotidiano* is what we face every day; it includes also how we face it."[241] Notice the vital *communal* dimension, which Luke's Jesus supports overall but which in fact is somewhat shadowed in the present context by the *individual* thrust mentioned above ("If any *one* [τις, *tis*] wants to come after me" [9:23]). But Latina Christians would never dream of carrying their crosses alone: that road leads only to death. Bearing one another's burdens—together, in vibrant community—is not just a nice motto for them, but the very stuff of living in a broken world. We might also note at this stage that even Jesus will accept cross-bearing aid, from a stranger no less (see discussion on 23:26).[242]

Third, Jesus's final words offer a tantalizing hope that "some standing here . . . will not taste death before they see the kingdom of God" (9:27). It is hard to reconcile "taking up the cross" with "not tasting death": how can any contact with a cross, metaphorical or literal, not involve some experience of bitter death? The paradoxes pile up. Yet, Jesus does not promise that these disciples will never die, only that in the immediate future they will "see" and "taste" the savory life of God's realm more palpably than the acrid decay of death.[243] Though still expect-

240. Barbara E. Reid, *Taking Up the Cross*, 4.

241. Isasi-Díaz, "Communication," 29; see also her *La Lucha*, 92–106.

242. David Lyle Jeffrey notes the significance of the "daily imperative" of cross-bearing for the Chinese church, which made Luke 9:23 a banner "year-verse" in 1998: "Chinese Christians know better than many what Basil the Great took to be self-evident, namely that 'readiness to die for Christ, the mortification of one's members on this earth, preparedness for every danger which might befall us on behalf of Christ's name . . . this is to take up one's cross (139; Basil, *Long Rules* 9.246–47).

243. On the epistemological associations of the "taste" term (γεύομαι, *geuomai*), similar to "see," note the definition in BDAG, 195: "to have perception of something either by mouth or by experience, especially in reference to relatively small quantity"; and more figuratively, "to experience something cognitively or emotionally, to come to know something." Heb 2:9 matches the specific notion of "tasting death" with reference to Jesus's substitutionary death

ing the visible return of the glorious Son of Humankind (9:26; cf. 17:22–24, 29–30; 21:25–28; 22:69) and the delectable climactic feast hosted by God's Messiah (cf. 13:29; 14:15–24; 22:28–30), such heavenly blessings can be partially but patently seen and tasted here and now, on earth. God's kingdom is already inaugurated in Christ as guarantee of the full beautiful (sight), bountiful (taste) reality to come.

How do the disciples respond to Jesus's stunning announcements in 9:21–27? Do they in fact hear, see, and taste what Jesus has said, shown, and dished up for them? The next scene depicts Peter, James, and John in a dramatic mountaintop encounter with the brilliantly transfigured Jesus, accompanied by Moses and Elijah (9:28–36). I concur with commentators who regard this epiphany as the primary, though not exhaustive, fulfillment of 9:27.[244] If any proximate experience of the disciples counts as glimpsing and tasting God's resplendent kingdom manifest in the Son of Humankind, it would surely be witnessing this unique predeath, lightning-charged (ἐξαστράπτων, *exastraptōn*), cloud-engulfed transfiguration "in glory" (9:29–31, 34–35).

But the brilliance of such glory is shadowed by its brevity, its blending with talk of "departure" (9:31), and its bridging into a tough battle with a vicious spirit "on the next day, when they come down from the mountain" (9:37–43a). In this juxtaposition of such opposite-yet-overlapping events, the developing characters of Jesus and the disciples shine through.

Transfiguring Jesus's Face and Clothes and Treating a Boy's Fits and Falls (9:28–43a)

Because of its exceptional elements that seem to interrupt Jesus's mission and flash forward to the final complex of Jesus's death-resurrection-ascension, the transfiguration is often treated as an isolated interlude. But in fact it closely links in Luke not only with Jesus's preceding preview of his suffering-and-glory destiny, but also with the succeeding scene, where Jesus liberates a father's young son from a convulsive condition. The following chart sketches the comparisons and contrasts of these paired miraculous episodes.

"for everyone." The writer of Hebrews does not, however, view Jesus's death as a "small" sample of the experience, but rather a total absorption in human "flesh and blood" to the very end (cf. 2:14–18). Though it is doubtful that Luke implies the substitutive force of Jesus's own death in 9:27, Hebrews provides a broader canonical perspective that Jesus's followers need not fear the poisonous sting of death because Jesus has drunk (tasted) the bitter cup in full.

244. For example, Vinson, 287, and Green, 376. Carroll sees this as a "possible" interpretation but prefers here to stress that "in a real sense God's reign is already present and powerfully at work in Jesus's ministry" (215).

	Jesus's transfiguration (9:28–36)	Boy's restoration (9:37–43)
Time:	"Now about eight days after these sayings" (9:28)[1]	"On the next day" (9:37)
Place:	"Jesus . . . went up on the mountain to pray" (9:28)	"when they had come down from the mountain" (9:37)
Characters:	Peter, John, James, Moses, and Elijah	Unnamed crowds, disciples, father, and boy
Fathers and sons:	*God*: "This is my Son, my Chosen; listen to him!" (9:35)	*Unnamed father*: "I beg you to look at my son; he is my only child" (9:38)
Physical transformations:	"The appearance of his face changed, and his clothes became dazzling white. . . . They saw his glory" (9:29, 32)	In a convulsive fit, "he foams at the mouth" (9:39); but he is healed by Jesus (9:42)
Vocal demonstrations:	From an "overshadowing" cloud, God affirms his Son Jesus (9:34–35)	Seizing a helpless boy, a violent demon shrieks and shakes his victim; Jesus rebukes the evil spirit (9:39, 42)
Addressing Jesus:	Disciples call him "Master ['Επιστάτα, *Epistata*]" (9:33)	The father calls him "Teacher [Διδάσκαλε, *Didaskale*]" (9:38)
Exit theme:	*Exodus*: "They . . . were speaking of his departure [ἔξοδον, *exodon*]" (9:31)	*Exorcism*: "I begged your disciples to cast it out [ἐκβάλωσιν, *ekbalōsin*]" (9:40)
Disciples' weaknesses:	Sleepiness; ignorance (9:32–33)	Impotence to help demonized boy (9:40)

1. Unlike the parallels in Matt 17:1 and Mark 9:2, which set Jesus's transfiguration six days after his first passion prediction, Luke marks the event *eight days* later. If one seeks some symbolic significance in the number (which may be overreaching; the detail may be incidental), the most likely surmise connects it to circumcision on the eighth day of a male infant's life, as experienced by Jesus in Luke 2:21. In the present case, Jesus's transfiguration previews his resurrection glory, that is, his emergence into *new life* (on Sunday, as it will happen, the first day of a new week, which equals the eighth day following the previous passion week). Barbara E. Reid ("Voices"), however, flatly contends that "no convincing explanation" has been offered for Luke's redacting of Mark's six days, leaving her to conclude that Luke takes "eight days" over from an independent source (23–24).

These episodes mark not only strategic developments in the spiritual pilgrimages of Jesus and the disciples, including key moments of knowing and "not knowing" (9:33), but also salient demonstrations of God's restorative, liberating mission in the world through Christ.

God: Word and Work (9:35–36, 42–43)

Each incident culminates with God.[245] Speaking from the cloud that overshadows the mountain, God has the last word, after which all "kept silent" in awestruck contemplation (9:36). While previewing God's ultimate sending of the Son of Humankind in lightning-radiated clouds (see above), the transfiguration also reprises the theophany in "thunder and lightning, as well as a thick cloud," on Mount Sinai, where God revealed the Torah to Moses (Exod 19:16–19; 24:15–18).[246] Now, with Moses again, God certifies Jesus's role as the expected "prophet like Moses" worthy of the people's full attention: "You shall heed such a prophet" (Deut 18:15; cf. Acts 3:22–23; 7:37–38); "Listen to him!" (Luke 9:35). But God also reaffirms the baptismal oracle identifying Jesus as *more* than a prophet, more than even the great Moses and Elijah: Jesus is uniquely God's "Son" and "Chosen One" (9:35; cf. 3:21–22). Aptly, after God verbally spotlights the Chosen Son Jesus, he is "found alone [μόνος, *monos*]," that is, without Moses and Elijah, who have exited the stage (9:36a). The "Chosen" or "Elect One" (ἐκλελεγμένος, *eklelegmenos* [9:35])[247] reinforces the "Beloved" appellation at the baptism and recalls the Spirit-anointed servant-prophet in Isa 42:1 (cf. 61:1; Luke 4:18–19). Such "chosen" language carries messianic associations, as Jewish leaders will mockingly apply to Jesus at his death: "Let him save himself if he is the Messiah of God, his chosen one [ἐκλεκτός, *eklektos*]!" (23:35). A terrible irony continues to build: this supreme Prophet, Servant, Son, Chosen One of God—the very embodiment of God's authoritative word—will "depart" from this world resisted and rejected by many of his own people, reminiscent of Moses's leadership struggles generations before (see Acts 7:23–29, 35–44).

The next scene ends with the audience's astonishment at "the greatness [μεγαλειότητι, *megaleiotēti*] of God" manifest in healing the demon-possessed boy who had been "dashed to the ground in convulsions" (9:42–43). The crowd thus echoes Mary's song of "magnifying" (μεγαλύνω, *megalynō* [1:46]) God's

245. Carroll's theocentric comment on the Gerasene demoniac incident culminating in Luke 8:39 ("declare how much God has done for you") is apposite here: "Luke reminds readers that Jesus's mission accomplishes the work of *God*. . . . Jesus's ministry of release, which brings salvation, accomplishes the purpose of God. . . . Luke's narrative is a story of salvation among God's people and also among Gentiles. First and last, it is a story about God and what God is doing in the world" (195 [emphasis original]).

246. For a thorough discussion of the "overshadowing cloud" associated with theophanies in Exodus and other literature, see Heil, *Transfiguration*, 129–48. For intertextual links of Luke's transfiguration account with the Exodus-Sinai theophany and the Deuteronomy prophet-like-Moses (Deut 18:15–19) traditions, see David M. Miller, "Seeing the Glory."

247. Perfect passive participle form ("having been chosen"), foregrounding the solid, permanent state of Jesus's divinely chosen/elected identity.

saving might and mercy on behalf of the lowly and powerless. Following close on the heels of Jesus's passion prediction and transfiguration, the ordeal of the demon-battered lad strikes particularly close to the heart of God as Father of the Chosen-Beloved Son destined to "undergo great suffering" (9:22) and a violent "departure" (9:31) from this world. A desperate father, pleading for the health of his son, his "only child" (μονογενής, *monogenēs* [9:38; cf. 7:12; 8:42]), naturally compels God's ministry through Jesus.

Jesus: Exodus and Exorcism (9:30–31, 37–42)

The characterization of Jesus in both stories closely relates to his "outgoing" or "exiting" activities. With Moses and Elijah on the mountain, Jesus discusses his "going out"/"departure" (ἔξοδος, *exodos* [9:31]) from this life; at the foot of the mountain, he instigates the "casting out" (ἐκβάλλω, *ekballō* [9:40]) of the demon threatening a young boy's life. Notions of progress and conflict color both exits. In the first case, the topic of Jesus's final destiny, uniquely described in Luke by the single term "exodus/departure," intimates a paradoxical nexus of death-resurrection-ascension-exaltation, ignominy giving way to glory, appropriate to Jesus's two conversation partners. Fundamentally, "exodus" evokes the history of God's delivering Israel from oppressive rule. We may assume, then, some typological parallel: as the God-authorized Moses led his people from Egyptian bondage and into a renewed bond (covenant) with Israel's Lord, so the God-anointed Jesus redeems his followers from evil powers, both spiritual and political, into a "new covenant" (cf. 22:20) with God governing God's righteous kingdom.[248]

But more pointedly, the mountaintop seminar now focuses on *Jesus's* exodus, not Israel's emancipation, though Jesus's experience certainly has vital connections with saving God's people. Of course, Moses personally participated in the original exodus, but that whole event was about *Israel's* escape, not Moses's: recall that Moses had already fled from Egypt to Midian, from where God commissioned him to go back and compel Pharaoh to release "my people" (Exod 2:11–15; 3:1–22). So what exactly is Jesus's personal exodus? In the present Lukan context, it must refer to the way of the cross, to Jesus's exit-departure from this life in *violent death* before resurrection (9:22–23). Such a self-sacrificing path will indeed issue in renewed life for Jesus and his followers (9:24), but at this point, Jesus diverges sharply from Moses, who, far from not losing his own life

248. On covenantal echoes in Luke's transfiguration account, see David M. Miller, "Seeing the Glory," 506–17.

in leading the exodus from Egypt, served as God's agent of killing (drowning) Israel's cruel overlords. Whereas Moses makes right through (God's) might (see victory song in Exod 15:1–19), Jesus's liberating mission runs through a Roman cross—on which *he dies*—triggering the excruciating-yet-invigorating "scandal" of power through weakness (cf. 1 Cor 1:18–25).

This contrast with Moses becomes only sharper as we consider his extraordinary personal exit-departure from this world—and also Elijah's centuries later.[249] Although both venerable prophets endured opposition from their own people and foreign oppressors, they did not meet violent ends, as other prophets did (cf. Luke 4:24, 28–29; 11:49–51; 13:33–34). Indeed, belief was rife that Moses and Elijah *never died* but were directly "translated" or "assumed" into heaven after completing their earthly missions. Thus they are uniquely qualified to "appear in glory" (9:31) with Jesus in advance of the general resurrection. The Bible attests to Elijah's experience of being suddenly "taken up [ἀνελήμφθη, *anelēmphthē*]" (2 Kgs 2:11 LXX) to heaven in a fiery chariot (cf. Sir 48:9; 1 Macc 2:58). But the circumstances surrounding Moses's "departure," though not so definitive, are equally suggestive. In the biblical account, Moses "dies"—while still in full health and strength—on the edge of the promised land near Mount Nebo "at the Lord's command," and he is mysteriously buried there—*by the Lord*—and "no one knows his burial place to this day" (Deut 34:5–7).[250] Such a hazy scene gave rise to a spate of Jewish traditions aligning Moses with Elijah (and Enoch [Gen 5:22]) as special figures seamlessly transported from earthly to heavenly spheres without the transitional phase of death. Philo, for example, references Moses's "pilgrimage from earth to heaven . . . when he was already being exalted [ἀναλαμβανόμενος, *analambanomenos*] and stood at the very barrier, ready at the [Father's] signal to direct his upward flight to heaven" (*Moses* 2.288–91).[251]

The prospect of Jesus's being taken up in glory fits Luke's interest in Jesus's ascension, including the use of ἀναλαμβάνω (*analambanō*) or cognate noun ἀνάλημψις (*analēmpsis*) (Luke 9:51; Acts 1:2, 11, 22; cf. Luke 24:41 [ἀναφέρω, *anapherō*]; Acts 2:33–34). But this "taking up in glory" integrally links with "taking up the cross" in the climactic "events that have been fulfilled among us"

249. I am indebted in this segment to the thorough analysis of relevant Moses and Elijah traditions in Heil, *Transfiguration*, 95–113.

250. "The Lord buried him" (Deut 34:6 CEB) identifies the singular subject of the Hebrew verb as "the Lord," following the natural flow from Deut 34:5 ("Moses, the Lord's servant died . . . according to the Lord's command," CEB). The LXX, however, switches to a third-person *plural* verb ("*they* buried him"), presumably to avoid directly involving the Lord in disposing of Moses's corpse.

251. Cited in Heil, *Transfiguration*, 111 (trans. Colson, LCL).

(Luke 1:1). Ascension comes *by way of crucifixion*, not bypassing it. John's Gospel virtually collapses these two events with a poignant wordplay on "lifting up" (ὑψόω, *hypsoō*), denoting both the physical hoisting of Jesus on the cross and his spiritual exalting in glory: "And I, when I am lifted up [ὑψωθῶ, *hypsōthō*] from the earth, will draw all people to myself" (John 12:32; cf. 3:13–14; 8:28). In Johannine perspective, Jesus's cross becomes a throne. While Luke connects Jesus's crucifixion and exaltation as a historical process, he does not conflate them like John, any more than he "translates" Jesus's departure into a Moses/Elijah-style reposting to heaven. Luke's Jesus will suffer, be rejected, and die at the hands of executioners. The cross will bear *down* on Jesus and kill him, and *from there* he will be taken *down* and buried (in a known place), and *from there* he will rise on the third day, and *then*, after forty days of instructing his followers, he will be taken *up* to heaven (see Acts 1:1–11).

The second scene, following the transfiguration, rudely jerks events back to the hard reality of human suffering and demonic oppression that Jesus must tackle. He clearly does not take off from the mountain with Moses and Elijah (with or without chariot) back to their presumably blissful heavenly stations, whatever those might be. From seeing God's magnificent glory and hearing God's assuring word, Jesus comes down and abruptly encounters "just then" ("look!" [καὶ ἰδού, *kai idou*]) a man shouting for his help amid a large crowd and an evil spirit "suddenly" ("look!" again [καὶ ἰδού, *kai idou*]) "seizing" the man's son and "all at once shrieking" as it convulses the poor child (9:37–39). The triumph and tranquility of the transfiguration are shattered, and Jesus does not simply take this whiplash in stride. Before healing the demon-possessed boy, he blurts out his most emotional, acrimonious retort thus far in Luke: "You faithless and perverse generation, how much longer must I be with you [all] and bear with you [all]?" (9:41).

The outburst against this stubborn "generation" suggests Jesus's frustration with the whole miserable lot of this present world—including crowds, disciples (see more below), father, son, and the demon harassing the boy—and his place within it. Though addressing "you [all]," Jesus does not so much target any one or group in particular as he reflects out loud on his own difficult, unrelenting battle against suffering and evil. "How long must I bear" this burden echoes laments to God by Moses (Num 11:10–15) and the psalmist (Pss 6:3–8; 13:1–4; 74:10–11; 80:4–6). Even the most faithful of God's servants come to a place of wondering whether they can hang on and complete the work they have to do. Jesus presses on ("Bring your son here" [Luke 9:41]), but not without *his own struggle*, no doubt heightened by the stark contrast with the previous ecstatic experience on the mountain. Peter's notion of building three tents for an extended retreat might not have been such a bad idea after all (9:33).

Disciples: Ignorance and Impotence (9:32–35, 40–41)

But in fact we do not know why Peter blurts out his construction proposal, since, as Luke reports, even Peter does "not know [μὴ εἰδώς, *mē eidōs*] what he said" (9:33). He knows that "it is good to be here," that Jesus wouldn't be glowing and Moses and Elijah wouldn't have shown up for just any occasion, but that is about as far as his understanding goes. Offering to make three tents (out of what materials?) may serve to honor the three dignitaries, or prolong the experience, or commemorate the event—all with some vague association with the Feast of Tabernacles/Tents (Sukkoth), marking Israel's wilderness wandering—or it may just reflect a nervous impulse to say and do something. Stirring from a sleepy state (9:32)[252] and addressing Jesus as "Master" (Ἐπιστάτα, *Epistata*) do not, as we have seen, promise the keenest of insight into Jesus's identity and purpose. Much more than "Master," the divine voice from the cloud reaffirms Jesus as the Chosen One, the Son of God. For Peter and his fellow disciples, however, this revelation only confirms their miring in a thick "cloud of unknowing"—until they, as Jesus's chosen/elect (ἐκλεξάμενος, *eklexamenos*) apostles (6:13 [in prayer on another mountain]), truly "listen to him," as God enjoins at the present moment (9:35) —rather than erupting in a flurry of impetuous speech and action. And above all at this stage, what they must keenly hear and deeply root in their hearts is the word about Jesus's deathly "departure," reinforcing the cross-bearing path he recently charted for himself—and them!

As Peter, James, and John are proving less than discerning on the mountain, the other nine disciples are proving less than dynamic below. Despite their recent success in healing and exorcising in Jesus's name (9:1, 6), they appear impotent to help the father's demon-possessed son: "I begged your disciples to cast it out, but they could not [οὐκ ἠδυνήθησαν, *ouk ēdynēthēsan*]" (9:40). It is this report from the desperate father that provokes Jesus's exasperated tirade against "you faithless and perverse generation" before liberating the tormented boy. While the "generation" reference suggests a wide audience (see above), the

252. The NRSV (main text) reading of 9:32 interprets the disciples' perception positively: "[They] were weighed down with sleep; but since they had stayed awake, they saw his glory." In other words, as Carroll comments, "Though fatigued, they fight off sleep and remain awake to see 'his glory'. . . . The disciples indeed see; they are qualified observers" (218). While the text can admit this rendering, it may also reflect a less flattering picture of the disciples as groggy or flat out asleep when the transfiguration begins and only belatedly seeing the scene "when they became *fully awake*" (NIV; see also NAB, NASB, NRSV alt. reading); on the meaning of the compound verb διαγρεγορέω (*diagregoreō*) as either "keep awake" or "awake fully," see BDAG, 227. The portrait of Jesus's followers as soporific attendants, lacking alertness, matches the later prayer scene on another mountain in 22:45–46.

most direct target is the feeble disciples. Jesus has already chided their lack of "faith" (πίστις, *pistis*) in the storm incident (8:25) and now seems frustrated with their continuing "faithless" (ἄπιστος, *apistos*) response. In both cases they fail to trust in Jesus's saving power operative for and through them. They have nothing to say for themselves this time, and Jesus offers no fuller instruction, like that Mark provides (Mark 9:28–29). Luke's Jesus takes care of the matter himself in short order, no doubt wondering "how long" it is going to take the disciples to grow into sufficient faith and knowledge to carry on his mission, even as he worries that he doesn't have much longer to "bear with them." Here and elsewhere, I focus on Jesus's emotions not simply to show his human side, but more substantively: his *core values*. As the Christian philosopher Robert Roberts stresses, emotions constitute our deepest "construals of concern," signaling what matters most to us, what drives our goals and actions.[253] The "frustrated" Jesus confirms his *core concern* with the disciples' growth and independence so they might effectively carry on his work after his "departure."

Previewing Jesus's Death and Preparing His Disciples (II) (9:43b–50)

Although Jesus's restoration of the convulsive boy naturally created a stir among "all" who witnessed this "astonishing" miracle (9:43a) and other "amazing" acts "he was continuing to do" (ἐποίει, *epoiei* [imperfect; 9:43b AT]), he keeps the focus on his disciples' training, especially (re)drawing their attention to his impending death and correcting their self-centered preoccupations. He begins by flagging his instruction as a matter of high aural importance: "Let these words sink into your ears" (9:44; cf. 8:8; 14:35). He then proceeds to echo the recent prediction of tragic destiny, though more briefly and with an added disturbing twist: "The Son of Humankind [ἀνθρώπου, *anthrōpou*] is going to be betrayed into the hands of human beings [ἀνθρώπων, *anthrōpōn*]" (9:44 AT). In a devastating travesty of love and justice, the divine-human one will be spurned by the human beings he has come to save. Jesus offers no details here concerning the operatives or schemes behind his anticipated betrayal, and thus far, the narrator has offered only the tantalizing hint that one of the twelve apostles, Judas Iscariot (listed last), would "become a traitor" (6:16). In any case, the specter of betrayal Jesus raises comes as a shock to the disciples, both short-circuiting their comprehension ("they did not understand this saying") and firing up

253. Roberts, *Emotions*, 141–51, 320; and *Spiritual Emotions*, 11–14, 23; cf. Vanhoozer, *Remythologizing*, 408–14; and the fuller discussion on "Passional Theology" in the closing "Integration" section to this volume.

their apprehension ("they were afraid to ask him about this saying") (9:45). The phobic response at least intimates some dawning sense of the ominous fate Jesus portends. But they prefer suppression to facing the truth. Maybe if they do not ask Jesus to elaborate, he will drop all this crazy talk about the Son of Humankind's demise. And by no means are they ready to consider that *one of them* might betray Jesus (cf. 22:21–23).

But from a theological perspective, the disciples' persisting ignorance (ἠγνόουν, *ēgnooun*) and hesitancy to press Jesus for further insight are not the most perplexing elements in the present text. For instance, God seems to play an oddly obstructionist role in the disciples' grasp of Jesus's statement: "its meaning was concealed from them, so that they could not perceive [αἴσθωνται, *aisthōntai*] it" (9:45).[254] How can the disciples hope to hear the crux of Jesus's message if their perceptual ears are plugged *by God* (implied in the divine passive)? More to the point, why does God *not want* them to perceive now? What purpose does concealment serve?

We tackled some of this taut tension between divine sovereignty and human responsibility in discussing 8:4–21, taking considerable comfort—after Jesus's jolting assertion that he speaks in parables "*so that* 'looking they may not perceive, and listening they may not understand'" (8:9–10, citing Isa 6:9–10)—in his overriding claim that every "hidden" or "secret" mystery will be uncovered (Luke 8:17). God ultimately aims to reveal, not conceal. But that doesn't preclude intermittent phases of divinely imposed blindness on the way to fuller insight. Saul of Tarsus provides the most dramatic example in Luke's writings. After being struck by the lightning blast of the risen Christ, Saul "could see nothing" for three days (Acts 9:3–9). The confusion, helplessness, and fear of blindness overwhelm Saul until the Lord directs a Damascene disciple named Ananias to instruct and lay healing hands upon Saul (9:10–18). And even then, he still has much to learn about his new vocation. Though Luke never spells out the precise purpose behind Saul's blinding, the trajectory of Saul/Paul's career suggests that the three-day blackout marks a liminal stage appropriate to radical transition from persecutor to proclaimer of Christ.[255] One does not make such a stunning turnabout without some dizzying hiatus. Disorientation precedes re-

254. The verb αἰσθάνομαι (*aisthanomai*), used only here in the NT, means, according to Louw and Nida (*Greek-English Lexicon*), "to have the capacity to perceive clearly and hence to understand the real nature of something" (1:384). Cognate nouns occur in Phil 1:9 and Heb 5:14. The Philippians usage appears in a context emphasizing progressive growth in spiritual knowledge: "your love will keep on growing more and more together with your knowledge and complete capacity for understanding [αἰσθήσει, *aisthēsei*]" (Louw and Nida, *Greek-English Lexicon*, 1:384).

255. On Saul's transformation through "liminal" states in Acts, see Spencer, *Journeying*, 106–9, and "Paul's Odyssey."

orientation; convolution creates an atmosphere for revolution. Notions of Saul's instantaneous, full-grown conversion, common in some popular theologies, do not fit the narrative of Acts or the nature of human experience.[256] Spiritual knowledge does not come in some preformed, easy step-by-step module. One often has to go through some "dark night of the soul" to gain perspective and readiness to understand God's truth.

Back to Jesus's disciples in Luke. While the behavioral change they need doesn't approach Saul's violent extremism, the attitudinal change they require is just as dramatic: in their own way, they would have found the concept of a crucified Messiah and Son of Humankind as alien and repugnant before Jesus's death as Saul does afterward. In both cases, that of the original apostles and of Saul/Paul, spiritual knowledge unfolds in personal encounters with the risen Christ *after a period of imposed deafness/darkness preparing them for radically new perception.*

That the disciples are still not ready to accept Jesus's self-giving, cross-bearing path becomes painfully evident in the next two vignettes, where they (1) compete with one another "as to which one of them was the greatest" (9:46); and (2) complain about some freelance exorcist "because he does not follow with us" (9:49). In both scenarios, the disciples promote and protect their own status. In turn, Jesus puts them in their places with respect to surprisingly positive figures: (1) a little child (9:46–48) and (2) a maverick minister (9:49–50).

Insignificant Child (9:46–48)

As the disciples demur from asking Jesus to explain his forecast of betrayal, they plow right into an internal dispute about their ranking in Jesus's organization. The juxtaposition could hardly be more awkward and insensitive: from the Son of Humankind's treacherous fate to his followers' petty jockeying for status. But such reveals the disciples' core "inner thoughts [διαλογισμὸν τῆς καρδίας, *dialogismon tēs kardias*]" (9:47), what drives them at this stage of the journey. And such motives are scarcely concealed from Jesus. Just as he perceived the misguided "inner thoughts/arguments" of the scribes and Pharisees in previous incidents (5:22; 6:8), he now knows (εἰδώς, *eidōs*) his disciples' true intentions.

Accordingly, Jesus proceeds to correct their skewed ambitions through a surprising live demonstration. He summons a "little child [παιδίον, *paidion*] and put it by his [own] side [παρ' ἑαυτῷ, *par' heautō*]" in a position of closest

256. On "conversion as journey" as a major conceptual metaphor in Acts, see Green, *Conversion*, 99–105.

proximity and authority (9:47). Matthew and Mark report that two apostles, James and John, even dare to ask for the top posts at Jesus's right and left hand (Matt 20:20–21; Mark 10:35–37). In any case, the idea is preposterous that an anonymous "little child"—a nobody, a powerless tyke with nothing to offer who might not even live into adulthood—stands as Jesus's right-hand "man" or chief lieutenant in God's kingdom. This is not Jesus's own son, his royal heir, but just an ordinary little one: the neuter παιδίον (*paidion*) even leaves open the child's gender (Jesus might have called a little girl to his side!). Lest we think that Jesus simply reinforces his commitment to help small children, like the father's epileptic boy (παῖς, *pais* [9:42]), he identifies with this child in the most personal and theological way: "Whoever welcomes this child in my name welcomes me [Jesus], and whoever welcomes me welcomes the one [God] who sent me" (9:48). In other words, God-Jesus-child forms an intimate "trinity," or side-by-side partnership. It doesn't get any "greater" than that! So Jesus addresses the disciples' desire for greatness, while shattering their conventional images of greatness. A new stream flows into the paradox cascade: "the least among you is the greatest" (9:48); the cross-bearing Lord, Messiah, and Savior is a small dependent child often carried by others.

Independent Exorcist (9:49–50)

In an odd non sequitur, the apostle John "answers" Jesus's lesson about greatness with a report about "someone" outside their circle casting out demons in Jesus's name. John and fellow insiders ("we"/"us") "tried to stop him," apparently with limited success. It seems that John, still absorbed in power rankings and political turf battles, appeals for "Master" (Ἐπιστάτα, *Epistata*) Jesus to do something about this maverick exorcist (9:49). This final "Master" address by the disciples in Luke follows the pattern of marking a perceptual deficiency on their part (cf. 5:5; 8:24, 45; 9:33), as Jesus crisply rebukes them: "Do not stop him; for whoever is not against you is for you" (9:50). Far from helping John and company squelch the competition, Jesus encourages them to embrace anyone who supports the liberating cause of God's realm.

"Do not stop [μὴ κωλύετε, *mē kōlyete*]" neatly encapsulates Jesus's inclusive mission policy operative throughout Luke and continuing into Acts. The negated verb connotes "not preventing/ hindering" those who seek to participate in God's kingdom. In the next major unit, Luke's Jesus chides a group of religious lawyers for "preventing" (ἐκωλύσατε, *ekōlysate*) others' access to God (11:52) and his own disciples (again) for trying to "stop little children [τὰ παιδία μὴ κωλύετε, *ta paidia mē kōlyete*]" from coming to him (18:15–17). Sadly, they continue to resist the program of accepting the "littlest" and "least" of humanity as Jesus's kingdom partners. In key moments of boundary-breaking outreach to Gentiles in Acts, an Ethiopian eunuch and a Roman centurion's household are "not prevented/withheld" (κωλύω, *kōlyō*) from being baptized into Christ's family and receiving the gift of the Holy Spirit (Acts 8:36; 10:47–48; 11:17). And indeed, the very last word in Luke's two-volume work declares the persisting proclamation of God's kingdom and Christ's gospel "without hindrance [ἀκωλύτως, *akōlytōs*]" (28:31).

Knowing God the Seeking Savior in the Travels and Parables of Jesus (9:51–19:44)

The first block of Jesus's ministry (4:14–9:50) featured his welcoming, liberating teaching and miracle-working in his native region of Galilee on behalf of the poor, bound, sick, and disabled (cf. 4:18–19; 7:21–22). However, Jesus's open-hearted outreach was not always reciprocated: in fact, this unit began with vehement rejection of Jesus's mission, including attempted murder (4:16–30), and ended with predictions of his violent death and patterns of the disciples' cliquish withdrawal from hungry masses, little children, and freelance liberators operating in Jesus's name (9:10–13, 21–27, 31, 44–50). In between, the course of Jesus's gracious extension of God's saving realm is routinely dotted with conflicts and challenges from various parties, including his own followers. Liberation does not come without confrontation; embrace and inclusivity constantly strain against counterweights of exclusion and inhospitality.[1] These *social* tensions of outreach and pushback intensify in the next unit, commonly dubbed the "Central Section" or "Travel Narrative" (9:51–19:44), enmeshed with other tensions surrounding *spatial*, *temporal*, *social*, and *perceptual* coordinates.

Spatial tension. Jesus's ministry expands southward across the Galilee border into Samaria en route to Jerusalem in Judea (9:51–53). The journey, however, is oddly protracted and meandering. Jesus may "set his face" in "resolute determination"[2] to get to Jerusalem (9:51, 53), but his feet do not seem to comply. He follows no set itinerary; beyond the general movement through Samaria to Jerusalem, the trek defies plotting on a map. From a writer who promised a carefully "ordered" narrative (1:1, 3), this travel unit appears to be a long aberration. But perhaps there is a method to the meandering, a design

1. I again appropriate the language of "embrace" and "exclusion" from Volf's major theological work, *Exclusion*.

2. Craig Evans, "He Set His Face," 100.

to the disarray. In his labyrinthine path of twists and turns, Jesus continues to identify with God's *wandering people* in their extensive experience of being tried and tested, formed and forged, into covenantal partnership with God and one another.[3]

Amid its geographic and formalist-literary vagaries, this winding narrative coheres around a driving theological-missional purpose: Jesus roams about *seeking to save those who have lost their way*. By definition, the "lost" have drifted off the straight-and-narrow path into perilous territory. They do not naturally congregate in city squares, holy sites, and cozy homes but must be sought out and invited in, one by one, from outlying "streets and alleys . . . highways and hedgerows" (14:21–23 NAB). Jesus wanders to find and save the wayward, wherever they are. This major theme crystallizes in a trio of parables at the heart of the Travel Narrative, in which Jesus affirms his mission of "welcoming sinners" (15:2) via the models of a shepherd, a woman, and a father pursuing and reclaiming a lost sheep, coin, and son, respectively (15:3–32). This seeking-saving theme frames the Son of Humankind's vocation at the beginning and toward the end of the unit.

> For the Son of Humankind has not come to destroy the lives of human beings but to save [σῶσαι, *sōsai*] them. (9:56)

> For the Son of Humankind came to seek out [ζητῆσαι, *zētēsai*] and to save [σῶσαι, *sōsai*] the lost. (19:10)[4]

Temporal tension. On the one hand, the languorous length of the journey in both story and discourse time suggests an extended campaign, as long as it takes to find the lost and fill the banquet halls of God's kingdom (cf. 13:29–30; 14:7–24). But on the other hand, this is no lazy, piddling venture. Every step of the long, winding road is taken with dead-serious urgency. Saving the lost is not a minor nudge back on the main path but a critical search-and-rescue mission from dire peril, a matter of life and death: "This son of mine was dead and is alive again; he was lost and is found!" (15:24; cf. 15:32).

3. Cf. commentary on 4:1–13 correlating Jesus's temptations with Israel's wilderness experience. For a sustained reading of the Travel Narrative as Jesus's journey with God's people patterned after Moses's prophetic leadership of Israel, see Moessner, *Lord of the Banquet*.

4. More specifically, this unit features *seeking* (ζητέω) God in prayer (11:9–10), signs (11:16, 29), a resting place (by an expelled demon [11:24]), God's kingdom (12:29, 31), fruit (by God [13:6, 7]), the door of salvation (13:24), a lost coin (15:8), security in life (17:33), and Jesus (by Zacchaeus [19:3]); and *saving* (σῴζω) a few persons (13:23), a Samaritan leper (17:19), anyone ("Who then can be saved?" [18:26]), a blind man (18:42), and Zacchaeus and other lost persons (19:10).

This tension is heightened by Jesus's own impending death. Though recent predictions of his violent demise included no specific timetable or destination, identifying his virulent opponents as "elders, chief priests, and scribes" most readily evokes a Jerusalem headquarters, especially for the priestly hierarchs (ἀρχιερεῖς, *archiereis* [9:22; cf. 19:47]). Thus the course Jesus decisively sets to Jerusalem (9:51)—where he hasn't been since childhood—is in fact a lethal collision course with hostile authorities, as he soon makes explicit: "Yet today, tomorrow, and the next day I must [δεῖ, *dei*] be on my way, because it is impossible for a prophet to be killed outside of Jerusalem" (13:33). So the Travel Narrative plots a kind of death march for Jesus, a martyr's farewell trek.

Jesus now journeys, day after day, under the shadow of the cross, delivering a fervent "last call" to heed God's saving word. But he doesn't rush it. Though committed to the cross-bearing path laid out for him, he drags his heels, as it were, not for his own sake, but to seek out and save as many lost ones as possible. Moreover, he makes the most of the extended journey to offer a final seminar to his disciples, instructing them in the "rules of the road" in God's realm, especially through the medium of *parables*, which proliferate in this unit. I will introduce Jesus's role as traveling storyteller more fully below.

Treating this long travel segment as Jesus's ominous "farewell tour" in which he offers "last calls" and "final seminars" pushes us to appreciate not simply Jesus's personal climactic ordeal, but also the consummative (eschatological) crisis Jesus poses to God's people and, indeed, the entire world, as the authorized agent and co-regent of God's saving domain. Again, temporal tension simmers: God's kingdom is palpably present already, here and now in the person and work of God's Messiah (11:20; 17:20–21) as a welcome-and-warning sign of God's complete restorative reign to come (12:35–48; 17:22–37; 19:11–27). This "already–not yet" balancing act pushes toward a tragic, gut-wrenching tug-of-war that overwhelms Jesus on the cusp of his entry into Jerusalem. "As he came near [ἤγγισεν, *ēngisen*] and saw the city, he wept over it . . . because you did not recognize/know [ἔγνως, *egnōs*] the time of your visitation from God" (19:41, 44). In Christ, God the king and God's kingdom have "come near" (cf. ἐγγίζω, *engizō* in 10:9, 11) as personally and powerfully as anyone could imagine. God makes a house call on Jerusalem, but the leaders and many of the people do not "recognize/know" that God has come to visit. And as a result of missing this divine redemptive appointment, they tragically set themselves up for another kind of visit on the horizon: the "crushing" destructive invasion of enemy forces (19:41–44). These patterns of inhospitality and ignorance merit further consideration in the swirl of social and perceptual tensions.

Social tension. As Jesus's journey to Jerusalem ends with his lamenting the city's failure to welcome God with open arms, so it begins with a Samaritan village's turning Jesus away *because* he was heading to Jerusalem (9:53). He appears to find no more hospitality in Samaria and Judea than he did in Galilee, confirming his virtual homeless existence with "nowhere to lay his head" (9:58). Several parables expose inhospitable figures (priest/Levite [10:25–37], wealthy landowner [12:13–21], Pharisaic leader [14:1–24], rich banqueter [16:19–31]) who turn a blind eye to nurturing those in need. As Jesus seeks to extend the "hospitality of God"[5] to the least and lost, he is criticized and ostracized (15:1–2). The divine-human Host receives shabby treatment as a guest—at least some of the time (9:51–56; 11:38; 13:14).

But at other times Jesus finds residential welcome stations along the road, though from questionable hosts such as the vocal woman Martha (10:38) and the chief tax collector Zacchaeus (19:6) (the same "welcome" verb, ὑποδέχομαι [*hypodechomai*], appears in each reference). Naming these hosts—a rare attribution for any character other than Jesus in this unit[6]—highlights their importance. The profile of the Pharisees also complicates the social dynamics of the Jerusalem trek. Though spearheading much of the pushback against Jesus's outreach to lost "sinners" ("the Pharisees . . . were grumbling . . . 'This fellow welcomes [προσδέχεται, *prosdechetai*] sinners and eats with them'" [15:2]), some Pharisees continue to invite Jesus into their homes for dinner (11:37; 14:1) and even warn him about a Herodian plot on his life (13:31). Of course, the Pharisees' dinner parties with Jesus do not prove to be the most congenial affairs (recall the hubbub around Simon's table in 7:36–50), not only because the hosts watch him like a hawk, but also because Jesus uses these occasions to blast narrow guest-lists, preferential seating arrangements, and woeful hypocrisy regarding professed love of God and neighbor (11:37–54; 14:1–24). Never a dull, docile moment at these meals! Generally, Jesus and the Pharisees are not so much enemies as vigorous debaters in symposia-like forums.

Perceptual tension. Luke's aim to solidify knowledge of God's saving purposes through Christ continues to develop amid shaky responses from Jesus's disciples, whose spiritual pilgrimage follows the bumpy, twisty contours of the journey to Jerusalem. James and John commence the trip with a gross misapprehension of Jesus's seeking-and-saving mission (9:54–56). Not long thereafter, we discover that the apostles do not even know how to pray yet, though one of them finally asks Jesus for instruction in this vital practice, which he provides (11:1–13). Further down the road, they at last perceive their deficiency and plead that Jesus "increase our faith!" (17:5). However, as Jesus again alerts his followers

5. Byrne, *Hospitality*; cf. Koenig, *Hospitality*, 85–123.

6. See also Lazarus—the *only* named character in a parable in another hospitality story (16:20, 23, 25)—though poor Lazarus suffers from another's *in*hospitality in this life.

to his destiny of "much suffering" and violent death (17:25; 18:31–33), they still "understood [συνῆκαν, *synēkan*] nothing about all these things . . . and they did not grasp/know [ἐγίνωσκον, *eginōskon*] what was said" (18:34). But then again, the thorny epistemological problem persists that the full meaning of Jesus's "message *has been hidden* [κεκρυμμένον, *kekrymmenon*—perfect tense] from them"—by God (18:34 AT). Beyond the disciples, other character groups—Samaritans, Pharisees, scribes, crowds—also "do . . . not know [οὐκ οἴδατε, *ouk oidate*] how to interpret the present time" (12:56) of God's visitation because to some degree such discernment is now "hidden [ἐκρύβη, *ekrybē*] from [their] eyes" (19:42).

Yet, however risky and cloudy the path to knowledge may continue to be, Jesus the Son maintains the surest and clearest perception of the Father's way *and* the singular responsibility to communicate this insight to others: "All things have been handed over to me by my Father; and no one knows [γινώσκει, *ginōskei*] who the Son is except the Father, or who the Father is except the Son and anyone to whom the Son chooses to reveal him" (10:22). Fortunately, the Father-Son communion—joined with the Holy Spirit, in whom Jesus rejoices (10:21; cf. 11:13)—ultimately chooses revelation, but again with a critical "hidden" twist: "I thank you, Father, Lord of heaven and earth, because you have *hidden* [ἀπέκρυψας, *apekrypsas*] these things from the wise and the intelligent and have *revealed* [ἀπεκάλυψας, *apekalypsas*] them to infants; yes, Father, for such was your gracious will" (10:21). The rhyming of the Greek verbs suggests the fine line between God's concealing and revealing, disguising and disclosing. We often see yet do not perceive; hear but do not understand (cf. 8:10)—especially we who regard ourselves as "wise and intelligent." God delights in flipping tables on standard wise/foolish, smart/simple guests in God's household. Faithful disciples must appreciate how truly "blessed" they are to see what God graciously makes known through his Son (10:23–24).

In this travel unit, Luke's Jesus conveys his provocative, unconventional knowledge of God's realm predominantly through the vivid medium of *parables*. Although Jesus has previously spoken a few parables (5:34–39; 6:39–49; 8:4–15), he utters many more, several unique to this Gospel, en route to Jerusalem. The parable genre perfectly suits Jesus's pedagogical purpose of disclosing the "gracious will" of God to "infants" longing for spiritual nurture, while disrupting pet dogmas of putative "wise" men (10:21). Though the lexical term and literary form "parable" (παραβολή, *parabolē*, lit. "throw alongside" as a comparative explanation) resist a concise glossary entry, a classic definition by C. H. Dodd aptly captures key elements: "a metaphor or simile drawn from nature or common life, arresting the hearer by its vividness or strangeness, and leaving the mind in sufficient doubt of its precise application to tease it into active thought."[7] Jesus's parables indeed reflect a "natural/common" environment and exert "strange/thought-teasing" influence on hearers. He draws on the mundane, everyday worlds of farming, family life, financial matters, and such (but not metaphysics) to make anything but a mundane point or moral platitude. As a kind of storytelling troubadour, Jesus entertains but also delivers a spark of doubt and jolt of mind toward "active thought" (Dodd) and, we might add, "thoughtful action" (as always in Luke, doing the word, not simply deliberating it).

To gain a sense of how densely Jesus's parables populate Luke's Travel Narrative,[8] I list the following with common descriptions (the parables have no set titles). In 6 and 8, I group together obvious parable clusters.

1. good Samaritan (10:30–35)
2. friend at midnight (11:5–8)
3. rich fool (12:16–21)
4. faithful and unfaithful slaves (12:35–48)
5. barren fig tree (13:6–9)
6. mustard seed and yeast (13:18–21)
7. great dinner (14:15–24)
8. lost sheep, coin, son (15:1–32)
9. dishonest manager (16:1–13)
10. rich man and Lazarus (16:19–31)
11. widow and unjust judge (18:1–8)
12. Pharisee and toll collector (18:9–14)
13. pounds (*minas*) (19:11–27)

Apart from nesting adjacent parables featuring little things with big growth potential (6) and lost and found things (8), more diffuse groupings cohere around common themes of wealth and poverty (3, 9–10), compassion and mercy (1, 8), judgment and justification (3–5, 9–13), prayer (2, 11, 12), women's work (6, 8, 11), household/estate management (4, 9, 13), and hospitality (1– 2, 7, 9–10). Moreover, along this sprawling journey where narrative threads sometimes wear thin, we never completely lose the trail and often detect key co-textual links between the parables and surrounding material. In other words, Luke does not just drop in parables willy-nilly to entertain the weary traveler.

7. Dodd, *Parables*, 16.

8. For those interested in statistics, parabolic material (mostly in the Travel Narrative) represents 52 percent of Luke's unique material ("L")—compared with 35 percent of Jesus's teaching in the Synoptics and 43 percent of Matthew's unique material ("M")—according to Snodgrass, *Stories*, 22; cf. Lischer, *Reading*, 5.

In the commentary, I aim to interpret the parables not as free-floating teaching-tales of the historical Jesus, but as "stories with intent"[9] not only for Jesus, but also for Luke's narrative. So, for example, I will explore the parable of the good Samaritan (10:30–35) within its immediate frame of Jesus's exchange with a legal scholar (10:25–29, 36–37) and the hospitality scene in Martha's home that follows (10:38–42); and the parables of the widow and unjust judge and of the Pharisee and tax collector (18:1–14) in light of Jesus's preceding discourse on the Son of Humankind's present and future mediation of God's reign (17:20–37).

Having previewed various tensions within and other aspects of Luke's Travel Narrative, we consider finally, by way of introduction, the vexed matter of this unit's overarching structure. I've already indicated that Luke is shy on geographic coordinates, but perhaps he follows another organizational model. I briefly discuss two proposals, which have some merit but overshoot their mark in my judgment, before sketching the loose schema I follow.[10]

First, some scholars have delineated an elaborate *Deuteronomic* pattern, casting Luke's Jesus as a prophet-teacher like Moses instructing God's wandering people in the curriculum of Deuteronomy. In this model, Deuteronomy does not simply represent "recommended reading" on the syllabus, but the core textbook Luke follows sequentially in constructing his Travel Narrative.[11] However, while Luke's Jesus has deeply reflected on Deuteronomy since his wilderness test (4:4, 8, 12) and continues throughout his Jerusalem journey to affirm Deuteronomy's covenantal commitment to loving and obeying "God alone" (Luke 10:15–28; 18:18–20/Deut 5:16–20; 6:4–6), the attempt to track Luke's entire central section as a running commentary (midrash) on the fifth Torah book overruns the evidence. Though Deuteronomy certainly represents a key intertext—for both comparison and contrast with Luke's narrative—it does not function as a point-by-point travel guide or sole scriptural resource informing this unit.[12]

The second model—plotting Luke's Travel Narrative on a complex *chiastic*

9. The title of the major work by Snodgrass (*Stories*), which consistently pays careful attention to the Gospel contexts of the parables and to correlations with Jesus's overall teaching; cf. the helpful survey of modern parable study in Gowler, *What Are They Saying?*

10. See Spencer, *Gospel of Luke*, 36–41, 48–49,

11. C. F. Evans, 34–36, 433–35, and "Central Section"; Drury, *Tradition*, 138–64; Goulder, *Evangelists' Calendar*, 95–101; Moessner, *Lord of the Banquet* and "Luke 9:1–50"; James A. Sanders, "Ethic of Election"; Craig Evans, "Luke 16:1–18."

12. Cf. the balanced conclusion of Craig Evans, "Luke 16:1–18," 133: "The [third] evangelist has produced a 'commentary' on Deuteronomy only in the most general sense. . . . Luke wishes his readers to study the materials of the central section in the light of the parallel passages and themes from Deuteronomy. Thus, the central section and Deuteronomy, set side by side, are mutually illuminating."

grid—also merits a qualified assessment.[13] Clear parallels between early and late parts of the journey (e.g., parables illustrating persistent prayer [11:5–8/18:1–8] and answers to "what must I do to inherit eternal life?" [10:25–28/18:18–22]) suggest a broad "ring" compositional arrangement;[14] and Jesus's extended emphasis on hosting the least and seeking the lost in chapters 14–15 packs a powerful thematic punch at the heart of the narrative. But trying to shoehorn every part of this sprawling unit into a chiastic structure and pinpoint *the* focal center pinches the interpretive process too tightly.

I propose a more general *dramatic* plotting of Luke's Travel Narrative in four "acts" or "stages," hinged on the few travel notes Luke does supply and tracking Jesus's slow but sure onward (and upward) "going" (πορεύομαι, *poreuomai*) to Jerusalem.[15]

> *Stage 1:* "When the days drew near for him to be taken up, he set his face to go [πορεύεσθαι, *poreuesthai*] to Jerusalem." (9:51)
>
> *Stage 2:* "Jesus went through [διεπορεύετο, *dieporeueto*] one town and village after another, teaching as he made his way [πορείαν, *poreian*] to Jerusalem. . . . 'Yet today, tomorrow, and the next day I must be on my way [πορεύεσθαι, *poreuesthai*], because it is impossible for a prophet to be killed outside Jerusalem.'" (13:22, 33)
>
> *Stage 3:* "On the way [πορεύεσθαι, *poreuesthai*] to Jerusalem Jesus was going through the region between Samaria and Galilee." (17:11)
>
> *Stage 4:* "Then he took the Twelve aside and said to them, 'See, we are going up to Jerusalem.'" (18:31)

The latter two stages are considerably shorter than the first two, conveying a stronger sense of urgency the closer Jesus gets to his ominous final fate in Jerusalem (note his vivid, final death prediction at the beginning of stage 4 in 18:31–32). However, as mentioned above, an atmosphere of conflict and struggle pervades the entire journey. The headings I assign to the four stages aim to highlight this tension.

> *Stage 1 (9:51–13:21)*: Refusing to Retaliate and Destroy in the Face of Rejection and Prejudice
>
> *Stage 2 (13:22–17:10)*: Longing to Gather and Protect in the Face of Opposition and Obstinacy

13. Talbert, 117–19; Blomberg, "Midrash, Chiasmus"; Bailey, *Poet and Peasant*, 79–85.
14. Cf. Douglas, *Thinking in Circles*.
15. See Spencer, *Gospel of Luke*, 152–54.

Stage 3 (17:11–18:30): Choosing to Restore and Welcome in the Face of Ingratitude and Otherness

Stage 4 (18:31–19:44): Pressing On to Suffer and Save in the Face of Injustice and Ignorance

Stage 1: Refusing to Retaliate and Destroy in the Face of Rejection and Prejudice (9:51–13:21)

For all the urgency ("the days drew near") and earnestness ("set his face") with which Jesus embarks on his journey to Jerusalem (9:51), these motivations are not enough to speed him upward to the Holy City along a smooth highway. From the outset he encounters hostility from some Samaritans who, in turn, draw vengeful "fire" from a hotheaded pair of Jesus's apostles (9:51–56). A bit further down the road, Jesus again addresses the problem of Samaritan-Jewish antipathy in a parable featuring a surprising Samaritan exemplar (10:25–37). Other groups among the crowds generally—or Pharisees and scribes more specifically—also attempt to block Jesus's way, sometimes with sharp invective and devious plotting. One summary of this opposition is typical: "The scribes and the Pharisees began to be very hostile toward [Jesus] and to cross-examine him about many things, lying in wait for him, to catch him in something he might say" (11:53–54).

The opening scene sets the basic tone for Jesus's reaction to rude treatment through this first stage.[16] Registering no rebuke of the Samaritans' inhospitality and repudiating the violent retaliatory scheme of James and John, Jesus leaves the door open for better future relations (cf. 10:33–37; 17:11–19). He comes and goes in peace, compassion, and mercy—but not in some naive, sentimental, rosy-colored, and mushy-minded sense. Though consistently eschewing fiery and bloody reprisals, when his and his ambassadors' benediction of "peace to this house" (10:5) is not properly received and reciprocated, Jesus is not shy about hurling sharp verbal warnings and "woes to hypocrites" (11:42–52; 12:1; 13:15). Though no gang leader or zealot fighter, Jesus remains a bold prophet refusing to promise "'peace, peace,' when there is no peace" (Jer 6:14; cf. Ezek 13:10; 1 Thess 5:3). While seeking to rescue and reconcile the lost, Jesus provokes as much "division" as "peace on earth" and, in its own way, "brings fire to earth" (12:49–51).

16. As in the Galilean unit (4:14–9:50), I give particular attention to the initial scenes in each subunit, since they set the thematic stage for what follows.

Inhospitable Samaritans and Vengeful Disciples (9:51–56)

Though Jesus will come to a lonely end on the cross, abandoned by friends and foes alike, his final journey to Jerusalem is a gregarious affair with his disciples (training expedition), certain Pharisees (table fellowship), and lost outsiders (search-and-rescue operation), among others. In this strategic opening scene, Jesus deals with three key groups at different points of proximity—people of Jerusalem (distant), Samaritans (immediate), and apostles (intimate)—each described in some relation to Jesus's "face":

- "He *set his face* [πρόσωπον ἐστήρισεν, *prosōpon estērisen*] to go to [the people of] Jerusalem" (9:51).
- "He sent [apostolic] messengers *before his face* [πρὸ προσώπου αὐτοῦ, *pro prosōpou autou*]" (9:52 AT).
- "[The Samaritans] did not receive him, because *his face* [πρόσωπον αὐτοῦ, *prosōpon autou*] was set toward Jerusalem" (9:53).

Setting His Face against the Hardened Jerusalemites (9:51, 53)

Luke modifies Jesus's "going" to Jerusalem with the striking idiom of "setting his face." Generally, this description resonates with both ancient physiognomic and modern biopsychological focus on facial features as markers of character and emotion. Cicero, for example, argued that "everything rests with the face, and the face in turn is under the power of the eyes . . . and the eyes are the index of the emotions" (*De. or.* 3.221–22). Cicero applied this logic in a polemic against a scheming Roman consul named Piso: "It was your eyes, eyebrows, forehead, in a word, your whole countenance, which is a kind of silent speech of the mind that pushed your fellow-men into delusion" (*Pis.* 1).[17] Jesus makes a similar observation later in the first travel segment: "Your eye is the lamp of your body. If your eye is healthy, your whole body is full of light; but if it is not healthy, your body is full of darkness" (11:34).

Later attempts to render more "scientific" physiognomic judgments involved measuring facial angles, proportions, and other structural features (e.g., distance between the eyes) to hypothesize a mathematical scale of beauty (and ugliness) correlating aesthetics and ethics, good (and bad) looks with good (and bad) characters: a moral twist on "what you see is

17. Citations of Cicero from Parsons, *Body*, 27; cf. throughout for a stimulating study of various Lukan characters in light of ancient physiognomic handbooks.

what you get."[18] More firmly grounded in empirical research than pseudoscience, Darwin concentrated on observing links between various facial *expressions* (not static features) and *emotional* (not moral) states in hundreds of cross-cultural and cross-species cases among humans and nonhuman animals.[19] Darwin's meticulous analysis resulted in a set of near-universal coordinates of expression and emotion, including facial images connected with both *resolve* (determination) and *rage*.[20] Concerning the former, he wrote: "The firm closure of the mouth tends to give an expression of determination or decision to the countenance. No determined man probably had an habitually gaping mouth. Hence also a small and weak lower jaw, which seems to indicate that the mouth is not habitually and firmly closed, is commonly thought to be characteristic of feebleness of character . . . the mouth would almost certainly be closed as soon as any determined resolution was taken." And similarly associated with rage: "The mouth is generally closed with firmness, showing fixed determination, and the teeth are clenched or ground together."[21]

Unfortunately, Luke does not give us a portrait of Jesus's face beyond its being "set." However, such language readily intimates a basic *set*tledness, fixity, resoluteness, or determination of purpose, which may lead us to imagine Jesus's pursed lips, clenched teeth, and jutted jaw. If we continue down the Darwinian trail, we might also wonder whether Jesus's face-revealing resolve also entails a measure of frustration, hardness, anger, and even rage. Our only previous clue to Jesus's countenance has been his extraordinary face-lift during the transfiguration event (9:29). Though including somber discussion about Jesus's upcoming "departure," the overall scene prefigures his "taking up" in glory (see above). No anger or rage in sight, it seems, only the warm glow of divine presence like that reflected in Moses's shining face upon descending Mount Sinai (Exod 34:29–35) or Stephen's "face of an angel" displayed before his synagogue interrogators (Acts 6:15). But Jesus's mountaintop metamorphosis was a unique preview of coming exaltation, glaringly contrasted with the suffering, cross-bearing mission he continued to undertake "down from the mountain," accompanied by frustration with this "faithless and perverse generation" (Luke 9:37, 41). As for Moses and Stephen: the glowing face of the former was more a

18. Cf. Etcoff, *Survival of the Prettiest*, 130–66.

19. Darwin, *Expression*, the first major work to employ the new technology of photography, combined with Darwin's acute observational skills.

20. Darwin's work on facial expressions and emotions has been refined and expanded by Paul Ekman, *Emotions Revealed*; cf. Ekman, *Emotion* and *Darwin*; Ekman and Rosenberg, *What the Face Reveals*.

21. Darwin, *Expression*, 231, 236.

source of fear than of comfort for the ancient Israelites (Exod 34:30), revealing his intimate fellowship with God, who had recently "burn[t] hot" against the "stiff-necked" people for their idolatrous worship (32:9–10). And the angelic face (mouth) of the latter soon spews a torrent of invective against "you stiff-necked people," in turn provoking his hearers' "enraged" teeth-grinding and stone-throwing (Acts 7:51–58). Faces can change expressions in an instant.

However Darwin might associate a "set face" with both resolve and rage, does Luke provide any hint of the steelier, more vehement side of Jesus's approach to Jerusalem? The particular verb for "set" (στηρίζω, *stērizō*) describing Jesus's countenance precisely echoes that of biblical prophets, especially Jeremiah and Ezekiel, called to "set their faces" in *judgment against unfaithful Jerusalem* during the era of Babylonian conquest. In Ezekiel, "Son of man, set your face upon/against" (NETS) functions as a virtual refrain for the prophet's denunciatory vocation to Israel/Jerusalem and surrounding nations (Ezek 6:2; 13:17; 14:8; 22:2, 7; 25:2; 28:21 [Tyre]; 29:2 [Egypt]; 38:2 [Gog]).[22] Note the following texts, which stress the prophets' face-setting against *Jerusalem*, threatening a judgment of *fire* delivered not with glee, but amid a cascade of *grief* for the people's woefully deficient *recognition* of the Lord.

> For I have set my face [ἐστήρικα τὸ πρόσωπόν μου, *estērika to prosōpon mou*] against this city [Jerusalem] for evil and not good. It shall be given over into the hands of the king of Babylon, and he shall burn it with fire. (Jer 21:10 NETS)

> This is what the Lord says: Like the wood of the vine among the trees of the forest, that which I have given to the fire for consumption, so I have given the inhabitants of Ierousalem. And I will give my face against them; they shall go out from the fire, and fire shall devour them, and they shall recognize [ἐπιγνώσονται, *epignōsontai*] that I am the Lord when I set my face [στηρίσαι με τὸ πρόσωπόν μου, *stērisai me to prosōpon mou*] against them. (Ezek 15:6–7 NETS)

> Therefore, prophesy, son of man, set your face [στήρισον τὸ πρόσωπόν σου, *stērison to prosōpon sou*] toward Ierousalem, and gaze upon their holy things, and you shall prophesy against the land of Israel, and you shall say to the land of Israel: Behold, I am against you and will draw my hand-knife out of its sheath and will utterly destroy the unjust and the lawless from

22. I am indebted to an important essay by Craig Evans, "He Set His Face" ("virtual refrain" appears on p. 100).

you. . . . And you, son of man, sigh . . . and in grief you shall groan before their eyes. (Ezek 21:2–6 NETS)

In Luke's present scene (9:51–56), the prospects of fiery judgment are directed against a Samaritan village, not Jerusalem, and are deterred by Jesus. But Jesus knows that Jerusalem's terrible destruction looms on the horizon, as we have already noted, because the religious leaders (especially) and the people will not fully "recognize" and receive God's gracious "visitation" in Christ. And in the passionate mold of Jeremiah and Ezekiel, Jesus will weep, grieve, and groan over the city's devastating fate (19:41–45).

In sum, prophetic intertexts, together with the framing contexts of Luke's Travel Narrative, establish a critical-judgmental, tragic-emotional tone suffusing the entire journey. If Jesus's face is set hard with adamantine indignation against a stubborn people who ultimately reject and kill him (cf. Isa 50:4–7), coursing beneath are rivers of anguished tears and waves of crushing grief poised to break through his stony stare and to make his pursed lips quiver.

Setting the Stage for Loving Enemy Samaritans (9:52–56)

Though Jesus sets his face against Jerusalem, not Samaria, the Samaritan village where Jesus seeks lodging sets their face against him "because his face was heading [πορευόμενον, *poreuomenon*] to Jerusalem" (9:53 AT). Simply put, the Samaritan people, with deep ancestral roots in north-central Israel (Samaria), hated the Jews in Jesus's time, anchored religiously and culturally in Jerusalem and the surrounding region of southern Israel (Judea). And the antipathy was mutual: Jews and Samaritans effectively regarded each other as enemies, with tensions exacerbated by their distinctive appropriations of Israel's heritage and their territorial proximity, forcing them to rub raw shoulders with one another. More specifically, various historical, social, and theological pressure points crystallized around the prime locus of Jewish-Samaritan conflict: the most holy place, the sacred mountain, where God meets God's people: the Samaritans looked to Mount Gerizim near Shechem; the Jews looked to Mount Zion in Jerusalem (see John 4:20; Josephus, *Ant.* 12.6–10; 13.74–79).[23] Temples were erected at both sites, though in Jesus's day only the Jerusalem temple was operative, since a century earlier John Hyrcanus, a Jewish Hasmonean ruler, had demolished the Gerizim sanctuary (*Ant.* 13.254–58). This action further fueled

23. See Pummer, *Samaritans*, iv–118; Purvis, "Samaritans and Judaism"; Spencer, *Portrait*, 73–75.

Samaritan animosity toward Jews, expressed in periodic violent attacks against Jewish travelers through their region en route to Jerusalem and the odd raid on the Jerusalem temple.[24] It is not surprising, then, that a Samaritan village refuses hospitality to the Jewish Jesus and company heading to Jerusalem. If these Samaritans have any inkling that Jesus aims to render *prophetic judgment* against Jerusalem, they perceive (rightly!) that he challenges his people empathetically from within, as one of them. The itinerant Jesus, for all his prophetic edge, remains a faithful Jerusalem-worshiping Jew, and that is enough to make him unwelcome in Samaritan territory.

It is surprising, however, that Jesus seeks to stay in a Samaritan village in the first place at potential risk to himself and his fellow travelers. He may come in peace, but he can't guarantee that the Samaritans will reciprocate: letting him in town could be a set-up for maltreatment. As it happens, the Samaritan villagers do not "receive" or "welcome" (δέχομαι, *dechomai*) him at all (Luke 9:53). But in turn, Jesus continues to defy convention and does not retaliate in any way, verbal or gestural (no "shaking the dust" in protest), but simply moves on "to another village" (in Samaria?), though Luke says nothing about the reception there (9:56). In any event, Jesus first seeks connection with a hostile neighboring people, and after they turn him away, he leaves the door open for conciliation down the line. Jesus thus practices his radical teaching: "Love your enemies . . . expecting nothing in return" (6:35).

Setting Straight a Pair of Misguided Apostles (9:54–56)

A brother pair of Jesus's disciples, however, is not so graciously inclined. James and John may have been among the apostolic advance team Jesus "sent [ἀπέστειλεν, *apesteilen*]" to arrange accommodations in the Samaritan village (9:52); if so, they may have been direct targets of the Samaritans' snub. In any case, they take the village's rejection very personally and prejudicially, in the full spirit of hostile Samaritan-Jewish relations proposing the rash reprisal of calling down heavenly fire on the Samaritans' inhospitable heads (9:54). So much for loving one's enemies!

Nevertheless, though out of step with Jesus's way at this juncture, James and John should not simply be dismissed as a couple of hotheaded thugs. Recall that they were among the privileged trio to witness Jesus's glorious transfigured face on the mountain (9:28–29), and they may well sense the prophetic-judgmental thrust of Jesus's current "set face." Jesus seems poised for power-

24. See Josephus, *Ant.* 15.118–36; 18.29–30; and *J.W.* 2.232–45; Spencer, *Portrait*, 56.

ful, decisive action in the pyrotechnic mold of biblical prophets, not only the fire-threatening Jeremiah and Ezekiel cited above, but more directly with the fire-summoning Elijah targeting *Samaritan* (northern kingdom) resisters of God's purpose on two occasions, the latter just before Elijah was "taken up" to heaven (1 Kgs 18:36–40; 2 Kgs 1:9–16; cf. 2:1).[25] Moreover, John the Baptist, acting in "the spirit and power of Elijah . . . to make ready a people prepared for the Lord," candidly forecast Jesus Messiah's baptismal mission of "Holy Spirit and fire," culminating in apocalyptic incineration of ungodly "chaff . . . with unquenchable fire" (Luke 1:17; 3:16–17). The script seems all set for fireworks, and James and John are ready to light the fuse. But they are *not* ready for Jesus's going off script and aborting the bombing mission.

In closely tracking the disciples' spiritual pilgrimage with Luke's Jesus, we have frequently noted the steep learning curve they negotiate with less than keen perception. But now, even as the attentive James and John pick up on important clues, they still find themselves the object of Jesus's rebuke. What's a poor disciple to do? As the divine voice exhorted them on the mountain, "Listen to Jesus": listen closely to everything he says and implies in vocal and body language, including subtle tensions as well as clear-cut orders. It is not easy to know Jesus intimately.

According to the best textual evidence, we do not know what Jesus says to James and John beyond a basic rebuff. Various ancient versions and church fathers fill in the gap with Jesus's commentary: "You do not know what spirit you are of, for the Son of Humankind has not come to destroy the lives of human beings but to save them" (9:56) If not original, this gloss puts appropriate words in Jesus's mouth for the present situation, emphasizing his primary *saving* rather than *destroying* purpose throughout this journey, echoing a similar purpose in 19:10 ("For the Son of Humankind came to seek out and to save the lost") and placing Jesus's hard-set approach of judgment in proper context. Jesus knows full well that destruction will come for many of God's people, that "only a few [might] be saved" (13:23) if they continue along their wayward course. But this will break Jesus's heart; he takes no joy in pronouncing or executing judgment. His hope is that his people will "repent," change their hearts and minds, and not "perish" (13:3, 5). He aims to hold back the fire as long as possible. The balance between judgment and mercy remains a delicate one, and James and John may be forgiven for tilting the wrong way concerning the Samaritans. If one is to err, however, it aligns better with Jesus's overarching mission to err on the side of mercy, compassion, and salvation than of judgment, retaliation, and destruction.

25. Of course, since Elijah appeared with Jesus (and Moses) on the mountain of transfiguration, he would naturally weigh heavy on the minds of James and John.

Jesus's Priorities and the Seventy(-Two)'s Preparations (9:57–10:24)

Undeterred by either inhospitable Samaritan villagers or belligerent brother-apostles, Jesus keeps "going along the road/way [ὁδῷ, *hodō*]" toward Jerusalem (9:57); and he continues to send a team "ahead of him" (again, "before his face") into "every town and place where he himself intended to go" (10:1). Given that Samaria lies between Galilee and Judea, it seems likely that Jesus keeps trying to enter other Samaritan villages. But as already noted, Luke provides no detailed roadmap and rarely identifies specific places. Oddly, in the present segment, Jesus cites Chorazin (Khirbet Karazah), Bethsaida, and Capernaum for their inhospitality (10:13–15). These are not, however, Samaritan sites, but rather towns along the northern shore of Lake Gennesaret, in or near Galilee, two of which Jesus visited earlier (Capernaum [4:23, 31; 7:1] and Bethsaida [9:10]). Mentioning these places now suggests a dramatic detour, whereby Jesus reverses course in a northeasterly trek around the upper tip of Lake Gennesaret, sixty miles or so out of his way, en route to trans-Jordanian territory. Avoiding further Samaritan tension is a reasonable move, but why not head due east across the Jordan River rather than go so far afield? Such "map-quests" should not preoccupy us unduly, however, since Luke is more concerned with broad geographic symbolism than with GPS precision.

Suddenly, Jesus's travel party expands considerably. Up to this point, Luke has dropped hints of a larger company of disciples beyond the Twelve, including women followers (8:1–3). Numbering the group at *seventy(-two)* now solidifies the image of a more substantial movement beyond a small band of associates (10:1, 17). We will consider the significance of this number below; for the moment, we simply register the escalation factor: Jesus keeps gathering followers and gaining steam on his way to Jerusalem, even in the midst of obstacles and opposition. The seventy(-two) ambassadors experience a mixed reception, confirming the "divided people" fallout from Jesus's mission (cf. 2:34). For Jesus's part, despite his strong restorative and reconciliatory heartbeat, he doesn't go out of his way to ease people's access to God's realm; the path to salvation has room for all to travel, but the entry point is narrow and the cost is high (cf. 13:22–24; 14:25–33; 18:22–30). In strategic teaching snippets flanking the central discussion of the Seventy(-Two)'s campaign, Jesus lays on the line what it takes to *follow* him (9:57–62) and draws a joyous, yet challenging, picture of who comes to *know* God's saving will and how they come to know it (10:21–24). As the number of disciples increase, the standards of discipleship get sharper and steeper. The passage unfolds as follows:

A Jesus, Son of Humankind: "Nowhere to Lay His Head" (9:57–62)
B The Seventy(-Two) Received in Peace (10:1–9)
C The Seventy(-Two) Rejected in Woe (10:10–16)
B′ The Seventy(-Two) Returning in Joy (10:17–20)
A′ Jesus, Son of the Creator-Father: "No One Knows" without Him (10:21–24)

Jesus, Son of Humankind: "Nowhere to Lay His Head" (9:57–62)

Whereas some Samaritan villagers wanted nothing to do with Jesus, other people of nondescript identity ("someone," "another") seek out Jesus's company and long to "follow" him, though with preconditions in a couple of cases. However, Jesus does not negotiate with would-be disciples. With unstinting authority, even audacity, Jesus claims absolute priority over his followers' lives: they must put him and his way "first" (πρῶτον, *prōton* [9:59, 61]), above everything and everyone, including otherwise good things and people. He utters no fiery curse against those with different priorities, but he cuts them no slack either. He quickly dispatches three prospective disciples.

Case #1 begins very promisingly: along the road, someone approaches Jesus and exclaims, "I will follow you wherever [ὅπου ἐάν, *hopou ean*] you go" (9:57). Here no apparent conditions qualify the commitment; this person seems willing to go "wherever" Jesus goes. But rather than immediately welcoming this enthusiastic seeker with open arms, Jesus clarifies that "wherever" doesn't mean a smorgasbord of locales and lodging-places as much as "nowhere" (οὐκ . . . ποῦ, *ouk . . . pou*) at all "to lay his head" (9:58). His "face" is so set on his Jerusalem destination that his "head" (κεφαλή, *kephalē*) will find no rest until he gets there (and soon his crucified head rests on a burial slab). In intimate solidarity with all humanity, the itinerant Son of Humankind embraces the drifters, the disrupted, and the displaced. As he was born in the double-dislocated, makeshift Bethlehem manger (see above on 2:1–20), so he lives and moves as a stranger and nomad, stopping here and there in hospitable oases, but making no permanent settlement until God's homeland is fully established on earth.[26] In the meantime, he leads his *exiled people* on a rough wilderness road toward that restored divine estate. By placing himself in the no-place of the suffering

26. Cf. Bertschmann, "Hosting," 34: "Despite Jesus' homeless and itinerant status, the gospels, including Luke, focus on meal scenes, not on overnight lodging extended to Jesus: Luke seems to be almost interested in *dissociating* Jesus from staying [long] in other people's homes" (emphasis original). This displaced, dissociated status is set early on from Jesus's birth in a provisional locale to counter the "no place" in the lodging house (2:7).

homeless, the Son of Humankind places himself lower than animals, such as den-dwelling foxes and nest-resting birds (9:58). Since the beginning in Eden, God has desired a fruitful home for all creation. It is thus profoundly unnatural and ungodly, a travesty and tragedy of the highest order, when some people dwell in palaces (cf. 7:25) built on the backs of the dispossessed. Jesus aims to redeem rootless exiles from below, from "nowhere."

Luke does not report whether the prospective follower joins or spurns Jesus's nomadic movement. But the choice before him is clear, though not comfortable. In any event, Jesus continues to recruit new followers along his wandering way.

In *case #2* Jesus issues the same simple, stark call to "another" individual as he did to Levi the tax collector: "Follow me" (9:58)—no prescribed itinerary or agenda beyond that of personal adherence to Jesus and his spontaneous leadership. Discipleship and faith (trust) come together in breathtaking submission to Jesus's sovereign authority. Caesar claimed no less, and Jesus cedes no scintilla of authority to him: only one who claims to be truly Lord, King, and Savior says "Follow me" *simpliciter* and brooks no excuses from would-be followers. As it happens, the current disciple-prospect, while acknowledging Jesus's status as Lord, asks for a temporary deferment on solid compassionate grounds: "first [πρῶτον, *prōton*] let me go and bury my father" (9:59). Who could argue with such a request, especially in a Jewish culture that deeply valued lifelong parental respect, culminating in honorable burial (Gen 50:1–14; Exod 20:12; Deut 5:16; Tob 1:16–18; 2:3–8; 4:1–4; 6:14)?

But in fact Jesus does veto this proposal with a ridiculous counterplan—"Let the dead bury their own dead" (as if they could!)—and a reinforced prophetic call: "As for you, go and proclaim the kingdom of God" (9:60). Jesus is not formulating a broad-based policy of public health or family values. For rhetorical effect, he exploits the absurd notion of dead bodies tending to themselves. The best thing anyone can do for their loved ones, dead or alive, is to advance the in-breaking reign of God, to the end of restoring all God's people, of refleshing and inspiriting the dry bones of "the whole house of Israel" (see Ezek 37:1–14).[27] As Luke's Jesus will affirm in his final week: "[God] is God not of the dead, but of the living; for to [God] all of them are alive" (Luke 20:38).

27. It is possible that the man is asking for permission to *re*bury his father, according to the custom of replacing desiccated bones, after the flesh has decayed, in boxes (ossuaries) or niches (*loculi*) with the remains of other family members. In this way, deceased loved ones are "gathered" with their ancestors. In any case, Jesus advocates leaving dead bones (and bodies) as they are and getting on with the urgent business of establishing God's restorative ("resurrection") domain; cf. discussion in McCane, *Roll Back*, 73–77, and "Let the Dead"; Spencer, "Follow Me," 150–52.

Case #3 features another prospective follower with a family-related proviso: "I will follow you, Lord; but let me first [πρῶτον, *prōton*] say farewell to those at my home" (9:61). Again, this request seems reasonable, all the more since a disciple of the cross-bearing Christ might never see his family again. But Jesus's face is set in full forward position, "plowing" ahead to prepare the ground for the seeding and flourishing of God's domain. No one who "looks back"—even temporarily for a good cause—no one not totally committed to laboring with Lord Jesus in God's field needs apply (9:62; cf. 10:2). There is a "fitness" requirement for following and working with Jesus: one must know one's "place" (the "fit" term [εὔθετος, *euthetos*] literally means "well-placed/put" [cf. 14:35]) and be able to stay the course in God's realm, walking in Jesus's footsteps. At this juncture Jesus fits, rather than breaks, Elijah's mold, when he curtly brushed off Elisha's request to kiss his father good-bye before following Elijah's prophetic path: "Then [Elijah] said [to Elisha]: 'Go back, for I am done with you'" (1 Kgs 19:20 NETS). But Elisha is not done with Elijah. The summoned prophet-disciple abruptly shifts plans from kissing his father to killing his oxen (with which he had been *plowing* when Elijah passed by), cooking them for his people with the kindling from the animals' wooden yokes, and leaving it all (burnt and consumed) to follow Elijah (19:21). Henceforth, Elisha would only plow, as it were, behind Elijah in God's field. A similar challenge faces Jesus's would-be disciple, but in this case, we're not told how he responds. Readers are left to fill in the gap not only in the story but also in their own discipleship experience.

The Seventy(-Two)'s Mission (10:1–20)

Only Luke reports this extra mission of Jesus's disciples, both mirroring and expanding that of the twelve apostles (9:1–6, 10; cf. Matt 10:1–15; Mark 6:7–13). This larger campaign, launched but not personally led by Jesus, foreshadows the early church's outreach in Acts. Sending "in pairs" (Luke 10:1) matches the partnering arrangement of Peter/John, Paul/Barnabas, Paul/Silas, Barnabas/John Mark, Priscilla/Aquila in Acts. Given women's involvement in Jesus's movement (8:1–3), it is possible that the present mission includes some male-female teams or even "sister" pairs (cf. 10:38–42; Rom 16:7, 12).[28] Just as Jesus's choice of the Twelve carries symbolic significance associated with restoring Israel's tribes, we

28. D'Angelo ("Reconstructing 'Real' Women") speculates that the traditions concerning Martha and Mary in Luke 10:38–42 and John 11:1–12:8 reflect "the memory of two famous women who formed a missionary partnership, like the pairs in Matt 10:1–4" (108; cf. 107–9).

assume some import behind a larger number of emissaries. A textual question arises, however, concerning whether Jesus commissions *seventy* or *seventy-two* disciples (thirty-five or thirty-six pairs). Strong manuscript evidence for and suggestive biblical allusions to *both* numbers complicate a hard-and-fast choice. The intertextual links are especially informative.

The postdiluvian catalog of all peoples on earth in Gen 10 comes to *seventy* in the Hebrew Bible (MT) and *seventy-two* in the Greek version (LXX). Likewise, early legends attributed the production of the Greek translation to *seventy-two* bilingual scholars, six representatives from each of Israel's twelve tribes, though some variants adjusted the number to *seventy*—hence, the Roman numeric designation LXX.[29] Rendering the Bible into the lingua franca of the Greco-Roman world made Israel's Scriptures accessible to a wider population, Jew and Gentile. So both the Genesis Table of Nations and the LXX attest to God's saving concern for all people. By expanding from twelve to seventy(-two) messengers, Luke's Jesus, though rooted in Jewish soil, prepares the way for his followers' evangelistic dispersion into the wider Hellenistic milieu reported in Acts.

But Luke's Jesus is not only concerned with the *catch and enlistment* of many disciples (cf. Luke 5:6–11), but also with their *care and discipline*. For the number seventy(-two) also recalls the staff of Spirit-imbued elders appointed to assist Moses in managing the burden of plaintive Israelites in the wilderness. In one tradition, at the advice of father-in-law Jethro, Moses selects an unspecified number of "able men" to settle petty disputes, leaving him free to handle major cases (Exod 18:13–27). Along with providing Moses much-needed relief, this arrangement permits "all these people [to] go to their home in peace" (18:23). In another model, the Lord commands Moses to gather *seventy* elders to help him handle the congregation's boiling displeasure over their meatless, manna-only desert diet (Num 11). In this scenario, however, Moses's assistants function not as pastoral-counselor judges promoting peace but as *prophetic-correctional judges* mediating the Spirit of the Lord's intense *anger*, which ultimately erupts in a "very great plague" against the ungrateful Israelites at a site morbidly memorialized as Kibroth-hattaavah, "Graves-of-craving" (Num 11:33–34). In addition to the official seventy elders stationed around the main community court (tent), *two* Spirit-inspired mavericks, Eldad and Medad, begin prophesying "in the camp." Far from condemning these independent judges, Moses commends them as exemplars: "Would that all the LORD's people were prophets, and that the LORD would put his spirit on them!" (11:26–29). In the meantime, *seventy-two* (total) messengers will do.

29. See Let. Aris. 32–51; Josephus, *Ant.* 12.39–57, 86; Justin Martyr, *Dial.* 68–71; Warren Carter, *Seven Events*, 30.

This mix of peaceful and penal judgment also characterizes the mission of Jesus's seventy(two) delegates. On the one hand, they bestow peace on a selected household, seeking in return a kindred "child of peace [υἱὸς εἰρήνης, *huios eirēnēs*]" who "shares the peace" in tangible acts of feeding and lodging (10:5–7 AT).[30] But this is a risky operation, not only because of the disciples' total dependence on others' hospitality (Jesus again dispatches them with no money or provisions [10:4; cf. 9:3]), but also because of itinerant preachers' sketchy reputations for bilking generous hosts and overstaying their welcome just before skipping town (Did. 11–13). Jesus expressly orders his emissaries not to hop from house to house, not to demand special treatment ("eating and drinking whatever they provide"), and by implication, to be "worthy" (ἄξιος, *axios*) of the hospitality they merit for valuable service they render (Luke 10:7–8). Such ministers bring substantive peace beyond the initial peace greeting—which can easily be hollow (cf. Jas 2:14–16)—imparting the holistic well-being (*shalom*) of God's realm, including curing the sick and freeing those tormented by Satan (Luke 10:9, 17–18). They serve as peaceful, seemingly weak *lambs*, but in that pacific role, they declaw *wolves*, defang *snakes*, and de-tail *scorpions* (10:3, 19). Ironically, the way of lamblike peace is the way of liberating power.[31]

But the mission has a shadow side: that of final reckoning ("at *the* judgment" [ἐν τῇ κρίσει, *en tē krisei*; 10:14]) and retribution for unrequited peace and unrepentant status quo (10:10–16). The palpable nearness of God's peaceable kingdom (10:11) demonstrated by Christ and his messengers demands decision. If not already a "child of peace," one must urgently undergo a change of heart and mind in that direction. To harden one's heart and choose against God's peace in the face of such powerful signs of God's saving-peacemaking realm is to secure one's place in Hades (10:15), the realm of death and devastation. Sodom, Tyre, and Sidon—notorious non-Israelite centers of pride, greed, and violence that catalyzed their own downfall (see Gen 19:12–28; Isa 23; Ezek 16:48–50; 26–28)—should have been so lucky to see what contemporary Chorazin, Bethsaida, and Capernaum have witnessed of God's beneficent work in Christ (Luke 10:12–15). As it happens, current Tyre and Sidon indeed have proven more receptive (6:17–19) than some Galilean places, including Jesus's hometown (4:16–30). Moreover, Bethsaida and Capernaum have not been as

30. The literal reading "son/child of peace" (vs. NRSV's "anyone who shares in peace") conveys a core peacemaking identity and commitment, rather than random gestures of hospitality. See Swartley, *Covenant of Peace*, 125–26n6; Klassen, "Child of Peace."

31. Cf. the apt comment on Jesus's statement in 10:18 by Swartley, *Covenant of Peace*, 125–26: "It is clear that this kingdom peace gospel is one of ultimate power. It carries with it the power to overthrow the forces of evil. . . . The peace gospel is God's way in Jesus and his followers to subdue evil."

hostile to Jesus's ministry as the present text suggests: in fact Capernaum has been cast as a foil to Nazareth's stubbornness (4:23, 31–42; 7:1–10), and Bethsaida was where Jesus debriefed the Twelve (after their mission) and then bestowed teaching, healing, and feeding blessings of God's kingdom upon the five thousand (9:10–17).

Luke's larger narrative thus deconstructs rigid binary oppositions of good places/bad places, good people/bad people; but in so doing it ratchets up both challenge and opportunity. Following God's way of peace demands persisting commitment: one peaceful response here or there does not a "child of peace" make. Conversely, long-standing patterns of hostility can be broken and fresh paths of peace pursued. It is too late for Satan and his minions. Jesus certifies their precipitous plummet from heavenly heights and unrelenting death-dealing schemes, which he continues to thwart (10:18–19). But for Capernaum and Tyre, Jew and Gentile, whatever their histories, good or bad, opportunity knocks with the thunderous force of God's powerful peace in these last days. Instead of the NRSV's question and negative answer, "Will you be exalted to heaven? No, you will be brought down to Hades," Jesus's stern warning to Capernaum may be taken as a double question: "You won't be exalted to heaven, will you? You won't be brought down to Hades, will you?" (10:15).[32] To be sure, persisting arrogant self-exaltation and violent exploitation of God's people lead to downfall into deathly shades, as with Satan and his ancient royal Babylonian avatar (Isa 14:12–15; see 14:3–22). But Jesus's present audiences do not have to perpetuate this vicious cycle, and Jesus sincerely hopes that they won't: "You *won't* keep ignoring these powerful signs of God's peaceful reign and clarion calls for repentance, will you?"

As Jesus tempers the seventy-(two) disciples' proffer of peace with a charge that they protest any rejection of such ministry (wiping the town's dust from their feet [10:10–11; cf. 9:5]), he also qualifies their response of joy over conquering demonic spirits. While such achievement is well and good—and constitutes a marked advance over some disciples' recent failure to help a demon-possessed boy (9:39–42)—it is not what Jesus deems most worthy of joy: "Nevertheless, do not rejoice at this, that the spirits submit to you, but rejoice that *your names are written in heaven*" (10:20). While Luke's story has repeatedly featured Jesus's domination over evil spirits, it has mentioned nothing about a heavenly record book. Still, the "heaven" reference resonates in the

32. I take the opening negative μή (*mē*) as applying to both of the ensuing parallel questions with aorist subjunctive verbs: ἕως οὐρανοῦ ὑψωθήσῃ/ἕως τοῦ ᾅδου καταβήσῃ (*heōs ouranou hypsōthēsē/heōs tou hadou katabēsē*). Such interrogative constructions typically imply a negative response: "You wouldn't do such and such, would you? Of course you wouldn't!"

present context: whereas those who spurn God's rule in Christ presumptuously vault themselves to heavenly status (10:15) and risk lightning-like discharge from God's heavenly realm (10:18), Christ's faithful messengers enjoy secure enrollment in God's heavenly register, now and in the age to come (cf. 18:28–30).

But why is this knowledge *better than*, more joyous than, the experience of subduing demons and liberating those they oppress? Perhaps the messengers are too enamored with the power rush they experienced at driving out demons—"in Jesus's name," of course—but with that name more ancillary than primary. Note the Greek word order of their report: "Lord, even the demons are subject *to us* [ἡμῖν, *hēmin*] in the name of you [σου, *sou*]" (10:17 AT). While Jesus frames their comment ("Lord"/"you"), the central action focuses *on them* ("us"), thus marking another imbalance in their spiritual development: without their vital connection to God's peaceful-powerful realm in Christ, they would have no ability to bring God's shalom to anyone. Focusing on the catchword "name," if the names of the seventy-(two) were not inscribed in God's heavenly scroll—authenticating their identities as God's own—then they would have no authority to use the name of God's Son, as some itinerant Jewish exorcists dallying with Jesus's name find out in Acts, to their deep embarrassment (Acts 19:13–17). Close relationship with God and Jesus constitutes a sine qua non of genuine peacemaking ministry. Before anyone can subdue evil forces, he or she must be *signed into* God's registry and *subject to* God's reign. A key prophetic intertext reinforces this link between inscription in God's book and subjection to God's will: "And the Lord took note and listened and wrote a *book of remembrance* before him for those who fear the Lord and *reverence his name*. And they shall be mine, says the Lord Almighty, in the day when I make them my acquisition, and I will choose them as a person chooses his son [υἱόν, *huion*] who is *subject to him*. And you shall turn and discern between the just and between the lawless and between the one who is *subject to God* and the one who is *not subject*" (Mal 3:16–18 NETS). A true "son [υἱός, *huios*] of peace" (Luke 10:6), able to "turn" others toward peace and justice, must first be a child-subject of the Father-Lord of heaven and earth, who wills peace and justice for all creation—as Jesus proceeds to explain in personal and doxological terms.

Jesus, Son of the Creator-Father: "No One Knows" without Him (10:21–24)

Jesus's correction of the messengers' joy by no means makes him a killjoy; quite the contrary, he simply aims to bring their joy into proper focus. Moreover, he chimes in with his own rejoicing "at that same hour." This text marks the only report of Jesus's personal joy in Luke,[33] making it a key indicator of Jesus's emotional life, all the more so because he rejoices here "in the Holy Spirit" while praying to his "Father, Lord of heaven and earth" (10:21). We are afforded a special glimpse into divine passion—into what excites the Triune God. If, as noted above (on 9:28–43a), emotions generally convey a person's deep-down interests, such is especially true of joy. We rejoice over momentous events and insights of keenest import to us.

So what sparks Jesus's joy? In short, Jesus rejoices in revelatory "things": in who knows God and what God knows; in who is in the know about vital matters of God's purpose for the world.[34] "I thank you, Father, Lord of heaven and earth, because you have hidden *these things* [ταῦτα, *tauta*] from the wise and the intelligent and have revealed them to infants. . . . *All things* [πάντα, *panta*] have been handed over to me by my Father; and no one knows who the Son is except the Father, or who the Father is except the Son and anyone to whom the Son chooses to reveal him" (10:21–22). The range of knowledge is panoramic, moving from "these things" Jesus has just explained to the seventy-(two) about their mission and identity (10:18–20) to "all things" in the universe created by God. And the experience of joyful knowing unfolds within a familial nesting network from Father → Son → infants and anyone else whom the Son chooses. The household is patriarchal, but ruled by the Father-God (paterfamilias), who shares everything with Son Jesus, who in turn opens the divine mind and heart to his little brothers and sisters ("infants"). In this family portrait, Jesus stands in the middle as both *receiver* and *revealer* of divine knowledge. In his faithful subjection to God (cf. John 5:19–21; 8:28–29; 1 Cor 15:24–28), the Son Jesus receives the fullness of God's revelation, out of which he then guides disciple-subjects as their Lord.

Jesus's open mediation mitigates oppressive hierarchy. In patronage terms, Jesus graciously *brokers* the vast wealth of God's knowledge, investing in the

33. The relatively few expressions of joy in Luke thus far involve (1) others' excitement over Jesus's birth (1:14; 2:10) and (2) Jesus's exhorting his disciples to rejoice in persecution (6:23) and to cultivate with deep roots the word-seed they initially receive with joy (8:13–15). On joy in Luke, see Dinkler, "Reflexity."

34. In line with the opening tenet of the Westminster Shorter Catechism (1647): "The chief end of man is to glorify God, and to enjoy him forever" (Pss 16:5–11; 144:15; Isa 12:2; Luke 2:10; Phil 4:4; Rev 21:3–4).

spiritual growth of "infants." As these little ones mature, they will yield some return on the investment (cf. 8:4–21); but divine revelation is not driven by cold calculation. The self-disclosure of the Triune God flows out of the pure joy and love of sharing with totally dependent infants, who can do little else but return a measure of that love and joy. Spiritual knowledge is wholly relational and gratuitous before it becomes practical or utilitarian. The first fruitful products of the Spirit's infusion, as Aquinas argues via Paul, are *holy passions for God*—"love, joy, peace" (Gal 5:22)—before practical service to God and others: "The love of God is poured forth in our hearts by the Holy Spirit who is given to us. The necessary result of this love is joy, because every lover rejoices at being united to the beloved. . . . So the consequence of this love is joy. And the perfection of joy is peace . . . because our desires rest altogether in [God]."[35]

Potential losers in this divine-human community of knowing and growing, loving and rejoicing, are "the wise and the intelligent" (Luke 10:21)—the sophisticates (σοφῶν, *sophōn*) and the scholastics (συνετῶν, *synetōn*)—by their own or others' estimation. Jesus by no means endorses foolishness and ignorance, but rather reinforces the Creator God's honor as the fountain of true wisdom and knowledge, which is grasped most deeply in humble relationship with God (cf. 1 Cor 1:18–31). In their first flush of enthusiasm, the seventy(-two) messengers risked becoming too wise and powerful in their eyes ("the demons are subjected to us!"). So Jesus gently and joyfully reminds them that their insight into the workings of God's kingdom comes only through their intimate connection with Christ. In this "blessed" experience, the disciples outpace "many prophets and kings" whose arrogant pretensions to wisdom and power have blocked their perceptions of God's wondrous realm. But with Jesus's benediction comes an implicit exhortation that the eyes and ears of Jesus's followers remain open to his relational revelation (Luke 10:23–24).

The Compassionate Samaritan Traveler and Complaining Host Martha (10:25–42)

The so-called parable of the good Samaritan has become such an iconic part of Jesus's teaching, both within the church and within the wider culture, as virtually to stand alone. But as with all of Jesus's teaching, it comes to us in

35. Aquinas, *ST* I-II, q. 70 a. 3, cited in Stump, "Aquinas," 102; cf. Stump's summation of Aquinas's view of emotions/passions: "The fruits of the Holy Spirit are a matter of having emotions, spiritual analogues to the passions, transformed in second-personal connection to God" (103; cf. 96–104).

narrative context, not as a separate file or single release.[36] While the historical Jesus may have told the tale several times in different settings, its fame owes to its unique place in Luke's Gospel. Jesus offers the parable (10:30–35) in response to the question of a religious legal expert ("lawyer") concerning "who is my neighbor" meriting the love that God enjoins (10:29, 36–37; Lev 19:17). More broadly, the tale slots within a fuller exchange about eternal life and covenantal love (Luke 10:25–28), tightly linked with Jesus's preceding message about seeing and understanding God's revelation: "Just then [and look!—καὶ ἰδού, *kai idou*] a lawyer stood up to test Jesus" (10:25). Jesus's extraordinary claim to know and reveal God's will to "infants" rather than those who seem wiser and more intelligent prompts the lawyer, a respected "wise" figure, to press for evidence of Jesus's understanding of the divine (eternal) realm. Jesus first turns the discussion right into the wheelhouse of the lawyer (νομικός, *nomikos*), namely, Torah interpretation: "*In the law* [νόμῳ, *nomō*], what is written? How do you read it?" (10:26 AT [following Greek word order]). He then *affirms* the lawyer's "orthodox" response, focusing on the double-love command to love God with one's whole being (Deut 6:5) and one's neighbor as oneself: "You have given the right [ὀρθῶς, *orthōs*] answer" (10:28).

Significantly, Jesus roots his intimate knowledge of the Father through the Spirit not simply in mystical, visionary experience (e.g., "I watched Satan fall from heaven" [10:18]), but also in *scriptural, lectionary* engagement: "What *is written* in the law? What do you *read* there?" (10:26). As Jesus himself discerns God's will through careful reflection on the biblical canon of Law, Prophets, and Writings (4:16–30; 24:25–27, 44–47), so he exhorts his interlocutors and followers to search the Scriptures to find God and to learn God's ways (24:25; cf. Acts 8:30–35; 17:11; John 5:39). But truly revelatory study of Scripture is far from a mechanical "search engine" compilation of terms, texts, and topics. God-knowing, life-giving encounter with Scripture flows out of openness to the fresh inspiration of God's Spirit and the "right" interpretation of God's Son. At this critical point Jesus pushes the legal scholar's knowledge: while he quotes the right Torah texts about loving God and neighbor as the dual-lane path to eternal life, his *interpretation* of the neighbor track is too narrow in Jesus's book. Jesus tells the parable of the good Samaritan as authoritative, expansive commentary on the law's instruction about neighborly love.

A careful co-textual reading of Jesus's famous parable also extends forward to the snippet about Jesus's visit with Martha and Mary (10:38–42)—a

36. Green ("Luke-Acts") notes—and laments—how popular Lukan parables like the good Samaritan and prodigal son have been routinely "sundered from their narrative service in the Third Gospel" in the history of interpretation (108).

famous story in its own right and also commonly treated as an isolated episode. But some commentators have sought to connect the two scenes. Charles Talbert, for example, juxtaposes the parable's Samaritan as a model of neighborly, active love, with sister Mary as an exemplar of godly, contemplative love.[37] I detect a stronger thread, however, between the Samaritan and *Martha* around the continuing theme of loving others, whether strangers on the road or friends in the home, through generous acts of hospitality. But Luke's Jesus makes this congenial point about helping others through some not-so-comfortable host figures. A "foreign" Samaritan should not help! A domestic woman should not harp! A "good Samaritan" was an oxymoron from a typical Jewish perspective, and a nagging woman did not make a "good choice" (cf. 10:42).

Compassionate Samaritan (10:25–37)

Luke discloses an ulterior motive behind the lawyer's neighbor-identity question: he was "wanting to justify [δικαιῶσαι, *dikaiōsai*] himself" as a faithful law observer and neighbor-lover (10:29). We need not impugn this desire as necessarily sinister or defective, though the lawyer does aim to "test/tempt" (ἐκπειράζω, *ekpeirazō*) Jesus in this discussion (10:25). Even so, he seems to respect Jesus's teaching on some level and to anticipate that it will confirm his righteous self-image. Moreover, the lawyer's longing for self-assurance need not entail a boastful, solipsistic justification or "works righteousness" apart from God's right-making grace. He does not seek to gain entry into God's covenantal family: as a Jew, a descendant of Abraham graciously chosen by God, his place among God's people is his *birthright*, not his achievement. However, *maintaining* that place and ensuring full "inheritance" of God's eternal life (cf. 10:25) correlate with his faithful commitment to God's covenant grounded in love for God and neighbor.[38] Accordingly, the lawyer wants Jesus to bolster his concept of neighborly love, about which he seems least confident and suspects Jesus's alternative view.

Although Luke never spells out the lawyer's profile of the beloved neighbor, it is reasonable to assume a common identification with fellow covenantal Israelites, including proselytes, and also Godfearers and "immigrants [who] live in your land with you" (Lev 19:33–34 CEB). But should these outsiders

37. Talbert, 120–26.

38. On Jesus's adherence to the central Jewish doctrine of "covenantal nomism," see E. P. Sanders, *Jesus*, 335–37; cf. N. T. Wright, *Justification*, 55–77.

become enemy combatants, foreign invaders, or hostile oppressors, then duties to love them as ourselves would not apply (see Deut 7:1–11). Loving one's own people, along with others who peacefully exist with them, hardly constitutes an unreasonable application of the commandment to love one's neighbor as oneself. But divine revelation mediated by Jesus stretches and even shatters natural reason from time to time. This is one of those times, as Jesus showcases a Samaritan as focal subject and object, prototype and target, of true neighborly love.

But before unpacking the shocking elements of the Samaritan parable, we should underscore that Jesus never challenges the lawyer's desire to *act rightly* or to *justify himself* as a neighbor-lover. Note well Jesus's final words: "Go and *do* likewise" (Luke 10:37). The lawyer's problem is not the pursuit of self-justification per se (cf. 12:57—"And why do you not judge for yourselves what is right [δίκαιον, *dikaion*]?"), but seeking it on restricted, prejudicial grounds, similar to those Jesus addresses in a later story: "He also told this parable to some who trusted in themselves that they were righteous [δίκαιοι, *dikaioi*] and *regarded others with contempt*" (18:9).

Jesus's present parable revolves around a case of dire need: an anonymous Jewish[39] traveler ("a certain person")[40] on the perilous highway from Jerusalem down to Jericho[41] falls prey to a band of thugs who strip and beat him within an inch of his life (lit. "half dead [ἡμιθανῆ, *hēmithanē*]" [10:30]). To put it mildly, the man could really use some neighborly love! But what neighbors can he count on in his precarious roadside station? As it happens ("by chance"), three neighbor candidates come along one by one, each *seeing* (ἰδών, *idōn*) the beaten man (10:31, 32, 33). What good fortune, it would seem, especially since the first two passersby are a priest and Levite, respectively, appointed ministers of God's law! But here the story takes a surprising turn, as each religious figure not only passes by the hapless victim, but does so by *choice*, not by chance, "on the other side" (10:31, 32). Jesus cites no motives for their neighborly negligence, and it is best not to fill in this gap, as commentators are wont to do. Jesus remains purposefully vague to undercut *any* reason that *anyone*, cleric or layperson, might give

39. Though Jesus does not specify the traveler's ethnic identity, the fact that he heads "down from Jerusalem" implies he is a Jew, along with the priest and Levite (who also "go down that road"), in contrast to the Samaritan, who is simply "traveling," without reference to Jerusalem.

40. Luke's Jesus often focuses on a generic "certain person" (ἄνθρωπός τις, *anthrōpos tis*) in his parables in order to maximize the application: this could be "anyone" of you or "someone" you know; see 13:19; 14:16; 15:11; 16:1, 19; 18:2 ("a certain city"); 19:12; 20:9; cf. 11:5; 15:3; 17:7.

41. The dangerous route from Jerusalem to Jericho runs about eighteen miles and descends some 3,200 feet (Tiede and Matthews, "Gospel according to Luke," 1785).

to "pass by" someone in need.[42] The victim's need and the Torah's mandate trump all excuses.[43]

With neighbor candidate number three, the parable escalates from surprising to shocking, as a Samaritan, who would never be labeled "good" in a typical Jewish neighborhood and in turn wouldn't be caught dead hanging out there (cf. 9:51–56)—and who was probably a despised Samaritan oil and wine *merchant* (traveling salesman, no less)[44]—eschews all social expectations and chooses to help the Jewish victim in a remarkable display of merciful love, at considerable personal cost.[45] *How* the Samaritan shows therapeutic (not forensic) "mercy" (ἔλεος, *eleos* [10:37]) is stunning, devoting his time, energy, and resources toward medical and convalescent aid in lavish, even imprudent, fashion. According to Oakman's calculations, the two denarii that the Samaritan hands over to the innkeeper amounts to a "substantial value" of "three weeks' worth of food" for the beaten individual;[46] and running an open tab for further expenses in a sketchy roadside tavern ("inn" [πανδοχεῖον, *pandocheion*]) is just asking to be fleeced.[47]

But the more critical point concerns *who* emerges as neighbor. As we have seen, that is what/who the lawyer wants to know ("who [τίς, *tis*] is my neigh-

42. What about a seminary student? In a fascinating study, psychologists John Darley and Daniel Batson ("From Jerusalem to Jericho") arranged (unbeknownst to the students) for seminarians to encounter a very ill-appearing man as they walked across campus to deliver a sermon on the good Samaritan parable. Did the preaching students stop to help? That all depended on how much time they thought they had before their scheduled sermon. Most offered aid if they were in no hurry; but among those informed they were running late, only 10 percent assisted the apparent sufferer! Cf. summary in Nisbett, *Mindware*, 37; Gilovich and Ross, *Wisest One*, 43–44.

43. The popular tendency among commentators and preachers to accentuate the priests' scruples regarding corpse impurity does not really factor into the story, especially since they are heading *away* from Jerusalem and the temple, where purity concerns are most critical. Jesus deliberately leaves open the motive of their neighbor neglect. Could it be fear, preoccupation, callous disregard? *Whatever* the excuse, it is no good reason to pass by the needy victim.

44. Oakman, "Was Jesus A Peasant?," 133; Gowler, *What Are They Saying?*, 77.

45. Vinson makes the keen observation that, in contrast to the family- and employment-forsaking, moneyless, hospitality-dependent itinerant mission of Jesus and his disciples (9:1–6; 10:1–12), the Samaritan "does carry money and supplies—good thing, too, or how could he have given first aid to the injured man, or paid for his stay in the inn? . . . he has a job, a family, he cannot stay even until the man is fully recovered. . . . [he] pays for health care, food, and lodging for a perfect stranger and promises to come back to make sure things go well" (355).

46. Oakman, "Buying Power," 44–45.

47. This roadside lodging place would have been closer to a brothel than a Holiday Inn. Cf. Strabo, *Geogr.* 12.8.17: "Moreover, it is said that once, when a brothel-keeper had taken lodging in the inns along with a large number of women, an earthquake took place by night, and that he, together with all the women, disappeared from sight" (cited in Oakman, "Was Jesus a Peasant?," 134; cf. 133–35; Gowler, *What Are They Saying?*, 77). The laughable irony of the Samaritan's action is that he is virtually asking to be robbed of his resources, as the mugged man was.

bor?" [10:29]) and precisely what/who Jesus targets in the question he throws back to the lawyer after the parable: "Which/who [τίς, *tis*] of these three . . . was a neighbor *of*[48] the man who fell into the hands of the robbers?" (10:36). The lawyer correctly identifies the Samaritan as the true neighbor, even though he chokes on the ethnic label, preferring the circumlocution, "the one who showed him mercy" (10:37a). The rhetorical dynamics, however, convey not simply that the Samaritan *acts* with neighborly love toward the Jewish mugging victim, but also that the Samaritan *is* himself a neighbor *to whom* love is required, just as he showed love.[49] "Go and do likewise" (10:37b) implies more than helping one's needy countryman, as the priest and Levite fail to do. It calls for aiding the foreigner, the stranger, as the Samaritan exemplifies, which means, mutatis mutandis, that if the half-dead traveler in the ditch happened to be a *Samaritan*, Jews must show *him* loving kindness![50]

Not just the resident immigrant, then, but also the transient immigrant (this is a travel story) and even the violent immigrant (recall Samaritan-Jewish hostilities, 9:51–56) are worthy of love. Loving your neighbor encompasses loving your enemy. This radical ethic of Jesus remains thoroughly rooted in the Jewish Scriptures, expanding the Torah's focus to be sure, but in line with—and likely dependent upon—the narrative theology of Chronicles, from the Writings (Ketuvim) section of the HB. An extraordinary chronicle of compassion amid the ravages of warfare between ancient Samaria (Israel/Ephraim) and Judah provides too many contacts with Jesus's parable to be mere coincidence (2 Chr 28:5–15).[51] Samaria/Israel's King Pekah and his "mighty warrior" Zichri massacre 120,000 Judeans, murder the son and right-hand men of Judah's King Ahaz, and capture 200,000 Judeans—men, women, and children—stripping them of their clothing and possessions. However, on the victory march back to Samaria

48. Here, against the NRSV and most modern versions that read "neighbor *to*," I follow Strahan's ("Jesus Teaches") more natural interpretation of the genitive participle as a possessive genitive: "neighbor *of the one who fell* [τοῦ ἐμπεσόντος, *tou empesontos*]" (84), fitting nicely with the earlier "possessive" (i.e., intensely personal rather than merely relative or transactional) uses: "love . . . *your* [σου, *sou*] neighbor" and "Who is *my* [μου, *mou*] neighbor?" (10:27, 29).

49. Van Elderen, "Another Look," 111–14; cf. Spencer, "2 Chronicles 28:5–15," 341–43.

50. Strahan ("Jesus Teaches," 84–86) and Mark Allan Powell (*What Do They Hear?*, 37) rightly stress that the parable invites readers' identification with the marginalized roadside victim, whom Jesus spotlights as the valuable object of neighborly love. What if we were in the ditch? How would we want to be treated? But whatever one's social location (not just priest and Levite types), the parable also pushes hearers to place themselves in the subject position of neighborly *lover* of an injured party, especially if that person is one's enemy or a member of an enemy group (a Samaritan type).

51. Spencer, "2 Chronicles 28:5–15"; Craig Evans, "Luke's Good Samaritan"; Scheffler, "Assaulted (Man)."

parading this humiliated mass of slaves, the prophet Oded and certain Samarian (Ephraimite) leaders protest the brutal treatment of these Judean captives, who represent their "kin(dred)" (28:8, 11, 15) as much as their enemies. In response, the captors halt the procession and appoint representatives to aid the war victims and escort them back to Judah. The details of their ministrations provide a template, though on much larger scale, for the "good" Samaritan's actions in Jesus's story, right down to the medicinal treatment, animal transport, and Jericho destination: "[They] took the captives, and with the booty they clothed all that were naked among them; they clothed them, gave them sandals, provided them with food and drink, and anointed them; and carrying all the feeble among them on donkeys, they brought them to their kindred at Jericho, the city of palm trees. Then they returned to Samaria" (28:15). Intertextually linked with the Chronicler's story, Jesus's parable about individual, boundary-breaking love of a neighbor-enemy assumes a national-political profile.[52]

Besides *what* the Samaritan does to *whom*, the issue of *why* he acts lovingly toward the victim also emerges in Jesus's tale. Though the motives for the priest and Levite's negligence are not identified, the Samaritan "came near" and aided the victim, rather than "pass[ing] by on the other side," *because* he "was moved with pity/compassion" upon seeing the afflicted man. Notice the contrasting perceptual responses, distinguished by the Samaritan's compassion:

> *Priest/Levite:* "Having seen [him], he passed by on the other side [ἰδὼν ἀντιπαρῆλθεν, *idōn antiparēlthen*]" (10:31, 32).
> *Samaritan:* "Having seen [him], he was moved with compassion [toward him] [ἰδὼν ἐσπλαγχνίσθη, *idōn esplanchnisthē*]" (10:33 AT).[53]

Far from being invariably disruptive, perturbing impulses to be checked by calm reason, emotions are vital movers/motivators toward salutary as well as deleterious ends, depending on the situation. They drive us, "move us" to action, and if rightly directed at the right time, as Aristotle argues regarding fear, they move us to do the right thing (*Eth. nic.* 3.7.5 [115b18–20]; cf. *Eth. eud.* 2.2.4–5 [1220b12–14]).[54] So it is with compassion: a "feeling with" (sym-

52. On "political compassion" and the parable of the good Samaritan, see O'Connell, *Compassion*, 183–207.

53. Here I change the NRSV's "pity" to "compassion." Though historically closely related in meaning, "pity" in modern English has skewed toward a negative tone of condescension ("I pity you poor fool"), not conveyed in various "pity" terms in ancient Greek; cf. Konstan, *Pity* and *Emotions*, 201–18.

54. On the "action readiness" or "action tendency" of emotions, see Frijda, *Laws of Emotion*, 3–46.

pathy) or deeper "feeling in" (empathy) another's painful experience, moving one to loving, care-giving action. The priest and Levite see the suffering man on the roadside, and whatever emotions they might have (fear? anxiety? disgust?), compassion is not strong enough, if present at all, to impel them to aid this "neighbor." By contrast, the Samaritan sees the same victim, identifies with him, feels the man's pain as his own, and is motivated to charitable assistance. Self-participating empathy drives other-benefiting ministry: "Love your neighbor *as yourself*" makes the vital "I-Thou" connection that spurs compassionate action.[55] Despite the volatile ethnic-religious differences between their peoples, the Samaritan becomes one with the Jew as object of God's love and subject of human vulnerability. As Jesus was earlier "moved with compassion [ἐσπλαγχνίσθη, *esplanchnisthē*]" (7:13 AT) toward the weeping bereaved widow—keenly sensing her terrible loss and grieving with her, though he had never met her before and himself was an unmarried male with no children—so the Samaritan is moved with fellow-feeling toward the Jewish victim to "come near" him and break through social-systemic barriers that otherwise foster neglect or maltreatment rather than compassionate service.

While compassion is undoubtedly useful in motivating neighborly love, is it *necessary*? Or put another way, does the absence of felt compassion for whatever reason, ranging from tepid, "banal" preoccupation with assigned duties[56] to blood-boiling antipathy, make loving action impossible to muster? Is the noncompassionate respondent somehow anesthetized, even legitimized, on some level? The philosopher-theologian Nicholas Wolterstorff worries that overreliance on sympathetic feeling blunts the moral imperative to therapeutic healing of all human beings by virtue of their being God's creation with inalienable rights to life and well-being. Compassion is ideal, but human hard-heartedness is real, whether evidenced by Serbian militants against Bosnian women, Nazi guards against Jews, or priest and Levite against a hapless half-dead traveler (Wolterstorff's examples). Wolsterstorff underscores the significance of *conviction* over compassion, which is to say, reason over passion:

> The affective side of the self cannot, all by itself, expand or even sustain human rights culture. Conviction must also be engaged—conviction of the

55. See Buber, *I and Thou*, 177–78: "Everything, from your own experience of looking day after day into the eyes of your 'neighbor' who needs you . . . but responds with the cold surprise of a stranger, to the melancholy of the holy men who repeatedly offered the great gift in vain—everything tells you that complete mutuality does not inhere in . . . life with one another. It is a form of grace for which one must always be prepared but on which one can never count."

56. On the "banality" of evil and evildoers, see Arendt, *Eichmann*; for discussion of this trenchant work, see Robin, *Fear*, 110–26; and Iris Marion Young, *Responsibility*, 75–93.

> right sort, of course, conviction that this human being has great worth. . . . Our Judaic and Christian heritage neither denies nor overlooks the flaws of humankind. . . . But in the face of all the empirical evidence it nonetheless declares that all of us have great and equal worth: the worth of being in the image of God and of being loved redemptively by God. It adds that God holds us accountable for how we treat each other—and for how we treat God. It is this framework of conviction that gave rise to our moral subculture of rights. If this framework erodes, I think we must expect that our moral subculture of rights will also eventually erode and that we will slide back into our tribalisms.[57]

Sage words, if a tad oversentimentalizing (de-rationalizing) the "affective side" of humanity. Ancient and contemporary philosophy, as we have seen, stresses the fundamentally *cognitive-evaluative* dimension of emotions. I think *and* feel, feel *and* think. Compassion is not some mushy sentiment that either hits me or not but is borne of considered engagement with hurting humanity. And conviction is not some mechanical adherence to an abstract idea, but a passionate commitment to God's law of love.

Complaining Martha (10:38–42)

Another passionate, hospitable character now emerges, though not in a story Jesus tells, but in an incident where he receives ministry. Though not yet in physical distress, stripped, and beaten like the victim in his parable, Jesus is a fellow traveler on a road leading to a violent end (9:22, 44; 18:31–33). The direction is reversed: Jesus heads *up to* Jerusalem instead of down from it, but he too will tread the perilous route via Jericho, his last stop before reaching Jerusalem (18:35; 19:1, 28).[58] His primary host is a woman named Martha, heretofore unknown in Luke's narrative, but someone who already knows and embraces Jesus as Lord (κύριος, *kyrios*), as she directly addresses him (10:40) and the narrator twice refers to him (10:39, 41).[59] She thus joins a motley company of those calling Jesus Lord: Elizabeth (1:43), John the Baptist (3:4), Peter (5:8), a

57. Wolterstorff, *Justice: Rights*, 392–93; cf. also his *Justice in Love*, 116–18, 131–33.

58. Jesus makes the third of his three passion predictions just before entering Jericho (18:31–35); among the three forecasts, this one accentuates most the suffering and beating Jesus anticipates before his death, reminiscent of the victim's attack in the parable.

59. See the thorough discussion of textual variants in Rowe (*Early Narrative Christology*, 142–49), affirming the internal narrative support for all three κύριος (*kyrios*) references, but admitting that Luke "could have written" Ἰησοῦς (*Iēsous*) in 10:39, 41 (149).

leper (5:12), centurion (via friends, 7:6), James and John (9:54), others among the Twelve and Seventy(-Two) (6:46; 10:17), and prospective disciples (9:59, 61) at various levels of recognizing his exalted position. I see no reason, however, to presume Martha's particularly deficient grasp of Jesus's lordship just because she lodges a complaint that Jesus does not accept.[60] She can be wrong on the issue while right about Jesus's identity: in fact, laments to the Lord typically assume the Lord's ability to make things right.

Martha demonstrates wholehearted, exemplary love for her Lord as *neighbor-traveler* by "welcoming [ὑπεδέξατο, *hypedexato*] him into her home" (AT)[61] and lavishing "much ministry [πολλὴν διακονίαν, *pollēn diakonian*]" upon him, which likely included customary diaconal ministrations, such as anointing his head with oil and providing basin and water for footwashing (cf. 7:44–46). Just before embarking on his Jerusalem journey, Jesus stressed that whoever "welcomes" (δέχομαι, *dechomai*) him effectively welcomes both the lowliest, neediest persons among them (modeled as a little child) and "the one who sent me," namely, *God* (9:46–48). Martha practices this theological ethic of hospitality, like the merciful Samaritan in the parable and unlike the vengeful James and John (9:49–50, 54–55).

Yet, Martha also shows a temperamental side. Human emotions are rarely pure and antiseptic but typically spark with—and sometimes against—one another.[62] Martha is a dedicated host who cares passionately about serving her Lord: it is not every day that God makes a house call in flesh and blood! And her zealous compassion trips a related, but not so congenial, emotion of *jealous frustration* toward sister Mary, who sits at Jesus's feet listening to his word without lifting a finger to help Martha—and toward Jesus as well, who seems content to let this unfair division of labor persist: "Lord, do not you care that my sister has abandoned me to do all the ministry [διακονεῖν, *diakonein*] by myself? Tell her then to help me!" (10:40 AT). While interpreters through the ages have bristled at this testy retort (that is no way to talk to the Lord!),[63] it is important to check emotional first responses to Martha in light of what she actually says and does in Luke's story. Consider these points:

60. Contra Rowe (*Early Narrative Christology*), who comments: "The distracted and busy Martha . . . addresses Jesus as κύριε, apparently without understanding the significance of her address" (149).

61. "Into her home," though lacking in some early manuscripts (P45, P75, B) is found in codices A and D and fits the scenario where Martha acts as the main host (homeowner).

62. On the chain-reaction "stream of emotional responses," see Ekman, *Emotions Revealed*, 69–71.

63. On the reception history of Martha's character in this story, see Constable, "Interpretation"; Heffner, "Meister Eckhart"; Gench, *Back to the Well*, 72–81; Spencer, *Salty Wives*, 173–84.

- Martha reinforces her "Lord" address with a plea that Jesus "tell" Mary what to do; though Martha appears to be the household head and no doubt has ordered her sister around many times before,[64] she acknowledges on this occasion that Jesus is the Lord-Host (as well as guest) with final say over the proceedings. Mary's not the only sister to respect Jesus's "word" (λόγος, *logos* [10:39]).
- The work of service/ministry (διακονεῖν, *diakonein*) that preoccupies Martha is precisely what she *should* be about—like all of Jesus's disciples, male and female, following the word and deed of their Lord who hosted the five thousand (9:11–17) and will identify himself at table as "the one who serves [ὁ διακονῶν, *ho diakonōn*]" (22:26–27).
- Martha's desire for help in ministry is hardly unreasonable. Since Jesus recently sent out the Seventy(-Two) in pairs, why should Martha have to work "alone" (μόνος, *monos*)? Moreover, the compound term she uses for "help" (συναντιλαμβάνομαι, *synantilambanomai*), meaning "to help by joining in an activity or effort"[65] or "to come to the aid of, to be of assistance,"[66] acquires a special resonance in contrast with characters' behavior in Jesus's preceding parable. Whereas the priest and the Levite pass by the helpless victim "on the *other/opposite side* [ἀντιπαρῆλθεν, *antiparēlthen*]" (10:31–32) to avoid any contact with him, Martha implores Jesus to send Mary *alongside* her to provide support. In other words, she asks Jesus to send her sister to her as a "good Samaritan."

Martha's complaint, therefore, should not be dismissed as trivial nagging, a kind of drip-drip water torture, as the stereotype has it, by an overwrought woman (Prov 19:13b; 27:15). She lodges a legitimate lament to the Lord, urging him to redress an unfair labor situation. How does he respond? To be sure, Jesus does not comply with her wishes; but neither does he excoriate her foolish conduct. In fact, in keeping with the theme of the Samaritan parable, Jesus's response may be viewed as *sympathetic* (compassionate) with Martha. His double "Martha, Martha" reflects sensitivity, not hostility (she and sister Mary are the only women Luke's Jesus calls by name). He then conveys his loving concern by exposing the *emotional roots* of her ministerial angst. He never rebukes her diaconal action (how could he, since *diakonia* constitutes the core of his own work?), but instead gently chides her attitude of excessive "worry, anxiety" (μεριμνάω, *merimnaō*) and "inner turmoil" (θορυβάζω, *thorybazō*) over

64. Luke says nothing about a brother (Lazarus) householder, as in John 12:1–2.

65. Louw-Nida, *Greek-English Lexicon*, 1:458–59

66. BDAG, 965.

getting everything done (Luke 10:41). Earlier, Jesus warned about the potential of "[anxious] cares [μεριμνῶν, *merimnōn*]" that choke the divine word (8:14). Martha, who takes Jesus's word quite seriously, runs the risk of stifling that word through her frustration over a worthy goal of hospitality.

Simply put, it is hard to hear the Lord's word clearly and respond to it faithfully when consumed with worry. Notice the counterexample of Mary, calmly sitting at Jesus's feet and attentively focused on his teaching (10:39). No angst here. No words, either, or any other activity: more of a passive (than passionate) still-life portrait, fixing Mary in her proper subordinate, quiescent place. The contrast with Martha's fraught state and forceful statement hardly favors women's vocal leadership. Remarkably, Martha is the first woman to speak directly in Luke's story since Mary of Nazareth's rebuke of twelve-year-old Jesus in 2:48.[67] And in both cases, women devoted to Jesus become very "anxious" and testily challenge his insensitive abandonment in one way (leaving mother Mary alarmed at his unexplained absence) or another (leaving Martha alone to do all the work).

As it happens, the mature Jesus's response to Martha proves more sensitive than the dismissive, adolescent answer he gave his mother (2:49). Jesus challenges Martha's anxiety for her own good: it is making her miserable and is not "needed" (NIV; Vulg. *necessarium*) in the present scenario. Jesus is not pounding on the table demanding quicker service (he does not live by bread alone). Just as important as the ministry of food is the ministry of word. Recall Jesus's nourishing blend of both forms of service to the multitude (9:11–17; cf. Acts 6:1–7). So Mary, for her part, is doing the "good [τὴν ἀγαθήν, *tēn agathēn*] thing"—not necessarily the "better" thing, as the NRSV and most versions have it[68]—from which Jesus will not pull her away. But by affirming Mary's present choice, Jesus does not discredit Martha's service. Martha, too, has made a "good" choice, except that she undermines her good work with a sour attitude. Jesus does not, in any case, feed the fire of sibling or ministerial rivalry, as if pitting Martha's inferior active/menial domesticity against Mary's superior contemplative/spiritual devotion.

But doesn't Jesus come close to enforcing such a hierarchy by asserting, "There is need of *only one thing*"—that is, the one thing Mary does? Yes, if that is the correct reading. But as Gordon Fee has persuasively argued, an alternative reading with strong manuscript attestation and greatest grammatical

67. The narrator credits the cured bleeding woman with a general report of her experience (8:47) but gives her no speaking lines.

68. Culy, Parsons, and Stigall translate τὴν ἀγαθὴν μερίδα ἐξελέξατο (*tēn agathēn merida exelexato*) as "made the right choice," while indicating that the phrase literally means "chose the good portion" (368, 371).

awkwardness (thus most liable to scribal emendation) appears more original: "You are worried and distracted by many things [πολλά, *polla*]. But *few things* [ὀλίγων, *oligōn*] *are needed, or one* [ἑνός, *henos*]."[69] The awkwardness emerges in the numbers: Jesus quickly jumps from "many" to "few" to "one," granting the "need/necessity" of the last two units ("few *or* one") (10:41–42). Jesus seeks to reduce the burden of Martha's "many" duties even as he endorses both her multiple ("few") acts of service and Mary's singular ("one") attention to his teaching. Overall, Augustine views the oneness in this text as a complementary unity between the two sisters, rather than preferring one over the other: "Both [Martha and Mary] were pleasing to the Lord, both amiable, both disciples . . . both innocent, both laudable—two lives in the same house and just *one fountain of life*. . . . Martha has to set sail in order that Mary can remain quietly in port."[70] John Calvin gets at the same point by stressing the limited focus of this brief scene, which scarcely represents a full portrait of either sister's spirituality: "Luke says that Mary took her station at Jesus's feet. Does this mean that she was doing this the whole of her life? Rather the Lord commanded that the time of a man who wishes to advance in Christ's school should be so divided up that he shall not be an attentive yet unpractising hearer but shall make use of what he has learnt. There is a time for hearing and a time for doing."[71]

Mary might have a "better" sense of the present moment, but if she really listens to Jesus, she will perceive his urgent call to active ministry. And while Martha might currently be so "distracted" by her overwhelming ministerial duties that she can't concentrate on Jesus's teaching, she acknowledges the authority of her Lord's word and may be as jealous of Mary's position (Martha would love to hear Jesus too!) as she is irked by her cumbersome workload. Jesus's calming (down) words effectively invite Martha to join the seminar. Dinner can wait.

The Praying Jesus and Shameless Host (11:1–13)

The setting shifts abruptly from Martha's house to an undisclosed location without a tight transition: it just "happens" (καὶ ἐγένετο, *kai egeneto*), continuing the episodic pattern of the Travel Narrative. The reposting to a "certain place [τόπῳ τινί, *topō tini*]" from Martha's residence in an unspecified town continues

69. Fee, "One Thing Is Needful?" None of the possible Greek readings has the term "only" (μόνος, *monos*) reinforcing "one."

70. Augustine's Sermon 104, cited in Heffner, "Meister Eckhart," 173–74; cf. Constable, "Interpretation," 18–19.

71. Citation from Calvin, *Harmony of the Gospels*, 89; cf. Gench, *Back to the Well*, 75–76.

the vague itinerary (11:1). Still, significant thematic threads hold together the meandering journey to Jerusalem and chart the way for Jesus and his disciples.

Since we find Jesus *praying* in this new place (11:1) and then teaching his disciples how they should pray, we might assume a prayer connection with the Martha/Mary episode. But while Mary appeared as contemplative, she did not engage in prayer per se, but rather in hearing Jesus's instruction. Nevertheless, ministries of "prayer and word" complement each other (cf. Acts 6:4), and prayer involves as much quiet, reflective listening as talking to the Lord. Moreover, Luke has repeatedly highlighted Jesus's personal practice of prayer, though the present passage marks the first time Jesus speaks *about* prayer.

In addition to reinforcing a prayer chain, Luke also continues to stress—and to link with praying and teaching—the ministry of *hospitality*, particularly related to physical nurture. Thereby, *Martha's* model service continues to shine. Notice the threefold emphasis on eating/feeding in Jesus's primer on prayer:

- "Give us each day our daily bread" (11:3—at the heart of the Lord's Prayer).
- "Friend, lend me three loaves of bread" (11:5—parable of the persistent host).
- "Is there anyone among you who, if your child asks for a fish, will give a snake instead of a fish?" (11:11).[72]

Another tie-in with Martha concerns the request for Jesus's action. Just as she pleaded with "Lord" Jesus that he attend to a pressing matter, so now "one of his disciples," after observing Jesus's prayer session, implores him, "*Lord*, teach us to pray, as John taught his disciples" (11:1). Though this request does not carry the frustrated emotional freight of Martha's entreaty, it does expose a curious gap in Jesus's discipleship training. John the Baptist had taught his followers to pray, as the Pharisees no doubt taught their students. Praying and fasting were major disciplines of Jewish spirituality (cf. 5:33; 18:11–12). Though Jesus temporarily released his disciples from fasting duties (5:34–35), he never suspended their practice of prayer and in fact regularly commended it by his own example. If the goal of discipleship, as we have been tracking across Luke's narrative, is to know God through Christ more fully and assuredly, then knowing how to commune with God in prayer constitutes a vital means to that end.

Why, then, does Luke's Jesus wait so long to introduce prayer into his curriculum, and only when one of his disciples asks for it? In his first major

72. Some manuscripts add "bread/stone" to the "fish/snake" contrast. Though this reading nicely reinforces the "bread" theme from 11:3, 5, it is probably a secondary harmonization with Matt 7:9 and/or the bread-and-fish menu of multitude feeding in Luke 9:13–16.

block of instruction (6:17–49), Jesus exhorted his followers to "pray for those who abuse you" (6:27) and to forgive one another (6:37). But these were subpoints in a larger discussion of community ethics (see above). Perhaps Jesus waits for the right "teachable moment" regarding fine points of prayer. The most recent opportune time for prayer instruction would have been on the mountain, where Jesus "took with him" Peter, James, and John for the express purpose of prayer (9:28). But when Jesus's praying catalyzed his glorious transfiguration and manifestation of Moses and Elijah, all Peter could think to propose was a tent-building project (9:32–33). Not a peep from him or the other two disciples along the lines of, "Lord, teach us to pray so we too can see the glory of God." Here the "active" life, focused on pointless activity, does seem to clash with "contemplative" prayer, which provides divine inspiration and direction for ministry. Maybe the disciples just weren't ready to receive Jesus's guidance about prayer until now.

Prayer Outlined (11:2–4)

Jesus answers the disciple's plea with a short model prayer, sketching key lines of communication with God the Father. Matthew's longer version follows the same train of thought in a more poetic, liturgical framework; it is no accident that Matthew's form has dominated public recital. But Luke's version has its own value as a more personalized path to prayer, starting simply with "Father" rather than the more elaborate "Our Father who art in heaven" (Matt 6:9 KJV), and may lay claim to being more original.[73] For the sake of analysis, I provide my own translation and layout of the Lord's Prayer in Luke, giving special attention to Greek verbs and word order.

FATHER:

A1 Let be honored [ἁγιασθήτω, *hagiasthētō*] your name

A2 Let come [ἐλθέτω, *elthetō*] your kingdom

B Our bread for this day's living give [δίδου, *didou*] us each day

C1 And forgive [ἄφες, *aphes*] us our shortcomings, for we ourselves also forgive [ἀφίομεν, *aphiomen*] each one indebted [ὀφείλοντι, *opheilonti*] to us

C2 And do not bring [μὴ εἰσενέγκῃς, *mē eisenenkēs*] us into a period of testing

73. See the concise comparative analysis of Matthew and Luke's versions of the Lord's Prayer in Stanton, *Gospels*, 6–11.

This five-part layout features a *daily bread* centerpiece (B) flanked by an introductory pair of *God-focused* concerns (A) and a concluding pair of *human-frailty* issues (C). The first pair also coheres grammatically by third-person imperative leads ("let be honored"; "let come"), and the last pair by the καί (*kai*)-conjunction ("and") + second-person mandates ("forgive"; "do not bring"). The centerpiece stands out by breaking the verb-first pattern with an article-noun-pronoun + attributive adjective in the lead position before the verb: woodenly, "*the bread-of-us for-this-day's living* give us each day." As "Father" heads the entire prayer, "bread," more specifically "daily bread," marks its hub. This structure might commend the breakfast table as an ideal, though by no means only, setting for this prayer.

Closer analysis of the substance of this prayer yields a rich tapestry of theological, ethical, ecumenical, political, socioeconomic, and juridical threads tightly woven into the spiritual fabric. First and foremost, Jesus's model casts prayer as a *theological* practice, addressed to and about *God*. While that observation may seem obvious, the study of prayer can easily reduce to a catalog of practical techniques and personal benefits, with little use for God beyond some "higher power" who happens to be a good Rogerian listener or genie-style wish-granter.[74] Luke's Jesus, however, grounds prayer in the God and Father of Jesus, Israel, and all creation. From the start, supplicants must *know* to whom they appeal, namely, no one less than the "merciful" Father (6:36), the "heavenly Father" (11:13), the "Lord of heaven and earth," who intimately knows and is known by Jesus the Son and *to whom Jesus himself prays* (10:21–22) and offers obedience (2:49). Remarkably, Jesus invites his followers as brothers and sisters (cf. 8:21) into the divine family circle with his—and their—Father. Jesus caps off his larger prayer lesson with assurance of the *Holy Spirit's* availability to the Father's children, thus sealing the divine-human familial bond (11:13). From beginning to end, prayer is the language of God's household, speaking to the heart of God the Father through the Holy Spirit, just as Jesus the Son prays ("Jesus rejoiced in the Holy Spirit and said, 'I thank you, Father'" [10:21; cf. 3:21–22]). Paul put it this way, with special focus on God's adopted children as heirs with Jesus the "begotten" Son: "For all who are led by the Spirit of God are children of God. . . . You have received a spirit of adoption. When we cry, 'Abba! Father!' it is that very Spirit bearing witness with our spirit that we are children of God, and if children, then heirs, heirs of God and joint heirs with Christ" (Rom 8:14–17; cf. 8:26–27; Gal 4:6).

74. This is not to deny the considerable physical and mental benefits of prayer (and meditation), supported, for example, by the research of neuroscientist Andrew Newberg and colleagues (*Why God*; *How Enlightenment*; *How God*). But the biblical focus of prayer trains on God, not primarily on human enrichment.

The priority of God in the Lord's Prayer pushes beyond the "Father" address into the first set of petitions. We pray to God *for* God, specifically, for God's name to be honored and for God's kingdom to arrive. God the Father is also the Creator-Ruler of all. To be sure, these divine manifestations benefit humanity, but our interests are not primarily in view, certainly not in a narrow, individualistic sense. Prayer is ultimately about God and God's world and our *responsible* (more than privileged) relationship to God within that world.[75] Early in the biblical story, this responsibility concentrates in Israel's covenantal faithfulness to God's way: "And you shall keep my commandments and do them. And you shall not profane *the name of the holy one* [τὸ ὄνομα τοῦ ἁγίου, *to onoma tou hagiou*], and I shall be *sanctified* [ἁγιασθήσομαι, *hagiasthēsomai*] among the sons of Israel; I am the Lord who *sanctified* [ἁγιάζων, *hagiazōn*] you, who brought you out of the land of Egypt to be your God; I am the Lord" (Lev 22:31–33 NETS). A stunning dynamic of reciprocal sanctification (honoring, holy making, consecrating, setting apart) emerges: as the Lord set free the Israelites from Egyptian servitude, so they in turn must set apart the Lord as their venerable covenant partner through loving compliance with the Lord's commands redounding to the glory of God's name (identity and reputation). As always, biblical theology compels an *ethical* response by God's people—but not only to exemplify their relationship with God.

Theological ethics moves beyond the ethnic, covenantal realm into global, *ecumenical* space, blessing "all the families of the earth," as stipulated by the original pact with Abraham (Gen 12:1–3; 18:17–18; 22:15–18) and strengthened by prophets like Ezekiel in connection with honoring the Lord's name: "This is what the Lord says: I do not act for you, O house of Israel, but rather on account of *my holy name*, which you profaned among the nations. . . . And I will *sanctify my great name* [ἁγιάσω τὸ ὄνομά μου τὸ μέγα, *hagiasō to onoma mou to mega*], which was profaned among the nations . . . and *the nations shall know* that I am the Lord when I am *hallowed* [ἁγιασθῆναι, *hagiasthēnai*] among you before their eyes" (Ezek 36:22–23 NETS). The Creator-Father-God desires that all peoples (nations) know the greatness of God's name: that is, the sum and substance of all that God is, has done, is doing, and will do for Israel and the world. In short, then, to pray that God's name be honored is to pray for worldwide acknowledgment of God's goodness and to commit oneself to exhibiting this goodness in Godlike loving treatment of others, near and far.

Jonathan Sacks, philosopher, theologian, and former chief rabbi of Great Britain, boldly propounds this ethical-ecumenical and moral-transnational

75. I draw heavily here on the trenchant chapter "Sanctifying the Name" in Sacks, *To Heal*, 57–70.

thrust of sanctifying God's name, grounded in Torah, Prophets, and rabbinic tradition, as a "metaprinciple of Judaism." He begins with an incisive question: "Why should God be concerned about how the nations perceive him? Truth is not made by public opinion. Faith is not the pursuit of popularity. What difference does it make whether the nations believe that God is powerful or powerless?"[76] The difference concerns God's obsession with blessing and transforming the "nations." God's love, the core of God's nature (God's name *is* Love), is not satisfied until all trust and thrive within God's loving embrace. And amazingly, God cannot accomplish that mission alone. God enlists God's people as partners in sanctifying God's name throughout the world through their compassionate, "sanctified" conduct worthy of God's name. As Sacks concludes:

> The concept of "sanctifying the name" introduces into ethics a simple but surprising principle. We are God's ambassadors on earth. The way we live affects how others see him. God needs us. The idea sounds paradoxical but it is true. Wittingly or unwittingly, the way we live tells a story. If we live well, becoming a blessing to others, we become witnesses to the transformative power of the divine presence. . . . As a radio converts waves into sound, so a holy life translates God's word into deed. We become his transmitters. That is why "sanctifying the name" is a metaprinciple of Judaism.[77]

This ethical-ecumenical stream of advancing God's name throughout the earth naturally flows into tumultuous *political* waters. God's name signifies not a static label or form of identification, but rather a dynamic shorthand for all that God does and desires—which is nothing less than ruling the world God created in justice, righteousness, love, and peace. As "Wonderful Counselor, Mighty God, Everlasting Father, Prince of Peace" (Isa 9:6), the name(s) of the Lord means that:

> His authority shall grow continually,
>   and there shall be endless peace
> for the throne of David and his kingdom.
>   He will establish and uphold it
> with justice and with righteousness
>   from this time onward and forevermore.
> The zeal of the LORD of hosts will do this.
>
> (Isa 9:7)

76. Sacks, *To Heal*, 61.
77. Sacks, *To Heal*, 67.

Where God's name is honored, God's rule is accepted and established, and all other claimants to imperial power are deterred and dethroned. To pray, then, "Your kingdom come"—an inextricable corollary to "Your name be hallowed"—is to pray for political revolution, a change in world order. Caesar's reign is already here, or so it seems. But God's reign *comes*, not in some distant utopian horizon or mythical singular moment, but here and there, now and then, to restore God's good order over all creation (cf. 11:20; 17:20–21); and when it comes, when it moves in, it pushes out the present powers of this evil age. God does not share a nameplate or governing seat with any other authority (see 16:13). The "zeal of the LORD of hosts" wins out.

Though set apart as sovereign over the world, the Creator-Father remains very much invested in the well-being of all God's children, God's collective family. Accordingly, the Lord's Prayer moves seamlessly into envisioning present-and-future life in the kingdom-household. This prayerful project is about the way of life in God's realm resulting from God's coming into the world, not our escape to some ethereal paradise in outer space; it is about heaven coming to earth, not our going to heaven. More important, it is about very particular transformations of earthly life highlighted in the balance of Jesus's Prayer, revolving around *social solidarity* ("our/us"), *economic security* (sufficient bread, released debt), and *spiritual sanctity* (forgiveness of sins, deliverance from evil). Though briefly stated, the final petitions in the Lord's Prayer represent no wistful plea for general world betterment: they get down to hard, brass tacks.

The *socioeconomic* dimension features prominently in the plea for daily bread and the pledge to remit others' debts. The importance of "the bread" (τὸν ἄρτον, *ton arton*) in first position in the line and center point in the prayer (see above) should not be minimized or spiritualized. This bread is not a metaphor for moral behavior or eternal life (as in Mark 8:14–21; John 6:25–51): this bread is natural grain, the staff of physical life, necessary for human bodily survival and in short supply for many in Jesus's day. Luke's interest in actual bread for the hungry poor persists (1:53; 6:1–5, 20–21; 9:10–17). The double "daily" emphasis ("bread for *this day's living* give us *each day*") reinforces the focus on basic sustenance. The initial, unusual "daily" term (ἐπιούσιον, *epiousion*) modifying "bread" appears only here and in parallel texts in ancient Greek literature (Matt 6:11; Did. 8:2) and was perhaps coined by Jesus. With its precise meaning uncertain, major interpretive options include bread:

- "necessary for existence" ("for being": ἐπί + οὐσία, *epi* + *ousia*)
- "for the current day"
- "for the next day"

- "for the coming day" (with particular tie-in to the "coming" kingdom)
- "which comes upon us [from the Father]."[78]

I incline toward the first two connotations, concerning provision of enough bread to sustain the present day's existence ("bread for this day's living" [AT]). The more future-oriented "next day" or "coming" time, including the time of the climactic messianic banquet, is less likely. When Luke refers to anticipated events "on the next day/night," he uses the feminine dative participle τῇ ἐπιούσῃ, *tē epiousē* + (optionally) the noun for "day" or "night" (both feminine) (Acts 7:26; 16:11; 20:15; 21:18; 23:11). The masculine adjective ἐπιούσιον (*epiousion*) in the Lord's Prayer modifies "bread," as we have noted, not "day," which comes at the end of the line in a phrase denoting "each day" or "daily" (καθ' ἡμέραν, *kath' hēmeran*). So the petition *builds up to* bread for tomorrow and "each day" after that, but begins with present-day nourishment "necessary for existence." (I opt for a progressive rather than redundant reading of the "double daily" language.) Crossan captures well the overall intent: "The meaning is enough for today, but also with assurance of the same tomorrow. It is a request that 'our daily bread' be never again exceptional or conditional as in the past, but always normal and unconditional in the present and the future."[79] In other words, the Lord's Prayer promotes a consistent, sustaining *way of life* in God's realm, at God's table in this case, for all God's children.

Most needful of this good news, the poor and needy pray this prayer most authentically. The emphasis on day-to-day dependence for basic bread appears superfluous for the rich and powerful with their stocked storehouses of grain. For them, the Lord's Prayer becomes less a personal petition than a *moral mandate* to share their abundance with those in daily need; they become the *means* of answered prayer as stewards of the Father's blessings (cf. 12:13–21). The Lord's Prayer effectively advances a communal agenda of equitably distributed resources on a daily rhythm that precludes hoarding and widening gaps between haves and have-nots. In accounting terms, the community's books should be balanced day by day to prevent deficits from developing. This arrangement evokes the wilderness provision of manna that God showered upon Israel *each morning*—sufficient for all *for that day* but useless to stockpile because of its current expiration (spoilage) date. An exceptional double portion—but no more—was provided on the sixth day, so they would not have to gather on the

78. For these various choices, see the extensive entry in BDAG, 376–77; and Hultgren ("Bread Petition"), who favors the last option: "the coming bread," treating ἐπιούσιον (*epiousion*) as a participle from ἐπιέναι (*epienai*)—"come upon"—modifying ἄρτον (*arton*) (48–53).

79. Crossan, *Greatest Prayer*, 138.

Sabbath (Exod 16). But this procedure only reinforced the people's dependence on God and their shared responsibility to one another. Only in this faithful relationship to God and neighbor would they find true rest and strength for the journey.[80] Jesus's bountiful feeding of the multitude in the desert—with twelve baskets of leftovers after everyone ate their fill—provided a foretaste of the consummative messianic banquet (9:12–17; cf. 13:29; 14:7–24). The Lord's Prayer deals with daily life in the interim, seeking sustaining bread on the road to the land of promise flowing with milk and honey.

Survival for the destitute scrounging for daily bread was made more precarious by the burden of crushing debt to landlords and other creditors, which could lead not only to foreclosure (with no land, how could they hope to feed their families?), but also to imprisonment until payment was rendered (already at rock bottom, how could they hope to find extra funds?) (cf. 7:41–42; 12:57–59). Jesus's Prayer addresses this dire socioeconomic situation with a plea for God's forgiveness/remission of our "sins," conjunctively ("for also") and emphatically ("we ourselves") linked with our forgiveness/remission of others' "debts."[81] In our discussion of Jesus's Jubilee program (4:16–30), we noted the semantic scope of ἀφίημι (*aphiēmi*) under the umbrella notion of "release/redemption/liberation," encompassing both atonement for sins (forgiveness) and annulment of debts (remission) and thus marking the economic realm as especially ripe for errant conduct. Any catalog of sins should place robbery, disinheritance, extortion, debt slavery, wage and price gouging, pimping, and other forms of avarice and aggrandizement at the top of the list (cf. Mark 7:21–23; Rom 1:29–32; 1 Cor 5:9–10; 6:9–11; 1 Tim 1:9–11). Life in God's family circle under God's gracious and just rule demands basic material-economic support of all spiritual brothers and sisters. The Lord's Prayer not merely suggests, but positively shatters, convenient spiritual-economic dualisms. Our experience of God's liberating mercy is ineluctably linked with loving treatment of one another as *free* people bound together in familial covenant, not by financial constraint.

The last petition, structurally paired with the plea for forgiveness/remission, seeks protective care from more *spiritual-juridical* than economic distress: relief from trials or tests rather than debts. At first blush, "Do not bring us into a period of testing [πειρασμόν, *peirasmon*]" strikes a dissonant chord, since that is precisely what the Spirit brought Jesus into after his baptism and what Luke suggested would continue to dog Jesus's spiritual journey: "[Jesus] was led by the

80. On the manna connection, see Crossan, *Greatest Prayer*, 139–40; Hultgren, "Bread Petition," 50–51.

81. Cf. Oakman, *Political Aims*, 99–102, and *Jesus and the Peasants*, 11–39, 199–242; Hanson and Oakman, *Palestine*, 119–20.

Spirit in the wilderness, where for forty days he was tested [πειραζόμενος, *peirazomenos*] by the devil. . . . When the devil had finished every test [πειρασμόν, *peirasmon*], he departed from him until an opportune time" (Luke 4:1–2, 13). Isn't such character testing a necessary part of spiritual formation and authentication? Must Jesus's followers not learn to overcome "rocky" tests of faith that inevitably come their way, so as not to choke the productive word they have received (8:14)? No doubt God's children face persisting trials, instigated by evil spirits and callous societal hierarchs; and given the biblical doctrine of God's sovereignty, in some sense God wills, allows, and utilizes these tests for the good of God's children. But that perspective is not meant to foster a masochistic, martyr complex glorifying human suffering and heroic stamina under a cheap banner of "no pain, no gain." Enough challenges to faith will come without seeking them.

There is nothing weak-minded or half-hearted about praying that God would minimize the painful tests we undergo. On the positive side, praying not to be led into menacing trials means praying *for* peace and justice to prevail in the world. Jesus himself will passionately pray at the eleventh hour for God to "remove the cup" of death and suffering from him (if God wills), and in the same scene he twice exhorts his disciples to "pray that you may not come into the time of trial [πειρασμόν, *peirasmon*]" (22:39–46). As it happens, Jesus does not escape this deadly ordeal, and his followers face their share of trials in Acts, however much they pray for peace. But the pattern is mixed. In Paul's case, while he must suffer much "for the sake of [Jesus's] name" (Acts 9:16)—including interrogation, imprisonment, and stoning—his friends often lead him *away* from hostile opposition (9:23–25; 17:4–10; 19:28–31; 23:12–35), and the Lord keeps him alive to bear continuing witness to Christ (18:9–10; 23:11; 27:23–25).[82]

One more issue regarding Luke's final line of the Lord's Prayer begs for interpretation: the *absence* of Matthew's reassuring addendum, "but rescue us from the evil one" (Matt 6:13).[83] If our prayer to be spared severe testing is denied (like Jesus's "remove this cup" plea), are we left to face these trials alone, in our own strength? Clearly not, as the experiences of Jesus and the apostles in Luke's two volumes attest. Moreover, the only other uses of "lead/bring into" (εἰσφέρω, *eispherō*) in Luke appear in contexts of the sufferer's deliverance through benevolent human and/or divine agency. The paralyzed man

82. Cf. Spencer, *Journeying*, 169–71.

83. Additions of "but rescue us from the evil one" to Luke 11:4 come from later scribes seeking to harmonize with Matt 6:13. The popular addendum to the Lord's Prayer ("Yours is the kingdom and the power . . ."), constituting further assurance of victory over temptation, is not original to Matthew (or Luke), perhaps deriving from 1 Chr 29:11–13; cf. discussion in Bruce M. Metzger, *Textual Commentary*, 13–14, 132.

was "carried" (φέρω, *pherō*) by four friends who "were trying to bring/carry him in [εἰσενεγκεῖν, *eisenenkein*—an infinitive form of εἰσφέρω, *eispherō*] and lay him before Jesus" (5:18); because of the large crowd, they had to lower him through the roof to Jesus, who promptly enabled the lame man to rise up and walk (5:17–25). A bit further along his Jerusalem journey, Jesus frankly tells his followers that they can expect to be "led/brought to" (εἰσφέρω, *eispherō*) judicial authorities by callous accusers (12:11). Here Jesus assumes that, at times, God will not answer prayers to escape trials, but he hastens to add that God's Spirit will guide the disciples through their ordeals: "Do not worry about how you are to defend yourselves or what you are to say; for the Holy Spirit will teach you at that very hour what you ought to say" (12:11–12). Luke's Jesus may not end his model prayer with a "rescue" clause, but he does conclude the larger prayer lesson with assurance that the Father will faithfully "give the Holy Spirit to those who ask him" (11:13). Among the Spirit's gifts are power and wisdom to endure and overcome evil forces in all their forms. Whatever and whoever might "lead us into testing," God's Spirit and fellow praying believers "go in" with us. We help bear each others' trial burdens.

Prayer Illustrated (11:5–13)

Jesus's prayer tutorial with the disciples ("Suppose one of *you*"; "So I say to *you*" [11:5, 9]) adds illustrative material focused on food, father, and family. A short parable features a *friend* seeking bread from a *neighbor-father* in order to feed a *traveler-friend* who's arrived at midnight. At this late hour, the neighbor—father of multiple children (no mother mentioned)—has already locked his door and retired, his "children are *with me* [μετ' ἐμοῦ, *met' emou*] in [the same] bed [τὴν κοίτην, *tēn koitēn*]," it seems (11:7), an indicator of a poor, though not destitute, village family.[84] He has enough bread for the next day, including some to share with a needy neighbor; but midnight is hardly the optimal time for charity, and the father tells the pleading friend to go away and leave him alone: "I cannot get up [now] and give you anything" (11:7). Though in our modern Western preoccupation with privacy and schedules, this seems like a perfectly reasonable (not coldhearted) response, in an ancient Middle Eastern setting, putting one's personal convenience ahead of helping a community neighbor—at whatever time of day or night—would have been considered rude and callous behavior in

84. Moxnes (*Economy*) groups the household in this parable among "peasants [that is] smallholders who own a piece of land and who work it themselves together with their family and perhaps with some hired help" (57).

the extreme. Friendship and attendant obligations were valued with sacrosanct seriousness, not to be trifled with.[85] Even so, as Danker suggests, the imagined scene verges on the farcical or slapstick: a groggy father climbing out of bed, trying not to jostle his children, and then stumbling to the cupboard and trying to open the door as quietly as possible. Though not at all amusing to the father in the story, Jesus's audience could scarcely suppress a chuckle.[86] They might laugh, however, more in derision than amusement at the sleepy father who failed to rise to the present occasion of hospitality, inconvenient though it be. Helping out a friend and fellow villager in an emergency is what we do around here. How dare he treat this as a bother!

In any case, the supplicant friend is not put off by the father's rebuff. Hospitality demands that he feed his traveler-friend, and he has "nothing to set before" his guest (11:6). He is clearly a man of little means (or maybe just poor management skills), with no surplus of food. What money he might have to purchase his family's next-day bread counts for nothing with the shops closed for the night. His neighbor is his only resource, and so he keeps pleading for help, despite the neighbor's (inhospitable) wish not to be bothered. The scenario sets up Jesus's punch line: "Because of [the petitioning friend's shameless] persistence [ἀναίδειαν, *anaideian*], [the father] will get up and give [the friend] whatever he needs" (11:8). Thus the friend obtains the daily (or rather, nightly) bread he seeks from the father.

Through this parable, Jesus depicts *how* his followers should pray to the Father, that is, with "shameless persistence."[87] English versions typically stress the element of "persistence" (NKJV, NRSV) or "importunity" (KJV), which may be implied (see below), but it is not the primary meaning of ἀναίδεια (*anaideia*). The term chiefly denotes "lack of sensitivity to what is proper, carelessness about the good opinion of others, shamelessness, impertinence, impudence, ignoring of convention."[88] By rudely awakening the father and disturbing his

85. See Bailey, *Poet and Peasant*, 121–24; Waetjen, "Subversion," 710–13; Brad H. Young, *Parables*, 45–46.

86. Danker, 230.

87. Barclay M. Newman, *Greek-English Dictionary*, 11.

88. BDAG, 63; cf. "brashness" (CEB); "shameless audacity" (NIV). In his article ("*ANAIDEIA*") and monograph (*Stories*, 438–39, 442–48), Snodgrass tracks ἀναίδεια (*anaideia*) in ancient Greek literature and discovers a preponderant negative connotation. It was not an admirable virtue; indeed, as Plutarch flatly put it, "God hates *anaideia*" (*Is. Os.* 363F–364A; cf. Dio Cassius, *Hist.* 45.16.1 [both cited in Snodgrass, "*ANAIDEIA*," 508–9]). Bailey (*Poet and Peasant*, 126–33) supports this "shameless" reading, though specifically applies it to the *sleeping man's* shame (as does Bernard Brandon Scott, *Hear*, 89), if he does not help his neighbor pleading for help. Though the shame of inhospitality to a traveler falls to some extent on the entire close-knit village (Bailey, *Poet and Peasant*, 122), I think that the host in the present story still bears the brunt of responsibility, as do Waetjen ("Subversion," 707–11) and Snodgrass ("*ANAIDEIA*," 509–10).

family in the dead of night, the needy friend shows a shameless disregard for his neighbor's well-being. Of course, the friend himself experiences an honor crisis, shamed by his inability to feed his late-arriving guest. And, as indicated above, the sleeper, by expected social standards of village life, should have been more willing to help from the start. But the primary shamelessness (tantamount to extreme shame*ful*ness) in Jesus's parable falls on the unprepared petitioning, nagging friend at the ungodly midnight hour. Ironically, yet necessarily, he risks shamelessly bothering his neighbor to remedy his own hospitality gaffe.[89]

We might again crack a smile, this time at the seeker's expense, as he scurries about in the dark currying disfavor one way or another. Yet, the man has to do what he has to do in a tough situation (as far as we know, he had no inkling that the traveler-friend would drop in on him at such a late hour), although it "subverts the social relationship of friendship"[90] more blatantly (and loudly!) than the sleepy father.

But what does this scenario have to do with seeking God? In interpreting Jesus's parables, we must exercise caution in identifying any story character *wholly* with God.[91] Parables illustrate suggestive aspects of God's nature and rule rather than provide definitive theological exposition. In this parable of the friend at midnight, Jesus reveals God via the father-figure not so much as a grumpy character to be approached gingerly at inconvenient hours, but rather as one who invites his children, whether snugly "in bed" with him or precariously "outside in the dark," to plead their case with boldness bordering on the shameless. Though using a different Greek term, Heb 4:16 makes a similar point: "Let us therefore approach the throne of grace with *boldness* [παρρησίας, *parrēsias*], so that we may receive mercy and find grace to help in time of need." But Jesus's tale also seems to imply an edgier theological concern about whether God is always "awake" to help or must be "roused" to action at certain times. The disciples experienced such angst during the storm on Lake Gennesaret (8:22–25). And the Psalter holds in tension the comforting affirmation that the Lord "who keeps Israel will neither slumber nor sleep" (Ps 121:4) with the fervent lament during periods of "disgrace/shame" (44:15): "Rouse yourself! Why do you sleep, O Lord? Awake, do not cast us off forever!" (44:23).[92]

89. Brad H. Young (*Parables*) likens the notion of the petitioner-friend's "shamelessness" to the Hebrew notion of chutzpah, suggesting "raw nerve," "brazen tenacity," "bold perseverance" (50).

90. Waetjen, "Subversion," 711.

91. The only direct appearance of "God" in a parable is in 12:20 (the rich fool).

92. Though he doesn't develop the point, Danker suggests, "To the biblically informed, the parable [in 11:5–8] was in effect a commentary on Psalm 44" (230).

In addition to the parable's theological illumination of praying to the Divine Father for daily bread, it also reinforces the communal element of sharing "our" bread. Note again the three overlapping circles of family, friends, and neighbors: (1) the *distant traveler-friend* who arrives unexpectedly, (2) the *host friend-neighbor* who secures bread for his traveler-guest at midnight from (3) another *friend-neighbor*, who also happens to be a caring *father*. The only way the traveler receives bread is through a network of social relations. Love of neighbor and provision of food take place in community within the tense tousle of honor and shame relations. As will become even more patent via a later parable in the Travel Narrative (18:1–8), this story blends the practice of prayer with a dogged, "shameless" advocacy of social justice. As Herman Waetjen concludes: "Impudence, effrontery, and dishonorable conduct are divinely legitimated in the pursuit of justice in all the arenas of social life. Although the story of the parable focuses on a villager petitioning a neighbor for bread, its world subversion is not to be limited to prayer. The metaphorical character of the parable validates a more comprehensive application that includes all the exchanges that may occur in the relationship between God and human beings as well as the association that human beings have with each other."[93]

Although the aspect of shamelessness predominates in the friend's late night house call, a secondary shade of *persistence* surfaces in Jesus's final comments about prayer. He conveys a threefold exhortation to "ask, seek, and knock," assuring a positive response in each case, in a series of present imperatives reinforced by present active participles: for example, "*Knock* . . . for everyone *knocking* the door will be opened" (11:9–10 AT). The present tenses foreground *continuing* action, with the effect: "Knock and *keep on knocking* . . . for everyone who *keeps on knocking*, the door will be opened"—precisely as portrayed in the parable. But the point is scarcely that we must badger an unsympathetic Father into hearing our pleas and meeting our needs. Persistent praying is about maintaining connecting and strengthening relationship with the Father, not about wearing God down with whiny nagging.[94] The loving Father remains eager to attend to the children's supplications through the sympathetic Spirit. As Jesus caps off his teaching about prayer, via a "lesser to greater" rabbinic technique of theological argument: if even flawed earthly fathers grant their children's food requests (only an insane parent would serve a child a snake or scorpion instead of a fish or egg), "*how much more* will the heavenly Father

93. Waetjen, "Subversion," 717.

94. See below on the parable of the widow and unjust judge, where I discuss the notion of bothersome, wearing-out action in 18:5, parallel to 11:7.

give the Holy Spirit to those who ask him!" (11:13). Whereas Matthew's parallel juxtaposes human fathers' providing foodstuffs with the heavenly Father's giving "*good things*" (Matt 7:11), Luke's Jesus focuses on the personal gift of the Holy Spirit, that is to say, on God's very self. At root, prayer is a theocentric practice: seeking, finding, and knowing God.

Demonic Occupants and Inhospitable Pharisees (11:14–54)

Jesus's journey to Jerusalem now hits a bumpier stretch, shifting from in-group fellowship with disciples (including Martha and Mary) and practical instruction about prayer and care in the Father's household to wider and tenser encounters with the *crowds* (ὄχλοι, *ochloi* [11:14, 27, 29; 12:1, 13]) and polemical engagement with certain *Pharisees and scribes* (12:37–39, 42–43, 53). The two main episodes framing this subsection continue to deal with household matters: the first, questioning the legitimacy of Jesus's place and power in God's household (11:14–26); the last, challenging Jesus's table etiquette, which in turn prompts his tirade of "woes" against hypocritical, inhospitable Pharisees and scribes (11:37–54). Spliced within these major conflict scenes are three briefer snippets of Jesus's teaching, still polemical in thrust but less targeted at particular accusers. In two of the three, women play a key role: a "woman in the crowd" cuing Jesus's reiteration of God's household as adherents to God's word (11:27–28), and the "queen of the South" standing as judge over all who spurn God's wisdom (11:31).

Defending Integrity and Alliance with God's Kingdom (11:14–26)
  Blessing All Who Hear God's Word (11:27–28)
  Desiring Signs of God's Kingdom (11:29–32)
  Judging Light and Darkness (11:33–36)
Denouncing Hypocrisy and Resistance of God's Wisdom (11:37–54)

How does this course of sharp rhetoric by Jesus, with the disciples receding to the background (until 12:1, 22), contribute to Luke's interest in knowing God more fully and firmly? Though not addressed directly, the disciple-learners still accompany Jesus and form part of the audience hearing his stern words. And any competent training program, certainly one preparing for arduous service, includes warnings about potential pitfalls and missteps. But Jesus does not simply rail against this "evil generation" (11:29) and put them in their place. He weaves into his judgments various positive dimensions of God's saving outreach to humanity:

- finger of God (11:20)
- word of God (11:28)
- justice and love of God (11:42)
- wisdom of God (11:49).

Condemnation (11:31–32) serves no purpose beyond bitter vindictiveness if not chiefly motivated to turn the misguided toward God's redemptive power (*finger*), directive path (*word*, *wisdom*), and restorative, right-making rule (*love*, *justice*).

Some among the throng of "this evil generation" remain skeptical and stubborn about Jesus's authority to reveal God, insisting that he produce "a sign from heaven" (11:16; also v. 29) authenticating God's kingdom. Jesus refuses to play their game, however, not because he is unwilling or unable to use such sign language, but because sufficient signs have already been provided through his dynamic exorcisms (11:19–20) and prophetic Scripture ("sign of Jonah" [11:29–30]). As Paul puts it, "What can be known about God is plain to [this evil generation], because God has shown it to them" (Rom 1:19). The problem is not lack of revelation (through Christ, creation, and Scripture) but lack of attention to what God has plainly disclosed.

Defending Integrity and Alliance with God's Kingdom (11:14–26)

Jesus moves directly from instructing about prayer to casting out a demon that had rendered its host speechless, both mute and deaf (11:14).[95] Again Jesus combines ministries of praying, teaching, and healing. The present healing act reinforces the importance of speaking and hearing God's word (without denying that those with permanent speech-and-hearing disabilities can also fruitfully engage God's word). But the focus quickly turns from the particular case to Jesus's overall exorcising mission: specifically, the source of his power over demons. "Some" in the crowd accuse Jesus of affiliating with "Beelzebul, the ruler of the demons,"[96] while "others" clamor for a real "sign from *heaven*," apparently attributing his dislocation of the deaf/mute demon to a nongodly source (11:15–16). These challenges serve the purpose of putting Jesus to the

95. Κωφός (*kōphos*) applies to both oral (1:22) and aural (7:22) incapacities.

96. The obscure name Beelzebul appears in the NT only in Matt 10:25; 12:24, 27; Mark 3:22; and Luke 11:15, 18, 19. Beyond the stated identification with Satan, "the ruler of demons," little is known about the precise etymological derivation and semantic nuance of Beelzebul. As a best guess, Stein ("Who the Devil?") proposes some pejorative association with the Canaanite god Baal via the common ancient "pattern of deliberate debasement of foreign deities into demons" (45).

"test" (πειράζω, *peirazō* [11:16]), just after he taught his followers to pray *not* to be steered into testing! Such inquiry may seem odd right after Jesus proved his demon-conquering mettle. But while his interlocutors are perhaps being perverse for perversity's sake, they could also be genuinely leery, even afraid, of Jesus. They were "amazed" at his exorcism (11:14); while this response is not to be equated with approbation, it may be laced with worry and fear. The prevailing worldview of the time included a pervasive sense of vulnerability to a host of volatile, malevolent forces, seen and unseen.[97] In the invisible realm teemed an army of "cosmic powers of this present darkness . . . spiritual forces of evil in the heavenly places" under the wily devil's control (Eph 6:11–12). "Principalities and powers" appearing helpful one minute could turn harmful the next. In this anxious environment, charismatic figures abounded, promising prophylactic and therapeutic relief through an olio of magical spells and stratagems, with varying degrees of success—and financial cost. There was no shortage of quacks and hucksters exploiting the vulnerable. Let the buyer beware![98]

Bolstering the practical wisdom of testing claimants to divine power is the scriptural warning from Deuteronomy, setting God's people apart from evil "nations" enslaved to "abhorrent practices" of diviners, soothsayers, sorcerers, spell-casters, mediums, and other dabblers in the occult (Deut 18:9–14). Security in the land depends upon exclusive loyalty to God and heeding God's word mediated through God's true prophet: the *prophet like Moses* (18:15–22). In Luke's view, Jesus fulfills this Moses-style prophet role as the consummate Savior-Liberator of God's people (Luke 7:16; Acts 3:22–23; 7:37).[99] But while some recognize Jesus's unique prophetic vocation (Luke 7:16), others remain dubious.

In the present scene, the problem is less the cautious reservation about Jesus's mission (it is prudent to "test the spirits") than the peculiar reasoning that Jesus's authority to expel demons derives from his alliance with their diabolical ruler. That poses a serious logical fallacy, as Jesus pithily exposes via familiar images of kingdom, desert, and household: "Every kingdom [βασιλεία, *basileia*] divided against itself becomes a desert [ἐρημοῦται, *erēmoutai*], and house [οἶκος, *oikos*] falls on house" (11:17). Why would Satan turn against himself, drive his minions out, and bring down his own kingdom/house? Only a true opponent of the Evil One would do that! By casting out demons, Jesus wields the very "finger of God" (11:20)—the same divine digit that Pharaoh's magic artists acknowledged as guiding Moses's superior power (Exod 8:16–19)

97. See Spencer, *Gospel of Luke*, 68–71.

98. On "magicians" and other "charismatics" in Luke's narrative and social worlds, see Garrett, *Demise*; Mitzi Smith, *Literary Construction*, 11–56; Spencer, *Portrait*, 88–131.

99. See Luke Timothy Johnson, *Prophetic Jesus*, 29–38; Moessner, *Lord of the Banquet*.

and that etched the stone Torah tablets given to Moses (Deut 9:10)—to enforce God's rule in a troubled world, emancipate God's people from bondage, and navigate them *through* the desert trek as the preeminent prophet like Moses.[100]

Jesus further combines kingdom and household in the image of the castle or palace (αὐλή, *aulē*) fortified by a strong ruler protecting his property (11:21–22). Such grand, gated residences housed ruling authorities like Herod Antipas in Galilee (cf. 7:25) and the high priest in Jerusalem (αὐλή, *aulē* = palace "courtyard" in 22:54–55), who were opposed to Jesus's way. In the present text, this palatial space metaphorically marks the realm of Satan, the cosmic evil liaison with corrupt earthly powers. Satan and his demonic troops are unquestionably "strong" and destructive, but not invincible. When attacked by the "more powerful" one (ἰσχυρότερος, *ischyroteros*)—as John the Baptist so touted Messiah Jesus (3:16)—Satan's malevolent kingdom begins to crumble and give way to God's right-making realm (11:22). Jesus's exorcisms exhibit clear signs of this incursion of God's rule and issue clarion calls to join forces with him in the surging cosmic battle: "Whoever is not with me is against me, and whoever does not gather with me scatters" (11:23).

Although the "stronger" Christ decisively "overpowers" Satan's defenses (11:22), persisting skirmishes and mopping-up operations delay full and final victory. Thus, in the interim, those liberated by Christ must maintain constant vigilance. Jesus continues to develop the household theme, with "house" now representing an individual formerly "occupied" by a demonic resident. Since the "unclean spirit has gone out," the "house" has been "swept and put in order" (11:24–25), which seems like a good thing. But in this case, the clean house signifies *emptiness and inertia*. The house is neat and tidy because nothing is happening there; nothing has filled the vacated space. Hence, Jesus warns, this dark void becomes prime territory for demonic *re*possession with *seven more* nasty cohorts, converting the swept "house" into a slum tenement of filthy inhabitants, so that "the last state of that person [place] is worse than the first (11:26). The implications are clear: deliverance must lead to discipleship, filling the freed life with the Holy ("Clean") Spirit and with acts of service to God and God's people. The "house" metaphor readily situates the individual in a communal context. Tweaking John Donne, we might say that "no one is a house entire of themselves" in God's realm. Each personal "house" becomes an active site of mutual fellowship and support, in the power of the Holy Spirit, to resist the onslaught of oppressive forces.

100. Cf. Spencer, *Portrait*, 107–15; Wall, "Finger of God."

Blessing All Who Hear God's Word (11:27–28)

"While [Jesus] was saying this" (about protecting oneself from returning demons), "a woman in the crowd" suddenly blurts out a benediction of Jesus's mother who carried and suckled him (11:27). What motivates her outburst is uncertain. Perhaps Jesus's reflections on household matters spark the woman's interest in Jesus's family, or perhaps she's simply overcome with the effects of Jesus's "blessed" power and wisdom. The beatification of Jesus's mother, reminiscent of Elizabeth's earlier announcement (1:42–45), does not express devotion to Mary as much as desire for intimate connection with Jesus akin to that enjoyed by Mary in pregnancy and nursing. Intimations of erotic love, associated with womb and breasts, should not be glossed over. We have already observed another woman's passionate physical expressions of love toward Jesus (7:36–50); moreover, various church *fathers* were not shy about imagining their intense love for Jesus as sexual stimulation of *their breasts*, patterned after the unabashed love lyrics in the Song of Songs.[101]

Jesus's response to the woman, while somewhat curt, is more expansive than dismissive, extending her maternal benediction to God's entire household, irrespective of biological kinship or gender: "Blessed rather [or 'much more' (μενοῦν, *menoun*—another 'lesser to greater' comparison; cf. 11:13)] are those who hear the word of God and obey it!" (11:28). This extended-family principle echoes 8:20–21 and enhances the present chapter's emphases on faithful, Spirit-driven activity in the Father's kingdom (11:1–26).

Desiring Signs of God's Kingdom (11:29–32)

As the crowds swell around Jesus, he returns to the penchant for dramatic signs among this "evil generation," now calling attention to biblical signs associated with the prophet Jonah and the people of Nineveh (Jonah 1–4) and the royal figures of King Solomon and the queen of the South (1 Kgs 10:1–13). As Jesus's exorcisms certify his mediation of God's liberating rule, these scriptural stories signify God's communication of transformative word and incisive wisdom throughout the world. On the flip side, however, which Jesus stresses here,

101. Song 1:13; 4:5; 7:3, 7–8; 8:8–10. Cf. Bernard of Clairveaux, *Sermons on the Song of Songs* 9.7: "While the bride is conversing about the Bridegroom, he . . . suddenly appears, yields to her desire by giving her a kiss. . . . The filling up of her breasts is a proof of this. For so great is the potency of that holy kiss, that no sooner has the bride received it than she conceives and her breasts grow rounded . . . with milky abundance. *Men with an urge to frequent prayer will have experience of what I say*" (cited in Moore, "Song," 330 [emphasis added]).

these signs also portend condemnation against those who fail to heed God's message. Counterpointing Jesus's affirmation of those who "hear the word of God and obey it" (Luke 11:28) is his denunciation of those who obstruct and repudiate this word. Moreover, the temporal scope expands from the present manifestation of God's reign ("the kingdom of God has come to you" [11:20]) to include God's final judgment of the world executed through the Son of Humankind (11:30–32).

As God's appointed eschatological judge (cf. Acts 17:30–31), Jesus the Son of Humankind is already lining up key witnesses against recalcitrant evildoers. In this scenario, the channels of God's word and wisdom, Jonah and Solomon, prove less significant than the receivers: the people of Nineveh and the queen of the South, who will "rise up at the judgment" as models of repentance (Ninevites) and receptivity (queen) to testify against this corrupt generation (Luke 11:31–32). Note well the surprising, "foreign" character of these exemplary witnesses: Ninevite men (ἄνδρες, *andres*) from the north (Assyria in Mesopotamia), typically cast as Israel's bitter enemies (cf. Nah 1–3); and a female ruler from the south (Sheba in Africa), who breaks the negative mold of alien queens and princesses in 1–2 Kings opposing God's prophets and leading Israel's kings astray (1 Kgs 11:1–8; 18:4; 19:1–3; 21:1–16; 2 Kgs 9:30–37). Far from contributing to Solomon's corruption (1 Kgs 11:1–8), the southern queen gave full ear to his God-given wisdom. Moreover, she took the initiative, making a long journey to seek out and take in this wisdom: "she came from the ends of the earth to listen to/hear [ἀκοῦσαι, *akousai*] the wisdom of Solomon" (Luke 11:31). Her aggressive, acoustic response ranks her among the "blessed" members of God's family (11:28).[102] Jesus's pairing of positive, "foreign," male and female exemplars who challenge Israel to a more faithful relationship with God recalls his earlier allusions to the Sidonian widow and Syrian officer Naaman (4:25–27). Once again, Jesus mines the Jewish Scriptures to highlight the expansive scope of God's realm, extending north and south (east and west [13:29]) to the ends of the earth (cf. Acts 1:8) to welcome all peoples, across gender and other status lines, into God's royal household.

While Jesus looks back to Israel's history and forward to the final judgment, he remains fully in the present moment as the supreme agent of God's kingdom to *this* generation. If the ancient Ninevites and queen of the South embraced God's way revealed through Jonah and Solomon, respectively—both of whom Scripture portrays as seriously flawed figures used by God—how much more should this current audience welcome God's word and wisdom embodied in Jesus the Son of Humankind, infinitely "greater than" Jonah and Solomon

102. See the extensive discussion of Luke's reference to the queen of the South in Spencer, *Salty Wives*, 230–45.

and intimately *here* (ὧδε, *hōde* [Luke 11:32])![103] The eschatological blessings and judgment of God's rule have been set in motion, here and now, in Jesus's mission.

Judging Light and Darkness (11:33–36)

Jesus further expounds his judgment theme via a common light/darkness trope. The focus shifts from aural to visual imagery, from ear to eye, which functioned in ancient anatomical thought as the "lamp of the body," emitting light rays pulsing *within* the body (rather than processing from without) to shine upon objects and to guide one's way.[104] As a moral-perceptual image, the eye betrays the quality of one's inner life (light). If it is "healthy," blazing clearly and brightly as a "lamp to [one's] feet and a light to [one's] path" mapped by God's word (Ps 119:105), the eye reveals an inner being (will, thoughts, emotions, "heart," "soul") suffused with benevolent power and purpose. Conversely, an "evil eye" shooting dark poison darts against neighbors and strangers alike betrays a stained heart full of malice and misery.[105]

But eyes can play tricks on us; appearances can be deceiving. Accordingly, Jesus, ever with a keen eye for seeing through the hidden and the hypocritical to the heart of the matter, warns: "Consider whether the light in you is not darkness" (11:35). That is, consider whether the sight you *presume* or *pretend* to have is true or skewed according to the definitive "eye chart" tracking your *attitudes* and *actions*. What dwells within, what fuels one's inner life, will come out in conduct, both verbal and behavioral (cf. Matt 15:10–20; Mark 7:14–23). This general caution against hypocrisy boils over in a scathing invective against a group of Pharisees and scribes in the ensuing dinner scene.

Denouncing Hypocrisy and Resistance of God's Wisdom (11:37–54)

Neither host nor guest approaches this affair loaded for battle. "While Jesus was speaking, a Pharisee invited him to dine with him," and Jesus cordially

103. Distinct from the parallel in Matt 12:40–41, Luke does not compare Jonah's three-day sojourn in the fish's belly with the Son of Humankind's three-day destiny "in the heart of the earth." Luke's analogy between Jonah and the Son of Humankind focuses exclusively on their preaching of repentance.

104. Plato, *Tim.* 45B–46A; Empedocles, frag. 84; Philo, *Abraham*, 150–56; for these and other references concerning the "extramission theory of vision," see Allison, "Eye Is the Lamp," building on Betz, "Matthew vi.22f."

105. On the "evil eye" in antiquity, see Elliott, "Paul"; Derrett, "Evil Eye."

accepted and "took his place at the table" (11:37). The scenario signals considerable common ground between this Pharisee and Jesus (table = fellowship) and a congenial forum for biblical-theological discussion (table talk). Luke reports no prior intent on this Pharisee's part to test or trap Jesus; he seems genuinely interested in Jesus's teaching. But soon the host does look askance at a peculiar (unexpected) aspect of Jesus's table manners, much as Simon the Pharisee had done (7:39). In this case, however, the issue is not whom Jesus welcomes at table but *how* he eats, specifically, with unwashed ("unbaptized"— οὐ . . . ἐβαπτίσθη, *ou . . . ebaptisthē*) hands (11:38). The concern is not with hygiene but with holiness or purity—*not* conceived as washing away sins (only God can do that) but as ritually setting one apart for fellowship with the holy God. Recall that the Pharisees envisioned the domestic table as sacred space, a microcosm of the Jerusalem temple, so to speak, where they hosted God and acknowledged God's holy presence in daily life. No written Torah legislation required hand-washing before meals, but this and other ablutions constituted a logical part of the Pharisees' oral traditions reinforcing holiness.[106]

Jesus has no particular axe to grind about washing up before dinner. He can take it or leave it. Remember that he earlier blasted Simon's inhospitable failure to provide washing-water (though for feet rather than hands), but only after Simon had criticized the "sinful" woman's bathing Jesus with her tears and kisses (Luke 7:39–45). Jesus is not antiwashing and certainly not antiholiness. But he does insist on the real thing, on a true match between ritual and behavior, symbol and character, inner and outer being. As John challenged those who sought baptism to show evidence of a changed life signified by the water rite (3:7–14), so Jesus exhorts his host and Pharisee-lawyer companions to synchronize their mealtime "baptizing" of hands with faithful, loving, and merciful conduct.

Somewhat surprisingly, however, Jesus's rhetoric rises to such a shrill pitch as to make John's preaching seem almost tame in comparison. Though Jesus refrains from labeling his audience as "vipers" (cf. 3:7), he calls them "fools"—shamefully unwise in the ways of God (11:40)[107]—a move designed to cut the Pharisees and legal experts to the quick. Jesus then excoriates them with a litany of six "woes" (11:42–52). Little wonder after this tirade that this group becomes "very hostile" to Jesus, and once he goes "outside" (pushed out by his insulted

106. See Borg, *Conflict*, 110–13; Spencer, *What Did Jesus Do?*, 93–94.

107. "Fools" (ἄφρονες, *aphrones*) represent the *un*wise, the antithesis of the "wise" (φρόνιμοι, *phronimoi*); cf. Jesus's exposure of violent resistance to messengers of the "Wisdom of God" later in this polemic (11:49–51).

host?), they "lie in ambush to pounce on something he might say" (11:53–54 AT).[108] At this juncture, Luke's Jesus markedly ramps up the debate with the leading interpreters of God's scriptural way.

The issues surrounding Jesus's six woes must be serious indeed to generate this much heat. We may analyze them in two sets of three, addressed to distinct-yet-related targets—Pharisees and lawyers—and focused on social/ministerial and pedagogical/epistemological matters, respectively. Jesus remains deeply concerned with how people act and treat one another and what they know and share with one another.

Social and ministerial ethics (Pharisees)	**Pedagogical and epistemological strategies (lawyers)**
1. Practicing charity (11:39–42)	1. Conveying Torah (11:45–46)
2. Seeking honor (11:43)	2. Receiving wisdom (11:47–51)
3. Exercising leadership (11:44)	3. Sharing knowledge (11:52)

Social and ministerial ethics. For all their admirable study and application of Torah to daily life, the Pharisees fail miserably as religious leaders, in Jesus's view, to translate their virtues and values to the wider community. In short, though staying within society rather than withdrawing like the Qumran sectarians, the Pharisees in Jesus's critique still seek more to establish their own private holiness havens than to promote the inclusive kingdom of God. Jesus first addresses their *economic* orientation: for all their attention to clean cups and dishes (and hands) and tithing obligations to the minute level of herbs and spices (no "tax loopholes"), the Pharisees remain motivated by "greed and wickedness" (11:39) to the neglect of core virtues of "justice and . . . love" toward all people (*woe #1* [11:42]).[109] Again, Jesus has no problem with their washing and tithing concerns ("these you ought to have practiced"), but if these actions truly bring the Pharisees closer to God, then they should trigger material manifestations of God's right-making love through "giving alms" to the poor out of the generous "contents"[110] of their hearts ("the core of who you are" [CEB]), as well as out of their cupboards and storehouses (cf. 12:33; Acts 9:36; 10:2–4, 31; 24:17).

108. On ἐνεδρεύω (*enedreuō*) as "lie in ambush," see Barclay M. Newman, *Concise Greek-English Dictionary*, 62; cf. Acts 23:21 for only other NT reference.

109. "Wickedness" (πονηρία, *ponēria*) in 11:39 relates to the "evil" (πονηρός, *ponēros*) eye in 11:34 (rendered rather mildly as "not healthy" in the NRSV). The "love of God" in 11:42 is best taken as a subjective genitive, signifying God's love toward those suffering injustice.

110. Τὰ ἐνόντα (*ta enonta*), lit. "the things being inside" (11:41); cf. BDAG, 334; Fitzmyer, 2:941, 947.

Next, Jesus addresses the Pharisees' *public* preoccupation with honor-rating as they jostle for prime places, or "the seat of honor" (lit. "first seat"—πρωτοκαθεδρίαν, *prōtokathedrian*) in both synagogue and market square (*woe #2* [11:43]). The problem is not honor-seeking per se, but rather the means and motive. The pursuit of true greatness runs down the path of humble service to the last and lowliest, such as little children, not self-promoting preening and currying of accolades (9:46–48; 22:24–27). The Pharisees (and Jesus's disciples!) are locked on this self-serving, social-climbing treadmill. Sadly, they "love" (ἀγαπᾶω, *agapaō* [11:43]) such personal honor most of all, rather than the Most High God of "justice and love," whose lordly character finds greatest expression in Jesus's self-emptying service to others (cf. 22:27).

Third, Jesus exposes the Pharisees' *didactic* deficiencies. As dedicated scholars and practitioners of Torah, they have a responsibility to guide the less learned in God's way. Unfortunately, though, they function "like unmarked graves" that "people walk over" unawares (*woe #3* [11:44]). This cemetery comparison, particularly invidious to Pharisees adhering to regulations governing contact with unclean corpses (see Lev 21:11; Num 5:2; 6:6–8; 19:11–20), digs deeper than the parallel in Matthew. Matthew's Jesus pushes the stark outer-inner discrepancies of these polished biblical scholars who "look beautiful" on first glance, like "whitewashed tombs," but cannot hide the rotting "filth" of their skeletal inner lives (Matt 23:27–28). Luke's Jesus keeps the grave image but doesn't give these Pharisees credit even for trying to play the game and impress others (outsiders) with their piety. They simply lie low, caring nothing about the masses that pass by or over them, whom they couldn't help anyway in their lifeless states. They seem only to use people as an audience to bask before and to boost their honor-rating (cf. the second woe). Otherwise, they couldn't care less whether anyone noticed them beyond their religious klatch; by the same token, they show no interest in guiding others' "walk" in God's life-giving way outlined in the Torah (Luke 11:44). As with the neglectful priest and Levite in the parable, Jesus may again hint at the banality of evil, the blithe, blind obsession of ideologues and functionaries alike with their own agendas and ambitions at the expense of the masses and in contradiction with the ideas (Torah in this case) they putatively espouse.[111] The two scenarios flip roles, however: in the parable, the religious personnel walk by the half-dead victim without lifting a finger; in the woe, the people walk over the "dead" Torah scholars without receiving an ounce of life-giving instruction.

Pedagogical and epistemological strategies. Jesus develops this teaching-learning, revealing-knowing crisis more fully in the next triad of woes,

111. See Arendt, *Eichmann* (cf. n. 56 above on Luke 10:25–37).

with particular focus on the "lawyers," closely aligned with Pharisees' interests but not necessarily affiliated with their party. As a νομικός (*nomikos*) earlier prompted "Teacher" Jesus to interpret the Torah's love command through the Samaritan parable (10:25–37), so a "lawyer" now provokes woes from Jesus, remarking, "Teacher, when you say these things, you insult us too" (11:45). He's right about that, as Jesus doesn't skip a beat in continuing his tirade with special application to Torah professionals. The lawyer's term for "insult" (ὑβρίζω, *hybrizō*) is a strong one, way beyond a needling gibe or constructive criticism. Luke's two other uses appear in contexts of cruel mocking and mistreating Jesus (18:32) and Paul (Acts 14:5) with deadly intent (cf. similar violent associations in Matt 22:6; 1 Thess 2:2). Eerily, Jesus seems more destructive than constructive in his woes. This is as vehement as Luke's Jesus gets. The rarity and intensity of this polemic signal the seriousness of the problem Jesus addresses. Nothing is more vital than leading people to know God and God's ways; conversely, nothing is more despicable than negligent stewards of this knowledge.

Jesus first upbraids the lawyers for loading up (φορτίζω, *phortizō*) people with back-breaking loads (φορτία, *phortia*) without so much as lifting a finger to assist them (*woe #4* [11:46]). In context, these "burdens" must be the panoply of the 613 Mosaic regulations, plus the myriad oral traditions interpreting them. Some envisaged Jewish covenantal law inscribing God's wisdom (see Sir 24) as a yoke placed on the necks of God's people, both heavy in import and responsibility and light in privilege and life-enriching potentiality (cf. Jer 5:5; Sir 6:23–31; 51:26; Acts 15:10; m. 'Abot 3:5; m. Ber. 2:2). Though a marvelous gift of God and incorporating provisions of mercy and forgiveness, the law could seem unbearable for the weak and wayward beset by the burdens of life and sin—which is to say, for everyone from time to time (cf. Acts 15:10). Accordingly, the solemn vocation of Torah teacher-scholars is not merely to impose and enforce the law, but also to explain its benefits and ease the path to obedience through patient, sympathetic leadership (cf. Matt 11:28–30). As Paul enjoined the Galatian churches, fraught with weighty tension over legal observance: "Bear one another's burdens, and in this way you will fulfill the law of Christ" (Gal 6:2). Unfortunately, however, the Torah specialists that Jesus encounters refuse to lend a "finger" to lighten their clients' loads. What a contrast with Jesus's lending the dynamic "finger of God" to liberate those beaten down by oppressive forces (Luke 11:20).

From exposing the lawyers' dereliction of pedagogical duty, Jesus turns to challenge their violent rejection of divine Wisdom's messengers (*woe #5* [11:47–51]). The scope also widens to identify the lawyers historically with the gamut of Israel's "ancestors" (11:48) and presently with the whole of "this generation" (11:51). Since creation, Woman Wisdom has revealed God to human beings through a host of prophetic emissaries crying out in the streets, calling people to heed God's word and walk in God's way:

> In every generation [Woman Wisdom] passes into holy souls
> and makes them friends of God, and prophets;
> for God loves nothing so much as the person who lives with wisdom.
> (Wis 7:22–23; cf. 7:22–8:1; Prov 1:20–33; 8:22–9:6).[112]

In this current generation, the "Wisdom of God" has sent her most personal and powerful prophet, Jesus the Son, along with his closest associates, John the baptizer and select apostles (Luke 2:40, 52; 7:33–35).[113] However, the tragic pattern of snubbing Wisdom's ambassadors, even to the point of shedding their innocent blood, persists from primeval to present-evil times, from A (Abel) to Z (Zechariah) in biblical history—from the beginning of the first HB book (Gen 4:1–8) to the ending of its last (2 Chr 24:20–22)—and continuing in the crucifixion of Jesus and persecutions of the apostles, presaged now by Jesus (Luke 11:49–51) and fulfilled in the balance of Luke and Acts. Opportunities for humans created in God's image to know God intimately have been wide open (nothing has been hidden!) across the generations in complementary divine manifestations of Father King and Mother Wisdom, in the comprehensive curricula of scriptural Law, Prophets, and Writings, and in compelling incarnations of God's way through Jesus the Prophet-Son and his delegates. What more could God have done, short of coercing love, which would cut the nerve of covenantal partnership? How can God bear the repeated, brutal rejection of God's ever-flowing stream of love and wisdom? What is there left to say but "Woe!"?

In a final, more pointed barb, summing up his overall frustration, Jesus rebukes the lawyers because they "have taken away the key of knowledge [κλεῖδα τῆς γνώσεως, *kleida tēs gnōseōs*]" (*woe #6* [11:52]). The problem is not in *losing* the key—they still have it, a whole set of master keys in fact from lessons of history, Scripture, prophets, and apostles highlighted above (cf. Rom 9:4–5)—but rather in not *using* it to enter into a fuller relationship with God and deeper understanding of God's realm for themselves and their tutees. In fact, in Jesus's judgment, these religious leaders have not simply abdicated their Torah-teaching, spiritual-directing vocations but have actively obstructed ("hin-

112. See Elizabeth A. Johnson, *Friends of God*, 40–45, and *She Who Is*, 86–100.

113. Whereas Matthew's Jesus directly sends divine emissaries ("Therefore *I send* you prophets, sages, and scribes, some of whom you will kill and crucify" [Matt 23:34]), in Luke, the "prophets and apostles," including Jesus himself, are sent by the personified "Wisdom of God" (Luke 11:49).

dered, prevented" [κωλύω, *kōlyō*]) people's path to knowing God (11:52). They seem to view knowledge (γνῶσις, *gnōsis*) of God more like a secret gnostic code for the initiated in-group rather than a gracious disclosure of revelation to all God's children. Lest we heap all the blame, however, for such smug protectionism on the lawyers and associates, we should recall Jesus's rebuke of his own disciples' proclivity to block outsiders' participation in Jesus's liberating mission ("Do not stop [κωλύετε, *kōlyete*] him" [9:49–50]), which will sadly extend to hindering little children's access to Jesus before journey's end (18:15–17; cf. Acts 8:36; 10:47; 11:17).

The Gracious Creator God and Anxious Human Creatures (12:1–34)[114]

Introduction and Transition (12:1–3)

"Meanwhile" Luke crisply introduces three transitions. First, Jesus's teaching now concentrates "first" on the disciples, with the crowds still present but more marginal. Ironically, the crowd, "gathered by the thousands [lit. 'the myriad'—τῶν μυριάδων, *tōn myriadōn*]," tramples over one another to hear Jesus (12:1a), thus impeding their desired goal. The people wind up blocking each other's paths to knowledge, albeit unwittingly, in contrast to the lawyers' calculated obstruction. Either way, "this generation" continues to struggle to find their way to God.

Second, Jesus reiterates the warning about the Pharisees' "hypocrisy," which he had just expounded at the dinner table. Now he compares their insidious cant to *yeast* (12:1b), a decaying ingredient that spreads its influence pervasively and surreptitiously. While yeast can work for good in making bread (13:20–21), in the Bible it often symbolizes infectious evil to be ferreted out, as the ancient Israelites removed all yeast (leaven) from their homes before the exodus, signifying repudiation of their despoiled, oppressed exile in Egypt (Exod 12:8, 15, 19–20, 33–34; cf. 1 Cor 5:6–8; Gal 5:7–9). Although the Pharisees attempt to "cover up" instead of root out their inner corruption, Jesus makes "known" (γινώσκω, *ginōskō*) their true character (Luke 12:2). His earlier point about God's concealing insight from self-touting "wise" and "intelligent" religious teachers (10:21) matches the Pharisee scholars' own blinkered misunderstanding of God's revelation. This "hiding" dialectic is similar to the "hardening" dilemma with Pharaoh: "I [God] will harden Pharaoh's heart" (Exod 4:21; 7:3; 9:12; 10:1, 20, 27; 11:10); "Pharaoh hardened his [own] heart" (8:15, 32).

114. See a closely related, detailed analysis of this passage in Spencer, "To Fear."

Third, Jesus subtly shifts the open-curtain scenario from the Pharisees back to the disciples via the reprised image of light shining in the darkness: "Whatever *you* [disciples] have said in the dark will be heard in the light" (Luke 12:3; cf. 11:33–36). He then reinforces this visual image with a verbal one: "Whatever *you* [disciples] have whispered behind closed doors will be proclaimed from the housetops" (12:3). These scenarios adumbrate the theme developed at length in 12:4–34. What Jesus now seeks to bring to light and out in the open is not unconscious, delusive pride and hypocrisy, but rather high-alert, hyper-sensitive *fear and anxiety*. Speaking "in the dark" and "whispering" (lit. "speaking in the ears") in closed-door "inner room" (ταμεῖον, *tameion* [cf. Matt 6:6; 24:26]) befit situations of intense vulnerability to outside threats. By evoking these feelings of insecurity, Jesus sets the stage for instructing his "friend"/"flock"-followers (Luke 12:4, 32) about what does and does not merit fear and worry (12:4–12, 22–34). In between he presents a parable addressing common anxieties about financial security and inevitable, yet temporally unpredictable, mortality (12:13–21).

We have already noted the deep-seated angst afflicting many ancients who perceived themselves as pawns in a volatile battle among cosmic and political powers. Jesus continues to assume this precarious environment, especially on the political front with threatening "synagogues," "rulers," and "authorities" (12:11). Otherwise, however, Jesus focuses more pointedly on *personal and practical* anxieties regarding "what you will eat," "what you will wear," how long you will live, when you will die, and what happens to you then (12:4–7, 19–31). Such cognitive-emotional fretting weighs heavily on the human species. Other animals, such as birds (12:6–7, 24), have instinctual physiological reactions of flight, fight, or freeze to perilous situations but lack the capacity in their tiny bird-brains to ruminate on their vulnerable lives. With humans' advanced brain power come enormous benefits, not least critical faculties for self-conscious knowing and thinking about what it means to know (epistemology). But such higher thinking also brings potential for greater stress: the capacity not simply to avert danger when it strikes, but to anticipate various forms it might take in the future, including ultimate experiences of *death and afterlife*, taps into deep veins of fear, anxiety, depression—and repression.[115] What we know (that we will die) can trigger considerable angst about what we do not know (when we will die and what happens afterward). Ignorance may not be all bliss, but it has its moments.

Jesus confronts this distress with a kind of cognitive therapy, addressing corrosive automatic thoughts and feelings, not with some miracle cure—no

115. Cf. Ernest Becker, *Denial*; Varki and Brower, *Denial*.

casting out of a demon of fear or spirit of worry—but with *correct thinking* about the way things are and will be. More specifically, Jesus admonishes his followers to engage in wise *theological thinking* about the *Creator God*, the Source and Sustainer of all life, plant (grains and lilies) and animal (sparrows, ravens, and humans). Jesus commands the disciples to "consider" (κατανοέω, *katanoeō* [12:24, 27]), that is, "to think about very carefully, to consider closely,"[116] this God-centered view of life and death, present and future. Consider this Creator God as Bird-Keeper, Landowner, Farmer, Gardener, Shepherd, Father—images of divine care running through 12:4–34. But we must also reckon with a more demanding (12:20) God of judgment with whom we have to do, in conjunction with the Holy Spirit, Son of Humankind, and "angels of God" (12:8). Peace and security come in compliance with God's way and solidarity with God's world. Self-absorbed resistance and independence can have fearful consequences. The key, with Jesus (like Aristotle), is to fear the right things for the right reasons at the right time (cf. *Rhet.* 2.1.9 [1378a], *Eth. nic.* 4.5 [1125b–1126a]).

God of Sparrows and Hairs (12:4–12)

Jesus calls his disciples to solemn attention with a triple "I tell you" preface (12:4, 5, 8), tempered, however, by the intimate "my friends" address (12:4), the only time Luke's Jesus so refers to his disciples. This is serious, personal business, a matter of life and death, for Jesus and his beloved followers. Specifically, Jesus discusses the apostles' impending unjust persecution, even martyrdom, at the hands of religious and political authorities, predicted in 9:23–24 and 11:49–50 (cf. 21:12–19) and realized in Acts. While such ominous prospects naturally engender apprehension, Jesus urges his associates to resist baseless panic ("Do not fear"/"Do not worry"), even as he alerts them to a legitimate cause for fear ("But I will warn you whom to fear") (12:4–5, 7, 11). His therapeutic approach is driven by *theological argument* to educate (not eradicate) proper emotional response. The logic unfolds in two paired lesser-to-greater considerations: the first focused on *fear*, the second on *care*.[117]

116. Louw and Nida, *Greek-English Lexicon*, 1:350.

117. On "fear" and "care" ("nurturing love") as two distinct "primal passions" or deeply rooted "primary process" emotional systems, see Panksepp and Biven, *Archaeology of Mind*, 1–38, 177–202, 283–310.

	Fear	Care
Lesser:	*Body-killers*: "Do not fear those who kill the body, and after that can do nothing more [lit. 'not having (ἐχόντων, *echontōn*) anything more to do']" (12:4).	*Sparrows*: "Are not five sparrows sold for two pennies? Yet not one of them is forgotten in God's sight" (12:6).
Greater:	*Hell-dispatcher*: "But I will warn you whom to fear: fear him who, after he has killed, has [ἔχοντα, *echonta*] authority to cast into hell. Yes, I tell you, fear him!" (12:5).	*Disciples*: "But even the hairs of your head are all counted. Do not be afraid; you are of more value than many sparrows" (12:7).

The "fear" pair of statements narrows the objects of dread from *multiple assaulters* ("those"), whose nefarious influence extends only to body-killing in this life, to the *singular death-dealer* ("him"), whose authority includes enforcing a permanent, postmortem punishment in hell. The "lesser" threats are earthly officials (12:11) who will arrest, interrogate, and charge Jesus's followers with capital crimes. But their power is neutralized by the "greater" one with unique authority over people's lives, deaths, and eternal destinies. This may seem like cold comfort, hardly an antidote to fear—more like going from the frying pan into the fire, literally, hellfire![118] Here Jesus seems to provide plenty of fuel for fire-and-brimstone preachers, unlike earlier where he nixed James and John's incendiary scheme (9:54–55).

Or maybe not. This "greater" Supreme Judge of whom Jesus warns is no doubt God the Creator of all. Satan, the only other possibility, might like to have all the miserable companions in hell he could muster, but Jesus regards Satan as already fallen under judgment (10:18; 11:18–22), not as the final judge. Still, it is important to register that Jesus refers to the terrifying, hell-casting God "implicitly,"[119] not overtly, as "the one/this one" (τόν/τοῦτον, *ton/touton*) to be feared. In this thick theocentric discourse, Jesus names God nine times—seven as "God" (θεός, *theos* [12:6, 8, 9, 20, 21, 24, 28]), twice as "Father" (πατήρ, *patēr* [12:30, 32])—but is careful not to overplay fearful-punitive elements. Rather, he begins with "God's" comforting watch care over sparrows (12:6) and ends with

118. Luke 12:5 is Luke's only reference to "hell," or Gehenna (γέεννα), associated historically with the valley of Hinnom outside Jerusalem, a site of occasional child sacrifice (2 Kgs 23:10; 2 Chr 28:3; 33:6; Jer 7:32–33; 19:6), and eschatologically with the fiery pit of punishment for the wicked (4 Ezra 7:36; Matt 5:22, 29–30; 18:9; 23:33).

119. Carroll, 264.

the "Father's" reassuring benevolence toward his "flock" (12:32) as definitive reasons to "not be afraid" (12:7, 32).

The transition from fearsome hell-dispatcher to winsome birdwatcher in the second pair of arguments may not be as abrupt or different as some have supposed.[120] Having authority or capacity to do something is not the same as using it. One who *could* kill bodies and then raise and consign them to a pit of perpetual fiery torture ("this one" *is* a terrifying cosmic power) *will not necessarily carry out* such horrific action, might not exercise the nuclear option, certainly not as a first response, on his creatures. Green catches well the spirit of Jesus's logic: "In hostile situations of life imperilment, God is the only one who should be feared, but the character of God is such that one need not fear him!"[121]

This divine character is poignantly manifest in the Creator's minute, material care for the lowliest of creatures, represented by the sparrow, and the least significant human body parts, represented by head hairs. Though sparrows rate low on the commercial index,[122] each one remains as firmly "before God" (ἐνώπιον τοῦ θεοῦ, *enōpion tou theou*), in God's attentive presence, as the archangel Gabriel (1:19; 12:6). God takes sympathetic account of the plight of each sparrow, whether it is sold for consumption or, as Matthew adds, simply "falls to the ground" (Matt 10:29). A strong ecotheological point emerges: if God remains carefully invested in the struggle of all creation, so should we.[123] But Luke's Jesus does not lead us down an ultra-Darwinian, hyperreductionist trail, placing all nature, including human nature, on a static, self-centered flat level.[124] With remarkable capacities for thought, language, and dialogic relationship with God, whose creative image they bear, humans have "more value" than the sparrows.[125] And since God cares for the common, vulnerable sparrow, "how much more" can we count on God's meticulous care for us, down to every

120. Tannehill, 202: "A fearsome God has authority to cast into hell. Then Jesus shifts abruptly to emphasize God's care for even the least creatures and God's greatest care for the disciples (vv. 6–7). These different descriptions of God have the common goal of overcoming fear of human opponents."

121. Green, 482.

122. "Penny" is a loose translation of ἀσσάριον (*assarion*), designating a Roman coin worth one-sixteenth of a denarius. So in Jesus's calculus, each sparrow is valued at one-fortieth of a denarius. See Troy Martin, "Time and Money," 69–73.

123. Cf. Elizabeth A. Johnson, *Quest*, 190: "The Creator Spirit dwells in compassionate solidarity with every living being that suffers, from the dinosaurs wiped out by an asteroid to the baby impala eaten by a lioness. Not a sparrow falls to the ground without eliciting a knowing suffering in the heart of God. Such an idea is not meant to glorify suffering. . . . Nature's crying out is met by the Spirit, who groans with the labor pains of all creation (Rom 8:22)."

124. See the richly detailed, incisive argument in Cunningham, *Darwin's Pious Idea*, 25–129.

125. On humans' special bearing of God's image, see Jeeves, *Minds*, 73–75, 189–91.

strand of hair on our heads, which tend to "fall out" the closer we get to death (12:7, 24; cf. 21:18; Acts 27:34)![126]

Hence, Jesus confronts his disciples' natural fear of death and decay with a subtle vision of life after death, which he soon develops more patently (12:8–12). In this more allusive approach, he clarifies the potential misconception that his followers need not fear those who can "only" kill the body because the body doesn't really matter in the long run, since, once rid of its somatic baggage, the spirit/soul is free to soar in heavenly bliss. Jesus effectively shatters such dualistic notions by asserting God's intimate interest in feathered and haired "friends," down to the last follicle. Augustine took this assurance as a sign that we will have full heads of hair in our afterlives on our resurrected bodies![127] The hope of renewed *bodies* heightens the value of bodily existence and lessens the fearful sting of death (and receding hairline).

But for all the sympathy God shows for human frailty and the promise of eternal security for God's much-valued embodied creatures, humans have a corresponding *capacity and responsibility* to "acknowledge" Jesus before hostile authorities, with dire consequences for failure to do so (12:8–9). For all the disjunction between the corrosive present age and the restorative age to come, a vital confessional-relational continuity with God stretches across time via Jesus the Son of Humankind (and attending angels) and the Holy Spirit. Publicly confessing one's loyal love now for God-in-Jesus before antagonistic rulers, even unto death, guarantees the Son of Humankind's advocacy both now and postmortem before God's heavenly angelic court (cf. 1 En. 99:3). Conversely, present public denial or equivocation warrants the Son of Humankind's future repudiation rather than defense.

The cosmic-eschatological horizon Jesus pictures most closely reflects the apocalyptic visions of Daniel and Revelation, complete with angels, the Son of Humankind as God's chief ruling-judging agent, and lethal crises fomented by usurpers of divine authority (see Dan 7:9–28; Rev 1:9–20; 14:14–20). In Daniel's day, the Hellenistic megalomaniac Antiochus IV arrogated to himself the divine status of "Epiphanes," or "God Manifest," and demanded worship from all his Jewish subjects, under penalty of death. Similarly, in John the seer's (and Luke's) time, various Roman emperors promoted their adoptive deifications and persecuted any who refused to acknowledge their claims, which for Jews and Christians was tantamount to blasphemous denial of the one true God.[128]

126. This "greater value" of human beings in Luke does not demand a narrow anthropocentrism, nor does it deny the interdependence of creatures made and nurtured by God. See the useful, though somewhat overplayed, ecotheological critique in Elvey, "Storing."

127. Augustine, *City of God* 22.19; cited in Just, 204.

128. On divine sonship in the Roman imperial cult, see Peppard, *Son of God*, 31–85.

Moreover, in both eras, a small but powerful cadre of Jewish elites collaborated with the imperial tyrants for political expediency.[129] But for Jesus the Son of Humankind, presaged by Daniel and proclaimed by John and Luke, there can be no truck with divine pretenders, however powerful they may seem. Acknowledged, unshakeable alliance with the true Creator God revealed in Son Jesus is nonnegotiable and, if it comes to that, worthy of martyrdom. To lose one's life in wholehearted communion with the Lord of life is to save it; to save one's life in double-minded segregation from the Lord of life is to lose it (cf. Luke 9:24–26).

Jesus thus appears to draw a bold theological and eschatological line in the sand. But as he concludes the present argument, the matter becomes more complicated, flickering back and forth between lighter and bolder fonts. A lighter note emerges in the proviso that "everyone who speaks a word against the Son of Humankind *will be forgiven*," only to be overwhelmed by the bolder addendum, "but whoever blasphemes against the Holy Spirit *will not be forgiven*" (12:10). Jarring paradoxes are nothing new for Luke's Jesus, but at first blush this set of parallel statements seems blatantly contradictory. The Son of Humankind Jesus and the Holy Spirit, though distinct persons, are united in fellowship with God. Jesus the divine-human is conceived in Mary's womb by the Spirit and filled with the Spirit at his baptism in filial love with God the Father (1:35; 3:21–22). To affirm one is to affirm the other; likewise, to offend one is to offend the other. So why can offensive speech against one (Son of Humankind) be forgiven, but not against the other (Holy Spirit)?

Closer examination, however, suggests a key distinction, again on the lines of a lesser/heavier contrast: one who "speaks a word against" is committing a lesser offense than one who "blasphemes against." The Triune God is not some petty insecure ruler who cannot abide a cross word. Quite the contrary, the biblical lament tradition encourages candid, even critical, dialogue as a means to growing in faith and knowledge of God. Luke's Jesus frequently responds to criticism, from disciples or scholars, with constructive ripostes, not ex cathedra bans on forgiveness. Blaspheming, however, connotes a more invidious and inveterate assault on divine honor by one who knows better, by one who has previously known God's gracious character but opts to turn defiantly against God's way. Blasphemy reflects adamant apostasy, the determined "denial" of the Creator-God-in-Christ-and-Spirit "before others," extending Jesus's warning

129. See 1 Macc 1:10–15; 2 Macc 4:7–22. Luke typically portrays the temple authorities (chief priests and elders) in some alliance with Roman and Herodian officials against the rule of God advanced by Jesus and his followers (Luke 9:22; 19:27; 22:3–6, 66–71; 23:35; Acts 4:1–3, 25–27; 5:17–18). The response among synagogue leaders, however, is more variable, with some welcoming Christ and his gospel (Luke 4:15, 42–44; 8:41, 51–56; Acts 18:8; 28:23–24).

from 12:9.[130] This offense "will not be forgiven," a genuinely terrifying prospect to which, however, hardened arrogant offenders are totally oblivious.

Divine figure	**Verbal offense**	**Juridical verdict**
Son of Humankind	*Light*: anyone who "speaks a word against [λόγον εἰς, *logon eis*]"	Forgiveness
Holy Spirit	*Heavy*: anyone who "blasphemes against [βλασφημήσαντι εἰς, *blasphēmēsanti eis*]"	No forgiveness

So as not to incite undue fear, the net of unforgivable blasphemy should not be cast too widely. Consider two cases. First, recall when the scribes and Pharisees raised serious questions about Jesus apparently "speaking blasphemies" because he claimed the divine prerogative as Son of Humankind to forgive sins (5:20–24). Though the Spirit is not mentioned, the collocation of blasphemy, Son of Humankind, and forgiveness suggests a potentially unpardonable offense against God's honor. But though Jesus pushed back against his critics, he pronounced no anathema. Did they get away with blasphemy, then? Actually, the religious scholars assessed blasphemy quite rightly: any human claiming authority to do what "God alone" can do is blaspheming God—*unless* that human being is in fact God incarnate, the most audacious claim anyone could dare make. The scribes and Pharisees were right not to swallow the inference that Jesus (or any prophet or so-called Messiah) fit that bill without serious examination. They did not, at this early juncture in Jesus's ministry, have enough evidence to accept his fully divine-human identity and then reject it. In fact, after Jesus's response they remained open to further insight (5:26).

Second, we take a brief peek ahead at that most infamous denial by Peter at Jesus's trial, beginning with the flat disavowal: "I do not know him" (22:57). If anyone qualifies as an established disciple who turns his back on Jesus in a public-official environment, it is Peter. Is this not a classic case of blasphemy-denial? Although Peter succumbs to fear of bodily harm from the authorities, he does not directly denounce Jesus's divine mission and definitively divorce himself from loving loyalty to Christ. Indeed, when Jesus's eyes met Peter's after the third denial, Peter "went out and wept bitterly" (22:62)—the mark of a deeply re-

130. On the correlation between blasphemy against the Spirit and public denial of Christ, see Green, 484; Tannehill, 203.

morseful devotee, not a stiff-necked apostate. And Peter eventually experiences full forgiveness and restoration, as Jesus predicted and prayed for (22:31–34).

If we want a bona fide example of a blasphemer-denier, I propose Herod Agrippa I in Acts 12:21–22.[131] The match is not perfect, however, in that Herod is not a disciple hauled before the authorities, but in fact a ruler who had the apostle James killed and planned the same fate for Peter (12:1–19). Herod aligns more with Antiochus and the Caesars in his delusions of divine grandeur, but also he is distinguished from them in his greater insider knowledge of Jewish faith and practice.[132] To whatever degree he had embraced the God of Israel, Herod publicly *repudiates* God in the most heinous way by basking in the glow of the crowd's adulation of his speech as "the voice of a god, and not of a mortal!" (12:22). This is blasphemy of the highest order and will not be tolerated (forgiven): "Immediately, *because he had not given the glory to God*, an angel of the Lord struck him down, and he was eaten by worms and died" (12:23). We cannot be certain of Herod's eternal destiny, but being served up to voracious worms suggests a garbage-heap, hellhole fate (cf. Isa 66:24; Jdt 16:17; Sir 7:17; Mark 9:48).

Finally, Jesus mitigates the terror of unforgiveable blasphemy against God's Spirit by assuring his "friends" that this same Spirit is on their side, ever present at times of inquisition to "teach you at that very hour what you ought to say" to remain faithful to God (12:12; cf. 21:12–19). Far from playing the role of adversary-tyrant, seeking to trap God's people in an unforgiveable slip of the tongue, the Spirit operates as advocate-teacher guiding them through prosecutorial ordeals. Such confidence of divine assistance helps Jesus's disciples "not to worry," provided they remain open-minded to the Spirit's instruction. But whereas the final accent falls on comfort, the frightening possibility of blaspheming-denying God in Christ stays on the table. Yet, such fear is not meant to paralyze God's emissaries, making them wary of saying a wrong word or taking a wrong step, but rather to galvanize them into dynamic speech and action around the core of Jesus's mission advancing God's right-making rule in the world.[133]

131. Carroll regards the Ananias-Sapphira incident in Acts 5:1–11 as the best illustration of Luke 12:8–12, since "the tragic outcome of the event (the deaths of both husband and wife) is consistent with a withholding of forgiveness," and their financial greed correlates with the ensuing parable in 12:13–21 (265–66). But whereas the couple's sudden deaths are intensely frightening to the community (Acts 5:5, 11), the narrative offers no comment about their eternal destinies; it does, however, report their decent burials (5:6, 10), minus worms or other degradations; cf. Spencer, "Scared to Death."

132. On the Herodian family's knowledge of Jewish traditions, see Luke 9:7–9; 23:6–12; Acts 26:2–3, 26–27.

133. On the potential of fearing a common threat to generate a "galvanizing moral electric-

God of Land and Grain (12:13–21)

What seems like an interruption and digression from "someone in the crowd" (12:13; cf. 11:27) Jesus uses to continue developing his therapeutic instruction about faithful devotion to the Creator God amid fearful prospects of life and death. A man presumes that Jesus, as a "teacher" of the law, might usefully weigh in on a legacy dispute (cf. Num 27:1–11; 36:5–12; Deut 21:15–17). Specifically, the man wants Jesus to order "my brother to divide [μερίσασθαι, *merisasthai*] the family inheritance with me" (Luke 12:13). This scenario casts Jesus not only in the role of judge but also in the place of *father*, the *patria potestas*, who had exclusive say over distribution of goods to heirs.[134] Jesus will soon discuss God's fatherly patronage over the "goods" of God's kingdom (12:29–32) and later relate a lengthy parable about a father and his two son-heirs (15:11–32). But for now, he curtly retorts to his interlocutor, "Man [ἄνθρωπε, *anthrōpe*—not 'Friend' as in NRSV and 12:4], who set me to be a judge or arbitrator [divider—μεριστήν, *meristēn*] over you?" (12:14).

In fact, as Son of Humankind, Jesus does have divine juridical authority over human affairs. The proper answer to Jesus's question is that *God* has made him judge. But as the ensuing statement and parable make plain, it is precisely God's perspective that this brother has lost sight of in his preoccupation with his own security and portfolio. Obsessive bean (and estate) counters risk operating from *fear* rather than faith, blind to God's rightful and compassionate ownership and oversight of creation. It is this blindness that the man should fear, not whether God will take care of him. And so Jesus continues, "Take care! [or better, 'Beware, Watch out!' (ὁρᾶτε, *orate*)]. Be on your guard against all kinds of greed [πλεονέξιας, *pleonexias*][135]; for one's life does not consist in the abundance of possessions" (12:15). Everyone owes his or her life to the Creator God, in whom one exists, consists, and persists. Within God's overarching good purpose for all creation, fear and anxiety have no fuel or foundation. But when one steps outside of God's realm and seeks to secure one's life through greedy accumulation, panic sets in.[136] When is enough enough? Have I amassed

---

ity . . . coursing through the body politic: an electricity of public resolve and civic commitment, fueling a more considered gravitas," see Robin, *Fear*, 157 (cf. 155–60).

134. Cf. Peppard, *Son of God*, 51: "The father [in the Roman world] had complete power over each child. . . . The power of the father was used most frequently not to administer beatings, but to distribute goods. For this reason, the power of the father came to a head, so to speak, in the matter of the family's inheritable goods."

135. Or "covetousness." On the pitfalls of this vice, especially its "insatiability," in Greek moral philosophy, see Malherbe, "Christianization."

136. Fear of God's presence after eating the forbidden fruit is the first reported human

enough for a comfortable retirement, however short or long that might be? How can I keep what I've saved from personal predators (tax officials, robbers, beggars, moochers, unscrupulous relatives) and impersonal depredations (bad weather, corrosive "moth and rust," deleterious free-market forces)?[137]

These nervous, self-reliant, and God-denying questions underlie Jesus's parable of the rich fool, as it is typically called. But it is not really the rich man's story. Along with God's stunning direct appearance in 12:20 (the only time Jesus introduces "God" within a parable), God implicitly plays the lead role throughout as Creator of land, grain, and humanity and as Lord of life and death. The part of best supporting actor is played by the *earth*, endowed with God's creative energy. Note well the subject of Jesus's opening statement: "*The land* [ἡ χώρα, *hē chōra*] of a certain rich man *brought forth a bumper crop* [εὐφόρησεν, *euphorēsen*]" (12:16 AT).[138] This sentence follows the primordial pattern, when the God-generated "earth brought forth vegetation: plants yielding seed of every kind, and trees of every kind bearing fruit with the seed in it" (Gen 1:11–12), and "the Lord God formed an earthling [אדם, *adam*] from the dust of the ground [אדמה, *adamah*]" (2:7 AT). Humans are naturally and integrally grounded in the God-made humus of the earth.

The rich man's foolishness aligns with his willful ignorance of the *source* of his abundant harvest, his arrogant presumption that *he* —not God and God's earth—is the creative subject of his life. It is a classic problem of *egoism*, which Jesus exposes in tedious redundancy, piling up eight first-person verbs (most in the future tense) and five first-person pronouns in three short verses (Luke 12:17–19). The rich man acts as the sole inhabitant of his circle of life, speaking to himself and "his life [ψυχή, *psychē*]"[139] as if he had complete

emotion in the Bible (and God does *not* allay their terror with "It is I, do not be afraid") (Gen 3:8–10); cf. Robin, *Fear*, 1–2, 7.

137. Adam Smith's classic vision that an "invisible hand" would steer self-interested, free-market competition toward maximum profits, which would then be reinvested and redistributed for the public good (*Wealth of Nations* 4.2), fails to account sufficiently for self-serving tendencies to hoard and profiteer at others' expense. See the thoughtful analysis of "A Rich Fool in the World of Adam Smith" in Verhey, *Remembering Jesus*, 243–52.

138. Rindge, *Jesus' Parable*, 162; contra Elvey's claim that in Luke 12 "the *agency* of the Earth in the provision of human life and sustenance is backgrounded" ("Storing," 10 [emphasis original]).

139. The KJV/NRSV rendering of ψυχή (*psychē*) as "soul" carries misleading dualistic-immaterialist baggage. The rich man is not speaking to some distinct "soulish" part of himself, but rather having an internal conversation with himself (his unitary, embodied self), as is common in Luke's parables: "I will say to my life/myself, 'Life/Self, what should I do?'" (12:17; cf. v. 20). Within this holistic model of personhood, however, we should not swing the pendulum so far as to deny introspective, "soul-searching" reflection on the part of ancient people. While Western psychological concepts of interiority have developed in various directions beyond (or should

control over it. He is totally wrapped up in own egoistic survival and fitness, which fundamentally drive human emotions and actions. But for Darwin and other broad-minded evolutionary theorists, individual selection does not tell the whole tale. Vital aspects of group, social, or multilevel selection have also forged human experience, at times against selfish interest.[140] Biologist and cultural anthropologist Christopher Boehm argues that, from its earliest stages, human moral development has entailed a complex struggle on a gradient of *egoism-nepotism-altruism*, not egoism by itself or even necessarily as the dominant force.[141] From the beginning, sharing with kin and cronies (nepotism) and more distant neighbors and strangers (altruism) has enhanced humans' ability to survive and thrive.

The parable's rich man, however, is stuck in a truncated, infantile—and ultimately self-defeating—morality, with no concern for family (including passing anything along to his heirs) or the wider community, least of all the poor who would benefit most from his surplus grain. Apart from neglecting to reciprocate God's and the earth's bountiful goodness to him, the rich man also discounts others' contributions to his fortune, such as tenant farmers, harvesters, and storehouse builders. He blithely functions as a narcissistic free rider on the system, presuming in his monologic mind that he has beaten the system and can "relax" on easy street from here on out (12:19). But as Boehm demonstrates from his and others' extensive fieldwork among "primitive" societies, free riders are never as free as they think. One way or another, the group will bite back and punish free riders for the good of all. Altruism—reciprocal generosity across status lines—wins out.[142]

Jesus makes no mention of social backlash toward the rich man in the parable, though we might imagine booing and hissing from peasant audiences. But Jesus does stress *someone's* "demanding" intervention in the man's life, actually, the demanding *of* his life in death (12:20). In fact, the present tense verb has a third person plural subject, literally "*they are demanding* [ἀπαιτοῦσιν, *apaitousin*] your life." Who are these unspecified "they"? Some have suggested angels (divine emis-

---

we say, beneath) earlier Middle Eastern perspectives, this does not warrant replacing one strict dualism (body/soul) with another (ancient East/modern West). As Dinkler ("Thoughts") sagely advises: "Our options are not either/or—soul or body, individualistic or communalistic, introspective or anti-introspective. Like human interactions more generally, ancient narrative depictions of the self are complex and often ambiguous. Characterizing all ancient Mediterranean people as 'anti-introspective' does not do justice to the 'diversity of opinion' on such matters found in the ancient texts themselves" (377); cf. Bovon, "Soul's Comeback."

140. Cunningham, *Darwin's Pious Idea*, 27–40, 66–67; Wilson, *Social Conquest*, 139–87.

141. Boehm, *Moral Origins*, 7–18, 49–74.

142. Boehm, *Moral Origins*, 64–70, 195–212.

saries) of death (cf. 16:22);[143] Carroll proposes (but does not elaborate) a possible link earlier in the chapter with "*those* [unidentified] who kill the body, and after that can do nothing more" (12:4);[144] still others highlight the grammatical point, in both Hebrew and Greek, that indefinite plural pronouns with active verbs can substitute for a singular agent ("they" = "someone") and a passive construction, including an implied *divine passive*, as in the present instance, where God speaks. We may thus read: "This night your life is demanded from you *by God*."[145] In any case, though God clearly controls the man's fate, we should not presume here, beyond the evidence of the story, some divine smiting (as with Herod Agrippa I), consignment to hell (cf. 12:5), or even quid pro quo retributive judgment for the man's miserliness. But a sharp stress does fall on human limitation, which evokes its own measure of fear, but toward healthy, constructive ends.

The verb "demand" (ἀπαιτέω, *apaiteō*) means "ask for something back, ask to be returned," typically in transactions of lending and borrowing (cf. 6:30; Deut 15:2–3; Sir 20:15). A creditor has the right to call in, ask for, "demand" payment on a loan, with or without interest. The concept is most apt for this accounting-obsessed rich man,[146] whose fortune was likely built through shrewd credit arrangements, including land foreclosures. What he has not accounted for, however, is that *he* has received his entire life and possessions on theological and terrestrial credit: everything comes from God and God's land and will all *revert back* to these life sources in *God's time*. Like all creation, the rich man lives on borrowed time and resources. He just doesn't know it, or better put, he *denies* knowledge of his finitude and dependence. And that makes him a damn fool.[147] His presumed arrogant control over his God-fashioned, earthbound life marks the same impudent attitude of the idolater exposed in the Wisdom of Solomon: "And, toiling perversely, he molds a futile god out of the same clay, he who a little before came into being out of the earth and after a while returns whence he was taken, when the soul [ψυχῆς, *psychēs*] which was lent him is demanded back [ἀπαιτηθείς, *apaitētheis*]" (Wis 15:8 NETS).

By failing to acknowledge the source of life, the rich man also has no proper sense of the *end* of life, either life's *goal* (teleology) or its *duration* (tem-

143. For example, Marshall, 524.

144. Carroll, 267.

145. Cf. Luke 6:38. See the clear discussion by Wallace (*Greek Grammar*), with the helpful English analogy: "I understand that *they* have discovered a cure for cancer" carries the idea: "I understand that a cure for cancer has been discovered [*by someone*]" (402; emphasis original in the first statement, added in the second). See further Fitzmyer, 2:974; Culy, Parsons, and Stigall, 423.

146. An image vividly portrayed in Rembrandt's *Rich Fool* painting, with the figure transfixed by the single coin he examines by candlelight; cf. Gowler, "Enthymematic."

147. Cf. Ernest Becker, *Denial*; Varki and Brower, *Denial*.

porality). The goal is inextricably linked with the divine source: birthed and blessed by God, human beings are called (demanded) to a life of "rich[ness] toward God [εἰς θεὸν πλουτῶν, *eis theon ploutōn*]" (12:21), which Bailey understands as "gathering riches *for* God" or "enriching God" (though not in the sense of "add[ing] to the perfection of God").[148] In his careful linguistic study, Joshua Noble sharpens the meaning of εἰς θεὸν πλουτῶν (*eis theon ploutōn*) as being "generous to God" materially-financially (with monetary "treasure," not some spiritualized form of gifting) by way of charitable contributions to the poor (cf. 12:33), precisely as stipulated in Prov 19:17: "Whoever is kind to the poor lends to the LORD."[149] Grain-piling for the rich man's cushy retirement is antithetical to almsgiving to the needy, with whom God personally identifies. Not only the meaning and purpose of earthly life, but also its length and opportunity for enjoying life's earthly possessions, are wholly determined by God's schedule, which we *cannot know* with precision. There is "a time to be born and a time to die," as another Solomon-styled sage reflects, with considerable attendant frustration: "What gain have the workers from their toil? . . . [God] has made everything suitable for its time; moreover he has put a sense of past and future into their minds, *yet they cannot find out* what God has done from the beginning to the end" (Eccl 3:1, 9–11; cf. 8:17).

So what to do about this vexed life, especially this business of working, producing, and accumulating wealth, which this wisdom writer, like his Solomon-prototype and Jesus's parable figure, had thrown himself into? Unlike the parable's rich fool and some wisdom traditions that equate prosperity with God's favor and long life, Qoheleth is under no illusions about forestalling death or transferring one's portfolio beyond the grave. In fact, he fights a rather fatalistic, depressive viewpoint about the utter "vanity" of earthly life that can be cut off in a moment, leaving behind one's possessions to be scrapped, stolen, or squandered by incompetent heirs or strangers (Eccl 2:18–26; 5:13–17; 6:1–6). In his more optimistic moments, however, he finds meaning in a philosophy of life that seems a mirror image of the rich fool's: "So I commend enjoyment, for there is nothing better for people under the sun than to eat, and drink, and enjoy themselves, for this will go with them in their toil through the days of life that God gives them under the sun. . . . Go eat your bread with enjoyment, and drink your wine with a merry heart; for God has long ago approved what you do" (8:15; 9:7). This perspective echoes the rich fool's plan of "relax, eat, drink,

148. Bailey, *Through Peasant Eyes*, 69–70.

149. Noble, "Rich." Regarding Luke 12:21, Noble concludes, "This verse is the most explicit reference in the NT to the idea of almsgiving not just as a means of compiling a treasure in heaven but also as a loan or gift made directly to God" (320); cf. Rom 10:12; Lucian, *Sat.* 24; Philostratus, *Vit. Apoll.* 4.8; Anderson, *Charity*, 62–66, and *Sin*, 146; Malherbe, "Christianization," 133–34.

be merry" (Luke 12:19), *except for the critical distinctions that Qoheleth* (1) counts on no speculative retirement plan "for many years" but instead commits himself to live joyfully in the present, "through the days of life," and, most important, (2) never loses sight of *God's* life-giving and life-approving sovereignty over human affairs. Although a recipe for joy (at least, as much joy as Qoheleth can muster), the element of fear persists. How can fear not persist to some degree in the face of our *unknowing* the plans of God? If you can't beat it, then, why not turn it into a *duty*? And so Qoheleth concludes: "The end of the matter: all has been heard. *Fear God*, and keep his commandments; for that is the *whole duty of everyone*. For God will bring every deed into judgment, including every secret thing, whether good or evil" (Eccl 12:13–14).[150]

God of Ravens and Lilies (12:22–34)

By ending on an ominous note of life suddenly cut short by the "demanding" God, Jesus's parable of the rich fool reinforces the fearful frustration in Ecclesiastes with mortality. But Jesus goes further than Qoheleth in seeking to mitigate anxiety by implicitly placing the vicissitudes of human existence within a cosmic network pulsing with divine creative energy. The incessant insecurity of loner self-reliance exemplified by the rich fool may be eased by a deep sense of dependence upon the Creator God and interdependence with God's earth and other earthlings. But Jesus also has more explicit therapeutic wisdom to offer fretful creatures in their daily embodied lives. The tragedy of the rich man lies as much in his failure to enjoy God's bounty in this life—*because* he was *obsessively worried* about taking care of himself—as in his unexpected death.[151]

"Therefore" (διὰ τοῦτο, *dia touto*), Jesus says, again punctuated with "I tell you": "Do not worry about your life [ψυχῇ, *psychē*], what you will eat, or about your body, what you will wear" (12:22). The parable's rich farmer had worried plenty about his food supply and finally reached the point where he thought he could relax, but tragically he thought wrong. But what can one do in a precarious, embodied world but scrape and claw, fight and fret, to make ends meet and satisfy basic needs for food and clothing (Jesus now adds this wardrobe concern)? And doesn't such pressure hit the poor majority harder than privileged elites like the rich land baron? At first, Jesus seems to offer a philosophical

150. For a more extensive investigation of Ecclesiastes and other illuminating intertexts (Sirach, 1 Enoch, Testament of Abraham, Lucian's *Dialogues*, Seneca's *Epistles*), see Rindge, *Jesus' Parable*, 43–157, and "Mortality and Enjoyment."

151. See Rindge, *Jesus' Parable*, 177–83.

platitude void of any real relief: "For life [ψυχή, *psychē*] is more than food, and the body more than clothing" (12:23). Fine, easy to say if you have daily bread (11:3) and suitable clothes: any life worth living is certainly not *less than* basic food, drink, and clothing (12:29–30). But Jesus's "more than" argument is meant to be expansive, not dismissive. By no means does "more than food/clothing" denigrate the sanctity of physical, somatic life; quite the contrary, it ennobles and extends it from an egocentric tunnel vision to a cosmic theological horizon encompassing all of God's creation. Once more, Jesus uses lesser-lighter/greater-heavier rhetoric to good effect with analogies from avian and botanical life.

The basic point is that God provides for nonhuman creatures without their developing ulcers stewing over their next meal or five-year business plan.[152] Again, since God cares for ordinary animals and plants, "how much more" should God care for "valued" human beings (12:24–28; cf. 12:7). Of course, nonhuman creatures have to "toil" in hunting and gathering (Jesus exaggerates for effect), but they do not worry about it, and they do not stockpile resources in "storehouse or barn" (12:24): they accept what is available, what God and God's earth supply, as we would say. They follow a daily rhythm, as Jesus advocates for his followers (9:23; 11:3; cf. Acts 2:46; 5:42). But the *particular* creatures Jesus features here provide some interesting twists on the theme.

Instead of sparrows, Jesus now showcases *ravens* (distinct from the generic "birds of the air" in Matt 6:26), hardly the most congenial avian species. As a bird of prey, the raven feeds on carrion, which scarcely serves as an appetizing analogy for human nourishment. Because of its bloody diet, the raven was off-limits (unclean) for human consumption, according to Jewish law (Lev 11:15; Deut 14:14); and it also served as a symbolic agent of terrible "eye-pecking" judgment against those who dishonored their parents (Prov 30:17) and against arrogant hypocrites who exploited innocent ones, who "*did not fear God* . . . and provoked and angered God" (Pss. Sol. 4:20–22 NETS). If God dispatches sharp-beaked ravens to gouge out the eyes of unjust oppressors who do not fear God, we might not think that God would care much about feeding or clothing these unclean monsters (the hungrier they are, the more vicious they will be). But God's bountiful kindness reaches all creatures, including "the ungrateful and the wicked" (Luke 6:35). Remarkably, the OT emphasizes God's nurturing ravenous fledglings:

> Who provides for the raven its prey,
>   when its young ones cry to God,
>   and wander about for lack of food?
>
> (Job 38:41)

152. Cf. Sapolsky, *Why Zebras Don't Get Ulcers.*

He gives to the animals their food,
  and to the young ravens when they cry.
His delight is not in the strength of the horse,
  nor his pleasure in the speed of a runner;
but the LORD takes pleasure in those who fear him,
  in those who hope in his steadfast love.

(Ps 147:9–11)[153]

The Psalms text stands out for associating these vulnerable young birds with those who positively *fear God and trust in God's love*. God "delights" in helping the weak and outcast over the strong and admired. The lowly ones know their place before a fearsome God; they know how easily they can be crushed by superior power. But they also know that God rules and judges rightly—for the right reasons at the right times, in the right spirit of steadfast love and mercy (cf. Luke 1:46–53). They also have a deeper sense of dependence on and greater capacity for hope in God's provision than those who foolishly claim self-sufficiency.

This biblical-psychological perspective does not simply equate fearing God with hope, trust, love, or even honor or respect, and it does not eliminate the terror component altogether.[154] Mixed, rather than pure, emotions typify the human condition.[155] "Perfect love" indeed "casts out fear" (1 John 4:18), but our love is never "perfect" or "complete" (τελεία, *teleia*) in this life and mingles with a variety of sentiments. God has nothing to fear because God is pure love (cf. 4:16); but in our imperfection and immaturity, we must maintain for our own good a salutary fear of God and of the deleterious consequences of going against God's way, even as that fear is mitigated by our perceptions, limited though they be, of God's perfect love.[156]

Before shifting examples from fauna (ravens) to flora (lilies), Jesus briefly challenges his audience in a more direct fashion, compelling them to admit how ineffectual worry is in enhancing their lives, whether in adding a single minute to their lifespan or inch to their stature, much less anything of bigger

153. Recall also, in an ironic twist on the predatory-polluted nature of ravens, that God employs ravens to *feed* the prophet Elijah (1 Kgs 17:4–6).

154. For classic, nuanced treatments of "fearing God" that retain a healthy sense of real fear (terror, dread), see Kierkegaard, *Fear*, 89–90, 94–95; and Bunyan, *Treatise*, 43, 45.

155. See Ekman, *Emotions Revealed*, 69–71, 105, 185–86, 211–12; Solomon, *True to Our Feelings*, 170–79; Rorty, "Plea for Ambivalence."

156. On beneficial, life-adaptive dimensions of fear (e.g., instinctive recoiling from snakes or snake-like objects until one can assess the threat level), see LeDoux, *Emotional Brain*, 128–34; Gavin de Becker, *Gift of Fear*; Whitehead, *Redeeming Fear*.

consequence (Luke 12:25–26). Modern psychologists might add that, far from bolstering one's life, excessive worry shortens and stunts one's progress.

If ravens epitomize predatory, polluted creatures under the Creator God's care, *lilies* grace the opposite end of the spectrum. Lily carvings adorned Israel's tabernacle and temple (Exod 25:31, 33–34; Num 8:4; 1 Kgs 7:8, 12; 2 Chr 4:5), the latter constructed by King Solomon, whom Jesus notes couldn't light a candle, for all his sartorial splendor, to the brilliantly decked-out lilies in nature (Luke 12:27). Beautiful lilies sprouting in the bleak desert further served as prophetic symbols for Israel's restoration from exile (Isa 35:1; Hos 14:5). Unlike mature ravens, who do have to exert some effort to eat, lilies "neither toil nor spin" for their basic sustenance or exceptional resplendence (Luke 12:27); and although they top the aesthetics chart, their utilitarian value is rather scant. They themselves may be nicely nourished, but they provide no grain for others' consumption; they are a "delight to the eyes" but not "good for food," to parody Eve's assessment of the forbidden garden tree. Lilies have a limited shelf life, sharing the evanescent, withering fate of all "grass of the field" (12:28) and, indeed, of all finite creatures, including the richest and most powerful humans, as Jesus's recent parable underscored (cf. Jas 1:9–11).

The Solomon-lily association also equivocates. On the one hand, in addition to the lilyworks in Solomon's temple, the Solomon persona in the Song of Songs enthralls his lover with his luscious lily lips (framed, as it happens, with *raven*-black hair [Song 5:11, 13]). On the other hand, at the height of his ostentation and opulence, the wise Solomon descends to the role of the fool, serving his own selfish desires and sowing seeds for the kingdom's schism (see 1 Kgs 11–12). He dies, like all mortals and grasses, leaving his resources to royal successors who mostly make things worse.

To sum up Jesus's broad lesser-to-greater argument: if God graciously provides for all creatures great and small, powerful and weak, rich and poor, pure and impure, pretty and ugly, "how much more" will God feed and clothe God's people. Jesus thus calls his followers to realize the futility of worry and the priority of relating to God in confident faith rather than cowering fear, of seeking (ζητέω, *zēteō*) the rule of God above everything else with assurance that the needs of daily life will be supplied (12:29–31). The seeking God and Christ (cf. ζητέω, *zēteō*, in 15:8; 19:10) must also be sought. In this meeting of divine and human desire, God's people flourish.

Conclusion: God of the Flock

Jesus crowns his extended teaching about life in God's world with a final exhortation addressed to his disciples via another natural image: "Do not be afraid, little *flock* [ποίμνιον, *poimnion*], for it is your Father's good pleasure [εὐδόκησεν, *eudokēsen*] to give you the kingdom" (12:32). The greater "value" of God's people should be appreciated without devaluing God's other creatures or denying the connection between all living things. Indeed, a robust theology of creation provides the antidote to paralyzing fear in a precarious environment. By comparing the disciples to *sheep—little* sheep at that—Jesus acknowledges their extreme vulnerability to going astray and being attacked by predators (cf. 15:3–6; Isa 53:6; John 10:1–18). Sheep, little or large, have good reason to fear for their lives in isolation. The lone wolf can make his way (partly by preying on weak sheep), but the lone lamb doesn't have a prayer. Sheep need connection and protection: connection with the flock and protection by attentive shepherds. Fortunately, Jesus's little flock is shepherded by no one less than God the Father, whose "pleasure" it is to give the sheep access to royal resources. This Paternal-Pastoral "pleasure" in Jesus's followers remarkably reflects the same intimate caring bond the Father expressed to Jesus the Son at his baptism: "You are my Beloved Son; it has been my pleasure to choose you [εὐδόκησα, *eudokēsa*]" (3:22 AT).[157] Fear and anxiety dissipate in the strong and loving arms of the good Father-Shepherd (cf. 15:4–7).

So we have nothing to fear, least of all from God, right? Not entirely. Although the larger text is framed with "Do not fear" admonitions (12:4, 32), in neither case is *God the object*. On the front end, Jesus tells his "friends" not to fear human attackers; on the back end, Jesus implicitly implores his "little flock" not to fear assault by predators or abandonment by caregivers, especially God the Father. But to say that we need not fear God's abandonment—as if God were a flighty, irresponsible parent or shepherd—is not the same as saying there is no continuing cause for fearing God. Jesus neither abrogates the "whole duty" to fear God enjoined by Qoheleth (Eccl. 12:13) nor amends the psalmist's claim that God "takes pleasure [εὐδοκεῖ, *eudokei*]" in those who fear him, as well as hope in his steadfast love (Ps 147 [146]:11 LXX]). Jesus lets his earlier double "fear God" warning stand (Luke 12:5). God still has the "authority to cast into hell" and is not afraid to use it, though God does not rush to such judgment and takes no delight in it. We might hope and pray that at the final restoration the

157. On the combined emotional-volitional valence of εὐδοκέω (*eudokeō*) as "pleasurable choosing" (or what we might call "euphoric selection"), see Peppard, *Son of God*, 106–12; and n. 130 above on 3:22.

Creator God chooses not to exercise his death-dealing, hell-casting option. As noted above, Jesus leaves open the eternal fate of the parable's self-centered rich fool. Perhaps he would yet be redeemed, with or without serving any time in Gehenna. Perhaps, but it is not wise to bet our lives on this idyllic postmortem prospect. In another Lukan parable, another insensitive rich man is assigned to afterlife in *Hades*, which is not quite the same as Gehenna, but is clearly no happy place (with its fiery torments) and seems to be a permanent residence (16:19–31). Of course, neither rich-man parable (nor any other passage in Luke) provides an apocalyptic tour of hell or heaven, pit or paradise, or any other extraterrestrial locale.[158] But the little information Luke does supply suggests there is a fearsome place of judgment to which God has full right to consign ungodly people.

Accordingly, God is worthy of ominous fear. But that truth does not warrant fear as the only or even primary emotional response due God. Fear of the right things at the right time is healthy and life-preserving. Best to fear and steer clear of poisonous snakes as a basic life-preserving policy (notwithstanding a few contrary NT texts [Mark 16:18; Luke 10:19; Acts 28:3–6]). God is no poisonous serpent (though God did send them once to kill many Israelites [Num 21:6]), but God is routinely compared in the Bible to *fire*, with potential for painful scorching if ignored or mishandled, but also for life-nurturing heating, cooking, and energy-producing. Rightly relating to the Creator God, who warms, feeds, cares, and enlivens, inspires trust and obedience, not dread and avoidance. But resisting God's way at every turn and ignoring God's claim on human life courts disaster, not because of God's capricious tendency to erupt in fiery anger, but because of humanity's presumptuous disregard of God's program for the flourishing of creation. Motivation for staying on the path of trust and obedience thus springs in part from judicious fear of being burnt by malevolent forces lurking off road.

Speaking of obedience, Jesus adds to his "do not fear" command a charge to "sell your possessions, and give alms" and not to "make purses" (12:33)—or by extension, barns or storehouses—to amass resources, to "store up treasures [θησαυρίζων, *thēsaurizōn*] for themselves," as the rich fool tried to do (12:21). Initially, this activity seems counterintuitive: selling your possessions and helping others seems to put you right back into a scary predicament of having nothing to live on! The business world would certainly question the prudence of this "foolish" move; and most believers, whatever their level of faith, would no doubt retain some ingrained fear of survival if they give too much to others. Of

158. On Luke's treatment of afterlife states, in careful dialogue with Second Temple Jewish texts, see Green, *Body*, 157–70.

course, Jesus's world is the realm of God, whose full "treasure chest" (θησαυρός, *thēsauros*) has been opened to God's people (12:33–34). Yet, God does not write each subject a blank check; rather, he calls all to share God's bounty: as each sells and shares in almsgiving, each depends on God's love working through others who reciprocate and redistribute God's royal resources.[159] What a wonderful utopian idea that the early church practiced for a while (Acts 2:44–45; 4:32–34)—but with natural anxiety always nipping at its heels. This side of paradise we must live—through wise cognitive-affective discernment and faithful obedience— in the creative tension of fearing *and* not fearing God amid the challenging vagaries of life.

Divided Households and Vulnerable "Sinners" (12:35–13:9)

Jesus shifts his pedagogical focus from a mix of challenge (fear God) and comfort (do not worry) in a precarious world (12:1–34) to a more purely challenging call to service, faithfulness, and repentance in a divided and volatile society. The transition from pastoral advice to the Father's "little flock" ("Do not be afraid" [12:32–34]) to urgent admonition to the master's slaves ("Be dressed for action" [12:35–36]) is rather abrupt, though prepared for somewhat by Jesus's economic orders ("sell your possessions and give alms" [12:33–34]). Also the "thief" (κλέπτης, *kleptēs*) image from 12:33 reappears in 12:39, though with a different slant. In any case, Jesus does not want his followers to be too comfortable, to "relax" too much (cf. 12:19), at this critical time of God's visitation.

Although Jesus primarily addresses his disciples, wider audiences continue to listen in and interject questions and comments (12:54; 13:1). At one point Peter asks: "Lord, are you telling this parable for us or for everyone?" (12:41). The fact that Jesus leaves this question hanging and proceeds with his teaching suggests that Peter poses a false dichotomy: Jesus broadcasts his word for anyone with ears to hear. In other respects, however, 12:35–13:9 constitutes the *most divisive* segment in Luke, headlined by Jesus's rare and stark self-definition: "Do you think that I have come to bring peace to the earth? [Actually, yes, since that is precisely what the angels announced in 2:14.] *No, I tell you, but rather division!*" (12:51). Jesus buttresses this statement by dividing humanity, at least on the surface, between masters and slaves (12:35–48), fathers and sons and other family relations (12:49–53), and repentant and recalcitrant sinners (13:1–9). Although closer examination will blur these binary oppositions

159. On the significance of almsgiving as heavenly treasure in Luke 12, in dialogue with Jewish wisdom texts, see Anderson, *Charity*, 62–66.

to a great extent, Jesus's sharp rhetoric serves to shock complacent hearers into keener alertness and more honest assessment. Formative *knowing* ("But know this"; Why do you "not know"?) and *thinking* ("Do you think?") remain integral to discipleship (12:39, 47–48, 51, 56; 13:2, 4).

While Jesus scarcely draws a transitional breath in this brisk segment of teaching, we may delineate three parts for the sake of analysis.

- Masters and Slaves: Knowing and Serving (12:35–48)
- Families and Societies: Knowing and Judging (12:49–59)
- Sufferers and Sinners: Knowing and Repenting (13:1–9).

The first two parts concern the *household* arena, which Luke has already featured in terms of parents, children, siblings, and in-laws (4:38–39; 7:11–15; 8:19–21, 40–56; 9:37–43; 10:38–42; 11:5–8). But except for the centurion's "highly valued" slave (7:2), whom Jesus heals but never meets, no other household slaves or servants have yet appeared.[160] From this point forward, however, elite households or estates with servant-staff increasingly populate the narrative landscape, especially in Jesus's parables (12:35–48; 14:15–24; 15:11–32; 16:1–13; 17:7–10; 19:11–27). And with them comes a hornet's nest of theological and ethical complications.

The experience of runaway slave and abolitionist leader Frederick Douglass in nineteenth-century America painfully exposes the problem relative to our current text. While still a slave in the summer of 1832, Douglass hoped that his master's conversion at a Methodist revival meeting would prompt him to release his slaves or at least to treat them more humanely. Quite the contrary, however, Douglass laments that his master's newfound "faith" only corrupted him further, cloaking oppression under an insidious guise of divine approval. In Douglass's haunting words: "Prior to his conversion, he relied upon his own depravity to shield and sustain him in his savage barbarity; but after his conversion, he found religious sanction and support for his slaveholding cruelty." A young female slave called Henny bore the brunt of the master's pseudo-faith-fueled violence, as she was subjected to terrible beatings under the banner of gospel proof-texting: "in justification of the bloody deed, he [the master] would quote this passage of Scripture—'He that knoweth his master's will, and doeth it not, shall be beaten with many stripes.'" That text is Luke 12:47.[161]

160. Thus far Luke has mostly used slave/servant language *metaphorically* (rather than legally) for ministers of God and Christ, especially women—Mary (1:38, 48), Simon's mother-in-law (4:39), Mary Magdalene and company (8:2–3), and Martha (10:40)—though diaconal work has also been implied for the twelve male disciples (9:12–17; cf. 22:24–27).

161. Cited in Meacham, *American Gospel*, 125 (from Douglass, *Narrative*, 44).

Citing a litany of discrete, decontextualized Bible verses to support an unbiblical and ungodly cause is nothing new, and at no time was this practice more evident in American biblical hermeneutics than during the bitter dispute over slavery. As Lincoln declared in his second inaugural: "Both read the same Bible, and pray to the same God; and each invokes His aid against the other. It may seem strange that any men should dare to ask a just God's assistance in wringing their bread from the sweat of other men's faces; but let us judge not, that we be not judged. The prayers of both could not be answered; that of neither has been answered fully."[162] A more particular caveat should govern the interpretation of Jesus's teaching: by sketching an image or scenario—like slaveholding—in a parable, he does not necessarily endorse that picture; he may use it as a point of contrast rather than comparison or to highlight tension between competing views. From the start, the fact that Luke's Jesus and most of his Galilean audience, including his disciples, are far from wealthy estate owners and slaveholders should give us pause concerning the exemplary nature of these household stories. As always, narrative biblical interpretation must be anchored in multilevel contexts: literary, social, cultural, and theological.

Before delving into the details of the present texts, it is useful to sketch a broad contextual framework of household structures and values in the first-century Roman world.

THE HOUSEHOLD OF CAESAR

Hierarchy of Honor and Power

emperor, supreme father (*pater patriae*)-lord-head of the realm

↓

household father-lord-head (*paterfamilias*)

↓

adult sons (elder over younger)

↓

household manager (could be a slave)

↓

wife/mother and children

↓

lower slaves/servants

This structure was rigidly hierarchical, a tight chain-of-command, with a premium on maximizing paternal (patriarchal-patronal) honor and power at the top of the ladder.

162. White, *Lincoln's Greatest Speech*, 100; cf. 100–20.

Against this worldly arrangement, Luke advances an alternative household in God's economy under the authority of the divine Father and Son but exercised in a dynamic fellowship of mutual love and service.

THE HOUSEHOLD OF GOD IN LUKE

Fellowship of Mutual Love and Service

God the Father-Lord-Head of all creation

↓

Jesus Christ the faithful "Elder" Son-Lord-Servant

↓

faithful disciples: mothers/sisters/brothers, slaves/servants

The more inclusive, more egalitarian bottom rung, inhabited by all "family" members who "hear the word of God and do it" (8:21; 11:28), begins to shake the whole ladder. The multidimensional portrait of Jesus—including lowly roles of cross-bearer and servant (9:21–24; 22:27), as well as loftier positions of Lord and Son of God and of Humankind—threatens to collapse the household hierarchy altogether: those who heed God the Father's word are "*my* mother and *my* brothers [and sisters]" (8:21).

Masters and Slaves: Knowing and Serving (12:35–48)

Jesus speaks here in loose, fluid parabolic fashion under the general banner of household management, but freely modulating among three particular scenarios of "readiness" (ἕτοιμος/ ἑτοιμάζω, *hetoimos/hetoimazō* [12:40, 47]):

- Household scenario 1: Ready to receive the master when he comes (12:35–38)
- Household scenario 2: Ready to stop a thief when he comes (12:39–40)
- Household scenario 3: Ready to be reviewed by the master when he comes (12:41–48).

In the first scenario, the master or lord (κύριος, *kyrios*) has left his estate to attend a wedding banquet hosted by a relative, friend, or prominent citizen in the community (but not a king or groom, as in the wedding-feast parables of Matt 22:1–14; 25:1–13). The timing of the master's return is uncertain (such celebrations can extend late into the night), but whatever the hour, "as soon as he comes and knocks," his slaves must be ready—with belts tightened and lamps lit—to tend to his needs (12:35–36, 38). But Jesus injects a stunning twist into the story. *If* the slaves are ready and alert, as their station demands they be, *then* the master will hike his cloak, cinch his belt,[163] and *serve his slaves* (12:37). With this announcement Jesus collapses the social ladder, reconfigures it into a table of mutual service, and virtually deconstructs binary codes of master and slave.

The second scenario also focuses on the behavior of the homeowner (οἰκοδεσπότης, *oikodespotēs* [12:39]), but now shifts to matters of security rather than hospitality. Although homes are sites of welcome and fellowship, they can also be targets of attack and disruption. Whereas in the previous scene, slaves must be ready to receive their master, here the master must be on guard *not* to receive a *thief*, especially if he's been tipped off about when the thief was coming. But of course thieves do not publish their schedules; their whole modus operandi depends on stealth and surprise. So Jesus presses upon the disciples: like the master (no servants have appeared yet), "you [all] must be ready" at all times, since you do not know the "hour" an invader might come (12:40).

Sage advice for any homeowner, large or small. But that is not Jesus's main point here. The bombshell explodes with Jesus's identification of the invader-thief with *himself* as the *Son of Humankind* (12:40). Though "thief" represents a common NT image for the Son of Humankind's sudden climactic appearance, with primary stress on its unexpected timing (Matt 24:42–44; 1 Thess 5:2–5; 2 Pet 3:10; Rev 3:3; 16:15), the thief's dispossessing aims remain part of the picture. As the agent of God's restorative and redistributive judgment, the Son of Humankind reverses fortunes in the interest of establishing true justice. Those complacently set in their "powerful" and "rich" ways will be rudely robbed by the surprising Son of Humankind *thief* (cf. Luke 1:51–53). Those with the most to lose socially and materially seem to be Jesus's main audience here. So how do his disciples, many of whom have left everything to follow Jesus and have nothing more for him to take, fit into this scenario? Peter, for one, would like to know: "Lord, are you telling this parable for us or for everyone?" (12:41).

Jesus answers with a third household vignette, which has application not only for Peter and company but for "everyone" (12:48). Now he depicts a larger estate owned by an absentee master/landlord (κύριος, *kyrios*) and superintended by a household manager (οἰκονόμος, *oikonomos*) who is also a slave (δοῦλος, *doulos*) and trusted foreman with authority over rank-in-file slaves and particular responsibility to see that these workers get their proper "food allowance." While assuming a typical household hierarchy, Jesus envisions an optimal operation in which a "faithful and prudent" manager tends

163. Luke uses the same verb (περιζώννυμι, *perizōnnymi*) to denote the slaves' and master's belt-gathering preparation for meal service in 12:35, 37, respectively—a fact obscured by the NRSV's different renderings: "dressed for action" (12:35) and "fasten his belt" (12:37).

to the interests of the master above him and the needs of the slaves below him (12:42–43). However, severe consequences will befall the manager should he lapse into "unfaithful" behavior, specifically, indolent self-indulgence and violent mistreatment of the slave-workers, during the master's absence. For whatever reason and however long the "master is delayed in coming," a time of stern reckoning will eventually dawn on an unexpected day. The master will "cut in two" (διχοτομέω, *dichotomeō*) his irresponsible steward, severing him from the household and divesting him of all associated benefits (12:45–46).[164]

The manager's fraudulent ethics is entwined with his faulty epistemology. He "does *not know* [οὐ γινώσκει, *ou ginōskei*]" the hour of his master's return (12:46). But rather than take this uncertainty as a warrant for constant readiness, he succumbs to complacent recklessness, imprudently presuming he has many years "to eat and drink and get drunk," with no accountability to his master (12:45–46; cf. the rich fool in 12:19–20). Beyond the temporal matter of *when* the master will return, Jesus extends the knowledge/ignorance problem to the vocational issue of *what* the master requires, sketching two subscenarios of responsibility and punishment.

- The slave who *knows* (γνούς, *gnous*) his master's will, but fails to do it, merits a heavy beating (12:47).
- The slave who *does not know* (μὴ γνούς, *mē gnous*) his master's will, and fails to do it, merits a lighter beating (12:48).

Stewardship of *knowledge* is as significant as stewardship of resources. *Knowing* disobedience—willful, brazen, intentional rebellion—courts the Lord's sternest judgment: "Whoever acts highhandedly [intentionally], whether a native or an alien, affronts the LORD, and shall be *cut off* from among the people. Because of having despised the word of the LORD and broken his commandment, such a person shall be utterly *cut off* and bear the guilt" (Num 15:30–31). Unintentional, inadvertent, unknowing transgression is less serious, but not trivial. It still constitutes unfaithfulness to the Lord, and once exposed, it demands repentance and forgiveness to maintain community standing (see Lev 4–5; Num 15:22–28; Luke 23:34; Acts 3:17–21; 17:30–31). "But I didn't know" is no excuse; ignorance remains blameworthy, not blissful.

Back to timing matters, Luke 12:35–48 introduces the critical issue of the *delay of the parousia*, referencing the interim period between Christ's ascension

164. I opt for a more socioeconomic "cutting off" penalty (see NRSV alternative note) rather than a physical "cutting in pieces" (NRSV main text) here and in Matt 24:51 (the only NT uses of διχοτομέω [*dichotomeō*]). However, the only LXX usage of the verb refers to the surgical dissection of a ram in a cultic context (Exod 29:17).

and promised return to earth. Though often dubbed the "second coming," the NT does not use such terminology: παρουσία (*parousia*) simply means "appearing" or "coming," with no numerical factor. In any case, most early Christians expected Lord Jesus's quick turnaround back to earth, and some began to fret over his *delayed return* as the years passed. Not knowing the "hour" of Christ's coming was tolerable, but they hadn't counted on waiting for years (cf. 1 Thess 4:13–5:10; 2 Pet 3:1–13). By Luke's time the delay had likely stretched into the fifth or sixth decade. We can only assume that questions surrounding this delay intensified, especially in the wake of Rome's brutal razing of Jerusalem in 70 CE.

Nevertheless, it is hard to determine the extent of Luke's concern with the parousia-delay problem.[165] Acts opens with the apostles' hopeful query to the risen Jesus: "Lord, is this the time when you will restore the kingdom to Israel?" (Acts 1:6). Jesus parries their question, however, with a striking assertion of their limited capacity for knowledge: "It is *not for you to know* [γνῶναι, *gnōnai*] the times or periods that the Father has set by his own authority" (1:7). In a narrative designed to solidify knowledge (Luke 1:4), some things remain beyond human understanding. Rather than worrying about God's timetable, Jesus's followers are to get on with God's mission in the world, as long as God wants it to last (Acts 1:8). In one sense, Jesus leaves them to it, as he departs into heaven, awaiting an eventual return at some unknown time (1:9–11). In another sense, however, Jesus by no means abandons his delegates *in the meantime*, but rather assures them of imminent infilling with the Holy Spirit (the "Spirit of Jesus" [16:7]) to empower their mission (1:8). Accordingly, Jesus's Spirit-imbued emissaries waste no time in pining for Jesus's coming (again), still less in indulging their own interests and mistreating one another in the interim. Their "eating and drinking" occurs in the context of worship, mutual fellowship, and relief ministry, overall proving themselves as faithful servant-managers of God's work (2:43–47; 11:27–30). Moreover, the exalted Jesus not only guides his witnesses "in Spirit." He also *comes personally* and *unexpectedly* at strategic points, especially to get the abusive Saul on the right track ("I am Jesus, whom you are persecuting" [9:5]). The Lord/Master *suddenly comes* to call his "chosen instrument" to account for his violent behavior, though rather than "cutting off" Saul, Jesus surprisingly transforms Saul and entrusts him with a wider mission (9:15–16).

The upshot of the household illustrations in Luke 12:35–48, in light of developments in Luke's second volume, stresses the responsibility of ever-faithful

165. Conzelmann (*Theology*) offered the classic argument that Luke's *chief purpose* in writing his two volumes was to accommodate the problem of the parousia's delay. Few scholars today accept Conzelmann's thoroughgoing de-eschatological approach to Luke. See the careful discussion of Luke's eschatology in Carroll, *Response*.

readiness by God's servants for the ever spiritually present Master/Lord, who may come more palpably, more personally, at any moment. Furthermore, narrative-theological space opens for *multiple comings* or visitations of the Lord-God-in-Christ, the Son of Humankind, between his first coming in a manger and final coming in the clouds (21:27; Acts 1:9–11). As Walter Rauschenbusch expressed the eschatological tension, "The kingdom of God is always but coming," thus diluting the notion of delay and demanding full engagement in God's restorative mission at all times.[166]

Families and Societies: Knowing and Judging (12:49–59)

Jesus stays in judgment mode, in terms of both challenging his audiences' misjudgments and pronouncing judgments on their clouded thinking. In each of three matters he briskly addresses—first to his disciples and the latter two including the crowds—Jesus poses to "you" (plural) a critical cognitive-perceptive question:

> Do *you think* [δοκεῖτε, *dokeite*] that I have to come to bring peace to the earth? (12:51)
> Why do *you not know* [οὐκ οἴδατε, *ouk oidate*] how to interpret the present time? (12:56)
> Why do *you not judge* [οὐ κρίνετε, *ou krinete*] for yourselves what is right? (12:57)

The first question, concerning why Jesus came to the "earth" globally or to the "land" of Israel locally (γῆ [*gē*] denotes both realms), drills to the core of Jesus's mission. Recall Jesus's positive evangelical agenda: "I must proclaim the good news [εὐαγγελίσασθαι, *euangelisasthai*] of the kingdom of God . . . for I was sent for this purpose" (4:43; cf. 4:18–21). But now, amid mounting opposition, Jesus's news is not uniformly "good" for everyone. In fact, he seems to flip the message on its head, now asserting that he has come "to throw/hurl [βαλεῖν, *balein*] fire on the earth" (12:49 AT), reminiscent of Elijah's displays of infernal judgment against the prophets of Baal (1 Kgs 18:30–40) and the delegates of idolatrous King Ahaziah (2 Kgs 1:5–12). While Luke's Jesus has appropriated the miraculous feeding and healing dimensions of Elijah's ministry (Luke 4:25–27; 7:11–17; 9:10–17), he has previously eschewed the fire-breathing side (9:51–56). But now he suddenly seems ready to set the world ablaze. Moreover, against

166. Rauschenbusch, *Christianity*, 338; cf. Christopher Evans, *Kingdom*.

the natal angelic anthem extolling Jesus's coming to bring "on earth peace" (2:14; cf. 1:79), which he has heretofore confirmed (7:50; 8:48), now he exhorts his followers *not to think* he's "come to bring peace to the earth . . . but rather division," specifically within close family units (12:51–53).

However, despite the sharp edge of Jesus's verbal dagger, it should be taken more as a "revised mission statement"[167] than a reversed one; or better yet, as a *realistic* appraisal of mixed responses of acceptance and rejection, alienation and reconciliation, that Jesus's mission elicits. The family split of "three against two and two against three" (12:52) describes a tightly contested environment of debate and tension. Such conflict has percolated throughout Luke's story. Though the angel forecast that John the Baptist would prepare Jesus's way by turning "the hearts of parents to their children" (1:17), John's message was laced with strong warnings against God's divisive, fiery judgment (3:9, 17). In Jesus's own family, though Mary faithfully "pondered" the significance of her special son (1:29; 2:19), her and Joseph's understanding remained incomplete (2:41–51). Mary experienced piercing turmoil (2:34–35), and Jesus's hometown sermon evoked murderous rage against "Joseph's son" (4:16–30). Jesus scarcely went out of his way to appease his Nazareth kin, since his family values extend to all "mother[s] and . . . brothers . . . who hear the word of God and do it" (8:21; cf. 11:27–28).

Images of fire and baptism reinforce the two-pronged thrust of Jesus's mission. After declaring his purpose to hurl fireballs on the earth, he admits the mounting "stress/distress" (συνέχομαι, *synechomai*) of "a baptism" that he himself must soon endure (12:50).[168] This marks an odd juxtaposition, both because water (baptism) quenches fire and because Jesus has already been baptized (3:21–22). But a vital point emerges from this tension: if, as seems likely, this new baptism refers to Jesus's impending immersion in death and burial (cf. Rom 6:1–11), then Jesus alludes to his own experience of human suffering as a means of dousing or diminishing the fires of judgment. Jesus is no remote firebomber. He is fully, "stressfully," engaged (immersed) with his people on earth within the fire. Moreover, returning to Jesus's water baptism, John heralded this act as a harbinger of the Messiah's ultimate mission to "baptize you with the

167. Carroll, 275.

168. Nine of the twelve NT uses of συνέχω (*synechō*)—lit. "hold together"—occur in Luke's writings, with a range of connotations. In the active voice, it can refer to crowds' *pressing* around Jesus (8:45) or guards' *holding* him in custody (22:63). In the passive, it can express, positively, being *captivated* by God's word (Acts 18:5) or, negatively, *beset* by physical disease (Luke 4:38; Acts 28:8) or emotional distress (Luke 8:37). The last meaning of being *stressed* or *pressed down* emotionally best fits the present context of 12:50: "to experience great psychological pressure and anxiety" (Louw and Nida, *Greek-English Lexicon*, 1:315; cf. Carroll, 273).

Holy Spirit and fire" (Luke 3:16). This dynamic confluence of water, fire, and Spirit also characterizes the mission of the church, inaugurated at Pentecost, to bring *both salvation and judgment* to the world in Jesus's name (Acts 1:4–5; 2:1–4, 17–21, 37–42).

Setting up his second question, Jesus now reflects on earth/land events via the crowd's perceptions of climate patterns (Luke 12:54–56). They keenly discern the threats of torrential rain from western clouds and "scorching heat" from southern winds. But apart from weather's notorious unpredictability (cf. 8:22–24), Jesus laments that the people's supposed ability "to interpret the appearance of earth and sky" does not carry over to their knowledge of the "present time" (καιρός, *kairos* [12:56]), the *significance* of God's momentous "today" (2:11; 4:21; 5:26; 19:5, 9; 23:42) revealed in Christ, distinct from simple clock/calendar time (χρόνος, *chronos*). Though obsessed with knowing how wet and hot a day will be (to plan and dress accordingly), they have no clue about embracing and bracing for the outpouring of water-and-fire by God's suffering Christ and seismic Spirit.

Jesus's third question urges a right response to the "present time" of God's revelation before this grace period gives way to costly judgment (12:57). He paints a legal scenario in which an aggressive litigant drags an opponent through the court system, extracting every "last penny" from the sued party. It is better, then, for the defendant to settle the matter "on the way [ἐν τῇ ὁδῷ, *en tē hodō*]," out of court (12:58). While Matthew's Jesus makes the same point to encourage conflict settlement privately among fellow believers (Matt 5:23–26), in Luke, the focus falls on reconciliation with the *adversarial Jesus*—the prophet-prosecutor charging the people to return to "the way [ὁδόν, *hodon*] of the Lord" (3:4; cf. 1:76–79; 9:52, 57; 10:38; 13:22, 33; 17:11) before the final day of reckoning.[169]

Sufferers and Sinners: Knowing and Repenting (13:1–9)

Set "at that very time" (13:1), this scene extends Jesus's discussion in 12:49–59 concerning right and wrong judgments.[170] The fallout from misjudging the pregnant "present time" (12:56) of God's right-making rule revealed in Jesus Messiah escalates from tragedies of family division (12:49–53) and personal deprivation (12:59) to capital punishment ("perish[ing]" [13:3, 5] and "cut[ting] down" [13:7, 9]), specifically: *who* merits it and *when* it will be executed. The

169. Johnson, 209.
170. Green, 513–14.

hard bottom line is that Jesus indicts "all" people as "sinners," "offenders" ("debtors"), and fruitless ones deserving destruction "unless they repent" (ματανοέω, *metanoeō* [13:3, 5]). He drives home this point in prophetic (13:1–5) and parabolic (13:6–9) responses to current headlines.

Two newsworthy "atrocity stories"[171]—one a terrorist act, the other a terrible accident—spark Jesus's challenge (13:1–5). The first involves the tyrannical execution of some Galilean worshipers in the Jerusalem temple by the Roman provincial governor, Pontius Pilate; the second recalls the accidental demise of eighteen hapless citizens of Jerusalem crushed by the collapse of the Siloam tower (cause unreported: structural defect? earthquake? enemy attack?). Both incidents are otherwise unknown, but there is no reason to doubt their veracity. Pilate's capacity for bloody assaults was well-known, and a watchtower near the pool of Siloam would have been a plausible means of safeguarding Jerusalem's water supply (cf. 2 Kgs 20:20; Isa 22:8–11; John 9:7).[172]

In the face of tragic misfortune, it is common, à la Job's friends adhering to a strict Deuteronomic theology (e.g., Deut 6:10–15; 8:11–20; 28:15–68), to blame the victim and assume some underlying disobedience provoking God's reprisal through enemy agents or natural disasters. But Jesus utterly rejects such thoughts, which he discerns that some in the audience *were* thinking ("Do you think?" [13:2, 4]). Comparative sinfulness had nothing to do with the fateful events: neither the murdered Galileans nor the crushed Jerusalemites merited their terrible ends because they were "worse offenders" than anyone else. Simmering prejudices against Galileans (including Jesus) or any other regional group as less devout than Jerusalem-dwelling Jews (see John 1:46; Acts 2:5–7) are as irrelevant as they are erroneous: after all, the Galileans in question were offering sacrifices to God in the temple when they were unjustly struck down.[173] The blame falls full force on *Pilate's* head, not the Galileans'.

But Jesus does not simply challenge naive connections of piety with good fortune or narrow constructions of merit-based ideology (they got what they deserved). More radically, he moves to shake everyone's security: the arbitrary cases of tragic death, while not owing to any particular wrongdoing by the victims, should alert "all" to the injurious consequences of universal human sinfulness. In solemn prophetic voice ("No, I tell you"), Jesus warns: "Unless you repent, you will all perish [just] as they did" (Luke 13:3, 5). A strict calculus of just deserts would claim the lives of all people, not least Pilate's, and not limited

171. Tannehill, 216.

172. Tiede and Matthews, "Gospel according to Luke," 1791.

173. Cf. González, 170: "Many Jews viewed Galileans as second-class Jews, somewhere between true Jews and heathenish Gentiles."

to a couple of random groups who happen to suffer premature violent deaths. Though recognizing the difference in scale, Justo González contemporizes the tower disaster in poignant terms: "Do you believe that those who perished in the Twin Towers were worse offenders than all others living in New York?" He then glosses Jesus's universalizing logic: "The surprising thing is not that so many die but that we still live. If it were a matter of sin, we would all be dead."[174]

As the New York City location carries special political weight in the modern world, so does Jerusalem in Luke's narrative world, especially as Jesus anticipates not only his unjust execution there (ordered by Pilate!), but also the eventual demolition of the holy city and its temple (9:22, 44; 13:33–34; 18:31–33; 19:41–44; 21:5–6, 20–24; 23:28–30). These are precarious times, and mantras of the inviolable "temple of the Lord, temple of the Lord, temple of the Lord" offer no more protection for God's people now than they did in Jeremiah's day *unless* accompanied by true repentance, particularly renewed loyalty to God and loving justice toward vulnerable outsiders, widows, and orphans (see Jer 7:1–15).[175] Jesus elaborates this prophetic charge to his people in parable form, pressing the urgency to repent sooner rather than later.

In depicting "a fig tree planted in [a] vineyard" (Luke 13:6), Jesus draws on familiar prophetic images of Israel as graciously rooted by God in the promised land to bear fruit for God's glory. The desired harvest chiefly yields loyal covenantal love toward God and neighbor expressed in acts of justice and mercy. However, Israel's history has been marred by repeated failure to fulfill its fruitful vocation, despite God's attentiveness as faithful owner and caretaker (Isa 5:1–7; Jer 8:8–13; Ezek 15:1–8; Hos 9:10; Mic 7:1–6). Jesus now alerts his people that they stand at another critical crossroad. Despite his and John's urgent calls to repent and bear fruit (Luke 3:7–14; 6:43–45; 8:4–15), many continue to resist the message and thereby risk divine judgment. As God used ancient Assyria and Babylon to "cut down" his recalcitrant people and get their attention, so the present threat of uprooting by Rome—accompanied by the downfall of Jerusalem and its temple—looms on the horizon. But there is still time, barely, for God's people to change their lives and the course of history. The long-suffering landowner (God), having already waited "three years" for figs, grants the gardener (Jesus) "one more year" for cultivating and fertilizing (13:7–8). The work of God in Jesus Messiah provides the most optimal environment for the growth of God's people. But God's patient nurture, while extensive, is not limitless. The window is fast closing; the "year of the Lord's favor" (4:19) is winding down. As

174. González, 171.

175. Note Jeremiah's specific denunciation of "shed[ding] innocent blood in this place" (Jer 7:6)—precisely what Pilate did centuries later, according to Luke 13:1.

Danker comments, "There can be no tampering with the grace of God. Luke's frequent reminder, 'Blessed are those who hear the word of God and keep it,' lurks in the shadow of this dramatic recital, which searches the nooks and crannies of all institutionalized religion."[176]

While the final judgment note rings loud and clear, Jesus's parable resists a knee-jerk "chop it down" response to failure—the tendency, as Eugene Peterson puts it, to "solve kingdom problems by amputation." Peterson further teases out the organic connection between decomposition (manure) and fruit-bearing as a sign of God's synergistic orchestration of "the silent energies that change death into life, the energies of resurrection."[177] We may add that the Greek terms for "manure" (κόπριον, *koprion*) and "fruit" (καρπός, *karpos*) evince a suggestive euphony (13:8–9).[178] Peterson, however, overplays the extent of God's patience in Jesus's thought ("Manure. God is not in a hurry").[179] Overall, manure commends the sure-but-slow death-and-life cycle, but here Jesus sets a firm (though figurative) "one-year" deadline. The divine clock (GOT) is fast winding down; the kingdom of God is at hand.

The Bent/Bound Woman and the Hospitable Farmer/Baker (13:10–21)

In this final segment of stage 1 of the Travel Narrative, the focus of Jesus's ministry veers from the crowds and disciples to individual characters he meets or speaks about in "one of the synagogues" (13:10). These persons—two women (one disabled, the other a baker) and a man (a farmer)—telescope attention from the larger economic world of masters/landowners and their managers, gardeners, and slaves to the smaller interests of everyday persons struggling to live or plying their trade.[180] The characters operate within precarious environments of *limited resources*[181]—pertaining in various respects to *size* (small, short, reduced, few), *strength* (weak, powerless, needy, shy), and/or *status* (low, poor, marginal, outcast)—which transmogrify, however, into experiences of dynamic health, growth, and stability in the realm of God mediated by Jesus.

176. Danker, 260.

177. Peterson, *Tell It Slant*, 73 (cf. 154).

178. Related sound plays echo in ἔκκοψον/ἐκκόψεις (*ekkopson/ekkopseis* ["chop down"]) and σκάψω (*skapsō* ["dig"]). The hope is that "cutting" can be prevented by "cultivation."

179. Peterson, *Tell It Slant*, 72.

180. On the links between the three stories and main characters in 13:10–21, see Gench, *Back to the Well*, 91–92; O'Toole, "Some Exegetical Reflections," 90–100; Hamm, "Freeing," 29–31.

181. On the first-century Mediterranean world as a "limited goods society," see Malina, *New Testament World*, 81–107; Moxnes, *Economy*, 76–98.

More pointedly, the three stories (one narrative, two short parables) all feature a remarkable *rise* from lowly, limited beginnings: a stooped-over woman to erect posture; a farmer's mustard seed into an upright tree; a baker woman's pinch of yeast into rising dough. Though typical "resurrection" terminology is absent, the thought-image "rises" up and dominates these scenes.

A Woman's Bent Back Raised Up to a Straight Position (13:10–17)

The scene opens in familiar terms: "Now he was teaching in one of the synagogues on the Sabbath" (13:10). As we have seen, Luke's Jesus uses Sabbath-synagogue forums to announce his Spirit-anointed program of liberating and healing acts (4:18–21) or to perform such acts on the spot (4:31–35; 6:6–8). Jesus's Sabbath words have proven to be as transformative as they are informative. But by representing words that *work*, these speech-acts have also sparked considerable conflict on the Lord's sacred day of rest (4:28–30, 36–37; 6:9–11).

It is not surprising, then, that the present scene evolves into a dramatic healing event, which sets off heated debate between Jesus and the synagogue leader. But for all its similarity with previous synagogue incidents, this case includes distinctive elements. While Jesus is teaching, a woman with a severely bent back—such that she "was quite unable to stand up straight" (13:11)—appears in the synagogue. Though her condition inhibits her from seeing much beyond the ground or looking anyone in the eye, Jesus notices her ("when [he] saw her") and promptly stops his lecture to "[call] her over . . . and free [her] from [her] ailment" with his liberating word (13:12). Her orthopedic disability is described in spiritual as well as physical terms as "a spirit that had crippled her," or more literally, "a spirit of weakness [ἀσθενείας, *astheneias*]" and a state of bondage to satanic control (13:11, 16). Though such a diagnosis might reflect popular opinion that the woman had somehow brought this infirmity on herself through her "weak" will or character—linking physiology and morality in the stereotypical "weaker" sex—Jesus makes no such misogynistic assumptions.[182] He simply recognizes her as a casualty of a "cosmic battle . . . engaged on this woman's back,"[183] much as the marauding Legion had wracked the mind and body of the Gerasene demoniac (8:26–39).

Her condition is compounded by its duration "for eighteen long years" (13:16; cf. v. 11). Luke specifies the length of a chronic malady in three other cases:

182. See the incisive discussion of "physiognomic misogyny" underlying this incident—and "undermined" by Jesus—in Parsons, *Body*, 85–89.

183. Gench, *Back to the Well*, 86.

the woman who suffered a draining bleeding disorder for twelve years (8:43); a beggar man lame from birth for over forty years (Acts 3:2; 4:22); and a paralyzed man named Aeneas, bedridden for eight years (9:33). The bent-over woman's eighteen-year affliction perhaps recalls periods of Israel's bone-crushing subjugation by the Moabites and Ammonites in the Judges era (Judg 3:14; 10:8).[184] Following this historical allusion, the woman's back also becomes a symbolic site of political-international (as well as cosmic-spiritual) oppression. In any event, Jesus moves to lift and liberate the woman from her back-breaking enslavement and thus fulfill Mary's marvelous vision of God's "lifting up the lowly" (Luke 1:52) and Jesus's messianic mission "to let the captive/oppressed go free" (4:18) and to raise rigid, rigor-mortised bodies to new life (cf. 7:14, 21–22; 8:54).[185] But while the woman herself and most of the audience praise God for this Jubilee moment (13:13, 17), not everyone is thrilled with Jesus's Sabbath activity.

As a group of Pharisees and scribes earlier objected to Jesus's Sabbath cure in a synagogue (6:6–10), so now the chief synagogue administrator is "indignant" in censuring Jesus's healing of the bent-over woman. Rather than take up the matter directly with Jesus, however, he repeatedly voices (imperfect ἔλεγεν, *elegen*—"kept saying") his criticism of Jesus "to the crowd" (13:14). The synagogue official thus worries more about the effect of Jesus's work on the congregation than on the liberated woman herself. This concern does not make the leader a callous man who cares nothing about helping the infirm; he simply believes that a bigger principle is at stake—nothing less than the rule of law.[186]

Once again the law in question is the Decalogue's Sabbath mandate to rest from a week's productive labor on the seventh day, as God rested from the good

184. Gench, *Back to the Well*, 86; Danker, 261. For a fascinating (and plausible) symbolic-numerical link with the name of Jesus and eighteen, see Parsons, *Body*, 89–95. In Luke 13:16 the span of the woman's disability is oddly identified as a sum of "ten and eight years" (δέκα καὶ ὀκτώ [*deka kai oktō*]—unlike the more usual single word δεκαοκτώ [*dekaoktō*] in 13:11). By the rules of gematria, assigning numerical values to letters, ι = 10 and η = 8; or ιη = 10 + 8, with these Greek letters being the first two letters of Ἰησοῦς, *Iēsous* (Jesus). A third-century papyrus (P45) of Luke 13:14, 16 renders both "Jesus" and "eighteen" by the abbreviation ιη (*iē*).

185. See also the context of eschatological restoration associated with the Son of Humankind's consummative return in Luke 21:28—"Stand up [ἀνακύψατε, *anakypsate*—the same verb also in 13:11] and raise your heads, because your redemption is drawing near"; and Acts 15:16—"After this I will return . . . and I will set it [David's house] up [ἀνορθώσω, *anorthōsō*—the same verb for the bent woman's "straightening" in Luke 13:13]." See Hamm, "Freeing," 33; Gench, *Back to the Well*, 87.

186. On synagogues in the Greco-Roman period, not only as places of "religious" activity such as prayer, biblical study, and fellowship, but also as established sites of public disputation about legal matters (similar to the city gate in early times) among leaders and the wider community ("crowds"), see Ryan, "Jesus and Synagogue Disputes" (cf. Sus 28–41; Josephus, *Life*, 277–303).

work of creation (Gen 2:1–3; Exod 20:8–11) and *not* as Pharaoh worked God's people to death as slaves (Deut 5:12–15). No day marks the sacred rhythms of GOT and JST more saliently than the Sabbath. The Torah specifies no exemptions for special types of Sabbath work, except for required priestly sacrifices (Num. 28:9–10; cf. Matt 12:5). Accordingly, some devout Jews assumed that no medical treatment should be offered on the Sabbath, except in life-threatening cases. The disabled woman had suffered for eighteen years; one more day would not kill her (see discussion on Luke 6:1–11).

But Jesus again firmly rejects this moral logic, not because he repudiates Sabbath law, but because of how he *interprets* it. He begins with a practical analogy regarding draft animals, which in fact should also be rested on the Sabbath (Exod 20:10; Deut 5:14). But they should also be cared for, which requires their owners to do basic *work* of animal husbandry on the Sabbath, such as untying (λύω, *lyō*) an ox or donkey from its manger and leading it to water (Luke 13:15). If such life-sustaining Sabbath work is acceptable on behalf of animals, "must [ἔδει, *edei*] not," then, this poor "daughter of Abraham," pressed down so long under the weight of her bowed back—akin to a beast of burden—"be set free [λυθῆναι, *lythēnai*]" from her oppression without further delay (13:16)? What better day than the life- and freedom-affirming Sabbath to release her burden and restore her health! What better day than the "today" of God's salvation, as we will also see with a physically challenged "son of Abraham" (19:9; cf. vv. 2–5)! The assembly couldn't agree more with Jesus, erupting with joy at all the "wonderful [honorable—ἐνδόξοις, *endoxois*] things that he was doing." Conversely, "all his opponents were put to shame [dishonored]" (13:17).

Although Jesus's argument may appear to run along a similar lesser-to-greater, beast-to-human track as 12:24 ("Of how much more value are you than the birds!"), in fact Jesus makes no value distinction here between ox/donkey and the woman. This does *not* constitute a *devaluation* of the woman, reducing her to a beast of burden, but rather an *elevation* of all God's creatures, human and nonhuman, as worthy of Sabbath care and dignity. While modern discussions of "animal rights" build upon sophisticated biological and psychological research, human sympathies with animals' physical and emotional needs were not unknown in antiquity. Martha Nussbaum describes one poignant case from ancient Roman history: "In 55 BCE the Roman leader Pompey staged a combat between humans and elephants. Surrounded in the arena, the animals perceived that they had no hope of escape. According to Pliny, they then 'entreated the crowd, trying to win their compassion with indescribable gestures, bewailing their plight with a sort of lamentation.' The audience, moved to pity and anger by their plight, rose to curse Pompey—feeling, writes Cicero, that the elephants had a relation of commonality [*societas*] with the human race."[187] Where societal leaders, whether Roman military or Jewish religious officials, seem less inclined from their powerful perches to compassion toward people or animals, the people themselves more readily sense the sympathetic bond of "commonality" among all God's creation.

A Farmer's Mustard Seed Raised Up to a Hospitable Tree (13:18–19)

As Wisdom's prophet-teacher, Jesus continues to observe the natural world, moving from zoology (ox/donkey) to botany (mustard seed [cf. fig tree in 13:6–9]). The broad scope of Jesus's thought reflects his vision for the realm of God encompassing all creation. Now he aims to reveal "what . . . the kingdom [realm, sphere] of God is like" via one element of that kingdom, a *mustard seed*. Jesus does not equate God's realm with nature (pantheism); note well the simile: God's kingdom "is *like*," is *homologous* to (ὅμοιος/ὁμιόω, *homoios*/*homioō*), not synonymous with (13:18–19). But Jesus does affirm the dynamic connection between God and the world God has made, even down to its tiniest components. Although unlike Matt 13:32//Mark 4:31, Luke does not specify that the mustard is the "smallest of all seeds" (which is technically not true anyway), the single mustard grain was proverbial for its little size disproportionate to its large yield (cf. Luke 17:6).

Jesus's short parable features the *tree* that sprouts up from the small seed and provides *nesting places for birds* (zoology again). In fact, a common Palestine species of mustard plant (*Brassica nigra* [black mustard]) could grow into a modest tree ten to fifteen feet tall (though most were shorter bushes) with thick enough trunk and branches to sustain small birds roosting and eating the tree's seeds.[188] Notably, Jesus's comparative picture does not highlight the benefits for *human* consumption of oils or sauces from the mustard crop. The concern is for birds' shelter and sustenance, or in other words, the mustard tree's *hospitality* to the fowls of the air. Of course, as in 12:4–7, 22–24, the Creator's care for birds implies care for creation, not least ("how much more") humans. But Jesus's interdependent cosmic-creational perspective, reinforced in the more literal "birds of the air/sky/heaven [οὐρανοῦ, *ouranou*]" (13:19), should not be reduced to a narrow anthropocentric grid. However small and imperceptible it may seem in a world beset by evil and hardship, God's work still pulses throughout the whole

187. Nussbaum, *Upheavals*, 89, and *Frontiers*, 325; Pliny, *Nat.* 8.7.20–21; Cicero, *Fam.* 7.1.3; Dio Cassius, *Hist.* 39.38. 2–4. Cf. Sorabji, *Animal Minds*, 124–27.

188. Koch, "Brassica nigra."

of God's realm—heaven and earth, plant and animal, beast and human—ready to burst forth in abundant provision and restoration (resurrection).

This little kingdom-parable sparks two further resonances: one from Ezekiel, the other from earlier in Luke. In place of a mustard seed Ezekiel develops the image of a small sprig snipped off by an eagle atop a tall cedar and its seed replanted in alien territory. This scenario reflects the experience of Ezekiel and fellow Judahite exiles: a small remnant cut off during Nebuchadnezzar's siege of Jerusalem and relocated in Babylon. While this "sprig" manages to take root and survive in a foreign land, it grows only into a "low" vine (Ezek 17:1–6). But such would not be its final state, as the prophet further envisions the day when the Lord would restore the "sprig" to its natural habitat and mountain height, with revolutionary results for Israel and the world.

> Thus says the Lord God:
> I myself will take a sprig
> from the lofty top of a cedar;
> I will set it out.
> I will break off a tender one
> from the topmost of its young twigs;
> I myself will plant it
> on a high and lofty mountain.
> On the mountain height of Israel
> I will plant it,
> in order that it may produce boughs and bear fruit,
> and become a noble cedar.
> *Under it every kind of bird will live;*
> in the shade of its branches will nest
> winged creatures of every kind.
> All the trees of the field shall know
> that I am the Lord.
> I bring low the high tree,
> I make high the low tree.
>
> (17:22–24)

Notice the echoes with Luke's high-low leveling scheme (Luke 1:48–52; 3:4–6; 6:17–26) and, more to the point of the present parable, the attracting of winged creatures to the "kingdom" tree's branches. Though Luke's Jesus speaks here in generic avian terms, Ezekiel's notation of "every kind of bird" offers suggestive creational and missional possibilities: *creational*, harking back to pairs of "every bird of every kind—every bird, every winged creature" preserved in the ark to begin a new world (Gen 7:14; cf. 1:21–22, 26, 28–30);[189] and *missional*, looking ahead to "all kinds of . . . birds of the air" (including "unclean" raptors) projected on Peter's screen-vision, calling him (and the church) to bring people from "every nation" into God's peaceful kingdom (Acts 10:12, 34–36; 11:4–6, 17–18). Though beginning as a sect with limited results among a small group of Jews, the kingdom of God in Christ promises—and demands—nothing less than universal, multiethnic hospitality in a renewed, fruitful heaven and earth.[190]

Jesus's mention of "birds of the air" more directly evokes his earlier words in the Travel Narrative, although the link is more contrastive than comparative: *unlike* the birds with their multiple nesting spots, "the Son of Humankind has *no place to lay his head*" (Luke 9:58 AT). As we have seen, this stark announcement sets the stage for a long trek of roughing it on the road. But prospects of hospitality smooth the way. As Jesus and his followers carry out their itinerant mission, they find welcome respite and refreshment in various homes (nests) (10:5–9, 38–42; 11:37; 14:1). Jesus also knows, however, that he is destined, as the Son of Humankind, to suffer and die: his final "nesting tree" will be a cross (9:22–24, 44; 18:31–33). But the story will not end there: "on the third day" Jesus will be raised to new life (9:22; 18:33) as "the first [of many] to rise from the dead . . . proclaim[ing] light both to our people and to the Gentiles" (Acts 26:23). The mysterious outworking of God's kingdom thus involves Jesus in paradoxical roles: as both chief *host-agent* of God's household and humble *guest-dependent*, identifying with the littlest, least, and last (9:47–48; 13:30). The suffering-serving Jesus embodies the parable's principle that from small, seemingly insignificant sources, abundant growth and gathering result. Jesus may be compared to both seed and bird, both giver and receiver of hospitable life in the symbiotic dynamics of saving creation.

A Baker Woman's Yeast Rises Up into a Bread Feast (13:20–21)

This parable functions in close tandem with the preceding, making a similar point about the operation of God's kingdom and serving Luke's penchant for pairing male/female protagonists. The following chart delineates the connections, while also hinting at some telling variations.

189. Gen 1:29–30 in fact closely juxtaposes "every tree" with "every bird of the air," suggesting an arboreal-avian symbiosis in creation.

190. Luke's version of the mustard seed in a "garden" (κῆπος, *kēpos*), in distinction from Matthew's "field" (ἀγρός, *agros* [Matt 13:31]), may have some Eden-like associations with restored, fruitful creation.

	Luke 13:18–19	Luke 13:20–21
Personal agent:	sower man	baker woman
Natural element:	mustard seed	yeast
Limited element:	small-sized seed thrown (βάλλω, *ballō*) into a garden	small amount of spoiled element (yeast) mixed in (lit. "hidden in" [ἐγκρύπτω, *enkryptō*]) the flour
Abundant result:	tree grows with branches for birds of the air to nest	50 lbs. of dough rises to produce 100 loaves of bread

The primary comparative element of God's realm—"It is like yeast [leaven]"—adds a notable feature of spoilage and infection to the small-sized dimension of the mustard seed. As we have seen, the Bible normally exploits yeast as a symbol of insidious evil to be expunged from God's people, like the hypocrisy of some Pharisees (cf. 12:1). Like yeast, evil has potent capacity to spread inexorably and exponentially, corrupting a large "batch" of people and institutions. The work of God exerts similar catalytic, contagious energy on everything it touches, but with a *polar opposite outcome*, namely, optimal *good* rather than evil. The result is bread for the world rather than poisonous fare. Moreover, Jesus may intimate the Creator God's ultimate power and purpose to *transform* evil (fungal yeast) into good (nourishing bread), on the order of Joseph's climactic Genesis assertion, reflecting on God's *sustaining feeding* of the people: "Even though you intended to do harm to me, God intended it for good, in order to preserve a numerous people, as he is doing today" (Gen 50:20).

The role of the baker woman as the *personal agent* manipulating the potent natural ingredient toward productive ends places her, like the male sower in the previous snippet, in comparison with *God*. The *kingdom* is like yeast (and a mustard seed). *God*, who creates, sustains, and rules the kingdom, is like the *baker woman* (and sowing man).[191] Casting God in female as well as male imagery affirms female dignity and equality with men (cf. Gen 1:27). And if anything, Luke's present male-female pairing tips the agential scale toward the woman. Whereas the male farmer simply "took and sowed [threw]" the mustard seed in the garden (no mention of digging/fertilizing as in Luke 13:7–8), the baker woman "took and mixed in" the yeast into "all [the whole—ὅλον, *holon*]" the dough. She *works* hands-on and hands-through the process. The verb for "mix in" is more literally "hide in" (ἐγκρύπτω, *enkryptō*), suggesting both the complete diffusion of the kingdom-yeast throughout the "whole" batch and its incognito operation. The naked eye cannot detect yeast within flour, except by its eventual rising effect on the dough. Except for chemists, few have any clue

191. See Barbara E. Reid, "Beyond Petty Pursuits," 285–87.

how the yeast does its "raising" work. In Luke's narrative designed to solidify knowledge of God's work, some things still *cannot be fully known*; some things remain mysterious, secret, hidden. While much can be known about God's realm, its ultimate efficacy remains counterintuitive to human perception and deeply rooted in God's inscrutable mind and in whomever God reveals it to (see 10:21–24; 12:1–3). Faith in God's saving purpose perseveres in the tension of knowing and unknowing.

And pressing through these less-than-limpid moments eventually yields abundant clarity and fruitfulness. In the present example, the woman kneads a small amount of yeast (though no exact measure is given)[192] into about fifty pounds of flour, producing a hundred loaves of bread![193] As a flock of birds nest (and feed) in the branches of a mustard tree sprouting from a single seed, so a host of banqueters feast on the bread served up by the yeast-plying baker woman. The hospitality of God's kingdom rises to prominence yet again in Luke's story with a key accent on servant ministry. The woman plays her conventional part in this household drama. Who else but a woman would make and serve the bread? But in fact this is not catering business as usual: this is feeding and serving in God's realm, where God and Son Jesus get their creative hands in the dough, work in the yeast, and serve it up to all who are hungry, with basketfuls left over (cf. 9:10–17). And they enlist *all* household members—male and female—as partners in mutual service and fellowship (8:1–3; 12:35–38, 41–42; 22:24–27).

Stage 2: Longing to Gather and Protect in the Face of Opposition and Obstinacy (13:22–17:10)

This stage begins with a reset of Jesus's broad itinerary: "Jesus went through one town and village after another as he made his way to Jerusalem" (13:22). Though Luke still provides no precise coordinates for the route, the Jerusalem goal stays firmly in view. And now, in no uncertain terms and with unstinting resolve, Jesus links this destination with his demise: "Yet today, tomorrow, and the next day I must be on my way, because it is impossible for a prophet to be

192. This lacuna may be significant in itself: the kingdom is not calibrated in a precise "recipe" formula. God supplies however much is needed to get the job done.

193. Barbara E. Reid ("Beyond Petty Pursuits") notes the fascinating interlink of the fifty pounds of flour amount in the offerings of Sarah (Gen 18:6), Gideon (Judg 6:19), and Hannah (1 Sam 1:24) in sacred contexts: "In each instance the large-scale baking prepares for a manifestation of God. So, too, the parable of Luke 13:20–21 portrays the work of a woman as a vehicle for divine revelation" (287).

killed outside Jerusalem" (13:33). Though voluntarily undertaken, Jesus's trek to Jerusalem remains a death march with mounting opposition along the way, yet also hope of vindication "on the third day" (13:32; cf. 9:22).

The Pharisees and scribal associates continue to represent major foils to Jesus's interests (14:1; 15:1–2; 16:14–15). Luke affixes a new pejorative label to the Pharisees as "lovers of money" (16:14), set against Jesus's generous God- and neighbor-loving path sympathetic to the poor and needy. The economy of God's kingdom, with pointed challenges to wealthy householders, represents the major theme of Jesus's teaching in this segment, especially in the form of parables (14:7–24, 28–33; 15:1–32; 16:1–13, 19–31). Yet, the Pharisees do not constitute the most serious threat to Jesus, nor do they bear the full brunt of Jesus's prophetic critique. In fact, the second leg of the journey opens with some Pharisees imploring Jesus to "get away from here, for Herod wants to kill you" (13:31). Though they may vigorously, even furiously (cf. 6:11), debate Jesus on the fine points of God's way, the Pharisees do not seek to kill him. They may be "watching him closely" with a wary eye, but they do so at Sabbath fellowship meals to which they invite him (14:1). They may ultimately reject Jesus as God's messianic prophet, as Israel has historically spurned God's messengers (cf. 11:47–54), but the Pharisees give Jesus a full hearing, if not always an entirely fair one, and are not out for his blood.

The murderous threat comes more from the *Herodian-political* front than the Pharisaic-religious side. More specifically, Herod Antipas, tetrarch of Galilee, seeks to kill Jesus, as he had exterminated Jesus's prophetic forerunner, John. Herod's paranoia about John's reincarnation as Jesus, Elijah, or another prophet (9:7–9) has only escalated. To be sure, Jesus seems to have journeyed outside Herod's actual Galilean jurisdiction, but not very far. Galilean-Samarian borderlands, where Jesus appears to be wandering (cf. 17:11), remain within Herod's reach. Plus, allied Herodian-Roman authority stretched across first-century Palestine. Down the road in Jerusalem, Antipas will cement his friendship with Pilate around a common annoyance with Jesus's subversive tendencies (23:6–12). But for his part Jesus will not now or later be intimidated by "that fox" Herod. He presses on, knowing full well that his journey will end in death (and resurrection); and in the meantime he continues his mission until "I finish my work" of conquering malevolent powers, whether "casting out demons and performing cures" or denouncing political oppression (13:32). As it happens, however, this segment features no exorcisms and only one short healing incident (14:1–6). Most of Jesus's ensuing saving-liberating work entails prophetic critique of social conventions and domination systems. Though no other mention of Herod occurs until the closing scenes in Jerusalem, we may presume along the way Jesus's persisting indictment of the tetrarch and all he represents.

Though Jesus's personal fate remains critical in the narrative, his primary focus falls on training his followers and reaching out to the wider populace. He delineates the demands of discipleship (14:25–35; 17:1–10) and demonstrates his concern to seek and save the lost and least. He desperately longs to bring all of God's people (1) into the banquet house (13:22–30; 14:1–24; 15:20–32), (2) under protective wing (13:34), (3) back home to secure shelter (15:1–32), and (4) into Abraham's eternal bosom (16:23–31). But a tragic undertone of resistance dogs Jesus's efforts: many are "not willing." From the start of this segment, Jesus laments this deep, willful disjunction: "How often I desired [ἠθέλησα, *ēthelēsa*] to gather your children . . . but you did not desire [ἠθελήσατε, *ēthelēsate*] [my protective care]" (13:34 AT). Though Jesus's heart and arms (wings) are open wide, only a few find their way into Jesus's saving presence (13:23). Though the realm of God's salvation extends to the tips of the world's four compass points (13:29), it must be willfully and actively *entered* via a *narrow* door (13:24), designed not to keep people out but to keep them on the God-centered track blazed by Jesus through whom, and only whom, salvation comes (cf. Acts 4:12). The way of God is both inclusive (all are welcome) and exclusive (in Christ alone).

In House and under Wing (13:22–35)

In this opening, theme-setting scene of stage 2, the image of "house" stands out as a critical kingdom boundary site: saving and protecting those within, while shutting out and abandoning those without.

> When once the owner of the house [οἰκοδεσπότης, *oikodespotēs*] has got up and shut the door, and you begin to stand outside [ἔξω, *exō*]. . . . (13:25)

> See, your house [οἶκος, *oikos*] is left/forsaken [ἀφίεται, *aphietai*] to/for you. (13:35)

Jesus depicts the first place as a *banquet house* where the owner prepares to host a stream of guests, but only those who enter the proper site at the proper time, that is, the "narrow door" before it shuts (13:22–30). The second place Jesus envisions as a *farm house* where a mother hen nurtures a brood of chicks, but only those that stay under her wing (13:31–35). Both houses typify the realm of God, the *house of the Lord*, closely associated with Jerusalem and the temple. But God's kingdom is not coterminous with these sacred sites, but rather reaches out to all points of the world. And if Jerusalem proves inhospitable to God's Messiah and people from far and wide, then it will find itself desolate again, as the biblical prophets warned on the cusp of Assyrian and Babylonian demolitions (cf. 13:28, 34). A tragic spirit of lament and judgment weighs heavily on Jesus at this juncture, dampening otherwise bright prospects of a great ingathering and homecoming (13:29, 34–35). A shocking upside-down configuration of God's household will result: "Indeed some are last who will be first, and some are first who will be last" (13:30).

The Host and the Banquet House (13:22–30)

The picture of table fellowship as a defining mark of God's household throughout Luke's narrative is particularly salient in the present context, following on the heels of the baker woman parable (13:20–21) and setting up a series of banquet/feeding tales (14:1–24; 15:1–2, 11–32; 16:19–25). The focus now falls not so much on *what* is eaten or *how* it is provided, but on *who* gathers at the table to enjoy God's bounty and *how* they get there. Regarding the "how" matter, Luke has thus far highlighted both (1) Jesus's dramatic provision of abundant bread and fish on special occasions (5:1–11; 9:10–17) and (2) the cryptic process of transforming "yeast" into kingdom "bread" (13:20–21). In each case, the operant work of God in Christ is paramount. But now the onus of agency shifts to human respondents who must *enter* the kingdom banquet hall via the prescribed route and door.[194]

Two verbs enhance the ingressive action: "*Strive* [ἀγωνίζεσθε, *agōnizesthe*] to enter . . . *seek* [ζητήσουσιν, *zētēsousin*] to enter" (13:24 AT). Both terms stress concerted effort and attention along a difficult course, with no cheap guarantees of success.[195] The first carries the stronger force, aptly captured in English by "agonize," derived from Greek. Originally, it connoted vigorous athletic training and straining toward a worthy, but hard won, goal. It valorized a fierce fight to the finish (cf. 1 Cor 9:25; 1 Tim 6:12; 2 Tim 4:7). Cognate nouns ἀγών (*agōn*) and ἀγωνία (*agōnia*) apply to Jesus's own agonizing struggle to complete his cross-bearing "race" (Heb 12:1–2; cf. Luke 22:44). The road to God's kingdom runs off the beaten path over rough, "narrow" terrain that exacts a heavy toll on persistent travelers.

"Seeking" may involve less pain than "striving," but no less perseverance. At the heart of stage 2 (and the entire Travel Narrative), a trio of parables

194. Jesus's brief introduction of "entering" language in 11:52 (see above) becomes more prominent now.

195. Rendering ζητέω (*zēteō*) as "try to" (NRSV, NIV) gets at the precariousness of entering (many will try and fail), but not the connotation of determined "seeking" or searching.

features a seeking shepherd, a sweeper woman, and a father dedicated to the arduous task of recovering, respectively, a lost sheep, coin, and son (15:3–32). These stories illustrate (and vindicate) Jesus's reaching out and retrieving, seeking and saving, lost "sinners" (15:1–2). Now, however, the seeking burden falls on the other foot: people must seek after and come to God via Christ. This travel image is more of a pilgrimage than a rescue mission. But sadly, many who assume they will gain entrance after their journey "will not be able" (13:24). They will find the door locked, and by this point no amount of knocking and pleading will stir the host to grant them access. They remain "outside" (ἔξω, *exō* [13:25, 28]), forever barred from the banquet. The only thing they will sink their teeth into is their own molars, as they grind and "gnash" in bitter frustration (13:24–28).[196]

What accounts for this stark rejection? Why does this "asking and knocking" not yield any food (contra 11:5–13)? Implied is a *temporal* problem: somehow these would-be entrants come too late; the hour has gone beyond the "midnight" interruption of the earlier parable (11:5), such that when this householder "has got up/rises up [ἐγερθῇ, *egerthē*]" (13:25) to answer the door, he refuses to open it for these tardy arrivers. But the bigger issue is the *relational-epistemological* problem that the host doubly emphasizes: "I do not know where you come from [οὐκ οἶδα (ὑμᾶς) πόθεν ἐστέ, *ouk oida (hymas) pothen este*]" (13:25, 27). The seekers claim to know him by previous association: "We ate and drank with you, and you taught in our streets" (13:26). But casual acquaintance does not guarantee loyalty to the host or fealty to his instruction; and only such *personal, faithful knowledge* truly binds the householder and his extended family around the banquet table. The feast celebrates a kinship of covenant and ethics. These inveterate "evildoers" ("workers of injustice [ἐργάται ἀδικίας, *ergatai adikias*]"), as the host identifies them, whose prior acquaintance has not led to any substantive change of character, have effectively disenfranchised themselves from the family. He does not know where they "come from [πόθεν, *pothen*]," which in this context has a connotation that is more dispositional than directional, akin to the modern English colloquialism "I don't know where you're coming from thinking or acting like that. But if that's where you're coming from—in thought and deed—you can't come in here!"

This is not to set up a closed, sectarian table, à la certain Essenes and Pharisees. People "will come/be present [ἥξουσιν, *hēxousin*]"[197] from north,

196. "Weeping and gnashing of teeth" is a common image of eternal, hellish judgment in Matthew (8:12; 13:42, 50; 22:13; 24:51; 25:30). In Luke, however, the only use of the phrase is in 13:28, with no patent application to afterlife punishment. Luke's main depiction of postmortem misery comes in 16:19–31.

197. BDAG, 435. This rendering is preferable to the NRSV, "Then they will come." The con-

south, east, and west to "eat in the kingdom of God" with the venerable patriarchs and prophets of old (13:29). The vision of a great universal banquet unites God's people across vast space (four compass points) and time (since founding father Abraham). While directional-geographic dimensions now come to the fore, relational-epistemological concerns still apply. Territorial demarcations often reflect divergent cultural and ideological perspectives (e.g., international East/West divides, national North/South conflicts in Irish and American histories). People indeed "come from" different places. But the God of all creation has never abandoned the covenantal purpose of blessing "all families of the earth" (Gen 12:1–3; 18:18; 22:15–18; cf. Gal 3:6–9) and being, through God's servant Israel, "a light to the nations" (Isa 42:6; 49:6; cf. Luke 2:29–32; Acts 13:47; 26:17–18, 22–23).

Jesus's message through this brief banquet tale carries heavy eschatological and christological freight. The sweeping spatiotemporal scope envisions a culmination—an "at last!"—of God's gracious goals for creation. Such consummative work has begun through the mission of Jesus Messiah as he "has come eating and drinking" (Luke 7:34), setting up tasting stations of God's royal eschatological feast throughout the land in anticipation of his ultimate role as exalted Lord seated at the head of God's table. In this position, he has the final say, as Savior and Judge, over who gets in and who does not. And the guest list flips as many tables as it fills: "Some are last who will be first, and some are first who will be last" (13:30). Tax collectors, sinners, and other unsavory characters who have come "to repentance" (5:32; cf. 7:34–35; 15:1–2; 19:1–10) may find themselves chatting with Abraham at the messianic table, while certain self-righteous types, with excessive dining scruples, may find themselves banging on a shut door to no avail. One must *know* the Lord-Host of God's kingdom to get into the grand banquet hall. And to know this Lord is to know his ways of welcoming the last and the lost.

The Fox and the Hen House (13:31–35)

The scene continues "at that very hour," but with a dramatic shift in focus to an immediate threat to Jesus's life (13:31) and to the imminent tragedy of Jerusalem's dispersion and the temple's desolation (13:34–35). More specifically, the plot revolves around two opposing figures cast in animal images of a fox and hen with clashing desires or wills (θέλω, *thelō*).

---

junction is simply "and" (καί, *kai*), not "then" (implying many comers *after* the false, late seekers are thrown out); the welcome guests are already present.

> "Get away from here, for Herod *wants* [θέλει, *thelei*] to kill you [Jesus]." He said to them [some Pharisees], "Go and tell that *fox* for me. . . ." (13:31)

> How often have I [Jesus] *desired* [ἠθέλησα, *ēthelēsa*] to gather your children together as a *hen* gathers her brood under her wings, and you were *not willing* [οὐκ ἠθελήσατε, *ouk ēthelēsate*]! (13:34)

The tetrarch Herod and Messiah Jesus represent two antithetical approaches to power. Herod's perplexed speculation about the beheaded John's recrudescence through Jesus (9:7–9) has mushroomed into an anxious plot to murder Jesus. The wills and ways of God's realm threaten to subvert the wills and ways of Herod's arena. Hence, Herod seeks to exterminate Jesus, as he did John.

But Jesus has no intention of backing down, changing course, or dying before his time in Jerusalem (not Herod's Galilee). Herod will throw in his two cents of opposition at Jesus's trial; though not explicitly insisting on the death penalty, he lifts no finger to stop Jesus's execution. In any case, the final judicial authority rests with Rome's military man, Pilate (23:8–25). Herod Antipas is but a petty puppet ruler over a mere quarter-kingdom. From Jesus's perspective, he's nothing but a pesky, predatory little *fox*—a malign epithet Jesus is not afraid to "tell" Herod. Any positive vulpine notions of wisdom, cleverness, or slyness are not in view. Jesus draws here on the common biblical portrait of foxes as sneaky spoilers of vineyards (Song 2:15) and exploitative looters of ruins (Ps 63:10; Ezek 13:4; Neh 4:3; 2 Esd 14:3). They are first on the disaster scene, not to offer relief, but to raid the remains. In the wake of Babylon's destruction of Jerusalem and the temple, the writer of Lamentations bewailed the desolate ground zero site as the haunt of scavenging foxes (Lam 5:18).[198] Of course, the slightly built foxes have no real power to effect the demolition; they just prey on the aftermath. Such is Jesus's biting image of the petty tyrant Herod Antipas.[199]

By the starkest of contrasts, God's Viceroy Jesus does not exploit the vulnerable for his own advantage but rather liberates them from demonic forces and physical maladies. And no one will deter him from continuing this salvific work "today, tomorrow, and the third day" (13:32, 33). Unlike Herod Antipas, luxuriating in his palace-den in lakeside Tiberias, Jesus persists in his itinerant seeking-and-saving mission, with not so much as a fox hole to call his own (see 9:58; cf. 7:25). He will not rest until he reaches Jerusalem, "the city that kills the

198. Though here and other places, the NRSV renders the Hebrew (שועל, *shu'al*) and Greek (ἀλώπηξ, *alōpēx*) as "jackal," these are standard terms for "fox," as in Luke 13:32.

199. On the character of Herod in Luke's narrative, see Darr, *Herod*; Dicken, *Herod* and "Herod."

prophets" (13:34). He, too, will be killed there. Herod will get his wish, but not until Jesus has done what he came to do. And even then, neither Herod nor any malevolent power will have the last word. For perceptive hearers/readers, Jesus's reference to "the third day" cues the hope of resurrection from the dead (9:22; 13:32; 18:33; 24:7, 21, 46; Acts 10:40).

While Jesus displays unflinching courage in the face of Herod's hostile pursuit, his dominant emotions at this juncture are sorrow and disappointment, not over his own fate, but over Jerusalem's people, who will spurn his protective care. His present lament over Jerusalem, at the start of the Travel Narrative's second leg (13:34–35), previews the weeping dirge at journey's end, on the edge of the city (19:41–44). He assumes the role of a *mother bird* (ὄρνις, *ornis*) longing to gather and guard her chicks under wing against predators. Having recently employed avian examples of Father-God's care for his creatures, including his human "flock" (12:22–32), and of the kingdom's "nesting" hospitality to creation (13:18–19), Jesus now presents himself as the chief ornithological-maternal agent of the Creator's redemptive purpose.[200] Though eyed by various raiders, including opportunistic "foxes," Jesus as "mother hen" is scarcely a weak, vulnerable figure. Ὄρνις (*ornis*) identifies the female gender but no particular species of bird, and the biblical portraits of protection under divine wings typically feature dominant birds, like eagles, not domestic chickens. For example:

> He sustained him in a desert land,
>   in a howling wilderness waste;
> he shielded him, cared for him,
>   guarded him as the apple of his eye.
> As an eagle stirs up its nest,
>   and hovers over its young;
> as it spreads its wings, takes them up,
>   and bears them aloft on its pinions
> the Lord alone guided him.
>
> (Deut 32:10–12)

> You who live in the shelter of the Most High,
>   who abide in the shadow of the Almighty,
> will say to the Lord, "My refuge and my fortress;
>   my God, in whom I trust."

200. See Elizabeth A. Johnson's discussion (*Ask the Beasts*, 139–43) of avian imagery and Wisdom within "the broad tradition of divine female power," drawing on Augustine, Syriac traditions of spirituality, and other early Christian sources.

For he will deliver you from the snare of the fowler
and from the deadly pestilence;
he will cover you with his pinions,
and under his wings you will find refuge.

(Ps 91:1–4)

The Lord-Eagle's mighty wings and pinions provide the offspring not only shelter from attack, but also training in flight: both protection and propulsion. The fox doesn't have a chance—*unless* the young brood wanders out from under wing.

And herein lays the tragedy that Jesus laments. The fox's evil desires are no match for the mother-eagle's desires to nurture her fledglings. But the chicks have their own penchants, and the awful fact Jesus senses is that the preponderance of Jerusalem's children is "not willing"—does not desire to come under her Mother-Messiah's wings. Jesus foresees their dire destiny of homeless desolation among the ruins, where they will be easy pickings for prowling foxes (Luke 13:34–35). The warning of a God-forsaken, bleak "house" ("Look, your house is left to you desolate [NIV]/abandoned [CEB]" [13:35]) recalls prophetic judgments against unfaithful Jerusalem and the Lord's house (temple), realized in the Babylonian siege (Jer 22:5; 26:6, 9). The reference to a mother bird's wings (πτέρυγα, *pteryga*) also subtly alludes to the temple as the locus of God's secure gathering of the people, as under a massive winged canopy. It was from the temple's pinnacle or wing-tip (πτερύγιον, *pterygion*) that Satan tempted Jesus to jump, outside of God's sanctuary. But Jesus refused to tempt the Lord's out-of-wing protection (Luke 4:9–12). Luke's Jesus has both stayed under God's wing through faithful temple worship (2:22–24, 41–49) and stretched out his own wings as an embodiment of God's place of refuge. But, as in Jeremiah's day, institutional temple security has become increasingly illusory, as priestly leaders preside more over a "den of robbers" (foxes!) than a haven of prayer and ministry, and the people go their own rebellious ways (cf. 19:45–46; Jer 7:1–11). They thus court terrible disaster, which in fact hits within a generation of Jesus's lament, when Rome razes Jerusalem and the temple in 70 CE. Since Luke likely writes a decade or so after this debacle, it would remain deeply etched in his audience's memory.[201] And modern readers should note well, cognizant of those who gather daily at the Wailing Wall ruin, that the temple remains "desolate" to this day.

But the crisis is not void of hope. As lament psalms press through to confidence in God's faithfulness, so Jesus's lament ends on a more positive,

201. See Tannehill, *Narrative Unity*, 2:93–94; Spencer, *Gospel of Luke*, 74–77.

though still challenging, note. In fact, he concludes with a Psalms citation, not of lament but of praise. He quotes from the Hallel album (Ps 113–18), aptly sung during Jerusalem pilgrimages, temple processions, and Passover celebrations, specifically associating *his* coming to Jerusalem with the people's exclamation: "Blessed is the one who comes in the name of the Lord" (Luke 13:35/Ps 118:26). Jesus virtually equates his coming with the Lord's blessed advent to the people in glorious salvation (see Ps 118:14, 21). But will they truly "see" and embrace this visitation? At the end of Jesus's journey many will indeed burst forth with this very Hallel, punctuated with a royal attribution: "Blessed is the *king* who comes in the name of the Lord" (Luke 19:38). But tragically this chorus will wane, prompting Jesus to lament over Jerusalem in more searing tones and to disrupt temple business with a forceful demonstration and prophetic critique (19:41–46). Soon paeans of praise will turn to pleas of "Crucify him, crucify him!" and mockeries of Jesus's saving mission (23:21, 35–39).

Still, the eschatological context of Jesus's teaching (see above) points to other "comings" of the Lord—including a consummative coming with "blessed" prospects of restoration for those ready to "see" at last. But counterstrains of judgment and responsibility also persist. When the Lord comes to rule his great household, to set his messianic table, and to spread his maternal wings, his children (brood) must acknowledge his lordship, enter his banquet hall, and take their rest under his sturdy canopy.

Sabbath Healing and Banquet Feeding (14:1–24)

As Jesus's healing the stooped woman on the Sabbath set the stage for a pair of hospitality parables (mustard seed and yeast) (13:10–21), so now another Sabbath cure, this time of a man with dropsy (14:1–6), prepares for another tandem of hospitality stories: first, concerning seating arrangements at a wedding banquet (14:7–11); second, concerning invitees to a large feast (14:12–24). Luke's Jesus continues to portray God's kingdom as a salutary realm of healing and feeding: a *hospital*, as it were, in both its modern sense of a healthcare center and its linguistic connection to household hospitality. Moreover, the banquet theme from 13:22–35 carries over into 14:1–24 in the setting of an actual dinner party Jesus attends, hosted by a "leader of the Pharisees" (14:1, 7, 12, 15). Now, however, Jesus is less concerned with how invitees respond (though see 14:17–20) than with where guests sit (14:7–11) and whom hosts invite (14:12–24).

Dropsy Cure (14:1–6)

Luke's Jesus rarely travels far without entering a home, eating a meal there, healing an afflicted person, and observing the weekly Sabbath, though often creating as much stir as rest. All these elements coalesce in the present snippet: a meal scene, a healing story, and a Sabbath controversy. The meal, hosted by a prominent Pharisee, naturally includes a company of fellow Pharisees. Jesus's presence at the affair, presumably by the host's invitation, sets the group to "watching him closely [παρατηρούμενοι, *paratēroumenoi*]" (14:1). While the term can connote positive, "careful attention" to Jesus's words and actions, Luke's usage always conveys a more sinister motive, as in an earlier Sabbath-healing scene, where "the scribes and the Pharisees watched him [παρετηροῦντο, *paretērounto*] . . . *so that they might find an accusation against him*" (6:7; cf. 20:20; Acts 9:24). This prosecutorial disposition toward Jesus seems at odds with the Pharisees' recent move to protect Jesus from Herod's attack (Luke 13:31). But the Pharisees are no great friends of Herodian officials in Luke, and their relationship with Jesus appears more like an in-house debate than a battle among hardcore enemies. The Pharisees want to correct Jesus at key points (and vice versa), not to kill him, though tensions could flare quite hot (6:11; 11:53). The fact that they continue to invite him to table conferences is a sign of respect, however begrudging at times. Though they oppose Jesus's tendency to fellowship with "sinner"types, the Pharisees do not strictly classify him with these outliers; otherwise, he would not be welcome at *their* tables.

The first issue at the current meal, involving a man suffering from dropsy or edema, constitutes the third Sabbath-healing incident, though the first in a home rather than synagogue (cf. 6:6–11; 13:10–17). In placement and language, the present incident most closely links with that surrounding the back-pained woman (13:10–17). Dropsy designates a serious condition of fluid retention around the heart and other bodily cavities, accompanied by a terribly ironic insatiable thirst for more liquids the body cannot process. This waterlogged (ὑδρωπικός, *hydrōpikos*) state offers horrible prospects of either self-drowning or bursting open. Like gout, the folkloric "king's disease," dropsy was widely associated in antiquity with the affluent and indulgent. Whatever its precise epidemiology, dropsy became an apt metaphor for the inexorable cravings of greed and consumption by the wealthy at the expense of the less fortunate—and ultimately of themselves. With no restraints on their rapaciousness, they would bloat themselves into oblivion.[202] If the hunched-over woman symbolizes cos-

202. See Stobaeus, *Flor.* 3.10.45; Philostratus, *Vit. Apoll.* 1.9; Ovid, *Fast.* 1.215–16; Horace,

mic-social oppression loaded up on her bent back (see above), the polysaturated man represents powerful agents of such oppression. While he may have enjoyed long years of self-indulgence on the backs of unfortunate victims, it may now be killing him from within. He may literally eat and drink himself to death.

Apart from Greco-Roman moral philosophers' associations of dropsy with avarice and self-aggrandizement, the Jewish historian Josephus makes a similar judgment with respect to Herod the Great, the father of Antipas the "fox."[203] Herod suffered at the end of his life from painful dropsy- and gout-like ailments, with thick pooling of fluids in his entrails and feet and an internal burning that fueled a ferocious appetite. In Josephus's view, such affliction served as appropriate punishment for Herod's impious and imperious reign, most egregiously evidenced in installing a large golden eagle over the main temple gate (*Ant.* 17.146–80). Whether intended as a symbol of God's or Rome's oversight of the temple, the crafted ornament represented, first and foremost, a Torah-forbidden graven image (like the golden calf) and a monument to Herod's opulent kingdom showcased in his massive temple renovation project. But as Herod's temple and eagle would not last a century, his bloated body would not last the year. Antipas would only continue in his father's swollen footsteps, albeit with only a quarter of his realm. And most tragically, while some faithful Jews resisted Herod the Great's golden eagle, at the cost of their lives (*Ant.* 17.149–67), the populace would largely spurn, as Luke's Jesus has just lamented, the hospitable-healing nurture in God's house provided by God's messianic mother-eagle (13:31–35).

Not to be missed, however, in Luke's present story—whatever the implicit critique of self-absorbed (and -absorbent) diners and however the man with dropsy happens to appear "in front of [ἔμπροσθεν, *emprosthen*]" Jesus[204]—is the fact that *Jesus heals the diseased man* (14:4). While scoring another point for the Sabbath's restorative purpose, Jesus does not merely use the man as another legal-object lesson. He also fulfills his commitment to keep "performing cures today and tomorrow" *in the face of Herod's opposition* (13:32), indeed, targeting the very ailment that killed this Herod's father. A striking redemptive note thus sounds at the outset of this new stage of Jesus's Jerusalem journey, signaling

---

Epod. 2.2.146–49; Seneca, *Helv.* 11.2–4; Plutarch, *Mor.* 523C, 524F; cited and discussed in Hartsock, "Healing," 349–52; cf. Braun, *Feasting*.

203. Hartsock ("Healing," 351–52) briefly mentions this Josephus text. I amplify and relate this example to Luke's critique of Herodian politics and economics.

204. It is not clear *why* the man with dropsy suddenly ("just then"/"look!" [ἰδού, *idou*]) appears before Jesus. Is he an invited guest, a drop-in (like the "sinful" woman in Luke 7), or perhaps a plant by the host to trigger a response from Jesus (see discussion in Hartsock, "Healing," 346–47)? In any case, his positioning "in front of" Jesus, whether at table or elsewhere in the house, is critical for direct encounter with Jesus.

that Jesus does not peremptorily exclude the wealthy and privileged from God's gracious care. As much as Luke's Jesus exemplifies liberation theology's "preference for the poor," he does not write off the rich. In fact, hope for a truly just and compassionate world must include transformation of high and low, rich and poor—a leveling of the field (6:17–19) alongside a great reversal of fortunes (1:52–53). Revolutionary overthrow of the establishment by the downtrodden too easily leads to violent backlash from both parties, not to world-mending and peacemaking. Though not without difficulty, powerful elites can be "saved" by God (see 18:24–26) and "sent . . . away" (14:4) on a changed, new way.[205]

Once again, Jesus intentionally pushes the envelope on the Sabbath. As in 6:9, he is the one who raises the legal question about Sabbath healing (14:3). In the face of the Pharisees' silence, he then proceeds to heal the man with dropsy and to justify his actions with analogies from family life and animal husbandry. Since anyone would naturally rescue "a child or an ox that has fallen into a well" on the Sabbath as much as (if not more than) on any other day, why object to relieving this man's painful condition today (14:5)?[206] The argument is similar to that offered concerning the bent-over woman, but with a telling twist. Rather than appealing to the normal *feeding/watering* of donkeys and oxen on the Sabbath (13:15), Jesus now references the *saving/extracting* of children and oxen from a well-pit. The former case enables thirsty animals to *drink* (ποτίζω, *potizō* [13:15]); the latter rescues the imperiled from *drowning*—an apt parallel to the fluid-soaked sufferer from dropsy.

Seating Chart (14:7–11)

After healing the dropsy sufferer, Jesus turns his attention to the arrangement of guests, typically in reclining position around a U-shaped table. He carefully "noticed" (ἐπέχω, *epechō* [14:7]) this set-up, however, not with detached, unbiased interest, as Sextus Empiricus and fellow Skeptics counseled, but with pointed critical judgment conveyed in parable form.[207] Though referring to a

205. After healing, restoring, or forgiving individuals, Luke's Jesus often sends them on their renewed way ("Go"), as in 5:14, 24; 7:50; 8:39, 48; 17:14, 19. Here, however, the dispatching (ἀπέλυσεν [*apelysen*, "released/sent off"; 14:4]) of the man cured from dropsy may also signal a demarcation from the other banqueters who remain set in their ways.

206. For a more consistent point of animal rescue, some copyists changed "child" (υἱός, *huios*) to "donkey" (ὄνος, *onos*) or "sheep" (πρόβατον, *probaton* [cf. Matt 12:11]); see Bruce M. Metzger, *Textual Commentary*, 138–39. Luke's "child" perhaps drives the point home more personally.

207. The verb ἐπέχω (*epechō*) means to "fix attention" (Acts 3:5), "to be mindful or espe-

"wedding banquet" (14:8) rather than to the more ordinary dinner party thrown by the Pharisee, Jesus's censure of the present scene can scarcely be missed. Whatever the festive occasion, invited guests should let the host determine their seats rather than jockey for the best, most honored spots closest to the host and other prominent persons. The host will have his way regardless, and the shame of being *dis*placed, *re*seated to a lower position is not worth the risk of presumptuous self-seating (14:9–10). It is an issue again of who's "first" (πρωτοκλισία, *prōtoklisia*, "first place," "place of honor") and "last" (ἔσχατος, *eschatos*) in status (14:8–9; cf. 13:30), depending on the host's sovereign—and sometimes surprising—choice. For the guests' part, they are better off taking the low road: "For all who exalt themselves will be humbled, and those who humble themselves will be exalted" (14:11; cf. 18:14).

Of course, Jesus is mainly concerned with the ethics of God's kingdom rather than the etiquette of wedding events. In this respect, he shares the Pharisees' commitment to the household table as a microcosm of God's realm. But Jesus's theological and communal values tend to be more disruptive (first/last inversions) and inclusive ("sinners" and such) than the Pharisees', and he dares to let them know so in the middle of their dinner parties!

Guest List (14:12–24)

Jesus turns from addressing the guests to challenging his host directly (not in a parable) about the cliquish makeup of his invitees. Whatever the meal occasion, earlier (breakfast/lunch [ἄριστον, *ariston*]) or later (supper [δεῖπνον, *deipnon*]) in the day, Jesus exhorts the host not to invite his A-list associates, but to reach out to O-list outcasts. With stunning specificity, Jesus delineates a quartet of contrasting groups (14:12–13; cf. 14:21).

"A" list **(*Do not* invite associates)**	**"O" list** **(*Do* invite outcasts)**
Friends	Poor
Brothers	Crippled
Relatives	Blind
Rich neighbors	Lame

cially observant, to hold toward" (BDAG, 362). It could also imply a more passive "holding back" or suspending judgment, which served as a virtual motto for Pyrrhonian Skeptics like Sextus Empiricus and (later) Montaigne (see the discussion of ἐπέχω [*epechō*] in Bakewell, *How to Live*, 123–33). In any case, Jesus is no Skeptic and finds no particular virtue in laissez-faire ideological fence-sitting. Though no dogmatic theologian, Jesus offers clear and challenging judgments about faith and practice.

Apart from the comfort level of associating with kin and other equals on the social ladder, the issue turns, in Jesus's view, on conventions of reciprocal honor and benefaction.[208] Social peers were expected to return (repay) favors of hospitality (14:12). Such "giving back" was not so much a matter of financial balance as of social equilibrium, maintaining one's "honor-rating" in the community. Failure to reciprocate an invited meal would be regarded as a serious snub, accruing shame to the original host or guests, depending on the delicate scale of current patron relations. If enough guests of unassailable high standing declined to repay their host for whatever reason (he put out a stingy spread; we never liked him anyway), they would besmirch the host's reputation; conversely, if the host enjoyed a secure social position, any guests who failed to reciprocate in a timely manner would suffer disgrace and risk blacklisting from further invitations.

Of course, the cluster of poor-crippled-blind-lame folk was automatically disqualified from this social game. Already relegated to the bottom of the ladder, they had nothing to offer in terms of status or goods. Though suitable targets of patronizing charity to the enhancement of benefactors' honor, they themselves had nothing to give back, no way to match hospitality. It is fine to send them help "out there" as long as they stay in their humble places. To invite them "in here" would only situate them where they do not—and cannot—belong in a tightly strung social system. *But that is precisely the system Jesus seeks to dismantle.* According to a fourfold taxonomy of moral actions used in neuroscience research, humans engage in self-serving behavior that has either (1) no effect or (2) a negative effect on others; or in other-serving actions that have either (3) a strong likelihood of reciprocation ("reciprocal altruism") or (4) no expected return ("genuine altruism").[209] Luke's Jesus clearly advocates the last altruistic option against prevailing ambitious and reciprocal aims of an agonistic society.

He exhorts elite diners, and them alone, to "humble *themselves*" (14:11). Calling the lowly and downtrodden to humility would only reinforce their position and further serve established hierarchical interests.[210] Moreover, the kind of humility Jesus demands of privileged classes pushes beyond philanthropic tokenism and solipsistic benefaction, as he prods his host to defy convention and put the disenfranchised and disabled at the top of his guest list "*because*

208. See Neyrey, "Ceremonies," 371–87; Malina and Rohrbaugh, *Social-Science Commentary*, 365.

209. Moll, Oliveira-Souza, and Zahn, "Neural Basis," 162; Sam Harris, *Moral Landscape*, 91–92.

210. In a provocative study of the Christ hymn in Phil 2:5–11 and other texts, Fredrickson (*Eros and the Christ*) cautions against a sweeping kenotic (self-emptying) ethic that "sets a moral standard of humility before the poor and marginalized, which they are, structurally, never able to live up to but to which they perpetually are held accountable by those who have power and privilege" (155).

[ὅτι, *hoti*] they cannot repay you" in this world's currency (14:14). As always, the prime goal of Luke's Jesus is *theological*, though with profound social and political ramifications. He's not a party planner, least of all for elite affairs. He's a kingdom promoter for *God*, as one astute dinner guest soon recognizes: "Blessed is anyone who will eat bread in the *kingdom of God!*" (14:15). This perception of divine blessedness follows from Jesus's comment that those who embrace the poor and company in this life will be blessed, even "repaid" in a sense, "*at the resurrection of the righteous*" (14:14). The table fellowship envisioned by Jesus advances God's right-making, "resurrecting" salvation for all persons, regardless of social position. Jesus's theology again carries eschatological force, in both the general sense of fulfilling God's ultimate redemptive purpose and the more particular vein of welcoming the "last/least" (ἔσχατοι, *eschatoi*) into God's liberating realm. Also hinted at is a final settling of accounts, a closing of the books on all debts, not least those racked up in a rigged honor-shame, tit-for-tat system. In God's economy, all glory and honor redounds to the righteous, resurrecting, benevolent Divine Patron and Lord.

Prompted by the guest's reference to God's blessed royal dinner, Jesus elaborates on the participants in this great banquet, turning the tables once more via another householder/host parable. Along with reprising the call to reach out to the poor-crippled-blind-lame where they live, he also expands the guest list to include other peripheral folk in more remote places. Moreover, beyond incorporating the lowly into the kingdom celebration, Jesus now *counterpoints* those on the margins with A-list associates who *decline the invitation* at the last minute with contrived excuses (14:17–20). Throughout this tale, Jesus carefully maps characters' locations with respect to the centralized host. It is thus helpful to chart basic lines of ancient urban geography radiating out from the center.

Power hub at the city's center
↓
disadvantaged inner city ghettos in narrow "streets and lanes" (14:21)
↓
walls and gates at the city's edge
↓
outside "roads and lanes" (14:23), dotted with the indigent, homeless, and other outcasts
↓
further outlying fields and estates owned by city bigwigs and served by tenant workers.[211]

211. Adapted from "Pre-Industrial City," a superb essay by Richard Rohrbaugh.

As the first order of business, the master in Jesus's story dispatches his slave to the invited guests—presumably the host's friends, family, and wealthy neighbors—to summon them to the prepared feast (14:16–17). But with their places set and the host's reputation on the line, these supposed confreres offer a belated "with regrets" RSVP, claiming (feigning) other more pressing duties and higher-priority companions. Specifically, three invitees prefer to be with their (1) land, (2) oxen, or (3) wife rather than with the wealthy banquet host (14:18–20). Such responses make very clear how the host rates in their eyes: below dirt, draft animals, and a domestic producer (all considered the patriarch's property). The first two cases intensify the snub with excuses of having to "go out [ἐξελθών, *exelthōn*]" (14:18) to see land and oxen in farms beyond the city walls, *away from* the center-city host. Moreover, the second would-be guest feels more compelled to "try out" or "test" (δοκιμάζω, *dokimazō* [14:19]) his new oxen team, a job befitting tenant plowboys, than to dine in a fellow master's urban villa. The final excuse may be the rudest by its lewd implication. This man begs off the dinner invitation in light of his "hav[ing] just been married" (14:20). Is his wife forbidding him from attending the banquet? That would be insulting for both husband and host. More likely, the husband is intimating (wink, wink) that he must "try out" his new bride in bed and prod her baby-making work.[212] However modern Western culture society might idealize heterosexual sex as men's greatest desire, in Greco-Roman antiquity the idea of doing one's conjugal duty didn't light a candle to dining with convivial male friends, especially when spiced with pleasant intercourse (verbal and otherwise) with engaging courtesans.[213] Jilting an elite male host in order to have sex with one's wife amounted to a stinging slap in the host's face.

This is one of those places where Deuteronomy especially informs Luke's Travel Narrative. The Torah allowed for deferring war-time deployment in cases of having (1) built a new home, but not dedicated it; (2) planted a new vineyard, but not sampled its fruit; and (3) become engaged to a woman, but not yet joined in marriage (Deut 20:5–7). Since "he might die in the battle" (20:7), the soldier is granted time beforehand to consummate blessings of home, land, and marriage. While the excuses offered in Jesus's parable closely echo the Deuteronomy exemptions, there are also marked differences. Deuteronomy's stipulations relate to *legitimate, God-sanctioned* property and family values. Israel was fighting as God's covenant people (God's household, God's spouse) for the

212. See Longenecker, "Humorous Jesus?," 184–89.

213. On the importance of male friendship in the ancient world, see Aristotle, *Eth. nic.* 8–9 (1155a–1172a); Konstan, *Friendship*; on banquet entertainment provided by women, see Corley, *Private Women*, 24–79.

promised land, for the right to sit peacefully "under their own vines and under their own fig trees" (Mic 4:4). So the deferments from battle—which "the LORD your God who goes with you [will] fight for you, to give you victory" (Deut 20:4)—were part and parcel of the Lord's purpose for Israel, the very things being fought for. And they applied to *all* God's people, to rank-in-file soldiers as much as officers.

By sharp contrast, the excuse-makers in Jesus's story engage in no battle, except for petty point-scoring in honor games. Their land, possessions, and families are secure, with ample resources to "buy" (ἀγοράζω, *agorazō*) more (Luke 14:18–19). They can afford, so they think, to demean the royal master and mar his reputation to their advantage. But recall that this is a story about the kingdom/banquet of God—the Creator-Redeemer God—to whom all, high and low, owe whatever territory, property, and family they have, whether they realize it or not. This God will not be mocked. Those who think they can make it on their own are free to try their luck. But they can expect no special wooing into the banquet hall. If and when they decide to "taste [the Master's] dinner," the kitchen will be closed (14:24; cf. 13:25–27). Their absence will only make more room for those who truly "strive for [God's] kingdom" (12:31) and trust God for their sustenance and salvation. So the gospel invitation is to "go out [ἔξελθε, *exelthe*]" (14:21, 23) to the urban unfortunates inhabiting the "streets and lanes" and, further still, to the walled-out pariahs loitering in the "roads and lanes [hedge paths]" in order to "compel people to come in [εἰσελθεῖν, *eiselthein*]" (14:23) to the Lord's central royal banquet house. The term for "hedge path" or "fence line" (φραγμός, *phragmos*), too loosely translated "lane" in NRSV, may refer to a wall or a fence itself, as in a rich Pauline ecclesiological passage announcing the demolition through Christ's death of the "dividing wall" (μεσότοιχον τοῦ φραγμοῦ, *mesotoichon tou phragmou*) separating Jews and Gentiles in God's household (Eph 2:14; cf. 2:11–22). Likewise, Jesus's parable in Luke may allude to the breakdown of ethnic (Jew/Gentile), as well as social (rich/poor), barriers in God's kingdom.

Counting the Cost and Carrying the Cross (14:25–35)

Having paused for dinner and pictured God's kingdom as a banquet house "filled" with people from all walks of life (14:23), Jesus resumes his journey more popular than ever, as "large crowds" tag along with him (14:25). But though he may appear to fulfill the "slave" role in the parable, inviting and compelling the masses into the master's (God's) household (14:17, 21–23), Jesus refuses to equate mere accompaniment with discipleship, curiosity with commitment. The time is ripe for more rigorous instruction to would-be followers, along the lines sketched at the start of each preceding leg of Jesus's trek (9:57–62; 13:22–29). Now Jesus stops, turns (στρέφω, *strεphō*), and spells out to the throng what it takes to follow him. Such a physical about-face marks a strategic "turning point" in the narrative, the fifth and last of these "turns" over the course of Jesus's ministry, before making two more during his last days. We chart here all seven occurrences.

Text	Setting	Addressees *Jesus "turned* [στραφείς, *strapheis*]" *toward:*	Issue Jesus addresses
Luke 7:9	Healing of centurion's servant in Capernaum	Jewish crowd following Jesus	Banner example of Gentile faith exceeding that of the Jews
Luke 7:44	Dinner at Simon the Pharisee's home	"Turns" to "sinner"-woman, but Jesus exhorts Simon to "see" her	"Sinner"-woman's loving hospitality superior to that of Simon
Luke 9:55	Samaritan village's inhospitality toward Jesus and disciples	Jesus's disciples James and John	Rebuking the vengeful request of James and John to call down fire on Samaritan village
Luke 10:23	Return of Jesus's seventy(-two) messengers	Jesus's seventy(-two) messengers "privately"	Jesus the Son's privileged revelation of the Father to disciples beyond that granted to "many prophets and kings"
Luke 14:25	On the crowded road to Jerusalem	"Large crowds" traveling along with Jesus	Costs of following Jesus's true way (discipleship)
Luke 22:61	Jesus's trial at the high priest's house	Peter, just after his threefold denial of Jesus	Peter "remembers" Jesus's prediction of denials (no accompanying words of Jesus)
Luke 23:28	On the road to Jesus's crucifixion	Women followers wailing, grieving for Jesus	Jesus's forecast of Jerusalem's destruction

One way or another, all these "turnings" by Jesus come at tense moments in the narrative, marking critical—and often surprising—distinctions between true and false perceivers, pursuers, and practitioners of the Lord's way. In the present situation, Jesus sharply demarcates between genuine and pretentious disciples. Before the crowds go any further with him, Jesus wants them to know the hard line they must cross and the heavy load they must carry. Journeying with Jesus Messiah is worth everything they might long for, but it will come at a cost, demanding everything they have. Jesus sets his audacious terms via three stipulations and three illustrations.

Stipulations (14:25–27, 33)

In frank, nonnegotiable fashion, Jesus lays out one attitude and two actions, without which no one can truly tread his way. All three demands, conveyed in present tense verbs, entail habitual dispositions or life patterns and reinforce a strict *via negativa*: a double-negative way concerning some other- or self-denying move one must *not not* make, without which one "*cannot* be my disciple [οὐ δύναται εἶναί μου μαθητής, *ou dynatai einai mou mathētēs*]."

- "Whoever comes to me and *does not hate* father and mother . . . yes, and even life itself, *cannot be my disciple*" (14:26).
- "Whoever *does not carry* the cross and follow me *cannot be my disciple*" (14:27).
- "So therefore, you [any of you] *cannot become my disciple* if you *do not give up* all your possessions" (14:33).

Glossed over in the above NRSV renderings is Jesus's sharply individual ("one's own [ἑαυτοῦ, *heatou*]") challenge, repeated four times: "hate *one's own* father . . . *one's own* life," "carry *one's own* cross," "give up *one's own* possessions." Jesus calls for deliberate self-conscious, self-sacrificing discipleship.

Christian interpreters may resort to all sorts of hermeneutical maneuvers to sand off the rough edges of Jesus's teaching. Surely "hate" (μισέω, *miseō*) is too strong, too strident an emotion to direct against one's kin, even if parents, siblings, and spouses can impede one's spiritual progress. How can the loving Jesus advocate misanthropic conduct, even if his own family obstructs his path from time to time (2:48–50; 4:16–30)? Heretofore, Jesus has advocated the inclusive scope of God's household beyond bloodlines without devolving into "hate" speech (8:19–21; 11:27–28). His language has been heating up on this matter, with recent talk of his mission's dividing family members against one another

(12:51–53), but until now, this tension has remained descriptive rather than prescriptive. Moreover, "hate" has been limited to others' hostile responses *to* Jesus and associates (1:71; 6:22; cf. 19:14; 21:17), the stock-in-trade of *enemies*, whom Jesus implored his disciples to *love and do good unto* in radical nonreciprocation of their vehemence (6:27). So Jesus's present call to hate family members must be exaggerated for effect, especially since he includes *children* in the mix (14:26). How could these innocents merit hateful opposition and abandonment? How could they now hinder discipleship when Jesus so honored a "little child" as if he or she were as worthy of welcome as Jesus himself or the Father who sent him (9:47–48; cf. 18:15–17)?

So we take refuge in hyperbole to take the sting out of Jesus's shocking demand. The thrust of Jesus's teaching commends the priority of putting the interests of God and God's household above all other relational obligations, as in Jesus's later statement: "No slave can serve two masters; for a slave will . . . hate [μισήσει, *misēsei*] the one and love the other. . . . You cannot [οὐ δύνασθε, *ou dynasthe*] serve God and wealth" (16:13). But again, the focus falls on a loving or hateful response *to the Master-Lord*, not to other household members, leaving 14:26 standing alone in Luke's narrative and, indeed, in the entire Christian canon. No other NT writer calls for *hating* "father and mother, wife and children, brothers and sisters" in order to serve God faithfully.[214] Rhetorically, a very fine line separates effective hyperbole from offensive polemic. Hate speech directed toward others, if ever appropriate for shock value, must be deployed with extreme care because of the extreme harm it can provoke.[215]

By the same token, incendiary hate speech must be carefully evaluated, resisting extremes of cavalier dismissal ("Oh, he didn't really mean it") and fanatical approval ("Yeah, let's hate 'em and leave 'em!"). Accordingly, instead of rushing to blunt the force of Luke's hate language as (simply) exaggerative, a more balanced, though no less challenging, reading gives full weight to the final target of Jesus's "hate"-list, which he cites with special emphasis: "yes, and even one's own life" (14:26 CEB).[216] While self-hate carries its own corrosive psychological baggage, as the culminating element in a series it puts

214. Though Paul certainly relativizes family ties in 1 Cor 7 for the higher priority of serving Christ, he uses no hate language. Likewise, the Johannine writer strongly exhorts readers not to "love the world or the things in the world" (1 John 2:15), but he never advocates hating unbelieving family members in particular. Moreover, though acknowledging that "the world hates you" as it hated Christ (John 15:18–25), such hatred is reciprocated with divine love (John 3:16; 1 John 4:7–12).

215. See Waldron, *Harm*; Aaron T. Beck, *Prisoners*.

216. "One's own life" (see also KJV, NAB, NIV) better translates the Greek—"the life of himself" (τὴν ψυχὴν ἑαυτοῦ, *tēn psychēn heautou*)—and avoids the sweeping antilife implications of the NRSV's "life itself."

the whole of Jesus's "hate"-message in perspective. Luke's Jesus is not a rough and rugged individualist pitting the independent, omnicompetent self against all familial and societal constraints. (His longest parable, which soon follows, makes precisely the opposite point: a maverick son finds what he needs only upon his humble *return* to the father he had rejected [15:11–32].) Although Jesus warns against narrow, self-serving egoistic and nepotistic attachments (cf. 9:23; 14:7–14), remember from the discussion above related to the parable of the rich fool (12:13–21) that such attachments can complement broader theistic, altruistic, and cosmic interests (loving God, all people, and all creation). Perhaps, then, we could tone down Jesus's *miso*-language by opting for paradox rather than hyperbole: we find/love our*selves* only when we lose/hate *self* (9:24). Yet, Jesus does not rush to that softer statement in the present context. In fact, he adds two other harder stipulations, which clarify, lest there be any doubt, what self-denial, self-"hatred," actually entails.

It involves nothing less than (1) carrying one's own cross and (2) surrendering all of one's possessions—both totalizing demands ratcheted up from previous admonitions. Jesus has already called *his current, closest disciples* to carry their crosses, as he himself will, but with a set of mitigating factors, like *saving* one's life through loss (9:23–27). But now he simply calls *the crowds* to a cross-bearing death march without recounting the benefits beyond following him. Jesus has also instructed his disciples to generous charity, including selling possessions to help the poor (6:30, 38; 12:33); but now he summons the crowd to divest themselves of *all* (πᾶσιν, *pasin*) possessions, with no added incentive of banking "treasures in heaven" and drawing on the bounty of God's kingdom (14:33; cf. 12:32–33). Luke's Jesus makes no attempt to curry the crowd's favor with political promises (which, as the true messianic agent of God's kingdom, he could actually deliver!). At this critical juncture in his mission, he stresses the steep price of discipleship, not its perquisites. Enthusiasts of a prosperity gospel or mass political movement will find little appeal here.[217]

217. In his classic work on mass movements, Eric Hoffer (*True Believer*) observes that disaffected, "frustrated" masses are primed to renounce their miserable lives to follow anti-family, anti-establishment leaders in fanatical hopes for a new regime. He includes the early Jesus movement in this pattern (36–37). In the present scene, however, Luke's Jesus accentuates the high cost of discipleship to deter, or at least to winnow, a massive following; throughout Luke, Jesus's relationship to the crowds (mobs) is more cautious, even oppositional at times, than courting.

Illustrations (14:28–32, 34–35)

Jesus elaborates on the cost of discipleship through three illustrations: from architecture (14:28–30), warfare (14:31–32), and agriculture (14:34–35).

Agent	Project	Resources	Results
Builder	Tower	Money/materials	Completion *or* incompletion and ridicule
King	Battle	Soldiers	Victory *or* defeat and treaty
Farmer	Harvest	Salt	Fertilization *or* uselessness and expulsion

Each scenario features some project, whose success hinges on properly assessing the cost of getting the job done. Inadequate cost analysis—whether of building materials, troop strength, or mineral potency—guarantees failure. Jesus's work illustrations reinforce his concept of discipleship as *mission*, establishing God's right-making realm on earth. The primary "student-learning" dimension of the "disciple" (μαθητής, *mathētēs*) designation always extends, in Jesus's understanding, to *practical outworking* or *service learning*. Knowing leads to doing (and vice versa).[218] Following involves imitative action of Jesus as Lord, not simply intellectual adherence to his teaching. And this action of kingdom-building, -fighting, and -planting is a costly undertaking, as all worthwhile projects are, demanding the totality of one's life, loyalty, and possessions. Far from discounting the price, these illustrations encourage taking the full measure of expenses before jumping into a journey one cannot finish (14:28–29).

This emphasis on sober cost-assessments to complete the work, while most patent in the tower venture, is also implied in the other two. A king facing battle must prudently prepare for the end game, whether achieving victory or suing for peace (14:31–32). A farmer must take hard stock of cultivating resources to produce the best crop. A certain amount of salt (in right balance) enriches soil and compost minerals. But if saline nutrients are degraded, the substance would not be "fit [εὔθετον, *eutheton*]" as fer-

218. I accept a holistic anthropology integrating cognitive, affective, volitive, and active engagement with the world. Christian philosopher James K. A. Smith (*Desiring*) largely agrees with this perspective, even as he stresses the epistemological primacy of deeply affective (affecting) embodied acts and arts: "Over time, rituals and practices—often in tandem with aesthetic phenomena like pictures and stories—mold and shape our precognitive disposition to the world by training our desires" (59). The frequent parables/illustrations of Luke's Jesus serve this imaginative, pedagogical purpose.

tilizer; since this unsalty salt is useless to help bring the harvest to fruition, workers must "throw it away" (14:35). This picture of unfitness evokes Jesus's ultimatum at the beginning of his journey, also couched in an agricultural image related to kingdom work: "No one who puts a hand to the plow and looks back *is fit* [εὔθετος, *euthetos*] for the kingdom of God" (9:62). Again, emphasis falls on the lack of potency to finish the task, to persevere until a fruitful end. To follow Jesus requires the right amount of salty grit and determination to tread the long rugged way of the cross. To teeter and toy with backtracking is to risk ossification into a useless pillar of salt ("Remember Lot's wife" [17:32]). A truly "fit" disciple cultivates the "good soil" of his or her heart with the right ingredients to nurture the "seed" of God's word so it might "bear fruit with patience endurance" (8:15). "Let anyone with ears to hear listen!" (14:35).

Seeking and Finding the Lost (15:1–32)

Demarcating who can and cannot join Jesus on his messianic journey—both on the road and in banquet-house stations—continues to dominate this leg of the Travel Narrative. Thus far Jesus has modulated between a *restrictive* approach that laments the many who eschew God's gracious ingathering ("only a few [will] be saved" [13:22–35]) and lays down stiff guidelines for faithful discipleship (14:25–33) and a more *inclusive* policy that seeks out and welcomes the scattered poor-crippled-blind-and-lame masses into the festal hall, with the few honor-obsessed elites missing out, if they so choose (14:1–24). Not surprisingly, then, after tempering the enthusiasm of the "large crowds" (14:25) tagging along with him, Jesus shifts back to his more embracive mode, this time defending his open commensality with "all the tax collectors and sinners" against the protestations of "the Pharisees and the scribes" (15:1–2). This is not the first (5:29–32; 7:34–50) or last (19:1–10) time Luke's Jesus defends his table fellowship with sinners, but it is his fullest account.

Jesus presents a triad of parables—two short snippets (15:3–7, 8–10) and one long drama (15:11–32)—featuring a diligent search for and jubilant finding of a valued "lost" entity: animal (sheep), object (coin), and person (son). Each story illustrates, the last one directly, a repentant "sinner's" restoration, celebrated by God and the angels (15:7, 10, 18–19). Although the climactic parable of the prodigal son, as it is commonly called, has received the lion's share of homiletic attention, its placement in a tight trio of "lost and found" scenarios should not be ignored. The following chart provides an overview of similar and distinctive elements.

	Lost sheep (15:3–7)	**Lost coin (15:8–10)**	**Lost son (15:11–32)**
Caretakers:	Male shepherd	Female housekeeper	Paternal landowner
Economic status:	Fairly well-off (100 sheep)	Not well-off (10 drachmas)	Well-off (estate with slaves)
Percentage of loss:	1% (1/100)	10% (1/10)	50% (1/2)
Place of loss:	Wilderness	House	Distant country
Reason for loss:	Straying sheep (ignorance)[1]	Careless coin holder (negligence)	Rebellious son (willful flight)
Rescue mission (hands on):	Shepherd leaves 99, goes after 1 lost sheep, lays it on his shoulders	Woman lights lamp, sweeps house, and searches carefully for lost coin	Father looks on horizon, meets returning son, runs to, hugs, and kisses him
Homecoming party:	Friends and neighbors	Friends and neighbors	Household servants, friends, and elder brother (maybe!)

1. Technically, Luke uses no "straying" language as in the Matt 18:12–13 parallel, but the sheep's lost state implies wayward movement (see discussion below).

Several observations emerge from this comparative sketch:

- The social worlds span gender and class boundaries, though with the poorer female figure occupying the smaller space between the wealthier male protagonists (alternately, the *central* position of the house-keeping woman may be viewed as tempering the flanking scenarios to some degree). Portraits of better-off male seekers more readily reflect the Pharisees and scribes Jesus addresses.
- The mathematical progression zooms from a negligible 1% to a substantial 50% loss. But numbers do not tell the whole tale. The lone lost sheep out of a large fold is still worth saving; a poor woman with a paltry ten-coin fund can scarcely afford to lose one; and even if the father had twelve sons, the loss of one would still be excruciating (recall Jacob's grief over the missing Joseph). But overall the progression from property (sheep/coin) to progeny with escalating percentages (and narrative length) heightens the poignancy of the closing parable.
- The lost are found in locations near and far, from house (woman's coin) to desert area (wandering sheep) to distant country (wayward son). The

remote sites evoke Israel's historic experiences of *exodus* and *exile*, anticipating God's bringing the people (back) home.[219]

- The lost ones' motivations vary from the sheep's ignorant roaming to the son's deliberate rebellion; of course, the inanimate coin has nothing to do with its lost state. The prodigal son is the only *knowing subject*, the only one who *determines* to go away and who (eventually) *discerns* his lost condition and *decides* to return home. Since Jesus addresses the problem of lost human beings (tax collectors and sinners), the last parable carries the most weight. But people can also be *like* sheep and coins, blithely drifting away from safekeeping with no malice aforethought or sense of impending peril. Moreover, these lost property cases place the greater *burden of loss* on the *personal caretaker* (shepherd, housekeeper).
- The search-and-rescuers are the *key agents* in each story through various actions and emotions. To be sure, the runaway son meets his father halfway, but the father's intense longing for the son's return should not be missed (see below). Also, each case features an intimate *hands-on* reclamation, by the shoulder-hoisting and leg-holding shepherd, the broom-sweeping and finger-clasping woman, and the arm-hugging and face-kissing father. Like no other part, the hand *extends* the outreach of one's *self*, implementing what the self *intends* about *tending* other selves and objects, for good or ill (good touch/bad touch). The hand, not least the hand of God, is the quintessential instrument of seeking and finding.[220]

Appreciating the thick texture of this parable cluster broadens a popular interpretive framework. The parable of the prodigal son has been commonly treated in modern evangelical-revivalist circles as the archetypal *evangelistic*, *individualistic*, and *moralistic* gospel story, trumpeting the call to each sinner-outsider to make a personal decision to repent, throw oneself on God's mercy, and be "saved."[221] The moralistic angle typically assumes a rather contradictory moralistic (indignant, dismissive) stance toward the elder brother (a Pharisee stand-in) for being too moralistic! That is, it all but cuts off the supposed self-righteous first son from the family for promoting a prejudicial "works" standard toward his immoral younger sibling.

219. On key connections between Luke's "lost and found" parables and Israel's story of exile and restoration, see N. T. Wright, *Jesus*, 125–33; Bailey, *Jacob* (see discussion below).

220. See Tallis, *Hand*; Spencer, "Woman's Touch," 79–81; Grayston, "Significance."

221. As Snodgrass (*Stories*) observes, however, the premodern "church most often understood the shepherd's going to find the sheep as a reference to the incarnation [of Christ] to recover lost humanity, with the ninety-nine understood as the angels" (130). For support, Snodgrass refers to Wailes, *Medieval Allegories*, 128–30.

A closer contextual reading, however, of this iconic parable shifts the tenor to more complex *soteriological*, *ecclesiological*, and *theological* themes. No explicit "save/salvation" language appears in Luke 15, but the salvific theme permeates the parable series in terms of *restoration to the community* (sheepfold, money purse, family estate) from which the lost had drifted. These stories are *not* about finding *new* recruits or increasing numbers, but rather about reclaiming residents and recouping deficits. Though the wayward son seeks forgiveness of sin, the father never formally declares absolution, not because he is unwilling or hesitant to grant it, but because he presumes forgiveness *as a given*. Forgiveness is simply understood and sumptuously overshadowed by joyous fellowship. Any expectation of the father's judicial demand ("What do you have to say for yourself? Let me hear your confession, my son!") is quickly squashed by the festive announcement, "Kill the fatted calf. Let's eat!" (15:23 AT). And the joy is not over remission of sins, but over restoration to family and resurrection to life: "This son of mine was dead and is alive again; he was lost and is found!" (15:24). Repentance—a change of mind, heart, and will (back) toward the father—*is* a critical factor in the son's return home. But again, the father makes no example of the boy's moral state, before or after his homecoming—as the elder son wishes the father would—and says nothing about the younger son's repentance *from sin*. In fact, the only repentance (μετάνοια, *metanoia*) language in Luke 15 comes from Jesus's applications of the first two parables, *likening* the sinner's turnaround to that of the retrieved *sheep* and *coin* (15:7, 10); in these analogous cases, the *willful* factor in both going astray and turning back is either extremely weak (sheep) or nonexistent (coin).

The protagonist *seeker-finder* images *God-in-Christ* as shepherd, sweeper woman, and father. These parables, then, are profoundly *theological*, revealing the loving, longing, restoring heart and will of God toward God's own. This divine nature is expressed in the father's gut-level "compassion" (σπλαγχνίζομαι, *splanchnizomai* [15:20]), and the scope of God's own extends to all creation: animal, material, and human. Such sympathetic outreach jealously claims and reclaims ownership, but not at the expense of freedom (the younger son is free to go his own way) and not in a tight-fisted, high-handed fashion. Indeed, it is the resentful, resistant elder son whom the father reassures: "Son, you are always with me, and all that is mine is yours" (15:31), a perfect gloss on Jesus's earlier statement: "Do not be afraid, little flock, for it is your father's pleasure to give you the kingdom" (12:32). Sovereignty goes hand in hand with generosity. Officious moralism is handcuffed by genuine altruism.

The deep-tissue bond between caretaker and cared-for, between seeker and lost ones, significantly enlarges our concept of *lostness* in these stories. In fact, being lost, at a loss, suffering loss may be viewed as the core experience of all the characters, not just those who have lost their way and risked losing their lives and utility, but also the overseers and community members who have *lost part of themselves* by losing one of their own. In a limited-goods/zero-sum mind-set, one person's loss is another's gain and vice versa. It is a win-lose game, pure and simple, with no draws.[222] Such is the viewpoint of the elder brother, who assesses the younger brother's inheritance payoff (before it was due him) and his subsequent undeserved restoration as a double loss for the father and the estate, which would pass to the oldest son's control. From this perspective, celebrating the thieving runaway's homecoming is tantamount to denigrating the faithful elder brother.

But from the father's, God's-eye view, the sense of loss and gain runs wider and deeper. The game is always rigged for a tie in the close-knit family community, and in God's universe, everyone is family. It is either *lose-lose* or *win-win*: "If one member suffers, all suffer together with it; if one member is honored, all rejoice together with it" (1 Cor 12:26). The younger brother's material gain of his trust fund was truly a devastating loss, not just because he squandered it, but because he used it to separate himself from the nurturing family fold. He *lost* family identity and security ("I am no longer worthy to be called your son" [Luke 15:21]). He became abjectly diminished, on the precipice of death, all but losing *himself*. Concurrently, the father and elder brother lost part of *themselves*, not simply their money: "this brother *of yours* was dead . . . he was lost" (15:32). We have all died a little and lost a lot through our son/brother's exile in a far country. It has been a devastating *lose-lose* arrangement—*until* the younger son returns, and sorrow gives way to joy. Now it is party time with music, dancing, and feasting *for everyone* in the household (15:25–26). It is a *win-win* proposition for the older brother as much as for the younger. In an economy of shared abundance operative in God's kingdom, there's plenty to go around; no one need be displaced or diminished by another's welcome: "[My oldest] Son, you are always with me, and all that is mine is yours" (15:31).[223]

The emotional fuel for this generous (and regenerative) economy, as noted above, is *compassion* or *sympathy*, a deep feeling-with others' experiences. Its close cousins are *grief* and *joy*: mourning loss (bereavement, diminishment) and feting return (recovery, enhancement). Its potentially wicked stepbrother is *anger*, the heart of which beats with retaliatory response to personal or communal *loss* (diminishment, belittlement). Aristotle succinctly characterizes anger (ὀργή, *orgē*) as motivated by "an *apparent slight/belittlement* [ὀλιγορία, *oligoria*] that was directed, without justification, against oneself or those near to one"

222. See Malina, *New Testament World*, 81–107; Moxnes, *Economy*, 76–98.

223. Evocative of the larger community of goods in Acts 2:41–47; 4:32–37.

(*Rhet.* 2.2.1 [1378a]).[224] The father in Jesus's parable teeters between grieving the younger son's absence and rejoicing over his presence, while the elder brother is trapped in the vice of anger (ὀργίζομαι, *orgizomai* [15:28]) over his *apparent slight*, his misperceived diminished status. Yet, the father seeks to restore the older son as well, pleading with him to join the celebration. The elder brother's salvation, left open in the story, rests on a proper, sympathetic sense of loss and gain, grief and joy.

Having spent some time with a panoramic analysis of Jesus's lost-and-found parables, we zoom in to unpack more particular dimensions of each story, paying special attention to the emotions and actions of the seeker-God figure.

The Shepherd and His Wandering Sheep (15:1–7)

Jesus immediately puts the onus on his murmuring Pharisee/scribe interlocutors: "So he told *them* this parable: 'Which *one of you*, having a hundred sheep?'" (15:3–4). Putting *them* in the position of a vocational shepherd (tending a whole flock) cuts two ways (cf. discussion on 2:8–20): *socially* identifying them with a lower-class occupation of nomads, far below their professional-legal position (none of them would dream of being actual shepherds), but *pastorally* associating them with leading and tending God's people as deputies of the iconic shepherd-king David appointed by the Divine Pastor: "The Lord is my shepherd" (Ps 23:1). In the first sense, Jesus puts his hearers on the "least" level with tax collectors and sinners; in the second sense, he recognizes their calling to the "greatest" level of caring service to all God's people, not least the "least," who need the most help. Either way, Jesus summons them to empathetic embrace of "sinner"-types, just as he has exhibited in his "welcoming" table fellowship.

Jesus assumes that the Pharisees/scribes are indeed capable of fulfilling their spiritual vocation. In a rhetorical tour de force, Jesus appeals to his critics' better natures and enlists them as allies. The negative interrogative construction, "Which one of you . . . does *not* leave the ninety-nine . . . and go after the one [sheep] that is lost until [it is found]?" (Luke 15:4), expects an affirmative answer: "Of course, we would do that; none of us would think of abandoning a poor, helpless lost one without trying to save it."[225] The case resembles that of doing whatever it takes to rescue an endangered child or ox on the Sabbath

224. See the discussion of Aristotle's treatment of anger in Fisher, *Vehement Passions*, 181–84; Konstan, *Emotions*, 41–48; Spencer, "Why Did the 'Leper'?," 116–17.

225. Cf. Snodgrass, *Stories*, 101.

(14:5; cf. 6:9; 13:15). Conversely, however, the prophetic biblical repertoire, well-known by Jesus and his interlocutors, also includes scathing critiques of Israel's leaders who function as voracious, unscrupulous shepherds, preying on their own people/flock (Jer 23:1–4; Ezek 34:1–10; Zech 10:2–3; 11:4–17). Given their generally bad, ruffian reputations, shepherds may be as prone to stray from the fold as the sheep under their charge. But while prophet-pastor Jesus no doubt implies a warning against fraudulent overseers of God's flock, his primary message seems more positive than pejorative, as if to say to the Pharisees/scribes: "While we all know how Israel's shepherds have failed in the past—even the great David (recall Nathan's parable of the ewe lamb [2 Sam 12:1–15])—I hope that you fervent advocates of God's way do not fit that counterfeit bill. You're better than that!"

Moreover, Jesus pointedly frames the loss of even a single sheep as the shepherd's burden: "Which one of you . . . *having lost* [ἀπολέσας, *apolesas*] one of the sheep?" (15:4 AT). This is not to suggest culpable negligence on the shepherd's part.[226] Sheep cannot be shackled or permanently penned up; they must have some freedom to graze and water. Even under the watchful eye of a band of shepherds, a lone sheep can easily stray from a large flock, particularly in "wilderness" conditions requiring frequent roaming to find sufficient pasture and water. In the present story, the chief shepherd accepts full responsibility for the lost sheep and goes into full rescue mode when he realizes it is missing. In the meantime, we need not think that he leaves the ninety-nine to fend for themselves, caring more for the maverick than for the many who stay close.[227] A flock this size would likely be managed by a team of chief overseer and undershepherds.[228] The flock remains in good hands while the lead shepherd seeks the lost member. This is a *good, faithful* shepherd whose goodness and faithfulness shine most brilliantly in *his recognition of loss* and *resolution to recover loss*.

Key resonances echo with the biblical mission of God and God's servant leaders (undershepherds). The God who led the beleaguered flock of Israel out of slavery into the wilderness, showed them unfailing love, and provided

226. Contra Bailey (*Jacob*, 65–72, and *Good Shepherd*, 107–44), who argues that Jesus first introduces a "bad" shepherd who "loses" a sheep; see the critique in Snodgrass, *Stories*, 105–9.

227. This thought revises my reading in *Salty Wives*, 43. There is "more joy" over the returned lost sheep because of the danger it was in, not because, as Gos. Thom. 107 puts it, the shepherd loved the stray "largest" sheep more than the ninety-nine that didn't wander off.

228. Multiple shepherds typically worked together, as in Luke 2:8, "watching over their flocks," particularly if the flocks were large, in the medium-to-large range of 100–300 sheep. In all likelihood, then, the parable assumes at least one associate shepherd staying behind to supervise the ninety-nine remaining animals; see Bailey, *Poet and Peasant*, 149–50; Brad H. Young, *Parables*, 192–93; Jeremias, *Parables*, 133–35; Bishop, "Parable of the Lost," 49–50.

them with ample food and water along their hard journey—this divine Pastor in fact *lost* the preponderance of the exodus generation in the desert, including his senior "associate pastor" Moses.[229] To be sure, these were a stubborn, rebellious bunch prone to wander (including Moses at a weak moment over a water dispute), but their failure was still the *Lord's loss*. As Moses reminded the Lord, the divine reputation was wrapped up in the fortune of the people. How God managed and nurtured Israel revealed God's power and character. At a particularly tense moment of Israelite obstinacy, sparking God's wrathful plan to "consume" the people—to write them off as a total loss—Moses pleads: "O LORD, why does your wrath burn hot against your people, whom you brought out of the land of Egypt. . . . Why should the Egyptians say, 'It was with evil intent that he brought them out to kill them in the [desert] mountains, and to consume them from the face of the earth?' Turn from your fierce wrath; change your mind, and do not bring disaster on your people." Moses proceeds to repeat the Lord's covenantal promise, dating back to Abraham, Isaac, and Jacob, to bless Israel "forever" (Exod 32:11–13). Accordingly, the Lord repents of ("changed his mind about" [32:14]) the terrible threat and reaffirms the passionate core of the divine pastoral heart:

> The LORD, the LORD,
> a God merciful and gracious,
> slow to anger,
> and abounding in steadfast love and faithfulness,
> keeping steadfast love for the thousandth generation,
> forgiving iniquity and transgression and sin.
>
> (34:6–7a)

The Lord overcomes the pain of loss with the pursuit of love.

As we have seen, Luke's Jesus also laments the *loss* of many beloved "children" he seeks to guard and guide, albeit through the image of a mother hen rather than that of a protective shepherd (Luke 13:34–35). More personally, the hint has already been dropped that one (Judas) of Jesus's twelve chosen apostles, his closest undershepherds, will betray him (6:16). And in effect he will *lose all* of them at his arrest and trial, contributing to his deep anguish (cf. 22:39–46, 61). But Jesus's desire to restore those who stray still predominates. Through prayerful commitment to reclamation (22:31–32), Jesus draws his feckless followers back into the fold, with one glaring exception. Unlike Peter, who "turned

229. As it happens, Moses was "keeping the flock" of his Midianite father-in-law (Exod 3:1) when the Lord called him to lead/shepherd God's people out of slavery.

back" (22:32), Judas "turned aside" to his own desolate place (Acts 1:25; cf. 1:16–20), a haunting monument to the tragedy of both divine and human loss.

In Jesus's parable, however, the movement runs from tragedy to comedy, painful absence to joyous retrieval, with no remainder. The bereft shepherd springs into action, scouring the wilderness "until he finds" the missing sheep (Luke 15:4). When he discovers the lost one, far from berating the dumb animal or beating it back to the fold, the shepherd takes matters into his own hands: lifting the sheep—all seventy to ninety pounds of it by most estimates—likely frozen in fear by this time, draping it across his shoulders and clasping his hands around the animal's fore- and hind-legs for transport back to camp.[230] Jesus thus evokes not merely a culturally accurate scene, but also a dramatically poignant one, where the shepherd himself works as a *beast of burden* bringing the lost back home. In the zoological iconography of Gospel interpretation, Luke has been traditionally associated with the strong yoke-bearing and baggage-lading *ox*, of particular relevance to the work and support of the poor.[231] In a daring mix of images, the present parable casts the God/Christ-figure as an *Ox-like Shepherd* sustaining his vulnerable sheep. "The Lord is my shepherd" rings so familiarly and soothingly. "The Lord is my ox" takes some getting used to but is well worth the adjustment.

The Woman and Her Wayward Coin (15:8–10)

As Jesus shifts from speaking about a male shepherd to a female house sweeper, he correspondingly shifts from direct address ("Which *one of you* [*men*], having a hundred sheep?") to the indirect, "Or *what woman* having ten silver coins?" (15:8). As some feminist critics have observed, this gendered rhetoric, which continues in the final parable (the two sons' mother is never mentioned), presumes a male audience within the narrative and male readers engaging it. The text thus compels women readers either to (1) look elsewhere (this is a private "men's only" text); (2) adopt the male point of view; or (3) employ a suspicious, resistant hermeneutic.[232] The androcentric and patriarchal perspectives of Luke 15 are patent. Since leaving the birth narratives, Luke's story gives little voice

230. See Brad H. Young, *Parables*, 192–93.

231. See the exposition of Luke's Jesus as "The Bearer of Burdens," inspired by the symbolic-animal association of the Third Gospel with the ox, in Burridge, *Four Gospels*, 101–32. In this fourfold tradition discussed by Burridge, Mark's Jesus is imaged as a lion, John's as an eagle, and Matthew's as a human.

232. See Durber, "Female Reader"; Moore, *Poststructuralism*, 50–52; Spencer, *Salty Wives*, 24–54.

to women characters and operates, with a few notable exceptions (8:1–3, 19–21, 43–48; 10:38–42; 11:27–28; 13:20–21), in a man's world. Of course, that *was* the dominant social world of Jesus and Luke's day, and in Luke 15 Jesus speaks the parables to and for the male Pharisees and scribes. So feminist-conscious women readers may well look askance at the tiny parable of the sweeper woman framed (fenced in) by larger stories of male seekers. Apart from the women-distancing rhetoric, the problem only compounds for modern readers who resist the stereotype of housecleaning as "women's work."[233]

But various other features resist a thoroughly resistant reading, aiming to *recover lost interpretive elements* in this parable supporting feminist interests. First, we should probe why Luke's Jesus includes a woman's story at this juncture. What point does he hope to score? Why would the male authorities he addresses care about this female figure, except maybe to keep her in her domestic place (which Jesus does) in "proper" relation to itinerant teachers like Jesus? But that is not their sticking point. They criticize Jesus for fraternizing with tax collectors (all male) and sinners (15:2). When Simon the Pharisee took issue with Jesus's contact with a "sinner"- woman, the problem in Simon's eyes was based more on virtue than on gender ("*what kind of woman* this is" [7:39]). He would have been just as exercised by Jesus's fellowship with a *male* "sinner." Elsewhere, among all the charges Jesus's opponents levy against him, associating with women, inside or outside the household realm, is not one of them.[234] In the present tale, the woman herself is no "sinner"; she seeks no sinful person, and she socializes only with women "friends and neighbors [φίλας καὶ γείτονας, *philas kai geitonas*]" (15:9).

So Jesus *need* not tell a woman's story to defend his mission. But he opts to in order to expound—and expand—the image of *God* as Seeker and Savior of the lost. God as shepherd and father conveys the idea clearly and convincingly. But these are familiar theological metaphors, easily absorbed by the Pharisees/scribes, who already regard themselves as faithful undershepherds and patriarchs of God's people. But what do God and these religious-legal officials have to do with a poor sweeper woman on hands and knees scraping to find a missing coin out of a measly ten-drachma savings account (Greek drachma =

233. Cf. Beauvoir, *Second Sex*, 474; Mainardi, "Politics of Housework"; Spencer, *Salty Wives*, 51–54.

234. See Schaberg, "Luke," 375; Freyne ("Jesus") proposes that (falsely) tagging Jesus as a "glutton and drunkard" (7:34) may include, by implication, his consorting with women in scurrilous, Dionysian-style banquets; in other words, the culinary slur may have been a tactic employed by Jesus's enemies to besmirch his association with women. While this is a plausible assumption, it is still remarkable that explicit complaints about Jesus's fellowship with women do not appear in the Gospels (except for the lone internal query in John 4:27 by *his male disciples*).

Roman denarius = day laborer's minimum wage)?[235] Jesus dares to claim that this woman in fact embodies the seeking-saving work of *God* as surely as do the shepherd and the father. God identifies with *her* as much as with male overseers. *She* has as much to teach male authorities about divine ministry as any shepherd or father (or king or warrior). To be sure, Jesus advocates no feminist labor revolution. This woman stays at home and sweeps the floor, as the woman in a previous parable kneads and bakes bread (13:20–21). But Jesus does call for a kind of counterkyriarchal[236] revolution in which *wealthy men* serve *with poor women* and *with God and God's Messiah* in the home, at table—an open table welcoming the least and lost. God as Sweeper and Baker Woman ennobles traditional women's work and challenges men to join in the action, as Jesus does.[237]

Second, speaking of God's action, the sweeper woman particularly illustrates the rigorous effort of *seeking* the lost. By contrast, the shepherd and father more dramatically demonstrate *restoring* actions after finding the lost. In a brief compass, Jesus highlights the woman's careful three-part search operation: whatever negligence she bears for her missing coin (again, Jesus states that "she loses" it) is more than compensated by her diligence in (1) lighting a lamp, (2) sweeping the house, and (3) "search[ing] carefully [ζητεῖ ἐπιμελῶς, *zētei epimelōs*]" until she finds it (15:8). The woman may lack the carrying strength of the shepherd and the purchasing power of the father, but she will not be outdone in her indomitable quest to track down and reclaim what's hers. As such, she embodies the dynamic agency of divine outreach, the hand of God that will not rest until it lays hold of its own.

Third, from a broader cultural perspective, we may celebrate more than the woman's industrious search. In a fascinating study informed by a five-month sojourn in Yemen and interviews with Arab-Christian female immigrants to the US from Egypt and Lebanon, Carol Schersten LaHurd reports that these women find Jesus's parable true to their experience and not the least demeaning or delimiting in its domestic orientation. From her biblical and sociological research, she concludes that the parable's searching housekeeper operates freely "by choice," not by coerced patriarchal confinement to private space. Indeed, it is within the domestic realm that some Middle Eastern women, then and

235. Schottroff (*Lydia's Impatient Sisters*, 91–100) associates the sweeper woman with other poor female workers struggling to survive in an ancient economy where women typically earned half of men's wages for the same labor; cf. Spencer, *Salty Wives*, 46–47.

236. Schüssler Fiorenza ("Introduction to Tenth Anniversary") "coined the neologism 'kyriarchal' . . . to mean a social-political system of domination and subordination that is based on the power and rule of the lord/master/father" (xix). The term has been widely adopted by feminist biblical scholars.

237. Again, see Barbara E. Reid's fine article "Beyond Petty Pursuits."

now, exert considerable leadership and influence by managing family finances, overseeing household maintenance, and raising children.[238]

Approaching the parable of the lost coin from another cultural angle, Linda Maloney marks a 1985 conference of feminist-liberation theologians in Buenos Aires as a critical moment when this little story "first came into its own." Out of their experience of intense social and political struggle (*lucha*), these theologians rallied around the sweeper woman's action as a manifesto for their interpretive practice. They discovered that biblical-theological "work," as Maloney puts it, "is contextual and concrete; it sees the ordinary and the everyday as the place God is revealed; it takes place 'in the house'—long a symbol of believing community. It is hard work; it is a struggle to find what has been lost in the darkness that has covered it for so many centuries. But it is also characterized by joy and celebration, and by hope: the hope that 'God is with us' (Mt 1.23). Like the woman in the parable, God has her skirts tucked up and is busy sweeping and searching, too."[239]

These positive social and theological appropriations of the sweeper woman *for women* provide an important check and balance to the first point above commending the woman as a model *for men* of all classes. While it is good for men to be so challenged, to join their sisters in ground-level service to God and one another, continued focus on male disciples can easily skew toward temporary, token service by men, even as women are kept in place to bear the brunt of the load. A male leader lights one lamp, sweeps out one corner of the house, cooks one meal, washes one set of dishes or pair of feet—and he's a hero! Cue the photo-op, standing proud with broom in one hand and towel in the other. Meanwhile, leave the little lady out of the picture, on her hands and knees on a mud-packed floor. Luke's expansive vision of God's kingdom, however, keeps pushing male disciples and religious leaders into the "greatest" vocation of humble service, even as it *lifts up* lowly, serving women as authoritative models of God's action, mediators of God's will, and managers of God's household (cf. 1:46–55).

The Father and His Wasteful Sons (15:11–32)

We have already suggested the core experience of loss by all three family figures (not only the runaway son) and the passionate quest for communal restoration.

238. LaHurd, "Re-viewing Luke 15." Of course, one might question how much independent, as opposed to internalized, choice women truly have in a rigid patriarchal social system; cf. Spencer, *Salty Wives*, 41–42.

239. Maloney, "Swept," 35.

We now explore a key dimension of loss as *waste*, again in relation to all three characters, including the father typifying the *wasteful God*. The focus on "waste" recovers a neglected theme. Though the traditional designation "prodigal son" remains, few English speakers use "prodigal" in daily language or have a clear idea of its meaning beyond something pejorative.[240] Its primary sense of "wasteful," which fits the report that the son "squandered his property" (15:13), has largely been lost, not to mention more positive nuances of "prodigal" associated with extravagant largesse, a profusion of gifts upon loved ones—"holy waste," as Tillich calls it.[241]

The prodigality of the younger son extends beyond unfortunate mismanagement or diminution of inherited funds to utter wasting of his *life* to the razor's edge of destitution and death. He expends the entire allotment of his father's livelihood (βίος, *bios*) "living dissolutely/wastefully/prodigally" (ζῶν ἀσώτως, *zōn asōtōs*),"[242] "squandering/scattering" (διασκορπίζω, *diaskorpizō*)[243] it abroad in a "distant" (μακράν, *makran*) land, far away from familial or neighborly networks of support, who would be loathe to help him anyway, since he had shamefully treated his father as if he were dead (cashing out his legacy) and cut himself off from the community in "self-imposed exile"[244] (15:12–13 AT). In a last-ditch move when "severe famine" strikes the foreign country, he hires himself out to a local pig farmer. But this move provides little aid; the pigs he feeds are more likely to survive than he is, as he begins "dying of hunger," and "no one gave him anything" (15:14–17). With his last threads of life unraveling, he "came *to himself* [εἰς ἑαυτόν, *heauton*]," what little self he has left, and purposes to return to "my father," whom he has disowned and disgraced. In his totally wasted state, however, he's in no position to make any more familial demands. All he has left is a heartfelt confession of sinfulness against heavenly and earthly authorities and a desperate petition for slave status in his father's household (15:17–19).[245] It is hard to imagine any more pathetic picture of homecoming in a

240. My informal surveys in seminary, university, and church classes over the years have proven widespread ignorance: most people think "prodigal" means something bad ("immoral, evil, sinful"), not more specifically wasteful.

241. "There is no creativity, divine or human, without the holy waste which comes out of the creative abundance of the heart and does not ask, 'What use is this?'" (Tillich, *New Being*, 48); cf. Haught, *Making Sense*, 36; Mark 14:3–9.

242. BDAG, 148.

243. Reminiscent of the parable of the lost sheep, the verb can apply to the scattering of a flock of sheep into perilous territory (see Matt 26:31 and Mark 14:27).

244. Bailey, *Jacob*, 209.

245. Bailey (*Jacob*, 166–67, 209) thinks that the prodigal initially formulates a "manipulative speech," rather than a sincere confession of sin, in 15:17–19 to worm his way back into his father's good graces. It is only in response to the father's loving embrace that the wayward son truly repents

Jewish context: a filthy, smelly, swine-slopper from far exile and near extinction trudging back and hoping against hope for some vestige of restoration.

This abject return sets up the prospect of a tense reunion, reminiscent of Jacob's anticipated meeting with elder brother Esau years after Jacob had cheated Esau out of their father's blessing and birthright. Major differences also appear, however, not least that Jacob multiplied his resources after leaving home and attempted to curry Esau's favor with lavish gifts (Gen 32:3–21), whereas the prodigal son has nothing but his tattered self and desperate plea to offer his father (moreover, the older brother, unlike Esau, still possesses his firstborn share of the estate).[246] By all social and moral conventions, ancient readers, along with the prodigal returnee, expect an irate reception from the father, probationary at best, exclusionary at worst. This traitorous, family- and nation-spurning son simply has *no right* to restorative justice: retribution, yes; restoration, no.[247] But astoundingly, the father eschews merited punishment for merciful pity, practicing a politics of compassion rather than condemnation.

Most remarkably, this heart- and mind-set does not reflect a spontaneous *change* of outlook, a burst of fresh emotion upon hearing the son's confession, but rather the consistent *disposition* (habit) of the father toward his son. Note well Jesus's language, set off in a genitive absolute construction: "But *while he was still far off* [μακρὰν ἀπέχοντος, *makran apechontos*], his father saw him and was filled with compassion" (15:20). Though the son separates himself from his father in blatant, blasphemous fashion, the father never lets the son go, never lets him out of his sight. His longing, compassionate vision follows his son's departure and stays trained on him all the way into the "far [μακράν] country" (and pig sty). The son's "being distant [ἀπέχοντος, *apechontos*]" from the father, while a physical reality, is an emotional illusion.[248] The father's indefatigable love bridges the distance, however far, approximating God's panoramic vision and passionate love for God's children.

Moreover, such emotion remains poised to spring into action. The father in Jesus's story is dramatically *moved* with compassion toward his return-

and proposes the scheme to become a hired hand (15:20–21). Though the prodigal undoubtedly comes to a deeper knowledge of himself upon meeting his father again, I still see his "coming to himself" in the far country as a decisive moment of realization and "conversion."

246. I am indebted to Bailey (*Jacob*) for the fruitful intertextual juxtaposition of the parable of the prodigal son in Luke 15:11–32 with the Jacob story in Gen 25–37, though I am not convinced that Jesus (or Luke) systematically "retold" (or rewrote) the Jacob saga.

247. For a stimulating treatment of this parable from a perspective of criminal justice or jurisprudence, see Marshall, *Compassionate Justice*, 192–245.

248. This intransitive meaning of ἀπέχω (*apechō*) combines with the adverb μακράν (*makran*) to double-mark the gap: "being *far distant*." The verb can signal spatial-geographic (Luke 7:6; 24:13; Matt 14:24) or volitional-emotional distance ("their hearts are far from me" [Matt 15:8//Mark 7:6]).

ing—yet *still far away*—son. The father does not wait for the son's arrival to reach out to him but rather erupts in a series of profuse gestures that can only be described as *wasteful*. The prodigal son is engulfed by the prodigal father: first in physical contact, then in regal clothing, and finally in festal celebration. Sandwiched *between* is the son's rehearsed legal confession, which the father never asks for or acknowledges. The confession is squeezed out by the father's bear hug, covered over by his best robe, and shouted down by the party's dance music. Notice the narrated order of events:

- Physical contact (running, hugging, kissing) (15:20)
- [*Legal confession (sinful, unworthy, disenfranchised)* (15:21)]
- Regal clothing (best robe, ring, sandals) (15:22)
- Festal celebration (fatted calf, music, dancing) (15:23–25)

The initial *contact* exceeds the limits of proper paternal behavior. The father wastes energy and dignity sprinting out to his son on the edge of the estate. Normally, no self-possessed, self-respecting elite male would be caught dead hiking up his outer garment and running anywhere in public (scurrying about is for children and slaves).[249] Then, without interrogating the returning rebel, without letting him say his confessional piece, and without insisting on a bath (imagine the filth and stench from the pig sty and long journey), the father embraces his son ("fell upon his neck" [15:20 KJV], a vivid Semitic idiom), and kisses him. The parallel with Esau's running-hugging-kissing reunion with Jacob is striking, except for the mutual weeping in the Genesis incident (Gen 33:4) and the fact that Esau is Jacob's brother, not father (we must wait for the elder brother's response in Jesus's parable). By all rights again, we might expect the offended party to charge at the younger man with an armed posse (Esau has 400 men [32:6]) and fall upon his worthless neck with a sword! And the only kiss we might imagine would be a mocking set-up for assault, like the kiss Judas will attempt to give Jesus (Luke 22:47–48). But the only lips and hands the father lays on the wasteful son are extensions of compassion and restoration, mirroring the loving ministrations of the sinner-woman to Jesus. Though the action moves *toward*, rather than from, the sinner in the parable, the intent and result are the same: effecting forgiveness and wholeness (cf. 7:36–38, 44–50). And unlike the woman's humble, hunched-over handling of Jesus's *feet*, the father's attention is directed straight up, in more

249. See Bailey, *Poet and Peasant*, 181–82, and *Jacob*, 166; cf. Aristotle, *Eth. nic.* 4.3 (1125a): "Slowness of movement seems to be the mark of the great-souled man" (trans. Bartlett and Collins). On the trope of the "running slave" (*servus currens*), applied to the Rhoda story in Acts 12:13–16, see Harrill, "Dramatic Function."

lateral than hierarchical arrangement, at the son's face, neck, and back (though he will soon take care of the son's battered feet). The focus on the father's *hands* is exquisitely illuminated in Rembrandt's portrait, featuring splayed fingers, at once outreaching and ingathering, applying palpable pressure, at once gently reassuring and firmly repossessing, across the son's back.[250] The son kneels with his weary head nestled in the father's abdomen—a reasonable and beautiful embellishment of Jesus's story—but perhaps too much. Just as the parable's father wastes no time allowing for the son's verbal confession, he insists on no genuflected submission. Fellowship is immediately and fully restored.

The exuberant pace of restoration continues with the *clothing* of the son (15:22). The father orders his attending slaves to bring "quickly [ταχύ, *tachy*]"—not a moment to waste—the "best/first [πρώτην, *prōtēn*]" robe (top of the line) for his back, a ring for his finger, and sandals for his feet. The fact that the father orders his slaves to serve "this son of mine" (15:24) shows that he in no way disavows the young man's filial status (despite "I am no longer worthy to be called your son" [15:21]) and has no intention of treating him as a hired hand. Adorning this son with the finest robe recalls the indulgent favor of Jacob toward Joseph, to the chagrin of jealous older brothers (Gen 37:3–4). With the parable's father, however, favored love also assumes the garb of a frivolous waste of rich, clean fabric on a poor, polluted body. By placing a ring, probably the household signet ring, on the prodigal's finger (lit. "a finger-ring on his hand"), the father fully reinstates the son into the family, accords him, as it were, the "right hand of fellowship" and unending covenant of loyal love. The provision of sandals completes the head-to-toe makeover and allows the father and son to *walk together*, on an equal social footing, from field to estate house.[251]

They proceed together to a *celebration* of the prodigal's return, complete with music, dancing, and feasting on the fatted calf (Luke 15:23–25). Here the most salient intertextual resonance counterpoints the greatest spiritual crisis in ancient Israel's wilderness journey. In that tragic event, the people physically stayed around the base of Mount Sinai while Moses went away, up to the mountaintop to commune with God. But though not traveling an inch, the people "were running wild" (Exod 32:25) in *feasting* and *dancing* before the image of a *calf* they had forged from the gold in their ear *rings* (32:2–6, 19). This was a celebration of rebellion against God, of casting off their spiritual "father" who

250. See the poignant and perceptive treatment of Luke's text and Rembrandt's painting *Return of the Prodigal* (ca. 1667) in Nouwen, *Return*.

251. Besides the father's hands, another prominent feature of Rembrandt's painting is the prodigal's feet (as he kneels): the left unshod showing the dirty, creased, and calloused sole; the right exposing a rough bare heel poking out of a tattered shoe. Deeply etched in these feet are the prodigal's hard journey and broken condition.

had redeemed "son" Israel from Egyptian bondage (cf. 4:22–23; Jer 31:9; Hos 11:1). But this celebration soon turned sour as an incensed Moses returned to his prodigal people, ground their calf-idol into dust, scattered it on the water, and forced the Israelites to drink the bitter brew (Exod 32:19–20). Moreover, he drew a line in the sand and mobilized his fellow Levites to execute some 3,000 rebels, thus restoring some spiritual order to the community, "each one at the cost of a son or a brother" (32:26–29). Yet, the Lord's anger was not completely assuaged: "The LORD sent a plague on the people, because they made the calf," and threatened to obliterate them (32:30–35). Spurred by Moses's intercession, however, the Lord relented from his wrath in favor of merciful and faithful compassion (34:6–7). The covenant was renewed—though with strict demands that the Israelites not "prostitute" themselves again with false gods and fashion idols (34:10–17)—and construction plans were quickly launched for a tabernacle devoted to proper worship of the Lord. To support this reconciliation project, the Israelites provided their most precious gold objects (including "signet rings and pendants") and finest fabrics (35:20–23).

It is striking how Jesus forges similar elements of rings, calf, food, music, and dancing into a parable of lavish (wasteful) restoration without mitigating judgments or provisos. He heads straight for the gracious, compassionate ending without extending the communal crisis. He *wastes* the opportunity to teach critical lessons of discipline and responsibility, not to mention fairness and justice; or better put perhaps, he deems these unsuitable talking points around the family banquet table at *this* setting. This is the time and place for celebration, not education. Paternal lectures about family values and reputations can wait.

But not in the mind of the *elder brother*. This gross waste of the father's love and the family's resources is not lost on him. Coming from the field and approaching the house, he hears the party in progress. Then, after learning the purpose of the affair, this brother "became angry and refused to go in [εἰσελθεῖν, *eiselthein*]" (Luke 15:28). He thus plays the Moses role, indignant over flagrant revelry that appears to honor the impudence and decadence of the prodigal son/brother. He even indicts his brother (with probable cause) because he "devoured" ("ate up" [κατεσθίω, *katesthiō*]) his father's "life/livelihood" (βίος, *bios*) "with *prostitutes*," reminiscent of the common scriptural charge against Israel, beginning in the aftermath of the golden-calf incident, for "prostitut[ing] themselves to their gods" (Exod 34:16).[252] The parable's father, however, does not indulge the elder's son jealous resentment ("you've never thrown a party for me and my friends") or bitter fraternal denunciation ("this son *of yours*" = "no

252. Other biblical examples imaging Israel's idolatry as prostitution include Num 25:1–2; Lev 17:7; 20:5–6; Deut 31:16; Judg 2:17; 8:33; Jer 3:1–5; 5:7–9; Ezek 16; Hos 2.

brother *of mine*"). But neither does he dispute this son's loyal obedience ("all these years I have been working like a slave for you, and I have never disobeyed your command" [Luke 15:29]). The father does not favor the younger son *over* the older (as Jacob favored Joseph) or suddenly "hate" the older brother out of preferential "love" for the younger (as Mal 1:2–3 and Rom 9:13 interpret the Jacob and Esau saga). In fact, the father equally reaches out to the older brother, for he "came out [ἐξελθών, *exelthōn*]" to the brother and "began to plead with him" to join the festivities (Luke 15:28). He does deliver a little lecture now, but it is all in the best interest of the older son and the entire family. The firstborn has nothing to lose here ("all that is mine is yours"), *except* the joy of reintegrating with a lost part of himself ("this brother *of yours* was dead") and reuniting with a fully restored community (15:31–32). The elder brother *wastes* a golden "must" moment of personal and communal resurrection and reconciliation: "We *had to/must* [ἔδει, *edei*] celebrate and rejoice, because this brother of yours was dead and has come to life; he was lost and has been found" (15:32).

Notably, Jesus leaves the response of the older son in the balance. Will he, this dutiful, resident brother, *come home* when it matters most? He must face his own self-imposed alienation from the father's compassionate heart. He, too, is beckoned to return from exile to full fellowship in the father's house. And so, by analogy, are the Pharisees and scribes whom Jesus addresses. As he indicts these religious scholars, he also invites them to come home again and join him in the great banquet for saints and sinners alike, for God's people near and far, sharing together in the gracious bounty of God's kingdom.

Money Lovers and God Servers (16:1–31)

The narrative boundary between Luke 15 and 16 is thin, as Jesus continues in parable-spinning mode, emphasizing themes of integrity and hospitality. Moreover, though the disciples reemerge as Jesus's main audience (16:1), the Pharisees are still listening and responding critically (16:14). Yet, for all that connects Luke 15 and 16, the latter chapter exhibits internal coherence with framing parables (16:1–13, 19–31) beginning with "there was a certain rich man [πλούσιος, *plousios*]" (16:1, 19 KJV), surrounding Jesus's brief discursive riposte to "the Pharisees, who were lovers of money" (φιλάργυροι, *philargyroi* [16:14]). While the slave-owning, trust-funding father from the "prodigal" parable was clearly a man of means, Jesus simply introduced him as "a [certain] man who had two sons" (15:11), not a "rich" one per se. Jesus now particularly targets the wealthy.

Overall, Jesus appears suspicious of financial gain, crystallized in the antithesis at the heart of the chapter: "You cannot serve God and wealth" (16:13).

Money-obsessed Pharisees (or anyone else) risk being not simply spiritually misguided but *theologically bankrupt*, utterly opposed to God and God's ways, like the rich man in the closing parable who suffers eternal separation from God ("a great chasm" [16:26]). Jesus moderates this condemnation somewhat, however, in the opening parable, where the top "rich man" is a more neutral figure wronged by his household manager (οἰκονόμος, *oikonomos*), who becomes the story's protagonist. Though an employee, he enjoys considerable authority and access to bountiful resources. But he winds up being fired for abusing his position and mismanaging his master's funds. So money brings him down, at least initially. But the manager then further manipulates financial dealings to secure his future and even to garner praise from his former master. Bottom line: Jesus casts this man as an ambiguous character, both "dishonest" (ἄδικος, *adikos*) and "prudent" (φρόνιμος, *phronimos*)—indeed, using his "dishonest wealth" to "make friends" who host him after his dismissal. In some sense this figure models what it takes to secure "eternal homes" (16:4, 8–9). Thus Jesus seems to endorse building up eternal capital *through* shrewd money management. This "rich man" parable and Jesus's commentary on it represent some of the most perplexing material in Luke's narrative. A full investigation appears below. But for now, we simply note that this first story, which "comes to us courtesy of the business school rather than the divinity school or chapel," as Richard Lischer quips,[253] suggests more salutary possibilities for moneyed folk than eternal torment in the flames of Hades (16:23–24).

Money is not the problem in and of itself. Neither it nor material things are inherently evil; in fact, all "goods," all "these things," may be properly valued as good gifts of the Creator God (see 12:30–32; 16:25). It comes down to stewardship of God's resources as a barometer of whom and what one *loves* the most.[254] More than most "things," wealth acquisition and management can consume one's life, one's "soul" (cf. 12:15, 19–20). It can arrogate voracious, dictatorial, faux-divine power as Mammon (Wealth), demanding absolute devotion to feed its insatiable interests.[255] Hence one cannot serve Mammon and God concurrently or love both Mammon and God wholeheartedly (16:13). But one can dethrone Mammon and make it subservient to God. One can serve and love God and God's people through generous monetary redistribution. One can "make friends" or "loved

253. Lischer, *Reading*, 100.

254. Cf. James K. A. Smith, *You Are What You Love*, 9: "It is not just that 'I know' some end or 'believe'" in some *telos*. More than that, I *long* for some end. I *want* something, and want it ultimately. It is my desires that define me. In short, you are what you love" (emphasis original).

255. The Greek μαμωνᾶς (*mamōnas*), used only in Luke 16:9, 11, 13 (and Matt 6:24) in the NT, derives from the Aramaic ממון (*mamon*) and the related Hebrew term for "money, wealth" used in the Hebrew of the Mishnah (m. 'Abot. 2:17) and at Qumran (1QS 6.2; CD 14.20); see Wilcox, "Mammon"; BDAG, 614–15.

ones" (φίλοι, *philoi*) by replacing "money-loving" (φιλάργυρος, *philargyros*) propensities with active commitments to love one's neighbors, strangers, and even enemies through money-sharing benevolence and hospitality (cf. 10:25–37).

Facing eviction from his master's household, the chief manager in the first parable brokers debt-reduction deals with his patron's clients so that these grateful "people may welcome [him] into their homes" (16:4). The rich man in the second parable has every opportunity to practice hospitality toward poor, infirm Lazarus who lay at his gate, longing for a few scraps from the sumptuous table (16:19–20). But in this case, Mammon's monstrous appetite wins out, squelching all chances of tending and befriending the needy neighbor.[256] Only in the afterlife does Lazarus receive the welcome he deserves as a beloved son of God through father Abraham (16:22–25).

In Luke 16 Jesus rates value in terms of *moral virtue*, not material fortune—virtue springing from (1) deep devotion to God's will ("God knows your hearts" [16:15]) manifest in (2) "faithful" (πιστός, *pistos*) and "true" (ἀληθινός, *alēthinos*) stewardship of God's resources (16:10–12) in accordance with (3) the way of God revealed in Scripture. This last point provides the linchpin in Jesus's argument with the Pharisees about the very foundation on which they base their faith and practice. As scholars of "the law and the prophets," they should know the "abomination" of false, fraudulent idolatry that compromises loving service to God and people (16:15–16). Though Jesus does not cite specific texts at this point, it is not hard to recall his affirmation of the double-love commandment and Sabbath/Jubilee legislation, advocating debt relief for the poor and beleaguered (Lev 19:17; 25:1–55; Deut 6:5; 15:1–18; Isa 58:1–14; 61:1–3; Luke 4:18–21; 10:25–28). By fleshing out and fulfilling God's scriptural revelation, Jesus walks the same path the Pharisees tread and, indeed, blazes the way for them, if they would just look and listen. He faithfully interprets the law and the prophets by incarnating their message. So the final word of father Abraham for the rich man's brothers in the parable rings as true for the money-loving Pharisees: "They have Moses and the prophets; they should listen to them" (16:29). And we might add: they should also notice how Jesus embodies this Mosaic and prophetic vision.

The Fraudulent Property Manager and Prudent Debt Settler (16:1–13)

As noted above, Jesus casts this parable's manager in puzzling contrasting tones as dishonest and prudent, wicked and wise (16:1–8a), and his commentary on

256. See the extensive sociopsychological and neuroscientific analysis of the core nurturing drives "tending and befriending" in Shelley E. Taylor, *Tending Instinct*.

the story exacerbates the tension between faithful service to God and stewardship of "dishonest wealth" (Mammon [16:8b-13]). We may find some help in sorting out Jesus's message through the "how much more" route: if a wasteful, fraudulent money manager can still act prudently and win his master's praise, *how much more* should a faithful, benevolent steward of God's blessings act wisely to God's glory. But in fact, Jesus advances no explicit "lesser to greater," "how much more [πόσῳ μᾶλλον, *posō mallon*]" argument here, as elsewhere in Luke (11:13; 12:24, 28). In fact, he makes more of a one-to-one, equivalent point: "Make friends for yourselves by means of dishonest wealth" (16:9), exactly as the parable's unscrupulous manager did; and Jesus's comparative argument points in an unexpected direction: "the children of this age are *more shrewd/prudent* [φρονιμώτεροι, *phronimōteroi*] . . . than are the children of light" (16:8).

Although Jesus's movement from the manager's reception into friends' earthly homes (16:4) to disciples' welcome into "*eternal*" (αἰώνιος, *aiōnios*) dwellings (16:9) ups the ante to the cosmic level, the currency for obtaining such eternal structures is still calculated in terms of "dishonest" Mammon, which is finite and perishable: it will be "gone" ("fail, cease" [ἐκλείπω, *ekleipō*]) (16:9). If that doesn't complicate the matter enough, Jesus actually calls these eternal residences "*tents*" (σκηνή, *skēnē*), setting up an apparent oxymoron: tents are portable, temporary (*not* "eternal") shelters more suited to desert travel than promised-land settlement. Jesus may well be trading in acrid irony, as if to say: "Go ahead and follow the lead of the crooked manager in the parable, if you dare, and bet your eternal soul on the friends you buy off and the security they provide. And see what it gets you!"[257]

To unravel this tangled passage obviously requires close attention to the internal language. But also, the more difficult a text seems, the more important it becomes to interpret it, not as an isolated phenomenon, but as part of a broader narrative. In addition to the ensuing co-texts in Luke 16, a set of previous parables treating similar themes provides a key informative network. Though not precluding some innovation in the present case, these related stories mark major lines of Luke's thought guiding us to and through this new parable concerning the dishonest manager. The following chart highlights links with four prior parables and their immediate narrative settings.[258]

257. Spencer, *Gospel of Luke*, 174; for other assessments of irony as a key element in Jesus's commentary on this parable, see Porter, "Parable"; and Trudinger, "Ire or Irony?"

258. The householder/manager parables in 12:41–48 and 19:11–27 also provide some links, but not as strong as the four presented in the chart. The immediately preceding parable of the prodigal son affords the closest connection, featuring comparative elements in all six charted categories. For a study focused on correlating the parables of the rich fool and the dishonest manager, see Schumacher, "Saving like a Fool."

	Two debtors (7:40–43)	**Friend at midnight (11:1–13)**	**Rich fool (12:16–21)**	**Prodigal son (15:11–32)**	**Dishonest/ prudent manager (16:1–13)**
Debt management:	Creditor *cancels* two substantal debts of 500/50 denarii	"Forgive us our sins, for we *forgive* everyone indebted to us" (11:4)		Father *ignores* the debt incurred by inheritance-wasting son	Manager-broker *reduces* two substantial debts from 100 to 50 and 80 measures
Love and friendship:	Debtor forgiven more loves the gracious creditor more	One friend/ neighbor imposes upon another for bread		Father shows compassion toward prodigal son	Debtors befriend manager-broker, who lessens their burden
Hospitality:	Parable illustrates sinner-woman's hospitality to Jesus not provided by Simon (7:44–46)	The friend/ neighbor needs bread to feed a traveler-friend who has come to visit	Landowner concerned about housing goods for present-life security but is bankrupt eternally	Father provides hearty welcome and lavish banquet for returning "sinner" son	Dismissed manager makes friends who will welcome him into their homes; Jesus speaks of hospitality in "eternal tents" (16:9)
Rich property owner:			"The land of a rich man produced abundantly" (12:16)	Father has substantial estate with hired hands and servant workers	"There was a rich man who had a manager" (16:1)
Self-analysis and scheme:		No self-analysis, but the unprepared host devises a resourceful scheme to obtain bread for his guest	The rich man "thought to himself, 'What should I do?'" (12:17) and devised a foolish retirement scheme that proved futile	"But when he came to himself" (15:17), the prodigal son devised a survival/ return scheme that proved unnecessary	"Then the manager said to himself, 'What will I do?'" (16:3) and devised a wise rehabilitation scheme that proved successful
Stewardship: waste and surplus:			The rich landowner stockpiled his surplus goods but lost/wasted them in death to unknown successors	The younger son "squandered" (διασκορπίζω, *diaskorpizō* [15:13]) his father's property yet graciously shared "all" his father's bounty	The manager "was squandering" (διασκορπίζω, *diaskorpizō*) his master's property yet shrewdly made friends to take care of himself

Related to the leitmotif of "waste" management in the prodigal story is that of *debt management* in several parables leading up to the present tale. Moreover, debt release associated with scriptural Jubilee traditions formed a major plank of Jesus's manifesto (see discussion on 4:16–30). In Luke's narrative and social worlds, *indebtedness* constitutes a critical problem in the human condition requiring relief, release, or redemption by creditors, brokers, or benefactors. It carries both literal/economic (debt = money owed) and figurative/moral (debt = sin committed) freight. Accordingly, holistic salvation is aptly conceived as remission of debts. In any case, in a context of economic scarcity and moral frailty, options for self-security or personal liberation (timely payment of debts) are severely limited. Everyone needs a little (or a lot of) grace. Just as I suggested that all three previous figures (father, younger and older sons) experienced some kind of waste, I contend that all three current characters—the rich landlord, his chief manager, and the master's tenants—incur some sense of *debt*.

From the start, the estate manager (οἰκονόμος, *oikonomos*) appears as a shady character brought up on charges of "squandering" (διασκορπίζω, *diaskorpizō*) his rich master's property (16:1), just as the prodigal son had done with his father's inheritance (15:13). We are not told how the steward mismanaged the owner's resources (poor investments? sloppy bookkeeping? lazy neglect? petty pilfering? reckless spending?), but at any rate, some type of fraudulent conduct mires him in deeper debt: beyond owing his job and home to the landlord, he also owes whatever deficits emerge from the audit of his accounts. Among various penalties the master may exact, including corporal punishment, legal action, imprisonment, and demotion to lower slave status (cf. 12:46–48; 19:22–27), he chooses simply to discharge the manager from his position and residence (16:2). While this may seem to let the steward off lightly, it amounts to a severe sentence of disgraceful expulsion. Contrary to the prodigal son, who *chooses* to leave his father's home and thereafter wastes the family's resources, the present manager is *forced* to leave *because* of his profligate practices. And he finds himself with very limited opportunities. Who will dare to hire him now with his reputation? Moreover, he himself admits he lacks the strength to dig as a common laborer and cannot bear the shame of begging for alms (16:3). He thus has no way of repaying his debts and no option to return to his former employer. The prodigal's survival plan to serve as one of his father's hired hands would not work for this weak-bodied former manager, and he also seems too proud to badger any friends for assistance, unlike the bread-seeking neighbor at midnight (cf. 11:7–8).[259] Whether he has any friends to turn to is also questionable at this point.

So, "what will [he] do, now" with his back against the wall (16:3)? In the absence of supporters, he desperately needs to "make friends." So he does, using the only skills he has, those related to financial administration. Capitalizing on his final moments of employment, the estate manager renegotiates the terms of his master's debtors (χρεοφειλέται, *chreopheiletai*)—probably tenant farmers who leased land and secured operation loans from the wealthy landlord[260]—reducing the promissory note of one by 50 percent and another by 20 percent (16:6–7). Through this generous brokerage, the manager thus puts these tenants in *his debt*, which he can call in, when thrown out on his ear, in the form of hospitality.

Though the steward employs a manipulative scheme to his advantage, he does not necessarily make an illicit, deceitful deal, compounding his previous fraudulent activities. Owners of large estates commonly gave considerable authority to local managers to handle business matters, while they, as largely absentee landlords, preoccupied themselves with civic and political affairs (cf. 12:42–48; 19:11–27). In particular, ancient real estate contracts from Pliny's letters (Italy) and Oxyrhynchus papyri (Egypt) attest to the common, aboveboard practice of landowners or steward-representatives *reducing* or *refinancing* tenants' debts to keep them cultivating the land, even during lean, deficit seasons beset by harsh climate, pestilence, or farmers' illnesses or injuries. In the long run, a stable workforce was more beneficial to owners and managers than repeated foreclosures on delinquent clients and pressures to find new tenants.[261]

In Jesus's parable, then, the debt-reducing manager can be seen not only as serving his own interests, but also those of the master. The lord (κύριος, *kyrios*) of the estate sincerely "commended/praised [ἐπῄνεσεν, *epēnesen*] the dishonest manager" for his sound strategy to retain clients (16:8).[262] The "dis-

259. I can't resist citing Lischer's (*Reading*) verbal dig modernizing the steward's "realistic self-assessment [of his limited career options and abilities]—one that continues to resonate with middle-management types, academics, and the clergy" (101).

260. See Ukpong, "Parable." For an alternative scenario of the debtors as *merchants* selling the rich man's supplies of oil and grain in the urban marketplace, see Herzog, *Parables*, 239–52.

261. See the superb article by Goodrich, "Voluntary Debt Remission." For example, Goodrich cites the contract from P.Oxy. 2351 between a landowner named Phatres and three tenant wheat farmers, in which "Phatres remitted nearly 35 percent of the arrears that his tenants owed in exchange for a lease extension and satisfactory payment of each future installment. . . . Phatres utilized his generosity to secure significant negotiating power, culminating in a new lease and thus his own financial longevity" (560).

262. The lord (κύριος, *kyrios*) of the parable (ending at 16:8a) is not to be identified *simpliciter* with Lord Jesus, who comments on his own story in 16:8b–13. Nonetheless, the close juxtapo-

honest/unjust" (ἀδικία, *adikia*) label applies to the manager's *former* conduct of squandering the rich man's property, for which he now makes some amends by this "prudent" transaction with the tenant farmers. In the give-and-take dynamics of this patronage system, the patron-master, though at the top of the ladder, acknowledges *his debt* to the (formerly) dishonest, dismissed manager for stabilizing the estate's long-term operations. The master repays this debt, as it were, by congratulating the steward for his wise debt-reduction scheme and thus restoring some of his tainted reputation.

In sum, the debt cycle in Jesus's parable runs as follows.

- The *manager-steward* incurs a heavy debt to the *landlord-master* by squandering his property. This moral (breach of trust) and financial debt cannot fully be repaid and demands dismissal.
- In response, the "dishonest," disenfranchised manager prudently reduces certain *tenant farmers'* debts, thus relieving them of some financial burden, as well as solidifying the master's work force.
- As a result, the *manager* places both *master* and *tenants* in his debt, which the former repays by commendation and the latter by accommodation.

Within the social-narrative framework of the parable, the characters play out the exchange economics of remitting others' debts as they themselves receive remission. On this plane, the parable illustrates the economics and spirituality of God's kingdom established in the Lord's Prayer: "Forgive us our sins, for we ourselves forgive everyone indebted to us" (11:4). But this remains a *partial, imperfect* analogy. For one thing, this manager merely *reduces* his clients' debt loads, while Luke's other stories charted above feature total cancellation of debts, large and small (7:41–42), and full reinstatement of fortune and position (the prodigal). Likewise, though the landlord in the present parable approves his manager's shrewd debt-reduction scheme, he neither forgives the earlier mismanagement nor restores the steward's job. For the tenants' part, while they receive some economic relief, they are still enmeshed in an exploitative system. Indeed, though easing their burden in the short run, more generous payment terms create a bigger honor (loyalty) debt to the landlord, not to mention more pressing obligation to make the monetary payments they still owe. Further-

---

sition between the lord of the "embedded" (metadiegetic) parable and the Lord of the "primary" (diegetic) narrative, as Ryan Schellenberg ("Which Master?") argues, blurs the boundaries between them amid persisting tensions. Schellenberg concludes: "Insofar as this Gospel describes the Lukan Lord as one eager to bring release from debt and restoration for 'sinners', the diegetic κύριος stands in judgment over his metadiegetic counterpart and vindicates the debt relief scheme of a prudent steward" (282).

more, the tenants must now also repay the broker-manager in terms of hospitality, which they can hardly expect to be reciprocated, since he has no home of his own and is unable (supposedly) to do any manual labor to assist his prospective hosts. In short, whatever benefits the tenants might receive from the manager's deal, they scarcely reach the level of full Sabbath-year debt-slave relief, complete with emancipation and liberal provision of goods enjoined in Deut 15:12–15.[263]

Jesus's commentary on the parable (Luke 16:8b-13) grants the manager's sagacious and gracious action *as far as it goes*. But he also exposes the limits of this economic plan and raises the discussion of discipleship and stewardship to the level of *eternal light*, which is to say, the cosmic realm of God, the Creator and Sustainer of light and life. Note three points.

First, Jesus grants the prudence of the debt-reducing, house-securing manager within the limited spheres of "this age" and "[this] generation" (16:8b). This present temporal (age) and social (generation) realm has great value as the sphere where Jesus has lived, moved, and worked in promoting God's kingdom. But it is not coterminous with God's realm, which encompasses "this age/generation" but extends infinitely beyond in eschatological scope ("the age to come" [18:30; cf. 20:34–35; 21:32–33]) and ethical force. As we have seen, "this generation" in Luke tilts more to the wicked-rebellious than the righteous-receptive pole (7:31; 9:41; 11:29–32, 50–51; 17:25; 21:32). But it has its wise, virtuous moments, which God's "children of light" do well not simply to emulate but to exceed. Though not stated, a "how much more" perspective seems evident: if creditors of "this generation" occasionally reduce some debts, how much more should bearers of God's compassionate light remit all forms of debt altogether.

Second, Jesus commands his disciples to use Mammon, as the manager does, for purposes of networking and friend-making. But there's a difference: ever alert to Mammon's "dishonest" traps, it must be invested not for its own sake—to multiply wealth and pad one's portfolio—but to solidify communal ties in "eternal tents [αἰωνίους σκηνάς, *aiōnious skēnas*]," which will sustain "true" life "when [Mammon] *is gone*" (16:9). Jesus cuts Mammon's value to the bone. It is, by nature, a deceitful, perishable commodity; however glittery it appears and however much accumulated, it is all subject to theft, moth-bite and other predations, not least the ultimate bankruptcy of death, as the earlier parable's

263. On the vicious, exploitative trap ensnaring the debtor-farmers, see Ukpong, "Parable." He puts the full blame, however, on the callous rich master rather than on the manager, who is also victimized by the estate baron: "Because he [the manager] is only an employee, and he is poor, he has no rights. He is therefore an object of exploitation by the rich man and a victim of the vagaries of the economic system of his society" (204). Following Goodrich ("Voluntary Debt Remission"), I view the landowner in somewhat more sympathetic and pragmatic business terms, though still the prime beneficiary of the hierarchical patronage system.

rich fool ruefully discovered (12:15–21, 33). Mammon has no *eternal* value. The manager in the present story obtains *temporal* lodgings through financial finagling, but these tenant homes cannot provide lasting security. The same could be said for the rich master's estate: it, too, will eventually erode. Nevertheless, Jesus contends that money still has its use as a *means* (not end) to building solid dwellings of *eternal tents*.

This strange housing plan, so described only here in the NT, neatly captures the tension of faithful living in "this age" when Jesus Messiah reignites God's heavenly rule on earth, anticipating its consummation in the "age to come." "Eternal tents" may be glossed as "heavenly earth nests" or "divine-human huts." "Tents" or "tabernacles" provide *portable* shelter for a *pilgrim* people, like (1) the ancient Israelites guided through the wilderness by God's sacred "tent of testimony [σκηνὴ τοῦ μαρτυρίου, *skēnē martyriou*]" (Acts 7:44); (2) the traveling Jesus, with "nowhere to lay his head" (Luke 9:58), and his followers en route to Jerusalem; and (3) Paul the tentmaker (σκηνοποιός, *skēnopoios* [Acts 18:3]) on Jesus's gospel mission across the Mediterranean world to Rome. God's journeying people have their feet firmly grounded in this world created by God, but they are not content with the world *as it is.* As the writer of Hebrews puts it, they are "strangers and foreigners on the earth . . . seeking a homeland"; they tread the earth in hope of a "better country . . . a heavenly one" (Heb 11:13–14, 16). They do not seek *escape* "up to" heaven (eternal tents are not heavenly mansions), but rather a *transformation* of the whole world according to God's just, right-making will, a complete *interpenetration* of heaven and earth. God's faithful people invest in this eternal realm here and now by establishing signposts, beachheads—*tent camps*—staking claims to God's coming redemptive (debt-freeing) kingdom. Peter got it half right when he proposed to build tents to commemorate God's transformative glory (Luke 9:33). But he completely missed the critical part of "tenting" or "tabernacling" *among* "this generation," *along* the path of "this age."[264]

How, then, does one go about investing in eternal tents? Not by forsaking the material world, but by *wisely using Mammon* for God's interests. The actions of the steward in Jesus's parable establish a precedent for his followers to expand upon. In God's economy managed by Lord Jesus, debts should be fully canceled, all possessions sold, and all proceeds distributed to the poor, forging an interdependent community of goods and services (12:33; 14:33). "No one claim[ed] private ownership" of anything, including property and residences; lands and homes were held "in common," ensuring a place of welcome and nurture on the

264. Cf. John 1:14: "And the Word became flesh and lived ['tabernacled'—ἐσκήνωσεν, *eskēnōsen*] among us."

journey (Acts 4:32). This divestment of all personal ("my") resources, far from translating into loss, guarantees a bountiful communal ("our") return. As Jesus will say to Peter, after encountering a rich ruler: "Truly I tell you, there is no one who has left house [as the disciples did] . . . for the sake of the kingdom of God, who will not get back very much more *in this age, and in the age to come eternal life*" (Luke 18:29–30).

While this vision of hospitality applies primarily to Jesus's disciples (16:1), it also reaches to the overhearing Pharisees (16:14) and, in retrospect, to Simon the Pharisee. Though having no house of his own, Jesus made friends of "tax collectors and sinners" by forgiving their sin-debts and eating with them (7:34; 15:1–2). Accordingly, he has been received into their homes, which effectively become his temporary residence or "eternal tent," where he further mediates God's love by receiving and forgiving debtors (5:27–32; cf. 19:1–10). But not everyone has been so hospitable. Recall the scene around Simon the Pharisee's table, when Jesus fully embraced and pardoned a debt-ridden "sinner"-woman. Simon, however, only minimally hospitable to Jesus from the start, shuddered at Jesus's welcoming this "kind of woman" into Simon's home, which in turn, prompted Jesus's pithy parable of debt cancellation (7:41–43). Revisiting this story in light of Jesus's present parable, we may cast his response to Simon as a challenge to transform his segregated house into an "eternal tent" where he acknowledged his own indebtedness to God, received God's forgiveness anew in Jesus Messiah, and befriended fellow debtors like the "sinner"-woman.

Third, Jesus sounds the theme of *faithfulness* (16:10–13), both connecting with and projecting beyond the prudent action of the parable's manager. Faithfulness is the proper exercise of stewardship: trustworthy management "of what belongs to another" (16:12). Convinced that all life and goods come from God, belong to God, and demand grateful, diligent care in honor of God, Luke's Jesus unpacks this worldview in both quantitative and qualitative terms. *Quantitatively*, he commends faithful stewardship of "very little" or the "least matter" (ἐλάχιστον, *elachiston*) as a prerequisite and barometer of one's ability to manage "much." As head steward of a rich man's estate, the parable's protagonist came to handle "much" money and resources (e.g., one hundred jugs of oil and bins of wheat owed by the two debtors). Presumably, however, he had worked his way up the ladder with responsible administration of lesser amounts (cf. 19:11–27). The landlord would have been foolish to appoint a chief manager who had squandered smaller assets. In God's realm, however, all Mammon transactions, big or small, have "very little" inherent value, given their potential for dishonest manipulation and Mammon's all-consuming, God-usurping force (16:13). Notice the parallelism Jesus draws between "very little" and "dishonest Mammon" in 16:10–11.

Whoever is faithful in a *very little*
  is faithful also in much.
Whoever is dishonest in a *very little*
  is dishonest also in much.
If then you have not been faithful with the *dishonest Mammon*,
  who will entrust to you the true [riches]?

Conversely, "much" (πολύ, *poly*) corresponds with "true/genuine" (ἀληθινόν, *alēthinon*) worth, that is, the just and righteous values of God's kingdom. Ultimately, Jesus stresses the *qualitative*, ethical dimension of stewardship. The manager in the parable proved to be both dishonest and prudent with his master's material goods: *dishonest* in the initial swindling, and *prudent* in the later debt-reduction. He thus remains a mixed character, altogether limited by his absorption in "little" money matters. But he also poses a basic challenge, a place to start, for disciples and Pharisees alike: faithfulness to God begins in *this world* with its economy, managing this world's resources resourcefully and beneficently as gifts of God.

The Pharisees and John the Baptist (16:14–18)

Though not the primary targets of Jesus's stewardship lesson, the Pharisees who "heard all this" take great offense at his Mammon-critical stance, as would any "lovers of money," a disposition hardly limited to Pharisees or other wealthy persons (the poor and dispossessed can also become obsessed with acquiring money) (16:14). Jesus rebuffs the Pharisees' present criticism not by directly defending or elaborating his radical economic policy, but by setting it in the framework of theological and ethical *knowledge* (economics meets epistemology), a major source of Pharisaic pride. In Jesus's view, the Pharisees overestimate their spiritual acumen, for they too smugly "justify [themselves] in the sight of others" (16:15a; cf. 10:29; 18:9) and too easily forget the ultimate standard of knowledge: "But *God knows* your hearts," which as with all flawed mortals, are infected by evil intentions, which are an "abomination" in God's sight (16:15b).

But God's people need not dwell in darkness, as the light of God's word, suffused in "the law and the prophets" (16:16), shines in perverse hearts. On this core scriptural principle, Jesus and the Pharisees—and John the Baptist (suddenly referenced again since last mentioned in 11:1)—couldn't agree more. But the Pharisees' scriptural practice has been lacking in comparison with John's and Jesus's missions. Here Jesus sets up a three-part chain: (1) beginning with "the law and the prophets," (2) "until [μέχρι, *mechri*] John came," and (3) "since then [ἀπὸ τότε, *apo tote*]" to the proclamation (εὐαγγελίζομαι, *euangelizomai*) of God's kingdom by John and Jesus (16:16; cf. 3:18; 4:18, 43; 7:22; 8:1; 20:1). Post-war twentieth-century scholarship, spearheaded by Hans Conzelmann, made much of this arrangement as the key to Luke's panoramic view of salvation history (*Heilsgeschichte*), sharply divided between old and new phases of God's work, between Law and Gospel, the former encapsulated in OT law and prophets ending with ("until") John the Baptist, and the latter inaugurated in the NT gospel program of Jesus Messiah.[265] But in recent decades, few scholars have accepted this sharply disjunctive scheme. Luke's narrative-historical perspective highlights the story of Jesus (and the early church) as continuing and consummating the story of Israel, or better put, the biblical story of God the Creator of the world and Covenanter with Israel. In schematic terms, rather than:

> [Law/Prophets (up to John)] ≠ [Gospel of God's kingdom (established by Jesus)],

we should envision:

> Law/Prophets → John the Prophet → Jesus the Prophet.

Jesus's commitment to uphold and fulfill all the Jewish Scriptures could hardly be made clearer than in his follow-up statement: "But it is easier for heaven and earth to pass away, than for one stroke of a letter in the law to be dropped" (16:17).[266]

John and Jesus proclaim and practice the way of God blazed in Torah and Prophets, not least, the way of dealing with wealth, to return to the focal issue. To reprise only the Jubilee example, the Law and Prophets mandate debt-release, poor-relief, and communal sharing rather than stockpiling of goods (Lev 25; Deut 15:1–18; Isa 58; 61:1–2). John propounded this theme of economic justice and redistribution, specifically to money-grubbing tax collectors and soldiers, in his "baptism of repentance" (3:1–8), and he practiced what he preached as an ascetic palace-challenging, luxury-eschewing prophet in solidarity with the "least in the kingdom of God" and at odds with "the Pharisees and the lawyers" who spurned his baptism "for themselves" (7:28–30). To an even greater extent,

265. On the central importance of Luke 16:16 for Conzelmann's scheme, see his *Theology of Luke*, 20–27, 112, 160–69, 185.

266. Cf. Matt 5:17–20; "one stroke" likely refers to minute markings of Hebrew letters where, for example, a small line extension distinguishes between *resh* (ר) and *dalet* (ד) or medial/final *nun* (נ/ן) and *pe* (פ/ף).

Jesus the Spirit-anointed prophet and Son of Humankind has incarnated, in word and deed, the core legal-prophetic principle of God's "evangelical" compassion for the destitute and disenfranchised. As he summarized his work to John's messengers: "Go and tell John what you have seen and heard: the blind receive their sight, the lame walk, the lepers are cleansed, the deaf hear, the dead are raised, the poor have good news brought to them [εὐαγγελίζονται, *euangelizontai*]. And blessed is anyone who takes no offense at me" (7:22–23). Unfortunately, the Pharisees—and others, including would-be followers—have continued to take offense at Jesus's mission, particularly his critique of wealth amassment, his call to give up all Mammon, and his outreach to the lowliest and neediest.

Jesus emphasizes the universal scope of God's realm encompassing "all/everyone" (πᾶς, pas), but with the strongest accent on "all" those commonly ostracized: the poor, the last, the least of all, such as "tax collectors and sinners," upon whom the Pharisees have fixated. In an unusual, enigmatic phrase, Jesus stresses that "everyone tries to enter [God's kingdom] by force" (16:16b). This NRSV rendering, however, marks an overreading with its "tries to enter" (not in the Greek), perhaps in the interest of softening the "forceful" theme. The aspect of force comes from the verb βιάζω (*biazō*), appearing only here and Matt 11:12, in both cases in the middle/passive form βιάζεται (*biazetai*). So the phrase may read as either "everyone forces themselves into it [God's kingdom]" or "everyone is forced into it." The nuances of the term's cognates and extra-NT usage suggest a notably robust, even violent, coercion. But a military conquest of God's kingdom makes no sense (what force could defeat God?), and except perhaps for the evangelical fishing image in 5:10 ("catching/netting" people), Jesus never hints at a violent round-up of converts or forced baptisms. It seems best, then, to take Jesus's expression more figuratively, but without sapping it of its strong "force."[267]

So Jesus stresses either that "everyone" (again, especially those ignored by the establishment) "is desperately, enthusiastically, fervently pushing their way into God's kingdom," "beating the door down," as it were, or that they are being

267. See the helpful layout of translation options for βιάζω (*biazō*) in BDAG, including more figurative nuances of "go after something with enthusiasm, seek fervently, try hard" and "constrain warmly" (175–76). Elsewhere Danker (282, also "Luke 16:16") argues that 16:16 reflects *the Pharisees' critique of Jesus's inclusive mission*, rather than Jesus's declarative pronouncement: in their eyes Jesus has shamefully "lowered the bar" for entry into God's realm, prompting a flood of "sinners" to think they can "take it by storm" (force their way into) without repentance. Though I tilt toward the traditional interpretation that Jesus directly affirms here a "forceful/compelling" of "all" into the kingdom (which would certainly irritate many Pharisees), Danker's reading fits the Pharisaic polemic evident elsewhere in this Gospel (5:29–32; 7:39–44; 15:1–2).

desperately, enthusiastically, fervently compelled to come in. Either way the emphasis falls on passionate physical and emotional engagement, as appropriate for kingdom matters of life and death. Jesus has already touted in a Pharisee's home the urgent approach of "compel[ling] people to come in" (albeit with a different verb [ἀναγκάζω, *anankazō*]) to God's banquet house, particularly "the poor, the crippled, the blind, and the lame" on society's extreme margins (14:23, 21). This project is what the Pharisees should be worked up about with Jesus, not his potential infringements on their economic privilege.

From focusing on scriptural ethics in relation to financial issues, Jesus now turns, rather abruptly it seems, to a brief statement about divorce and remarriage (16:18). But though this dominical saying, related to other Synoptic teaching on marriage (Matt 5:27–32; 19:1–12; Mark 10:1–12), may appear spliced in with little concern for context, in fact it continues the train of Jesus's economic reflections based on the Law and the Prophets. Interpreters of the Jewish Scriptures must adjudicate among different perspectives on divorce:

- The Genesis creational foundation of marriage as an indissoluble "one flesh" union (Gen 2:23–24).
- The Deuteronomic legal provision whereby a man may dismiss his wife "because he finds something objectionable about her"; he must certify for her "a bill of divorce," permitting her to remarry, but the original husband can never take her back (Deut 24:1–4).
- The late prophetic reclamation of marriage as a unitary, unbreakable flesh-and-spirit covenant, since "I hate divorce, says the LORD, the God of Israel" (Mal 2:16).

The Deuteronomic loophole created an opportunity for some Jewish scholars, like some Pharisees (cf. Matt 19:3, 7; Mark 10:2–4), to allow men considerable latitude to initiate divorce on all sorts of grounds (lawyers can have a field day with "something objectionable").[268] While we have no hard data about divorce rates among first-century Jews, it appears that divorce was primarily a husband's prerogative,[269] for a range of reasons, with enormous consequences

268. Early rabbinic interpretations of grounds for divorce spanned from loose views of "objectionable/indecent" wifely behavior, including deficient culinary skills and physical beauty (cf. m. Giṭ. 9:10), to stricter criteria focused on sexual transgressions, including but not limited to adultery. Sigal (*Halakhah*) aptly concludes: "In sum, then, the *halakhah* of divorce practiced by the diverse communities of a many-faceted Judaism was in no way monolithic. There was no orthodoxy and no orthopraxy" (142); cf. Spencer, "Scripture," 374–75.

269. On the dominant patriarchal management of divorce in ancient Jewish households, see Sir 7:26; 25:24–26; 42:9–10; Jos. *Ant.* 15.259–60. Some early Jewish sources, however, acknowledge

for the expelled wife—not least her *economic welfare*. Within the patriarchal household, the wife's very sustenance depended on her husband's provision. Divorce could place her in a highly vulnerable "no-man's" land—hence, Deuteronomy's insistence on an official divorce certificate, allowing the woman to remarry, but not return to her first husband for further exploitation. A new, benevolent husband, should she be lucky enough to find one, could support her. But this outcome was by no means guaranteed, since, bill or no bill, a divorced woman could carry a stigma of "damaged goods." Divorce and remarriage, then, represented critical *scriptural* and *financial* issues for women in early Jewish life.

Luke's Jesus is in no mood to debate the fine points of Jewish divorce legislation. He cuts to the chase in favor of protecting a woman's marital-economic rights (Luke 16:18). Addressing the male Pharisees, he flatly prohibits them from divorcing their wives, marrying another for any reason (no "exceptive" clause here concerning an unchaste wife as in Matt 5:32; 19:9), or marrying a previously divorced woman—equating all such practices with adultery. This brief statement hardly constitutes a policy manual on marriage and divorce. Many critical issues are left unconsidered, such as a wife's suffering at the hands of an abusive husband, in which case her very survival may depend on getting out. Jesus does not address women at all here, nor does he consider their agency or perspective. But within its literary and cultural setting, Jesus at least presses the male religious teachers to support a biblical hermeneutic that protects and provides for vulnerable women *economically*. Whether a man serves God or Mammon is as evident in his treatment of his wife as in any other societal relationship.

The Purpled Rich Man and Poor Beggar Lazarus (16:19–31)

Jesus's extended peroration on the pitfalls of idolatrous Mammon culminates in a lengthy parable contrasting the experiences of a rich man and a poor beggar. He portrays an unbridgeable gap—a "great chasm [χάσμα μέγα, *chasma mega*]" (16:26)—between extreme examples of wealth and poverty in the framework of three symbolic boundary markers, tracked from life to afterlife:

1. The rich man's *gate* (πυλών, *pylōn*) (16:19–21)
2. Abraham's *bosom* (κόλπος, *kolpos*) (16:22–26)
3. The realm of the *dead* (νεκρῶν, *nekrōn*) (16:27–31).

---

women's reciprocal rights and duties in marriage, divorce, and sexuality (Philo, *Spec. Laws* 3.80–82; CD 5:9–10; 1 Cor 7:2–5, 10–16); see the discussion in Sigal, *Halakhah*, 127–43.

Passage to and from Abraham's bosom (2) is impossible in the afterlife, however much an outsider might want to get there (16:26). The other boundaries (1, 3) are not so absolutely fixed, but they are rarely broken down.

Consider first the stark scenarios on either side of the rich man's *gate* (16:19–21).

	Rich man	Poor man
Position:	Inside	Outside
Name:	Anonymous	Lazarus
Clothing:	Purple finery	Purpuric sores
Diet:	Daily feasting	Perpetual hunger

Inside his palatial gated villa, this wealthy man enjoys as grand a material life as one might imagine, bedecked in the finest linen and purple fabrics, befitting royalty, and gorging himself "every day" on the richest foods (16:19). The supplication "Give us each day our daily bread" (11:3) would make no sense to him. But just outside his gate lay poor Lazarus, whose daily existence barely qualifies as such. He can't even score a few crumbs from the rich man's table or a cast-off rag to wear. He suffers on the brink of starvation covered in nothing but his own sores, which may have a bruised, purplish-stained cast, in humiliating contrast to the rich man's satiny purple robes.[270] Any restful associations of Lazarus's being "laid" at the villa's gate dissipate with a likelier rendering of the verb: "he had been *thrown/cast out* [ἐβέβλητο, *ebeblēto*] at the gate" (16:20 AT). This is hell on earth, made all the more hellish by its close proximity to such abundance. But the rich man, who could scarcely miss noticing this pathetic figure as he traversed in and out of his gate, lifted no finger to help him. Lazarus has nothing in this world except scavenging dogs to lick his sores (16:21). At least they provide some medical attention, though only out of grisly taste for blood and pus; like the pigs in the prodigal story, they actually eat better than the poor human character.

Lazarus does have one thing in this story the rich man doesn't: a name! In fact, this is the only Gospel parable featuring a named character. Jesus thus personalizes this poor figure, urging his audience to *see him, take full notice,* and not blithely pass by like the rich man (cf. 10:31–32). The specific name may carry a double thrust: on the one hand, evoking the Hebrew Eleazar (אלעזר, *ʾeleaʿzar*), meaning "God helps" (when no one else cares, God's compassion remains firm); but on the other hand, taking the first syllable as לא (*lo*ʾ) ("not") together with

270. On Lazarus's "purpuric body," see Hatcher, "In Gold," 278.

עזר (*'zar*) ("help"), meaning "not helped."[271] Both could work: *not helped* by anyone in this world, Lazarus will be *helped by God* in the world to come.

The story shifts to a remarkable inversion of fortunes (16:22–26). Lazarus dies—no surprise, as he was already on death's door—but now, rather than be cast off by a callous society, he is "carried away"[272] by angels "to be with Abraham," the great father of God's people. Moreover, he doesn't simply land in Abraham's vicinity or just outside his gate, but "by his side" or, more intimately, "*into his bosom* [εἰς τὸν κόλπον, *eis ton kolpon*]." Κόλπος (*kolpos*) denotes a pouchlike place of physical nurture, such as the lap (6:38) or chest, where loose garments gather in pocket-folds.[273] So we may envision Lazarus in the child's pose of sitting in Abraham's lap or, more aptly in the present story, reclining in customary eating posture with his head resting back on Abraham's chest at God's great royal banquet (cf. 13:28–29). Lazarus thus takes his place as beloved "son of Abraham" (cf. 3:8; 13:16; 19:9), with the opportunity to feast sumptuously for all eternity. Incorporating vivid imagery from John's Gospel, we may compare Lazarus's eternal succor to that enjoyed by Jesus in relation to God ("God the only Son, who is close to the father's heart [bosom—κόλπον, *kolpon*)]" (John 1:18) and by the disciple "whom Jesus loved" lolling back on Jesus's bosom [κόλπῳ, *kolpō*] at the Last Supper (13:23).

In relation to the two preceding parables, Lazarus experiences (1) an embracive, festive reception of a tattered, starving "son," like the prodigal, yet with the important distinction that Lazarus had not lost his way in moral rebellion and doesn't need to "decide" to come home (he needs rescuing and "carrying" home, more like the lost sheep); and (2) an eternal place of hospitality in father Abraham's realm—evocative of the "eternal tents" that Jesus mentioned in conjunction with the dismissed manager (16:9) and Abraham's tent in the oak grove where he hosted three divine messengers (Gen 18:1–8)[274]—yet in this case an intimate, heavenly abode in the tentlike folds of Abraham's cloak. Moreover, Lazarus doesn't need to "make friends" (Luke 16:9) with anyone—with money he doesn't have!—to secure this destination, since God has graciously befriended and welcomed him home.

As it happens, the rich man also dies, a while later than Lazarus, but just as surely. The fact that he receives a decent burial (16:22), a dignity no doubt

271. See Thayer, *Greek-English Lexicon*, 367.

272. The compound verb ἀποφέρω (*apopherō*) might connote "carry *back* [home]," that is, "carry to where he belongs," as Van der Horst suggests ("Abraham's Bosom," 142–44); cf. the "carrying [back]" of therapeutic cloths that had contacted Paul's "skin" to the infirm (Acts 19:12); O'Kane, "Bosom," 492n15.

273. Hatcher, "In Gold," 279; O'Kane, "Bosom," 489–90.

274. Hatcher, "In Gold," 279.

denied to Lazarus, does him no good beyond memorializing a (false) sense of honor. Death is the great equalizer, as Qoheleth and the rich fool in Jesus's parable came to know. But the wealthy snob in the present story is slow to get the point. In one sense, the gap between him and Lazarus has collapsed: they both enter the afterlife with no possessions, no resources. But in another sense, the gulf only hardens, becomes permanently "fixed/established [ἐστήρικται, *estēriktai* (perfect tense)]." Even more shocking to the rich man, the sides have been switched, with him agonizing in the flames of Hades while Lazarus basks in Abraham's bosom. There must be some serious mix-up, prompting the rich man to play true to form and *presume* on his familial bond with Abraham and right to menial service by Lazarus: "*Father* Abraham . . . *send* [πέμψον, *pempson* (imperative)] Lazarus to dip the tip of his finger in water and cool my tongue" (16:24). His calling Lazarus by name shows that he recognizes this one he had habitually neglected. But the rich man continues to accord no respect to the poor beggar; even now, beyond the grave, if Lazarus is good for anything, it is to *help the rich man in his discomfort*!

Abraham tries to set him straight, tenderly it must be said, addressing the rich man as "child," but firmly. Life and afterlife, earth and heaven, track across an interconnected, space-time continuum in God's universe. The rich man, for all his claiming of Abrahamic heritage, has not *acted like* a child of Abraham and Abraham's God (cf. 3:8–9), particularly in *alienating himself* from poor fellow children (brothers) like Lazarus. By neglecting Lazarus, the rich man has effectively segregated himself from God's household and stoked the flames of his own hellish destiny. He is not so much consigned to Hades by divine judgment as confined there by his self-absorbed myopia.[275]

The rich man thus suffers from a destructive dearth of proper *self-knowledge* evidenced in a dismissive distortion of *neighbor-knowledge* and, ultimately, in a practical devaluation of *Scripture-knowledge* (16:27–31). For all his social prestige and economic prosperity, he is epistemologically and ethically destitute. He has no moral purchase on "good" and "evil" because he has no appreciation

275. In a sharp "feminine" (which she prefers to "feminist") challenge to this story, philosopher and education theorist Nel Noddings (*Caring*) decries the callous judgment of "harsh father" Abraham (God's surrogate) against one of his needy children, a stance no decent mother could conceive of taking: "This is not the love of the mother, for even in despair she would cast herself across the chasm to relieve the suffering of her child. If he calls her, she will respond. Even the wickedest, if he calls, she must meet as one-caring. Now, I ask again, what ethical need has woman for God?" (97–98). Though I appreciate this maternal critique (similar to that of the missing mother in the prodigal tale), it underplays the emphasis I've highlighted on the mature man-"child's" personal responsibility, not to mention the tragedy of Mother-Christ's frustrated longing to protect her "chicks" when they simply refuse to follow her way (Luke 13:34–35).

for their inextricable linkage to one's material management of "good/evil *things* [τὰ ἀγαθά/τὰ κακά, *ta agatha/ta kaka* (16:25)]" (like food, clothing, bodily pain, disease) to promote his and *his neighbors'* embodied flourishing.[276] But still he pushes his case, daring once more to presume on Abraham's paternal favor and Lazarus's servile status, impelling "Father" Abraham to "send" (πέμπω, *pempō* again) Lazarus to the rich man's five living brothers to persuade them to "repent" (16:27–30). While at least showing some concern for others, he constricts his benevolent circle to the male members of his immediate family (he never calls Lazarus "brother"). And though acknowledging his brothers' need for repentance, the rich man never confesses his own sin, even in his torment, or specifies what transformative action his brothers should take. Somehow he thinks that Lazarus's postmortem epiphany will jolt them into some change of behavior, whatever that might be. We might envision an opportunity to redress the former mistreatment of Lazarus, to welcome him at last inside the gate at the family table. But the rich man proves more interested in what Lazarus can do for his brothers than what they can do for him. In this scheme, Lazarus functions as little more than a fire insurance agent, dispatched to "warn" the five brothers "so that they will not also come to this place of torment" (16:28).

In any case, father Abraham is no more disposed to grant this second request than the first. Lazarus isn't going anywhere, whether across to Hades or back to his former world for the rich man's sake. They have all the revelation they need in the *scriptural law and prophets*, the road map of God's way and manual of God's realm, laying out with abundant clarity God's concern for the poor. Repentance by the rich man's brothers or anyone else begins with adherence to God's just and merciful word. Fair enough, but surely a personal postresurrection witness would speed the repentance process along? Not necessarily, in Abraham's view: "If they do not listen to Moses and the prophets, neither will they be convinced even if someone rises from the dead" (16:31). The evidentiary value of postresurrection appearances is more limited than we might appreciate, not least because of humans' capacity for delusion and lack of acuity in discerning the "thin" thresholds between visible and invisible, immanent and transcendent reality.[277] If one can't read the patent words of Scripture, it is doubtful one will have better luck with *rightly* reading otherworldly visions. Indeed, Scripture provides fundamental and critical checks on fanciful

276. In a stimulating study, Brookins ("Dispute") contrasts Luke's integrated view of ethics and embodied life in this parable with Stoic virtues of good and evil markedly detached from variable, "indifferent" (ἀδιάφορα, *adiaphora*) material, epidemiological, and emotional elements.

277. On "thin places," drawn from Celtic spirituality, where invisible divine reality shines through the visible world, see Borg, *Heart*, 155–63; Newell, *Rebirthing*, 46, 59.

flights of spiritual imagination, not in an "imperious way" like an "academic magisterium," but through the inspired (inspirited) guidance of the Holy Spirit.[278]

This provocative closing statement about the ambiguous testimony of someone raised from the dead alerts us to potential difficulties in spreading the gospel of Jesus's resurrection. He has already predicted that he will die and "on the third day be raised" (9:22), but his closest followers have shown little sign of accepting this destiny, still less of understanding its significance. Many Jews—including the Pharisees—believed in a *general resurrection* of God's children at the end of the age, but this hope did not typically extend to interim resurrections or to prophetic missions *back to* the present world (Moses and Elijah's mountaintop discussion with Jesus is unique). As Luke's final chapter demonstrates, Jesus's own postresurrection appearances are not met with instant recognition. Moreover, the risen Jesus will reiterate the present parable's conclusion concerning the revelatory primacy of holy writ: "Oh, how foolish you are, and how slow of heart to believe all that the prophets have declared! . . . Then beginning with Moses and all the prophets, he interpreted to them the things about himself in all the scriptures" (24:25, 27; cf. vv. 44–47).

Forgiving Disciples and Serving Apostles (17:1–10)

This passage, like 16:16–18, has often been viewed as a random olio of teachings bearing little connection to its narrative setting. Luke knew these sayings from the Synoptic tradition (cf. Matt 17:20; 18:6–7, 21–22; Mark 9:42; 11:22–23) but supposedly didn't know how to weave them into his story. But closer examination again uncovers a more "orderly account" (1:3) and logical progression. For example, the theme of *repentance*, highlighted in the "lost" parables (15:7, 10, 21) and at the end of the directly preceding story (16:30–31), carries over into 17:3–4. Likewise, issues of *brotherly relations* (ἀδελφός, *adelphos* [17:3]), *debt forgiveness* (17:4), *faith/faithfulness* (17:5), and *table fellowship* (17:7–10) figured prominently in Luke 15–16. Luke continues to develop these key themes (not merely catchword links) in 17:1–10.

Jesus shifts his prime attention back to the disciples (17:1), with particular aim at the apostles (17:5), his twelve chosen delegates (cf. 6:13; 9:10–12). Overall, however, Jesus's tone remains critical, warning ("Woe"/"Be on your guard" [17:3]) and exhorting ("So you also, when you have done all that you were ordered to do . . ." [17:10]) his disciples and apostles as much as he has challenged the scribes and Pharisees. Jesus's followers may well have thought

278. Webster, *Holy Scripture*, 128; cf. 2 Tim 3:15–17.

themselves exempt from his polemic against wealthy Pharisees. Surely they who left their homes and businesses for the sake of God's realm are on the side of poor Lazarus and father Abraham. Surely they tread the straight and narrow way of the Law and Prophets. What need do they have for repentance? From Jesus's perspective, however, his own people—including the Twelve—run just as much risk as the Pharisees of falling into the trap of self-justification (cf. 16:13–14). Before journeying any further, Jesus calls his confidants to stop and take stock of roadblocks and pitfalls in their own lives.

Forgiving Disciples (17:1–4)

Actually, Jesus first warns the disciples about *being stumbling blocks* to others, especially "one of these little ones [μικρῶν, *mikrōn*]" (17:2). However high they may advance in God's kingdom, they must never do anything to offend or oppress those reckoned "least" or "littlest" by any measure. For in God's economy the so-called least (μικροί, *mikroi*) rank as the greatest and worthiest of hospitable attention on the same level as Jesus and God (7:28; 9:48). The disciples have been slow to grasp this radical egalitarian ethic, and Jesus has no intention of letting the point slide. He punctuates it with a shocking penal image: mistreatment of "little ones" deserves a punishment worse than being thrown overboard into the chaotic sea with a massive millstone as a noose (modern Mafia equivalent: thrown into the river in concrete boots) (17:2). A hyperbole, to be sure—but one that sinks home—with particular focus on intracommunal, interdisciple relations.

In a sense, all disciples are "little ones" who have humbly acknowledged their sinfulness (cf. 5:8) and frailty before God and received God's uplifting, forgiving grace. Accordingly, they are called to fellowship with other forgiven "little ones," who continue to falter and offend, thereby needing forgiveness and restoration *from one another*. God's kingdom becomes a community of reconciliation, a lighthouse of forgiveness to an embittered world: forgiving as we ourselves have been forgiven (11:4). Such forgiveness is not cheap, however: a wayward "brother" must be shown the error of his ways ("rebuke the offender") and spurred toward a change of conduct ("repentance") (17:3). But neither is it chintzy: no "three strikes you're out" policy; if the brother stumbles "seven times a day" and repents each time, "you must forgive" every time (17:4).

The fraternal context and concern for repentance/forgiveness challenge the disciples (as much as the Pharisees) to examine themselves in light of Jesus's recent parabolic teaching. How would *they* respond to the returning younger brother who had wasted family resources? Would *they* react more like the father or the elder brother? Would *they* merely reduce their debtors' accounts, like the dismissed manager in the next parable, or remit them altogether? Are *they* as keenly observant of the Torah/prophet Jubilee ethic as they think they are? Is Lazarus welcome at *their* table as a true brother, and are *they* encouraging their tighter-knit brothers, as the rich man belatedly wished he had, to repent and follow the scriptural path of hospitable ministry? The shoe often pinches hardest on local levels of familial, congregational, and neighborhood relations. But God's creational purpose and covenantal plan to bless "all the families of the earth" through father Abraham (Gen 12:3) extends the conciliatory vision to national and international horizons, such as those that theologians and other thinkers have advocated, for example, in violently segregated Balkan, South African, Northern Irish, Israeli-Palestinian, and US contexts.[279]

Serving Apostles (17:5–10)

In response to Jesus's summons to forgive others, the apostles pipe up with a curious request: "Increase our faith!" (17:5). Though ostensibly a welcome petition, especially in view of the apostles' prior deficiencies in faith (8:22–25; 9:37–42), it may not spring from altogether pure motives. For one thing, their faith plea follows abruptly on the heels of Jesus's forgiveness mandate, as if to change the uncomfortable subject: "Forgiving others is well and good, Lord, but we're more interested in performing greater feats of faith" (cf. 10:17). Jesus's chosen twelve right-hand men tend to think more highly of themselves than they ought and to seek greater signs of their authority rather than more opportunities to love others as themselves (9:10–17, 32–43, 49–50; 22:24–30). In the present case, they assume they have a strong faith foundation on which to build, meriting an "increase" in faith and responsibility; having proven faithful in little, they deem themselves ready to be faithful in more (cf. 12:48; 16:10–12).

But Jesus is not so sanguine about the apostles' faith prospects yet. He responds with a conditional statement, the first part (protasis) posing: "*If* you have faith [εἰ ἔχετε, *ei echete*] as [small as] a mustard grain" (17:6 AT). This is *not* a contrary-to-fact clause ("If you had faith, which you obviously do not"). Jesus grants, for the sake of argument, that the apostles *do have faith*, at least a modicum, a tiny mustard seed's worth. And that amount is quite sufficient; in God's realm, faith is not measured in quantitative, worldly terms (cf. 13:20–21).

279. Cf. Volf, *Exclusion* (Balkans); Tutu, *No Future* (South Africa); Luskin, *Forgive* (Northern Ireland); Ateek, *Palestinian Christian Cry*; King, *Strength*, 43–52 (US). See discussion below on Jesus's prayer of forgiveness from the cross (Luke 23:34).

The calculus of faith/faithfulness factors not how much one has but what one does with whatever one has; and in fact one can do amazing things with a little faith. In the conclusion (apodosis) to the condition, Jesus claims that if the apostles have even a speck of faith, *then* they "could say to this mulberry tree, 'Be uprooted and planted in the sea,' and it would obey you" (17:6).[280]

To be sure, Jesus chooses an odd example. Why would he or his apostles care about nautical reforestation? Transplanting a mulberry tree in the ocean seems more like the violent act of a hurricane than a benevolent act of faith. At least Jesus stops talking about drowning the disciples in the sea! Obviously he again exploits a hyperbolic sea scenario for effect. The literal action is beside the point (no walking the plank; no flying trees). Faithful living in an unstable, chaotic world and exercising faith to make right, to "uproot and replant," a topsy-turvy world (cf. 3:4–6; Acts 17:6): that is what matters. The apostles must seriously assess why they want more faith and how they are exercising the faith they already have. In short: why are they following Jesus?

Now that he has their attention, Jesus clarifies the thrust of the apostles' mission, which is not faith for faith's sake or tree-moving faith as a status-boosting spectacle, but rather faithful *service* to the Lord. Once more Jesus spins an illuminating parable: "Who among you [Twelve] would say to your slave who has just come in from plowing or tending sheep in the field . . . ?" (17:7). Jesus hooks the apostles from the start, playing to their sense of privileged leadership over other disciple-servants imaged again as those who plow fields and pastor sheep (cf. 8:4–15; 9:62; 15:3–7). He casts them as masters, though in actuality no apostle owned slaves or belonged to elite society. But no doubt they enjoy the role-playing, all the more so as Jesus appears to fluff their lordly pillows. No typical master would greet a hard-working slave at day's end with a "thank you," much less an offer to serve supper to his underling (17:7–9). A slave's work is never done. The day shift in the fields or pastures gives way to the night shift in the house preparing and serving dinner *for* the master.

We have already seen that, while Jesus often depicts master-slave relations for illustrative purposes without explicitly denouncing the socioeconomic system, he also drops some deconstructive signs through role reversals, such as the master who, returning late at night to awaiting slaves, promptly "fastens his belt" and *serves them* at table (12:35–38). The apostles heard that story, though Peter did query whether it was meant "for us or for everyone" (12:41). In any case, it is doubtful that they register Jesus's cue in the present parable. To para-

280. The most common mulberry or sycamine (συκάμινος, *sykaminos*) tree in the Middle East is the hardy black mulberry variety, which grows about thirty feet high with a "stout trunk" (Moldenke and Moldenke, *Plants*, 140-41).

phrase: "Would any of you master-types thank your hard-working slaves and don your aprons to serve them? *Would you not rather* insist the slaves get busy fixing your supper?" (17:7-9).[281] Assuming that is exactly what the apostles would prefer and hearing no objections, Jesus suddenly shifts their roles and pulls the rug out from under them: "So *you also*, when *you* have done all that you were ordered to do, say, '*We are worthless slaves*; *we* have done only what *we* ought to have done!'" (17:10).

Wait a second! What just happened? Stunningly, after inviting the apostles to indulge in their inflated kyriarchal self-image, Jesus reminds them of their true calling—the calling of all followers of the Servant-Lord—as *servants of all*. They are "worthless [ἀχρεῖοι, *achreioi*] slaves" at that—not good-for-nothing lowlifes (though earthly masters might treat their slaves thus)—yet ones working not for pay but out of indebtedness to an overlord: doing "what we ought/owe [ὠφείλομεν, *ōpheilomen*]." As discussed above concerning the dishonest/prudent manager, earthly creditors may abuse or manipulate their debtors for their own interests, getting as much "worth" out of bound servants as they can. But the God whose kingdom the apostles serve and the Christ who models servant ministry exercise an altogether *gracious, benevolent lordship* that seeks the good of its subjects and forgives their debts in a bond of faithful love. As Christ's chief ambassadors, the apostles find their greatest worth in serving God and God's people: the higher the position, the greater the responsibility for service and the heavier sense of duty (9:48; 22:24–27).

The astute homiletics scholar Richard Lischer incisively captures the thrust of Christian ministerial duty in light of Luke's parable:

> Hello, my name is Richard. I'll be your server this morning. And when you are sick, I'll kneel beside your hospital bed and pray for you; and when you are sad or angry, I'll sit at your kitchen table and listen; and when you are hungry and thirsty for redemption, I'll meet you at the table and ask, "Would you like to hear about our specials?" "The body of Christ given for you, the blood of Christ shed for you." No need to thank me. It is almost bad form to do so. I am only the servant. It is my duty.[282]

The little story in 17:7–9 may function not only to reinforce the nexus between leadership and service in God's kingdom, but also to neutralize distinctions

281. Lischer (*Reading*) offers an apt modern parallel: "What is true of the world of the waiter, worker, and maid applies also to the hairdresser, garage mechanic, grocery clerk, and flight attendant. Who among us will say to any of them, 'Why do not you sit down and rest? Let me help you'" (144).

282. Lischer, *Reading*, 145.

between *types of service*, especially between itinerant evangelism and residential hospitality.[283] Despite Jesus's merging of preaching and feeding, sowing the word and serving at table, the apostles prefer public performance and being catered to upon returning from their missions (cf. 9:10–17; Acts 6:1–6).[284] As Paul Minear discerns the purpose of the present tale: "The parable presupposes that the apostolic evangelists have a penchant for claiming that their work is finished when they come from the field into the house; they also have a tendency to assign priority and superiority to their 'field work.' The parable counters this tendency with the insistence that the same servants must fulfill both extramural and intramural duties to their lord"—"the double obligation of the apostle both to wait on table and to preach the word."[285]

Stage 3: Choosing to Restore and Welcome in the Face of Ingratitude and Otherness (17:11–18:30)

At the start of the Travel Narrative's third stage, we read that Jesus is still making his "way to Jerusalem," without learning much more about his precise whereabouts. He continues roaming "between" or "in the middle of [διὰ μέσον, *dia meson*]" the bordering regions of Samaria and Galilee (17:11). But Luke remains more concerned about *social* cartography than GPS tracking. Throughout his journey, Jesus purposes to seek and to save the lost, to retrieve and restore God's people—to act as *go-between*—reconciling conflicting groups such as Zion-oriented Jews and Gerizim-directed Samaritans. Although Jesus's first move toward Jewish-Samaritan détente faltered (9:51–56), he pressed on in the parable of the compassionate Samaritan (10:30–37) and now in a healing incident involving a mixed group of Jewish and Samaritan lepers (17:12–19), in which one cured Samaritan leper "turns/returns" (ὑποστρέφω, *hypostrephō*) to praise God and thank Jesus (17:15–18).

This opening incident again previews key themes to follow in this leg of the journey. Restoration of outsiders at odds with establishment figures, like judges (18:1–8) and rulers (18:18–26), takes top priority. After showcasing Jesus's outreach to Samaritans and lepers, stage 3 features Jesus's concern for widows (18:1–8), tax collectors (18:9–14), and children (18:15–17), along with Pharisees (17:20–21; 18:9–14) and disciples (17:22; 18:28–30)—all character-types

283. On this division and conflict between itinerant and residential forms of ministry in the early church, see 2 John 7–10; 3 John 9–10; 2 Tim 3:6–9; Did. 11:1–2; cf. Theissen, *Sociology*, 8–23; Koenig, *Hospitality*, 85–123.

284. See Spencer, *Portrait*, 199–211, and "Neglected Widows."

285. Minear, "Note," 85, 86.

previously embraced and/or challenged by Luke's Jesus. The recurrence of these diverse, and often divided, figures and the snail-like progress to Jerusalem suggest the difficulty of overcoming long-standing prejudices and hierarchies, demanding indefatigable persistence. The path to peace is long and hard.

The goal of such conciliatory work is not merely a cease-fire or absence of conflict, but nothing less than *holistic salvation*, as confirmed in Jesus's final word to the grateful Samaritan leper, reminiscent of previous statements to healed and forgiven persons: "Get up and go on your way; your faith has made you well/whole/saved [σέσωκεν, *sesōken*] you" (17:19; cf. 7:9–10, 50; 8:47–48). Such salvation also remains possible, though admittedly harder, for self-assured, wealthy rulers (18:24–25). But Jesus insists that God, who specializes in treating "impossible" cases, can soften hard hearts and save elites and unfortunates alike (18:27). "Then who can be saved [σωθῆναι, *sōthēnai*]?" (18:26). Answer: *anyone*, since God is the Savior (σωτήρ, *sōtēr*), as Mary intoned (1:47).

Grateful and Ungrateful Lepers (17:11–19)

In the precarious borderlands between Samaria and Galilee, Jesus "entered a [certain] village [τινα κώμην, *tina kōmēn*)" of unspecified demographics (17:12). With the probability of some Samaritan population in the area, however, we expect some opposition to the Jerusalem-bound Jesus, based on his earlier aborted foray into an unwelcoming Samaritan town (9:51–56). Despite his engaging parable about a model, magnanimous Samaritan traveler, Jesus has thus far healed no Samaritan, dined in no Samaritan home, and enlisted no Samaritan disciple; and no Samaritan has commended him. But that is all about to change.

Ten Receive God's Healing (17:11–14)

This time Jesus has no problem entering a village. But his initial greeters are scarcely city officials or respectable citizens. He is first approached by a company of ten lepers, including at least one Samaritan (17:12, 16). Early in his ministry, Jesus happily received a lone individual "covered with leprosy," cured him by touch, and sent him to the priests for certification (5:12–15). Likewise, he heals the present group of lepers and dispatches them to the priests for examination (17:14). But some key distinctions also emerge. Unlike the previous leper, who bowed down at Jesus's feet (5:12), the current company encounters Jesus while still maintaining a safe "distance" (πόρρωθεν, *porrōthen*) from him, close enough to plead for help but far enough to avoid contact, as proscribed by Mosaic law. Furthermore, whereas the earlier leper addressed Jesus as Lord (κύριε, *kyrie* [5:12]), these lepers call him by name and a different title: "Jesus, Master [ἐπιστάτα, *epistata*]" (17:13). To whatever extent the first man understood Jesus's lordship, he used the higher christological title. The latter group, however, opts for a lesser, though still respectful, designation: the same "Master" term Peter and other disciples use in situations of fear and doubt, drawing Jesus's corrective retort (see above on 5:5; 8:24, 45; 9:33). We're not sure what to expect now. Given Jesus's compassionate outreach to lepers, will he call these ten closer and lay healing hands on them? However he cures them, will he also chide their lack of faith and commitment, evidenced in "keeping their distance" and their somewhat lukewarm "Master" address?

As it happens, "when he saw them" (and presumably heard them), rather than inviting them to come closer, Jesus promptly sends the lepers away to the priests (17:14). But the only reason for lepers to go to cultic-legal authorities is for inspection and reinstatement into society, and, curiously, Jesus *has not yet* cured their skin diseases. The cure ("cleansing") occurs only "as they went [ἐν τῷ ὑπάγειν αὐτούς, *en tō hypagein autous*]" (17:14)—that is, *in the process of their going* to the priests. This procedure is significant for two reasons.

First, Jesus's seeing the lepers and responding to their need *at a distance*, far from being an arms-length, half-hearted gesture, recalls the parable father's merciful response to his wayward son: "While he was *still far off*, his father saw him and was filled with compassion" (15:20). By social definition, lepers are outcasts, far from the hearth of a loving household. Any *Samaritan* lepers would be judged as doubly exiled in traditional Jewish eyes. As the Master of God's household, however, Jesus reaches out to these lepers by word (rather than hand this time) and invites them to wholeness and homecoming through proper legal channels.

Second, the healing process in this incident further develops Luke's understanding of faith/faithfulness along the lines of the *obedience of faith*, to borrow from Paul (Rom 1:5; 16:26), or *faith evidenced in action*, as James assesses the faithful works of Abraham and Rahab (Jas 2:18–26). The ten lepers must trust Jesus's word and act upon it *before* seeing tangible results. They must "walk by faith" (2 Cor 5:7), or in language more fitting Luke's narrative, they, like Jesus and his followers, must *journey by faith* along a rough, narrow road, seeking and finding rest and restoration "on the way."

One Returns to Give Thanks (17:15–19)

But the faithful journey demands more than obeying the Lord's word, receiving the Lord's blessing, and proceeding along one's way. As the trio of prophetic hymns signaled at the beginning of Luke (1:46–55, 67–79; 2:28–32), the way of God in Christ is a *worshipful* way, a pilgrimage of praise to God and Christ, not because their egos need stroking, but because God's people need sustaining on the journey by joyful reliance on the Creator God, the Messiah Son, and the Holy Spirit. The goal is not merely regaining lost health, but maintaining and strengthening wholeness in grateful fellowship with God and God's community. Recent studies of the "science of gratitude," demonstrating the benefits of a thankful disposition, reinforce what the Psalms and a robust theology of worship have long understood.[286]

With an inflated sense of self-importance, however, humans are not naturally inclined to thank others. Recall Jesus's recent point about the absurdity of masters' thanking their slaves (17:9). This pattern follows with ten cured lepers (though here the flow of gratitude runs toward the benevolent "Master" Jesus)—with one notable exception. One healed leper delays his priestly visit and returns to praise (δοξάζω, *doxazō*) God and thank (εὐχαριστέω, *eucharisteō*) Jesus (17:15–16).[287] In turn, Jesus accepts his grateful response and laments the absence of the "other nine" (17:17–18), though he doesn't threaten to rescind their healing, since they were, after all, simply following his instructions to go and show themselves to the priests. Moreover, while some beneficiaries of Jesus's aid have responded by praising God (7:16; 9:43; 13:13), Jesus has never solicited a "thank you" for his ministry. Yet, his obvious puzzlement over the nine's not returning with the one thankful client implies some disappointment over their more tenuous connection to God's realm: though physically and socially restored, they opt to "keep their distance" from Jesus's way.

What most sets apart the lone leper, however, and makes his gratitude more remarkable, is his identity as a *Samaritan*, whom Jesus further dubs as a "foreigner" or "foreign breed," as Dennis Hamm renders the term ἀλλογενής (*allogenēs*), used only here (17:18) in the NT and hauntingly matching the "No Trespassing" signs in the Jerusalem temple, inscribed in Hebrew, Latin, and Greek, prohibiting access to any ἀλλογενῆ (*allogenē*)—on "pain of death"—

286. Emmons, *Thanks!*; Emmons and McCollough, *Psychology of Gratitude*; Frank, *Success*, 98–103; cf. Roberts, *Spiritual Emotions*, 130–47.

287. Hamm ("What the Samaritan Leper Sees," 283) notes the striking parallel with the shepherds' response to meeting Jesus in the nativity scene: "The shepherds returned, glorifying and praising God for all they had heard and seen" (Luke 2:20).

from the Court of the Gentiles into inner, sacred precincts.[288] We should remember that the ethnic-genetic relationship between Samaritans and Jews, while disputed, is much closer than between both groups and Gentiles. But "foreigner" is a slippery label for all types of alien "others" (ἄλλοι, *alloi*). Here Luke's Jesus uses the term in the sense that many Jews applied to Samaritans. But he immediately deconstructs it. Though considered "foreign" to God's kingdom by Jerusalem-centered Jews, this Samaritan has proved himself more faithful to God's way than many of Jesus's compatriots. We do not know whether all nine other lepers were Jews, but the narrative dynamics demand that at least some, even most, were Jews in this border zone between Galilee and Samaria. While their common leprous condition nullified ethnic social distinctions, sadly, after their healing, old prejudices come back to life—*except* (εἰ μή, *ei mē*) for one Samaritan who returns to praise the God of Israel (including Samaria) and the Jewish Messiah Jesus. He alone grasps the big restoration picture; he alone demonstrates a full measure of *faith* (πίστις, *pistis* [17:19]), not unlike the "foreign" centurion Jesus dealt with earlier (7:9).

In an ironic twist, the grateful Samaritan turns back *to* rather than turning his back *from* the Lord, as Jesus has warned his followers not to do (9:62; cf. 17:31–32). In another apparently surprising move, Jesus tells the thankful, faithful Samaritan to "go on your way" in his "saved" condition (17:19). Why not, "Come and follow me?" For one thing, the Samaritan still needs to see the priest to be fully reincorporated into society (both Jesus and the Samaritans were Torah observant).[289] Perhaps also Jesus does not wish to complicate this Samaritan's life unduly by bringing him to Jerusalem. But most important, the way of God led by Luke's Jesus is principally a communal, ethical, and spiritual path through the world, illustrated by, but not limited to, Jesus's literal journey to Jerusalem or any other locale. The way of the restored Samaritan leper—solidified and nurtured by worship and gratitude to God and Jesus—marks the true way of God's kingdom.[290]

288. Hamm, "What the Samaritan Leper Sees," 273, 284–85; see Josephus, *Ant.* 15.417; BDAG, 46.

289. I. Howard Marshall suggests that the plural "priests" (ἱερεῖς, *hiereis*) in 17:14 indicates that "each man would go to the appropriate priest," that is, to either Jewish (Jerusalem) or Samaritan (Shechem/Gerizim) officials (651). Though sharing common devotion to Torah regulations, Jews and Samaritans worshiped at different holy sites superintended by different priestly leaders.

290. Hamm ("What the Samaritan Leper Sees") observes that Luke's description of the Samaritan's faith in action evinces a "high Christology," virtually equating "praising God" (17:15, 18) with "thanking Jesus" (17:16) (284, 286–87). This divine linkage is solidified by the fact that all other uses of εὐχαριστέω (*eucharisteō*) in Luke and Acts are directed *to God* (18:11; 22:17, 19; Acts 27:35; 28:15).

Keen and Dull Observers (17:20–37)

Having ministered to ten lepers, particularly one exceptional Samaritan among them, Jesus resumes his alternating discussions with the Pharisees (17:20–21) and his own disciples (17:22–37).[291] But the healing incident should not be viewed as an intrusive aberration; neither should the Pharisees' ensuing question about God's kingdom be taken as disjunctive. The word "once," beginning 17:20 in the NRSV and NIV ("Once [upon a time] Jesus was asked by the Pharisees") is not in the Greek and creates an unwarranted awkward transition. As Jesus's main interlocutors throughout the Travel Narrative, the Pharisees and Jesus's disciples may be regarded as *implied observers* of the leper incident, which then, in its strategic position at the head of stage 3, introduces the discussion that follows. More pointedly, the Samaritan leper models the perception, faith, and practice expected of faithful pilgrims, including the Pharisees. The *perceptive* dimension remains salient in Jesus's traveling seminar aimed at solidifying experiential knowledge of God's rule among Pharisees, other legal scholars, and his own disciples. In formulaic terms, keen seeing = true knowing/perceiving → faithful action: "When [Jesus] *saw* [ἰδών, *idōn*] them [the pleading ten lepers]," he perceived (grasped, internalized) their need and moved to help them; likewise, when the Samaritan leper "*saw* [ἰδών, *idōn*] that he was healed," he perceived (grasped, internalized) his changed condition and moved to praise God and thank Jesus personally (17:14–15). The Pharisees and the disciples, however, prove not to be such keen observers.

The Pharisees and the Kingdom of God (17:20–21)

The Pharisees raise the basic temporal question about God's dominion that has preoccupied many Jews and Christians to the present day, asking "*when* [πότε, *pote*] the kingdom of God was coming" (17:20a). This concern aligns with other queries about signs and times from the crowds and Jesus's disciples (11:16, 29–30; 21:7; Acts 1:6). Inquiring minds want to know *when* God's way will finally win. Surprisingly, given the recent emphasis on perception, Jesus first responds negatively, indicating that God's coming kingdom is *not* discernible

291. Green nicely sums up the modulation and interconnection between Pharisees and disciples, especially in Luke 15–17: "The move back and forth between Pharisees (along with legal experts) and disciples has been normal fare in chs. 15–17, highlighting the permeable quality of the perimeter separating the two. The Pharisees continue to be instructed by Jesus, for they may yet respond to his message; the disciples continue in their susceptibility to the miscalculations concerning the purpose of God otherwise characteristic of the Pharisees" (631).

by *observation* (παρατήρησις, *paratērēsis* [Luke 17:20b]). It *cannot be seen*, at least not on the level the Pharisees are looking. The term connotes *close examination*, which seems like a good, attentive response. But Luke's two uses of the cognate verb παρατηρέω (*paratēreō*) reference the Pharisees' *sinister inspection* of Jesus, in hopes of catching him in medical malpractice of Sabbath law (6:7; 14:1). Careful attention to Jesus's deeds is admirable, but it can still miss the point. Seeing is not always perceiving. One can look intently at the right thing for the wrong reason. So when Jesus healed the man's withered hand (6:6–10) and another's dropsy (14:1–6), the Pharisees clearly observed the therapeutic events but totally misread their significance as transgressing God's law rather than expressing God's re-creative reign.

In the present situation, they fall into a similar epistemological trap, seeing but not perceiving the *sign*ificance of Jesus's miracles as evidence of God's restorative work. They want something special to pop "here" or "there," when Jesus has already revealed God's dynamic realm "among/within you [ἐντὸς ὑμῶν, *entos hymōn*]," within their midst, right under their noses (17:21).[292] What more evidence could they want than curing a group of lepers and sparking faithful devotion to God by a Samaritan? These are patent signs of God's rule manifest "today": "the lepers are cleansed" (7:22); "foreigners" are bowing before the true God and God's Messiah.

Though granting that God's rule unfolds inexorably in creation beneath the surface of naked phenomena (cf. 13:18–21), in Luke's theological story the realized immanence (it is here now), along with expected imminence (it is coming soon), of God's reign in the world is manifest most clearly in the palpable *saving acts* of Christ and in Christ's name. "Kingdom of God" constitutes a living, embodied transformative reality, not a grand utopian idea, abstract philosophical concept, or antiseptic celestial wonderland. It brings God's peace and healing power house to house, town to town. In this grounded, dust-on-the-feet, salvific mission, the kingdom of God has not only "come near" (ἤγγικεν, *ēngiken* [10:9, 11]) but has

292. The precise meaning of ἐντός (*entos*) is highly debated between the options of "within" (personal-psychological) and "among" (social-environmental). BDAG acknowledges that the term can "pertain to a specific area inside something, *inside, within, within the limits of*," such as "within your heart" (Pss 38:4; 102:1; 109:22); in Luke 17:21, however, "the sense *among you, in your midst*, either now or suddenly in the near future" seems more apt (340). For patristic interpretations, see Baarda ("Luke 17,21"), who argues that the Syrian church father Ephraem applied both meanings: "within" in his Diatessaron and "among" from the *Vetus Syra*, which "he adopted in the hymns against the heretics" (293); and Michaels ("Almsgiving"), who favors Tertullian's ethical reading of "within you" in Luke 17:21 as "'in your hands' or 'within your power,' in the sense that the Pharisees, as 'lovers of money' (Luke 16:14), had the opportunity to open their hands in reckless generosity to the poor" (481; cf. Luke 11:41; 18:18–27; Tertullian, *Marc.* 4.35–36).

arrived in some measure. It is already releasing the oppressed from evil, harmful forces and drawing them, here and now, into the orbit of the gracious, right-making realm of God: "But if it is by the finger of God that I cast out the demons, then the kingdom has come to/upon/unto you [ἐφ' ὑμᾶς, *eph' hymas*]" (11:20). Jesus's matter-of-fact statement in 17:21, following the healing of the ten lepers, that "the kingdom of God within/among you [simply] *is* [ἐστιν, *estin*]" (AT, reflecting Greek word order) conveys an even more immanent and pervasive sense of God's active rule in the present world. Jesus thus invites the Pharisees' participation in God's manifest saving work here and now. To fixate too much on the future, on "when" God will finally take care of business, betrays not only ignorance of what God *is* doing but also *ingratitude*, like the nine cured lepers. Put positively, praise and thanksgiving are portals into God's kingdom and prompts to participate in its restorative work in the world.

Luke's belief in God's saving interventions in the world through Christ raises a core theological problem for many moderns presuming a closed environment bound by natural laws of cause and effect. If lepers get well, it is because biological healing processes kick in, with or without medical aid. External supernatural powers interfering in this system, whether for good (deities) or ill (demons), are ruled out from the start. One may hold this noninterventionist view along with believing in a Creator-Designer of the whole system, provided that this Prime Mover thereafter lets the universe run on its own steam. Such is the Deist option. But Luke was no Deist. For him, the Lord of heaven and earth continues to be a personal agent involved in the created world through the divine-incarnate Son and the dynamic Holy Spirit. Such involvement entails supernatural influence "within/ among," not simply a fuzzy presence around or amid, us and all things. Luke's God does not merely coach or cheer us to hang in there and do what we can. God continues to create, rule, and work out God's saving purpose.

So Luke is no modern. No news in that. But are we moderns and postmoderns among "the wise and the intelligent," as we like to think (cf. 10:21)? This is not the place to wrestle with all the implications of God's work in the world, particularly why God seems to act in some cases and not others (the theodicy problem). But can we at least posit a personal, agential God operative in some ways within and through us and our environment? The philosopher-theologian Frank Kirkpatrick believes we can on the simple yet profound analogy of human activity in the world, that is, "the way in which human agents jostle each other within the common ontological space of their actions."[293] Though subject to the thick web of physical laws that envelop them, humans routinely

293. Kirkpatrick, *Mystery*, 118.

adjust, disrupt, and "jostle" the outworking of these laws in ways large (flying to the moon, wrecking the ecosystem) and small (swatting a fly, catching a baseball), affecting the course of events by acts of will and power.[294] Succinctly put: "When I act, I do something that overrides or supervenes upon the laws of nature that, in the absence of my action, would produce a result that is completely caused by non-agential forces."[295]

It then reasonably follows, in Kirkpatrick's view: "If human action can 'intervene' into the causal structures of the world without causing theological or metaphysical apoplexy that such human action is an inexplicable 'ripping' into or a threat to our understanding of worldly events, then why should divine actions evoke such consternation when they, like all actions, intervene in the *otherwise* closed causal nexus?"[296] Overall, Kirkpatrick prefers to speak of God's "supervening" in the world, since God can and, from time to time, does bring superlative divine power to bear upon earthly events and processes. But the point still holds that God, like humans, except to a greater degree and higher good, transforms the world without destroying it, operates on and in it without obliterating it. In Christian terms, this analogous divine and human activity coalesces in the divine-human Christ, the consummate agent of God's rule in the world.

In sum, the pithy announcement of Luke's Jesus that "the kingdom of God is among/within you" (Luke 17:21)—with its tantalizing preposition ἐντός (*entos*), meaning "among/within"—may be elaborated in a surfeit of philosophical terms: "The divine act must preside over, ramify in, unify, deploy, pervade, supervene, be superordinate over, and govern all that falls under its sway and exercise of power. God's act 'enframes' all that is unified within it and grounds the powers that act at subordinate level within the structures that are being unified and deployed."[297] This key "deployment" concept, which Kirkpatrick derives from Edward Pols, is notably distinct from *employment*.[298] In Christian theological terms, the world and we humans within it do *not employ* God as a superservant to cure our ills and feather our nests. God does not work for

294. Of course, as Kirkpatrick (*Mystery*) acknowledges, those who categorically deny human free will would disagree: "This kind of intervention seems unproblematic unless one assumes [as Kirkpatrick does not] that there are *no* free actions; every occurrence being exhaustively determined by causal law" (119 [emphasis original]).

295. Kirkpatrick, *Mystery*, 123.

296. Kirkpatrick, *Mystery*, 113 (emphasis original).

297. Kirkpatrick, *Mystery*, 109. Kirkpatrick mounts no biblical argument (the application to Luke is mine); he primarily dialogues with philosophers Edward Pols, John MacMurray, and Raymond Tallis.

298. Kirkpatrick, *Mystery*, 96, 110; see Pols, *Meditation*.

us. God *deploys* the world and us humans, works upon, within, through, and among us to fulfill God's good purposes.

So Luke's Jesus avers that evidence of God's saving kingdom *is*, in fact, here and there, for those with perceptive eyes and grateful hearts to recognize. But only a naive idealist would claim that God's salutary rule has been fully established here, there, *and everywhere.* A lot more than ten lepers continue to suffer in this world; the vast majority of sufferers remain uncleansed. Most first-century Samaritans and Jews still wanted to wipe each other out. Evil powers still wield considerable authority and wreak terrible havoc. The "here already" of God's restorative work in Christ inspires hopeful endurance, but it leaves a lot of "not yet" to be realized. And no one is more aware than clear-eyed, realistic Jesus of the "much suffering" (17:25) that still plagues this world and of the necessity for God to "come" (again and again) and complete the world-renewing project. He now addresses his disciples (with Pharisees in the background) to alert them to these future comings and troubling state of affairs in the meantime.

The Disciples and the Coming Son of Humankind (17:22–37)

In prophetic-apocalyptic mode, Jesus speaks candidly about coming days of hardship. Things are going to get worse before they are made right once and for all. As time and history march on, the clear light of God's saving operations through Jesus the incarnate Son of God, a.k.a. the Son of Humankind, will temporarily dim, leaving his followers pining to see just "one [more] of the days of the Son of Humankind" which they have enjoyed during Jesus's life; but ominously, "[they] will *not* see it" (17:22).[299] What accounts for this stunning optical shift: now you see it (17:20–21), now you don't (17:22)?

Luke's Jesus has already broached this topic, but with little understanding by his disciples. So he tries again. Jesus's historical, embodied fulfillment of the eschatological, Danielic Son of Humankind redeeming God's people from oppressive rule will unfold across variable "days" (plural) up to "the [singular, climactic, apocalyptic] day that the Son of Humankind is revealed [ἀποκαλύπτεται, *apokalyptetai*]" (17:30).[300] The present "days" in Jesus's com-

299. Here I interpret "one of these days" as a retrospective typical day in Jesus's earthly ministry to which beleaguered followers will long to return. Alternatively, John Carroll (*Response*) takes a prospective angle in which believers "will be eager for just one of the days of bliss" that will mark the coming, future kingdom (92n211).

300. Some ancient witnesses (א, A, L) also attest to the "day" of the Son of Humankind in 17:24—"so will the Son of Man be *in his day*." However, "in his day" is lacking in other key manuscripts (P75, B, D), suggesting that the phrase could have been added to harmonize with 17:30.

pany have been glorious, as Peter, James, and John could attest from their vision of Jesus's transfiguration. But that dramatic event should have also taught them, *if* they were looking and listening carefully, that God's complete world-transformation through God's Son would proceed more deliberately and precariously than they expected. Full restoration of God's creation would occur only after "his *exodus*" (9:31 NAB), after passing through chaotic waters and emerging to renewed life on the other side. The Son of Humankind brings ultimate deliverance not simply from "on high" but from *within* the turbulent storm *among* his distressed people, absorbing their pain and vulnerability, even to the point of death.

So the present *days* of the Son of Humankind's saving acts portend the final *day* of restoration, but only via the essential bridge of suffering and death traversed first by the Son himself and then his followers. Oh to leap right from these marvelous days of leper-cleansing and Samaritan-turning to the great day of universal health and international peace! "*But first* [πρῶτον, *prōton*], he"—Jesus, the Son of Humankind—"*must* [δεῖ, *dei*] *endure much suffering and be rejected* by this generation" (17:25; cf. 9:22, 44–45). There is no other way of salvation except within, among, and out of the depths of despair and death. What, then, are the disciples to do in the meantime, in these hard interim days to come? Following the perception theme, what should they see and know about the course of God's kingdom to guide their faithful service of God in the convulsive transitional world?

First, their vision must remain *focused*. However much they might long for Jesus's consummative return, they must not dash about willy-nilly, chasing hyped-up reports of God's triumphant visitation "there" and "here" (17:23). They can rest assured that God's rule remains active within/among them where they are, even in Jesus's physical absence. Though not emphasized in the present text, Luke's Jesus stresses the Holy Spirit's ongoing operation within/among God's people (11:13; 12:11–12), especially at the threshold of his ascension (24:49; Acts 1:1–8). Even as they do *not know* "the times or periods" God has marked out for the final establishment of the kingdom, Jesus's followers *can know* they will be empowered by God's Spirit throughout the span, short or long, between Jesus's departure and return (Acts 1:6–11). Also, they should know that when the Son of Humankind comes at the final restoration, it will be a cosmic cataclysm, involving upheaval (judgment) and renewal (salvation) that no one can miss or escape. No need to look here or there, since it will be manifest everywhere in pyrotechnic brilliance, "as the lightning flashes and lights up the sky from one side to the other" (Luke 17:24).

But neither is there any call to look transfixed at the sky, waiting for Jesus to come blasting back (cf. Acts 1:10–11). It will happen when it happens. In the meantime, attention must remain trained on living out these days on earth in light of both God's immanent rule being worked out here and now and its transcendent culmination in the age to come. As the German-American Baptist theologian, pastor, and reformer Walter Rauschenbusch encapsulates this tension at the conclusion of *Christianity and the Social Crisis*, "The kingdom of God is always but coming." He was under no illusions about establishing a global utopian community: "At best there is always but an approximation to a perfect social order." But this realization, far from dispiriting Rauschenbusch, only spurred him and his "social gospel" allies to greater involvement in God's way of justice and wholeness in contemporary society: "But every approximation to [God's kingdom] is worthwhile. Every step toward personal purity and peace, though it only makes the consciousness of imperfection more poignant, carries its own exceeding great reward, and everlasting pilgrimage toward the kingdom of God is better than contented stability in the tents of wickedness."[301]

In his own way, Luke's Jesus makes the same point with reference to the *days of Noah and Lot* as prototypical of the interim days preceding the final day of reckoning and renovating. Though Rauschenbusch does not make the connection, "contented stability in the tents of wickedness" perfectly describes the worlds of Noah and Lot. While these worlds conjure up images of violence, immorality, and other forms of gross "wickedness" (Gen 6:1–13; 13:13; 18:20–33; 19:4–11; Wis 10:6–8; 2 Pet 2:4–8), Jesus in fact focuses more on the "contented stability" of these societies in their eyes, rocking along with the business as usual of "eating and drinking, and marrying and being given in marriage, . . . buying and selling, planting and building" (Luke 17:27–28), impervious to God's rule and impending judgment on their false security. Likewise, Jesus's followers risk drifting into careless and carefree routines, losing focus on the urgent business of God's always-but-coming kingdom, especially during the long haul between Jesus's first and final advents. Hence, Jesus's repeated calls to faithfulness and alertness (8:18; 10:23–24; 12:35–48; 13:22–30; 16:10–12).

Second, the "days of Lot" analogy leads to another perceptual-motivational concern: not only to remain focused on pressing kingdom matters here and now, but also to look and to *move forward* (no turning back). The way of discipleship, as plotted in Luke's two volumes, is an advancing *journey* led by Christ and the Spirit through and out to the world,[302] or in Rauschenbusch's terms, an "everlasting pilgrimage."[303] The only backtracking permitted is that modeled

301. Rauschenbusch, *Christianity*, 338.

302. See the discussion of Luke's "spiritual theology" in the concluding "Integration" section.

303. Note that both Luke's Gospel and Acts feature festival pilgrimages to Jerusalem from the outset: Luke 2:41–52 (Passover); Acts 2:1–13 (Pentecost).

by the Samaritan leper: turning back to God/Christ in praise/thanksgiving and then proceeding on one's faithful way (17:15–19). The antitype is Lot's wife, who halted in her flight from firebombed Sodom, looked back, and became a petrified salt block. Her well-known experience is worth contemplating. Though Jesus does not elaborate at length, his exhortation to "remember" her (17:32) culminates a kind of midrash on the story of Lot's wife around the theme of discipleship.[304] Notice the following connections:

- *9:21–25.* Right after first predicting the suffering and death of the Son of Humankind (9:22), Jesus pronounced cross-bearing as a necessary condition of discipleship and paradoxical pathway to salvation: "For those who want to save their life will lose it, and those who lose their life for my sake will save it. What does it profit them if they gain the whole world, but lose or forfeit themselves?" (9:24–25). By stopping, looking back, and emotionally clinging to her "whole world" going up in smoke, Lot's wife loses not only that world but her life as well. Unwilling to move forward, she becomes frozen in place. Longing "to [re]make [her] life secure," she winds up losing it altogether (17:33).
- *9:57–62.* Jesus's God-directed way was anything but settled and secure around traditional havens of home and family. The Son of Humankind "has nowhere to lay his head" (9:58) and brooks no kinship commitments above God's transnatural household, including to one's biological parents, dead or alive (9:59–61). The faithful disciple answers Christ's audacious call to drop everything and "follow me" (cf. 5:27–28). No one who begins the journey and "*looks back* is fit for the kingdom of God" (9:62). Since the Bible does not disclose what motivates Lot's wife to look back on smoldering Sodom, we need not assume her addiction to the city's wicked elements, whatever those might have been. It is sufficient and most natural to posit her close connectedness with the maternal, material, social, quotidian world she's been forced to flee but cannot bring herself to abandon, even if it costs her life. We can easily imagine her lamenting the loss of other family and friends in the burning city, along with her home and possessions, and daily routines of shopping, cooking, dining, sewing, sweeping, gossiping, and so on.[305] But though Luke's Jesus is normally sympathetic to "daily bread" concerns, especially for the poor (which Lot's

304. For a fuller treatment of the reception history of the story of Lot's wife and its links with Luke's narrative, see Spencer, *Salty Wives*, 245–63.

305. For examples of poets and feminist interpreters who appreciate more than excoriate the devotion of Lot's wife to mundane and familial interests, see Spencer, *Salty Wives*, 256–59.

family was not!),[306] he now cautions his disciples against becoming, like Lot's wife, so enmeshed in ordinary business (eating/drinking, buying/selling) as to miss God's renewing movement in the world. Tragically fixed on the settled, static realm of Sodom, Lot's wife becomes "unfit"—permanently ossified—for the propulsive, dynamic realm of God.

- *10:11–12.* Jesus advised his seventy(-two) emissaries not to linger in hostile towns, but rather to (1) shake the dust off their feet in protest; (2) levy a sentence of judgment, "Yet know this: the kingdom of God has come near" (10:11); and (3) leave final reprisals to God "on that day" of reckoning, when "it will be more tolerable for *Sodom* than for that town" (10:12). Note again that Sodom's sin has less to do with overt evil acts than with lack of readiness to welcome God and God's agents. Lot distinguished himself from the mob by hosting, rather than sexually harassing, the angelic visitors, but then he despicably offered his daughters' bodies to appease the rapacious gang (Gen 19:1–8). He eventually left the condemned city, shaking the dust from his feet as it were, but only after "lingering" and being dragged away by the angels (19:15–16). For her part, Lot's wife simply accompanies her husband's exit in the Genesis story, though early Jewish traditions blame her for the earlier fiasco by "sinning in connection with salt" (Gen. Rab. 50:4; 51:5; Tg. Ps.-J. Gen 19:26). That is, failing to stock her cupboard with sufficient cooking salt, she goes begging to her neighbors and, in the process, blabbing about the "male" guests' arrival. Her salty gossip thus alerts the town ruffians to the visitors' presence, and her salt-pillar fate serves her right. Be that as it may, her halting and looking back at Sodom make her complicit in Lot's lingering and suggest a deeper longing for Sodom's hard-set ways than for the pilgrim path of God's righteous rule.
- *14:25–35.* Here Jesus assessed the cost of discipleship in the starkest terms: unless one chooses to "hate" encumbering family members, all possessions, "and even life itself," one cannot be a true follower of God's way (14:26, 33). Such a high price Lot's wife—and most other people—are not willing to pay. For her resistance, however, she pays with her salt-encrusted life—not the good "salt-of-the earth" kind of life,[307] but rather the stale, tasteless kind "fit" for nothing, even the dung heap. Such is the antidisciple with ears blocked against God's word and eyes locked on the

306. On the relatively well-off socioeconomic status of Lot's family, see Spencer, *Salty Wives*, 251–53.

307. See Matt 5:13, "You are the salt of the earth." Oddly, however, Irenaeus co-opts Lot's wife's "pillar of salt" as an image of the enduring *church* in the world, "the foundation of the faith" (*Haer.* 4.31.3; see Spencer, *Salty Wives*, 256).

world's transitory pursuits (Luke 14:34–35). The particular call to abandon all possessions (14:33)—letting them burn, as it were (though elsewhere, Jesus advocates *selling* everything and giving proceeds to the poor [12:33; 18:22])—resonates with Jesus's warning against trying to secure personal belongings in cataclysmic times, like the days of Lot and those precipitating the Son of Humankind's return (17:31). Attempts to save and hold on to perishable goods risks loss of life and limb, as Lot's wife, fixated on her besieged city, house, and furnishings, forfeits her salvation (17:33).

Jesus punctuates ("I tell you") his instruction concerning interim suffering and ultimate reckoning with another assessment of a *divided people*[308] (cf. 12:49–53): some remain faithful and some fall away; some look ahead and some look down; some are "taken" and some are "left [behind]" right up to "that night" of the climactic day of the Son of Humankind's "revelation" (17:34–35). The "taken/left behind" dichotomy, though clearly contrasting two fates, is ambiguous about the respective outcomes. "Taken" or "taken alongside" (παραλαμβάνω, *paralambanō*) to what end: salvation (rescue) or judgment (arrest)? "Left behind" or simply "left" or "let go" (ἀφίημι, *aphiēmi*) to what end: salvation (release, let off the hook) or judgment (abandonment, rejection)? The Lot/Sodom analogy favors taken *away* to safety from the death that befalls those left *behind*,[309] but this story sets no precise agenda of end-time events (which would get awkward if extended to the strange relations between Lot and daughters after being "saved" [Gen 19:30–38]).

Overall, Jesus's language is allusive rather than definitive: he gives no exact accounting of humanity, a 50/50 split, *one* taken for *one* left. He also provides no spatial coordinates for human destinies: the "saved" taken *up* in heavenly rapture, the "damned" left *behind* in hell on earth. In fact, Luke's Jesus uses no specific "up" or "behind" language in this text, much less "heaven" or "hell."[310] His point follows the comparisons with the days of Noah and of Lot. As then, when the Son of Humankind reappears, people will be engaging in *ordinary, everyday* activities, in this case *reclining* in bed and *grinding* at the mill, basic human pursuits of rest and sex ("two in one bed"), work and food (17:34–35). Nothing wrong with these activities—indeed, life in this world depends on them—but they must not be divorced from the top-priority business of God's realm operating within, among, and above these things.

308. See "Divided People," a classic article by Jervell.

309. Carroll, 352.

310. Exposing the flimsy biblical evidence for dispensational "rapture" theology (popularized in the *Left Behind* novel series), see Rossing, *Rapture*; Hill, *In God's Time*, 199–209.

Resting (think Sabbath), having sex (marrying/giving in marriage), working (think Sabbath again) and feeding/eating (central to Jesus's mission) must all be practiced by Jesus's disciples, male and female,[311] in faithful obedience to God's rule and in forward response to God's leadership, ready to move bed, home, job, and table on a dime, to be "taken" into God's saving mission to (*not* out of) the world.

Heady stuff for the disciples to grasp, and they do not seem much more perceptive than the Pharisees. Whereas the Pharisees were stuck on "when" the kingdom would come, the disciples now lodge a banal "*Where*, Lord?" query in response to Jesus's extended comments about God's reign (17:37). Preoccupations with set times and places—which are "not for [us] to know" (Acts 1:7—seem irresistible for millennial kingdom seekers across Christian history.[312] With some exasperation, it seems, Jesus answers with a curt observation as obvious as it is ominous: "Where the corpse is, there the vultures will gather" (17:37). Actually, Luke's text reads, "Where *the body* [τὸ σῶμα, *to sōma*] is," not *corpse* (πτῶμα, *ptōma*), as in Matt 24:28, though vultures in any case prefer to congregate around *dead* bodies. So Jesus utters a truism: when a group of vultures huddle on the ground, it is a good bet that road-kill has drawn them there. No secret there, just as there will be no missing the Son of Humankind's final gathering of his people. When and where it happens will be clear at *that* time and place; in the interim, the disciples need to keep alert and keep attending to kingdom affairs. But is Jesus comparing himself to a predatory vulture or eagle (ἀετός [*aetos*] denotes both raptors) feasting on bloody corpses in the tumultuous final days? After the world deluge and Sodom conflagration, Noah and Lot, respectively, got drunk and were disgraced by their children (Gen 9:20–27; 19:30–38); but nobody cannibalized any corpses in those horrible days. More to the point, Jesus the mother hen who longs to gather his chicks (Luke 13:34) is the antipode of a bloodthirsty carrion feeder.

Perhaps, then, Jesus's violent scenario simply reinforces his stark appraisal of intensified suffering before redemption's grand finale; recall that the Son of Humankind *himself* will suffer much and become a corpse before returning in glory (17:25). But the picture of a dominant bird of prey may also evoke a major image of Rome's mighty military machine—the golden

311. The pair of examples in 17:34–35 follows Luke's penchant for juxtaposing male and female characters, with an interesting twist: *not* a man and woman together in bed and at the millstone, respectively, *but* rather *two men* reclining followed by *two women* grinding meal. The cardinal pronouns are key: *one man* (εἷς, *heis*) taken from bed, the *other man* (ἕτερος, *heteros*) left; then *one woman* (μία, *mia*) taken from the millstone, the *other woman* (ἑτέρα, *hetera*) left.

312. Like the Münster Anabaptists (1534–35) or the Adventists/Branch Davidians of Waco, Texas (1993); on millenarian movements, see Allison, *Jesus*, 78–94; Moltmann, *Coming*, 109–255.

eagle—which will kill Jesus[313] as it has and will many others, culminating in the brutal devastation of Jerusalem within a generation.[314] The great roads of the Roman Empire are paved over the corpses (road-kill) of any who stood in its way. This (and other) kingdom(s) of cruel conquest will cause untold suffering until the empire of God and Son of Humankind establishes the way of peace and justice for all.

Justified Plaintiffs and Self-Justifying Judges (18:1–14)

Jesus shifts again into storytelling mode to reinforce, not to relieve, the tension of his teaching. The issue of preparedness during the tough times before the Son of Humankind's return remains central, as the hinge query between the ensuing two parables demonstrates: "And yet, when the Son of Humankind comes, will he find faith/faithfulness [πίστιν, *pistin*] on earth" (18:8)? This challenge is not for unbelievers, but for disciples and Pharisees, whom Jesus continues to press about their levels of faith/faithfulness. Will they tenaciously pursue God's right way and promote God's just rule in the face of opposition and hardship? The use of the adversative conjunction πλήν (*plēn*, "yet, nevertheless") and the interrogative particle ἆρα (*ara*) convey a sense of urgency, laced with some anxiety, about the outcome. The latter, untranslatable particle "functions as a 'marker of a negative response to questions, usually implying anxiety or impatience,'"[315] or "a tone of suspense . . . in interrogation . . . with the onus for a correct answer put on the addressee . . . will he find (the necessary) faith?"[316] The seeking-finding Jesus (15:1–32; 19:10) is genuinely concerned about what he will "find on earth" when he returns.

But Jesus does more than limply challenge his followers to hang in there, even as he doubts their durability. Because of the difficulty of the journey and

313. Since Luke 17:37 reads, "Where *the body* [τὸ σῶμα, *to sōma*] is, there will the eagles be gathered" (AT), Lang ("Where the Body Is") sees the primary reference to *Jesus's attacked and crucified body*, alluded to in 17:25 and carried out by Roman "hostile, capturing forces" (symbolized by "eagles") as the narrative unfolds (336).

314. On the image of the rapacious Roman eagle, related to the parallel text in Matt 24:28, see the following studies by Warren Carter: *Matthew and Empire*, 87–88; "Are There Imperial Texts?"; and *Seven Events*, 74, 77, 87. In Matthew's context, however, Carter interprets Jesus's statement as predicting the apocalyptic destruction *of* Roman forces at the Son of Humankind's climactic parousia: the annihilation of "Roman troops ('the corpse') with fallen eagle standards scattered among them" (*Matthew and Empire*, 87).

315. Culy, Parson, and Stigall, 566; citing Louw and Nida, *Greek-English Lexicon*, 1:666 (cf. Acts 8:30; Gal 2:17).

316. BDAG, 127.

frailty of believers, Jesus discloses a vital secret to endurance: "their need to *pray always* and not to lose heart" (18:1). Both parables illustrate the importance of prayer: the first one more obliquely (18:2–5); the second directly featuring prayers of two men in the temple (18:10–14). Just as Jesus's habit of prayer has sustained him throughout his embattled ministry (3:21–22; 6:12; 9:28–29; 11:1–4; cf. 22:39–46; 23:34, 46), so disciples must follow suit, especially during the trying days to come (cf. 22:40, 46). Such spiritual discipline, however, is not simply private communion with God to bolster trust (faith) in God's personal care, but rather a regimen of strength conditioning for public action (faithfulness) promoting God's *justice* in a corrupt, callous world.

The "justice" word group ([ἐκ]δικ-, [*ek*]*dik*-)—related to judges and judgments, justifiers and justifications, including negative agents of self-justification and injustice—is prominent in both parables (18:3, 5–9, 11, 14). In the first, a mistreated widow pleads for justice (ἐκδίκησον, *ekdikēson*) against an unjust adversary (ἀντίδικος, *antidikos*) (18:3). She eventually wins her case through fierce persistence (faithfulness) before an "unjust judge [κριτὴς τῆς ἀδικίας, *kritēs tēs adikias*]" (18:6). The second story targets those "who trusted in themselves that they were righteous/just [δίκαιοι, *dikaioi*]" and boosted their self-justification by looking on others "with contempt" (18:9). Since the Pharisees and legal experts have been particularly prone to this self-justifying tendency in Luke (10:29; 16:15), it is not so strange to see a praying Pharisee and tax collector in the parable, with the repentant latter figure, typically excluded from the Pharisees' circle, becoming "justified [δεδικαιωμένος, *dedikaiōmenos*]" by God (18:14; cf. 5:29–32; 7:29–30; 15:1–2). Though I argue below that this tale does not necessarily pit the two characters against each other (the Pharisee may not be such a bad guy), the issue of justification remains key.

Along with the motivational connection between faithful prayer and just action is a vital *emotional* component. Prayer moves the heart as well as the mind, and justice must move beyond a clinically "fair" application of the law if it is to be genuinely restorative, which is precisely what the widow and tax collector need, though for different reasons.[317] Not simply internal feelings affecting our moods, emotions are dynamic "action tendencies," powerful drivers

317. On the critical intersection of law, emotion, and justice, see the works of the philosophers John Deigh (*Emotions*, 136–58) and Martha Nussbaum (*Hiding*, 1–70; *From Disgust*; *Political Emotions*); of the research psychologist Lisa Feldman Barrett (*How Emotions Are Made*, 219–51); and related to biblical law, see Thomas Kazen, *Emotions*. Cf. the comment from neuroscientist and philosopher Sam Harris (*Moral Landscape*): "Fairness is not merely an abstract principle—it is a felt experience. We all know this from the inside, of course, but neuroimaging has also shown that fairness drives reward-related activity in the brain, while accepting unfair proposals requires the regulation of negative emotion" (79).

of human (and divine) behavior.[318] The judge in the first story prides himself on his (alleged) strict impartiality, not being swayed by soft sentiments of "respect/regard for others" (18:2, 4). But the desperate widow needs more respect than she's been receiving from the economic and judicial system. She needs someone to *feel* her plight enough to *do* something about it, and as it happens, she does everything in her power to make the judge feel her concern and finally grant her justice. Likewise, the tax collector passionately pleads with God on an emotional-action level, "Be merciful to me, a sinner!" (18:13). That is, "Have a heart, God! Feel the pain of my guilt and act to alleviate it through your forgiving love." The two cases are not identical. Unlike the unjust judge, the just God is predisposed to merciful action; and unlike the exploited widow, the tax collector is truly blameworthy. Yet, both feature deep emotional engagement in pursuit of justice/justification. Both plaintiffs seek *sympathetic/compassionate restoration* by powerful judges, a "feeling with" their anguished condition that prompts making things right.

To sharpen the picture, it is not simply *feeling what* someone feels or *knowing how* they feel, even from personal experience. That emotion is more properly called *empathy*, which, as the psychologist and philosopher Paul Bloom contends, should be distinguished from *sympathy/compassion*, which reflects more deeply relational feelings *with* (sym-/com-) a fellow sufferer motivating benevolent outreach.[319] Merely knowing how it feels to walk in someone else's tattered shoes does not guarantee buying the poor pedestrian new shoes. Having walked in those same shoes may evoke a kind of empathetic *horror* to never go that way again or have anything to do with shoddily shod folks.[320] "I may have been down that rough road before, but I am not like that anymore, and I do not like those who are still stuck there." This may or may not represent the attitude of the parable's Pharisee who thanks God, "I am not like other people . . . or even like this tax collector" (18:11). In any case, the social emotion of empathy can spur either positive-restorative (sympathetic) or negative-recoiling (antipathetic) actions toward disadvantaged persons.

If empathy is morally ambiguous, the emotion of *disgust* or *contempt* toward other people is utterly reprehensible to Luke's Jesus. Note again the pivotal

318. According to the Dutch psychology scholar Nico Frijda, "All emotion . . . involve[s] some change in action readiness: (a) in readiness to go at it or away from it or to shift attention; (b) in sheer excitement, which can be understood as being ready for action but not knowing what actions; (c) in being stopped in one's tracks or in loss of interest" ("Laws of Emotion," 351; cf. Frijda, *Laws of Emotion*, 3–46; Elster, "Emotion," 151–55).

319. Bloom, *Just Babies*, 33–57, and "Against Empathy."

320. Or as Bloom (*Just Babies*, 46) indicates, empathy may spark a delicious Schadenfreude bordering on sadism, a reveling in feeling others' unfortunate pain.

statement between parables disclosing Jesus's aim to challenge self-justifying types who "regarded others *with contempt* [ἐξουθενοῦντας, *exouthenountas*]," or "looked on everyone else with disgust" (CEB) (18:9). The participle derives from "nothing" (οὐθέν, *outhen*), that is, devaluing and treating others as if they were "nothing, nobody, of no account." The same term applies to the vehement abuse Jesus receives from religious and political authorities before being sentenced to crucifixion (23:11; cf. Acts 4:11).[321] Feeling disgust toward an individual or group and judging them as disgusting (the cognitive-appraisal element of emotions) bans these "nothings" from one's "moral circle" and justifies negligent or violent actions against them, just as one might swat an annoying gnat or bloodsucking mosquito.[322] Disgusting creatures are not human and thus deserve inhuman treatment.[323] Lepers fit this bill in many cultures, all the more for their ugly oozing of contaminant bodily fluids,[324] as do despised ethnic-national entities for (variable) reasons "justifying" genocidal "cleansing." As we have seen, some first-century Jews and Samaritans would regard each other as contemptible, subhuman parasites worthy of destruction. Likewise, the callous judge in the first parable couldn't care less about a needy widow, especially this one who keeps bothering him like a pesky gnat (he would happily get rid of her if he could) (18:4–5); and many Jews in Jesus's world loathed tax collectors (with good reason) as despicable, money-sucking traitors (though whether the parable's Pharisee has such disgust remains an open question [see below]).

But in all these potentially "disgusting" cases—involving lepers, Samaritans, widows, and tax collectors (17:11–18:14)—Luke's Jesus creates an "expanding circle," to borrow the image of the bioethicist Peter Singer, of merciful concern and action. Indeed, Singer places this expanding circle at the heart of religious ethics and moral philosophy across traditions and cultures, including the early rabbis Jesus of Nazareth and Hillel the Pharisee in their central formulations of the Golden Rule and love commandments (cf. 6:31; 10:25–28; Matt 7:12; 22:34–40; Mark 12:28–34; b. Šabb. 31a).[325]

321. On ἐξουθενέω (*exoutheneō*) in this context, see BDAG, 352: "to regard another as of no significance and therefore worthy of maltreatment."

322. On the developmental notion of the expanding "moral circle," derived from William Lecky (*History of European Morals*) and Peter Singer (*Expanding Circle*), see Bloom, *Just Babies*, 194–205.

323. On the moral and social implications of disgust, see Rozin et al., "CAD Triad Hypothesis"; Rozin, Haidt, and McCauley, "Disgust"; Nussbaum, *Hiding*, 71–172; Bloom, *Just Babies*, 131–57; Richard Beck, *Unclean*.

324. Although biblical law regulated "polluting" bodily seepages (oozings) from lepers, menstruants, and ejaculators, it did not permanently ostracize such folk from the community; to the contrary, it provided clear guidelines for "purification" and restoration.

325. Singer, *Expanding Circle*, 135–36; cf. Bloom, *Just Babies*, 194–95, 211–13. According well

We now turn to unpack more fully the two legal-emotional parable scenes in relation to core themes of prayer and justice.

The Justice-Seeking Widow and the Unjust Judge (18:1–8)

In lieu of providing a detailed dossier on the widow's case, Jesus simply places her in a terrible squeeze between an unjust, oppressive antagonist (ἀντίδικος, *antidikos*) and an unjust (ἀδικία, *adikia*), dispassionate judge. We can reasonably assume, however, that the widow finds herself embroiled in some dispute over property rights and the economic support due her after her husband's death. In a heavily impoverished society, most widows would be vulnerable without a male provider. But even those from wealthier families might have to fight for their estates (greater resources attract more predators) against *other family members*, especially greedy male relatives (brothers, uncles, even sons) desiring a bigger slice of the paterfamilias's pie. We do not know the parable widow's socioeconomic status, but poor or rich, her adversary might be a close male kin.[326] Alternatively, Jesus soon exposes the *scribes*—the main documentary officers preparing real estate deeds and wills—for using their clerical positions to "devour widows' houses" and trying to cover up their injustice with pretentious "long prayers" (20:47).

Whoever aims to take advantage of her vulnerable position, the widow seeks justice in the city's courts. She represents herself (no supporting advocates) before a magistrate "who neither feared God nor had respect for people" (18:2). On the surface, as suggested above, this judge might be thought to model objectivity and impartiality, analyzing each case on its own legal merits free from social and religious biases. Scriptural jurisprudence asserts that "God shows no partiality" (Acts 10:34; Rom 2:11; cf. Sir 35:15), or "is no respecter of persons" (Acts 10:34 KJV), and that Godlike judges should give fair and equal attention to the poor and rich (Lev 19:15). But the judge in Jesus's story does not fear the biblical God. Yet, as an apparently non-Jewish Roman judge,[327] he would still be held to a standard of judicial impartiality, including a broad

---

with Jesus's moral teaching is Hillel's famous formulation: "What is hateful to you, do not do to your neighbor; that is the whole Torah, while the rest is commentary" (b. Šabb. 31a).

326. See the detailed discussion of this "savvy widow," including her socioeconomic status, in Spencer, *Salty Wives*, 264–314.

327. As in the property case brought before a Roman judge in the early second century CE by Babatha, a Jewish widow, evidenced in the papyri legal documents from the Cave of Letters; see Spencer, *Salty Wives*, 271–78. For an alternative view, envisioning a local Jewish court before a "Torah judge," see Herzog, *Parables*, 226–28.

tolerance for all religions. But as in most legal systems, the reality is far from ideal. Livy impugns one Roman consul who "had been proud and headstrong . . . and lacked all proper reverence, not only for the laws and for the senate's majesty, but even for the gods. . . . It was therefore sufficiently apparent that, seeking no counsel, either divine or human, he would manage everything with recklessness and headlong haste" (*Ab urbe cond.* 22.3.3–4).[328] If any doubt lingers about the parable judge's moral character, it is soon resolved in Jesus's labeling him "unjust" (18:6). The judge's nonpreferential, nonpartisan stance is in fact an apathetic, noncaring position concerning the interests of God and people. All he cares about in the present case is his own reputation and security, not the cause of the widow, unless it suits him. And she does nothing to ingratiate herself: she employs no flattery, offers no bribe, and makes a royal nuisance of herself.

But the widow brilliantly works the system and the judge's solipsism to her advantage. She keeps "continually coming," day after day, to plead her case before this recalcitrant judge. She aims to see this matter through (lit. "to the end" [εἰς τέλος, *eis telos*]), however long it takes. She will bother—literally, "bring about trouble for me [παρέχειν μοι κόπον, *parechein moi kopon*]"—until he relents (18:5), just as the friend in an earlier parable pestered (same Greek phrase) his sleeping neighbor until he got up and filled his bread order (11:7). The widow's persistent strategy works: eventually, the judge decides to "grant her justice" (18:5), not out of compassion for her, but to get her off his back.

But why does he allow it to go this far? Why doesn't he just hold her in contempt of court (reinforcing the contempt theme) and refuse to keep hearing—and dismissing—her pleas? Perhaps he must keep up some appearances. She is a "weak" widow, after all; he can't appear too callous in public, too insensitive to this poor woman; so best to humor the little lady awhile. But she goes on too long and makes quite a scene to boot when she approaches the judicial bench. The judge's complaint that the widow seems determined to "wear me out [ὑπωπιάζῃ με, *hypōpiazē me*]" (18:5) reinforces the nuisance factor but glosses over a more demonstrative dimension of the widow's behavior. The verb means "strike under the eye," like a boxer in the ring (cf. 1 Cor 9:27). The picture Jesus evokes, at once comical and shocking, is of the widow woman punctuating her pleas with flailing arms and shaking fists in the judge's face, threatening to land the odd punch and give the man a black eye! Whether such action should be taken literally, with the judge sporting a shiner about town, or figuratively,

328. Livy translation by Benjamin Foster (LCL); for this reference and similar opinions from Dionysius of Halicarnassus and Josephus, see Fitzmyer, 1:1178; Danker, 294–95; Cotter, "Parable of Feisty Widow," 331–32.

taking a hit to his reputation, he faces serious public *shaming* ("embarrassing" [CEB]) by this pesky, pugilistic widow.[329] Imagine the jokes and jibes he would suffer for not being able to control a poor woman. Better to cut his losses and give her what she wants.

Good for this passionate, proactive widow, who does whatever it takes to obtain justice for herself. There remains, however, a problematic undertow from theological and feminist perspectives. *Theologically*, the system remains badly flawed: a vulnerable widow should not have to fight her way to justice. She, along with orphans and other poor unfortunates, enjoys *God's preferential favor* and *affirmative action*. Without apology, God has a soft spot for needy widows, counterbalancing their often weak position and harsh treatment in society (Exod 22:21–24; Deut 10:17–18; 24:17–22; 27:19; Ps 68:5).[330] Accordingly, exploitative judicial authorities who resist God's compassionate rule, including those within Israel from time to time (Isa 1:16–17, 23; Jer 7:5–7; Zech 7:8–12), must themselves be staunchly resisted by all God's people, not only by those unfortunates suffering injustice like the parable's widow. From a *feminist* standpoint, while the widow's vocal agency and vehement action appear commendable, they come at the expense of a *nagging* stereotype, like Delilah or the insufferable wife in Proverbs who wears her husband down drip by drip (Judg 16:4–22; Prov 21:9; 25:24; 27:15). Women can get what they want if they bitch and pitch enough of a fit.

Acknowledging these difficulties, we can still admire the parable widow's fervent, persistent pursuit of justice in the face of opposition. But what does her story have to do with prayerful devotion (18:1) or faithful action until the Son of Humankind returns to earth (18:8)? The widow never prays to God in the story. If she's prayed before, it hasn't done her much good, since she remains oppressed and forced to seek justice in the state courts. She makes no reference to God. Ironically, the only character to speak of God is the parable's non-God-fearing judge (18:2, 4). The widow appears completely on her own, independent of supportive family or deity. Nonetheless, Luke's Jesus appropriates the widow's tale for spiritual (prayer) and ethical (faithfulness) purposes.

After narrating the brief parable where the widow does not pray, Jesus promptly makes a prayer application (as expected from 18:1): "And the Lord

329. After surveying ὑπωπιάζω (*hypōpiazō*) in ancient Greek literature, Cotter ("Parable of Feisty Widow") concludes that "the verb must be translated *literally* every time if the metaphor is to work" (339 [emphasis original]); in other words, even in a figurative application, the punch of the image should not be pulled or its force blunted.

330. Cf. Green, 639: "The God who liberated Israel from Egypt is the God who directs his people to show special regard toward, *partiality* on behalf of, the oppressed among them—specifically for the alien, the orphans, and the widow" (emphasis original).

said, 'Listen to what the unjust judge says. And will not God grant justice to his chosen ones who cry to him day and night? Will he delay long in helping them? I tell you, he will quickly grant justice to them'" (18:6–8a). On one level, the connection between praying and promoting justice is clear enough: as the beset widow persistently pleaded for and eventually secured justice for herself, so God's people who relentlessly "cry to [God] day and night" will gain God's swift justice on their behalf. Jesus offered similar assurances through scenarios of the importunate neighbor and the supplicant child (11:5–8, 11–13). Moreover, his lesson about God's response to petitioners again trades on contrast with the parable's characters. Though Jesus initially exhorts, "Listen to what the unjust judge says," he certainly does not view this figure as a stand-in for God. Though using no explicit "how much more" formula, as in 11:13, he no doubt implies here that if this callous earthly judge finally does right by this pleading widow, *how much more* does God attend to cries for justice or *how much less* does God make sufferers wait for enacted justice? Indeed, God moves "quickly," unlike the parable's obstinate, dilatory magistrate. Note Jesus's emphatic double negative question, assuming a robust, positive answer: "Will not [by all means] [οὐ μή, *ou mē*] God grant justice?" (18:7). Of course the just God will. How could God *not*?![331]

But the matter is more complicated than that. To some degree, the parable, as it stands, keeps posing a nagging problem of theodicy—the justification of *God*. Again we wonder: did the widow pray for God's help (a likely assumption) before filing suit as a last resort? If so, why did God *not* take care of her situation? Where is God *in this story*, except in dismissal by the impudent judge? Less speculatively, this widow's predicament evokes the uncomfortable fact that many widows and other sufferers among God's children do not receive God's *speedy* help. "How long, O Lord?" reverberates in the biblical lament tradition. So does Luke's Jesus just swat that complaint away with a cheap platitude? Unlikely, given his keen awareness that he himself "must endure much [long] suffering" (17:25) before fully realizing God's justice.

To better understand Jesus's commentary on the parable, we must carefully break down 18:7–8a. My translation diverts from the NRSV and other versions at key points:[332]

331. See Culy, Parsons, and Stigall, 560: "So won't God certainly give justice to his chosen ones who cry out to him?" (cf. 564). This double-negative + subjunctive form of interrogative is rare in the NT, though see a similar case in John 18:11, expecting a positive answer: "Am I not to drink the cup that the Father has given me? [Of course I will!]" (see Porter, *Idioms*, 279).

332. Adapted from Spencer, *Salty Wives*, 296–302.

Rhetorical question: But will God not by all means [οὐ μή, *ou mē*] grant justice [ποιήσῃ τὴν ἐκδίκησιν, *poiēsē tēn ekdikēsin*] for his chosen ones who keep crying out to him day and night?
Realistic statement: And God is patient [μακροθυμεῖ, *makrothymei*] with them.
Optimistic punch line: I tell you that God will grant justice [ἐκδίκησιν, *ekdikēsin*] for them suddenly [ἐν τάχει, *en tachei*].

The middle line (realistic statement) represents my starkest deviation from other translations:

- NRSV: Will he delay long in helping them?
- NIV: Will he keep putting them off?
- CEB: Will he be slow to help them?
- NAB: Will he be slow to answer them?

In my judgment, the "and" (καί, *kai*) conjunction in the middle line, combined with a tense-and-mood shift from the aorist subjunctive "will/might grant" (ποιήσῃ, *poiēsē*) in the previous line to the present indicative "is patient" (μακροθυμεῖ, *makrothymei*) in the middle line, *breaks the interrogative flow*. Thus Jesus modulates to a declarative statement, focused on the Lord's *patience*, which is the basic meaning of μακροθυμία/-έω (*makrothymia/-eō*).

In the present context, this conventional affirmation of God's forbearance takes on a provocative double edge: stressing that (1) like a good parent, God patiently hears children's round-the-clock cries; that is, God is a good and kind listener, in no way bothered by persistent pleas (contra the unjust judge),[333] while

333. Culy, Parsons, and Stigall (565) favor the "patience" reading, but with a slightly different emphasis by way of comparing Luke 18:7–8 with Jas 5:7 ("The farmer waits for the precious crop . . . being patient [μακροθυμῶν, *makrothymōn*] with it until it receives the early and late rains"). In both cases, the subject (God/farmer) patiently waits "upon/for" (ἐπί, *epi*) the response of others (needy petitioners/growing crops). The parallel breaks down somewhat, however, in that the farmer in James represents not the patient Lord but *beleaguered believers* who must "be patient [μακροθυμήσατε, *makrothymēsate*]" in waiting for "*the Lord* to come again" (5:7a), whereas in Luke, God's patience (slowness) is directed toward supplicants. Thus, a clear *eschatological* horizon links the gospel and epistolary texts, but one that bolsters as much as mitigates the problem of the Lord's *delayed (slow)* intervention.

Moreover, whereas Culy and company take the ἐπ' αὐτοῖς (*ep' autois*) in Luke 18:7 to mean that "God is patient in waiting [*for them*, that is,] *for his children* to bring their needs to him in prayer" (560, 565; emphasis added), I lean toward taking the prepositional phrase in the sense of God's (sometimes) tardy waiting *on them* or dealing *with them*. No one (including God) needs to wait for the widow's cry for help; her problem is getting someone (including God?) to listen and act on her behalf!

also suggesting that (2) this patient God will not necessarily grant petitioners' wishes or actively intervene on their behalf; that is, the statement may convey "and the Lord *is slow to help them*,"[334] as many lamenters (à la the parable's widow) would concur. The virtue of patience diminishes when decisive action seems demanded. Jesus thus applies a dose of spiritual reality: God often does *not* move as swiftly as we would like or expect.

But isn't this hint of the Lord's slow response effectively undone by the punch line that God "will *quickly* grant justice"? However sluggish God's work *may seem* from time to time, God remains committed to *swift* justice on God's schedule. Perhaps, but periods of harsh exile have historically stretched out for generations, provoking the desperate "How long?" pleas. Again, I propose a different interpretation, rendering ἐν τάχει (*en tachei*) as "suddenly" rather than "quickly." Still stressing the sense of rapid response *when* it comes, "suddenly" also allows for delay in answering the call. Make no mistake: God's just reign has and will *suddenly* irrupt in "signs and wonders" at various points (Acts 2:19, 43; 4:22, 30; 5:12; 6:8) and will ultimately shake and remake the cosmos to its core (Luke 17:20–37). But remember that *first* the Son of Humankind and God's people "must endure" a season of onerous adversity (17:25).

Two uses of ἐν τάχει (*en tachei*) in Acts related to prayer conjoin occasional, sudden signs of God's deliverance with rapid, decisive action by God's human agents. First, at the eleventh hour on "the very night" the imprisoned Peter expected to be executed, he is suddenly awakened by the Lord's angel and told to get up and out "quickly" (ἐν τάχει, *en tachei* [Acts 12:7]). Throughout his incarceration, "the church *prayed fervently* to God for him" (12:5), but their pleas are not answered *until* God acts *suddenly* (and not a moment too soon), which then prompts Peter to move swiftly.

Second, amid the turmoil of Paul's early ministry, he has a visionary encounter with the risen Jesus "while . . . *praying* in the temple." In this trance, Jesus exhorts Paul to "get out of Jerusalem *quickly* [ἐν τάχει, *en tachei*]" (Acts 22:17–18) in order to escape violent opposition. But far from going into a witness protection program, he is suddenly sent to proclaim the gospel to the Gentiles, where he has considerable success but hardly a smooth ride. Indeed, he recounts this past vision to an angry Jewish mob falsely accusing him of bringing a Gentile into the temple's inner precincts (21:27–22:29). For the balance of Acts, Paul remains in Roman custody and undergoes a battery of trials for disturb-

334. Barclay M. Newman (*Greek-English Dictionary*, 113) suggests this as a possible rendering (along with "delay to help them") of Luke 18:7; actually, there is no separate word for "help" in this Greek verse (Newman takes it as implied in "be patient"), which may hint that help is not automatically, immediately, or easily come by in response to persistent pleading.

ing the peace. Overall, Paul's perilous mission combines (1) prayer, (2) divine intervention, (3) rapid response, and (4) persisting hardships. Dramatic signs of salvation suddenly appear now and then, spurring Paul to swift movement into new arenas of opportunity *and* hostility.

Outside of Luke's writings, the most instructive intertext appears in Sir 35:14–26, which bears striking linguistic, structural, and thematic resemblances—along with key differences—to the widow's case in Luke 18:1–8.[335]

> [14] Do not offer a bribe, for he will not accept it,
> [15] and do not be intent on an unrighteous [ἀδίκῳ, *adikō*] sacrifice;
> because the Lord is judge [κριτής, *kritēs*],
> and with him there is no reputation of person.
> [16] He will not receive a person against a poor person,
> and he will listen to the petition of one who is wronged [ἠδικημένου, *ēdikēmenou*].
> [17] He will never ignore an orphan's supplication,
> nor a widow [χήραν, *chēran*] if she pours out speech.
> [18] Do not a widow's [χήρας, *chēras*] tears run down upon her cheek,
> [19] and is not her cry against [καταβόησις, *kataboēsis*] the one who drew them down?
> [20] One who serves with goodwill will be accepted,
> and his petition will reach to the clouds.
> [21] A humble person's prayer [προσευχή, *proseuchē*] passed through the clouds,
> and until it draws near, it will never relent,
> and it will never desist until the Most High takes notice.
> [22] And he will adjudicate for righteous persons [δικαίοις, *dikaiois*], and will execute [ποιήσει, *poiēsei*] judgment.
> And the Lord will never be slow [οὐ μὴ βραδύνῃ, *ou mē bradynē*],
> nor will he will ever be patient regarding them [οὐδὲ μὴ μακροθυμήσῃ ἐπ' αὐτοῖς, *oude mē makrothymēsē ep' autois*]
> until he crushes the loins of unmerciful persons
> [23] and will repay vengeance [ἐκδίκησιν, *ekdikēsin*] upon the nations;
> until he removes the multitude of insolent persons
> and will shatter the scepters of unrighteous persons [ἀδίκων, *adikōn*],
> [24] until he repays a person according to his deeds
> and the works of human beings according to their notions,

335. See the detailed study by Dumoulin, "Parabole"; Bailey, *Through Peasant Eyes*, 127–30, and *Jesus*, 261–63; cf. Spencer, *Salty Wives*, 299–301.

25 until he judges the case of his people
and will gladden them with his mercy.
26 Timely is his mercy in a time of distress,
as are clouds of rain in a time of drought.

(Sir 35:14–26 NETS)

This text seems to offer the perfect template for Jesus's parable and commentary with similar characters and plot: a wronged widow pleading her case before a judge favoring "no reputation of person" (35:15). But the settings are markedly different. In Sirach the entire scene plays out in a *heavenly courtroom* where the widow's prayerful cries "reach to the clouds" and to the ears of the divine magistrate ("the Lord is judge") (35:20, 15), with no countervailing *earthly courtroom* scene, as in Jesus's parable, before a hardened secular judge. Without this this-worldly judicial complication, the Sirach drama unfolds without a hitch. Yes, the widow (and the poor, orphaned, and humble) suffers hurtful earthly opposition, provoking her stream of tearful cries to God against her persecutors; and yes, she may need to persist ("never relent," "never desist") in her praying "until the Most High takes notice" (35:21). But respond God most assuredly will, and not with any pokey pace: "the Lord will never be slow, nor will he ever be patient regarding them (οὐδὲ μὴ μακροθυμήσῃ ἐπ' αὐτοῖς, *oude mē makrothymēsē ep' autois*)" (35:22). Nothing slack about this Lord. He will by no means be slow/patient in dealing with "them," which, in light of what follows, refers primarily to those "unmerciful," "insolent," and "unrighteous" vultures of widows and company (35:22b–23).[336] The Lord will hit the warpath to wreak retributive justice (ἐκδίκησιν, *ekdikēsin*) on all, including nations, who oppress God's people. The Sirach story moves in "timely" fashion, swiftly and decisively, from the widow's plight and prayer to a grand apocalyptic vision of restored global order (35:22–26).

In broad strokes, Luke's Jesus concurs with this cosmic hope of God's sovereign, righteous reign. But in the midst of a colonized people, replete with disadvantaged widows, orphans, and poor peasants, and himself en route to a Roman cross in ill-fated Jerusalem, this Jesus the Son of Humankind has more genuine sympathy for the hard human situation than does the aristocratic Jesus Ben Sira.[337] Thus Jesus thickens the plot with this thorny parable and its crusty widow. She is way beyond tears now: she's just plain mad, with nothing to lose.

336. Dumoulin, "Parabole," 175–77.

337. Cf. James Metzger, "God," 50–51: "Employing an optic of suffering and foregrounding intertexts in which God is portrayed unfavorably, I have argued that in Luke 11:5–13 and 18:1–8 Jesus acknowledges a negative experience of the deity among some of Roman Palestine's 'poor . . . captives . . . blind . . . [and] oppressed' (4:18–19)."

Her head is not remotely in Sirach's "clouds" but firmly in the trenches. She's not looking for world peace or cosmic justice; first, she herself must survive: "Grant *me* justice." She's not trying to overthrow the Roman government, crusade for judicial reform, or even impeach this corrupt judge. She just wants her fair shake. She shamelessly threatens to shame this unjust official, to blacken his eye, but she calls down no fire from heaven on his head, and he receives no angelic smackdown. Overall, she's given up on speedy trials, quick fixes, magic bullets, and celestial thunderbolts and ultimately wins her case with her irrepressible will and wits. She takes matters into her own capable hands.[338]

Everything about this parable screams *delay*—in direct contrast to the Sirach text. Jesus's commentary confirms this point and extends it to the practice of prayer, flipping Sirach's language on its head: "God *is* patient," slow-acting toward God's beloved yet besieged people who cry out to him day and night (Luke 18:7).[339] In Israel's wisdom tradition, Jesus is closer to Job than Ben Sira.[340] No use denying or soft-pedaling it. *Delay*—including *divine* delay—is a lamentable conundrum of daily life for God's children. Yes, the just rule of God is dawning "today" in Jesus's liberating mission (cf. 4:18–21), but *not yet* with consummate brightness. Yes, the "kingdom of God *is* among you" as a sign of the full restoration to come, *but first*, the innocent Son of Humankind will be unjustly crucified and rejected by many compatriots in an unspeakable *travesty of justice* (17:21–25). The final "day" of justice is postponed.

Thus we return to the critical question of enduring faith-in-action, that is, *faithfulness* during the hard interim times. Whatever the duration of the delay, short or long: will the Son of Humankind find any faithful followers left when he returns to earth (18:8b)? Jesus's wistful plea eerily evokes Abraham's bargaining with God over Sodom's judgment in the days of Lot: "Suppose fifty, forty-five . . . ten righteous/just [δίκαιοι, *dikaioi*] persons *are found* there: will you still judge and destroy the city?" (Gen 18:23–33 AT). But not even a small quota of righteous persons *is* found; it is even doubtful that Lot's spared family truly qualifies as righteous. These "days of Lot," paradigmatic, as Jesus has argued, of the interim before the Son of Humankind's coming, are conspicuous by their dearth of faith/faithfulness on earth. Will anyone buck the business-as-usual system and stand up for the cause of justice in a callous world?

338. Cf. Curkpatrick, "Parable," 31: "The widow of Luke's parable takes Yahweh's responsibility into her own hands. Like the prophets, she champions the cause of justice. . . . In Luke's parable, the widow does not wait for Yahweh to execute justice. She takes the issue into her own hands."

339. Whereas Sirach speaks of the Lord's *not* being patient (dilatory) with *unjust* persons ("them"), Luke refers positively to God's being patient (dilatory) with God's *chosen* people; cf. Dumoulin, "Parabole," 176–77.

340. On Job as a key intertext, see James Metzger, "God," 36–37, 47–50.

It is precisely at this point that the parable's widow stands out, not only as an oblique illustration of persistent prayer, but more directly, as a model of fervent, faithful pursuit of justice. In fact, the definite article may highlight the widow as *the* model of faithfulness: "Will [the Son of Humankind] find *the faith/faithful one* [τὴν πίστιν, *tēn pistin*] on earth?" (Luke 18:8). As Green comments, "According to the Greek text of v. 8, Jesus's question is not concerned with 'faith' (in general) but with '*the* faith'—that is, that manner of faith demonstrated by the widow in the antecedent parable."[341] The widow showcases that rare and special faith Jesus seeks, which moves with brisk dispatch and bold determination to bring God's justice on earth. This is no clueless, helpless woman mired in the grime of an oppressive society. She tackles injustice head-on and hands-on as an agent of God's realm. And she's no secret agent: she marches on city hall, as it were, publicly challenging the unjust local regime. Luke's narrative—parable plus commentary—cements her gutsy performance on center stage.

To summarize my take on 18:1–8: God's distressed people, beset by exploitative forces, bombard heaven with pleas for justice and deliverance; God patiently and sympathetically hears their cries (waits "upon them"), but for inscrutable reasons often seems too slow-acting to rectify the situation. The longer the wait, the more God's supplicants move in their "optic of suffering"[342] toward honest, impassioned, fist-shaking lament, without abandoning hope; indeed, hope tenaciously believes that God can and will be roused to put things to rights suddenly, climactically, once-for-all. Even so, Lord—even after much suffering and long delay—come quickly! (Rev. 22:20). Thus the theodicy problem is addressed, though not completely erased. In these challenging interim days, experiencing the justice of God requires persistent praying and working as long as it takes, with no illusions of quick and easy solutions.

341. Green, 637; cf. James Metzger, "God," 50n60.

342. I draw this apt phrase from James Metzger, "God," 53–55 (the fuller title is "God as F(r)iend?"). This thoughtful study takes a similar approach to mine, though it draws heavily on process theology and suggests the potential for God's "moral transformation," which frustrated human sufferers can spark within God. While affirming Metzger's endorsement of candid, plaintive, even angry conversation with God, I do not see the purpose of prayer illustrated in the widow parable as changing God's character. The theological problem is principally temporal (delay), not moral. God's fundamental commitment to justice remains constant. *Challenging* God through passionate lament to be true to God's just nature is different than *changing* God's moral perspective.

The Praying Pharisee and the Justified Tax Collector (18:9–14)

In the transitional statement between Jesus's parables in Luke 18, it is worth noticing two little words. First, "he *also* [καί, *kai*] told this parable," reinforcing the thematic connection between the tale of a widow's judicial case and the ensuing story about judging self and others. Second, "he also told this parable to *some* [τινας, *tinas*]" (18:9) of those who tend to be self-justifying and other-condemning. Presumably, the audience still includes Jesus's disciples and a group of Pharisees. As we have seen, however, law-focused Pharisees have been especially prone to self-justification (10:29; 16:15) and to segregation from tax collectors/sinners, whom John and Jesus welcome (5:30; 7:29–30; 15:1–2). This pattern sets up the parable juxtaposing a Pharisee and a tax collector praying in the temple. Yet, while Luke's Jesus clearly targets *some* Pharisees in some fashion, the parable need not be read as a blanket denunciation of Pharisaic piety, reduced to rank hypocrisy, as the adjective "pharisaic" connotes in modern parlance. As with most of Jesus's parables, this one carries a stinging challenge to all its hearers, not least to religious devotees like the Pharisees *and* Jesus's adherents. Let anyone with ears to hear, hear! But *some* merit more indictment than others, depending on their degree of faithfulness to God's love-centered law.

The story can cut different ways. The attitudes and emotions of the praying Pharisee are ambiguous. They admit either positive or negative interpretations, suiting Jesus's aim that hearers reflect critically on their motivations in prayer. Although the conventional reading regards the parable's Pharisee as a self-righteous, negative foil to the humble tax collector, I am increasingly inclined toward a more congenial appraisal via caricature that stresses the strange *solidarity*, rather than polarity, of the Pharisee and tax collector, allowing *both* figures to go "home justified" (18:14). But again, the case is not cut and dried. The following chart breaks down the positive and negative options.

	Pharisee (negative)	**Pharisee (positive)**	**Tax collector**
Setting:	Temple	Temple	Temple
Position:	"Standing by himself" (18:11) in proud self-preoccupation — too good to pray with anyone else	"Standing by himself" to focus full attention on God and not disturb others	"Standing far off" (18:13), also by himself, but in humble self-deprecation—too bad to pray with anyone else

	Pharisee (negative)	Pharisee (positive)	Tax collector
Posture:	Implied raised head and hands to heaven? Theatric show of piety	Implied raised head and hands to heaven? Openness to God and expression of praise	Bowed head and beaten breast
Addressee:	God—but more concerned about himself; God is just another audience	God—a sincere acknowledgment of God's authority	God—a sincere acknowledgment of God's authority
Content:	*Thanksgiving*—really self-congratulation and other-denunciation; "I-itis"; prayer just a platform for puffery	*Thanksgiving*—sincere gratitude for God's power and grace to do good (fasting, tithing) and avoid evil; "By the grace of God, there go I"	*Confession*—plea for God's mercy and forgiveness; acknowledgment that he is a sinner
Result:	Goes home *not* justified/in-the-right "*rather than* the other [παρ' ἐκεῖνον, *par' ekeinon*]" (18:14)	Goes home justified/in-the-right "*beside/along with* that one [παρ' ἐκεῖνον, *par' ekeinon*]" (18:14)	Goes home justified/in-the-right

"Two men went up to the temple to pray, one a Pharisee and the other a tax collector" (18:10). So Jesus sets the tale of two supplicants. On the one hand, the picture is unremarkable: as the house of God, the temple is above all a "house of prayer" (cf. 19:46; Isa 56:7). On the other hand, while both figures are doing the right thing in the right place, one is a more surprising participant. Pharisees were known for their devotion to prayer and piety; tax collectors, not so much. We expect the latter at a toll booth or customs house (5:27), not in the temple. But here one is, engaging in penitential prayer with the Pharisee. But saying it like this is not quite right, is it? The two men are both praying in the temple precincts, but not really *with* each other or in the same way.

Their position and posture differ, except that both pray while "standing" (ἵστημι, *histēmi* [18:11, 13]), a standard prayer position (like kneeling) and not an automatic indicator of pride or stiff-necked obstinacy. To be sure, the tax collector appears more humble with his bowed head ("would not even look up to heaven" [18:13]) and beaten breast, but he remains standing through it all.[343] For the Pharisee's part, his standing to pray need not reflect a haughty heart or showy display.[344] Neither would his upward look or raised hands, if we infer these gestures (not specified in the text) in contradistinction to those of the tax collector. The Pharisee could simply be demonstrating his outreach to God and offering God due praise and thanksgiving ("God, I thank you" [18:11]).

Still, however, Jesus differentiates between the two figures: the Pharisee stands *by himself* (πρὸς ἑαυτόν, *pros heauton*) and the tax collector *far off* (μακρόθεν, *makrothen*).The Pharisee's orientation toward "himself" recalls the self-absorbed rich fool (12:17–19), and the sinful tax collector's isolation "far off" matches the prodigal's distant self-exile (μακράν, *makran* [15:13, 20]). But the parallels are not exact. The present parable's setting in the temple, rather than on a land baron's estate (rich fool) or in remote Gentile territory (prodigal), and the presentation of both praying characters distinguish this story. The tax collector may *feel* far away from God *within* God's house, but he in fact finds merciful welcome there, a renewed sense of belonging—of homecoming and home-going (he "went down to his home justified" [18:14]). The Pharisee's praying alone need not betray a standoffish arrogance or contempt for less pious worshipers. He may simply want to pray privately without distraction, as Jesus does from time to time, though in more remote sites than the temple (6:12; 9:28; 22:39–41).[345] Moreover, the Pharisee remains aware of other supplicants, particularly the tax collector, however "far off" he might be, and never suggests that this "sinner" has no right to be praying there (what better place to "get right" than in the temple, the focal place of atonement?).[346] Ah, but the Pharisee doesn't just notice the tax collector; he actually mentions him in his prayer, and not in a nice way. In fact, it is right at this point that his condescending attitude toward contemptible sinners raises its ugly head. Or so it seems.

343. I've been in two productions of *Godspell* in my adult life, both of which dramatized this parable with the tax collector actor falling to his/her knees and assuming a most abased posture: a popular image, but contrary to Luke's text.

344. In Matt 6:5 Jesus criticizes those "hypocrites" who "love to stand and pray in the synagogues and at the street corners, so that they may be seen by others." The problem, however, is not the posture (standing) but the placement (street corners) and, especially, the purpose (to attract people's attention and admiration).

345. Friedrichsen ("Temple") suggests that "the Pharisee moved farther into the temple precincts [Court of Israel] than the tax collector" (109), perhaps indicating his desire to be as close to God's holiest place as possible; cf. Fitzmyer, 2:1186.

346. Levine, *Short Stories*, 190; Hamm ("Tamid," 223–24) notes that the verb ἱλάσκομαι (*hilaskomai*) in the tax collector's petition, "God, *be merciful to* [propitiate] me" (18:13), was associated with the morning and afternoon daily burnt-offerings for atonement *in the temple* (cf. Exod 30:16; Deut 21:8; Heb 2:17).

"God I thank you that I am *not like* other people: thieves, rogues, adulterers, or *even like this tax collector*" (18:11). So prays the Pharisee, twisting admirable thanksgiving to God into a despicable litany of self-adulation and other-denunciation, with the tax collector at the bottom of a heap of lowlifes manifestly "not like" the Pharisee. Such is the common reading: the Pharisee represents the self-justifying bigot who boosts his inflated ego at the expense of disgusting antitypes. Perhaps. But alternatively, the Pharisee *in this story*, to say nothing of many devout historical Pharisees, may *himself* support the point in a *positive* fashion. The opening "eucharistic" expression—"God, I thank you [εὐχαριστῶ, *eucharistō*]"—need not reflect a pretentious cover for spiritual snobbery. Rather, it may mark a sincere acknowledgment of God's grace in steering him into "paths of righteousness for his name's sake" (Ps 23:3 KJV) and away from ways of wickedness traversed by tax collectors and other rogues (Ps 1). Why not gloss the Pharisee's prayer with the popular phrase "But for the grace of God there go I,"[347] echoing Paul the Pharisee's confession, "By the grace of God I am what I am [and I do what I do]" (1 Cor 15:10)? Likewise, the parable Pharisee's comment about fasting twice a week and tithing "all" his assets—both unassailably *good* and *above average* practices—need not be taken as boastful preening, but rather as grateful counting of God's blessings.

Indeed, Deuteronomy (recall the influence of this book on shaping Luke's Travel Narrative) *commands* recitative prayer to God *after tithing*:

> When you have finished paying all the tithe of your produce . . . giving it to the Levites, the aliens, the orphans, and the widows, so that they may eat their fill within your towns, then *you shall say before the Lord your God*: "I have removed the sacred portion from the house, and I have given it to the Levites, the resident aliens, the orphans, and the widows, in accordance with your entire commandment that you commanded me; I have neither transgressed nor forgotten any of your commandments. . . . Look down from your holy habitation, from heaven, and bless your people Israel." (Deut 26:12–15)[348]

Note well that such confession to God of one's good tithing works stresses *giving these tithes to the most vulnerable members of society* (as well as to God or, better put, on God's behalf) as the basis for God's blessing the entire community ("your people Israel"), not crowing about helping others to boost the

347. Friedrichsen, "Temple," 94; Levine, *Short Stories*, 194.

348. On this important Deuteronomy connection, see Holmgren, "Pharisee"; Levine, *Short Stories*, 187–88.

reputation of the benefactor. Though the praying Pharisee in the parable does not specifically thank God for using his tithes (and fasting) to aid the needy, there's no reason *not* to assume this charitable implication. By the same token, though the penitent tax collector does not spell out a program of helping the poor and restoring funds to those he's cheated (as chief tax collector Zacchaeus soon does [19:8]), we may presume that Luke's Jesus would certainly demand such "repentant" actions of him (cf. 3:12–13; 5:27–32; 19:7–10). Whether the Pharisee's "sacrifices" (cf. Heb 13:15–16) of money (tithes) and food (fasting) should also be seen as vicariously atoning for the community's "sinners"—like this tax collector!—is possible and intriguing,[349] but not in my judgment sufficiently hinted in Luke's immediate or overall context.

To be sure, if we grant the Pharisee's positive portrayal in Jesus's parable, we must also acknowledge its hyperbolic hue. Here we meet not just a good Pharisee, but a great one, a virtual "saint,"[350] an "over the top, overblown"[351] paragon whose tithing (on everything) and fasting (biweekly) go well beyond the call of duty and practicality (of course, so does Jesus's demand in this same chapter to "sell all that you own and distribute the money to the poor" [18:22; cf. 12:33; 14:26, 33]). As elsewhere, Jesus clearly trades for effect in extreme, exceptional *caricature*, but caricature does not equate with charlatan; hyperbole does not equal hypocrisy. Though an "overdrawn" character who might well "have brought a smile even to the faces of real Pharisee bystanders,"[352] he is no blatant fraud or "fake Pharisee."[353] Moreover, the tax collector is just as overblown in his own right with his hyperbolic claim to be "*the* sinner [τῷ ἁμαρτωλῷ, *tō hamartōlō*]... *par excellence* ... the worst of all sinners"[354] and his histrionic head-bowing, mercy-pleading, and breast-beating (characteristic of female mourners [cf. 23:27]) in the temple.[355] We have met some apparently penitent tax collectors at the Jordan River with John and at a household table with Jesus and Levi (3:12–13; 5:27–32; 7:29), but not in the temple and not in dramatic mode. If we do presume that the praying Pharisee is putting on airs

349. See Friedrichsen, "Temple," 110–19; Levine, *Short Stories*, 188; similarly Farris ("Tale") suggests that the Pharisee's supererogative tithes and fasts were acts of "intercession" or "contrition on behalf of ... the people who were not like the Pharisee: the swindlers, hypocrites, and adulterers" (28–29).

350. Levine, *Short Stories*, 188.

351. Doran, "Pharisee," 267, 269.

352. Doran, "Pharisee," 267, 270.

353. Peterson, *Tell It Slant*, 137.

354. Wallace, *Greek Grammar*, 223.

355. On Jesus's caricature of both parable figures, see Holmgren, "Pharisee," 252–53; Levine, *Short Stories*, 171; Doran, "Pharisee," 267–70.

for personal gain, then we should suspect similar machinations from the tax collector, if not more so, in light of his profession's propensity for traitorous, exploitative practices. Amy-Jill Levine provocatively queries: "The tax collector works for the government that abuses the Temple system. Will he abuse it as well by making it his own personal bank, with an automatic withdrawal of forgiveness?"[356] Whether tilting to a more positive or a more negative pole of characterization (caricature-ization), the parable allows for as much *associative* as antithetical juxtaposition of the two figures.

In any case, however we might "justify" the respective prayers of the Pharisee and tax collector, does it not come crashing down at Jesus's dichotomous punch line: "I tell you, this man [tax collector] went down to his home justified *rather than* the other [Pharisee]"? (18:14). The humble, sin-confessing tax collector is exalted, while the exalted, self-congratulating Pharisee is humbled. It all depends on the prepositional phrase παρ' ἐκεῖνον (*par' ekeinon*); and again, Jesus's language is ambiguous, perhaps deliberately so. The prepositional construction παρά (*para*) + the accusative case admits multiple meanings:[357]

- *Contrastive*: "rather than" (NRSV, CEB, NIV, NASB) or "against, contrary to"
- *Comparative*: "more than/in comparison to"[358]
- *Causative*: "because of/on account of"[359]
- *Connective*: "beside/alongside of/next to"

The final *connective* (associative) meaning, advocated in Levine's trenchant study of this parable, merits much more consideration than it has been given.[360] Accordingly, Jesus may suggest that the repentant tax collector goes

356. Levine, *Short Stories*, 174 (cf. 175).

357. Wallace (*Greek Grammar*, 378) identifies three semantic spheres of παρά (*para*) + accusative: (1) spatial—"by, alongside of, near, on"; (2) comparison—"in comparison to, more than"; (3) opposition—"against, contrary to." He includes no "causative" nuance, as I do below.

358. Doran, "Pharisee," 265–66; cf. Nolland, 2:878: "Without the Lukan framework it would seem more natural to take παρ' ἐκεῖνον as 'more than' than as 'rather than,' but the Lukan frame encourages a sharper contrast, and so I have translated as 'rather than' (despite the 'more than' required in 13:2, 4)." Quoting BDAG (758), Wallace (*Greek Grammar*) notes in relation to Luke 18:14 that, while παρά (*para*) + accusative frequently conveys a comparative relationship ("more than"), "one member [of the comparison] may receive so little attention as to pass from consideration entirely, so that the 'more than' becomes *instead of, rather than, to the exclusion of*" (297n10 [emphasis original]).

359. Friedrichsen, "Temple," 116–17 (tied in with his reading of the Pharisee's good deeds as vicariously atoning for the tax collector).

360. Levine, *Short Stories*, 192–93. The virtual neglect of this reading is all the more puzzling

home justified "along with" the genuinely righteous (because of God's grace) Pharisee, instead of setting up stark status reversals ("rather than"), namely, the former's gain of God's justification and the latter's loss of the same, despite (or because of) his self-justification. Or perhaps Jesus keeps both options on the table to punctuate his challenge. Which type of Pharisee, disciple (or other religious devotee) will you be: one who blesses God as the fountain of all righteousness, or one who trifles with prayer as a pretense for self-promotion? Regarding your attitude toward others: Will you accept penitent tax collectors among God's justified people "rather than" look down on them with disgust? Will you go "along with" them in solidarity from God's house to your homes? Better yet: Why not invite them to your homes as a foretaste of God's great restorative banquet?[361] And to flip the tables, especially in light of Christianity's long-standing Gentile dominance and anti-Judaic strains: will we Christians today welcome faithful and/or penitent Jews, whether of the "Pharisee" or "tax collector" type (both were Jews in their original context), around God's table and diligently strive in our preaching and teaching of this parable not to justify ourselves by regarding Jews, ancient or modern, with contempt.[362]

Welcomed Children and a Challenged Ruler (18:15–30)

Having stressed both the present reality and the future consummation of God's kingdom (17:20–18:8), Luke's Jesus now focuses on *admission requirements*: *Who* can enter God's saving realm, and *how* must they come in? (cf. 18:16–17, 24–27). The candidates for membership presented to Jesus couldn't be more different: on the one hand, infants and little children (18:15–17); on the other, a wealthy and pious ruler (18:18–30). Jesus's judgments also prove distinctive, not to mention disturbing. Conventional wisdom might disqualify little ones until

in light of the fact that the spatial "alongside" sense of παρά (*para*) is by no means obscure or exceptional (as in numerous *para*-compounds in Greek and English).

361. I no longer see a stark social-spatial dichotomy in Luke's narratives between temple and home, as I argued in *Journeying* (38–39), following Elliott, "Temple versus Household" (based in large measure on the present parable [215–17]). Like the Pharisees, Luke envisions people's homes as microcosms of God's house/household epitomized in the sacred temple. All creation is God's residential realm, a locus for prayer and fellowship for all peoples. To be sure, all instantiations of God's "house," including the temple, can become corrupted in various ways, necessitating repentance and reform. But such opportunities for renewal are part and parcel of the entire system in a broken world.

362. See Salmon, *Preaching*; and Levine's (*Short Stories*) biting rhetorical question: "Why is that so many interpreters find both compelling and congenial readings that damn figures identified with Jews and Judaism?" (192).

they grow up (what do they know? what use are they now?) and embrace the law-abiding official who has somehow not allowed his position and prosperity to dilute his faithfulness to God (Jesus does not dispute the man's Torah piety). But Jesus again bucks convention, approving the children as model kingdom entrants and refusing the rich ruler's application, pending satisfaction of an additional, arduous requirement.

The shockwaves of Jesus's stunning admissions policy radiate beyond the present characters to all would-be participants in God's realm, including Jesus's chosen associates. In fact, these disciples become the targets of Jesus's "Truly I tell you" punch lines (18:17, 29), since they are the ones (not the Pharisees) who try to *block* the children's coming to Jesus and who *query* his rough response to the seeker-ruler (18:15, 26). Though kingdom insiders, they still have much to learn about others' place in God's household. Once again, Jesus's teaching resists simplistic categories. Whereas he completely reverses the disciples' dismissive judgments about little ones, his dealings with the wealthy official prove more nuanced than the disciples—and many interpreters—think. A robust theological reading refuses to shut the door on this ruler prematurely, since "what is impossible for mortals is possible for God" (18:27).

Do Not Obstruct the Blessing of Children (18:15–17)

Proceeding from a parable depicting God's welcome of humble, thankful petitioners (18:9–14), Luke presents a scene in which "people"[363] bring infants to Jesus so he might graciously touch them. Who could be more humble and in need of blessing than these babes (cf. 10:21)? Yet, they might also be regarded as insignificant *nobodies* and irritating *nuisances* impeding important people, like Jesus, from their work.[364] Jesus nears the culmination of his urgent kingdom mission; this is no time for babysitting. So think Jesus's disciples, so much

363. Thus the NRSV reflects the generic third person plural pronoun "they" embedded in the verb προσέφερον, *prosepheron*. Somewhat unusually, no mention is made of mother or father, thus raising the possibility that some of these infants have been abandoned by their parents.

364. This is not to deny the high value placed on children in Jewish families as precious gifts from God (see Strange, *Children*, 9–18, 46–60). Nonetheless, attitudes toward infants (esp. female babies) were more mixed in the wider Greco-Roman world, and in any case, infants, requiring much attention and resources and subject to high mortality risk in antiquity, would greatly complicate the travel and mission of Jesus. In the disciples' view, the kingdom-building Messiah en route to Jerusalem should scarcely be bothered with these little ones, who might not even survive the journey anyway. On God's realm as a "kingdom of nobodies and nuisances," see Crossan, *Jesus*, 54–64, and *Historical Jesus*, 266–68; Caputo, *Weakness*, 30–38, 45–47, 60, 107 (cf. 1 Cor 1:26–28).

so that they "sternly ordered" (ἐπιτιμάω, *epitimaō*) the infant bearers to stop and desist their interfering activity (18:15). Heretofore, this term has applied to *Jesus's* stiff "rebuke" of *evil spirits* (4:35, 41; 9:42), *high fever* (4:39) and *violent weather* (8:24) threatening the welfare of men and women; and twice he has also "rebuked" his own disciples: first, for not grasping his messianic identification with suffering humanity (9:20–22); and second, for proposing a brutal reprisal against an inhospitable Samaritan village (9:55). In all these instances, Jesus issues a stern rebuttal to forces or followers obstructing his compassionate outreach to the afflicted and alienated.

With the disciples' dismissal of infants so woefully out of step with Jesus's aims, it comes as no surprise that he countermands their blockade order: "Let the little children [παιδία, *paidia*] come to me, and do not stop [μὴ κωλύετε, *mē kōlyete*] them; for it is to such as these that the kingdom of God belongs" (18:16). This response should not come as news to Jesus's followers. Just before embarking on the Jerusalem journey, Jesus received a little child (παιδίον, *paidion*) and announced that anyone who welcomed such a person welcomed Jesus himself and attained true greatness (9:47–48). But no sooner had Jesus made the point than John, speaking on behalf of his brother-apostles, proudly reported their stern repudiation of an exorcist using Jesus's name without proper authorization. So again they draw Jesus's retort: "Do not stop [μὴ κωλύετε, *mē kōlyete*] him [the exorcist]; for whoever is not against you is for you" (9:50). Though they have traveled much further with Jesus since that moment, the disciples must still be stopped from stopping the inclusion of others among the citizens of God's realm. Indeed, they must face the sober fact that those they try to stop—like these little children—represent the *standard* entrants into God's community by which all others are judged: "Whoever does not receive the kingdom of God as a little child will never enter it" (18:17).

Do Not Limit the Saving Will of God (18:18–30)

The next person who approaches Jesus is no child in age or status. He is introduced as a "certain ruler," an authority figure of advanced standing and probably years. Luke never calls him a "young man" (as in Matt 19:22), which in any case ill fits someone reflecting back on his early years ("since my youth" [Luke 18:21]). He appears to be a respected community *elder*. But however mature and influential he might be, his place in God's realm depends on his faithful identification with a "little child" (18:17). The disciples' recent failure in this regard primes us to expect more resistance from this ruler, especially when we learn that he is *very rich* (18:23). But Luke holds back this economic datum until later in the story. To be sure, the man's wealth becomes the key sticking point hindering his joining Jesus's movement. But his discussion with Jesus up to that point, his demeanor at the moment of decision, and Jesus's final response all suggest the rich ruler is not as far from God's kingdom (cf. Mark 12:34) as we might think.

The ruler addresses Jesus with high respect as "Good Teacher" and asks the vital question: "What must I do to inherit eternal life?" (Luke 18:18). This question closely echoes a legal scholar's earlier opening gambit with Jesus (10:25), except that the ruler adds the virtuous descriptor "good" (ἀγαθέ, *agathe*), and the narrator omits any mention of him seeking to "test Jesus." "Good Teacher" may not rise to the level of "Messiah" or "Lord," but it is loftier than plain "Teacher," which in itself is not disrespectful but can coordinate with a certain wariness of Jesus's authority (7:40; 8:49; 9:38; 11:45; 12:13; 19:39; 20:21, 28, 39). Still, Jesus pounces on the ruler's "good" address: "Why do you call me good? No one is good except the one God [εἷς ὁ θεός, *heis ho theos*]" (18:19 CEB). The surprise here comes less from Jesus's rebuke of a sincere seeker (he often sets inquirers back on their heels) than from his apparent self-distancing from God, marking an awkward, even unorthodox, christological moment.

Matthew, for one, seems concerned, assuming Mark as his main source. While Luke adopts Mark's text without change, Matthew redacts both the rich man's question and Jesus's response, shifting the "good" away from Jesus's identity to the man's activity:

- *Question*: "Teacher, what *good deed* [ἀγαθόν, *agathon*] must I do to have eternal life?"
- *Answer*: "Why do you ask me about *what is good* [του ἀγαθοῦ, *tou agathou*]? There is only one who is *good* [ὁ ἀγαθός, *ho agathos*]" (Matt 19:16–17).

But this massaging of a christological problem, if that is what Matthew is doing,[365] is not necessary. For Luke (and Mark), the issue is less about Jesus's self-understanding as God's intimate Son—which Jesus affirms in Luke 10:21–23—than about his Jewish view of God. The crux is *theological* more than christological. Luke's Jesus accepts the Torah's *Shema*, Israel's classic confession of faith: "Hear, O Israel: The Lord our God, the Lord is one" (Deut 6:4 NIV, NASB). Accordingly, Jesus tests the ruler's orthodoxy and begins to answer his question about

365. Matthew places greater emphasis on "good deeds" than other Gospels do (5:16; 7:17–19; 11:19; 12:34–35; 13:37–38; 25:21, 23, 31–46; 26:10), without any Protestant angst about "works righteousness"; hence, the focus here (Matt 19:16–17) may be more ethical than christological.

inheriting eternal life, which is to say, experiencing the fullness of God's life. Jesus essentially outlines the same path to life presented earlier to the lawyer: the way of Torah, God's gift of life grounded on twin pillars of consuming love for God and considerate love of neighbor —"Do this, and you will live" (10:28). The first half of the Decalogue details basic expressions of loving the one good God (Exod 20:2–11; Deut 5:6–15). Though Jesus does not enumerate these theological requirements to the ruler (likely because he discerns his faithfulness on these matters), he leaves no doubt as to their foundational importance: apart from God, there is no life, certainly no *good* life.

Jesus does, however, break down the obligations of neighborly love listed in the second part of the Decalogue, citing prohibitions of adultery, murder, theft, and false testimony, and the affirmation of honoring parents (cf. Exod 20:12–17; Deut 5:16–21). Yet, he cites these mandates, not to indict the ruler on any of them, but to commend his knowledge of the law: "You know [οἶδας, *oidas*] the commandments" (Luke 18:20). And this is no mere intellectual knowledge without practice. Upon hearing the ruler's claim to have kept all these things "since my youth," Jesus offers no rebuttal (18:21). By all accounts, the ruler is a dedicated law-observant Jew, a man after Jesus's own heart in many respects. If he were trying to justify himself (which is not indicated here), he would seem to have good grounds for doing so.

But that is not the end of the matter regarding neighborly love. While Jesus pressed the lawyer, via a vivid parable, to include Samaritans among God's love-worthy people (10:25–37), Jesus presents a more radical, direct challenge to the ruler: "You still lack one thing. Sell everything you have, and disburse it all to the poor, and you will have treasure in heaven. Then come, follow me" (18:22 AT).[366] This call to economic divestment and redistribution to poor neighbors is no new criterion for discipleship. Jesus laid out these same requirements (costs) to the swelling throng that began tagging along (14:25, 33; cf. 12:33–34). But those crowds represented a fickle bunch, with varying degrees of attachment to the law and to Jesus. Now we learn that Jesus does not mitigate the demands of discipleship for any individuals, however "good" they might be. No exemptions for this model ruler. Moreover, this case reinforces Jesus's charitable concern for all poor people in God's universal realm, not only those in his inner circle. Luke's Jesus does not strictly advocate a community pooling of goods, as practiced by the early church and Qumran sect (Acts 2:44–45; 4:32, 34; 1QS 1.11–12; 5.2; 6.18–23). He does *not* tell the ruler to sell everything and give the proceeds *to him and his poor followers*.

366. The stress on (only) *one* (ἕν, *hen*) thing the man lacks again assumes the man's otherwise commendable piety.

The responses that ensue to Jesus's challenge by both the ruler and Jesus are emotion-laden, rich with pathos—not reductive, calculating decisions. The ruler "became sad" when he "heard" Jesus's sell-all proposition, entangled with the fact that the man was "very rich" (as we just now learn [18:23]). Before we unpack this "sad" reaction, two matters merit attention. First, Luke registers only the ruler's emotional struggle, *not* that he decisively "went/turned away [ἀπῆλθεν, *apēlthen*]" from Jesus, reported in Matt 19:22//Mark 10:22; the possibility of overcoming his angst and deciding to follow Jesus—on Jesus's stringent terms—remains open. Second, though a major contributing factor to his reaction, the man's opulence is not wholly determinative. Rather than stating that the ruler "became sad *because* [ὅτι, *hoti*] he was very rich," Luke (also Matthew and Mark) presents two closely linked, yet independent, clauses: "he became sad; *for* [γάρ, *gar*] he was very rich." This wording allows for more complex cognitive-affective processing of Jesus's summons than a knee-jerk outburst, on the order of "No way am I giving up my whole fortune for the poor—are you crazy?!"

Of course, Luke provides no deep psychological analysis of the ruler. We know that he's sad and that this has something to do with Jesus's charge and the man's wealth. So we must not overspeculate. But using a disciplined imagination grounded in the scene at hand and in basic human emotional experience, we may sketch a more detailed interpretive landscape. The key affective term translated rather blandly as "sad" (NRSV, CEB) is the intensive adjective περίλυπος (*perilypos*), meaning, at the very least, "quite sad" (NAB) or "very sad" (NIV, NASB), but closer to the mark would be "deeply grieving" (BDAG), "grief-stricken," or "deeply distressed." The painful *grief* element should be taken seriously. Luke's only other use of the λυπ- (*lyp*-) word group occurs with reference to Peter, James, and John's exhausting "grief" (λύπη, *lypē*) over the imminent prospects of Jesus's arrest and death (see discussion on Luke 22:45). Matthew and Mark, however, use the full περίλυπος (*perilypos*) form in the same incident to describe *Jesus's* intense grief over his ominous fate (Matt 26:38//Mark 14:34).

Though most poignantly felt in situations of lost life, whether one's own or a loved one's, soon expected or recently experienced, other significant losses, perceived or actual, can also trigger heavy grief, such as Cain's shocking loss of God's highest favor: "On Kain and on his offerings [God] was not intent. And it distressed Kain exceedingly [ἐλύπησεν, *elypēsen*], and he collapsed in countenance. And the Lord God said to Kain, 'Why have you become deeply grieved [περίλυπος, *perilypos*], and why has your countenance collapsed?'" (Gen 4:5–6 NETS). Cain's fratricidal response also bears witness to the potential messy entwinement of *grief* (λύπη, *lypē*) with *anger* (ὀργή, *orgē*) (cf. Neh 5:6; Esth 1:12;

2:21; Sir 4:2; Tob 3:1; Mark 3:5).[367] The pain of loss not only fells one's face, but can also fire up one's fury. Deep loss is hard to bear.

The tumultuous power of grief (and other emotions) has been freshly investigated in recent decades by scholars in the humanities and sciences, combining rigorous analytic and reflective poetic sensibilities. The neuroscientist and molecular biologist Giovanni Frazzetto describes the agonizing "cascade of grief" in relation to physical and psychological hurt: "The physical pain sensed when we stub a toe or hit a wall is the effect of a *collision* that damages our tissue. The pain of loss or the breaking of an emotional bond, on the other hand, is the consequence of a physical *separation*. Something departs from our surroundings and from our lives. All the same its disappearance hurts us, causing pain just as would colliding with the wall."[368] In her seminal work on emotion *Upheavals of Thought*, based on her 1993 Gifford Lectures, philosopher Martha Nussbaum deeply probes her personal experience of grief:

> When I grieve, I do not first of all coolly embrace the proposition, "My wonderful mother is dead," and then set about grieving. No, the real, full recognition of that terrible event . . . *is* the upheaval. It is as I described it: like putting a nail into your stomach. The appearance that she is dead sits there . . . asking me what I am going to do with it. . . . If I go up to embrace the death image, if I take it into myself as the way things are, it is at that very moment, in that cognitive act itself, that I am putting the world's nail into my own insides. That is not preparation for upheaval, that is upheaval itself. That very act of assent is itself a tearing of my self-sufficient condition. Knowing can be violent, given the truths that are there to be known.[369]

Informing Nussbaum's subjective experience is her critical analysis of Chrysippus, an early proponent of Greek Stoic philosophy. At root, Chrysippus acknowledged grief's apt response to matters of vital, rather than trivial, concern. According to Nussbaum, "Chrysippus plausibly said that grief . . . contains not only the judgment that an important part of my life is gone, but that *it is right* to be upset about that: it makes a truth-claim about its own evaluations. It asserts the real value of the object, it says that getting upset is a response to something really important, not just a whim." Because grief is so intimately attached to a lost, prized "object," it represents a "wrenching, tearing

367. In fact, the LXX of Gen 4:5–6 reinforces the anger-grief connection by using λυπέω/περίλυπος (*lypeō/perilypos*) to render the Hebrew חרה (*ḥarah*), "to burn (with anger)"; cf. Jonah 4:1, 4, 9; Schlimm, *Fratricide*, 197–98.

368. Frazzetto, *Joy*, 120 (emphasis original).

369. Nussbaum, *Upheavals*, 45 (emphasis original).

violation of [one's] self-sufficiency and . . . undisturbed condition. The passion is a 'very violent motion' that carries us along, 'pushing us violently' toward action."[370] While it tends to dissipate over time, it initially delivers a thunder punch to the gut; or in Chrysippus's terms (cited by Nussbaum), it is "*prosphaton* [πρόσφατον]: not yet spoiled or digested, 'fresh.' . . . The 'fresh' acceptance is something tearing and wrenching. Since it concerns [one's] deepest values and projects, it upsets everything in me, all the cognitive structures of hope, cherishing, and expectation . . . built up around those values."[371]

I propose that the ruler's deep grief response to Jesus's "one thing you lack" challenge signals a gut-wrenching, painfully raw ("fresh") cognitive-affective "collision." It slams him against the wall and shakes him to his core, demanding that he come to grips with the terrible decision Jesus imposes. Neither he nor Jesus is playing any games: this is dire business, a matter of (eternal) life and death. This is not a wealthy character known from Jesus's parables: not the stockpiling rich fool (12:16–21), not the calculating estate-owner (16:1–8), and even less, the callous elite who ignored poor Lazarus (16:19–31). The present ruler struggles, as any normal mortal would do, with the nuclear option of giving *everything* he has to the poor, beyond the Torah principle of aiding the poor however one can. Deuteronomic instruction, alluded to throughout the Travel Narrative, is relevant here: "Giving you shall give to him, and you shall lend him a loan whatever he needs, and *you shall not be grieved* [λυπηθήσῃ, *lypēthēsē*] in your heart when you give to him, because through this thing the Lord your God will bless you in all your works and in all to which you may put your hand. For the needy shall not fail from the earth" (Deut 15:10–11 NETS). As genuinely law-observant, the rich ruler would know this teaching and in all likelihood have practiced it. But Jesus's *total divestment* policy ratchets up Deuteronomy to the max.

The ruler does not grieve over the call to help the poor; he does not begrudge anyone a life-sustaining portion of his resources. Rather, he grieves intensely over the complete gutting of his means that Jesus calls for, the gut-punching *loss* of his entire fortune for the poor's sake, which is tantamount to becoming the lowest of the poor to aid the poor. Of course, Jesus asks nothing of the ruler that he, Jesus, has not exemplified. As Paul says concerning "our Lord Jesus Christ . . . though he was rich, yet for your sakes he became poor, so that by his poverty you might become rich" (2 Cor 8:9). Fine, but the transition from abundant wealth to abject poverty is a grief-worthy shock to the system under any reckoning. If the ruler had not been so aggrieved, he would not have taken Jesus seriously.

370. Nussbaum, *Therapy*, 380 (emphasis original).
371. Nussbaum, *Therapy*, 381–82.

But taking Jesus seriously and struggling with the "violent," "colliding" force of Jesus's ethic does not equate to following his way. Nor does it eliminate the possible mixing of raw anger with the grief: "How dare Jesus make such an imperious demand and not appreciate the generous charity I do offer!" (my interjection; the ruler never says this). But it does give the ruler credit for a deeply engaged rational-emotional response, as opposed to a flippant dismissal. He does not stomp off in a huff. Furthermore, I suggest that the palpable prospect of *significant loss* concerns not only, or even primarily, monetary deficit, though this factor surely contributes to the man's swirl of thoughts and feelings. But recall his leading question about *inheriting eternal life*, which he believes that Jesus can illuminate. Now that Jesus has answered, the ruler must confront the steep price tag Jesus puts on eternal life. He *loses* one way or another: either all his possessions or the prospect of eternal life. No wonder he's consumed by grief. Of course, we can glibly quote Jesus's earlier assessment: "Those who want to save their life will lose it, and those who lose their life for my sake will save it. What does it profit them if they gain the whole world, but lose or forfeit themselves?" (9:24–25). In those terms, the trade-off is evident, but by no means *easy*. It is a *hard* deal to accept, and Jesus knows it.[372]

Jesus does not leave the ruler dangling in his terrible grief, though his pastoral response is not altogether comforting. But neither is it unsympathetic. He first "looked at" the ruler (Luke 18:24).[373] Though we know the power of the eyes to convey inner thoughts and feelings (cf. 11:34–36), we are not told what kind of knowing "look" Jesus gives here. Is it soft and kind, appreciating the ruler's struggle; or hard and piercing, pressing him to overcome his unhealthy attachment to earthly riches? In any case, Jesus does not turn away from the man. Though he proceeds to speak about "those who have wealth" as a group, Jesus continues to engage the individual before him, acknowledging "how hard" it is for this ruler and those like him "to enter the kingdom of God"—so hard, in fact, that they would have better luck squeezing a gangly, lumpy camel through the eye of a needle! (18:24–25).

372. Cf. the concluding statements in Spinoza, *Ethics* (trans. Curley): "Of course, what is found so rarely must be hard. For if salvation were at hand, and could be found without great effort, how could nearly everyone neglect it? But all things excellent are as difficult as they are rare" (2:308).

373. Some ancient texts add περίλυπον γενόμενον (*perilypon genomenon*) at various places in 18:24 ("Jesus looked at him *who had deeply grieved*"), reinforcing the description of the ruler's grief-reaction in the previous verse. Teetering between the solid witnesses (א, B, L) that omit the extra "grief" phrase and "Luke's penchant of repeating a word or phrase in adjacent passages," the UBS committee opted to retain the phrase, albeit in brackets (Bruce Metzger, *Textual Commentary*, 143; cf. Cadbury, "Four Features," 88–97).

The image is patently absurd (and not a little funny), not some object lesson about shedding one's material baggage as might be necessary to get a pack animal through a narrow gate.[374] However much one strips down a camel's load, however much weight it loses, it is *never* going through a needle's tiny aperture (it is hard enough to get a thread through!). This is a picture of *impossibility*, not merely difficulty.[375] That seems like bad news for the ruler, adding the insult of hopelessness to the injury of grief. God's realm of eternal life seems forever barred to rich folk, and Jesus aims for that hard truth to sink deeper into this man's heart. It is *impossible* for him to secure God's life on his own. Once entangled with Mammon for whatever reason (even apparently benign sources like hard work, frugal management, or good fortune), there's nothing anyone can do, even with extreme effort, to extricate oneself from its clutches. In a sense, then, Jesus does not so much blame the rich ruler as feel the pain of his impossible predicament. But while this response may count as empathy (as defined above), it has not yet moved to *sympathetic compassion* that seeks to help and to save, as the wider audience, including Jesus's disciples, patently discern, asking: "Then who can be saved?" (18:26).

This question creates a wider frame of application than to wealthy persons only. Though most in Jesus's audience would not qualify as well-heeled, they rightly recognize their own attachment to whatever resources they do possess; by necessity, the poor might even cling more tenaciously to the little they have (though contemporary studies also evidence how remarkably generous the poor can be). In any case, this matter of selling *all* is hard for *everyone* to handle. Plus, if *this particular rich man*—devout, honorable, and probably charitable—is brought to paralyzing grief by Jesus's demand, then what hope is there for any of us? That is the critical issue Jesus has been driving at throughout this discussion, setting up his climactic pronouncement for rich and poor alike: "What is impossible for mortals is possible for God." Or alternatively, "The things utterly beyond the power [ἀδύνατα, *adynata*] of human beings, are well within the power [δυνατά, *dynata*] of God to achieve" (18:27 AT). God is the only "Savior" (cf. 1:47) of humankind. No mortal, rich or poor, can give one's life sufficiently to gain God's eternal life, which is God's alone to give.

Thankfully, for this rich ruler as much as for anyone else, God's transforming work of salvation has flourished with fresh "possibility" in the mission

374. Popular devotional applications suggesting that a camel *could* make it through one particular city entrance (a so-called Needle Gate) *if* it knelt down on all four knees with all baggage removed rest on spurious historical evidence and ignore the *intentional impossibility* behind Jesus's imagined scene.

375. On the importance of the impossible in Jesus's vision of God's kingdom, see Caputo, *What Would Jesus Deconstruct?*, 45–46, 66–73, 84–86.

of Jesus Messiah. Witness Jesus's closest followers, as Peter represents them: "Look, we have left our homes and followed you" (18:28). Though this statement could be read as a sample of Petrine bravado, in the absence of rebuke it is better seen as an honest confession. Though not rich on the ruler's scale, Jesus's disciples did have businesses, families, and some possessions, which they abruptly abandoned in response to the brazen "Follow me!" summons of an itinerant preacher from Nazareth (5:9–11, 27–28).[376] While Peter, James, and John were partly motivated by Jesus's amazing control of fish (5:1–9), they hardly had enough evidence to warrant giving up everything for him and were told only that they would be "catching people" (5:10), not sacrificing everything for the poor. Moreover, they had scant time to think through the implications of following Jesus with total abandon. But leave everything they did (5:11), not because of their superior piety or prescience, but because of God's compelling grace and power manifest in Jesus's word and deed. By any natural assessment, a crew of hard-working Galilean fishermen, tax collectors (Levi in 5:27–28), and other ordinary folk would be the last people we might expect betting their whole lives on Jesus of Nazareth as the anointed co-regent of God's realm.

By following Jesus, these disciples embarked on a "life" venture they never dreamed possible, which Jesus now explicates not simply as "eternal life in the age to come," but also as rich, restorative life "in this age" in God's royal community. A compensatory principle applies. By leaving behind "house or wife or brothers or parents or children," they "*get back* [ἀπολάβῃ, *apolabē*] very much more" in terms of spiritual family and benefits—indeed, the full resources of God's bountiful kingdom (18:29–30; cf. 8:19–21; 11:27–28; 12:32–34). God makes "possible" their surviving—and thriving—through the generous fellowship of God's household. In this respect, the "impossible" calculus of loss becomes gain. Jesus's disciples have begun to grasp this point, though they still have much to learn, as the next scene demonstrates (18:31–34). The rich ruler just now confronts this exciting, though undeniably wrenching, perspective. The hope—and still live *possibility*—is that the dynamic, gracious God will overwhelm the man's crisis of grief and propel him to join Jesus's journey.

Stage 4: Pressing On to Suffer and Save in the Face of Injustice and Ignorance (18:31–19:44)

Jesus's announcement to the Twelve, "See, we are going up to Jerusalem" (18:31), signals the beginning of the last and shortest leg of the journey. Placing this

376. See Spencer, "Follow Me."

travel note on the lips of Jesus, punctuated by his "See/Look" (ἰδού, *idou*) exclamation, reinforces the nearness (at last!) of the destination. This anticipation heightens with pinpointing a location (finally!)—the city of Jericho, some twenty miles northeast of Jerusalem (18:35; 19:1)—and providing regular updates: "he was near Jerusalem" (19:11); "going up to Jerusalem" (19:28); "he came near and saw the city" (19:41). The Jericho-Jerusalem route recalls the setting for Jesus's good Samaritan parable early in the Travel Narrative, stressing the dangerous pitfalls of this highway and opportunities for compassionate ministry (10:30–35). Jesus now treads this path himself.

Jesus's awareness of the perilous fate awaiting him in Jerusalem dominates the opening scene (18:31–34) and sets the tone for what follows. In this surging crisis mode, issues of *power* and *perception* come to the fore, particularly problems of *injustice* (misuse of power) and *ignorance* (lack of perception). Jesus again informs the Twelve that ruling powers of state will soon seize, mock, and kill him (18:32–33). Jesus will fall victim to injustice. What does this tragic destiny mean for his mission as co-regent of God's kingdom and consummative heir of David's throne? The prospect that "on the third day he will rise again" (18:33) sounds more promising but does not allay the turmoil of Jesus's violent death. How does the impending imperial brutality against Jesus impinge on his dealing with a suspicious Jewish agent of Rome, the tax collector Zacchaeus, a *rich chief official*, no less (19:2)? Will Jesus be more cautious now about fraternizing with tax agents? In his final parable on the road, Jesus considers the established networks of "royal power" (19:12), pulling no punches about its harsh reprisals against any who buck the system (19:22–27). Then, as he brazenly approaches Jerusalem in a manner evoking Solomon's enthronement, inspiring shouts of kingly acclamation (19:28–38), Jesus suddenly breaks down—in unmanly, unkingly fashion—despondently weeping over the city he's about to enter (19:41–44). What kind of king is Jesus in the face of unjust powers arrayed against him?

Moreover, how do the Twelve (18:31; 19:29), the crowds (18:36; 19:3), the Pharisees (19:39), and the people of Jerusalem (19:41–44) negotiate Jesus's messianic mission in the face of complex power politics? Here the hermeneutical and epistemological challenge emerges again with particular force—and frustration. One way or another, all of Jesus's constituencies, from the most intimate to the most distant, have blind spots. They do not know; they do not perceive. Framing this final segment of the Travel Narrative are references to veiled understanding at this critical juncture. In both cases knowledge is said to be "cryptic" (κρύπτω, *kryptō*) or "hidden" from certain groups: first, the twelve apostles, and last, personified Jerusalem.

- *The Twelve*: "But they understood nothing about all these things; in fact, what he said *was hidden* [κεκρυμμένον, *kekrymmenon*] from them, and they did not grasp/ know [ἐγίνωσκον, *eginōskon*] what was said" (18:34).
- *Jerusalem*: "If you, even you, had only recognized/known [ἔγνως, *egnōs*] on this day the things that make for peace! But now they *are hidden* [ἐκρύβη, *ekrybē*] from your eyes" (19:42).

The passive constructions raise the issue of responsibility. If we take God as the implied subject (divine passive), God appears to be purposefully hiding spiritual knowledge from the Twelve and Jerusalem. This is not the first time Jesus's disciples have been obstructed in their education: "But they did not understand/know [ἠγνόουν, *ēgnooun*] this saying: its meaning *was concealed* from them, so that they could not perceive it" (9:45). These implications of God's veiling action chafe against Jesus's earlier lament concerning the people's willful obstinacy (13:34), to say nothing of promises that "nothing is hidden [κρυπτόν, *krypton*] that will not be disclosed, nor is anything secret/not known [οὐ μὴ γνωσθῇ, *ou mē gnōsthē*] that will not become known and come to light" (8:17; 12:2; cf. 10:21–24).

With other biblical writers, Luke lives with the tension of divine sovereignty and human responsibility without offering a neat and tidy resolution. While this delicate balance undermines extreme claims that God fiendishly hides the truth from those open to see it, it does tip the scale toward the primacy of divine revelation. If God the Father and Christ the Son—God's prime Revealer (10:22)—do not disclose divine truth, then flawed and finite human beings will not, cannot, find it on their own. Fortunately, the biblical God wants to be known as intimately as this God knows all people. God is open and outreaching, not reserved and reclusive. God does not hide God's self from view, but when people close their eyes and turn their backs on God's most personal self-revelation in Christ, this choice affects God deeply. Any dedicated teacher knows something of the personal struggle with failing students, even with those who couldn't care less. The best teachers feel some responsibility for those who do not "get it." What might they have done to make things clearer or more persuasive? It is *as if they hid* the master key to knowledge (cf. 11:52). It gnaws at the teacher's gut. It may even trigger anguished tears, like those that Jesus pours out over the willful ignorance of the city of Jerusalem (19:41–42).

Within this depressing frame, however, of blindness to God's will by Jesus's closest followers, as well as by the denizens of Jerusalem, light continues to radiate in the intervening material. The revealing Christ outshines the concealing counterpart in stunning fashion. In a related pair of incidents near and within Jericho, Jesus enables two sight-impaired men—one because of blindness, the other because of shortness—to see Jesus not only physically, but also perceptively and salvifically: the blind man comes to saving (σῴζω, *sōzō*) faith in Jesus and follows him (18:42–43); the diminutive tax collector comes to host Jesus and receive his blessing of salvation (σωτηρία, *sōtēria* [19:9]). We should also notice, however, that as both scenes highlight Jesus's revelatory purpose, they also emphasize the strong drive of the two sight-limited characters to see Jesus. Their seeking initiative meets Jesus's seeking-and-saving intention (cf. 19:10). To be sure, others persist in trying to block the path to recognition, whether bystanders shouting down the blind man (18:39), crowds grumbling about the "sinner" tax collector (19:7), or Pharisees resisting the people's adulation of Jesus (19:39). But not only do the seekers surmount these obstructive critics, Jesus announces in the last instance that even *the rocks* on the roadside are poised to praise him as God's anointed king (19:40). Nature, as God's creation, knows better the work of God in Christ than some people. Actual rocks prove more open to God's will than some hard, rock-hearted religious experts (cf. 8:13).

Final Prediction of Execution and Resurrection (18:31–34)

Just before setting out on the Jerusalem trek, Jesus twice informed his disciples of the Son of Humankind's destiny of suffering, betrayal, execution, and resurrection (9:22, 44). At the beginning of stage 2, Jesus specified that these tragic events would unfold in Jerusalem, where he "must" go to meet the same violent end that Israel's prophets often experienced (13:33–34). The disciples, however, have not apprehended these ominous disclosures about Jesus's fate, which run so counter to their immediate dreams of greatness (9:45–48). Now as the long trek to Jerusalem winds down, Jesus reprises his morbid forecast, with additional flourishes.

Beyond his previous predictions, he adds that the terrible fate awaiting him not only mirrors the rough treatment Israel's prophets personally received in Jerusalem, but also fulfills "everything that is written . . . by the prophets" in the Jewish Scriptures (18:31). Though citing no specific texts, Jesus assures his confidants that the harsh trials he will soon endure somehow fit into God's comprehensive ("everything") plan for humanity outlined in the Bible. But then he hits them with more grisly details about coming events. Not only will "human hands" generally (9:44) and Jewish religious leaders more particularly (9:22) attack the Son of Humankind, but they will also conspire with "the Gentiles," that is, the *Roman military-judicial au-*

thorities, who will carry out Jesus's execution. And they will show no mercy, running Jesus through a battery of mockeries, insults, spittings, and floggings en route to killing him. Jesus does mention again, almost as an afterthought, that "on the third day he will rise again"; but the main message he leaves ringing in his disciples' ears concerns his imminent torturous demise (18:32–33).

What are they supposed to do with this shocking information? How should they process it? Despite Jesus's earlier previews of his arrest and execution, it is not surprising that the disciples still "understood nothing about all these things" (18:34), if for no other reason than the prospects are just too horrible to contemplate. Repression trumps recognition. Moreover, we might chide the Twelve for not knowing better the prophetic Scriptures that Jesus references, but in all honesty, the notion of a dead Messiah or Son of Humankind is far from obvious there. Though veneration of Jewish martyrs became popular after the Maccabean Revolt (2 Macc 6–7; 4 Macc 6–18), the notion of a *crucified Messiah* had no patent precedents or proponents in early Jewish thought, as far as we know. In this respect, Jesus's messianic mission appears unique. Another problem to consider: if the disciples somehow come to realize the unthinkable course Jesus charts for himself, what would they do about it? What *could* they do if this is God's plan that "must" be done? Would they flee, try to divert Jesus's death march, hatch some plan of counterattack, futile though it would be against Roman troops? Their ignorance spares them further consternation, at least for awhile. Maybe God's blocking (hiding) their understanding is an act of mercy, sparing them mind-blowing distress if they'd taken it all in at this juncture.

Of course, from the later vantage point of the disciples and Luke's readers, Jesus's death comes into much clearer perspective. God's raising Jesus from the dead and outpouring of the Spirit make all the difference (Acts 2:14–36; 3:13–26). Scriptural images surrounding Isaiah's suffering servant and the unjustly persecuted righteous figures in the Psalms begin to appear in a new christological light. But in the story time of Luke's Gospel, in those tense days *before* Jesus's death and resurrection, these insights about a God-ordained, salvation-centered *crucifixion* would have been virtually inconceivable for Jesus's followers. And even *after* the first Easter, the experience of Christ's violent death remains hard to swallow. Paul candidly admits that the extraordinary saving gospel of "Christ crucified" remains a "stumbling block [σκάνδαλον, *skandalon*] to Jews and foolishness [μωρίαν, *mōrian*] to Gentiles" (1 Cor 1:23), cutting across all commonsense conceptions of power and wisdom (1:18–31). What is more scandalous and moronic than a Messiah/Savior dying in the most ignominious way as an enemy of the state?

The resurrection of Jesus, subsequent success of the church, and sophisticated theologizing about Christ's atoning sacrifice do not—must not—romanticize away the horrible offense of crucifixion. As Jürgen Moltmann approvingly cites H. J. Iwand, "The cross is the utterly incommensurable factor in the revelation of God. We have become far too used to it. We have surrounded the scandal of the cross with roses." Continuing in Moltmann's own words, "What interest can the religious longing for fellowship with God have in the crucifixion of its God, and his powerlessness and abandonment in absolute death? In spite of all the 'roses' which the needs of religion and theological interpretation have draped round the cross, the cross is the really irreligious thing in Christian faith." It is "radical" and "dangerous."[377]

> The "religion of the cross," if faith on this basis can ever be so called, does not elevate and edify in the usual sense, but scandalizes; and most of all it scandalizes one's "co-religionists" in one's own circle. But by this scandal, it brings liberation into a world which is not free. For ultimately, in a civilization which is constructed on the principle of achievement and enjoyment, and therefore makes pain and death a private matter, excluded from its public life, so that in the final issue the world must no longer be experienced as offering resistance, there is nothing so unpopular as for the crucified God to be made a present reality through faith.[378]

By any honest reckoning, then, Jesus's death mission *should be hard to grasp*!

Jesus Sightings by a Blind Man and a Tax Collector (18:35–19:10)

In marked contrast to the Twelve's persisting perceptual blindness concerning Jesus's death and resurrection, two men encountering Jesus for the first time overcome their somatic-visual disabilities to *see Jesus* in a fresh light—physically and spiritually—with Jesus's revelatory help. Despite their opposite social locations—one an unnamed, homeless blind beggar, the other a wealthy chief tax collector and homeowner named Zacchaeus—Luke coordinates their seeking, sighting, and saving experiences with Jesus, as the following chart illustrates, reinforcing the Son of Humankind's inclusive outreach to all types of "lost" people (19:10).

377. Moltmann, *Crucified God*, 36, 37–38.
378. Moltmann, *Crucified God*, 39.

	A blind man sees Jesus (18:35–43)	**A tax collector sees Jesus (19:1–10)**
Initial setting:	Roadside near Jericho	Sycamore tree in Jericho
Visual disability:	Total blindness	Short stature
Social status:	Poor beggar	Wealthy tax official
Determined outreach to Jesus:	Shouting loudly to "Jesus, Son of David" (18:38)	Running ahead and climbing up a tree
Obstruction by the crowd:	Sternly ordering the blind man to keep quiet	Blocking Zacchaeus's way and grumbling about his "sinner" reputation
Response to Jesus's lordship:	"*Lord*, let me see again" (18:41)	"Look, half of my possessions, *Lord*, I will give to the poor, and if I have defrauded anyone of anything, I will pay back four times as much" (19:8)
Jesus's saving response:	"Receive your sight; your faith has *saved* [σέσωκεν, *sesōken*] you" (18:42)	"Today *salvation* [σωτηρία, *sōtēria*] has come to this house, because he too is a son of Abraham" (19:9)
Final setting:	Following Jesus on his journey	Fellowship with Jesus in Zacchaeus's house

As these stories solidify the seeking-and-saving thrust of Jesus's mission (19:10), they highlight the seeking *of* Jesus (object) by the blind man and tax collector as much as their being sought *by* Jesus (subject) in the face of obstructive crowds. After tracking key aspects of setting, I focus on three character groups in these related incidents: stoppers, seekers, and Savior Jesus.

Settings (18:35; 19:1)

The two stories share a general locale "in the vicinity of Jericho."[379] Scholars have fretted over why Luke shifts Mark's placement of the blind man's healing

379. On "when he was in the vicinity of Jericho" as the best translation of ἐν τῷ ἐγγίζειν αὐτὸν εἰς Ἰεριχώ (*en tō engizein auton eis Ierichō*) in 18:35, rather than "as he approached Jericho" (NRSV), see Porter, "In the Vicinity." Part of the argument hinges on the parallel use of ἐγγίζω (*engizō*) in 18:40 as a verb of location rather than motion; the genitive absolute in 18:40 (ἐγγίσαντος . . . αὐτοῦ, *engisantos . . . autou*) marks the spatial nearness (not movement) of the blind man to Jesus: "when he was near," *not* "when/while he was approaching" (here Porter follows Moule, *Idioms*, 67–69).

as Jesus and company "were *leaving* Jericho" (Mark 10:46) to an earlier spot in the city's environs *before* Jesus meets Zacchaeus.[380] The simplest explanation relates to Luke's close narrative linking of the two episodes: Mark has no Zacchaeus story, and keeping the blind man on the exit road distances him from Jericho. But that begs the key question: Why Jericho, or better, the road through Jericho, as the focal site?

Some have suggested an intertextual connection with Elijah's final journey *through Jericho*, just before crossing the Jordan River and being taken up to heaven (2 Kgs 2:1–12 [the Jericho reference is in v. 4). To be sure, Luke often parallels the prophetic missions of Jesus and Elijah, not least in their ascents into heaven, though Jesus rides no chariot of fire and does not bypass death.[381] But I think the stronger connection at this Jericho junction in Luke is with *Elisha's* persistent following of Elijah (discussed below). I further suggest that the primary Jericho link is co-textual, arcing back to the parable of four travelers on the Jerusalem-Jericho road: one (victim) robbed, beaten, and left for dead; two (priest and Levite) who pass by the victim; and one (Samaritan) who stops, treats the victim's wounds, and carries him to a nearby inn (in Jericho?). Though heading in the opposite direction on the Jerusalem-Jericho highway from Jesus and his party, the parable's characters fit the same categories we find in Luke 18–19: (1) a person in dire need of roadside assistance (blind beggar in 18:35; Zacchaeus, too, suffers in his own way); (2) those who distance themselves from the needy (18:39; 19:7); and (3) one (Jesus himself now) who adjusts his itinerary and ministers to the afflicted. Though not crossing ethnic-national boundaries, as the parable's Samaritan does, Jesus breaks down physical, social, and economic barriers separating him and many other Jews from a blind homeless person and a despised tax collector (the latter's serving Roman-Herodian political interests involves some ethnic-national factors). Even as his own death draws near, Jesus stands out as "the one who showed . . . mercy" (cf. 10:37).

The internal setting of the present Jericho stories may be more specifically tracked in two moving parts, from "initial" to "final" situations, as charted above. The blind man does not stay on the roadside after Jesus heals him; neither does he simply go in peace on his own way (cf. 7:50; 8:39, 48; 17:19). Rather, "immediately he regained his sight and *followed [Jesus]*" (18:43) in "typical disciple" fashion.[382] In Zacchaeus's case, the action moves from his distant, precar-

380. See discussion in Porter, "In the Vicinity," 91–95; Brookins, "Luke's Use," 71, 76–79.

381. On Luke's appropriation of the Elijah narratives in his portrait of Jesus, see multiple studies by Brodie, *Crucial Bridge*, 82–86, also "Luke-Acts" and "Departure." See also Croatto, "Jesus, Prophet like Elijah"; and Craig Evans, "Function of Elijah/Elisha Narratives." On the Elijah-Jericho link with the present scene in Luke 18:35–43, see Brookins, "Luke's Use," 76–79.

382. Brookins, "Luke's Use," 84–85.

ious, and embarrassing (see below) treetop perch to the more intimate setting of his home, where Jesus "must" stay (19:5, 9). As Jesus's outreach to the blind man results in followship, so his interest in Zacchaeus results in fellowship. Such experiences demonstrate Jesus's commitment to life-changing discipleship and ministry, not merely random, hit-and-run acts of kindness (here again a bridge joins Jesus and the parable's Samaritan, who transports the victim to an inn and pays for his long-term care [10:34–35]).

Stoppers (18:39–40; 19:3–7)

As if the blind man and tax collector do not have enough obstacles to meeting Jesus with their visual disabilities, they must also contend with verbal impediments from others. In the first case, as the blind man begins to plead loudly for Jesus's aid, some "leading the procession [προάγοντες, *proagontes*]" (CEB) of the travel party "sternly ordered [ἐπετίμων, *epetimōn*] [the blind man] to be quiet" (18:39). These frontrunners clearing Jesus's path have not grasped the compassionate purpose of Jesus's way.[383] They seek to silence the blind man with the same gag order Jesus has issued several times to irksome demons and other harmful forces (4:35, 39, 41, 8:24; 9:42) and twice to his disciples: rebuking Peter's truncated view of Jesus's messianic identity (9:20–22) and chiding James and John for their vengeful plan to torch an inhospitable Samaritan village (9:54–55). But the blind man has no demon, is scarcely expected to know the full scope of Jesus's mission, and desires to see Jesus rather than turn him away. There is no good reason to silence him, only cruel prejudice against a loudmouth, disabled roadside beggar. Those aiming to stop the blind man are at cross purposes with Jesus, just like his disciples when they "sternly ordered [ἐπετίμων, *epetimōn*]" that people stop bringing infants to Jesus (18:15). Also like then, Jesus surmounts the obstructionists with his sharp counterorder that the needy person "be brought to him" (18:40).

The crowd also blocks Zacchaeus's path to Jesus by its sheer size, numerically and physically, since most would be taller than the abnormally diminutive tax collector (19:3). But more sinister cultural and moral elements also come into view. Greco-Roman physiognomy tended to correlate anatomical deficiencies with character flaws. Marked shortness of stature for adults, from extreme cases of congenital dwarfism to lesser height challenges, often equated with

383. Brookins ("Luke's Use," 83–84) links these *foregoers* (προάγοντες, *proagontes*) with those who seek to stand out in *first* positions, out of step with the servant model of greatness advocated by Luke's Jesus.

"small-spiritedness," "small-mindedness," or various other moral shortcomings. Heroic figures with diminutive bodies, like Caesar Augustus and the apostle Paul, were excused only because of their otherwise (airbrushed?) well-proportioned, fitly arranged physiques (Suetonius, *Aug.* 9; Acts of Paul and Thecla 3).[384] Zacchaeus, however, seems to have nothing to compensate his despicable shortness. In all likelihood, Luke's implied audience regards Zacchaeus as an object of riotous ridicule, the brunt of merciless "short jokes." This mockery would easily slide into moral opprobrium; though childlike in size, a vertically challenged man like Zacchaeus is not innocent in the crowd's eyes. He disgraces his name (based on the Hebrew "innocent") and his people, shortchanging them of their limited financial resources in his exploitative and traitorous collecting for Roman coffers. Though a top ruling officer (ἀρχιτελώνης, *architelōnēs*) in his profession, he ranks among the "least" (μικρός, *mikros*) in social value (cf. 7:28; 9:48; 17:2). The crowd simply labels him a "sinner-man" (ἁμαρτωλῷ ἀνδρί, *hamartōlō andri* [19:7; cf. 5:8; 7:37]). In short, as Cyril of Alexandria comments, Zacchaeus "was little of stature, not merely in a bodily point of view, but also spiritually."[385] He thus appears as the antitype of Luke's Jesus, who "grew and became strong . . . and increased in wisdom and in years/stature [ἡλικίᾳ, *hēlikia*], and in divine and human favor (2:40, 52).[386] But again Jesus overcomes the crowd's resistance to a social outcast, welcoming little ("least") Zacchaeus into God's saving realm.

Seekers (18:38–39, 41; 19:3–10)

But Jesus does not blaze the path to salvation alone. The blind man and tax collector each meet him halfway, seeking him as intensely as he seeks them: the former with his lungs, the latter with his legs. The blind man refuses to be deterred by the shushing crowd, meeting their demand for silence with "much more" (πολλῷ μᾶλλον, *pollō mallon*) shouting (18:39). He effectively shouts

384. Parsons, *Body*, 98–99. I am indebted throughout this section to Parsons's groundbreaking work on physiognomic features of Luke's narratives.

385. Cyril of Alexandria, Homily 127, as cited in Parsons, *Body*, 100.

386. The noun ἡλικία (*hēlikia*) can denote a chronological (age) or an anatomical (height) measure; both would be appropriate in 2:52, 12:25, and possibly 19:3; Luke may suggest that Zacchaeus was *both* young and short. Green (669–70), however, prefers a reference to Zacchaeus's youthful age. I argue conversely for a main focus on his diminutive height, reinforced by the adjective μικρός (*mikros*, "little/small" [19:3]) and reinforcing the visual-limitation theme and the man's low status (stature) in the people's eyes. Cf. Parsons (*Body*, 100–105), though I am not so sure Luke necessarily implies Zacchaeus's "pathological dwarfism" (101–4).

them down, resonant with Elisha's retort to fellow prophets who discourage him from following Elijah to Jericho with Elijah's departure imminent. To the prophets' inhibiting query, "Do you know that today the LORD will take your master away from you?" Elisha curtly replies, "Yes, I know; *be silent*" (2 Kgs 2:3) and continues pursuing his mentor.[387]

Luke's blind man is not concerned about anyone but himself and Jesus, directly addressing Jesus as "Son of David" and pleading for his mercy (18:38). This appeal to Jesus's Davidic heritage, with its royal messianic associations, shows deeper insight into Jesus's identity than that expressed by other supplicants, like the ten lepers ("Jesus, Master, have mercy on us!" [17:13]). Indeed, no one since Gabriel (explicitly) in the birth announcements (1:32; 2:9–11; cf. 1:27; 2:4; 3:31) and God (implicitly) at Jesus's baptism and transfiguration ("This is my Son" [3:22; 9:35—Davidic echo via Ps 2:7]) has declared Jesus's Davidic kingship. How the blind man came to this knowledge is anyone's guess (perhaps the Judean shepherds' report spread to Jericho; cf. Luke 2:11, 17–20). In any case, the blind man remarkably recognizes (sees!) Jesus's exalted role in God's kingdom and understands its merciful, restorative ("Let me see again") purpose.[388] Beyond extolling Jesus as "Son of David," he ultimately addresses Jesus as "Lord" (18:41), which in the present context seems to rise above a basic term of respect ("Sir") toward a sense of Jesus's divine-regal honor ("Lord God"). The persistent, vociferous acclamation of Jesus's blessed lordship and kingship in the face of opposition prepares the way—which the healed blind man will join (18:43)—for his royal entry into Jerusalem (19:37–40).

The undersized Zacchaeus surmounts the pressing crowd's blockade around Jesus by running ahead of the procession and scurrying up a sycamore tree to espy Jesus, and then scurrying back down when Jesus meets his eye and invites himself to the tax collector's home (19:3–6). All this energy evinces Zacchaeus's "*seeking to see* [ἐζήτει ἰδεῖν, *ezētei idein*] who Jesus was" (19:3 NAB), even at the risk of fueling people's already low opinion of him. For the sight of a tiny man scampering up a tree like an excited toddler or wild monkey could scarcely fail to bring howls of derision.[389] He enacts a public freak show. But

387. The match is not perfect, since Elijah also tells his protégé to stay put because "the LORD has sent me to Jericho"; even so, Elisha equally rebuffs Elijah's impediment in no uncertain terms: "As the LORD lives and as you yourself live, I will not leave you" (2 Kgs 2:4).

388. Although the Greco-Roman world credited some special blind persons with heightened powers of wisdom and in-"sight" (see Beavis, "From the Margin," 25–27, 36–38), the crowds in the present story certainly do not acknowledge this blind beggar's acumen. Only Jesus grants that.

389. Parsons (*Body*, 104) suggests a broad cultural-mythological association with the infamous legendary Cercopes brother-team of highway robbers zapped into apes by Jupiter (Ovid, *Metam.*, 14.90–100; Diodorus Siculus, *Bibl. hist.* 3.35.5) and depicted in popular art as ridiculous short figures with apelike faces.

no matter; Zacchaeus has his eye on a higher purpose, a meeting of the eye and mind with Jesus the Lord and Savior of humankind. It is perhaps even more remarkable than with the blind man that Zacchaeus, a person of much greater wealth and authority, also calls Jesus Lord (19:8). However much his social standing is diminished by his size and occupation, he's still considerably better off than the blind beggar.

The most astounding aspects of Zacchaeus's response to Jesus, however, are his hospitable reception and charitable confession. When Jesus brazenly invites himself over to Zacchaeus's house, for an extended stay no less ("I *must stay/remain* [δεῖ με μεῖναι, *dei me meinai*] at your house today"), the tax collector promptly "hurried [σπεύσας, *speusas*] down and was happy/joyous to welcome [ὑπεδέξατο . . . χαίρων, *hypedexato . . . chairōn*]" Jesus into his residence (19:5–6). This enthusiastic reception mirrors:

1. the shepherds' hasty (σπεύσαντες, *speusantes*) pursuit of the Christ-child (2:16);
2. Martha's welcome (ὑπεδέχατο, *hypedexato*) of Jesus into her home (10:38); and especially
3. the shepherd, sweeper woman, and father's joyous (χαίρω/χαρά, *chairō/chara*) seek-and-find missions, respectively, for their lost sheep, coin, and son (15:5–7, 9–10, 32; the father further matches Zacchaeus's *running* actions [15:20]).

This last comparison pairs Zacchaeus with the *diligent seekers* of the lost—ironically putting the sought-for Jesus in the "lost" position—as much as with the *penitent sinner* (prodigal) coming home.

Once inside his house with Jesus, Zacchaeus continues to assert himself, even as he acknowledges Jesus as Lord. He *stands* (σταθείς, *statheis*)—as tall as he can!—and announces his extraordinary commitment to give half of his resources to the poor and to restore fourfold to anyone he might have defrauded (19:8).[390] He does not bow, beg, or declare his unworthiness to stand

390. Green ("Cognitive") suggests various ways to interpret the location of Zacchaeus's "standing": "Does Zacchaeus 'stand up' (as if they had been sharing a meal in his home) or 'stand still' (as if they were still on the way to his home) or 'stand firm' (wherever, as if he were taking a stand against those who malign him as a sinner)?" (110). The parallel in 18:40, where Jesus "*stood still* [σταθείς, *statheis*]," that is, stopped his journey, to attend to the blind man may suggest a similar situation with Zacchaeus, though I incline more to the "stand up" option in his home, given the preceding narrator's report that Zacchaeus was "happy to welcome [Jesus]" and the crowd's complaint that Jesus "entered [εἰσῆλθεν, *eisēlthen*]" this sinner's residence as a guest (19:6–7 AT). In any case, Zacchaeus appears to take a confident, assertive stance, despite his small stature.

before Jesus, as the centurion did (7:6–8). He does not answer any question from Jesus, as the blind man did (18:41). In his home, Zacchaeus has the first word, to which Jesus responds. So what prompts Zacchaeus to speak up as he does? Is he offering a confession of (1) *sinfulness*, repenting of his old self-aggrandizing way of life, or of (2) *faithfulness*, confirming his fellowship with Jesus's self-emptying way?[391] The first option better fits the general "sinner" reputation of tax collectors and the call to repentance John and Jesus issue them (3:12–13; 5:29–32). But Jesus does not summon Zacchaeus to repent, unless by implication in his urgent ("must") self-invitation to Zacchaeus's house. But that interpretation stretches the language here, and in any case, Jesus's "Repent!" mandate is not limited to tax collectors in Luke (13:1–5). Moreover, it is not Jesus, but the Jericho crowd—hardly a reliable bunch—who slaps the "sinner" brand on Zacchaeus (19:7).

The second option, more focused on confirmation than conversion, finds some support in the present tense verbs Zacchaeus employs, literally: "I give/am giving [δίδωμι, *didōmi*] to the poor . . . I give back/am giving back [ἀποδίδωμι, *apodidōmi*] [to any I might have shortchanged]" (19:8). Though the grammar does not rule out a fresh decision and future pledge—from this present moment "I will give/I will pay back" (NRSV)—it more naturally conveys a pattern of generosity and honesty Zacchaeus had already begun to practice. Whatever anyone else may say about him, he affirms that "giving" *is* his way of life. But why does he feel the need to confess this to Jesus: to set the record straight? to impress Jesus with his goodness? to express solidarity with Jesus?

The best explanation may relate to the recent experience of another rich official who seeks Jesus. Recall that this was a good, law-observant man who "became sad" (18:23) over Jesus's charge that he sell *everything* he owned on behalf of the poor, prompting discussion about how hard it is for the wealthy to be saved (18:26–30). While Luke never specifies that Zacchaeus knew about this exchange, the close narrative juxtaposition of two rich men and their attitudes toward poor relief begs for attention. Whatever level of faithfulness Zacchaeus had attained, it is doubtful he could match the other rich official's history of law-keeping "since my youth" (18:21); the tax collector's fourfold restitution policy implies that during some phase of his career he *had* engaged in typical overcharging practices of his profession, though not necessarily with intentionality (inadvertent clerical errors are possible or correcting for his tax-collecting

391. The debate may be cast in terms of "resolve" (conversion and pledge of repentance via a futuristic present) vs. "defense" (confirmation of established conduct and commitments via a customary/iterative present). Arguing for the "resolve" side, see Hamm, "Luke 19:8" and "Zacchaeus"; for the "defense," see Mitchell, "Zacchaeus" and "Use of συκοφαντεῖν."

employees' misappropriations).[392] More critically, though Zacchaeus claims an impressive percentage of charitable giving, *half* of one's possessions is still that much short of the "all" that Jesus required of the rich ruler and that another tax collector Levi had actually surrendered: "He got up [from his tax booth], *left everything*, and followed [Jesus]" (5:28). So where does that leave Zacchaeus? Perhaps he braces himself for Jesus's "but one thing you lack" response. But it doesn't come (see below). Remarkably, Zacchaeus's place in God's kingdom already seems secure.

Whether Zacchaeus begins or bolsters his commitment to charity and justice in the present story, he further shatters the sinister "sinner" stereotype of tax collectors. As a chief revenue officer and the last taxman mentioned in Luke's narrative, he culminates the trajectory running from those seeking John's baptism (3:12; 7:29) to Levi (5:27–32) and other tax collectors (7:34; 15:1) who received God's welcome and embraced God's way in Christ.

Savior (18:40–43; 19:5–10)

Though the Jesus-seeking efforts of the blind man and tax collector should not be missed, Jesus himself remains the chief Seeker and Savior of those struggling to find their way in God's restorative realm (19:10). In both cases, Jesus adjusts his journey to attend to the needy seekers' salvation with aggressive therapy as directive as it is ameliorative.

In contrast to the pushy group that aims to silence and ignore the blind man, Jesus "stood still and *ordered* [ἐκέλευσεν, *ekeleusen*] the man to be brought to him" (18:40). He then invites the man to verbalize his request for sight, which Jesus then grants in *imperative* form, as if commanding the man's optical system: "Receive your sight [ἀνάβλεψον, *anablepson*]" (18:42). He uses a compound of "see," better rendered "see *again*." The verb appears three times in rapid succession in the present vignette, focalized, for maximum emphasis, through three narrative voices:

- *Blind man*: "Lord, let me see again [ἀναβλέψω, *anablepsō*]."
- *Jesus*: "See again! [ἀνάβλεψον, *anablepson*].
- *Narrator*: "Immediately he saw again [ἀνέβλεψεν, *aneblepsen*]" (18:41–43 AT).

Apart from the diagnostic clarification that the blind man had previously been sighted (i.e., not born blind), the more significant point concerns sight

392. See Mitchell, "Use of συκοφαντεῖν."

recovery as a key metaphor of holistic, *restorative* salvation ("your faith *has saved you*" [18:42]) at the heart of Jesus's mission.[393] This man's healing realizes the vision of Jesus's Spirit-anointed work of liberation inspired by Isaiah and inaugurated in the Nazareth synagogue: "The Spirit . . . has sent me to proclaim release to the captives and *recovery of sight* [ἀνάβλεψιν, *anablepsin*] *to the blind* (4:18; cf. 7:22; Isa 61:1 LXX). In the midst of limited spiritual perception and obstruction of Jesus's way, even by his closest followers, his redemptive march presses on.

Passing through Jericho still surrounded by stifling crowds, Jesus again stops to engage one bystander or, rather, tree-sitter. His interaction with Zacchaeus unfolds in three rapid steps. First, he "looked up [ἀναβλέψας, *anablepsas*]" to meet Zacchaeus's eye (19:5). This is the same verb that conveyed the blind man's sight renewal (the ἀνα- [*ana-*] prefix denotes both "above" and "again"), intimating a restorative purpose behind Jesus's interest in the tax collector. Moreover, whereas Jericho society typically *looked down* on Zacchaeus physically and figuratively, Jesus *looks up* to him not just physically but also, by implication, respectfully for his determination to see Jesus. Accordingly, Jesus disrupts conventional up/down hierarchies (cf. 1:52; 3:5; 6:17–26; 7:28; 9:46–48; 14:7–11; 18:14). And he continues shaking the social ladder in his second move, commanding the perched tax collector to *come down* posthaste and prepare for Jesus's urgent ("must") visit to his home (19:5). Jesus brings Zacchaeus down to size and effectively commandeers his home. Though Jesus repudiates the crowd's disdain for Zacchaeus, he accords the wealthy tax manager no special treatment. Jesus is the only one in this scene with true lordly authority (cf. 19:8). Yet, he does not exploit this status for his own personal advantage, as becomes evident in the climactic final step, when Jesus comes to Zacchaeus's home.

Though Jesus presumptuously invites himself over, he does not insist on being served by Zacchaeus or accommodated in any way. As we have seen, he allows Zacchaeus to open the discussion and set the agenda. To the tax collector's confession of his charitable and reparative practices, Jesus responds: "Today salvation has come to this house, because he too is a son of Abraham" (19:9). Jesus affirms, against popular prejudicial opinion, that this tax collector's residence is in fact a safe house, a haven of God's salvation, a branch office of God's restorative kingdom;[394] and that Zacchaeus himself enjoys solidarity with God's covenant people, the true children of Abraham: like the poor beg-

393. See Brookins, "Luke's Use," 80–81; Hartsock, *Sight*; Hamm, "Sight"; Culpepper, "Seeing."

394. Jesus's comment that salvation has come to Zacchaeus's "house" naturally extends to his "household" (also conveyed by οἶκος [*oikos*]); given this chief tax collector's wealth, we may assume a company of relatives and servants under the household head's umbrella of salvation, as with the households of Cornelius, Lydia, and the Philippian jailer in Acts 11:14–15; 16:15; and 16:31–34, respectively; cf. Matson, *Household Conversion*.

gar Lazarus in Abraham's bosom (16:22), the "last" pilgrims to God's banquet house with Abraham and sons (13:28–30), the liberated and "uplifted" bent-over woman ("daughter of Abraham" [13:16]), and the repentant, "fruit-bearing" seekers baptized by John into Abraham's family (3:7–14).[395]

These examples offer a mix of passive (Lazarus, stooped woman) and more active (diners, baptismal candidates) participants in the salvation experience. Of course, salvation is ultimately God's work, but it remains a realm humans must "enter" (18:24–25). As discussed above, Zacchaeus takes a proactive role in the restorative process. But he still recognizes the need to "see Jesus," God's chief saving agent, in order to solidify his place in God's realm. In sympathetic solidarity with humanity as Savior and Judge, Jesus the Son of Humankind has the final word on God's salvation, which he unequivocally pronounces in Zacchaeus's favor—"Today!" (19:9). Recall that this key temporal marker in Luke is less a slot on the calendar than the sign of a new era: the banner day of God's salvation has dawned in the mission of Jesus Messiah, and Zacchaeus enjoys full rights of participation and celebration. Jesus does not audit Zacchaeus's charitable contributions. Percentages, whether 10 percent (Pharisee's tithe), 50 percent (Zacchaeus), or 100 percemt (rich ruler), are evidential more than effectual. Salvation is not a numbers game. It is a work of God's grace and power, of God's effecting a radical change of heart and mind that humans find impossible to achieve on their own (cf. 18:26–27). Zacchaeus's testimony of compassionate and just action, which Jesus validates, provides sufficient evidence of God's "impossible" transformation of this wealthy tax official.

Royal Lambasting and Lamenting (19:11–44)

At long last, after many twists and turns along the journey, Jesus makes his final approach to Jerusalem. The end is very *near* now, and Jesus speaks and acts accordingly, with keen awareness of the holy city's historic significance.

> He went on to tell a parable, because he was *near* [ἐγγύς, *engys*] *Jerusalem.* (19:11)

395. Parsons (*Body*) draws a memorable connection between the "upraising" experiences of the bent-over woman and Zacchaeus as daughter/son of Abraham, in light of the Baptist's pronouncement that "God is able from these stones to raise up children to Abraham" (3:8): "In the Third Gospel, God has taken two 'stones,' one badly misshapen and the other undersized, and raised from them a son and daughter of Abraham" (108). We might also associate the Baptist's image of "cutting down" unfruitful trees (3:9) with Zacchaeus's scurrying down from the sycamore tree (19:6) to announce his commitment to God's gracious, redemptive path.

> He went on ahead, going up to *Jerusalem.* (19:28)
>
> When he had *come near* [ἤγγισεν, *ēngisen*] Bethphage and Bethany [on the outskirts of Jerusalem],[396] he sent two of the disciples. (19:29)
>
> As he *came near* [ἤγγισεν, *ēngisen*] and saw the city [Jerusalem], he wept over it. (19:41)

These last steps of Jesus's trek unfold in two dramatic parts: first, he *tells a parabolic tale* (19:11–27); then he *shows a symbolic act* (19:28–44). Both scenes feature three elements of royal activity (βασιλεία, -λεύς, -λεύω, *basileia, -leus, -leuō* [19:14, 15, 27, 38]): how the king and his chief agents (1) attain their *position,* (2) exercise their *power*, and (3) express their *passion.*

The parable features a high-born nobleman (εὐγενής, *eugenēs*) who travels to a "distant country" and obtains an appointment from the supreme ruler to serve as client-king over his local region (19:12). Upon returning home with royal authority, this hierarch acts as sovereign judge over his subjects, rewarding his slaves who multiplied his assets and punishing the one slacker who turned no profit, as well as those who resisted his promotion. The ruler brooks no opposition and accepts no excuses. He is by his own and others' admission a "harsh [αὐστηρός, *austēros*] man"—a stern, austere, exacting, cut-and-dried operator[397]—who takes every economic advantage he can, grabbing money he didn't deposit and crops he didn't plant (19:21–22). The king's harshness becomes particularly evident in his vengeful reprisals, demoting and divesting the unprofitable slave and having his political foes slaughtered "in my presence" (19:27).

Since four different subjects address this royal figure in Jesus's story as "Lord" (19:16, 18, 20, 25), a clear connection is forged with Jesus's own experience in the ensuing scene, where he comes into Jerusalem amid shouts of "Blessed is the king who comes in the name of the Lord!" (19:38). But the *point* of that connection is not so clear. Beyond matching his parable's protagonist as a traveling kingly/lordly personage, Jesus's personal enactment of that role is quite different:

- He does not attain his royal *position* by lobbying for it in some "distant country"; rather, he comes from a lowly manger birth in Judean Bethlehem and an upbringing in Galilean Nazareth.

396. Both are villages within two miles of the Mount of Olives on the eastern edge of Jerusalem; see Rousseau and Arav, *Jesus*, 15–16, 18–19.

397. The term, originally related to "becoming dry, stale," here suggests the "imagery of a tough, uncompromising, punctilious financier" (BDAG, 151–52).

- Apart from commandeering a colt for transport (19:30–34), he flaunts no executive *power* before the people, although they joyously praise him for "deeds of power," which have all been benevolent in Luke (19:37); when some Pharisees petition him to "order" the audience to cease their adulation, he refuses to grant their request but unleashes no invective or threats of punishment against them (19:39–40).
- Indeed, when he takes the measure of Jerusalem with poignant realization of the crushing violence it will soon experience from "enemies" (not from Jesus), he is overcome with the *passion* of grief, not glee, even though the city has sealed its fate "because [it] did not recognize the time of [its] visitation from God" (19:44).

This last part of the Travel Narrative marks a critical time to assess our *knowledge* of Luke's Jesus, a kind of prefinal exam. The parable's angry client-king lashes out at the one unsuccessful slave: "*You knew* [ᾔδεις, *ēdeis*], did you, that I was a harsh man?" (19:22). Although Luke's Jesus has been quite demanding in his calls to discipleship and challenges to stewardship, he has consistently led his followers in a spirit of compassion, generosity, and redistributive justice, eschewing brutal retaliation at every turn. The Lord in the parable is *not* the Lord Jesus we have come to know in Luke's narrative and *not* the Lord Jesus who cries over Jerusalem and faces imminent death there.

But this is not the full or final story. Jesus has already forecast his resurrection (9:22; 18:33) and return in supreme power on the Son of Humankind's climactic day (17:24–30). Will he not then, after a period of earthly absence in the heavenly sphere and having received all royal authority from God the Father-King, return to compensate his stewards according to their faithfulness and obliterate his enemies (cf. 12:41–48)? The two seemingly distinct kings in Jesus's parable and personal drama in 19:11–44 may in fact represent two sides of the one King Jesus *at different stages* in his messianic career: on the one hand, the distant, delayed, yet ultimately victorious King at the end of the age; on the other hand, the imminent, rejected, and finally crucified "King of the Jews" (23:37–38) by week's end.

This two-stage tracking of Luke's King Jesus has dominated the history of interpretation.[398] But increasingly scholars have advocated a different approach,

398. A notable exception to this pattern is represented by Luke Timothy Johnson ("Kingship"), who eschews a long historical "delay" element (lacking in Luke's parable) and focuses on the immediate fulfillment (19:11) in Jesus's royal entry into Jerusalem of the promised kingdom illustrated in the story of the pounds. As Luke's Jesus manifests his role as co-regent of God's "transcendent" (153, 155–56) kingdom in his final week, he is sadly rejected by the Jewish leaders

an opposite one, in fact, that views the client-king in Jesus's parable as an *antitype* or *antichrist* to the true messianic King Jesus. By juxtaposition, then, Luke sets up polar contrasting models of kingly rule.[399] The following discussion supports this newer perspective.

The Client-King Comes in a Tirade: The Tyrannical Entry (19:11–27)

The narrator bridges from Jesus's encounter with Zacchaeus to Jesus's monetary parable with the phrase: "As they were listening to this" (19:11), that is, the conversation that just unfolded in Zacchaeus's house (19:8–10). But who are "they" who now compose the main audience for Jesus's parable? Luke recounts a private, one-to-one exchange between Zacchaeus and Jesus. Now in quick retrospect, we learn that others ("they") in the background witness this dialogue. Since it is unlikely that any members of the accusatory crowd would follow Jesus into the despised tax collector's home, the attending group must be Jesus's disciples.

The narrator further explicates that Jesus tells the ensuing parable for two reasons: "*because* [διά, *dia*] he was near Jerusalem, and *because* [ὅτι, *hoti*] they [the disciples] supposed that the kingdom of God was to appear immediately" (19:11). Although we still do not know the precise contours of the disciples' messianic-kingdom perspective, we do know that they have not been in lockstep with Jesus's vision, which includes suffering, rejection, and crucifixion in Jerusalem (18:31–34). They have preferred the glory-victory dimensions of Jesus's work over the suffering-serving modes (9:10–36, 43–48; 17:7–10). Likely, then, their blurry eyes remain fixed on their narrow spatio-temporal target: if God's kingdom, the signs of which have been powerfully present throughout Jesus's journey, is going to reach its apex anywhere, it is going to be "up" in *Jerusalem*, God's holy city; and since Jesus Messiah, having long "set his face" in this direction (9:51, 53), is suddenly on the edge of this destination, expectation would naturally soar that God's kingdom is on the brink of *immediate* or at least *imminent* finality. Luke often uses "im-

---

in Jerusalem, as the "citizens of his country" spurned the noble-royal figure in the parable (19:14). This reading, however, while giving proper attention to the tight plotting of Jesus's parable and kingly procession in Luke's narrative, fails to appreciate the purposeful *disjunction* between the two scenes, particularly concerning the radically distinct *characters* of the royal protagonists (see more below).

399. On this parable as a dramatic "parody" of Jesus's countervision of God's kingdom, see Culpepper, 361–64; Vinson, 593–99, and "Minas Touch"; cf. Parsons, 280–85; Schottroff, *Parables*, 183–87.

mediately/right away/at once" (παραχρῆμα, *parachrēma*), much like "today," to mark notable signs of God's redemptive realm (1:64; 4:39; 5:25; 8:44, 47, 55; 13:13; 18:43).

The disciples' burning hope, however, that Jesus will soon consummate God's rule, centered in the nation of Israel and capital of Jerusalem, becomes crushed with Jesus's tragic death ("we had hoped that he was the one to redeem Israel" [24:21]), only to reignite after his resurrection: "Lord, is this the time when you will restore the kingdom to Israel?" (Acts 1:6). While Jesus's messianic mission stays on course with abundant breakthroughs of God's saving work here and now (Luke 11:20; 17:20–21), it is in fact *not yet* the place or time for climactic, cosmic (much less nationalistic) restoration of God's dominion. So Jesus's followers have much to learn about the realization of God's kingdom on earth through the soon-to-be crucified, resurrected, and exalted Christ, awaiting another advent (see Acts 1:6–11).

By the time of Luke's first readers, the *delay* of Christ's final appearing (*parousia*) had stretched a generation or longer, further complicating any sense of "immediate" completion of God's kingdom enterprise.[400] But this delay problem begins early in Jesus's story, pressing as hard on his disciples *before* his death as after, perhaps more so since the prospect of death by crucifixion posed such an unthinkable shattering of messianic dreams and such a depressing realization that wicked worldly kingdoms, particularly Rome's, would appear to maintain the upper hand—with which they would nail Jesus to a cross! If God's kingdom really is breaking in and moving forward in Christ, it must do so in protracted *combat with* and *counterpoint to* persisting evil powers. At this critical juncture, then, Luke's Jesus aims to paint in bold strokes the harsh realities of *ungodly royal rule*, with which he and his disciples must contend, as frontispiece to the counterdrama of God's righteous realm enacted by Jesus's Jerusalem entry.

Enmeshed, therefore, in this thick narrative, theological, and sociopolitical context, Jesus's parable best represents a vivid portrait of the dominant enemy of God's people, of the *antichrist* way of ruling the world. As noted above, this political reading reflects a minority interpretation against the more popular reading of Jesus's parable as an allegory of his return to earth in final judgment. The following chart outlines the main "fictive" characters/elements in the central column, with correspondent "real" figures from the two readings on either side.

400. See Spencer, *Gospel of Luke*, 65–68.

Popular reading: Celestial scenario	Characters/elements	Political reading: Imperial scenario
Exalted/ascended Jesus	Nobleman	Herodian official
Heaven	Far country	Rome
God	Supreme king	Caesar
Christian stewards/servants (metaphoric)	Slaves	Herodian servants (actual slaves)
Jews rejecting Jesus as Messiah	Embassy	Palestinian Jewish leaders
Returning Jesus (second coming)	Lord	Herodian client-king (Archelaus)
Faithful/resourceful Christian stewards gaining heavenly rewards	Two productive slaves promoted	Herodian cronies, profiteers, and city officials controlling the economy
Unfaithful/irresponsible (pseudo)-Christian steward	One unproductive slave divested	Passive resisters of Herodian rule losing property and suffering poverty
Unbelievers in Christ consigned to eternal death	Slaughtered enemies	Political dissidents executed as enemies of state

If one assumes from the start that the parable illustrates God's kingdom in a straightforward sense and that the protagonist "nobleman" represents Jesus's going (back) to God in heaven "to get royal power for himself" (back) on earth, then all the other elements line up accordingly. But there are problems with this start, which only exacerbate as the story unfolds toward its violent retributive denouement.

First, we have learned to be cautious about seeing parable figures as clear-cut stand-ins for God or Christ. These stories provide *indirect* instruction about God's kingdom through similes ("like"), uneven comparisons (lesser/greater), ironies, and parodies (*good* Samaritan; *unjust* judge). In any case, Jesus's parables are not primarily self-portraits.

Second, a "distant/far [μακράν, *makran*] country" (19:12), far from evoking heavenly environs in Luke, recalls the polluted realm of sin and shame, opposed to God, occupied by the prodigal son before returning home (15:13, 20).[401]

Third, Luke's Jesus has already received royal power from God, attested by heavenly messengers and dynamically exercised on earth (1:32–33, 69; 2:11;

401. Culpepper, 362; Vinson, "Minas Touch," 74.

11:20). He does not need to go away to heaven to receive more power, as if his earthly mission were probationary or preliminary.

Fourth, while the present parable's ruler leaves his territory in the hands of slave-managers, there is no indication that his return with enhanced authority was *delayed* beyond normal expectations, as reported of other long-absentee estate lords (12:45; 20:9; cf. Matt 24:48; 25:5, 19). Luke's nobleman-become-king simply "returns" (Luke 19:12, 15) at an unremarkable time.[402]

Fifth, the present story's stewardship focus strictly concerns financial management, with no additional interest in supervising other slaves (12:41–48) or debtors (7:41–43; 16:1–13). This ruler cares only about the return on his monetary investment of a mina (μνᾶ, *mna* or *mina* = 100 denarii) and asks nothing about *how* two slaves manage to turn a ridiculous 1000 percent and 500 percent profit (we could suspect some deceitful practice, to which the ruler turns a blind eye) (19:15–19).[403] Plus, his only interest in the pathetic slave who stashes his mina in a flimsy napkin is why he didn't at least deposit it in an interest-bearing account (19:20–23)! The bottom line is all that matters for this wealthy client-king. He gives none of the earlier rich ruler's thought for eternal business and wastes no emotion brooding over selling all to help the poor (cf. 18:18–25); likewise, he displays none of the commitments of opulent Zacchaeus to economic redistribution and reparation (19:8). Other parables portray wealthy elites as utterly oblivious to others' welfare right up to their deaths (12:13–21; 16:19–31). It is hard to see, even on a metaphoric level, how the present parable's aristocrat could convey anything positive about Christ.

Sixth, further probing money matters, the maverick slave's mismanagement is not so clear. He does not squander the money, as the prodigal son and dishonest steward did. Rather, he secures his master's asset and immediately returns it—"Here is your mina"—albeit with commentary about the master's unscrupulous character (19:20–21). To be sure, fearing risk and reprisal, he doesn't attempt to trade the mina for profit as the master ordered (19:15). But in a more fundamental sense, by keeping the coin in a napkin and readily handing it back, he wants nothing to do with it. In fact, this action may hint at non-violent protest or sardonic payback, similar to that Jesus soon lodges regarding

402. Vinson, "Minas Touch," 73.

403. Cf. Vinson, "Minas Touch," 74–75: "How do you increase your capital ten-fold in a short time? Luke leaves it to the audience's imagination, but clearly something shady happened. There was no ancient stock market or buying of oil futures; ordinary money-lenders could hardly get away with charging 1,000% interest. . . . In their world, such a huge return could only have come at someone else's expense, and bribery, influence-peddling, or outright theft would probably strike the audience as likely."

Caesar's coinage (see discussion on 20:20–26). Let the harsh master have back his ill-gotten gains; this one slave wants no part of it.[404]

Seventh, the point about rewarding service voiced by the *story's Lord*—"I tell you, to all those who have, more will be given; but from those who have nothing, even what they have will be taken away" (19:26)—while superficially comparable with *Jesus's commentary* on previous management parables, actually parodies Jesus's words, which stress (1) responsibility more than reward: "To whom much is given, much will be required" (12:48); and (2) faithfulness in "very little" affairs (including money matters) in the interest of justice rather than dishonesty, mercy rather than profiteering: "If then you have not been faithful with the dishonest wealth, who will entrust to you the true riches?" (16:11; cf. vv. 9–13).

Eighth, the local "citizens" who despise the nobleman and seek to block his promotion provide only a partial match with Jewish leaders who resist Jesus's kingdom pursuits. The most glaring difference is that, whereas the people's antiking campaign in the parable proves completely futile, in Jesus's case, the priestly officials collude with Roman authorities to have this would-be "King of the Jews" *executed*. To be sure, while Jesus's death soon gives way to resurrection and exaltation in Luke's drama, the cross is hardly a trivial inconvenience. It forever affects the character of Jesus's reign in God's kingdom. The forthcoming parable of the wicked tenants who *kill* the absentee vineyard-owner's *beloved son* (20:9–19) provides that missing link from the case of the nobleman-king, who loses nothing.

Last, but by no means least, the brutal judgment of the parable's client-king ill fits Luke's characterization of Jesus Messiah. While Jesus may pronounce dreadful judgment on those who ultimately reject God's authority (cf. 12:4–5, 8–10), he does so in the parental/pastoral context of generous care for his subjects/children/sheep: "Do not be afraid, little flock, for it is your Father's pleasure to give you the kingdom" (12:32). The parable's scenario concerning the so-called wicked slave terrified of his harsh master—whose austere authority he *fully acknowledges* (19:20–21)—rubs against the grain of God's gracious, bountiful kingdom. Moreover, the sadistic slaughter "in my presence" of the king's hateful (μισέω, *miseō*) enemies (ἐχθρός, *echthros*) (19:14, 27) could scarcely be more antithetical to Jesus's radical ethic: "Love your enemies [ἐχθρούς, *echthrous*], do good to those who hate [μισοῦσιν, *misousin*] you" (6:27).[405] Of

404. See van Eck, "Social Memory," 210–11; Rohrbaugh, "Peasant Reading."

405. In his reading of correspondence between Jesus's kingship parable and Jesus's authoritative mediation of God's kingdom, Luke Timothy Johnson ("Kingship") acknowledges: "Not everything fits exactly. One cannot push the 'slaughtering,' for example. . . . Luke is not working with needlepoint obsessiveness" (158). That may be fine to a point; but the final point of murdering

course, one might assume that the *returning* Christ-King will transmogrify into a violent retributive tyrant (no more Mr. Nice Guy), but the stain of vindictive blood would taint, if not utterly obliterate, everything Jesus stood for during his earthly ministry, culminating in *shedding his own blood* to seal "the new covenant" (22:20).

As much as the account of royal power in Jesus's parable diverges from his own management of God's realm, it closely converges with a "cultural-type scene"[406] played out again and again in imperial politics. Appointments of regional client-kings were the prerogative of the sovereign emperor. Whether for show of fairness or genuine regard for public opinion, Caesar would entertain various candidates and lobbyists before making his decision. Upon receiving royal authority, the winner would return to his district and typically cement his imperial mandate with harsh reprisals against his opponents.

One example reported by Josephus from first-century Palestinian politics offers a striking parallel to Luke's minas parable (*Ant.* 17.206–344; cf. *J.W.* 2.80–100). The succession battles in the wake of Herod the Great's death brought sons Archelaus and Antipas to Rome to appeal for Caesar's patronage. Archelaus had the greater testamentary claim and initial support from Jewish leaders who hoped he would rule in a more moderate fashion than his tyrannical father. However, when a group protested the harsh policies of the deceased Herod at Passover, Archelaus had them slaughtered—all three thousand of them! So much for moderation. This vicious retaliation prompted fifty ambassadors to travel to Rome and join with eight thousand resident Jews in lobbying against Archelaus's royal appointment: "How then could they avoid the just hatred of [Archelaus], who, to the rest of his barbarity, has added this [slaughter of the three thousand] . . . that they opposed and contradicted in the exercise of his authority?" (*Ant.* 17.313 [trans. Whiston]). Not surprisingly, Caesar sided with Archelaus against the Jewish embassy, though he limited Archelaus's position to ethnarch over Judea and Samaria, about half of Herod's kingdom. Moreover, after further accusations of Archelaus's "barbarous and tyrannical" actions, Caesar banished him to Vienna and placed Judea and Samaria under direct Roman military rule (*Ant.* 17.339–44). Whether Luke's first readers connected the nobleman-king with Archelaus, they would doubtless have heard the parable as an emblematic report of wicked royal affairs.[407]

---

one's enemies in cold blood—at sword (not needle) point!—seems to be a sharp sticking point indeed, not so facilely flicked away as a metaphor for being "cut off from the people" (which is bad enough even without bloodshed). This is not the way of loving one's enemies.

406. Culpepper, 363; Vinson, "Minas Touch," 74n23. Similarly, Parsons speaks of the familiar rhetorical "*topos* of the evil tyrant" (280–81).

407. For further analysis of Josephus's accounts of Archelaus in relation to this parable,

The Client-King Comes in Tears: The Non-Triumphal Entry (19:28–44)

Against this backdrop of a malevolent king, Jesus plays a very different royal role in approaching Jerusalem as the "blessed" king "who comes in the name of the Lord" (19:38). Though traditionally called his triumphal entry, Jesus's final ascent into the holy city seems, at most, a pale imitation of an imperial victory parade. He comes riding no warhorse or chariot, borne on no litter or palanquin, attended by no heroic soldiers or conquered slaves, hoisting no image-bearing standards, and buoyed by no trumpet fanfare. Unlike the client-king in the preceding parable, Jesus issues no orders and makes no summons, except for a colt to ride on, and he exacts no vengeance on his enemies. Jesus comes as king all right—the rightful heir to David's throne and God's anointed Son—but he comes to reinforce a way of ruling that differs radically from that of "all the kingdoms of the world" (cf. 4:5). Actually, this new way is steeped in venerable scriptural traditions, which Israel has sometimes followed, but more often spurned under the haughty leadership of idolatrous kings or forfeited under the heavy hand of foreign despots. But Jesus Messiah treads the old way anew, embodying and enacting the righteous rule of God. We may track this royal drama in relation to two *mounts* scripted by the prophet Zechariah and two emotional *outbursts* echoed in the Psalms and Prophets.

First, Jesus starts his final approach "at the place called the *Mount of Olives*," on the eastern side of Jerusalem (19:29). Postexilic Zechariah envisioned this mountain as the Lord's apocalyptic base of operations, from where he would defeat the rapacious nations occupying Jerusalem and stake his claim to

---

see Schultz, "Jesus as Archelaus"; and van Eck, "Social Memory." Schultz persuasively argues that the setting for Jesus's speaking this parable en route from Jericho to Jerusalem sparks memory of Archelaus's reign, since according to Josephus (*Ant.* 17.340), Archelaus refurbished Herod the Great's palace in Jericho and also constructed a new city to promote his own honor in the vicinity (112–19). In my view, however, Schultz wrongly concludes that Luke's Jesus appeals to the Archelaus scenario to reinforce his—Jesus's—message of judgment: "By crafting the parable with an Archelaus motif, Jesus used a poignant reminder of the seriousness of one's position vis-à-vis the Kingdom of God, no matter when it would be manifest: 'Jesus, the king-judge, will bring reward or punishment according to the attitude that one has taken towards him. This goes for his disciples as well as his enemies'" (127 [citing Denaux, "Parable," 85).

By contrast, van Eck (rightly) interprets Jesus's use of Archelaus as a violent, voracious antitype to the peaceful, gracious aims of God's reign: "Jesus is telling a parable not about two good slaves and one bad slave, but about the exploitative normalcies that were an integral part of first-century Palestine—elite who on a constant basis were looking for more honor, power, and privilege and using their power to exploit. In the words of Schottroff, 'The narrative is absolutely clear. It describes the economic and political structure of an exploitative kingship'" ("Social Memory," 210 [citing Schottroff, *Parables*, 185]).

universal rule: "And the Lord will become king over all the earth; on that day the Lord will be one and his name one" (Zech 14:9 NETS [cf. vv. 1–8]). No doubt inspired by this vision, a popular first-century prophet from Egypt marshaled a sizable mob at the Mount of Olives, from where he planned a Joshua-style, wall-smashing campaign into Jerusalem to oust the Roman overlords and place himself in power. Governor Felix, however, got wind of this plot and forcibly put down the rebellion (Josephus, *Ant.* 20.169–72; *War* 2.261–63; Acts 21:38). If Luke's Jesus taps into these royal-apocalyptic Olivet traditions, he drains the militant might out of them. He has assembled no army, planned no attack, and adjusted no forecast of his death in Jerusalem. He happily accepts the mantle of kingship ascribed by the jubilant crowds but has no illusions of displacing Roman-Herodian rule at this time.

His only flexing of imperious authority comes behind the scenes in procuring a mode of transport into the city, a rather simple one at that: a young "colt that has never been ridden," a portable *mount* for him to sit atop (19:30). He has no royal stable of steeds to draw from. In fact, he doesn't have a single animal of his own. But rather than buying or borrowing one, he commandeers a colt from a nearby village. Or rather, Jesus dispatches two disciples to find his required ride, which he seems to know will be tethered in place, as if prearranged (19:29–30). Luke narrates this clairvoyance of Jesus with little flourish. It is a simple matter of fact: this king, the Son of the Divine "Father, Lord of heaven and earth" (10:21), *knows* and *owns* all creatures great and small (cf. 12:6–7, 24–28). Normally Jesus doesn't go around flaunting this creational authority for his own benefit (cf. 4:1–13). But this time is special; this time he "needs" a particular colt, and such need is the only rationale given to the animal's owners when the disciples untie it (19:31, 34). The brief repeated statement, "the Lord *has need* [χρείαν ἔχει, *chreian echei*] of it" (19:31, 34 AT), is a remarkable expression of both authority and humility. This Lord-King has a sovereign right to appropriate his subjects' property for himself.[408] But the admission that he *has a need* also conveys a sense of acknowledged dependence on others and their valued contribution to his rule. This needy Lord Jesus, characteristically devoted to meeting others' needs (χρεία, *chreia* [5:31; 9:11]), again contrasts starkly with the blustering nobleman-king, known for "taking what [he] did not deposit and reaping what [he] did not sow" (19:21–22).

The question remains, however, why did Jesus need to ride this never-ridden colt into Jerusalem? Why doesn't he just keep walking? Zechariah again

408. Luke eliminates the pledge in Mark 11:3 to "send [the animal] back here immediately" to its owners after Jesus has used it. Luke's Jesus does not simply borrow the colt; he commandeers it as his own, as is his royal right.

comes into play. Though Luke does not explicitly cite Zech 9:9 (as in Matt 21:4–5; John 12:14–15), this text doubtless shapes the present scene: "Rejoice greatly, O daughter Sion! Proclaim, O daughter Ierousalem! Behold, your king comes to you, just and salvific is he, meek and riding on a beast of burden and a young foal [πῶλον νέον, *pōlon neon*]" (NETS). This allusion suggests that the never-ridden "colt" or "foal" (πῶλον, *pōlon*) chosen by Jesus is a young donkey ("beast of burden") rather than a horse (cf. Zech 9:9 MT; Matt 21:2–5; John 12:14–15). It is a pack animal of the common people, a "meek" creature of peace in contrast to stately cavalry horses supporting military commanders and pulling chariots. In Zechariah's vision, the peacemaking king enters Jerusalem on this humble mount only *after* he obliterates all foreign, invasive chariots and cavalry (Zech 9:10). One can be sure this king rode no little donkey *in battle*!

But Luke's Jesus bypasses this militaristic prelude to royal entry. While he has been establishing God's rule through powerful "just and saving [δίκαιος καὶ σῷζων, *dikaios kai sōzōn*]" (Zech 9:10 LXX) acts, driving out evil forces oppressing God's people, he has done so without shedding a drop of blood. He enters a Jerusalem still policed by Roman garrisons and issues no call to arms against them. He comes as Israel's anointed Davidic ruler, reminiscent of Solomon's inaugural procession on David's mule (only half-donkey, but again, no noble steed [1 Kgs 1:33, 38, 44]), but still with marked differences: Jesus comes to no free political center of Israel's united monarchy and has no plans of murdering rival claimants to the throne (Solomon's first order of business was eliminating half-brother Adonijah [1 Kgs 2:19–25]), still less of amassing "forty thousand stalls of horses for his chariots, and twelve thousand horsemen" (1 Kgs 4:26–28). Luke's Jesus is "greater than Solomon" (Luke 11:31)—and Caesar, Herod, and all other earthly rulers—because of a radically different concept of rule grounded in humble service and peacemaking rather than power politics and warfare (cf. 9:46–48; 22:24–27). He has no truck with "colonial mimicry."[409] Jesus advances the qualitatively superior kingdom of *God*—the loving, sustaining, merciful God of Israel and the world. Jesus is wholly devoted to serving this one God in God's way. Such consecration may coordinate with the choice of a young, never ridden (unbridled, unyoked) colt, typical of animals used in Israel's sacred rites (Num 19:2; Deut 21:3; 1 Sam 6:7). More basically, however, this fresh, unused

409. Though, of course, Luke still ascribes ultimate authority to Jesus, the true Lord and King, appropriating (co-opting) Caesar's language even as he subverts Caesarean/Herodian ruling aims and styles. "Colonial mimicry" thus remains a dangerous hybrid concept, always threatening to collapse on itself by reduplicating imperial oppression under a different name. For critical discussions in relation to Mark's Jesus, based on the seminal work of Homi Bhabha, see Liew, "Postcolonial Criticism," and Abraham Smith, "Cultural Studies," 198–206.

mount suggests the *unique* character of Jesus's reign. No other king has done it this way before.

Having considered the two "mounts" of Jesus's approach to Jerusalem, we now turn to two *outbursts*: one from the "multitude of the disciples" (19:38), the other from Jesus himself (19:41–44)—with distinct emotional tenors. First, the retinue around Jesus place their coats or outer garments (ἱμάτια, *himatia*) on the colt as a saddle for Jesus and on the pathway as a carpet into the city. These gestures are entirely initiated by the attendants (they even "set Jesus on" the donkey [19:35]) in spontaneous fashion. This is no preplanned procession, as a city might organize for an imperial visit. Except in the matter of securing the colt, Jesus has issued no orders or stage directions for a grand entrance; he may anticipate the crowd's response, but he does not orchestrate it or play to the audience: no hand-waving, chest-thumping, or other forms of public preening.

Having shed their coats, the excited throng bursts forth in jubilant praise to God, echoing Ps 118:26 and Jesus's forecast in Luke 13:35, but with telling additions. "Blessed is the one who comes in the name of the LORD" now becomes "Blessed is *the king* who comes in the name of the Lord" (19:38a), thus punctuating the royal character of Jesus's entry. Moreover, the second line of the chorus—"Peace in heaven, and glory in the highest realms [ὑψίστοις, *hypsistois*]" (19:38b AT)—replaces the psalmist's "We bless you from the house of the LORD." In other words, Luke shifts the temple (house of the Lord) orientation of Ps 118:26 to a higher celestial arena. As soon becomes evident, the Jerusalem temple, in Luke's view, now fosters more conflict and corruption than peace and justice (19:45–21:38), made all the worse because its leaders will not recognize the time of God's gracious "visitation" in co-regent Jesus Messiah (19:44). At this stage, ordinary folk side with the heavenly chorus against the temple establishment, echoing the angels' thunderous annunciation to the shepherds at Jesus's birth: "Glory to God in the highest, and on earth peace!" (2:14). The kingdom of God in Luke finds its deepest welcome among heavenly messengers, nightshift nomads, and coat-strewing commoners, hailing King Jesus born in a manger and borne by a donkey: a marvelous motley community of heavenly and earthly creatures joined together under the peaceful rule of God and Christ—and set against all oppressive powers, secular and religious.

Though not city officials or priestly authorities, some Pharisees voice their discomfort with the present proceedings. We have tracked the Pharisees' ambivalent responses to Jesus to this point. Here, though not denouncing Jesus's royal entry outright, they do press the "Teacher" (not "King") to command his disciples to desist their outburst (19:39). We do not know precisely what drives these Pharisees. Are they concerned about Roman reprisals against a politically charged demonstration? Offended by excessive, bordering on blasphemous, acclamations of Jesus's authority?[410] At any rate, they fit the pattern of those who obstruct Jesus's way and squelch the good news of God's kingdom (cf. 9:49–50; 18:15–17, 35–40). And once again, Jesus pushes back. Beyond refusing to mute his disciples' praise to God, Jesus announces, "I tell you, if these were silent, the stones would shout out" (19:40). Even the inanimate rocks yearn to participate in the cosmic royal drama, along with celestial and human bodies (and do not forget the donkey!). But some stones have special significance in the present story, namely, those fitted into the formidable city walls and magnificent temple structures, recently refurbished by Herod the Great. Terrible, tragic irony enters the picture: while these great stones know well their divine Maker and Master, their witness has been throttled by worldly overlords both apathetic and antagonistic to God's rule; and consequently, as if in a state of frustrated grief, these rocks will soon dislodge and fall apart, not "one stone [left] upon another" (19:44).

And so the scene dramatically shifts from joyous adulation to grievous lament, with Jesus bursting forth as the lead mourner. He can no longer play the triumphal role, even in his low-key way. He *knows* the awful fate that awaits the beautiful stones and entire city of Jerusalem (including children), because they—the leaders and people who follow them —*do not recognize/know* (οὐκ ἔγνως, *ouk egnōs* [19:44]) the dire emergency at hand and the critical challenge issued by the prophet-king Jesus to turn back in submission to God's rule. Jesus knows that Jerusalem, in its persisting blindness and unfaithfulness, will soon fall prey to crushing enemy attack. Like Babylon six centuries earlier, Rome will brutally flatten the holy city and its temple. Luke's Jesus sees this ominous writing on the wall, which by Luke's day had become bitter reality in Rome's wall-shattering demolition of Jerusalem in 70 CE.

So the "peace in heaven" extolled by Jesus's entourage is not as close to the earthly horizon as the singers hope. Jesus knows that their praise will turn to lament, their joy to mourning, in tragic fulfillment of his earlier "woe," without the flip-side "blessing" of weeping transformed into laughing (6:21, 25). This is no laughing matter in any respect, and it is more than Jesus can take. He takes no delight, justified or perverse, in judgment against his resisters, be they ignorant or defiant. Again, he proves antithetical to the preceding parable's vengeful nobleman-king. If there's anything Jesus could do to change Jerusalem's collective mind and avert its looming disaster, he would do it.

410. Cf. Danker, 313: "[The Pharisees] are typical of leaders who are allergic to demonstrations or what they term 'emotional outbursts'; they much prefer 'orderly' discussion, which practically guarantees hardening of institutional arteries and obsolescence of the gospel."

But all he can do for now is break down physically and grammatically. He can't even speak straight: "If you had known on this day, even you, the things of peace; but now" (19:42 AT, following the halting Greek word order). So begins a stuttering lament expressed in "fractured syntax"[411] that "throbs with the agitation of his heart"[412]—"short, choppy sentences" conveying a vivid sense of spontaneous, emotional outburst.[413] As his words fall apart, his tears fall down—both acts mirroring the dire destiny of the city's stones. Maintaining no stoic, stiff upper lip expected of tough kings, Jesus unashamedly—still in the public spotlight of his procession—bursts forth with indecorous (shameful) *weeping* (κλαίω, *klaiō*), the typical eruption of bereft *women* (cf. 7:13, 38; 23:28; Act 9:39), not confident rulers.[414] But such turbulent emotion also characterizes prophets in the face of ignorance and recalcitrance from God's people. Witness Jeremiah, during Babylon's siege against Jerusalem, yearning "that my head were a spring of water, and my eyes a fountain of tears, so that I might weep day and night for the slain of my poor people!" (Jer 9:1; cf. 13:17; 22:10);[415] and Paul, wrestling with his compatriots' limited acceptance of Jesus Messiah in "great sorrow and unceasing anguish in my heart . . . wish[ing] that I myself were accursed and cut off from Christ for the sake of my own people" (Rom 9:2–3). Such impassioned sympathy marks real men of God.[416]

411. Tiede, *Prophecy*, 79, 86.

412. Danker, 314.

413. Tannehill, 285; cf. Voorwinde, *Jesus' Emotions*, 149–50; Wilson, *Unmanly Men*, 218; Voorwinde associates the "broken grammar" of Luke 19:42 with the technique of *aposiopesis*, which (citing Robertson, *Grammar*, 1203), is "a conscious suppression of part of a sentence under the influence of a strong emotion like anger, fear, pity. . . . What differentiates [aposiopesis] from ellipses or abbreviations of other clauses . . . is the passion" (149 [cf. BDF, 255].

414. Though Shelly Matthews ("Weeping") acknowledges Jesus's dramatic emotional performance here, including the fact that "κλαίω [*klaiō*] is a stronger word [than δακρύω, *dakryō*], expressing a more vivid emotional display, since it indicates audible cries as well as the shedding of tears" (384), she argues that this otherwise anomalous portrait of a mushy Jesus, typically virile and stoic in Luke, actually fits a noble heroic Greco-Roman pattern of generals dutifully weeping over cities they are about to destroy, so as to prove that their impending violence is not driven by uncontrollable rage. However, apart from the obvious distinction, which Matthews acknowledges, that Luke's Jesus is no conquering military commander, she ignores Jesus's palpably weak, draining, overwhelming, broken state—evidenced not least in the broken syntax, which hardly strikes a dignified, domineering pose of a triumphal hero.

415. On the close Jeremiah link with Luke 19:41–44, see Tiede, *Prophecy*, 78–84. Tiede astutely observes that Jesus's Jeremiah-evoking weeping "produces a striking effect, intensifying the rhetoric and pathos by reminiscence of a previous tragedy that is about to be repeated" (82); cf. Wilson, *Unmanly Men*, 217–18; Fisk, "See My Tears," 170–75.

416. And not only for Israel: God even "drenches" devastated Moabite territory "with my tears" (Isa 16:9; cf. Jer 48:36); see Elizabeth A. Johnson, *Ask the Beasts*, 192.

Knowing God the Suffering Savior in the Death and Resurrection of Jesus (19:45–24:53)

At last Jesus enters Jerusalem, culminating the long journey to which he "set his face" in 9:51. The only other times Luke's Jesus came to the holy city were during his childhood: (1) his dedication in the temple as an infant in the presence of elderly prophets (2:22–24) and (2) his discussion in the temple (at Passover) as a precocious twelve-year-old with the established teachers (2:41–46). Both incidents sparked dramatic responses: (1) blessing from prophets Simeon and Anna (2:25–38) and (2) amazement from temple scholars and general audience, on the one hand, and consternation from parents Mary and Joseph, on the other (2:47–50). Now, as Luke's story draws to a close, the mature Jesus again comes to Jerusalem at Passover (22:1, 7–15) and teaches in the temple (19:47; 20:1; 21:37–38). But while the people continue to listen appreciatively, the temple authorities become increasingly antagonistic, to the point of hatching a plot against Jesus's life (19:47–48; 20:19).

But they do not act alone. The priestly hierarchs collude with one of Jesus's chosen apostles, Judas Iscariot, who in turn succumbs to Satan's nefarious influence (22:2–6), and with the Roman governor, Pontius Pilate (assisted by Herod Antipas), and his soldiers, who carry out Jesus's crucifixion (23:1–49). Along the way, the chief spokesman among Jesus's followers, Simon Peter, opts not to speak up for Jesus; in fact, he directly denies he even knows Jesus (22:54–62). Other disciples, including women who followed from Galilee, prove only slightly more supportive, observing Jesus's crucifixion "at a distance" (23:49). Finally, adding insult to injury, even "crowds" of Jerusalem citizens and visitors, some of whom had extolled his Jesus's entry (19:37), turn into a bloodthirsty mob crying for his execution (23:18–25).

We may group this wide cast of characters in Luke's closing chapters—sometimes aligned with Jesus but ultimately contributing to his death or watching helplessly as he dies—into three categories: Disciples, Authorities, People.

Active Accomplices and Passive Attendants to Jesus's Death

Disciples: Jesus's followers	Authorities: Jewish, Roman, Herodian	People: Jerusalem populace
Twelve apostles	Jewish "chief priests, the scribes, and the leaders/ first-ones [πρῶτοι, *prōtoi*]" (19:47); "assembly of the elders" (22:66); "leaders/ rulers [ἄρχοντες, *archontes*]" (23:13, 35)	"The people" (ὁ λαός, *ho laos* [20:1, 9, 26, 45; 21:38; 22:2, 66; 23:13–14, 27, 35])
Judas Iscariot (driven by Satan) (22:3)	Temple police (22:4, 52) and high priest's servants (22:54–59)	"Rich people" (πλούσιοι, *plousioi* [21:1])
Simon Peter (influenced by Satan) (22:31)	Pontius Pilate	"Crowds" (ὄχλοι, *ochloi* [22:6, 47; 23:48])
Galilean women	Centurion and Roman soldiers	"Multitude," "assembly" (πλῆθος *plēthos* [23:1, 27])
Other "acquaintances"; larger group of followers (συνακολουθοῦσαι, *syn-akolouthousai* [23:49])	Herod Antipas	"Daughters of Jerusalem" (mourners at Jesus's death; of uncertain relationship to him) (23:28)
Cleopas and companion (24:13–20)		Two criminals crucified beside Jesus (23:39)

In the swirl of these numerous characters determining his fate, however, Jesus is no passive pawn. To a great extent, Jesus pushes the envelope, provoking a decision for or against him—mostly against! From his first action in the temple (19:45–46), it becomes clear that he is making no social call on Jerusalem or moseying in for a casual Passover celebration. Jesus undertakes a divinely authorized "visitation" (ἐπισκοπή, *episkopē*), as he just tearfully announced on the city's edge (19:44); in other words, he's making a solemn house call on God's city and temple as the chief agent of God's judgment.[1] In this mode, as discussed above, Jesus visits Jerusalem not only as a king like David, but also as a prophet like Jeremiah, warning and weeping over God's people who "did not recognize/ know" the serious time at hand (19:44).

1. On "day/time of visitation [ἐπισκοπή, *episkopē*]" as an appointed occasion of divine reckoning, see Isa 10:3; Jer 6:15; 10:15; Wis 3:7; 1 Pet 2:12.

In fact, Jesus's role as God's ultimate, eschatological *prophet*, enacted throughout the course of his ministry (4:16–30; 7:16, 39; 13:33), predominates over his royal vocation in these closing chapters. Soon after his death, two of Jesus's followers encapsulate his prime identity: "Jesus of Nazareth . . . a *prophet mighty in deed and word* before God and all the people" (24:19). As Israel's prophets of old, Jesus comes speaking God's truth to political power—including *religious* political power—exposing complacent ignorance and effecting radical change of a misguided society on the cusp of destruction. The "hidden" dimensions of God's reign, to which Luke's Jesus has alluded, are now coming into full light (cf. 8:10, 17; 9:44–45; 10:21–24; 12:1–3; 13:20–21; 18:31–34). Jesus pulls no punches now, as his initial temple "visit" demonstrates with his driving out of the sellers and denunciation of the current temple system in the bold language of Isaiah and Jeremiah (19:45–46). This startling scene sets the stage for an extended series of debates, which we may entitle, from Jesus's prophetic perspective, "Challenging the Temple Establishment" (19:45–21:38).

However, the brighter that Jesus shines the light, the more blinding it becomes to those who "have eyes, but do not see" (Jer 5:21), who "look, but not perceive" (Mark 4:12; cf. Luke 8:10; 10:24; 11:33–35), who stubbornly resist *knowing the truth* staring them in their faces. Such blindness soon begets belligerence, as the exposed temple leaders begin to conspire "for a way to kill [Jesus]" (19:47). By week's end, their plot succeeds. This hostile response comes as no surprise to Jesus. He knows the fate awaiting him, having predicted it multiple times as the way of God's emissaries: "It is impossible for a prophet to be killed outside of Jerusalem" (13:34; cf. 9:22, 44; 11:47–51; 18:31–33). That is the "way" of things (13:33).

But this prophetic path is not all gloom and doom. However sharp the protest, it always breaks through to comfort (Isa 40:1–3); however dim the prospects may seem, the light of God's hope never dies. Human corruption never usurps the divine purpose of salvation. For Luke's Jesus, death gives way to new life, crucifixion to resurrection. But *crucially* (in the full sense of that word related to "crucify"), the gospel story of God's saving hope is not simply a resurrection rescue *from* death and darkness, a fortunate escape *from* a desperate situation. More accurately, Jesus's "third-day" resurrection caps a saving process enacted across the days (the eschatological "today") of Jesus's ministry all the way *through* his final trials and crucifixion. Remarkably and paradoxically, the cross is not so much an impediment to God's salvific plan as an implementation of it. Far from being a regrettable detour, it is the indispensable gateway. It is the *crux* of the saving matter *qua cross*—in all of its raw, unvarnished horror as a brutal instrument of state execution—before it became "gilded . . . with the expectations and ideas of salvation" promulgated by state religion for popular consumption.[2]

Although Luke's Gospel expounds no theory of atonement per se involving sacrifice for sin, it presents a dramatic narrative of the *saving significance of Jesus's trials and death* nonpareil in Gospel literature. Unique examples of Jesus's redemptive work, operating *through* his calamitous final days up to his last gasps of breath on the cross, include:

- *Last Supper*: Knowing that Peter would repeatedly deny knowing him, Jesus prays for the restoration of Peter's faith, leading in turn to his ministry of "strengthening" fellow disciples after Jesus's departure (22:31–34).
- *Arrest*: After one of his followers slices off the ear of a member of the high priest's arrest party, Jesus promptly touches and heals the maimed man (22:50–51).
- *Crucifixion*: In the face of repeated taunts about his saving efficacy from religious leaders, Roman soldiers, and one of the criminals dying beside him, Jesus prays for the forgiveness of his tormentors and answers the prayer of the other criminal for merciful consideration in Jesus's kingdom (23:32–43).

In short, Luke's Jesus keeps mediating God's salvation *through* his suffering, reminiscent of Isaiah's suffering servant (see Luke 22:37/Isa 53:12) and prototypical for St. Francis of Assisi, whose "starting place was human suffering instead of human sinfulness, and God's identification with that suffering in Jesus."[3] Luke's Jesus "*must suffer* [ἔδει παθεῖν, *edei pathein*]" (24:26 AT) the depths of human suffering in order to reveal the fullness of God's compassionate salvation. The Passover (πάσχα, *pascha*) setting for Jesus's passion, as tradition designates his last week, provides the perfect stage for this redemptive "suffering" (πάσχω, *paschō*). As Passover commemorates God's sympathetic attention to the anguished cries of God's people in advance of the Exodus ("I know their sufferings" [Exod 3:7]), so Jesus embodies God's personal concern for human affliction en route to the resurrection. Notably, such concern also encompasses the oppressors of Jesus and his fickle associates. He responds in saving, restoring, healing, and forgiving fashion *to* his persecutors and defectors, incarnating his policy of loving one's enemies (Luke 6:27–36).

Some, however, support and follow Jesus's cross-bearing path, albeit in limited ways. Roman soldiers force one Simon of Cyrene to literally carry Jesus's

2. Moltmann, *Crucified God*, 40.

3. Rohr, *Eager to Love*, 83.

cross "behind/after [ὄπισθεν, *opisthen*]" him, a task that he executes without objection (23:26). Of course, he has little choice in the matter, but still he winds up assisting Jesus, sharing in his suffering, and taking up the cross, as Jesus prescribed for all his adherents (9:23). Likewise, "a great number of people followed" Jesus to the cross, matching the throng who had just clamored for his death sentence. Surely most tag along to witness the bloody spectacle, but Luke's use of the basic discipleship term "follow"—in sentence-initial emphatic position (ἠκολούθει, *ēkolouthei* [23:27])—intimates a possible change in heart among some. In particular, we may surmise that the wailing women who accompany the death march are not simply fulfilling general mourning duties but are somehow moved to grieve *Jesus's* death in particular: they are "wailing *for him*" (23:27). More patently, in the throes of Jesus's execution, two surprising figures—one of the criminals hanging next to Jesus and the Roman officer overseeing events—erupt in unexpected, wholehearted endorsement of Jesus's character and mission (23:40–43, 47). Less positively, but still passionately, "all the crowds who had gathered there for this spectacle" for whatever reason beat their breasts in bereavement (like the daughters of Jerusalem) as they head home (23:48).

But there is more: the complex of saving events continues through Jesus's burial and resurrection. After Jesus expires, another unexpected supporting figure emerges: one Joseph of Arimathea, a member of the supreme Jewish court. Just as not all Roman officers remain blind to Jesus's significance (witness the centurion at the cross), not all Jewish leaders oppose Jesus. This Joseph "had not agreed to their plan and action" (23:51) and at least tries now to compensate for this travesty of justice by giving the crucified Jesus a decent burial. Furthermore, the Galilean women disciples who had attended Jesus's death "from a distance" now move close again, locating the tomb where Joseph places Jesus's body and returning at the crack of dawn on Sunday to anoint it. As such, they put themselves in position to be the first to discover Jesus's empty tomb and to learn and testify about his resurrection (23:49, 54–56; 24:1–10). Soon other disciples come into the orbit of the risen Christ, seeing him alive here and there before his heavenly ascension (24:13–42). With still much to grasp, the disciples' pilgrimage toward renewed hope, restored faith, and reenergized mission takes a giant leap forward.

Using the same categories as above, I list examples of positive adherence to the way of the crucified-risen Lord.

Active Sympathizers and Restored Supporters of the Dying and Risen Jesus

Disciples: Jesus's followers	Authorities: Roman and Jewish	People: General Jerusalem populace
Simon Peter (22:31–34)	Centurion at the cross (23:47)	Simon of Cyrene (cross-bearer) (23:26)
Mary Magdalene, Joanna, and other Galilean women at empty tomb (23:55–24:10)	Joseph of Arimathea at the tomb (23:50–53)	Wailing "daughters of Jerusalem" among "followers" to the cross (23:27–28)
Cleopas and companion (24:13–32)		Plaintive criminal on the cross (23:40–43)
Eleven apostles (sans Judas) and their companions (24:33–53)		"A great number of the people [πλῆθος τοῦ λαοῦ, *plēthos tou laou*]" who "follow" Jesus to the cross (23:27) and "crowds" (ὄχλοι, *ochloi*) who leave grieving (23:48)

After "Challenging the Temple Establishment," Jesus's sympathetic way of salvation in Luke's concluding scenes may be entitled, "Incarnating the World's Suffering" (22:1–24:53), epitomized in his Last Supper announcement, underscoring his palpable flesh-and-blood participation in mortal affliction: "This is my [broken] body. . . . This . . . is the new covenant in my [outpoured] blood" (22:19–20). As comfortable (and complacent) as modern Christians might be with these "words of institution" and with Jesus's sharing our sufferings, we must not minimize the serious epistemological (cognitive dissonance) and theological (theodicy) crises that Jesus's crucifixion fomented for his followers. Cleopas and companion poignantly pinpoint the problem as they trudge home to Emmaus after Jesus's tragic demise in Jerusalem: "But we had hoped that he"—this "Jesus of Nazareth . . . a prophet mighty in deed and word [yet] . . . condemned to death and crucified"—"was the one to redeem Israel" (24:19–21). They speak these words unwittingly to the risen Jesus, whom they "were kept from recognizing [ἐπιγνῶναι, *epignōnai*]" walking alongside them (24:16) and whom they chide as "the only stranger in Jerusalem who *does not know* [ἔγνως, *egnōs*] the things that have taken place there in these days" (24:18), which only accentuates the depths of their dissonance. It is simply unthinkable that the Messiah would die, even less that he be crucified. By all accounts, that looks like a *futile and failed* Messiah unworthy of faith and discipleship. Though Cleopas and friend doubtless believed, with many Jews, in a general resurrection at the end of the age, they could not conceive, despite Jesus's predictions, of the Messiah's third-day resurrection. Without considerable revelatory help, they just couldn't get beyond the scandal of a crucified Messiah to see any salutary possibilities.

Fortunately, the risen Jesus does not string along the depressed pair of disciples for long, soon revealing himself in word and sacrament, Scripture-opening and bread-breaking, as the life-giving Messiah who "should suffer . . . and then enter into his glory" (24:26). Still, much remains to be desired in terms of clarity and solidity of knowledge. Though Jesus rebukes the Emmaus couple as "foolish" and "slow of heart to believe" the Scriptures (24:25), it is not at all obvious what texts Jesus has in mind (he doesn't cite any); and no sooner had they "recognized [ἐπέγνωσαν, *epegnōsan*]" Jesus than "he vanished from their sight" (24:31). No chance for extended fellowship or a biblical studies seminar with the risen Jesus.

Though examples of exemplary suffering servants, righteous persecuted ones, and faithful martyrs appear in sacred Jewish history, nothing clearly anticipates a *crucified-risen Messiah.*

- Isaiah's suffering servant is destined to "make many righteous and . . . bear the iniquities" of God's people (Isa 53:11) through his sacrificial death and afterlife ("he shall see his offspring, and shall prolong his days" [53:10]); but there is no *direct* connection to crucifixion and (imminent) resurrection, still less to any messianic (royal, Davidic, Son of God) figure.[4]
- The psalmist's righteous sufferer, who faces terrible mistreatment from wicked opponents, may take on a Davidic persona in seeking God's "faithful help [to] rescue me from sinking in the mire; let me be delivered from my enemies. . . . Do not let . . . the Pit close its mouth over me" (Ps 69:13–15); but the focus falls more on rescue before death's jaws consume this figure than on revival after death.
- The Maccabean martyrs—Eleazar the scribe and a mother and seven sons—who nobly choose torturous death at the hands of the Greek-Syrian tyrant Antiochus IV over compromising their commitment to God's law, entrust themselves to God's life-renewing care. As the mother exhorts

4. The Servant's dominant "afterlife" hope in Isa 53, as typical in OT thought, seems to be *through "his offspring"* (v. 10) rather than in a distinctive personal resurrection.

> her sons: "Therefore the Creator of the world, who shaped the beginning of humankind and devised the origin of all things, will in his mercy give life and breath back to you again, since you now forget yourselves for the sake of his laws" (2 Macc 7:23; cf. 7:27–29); yet this promise of immortality (cf. 4 Macc 9:22; 14:4–5; 16:13; 17:12; 18:23) for these faithful martyrs does not make them Messiahs or obviate the need for Mattathias and sons to launch a *violent fight for national freedom*.

Anticipating further comments below about models of faithful sufferers in Luke's passion narrative, I simply note here that, while none provides a precise prototype for the suffering Jesus, Isaiah's servant offers the most apt precedent and the Maccabean martyrs the least.[5] Eschewing, or at least downplaying, Jesus's martyr role in Luke runs against a common interpretive line stressing Jesus's stoic, nonemotional, self- and God-confident approach to his trials and execution.[6] While Jesus periodically displays some of these features during his final week, they do not reflect the whole picture. I will argue that the passion of Luke's Jesus features a truly *passionate* Jesus, agonizing over the perilous path laid out before him.[7] Though he comes *through* the struggle to accept the necessity of death, he travels no easy road. His prayer on the Mount of Olives, with or without the textually disputed blood-like sweat (22:43–44), is not as stoic as some commentators think. Jesus truly wrestles with God about drinking the bitter "cup" set out for him (22:39–46). He who wept on the outskirts of Jerusalem doesn't turn off his emotions when he enters the city. And though challenging the authorities along the way, he does not deliver some blistering apologetic against his prosecutors, like that of the Maccabean brothers (4 Macc 9:1–9) or Stephen, for that matter, in Acts 6:8–8:1. Though the death scenes of Jesus and Stephen evince some notable parallels, we must not overimpose Stephen's martyrdom back on to Jesus's death. Along with voicing no extensive defense speech like Stephen's, Jesus shows no glowing angelic face and sees no open heaven at his trial or execution (cf. Acts 6:15; 7:55–56). Jesus's facial change happens earlier at the transfiguration (Luke 9:29), and his celestial vision comes later at the ascension (24:51; Acts 1:9–11).

5. See 22:37; Acts 8:32–33; Green, "Was It Not Necessary," 80–85, and "Jesus," 41–43.

6. For example, Neyrey, "Absence" and *Passion*, 49–65; Talbert, 212–18; Moltmann (*Crucified God*) credits Luke (but only by *misreading* Luke in my judgment) with creating "the pattern of martyr Christology" that features "Jesus as the archetype or example of faith under temptation" (148). Such a view has dominated Christian theology. On historical and theological grounds, Moltmann rejects this view (unfairly attributed to Luke, in my view) in favor of Matthew's and Mark's abandonment/forsakenness emphasis.

7. See Spencer, *Dancing Girls*, 120–37; Wilson, *Unmanly Men*, 190–242.

In sum, Luke must marshal all of his narrative-rhetorical skills to persuade readers of the integral necessity of Jesus's crucifixion in fulfilling God's purpose to restore a broken world. To *know the solidity* (Luke 1:4) of God's cruciform paradigm for the world's redemption is the ultimate epistemological challenge. As always in Luke, such knowledge is as much experiential and existential as it is intellectual and perceptual. The saving way of the cross is the day-by-day, dying-and-living way of God's Messiah Jesus (and followers), reinforced in Luke's final chapters in a vivid three-dimensional portrait:

- Jesus's *person*, incarnating the world's suffering in flesh and blood
- Jesus's *passions*, across the spectrum from anger to love, agony to peace, grief to hope
- Jesus's *practices*, chiefly prayer, Scripture-interpreting, and bread-breaking.

These aspects of Jesus's character-in-action provide frameworks, not formulas, for spiritual formation. Luke presents a tension-filled narrative of Jesus's cross-bearing spirituality, not a manual of spiritual disciplines. But for those with eyes to see and ears to hear, Luke's passion narrative floods fresh light and rips open the curtain (23:45) into vast horizons of God's cosmic vision of salvation.

Challenging the Temple Establishment (19:45–21:38)

Parallel statements frame this section and set the agenda for Jesus's next few days: "Every day he was teaching in the temple" (19:47; 21:37). Jesus comes to Jerusalem to "teach" (διδάσκω, *didaskō*) the people (cf. 20:1, 21); accordingly, audiences address him as "Teacher" (διδάσκαλος, *didaskalos* [19:39; 20:21, 28, 39; 21:7]). But the extended framing passages highlight that he comes as no ordinary teacher simply regurgitating traditional lessons.

> Every day he was teaching in the temple. The chief priests, the scribes, and the leaders of the people kept looking for a way to kill him; but they did not find anything they could do, for all the people were spellbound by what they heard. (19:47–48)

> Every day he was teaching in the temple, and at night he would go out and spend the night on the Mount of Olives, as it was called. And all the people would get up early in the morning to listen to him in the temple. (21:37–38)

Simply put: the temple leaders want to get rid of Teacher Jesus, and the laypeople can't get enough of him. The two responses are related. The surging popularity of the maverick teacher Jesus—a Galilean upstart with no priestly credentials or patronage—naturally sparks concern among the religious authorities, both pastorally for the people's welfare and jealously for their own political power (cf. Acts 5:17). The latter, more sinister, interest predominates in Luke's story, as the chief priests plot not simply to correct or curtail Jesus's influence, but to eliminate him altogether. On the other side, the people's mesmerized attraction to Jesus owes in no small measure to his distinctiveness from the current clerical establishment. They would not rise "early in the morning" (Luke 21:38) to hear the present temple faculty lecture, as these banal teachers mostly failed to inspire the beleaguered populace. Jesus, however, teaches with fresh authority (4:32, 36; 20:1–8), compelling insight, and spellbinding promise. The word translated "spellbound" in 19:48 (ἐκκρεμάννυμι, *ekkremannymi*) literally means "hang down," which translates nicely into the English idiom, "they hung on his every word" (NAB, NASB, NIV).

This portrait of Jesus as an authoritative, provocative teacher elides into his role as God's *prophet*, though this term will not designate him until 24:19 (Jesus calls his forerunner John "prophet" in 20:6). He is a prophet-teacher, as we have stressed, along the lines of Jeremiah and company (though Jesus was not a priest like Jeremiah), on the edge of the religious establishment and aligned with the marginalized majority. He comes into the temple precincts, as Jeremiah did, preaching his iconoclastic message of repentance, reform, and restoration of a corrupt system. But he makes no permanent home in the temple, which at present, is not a true "house of prayer" for God's people (19:46, echoing Isa 56:7). Each night during Passover week, Jesus returns to the Mount of Olives, the same place, loaded with eschatological significance (see above on 19:28–44), whence he entered Jerusalem and wept over it. Unlike the other Gospels, which lodge Jesus in a friendly Bethany suburban home (Simon the leper's in Mark 11:1, 11–12; 14:3–9; Matt 21:1, 26:6–13; Martha, Mary, and Lazarus's in John 12:1–8), Luke suggests that he simply camps out each evening on the Olivet mountainside. To the end, Luke's Jesus remains the itinerant prophet-teacher, the unsettled spiritual pilgrim, the restless journeyman through desert and mountain terrain, the king with "no place in the lodging-house" (2:7 AT), the "Son of Humankind [who] has nowhere to lay his head" (9:58). The divine realm he inhabits is as big as all creation and seeks the salvation of the "whole earth [πάσης τῆς γῆς, *pasēs tēs gēs*]" (21:35).

In classic prophetic-didactic fashion, Jesus's temple challenges unfold in a series of demonstrations (symbolic dramas), interrogations (rhetorical debates), and prognostications (prophetic forecasts).

- Demonstration: Casting Out Sellers from the Temple (19:45–48)
- Interrogation: Questions and Answers (20:1–44)
- Demonstration: Pointing Out a Contributor in the Temple (20:45–21:4)
- Prognostication: Signs and Events (21:5–38)

Thus Jesus culminates his vocation as an effectual prophet in deed and word. His acts of driving out the selling functionaries (19:45–48) and pointing out the contributing widow (20:45–21:4) both concern temple "business" in the hard economic sense and function as strategic visual aids for Jesus's forthtelling (20:1–44) and foretelling (21:5–38) messages.

Demonstration: Casting Out Sellers from the Temple (19:45–48)

Wasting no time scouting the place before his demonstration the next morning (as in Mark 11:11–12), Luke's Jesus proceeds directly into the temple and takes action. Luke provides the sparsest account of this startling scene, simply reporting that Jesus "began to drive out those who were selling things there" (Luke 19:45) and then offered an interpretive couplet from Isaiah and Jeremiah. The other three canonical Gospels additionally feature Jesus's overturning the temple merchants' tables (Matt 21:12//Mark 11:15//John 2:15). Mark also recounts Jesus's protest against carrying "anything through the temple" (Mark 11:16); and John spices the scene with Jesus's brandishing a makeshift whip, dumping out the moneychangers' coin boxes, and lamenting the desecration of "my Father's house," turning it into "a marketplace/emporium [ἐμπόριον, *emporion*]" (John 2:16). The comparative terseness of Luke's account, however, does not minimize the incident's dramatic significance. Its concentrated expression of Jesus's censure of current temple "business" packs its own explosive punch.

Emphasis falls on two present-tense verbs suggesting iterative action: *expelling* (ἐκβάλλω, *ekballō*) and *selling* (πωλέω, *pōleō*). The first term carries strong oppositional connotations, as in the Nazareth community's attempt to "throw out" Jesus from the city and over a cliff (Luke 4:29; cf. 6:22) and in Jesus's works of "casting out" demons from persons (4:41; 11:14–15, 18–19; 13:32). Now Jesus "drives out" out those selling merchandise in the temple compound. But though he acts in a forceful manner and aims to liberate the temple from corrupting influence, he does not dispatch the sellers over the precipice (the Temple Mount) (cf. 4:29; 8:32–33). Furthermore, he does not necessarily target the sellers as evildoers responsible for temple decadence. Rather than hawkers of various wares and souvenirs to tourists for personal profit, these merchants most likely are sellers of animals (lambs, goats, turtledoves, pigeons) authorized for sacrifice in the temple. They thus function as essential temple personnel, ensuring proper, holy offerings, "as it is written in the law of the Lord" (2:23). Enjoying a virtual monopoly on the stock of "clean" sacrificial animals, which must be paid in Tyrian currency (no Roman coins with Caesar's image), the sellers *may* engage in price gouging and exchange-rate inflating (colluding with moneychangers [cf. Mark 11:15]). But Luke's Jesus is more interested in indicting the entire temple system of his day, spearheaded by sacerdotal executives, than in rooting out a few corrupt members of the sales force.[8]

It is no accident that the "chief priests, the scribes, and the leaders of the people" plot to kill Jesus after his disturbing demonstration (19:47). They get the point: they know he's attacking the whole institution they oversee, threatening to place it under new management supervised by God's faithful Son and Servant Jesus; and they know that the people might happily support this takeover. So the "selling" activity that Jesus targets may be less a problem of shady business than one of business as usual, like the perfunctory "selling" during the days of Lot, which will also characterize the times preceding God's final judgment (cf. 17:28–30). Jesus may even be forcing the sellers out for their own good (as the angel did with Lot's family), compelling them to escape the disastrous fate awaiting the recalcitrant temple establishment (cf. 21:5–6).

Jesus's prophetic purpose drives home theological and ethical convictions reinforced by two scriptural ("it is written") citations. First, the *theological* point from Isa 56:7: "My house shall be a house of prayer" (Luke 19:46a). The Lord God, speaking through the prophets Isaiah and Jesus, reaffirms the temple as "*my* house," *God's* holy place, set apart for worship and fellowship with Israel's God (cf. 2 Sam 7:13; 1 Kgs 8:10–13). While the Isaiah text goes on to acclaim the universality of God's temple-house as saving refuge "for all the nations/ peoples" (Isa 56:7/Mark 11:17), Luke's Jesus, while sympathetic with this international perspective, focuses on God's exclusive proprietorship of the sanctuary. Temple administrators, from the highest leaders to the lowest functionaries, serve at God's pleasure, as God's stewards in a sacred trust. Violation of that trust constitutes grounds for dismissal and suspension of temple activity until divine order is restored.

8. For helpful discussions of the temple monetary system related to the "business" of sacrifice (and Jesus's reaction to the money-changers), see E. P. Sanders, *Jesus*, 63–71, and *Judaism*, 85–92; Hanson and Oakman, *Palestine*, 135–46; N. T. Wright, *Jesus*, 406–28. For a different angle, arguing that Jesus in fact was opposed to any trading in the temple precincts as a crass commercialization of solemn acts of sacrificial worship—following the view of many Pharisees and the eschatological vision of Zech 14:21 ("And there shall no longer be traders in the house of the LORD on that day")—see Chilton, *Rabbi Jesus*, 213–30.

Second, the *ethical* point, inextricably entwined with theology: exclusive love for God goes hand in hand with inclusive love for God's people manifest in acts of justice and mercy (Luke 6:36; 10:27–28). Though Jesus could continue drawing on Isaiah for his ethical indictment (Isa 58 packs plenty ethical punch), he shifts to Jeremiah's haunting image: "but you have made [my house] a den of robbers" (Luke 19:46b/Jer 7:11). Since Jeremiah spoke these words at "the gate of the LORD's house" (7:2), they carry particular force for Jesus's present setting. The damning picture is of God's glorious house shamefully remodeled into a "den of robbers," or "cave for criminals [σπήλαιον λῃστῶν, *spēlaion lēstōn*],"[9] a secret hideout for lawbreakers on the lam from authorities—except in this case the authorities host the thugs in the temple! The temple officials both promote unjust, ungodly activity within God's house and provide a safe haven for oppressors of the most vulnerable in society rather than a sanctuary for the oppressed.

Jeremiah's larger temple sermon spells out specific crimes of injustice and idolatry perpetrated by the temple "robber" gang: they "oppress the alien, the orphan, and the widow . . . shed innocent blood in this place . . . go after other gods to your own hurt. . . . Will you steal, murder, commit adultery, swear falsely, make offerings to Baal, and go after other gods that you have not known?" (Jer 7:6, 9). The problem compounds with the delusional mind-set that the temple institution acts like a prophylactic talisman guaranteeing peace in the land and, furthermore, is simply too big and important to fail, irrespective of faith and practice.[10] But one can cry "the temple of the LORD" mantra all day long and reflect mere "deceptive words" if not matched by righteous conduct (7:3–4, 8–11). However much God has sanctified the temple and desires to dwell there, God is by no means bound to this or any other locale unworthy of God's holy presence: "The Most High does not dwell in houses made with human hands" (Acts 7:48; 1 Kgs 8:27–30; Isa 66:1–2; cf. Acts 17:24). Like Jeremiah, Jesus throws down the gauntlet (as he throws out the merchants) in direct challenge to the temple establishment and implies notice (made explicit in Luke 21:5–6) of the temple's dismantlement, absent a major systemic overhaul. But tragically, as the Jerusalem leaders harassed Jeremiah rather than heeded his warning, so the chief priests and cronies "kept looking for a way to kill" Jesus from this moment on (19:47; cf. Jer 20:1–6; 32:1–5; 37:11–38:6).

9. Or as Chilton (*Rabbi Jesus*) puts it: "cave of thugs" (213, 230).

10. Cf. N. T. Wright, *Jesus*, 420: "The temple had become in Jesus's day as in Jeremiah's, the talisman of nationalist violence, the guarantee that YHWH would act for Israel and would defend her against her enemies."

Interrogation: Questions and Answers (20:1–44)

Though now under the priestly authorities' conspiratorial eye, Jesus keeps coming to the temple precincts each day to teach the people, who so far remain intrigued by his bold message (19:48). In no way apologizing for his initial outburst, Jesus does, however, refrain from other shocking demonstrations like driving out the temple merchants. This calmer demeanor may disappoint some curiosity seekers longing to see another spectacle, but Jesus still attracts positive attention with his poignant words. And why not, since he keeps "evangelizing" (εὐαγγελίζω, *euangelizō*) or "gospelizing"[11] the masses, who desperately need to hear good news of blessing and salvation (20:1)? The mission and message of Luke's Jesus remain gospel-centered to the end, even in the face of personal death threats.

Given the crowds' enthrallment with Jesus (19:48; 20:19), the religious leaders must tread carefully in plotting against him. So they or their appointed "spies" attempt to "trap [Jesus] by what he said, so as to hand him over to the jurisdiction and authority of the [Roman] governor" (20:20). They pose various loaded questions, which Jesus deftly parries, but which inevitably turn his prophetic rhetoric from evangelistic (benevolence) to apologetic (defense) mode. Again, the temple elites obstruct the people's salvation to safeguard their own political interests.

To clarify the players' identities, Jesus's current antagonists are the chief priests, scribes, and elders (20:1; cf. 19:47; 20:19) aligned with the aristocratic Sadducee party (20:27) and the clerical temple hierarchy. Luke implicates *no Pharisees* (lay scholar-reformers) in the final plot against Jesus's life and schemes to entrap him in seditious speech. Though earlier some Pharisees "were filled with fury" at Jesus's audacious Sabbath conduct in the synagogue (6:11) and, together with some scribes, "began to be very hostile toward him and to cross-examine him about many things" in response to his "woes" against them (11:53–54), their overall resistance has since tempered. In the Pharisees' last appearance in Luke, they urge Jesus as he approaches Jerusalem to stifle his followers' royal acclamation (19:39) (they might even be warning Jesus of imperial crackdowns against kingly promoters, just as they alerted him to Herod's murderous plan [13:31]). Unlike Synoptic accounts of Jesus's final week, where some Pharisees collude with Herodians to try to indict Jesus for tax evasion (Matt 22:15–22; Mark 12:13–17), Luke presents the instigators as direct agents of the priestly officials (Luke 20:19–20).[12]

11. Bird's felicitous coinage in *Evangelical Theology*, 30–31.

12. Matthew also has the Pharisees pose the question of the greatest commandment in

At the core of the temple debates is the issue of Jesus's *authority* (ἐξουσία, *exousia* [20:2, 8]), both its *source* and its *scope* in connection with other authorities: popular (John the Baptist [20:1–8]), political (Caesar [20:20–26]), and scriptural (Moses and David [20:27–44]). Of course, the chief priests are principally concerned with maintaining and bolstering *their own authority* as guardians of Jewish tradition, adjudicators of Mosaic law, and peacemakers with Roman overlords in the face of upstart rabble-rousers and world-shaking prophets like John and Jesus. Put another way, the temple disputes reflect a crisis of faith, not just in the narrower intellectual and doctrinal sense of belief (is Jesus the Messiah or not?), but in the wider judicial and personal sense of *trust*. Jesus and the priestly officials wage a critical war of trust in the temple courts for the hearts and minds of God's people. Whom can we really trust with our lives? Who is worthy of trust, and why? Who truly has the people's best interests at heart?

Philosophical and psychological assessments of trust-building and trustworthiness often start with the factor of competence or ability.[13] Does the one seeking our trust have what it takes to deliver the goods in terms of skills and resources? Authority based merely on position or status, especially inherited (ascribed) status, as with the temple elites, wears thin in the absence of proven competence. The pedigreed priests, ruling in Jerusalem in collaboration with Rome, may manage the temple's vast resources, but how efficiently and for whose benefit? How faithfully do they discharge their duty as stewards of God's house? Questions concerning the trustworthiness of the temple establishment arose from various quarters in Jesus's era, including from rival priests, like those who formed the apocalyptic sect at Qumran in direct opposition to corrupt Jerusalem leadership. For Jesus's part, though no priest, he takes his challenge directly to the people and the temple authorities on their own turf, demonstrating his trustworthy *achieved honor*, matching by evidential words and deeds his *ascribed authority* as God's Son.[14]

Apart from the core factor of competence, other elements complicate the trust-building (or trust-eroding) process, as David DeSteno argues from substantial psychological research.[15]

22:34–39 (Luke deals with that issue in 10:25–37). Moreover, though some earlier texts in Luke present the Pharisees and scribes together, now the scribes are allied with the Sadducees and priests (19:47; 20:19, 46).

13. For example, Solomon and Flores, *Building Trust*, 83–86, 93; DeSteno, *Truth*, 30–33, 69–77, 171–75.

14. On ascribed (inherited) and acquired (achieved) honor, see Malina and Neyrey, "Honor and Shame," 27–29.

15. DeSteno, *Truth*, 31–34 and throughout. The specific category labels are mine, derived

- *Moral integrity*, that is, matters of virtue, like goodness, generosity, and compassion, which are independent from competence. Character is vital for trust: the most skilled surgeon knows the most efficient ways to kill as well as help (bedside manner also plays a key role in patient trust); then again, the purest soul on earth might be useless in a crisis requiring special competence (in a hurricane, I would want Mother Teresa praying, but not piloting a plane).
- *Personal familiarity*. People are more likely to trust those they know over strangers, even strange *experts*; but there are obvious limits: I would not trust my lifelong best friend with my heart transplant if he had no training in cardiology.
- *Emotional impressionability*. Humans are, by design, heavily dependent on first impressions, "gut" feelings registered on a subconscious level before cognitive evaluation. To conduct a full examination of every new person or idea we encounter would paralyze human functioning. But conversely, though "gut checks" may be useful initial gauges of reliability, they can still deceive and should be counterchecked by critical analysis.
- *Historical consistency*. Those who seek our trust run on their past record, and we naturally look for long-term patterns of trustworthy behavior as pledges of continued reliability. But again, these can be tricky barometers, and not only because self-promoters might pad their resumes and embellish their achievements. Even those with spotless records may not be up to the demands of some present or future task for various reasons, such as the newness or complexity of the project or the waning skills of the trust-seeker.

These broad elements of trust help us negotiate the thick rhetorical and theological textures of the temple disputes in Luke 20 involving faith/faithfulness (trust/trustworthiness) in and of Christ. Jesus's debate performance in the temple constitutes a rhetorical tour de force. Though soon becoming much more reticent at his shotgun trials before the high priest and Roman governor, here he pulls out all the stops, appealing to the welter of cognitive, affective, volitional, and social forces that swirl together in forging human trust and commitment. The goal of ancient rhetoric was not merely to entertain or to enhance an argument with clever flourishes, but fundamentally to captivate the whole person with the living truth being proclaimed.[16] A comparable ho-

---

from DeSteno's argument. See my discussion of DeSteno's work on trust and that of other psychologists and philosophers in Spencer, "Your Faith."

16. For a solid introduction, see Witherington, *New Testament Rhetoric*, 1–43.

lism is part and parcel of the "dynamics of faith," as Tillich contends, beyond a mechanical-intellectual assent to a set of beliefs. "In the act of faith every nerve of man's body, every striving of man's soul, every function of man's spirit participates. But body, soul, spirit, are not three parts of man. They are dimensions of man's being, always within each other, for man is a unity and not composed of parts. Faith, therefore, is not a matter of the mind in isolation, or of the soul in contrast to the body . . . but is the centered movement of the whole personality toward something of ultimate meaning and significance."[17] Tillich goes on to gloss "ultimate concern," the essence of faith in his view, as "passionate concern . . . a matter of infinite passion."[18] This dynamic integration of emotional, volitional, intellectual, physical, and relational elements understands and experiences faith as *authentic trust*.[19]

We now investigate how Luke's Jesus solidifies his status as the supremely trustworthy mediator of God's realm in a series of exchanges with temple authorities.

Jesus and John the Baptist (20:1–8)

The chief priests and associates interrupt Jesus's teaching session with a double interrogative concerning the source of Jesus's authority delivered with imperatival force: "Tell [εἰπόν, *eipon*] us, by what authority are you doing these things? Who is it that gave you this authority?" (20:2). From the start, the temple leaders assert *their* authority by trying to intimidate Jesus and put him back on his heels. They challenge the validity not only of his teaching but also of all "these things" he's been "doing," no doubt particularly evoking his recent temple flare-up. But he doesn't budge an inch and in fact, without skipping a beat, returns their volley with a query and countermand: "I will also ask you a question, and you tell [εἴπατε, *eipate*] me" (20:3).

Jesus proceeds to take the onus off himself and on to his predecessor, the deceased John the Baptist: "Did the baptism of John come from heaven, or was it of human origin?" (20:4). By shrewdly taking charge of the debate and

17. Tillich, *Dynamics*, 123; cf. Clifford Williams (*Existential Reasons*, 170–74) for a helpful integration of Thomistic (belief) and Kierkegaardian (relationship) elements of faith, along with emotional aspects.

18. Tillich, *Dynamics*, 123.

19. On the vital balance of intellectual, volitional, and emotional elements in faith—and the distortions when one aspect is overemphasized to the neglect of the others—see Tillich, *Dynamics*, 35–46. For an extended discussion of "authentic trust," though not applied primarily to religious faith, see Solomon and Flores, *Building Trust*, 91–151.

deflecting his prosecutors' attention to another figure, Jesus reframes the authority discussion in key respects. First, by not jumping to defend his personal authority, he introduces an element of *humility*. Rather than burst out, no doubt to much crowd applause, "I am the greatest prophet who's ever lived" (a claim supported by Luke's narrative), Jesus is content to spotlight another authoritative prophet who baptized him and helped to launch his gospel mission. Jesus is not at all shamed by John's imprisonment and beheading (3:18–20; 9:7–9); despite appearances, John is no failed prophet: "I tell you, among those born of women no one is greater than John" (7:28). Obviously evaluations of authority operate differently in God's kingdom than in worldly realms.

Second, by posing the question of a "heavenly" source of authority, Jesus affirms the established principle that a true prophet serves as God's chosen delegate (cf. Deut 18:15–22). Only God can authenticate prophetic ministry, which is precisely why Luke has taken such pains to demonstrate John's and Jesus's divine authorizations. God's Spirit shaped and set apart both figures in their mothers' wombs (1:15, 31–35, 41–42), and God's Scripture sketched their prophetic vocations (3:4–6; 4:16–21). Jesus's authority has been further vindicated by God's direct voice and the Spirit's "bodily" presence at his baptism (3:21–22) and by his gracious and mighty deeds and words (24:19) thereafter among the people. In Luke's story, both John and Jesus demonstrate *moral integrity* and *historical consistency* in speech and action worthy of trust in God's kingdom. Those who withhold such trust thus find themselves resisting God (cf. Acts 5:38–39; 11:15–17). In the present case, if by chance Jesus's interlocutors now concede John's divine authorization after previously refusing to heed his message (Luke 7:29–30), they effectively incriminate themselves (20:5).

Third, however, Jesus raises the issue of a "human [ἀνθρώπων, *anthrōpōn*]" source of prophetic validation, not only as an alternative to divine authority, but also an auxiliary to it. God's authority remains foremost and firm, despite the all-too-common popular rejection of God's emissaries, like the Nazareth citizens' spurning of Jesus (4:16–30). God's sovereignty does not rise and fall with polling numbers. But massive sclerotic resistance to God's messengers scarcely enhances God's authority and certainly throttles effectual witness to it. In positive terms, faithful reception of God's prophetic word supports and solidifies God's honor. Though the prophets John and Jesus have met stiff opposition from various quarters, most antagonism has come from religious and political leaders. The wider populace has generally shown more openness to prophetic calls to repentance and renewal, though admittedly at various levels of trust from curious amazement to committed discipleship; and they are not beyond fickle reversal against God's witnesses if they sense their interests being threatened (again recall Jesus's hometown fiasco). Still, John's baptismal message attracted widespread adherence and conviction that "John was a [true] prophet," as Jesus now reminds the temple rulers (20:6; cf. "all the people" here and 3:21); and Jesus's powerful mediation of God's reign has been amply attested by grateful recipients throughout Luke's narrative. Accordingly, such human responses redound to God's glory and bolster God's authority ("declare how much God has done for you" [8:39]; "praising God" [13:13]; "praising God/praise to God [17:15, 18]).

Trust factors of *emotional impressionability* and *personal familiarity* discussed above come into play here. Firsthand the people have felt, seen, and thereby *known* God's dynamic, authoritative, embodied presence among them in the charismatic prophets John and Jesus. Such passionate experience is precisely what the temple leaders "did *not* know," as Jesus shrewdly gets them to admit (20:7). By way of appeal to John's authority, Jesus has his interlocutors between a rock and hard place, at odds with both God and the people. And he toys with them by implicitly claiming that if they can't handle John, they are not worth serious engagement about the work of God's kingdom: "Neither will I tell you by what authority I am doing these things" (20:8).[20]

But after scoring these debate points, Jesus does elaborate on his divine authority—as God's "beloved son," no less (20:13)—and the priests' misguided concern to protect their own authority. He still opts for a more oblique than obvious mode of argument, this time by way of a parable. But by the time he's through, there's little mystery left: the temple hierarchs "realized/knew [ἔγνωσαν, *egnōsan*]" full well that Jesus is denouncing them, pushing their ire against him to the boiling point (20:19).

Jesus and the Vineyard Owner (20:9–19)

This parable begins in familiar fashion: "A man planted a vineyard and leased it to tenants" (20:9). It recalls Jesus's earlier horticultural tale involving "a man [who] had a fig tree planted in his vineyard" (13:6), which in turn trades

20. I have unpacked Jesus's argument in terms of reframing conventional views of authority, with a sharp critique of present temple rulers. In Tillich's (*New Being*, 79–91) trenchant sermon "By What Authority?" on Luke 20:1–8, he presses a somewhat more radical, antiestablishment position undercutting all notions of authority outside God's: "There is something in the Christian message which is opposed to established authority. There is something in the Christian experience which revolts against subjection to even the greatest and holiest experiences of the past. . . . That which makes an answer [to the question in 20:2] impossible is the nature of an authority which derives from God and not man. The place where God gives authority to a man cannot be circumscribed" (88).

on Isaiah's classic Song of the Vineyard (Isa 5:1–7). For those steeped in biblical imagery—like Jesus, the chief priests, and many of the people—the code is readily cracked: God planted the Israelite nation as a prized vineyard in fertile territory. The story features God's gracious covenant with Abraham and his descendants in the land of promise (Gen 12:1–3; Luke 1:54–55). God initiates the deal (election) and cultivates the land for "beloved" Israel's flourishing and fruit-bearing for God's glory and the world's good (Isa 5:1–4; Luke 13:8). God the Master Gardener desires a return on God's investment, not as a calculating businessman, but as loving Creator and Covenanter. But God does not micromanage "tenant" Israel, any more than God micromanaged the first humans in Eden. Rather, God *entrusts* the people as managerial partners, as responsible stewards, to care for the world and multiply its creative resources for the mutual benefit of all (cf. Gen 1:26–31). Over the centuries, however, Israel has often failed to be a trustworthy steward of God's steadfast love, thus provoking God's periodic discipline (after extraordinary patience), extending at times to Israel's radical uprooting from the land. In this regard, Israel's trust level as covenant partner has suffered because of its historical *in*consistency. Prospects of present and future trustworthiness remain precarious, though not impossible, in light of God's transformative power and restorative love.

Luke's Jesus now updates this macrobiblical story in relation to his and the temple leaders' current divine vocations. Compared with Isaiah's Song of the Vineyard and his own parable of the barren fig tree (Luke 13:6–9), Jesus now focuses less on preparations of the vineyard owner (God) than on assessments of the owner's business by particular *tenants and accountants* (not the nation). The owner leases his vineyard to a group of tenants and leaves them to manage it "for a long time" (20:9). Here the tenants are stand-ins for priestly officials (as they recognize in 20:19), not the general populace. This image would hit the chief priests hard for a number of reasons, not least their implied status demotion from wealthy estate owners and superintendents of temple property.[21] They were accustomed to commanding tenants and servants, to ruling and owning, not to *being* sharecroppers! But Jesus precisely aims to level them down, to temper their sociology with a strong dose of theology. God is the gracious Creator, Sustainer, Lord, and Master of every parcel of the world, not least the promised land of Israel and sacred mount of God's temple-house. All creatures, then—especially the leaders of God's chosen servant Israel—are God's tenants. Because of God's covenantal bond of love, these are not God's oppressed slaves, but God's tenant-managers/stewards, laboring together with God. Those with

21. See Hanson and Oakman, *Palestine*, 99–129.

higher managerial responsibility are all the more answerable to God for their stewardship of God's bounty.

So how are the present *tenant-leaders* doing? Jesus's parable evaluates their performance according to their treatment of the vineyard owner's special emissary-accountants. A series of four audits unfolds, the first three involving trusted "slaves" and the last the owner's "beloved son," each seeking to procure the owner's rightful "share of the produce of the vineyard" (20:10). The master proves remarkably patient and persistent, affording multiple opportunities for the tenant-managers to prove their fruitfulness. Time after time, however, the tenants brutally spurn the collectors and mock the owner's trust and authority (20:10–15). Interpreters commonly regard the three slave-accountants as types of the prophets (including John), the apostles (looking ahead to Acts), and possibly angelic messengers, like Gabriel—all resisted by the temple establishment in Luke and Acts. Though that approach is reasonable, I suggest a related but more comprehensive picture based on the tripartite division of Scripture outlined in Luke 24:44: "[1] the law of Moses, [2] the prophets, and [3] the psalms."

In "many and various ways" (Heb 1:1), God has *sent word* detailing the covenant's manifold privileges and responsibilities. This accumulated revelation has been passed on for generations in authoritative written (scriptural) collections of legal, prophetic, and doxological material. God "has not left himself without a witness" (Acts 14:17)—abundant witness at that—in natural and biblical form, in both creation sustained by God and Scripture inspired by God. On the scriptural side, Luke's Jesus appeals to all three segments in his temple teaching: (1) Mosaic Law (Torah) (Exod 3:6/Luke 20:37); (2) Prophets (Isa 56:7; Jer 7:11/Luke 19:46); and (3) Psalms (Ps 118:22/Luke 20:17; Ps 110:1/Luke 20:42–43). For their part, however, the Sadducee priests subscribe to the canonical authority *only* of the Torah or Pentateuch (Genesis–Deuteronomy) and then, from Jesus's perspective, only in tendentious fashion (cf. 20:27–40).[22] They thus truncate and manipulate God's word for their own purposes, or in terms of the current parable, they reject all three of God's servant-messengers that call them to account for their contractual (covenantal) obligations.

Apart from the priestly officials' obstinate response to God's threefold scriptural witness is their even more shocking treatment of God's *Son*, the consummate incarnate Word and "heir of all things" sent to God's people "in these last days" (Heb 1:2; cf. John 1:14). Such early christological language is barely veiled in the tenants-parable (this is not one of Jesus's more obscure tales). After his tenants' rejection of the three slave-accountants, the vineyard owner faces a personal crisis: "What shall I do [now]?" (20:13; another internal deliberative

22. On the distinctive convictions of the Sadducees, see Josephus, *Ant.* 13.297–98; 18.16–17.

soliloquy; cf. 12:17–19; 15:17–19; 16:3–4; 18:4–5).[23] He answers himself with the monumental decision to "send my *beloved son* [τὸν υἱόν μου τὸν ἀγαπητόν, *ton huion mou ton agapēton*]; perhaps [ἴσως, *isōs*] they will respect [ἐντραπήσονται *entrapēsontai*] him" (20:13). Oddly enough, this is the only occurrence of this "perhaps" term in the NT, and its significance here should not be missed, as it reflects the desperate hope—but no guarantee—that the will of the vineyard owner may finally be honored. For all his lordly authority, he does *not know* for sure that his plan will work; he *cannot make* it happen by sheer force of his will. And what a risk he takes in the process—the risk of his beloved son's life, no less—a "chilling response" bordering on callousness toward his son in order that the father "perhaps" might recoup his lost honor and resources (do these matter more than his son's life?),[24] or "perhaps" just an incredibly naive response, failing to appreciate the evil aims his thuggish tenants have already demonstrated.[25] In the brisk flow of the tense story, however, we more immediately sense the estate owner's embroilment in an existential crisis,[26] which only intensifies, since in fact his tenants do not respect the son at all, aligning themselves with the unjust judge in another parable who evidences "no fear of God and no respect [ἐντρέπομαι, *entrepomai*] for anyone" (18:4; cf. 18:2). Their insolence pushes to the extreme of murder, precisely because they know "this is the heir" and prime obstacle to their usurping ownership of the vineyard (20:14).

Luke's readers should immediately recognize the "beloved son" as representing Jesus, so affirmed by God at Jesus's baptism (3:21–22; cf. 9:34–35). Though not trumpeted publicly by Jesus himself during his ministry, the critical matter of his divine sonship becomes a major bone of contention with the priestly authorities in his final days, ultimately sealing their lethal plot against him (20:41–44; 22:70–71). Just as they fail to recognize God's rule over the land

23. On internal monologues in Luke's parables, see Dinkler, *Silent Statements* and "Thoughts"; Sellew, "Interior Monologue."

24. Sellew, "Interior Monologue," 248; cf. Bernard Brandon Scott (*Hear*) on the story as a "shame-honor challenge" in which the vineyard owner's "strategy is that his honor as represented by his son will bring the tenants to their senses" (250).

25. Hultgren (*Parables*) claims that this scenario is not so bizarre or absurd as it might appear, since the son "could have been accompanied by a retinue" and in any case would plausibly have been dispatched by the father "to get the matter cleared up once and for all" (362). Perhaps, but the "perhaps" in Luke's version indicates that the father is *not* so certain the matter will be taken care of, and in fact the son *in the story* is sent (foolishly) alone. See the discussion in Dinkler, "Thoughts," 391–93, 397–98.

26. Cf. Dinkler, "Thoughts," 397: "The vineyard owner's self-talk deepens the dramatic irony of that scene: his wondering what to do . . . and his use of the 'perhaps' . . . suggest that he does not know that his 'beloved' . . . son will be killed."

and temple, they fail to acknowledge Jesus's authority as rightful heir to God's kingdom. Likewise, however, this perceptual failure of Israel's leaders signals a concomitant failure of God's saving mission in his messianic Son—*perhaps.* That little "perhaps" opens up a haunting, precarious space for God's disappointment and Israel's (and the world's) disgrace, while also clinging to a hopeful (against hope) potentiality of reversal and renewal. Drawing on Derrida's *Peut-être—il faut toujours peut-être pour . . .* ("Perhaps—one must always say perhaps for . . ."), the philosopher-theologian John Caputo advances a provocative "theology of perhaps" rooted in "the language of indecision and of the suspension of judgment," extending even to God in a potentially (perhaps) optimistic and reconstructive deconstructionist sense, but certainly not in a hypernihilistic defeatism: "The possibility of the impossible is one of God's most venerated biblical names, the proper referent, if there is such a thing, of 'perhaps,' maybe even of God, perhaps."[27]

In their present tunnel vision, the only thing the temple leaders do recognize clearly, as noted above, is that Jesus "told this parable against them" (20:19), which ironically stokes their desire to fulfill it, that is, to keep searching for a way to eliminate him without inciting the people to riot. In Jesus's view, however, it is not the people's judgment the priests should fear the most. The loving, long-suffering, covenant-making God will not ultimately be mocked, as Jesus stresses via the parable's ending and his ensuing midrash on a Psalms text. After the unjust killing of his beloved son, the vineyard owner plans to "destroy those tenants and give the vineyard to others" (20:16). Caught up in Jesus's electrifying story, the general audience blurts out in shock, "May this never happen!" (CEB) or, more colloquially, "Heaven forbid!" (NRSV); "God forbid!" (KJV) (μὴ γένοιτο, *mē genoito* [20:16; cf. Rom 3:4, 6, 31; 6:2, 15; 7:7, 13; 9:14; 11:1, 11; Gal 2:17; 3:21; 6:14]). If the chief priests join this stunned chorus, they may evince some subconscious twinge of guilt or, more likely, a sense of horror that Jesus would suggest a terrible outcome. It only gets worse as Jesus "looked at them," cites Ps 118:22, and offers a sharp comment on the text (Luke 20:17–18). The statement—"the stone that the builders rejected has become the cornerstone"—reflects the psalmist's joy over the Lord's marvelous "salvation" from terrible "distress" amid the people's praise of the blessed one "who comes in the name of the LORD" into "the house of the LORD" (Ps 118:5, 21, 26). This scenario recently came to life in Luke's story, as the crowd jubilantly applied (and adapted) "Blessed is the king who comes in the name of the Lord!" *to Jesus*

27. Caputo, *Insistence* (citations from 3, 11; cf. 3–23); though engaging with various NT texts, Caputo makes no reference to this one "perhaps" usage in Luke 20:13. My "hoping against hope" remark comes from the title of Caputo's latest book, but also from Paul in Rom 4:18.

as he approached Jerusalem (Luke 19:38; cf. 13:35). But as the people's rejoicing soon gave way to Jesus's weeping (19:41–44), so now in the Lord's house Jesus appropriates Psalm 118 as a tragic lament rather than a salvation song.

The "rejecters" of the sacred "cornerstone" in God's temple are those most invested in its business—the "builders," the tenant-managers, the religious leaders—subverting God's blessed work *within* God's house. Consequently, as Jesus now warns the officials, this holy place they have so blatantly deformed into a robber's den is destined in fact (not just perhaps) to crash down upon them. More personally, the appointed Lord of God's house—the living "cornerstone," the beloved Son, Jesus Messiah—whom the chief priests vehemently resist, will ultimately block their schemes and crush their power (20:18). This will not be the end of God's house: it will (hopefully, perhaps) be renewed, restored, and given to others (20:16) who will find true refuge and exercise faithful service in God's Christ-anchored household. But this will be the end of the present, unrepentant temple rulers. No wonder they are so upset with Jesus.

Jesus and the Emperor (20:20–26)

More incensed than ever at Jesus but still cognizant of his enthusiastic support among the people, the chief priests shift tactics to distance themselves from the fray. Rather than interrogate Jesus directly, they plant ringers in the audience to pose loaded questions to Jesus, hoping to provoke some seditious speech against Rome (20:20). Moreover, they now open with the gambit of *captatio benevolentiae* ("benevolent capture" or "polite entrapment"), as the ancient rhetoricians advised, or *cordial hypocrisy*, as modern philosophers Solomon and Flores label this trust-corroding phenomenon of public discourse.[28] It features "pretend[ing] to be honest" (20:20) and flattery, buttering up one's opponent to break down his defenses (cf. the English interjection, "with all due respect," belying blatant disrespectful intent). Jesus's questioners lay it on thick here: "Teacher, we know [οἴδαμεν, *oidamen*] that you are right in what you say and teach, and you show deference to no one, but teach the way of God in accordance with truth" (20:21). Ironically, this is precisely the solid gospel truth about Jesus (Luke couldn't have put it better himself). But the priestly agents do not mean a word of it; they "know" nothing of the kind; they are just trying to manipulate Jesus's emotional state. But Jesus is clued in to their game ("he perceived their craftiness" [20:23]) and trumps them—silences them in fact

28. Solomon and Flores, *Building Trust*, 4, 13, 36, 58–59, 113, 121.

(20:26)—with his own rhetorical skill, which he employs to make a subtle, yet significant, theological point.

The issue at hand is law-based and clear-cut: "Is it lawful for us to pay taxes to the emperor, or not?" (20:22). The question cuts two ways. First, on the Roman side, taxation constitutes a direct extension of Caesar's authority; accordingly, tax payment endorses that authority, just as tax resistance repudiates it. Second, though not secondary for God's people, Jewish law confesses God's supreme right to various taxes, tithes, and offerings as returns on God's entrusted bounty. And of special import in the present setting, the temple establishment, with its vast treasury and sacrificial system, served as the primary collector and manager of God's resources (cf. 21:1–4). These two economic realms—Caesar's and God's—represent irreconcilable conflicts of interest (cf. 16:13). Early in Jesus's life (6 CE) a fellow Galilean named Judas thought the conflict to be so severe that he instigated a tax rebellion against Rome, regarding tribute payment to any authority but God, the "only Ruler and Lord," as an unlawful act of blasphemy and idolatry. Rome had no patience for his or anyone else's antitax convictions and promptly moved to squelch the revolt (Josephus, *Ant* 18.3–9, 23–25; *J.W.* 2.118).[29] Jesus's current opponents bet that he will betray similar anti-Roman sentiments or, conversely, be too soft on Roman taxes and lose support of the common people chafing under a heavy financial burden. Either way, they think they've got him.

But not so fast. Jesus offers a remarkable show-and-tell response, at once clever and challenging. He first invites his questioners to "show me a denarius" (Luke 20:24), that is, the common coinage used to pay the imperial tax. He has no denarius of his own, which in itself demonstrates Jesus's priorities (cf. 9:3; 10:4). He then cuts to the chase in asking his interrogators to identify the "image" or "icon" (εἰκών, *eikōn*) and "inscription" (ἐπιγραφή, *epigraphē*) engraved on the coin. Their stark one-word reply, "Caesar's [Καίσαρος, *Kaisaros*]," says it all (20:24 NIV, CEB). They thus incriminate themselves. Every Roman denarius amounts to a miniature idol to Caesar. The inscription ringing the raised head of the emperor would have been: "Tiberius Caesar Augustus, son of the Divine Augustus."[30] The coin thus flies in the face of Jewish Scripture prohibiting any graven images to God (Exod 20:4; Deut 5:8; 6:4)—all the more so to human rulers pretending to divine status or sonship. In broader theological perspective, not detailed in the current text, "son/daughter of God" and "image of God" properly apply in a general sense to all God's children created in God's likeness

29. On Judas the Galilean's tax-resistance movement, see Horsley and Hanson, *Bandits*, 190–92.

30. See Herzog, "Dissembling," 346–47; Oster, "Show Me."

(Gen 1:26–27; 5:1), and in a more particular and primary sense, to Christ Jesus, "the image [εἰκών, *eikōn*] of the invisible God, the firstborn of all creation" (Col 1:15; cf. Rom 8:29), the "exact imprint [χαρακτήρ *charaktēr*] of God's very being" (Heb 1:3). By both his pompous distance from common humanity and his presumptuous alliance with supreme deity, Caesar and his coins mock the sacred biblical doctrine of God's image. By dramatic contrast, Jesus, as the authorized agent of God's realm, has been gloriously manifest as the consummate "son of Adam, son of God" (Luke 3:38).

So what about paying taxes to Rome with this corrupt imaged and inscribed denarius? Does that not amount to blasphemous denial of God's sovereignty, as Judas the Galilean claimed? While Jesus of Nazareth no doubt concurs with Judas in principle, he makes the point more obliquely, though no less provocatively. Since the denarius is the emperor's property, Jesus advocates giving it back to him; and by the same token, Jesus calls for giving God all that is God's (20:25). Jesus brilliantly invokes a merit system, giving what is due, no more and no less. Who can argue with that? But think through the implications. Giving Caesar's money *back* to him may carry the subtext: "What's this filthy coinage doing in your hands and purses! Get rid of it, and along with it, your complicity in Caesar's idolatrous and unjust economy." Or more personally: "Give the emperor what he really deserves; let him have what's coming to him!"[31] Jesus stops short of calling for rebellion, but he dances right on the edge. In any case, this is no banal advice not to rock the imperial boat, to be a good citizen and pay your taxes on time. It sets up the Roman emperor as the illegitimate competitor to the Creator God, to whom all things owe their existence and sustenance.

Accordingly, all things are *due God*—all glory and power, all goods and possessions (of which the annual temple tax is a mere token)—above that demanded by any other so-called authority. In slightly more subtle language, Jesus's statement is tantamount to Peter and the apostles' before the high priest's court: "We must obey God rather than any human authority" (Acts 5:29), a point, by the way, endorsed by the prominent Pharisee teacher Gamaliel (5:33–39). While Jesus and his apostles aim to confess theological integrity more than construct economic policy, their vision of a theocratic realm penetrates all aspects of personal, social, and political life. Jesus's concise articulation of

31. See N. T. Wright, *Jesus*, 502–7; Spencer, *What Did Jesus Do?*, 142–43; Horsley, *Jesus and Empire*, 98–99, and *Covenant Economics*, 133: "Everyone listening knew that 'the things that are God's' meant basically everything, and that according to the covenantal commandments nothing belonged to Caesar. Jesus is saying in so many words that the people do not owe Caesar anything, that the tribute is utterly contrary to the people's covenant with God."

that vision ultimately drops the jaws and shuts the mouths of his interrogators: "being amazed by his answer, they became silent" (Luke 20:26).

Jesus and Moses (20:27–40)

After Jesus cleverly parries the trap question concerning Roman taxation and imperial authority and counters with a piercing thrust, his opponents shift to the politically safer territory of Scripture interpretation and more speculative topic of afterlife. They still want to undermine Jesus's authority and the people's trust in him, but they now restrict the battle to internal Jewish affairs and leave Caesar out of it. The temple leaders serve, if not at the pleasure of Rome, at least as imperial clients responsible for tamping down popular rabble rousers like Jesus. If anti-Roman sentiment gets out of hand, the chief priests will soon be out of a job.

This time Luke identifies the interrogators as "some Sadducees," the religious party most closely aligned with the wealthy temple rulers (Acts 4:1; 5:17; Josephus, *Ant.* 13.298). These "some" are likely lower-level assistants of the chief priests and elders. In marked distinction from the Pharisees and other Jewish groups, the Sadducees adhered to the strict written canon of the Torah, apart from any later oral, traditional interpretations, and denied belief in bodily resurrection and the unseen world of spirit-beings (Luke 20:27; Acts 4:1–2; 23:6–10; *Ant.* 13.293, 297–98; 18.16–17; *J.W.* 2.164–65).[32] In the present scene, they hope to expose Jesus's erroneous views on these issues and to embarrass him as a tongue-tied, upstart teacher. Their strategy focuses on applying Mosaic case law to a hypothetical afterlife scenario (Luke 20:27–33). The law stipulates that the brother of a childless widow's deceased husband must take the bereft woman into his household; in this arrangement of *levirate marriage*, the ensuing offspring of the brother-in-law (*levir*) and widow perpetuate the line of the dead brother/husband (Deut 25:5–10; cf. Gen 38). That is clear enough. But matters become more complicated in cases of multiple levirate unions, especially in some imagined final resurrection state.

Since young women typically married older men in ancient Jewish society and male mortality averaged around forty years of age, it was not uncommon for wives to be widowed more than once. Now the Sadducees' present example of *seven* total marriages to brothers-in-law borders on the absurd, which suits their purpose of accentuating the ridiculousness, in their view, of a general resurrection from the dead. Just think of the social chaos in heaven: whether a

32. See Saldarini, *Pharisees.*

woman had two, seven, or seventy legitimate husbands in her earthly life, which *one* would she spend eternity with? And what are the poor men supposed to do? In the Sadducees' minds, this decidedly unheavenly confusion argues against afterlife. Or maybe they do not pose this as a serious argument, but just want to see Jesus squirm and fumble to find a cogent response.

But yet again he frustrates his opponents, this time with a two-pronged counterargument: first, correcting the Sadducees' specious picture of resurrection life; second, expounding the scriptural basis for belief in resurrection. Jesus begins by dismantling the faulty premise of the concocted marital scenario. In "that age"—the eternal age to come—all marriage ties will be obsolete, along with everything that goes with marriage: sex, child-raising, divorce, and widowhood. All will live forever as "children of God . . . children of the resurrection" (lit. "sons [υἱοί, *huioi*] of God/resurrection") in an asexual, angel-like state (20:36).[33] The business of marrying and giving in marriage, with all its entanglements both joyous and sorrowful, is restricted to life in "this age" (20:34).

Apart from rendering moot the Sadducees' seven-time widow case, Luke's Jesus, according to some scholars, also betrays an idealistic preference for single, celibate life in *this age*, here and now, especially given the climactic irruption of God's kingdom.[34] Preoccupation with mundane matters of marital life dulls attention to the priorities of God's realm, to preparing for God's ultimate visitation through the Son of Humankind (cf. 17:27–30). Perhaps, too, like Paul in 1 Cor 7, Luke's Jesus desires to spare his followers "anxieties" and "distress in this life" that marriage brings, especially in the apocalyptic throes of transition from this present evil age to the eternal righteous age (1 Cor 7:26–35). Supporting a few isolated pronouncements, the practice of Jesus and his followers in Luke and Acts also conjoins ascetic behavior with apocalyptic mind-set: Jesus him-

33. I think the NRSV is right to render "sons of God/resurrection" as "children of God/resurrection" here, not simply to satisfy modern interests of inclusivity, but to reflect a nongendered or beyond-gender view of life in the coming age. Though males (fathers, sons) represented the normative gender in patriarchal society, Jesus does not conceive the apocalyptic kingdom to come as an all-male club where "saved" women are transformed into perfect males. Everyone, male and female, will be "like angels." Though angels assume male forms in the Bible from time to time and are identified as "men," these are anthropomorphic, not essentialist, descriptors, just as God the Father ("he") is not biologically male. The risen-exalted Christ poses a more ambiguous case perhaps. He certainly remains a divine-human/incarnate being (Luke 24:37–43) in his postresurrection state, but with certain transcendent characteristics (e.g., not bound by earthly spatial boundaries). Though a male in his earthly life, gender and sexuality do not seem to be prime identity factors after his resurrection.

34. For example, multiple analyses by Seim: *Double Message*, 39–57, 185–248; "Gospel of Luke," 735–39, 755–61; "Children"; and Dale B. Martin, *Sex*, 106–9; see my critical assessment in Spencer, *Salty Wives*, 9–12.

self never marries; he calls his disciples to abandon ("hate") family members, including "wife and children" (14:26); and most women associated with his movement appear unattached to husbands and children and exclusively devoted to God's household (e.g., 8:1–3; cf. 8:21; 10:38–42; 11:27–28).

Nevertheless, as we have seen, Luke's narrative encompasses a wide range of characters and actions under an inclusive umbrella. Though affirming unmarried and/or childless men and women as faithful ministers in God's kingdom, Luke does not privilege them over married disciples or denigrate spouses' and parents' contributions in this earthly realm. While capable of functioning at the highest spiritual level separately from their husbands, Mary and Elizabeth do not leave their mates or children. The temporarily mute Zechariah eventually joins his Spirit-filled voice with wife Elizabeth's and Mary's (1:67–76). On the parenting front, though Jesus early on asserts his independence from his earthly mother and stepfather, he still remains "obedient to them" (2:51) into adulthood, benefiting from their training and wisdom (2:41–52). Back to wives, the upper-crust Joanna, who follows Jesus and helps finance his mission, is scarcely under her Herodian husband's thumb in Tiberias; but she is still called "the wife of Chuza" and never divorces him as far as we know (8:1–3; 24:10).[35] In Acts, though Priscilla takes the lead in teaching Apollos and assisting Paul, she is never mentioned apart from husband Aquila (Acts 18:2, 18–21, 26). Marriage does not necessarily encumber dynamic service to the Lord.[36]

Returning to the immediate dispute with the Sadducees, Jesus proceeds (second) to address resurrection life on scriptural grounds granted by the Sadducees. They agree on the fundamental authority of Torah. To be sure, Moses never explicitly mentions the general "resurrection of the dead." Indeed, the topic receives scant attention throughout the Hebrew Bible, with the clearest reference appearing in the latest writing (Dan 12:2–3).[37] But in good rabbinic form, Jesus draws key inferences from biblical texts, in this case from Moses's famous burning bush theophany in Exodus. In that strategic moment—when

35. See the full discussion of Joanna's social location in Spencer, *Salty Wives*, 101–44.

36. Likewise sexuality, with mutual consent and satisfaction, is encouraged by Paul within marriage (1 Cor 7:1–5); if some in Corinth were arguing for so-called spiritual/celibate marriage (7:1), Paul was not. As for Luke, see the discussion of 7:36–50 above, suggesting Jesus's personal affirmation of and indulgence in a form of intimate, erotic passion with the anointing woman (though not involving explicit intercourse).

37. Though not as explicit as Dan 12:2–3 regarding the general eschatological resurrection, powerful allusions to resurrection are more prominent in the HB/OT than often assumed (e.g., Abraham's offering of Isaac [Gen 22:1–19], Elisha's raising the Shunammite widow's son [2 Kgs 4:1–37], and Ezekiel's vision of Israel's revivified bones [Ezek 37:1–14]), as brilliantly analyzed by Levenson, *Resurrection*; and Madigan and Levenson, *Resurrection*.

the Lord reveals the divine name (I Am) to Moses and calls him to redeem the nation from Egyptian bondage—the Lord further self-identifies: "I am the God of your father, the God of Abraham, the God of Isaac, and the God of Jacob" (Exod 3:6). In Jesus's view, this statement attests to the eternal, *living* relationship of God with patriarchs Abraham, Isaac, and Jacob—*not* a dusty relic of past history. Accordingly, the founding fathers of God's people, long since passed from this age, must have been raised to new life, confirming that the Lord is "God not of the dead, but of the living; for to him all of them are alive" (Luke 20:38). A similar reading emerges in the roughly contemporary Hellenistic-Jewish book of 4 Maccabees, which discloses the resurrection faith of the Maccabean martyrs, who "believe that they, like our patriarchs Abraham and Isaac and Jacob, do not die to God, but live to God" (4 Macc 7:19).

This commanding theological argument of Jesus based on Moses's experience proves to be the clincher in the temple debates. No more questions follow from his opponents. In fact, some scribes can't contain their admiration of Jesus, announcing: "Teacher, you have spoken well" (20:39). This response hardly means that Jesus has won over all the religious leaders. But he has put them in their place for the moment. Far from basking in his victory, however, Jesus keeps pushing his case against the temple establishment and for the just cause of God's realm. This is a time of epochal crisis on the brink of the "age to come," a time of inescapable decision for God's people and their leaders.

Jesus and David (20:41–44)

Having been on the defensive, Jesus now turns to the offense, questioning his opponents regarding the Messiah's heritage as David's son. The royal Davidic link was a staple of early Jewish messianic thought, drawn from texts like Ps 2:1–9, 2 Sam 7:13–16, and Isa 9:6–7, and affirmed by Luke in relation to Jesus (Luke 1:32–33, 69; 2:11; 3:31; 18:38–39). Oddly, then, Jesus queries *how* this Davidic lineage works, more specifically: "How can *they say* that the Messiah is David's son?" (20:41). Although this messianic portrait seems to be something that "they" (including Jesus's interlocutors) get right, Jesus challenges their understanding on the basis of another Psalm text. In Ps 110:1 "David himself" announces: "The Lord said to my Lord, 'Sit at my right hand, until I make your enemies your footstool'" (Luke 20:42–43).[38] This language of lordship seems

38. To complicate matters, this text was not a common source of early Jewish reflection on a royal Davidic Messiah. As Fitzmyer notes, "There is simply no evidence of the Davidic messianic interpretation of Psalm 110 in pre-Christian Palestinian Judaism" (2:1311; cf. Rowe, *Early Narra-*

to contradict that of sonship in Ps 2:7: how can David call the exalted Messiah both lord and son? (20:44). Thus Jesus leaves the matter—but to what end?

While it is possible that after winning the previous rounds of debate Jesus decides to have a little fun with his interrogators by posing a clever exegetical riddle, the urgency of the hour suggests a more serious tack. Consider the following implications. First, on a basic level, Luke's Jesus encourages more careful engagement with Scripture by the religious establishment, taking into account Psalms as well as Torah and wrestling with, rather than glossing over, apparent discrepancies within the canon.

Second, Jesus invites a more dynamic understanding of "Lord/lord," "Messiah," and "Son/son" in divine and human relations. On a strictly biological-lineal level, David could only refer to Solomon and subsequent descendants up to the Messiah as his "sons," and they in turn refer to David as their ancestral father and lord; such is the "house of David" (cf. 2 Sam 7:16; Luke 1:27; 2:4). But the larger theological framework disrupts this family dynasty, since the Lord *God*, Israel's true King, has adopted, appointed, and anointed (christened) David and successors as *sons*; hence David *himself* is from the start both king and subject, lord and son within the orbit of God's supreme rule. In this dynamic divine realm, it is thus no great step for David to acknowledge not only the Lord God's sovereignty, but also the Lord's consummate Messiah—the most highly exalted Son of God and of David destined to reign over the entire world—as "my [David's] Lord." Of course, in Luke's scheme, "my Lord" and Messiah from David's house is *Jesus*, whom the Spirit-filled Elizabeth also proclaims, while he's still in Mary's womb, as "my Lord" (1:43).[39] Jesus thus fulfills multiple relational roles generated by God's Spirit as "Christ [Messiah] the Lord" (2:11) and triadic S/son of (1) the Most High God, (2) the Israelite king David, and (3) Mary of Nazareth. While it is doubtful that Jesus's temple audience could sort out all these connections on the spot, perceptive readers of Luke should pick up the clues.

Third, knowing readers will also sense an allusion to resurrection-exaltation, continuing the concern of the preceding passage (20:27–29), but applying it more particularly to the anticipated risen-exalted Lord and Christ. To be sure, the psalmist's vision of "my lord's" sitting at the Lord God's right hand with enemies under foot need not entail the "lord's" *death* in battle and *subsequent* resurrection and ascension. Indeed, the ensuing picture in Psalm 110 stresses God's *coming to* his appointed priest-king (lord) "in the midst of your foes"

tive Christology, 172n55). Interest in this psalm at Qumran focuses on the priestly descendant of *Melchizedek* from Ps 110:4 (11Q13; cf. Heb 5:6; 7:1–22 [applied to Jesus]).

39. Rowe, *Early Narrative Christology*, 175.

(110:2), empowering him to lead the people to victory over oppressive earthly rulers. As much as the Lord God exalts his lordly partner to his right hand, "the Lord [God, God's self] is [also] at *your [my lord's] right hand*" (110:5). The implied connection, then, with the risen-ascended Lord *Jesus* Christ *adds the link of crucifixion* to the prophetic chain of events. The lord's execution was the furthest thing from the psalmist's mind. The death of the Messiah, predicted by Jesus and necessary for resurrection (Luke 9:21–23; 18:31–33), remains the piece of the puzzle that doesn't easily fit, especially when it takes on the jagged shape of the cross.

Yet, early in the book of Acts, Luke follows Paul and the writer of Hebrews in explicitly slotting the crucified-and-risen Jesus into the exalted picture of Psalm 110:

> For David did not ascend into the heavens, but he himself says,
>
> "The Lord said to my Lord,
> 'Sit at my right hand,
> until I make your enemies your footstool.'"
>
> Therefore let the entire house of Israel know with certainty that God has made him both *Lord and Messiah, this Jesus whom you crucified.*
> (Acts 2:34–36; cf. 1 Cor 15:25–27; Heb 1:3–4, 13).

Thus Psalm 110:1, with the added cross factor, becomes a linchpin in Luke's apologetic, leading his God-loving readers to "*know with certainty/solidity* [ἀσφαλῶς οὖν γινωσκέτω, *asphalōs oun ginōsketō*]" (Acts 2:36)—echoing the purpose clause of Luke's prologue (1:4)—that God has exalted Jesus of Nazareth *through his suffering and crucifixion* as Israel's and the world's Lord and Messiah (cf. Phil 2:5–11). The Jewish Scriptures, freshly interpreted in light of the complex Christ event and the Spirit's outpouring, are *fundamental*, not auxiliary, for Luke's theological epistemology.

Again, within the immediate setting of Jesus's temple disputes, we can scarcely expect his audience to understand fully his enigmatic usage of Ps 110:1. Without Peter's Pentecost sermon in Acts 2, we would be hard pressed to grasp Jesus's point. So what purpose might Jesus's query about David's son and the Messiah serve in the present story? It may be that Luke offers a glimpse of Jesus's thinking out loud to himself, as it were, about his imminent fate. He's already won the temple debate, but he knows it will not forestall his execution. He also believes, as he's previously forecast, that he will be raised from the dead. But he has not expounded on his postmortem existence; and very soon he wrestles with God about the necessity of his death (22:39–44). Luke's Jesus struggles with his vocation as crucified Lord and Messiah. Even he, especially he, must know with certainty that he's on the right path. Leading the way for God's people, he treads the same paths to solid divine knowledge, namely, the paths of Scripture (like Ps 110:1) and prayer (see more below).

Demonstration: Pointing Out a Contributor in the Temple (20:45–21:4)

From his debate with temple representatives and his brief inquiry into Davidic-messianic identity, Jesus returns to dynamic prophetic form in denouncing the scribal officials for their predatory economic practices of "devour[ing] widows' houses" (20:47). He then illustrates this point by calling attention to a poor widow in the very act of surrendering her last two coins to the corrupt temple system. A sharp divide separates the scribes and their wealthy cronies, on the one hand, and the destitute widow, on the other: the former meriting "greater condemnation" (20:47), and the latter contributing "more than all" the rest (21:3). While the demonstration involving the widow is much less disruptive than Jesus's driving out the sellers, it is no less revelatory of the present temple's devolution into an exploitative "den of robbers."

Devouring—and Exhibitionist—Scribes (20:45–47)

The three main audiences of Jesus's temple discourse remain in view, as he speaks "in the hearing of all the [1] *people* [λαοῦ, *laou*] . . . to the [2] *disciples* [μαθηταῖς, *mathētais*]" about "the [3] *scribes* [γραμματέων, *grammateōn*]" (20:45–46). Though the scribes are the main targets of Jesus's critique, the larger crowd and Jesus's followers must also "beware" or "pay attention to [προσέχετε, *prosechete*]" potential snares of hypocrisy (20:46). Earlier in Luke, the scribes aligned with the Pharisees in various legal-scriptural disputes with Jesus (5:21, 30; 6:7; 11:53; 15:2). But more recently, they have associated with the temple establishment of chief priests and elders violently opposed to Jesus (19:47; 20:1, 19, 39; cf. 9:22; 22:2, 66; 23:10), with the exception of "some" scribes who publicly commended Jesus's clever response about resurrection (assuming "Teacher, you have spoken well" [20:39] was a genuine compliment rather than a smokescreen to cover up the Sadducees' embarrassment). Unlike the Pharisees, the scribes possessed more official legal authority to draw up contracts and manage land, estate, and other financial business. They thus functioned not only as religious teachers, but also as professional lawyers in the more modern sense.

It is in this capacity as inheritance and estate lawyers that the scribes draw Jesus's most damning indictment, exposing their rapacious raiding of widows' houses. The term for "devour" or "eat up" (κατεσθίω, *katesthiō*) appears two other times in Luke, both in negative parable contexts: the birds' eating up the seed strewn along the path, symbolizing the devil's snatching God's word from hardened hearts (8:5; cf. 8:12), and the prodigal son's "gobbling up [his father's] estate on prostitutes" (CEB), as the elder brother so crassly puts it (15:30). Jesus thus puts the scribes' exploitation of widows on a par with the work of Satan and immoral sinners, not to mention the widow-oppressing judge and adversary in another parable (18:2–5). The link with the prodigal's devouring his father's "livelihood" (βίος, *bios* [15:30]) strongly resonates with the scribes' milking widows out of their inheritances, with the glaring exception that the son squandered his inheritance on his own and was graciously welcomed back home, while the scribes callously profit at the widows' expense, leaving these women homeless and destitute. Because of their legal expertise in property settlements, they stand in prime position to take advantage of widows at their most vulnerable moments of loss and stress; and in Jesus's view, the lawyers shamelessly exploit these nefarious opportunities every chance they get.

Moreover, what makes the scribes' fraudulent schemes even worse is their brazen cloaking behind public social and religious activities. They hide in plain sight of marketplaces, synagogues, and banquet halls, among which they strut in long robes, curry popular acclaim, and pray long, grandiose prayers (20:46–47). But these "long [μακρά, *makra*]" pretentious performances really demonstrate the scribes' "distant" drift from God as surely as the prodigal son in a "far [μακράν, *makran*] country" (15:13). Unlike the prodigal, however, the scribes play out their ungodly drama *within* traditional social and sacred spaces, including no doubt the temple, as well as local synagogues. They thus make a mockery of God's sanctified "house of prayer" and haven of justice for widows and other vulnerable persons. Though Jesus does not cite Isaiah and Jeremiah again (cf. 19:46), he continues to channel their prophetic polemic.

Devoted—and Exploited—Widow (21:1–4)

The temple scene continues with both a wider and narrower focus: wider, in Jesus's observation of "rich people" (πλούσιοι, *plousioi*) generally (including scribes and other temple officials), contributing their offerings to the temple treasury; and narrower, spotlighting one particular poor widow, throwing her last two coins into the "treasury" (21:1–2), or "offering box" (γαζοφυλάκιον, *gazophylakion*).[40] The designation of these coins as λεπτά (*lepta*) indicates their "small, thin" shape appropriate to their miniscule monetary value, the smallest unit in circulation.[41] As such, they reflect the likely shriveled, gaunt condition of the impoverished widow, now made even poorer by her offering. She has, in cold, hard terms, given away "all she had to live on"—her entire "livelihood" (βίος, *bios* [21:4])—not to dissolute ventures, as the prodigal did, but to the temple system, which should represent giving to God!

Contrary to popular opinion, Jesus does not commend this widow's sacrificial behavior per se. He simply observes it and notes the obviously greater proportional cost to her than the larger amounts given by the rich (21:3–4). Technically, the widow meets Jesus's demand for his followers to liquidate all their possessions and give the proceeds to the poor (14:33; 18:22; cf. 19:8), though Jesus issues no call to this woman (he only speaks *about* her), and we're given no indication that she knows anything about Jesus. We're also not privy to what motivates this widow's giving, though we may reasonably surmise it reflects her devotion to and dependence upon God, a total throwing of herself, her *life*, on God's mercy. But a terrible, tragic irony mars this picture of the woman's faithfulness, since the appointed stewards (scribes, priests, elders) of God's gifts collected in the temple treasury have betrayed their calling and abused their power to boost their own economic interests on the backs of the poor entrusted to their care. So the widow in the present scene winds up playing right into the hands of her exploiters. They have now extracted everything they can from her; she is now effectively dead to them (good riddance) and all but literally dead with no resources to sustain her.

This brief story leaves us with a number of disturbing ethical questions, including, from the *widow's* side: How could she so foolishly give her last "dime" to a corrupt financial institution? Hadn't she seen how other widows lost their homes and shirts to unscrupulous scribes? Did she perhaps fall prey to some "prosperity gospel," naively thinking that the more she gave, the more she would gain (a favorite ploy of greedy propagandists then and now)? Wouldn't she have been better off, given the current deplorable state of temple administration, taking her chances in the secular courts, like the savvy widow in Jesus's parable? And on *Jesus's* side: Why does he merely notice her plight without taking action to remedy it? Why does he treat her as an object lesson and then let her go on her destitute way? Why doesn't he upend the collection box and make a little more prophetic noise here?[42]

40. Louw and Nida, *Greek-English Lexicon*, 1:71; cf. "collection box" (CEB).

41. See BDAG, 592.

42. See Seim, "Feminist Criticism," 73: "[The widow's] might is her mites as the system

These questions all push beyond the text and arise from silences within the text—which doesn't disqualify them. Narrative gaps invite critical theological and ethical probes, especially in relation to emphases within the overall story. But immediate context provides the most decisive interpretive key, and in the current case, the "greater condemnation" of the scribes and other temple hierarchs is primary (20:47). Jesus wants the entire temple assembly to see and to know what hypocritical actions these officials undertake and, most important, *whom* they adversely affect. This widow becomes the poster figure for the present temple's bankrupt state. Secondarily—but increasingly significant as the narrative ensues—the widow foreshadows Jesus's own plight, as the religious and political authorities strip him of every last thing he has until claiming his very life. Jesus will die in empathetic solidarity with this widow and all other lowly sufferers in society.[43]

Prognostication: Signs and Events (21:5–38)

From his prophetic critique of the temple scene he has just witnessed ("[he] *saw* rich people . . . he also *saw* a poor widow" [21:1–2]), Jesus proceeds to sketch the ominous future he sees for the temple, Jerusalem, and God's people. Following Israel's biblical prophets, Jesus warns about dire imminent consequences for persisting evil behavior. Divinely authorized seers are not armchair dreamers, still less theoretical cosmologists, speculating about the faraway fate of the world, whether in catastrophic or idyllic terms. Thoroughly entrenched in current events and pressing threats, they often spark violent pushback for being too revealing, too prescient, too intrepid in speaking truth to powers that be.

Building on earlier forecasts (13:33–35; 17:22–37; 18:31–34; 19:41–44), Luke's Jesus now offers his fullest and frankest prophecy of approaching events, focusing on the (1) cataclysmic destruction of Jerusalem (21:5–24) and (2) climactic appearing of the Son of Humankind (21:25–38). Though neither will happen before Jesus's death, he *sees* the inexorable forces set in motion. Still, history judges prophecy; the proof of the prophet is in the actualization of his announcements:

---

would remain hidden without the widow and her offering—which is also her allegiance to the system that exploits her. Hers is the contrasting prism that clarifies the distortion, and with her very action she expresses the need of an ethic of prophetic justice"; cf. 72–73, engaging with the essay by Althea Miller Spencer ("Lucy Bailey"), which seeks to bridge the horizon between Luke 20:47–21:4 and a poor, elderly woman named Lucy Bailey, who, though economically destitute, bore powerful witness to God in her Jamaican congregation.

43. The pioneering study of Addison Wright ("Widow's Mites") has sparked much of the newer critical reading of this story.

Do they come true? (Deut 18:21–22; Jer 28:5–16). How, then, does Jesus fare? On the one hand, within a generation, the same Roman imperial machine that kills Jesus will brutally put down a Jewish revolt and raze Jerusalem and its temple (66–70 CE). On the other hand, Jesus will not come again as the Son of Humankind, at least not temporally within "this [present] generation" (21:32) and dramatically "in a cloud with power and great glory" (21:27). To complicate matters further, Luke probably penned his Gospel 80–90 CE *in between* the two watershed events: after the Jewish War and before Jesus's return. The devastation of God's sanctuary haunted the memories of Jewish survivors and Gentile sympathizers (Godfearers), including those who followed Christ. The vise grip of Rome seemed stronger than ever, and the coming of God's kingdom seemed in serious doubt. How to cope, then? Christians like Luke could find assurance in the fact that Jesus had predicted Jerusalem's fall as a prelude to the Son of Humankind's ultimate advent. Since he was right about the former tragedy, we can trust that he will soon launch the final victory.

Yes, but the problem remains that, since Luke writes after the fact, he might have taken poetic license and put the predictive words (falsely) on Jesus's lips—reflecting more "prophecy historicized" rather than "history [truly] remembered."[44] It is reasonable, however, to take a more dialectic than dichotomous interpretive approach. As narrative-theological history, not a mere chronicle of events, Luke's Gospel reflects two horizons: on the one pole, the past, pre-Easter earthly life of Jesus; on the other pole, the present, post-Easter Jesus experienced in Luke's faith community.[45] These horizons arc together and mutually inform each other within Luke's *one story* of Jesus, albeit with gaps and tensions along the way. But given Luke's literary artistry, these disjunctions function more to maintain suspense and thicken the plot than to reveal cut-and-paste redactional seams. While one passage or another might reflect one perspective, past or present, more strongly than the other, overall Luke has fashioned a carefully interlaced narrative tapestry. On the issue of Jesus's forecasting Jerusalem's fall, such prescience does not strain the limits of belief. It would require no clairvoyant wizardry to read the signs of the times. It would, however, demand considerable political and theological astuteness, and above all courage, to warn of impending national disaster in the temple precincts, just as Jeremiah did six centuries earlier on the brink of Babylonian conquest.

Nevertheless, granting Jesus's accurate forecast of Jerusalem's destruction does not validate his yet unfulfilled prediction of the Son of Humankind's glo-

44. See Crossan's use of this terminology, in predominant favor of the passion narratives as "prophecy historicized," in *Who Killed Jesus?*, 1–38.

45. See the judicious, balanced view of Raymond Brown (against Crossan) in *Death*, 1:13–24.

rious παρουσία (*parousia*, "coming, appearing"), especially the longer it delays. Redemptive hope needs to be buoyed, particularly during protracted periods of intense suffering. The point that "it is not for you to know the times or periods [of kingdom restoration] that the Father has set by his own authority" (Acts 1:7), while a useful reminder of God's sovereignty, only fuels fervent laments of "How long, O Lord?" during hard times. Ignorance of God's schedule (GOT) is not bliss. But Pastor Luke does not leave his readers with some vapid appeal to hang in there as long as it takes in Jesus's absence. Though in one sense, at the time of Luke's writing, Jesus has ascended to heaven awaiting his climactic return to earth, in another sense, the living Jesus remains very much present through the sacred social media of Scripture study, table fellowship, and Spirit filling (Luke 24:25–35; Acts 1:5–9; 2:1–4, 32–33, 41–47). In addition, Jesus even makes an occasional personal visit to earth, dramatically shaping the course of human history.

The banner example involves Stephen's execution supervised by Saul, the archterrorist of the early church. In the final moments of Stephen's ill-fated trial, he catches a vision of Jesus the Son of Humankind standing (not sitting!) at God's right hand (7:56), poised both to welcome Stephen home and to "come down" and save his persecuted people. Soon Jesus *himself* ("I am Jesus, whom you are persecuting" [9:5]) appears in blazing heavenly light (though no clouds) to Saul, convincing him of Jesus's true identity as Lord and Messiah and commissioning him to evangelize Jews and Gentiles across the empire (9:1–15). In his writings, Saul, a.k.a. Paul the apostle, regards this experience as an apocalyptic encounter with the risen Christ, a "revelation" or "revealing" (ἀποκάλυψις/-λύπτω, *apokalypsis/-lyptō* [Gal 1:12, 16]), turning his world upside down and, through his witness to Christ, shaking the Western world for all time (cf. Acts 17:6). In Luke's and Paul's perspectives, Jesus the Son of Humankind is not some distant absentee Lord. Rather, he remains actively present by his Spirit and even personally *comes* now and then, making strategic visits advancing his restorative kingdom. We still anticipate a consummative parousia in vital hope because of Jesus's perpetual care and periodic "coming" here and now to palliate our pain and suffering. To repeat Rauschenbusch's claim, "God's kingdom is always but coming" (cf. Luke 17:22–37).

As Luke and other early Christians came to see and know in hindsight what Jesus sees and knows in foresight concerning the terrible trials of God's people and redemptive coming(s) of the Son of Humankind, so all readers of Jesus's temple discourse must come to see and know the significance of these events for themselves. Within his speech, Luke's Jesus repeatedly stresses this perceptual-epistemological experience:

> As for these things that *you see* [θεωρεῖτε, *theōreite*], the days will come. (21:6)
>
> *Beware* [*Look*] [βλέπετε, *blepete*] that you are not led astray. (21:8)
>
> When *you see* [ἴδητε, *idēte*] Jerusalem surrounded by armies, then *know* [γνῶτε, *gnōte*] that its desolation has come near. (21:20)
>
> Then *they will see* [ὄψονται, *opsontai*] the Son of Humankind coming in a cloud. (21:27)
>
> *Look* [ἴδετε, *idete*] at the fig tree and all the trees; as soon as they sprout leaves, *you can see* [βλέποντες, *blepontes*] *for yourselves* and *know* [γινώσκετε, *ginōskete*] that summer is already near. (21:29–30)
>
> So also, when *you see* [ἴδητε, *idēte*] these things taking place, *you know* [γινώσκετε, *ginōskete*] that the kingdom of God is near. (21:31)

Appropriately, Jesus concludes his temple teaching with exhortations to "be on guard/pay attention [προσέχετε, *prosechete*]" (21:34; cf. 20:46) and "be alert at all times" (21:36) in the coming days and years. To be forewarned is to be forearmed; perception is key to preparation.

Cataclysmic Assault on Jerusalem and the Temple (21:5–24)

In Jesus's multilayered discourse, he speaks both generally to the people about the looming disaster in Jerusalem and more particularly to his followers about how the crisis affects them and how they can endure it. Structurally, the descriptive sketches of the ominous signs of Jerusalem's fall (21:5–11, 20–24) envelop the prescriptive advice given to Jesus's disciples (21:12–19), formally illustrating the hard times surrounding them like armies (21:20).

Jesus's forecast of Jerusalem's fate follows spectators' observations about the "beautiful stones and gifts dedicated to God" adorning the temple compound (21:5). Such wide-eyed sightseeing would have been commonplace, especially for Passover pilgrims unaccustomed to regular temple viewing. But Jesus promptly deconstructs the beautiful scene by reprising his prediction, first announced through tears on the edge of Jerusalem, that "not one *stone* will be left upon another" in this magnificent structure (21:6; cf. 19:44). These stones include colossal square limestone boulders (ashlars) weighing up to eighty tons, quarried, cut, and arranged by Herod the Great's engineers.[46] Jesus's reference to these stones' demolition also recalls his recent Isaiah allusion to the builders' "rejected" stone, which "will crush anyone on whom it falls" (20:17–18).The mention of glittering *gifts* offered to God harkens back to the antecedent scene where Jesus contrasts elaborate gifts of the wealthy with the tiny, but total, offering of the poor widow to the temple treasury (21:1–4). The critical issue, in Jesus's view, focuses not on the amount or ostentation of the gifts, but on their true *object* and *consecration*. Because priestly officials have not faithfully managed the temple as *God's house* of prayer and justice, but rather have served their own social and economic interests, all these extravagant adornments will be for naught; however lovely on the outside, the system will collapse from the cancer within as much as much from conquerors without.

In response to this doomsday forecast, "they" (general audience) naturally ask Jesus about warning signs and timetables (21:7). He first answers with a caution, concentrating less on *when* and *what* (signs) and more on *whom* they should heed in this dire crisis. In the political powder keg of first-century Roman Palestine, there seemed to be no end of apocalyptic prophets, messianic promoters, and zealous rebels claiming divine mandate ("I am he/I am" [ἐγώ εἰμι, *egō eimi*]) and manifest destiny ("The time is near" [21:8]).[47] Difficult times bring out all sorts of would-be sages and saviors, many with self-aggrandizing, predatory designs. Though operating outside the system, pseudomessiahs could prove as exploitative as the scribes and other officials within the temple establishment. Jesus flatly warns his hearers, "Beware that you are not led astray. . . . Do not go after them" (21:8). Of course, Jesus has also claimed divine authority for himself and proclaimed the nearness of God's realm (10:9; 17:20–21; cf. 21:20, 28). It comes down again to a matter of *trust*. Luke continues to mount his case that Jesus is the one true prophet, Son, and Messiah of God worthy of trust, not least in times of upheaval.

After charging his audience not to fall for false messiahs, Jesus proceeds to address the times and signs. In apocalyptic worldviews, trials and tribulations typically build over time (though relatively short time), culminating in world-shattering events. Cataclysmic disasters do not strike out of the blue; those who know the signs have time (though not a lot) to prepare and perhaps forestall the "end." The signs Jesus sketches pointing to Jerusalem's destruction are boilerplate crises characteristic of any era: natural phenomena such as earthquakes, famines, plagues; "heavenly" turbulences (tempests, tornados, tsunamis); and international conflicts leading to wars and revolts (21:9–11). But

46. See Ritmeyer, "Herod's Temple," 46–48; Josephus, *Ant.* 15.392–425.

47. See Horsley and Hanson, *Bandits*; Horsley, *Jesus and the Spiral*; Gray, *Prophetic Figures*.

the new terrifying part of Jesus's message is that all these horrible events are about to converge on Jerusalem and the temple because of leaders' repeated spurning of God's reign. As the theopolitical center (navel) of the universe in biblical thought, the fate of Jerusalem is inextricably tied to world events, more specifically, to God's purposes for all creation. All politics may be local, but Jerusalem's local affairs have universal ramifications.

In the horizon of the near future, the picture of the holy polis and cosmos is not a pretty one. Jesus paints with chilling strokes the anticipated "desolation" of Jerusalem as Gentile (Roman) armies will "trample" it down, chop down myriad citizens by the sword, and hurl survivors into harsh exile. The effects of these tragic "days of vengeance" will radiate out from Jerusalem to Judea to the ends of the world, catalyzing "great distress on the earth" (21:20–24). Josephus's account in *Jewish War* confirms the Titus-led Romans' "barbarous cruelty" against Jerusalem's temple and people Passover in 70 CE (*J.W.* 6.432).

> While the holy house was on fire, everything was plundered that came to hand, and ten thousand of those that were caught were killed; nor was there a commiseration of any age, or any reverence of gravity, but children, and old men, and profane persons, and priests were all killed in the same manner. . . . The flame was also carried a long way, and made an echo, together with the groans of those that were killed. (*J.W.* 6.271–72)

> Now this vast multitude is indeed collected out of remote places, but the entire nation was now shut by fate as in prison, and the Roman army encompassed the city when it was crowded with inhabitants. Accordingly, the multitude of those that therein perished exceeded all the destructions that either men or God ever brought upon the world; for, to speak only of what was publicly known, the Romans killed some of them, some they carried captive. . . . There were . . . found killed there above two thousand persons, partly by their own hands, and partly by one another, but chiefly destroyed by the famine. . . . they would go in among the dead bodies that lay on heaps, and tread upon them. (*J.W.* 6.428–31 [trans. Whiston])

Moreover, as Jesus, Luke, and Josephus knew all too well, the horror of this assault on Jerusalem was compounded by a long and bitter history of invasions. Josephus specifically notes that the debacle of 70 CE was the *sixth time* David's Jerusalem had been devastated by an invading army, starting with Nebuchadnezzar and the Babylonians and followed by Shishak and the Egyptians, Antiochus and the Syrian Greeks, Pompey and the Romans, and Herod the Great (*J.W.* 6.435–37). These takeovers varied in their levels of havoc

(Herod's conquest led to the temple's grand refurbishment). Burning the city, razing the temple, killing citizens, and exiling survivors by Titus and his Roman legions most closely matched the Babylonian conquest in the early sixth century BCE—the tragedy of Israel's past most lamented by Deuteronomic historians (2 Kgs 24–25; cf. "vengeance" and "day of . . . calamity" in Deut 32:35), prophets (Jer 39:1–10; 52:1–30; Ezek 4–16; 22:1–31; 33:21–33), and the Chronicler (2 Chr 36:5–21; cf. Ezra 3:12–13; 4:11–24; Neh 1:1–4). But the more recent threat of the Hellenizing zealot Antiochus IV against Jerusalem and the entire Jewish way of life in the second-century BCE, though ultimately averted by Maccabean freedom fighters, also remained seared in the national memory, as attested in Daniel and 1–2 Maccabees. How could Israel possibly bear another seismic disruption of its capital, temple, and religiopolitical identity?

Like his biblical-prophetic forebears, Luke's Jesus offers a message of hope *beyond* doom, a grand restorative "End" redeeming the seeming "end" of Jerusalem's demise (Luke 21:25–28 [see discussion below]). But *before* that, as one who first *suffers* as the Son of Humankind, Jesus advises his followers about how to endure the suffering they will experience in the turbulent interim *before* the collapse of Jerusalem and climax of God's redemptive plan. Jesus frankly informs them that others, including close family and friends, will betray them to Roman and Jewish authorities, resulting in persecution for many and martyrdom for some (21:12–17). They should not be surprised by these developments, not only because of Jesus's predictive words, but also because of his own looming experience of betrayal, mistreatment, and crucifixion. The book of Acts details various examples of disciples' arrests, beatings, imprisonments, and deaths—all faced, however, with courage and commitment (reversing their cowardice in Luke's Gospel), not unlike the Danielic heroes and Maccabean martyrs. Luke's Jesus offers a critical key to their boldness: not some advanced strength-training or mental preparation, but the immediate revelation provided during times of trial: "I will give you words and a wisdom that none of your opponents will be able to withstand or contradict" (21:15).

This is a remarkable promise for at least two reasons. First, Jesus effectively dubs his disciples as inspired prophets and sages—a mouthpiece (lit. "I will give you a mouth [στόμα, *stoma*]") for the all-wise God (cf. Exod 4:10–16; Deut 18:18; Jer 1:9; Ezek 2:2–3:11). Jesus does not call his followers to armed resistance, as Mattathias the priest did against Antiochus IV. The only weapons of Jesus's emissaries are the *words* of God; they fight by speaking truth to power. Such words will not necessarily protect them from death. In fact, they may provoke the authorities to violent retaliation, as with Stephen. Unable to "withstand the wisdom and the Spirit with which he spoke" (Acts 6:10), the priestly council became incensed with Stephen and incited a mob to stone him to death—but not before he bore powerful witness to the panorama of God's revelation to Israel, capping in the death, resurrection, and exaltation of Jesus the Righteous One (7:52) and Son of Humankind (7:56) (cf. 6:8–8:1).

Second, Jesus stresses his continuing personal guidance: "*I will give* [ἐγὼ . . . δώσω, *egō . . . dōsō*] you a mouth and a wisdom." Earlier in a parallel forecast of the disciples' interrogations before hostile courts, Jesus promised that "the *Holy Spirit* will teach you at that very hour what you ought to say" (Luke 12:12). Now Jesus closely affiliates himself with God's Spirit and envisions his active, ongoing Spirit-presence with his witnesses after his physical departure. Jesus *himself* will still be with his followers and speak through them on the spot (not simply as they recall his teachings). This phenomenon, which no doubt many harassed believers had confirmed in the generations up to and beyond the first Jewish War, further solidifies the community's sense of Jesus's abiding post-Easter intimacy with and advocacy for them. The hope of his return, then, is not so much for reunion after a long absence as for radiation of God's saving power in Christ throughout the world.

Climactic Advent of the Son of Humankind (21:25–38)

Jesus now announces his final coming in close association with the terrible events preceding and including Rome's devastating assault on Jerusalem. This cluster of cataclysmic disruptions—shaking the whole cosmos and its regnant "powers" spanning heaven and earth (21:25–26, 33, 35)—signals that the irruption and extension of a completely new order, the redemptive reign of God, is *near* (ἐγγίζω/ἐγγύς, *engizō/engys* [21:28, 30]). Jesus once again uses the illustration of a fig tree, though to different effect. The earlier lesson compared Israel to a *barren* fig tree given one last chance, under God's cultivating care, to bear fruit before being chopped down (13:6–9). Now Jesus speaks of a *blossoming* fig tree poised to bear summer fruit in relation not only to Israel, but also encompassing the entire world: "the fig tree *and all the trees*" (21:29). The worst result of the previous parable has already taken place: fruitless Israel has been traumatically "cut down" by ravaging forces. But thankfully, that is not its ultimate "end," because as surely as budding trees harbinger a summer harvest, the sprouting of devastating events, including the explosive demise of Jerusalem, portends the imminence of God's restorative realm within a generation (21:29–33).

How will God's kingdom finally be manifest? As he draws on the prophets' "sign language" of celestial shakings, environmental disasters, and international battles converging on Jerusalem (Isa 13:10; 17:12–14; 24:17–20; Ezek 32:7; 38:14–23; Joel 2:28–30; Zech 12:1–3), Jesus alludes to Daniel's human-like son

(Son of Humankind) "coming with the clouds of heaven" as the climactic agent of God's redemptive rule (Dan 7:13; Luke 21:27–28). Heretofore, Luke's Jesus has assumed the Son of Humankind mantle both as instrument of divine authority and embodiment of the human condition, especially human suffering:

> The Son of Humankind has [divine] authority on earth to forgive sins. (5:24)
>
> The Son of Humankind has come eating and drinking. (7:34)
>
> The Son of Humankind must undergo great suffering . . . and be killed. (9:22)
>
> The Son of Humankind is going to be betrayed into human hands. (9:44)
>
> The Son of Humankind has nowhere to lay his head. (9:58)
>
> The Son of Humankind . . . must endure much suffering and be rejected by this generation. (17:24–25)
>
> The Son of Humankind . . . will be mocked and insulted and spat upon. After they have flogged him, they will kill him. (18:31–33)

In his dynamic and sympathetic earthly ministry culminating in crucifixion, Jesus the Son of Humankind brings God's reign closer to hand: this kingdom "has come to you" (11:20) and "is among/within you" (17:21). But these salutary signs remain embryonic of the full-fledged kingdom to come. The Son of Humankind has come to earth as son of God and Adam (3:38) via Mary's womb and Bethlehem's manger—not yet on clouds of heaven to Jerusalem (though hinted in the transfiguration "cloud" [9:34–35]); and his earthly life ends hanging from a cross, not sitting on a throne (though he rises and returns to heaven in a "cloud" [Acts 1:9–10; Luke 24:51]).

Hence, Jesus's *full*-fillment of Daniel's Son of Humankind must include a second act, a second coming, as he already suggested (9:26; 17:22–30) and now reinforces in his last temple discourse. In this anticipated return "with power and great glory" (21:27), Jesus will come as "*the* Son of Humankind" (not simply "like" a human figure) to restore his suffering people *with whom* he has intimately suffered. He will thus ultimately establish God's reign from *below*, on the ground with solidarity and sympathy for the oppressed; and from *above*, on the clouds with power and glory. He will come to save his people and judge the inhumane empires that have trampled Israel and the world. The dynasty of unjust, "beastly" kingdoms from Babylon to Media to Persia to Greece to Syria (Dan 7:1–12)—and now Rome—will be forever shattered so that God's kingdom might flourish unfettered.

Still, however, all this hopeful theology of God's righteous reign, Christology of Jesus's divine incarnation, and soteriology of universal redemption bump up against the nagging inconvenience of hard *chronology*. Granted, God's eternal calendar (GOT) is beyond our comprehension (cf. Eccl 3:11; 2 Pet 3:8), but Luke's Jesus speaks of "near" in human language that soon creates dissonance. The "delay of the parousia" becomes problematic for the church early on, even before the fall of Jerusalem (cf. 1 Thess 4:13–5:11). By Luke's day, a decade or so after the final sign of Jerusalem's demise falls into place, the issue becomes more acute, but not insurmountable, since Luke writes *within a single generation* of the Jewish War. No doubt more difficult years had passed without the Son of Humankind's coming than Luke and other Christians would wish, but at least they can muster hope that Christ's return remains "near" and manage to press on in the meantime. But two millennia further down the road where we sit, it has gotten exponentially tougher.

But perhaps all this calculating, all this assessing the present and future "age" or "generation," misses the point as much as narrower date-and-hour setting. As noted above, classic biblical announcements of national disaster typically pressed ahead to envision in the not-too-distant future (seventy years was a common target) God's faithful restoration of land, people, and temple: in other words, a climactic redemptive "End" after what seemed to be the "end" of their world. The high watermarks of these audacious hopes crest in Isa 35, 40–66, Dan 7–12, and memorable images like Jeremiah's new covenant (31:31–34) and field purchase during the siege of Jerusalem (32:1–15) and Ezekiel's valley of restored dry bones (37:1–14) and magnificent new temple (40–48). But these hopes of a grand finale were only partially realized at best within the "near" seventy-or-so-year future, leading to revisions of expectations and reconfigurations of end-time events (cf. Hag 2:1–8). Even the stunning Maccabean victory proved short-lived, soon ceding to fresh messianic visions in the face of Rome's imperial onslaught.

Biblical eschatology runs in linear and cyclical tension, unfolding a series of beginnings and endings, commencements and climaxes—with plenty of evil and suffering in the interim phases. This general pattern applies as much to God's rule in the first-century, Roman-dominated world of Israel and the church as in prior generations of God's people, even though, as Luke believes, the particular incarnation in Jesus Messiah represents the fullest manifestation of God's kingdom ever to appear on earth. Even that "near" day of Restoration announced by Jesus is still "not yet" and will be preceded (yet again) by terrible hardship before reaching another "end." John Goldingay aptly positions the eschatology of Luke and other NT writers within the broad sweep of biblical prophetic history:

> Their distinctive Christian angle is to present the story of Jesus as another, and climactic, intervention of the One on High who appears in Dan 7. Like the visions in Daniel, these New Testament middle narratives describe this intervention *as if* it brings the ultimate End, *but it does not do so*. They recognize this point, in that they incorporate their own account of events that follow Jesus's death and resurrection and of situations that arise. They know that there will yet come the crisis that was historically constituted by the fall of Jerusalem, but that this crisis, too, will not be the end.[48]

In a similar vein, Jürgen Moltmann tracks what he calls a "biblical catastrophe theology" from the Genesis flood to the Babylonian conquest to Jesus's crucifixion to Revelation's apocalypse and then arcs that theology into the contemporary horizon of World War II (including Auschwitz) and global terrorism (including 9/11).[49] Out of these debacles, however, new hope and life emerge as evidence of God's undying faithfulness to God's creation: "In every end a new beginning lies hidden. It will find you if you look for it. Do not lose heart!"[50] For all its academic erudition, Moltmann's theology is no ivory tower speculation. It is deeply personal, forged out of early life crises, including "Operation Gomorrah" in 1943, when the Royal Air Force bombarded his hometown of Hamburg, Germany, killing 40,000 citizens. The seventeen-year-old Moltmann miraculously survived this attack, while his anti-aircraft battery mate and school friend was blown to bits next to him.[51] Moreover, for all his deserved reputation as the great modern "theologian of hope," Moltmann is no naive positive thinker or pie-in-the sky dreamer. He knows all too well the

48. Goldingay, *Do We Need the New Testament?*, 89 (emphasis added). Goldingay distinguishes the scope of "short," "middle," and "grand" narratives mutually informing biblical theology: "The two Testaments contain many short narratives expressing theological insights: stories about Israel, about individual Israelites, about Jesus and about the infant church. They also imply a grand theological narrative, which the creeds aim to encapsulate. But in addition, the two Testaments include a series of extensive explicit or implicit middle narratives, which form a key way in which the Scriptures do theology" (71). Luke's tensive eschatological drama represents one of these key middle narratives.

49. Moltmann, *In the End*, 33–52.

50. Moltmann, *In the End*, 35.

51. Moltmann, *In the End*, 33–34, and *Broad Place*, 13–18.

recurring experience of catastrophic suffering that hope must endure en route to renewal. Biblical hope rooted in salvation history dares to look beyond disastrous "ends" for fresh beginnings but remains wary of accepting any new development as the ultimate "End" of God's redemptive plan. We hope and pray for God's final restoration of all things, but we do so in the crucible of continued "groaning" (Rom 8:22) and difficult interim endings that not only spark brighter beginnings but also transmogrify into other disastrous "endings" before the climactic-salvific "End."

Knowing this long pattern of beginnings and endings, Luke's Jesus again turns to instruct his followers concerning their conduct in the interim between his departure (ca. 30 CE), the destruction of Jerusalem (70 CE), and the consummative descent of the Son of Humankind, whenever that happens. He particularly enjoins careful attentiveness, crystallized in two imperatives: "Be on guard" (21:34) and "Be alert at all times" (21:36). This time the call is not visual: there's no need to see/look for the Son of Humankind's glorious comeback (cf. Acts 1:11). When he appears in the clouds, no one will miss it (Luke 17:24). Rather, one must be on guard/alert in diligently attending to God's rule on earth when(ever) the Son of Humankind arrives: "When the Son of Humankind comes, will he find faith(fulness) on earth?" (18:8). Such dutifulness in the tumultuous interim period entails serving the interests of God's right-making, merciful kingdom here and now, confronting forces of evil and injustice in God's name, and not bogging down in escapist numbing of harsh realities through "dissipation and drunkenness" or excessive preoccupation with "worries of this life" (21:34). The business of God's realm takes priority over business as usual (cf. 17:26–30).

Jesus does, however, encourage one escapist practice: "*praying* that you may have the strength to *escape* [ἐκφυγεῖν *ekphygein*] all these things that will take place, and to stand before the Son of Humankind" (21:36). The discipline of prayer as a source of divine power and wisdom during trying times is a spiritual staple in Luke, exemplified in Jesus's own practice and teaching (3:21; 6:12; 9:28; 11:1–13; 22:31–32, 39–46; 23:34, 46). Praying for "escape" does not chiefly aim to secure exit from harm's way (though there's nothing wrong with that [cf. 11:4; 22:42]), but rather to endure the crisis through God's strength (cf. 22:43) and surmount undertows of distraction and defection roiling in the maelstrom of "all these [turbulent] things." Ultimately, Jesus's followers must remain ready to "stand before the Son of Humankind" in faithful integrity when he comes, since he will judge the world "in righteousness" as part and parcel of his restorative project (Acts 17:31; cf. Luke 12:8–10). Saving and judging coalesce in God's just purpose for the world. Redemption offers no cheap pass; believers and unbelievers alike must reckon with God's co-regent Christ.

Incarnating the World's Suffering (22:1–24:53)

Although unabashedly promoting Jesus as regnant Lord and Christ, righteous Judge, and restorative Son of Humankind, Luke never allows this portrait to slip into chest-thumping triumphalism. From his nativity, Jesus "is destined . . . to be a sign that will be opposed" (2:34). Now, in these closing chapters, his vocation as *suffering Savior* comes to a head. Among the disastrous omens preceding final redemption, Jesus's imminent death stands out as the most critical sign, the most salient catastrophic event blazing the trail to the realized "End" of God's saving plan. As God's chief redemptive agent, Jesus will not descend on the clouds of heaven as world-restoring Son of Humankind until he first ascends the cross of Golgotha, "opposed" by authorities, disciples, and crowds alike, dying stripped and alone. He will not stand as Supreme Ruler and Judge until he dies as suffering slave and criminal. Indeed, the link between these experiences is more causal than circumstantial: Jesus's suffering-and-dying *entitles* him to rule-and-judge. He will rule and judge the world "in righteousness" *because* he knows in his bones the depths of human and creational agony crying out for healing and restoration. He *incarnates* this suffering in broken flesh and drained blood (22:19–20, 44), the signs of which remain etched in his hands and feet after his resurrection (24:38–40). The Son of Humankind forever bears the scars of violent suffering and death. It is before this Suffering One all must stand and give account.

Luke explicates this *crucial* theology in narrative rather than discursive form, unfolding Jesus's passion in great detail. Through this extended account, where "story time" crawls at an excruciating pace, readers are meant to sympathize, to "feel with" Jesus's ordeal at a visceral level. Though a large cast of characters swirls around Jesus in his last days, the spotlight remains trained on him: his person, his passions, and his practices (as outlined above). Luke's Jesus both models *how* his followers should live in the impending period of "great distress on the earth" (21:23) and manifests *why* Lord and Savior Jesus is uniquely qualified to see them through the crisis.

In tragic-ironic fashion, however, Jesus's confidants contribute to his grief, even as they grieve his fate (22:45; 23:27–28; 24:19–21). Bracketing the central drama of Jesus's trials and death at the hands of Jewish and Roman authorities are sequences of tense dealings with his own disciples, first involving their betrayals and denials, and finally their confusion and disbelief. Jesus's post-resurrection interactions with his associates distress *him* (24:25–26, 38).

- Suffering the Disciples' Tragic Betrayals and Denials (22:1–62)
- Suffering the Authorities' Mock Trials and Death Verdict (22:63–23:49)
- Suffering the Disciples' Persistent Confusion and Disbelief (23:50–24:53).

Arguably, human suffering cuts deepest in the relational, rather than purely physical, sphere. Nothing hurts quite like the pain inflicted by other people, especially those we love, which may involve an array of psychological damage along with physical abuse. Not to minimize the poignant portrayal of Jesus's torturous beating and crucifixion, we should note that Luke does not elaborate the grisly details and in fact gives more play to the injurious effects of the disciples' conduct *on Jesus* and, in turn, how he graciously responds to their mistreatment and misunderstanding of him. This *relationship* between Jesus and his people—forged in the crucible of suffering—remains primary.

Suffering the Disciples' Tragic Betrayals and Denials (22:1–62)

Through faithful mercy, love, and power, Jesus solidifies his relationship with his disciples before his ascension, preparing them to take greater responsibility for advancing God's realm. But they do not make it easy. Indeed, they break Jesus's heart and fray the ties that bind at his most critical hours—when he needs them most—to say nothing of their ongoing need for him. Trust between Jesus and the twelve apostles hits rock bottom with Judas's betrayal and Peter's denials, along with the others' self-centered and soporific insensitivity to the crisis at hand. While their trust (faith) in Jesus teeters as his terrible fate finally dawns upon them, Jesus's trust (faith) in them also shatters in pieces. Christian believers focused on professing faith in Christ, who offered himself as a sacrifice for sinful, suffering humanity, often overlook the vital reciprocal dimension of the faith *of* Christ *in* his followers. As God has long partnered with Israel to bless the world and bring "light to the nations" (Isa 42:6; 49:6; Luke 2:32; Acts 13:47), so Jesus extends that redemptive covenantal bond with the Twelve, the symbolic representatives of Israel (cf. Luke 22:30). As Jesus intimately collaborates with his divine Father and Spirit in this saving mission, he also seeks human cooperation. This divine-human *communal* project demands *mutual trust and trustworthiness*, which the apostles, for their part, miserably fail to sustain.

The categories sketched above pertaining to (mis)trust between Jesus and the religious authorities also apply in relation to his disciples:

- Flashes of ministerial competence demonstrated by the Twelve in "bringing the good news and curing diseases everywhere" (9:6; cf. 10:17) only go so far, not just because they also have occasional lapses in ability (9:40), but more critically, because their *moral integrity* remains suspect. In particular, their ambitious preoccupations with "which one of them was the greatest" (9:46; 22:24–27) betray their untrustworthiness as ambassadors of Christ's self-emptying, servant-grounded mission.

- The Twelve's close *personal familiarity* with Jesus since he called them to follow and chose them as "apostles" (6:13) has naturally forged a special bond of mutual trust. As in any intimate relationship, there have been testy moments, but not enough to demolish the fundamental trust that has been built. But because of the established trust among friends and confidants, when one party violates that good faith with shocking turncoat behavior, it cuts to the quick of the relationship and to the heart of the hurt party.
- Hence, *emotional impressionability*, a key component in negotiating levels of trust, surges during times of personal and social crisis. In Luke's suspenseful "passion" scenes, emotions of anxiety and grief, fear and disappointment, come to a head on *both sides*, for both Jesus and his feckless disciples. Along with explicit indications of these emotions (22:43–45, 61–62), we may reasonably assume other feelings rumbling below the surface.
- The pattern of *historical consistency* cuts two ways in faith formation between Jesus and the Twelve. "Consistency" has scarcely been the hallmark of the apostles' behavior, as their numerous weaknesses and misperceptions of Jesus's mission attest. But for all their bungling, the fact that "they left everything and followed" Jesus (5:11) cannot be gainsaid as evidence of exceptional trust. In any case, bonds of trust must be persistently nurtured in the throes of new challenges. Though past conduct provides a broad barometer for future responses, in the matter of trustworthiness, past fealty does not guarantee perpetual commitment, especially in *immediate, short-term* crises.[52] In explosive new ordeals, all bets are off. When Jesus's life is on the line and his messianic chips are down, his apostles hedge their bets and cut their losses—at Jesus's expense.

Sustaining Jesus during this crisis of trust are core spiritual disciplines of *prayer* (22:32, 39–46) and *Scripture reflection* (22:37) and also a keen *prescience* about "the time of trial" (22:40, 46) and "hour . . . of darkness" (22:53). He knows and announces his apostles' betrayals and denials beforehand (22:22–23, 31–34), which, despite their confusion and objections, come to pass, further evidencing

52. Cf. DeSteno, *Truth*, 198: "In any one instance, a person's decision to cooperate with or exploit another will be determined by the short- versus long-term trade-offs in question, not his or her past behavior. This truism doesn't mean, however, that reputation is completely useless" (cf. 23–25, 32).

his prophetic authority (22:47–62). As the world and his friends turn against him, even as he is (falsely) "counted among the lawless" (22:37), Jesus remains a faithful servant to God. And remarkably, he continues to nurture both his unfaithful followers—serving and praying for them in their weakest moments (22:14–27, 31–34)—and his enemies, healing a painful wound suffered by a member of the squad arresting Jesus (22:50–51). Luke's Jesus remains worthy of trust to the end.

What most drives Jesus's actions and attitudes, however, at this critical junction is the overriding *will of God* for him to fully drink the cup of suffering in the process of restoring a broken world (22:42). Jesus's (1) foreknowledge of Judas's scheme and Peter's shame, (2) advance preparation for eating the last Passover meal (22:8–13), (3) sense of Scripture "being fulfilled" (22:37), and (4) acceptance of the momentous "hour" at hand (22:53) all attest to an orderly divine plotting of events enveloping panicky human responses and apparent chaos. This is not to say that Jesus blithely consents to this saving-through-suffering plan. Just because he knows what he must do and what must happen does not mean he enjoys or prefers it. Indeed, because he knows the full terrible truth, with no illusions, of what awaits him, he honestly chafes against it and asks his Father to halt the cascade of his brutal sufferings at the eleventh hour (22:42). Alas, however, the die is cast and the plan remains set, not because of some callous disregard or bloodlust on God's part, but because of the massive entrenched, systemic violence and injustice that must be rooted out from within.

The narrative structure of these tragic events also unfolds in an orderly fashion, framed by Judas's treacherous deal with the priestly leaders and Peter's denials in the high priest's courtyard, with alternating attention to the two disciples in between.

Judas's Betrayal with the Chief Priests (22:1–6)
  Peter's preparation (with John) for the Passover (22:8)
  Judas's betrayal predicted (22:21–22)
  Peter's denials predicted (22:31–34)
  Judas's betrayal enacted (22:47–48)
Peter's Denials in the High Priest's Courtyard (22:54–62)

Though singled out, Judas and Peter hardly bear all the blame. The entire company of twelve apostles proves woefully out of step with Jesus's concerns in two major scenes in lofty settings:

Jesus's Last Meal in an Upstairs Room (22:7–38)
Jesus's Agony and Arrest on the Mount of Olives (22:39–53)

The "high" Jerusalem locales of an upper-story room and symbolic-rich mountain suggest occasions of significant divine-human encounters amid the "low" depressions of angst and grief.

Judas's Betrayal with the Chief Priests (22:1–6)

Passover commemorates the liberation of ancient Israelites from centuries of Egyptian slavery at the horrible cost of every firstborn Egyptian child's life (tenth plague) and of Pharaoh's army drowned in the Red Sea. These oppressive enemies of Israel, though given every opportunity to let God's people go, relented only under the pressure of violent defeat. Now, in Luke's story, as the annual Passover "was near" (22:1), Israel again finds itself under harsh foreign domination, albeit in its own land with some latitude (not abject slavery); and the religious leaders seek to eliminate a major threat, as they perceive it, to their freedom. But in a terrible ironic twist, they want to get rid of Jesus the Galilean, not some Roman official or legion. This one who "came to seek out [ζητῆσαι, *zētēsai*] and to save the lost" throughout Israel (19:10; cf. 15:1–32), providing a new lease on life, the temple authorities are now "looking for a way [seeking—ἐζήτουν, *ezētoun*] to put . . . to death" (22:2). "Seeking" the blessings of God's kingdom mediated through Jesus Messiah—in other words, seeking God in Jesus as Jesus "seeks" to restore the lost to God—is central to Luke's theological missiology (5:18; 6:19; 12:31; 19:3). Since the narrow road and door to God's eternal life open to those who seek and follow Jesus's leadership (cf. 10:25; 13:22–24; 18:18), one can scarcely imagine a greater obstacle to God's saving way than seeking Jesus's life with murderous intent.

Why do the chief priests persist in their desire not merely to resist Jesus but to kill him (19:47; 20:19 [also with ζητέω, *zēteō*])? He has spoken against them and challenged their authority but has mounted no coup and taken up no arms. The powerful motivation of *fear* again comes to the fore, specifically directed toward "the people," or by extension, toward the people's feelings about Jesus (22:2). The fear factor has subtly modified since its last mention. During the temple debates, the angry authorities refrained from seizing and sentencing Jesus for fear of provoking a riot among the people mesmerized by his teaching (20:19; cf. 19:47–48). Now, however, the temple leaders' aim to kill Jesus has intensified precisely "*because* they were afraid of the people" (22:2 CEB).[53] Popular interest in Jesus has escalated to the point where authorities now worry

53. The NRSV and most other versions opt for the customary, blander rendering of the conjunction γάρ (*gar*) as "for." But in the context here, the CEB rightly captures its causative force.

about an uprising *if they do not eliminate Jesus*. The more he keeps operating in the charged atmosphere of Passover, the more the religious hierarchs fear they will lose control of the situation and be displaced by militant crowds and/or Roman troops. In their anxious minds, the risk of letting Jesus live has become greater than the risk of killing him. In any case, as fear typically springs from threats of loss and personal insecurity, the chief priests and scribes fear the loss of their temple turf, which has boosted their dominant prosperity and power; and rather than flee or freeze, they choose to fight for their territory.

But it remains a delicate situation best handled in a clandestine rather than a frontal assault. As if made to order, Judas Iscariot, "one of the twelve," comes to the temple priests and police officers with a secret plan to hand over Jesus (22:3–4). Thus a member of Jesus's innermost circle instigates a betrayal plot. The experience of bitter treachery "even by parents and brothers, by relatives and friends," which Jesus predicted for the apostles during the coming days of crisis (21:16), is first perpetrated by one of these apostles against Jesus himself.

What possesses Judas to turn against Jesus? Though we have known since the original roll-call of the Twelve that Judas "became a traitor" (6:16), nothing in the narrative to this point has signaled how or why this would happen. In fact, Judas's name has not been mentioned between 6:16 and 22:3. He has simply been lumped in with the apostolic group, without distinction, in their good and bad times; we have no substantive cause to suspect him more than anyone else. Theories about motive—cowardice, disappointment over Jesus's nonviolent strategy, overzealous attempt to force Jesus's hand, even to push him on his saving way to the cross (someone had to do it)—remain speculative and distractive in the absence of clear evidence. Luke suggests none of these options. From his perspective, what possesses Judas to betray Jesus is actual *possession* by the Evil One: "Then Satan entered into Judas called Iscariot" (22:3). Is Judas somehow more open to satanic influence, more inclined to disloyalty than the other apostles? Perhaps, but again Luke doesn't say that. Judas "consented" to the financial deal offered by the authorities (he's a willing participant, not simply the devil's puppet), but this move is something first "agreed to" among the officials themselves, not a condition set by Judas (22:5–6).[54] He may well have been hoping for a payout and thus spurred by greed, but again that goes beyond Luke's account.[55] The temple leaders prove to be the more passionate partners with Satan in Jesus's demise, as their fear turns to joy at the prospect

54. The verb συνέθεντο (*synethento*) is an aorist middle form, suggesting "agree among/for themselves." Moreover, as Culy, Parsons, and Stigall note, "The συν- here must refer to agreement among the Jewish leaders rather than between them and Judas" (664).

55. The image of Judas as a greedy moneygrubber owes primarily to the Fourth Gospel's parenthetical remark about Judas as the group's unscrupulous treasurer (John 12:6; cf. vv. 4–5).

of exploiting Judas for their ends (ἐχάρησαν, *echarēsan*—"they were greatly pleased" or "were delighted" [22:5 NIV, CEB]). With some "consent" to be sure, Judas is ultimately caught in the lockjaws of cosmic and cultic powers beyond his control.

With the plot hatched, Judas now "began to look for" (or "was seeking" [ἐζήτει, *ezētei*]) Jesus for nefarious rather than salutary purposes, particularly the right "opportunity [εὐκαιρίαν, *eukairian*]" to deliver him to the temple police (22:6). Here again, the specter of Satan lurks over the proceedings. After testing Jesus after his baptism, the devil let him be "until an opportune time [καιροῦ, *kairou*]" (4:13). In the meantime, Jesus and his followers have liberated many from Satan's clutches (4:31–37; 8:26–39; 9:1–6, 37–43; 10:17–20; 11:14–23; 13:16); but now Satan seizes the "opportunity" through Judas and others to make a comeback and put an end to Jesus. The war wages on a cosmic spiritual and political battlefield for the hearts of all people and the wellsprings of all creation.

Jesus's Last Meal in an Upstairs Room (22:7–38)

In a helpful note, Louw and Nida sketch three meanings for πάσχα, *pascha* (Passover), from general to specific: (1) the entire, weeklong annual *festival* of Passover (also known as the feast of Unleavened Bread); (2) the Passover *lamb* sacrificed at a designated time during the festival; and (3) the Passover *meal* eaten in private dwellings in the evening after the lamb-offering in the temple.[56] In Luke's story, we have come to the Passover "day," featuring lamb and meal ceremonies (22:7), with momentous consequence for Jesus and his disciples on "this day" (22:34).[57] The spotlight falls on table fellowship at the meal rather than the temple sacrifice of the lamb; moreover, no lamb is on the menu. As a dark curtain has fallen over the temple system, Jesus turns his attention to the more private realm of his adopted family of God-followers, though with profound public implications. In a borrowed Jerusalem "house" (οἰκία, *oikia* [22:10]), specifically, in an upstairs "guest room" (22:11), Jesus conducts his last symposium with the apostles (before his death), involving a richly symbolic supper and equally charged conversation.

Jesus frames his final instructions with very practical concerns about the disciples' provisions during these challenging times: first, the immediate provi-

56. Louw and Nida, *Greek-English Lexicon*, 1:42.

57. Luke's specification in 22:7 of "the [singular] day of Unleavened Bread" reflects "inexact usage," as Tiede and Matthews ("Gospel according to Luke") note, since "unleavened bread was eaten all seven days of the Passover festival (see Exod 12:14–20)" (1805–6). Moreover, Luke does not use the term for the sacrificed "lamb" here; the animal is implied in the πάσχα (*pascha*) language.

sions to celebrate the Passover meal (22:7–13); and last, the imminent provisions to face the "lawless" events about to transpire (22:35–38). Grasping the short- and long-term picture, Jesus's future vision is both realistic and optimistic, fully aware of the intense suffering awaiting him and his followers, yet brimming with hope of the ultimate "fulfillment" (filling full) of God's kingdom (22:16, 18). Likewise, Jesus assesses his chosen emissaries with both clear- and bright-eyed judgment. Their character deficiencies—ranging across a spectrum of surreptitious disloyalty (22:21–23), overweening ambition (22:24–27), false bravado (22:33–34), and gross miscalculation (22:35–38)—are on shocking display during the Last Supper. Yet, for all their manifest shortcomings, Jesus proffers his life for these fickle followers (22:19–20), promises them honored positions in God's realm (22:28–30), and prays for their renewed strength (22:31–32).

Though Jesus normally employs no advance team to manage his itinerary, he does periodically send messengers ahead, notably (1) at the beginning of his Jerusalem journey, to secure lodging in a Samaritan village (9:52) and prepare his gospel mission in various towns (10:1–9); (2) at the end, to procure a colt for Jesus's ride into Jerusalem (19:29–34); and (3) now, a site to eat the Passover meal (22:8–13). All these occasions confirm Jesus's dependence on others' hospitality: he owns nothing in any place and has limited resources for payment. As Lord of God's realm, Jesus has the right to commandeer any goods and services he wants, but as he has demonstrated since the temptation scene, he refuses to take advantage of his authority for lavish personal accommodations and accessories. He acquires only modest things, like a colt, because he "needs" them (19:34). Though God's Son and heir of all creation, not least God's holy city and house in Jerusalem, Jesus does not exploit the property and riches he rightfully "owns" for his own benefit. Such conspicuous consumption, at others' expense, marks the economic tyranny of Roman, Herodian, and temple rulers from which Jesus aims to liberate God's people.

In the present case, why does Jesus "need" a home dining-place in Jerusalem? His campsite on the Mount of Olives won't do for this occasion, requiring a table and provisions simulating the first Passover. Though this sacred meal need not be eaten within Jerusalem's limits, Jesus's inner city choice doubtless reflects his claim as Son of God (and David) to the royal capital. Yet, Jesus seeks no palace or villa in the holy city, but rather dispatches Peter and John to gain access (which Jesus somehow prearranged) to a temporary space in a large upper-floor "guest room" (κατάλυμα, *katalyma*). The process unfolds, however, per Jesus's instructions, in a mysterious way: he tells the apostolic pair to rendezvous with "a man carrying a jar of water," who will lead them to a homeowner, to whom they must say, "The teacher asks you, 'Where is the guest room, where I may eat the Passover with my disciples?'" In turn, the owner will show them the upstairs space furnished for their use (22:10–12). This plan involving anonymous confederates and a password phrase securing access to a "safe house" reads like a spy mission, which it virtually is. Jesus is a marked man now and must tread carefully in Jerusalem. Knowing his time is short, he longs to spend this crucial Passover "hour" (22:14) with his associates unmolested. As all these preparations fall into place for this Last Supper, just "as he had told them" (22:13), Jesus's prophetic word remains a bulwark in the midst of chaos.

But a tragic sense of *exile* still colors these proceedings, all the more distressing because of its context of alienation *within* the land of Israel and the city of Jerusalem. The situation has improved only slightly since Jesus's birth. He was laid in a Bethlehem manger, displaced from the more suitable "lodging/guest room" (κατάλυμα, *katalyma* [2:7]), and visited by nomadic shepherds; now he spends part of his final evening with a group of itinerant Galilean disciples *in* a Jerusalem κατάλυμα (*katalyma* [22:11]), but he doesn't own the place and must go there in secret. Sadly, God's Messiah Jesus is all but homeless within the holy land and city. Yet, the temporary domiciles for food and fellowship that Jesus finds along the way provide potential home bases for the restoration of God's realm, "from house to house" (Acts 20:20).[58]

As the "hour" arrives, Jesus takes his place at the upper-room table as master of ceremonies, honored host, and also, as he soon makes clear, chief servant (22:27). Initially, he sets the emotional tone for this meal in a poignant statement unique to Luke: "I have earnestly desired to eat this Passover with you before I suffer" (22:15). This strong self-expression of desire by Jesus literally reads: "I have deeply desired with desire [ἐπιθυμίᾳ ἐπεθύμησα, *epithymia epethymēsa*]," that is, "I have fervently longed" (AT). As we have seen, modern philosophers stress that emotions typically reveal what we care about most. It is hardly surprising at this stage that Luke's Jesus longs for this last supper with his disciples, not because he's famished, desperately aching for food—like the prodigal in the pig pen or Lazarus at the rich man's gate (both cases of pining [ἐπιθυμέω, *epithymeō*] for food [15:16; 16:21])—but because the meal table represents a primary site of ministry to the hungry and fellowship with the homeless. He truly cares about sharing food, talk, and his very life with all types of people—the poor, the sinful, the Pharisees, and, of course, his beloved

58. The room where Jesus and his disciples eat the Last Supper is located "upstairs" (ἀνάγαιον, *anagaion* [Luke 22:12]); likewise, after Jesus's ascension the early group of believers first congregates in "the room upstairs (ὑπερῷον, *hyperōon*) where they were staying . . . devoting themselves to prayer" (Acts 1:13–14). Though using different terminology, the "upstairs" lodging in Jerusalem links the two experiences and sets the stage for the house-church movement in Acts as the main locus of fellowship, including the breaking of bread (2:46–47; 5:42).

followers. At table Jesus most intimately communicates and incarnates God's love for all, especially those who suffer (like the prodigal and Lazarus). He eats in joy amid the pain. In the current setting, his desire to eat with his apostles *before* he suffers and dies reflects not only a pragmatic reality, but also a sympathetic identity with his fellow-sufferers and commitment to prepare them for the grief and trials that lie ahead. At root Jesus cultivates hope with his double reference to eating this Passover again at the consummation of God's kingdom (22:16, 18). So this is not his *last* supper at all, but rather a foretaste of the eschatological messianic banquet for all God's people, celebrating the renewal of all creation.

This meal also provides a vital ingredient for enduring hard times of brokenness and depletion until the final restoration. Jesus imbues the Passover supper with fresh memorial significance. By no means replacing the foundational memory of God's liberation of Israel from slavery, Jesus enriches this experience with a personal focus: "Do this in remembrance *of me*" (22:19; cf. 1 Cor 11:24–25). Jesus takes into himself the sufferings of his people and takes upon himself the burden of redemption. And as with Israel's exodus of old, remembering Jesus's new "exodus" (9:31) involves much more than simple recollection or nostalgia; this is full-fledged sacramental memory: intimate, imaginative involvement with the past, as if one is living and feeling it anew in the present. In the Lord's Supper, Jesus's followers are truly with him, and he with them in his entire passion—and not just once a year at Passover, but "day by day" (Acts 2:46) or "as often as you eat" it (1 Cor 11:26)—until the Lord comes again. In this meal, Jesus's friends know and feel his sympathetic presence and power with them.

Jesus more deeply internalizes this nurturing experience by identifying with elements of the Passover meal: the *loaf of bread* "is *my body* which is given for you"; the *cup of wine* "is the new covenant in *my blood* [poured out for you]" (Luke 22:19–20). Communion with Christ is thus wholly incarnate—not just in Jesus, but in his followers, too—as they take his flesh and blood into their innermost, flesh-and-blood beings. Bodies in pain particularly matter to God: the body of his crucified Son, the bodies of all human beings subject to disease and death.

Another distinctive component of Luke's Last Supper account is the decanting of *two cups*, one before distributing the bread and one "after supper" (22:17, 20). While drinking multiple cups of wine was not unusual at Passover feasts, all other NT accounts of the Lord's Supper have *one cup* after the bread (part of the meal in Matt 26:26–27//Mark 14:22–23; "after supper" in 1 Cor 11:25). Assuming that Luke's orderly narrative has not suddenly become jumbled and accepting the longer, distinctive, more awkward double-cup (cup-bread-cup) reading,[59] we probe possible purposes behind Luke's special version. Perhaps through a common framing arrangement, with the two cups flanking the loaf, Luke gives central emphasis to eating bread with Jesus and thereby sharing his bodily life and ministry; overall in Luke's narratives, bread constitutes the main element in Jesus's revelatory table fellowship (9:12–17; 11:3; 13:20–21; 24:30–31; Acts 2:42, 46; 20:7, 11; 27:35).[60]

Alternatively or complementarily, Luke's separation of drinking (first cup) and pouring (second cup) actions conjoined in the other accounts may accord special significance to Jesus's postprandial *outpouring*. Matthew and Mark identify the *imbibed* wine with Jesus's "blood of the covenant, which is *poured out* for many" (Matt 26:28//Mark 14:24). Luke retains the symbolic picture of a blood covenant but more directly connects it with *outpoured*, rather than imbibed wine: "This cup that is *poured out* for you is the new covenant in my blood" (Luke 22:20). Simply schematized, though the Synoptics all mix the same brew, as it were, of outpoured and imbibed wine with Jesus's covenantal blood, in Matthew and Mark the formula runs "drunk wine = Jesus's blood → to be poured out," whereas in Luke it is "poured-out wine [after earlier drunk cup] = Jesus's poured-out blood." Since Luke does not report sharing or drinking this second cup, we might visualize it poured out *on the table or floor* as a decanted "offering to God," as Tannehill suggests, evoking the sprinkled and outpoured sacrificial blood offerings on the temple altar.[61] In this vein, Jesus's out-bleeding seals a renewed redemptive covenant with God's people (cf. Jer 31:31–34) and, indeed, with all creation—the earth into which Jesus's lifeblood will seep.

Immediately following and interrupting his jarring drama of outpoured wine and blood—which the disciples have no time to process—Jesus suddenly interjects, "But look here [πλὴν ἰδού, *plēn idou*]: the hand of my betrayer with me on the table!" (22:21 AT, following Greek word order). This abrupt shift to an apostle's "hand" on the table "with" Jesus after his shocking comments about his sacrificed body and blood aims to hit his followers hard. With all he has given

59. See the careful discussion supporting this reading in Omanson, *Textual Guide* (147–49), partly based on the overwhelming external evidence: "The longer, or traditional, text of cup-bread-cup is read by all Greek manuscripts except D and by most of the ancient versions and Fathers" (147); for a counter (and weaker) view, heavily based on presuming the non-Lukan origin of "given *for you*/poured out *for you*" in 22:19b–20 (interpolating an atonement view of Jesus's death), see Ehrman, *Misquoting Jesus*, 165–67.

60. Luke's Jesus punctuates his statement about the bread (not the cup) with only "Do this in remembrance of me" (22:19b), unlike the tradition handed down to Paul in 1 Cor 11:24–25, which appends the "remembrance" clause to both the bread and the cup pronouncements.

61. Tannehill (315–16), citing Lev 4:18, 25, 30, 34; Num 28:7–9, 14, 24; Sir 50:15 as possible parallels; cf. Spencer, *Dancing Girls*, 132–33.

and will give "for" them (22:19–20), what "hand" will they lend for him in his direst hours? What service can Jesus count on from these "hands," which have just taken nourishing wine and bread from his blessed hands? Sadly, not much. In fact, Jesus drops the bombshell that one of them now "with me" has already turned against him with plans to "hand him over" to the authorities. Of course, we already know, as Jesus does, that this betrayer is Judas (22:1–6), but the other apostles remain clueless, and Judas isn't telling. Jesus thus forces their hands (and hearts), compelling them to assess honestly their commitments at this trying time. Unlike in Matthew and Mark, however, the Twelve in Luke do not turn the searchlight inward, even in protest, "Surely not I, Lord?" (Matt 26:22//Mark 14:19). Rather, they suspect each other, "argu[ing]" (CEB) about "which one *of them* [αὐτῶν, *autōn*] it could be who would do this" (Luke 22:23). They are more given to hypocritical judgment of others than to internal self-examination. And like some Pharisees subject to the same hypocritical disposition, the apostles draw Jesus's denunciatory "Woe!" (22:22; cf. 11:37–52). Actually the "woe" falls on the most direct betrayer (Judas), but the fact that the other eleven also turn their backs on Jesus implicates them also. Though Jesus's arrest and execution are "determined" within the "horizon" (ὁρίζω, *horizō*) of God's plan (22:22)—the onus of personal guilt and responsibility remains on human perpetrators, particularly those religious leaders and disciples who should know better.

Completely callous to how Jesus's disclosure of a traitor might affect *him*, the apostles continue to show their true self-advancing, competitive colors by switching the topic from which one of them is most dangerous to which one is *greatest*, worthy of ruling the others (22:24)—the same issue, pathetically, they debated much earlier, after Jesus first predicted that the "Son of Humankind is going to be betrayed into human hands" (9:44). Clearly, they have made no progress. So Jesus tries again, this time aligning their lofty ambitions with oppressive worldly kingdoms, opposed to God's realm. The "kings of the Gentiles"—like Pharaoh of old and Caesar now—and their cronies crave highest honors and broadest powers over their subjects. Their good works on others' behalf boost their reputations as "benefactors" (εὐεργέται, *euergetai* [lit. "do-gooders"; 22:25]), an established "title of princes and other honored persons, especially those recognized for their civic contributions."[62] Names and titles carved on public buildings and monuments throughout the land bear imposing witness to such self-aggrandizing largesse.

But this is absolutely not the way of beneficent ministry Jesus embodies and advocates among his apostles: "*But you* [ὑμεῖς δέ, *hymeis de*] are not to be

62. BDAG, 405; see also Danker's rich studies of benefaction in Luke's world: 348, also *Benefactor* and *Luke*, 5–17.

like that" (22:26 NIV).[63] The problem, in Jesus's view, is not with the desire for greatness, but with its definition. By all means, be passionate about *true* greatness that leads and lords *from below*—from sympathetic identification with the "youngest" (νεώτερος, *neōteros*)—that is, the children, those most vulnerable and unable to reciprocate in society (cf. 9:46–48; 18:15–17)—and lowliest among us (22:26). In a word, authentic greatness in God's realm is about humble *service* (διακονία, *diakonia*) at table and other venues. In a more personalized word, culminating in Jesus's most revealing "I am" statement in Luke's Gospel: "I am among you as [the] *one who serves* [ὁ διακονῶν, *ho diakonōn*]" (22:27)—as he just marvelously illustrated at supper.

With the Twelve's glaring misapprehension of the core diaconal thrust of Jesus's mission in these final hours before his betrayal and death, one might forgive Jesus for writing this gang off as hopeless failures. If they still do not get what he's all about, when will they ever? But in fact, Jesus persists in believing in them, however untrustworthy they presently appear and however weak their faith in him may be.[64] In perhaps the most shocking statement Luke's Jesus makes about the Twelve, following his most revealing "I am" pronouncement, he says: "You are those who have stood by me in my trials" (22:28). Really now! He has just announced one of them will betray him and rebuked the whole group for their selfish preoccupations; and he's about to expose Simon Peter's impending public disavowals (22:34). The NRSV rendering "stood by me" may be a tad strong, as the verb (διαμένω, *diamenō*) denotes "continuing" or "remaining" with someone. But even so, its usage in a perfect (participle) form (διαμεμενηκότες, *diamemenēkotes*) reinforces a sense of past loyalty to Jesus sustained up to the present moment. The Twelve have stayed with and continue to support him. So Jesus claims—apparently by faith, since his apostles have shown and will show mixed fealty to him at best.

The "faith/trust" point is critical here, not as some kind of wishful fantasy or reverse psychology trick, but as the foundation of hope in God's restored realm. It is the *faith of Jesus in God* on behalf of his dozen delegates, who represent God's people, which sustains the vision of God's redemptive purpose through severe trials and failures. As God's beloved and trusted Son who trusts fully in his Father's love and power, Jesus may be trusted to see his

63. The NIV reflects the emphatic first position of the plural "you" subject in Greek.

64. On the relational and reciprocal aspects of faith/trust in the Greco-Roman world and the NT—including between authorities (like God and Jesus) and their subjects—see the important study of Teresa Morgan, *Roman Faith*. For example, in the NT "*pistis* . . . articulate[s] the tripartite relationship between God, Christ, and humanity, putting Christ in the centre of a nexus of faithfulness, trustworthiness, and trust which runs in all directions between God and Christ, Christ and humanity, and humanity and God" (281).

disciples through present and future crises to the ultimate realization of God's kingdom: "I confer on you, *just as my Father has conferred on me*, a kingdom, *so that* [ἵνα, *hina*] you may eat and drink at my table in my kingdom, and you will sit on thrones judging the twelve tribes of Israel" (22:29–30). Notably, the verb for "confer" (διατίθημι, *diatithēmi*) is cognate with the noun for "covenant" (διαθήκη, *diathēkē*) Jesus just used at the Last Supper (22:20; cf. Acts 3:25). As covenant initiator and renewer and co-regent of God's realm, Jesus guarantees the covenant's solidity and consummation with his outpoured blood, the supreme sign of sacrificial service and crucial criterion of righteous judgment.

Lest the Twelve bask too long, however, in their secure positions at the Messiah's banquet table and judicial court, Jesus again jerks them to fresh attention regarding their present struggles. This time he singles out Simon as the group's chief representative with a double-address and another "look!" interjection: "Simon, Simon, look!" (22:31 CEB). The imperative ἰδού (*idou*), with stronger visual than aural connotations ("look/see!" is better than NRSV's "listen!") echoes Jesus's use of the same term to expose the betrayer in 22:21. Now the stress falls on all the apostles' vulnerability to Satan's "sifting" trials, with special attention to Simon's crumbling under pressure before morning light, thrice denying he knows Jesus (22:31–34). Satan's "demanding/asking for" (ἐξαιτέομαι, *exaiteomai* [the only NT occurrence]) and being granted the right, presumably by God, "to sift all of you like wheat" recalls both Job's terrible testing ordeal, launched by Satan with God's permission (Job 1:6–12; 2:1–8), and John the Baptist's announcement of Jesus's ultimate judgment: "The shovel he uses to sift the wheat from the husks is in his hands. He will clean out his threshing area and bring the wheat into his barn. But he will burn the husk with a fire that can't be put out" (Luke 3:17 CEB).

This eerie alliance between God, Jesus, and Satan (at limited times), in sorting out the true characters of God's people through suffering, poses a major conundrum in the classic problem of evil. Why doesn't God "just say 'No!'" to Satan's demands to take a whack at God's servants? "Leave my people alone!" While the book of Job wrestles with this dilemma at some length, Luke's Jesus simply accepts the situation and devotes his energy to turning Satan's diabolical schemes into character-building and strengthening exercises. Jesus remains fully committed to his followers' faithful success through the same medium of dynamic *prayer* that has sustained and will see him through to the end: "I have prayed for you [Simon] that your own faith may not fail." But then, Jesus amazingly entrusts the restoration of the other apostles *to* Simon: "and you [Simon], when once you have turned back, strengthen your brothers" (22:32). Note well that Jesus knows that his beloved "Simon, Simon" (cf. "Martha, Martha" in her moment of distress [10:41]) will falter along with other followers.

He will initially prove shakier than "rock" solid (no "Peter" nickname here) and must be "converted back" (ἐπιστρέφω, *epistrephō*) to firm faith so he may then restore his brother-apostles. Trust between Jesus and his associates builds and buttresses over time in a network of partner relationships nurtured by habits of confession, forgiveness, and repentance, or, in a word: *conversion(s)*. Simon will indeed turn back to his solid Petrine place of leadership early in Acts, but it will not be the last "conversion" he experiences (see Acts 10:1–11:18; 15:6–11).[65]

Rather than taking solace in Jesus's announcement, however, Simon bristles at the insinuation that he would ever fail Jesus in the first place. So he trumpets, "Lord, I am ready to go with you to prison and to death!" (22:33). No doubt well-intentioned in his bravado, Simon nonetheless falls prey to a common psychological syndrome of "forward-looking myopia"—the tendency to underestimate the severity of a future trial and overestimate one's capacities to manage it. This pattern ties in with "willpower depletion."[66] Humans have a finite reservoir of willpower or self-control, progressively weakened under the stress of multiple decisions and, especially, choices to deny one's immediate pleasure. In the more controlled environment of, say, a cozy (Passover) meal with intimates, willpower claims tend to outstretch follow-through in more demanding situations, like being arrested by the police and arraigned before a judge (22:47–62).[67] Fully cognizant of this behavioral tendency, Jesus meets Peter's boast of undying loyalty with the bald facts of Peter's three denials before the morning rooster crows (22:34).

As Jesus's first "Look!" exclamation focused on Judas's betrayal, followed by the apostles' misguided dispute about kingdom greatness, his second "Look!" pointing to Simon's denials leads to the apostles' misunderstanding of kingdom provisions. Finally, a third "Look!"—this time directed to Jesus by the Twelve—caps off the Passover table talk.

Look! One of you will betray me (22:21–23).
  Apostles' conflict about their position (22:24–30)
Look! Simon, you will deny me (22:31–33).
  Apostles' confusion over their provision (22:34–36)
Look! Lord, here are two swords (22:38).

65. On conversion as a lifelong, transformative, and reformative "journey" in Luke's understanding, rather than a once-for-all, singular event, see the stimulating study of Green, *Conversion*. Specifically applied to Peter's "conversionary life" through Luke-Acts, see 88–99.

66. See DeSteno, *Truth*, 213–21; Gilbert, *Stumbling*, 18–25, 134–38, 192–97; Gilbert and Wilson, "Prospection"; Baumeister and Tierney, *Willpower*; McGonigal, *Willpower*.

67. A simple example playing off the meal-time setting: after a fully satisfying gourmet meal, announced plans to go on a strict yearlong diet are hardly to be trusted.

This threefold "Look!" (ἰδού, *idou*) scheme helps us understand the puzzling *sword* passage (22:35–38) as part of the apostles' asynchrony with Jesus's mission. Entwined in their woeful web of (1) betrayal and (2) denial is a viral strain of (3) violence (sword [μάκαιρα, *makaira*] = metonym for brutal death [Rom 8:36] or war [Gen 31:26 LXX]).[68]

Jesus continues to temper shocking disclosures with encouraging succor. After forecasting his associates' impending treachery and cowardice, he takes them back to better times of faithful service, advancing God's restorative realm through healings and exorcisms (Luke 22:35; 9:1–6; 10:1–12, 17–19). They carried out these earlier missions in difficult circumstances, without taking any money or extra provisions. They went out, per Jesus's instructions, entirely on faith, dependent on others' hospitality; and they *lacked for nothing*, as the apostles' now reaffirm without qualification (22:35). Sent out as "lambs into the midst of wolves" (10:3), they not only survived, but thrived, in mediating God's peaceable kingdom (10:5–6).

With this history of faithful, peaceful service to God and the afflicted in turbulent times, the apostles may reasonably hope for continued success and sustenance. But remember that past trust, though influential, is no airtight guarantee of future confidence in fresh crises. So Jesus, after reviewing his disciples' previous lessons, tests their faith in the current situation. Difficult hours and days keep coming—and intensifying. Like Isaiah's suffering servant, Jesus will soon unjustly be "counted among the lawless [ἀνόμων, *anomōn*]" (22:37/Isa 53:12), and his followers will also be enmeshed in this "lawless" age, where violent anarchy seems to prevail over God's gracious monarchy. So Jesus proposes a change of tactics, suggesting that his emissaries abandon their former (successful) barebones pacifist strategy and dip into their moneybags to buy swords! It is time for a Maccabean-style revolt or at least the "right to carry" arms for self-defense.

Not for the first time we respond to Jesus's Passover message with, "Really now?" He suddenly authorizes a military campaign to drive out the temple rulers (not just a few animal sellers), Roman overlords, or both from Jerusalem? To fight sword with sword (cf. 21:24)? Apart from the absurdity of his ragtag band becoming a well-oiled, swashbuckling fighting machine capable of defeating Roman legions, this new martial policy militates against everything Luke's Jesus has advocated, not least the manifesto to "love your enemies, do good, and lend, expecting nothing in return" (6:35). Of course, more desperate times might call for more desperate measures. But things have been pretty desperate throughout Jesus's ministry, and he has been under no illusions about how it all would end for him. Jesus's call to arms, then, contradicts his entire kingdom mission; and by explicitly recalling his apostles' prior *peaceful* victories over evil forces,

68. BDAG, 623.

armed with nothing more than God's saving word, he purposefully highlights the contradiction of sword armament. Since his confidants have shown tendencies toward violent reprisal (9:54–55) and have at least one "Zealot" among them (6:15), not to mention their persisting befuddlement over Jesus's cross-bearing way, he *tests* them with his sword talk to see if they have made any progress.

Sadly, they have not. They fail the test. They promptly and enthusiastically ("Look, Jesus!") take the bait and brandish two swords they have already procured and concealed (or so they think) from Jesus.[69] This is a pathetic response on two counts: one, a pair of daggers does not an army make, counting for virtually nothing against the Roman juggernaut or against a lawless mob; and two, it demonstrates how clueless the disciples remain about the nonviolent, benevolent thrust of God's reign. This is more than Jesus can bear. In the face of the apostles' persisting dullness at this critical juncture, the only response he can muster is "It is enough" (22:38). Again, we may detect a double meaning: on the one hand, a bit of ironic sarcasm—"Yeah, right, two swords will really get the job done, won't they!"; on the other, a frustrated brush off—"Enough of that!" (CEB). "No use talking about this anymore."

While this commentary chiefly aims to explicate Luke's final-form, narrative-theological message without sifting layers of tradition and redaction, I briefly engage here with a recent provocative historical hypothesis concerning Jesus's apocalyptic, zealot-style movement, culminating in his leading an *armed band* into Jerusalem. Dale Martin reconstructs the final events of Jesus's life around a militant, sword-wielding charge into the holy city with the intent of defeating Rome, displacing Jewish client-rulers, destroying the temple, and ushering in God's righteous kingdom.[70] Not being "crazy," however, as Martin puts it,[71] Jesus knew that he and his little gang could scarcely win the battle alone; hence, he anticipated joining forces with a mighty angelic host in the decisive apocalyptic battle, similar to that envisioned in the Qumran *War Scroll*. In effect, then, Jesus actually did summon his Father to send "twelve legions of angels" (see Matt 26:53), led by

69. Though it is possible that the disciples' swords are shorter, dagger-style weapons more easily concealed under clothing, the term μάχαιρα (*machaira*) typically denotes a larger battle sword, as in the Maccabean literature (1 Macc 3:12; 4:6; 10:85; 2 Macc 5:2) and, most significantly for our interests, in Luke 21:24 (cf. 22:49, 52; Acts 12:2; 16:27). Josephus (*Life* 293) distinguishes between the "sword" (μάχαιρα, *machaira*) he carries and the "daggers" (ξιφίδια, *xiphidia*) his pair of bodyguards hide under their garments. See the discussion in Dale B. Martin ("Response," 2–3), who also notes the much rarer usage of μάχαιρα (*machaira*) as "knife," particularly in a sacrificial setting, against the argument of Fredriksen ("Arms," 323–24), who suggests that, like many male Passover pilgrims, Jesus's disciples bore "sacrificial knives" for slaughtering the paschal lamb.

70. Dale B. Martin, "Jesus."

71. Dale B. Martin, "Jesus," 17.

either a heavenly Messiah or General Jesus Messiah. Of course, this plan failed miserably with Jesus's death and Jerusalem's (later) destruction, thus prompting an apologetic crisis among the Gospel writers. For his part in Martin's scheme, Luke covered up Jesus's failed apocalyptic military campaign by *disarming* him and concocting an antisword stance against his zealous followers, whose revolutionary ambitions, in any case, far outstripped their courage and capabilities.

Though Martin offers an intriguing proposal, it is not convincing. Apart from debates about who might and might not legally carry swords in ancient Roman cities or the likelihood of Jewish males "packing heat" for self-protection or other reasons at Passover,[72] and whether Luke is more pro- or anti-Roman or something in between, I do not think that Luke (or any other Evangelist), has fabricated Jesus's program of nonviolent protest in this age, whatever his expectations of final apocalyptic victory. Early on, Jesus forged his agenda around the radical call to "love your enemies" and eschew violent retaliatory responses (Luke 6:27–36; cf. Matt 5:38–48).[73] Because of its shocking, distinctive flavor (nonpareil in the OT or DSS), most historians regard Jesus's pacifist policy as authentic. In his final hours, he must contend with more hostile, Zealot-minded associates, anxious to draw enemy blood with their swords (see further Luke 22:49–51). But he does not contend with any personal bloodthirsty desires. He has no crisis of conscience concerning whether to launch a siege on Jerusalem, with or without angelic reinforcements. He comes in love, tough love to be sure, but he has certainly not come to fight. Quite the contrary, he has come to die, and *that* is what most churns his will and emotions, as the next scene vividly demonstrates. And it is *there* that he receives angelic aid—in the form of internal strength, not military force (22:43).

Jesus's Agony and Arrest on the Mount of Olives (22:39–53)

From the upper room in Jerusalem, Jesus returns again with his apostles to the Mount of Olives on the city's eastern edge (22:39), the site from which he made his emotional (weeping) entry (19:37–44) and to which he returns each evening for rest and reflection (21:37). Now, on his last evening of (prerisen) life, his emotions roil again, allowing him no rest (unlike his dozing disciples) (22:40–46). In fact, Jesus's night of anguished struggle over his fate will be interrupted by his arrest at the hands of the temple police, guided by Judas and led by the chief priests (22:47–53).

72. See the debate in *JSNT* with Dale B. Martin's "Jesus" by Fredriksen ("Arms") and Downing ("Dale Martin's Swords"), and then Martin's counterarguments ("Response").

73. See Downing, "Dale Martin's Swords," 33–34.

One line of thought, however, based in large measure on excising Jesus's "agony" on text-critical grounds or interpreting it in terms that are more virile than vulnerable (22:43–44), stresses Luke's aim to feature Jesus's "*absence* of emotions" in this scene, in contrast to Mark's presentation and in concert with Luke's presumed portrait of Jesus as a stoic, Maccabean-type martyr.[74] I continue, however, to challenge this dispassionate characterization of Luke's Jesus for various reasons, including but not solely dependent on accepting the "agony" text as authentic. Though this passage remains disputed, an impressive array of scholars favors its Lukan provenance, bolstered by reassessments of the manuscript evidence (highlighting early witnesses) and reaffirmations of its coherence with Luke's theology.[75]

My reading of Jesus's prayer and arrest on the Mount of Olives as an "emotional episode"[76] takes into account the centrality of emotions to human experience, emphasized by a spate of fresh research across the humanities and sciences in recent decades.[77] Busting down the long-standing barrier between cool reason and hot passion in Western thought, this research demonstrates the tight integration of emotions with physical feelings, cognitive appraisals, motivated (re)actions, social relations, and value concerns: in short, the total, holistic expression of sensation-thought-will-action networked in the brain and worked out *in* the entire body and *between* other embodied persons and the environment.[78]

74. Neyrey, "Absence" and *Passion*, 49–65 (cf. n. 6 above in this segment on Luke 19:45–24:53). Neyrey accepts the authenticity of the "agony" text but argues for its athletic interpretation (see below).

75. See, e.g., Brown, *Death*, 1:184–90; Green, "Jesus," 35–37; Tuckett, "Luke 22,43–44." Clivaz ("Angel," 425–32) plausibly proposes that one of the earliest witnesses lacking the "agony" passage—the early-third-century P69 from Oxyrhynchus, Egypt—represents a *deliberate omission* by gnostic-oriented Marcionite scribes.

76. See Price, *Emotion*, 25–27, 38.

77. See Spencer, "Getting a Feel," and, applied to biblical literature, Spencer, *Mixed Feelings*, a volume of interdisciplinary essays.

78. See Spencer, "Why Did the 'Leper'?," 110–18, and "Getting a Feel." For a recent theory of mind that emphasizes both "in and between" aspects, see Siegel, *Mind*; e.g.: "By *mind*, I mean all that relates to our subjective felt experience of being alive, from feelings to thoughts, from intellectual ideas to inner sensory immersions before and beneath words, to our felt connections to other people and our planet" (1 [emphasis original]). "The mind is within us—within the whole body—and between us. It is within our connections to one another, and even to our larger environment, our planet" (14). See further the incisive capsule of multiplex human experience provided by the noted Lukan scholar Green (*Conversion*), deeply informed by cognitive science and neurobiology: "If what makes us singularly human are the properties and capacities that have the complex human brain as their anatomical basis, then there can be no formation or transformation that is not fully embodied. To push further, if the neurobiological systems that shape how we think, feel, believe, and behave are continuously sculpted in the context of our social experiences, then in a profound sense we can speak of personal formation and reformation only in relational terms; that is, our autobiographical selves are formed within a nest of relationships, a community" (123–24n1).

The following chart correlates elements of this integrated system with experiences of Jesus and his disciples just before and during Jesus's arrest, triggered by three core emotions: (1) Jesus's "*anguish* [ἀγωνίᾳ, *agōnia*]" (22:44); (2) the disciples' "*grief* [λύπη, *lypē*]" (22:45); and (3) Jesus's *frustration* with various parties, implied in his verbal responses to their actions (22:46–53).

Emotion	Physical feeling	Cognitive appraisal	Motivated (re)action	Social relation	Value concern
Jesus's *anguish*	Intense sweat	Awareness of imminent death	Conflict of wills between Jesus and his Father	Jesus and his Father	Life
The Eleven's *grief*	Sleepiness	Loss of: Beloved leader, Messianic dreams, Future purpose, Honor	Sleep	Jesus and his apostles	Messianic hope; honor status
Jesus's *frustration* with:					
The Eleven	Sleepiness	Linking sleep with weakness	Jesus teaches the Eleven	Jesus and apostles	Endurance
Judas	Kiss	Hypocrisy of kiss	Jesus pulls back from kiss	Jesus and betrayer	Loyalty
The Eleven	One cuts off ear of enemy	Jesus opposes swordplay	Jesus heals cut ear	Jesus, Eleven, and enemies	Mercy
Arrest party	Laying on hands (by police)	Awareness of "dark hour"	Jesus submits to arrest	Jesus and enemies	Justice

Taking each focal emotion in turn, consider first Jesus's *anguish*. Burdened by his impending death and bereft of his friends' support, Jesus nonetheless takes the Eleven (Judas has slipped away) to pray with him on the Mount of Olives. Displaying an unreciprocated concern for their welfare, Jesus exhorts the Eleven, "Pray that you may not come into the time of trial" (22:40), echoing the last petition in the Lord's Prayer (11:4). Jesus wants his disciples to be as close to God and as far from trouble as possible in these dire hours. But he's also worried about himself, all the more so in his increasing state of aloneness. In a dramatic picture of this isolation, he in fact does not pray *with* his apostles, but rather "withdrew from them about a stone's throw" (22:41) to commune privately with his Father. This "stone's throw" measure (only in Luke) not only accentuates Jesus's distance from his associates (one can throw a stone a long way), but also intimates his distress over the temple and city's devastating fate ("all [stones] will be thrown down" [21:6; cf. 19:44; 20:17–18]). The weight of the world crashes down on Jesus's body and spirit—and he's not sure he can take it. Hence he himself prays for escape from trial, as he just encouraged the apostles to do (22:40) along the lines of the model prayer he taught and exemplified (it is *his* prayer, after all): "Father, if you are willing [βούλει, *boulei*], remove this cup [of suffering and death] from me" (22:42).[79] In other words: "Father, lead me not into this terrible trial" (cf. 11:4).

Though Jesus clearly expresses some aversion to crucifixion, many interpreters, as noted above, have questioned the intensity of Jesus's struggle and apparent resistance to God's will or purpose (βούλομαι/βουλή, *boulomai/boulē*), especially in Luke.[80] In this view, Jesus more clarifies and confirms the plan rather than chafes against it. Luke does not follow Mark's prefacing Jesus's prayer with a report that he "began to be distressed and agitated," confirmed by Jesus's own confession: "I am deeply grieved, even to death" (Mark 14:33–34). Luke's mention of Jesus's anguish/agony only comes *after* an angel *strengthens* him and he prays "more earnestly" (Luke 22:43–44); and in any case, the Greek notion of ἀγωνία (*agōnia*, related to ἀγών [*agōn*]) more connoted masculine,

79. The Greek construction underlying "If you are willing"—εἰ βούλει (*ei boulei*)—marks a first-class condition (εἰ [*ei*] + present indicative), which assumes the reality of the condition for the sake of the argument. In the present context it might push the meaning toward "*Since* you are willing," though this judgment is contextual, not strictly grammatical. See the discussion in Wallace, *Greek Grammar*, 689–84.

80. Kevin Madigan ("Ancient") provides a superb analysis of the tortured reception history of Jesus's Gethsemane crisis, noting that "it was a plague and embarrassment to patristic and medieval interpreters. Few narratives in the New Testament were so inimical to received christological assumptions" (157). Madigan focuses, however, on ameliorating interpretations of Matthew's and Mark's stark reports of the incident, arguing that Luke in fact kicks off the revisionist strategy: "In the hands of Luke, the grieving and fearful Jesus is transformed into a Socratic figure of equanimity and poise in the face of death, one whose soul not even the most appalling suffering can vex" (161). Such a narrow, heroic Socratic reading of Luke is precisely what I challenge. On βουλή τοῦ θεοῦ (*boulē tou theou*), "God's purpose" (Luke 7:30; Acts 2:23; 4:28; 5:38; 13:36; 20:27), as marking the "unifying purpose" driving Luke's two-volume narrative, see Tannehill, *Narrative Unity*, 1:21.

muscular martial or athletic vigor than emotional pain and weakness. Far from reflecting a psychic meltdown, Jesus's blood-like *sweat* (not tears!) evidences blood- (and adrenaline-) pumping energy for combat or competition. It's the stuff of staunch religious martyrs like Eleazar in the Maccabean era, who "steered the ship of religion over the sea of the emotions . . . setting his mind firm like a jutting cliff . . . [breaking] the maddening waves of the emotions" and modeled an indomitable commitment to God's law, "shield[ing] it with [his] own *blood and noble sweat* in sufferings even to death" (4 Macc 7:1–8; cf. 6:11);[81] or like the apostle Paul, who "fought [ἠγώνισμαι, *ēgōnismai*] the good fight [ἀγῶνα, *agōna*]" to the end (2 Tim 4:7; cf. 1 Tim 6:12). Nothing mushy or gushy here, as Luke's Jesus faces his terrible fate "like a man," like a heroic warrior or gladiator, in full control of his physical and mental faculties.[82]

While this rational, masculine, self-controlled dimension of the agonistic Jesus captures part of his experience, as with most rigid binaries (reason/emotion, male/female, equanimity/ hysteria), the picture is skewed. Luke's Jesus is certainly not irrational, gender-confused, or panic-stricken. But neither is he a paragon of pure Stoic placidity. As Claire Clivaz astutely comments: "For most readers in antiquity, Jesus's demand that the cup pass from him was the most shocking element in the Gethsemane story. Ancient readers expected that an individual confronting death should make a noble speech, or at least maintain a dignified silence that could be interpreted as proof of that individual's sensibility."[83] Luke's Jesus, like Matthew's and Mark's, lodges a desperate plea, an agonizing supplication—not a noble oration.

In Hellenistic Greek, ἀγωνία (*agōnia*) suggests intense inner turmoil as much as outer conflict, "a state of great mental and emotional grief and anxiety—'anguish, intense sorrow.'"[84] Even the Maccabean literature that so valorizes impassible courage attests to this emotional distress, albeit among the people and priests of Jerusalem, not the martyrs and freedom fighters. When the Greek-Syrian officer Heliodorus set about to plunder the temple treasury,

> There was no little distress [ἀγωνία, *agōnia*] through the whole city. The priests prostrated themselves before the altar . . . and called toward heaven. . . . To see the appearance of the high priest was to be wounded at heart, for his face and the change in his color disclosed the anguish of his

81. Adducing these and other references in support of his "*agonia*-as-combat" argument, see Neyrey, *Passion*, 63–65.

82. On the dominant theme of masculine self-control and emotional regulation in 4 Maccabees, see Moore and Anderson, "Taking It like a Man."

83. Clivaz, "Angel," 428–29.

84. Louw and Nida, *Greek-English Lexicon*, 1:319.

> soul [ψυχὴν ἀγωνίαν, *psychēn agōnian*]. For terror and bodily trembling had come over the man, which plainly showed to those who looked at him the pain lodged in his heart. People also hurried out of their houses in crowds to make a general supplication. . . . Women, girded with sackcloth under their breasts, thronged the streets. Some of the young women . . . ran together to the gates, and some to the walls, while others peered out of the windows. And holding up their hands to heaven, they all made supplication. (2 Macc 3:14–20)

The author then summarily derides all of these histrionics: "There was something pitiable in the prostration of the whole populace and the anxiety of the high priest in his great anguish" (2 Macc 3:21). Real men and real leaders of God's people wouldn't be caught dead in such pathetic "agony," choosing rather to fight God's enemies and die bravely, if need be.[85]

But "pitiable" though it may be, such expression of emotional anguish is very natural, very human, and very Jesus. With priests and populace—women and men—in Israel's history, Luke's Jesus pours out his heart to God, kneeling down in intense ("more earnestly"), soul-wrenching, pore-draining[86] supplication for relief from pain and suffering.[87] He candidly pleads for another way to accomplish God's will, a way out of death, not because of weak-kneed preference for ease and comfort, but because of strong-willed commitment to *life*.

85. Ἀγωνία (*agōnia*) is never attributed to the Maccabean fighters and martyrs, though ἀγών/ἀγωνίζομαι (*agōn/agōnizomai*) frequently applies to their engagement in competitive, heroic battle.

86. Michael Pope ("Downward Motion") argues persuasively that the flow of Jesus's sweat indicated by the participle καταβαίνοντες (*katabainontes*) in 22:44 more accurately denotes a "coursing/streaming down" of perspiration along the surface of the skin in a "gradual descent" to the ground rather than a "falling down" (in most English versions) of sweat drops in a "gravitational free fall" (261, 265–66). Though providing a more physiologically correct picture, however, Pope's interpretive corollary squeezes the image too tightly. In his view, Jesus's flow of sweat in a "measured," "more restrained and gradual rate" comports with his calm kneeling down (*not* "throwing himself down" as in Mark 14:35) to depict him "not as overwhelmed but as composed," thoroughly self-controlled (265–66, 280). But "kneeling" (lit. "placing [down] his knees" [θεὶς τὰ γόνατα, *theis ta gonata*]) in Luke 22:41 tells us nothing about the force of the action (we might easily assume "dropping/falling" to his knees), and in any case, praying "more earnestly" in a kneeling (though not prostrate) posture in a lather of sweat, whatever its precise "downward motion," hardly suggests a placid response to the crisis at hand.

87. On Jesus's "unmanly" emotional response here, see the excellent excursus in Wilson, *Unmanly Men*, 219–22. But Wilson also notes the important link between Jesus's "more fervent/earnest" (ἐκτενέστερον, *ektenesteron*), anguished praying in Luke 22:44 and other occasions of people, men and women, crying out to God "fervently" (ἐκτενῶς, *ektenōs*) in times of crisis in the LXX and NT (Joel 1:14; Jonah 3:8; Jdt 4:12; 3 Macc 5:9; Acts 12:5).

His entire being and behavior—his body, will, thoughts, feelings, words, and deeds—have all been in the service of a *life mission*, of restoring and enhancing others' lives. This core value is motivated by the complex emotion of love for God, the Source of all life, "with all your heart, and with all your soul, and with all your strength, and with all your mind"; and love for "your neighbor *as yourself*." Follow this path, "and you *will live*" (Luke 10:27–28; Deut 6:5; Lev 19:18).

Luke's Jesus has not simply taught this philosophy of life but has lived it himself—including the part about healthy *self-love*. Deep, grateful love for *his own life* generated by his Father, the Spirit, and Mary has driven his life-saving vocation. While Jesus also knows at gut-level that fresh life bursts from death, that saving one's own and others' lives proceeds from self-giving and self-losing (9:23–25), he never perverts this paradox into masochistic lust for personal pain or martyr glory. When it comes down to the eleventh hour, to the imminent culmination of his "suffering" or "passion" (πάσχω, *paschō*),[88] his passion for life boils over in agonizing resistance to death. His fervent will for life collides with his Father's present will for his Son's death, a clash all the more distressing because of God's very nature of eternal life and love. This is no small struggle within the united heart of the divine Son and Father. It is gut-wrenching, unimaginably *agonizing*. And Luke makes no attempt to chronicle the debate, reporting no response at all from Jesus's Father. God remains eerily silent. Jesus simply expresses his ultimate submission to God's will against his own: "Not my will but yours be done"; the cup of poison must still be drunk (22:42). But though Jesus finally agrees with God's purpose, he does not do so tranquilly. He keeps "praying through," as the expression goes, this ordeal—sweating, wrestling, agitating in prayer.

Though Jesus's Father does not speak or appear at Olivet, as at the baptism and transfiguration sites (3:21–22; 9:34–35), an "angel from heaven" comes to "give him strength" (ἐνισχύω, *enischyō* [22:43]). So Jesus is not without divine aid. But this angel brandishes no sword (cf. Josh 5:13–15) and betokens no angelic army to wage apocalyptic war. Rather, this divine agent supplies internal strength that Jesus *needs* in his time of turmoil. As Green has persuasively argued, this nurturing represents part of "a great mural in which Jesus is pictured as the Servant of the Lord," particularly as depicted in Isaiah.[89] For example, in addressing the exiled nation as collective Servant, the Lord says: "You are my servant; I have chosen you and not forsaken you; do not fear, for I am with you

88. William V. Harris (*Restraining Rage*) notes that by the fourth century BCE πάσχω (*paschō*), "the principal verb for suffering . . . came to include the specialized meaning of 'experience emotionally', while in the same period the noun *pathos* came to mean 'passion' or 'emotion'" (342).

89. Green, "Jesus," 42.

. . . for I am your God who has *strengthened* [ἐνισχύσας, *enischysas*] you, and I have helped you, and I have made you secure with my righteous right hand" (Isa 41:9–10 NETS); and again: "I, the Lord God, have called you in righteousness, and I will take hold of your hand and *strengthen* [ἐνισχύσω, *enischysō*] you" (42:6 NETS). God's beloved Son Jesus, who embodies all the hopes and dreams of God's chosen corporate "son" Israel, is not spared the pain and agony of God's people in this "lawless" age; but he is divinely strengthened to bear this suffering on their behalf (cf. Isa 53:3–8, 11–12; Luke 22:37; Acts 8:32–35).

And what about Jesus's chosen apostles? After probing Jesus's anguish, we consider, second, the emotion of *grief* that overcomes the Eleven and induces their minds and bodies into anesthetic sleep (22:45). They cannot even bear the consciousness of prayer. Only Luke describes the disciples' emotional state in this scene. Since the "grief" term Luke uses (λύπη, *lypē*) is cognate with the grieving language Mark and Matthew employ for *Jesus's* emotions (λυπέω/περίλυπος, *lypeō/perilypos* [Mark 14:34//Matt 26:37, 38]), scholars who argue for a more stalwart portrait often claim that Luke has deliberately transferred Jesus's grief to the apostles, already known to be weak. But as we have seen, Jesus's "anguish" or "agony" conveys considerable angst similar in emotional tenor to "grief" or "despair." By the same token, classics scholar William Harris places λύπ- (*lyp*-) words among various ancient "Greek terms which can border on meaning depression" and cover an experiential range from "physical pain . . . to psychological distress."[90] While the grief of the Eleven has a deep analgesic physical effect (sleep), the pain is primarily psychosocial. But Luke again stints on details, leaving us guessing what the disciples are grieving about. Cognitive appraisals can be difficult to sort out in the throes of grief, but on reflection, they typically focus on the *loss* of a cherished person or purpose. Again, though certainty eludes us, it is not hard to imagine the apostles' swirling sense of loss over (1) their beloved Lord's life, (2) his—and their—messianic dreams, (3) their broader future (what are they going to do now?), and (4) their honor.

Of course Jesus has not died yet, but it seems that the ominous demise he has long predicted and recently dramatized at the Last Supper finally begins dawning on his disciples. They start to realize the terminal diagnosis and commence the grieving process, likely with repressive denial pushing toward depression that cannot bear contemplation and expression; hence they succumb to the stupor of sleep.[91] Apart from anticipating the loss of their beloved

90. William V. Harris, *Restraining Rage*, 17, 342.

91. I admit to pushing the psychological analysis of the disciples here along the lines of the five stages of grief (denial, anger, bargaining, depression, acceptance) in the classic (though modern) work of Kübler-Ross, *On Death*. I use her scheme as a suggestive framework, not a straitjacket.

Teacher and Lord, the apostles also face the death of the messianic hope they pinned on Jesus to secure their and all Israel's future. It would be hard to overestimate the nuclear emotional force of this hope (cf. 24:21) within a corps of poor Galileans, suffering under Roman rule, who had left everything to follow Jesus. Such dashed hope cannot help but trigger intense psychophysical pain and distress (λύπη, *lypē*).

Perhaps the apostles' present grief is most sharply *self*-directed at their loss of *honor*. Another classics scholar, David Konstan, who otherwise downplays grief's cognitive, motivational, and social dimensions in the ancient Greek world, grants an exceptional case: "Of course, loss can be the consequence of an action, as where someone, through deliberate aggression or culpable negligence, brings about the death of another (along with damage to one's public self or reputation)."[92] Even here, Konstan focuses on "someone" *else* who causes our loved one's death, thus indirectly provoking our grief; as for what we feel toward the murderous party, our primary emotion inclines more to anger than grief (though these sentiments can easily intertwine). But lovers can also turn against their loved ones—through betrayal, denial, or desertion—for various reasons, frequently impulsive and, afterward, regrettable. Perhaps, then, we should understand the apostles' emotional state as a cocktail of anger and grief toward Jesus, on the one hand, who seems to be surrendering and letting them down, but also on the other hand, toward *themselves* as they confront their personal shame and guilt.

At supper, Jesus shockingly exposed their treachery and fickleness. The traitor Judas has since slipped away from the group. The denier Peter doth protest so much that he seems to betray underlying self-doubt about his readiness to join Jesus in prison and death (22:33); and we can only imagine the surging qualms and fears of the other ten. A creeping panic concerning *honor*—a core emotional and social value in antiquity, especially among men—no doubt sets in.[93] The disciples' blame in abetting Jesus's demise and threatening his whole movement would seal their shame, their loss of face, shrouded in grief. Also, however, as their grief pushes past initial repression (denial) to more abject humiliation, it would prompt them to begin facing up to their shortcomings, a necessary step to true repentance.[94]

92. Konstan, *Emotions*, 248 (cf. 244–58). As it happens, Aristotle has no entry for "grief" among his catalog of emotions discussed in his *Rhetoric*. For a remarkably personal as well as philosophically sophisticated (including interaction with Greco-Roman philosophy) treatment of grief, with special focus on its cognitive-affective dimensions, see Nussbaum, *Upheavals*, 19–88.

93. See Malina, *New Testament World*, 27–57; Malina and Neyrey, "Honor and Shame"; deSilva, *Honor*, 23–93, and *Hope*.

94. See Brueggemann (*Reality*), expounding the "three urgent prophetic tasks" enjoined by

The third emotional strain in the Olivet incident features Jesus's *frustration* with various agents, implied in his verbal responses to the deficient actions of others. Eschewing simple objections, Jesus launches a rhetorical tour de force charged with interrogative, declarative, imperative, and exclamatory challenges, laced with tinges of his own bewilderment with unfolding events, even as he expects them. Knowing that his apostles and the temple authorities will prove untrustworthy does not diminish Jesus's frustration and disappointment with them. Emotion drives cognition, passion stimulates perception, as much as the other way around.[95] Notice Jesus's four-pronged polemic:

1. *To the Eleven*: "Why are you sleeping? Get up and pray that you may not come into the time of trial" (22:46). Jesus does not rebuke his associates' emotion of grief, but rather their action-response of sleep to quell their despair. But they cannot sleep off the problem. Instead, they must *pray through* it, even to escape it if possible, as Jesus had advised them to pray (22:40; cf. 11:4), but not in naive optimism. For Luke, as typical of biblical spirituality, prayer is not dreamy wishful thinking, but a passionate engagement with God about the realities of life, ensuring that God's people not "come into the time of trial" unaware and unprepared, if and when that time comes. It is also the bedrock of *communal strengthening*, praying *for and with* one another for persevering power and deliverance (cf. 11:1–13; Acts 2:42; 4:23–31; 12:12). As frustrated as Jesus is for the disciples' sake, he also implicitly bemoans their lack of supporting *his* prayerful struggle with God at this woeful hour.[96]

2. *To Judas*: "Is it with a kiss that you are betraying the Son of Humankind?" (22:48). Calling Judas out by single name (not the gentler double-address with Martha [10:41] and Simon [22:31])[97] as he "approached Jesus to kiss him" (22:47) and hand him over to the arrest squad he has brought to the Olivet

---

the biblical prophets in the maelstrom of national disaster: "(1) the assertion of critical *reality* in the face of an ideology of chosenness, (2) voiced *grief* in the face of denial, and (3) buoyant *hope* as a counter to despair" (2 [emphasis added]).

95. See Seigworth and Gregg, "Inventory," 2–3: "Affect and cognition are never fully separable—if for no other reason than that thought is itself a body, embodied." Cf. Kotrosits, *Rethinking*, 3: "Thinking and feeling are hopelessly interwoven experiences. . . . My choice of the word 'sense' [as in 'making sense'] . . . implies both cognition and emotion."

96. Admittedly, Luke compresses Matthew's and Mark's threefold encounter with sleepy disciples; and only Matt 26:40 stresses (in the second exchange), "Could you not stay awake *with me* one hour?" No doubt Jesus's curt command in Luke 22:46, "Stand, pray" (AT—no "and" in Greek—ἀναστάντες προσεύχεσθε [*anastantes proseuchesthe*) implies "pray *with me as I have prayed*"; but lamentably, Jesus remains bereft of the disciples' support, as the time for prayer is "suddenly" preempted by the arrest party's arrival (22:47).

97. As Brown (*Death*, 1:259) notes, this marks the only occasion in the Gospel tradition where Jesus addresses Judas by name.

camp, Jesus rebuffs the intended kiss with a sarcastic question. We may also envision some accompanying physical reaction, like pulling his cheek away or turning his head as he speaks. In any case, as Jesus sees his betrayer coming in for a kiss, he edgily laments the travesty of this customary affectionate gesture. "Are you actually marking and selling me out to the authorities *with a kiss*, like ones we have regularly exchanged in warm greeting throughout this discipleship journey?" Rather than heartfelt love kisses, with which the woman lavished Jesus's feet (7:38, 45) and the father doused the returning prodigal's face (15:20), Judas's (attempted) kiss signifies treachery, which Jesus cannot help but *feel* on an emotional level.[98] Whatever other feelings may flood Jesus at this dark moment, certainly frustration and disappointment with Judas are among them.

3. *To the Eleven*: "No more of this!" (22:51). If the other apostles are not fully awake when Jesus stirs them, they come to full alert when Judas arrives with the temple police. But that doesn't mean they are spiritually attuned to the situation, as they immediately revert back to misapprehending Jesus's (anti-)sword policy (cf. 22:35–38). "Lord, should we strike [now] with the sword?" they plead (22:49). Without waiting for an answer from commander-in-chief Jesus, one of them springs into action and slices off the right ear of the high priest's slave-soldier (22:50).[99] In turn, before this escalates into a massacre of him and the Eleven, Jesus defuses the situation with a curt rebuke of his apostles and miraculous cure of the slave. The statement, "No more of this! [ἐᾶτε ἕως τούτου, *eate heōs toutou*]" (22:51), according to Louw and Nida, represents "an idiom, literally 'to leave off until,' to cease from what one is doing, with the implication of strong admonition— 'stop, quit, cease' . . . 'stop this.'"[100] It may also imply another derisive rhetorical question: "You're allowing [ἐᾶτε, *eate*] this violence after all I've said and shown to the contrary? You're going this far [ἕως τούτου, *heōs toutou*] with your misguided zeal?" Jesus's therapeutic action involves physical feeling—healing touch of the damaged ear—and perhaps implied compassion, too (cf. 7:13–14). In any event, it demonstrates Jesus's loving response to an enemy.

This latter rhetorical reading allows for more common meanings of ἐάω, *eaō* ("permit, allow") and ἕως, *heōs* ("until, as far as"), though still with a sardonic, critical force. David Matson follows this linguistic line ("permit until this"), but in a more straightforward sense of permitting God's will for Jesus's

98. See Spencer, *Dancing Girls*, 126–29.

99. The term ὠτίον (*ōtion*), the diminutive of οὖς (*ous*), can mean "outer ear," "earlet" (part of the ear, perhaps the lobe). Danker comments that "this rhetorical touch adds a note of pathos to the scene" (357). I suggest it also adds another dash of sarcasm: apart from having a pathetic arsenal of only two swords, the disciples are not very good at using them, managing only to nick a little portion of the enemy's ear—more annoyance than attack.

100. Louw and Nida, *Greek-English Lexicon*, 1:659 (punctuation adjusted).

death to ensue without obstruction ("allow the arrest to continue") and less an undertone of prohibiting the disciples' violent strategy as the primary target of Jesus's response. In this view, Luke's Jesus advocates more "divine determinacy" than principled pacifism; likewise, his healing the soldier's severed ear at this juncture reflects his calm "control of the situation" more than his love of enemies.[101] Although I grant the "necessity" (δεῖ, *dei*) of Jesus's death as constitutive of God's plan in Luke and Acts and can see "let this plan proceed" as part of the overall thrust of the arrest scene, I do not see this perspective prevailing over or substituting for Jesus's dramatic "love your enemy" demonstration (culminating in his "Father forgive them" plea on the cross in 23:34 [see discussion below]) or his sarcastic rebuke of his disciples' pathetic militaristic crusade ("It is enough!" in 22:38 and "No more of this!" or "Is this the violent way you're still allowing [pushing]?" in 22:51 strike similar mocking tones). Coming off his intense struggle with the divine will and his followers' persisting obtuseness, Jesus maintains a critical edge, even as he accepts his cross-bound fate.

4. *To the arrest party*: "Have you come out with swords and clubs as if I were a bandit? When I was with you day after day in the temple, you did not lay hands on me. But this is your hour, and the power of darkness!" (22:52–53). The grim "hour" has struck; the die is cast. No turning back now. As predicted, the Lord's servant Jesus is numbered among the lawless ones, specifically treated here as a "bandit" or political rebel (λῃστής, *lēstēs*) corralled by a sword- and club-wielding posse. Jesus peacefully surrenders, but not before getting in one last verbal-emotional jab. How sad and disappointing that his arresters—led by the "chief priests, the officers of the temple police, and the elders" (Judas is just their pawn) (22:52)—so misuse their religious authority to subdue him with "swords and clubs," though he carries no weapons, condemns his followers for doing so, and cleans up their bloody mistakes (healing the slave's ear). The supposed custodians of God's people and house match peace with violence. That is how bad it has gotten. And they are slinking around on secret nocturnal missions to boot, too afraid of the people's resistance to seize Jesus in the light of day in the temple. So much for genuine concern for the people's welfare. So much for religious "power" when it aligns with "darkness" (22:53).

Peter's Denials in the High Priest's Courtyard (22:54–62)

The arrested Jesus is brought directly for interrogation to the high priest's official "house" (more like a palace) by the temple police. Apparently content to nab the

101. Matson, "Pacifist?," 165–68.

ringleader Jesus, they let his eleven deputies go. Peter, however, chooses to tag along, but at a safe physical "distance" (μακρόθεν, *makrothen*) that soon betokens the social and spiritual separation from Jesus that Peter adamantly invokes (22:54).[102] In the flow of the narrative, Peter goes on trial before Jesus does.

Along with the "distance" factor, Luke accentuates the spatial-perceptual setting in which Peter finds himself: "in the middle [μέσῳ, mesō] of the courtyard" (outside the main structure where Jesus is being held), "seated together in the middle [μέσος, mesos] of them" (among the high priest's servant staff and lower-ranking policemen; 22:55 AT). The group has gathered near a lit fire in the courtyard on a dark and chilly night. The stage is ominously set for Peter's performance, which exposes in piercing firelight whom he's really with, what and whom he really knows, how he sees the present crisis, and whether he's ready to stand up and apart from the crowd or simply blend in the middle. Of course, Jesus has already scripted Peter's lying lines, and Peter plays his part right to form. Three people in the courtyard company—one a slave-girl and two nondescript men—put Peter on the spot, eying and fingering him as one of Jesus's associates. The slave-girl "stared [ἀτενίσασα, *atenisasa*]"[103] at him in deep suspicion before revealing his affiliation with Jesus; the first man then "sees [ἰδών, *idōn*]" Peter and makes the same accusation. Under the spotlight of blazing fire and boring eyes, Peter crumbles, falsely and vociferously denying all knowledge of Jesus three times over, during more than an hour of elapsed time (he has time to think about it, yet sticks to his story).

- "Woman, I do not know [οὐκ οἶδα, *ouk oida*] him" (22:57).
- "Man, I am not [οὐκ εἰμί, *ouk eimi*] [one of them]" (22:58).
- "Man, I do not know [οὐκ οἶδα, *ouk oida*] what you are talking about [claiming that I am a Galilean with Jesus]" (22:60).

As customary in Greek, the "not" term precedes the verb. In Peter's initial denial, it is the first word he says (delaying the vocative address until the end), as if to emphasize: "Not, no way [Οὐκ, *Ouk*]! I do not know him, woman."

102. The same "far away/off" position of the callous rich man in Hades without recourse (16:23) and of the sinful tax collector in the temple, who, however, is reconciled to God (18:13–14). Which way will Peter ultimately go?

103. Ἀτενίζω (*atenizō*) is a favorite Lukan word, marking intense eye-locking, attention-fixing encounters at strategic moments in the two-volume narrative, including the Nazareth synagogue audience's fixing on Jesus's pivotal interpretation of the Isaiah reading (4:20) and Peter's determined gaze on the lame beggar by the temple gate in preparation for healing him in Jesus's name (Acts 3:4; cf. 1:10; 3:12; 6:15; 7:55; 10:4; 11:6; 13:9; 14:9; 23:1). Now, in the high priest's courtyard, however, Peter himself is put on the spot by the slave girl, who exposes his weakness.

Peter's self-control and willpower, already taxed to the limit, are completely shot. However much he may want to make good on his earlier promise to stick by Jesus (22:33), he lacks the inner fortitude to hold on, as well as sufficient attunement to the Spirit's strength- and wisdom-giving resources (cf. 12:11–12; 21:14–19; Acts 6:10). To put Paul's words in Peter's mouth: "I do not do the good I want, but the evil I do not want is what I do [and say]" (Rom 7:19). But in Luke's story, it is *Jesus's words* that Peter "remembered" (Luke 22:61).[104] Having repressed Jesus's forecast of Peter's disavowals, this haunting memory now erupts into painful consciousness, triggered by the vocal rooster crow Jesus predicted and the visual laser look Jesus now "turns" and gives him (Luke 22:60–61). This withering "look" (ἐμβλέπω, *emblepō* [intensified verb form]) Jesus shoots his leading apostle at this critical "turning [στραφείς, *strapheis*] point"[105] matches the gaze he fired at the temple authorities after they objected to his parable targeting their rejection of God's Son (20:17).

Only Luke reports Jesus's optical response to Peter's denials. However brief and awkward this reaction might be (how precisely does Jesus inside the high priest's house overhear and lock eyes with Peter out in the courtyard?), it makes for an emotionally wrenching encounter. Though Luke does not spell out the nuances of Jesus's "ocular agency" in this scene, "extramitting" his inner passions to piercing effect (and affect),[106] we may surmise a complex mix of more frustration and disappointment with a measure of sympathy and reassurance (Jesus knew this was coming, and he had already prayed for Peter's restoration [22:31–33]). But whatever the case with Jesus, we know exactly how Peter feels. Upon remembering his Lord's words and meeting his eyes, Peter's dam bursts: "He went out and wept bitterly" (22:62).

Suffering the Authorities' Mock Trials and Death Verdict (22:63–23:49)

The authorities' "hour" and "power of darkness" (22:53) over Jesus actually spans several hours, from the day's dawning (22:66) to three o'clock in the

104. Earlier this same evening, Jesus exhorted his followers to reenact his bread-breaking Last Supper "in remembrance of me," specifically remembering his broken body (22:19). In a tragic-ironic twist, Peter first "remembers" Jesus's forecast of Peter's betrayal (22:34), which signals his passive-aggressive participation in Jesus's death.

105. See discussion/chart above concerning seven key "turning points" in the commentary on 14:24–35 (p. 374).

106. On "ocular agency," see Wilson, "Sight," 152; on "extramission," see Allison, "Eye Is the Lamp" (cf. discussion above on 11:34–36).

afternoon (23:44). The events of these hours move briskly, however, in Luke's narrative and culminate in an anomalous and apocalyptic period of darkness "over the whole land" from noon to three, as Jesus dies on the cross (23:44). A dark time, indeed.

After Peter's ignominious exit, Jesus undergoes his trials and crucifixion alone. Some sympathetic parties do appear at his execution, including some mourning "daughters of Jerusalem" (23:27–28) and "everyone who knew him" (CEB), particularly the Galilean female disciples (23:49). Apart from these women, however, the "everyone" group of Jesus's "acquaintances" (NRSV) or "know-ers" (γνωστοί, *gnōstoi*) is vague and possibly ironic (who really "knows" Jesus at this point?); and at any rate, they attend Jesus's crucifixion only "at a distance" (μακρόθεν, *makrothen*), matching Peter's aloof position (22:54), though not his outright repudiation of Jesus (23:49). Beyond these acquaintances, three surprising men emerge in the final scene as *new* allies of Jesus on some level: (1) *Simon of Cyrene*, who carries Jesus's cross (23:26); (2) *one of the criminals* crucified with Jesus, who pleads for Jesus's mercy (23:40–42); and (3) *the centurion* supervising the crucifixion, who proclaims Jesus's innocence (23:47).

This triadic pattern fits a major organizing scheme in Luke's account of the events surrounding Jesus's trials and death.

Three venues

- Jewish Supreme Court (22:63–71)
- Pilate's tribunal (23:1–25)
- Skull Place (23:26–49)

Three judicial parties

- Chief priests and other council members (22:63–71)
- Pontius Pilate (23:1–6, 13–25)
- Herod Antipas (23:7–12)

Three assertions of Jesus's innocence by Pilate

- "I find no basis for an accusation against this man" (23:4).
- "I . . . have not found this man guilty" (23:14).
- "I have found in him no ground for the sentence of death" (23:22).

Three statements of Pilate's intent to release Jesus

- "I will therefore have him flogged and release him" (23:16).
- "Pilate, wanting to release Jesus, addressed them again" (23:20).
- "*A third time* he said to them, . . . 'I will therefore have him flogged and then release him'" (23:22).

Three surprising allies of the crucified Jesus

- Simon of Cyrene (23:26)
- Criminal crucified with Jesus (23:40–42)
- Centurion (23:47)

Three taunts regarding Jesus's saving mission

- Leaders: "He saved others; let him save himself if he is the Messiah of God" (23:35).
- Soldiers: "If you are the King of the Jews, save yourself!" (23:37).
- Criminal crucified with Jesus: "Are you not the Messiah? Save yourself and us!" (23:39).

Three sayings of Jesus from the cross

- "Father, forgive them; for they do not know what they are doing" (23:34).
- "Truly I tell you, today you will be with me in Paradise" (23:43).
- "Father, into your hands I commend my spirit" (23:46).

In the web of these trials and taunts, Jesus experiences an all-out assault not simply on his body, but on the core of his identity and vocation as God's chosen Prophet (22:64), Messiah (22:67; 23:2, 35, 39), Son of God (22:70–71), Son of Humankind (22:69), King of the Jews (23:2, 37–38), and Savior of the world (23:35, 37, 39). Through it all, Luke's Jesus firmly defends his integrity, but more through demonstration than declamation. He spent most of his rhetorical energy in the temple debates. Now he makes no grand forensic speeches, like those Stephen and Paul utter in Acts; his comments are terse and occasionally nonexistent ("Jesus gave [Herod] no answer" [23:9]) and as likely to be prayerful (23:34, 46) as preachy. Nevertheless, Jesus says enough and conveys even more through his dying demeanor (*ars moriendi*) to compel the penitent criminal's affirmation of Jesus's indomitable saving power, the centurion's exclamation of his virtuous character, and the spectators' lamentation over the travesty of justice he endured (23:40–48). Though not a model, dispassionate Socratic or Stoic martyr (see above), Jesus does bear exemplary witness throughout his passion, even to the point of death. This is how God's true Messiah dies for his people.

Examined at the Supreme Jewish Court (22:63–71)

After harassing Jesus during the night at the high priest's house, the guards holding Jesus haul him in the morning to the meeting place of the high Jewish council, or Sanhedrin (συνέδριον, *synedrion* [judges "sitting down together"]).

This "high court was . . . the supreme legislative, judicial, and executive body of leading citizens meeting in a council chamber at the center of the city, near the temple."[107] Though the precise composition of this tribunal in Jesus's day is hard to determine, it certainly included "chief priests, scribes, and elders," as Luke reports, presided over by the high priest. While Acts numbers some Pharisees along with the dominant Sadducees in this body (Acts 5:33; 23:6–10), Luke names no party-groups at Jesus's interrogation.

These hearings unfold as more of a shotgun affair than a formal trial, carried out in haste and hostility with little concern for due process. In rapid fire, the police and council progressively challenge Jesus's claims to be the anointed prophet (22:64) → Messiah (22:67) → Son of Humankind (22:69) → Son of God (22:70). (Jesus interjects Son of Humankind on his own, without being specifically asked.) We may detect here an escalating scale of connection with divine authority, culminating with "Son of God" as the clinching blasphemous claim to intimacy with God. Jesus's responses, though constituting no elaborate apologia, communicate enough to confirm the council's suspicions.

Prophet: Among the "many . . . insults" the guards add to injuries they inflict on Jesus's body, they mock him in a cruel game of blind-man's bluff (22:63-65). Repeatedly striking the blindfolded Jesus (likely with fists and clubs) and insisting that he identify the strikers, they deride his reputation as a prophetic seer (the visual motif continues). But true prophetic insight is not child's play or a parlor trick. Jesus sees and knows the whole story unfolding in this hour of darkness beyond the ken of these abusive policemen. He will not dignify their brutality with a response.

Messiah: The high-priestly council demands a straight answer from Jesus about his claim to be the Messiah. Is he or isn't he—Yes or No? (22:67). Significantly, though Luke has proclaimed Jesus Messiah (Christ) from the beginning (2:11; 3:15–17), Jesus has not promoted himself as such: no "I am the Messiah, follow me!" stump speeches. When the imprisoned John sent messengers to inquire if Jesus was "the one to come," Jesus offered no direct Yes answer, but rather a short resume of his saving deeds and gospel for others' sake; his record, not his rhetoric, validates his messianic vocation (7:18–23). When Peter correctly answered Jesus's query "But who do you say that I am?" with "the Messiah of God" (9:20), Jesus did not confirm or congratulate him, but rather proceeded to prohibit any witness to his messiahship and to predict his rejection and execution by the authorities as *suffering Son of Humankind*. This suffering servant of God and humankind represents Jesus's main self-profile in Luke. Since he doesn't expect the Supreme Court to grasp this role any better than his disciples

107. Saldarini, "Sanhedrin," 5:976.

did or to engage in honest debate on the matter, he declines to answer their Messiah question (22:67–68). Instead, he offers a stunning addendum about the Son of Humankind.

Son of Humankind: Skipping past his final suffering—not because he hopes to evade it, but because he takes it for granted—Jesus asserts that "from now on the Son of Humankind will be seated at the right hand of the power of God" (22:69). Actually, "from now on [ἀπὸ τοῦ νῦν, *apo tou nyn*]" *includes* the present mockeries, beatings, and inquisitions leading to crucifixion, subsuming these afflictions among a complex of events revealing Jesus's exalted position at God's right hand. Subtly, but surely, Luke's Jesus perceives his experience as the *crucified* Christ not as a tragic accident but as an integral expression of God's power—power *in and through suffering.* A "scandal" no doubt, as Paul puts it in 1 Cor 1:23–24 (CEB), which Luke's Jesus only intensifies before the Jewish authorities by identifying with a three-dimensional portrait of suffering Messiah, Danielic Son of Humankind (Dan 7:13–14), and psalmist-Davidic ruler seated at God's right hand (Ps 110:1; cf. Acts 2:34). He thus pushes beyond a claim to be God's "right-hand man," as we might say; and the added "power of God [τῆς δυνάμεως τοῦ θεοῦ, *tēs dynameōs tou theou* [22:69]) element suggests more than basic access to God's resources. In ancient Jewish thought, "right hand" and "power" signified God's entire being-in-action (cf. Acts 4:27–30; 8:10). Jesus thus claims full equality with God, *right now* and for eternity.

Son of God: Detecting a bald assertion of deity in Jesus's words, the high-court judges retort as a body ("all [πάντες, *pantes*] of them") with their final prosecutorial query: "You, then, are you [in fact] the Son of God?" (22:70 AT). Though "Son of God" can refer to a variety of beings (angels, Israel, adopted children of God), here it no doubt merges a functional designation of the Davidic Messiah (2 Sam 7:13–14; Ps 2:6–9) with an ontological affiliation with God's mind and nature (cf. Luke 10:22).[108] "So tell us straight out," the council effectively demands of Jesus, "Are you claiming to be God? How dare you!" Again maintaining his independent judicial authority, Jesus opts for an oblique—and frankly, insolent—response. But its thrust is clear: "You say that I am [ἐγώ εἰμι, *egō eimi*]"—I am, echoing the divine name disclosed to Moses (Exod 3:14). That is blatant blasphemy to the council's ears, punishable by death (Luke 22:70–71). But under the present Roman rule, the council can't legally execute criminals on their own authority. So without delay, they "rise as a body," a body raging with self-righteous indignation, to bring Jesus to Governor Pilate (23:1).

108. See Spencer, "Son of God," 2:308–13.

Examined at Pilate's Tribunal (23:1–25)

The chapter division is unfortunate here, as it blunts the seamless movement from the high priest's house to Pilate's court (linked by the simple "and" [καί, *kai*] at the beginning of 23:1). This literary link hints at a political bond. For all of the Roman governor's apparent resistance to the chief priests' charges against Jesus, Pilate ultimately serves their interests, as they serve his. They work in cahoots with each other and with Herod Antipas, who is in town from Galilee for Passover. Only Luke reports Pilate's enlistment of Herod in Jesus's trial; and again, though these two might not have seen eye to eye on many issues, they come together (with the priestly council) in friendly agreement against Jesus (23:12). In this case, the enemy (Jesus) of my enemy is my enemy: at least "we" (Pilate, Herod, chief priests) can conspire together against this one who threatens "our" common interests.

As Pilate recruits Herod, the Jewish authorities manipulate the wider populace (23:13) and even attempt to co-opt one Barabbas, a current death row prisoner accused of murder and insurrection. The Jewish prosecutors negotiate a prisoner exchange, demanding that Pilate free Barabbas and kill Jesus (23:18). As long as Pilate gets to show some punitive muscle and crucify an anti-imperial rebel, why should he care whether it is Barabbas or Jesus?[109] But oddly enough, Pilate does seem to care, at least for a while, as he tries to dissuade Jesus's accusers; apparently, in Pilate's view, the evidence against Jesus doesn't rise to the level of Barabbas's treachery. Even so, Luke's Pilate wastes no great energy with any deliberative hand-wringing (or hand-washing. as in Matt 27:24). If the Jewish officials and people want Jesus's blood, that is fine with him: "So Pilate gave his verdict that their demand should be granted" (23:24). He "released" Barabbas in lieu of Jesus, thus unwittingly signifying a redemptive feature of Jesus's death beyond anything Pilate or the chief priests imagine. Amid widespread, ignorant resistance to Jesus's saving mission, even unto death, in Luke's narrative, discerning readers may pick up ironic hints of the gospel's persisting efficacy.

In addition to the Barabbas factor (discussed below), other surprising confirmations of Jesus's mediation of God's saving rule emerge during these final interrogations. Though less motivated by truth and justice than by expedience (Pilate) and curiosity (Herod), these imperial judicial agents often reveal more about Jesus than they know, as we track in the *three scenes* of Pilate's one-act legal drama, terminating in the death sentence against Jesus.

109. On Pilate's reputation for violent reprisals, see Luke 13:1; Josephus, *Ant.* 18.55–63, 85–89; *J.W.* 2.168–77; Warren Carter, *Pontius Pilate*, 1–40, 104–5.

Scene 1 (23:1–5) focuses on Jesus's putative threat to Rome's political hegemony. The Jewish authorities thus play to Pilate's interests. Knowing the Roman governor's disinterest in theological fine points about Jewish prophetic, messianic, and other religious vocations—except as they might disrupt imperial security—the priestly plaintiffs attempt to paint Jesus as a traitorous royal claimant ("anointed/messianic king [χριστὸν βασιλέα, *christon basilea*]" [23:2 AT]), tax-rebel and rabble-rouser (23:2, 5): hence, another insurrectionist on the order of Barabbas, Theudas, or Judas the Galilean (cf. Acts 5:36–37). In the framework of Luke's story, however, this branding Jesus as one "perverting our nation [ἔθνος, *ethnos* (Israel and/or Rome)]" sticks only if Pilate buys the Sanhedrin's perversion of the truth. The council trumps up each charge., since Luke's Jesus, for all his popularity with the crowd, has *not* fueled a campaign to (1) promote his worldly-kingly status (cf. 4:5–8), (2) prohibit tax payment to Caesar (cf. 20:20–26), or (3) provoke armed revolt against Rome (cf. 22:35–38, 47–51). Yet, though failing to meet evidential standards, Jesus's prosecutors mount a fair case—more than they know!—for Jesus's revolutionary advance of a *new regime*, the very reign of God, to whom Jesus grants sovereign rule and pledges total allegiance.

Apparently sensing more of an inner-Jewish legal dispute and power struggle than a real threat to Caesar's rule (cf. Acts 18:14–16), Pilate plays out his judicial role in rather lackadaisical fashion, simply asking Jesus, "Are you the king of the Jews?" (23:3), with no great worry that Jesus might seriously claim to be emperor or king of the world. Herod the Great, after all, had been regarded as king of Judea (cf. 1:5), while still being loyal to Rome and collecting taxes for the empire. Moreover, Jesus's terse answer, "You say so" (23:3), while not repudiating the question (again, Luke happily extols Jesus as God's chosen king of Israel and the world), doesn't vex Pilate in the least. Jesus offers no grandstanding defense, no "Death to Caesar!" rant, no crowd-stoking call to protest. So Pilate sloughs off the charges, though with an extra dash of emphasis: "I find *no basis for an accusation* [οὐδὲν . . αἴτιον, *ouden . . . aition*] against this man" (23:4). Such a pronouncement should not be viewed as boosting Jesus's reputation, about which Pilate couldn't care less, but rather as reinforcing the governor's absolute judicial authority. Prefect Pilate is happy to remind the Sanhedrin of its subordinate place in Judean affairs any chance he gets.

Detecting Pilate's cavalier dismissal of their case against Jesus, the chief priests and their confederates push the issue further, highlighting Jesus's Galilean origins and agitating influence "throughout all Judea" (23:5). Again, it is doubtful that Pilate buys their sweeping claims (*all* Judea? how had this escaped Pilate's notice until now?); but Jesus's Galilean roots render him more suspicious, since this region has been a hotbed of resistance (cf. Judas the Galilean) outside Pilate's jurisdiction, and Pilate has already proven his willingness to slaughter Galilean pilgrims in Jerusalem (13:1–2). Best to delve more deeply into Jesus's record, and who better to help than the Galilean tetrarch, Herod Antipas, who happens to be in town for Passover? Ever the opportunist, Pilate sends Jesus to Herod for a second opinion. There is no love lost between Herod and Pilate, and Jerusalem is unequivocally Pilate's turf, but a little diplomatic wheel-greasing never hurts. In any case, Pilate is less interested in giving Jesus a fair trial than in feathering his own political nest. No need to overantagonize the temple hierarchy or Herod Antipas. Pilate retains the right of final judgment, but if he can mollify testy local officials in the process, so much the better.

Scene 2 (23:6–12) covers Jesus's examination by Herod and dispatch back to Pilate. Oddly enough, in light of Herod's earlier reported aim to *kill* Jesus (13:31), as he had eliminated Jesus's baptizing friend John (3:19–20; 9:7–9), this sudden opportunity to meet Jesus seems to make Herod's day in a more positive sense. He is "very glad" or "super-elated [ἐχάρη λίαν, *echarē lian*]" to see Jesus and particularly primed to see him perform some miraculous sign (23:8). Yet, as elsewhere in Luke, this interest in Jesus's signs stems from dubious motives rather than sincere faith in Jesus's divine power (cf. 11:16, 29). In Herod's case, he seems driven more by curiosity or frivolity than any concern for justice or spirituality. The Passover festival, for all its solemn sacrifices, was also a week of celebratory activities; to spice it up with magic tricks from this so-called prophet and sage from Herod's Galilean district would be icing on the cake. Furthermore, this also gives Herod a golden chance to "question [Jesus] at some length" (23:9a) under more secure conditions in Jerusalem, without worry of strong resistance from Galilean crowds sympathetic to Jesus (and John).

But Jesus is in no mood to play to the whims of that pesky fox Herod (13:32). If Herod were so interested in Jesus's signs, he had plenty of time to investigate Jesus's daily "casting out demons and performing cures" during his Galilean mission (13:32). Such miracles functioned to liberate the oppressed and alleviate the infirm, not to tickle the tetrarch's fancy. So Jesus will perform nothing for Herod and, more than that, will say nothing ("Jesus gave him no answer" [23:9b]). Of course, Herod and the priestly officials who followed the proceedings to Herod's residence take Jesus's nonresponse as an act of insolence, which in fact it is. Jesus will not dignify his accusers or Herod with a response. In turn, if Jesus is not going to entertain them, Herod and his henchmen will make their own fun with Jesus, hurling insults as they stage a little dress-up charade: in mock investiture, Herod places "an elegant robe on [Jesus]"—maybe one of Herod's old robes that had lost some of its shine and "softness" (cf. 7:25)—"and sent him back to Pilate" (23:11).

Raymond Brown opts to separate Herod's mocking and clothing gestures, represented in adjacent aorist participles (ἐμπαίξας περιβαλών, *empaixas peribalōn*), taking the second ("having clothed") as a favorable adornment to placate Pilate. In other words, though Herod has no great affection for Jesus, he's in no position to buck Pilate's preliminary judgment; accordingly, he dispatches Jesus back to Pilate donned with a brilliant cloak (ἐσθής λαμπρά, *esthēs lampra*), not with a royal purple robe, so that "Pilate will interpret Herod's sending Jesus back as a sign of Jesus's innocence. . . . Luke shows a Herod who is acting to please Pilate; undoubtedly he would have judged another way if that were to his advantage."[110] While I agree that Herod plays his political cards as shrewdly as he can, I think Pilate does the same: both treat Jesus as a pawn in their schemes. Neither has any sincere conviction about Jesus's innocence, even as both remain wary of ceding too quickly to the temple leaders' demands for Jesus's execution. Herod knows as well as anyone how Pilate feels about upstart Galileans and that Pilate would not object to—and probably be amused by—Jesus's fancy garment, so out of character for this poor, itinerant preacher.

Grammatically, it makes good sense to regard Herod's acts of mocking and clothing as mutually reinforcing rather than disjunctive;[111] and it strains the logic of the scene to see Herod shifting from mockery to flattery, even if the supposedly "innocent" enrobing of Jesus intends to support Pilate's decision. To be sure, as Brown notes, Luke's only other usage of this "splendid garment" terminology occurs in Acts 10:30, where Cornelius (a Roman officer!) references the authentic angelic vision he received from "a man in dazzling clothes [ἐσθῆτι λαμπρᾷ, *esthēti lampra*]."[112] But Luke's aggregate of Herodian leaders is no ally of angels (see esp. Acts 12:6–7, 20–23), except perhaps in an unwitting, ironic function that Luke exploits tongue-in-cheek. Herod's mock-up of Jesus in a "dazzling robe" indeed advertises Jesus's heavenly glory and divine-angelic approbation, but in a fashion of which Herod and Pilate remain entirely ignorant.

Ultimately, as noted above, Herod's ill-treatment of Jesus winds up endearing the tetrarch to Pilate. I imagine, in light of Luke's (and others') portraits of Pilate's sinister character (cf. 13:1–2; 23:24–25; Acts 4:25–27), the Roman

110. Brown, *Death*, 1:775, 777.

111. Cf. Culy, Parsons, and Stigall, 708–9: "The participle [περιβαλών, *peribalōn*] could conceivably express the means of [the two preceding participles]: 'after Herod had [also] treated him with contempt [ἐξουθενήσας, *exouthenēsas*] . . . and made fun of him [ἐμπαίξας, *empaixas*] by putting elegant clothes [περιβαλών, *peribalōn*] on him.'" They cite Marshall's commentary (867) supporting this "epexegetic" coherence of the three participles.

112. Brown, *Death*, 1:774; cf. "dazzling clothes" (ἐσθῆτι ἀστραπτούσῃ, *esthēti astraptousē*) of two attendant "men" at Jesus's empty tomb (Luke 24:4).

governor laughing his head off when Jesus returns donning this fancy get-up. However much he pronounces Jesus's "innocence," Pilate, like other Roman prefects, is always up for lampooning any would-be king other than Caesar. (The other Gospels depict *Pilate's men* orchestrating Jesus's costume in a fancy cloak and crown of thorns: Matt 27:27–31 [adding a reed scepter in his hand]; Mark 15:16–20; John 19:1–5.)

The transformed relationship of Herod and Pilate from "enemies" (ἐχθροί, *echthroi*) to "friends" (φίλοι, *philoi*) through their encounter with the suffering Jesus implies two further ironic elements. One, it hints at Jesus's reconciling judicial role between hostile parties and his redemptive outreach as "friend of . . . sinners" (7:34; cf. 5:29–32; 15:2; 19:7), that is, "sinners" at enmity with God and people, though of course Pilate and Herod would consciously grant no such authority to Jesus. And two, this pair's status upgrade from enemies to friends results from their now greater bond over common enemy Jesus, whose signature social ethic demanded *love for enemies and doing good to those who hate you* (6:27–35). Their so-called friendship, then, stoked by mocking and mistreating a hated enemy, is a total sham, miles from any true experience of saving love. Only Jesus, the designated "enemy" in these trials, evinces any authentic love for enemies—thus far, by passive, nonviolent response—but soon by active praying for his executioners and by welcoming the repentant criminal crucified with him into God's kingdom (see 23:34, 42–43).

Scene 3 (23:13–25) presents the closing arguments for and against Jesus, culminating in Pilate's authorizing Jesus's public state execution. The elite Jewish prosecutors remain firm in their vehement opposition to Jesus and have now marshaled the full-throated support of "the people" (ὁ λάος, *ho laos* [23:13]). "All shout[ing] out together," this official and popular Jewish coalition repeatedly clamors for Jesus's crucifixion (23:18, 21, 23), and as noted above, they seek to force Pilate's hand by proposing a prisoner substitution: "Away with this fellow [Jesus]! Release Barabbas for us!" (23:18).

It is not clear why this Barabbas deal should carry any weight with Pilate, who continues to insist, now with Herod's presumed backing,[113] that Jesus "has done nothing to deserve death" (23:15, 22). Recall that Barabbas is a convicted insurrectionist and murderer (23:19, 25). Though the "kingdom"-promoting Jesus fits the bill of a political radical, he has resorted to no violent measures to further his revolution, beyond his little temple outburst (19:45); but he didn't injure anyone in that demonstration, and indeed, far from killing anyone any-

113. To be precise, Herod never explicitly pronounces on Jesus's guilt one way or another; he simply mocks him, dresses him up, and sends him back to Pilate, who then *interprets* this sending back as tacit agreement with Pilate's judgment (23:15a).

time in his life—whether in self-defense, "righteous" revolt, or any other reason, good or bad—Jesus has given people *new life*, even from the dead! (7:14–15, 22; 8:49–56; Herod even entertained the rumor that Jesus reincarnated the beheaded John [9:7–9]). A murder rap is preposterous for Jesus.

The other three canonical Gospels ground the call for Barabbas's release in an annual Passover custom of pardoning one prisoner at the Jews' behest (Matt 27:15–17//Mark 15:6–9//John 18:38–40). Never hurts to throw a bone to subjugated peoples, especially at such a potentially incendiary celebration of national freedom as Passover. Pilate might comply with this custom to prove he's no hardhearted Pharaoh-style slave master; he could graciously free a prisoner now and then, provided that it didn't disrupt the status quo too much. But as it happens, we have no clear external evidence of this Passover amnesty tradition in Jerusalem during Pilate's or any other regime.[114] If it did exist, it might function either as a single-option arrangement, focused on *one* prisoner the people proposed for release, or a bargaining process over *two* (or more) candidates. These Gospels expose Pilate's attempt to manipulate the custom by presenting the people with a Jesus or Barabbas *choice*, amounting to an exchange of one life for another. He underestimates, however, the chief priests' hostility against Jesus, prompting their preference for Barabbas's release (Matt 27:17–18//Mark 15:9–11//John 18:39–40).

By notable contrast with the other NT Gospels, Luke makes *no reference* to the Passover custom of pardoning a convict (perhaps because of its shaky historical foundation) and dissociates the issue from Pilate's scheming. In Luke, the *priestly-led mob initiates*—and insists upon—the Jesus/Barabbas swap. This scheme raises two critical issues: one sociological, the other soteriological.

Sociologically, Luke seems to place the heavier blame for Jesus's death sentence on the unreasonable, unjust Jewish side versus the more considerate Roman stance. Since the text offers no explanation for the assembly's favoring Barabbas (a Robin Hood social bandit championing the poor?[115] a popular, swashbuckling political rebel?), those calling for Jesus's death in Barabbas's place appear purely—and perversely—motivated by hatred toward the nonmilitant, nonmurderous Jesus—more anti-Jesus than pro-Barabbas.[116] This scenario may

114. On wider evidence in the ancient Near Eastern and Greek worlds of the custom of prisoner release at a major festival, which Mark might have exploited to "lend an aura of authenticity" to his Barabbas account, see Merritt, "Jesus Barabbas," 68. But again, as Merritt admits, evidence is lacking for such a custom in Roman Judea; cf. Bond, "Barabbas," 59–60.

115. See Wilkins, "Barabbas."

116. Apart from the fact that Luke does not specify the mob's motive in clamoring for Barabbas's release or the full dossier of his traitorous crimes beyond "murder" (23:19), we have no additional evidence for this Barabbas outside the four Gospels; cf. Wilkins, "Barabbas."

seem to exemplify Luke's pro-Roman, anti-Jewish polemic.[117] But as with many issues in Luke's complex narrative, the matter is not so clear-cut. We should note again that Luke has already confirmed Pilate's penchant for violence: a governor who goes so far as to swirl the blood of Galilean worshipers with that of the sacrifices they offer is no sweetheart or model of due process (13:1–2). Hence, my reluctance to take at face value Pilate's sudden insistence on fair treatment for an alleged Galilean agitator.

Likewise, with respect to the Jews, while Luke consistently paints priestly leaders (Sadducees) with a broad baleful brush, his portrait of the Jewish people is more nuanced.[118] In particular, this sudden "all together" collaboration of crowds and clergy (23:13, 18) doesn't quite ring true in Luke's story. Just a few days earlier, Jesus entered Jerusalem to the strains of joyous acclamation by "the whole multitude" of enthusiastic supporters (19:37). Then in the following days "all the people" happily listened to Jesus's teaching in the temple, "spellbound" by his arguments against the priestly authorities to such an extent that these rulers feared the people, that is, feared a massive uproar of public opinion against the establishment (19:48; 20:19; cf. 20:45–47). While we might easily believe that the Sadducee Jewish hierarchs could muster some mob to bolster their prosecution of Jesus before Pilate and Herod, the prospect of suddenly winning over the entire throng of Passover pilgrims, many of whom delighted in Jesus's antiestablishment teaching, doesn't compute within Luke's narrative logic. To be sure, Luke's loose usage of "all" (πᾶς, *pas*) language, here and elsewhere, muddies the waters, but only for mathematical literalists. For Luke, "all" rarely equals 100 percent, functioning more as a rhetorical signal of common purpose for various groups. Accordingly, in the present trial setting, "all" Jews *in this focal scene*—led by the chief priests—virulently oppose Jesus and shoulder part of the blame for Jesus's death. But hereby Luke scarcely indicts the whole Jewish population, especially since all of the Jewish Jesus's current followers are Jews and fifty days later, at the next Jewish feast (Pentecost), thousands more Jews join his movement (see Acts 2:41–42; cf. 4:1–4).

Soteriologically, amid all the nefarious political machinations in sentencing Jesus to death, someone still gets "saved": Barabbas is "released/set free"

117. See Jack T. Sanders's (*Jews*) attempt to mount an extended case for thoroughgoing, "monolithic anti-Judaism" (303). See the critique in Spencer, Review of Sanders.

118. See the more complicated, dialectic treatments of the "Jewish question" in Luke's narratives, resisting extreme pro-/anti-Jewish polarities, in Tyson, *Luke-Acts* (excepting that of Jack T. Sanders's essay, excerpted from his *Jews*); Tyson, *Images*: "Do the images that are embedded in Luke-Acts convey to the implied reader positive or negative impressions of Jewish religious life and the Jewish people? The answer, of course, is that they convey both" (187); Brawley, *Luke-Acts*; Schmidt, "Anti-Judaism"; Levine, "Matthew," 92–98.

(ἀπολύω, *apolyō*) from prison and execution as Jesus is "handed over/betrayed" (παραδίδωμι, *paradidōmi*) to crucifixion (23:25). Such an exchange scarcely sustains a full-fledged doctrine of substitutionary atonement. At the Last Supper, Jesus spoke of his broken body and outpoured blood "for you/on your behalf [τὸ ὑπὲρ ὑμῶν, *to hyper hymōn*]" (22:19, 20]), but such benefit does not necessarily entail dying *in your place*; and Luke never states that the Son of Humankind will "give his life a ransom [λύτρον, *lytron*] for many" (Mark 10:45). But narrative theology works by ironic allusion as much as by didactic prescription. Accordingly, the "this one" (Jesus) for "that one" (Barabbas) *substitution* begs for attention, especially in Luke's passion narrative, which stresses Jesus's ongoing saving ministry for "sinners" and "enemies" from his arrest (healing the slave's severed ear [22:50–51]) to his crucifixion (redeeming a convicted criminal [23:40–43]).

Compared with these other beneficiaries of salvation, Barabbas stands out as a *named* character, otherwise unknown in the historical record, but potentially significant in symbolic-theological terms. The name is Aramaic for "son of [*bar*] a father [*abba*]." It is impossible to prove that Luke exploits the meaning of this moniker, but some names carry symbolic freight in Luke's writings, including another "Bar-" name, or rather nickname, "Barnabas," which Luke interprets for his Greek readers as "son of encouragement," in line with Joseph "Barney's" character-in-action throughout Acts (Acts 4:36). Other Jewish "Bar"-figures also appear—Joseph Barsabbas (1:23), Bar-Jesus/Elymas (13:6, 8), and Judas Barsabbas (15:22)—suggesting that Luke expects his readers to recognize the common Aramaic "son of-" nomenclature. So what might Luke have in mind with the Barabbas reference on the brink of Jesus's death?

Whereas Mark and Matthew accentuate the sharp *contrast* between Barabbas and Jesus, Luke's juxtaposition of the two men appears more *connective*. In Mark only, Jesus addresses God as "Abba Father [Αββα ὁ πατήρ, *Abba ho patēr*]" (Mark 14:36 [at Gethsemane]), intimating his unique identity as "Son of God-the-Father" distinct from ordinary "sons of fathers." Though Mark does not thereby deny Jesus's humanity or other humans' graced status as God's children, he does exalt Jesus in the Father's royal family above all other "sons," such as Barabbas. As for Matthew, the fuller name *Jesus* Barabbas is likely original in Matt 27:16–17, despite its slim external attestation. The third-century church father Origen observed that "many copies" *omitted* the "Jesus" association with Barabbas, and rightly so in Origen's view, since "we know that no one who is a sinner [is called] Jesus." Evidently, then, many scribes scrubbed the *original* "Jesus" reference to preserve orthodoxy.[119] But Matthew's text can serve its own

119. See the Origen citation and discussion of this Matthean reference in Omanson, *Textual Guide*, 49; cf. Bond, "Barabbas," 60; Wilkins, "Barabbas."

"orthodox" purpose just fine by posing a dramatic either/or choice between the false/true "Jesus" (= "Savior" in 1:21) and s/Son of a/the f/Father: "Whom do you want me to release for you, Jesus Barabbas *or* Jesus who is called the Messiah?" (27:17).

As for Luke's Jesus, however, he calls and prays only to God as πάτηρ (*patēr* = Greek "Father" [Luke 2:49; 6:36; 10:21–22; 11:2, 13; 12:30, 32; 22:29, 42; 23:34, 46, 49]), with no transliterated Aramaic αββα (*abba*) equivalent, as in Mark, and he further encourages his followers to pray as he does, "Father [πάτερ, *pater*], hallowed be your name" (11:2). Luke also draws no contrast between two "Jesus" figures; in fact neither Pilate nor the Jewish accusers mention Jesus by name in this final trial scene: "Away with this fellow/one [τοῦτον, *touton*]! Release Barabbas for us!" (23:18).

Hence, I propose that Luke's language leans closer to the *interconnection* and *interchangeableness* of Jesus and Barabbas: "this one or that one," even "this one *for* that one"—it makes no difference. Though the Jewish prosecutors and Pilate disagree about which figure poses the greater security threat, as long as one rebel is executed, the state sends its message and maintains order. To appease the Jewish leaders, Pilate soon selects Jesus as the one to die instead of the other human "son," Barabbas. Recall that Luke has emphasized Jesus the Son of Humankind's solidarity with all people (Jews and Gentiles) descended from Adam (3:38) and destined to die (9:22, 44; 18:31–33). But recall, too, in Luke's thickening plot, that Jesus undergoes total immersion in the human condition, even unto death, as one *above* and *apart from*, as well as among, human beings: as God's unique "Beloved Son" (3:22) conceived in Mary by the Holy Spirit (thus only the "supposed" son of Joseph [3:23 CEB, KJV]) and appointed to rise from the dead (9:22; 18:33) and raise up broken, fallen humanity with him to renewed life. Moreover, as Son of Humankind, Jesus not only sympathizes with fellow human sufferers, but also serves as the divine kingdom agent appointed to liberate God's people. In sum, Jesus effectively dies to redeem Barabbas the "rebel-murderer" and all other *abba*-sired "sinners."[120]

120. Luke's "substitutionary" redemptive point, ironically conveyed by Governor Pilate, is similar (though more subtle) to that offered by High Priest Caiaphas in the Fourth Gospel: "It is better for you to have one man die for the people than to have the whole nation destroyed. . . . [Thus unwittingly] he prophesied that Jesus was about to die for the nation, and not for the nation only, but to gather into one the dispersed children of God" (John 11:50–52).

Executed at Skull Place (23:26–49)

Luke stresses Jesus's isolation in death, though not to the same degree as Mark. Luke omits Mark's stark statement at the arrest, "All of them deserted him and fled" (Mark 14:50), and the searing lament from the cross, "My God, my God, why have you forsaken me?" (15:34). Nonetheless, Luke locates a group of Jesus's "acquaintances . . . at a *distance*" (Luke 23:49) from his crucifixion site, with no mention of any apostles among this company, effectively implicating them all with betrayer Judas and denier Peter. The Roman execution squad, Jewish authorities, and death-clamoring rabble among the crowd do their dirty business unimpeded. In short, Luke's Jesus bears the full brunt of death in his broken and bloody body, as crucifixion necessarily entails. Though we might credit the soldiers' offer of "sour wine" (ὄξος, *oxos*) as a palliative gesture, it is accompanied by mocking and affords no great comfort under the circumstances; also there's no report that Jesus accepts the drink (23:36).[121]

In the throes of Jesus's final suffering and isolation, however, we find a remarkable outpouring of *sympathy* in the literal and bilateral sense of "suffering with": Jesus suffering with condemned criminals and even interceding for one in particular and for all his antagonists in general (23:34, 39–43); and conversely, others suffering and sympathizing *with Jesus* in various capacities, including (1) a man who carries Jesus's cross for him (23:26), (2) a company of breast-beating mourners over Jesus's fate (23:27–28, 48), (3) God the Father, to whom Jesus prays (23:34, 46), and even (4) the centurion overseeing the execution, who suddenly sees Jesus in a new light the moment Jesus expires (23:47). In Luke's narrative theology, Jesus's death represents not only his intense, corporeal, personal engagement with suffering, but also his embracive, corporate, communal experience of suffering with all fragile, finite human flesh. Jesus the Son of Humankind dies as he has lived, as a full-fledged human being in solidarity with all humankind. Accordingly, by unmitigated *realization* and *representation* of the human condition, he paves the way for *restoration* of broken humanity and *reconciliation* of estranged humanity from God, one another, and the world. Luke's Jesus mediates God's purpose of saving atonement, though not as much in a forensic (legal) or cultic (sacrificial) sense as in a cosmic (eschatological) and communal (ecclesial) vein. The dying Jesus bridges the divide between the human and divine realms, the guilty and innocent, the beaten and Father-loved (23:34, 46), earth and heaven, Skull Place and Paradise (23:33, 43).[122]

121. See Spencer, *What Did Jesus Do?*, 115–19.

122. On the significant element of *reconciliation* in atonement theology, see Adam Johnson, *Atonement*: "The doctrine of the atonement is a conceptually unified account of how the life, death

As we unpack Luke's account of Jesus's crucifixion, we seek again to *see* and *know* the significance of this crucial event with the participating and observing characters. Luke uniquely labels Jesus's death as "this spectacle [θεωρίαν, *theōrian*]" that the crowds "saw" or "watched" (θεωρέω, *theōreō* [23:48]), like a grisly, beastly mauling of traitors or other disreputable lowlifes in a public theater (θέατρον, *theatron*).[123] Paul notes that "God has shown that we apostles . . . are like prisoners sentenced to death, because we have become a *spectacle* [θέατρον, *theatron*] in the world, both to angels and to humans" (1 Cor 4:9 CEB). In this exposed scenario, the apostles reenact the drama of Jesus's death. In Luke's portrayal, how do viewers within the story *perceive* Jesus's crucifixion? Do they *know* what is truly—truthfully—taking place? Jesus prays for his executioners' forgiveness, because "they *do not know* [οὐ . . . οἴδασιν, *ou . . . oidasin*] what they are doing" (23:34). But Luke expects more from Jesus's followers and "*knowing* acquaintances/knowing ones [γνωστοί, *gnōstoi*] (23:49), who already have some insight into his mission and identity.

We may divide also the crucifixion act into three scenes.

Scene 1 (23:26–31) functions as a *prelude*. As "they led [Jesus] away" to the place of crucifixion (23:26), presumably referring to Pilate's soldiers who will carry out the execution (cf. 23:36–37, 47),[124] two additional characters enter the scene: one, Simon of Cyrene, commandeered by the soldiers (23:26); the other, a group of Jerusalem women, addressed by Jesus (23:28). The first-century city of Cyrene, located on the African-Mediterranean coast of Cyrenaica (modern Libya), contained a substantial Diaspora Jewish population. Hence, it is not unusual to find a Jewish-Cyrenean pilgrim to Jerusalem at Passover (note Libyans from Cyrene at Pentecost in Acts 2:10; cf. 6:9; 11:20). But it is surprising that the crucifixion squad suddenly "seized" this random Cyrenean called Simon (otherwise unknown) entering the city "from the countryside" (CEB) and forces him to carry Jesus's cross and walk "behind" him to Skull/Cranium

---

and resurrection of Jesus Christ are effective for the reconciliation of all things to God (Col 1:20)" (37). Johnson specifically stresses the "ethnic" (anthropological, social) and "cosmic" dimensions of this reconciliation (see 11, 153–55, 172–73).

123. See Wilson, "Sight" and *Unmanly Men*, 170, 233–34.

124. Laurie Brink (*Soldiers*, 103–9) argues that Luke greatly underplays the role of Pilate's Roman soldiers in Jesus's execution as part of a more pro-Roman agenda, shifting the responsibility for Jesus's maltreatment onto Herod's soldiers in the earlier trial scene (23:11); accordingly, Luke casts the crucifixion squad as an ambiguous "they" (23:26). This reading, however, overplays Luke's supposed redaction of Mark. First-century readers would clearly register that the cross was the quintessential *Roman* instrument of capital punishment carried out by *Roman* officials (Pilate and a centurion [23:47]) and their functionaries ("soldiers" in 23:36). However initially ambivalent Pilate might appear to be, his ultimate verdict of crucifixion constitutes final and forceful assertion of *Roman* state authority.

Place (τόπον . . . Κρανίον, *topon . . . Kranion*) (Luke 23:26, 33). Though the verb ἐπιλαμβάνομαι (*epilambanomai* [here translated "seized"]) can connote "hold" or "embrace" in a positive sense, as Jesus "takes hold" of the little child or man with dropsy (9:47; 14:4), it more commonly applies to sinister "entrapment" (20:20, 26) or police "arrest" (Acts 16:19; 17:19; 18:17; 21:30, 33). Simon does not volunteer for cross-carrying duty; the soldiers conscript him into temporary service. Luke does not specify why Simon's services are required, but we may surmise that Jesus is simply too weak from his trial ordeal to bear his own cross.

In any event, this little incident carries two ironic-symbolic implications. First, the soldiers effectively cast Simon of Cyrene as a disciple of Jesus, taking up one's cross and following "behind/after" (ὄπισθεν, *opisthen*) him, as Jesus required: "If anyone wants to come after [ὀπίσω, *opisō*] me, let him deny himself, take up his cross daily, and follow me" (Luke 9:23 AT). Though we do not know whether this Simon follows Jesus (in faith) beyond this accidental involvement, he sets the narrative stage for later Cyrenean believers (Acts 11:20; 13:1) and a namesake African-Christian prophet-teacher ("Simeon who was called Niger" [13:1]); and more immediately, he stands in stark contrast to Jesus's confidants (not least *Simon* Peter), who forsake their Lord at his dire, cross-carrying hour.

Second, we should take due note that Jesus *needs help in carrying his own cross*. This is hardly a slight against Jesus's character, given all that he endures, though the Fourth Evangelist feels compelled to provide a more self-sufficient portrait of "Jesus . . . carrying the cross *by himself* [ἑαυτῷ, *heautō*]" (John 19:16–17). Via Simon of Cyrene, Luke hints at the *shared, communal practice of cross-bearing*, even for Jesus. Though in one sense "all must carry their own loads" (Gal 6:5), in another vital sense, Jesus's followers are not heroic, maverick individualists, but rather, interdependent beings who "bear one another's burdens, and in this way . . . fulfill the law of Christ" (Gal 6:2). If Jesus needed help carrying his cross, how much more do his disciples need the support of Christ's Spirit and partner-pilgrims? Thereby we share *together* the sufferings of Christ (cf. Rom 8:16–17; Phil 3:10; Col 1:24).[125]

As Simon of Cyrene carries the cross behind Jesus, so a "great number/plethora [πολὺ πλῆθος, *poly plēthos*] of the people followed him" to Skull Place (Luke 23:27). Even in death, Jesus commands a large entourage; but it is not a happy band, as a group of women in particular follow (ἀκολουθέω, *akoloutheō* [like disciples]) in deep and loud mourning for their Lord. A short yet poignant scene ensues, unique to Luke, marking Jesus's final strategic "turning [στραφείς, *strapheis*]," this time to the grieving women, whom he addresses with compassionate concern, laced with grim warning (23:28–31). As an overture to Jesus's

125. On cross-bearing as a communal practice, see Hays, *Moral Vision*, 196–97.

farewell utterances from the cross, these words further reflect his sympathetic interest in others' needs, even in his most desperate hour, as he urges the women to weep not for him, but rather "for yourselves and for your children" (23:28). Jesus has come to grips with his own demise, which, as horrible as it will be, will issue in new life; but he also knows that this personal resurrection, however portentous for realizing God's reign, will not bring immediate relief for all God's people. Indeed, in the short run, as Jesus has announced (19:41–44; 21:5–24), things will only get worse for Jerusalem's citizens in particular, including the "daughters of Jerusalem," as he now identifies these wailing women.

Jesus again keenly perceives that the violent arm of Rome, about to strike down his own life, will soon come crashing down on Jerusalem with colossal force and devastation. Perhaps Jesus's puzzling final query reflects this escalating trauma: "For if they do this when the wood is green, what will happen when it is dry?" (23:31). Wood burns more brightly, quickly, and thoroughly when dry rather than green. The "green" wood of Jesus's cross will compound, as it were, into the "dry" deadwood of Jerusalem's people and temple in the coming conflagration ignited by Roman firepower. A "dry tree/root" is also a prophetic biblical image of childlessness pertaining to eunuchs (Isa 56:3) and either infertile or miscarrying women (Hos 9:16), resonating with Jesus's present warning to the Jerusalem daughters about the perilous prospects of producing and protecting children during the coming crisis (Luke 23:28–29).[126]

Jesus himself has already wept over this terrible prospect, all the more tragic because the Jewish officials have failed to resist oppressive Roman rule and to "recognize the time of [God's] visitation" in Christ (19:41–44). While some rank-in-file citizens have supported their leaders' recalcitrance, not all have fallen in line, certainly not the least and lowliest, including "daughters" and (other) children under patriarchal domination. It is a woeful truism that innocent women and children suffer egregiously as "collateral damage" in the all-too-real war games played by men. Though often having little power to stem the violent tide, women can weep in the face of brutal injustice, not simply in desperate sadness, but also in passionate *protest*, in purposive *lament*.[127] More-

126. See Pitre, "Blessing," 71. This is not to say, however, that Luke's Jesus fully endorses the strong judgment component of God's people in Hosea's text, which goes so far to say that *God* "will kill the cherished offspring of their womb" because of their rebellion against God (Hos 9:16).

127. Though Matthews ("Weeping") appreciates the protest/resistance element in the lament tradition, particularly as a means of "women's agency" amid bereavement, she argues that Luke's Jesus in fact *denies* weeping women this power in the present scene: "[Jesus's] rebuke deprives the daughters of Jerusalem of an opportunity to express grief and protest in the face of the unjust execution of their friend (and masks traditions of Jesus's female companions doing just that)" (400; cf. 396–400). To buttress this point, however, Matthews overplays (1) Luke's redactional

over, in the present case, they weep *together* over Jesus's unjust treatment, as he has wept *with them* and now turns *to them*, walks *their way* of suffering, and feels the pain of *their bleak future*, which will trigger only a greater torrent of tears. Luke's apocalyptic Jesus has by no means abandoned hope in God's righteous rule (for Israel), as he soon reaffirms from the cross. Paradise, however, does not lie at the end of a yellow-brick road, but only via a cruciform course through the darkest shadows of death (23:42–43). The redemptive "day of the Lord" dawns out of the destructive floods and fires of evil realms, like those in Noah's world, Sodom city (cf. 17:25–32)—and Rome's empire.

So what, then, should God's women (and men) do in the infernal interim period, except weep, pray, and pursue what justice they can before unjust authorities (which is far from a weak, resigned response, as the case of the determined widow in 18:1–8 exemplifies)? Perhaps they can mitigate their woes by being single, celibate, and childless; then, at least, they need worry only about themselves. Is this what Jesus means by the strange benediction he pronounces for the turbulent coming days: "Blessed are the barren, and the wombs that never bore, and the breasts that never nursed" (23:29)? Is this part of Luke's apocalyptic-ascetic ideal of discipleship, similar to the celibate, single life Paul advocates (but doesn't demand) for the Corinthians to spare them undue "anxieties . . . about the affairs of the world" during the period of intense crisis before Christ's climactic return (1 Cor 7:32–33; cf. 7:1–40)? Does this asexual, nonnatural-familial existence get a jump on the eternal age to come in God's spiritual family (cf. Luke 20:34–36), allowing for more concentrated attention on "the affairs of the Lord" (1 Cor 7:34) and less distraction by normal practices of "marrying and being given in marriage" leading to childbearing, as if this

---

omission of the Bethany woman's "memorialized" preburial anointing of Jesus (Matt 26:6–13// Mark 14:3–9) (Luke has his own agential "weeping" anointing woman strongly commended by Jesus in 7:36–50); (2) Jesus's supposed macho-heroic aim behind "Do not weep for me [Women]" (to the neglect of his sympathetic engagement [see above on 19:41–44]); and (3) Luke's supposed anti-Judaic perspective on the fall of Jerusalem as thoroughly merited judgment void of tragic pathos ("[The daughters of Jerusalem] are . . . exhorted to weep over the deserved destruction of the city they represent" [400]).

Pitre ("Blessing," 71–72) adduces Jer 16:1–4, 9 as another prophetic parallel to the terrible ordeal facing parents and their children in the coming (Babylonian) invasion of Jerusalem. Here, however, the Lord tells Jeremiah: "They shall die of deadly diseases. They *shall not be lamented*, nor shall they be buried; they shall become like dung on the surface of the ground" (16:4). Though Jeremiah and his people seem utterly bereft and completely hopeless, the prophet's otherwise famous "weeping" typically carries more vigorous notions of lament-as-protest and flickers of hope. I suggest, particularly on the basis of the persistent-widow story in Luke 18:1–8 (see discussion above), that Luke envisions vulnerable, violated women not simply as victims, but as forceful agents of faithful protest and proaction, with or without weeping.

present age would endure for generations (cf. Luke 17:27; 21:23)? And given the often oppressive environment of patriarchal households for women, would Jesus's endorsement of women's singlehood not liberate them to some degree and put them on a more equal footing to male disciples?

Though Luke's Gospel welcomes all types of women—including widows and other unmarried women, with or without children—in the spiritual, fictive family of God transcending natural-biological ties, it does not, to reprise my comments on the marriage-afterlife debate (20:27–40), advance a thorough-going ascetic ethic, as some interpreters argue.[128] It is important to note in Jesus's address to the daughters of Jerusalem at this critical moment that he does *not* actually commend barrenness or childlessness as a "blessed" condition in the difficult coming days. He says, instead, that this sterile notion of "blessedness" will reflect general public opinion as hardship escalates: what "*they* will say [ἐροῦσιν, *erousin*]," *not* what "*you* daughters" ought to say (23:29). He then follows with another desperate plea, which "*they* will begin [ἄρξονται, *arxontai*]" to utter, typical of disaster scenarios and amounting to hopeless suicide: "Fall on us" and "Cover us," they will say to the mountains and hills (23:30; cf. Hos 10:8; Rev 6:16).

To say the least, this is a perverted view of "blessed" life, especially for a Gospel story that begins with two wondrous births—one to a longtime *barren* woman—generated by God's life-giving Spirit in seemingly "impossible" situations (Luke 1:37) and ends with Jesus's resurrection from the dead.[129] Again, Luke peddles no cheap optimism. In the present encounter with the daughters of Jerusalem, the crucifixion-bound Jesus fully acknowledges the stark reality of human suffering worthy of profound lament. But he does not encourage abject defeatism. Whatever *they* (out there) might think and say about the world does not match the alternative, right-making truth of God's life-giving kingdom manifest in God's dying-and-rising Son.

Scene 2 (23:32–46) depicts the three-hour *crucifixion* itself (23:44), structured around three sayings of Jesus, unique to Luke, enveloping three taunts by different parties, deriding Jesus's *saving* power as putative Messiah-King of the Jews. While the cross itself never speaks (as it does in the apocryphal Gospel of

128. See n. 34 above in discussion of 20:27–40. On the present text (23:28–31) as part of Luke's ascetic agenda, see Seim, *Double Message*, 205–8. See also Pitre ("Blessing") on the historical Jesus's "apocalyptic asceticism" in this and parallel Gospel texts, warning about the precariousness of having children in the present age on the precipice of severe tribulation, followed by eternal cessation of childbearing in the age to come.

129. To say nothing of the venerable biblical tradition of children as among the most blessed of God's gifts (Gen 1:28; 33:5; 48:9; Ps 127:3–5; Prov 17:6; Isa 54:1), unequivocally confirmed by Jesus in Luke 18:15–17.

Peter), dialogue pervades Luke's crucifixion narrative; and in these exchanges the theological significance of Jesus's death comes to light in both dominical (from Jesus's authoritative lips) and ironical (from opponents' mouths) form.

Jesus's first saying:	Forgiveness of cruel enemies	"Father, forgive them; for they do not know what they are doing" (23:34).
Enemies' first taunt:	Jewish rulers mock Jesus's messiahship	"He *saved* others; let him *save* himself if he is the Messiah of God, his chosen one!" (23:35).
Enemies' second taunt:	Roman soldiers mock Jesus's kingship	"If you are the King of the Jews, *save* yourself!" (23:37).
Enemies' third taunt:	One criminal mocks Jesus's messiahship	"Are you not the Messiah? *Save* yourself and us!" (23:39).
Jesus's second saying:	Fellowship with criminal sinner	"Truly I tell you, today you will be with me in Paradise" (23:43).
Jesus's third saying:	Faithfulness of crucified Messiah	"Father, into your hands I commend my spirit" (23:46).

The *first saying*, involving Jesus's intercession on behalf of his persecutors, has deeply informed Christian faith and practice through the centuries. Its importance relates not only to its forgiveness theme in such a crucial historical and theological context, but also to its literary prominence at the head of Luke's crucifixion scene, as if he inscribes the superscription, "Father, Forgive Them" (23:34) over the mock—yet truthful!—inscription at Jesus's head, "This Is the King of the Jews" (23:38). However ignorant minds might misconstrue Jesus's death, Luke wants readers to know that it showcases the indomitable saving-forgiving purpose of God. This is how God rules through Jesus the Christ: in redemptive love, not vindictive terror.

Such a breathtaking picture of the gospel's power to save and forgive (cf. 1:77; 7:47–50; 24:44–47) inspires faith, gratitude, awe—and not a little anxiety and ambiguity. To thoughtful and faithful minds, not at all ignorant or recalcitrant, the "Father, forgive them" plea raises as many questions as answers, not least concerning the scope of Jesus's prayer in both its immediate setting and its broader significance for Christian ethics and spirituality. Are disciples of Jesus called to forgive all offenders, regardless of how cruel or unjust, from the get-go? Is any alternative response a moral and spiritual failure, apostasy from Jesus's way, an insidious, if unwitting, alignment with forces of hate rather than love? These and other questions have provoked persistent wrestling with the "*limits* of forgiveness," as evidenced in two recent case studies of forgiveness focused on Luke 23:34a: Maria Mayo's *The Limits of Forgiveness: Case Studies in the Distortion of a Biblical Ideal* (2015),[130] and Joshua Marshall Strahan's *The Limits of a Text: Luke 23:34a as a Case Study in Theological Interpretation* (2012).

We first confront a potential *textual* limit. Despite its honored place in the Christian tradition, modern textual critics debate its originality in Luke's narrative. This issue does not undo centuries of interpretation. As Raymond Brown comments, regardless of their precise origin, "the long use of these words by Christians means they have acquired normative authority."[131] Moreover, textual critics often note that, whether or not the forgiveness petition from the cross derives from Luke or a scribal interpolator, it rings true with Jesus's authentic teaching.[132] Even so, a tenable, though not dogmatic, case can be made for the statement's foundation in Luke. Early manuscript testimony is admittedly mixed, prompting Strahan's cautious conclusion, "The external evidence is too ambiguous to warrant a claim of unoriginality."[133] Of course, a counterclaim of originality would be just as tenuous on the same grounds. But the tight internal fit, "conforming to Lukan style and theology," tips the balance in favor of an authentic Lukan text.[134] Luke amply attests Jesus's commitment to the practice of forgiveness (5:20–24; 7:47–49; 11:4; 17:3–4; 24:46–47); and the emphasis on "ignorant" antagonism to Jesus and his plea to forgive persecutors sets the stage for apostolic preaching in Acts (3:17; 13:27–28; cf. 17:30) and a similar prayer by the dying Stephen (7:60).[135] It is altogether fitting that Luke's major theme of redemption—including liberating forgiveness (ἄφεσις, *aphesis* [cf. 4:18])—through the suffering Messiah Jesus finds its crowning expression in his words from the cross.

A second limit is *referential*: who are "them/they" that Jesus prays for? The most immediate antecedent is the "they" who ushered him to Skull Place and "crucified [ἐσταύρωσαν, *estaurōsan*] Jesus there" (23:33). Most directly, as noted above, these handlers and executioners are Pilate's soldiers. Augustine, however,

130. Mayo, *Limits*, 159–205 (ch. 4).

131. Brown, *Death*, 2:980.

132. See Bruce Metzger, *Textual Commentary*, 154; Omanson, *Textual Guide*, 152.

133. Strahan, *Limits*, 27; cf. Carroll, 465.

134. Strahan, *Limits*, 27 (see 8–27 for full text-critical analysis); Mayo, *Limits*, 201–5.

135. Here I modify my position in Spencer ("Forgiveness"): "Though likely not included in Luke's original work, it has the ring of an authentic saying of Jesus and fits well in its context" (287). I would now say: "probably included." One can argue the opposite way with the Stephen prayer ("Lord, do not hold this sin against them" [Acts 7:60]), easily imagining a scribe adding a similar petition for Jesus on the cross, so that Jesus would not be upstaged by Stephen's magnanimity. But on internal grounds, it is more likely in this case, as in many others in Luke's two-volume work, that the portrait of Jesus in the Gospel sets the stage for parallels with his followers in Acts.

represents a common interpretation targeting the "godless Jews" who had clamored for Jesus's death: while Jesus's own people "were raging . . . he was praying."[136] The general, third-person plural pronoun "them [αὐτοῖς, *autois*]" allows for a broad scope of offenders needing forgiveness, though stretching "them" to all sinful humanity (a popular preaching move) stretches the bounds of Luke's narrative. The series of exchanged sayings charted above warrants inferring that the dying Jesus prays for three "enemies" who explicitly taunt him: the Roman soldiers, the Jewish leaders, and one of the criminals hanging alongside him. But including the "people" (λαός, *laos*) of Jerusalem (and Israel) at large is less certain.

Though some "people" have joined the priestly leaders in demanding Jesus's death (23:13, 18–23), others, as stressed above, "followed" him in great numbers to the cross, including sympathetic "daughters of Jerusalem" (23:27–28 [cf. λαός, *laos* in v. 27]). Once at Skull Place, the "people" are cast simply as ones who "stood by, watching [θεωρῶν, *theōrōn*]," in distinction from leaders who "scoffed" (23:35). Though we might assume guilt by association, we hear no further cries of "Crucify him!" from the crowd; and after they "saw/watched [θεωρήσαντες, *theōrēsantes*]" this "spectacle" unfold, they returned home "beating their breasts" (23:48), just like the mourning women (23:27). Space thus opens for the people's change of heart toward Jesus. Indeed, Augustine views this hopeful prospect as the purpose of Jesus's prayer: "When he was praying as he hung on the cross, he could see and foresee. He could see all his enemies. He could foresee that many of them would become his friends. That is why he was interceding for them all."[137]

This suggestion concerning the aims and effects of Jesus's "forgive them" plea brings us to the third limiting factor, concerning *ethical-theological* frameworks with political, pastoral, and personal implications. To concretize and contextualize the issue in recent times: does Jesus's example demand unequivocal, unconditional, and unilateral forgiveness by countless victims of:

- apartheid in South Africa toward their attackers;[138]
- targets of ethnic cleansing in the former Yugoslavia;[139]
- segregation and violence in African-American communities toward their oppressors in 1950–60s civil rights conflicts[140] (horrifically reincarnated

136. Cited in Just, 361 (from Augustine, *Sermon* 382.2).

137. Just, 361.

138. See Tutu, *No Future*; Mayo, *Limits*, 97–157; Burridge, *Imitating Jesus*, 347–409; Nussbaum, *Anger*, 211–46.

139. See Volf, *Exclusion*, 119–25, and *Free of Charge*.

140. See Martin Luther King's sermon "Love in Action," in *Strength to Love*, 31–41; and the discussion in Strahan, *Limits*, 114–19.

in too recent memory by Dylan Roof's cold-blooded slaughter of nine members of "Mother Emanuel" A.M.E. Church in Charleston, SC, during a Wednesday evening Bible study and prayer meeting [June 17, 2015]);[141]
- battered women across the world toward abusive husbands, fathers, boyfriends, rapists, and other perpetrators of violence?[142]

"Forgive your enemies unconditionally, as God's Son Jesus said and did—even while you're being attacked—as well as afterward." Is that the ethical-theological message of this text?

Not so fast, argues Maria Mayo, attending carefully to limits of language and context. Luke's Jesus certainly affirms forgiveness of sinners, love of enemies, and prayer "for those who abuse you" (6:28). But that does not necessarily translate by some associative property into a clear-cut call to active or attitudinal forgiveness of enemies. That is, the words can't simply be boiled down to a pat "Forgive Your Enemies" banner motto or blank check, which Jesus never explicitly mandates. The Lord's Prayer comes closest, connecting "our" daily petition for forgiveness with the practice of "forgiv[ing] everyone indebted to us" (11:4). But this prayer operates first and foremost in a nurturing *ecclesial* context ("our/we/us") with a strong *economic* edge related to *debt* remission, rather than violent damage exemption. In any case, with both the Lord's Prayer and Jesus's intercession from the cross, Mayo stresses that these are in fact pleas for *God* to forgive, independent from our feelings or gestures of forgiveness toward others, except in the case of debt release. So we cannot confidently say that Jesus himself forgives his executioners on the spot, only that he prays for God to do so. Furthermore, Mayo entertains the notion that Luke's Jesus may well *struggle* with his natural responses to brutal assault: "The image of Jesus struggling with forgiveness in the face of violence can be an empowering one for victims who also struggle. . . . Thus instead of an impossible example for victims to imitate, Jesus choosing to pray on the cross becomes a model for victims to reclaim their agency by choosing *not* to forgive their abusers."[143] Pray for abusers, if at all possible—yes; but forgive them?—not required. Pray for God to forgive (and redeem) abusers, not to wreak vengeance upon them—yes. Do not retaliate against them, meeting violence with violence—yes again. But personally and passionately forgiving them?—maybe not. That is God's business.

141. Some of the victims' loved ones responded with a breathtaking display of forgiveness toward Roof, even when confronting him face-to-face by televised feed in court. See Von Drehle, Newton-Small, and Rhodan, "Murder"; Nussbaum, *Anger*, 77–78.

142. See Mayo, *Limits*, 159–65, 185–205; Jimmy Carter, *Call*.

143. Mayo, *Limits*, 186 (emphasis original).

While I sincerely appreciate Mayo's pastoral concerns, I believe she pushes her theological exegesis too far, cutting too fine a distinction between prayer and practice, certainly with respect to Luke's Jesus. His filial intimacy with God the Father intimates a mutual, dynamic partnership through the Spirit of heart, mind, will, and action. Recall the prayerful proclamation that Jesus joyfully uttered "in the Holy Spirit": "All things have been handed over to me by my Father; and no one knows who the Son is except the Father, or who the Father is except the Son" (10:21–22). One of the divine "things handed over" to Jesus is the "authority on earth to forgive sins" (5:24), which he now exercises on the cross—in full fellowship with God—toward his persecutors. Jesus does not pass the buck to the Father, praying for God to do what Jesus cannot yet bring himself to do, namely, forgive his torturers. This is not to say that the incarnate Son just tosses off this prayer as easy as you please while hanging on the cross, still less that he provides a breezy model for *our* practice of forgiveness. Though Jesus's emotional state while uttering these words of forgiveness is not elaborated, he is no dispassionate martyr, as we have already seen. This one who wept over Jerusalem, sweat, as it were, globules of blood at Olivet, and poignantly engaged with the distraught "daughters of Jerusalem" has not suddenly flicked a Stoic switch and shifted into impassible mode. A goodly measure of human *struggle* to forgive fits Luke's passion narrative, as we have seen, with more or less emotional angst.[144] Augustine hits the right note here: "He prayed as man, and as God with the Father he heard the prayer."[145] Oddly, Mayo interprets this Augustinian comment as *separating* rather than uniting human-divine action. I think, however, that this language more readily connotes a deft negotiation

144. Mayo rightly warns that modern, popular (mis)appropriations of biblical concepts of forgiveness are "often idealized and laden with emotional freight" (212)—that is, with fervent feelings of sorrow, remorse, sacrificial love, and the like. Biblical views of repentance and forgiveness are commonly linked to practices and rituals like debt-release, fasting, and baptism, which are more transactional than emotional, not requiring some intensely *felt* heart-strains on the part of the plaintiff or adjudicator (see Mayo, *Limits*, 11–12; Konstan, *Before Forgiveness*; Lambert, *How Repentance* and "Mourning"). But while the biblical world put less emphasis than modern Western thought on separate, interiorized, psychological experience, it was scarcely anti- or non-emotional, void of basic human feelings. Rather, it *incorporated* (integrated) affective responses with physiological, cognitive, volitive, associative (relational) aspects of *holistic-embodied* life—a unitary way of life that recent interdisciplinary study of emotions is increasingly validating (see Spencer, "Getting a Feel"; Olson, "Emotion"). Note Green's (*Conversion*) apt summary of John the Baptist's correlated "conversionary" mission of baptism, repentance, and forgiveness in Luke 3:1–20: "John has begun to map the patterns of thinking, feeling, believing, and behaving that deserve the label 'conversionary.' . . . Such patterns reach into the day-to-day interactions and affairs of life. Conversion is embodied" (84; cf. 45–86).

145. Cited in Just, 361 (from Augustine, *Sermon* 382.2).

of the trinitarian bond between Father and Son (and Spirit), respecting the integrity of the fully human Jesus (body, will, emotions) in integral, intimate fellowship with God: "as man *and* as God."[146] Though Luke never formulates the Trinity in philosophical terms, his narrative supports such a dynamic, mutual-relational view of God.[147]

Other vital issues arising from the dying Jesus's intercession concern related elements of *ignorance* and *repentance*, the former leaving the door open for the latter. "They do not know [οὐ . . . οἴδασιν, *ou . . . oidasin*] what they are doing" (23:34) and "you acted in ignorance [ἄγνοιαν, *agnoian*]" (Acts 3:17; cf. 17:30) likely draw on the Torah distinction in sins between those that are "unintentional" (ignorant) and those that are "deliberate" (CEB), "defiant" (NIV, NJPS), "high-handed" (NRSV) (Num 15:30; cf. 15:22–31; Lev 4:13–21; 5:18 [ἄγνοια, *agnoia*, LXX]).[148] Unwitting, "ignorant" transgressions, though no less blameworthy, are wholly forgivable—within the "whole congregation" (Lev 4:13; Num 15:24–26)—following prescribed practices of atonement; by contrast, "whoever acts high-handedly, whether a native or an alien, affronts the Lord, and shall be cut off from among the people" (Num 15:30). Origen specifically regarded Jesus's prayer from the cross as "confirming" Levitical instruction about sins of the community committed "through ignorance" (*Homilies on Leviticus* 2.1.5).[149]

Volitional variations motivating behavior also figure prominently in Aristotle's ethics: "Since virtue concerns passions as well as actions, and voluntary [actions] elicit praise and blame, whereas involuntary ones elicit forgiveness and sometimes even pity, it is perhaps necessary for those who are examining virtue to define the voluntary and the involuntary" (*Eth. nic.* 3.1 [1109b.30–34]). He further subdivides the latter category into *in*voluntary misdeeds committed "*in* ignorance" and *non*voluntary ones committed "*on account of* ignorance": the former accompanied by feelings of "pain, regret, and disgust at the action" (at least afterward, if not before); the latter involving no such pangs, "for [in this case] the ignorance involved in one's choice *is the cause*, not of what is involuntary, but of one's corruption." Accordingly, with truly *in*voluntary acts accompanied by some remorse, "there is both pity and forgiveness"; conversely, a cold ignorance devoid of compunction merits no compassion (*Eth. nic.* 3.1 [1110b.18–1111a.2]).[150]

146. On Augustine's complex understanding of the Trinity in *De Trinitate* and other works, see LaCugna, *God for Us*, 81–109.

147. See the section "Trinitarian Theology" in the concluding "Integration."

148. See Carras, "Pentateuchal Echo"; Strahan, *Limits*, 39.

149. Strahan, *Limits*, 39, 94.

150. Aristotle, *Aristotle's* Nicomachean Ethics, trans. Bartlett and Collins (emphasis added to quotations).

What can we say, then, about the particular "ignorance" of Jesus's torturers, both cognitively and affectively? Though cruel cries for Jesus's crucifixion may appear as "high-handed" or "defiant" as any action could be, they do not automatically disclose bald, calculated intent. Mob action can suddenly erupt without careful deliberation. Since even Jesus's closest disciples remain bewildered about his suffering and death, how can anyone at this stage, least of all Jesus's persecutors, really *know* what all is happening here in the grand purpose of God? How can they fully know what they are doing? Strahan perceptively chalks up present ignorance to "essentially a misperception of Jesus's paradoxical ministry and identity—exemplified by the cross . . . linked with unillumined minds, unillumined readings of Scripture, and God fulfilling his purposes."[151] In hindsight, after further wrestling with Scripture, troubling events may come into clearer perspective, leading to repentance and renewal. But such clarity can take considerable time and effort, as with Jesus's early followers coming to grips with the paradoxical and scandalous truth (reality) of the crucified Messiah and dying Savior.

Interlacing whatever thoughts might be swirling through—and limiting—the "ignorant" minds of Jesus's executioners, what *feelings* might also be affecting (and affected by) their cruel actions? Is there any hint of remorse or angst that might blossom into a change of heart, mind, and life (= repentance) worthy of forgiveness, as Aristotle—and Luke—would have it?[152] No other Gospel writer ties repentance and forgiveness so closely together in a cause-and-effect, condition-and-result nexus: "If another disciple sins, you must rebuke the offender, and *if there is repentance*, you must forgive. And if the same person sins against you seven times a day, and turns back to you seven times and says, '*I repent*,' you must forgive" (17:3–4).[153] Unlimited forgiveness numerically—but *not* unconditionally. Repentance is a sine qua non for forgiveness in Luke's narrative (cf. 3:3; 5:32; 13:1–5; 24:47; Acts 2:38; 3:19; 17:30). So where does that leave Jesus's enemies, for whom he petitions forgiveness? Just as we are not privy to Jesus's precise feelings about his attackers (praying for their forgiveness may or may not entail felt sympathy), so we have no profile of their emotional state. But their reported actions suggest callous hearts beating, as it were, in sync with ignorant minds. Immediately ensuing responses to Jesus's saving mission—(1) Jewish leaders "scoffed" (23:35), (2) Roman soldiers "mocked" (and apparently gambled for Jesus's clothes [the subject is unspecified]) (23:36), and

151. Strahan, *Limits*, 86.

152. See n. 144 in this unit on emotional aspects of repentance, forgiveness, and conversion.

153. The parallel in Matt 18:21–22 does not include the "repentance" condition.

(3) one criminal "kept deriding" (23:39)—hardly signal any sense of regret or potential for repentance, coordinate with Jesus's forgiveness and salvation. Regardless of how Jesus or God might "feel" about them (again, we do not know) and Jesus's plea for their forgiveness, we are not left brimming with hope for their redemption.

And yet, even with these dim prospects of repentance on the part of some leaders, soldiers, and one criminal, Luke's Jesus, *for his part*, still *offers* them God's forgiveness, perhaps to spur them to reconsider their position down the line, but certainly to assert his conciliatory nature to the end. As he lived in love, he resolutely refuses to die in hate toward his persecutors. Though bound to the terrible cross in death, he remains free from the corrosive pain of bitterness. Though he cannot coerce his enemies' reconciliation to him (forced compliance is vindictive, not redemptive), he can create space for them to come to know (not remain ignorant of) and follow God's way of salvation in Christ, which they presently impugn ("Save yourself!" [23:37]).[154]

But once more I hasten to stress that "they," while wide in scope, is not a uniform entity. Luke consistently resists sweeping character stereotypes and appreciates differing, divided responses to God and God's Messiah. As we have seen, Luke has already separated out, to some extent, the "bystander-people" from the leaders (23:35); and he now highlights an exceptional case of a repentant sinner addressed in Jesus's next words from the cross.

In his *second saying*, Jesus responds to the words of the other criminal, who in fact says more than any other character, including Jesus, in the crucifixion scene. This criminal directs his comments, first, as a rejoinder to the first criminal's derision of Jesus's saving ability; and second, as a request for Jesus's deliverance (23:40–42). In rebuking the other criminal, this one acknowledges God's authority ("Do you not fear God?") and admits both malefactors' guilt and just punishment ("We are getting what we deserve for our deeds"). We know nothing about this man's religious background or, indeed, his criminal record; he and his associate are simply designated κακοῦργοι (*kakourgoi*), "evildoers" (23:32, 39). But at least at this eleventh hour he makes a true confession of God-fearing faith and personal sin; in other words, he speaks in truth, not ignorance. Whether he also *repents* is harder to determine, especially since he has scant opportunity to demonstrate a changed life. But his present disposition inclines toward "conversion,"[155] and his plea (prayer) to Jesus reflects the

154. Many thanks to Craig Noll for nudging me to write this paragraph, where I attempt to grapple with the complexities of forgiveness and reconciliation more carefully.

155. Green (*Conversion*) slots the experience of this criminal in the category of "'prior conversions'... in which people in Luke's narrative behave as people who have already aligned themselves with God's kingdom." More specifically: "Luke says nothing of the criminal's conversion,

hopeful prospect of postmortem participation in Jesus's realm: "Remember me when you come into your kingdom" (23:42).

Though what this criminal knows about Jesus's character—beyond perceiving his innocence ("this man has done nothing wrong" [23:41])—and kingdom remains uncertain, in Luke's terms, the βασιλεία (*basileia*) of God mediated by Jesus Messiah represents a right-making, justice-doing, world-mending, peace-waging *way of life* on earth (11:2, 20; 17:21), as in heaven (12:32–33; 18:22–30; 19:38). On these terms, this criminal seeks a transformed life in fellowship with "King" Jesus ("Remember me"), grounded in God's forgiving and empowering love. Indeed, the present sequence of Luke's "orderly account" suggests that this evildoer (sinner), who first encounters Jesus on their way to Skull Place, primarily perceives and believes Jesus's trustworthiness by his preceding *prayer of forgiveness* for his persecutors. Such words prompt the criminal's confessional response and attest to Jesus's grace and power to move transgressors from perilous ignorance to saving knowledge.

Jesus confirms and completes this saving cycle in his solemn answer to the criminal's plea: "Truly I tell you, today you will be with me in Paradise" (23:43). The brevity of this remarkable pronouncement belies its temporal, social, and spatial significance.

Temporally, the prominent "today" (σήμερον, *sēmeron*) signals both (1) Jesus's immediate, *local-historical* perspective on this crucial moment extending through and beyond the "dark" interruption of death (cf. 23:44) to the "light" of afterlife this very day; these grim hours of crucifixion, for all their horror, neither forfeit all traces of goodness this day nor foreclose the prospect of hopeful days to come; and (2) Jesus's transcendent, *eschatological* outlook, in which the "whole purpose" (cf. Acts 20:27) of God's saving realm is realized in the eternal "today" of Christ's liberating work (cf. Luke 2:11; 4:21; 5:26; 13:32–33; 19:5, 9).

Socially, Jesus's next two words in Greek after "today" remarkably assure the criminal not simply of remembrance but also of *presence* with Jesus: "Today, *with me* [μετ' ἐμοῦ, *met' emou*], you will be" (Greek word order). Such experiences evoke the Lord's Supper, which Jesus's followers celebrate "in *remembrance*" of him and in spiritual table-fellowship *with him* "until the kingdom of God comes" (22:18).

---

suggesting that he, like the woman from the city [7:36–50], occupies the margins of conventional society yet has (already) aligned himself with Jesus. But this is presupposed, not recounted, by the account Luke gives us" (48). Inferring some prior, unnarrated encounter with Jesus by the criminal prior to their crucifixions stretches the imagination beyond the case of the anointing woman. Thus, I think the criminal's case also fits another of Green's helpful categories: "potential conversions," setting forth "the possibility of a change of heart and life, but Luke's narrative account comes to premature conclusions before the stories are finished" (47–48). Of course, death has a way of shutting the story down; but the paradise factor opens up a "potential" future.

But on the cross Jesus pledges that this man suspended next to him will be forever "with me" literally and palpably, not just in symbol and memory. As they "hang together," as it were, in death, so they will remain united in God/Christ's kingdom.

Jesus solidifies their communal fellowship by a *spatial* setting "in Paradise [παραδείσῳ, *paradeisō*]." This locale does not so much limit Jesus's kingdom to a particular territory as orient it to a type of environment. A Persian loanword, "Paradise" evokes an idyllic garden atmosphere. The three transliterated uses in the HB designate a luscious royal garden or "King's Park" (Neh 2:8 NJPS; Eccl 2:5), or a lover's exquisite body ("Your channel is an *orchard* of pomegranates with all choicest fruits" [Song 4:13]). But numerous times the LXX refers to the primordial garden of Eden (Gen 2:8–10, 15–16; 3:1–3, 8, 10, 23–24; Joel 2:3), the "garden of the Lord/God" (Gen 13:10; Isa 51:3; Ezek 28:13; 31:8–9), or the faithful people of Israel/Zion (Isa 51:3; Pss. Sol. 14:3) as "Paradise," shading into notions of an idyllic place of blessing and postresurrection life for the righteous, an eternally restored Eden—eschatology renewing protology—in early Jewish apocalyptic writings (1 En. 32:3–6; 2 En. 8:1–3; 42:3–4; 4 Ezra 8:52; Apoc. Mos. 38:5; 40:2; Apoc. Ab. 21; T. Levi 18:10–11; 2 Cor 12:4; Rev 2:7).[156]

For Luke, "Paradise" seems to function as the blissful afterlife counterpart to the distressful Hades (Luke 10:15; 16:23–24). On a broader intertextual level, however, it may also develop an Isaianic picture of communal restoration, especially since Luke's Jesus recently linked his death among criminals with Isaiah's suffering servant numbered among the "lawless" (22:37/Isa 53:12). Notice the Greek Isaiah's framework of "paradise lost" and "regained":

> But the lawless and the sinners shall be crushed together,
>   and those who forsake the Lord shall be brought to an end.
> For they shall be ashamed because of their idols,
>   which they themselves wanted,
> and they were embarrassed because of their gardens,
>   which they desired.
> For they shall be like a terebinth
>   that has shed its leaves
> and like an orchard [παράδεισος *paradeisos*] that has no water.
> (Isa 1:28–30 NETS)

> And I will comfort you now, Sion;
> I will comfort all her desolate places,

156. See Charlesworth, "Paradise"; on the fluidity of location: "Paradise is . . . situated in different [earthly and heavenly] places according to early Jewish documents" (154).

> and I will make her desolate places
> like the garden [παράδεισον, *paradeison*] of the Lord;
> in her they will find joy and gladness,
> confession and the voice of praise.
>
> (Isa 51:3, NETS).

The desolate picture of lawless, faithless Israel languishing in a parched, pseudo-"paradise that has no water" at the beginning of Isaiah gives way to postexilic hopes of lush, paradisiacal restoration brimming with "joy and gladness" in later portions of the book (cf. Isa 35:1–2; 43:18–19; 58:11–12). In this prophetic-national schema, Jesus's ushering the supplicant "lawless" criminal into his kingdom Paradise represents his determined will to bring all his people through the deathly, desert shadows of blindness and faithlessness to the delightful, regal garden of God's forgiveness and salvation.

The dying Jesus's *third saying*, uttered in a "loud voice," signals the actual moment of expiration under a meteorological veil of darkness punctuated by a "schism" (σχίζω, *schizō*) in the material veil of the temple (23:44–46). These signs mark cosmic and cultic upheavals, the onset of terrible natural and national (Jerusalem and temple) distresses, which, however, as Jesus previously averred, also portend that "redemption is drawing near" with the Son of Humankind's return in "power and great glory" (21:28, 27). The God of Israel and all creation, the God who rightfully dwells in the Jerusalem temple (note "my house" in 19:46 [cf. Acts 7:47]) and throughout the world in temples not "made with human hands" (Acts 7:48; 17:24), will redeem God's land and people through the crucified Son, Lord, and Christ.

In this spirit of hope amid the horror of suffering, Jesus prays again to his "Father," pleading this time in the language of the innocent persecuted psalmist: "Into your hands I commend my spirit" (Luke 23:46; Ps 31:5). The verb for "commend" or "entrust" (παρατίθημι, *paratithēmi*) conveys the action of "placing/setting before," as in several feeding examples ("putting food before" [Luke 9:16; 10:8; 11:6; Acts 16:34]). But the context of Jesus's putting/entrusting himself into the Father's hands fits closer to two Pauline mission situations in Acts:

> After they had appointed elders for them in each church, with prayer and fasting they entrusted [παρέθεντο, *parethento*] them to the Lord in whom they had come to believe. (Acts 14:23)

> And now I commend [παρατίθεμαι, *paratithemai*] you to God and to the message of his grace, a message that is able to build you up and to give you the inheritance among all who are sanctified. (Acts 20:32)

In each case, Luke's Paul entrusts the care, growth, and destiny of ecclesial mission delegates to God's direct nurture. The latter passage is part of Paul's fraught, final farewell to the elders of the Ephesian church, laden with forebodings of his imminent trials and demise (20:22–24, 36–38). Similarly, in the last throes of his life, with matters out of his own cross-bound hands, Luke's Jesus entrusts himself to his Father's care. Though this move reflects Jesus's hopeful faith in God's powerful love to ferry him through the maelstrom of death to the peaceful shores of Paradise, it also conveys, in parallel with Paul's prayers, Jesus's unflagging desire for the vigorous perpetuation of God's *mission*. Jesus is planning no leisurely retirement in an eternal-celestial garden resort. His "King's Park" is a dynamic working enterprise, aiming to establish God's flourishing realm for all God's creation in heaven and earth.

Lingering a moment longer, however, with these final words, we should not overplay the comforting, confident tone of his "trustful" prayer to the exclusion of tense, even tortured, counterstrains. Recall that Jesus utters this last-gasp plea in a gut-wrenching, ear-splitting "loud voice," consonant with the temple curtain's fabric-rending screech. Once again, though not knowing Jesus's precise emotional state, we should not deny his agonizing struggle with death.[157] At the very least, his concluding prayer of entrustment to the Father does not simply sound a triumphal shout of victory, still less a gentle lullaby into that good night.

Scene 3 (23:47–49) functions as *postlude* to Jesus's crucifixion, delineating various responses to this "spectacle" briefly referenced above. We now track these reactions more carefully in three segments:

Characters	**Responses**
Centurion	"Having seen [ἰδών, *idōn*]" what happened, praises God, declares Jesus's "innocence [δίκαιος, *dikaios*]"
Crowds	Return home, "having watched [θεωρήσαντες, *theōrēsantes*]" the spectacle, beating their breasts
"Acquaintances (γνωστοί, *gnōstoi*)"—including Galilean women	Stand at a distance (μακρόθεν, *makrothen*) "observing [ὁρῶσαι, *horōsai*]"

157. Mayo (*Limits*) regards this final plea "as the most convincing evidence that Jesus experienced pain and struggled on the cross. . . . This last request does not reflect a calm and composed Jesus. . . . While he entrusts his spirit to God, the shouting portrays Jesus as pleading for rescue as much as it indicates acceptance of his fate" (181–82).

A natural progression unfolds related to physical proximity and spiritual perspicacity: the closer to the cross, the greater level of perception. But the particular characters that fit this pattern at Skull Place *invert* normal expectations.

The Roman *centurion* supervising the crucifixion squad and thus (presumably) near the cross is the last person we expect to respond favorably to Jesus. But in fact, upon seeing "what had taken place"—that is, the entire execution scene up to Jesus's last breath, including, no doubt, hearing Jesus's words—the centurion glorifies God and exclaims Jesus's "real," "ontic" (ὄντως, *ontōs* ["certainly" NRSV]) guiltlessness (23:47). Somehow Jesus's words and demeanor *affect* this officer. Somehow he senses God's righteous work amid this heinous travesty of justice—which he, the soldier, has executed! Accordingly, he experiences some change of heart, will, and mind (repentance), but we do not know the extent of his new knowledge about Jesus, still less about any faith commitment. Nothing warrants a quixotic assumption that he suddenly throws off his military gear, resigns his commission, and devotes his life to Jesus's way. At best, this is a partial conversion.[158] But it still offers hope of further knowledge and growth—of cognitive and behavioral plasticity[159]—transcending the stereotype of brutal, bullying soldiers.[160] This pattern coordinates with other positive portrayals of centurions in Luke and Acts, especially the synagogue-supporting, Jesus-honoring centurion at Capernaum (Luke 7:1–10) and the God-fearing, Spirit-receiving centurion (Cornelius) at Caesarea (Acts 10). But the centurion enforcing the state's death penalty, who abruptly reverses his opinion about Jesus at the cross, stands out as the most unusual Roman officer in Luke's account. These examples scarcely signal a Christianized Roman Empire, but they do tout the amazing redemptive potential of Jesus's life and death.

The general *crowds* of Jewish spectators ringing the ghastly crucifixion scene, just beyond the soldiers, are also deeply moved by what they witness. But they speak no words, communicating instead with their feet ("they returned home") and their fists ("beating their breasts") (23:48). Again, though we should not read too much cognitive or affective change into this silent response, the physical gestures of not lingering, "returning [ὑπέστρεφον, *hypestrephon*] [home]," and lamenting suggest some dissociation from the priestly

158. I use "partial" as an ad hoc category for "conversion." It doesn't quite fit either of Green's (*Conversion*) "potential" or "prior" types (47–49); Green does not mention this centurion's case at all.

159. See Doidge, *Brain That Changes* and *Brain's Way*; Costandi, *Neuroplasticity*; Sapolsky, *Behave*, 137–53; applied to biblical-theological study, see Green, *Body*, 115–22, and *Conversion*, 40–43.

160. See Brink (*Soldiers*), which, per the subtitle—*Engaging, Contradicting, and Transcending the Stereotypes*—focuses on Roman military personnel in Luke's narratives.

leaders and some tinge of penitential regret over their earlier maniacal "Crucify him!" cries (cf. 23:13–23). Though Luke uses a different verb here for the crowds' breast-beating (τύπτω, *typtō*) than for the Jerusalem daughters' (κόπτω, *koptō* [23:27]), the meaning is synonymous, and the mourning sympathetic. In any case, if forgiveness is predicated on some awareness of wrongdoing (see above), the general "bystanders" (cf. 23:35) seem to leave Skull Place in a forgivable posture.

In a terrible ironic twist, the *acquaintances* who "know" (γνωστοί, *gnōstoi*) Jesus and support him on some level watch him die from the *farthest* vantage point: "at a distance" (23:49). At this point, their "knowledge" does not translate into faithful fellowship. The use of general terms ("all his acquaintances" [NRSV, NASB], "all those who knew him" [NIV, CEB]), rather than the more selective "disciples" or "apostles," raises doubts about whether any member of the Twelve is present. Moreover, the "distant" (μακρόθεν, *makrothen*) placement of those looking on from the periphery eerily aligns them via the same term with (1) the tormented rich man in Hades far from Abraham's bosom (16:23), (2) the sinful tax collector far from the pious Pharisee in the temple (he also "beat his breast" [τύπτω, *typtō*] in conjunction with pleading for God's mercy [18:13]), and (3) the cowardly apostle Peter following far behind Jesus's arrest party, just before denying that he knows Jesus at all (22:54). Significantly, the latter two cases lead to forgiveness and restoration (though it takes time for Peter to get there); the gulf is bridged in this life, unlike with the rich man permanently fixed in the afterlife. But for now, the distance is disheartening and unworthy of "knowing" discipleship. It doesn't even include possible signs of grief or remorse, like the breast-pounding Jerusalem women and crowds (and the parable's praying tax collector). Jesus's "acquaintances" just stand there, far off, frozen as it were in fear, frustration, or maybe just empty numbness. Who knows?

The *women*, though implicated in the overall "distant" group, also stand out as those who "followed" Jesus "from Galilee" (cf. 8:1–3).[161] They have proven their commitment to Christ by leaving their Galilean homes and families; but then so have the male apostles (5:11). The women have no part, however, in outright betraying or denying Jesus. Moreover, only they among Jesus's associates stationed far from the cross are explicitly said to be "watching [ὁρῶσαι, *horōsai* (a feminine participle)] these things" (23:49), that is, maintaining some perceptual connection with the dying Jesus. Though the analogy is imperfect, "seeing" Jesus across the horizon may reflect their longing for him akin to the

161. These Galilean women are thus distinguished from the weeping "daughters of Jerusalem" in 23:27–28, a wider group of mourners along Jesus's route to Skull Place. Moreover, Luke does not explicitly portray these female disciples as crying here or anywhere else in this Gospel.

love-inspired father of the prodigal who "saw" (ὁράω, *horaō*) his lost son "while he was still far off [μακράν, *makran*]" (15:20). Of course, Jesus has not run away or removed himself from his (spiritual) family (though he suffers, in a way, the prodigal's destitution and "death" [cf. 15:24, 32]); and the women do not run headlong toward the debilitated Jesus to affirm their love. But the stage is set for these Galilean women to follow Jesus's body to its burial place so they might anoint it and pay Jesus their deepest last respects (23:55–24:1). No one else—not the male apostles, not anyone in Jesus's wider acquaintance circle—seeks to maintain such passionate connection with Jesus to the very end. Though these "distant" women doubtless fight their own fears and confusion (cf. 24:5), they also fight to overcome these barriers, to bridge this distance, and become the *first* to "know with solidity" (cf. 1:4) the truth of their crucified Lord's resurrection (24:5–10, 22–24). To these and other final experiences of Jesus in Luke's Gospel we now turn.

Suffering the Disciples' Persistent Confusion and Disbelief (23:50–24:53)

With Jesus's passage from life to death, especially with such an agonizing, torturous finale, we might say, as we often do in such situations: "Well, at least he's not suffering anymore; he can now rest in peace." Of course, as knowing readers of Luke, we can say more than that, anticipating not merely Jesus's peaceful postmortem repose (in Paradise), but his powerful resurrection on the third day, as he predicted (9:22; 18:33). Luke's Gospel indeed closes with dramatic testimony of the third-day, revivified Jesus (24:6–7), though, like the other NT Gospels, it says nothing about the mechanics of resurrection or what Jesus does or feels during the weekend interim. Furthermore, Luke concludes, as it begins, with benedictions of "peace" and tidings of "great joy" (24:36, 41, 52; cf. 1:41–45, 58, 79; 2:10–14, 20, 29). All's well that ends well.

But all in fact is not as well as it could be. Luke provides no fairy tale ending. As in the story's opening, so in its ending, signs of hope, joy, and peace buck against persisting strains of doubt, fear, and confusion on the part of Jesus's followers, in turn sparking some consternation *within Jesus himself.* Note the edgy tone with which the risen Jesus addresses a pair of disciples, Cleopas and an unnamed companion, whose despair blinds them to Jesus's living presence among them: "Oh, how foolish you are, and how slow of heart to believe all that the prophets have declared! Was it not necessary that the Messiah should suffer these things and then enter into his glory?" (24:25–26). To some degree, their willful ignorance, as Jesus deems it, of his messianic vocation of glory through suffering—which he (and the Scriptures) have outlined—causes Jesus further pain and suffering, the roiling frustration of *not being known*, not being seen for who he truly is, but rather as a "stranger" (24:18).

Cleopas and associate (wife?) are not the only adherents who struggle with the truth of the risen Jesus, failing to recognize and understand him. As noted above, the Galilean women *first* discern and declare Jesus's risen status; they "remembered" his forecast of resurrection and related the wondrous events at the empty tomb to the apostles (24:8–10). But even they must work through their initial turmoil and terror and have their memories jogged by divine messengers (24:4–6). The male apostles then receive the women's testimony with derisive skepticism; even when Peter runs to the tomb and confirms its vacancy, the best reaction he can muster is amazement, not faith in the risen Christ (24:10–12). The Eleven and affiliates do not respond much better when Cleopas and friend report their encounter with the living Jesus, even though the apostles now claim to believe that "the Lord has risen indeed" on the basis of a private appearance to Simon (Peter) not narrated in Luke (24:33–35). But when Jesus suddenly pops into their midst, they meet his "Peace be with you" greeting with their persisting fears, doubts, and misjudgments of this experience as a ghostly apparition rather than a real appearance of the risen incarnate Jesus (24:36–41). It takes a substantial show-and-tell lesson from Jesus to assure them of his identity and to assign them their evangelical mission "in his name to all nations" (24:47).

Ultimately, Jesus's followers—the Galilean women, Emmaus couple, eleven apostles, and others—come to know the risen Messiah *through divine guidance and revelation*. Left to their own thoughts and emotions, they would have missed the boat. Though Jesus is no "ghost" or mere "spirit" (πνεῦμα, *pneuma* [24:37]) but a whole-bodied resurrected person (24:39–43), it takes *spiritual insight* beyond purely natural intelligence to grasp the solid truth concerning the crucified-risen Lord. But the disciples in Luke (and by extension, future generations of Jesus's adherents) are not arbitrarily at the mercy of divine prerogative, perchance finding themselves in the know—or not! Luke's final chapter charts clear *paths of knowledge* or *means of revelation* that seekers may access—still requiring the aid of the Spirit and Spirit-inspired tour guides (cf. Acts 8:30–31)—but in an active, participatory process rather than a passive, automatic program.

Luke's two fundamental paths, means, or "sacraments" mediating the presence of Christ are *word* and *bread* or, more fully, "opening the scriptures" (24:32; cf. 24:26–27, 44–47) and "breaking of the bread" (24:35; cf. 24:30–31, 41–42), or *biblical scholarship* and *table fellowship* in the broadest senses: "scholarship" as serious Scripture study by any interested party (including, but not limited to professional scholars) and "fellowship" as open communion with saints and sinners in partaking of God's life-giving provisions (including, but not limited to, the bread and wine of the Lord's Supper). To use categories anachronistic to Luke, we might say that his Gospel waves both Protestant "Word" and Catholic "Mass" banners, showcasing both the Holy Bible on the pulpit and sacred Eucharistic elements on the altar, while also bringing God's word and bread to highway and household.[162]

The crucified-risen Jesus holds the key to this whole revelatory operation as its focal *subject* (the one seeing, knowing, and disclosing God) and *object* (the one seen and known). Jesus Messiah stands as the supremely authorized interpreter of the divine word, the sacred Scriptures, which are in fact "about himself" and all the things that "must/should"—"of necessity" (ἔδει, *edei*)—happen to and through him in God's plan (24:26). A christological compass guides Luke's biblical hermeneutics. Likewise, Jesus sits as the centerpiece of the table: the chief host, guest, and servant of the sacramental meal. He "took bread, blessed and broke it, and gave it" (24:30), recalling both his feeding the hungry masses (9:10–17) and his final self-offering of body and blood "for you all," as a guarantee of the "new covenant" bond between God and God's people (22:14–20). "In the breaking of the bread" the crucified-risen Lord was "made known [ἐγνώσθη, *egnōsthē*]" (24:35).

Luke's postmortem and postresurrection narrative unfolds in three main acts involving various characters and settings in and around Jerusalem, including the Judean villages of Arimathea (23:51), Emmaus (24:13), and Bethany (24:50). Though Jerusalem clearly remains the hub of activity, as in the beginning of Luke (cf. temple references in 1:9 and 24:53), considerable movement in and out of the holy city (23:51, 55–56; 24:1, 9, 12, 13, 28, 33, 50, 52) reinforces Luke's journey motif in the interest of charting God's centrifugal saving mission in Christ "to all nations, beginning from Jerusalem" (24:47; cf. Acts 1:8).

At the Tomb with Joseph of Arimathea and the Women of Galilee (23:50–24:12)

As processes surrounding reproduction and birth were taken very seriously in Jewish law and society, so were customs pertaining to preparation and burial of the dead; both front and back portals of life and death were highly regulated. Accordingly, as Jesus's parents complied with laws of circumcision, purification, and dedication after Jesus's birth (2:21–27), so we expect similar scrupulosity in handling Jesus's dead body. But this matter is fraught with complications, since

162. See a fuller discussion in the section "Creational Theology" of the final "Integration."

Jesus dies in ignominy as a criminal of the state. Mosaic law required that even a publicly executed malefactor, "hung on a tree," be taken down before sundown and given a decent burial, lest the land be corrupted with this exposed object of "God's curse" (Deut 21:22–23; cf. Josh 8:29; 10:26–27). The cruel alternative leaves the suspended corpse for wild raptors and dogs to ravage (cf. 2 Sam 21:9–10) before discarding the mangled body in a shallow grave or ditch for further molestation. Such was a common fate of crucifixion victims in the Roman penal system: the more gruesome the end, the greater the deterrent to would-be enemies (though Rome could make some concessions for Jewish burial customs in Judea).[163] Family members or friends could try their luck pleading for loved ones' bodies, but in Jesus's case, no relatives are present (remember that even "acquaintances" keep their distance); and in any event, neither they nor any Galilean associates carry enough clout to command favors from Roman officers. The women from Galilee, including the named Mary Magdalene, Joanna, and Mary the mother of James (but *not* Jesus's mother Mary, as in John 19:25–27), remain most committed to caring for Jesus's dead body (23:49, 55–56; 24:10), but they can scarcely take matters into their own hands. So how can Jesus's crucified body receive proper treatment?

Enter an unexpected patron, one Joseph from Arimathea, a nearby Judean town, according to Luke, though otherwise unknown. Remarkably, he goes directly to Pilate, successfully petitions for Jesus's body, duly prepares it for burial, and before day's end places it "in a rock-hewn tomb where no one had ever been laid" (23:53). The urgent timing is critical, since it was late in the afternoon before the sacred Sabbath begins (at sunset) (23:54), and any corpse contact would defile the handler for seven days (cf. Num 19:11–22; 31:19). So who is this amazing Joseph, appearing only in these few verses in Luke (and parallels), and what does his strategic role in Jesus's burial signify? Several aspects stand out in relation to other characters and interests, especially from the birth narratives.

- Joseph of Arimathea is introduced as a virtuous man, of "good and righteous" character (23:50), the "righteous" (δίκαιος, *dikaios*) attribute mirroring that of Zechariah, Elizabeth, and Simeon in the nativity stories (1:6; 2:25) and of the crucified Jesus a few verses before (23:47).
- Joseph is further identified as a "member of the council [βουλευτής, *bouleutēs*]," or Jewish Supreme Court (Sanhedrin), headed by the chief priests, who prosecuted Jesus before Pilate and Herod. We now learn, however, that Joseph of Arimathea had not consented "to their plan [βουλῇ, *boulē*]

163. See McCane, *Roll Back*, 89–108; Craig Evans, *Jesus*, 113–40; Crossan, *Who Killed Jesus?*, 160–88.

and action" (23:51).[164] Though outvoted on Jesus's death sentence, Joseph boldly supports Jesus by petitioning Pilate for his corpse (23:52). So not all Jewish authorities oppose God's Jesus-centered "plan." Early in Acts, another councilor, a Pharisee named Gamaliel, also remains open to the divine origin of the "plan" (βουλή, *boulē*) of salvation rooted in the crucified-risen Christ, proclaimed by Jesus's apostles (Acts 5:38–39).

- Joseph's advocacy for Jesus edges beyond a legal "not guilty" decision toward a more devotional affinity, given that "he was waiting expectantly for the kingdom of God" (Luke 23:51), aligning with the dispositions of Simeon, of Anna, of "all who were looking for the redemption of Jerusalem [and Israel]" at the time of Jesus's birth (2:25, 38), and, most proximately, of the criminal on the cross acknowledging Jesus's transcendent kingdom, extending beyond death (23:42). Again, we cannot assume from Luke's Gospel that Joseph has become a full-fledged convert, true disciple (Matt 27:57), or even "secret" disciple (John 19:38). But Joseph does publicly and actively embrace Jesus (literally taking him in his arms) in his weakest and most shameful state.[165] That is more than the apostles and other disciples, except the Galilean women, do.
- Joseph demonstrates his solicitous care of Jesus's body in a threefold process: "he [1] took it down, [2] wrapped it in a linen cloth, and [3] laid it in a rock-hewn tomb" (23:53). Such hands-on treatment broadly recalls that of the Samaritan toward the half-dead victim on the Jerusalem-Jericho road (10:33–35). More directly applied to Jesus, however, Joseph of Arimathea's handling of his bloody, lifeless body provides an eerie juxtaposition with Mary of Nazareth, who "wrapped" his (bloody) newborn body in strips of cloth and "laid" it in a manger (2:7).[166] This arcing connection between Jesus's birth and death reinforces his identification with human vulnerability and suffering from start to finish as central to God's plan of salvation (cf. 2:29–35) and also, within this incarnation plan, Jesus's *dependence on others' bodily care* to fulfill his mission. Though intimately partnered with God the Father and full of the Holy Spirit, the Son of Humankind is not

164. Only Luke among the canonical Gospels makes this dissent of Joseph explicit (cf. Matt 27:57–61; Mark 15:42–47; John 19:38–42).

165. William Lyons (*Joseph*) unpacks the rich reception history of Joseph of Arimathea from the NT through the twentieth century in terms of a dialectic between "an *active* man, looking at examples of his bravery, his wealth and influence, his masculinity, his sanctification, and his dominance over others; and . . . a *passive man*, looking at examples of his guilt, his fear, his secretiveness, his malleability, and his submissiveness to those who have appropriated him" (7 [emphasis original]).

166. See Johnson, 53.

self-sufficient. He needs mother Mary to bear and nurse him, Simon of Cyrene to bear his cross, and Joseph of Arimathea to bury him. Though Lord and Co-regent of God's realm, Jesus Messiah cares for—and is cared for by—the faithful community in mutual restorative service.

- Only Luke and John stress that Joseph of Arimathea places Jesus in a "rock-hewn tomb *where no one had ever been laid*" (23:53; John 19:41). The significance of this unused sepulcher is not clear. The resonance with Jesus's entry into Jerusalem on "a colt that has never been ridden" (Luke 19:30) perhaps evokes similar associations with purity (undefiled space) and royalty (unrivaled status). Or perhaps the new "stone cut" (λαξευτός, *laxeutos*) tomb suggests Joseph's wealth (cf. "rich man" in Matt 27:57) and willingness to use it in providing for the poor, in this case, Jesus. But maybe the import of this vacant tomb simply lies in Jesus's being laid to rest *alone*, without the "companionship" of other dead bodies, typically those of relatives in other slab compartments or in ossuaries (bone boxes).[167] While this isolation might suit Jesus's unique position as Lord and Christ, it also signifies his tragic abandonment by his "family" of followers (cf. 8:21), more "far" than near in his direst hours, as we have seen. In their place, however, a new and surprising cadre of sympathizers has arisen—a Cyrenean pilgrim, a Jerusalemite group of women, a Roman centurion, and an Arimathean councilor—portending the redemptive power of Jesus's death for all people.

Consider further *Galilean women disciples*, who resist their distancing discomfort with the crucified Jesus and "followed [after] [κατακολουθήσασαι, *katakolouthēsasai*]" (23:55) his deceased body (superintended by Joseph), just as they had "followed" (συνακολουθέω, *synakoloutheō*) his live body from Galilee (23:49) and "*saw* the tomb and how his body was laid" (23:55) in advance of returning with oils and spices at dawn (Sunday) after the Sabbath (24:1). While all four Gospels then feature these women's distinguished roles as the first to know and bear witness to Jesus's empty tomb and resurrection, curiously Paul and other NT writers never mention them (cf. 1 Cor 15:3–8). Among all the "things/words [λόγων, *logōn*]" Luke wants Theophilus and others readers to "know with solidity" (Luke 1:4), the fact of the crucified-risen Jesus's saving rule as living Lord is paramount. He would agree with Paul's

167. Lyon (*Joseph*) suggests that Luke adds the note about the "unused [tomb], presumably . . . to remove the potential ambiguity of Mark's account as to the presence of other bodies" (16). But he does not elaborate on the significance of this fact. On ossuaries in ancient Palestine, see McCane, *Roll Back*; Craig Evans, *Jesus*, 97–102, 113–27, 145–47.

desire "to know Christ and the power of his resurrection" (Phil 3:10; cf. 3:8) as the primary goal for Christian discipleship and flourishing. Unlike Paul, however, Luke highlights the Galilean women as principal models for such knowledge.

As noted above, the women's path to knowing the living Christ is far from smooth; and we now observe that they are not initially guided by scriptural scholarship and table fellowship that prove so illuminating later in Luke 24. While the women *may* participate in these eye-opening experiences (see below), they first benefit from more *specialized revelation*, aided by divine messengers, as with Zechariah, Mary, and the shepherds. Still, however, like their counterparts involved in Jesus's (and John's) birth, the Galilean women must actively engage with revelation to grasp its significance. We may summarize their perceptual process—not as fixed formula, but as instructive example—as follows:

Presence and preparation (23:55–24:1). Though the women have every intention of anointing Jesus's body on the third day—and thus do not anticipate his resurrection—they at least remain as close to him as they dare and act as dutifully as they can. They locate Jesus's tomb on Friday afternoon and return there early Sunday morning with "prepared" unguents for his corpse. Unlike the absent and inattentive disciples, the women put themselves in a position to receive further insight.

Confusion and consternation (24:2–5a). When confronted with evidence of Jesus's resurrection—in the form of a displaced tombstone, vacant tomb, and pair of "men" (24:4) or "angels" (24:23) in gleaming garments[168]—the women do not initially perceive its significance. Of course, the clues could point elsewhere, such as to grave-robbing (cf. Matt 28:11–15), though the dazzling "men" are unlikely thieves. But whatever options run through the women's minds, they could scarcely sort them out. Luke reports that they are cognitively "perplexed [ἀπορεῖσθαι, *aporeisthai*]," or "in a confused state of mind . . . be at a loss,"[169] emotionally "terrified [ἐμφόβων, *emphobōn*], and physically overwhelmed ("bowed their faces to the ground") (24:4–5): all perfectly natural reactions in the face of dissonant circumstances, compounded by the extraordinary trauma still engulfing the women. In other words, they respond as normal human beings, not weak women. In the face of the past three days' harrowing events, they proceed through a modified cycle of "flight" (keeping their "distance"), "fight" (clinging to Jesus's body as best they can), and "freeze" (feet and faces stuck

168. On special divine messengers or "angels" (24:24) called "men," see Abraham's visitors in Gen 18:1–22 and Paul's vision of a "man of Macedonia" in Acts 16:9.

169. BDAG, 119.

to the ground).[170] But again, at least they engage in the process and struggle through the ordeal, rather than ceding to total escapism or denial.

Remembrance and report (24:5b–10). The distraught and stunned women receive the insight they need from the two divine spokesmen. Though spotlighted in dazzling attire, these messengers focus not on themselves, but exclusively on *Jesus's prior word*, spoken "to you [all], while he was still in Galilee" concerning the Son of Humankind's impending crucifixion and resurrection on the third day (24:6; cf. 9:22). Here the christological principle of interpretation concentrates on Jesus's prophetic words. The messengers' urging the women to "remember" Jesus's message confirms in retrospect (analepsis) their continued accompaniment of Jesus and the Twelve since 8:1–3 (though they have not been mentioned since!), reinforced by repeating the names of Mary Magdalene and Joanna (8:2–3; 24:10).[171] To their credit, these women indeed break through their cognitive-affective haze to "remember" Jesus's words and also break out of their physical paralysis to report to the eleven apostles what they have seen, heard, recalled, and by all accounts, now *believe* concerning the risen Christ. Now well ahead of the spiritual knowledge curve, they also find their own independent feet and voice in witnessing to the resurrection. As Seim stresses, whereas Mark treats the women at the tomb like "errand girls," dispatched by an angelic "young man" to tell "the disciples and Peter" (Mark 16:7), Luke features "their own spontaneous initiative as a continuation of what they themselves have heard and remembered."[172]

Dismissal and displacement (24:11–12). Yet, the women's struggle to solidify their faith in the crucified-risen Lord is not over, as their perseverance and perception are set in stark relief against the ridicule and rivalry of the Eleven. Beyond a healthy, cautious desire to verify the women's testimony for themselves, the male apostles utterly dismiss their report as an "idle tale" (24:11 NRSV, KJV). The derisive term "idle" (λῆρος, *lēros*) connotes sheer "nonsense" (CEB, NAB, NASB, NIV), "that which is totally devoid of anything worthwhile

170. On various passive and active responses to fear, anxiety, and trauma from a neuroscience perspective, see Frazzetto, *Joy*, 89–113.

171. While Luke's belated, retrospective connection between the Galilean women in Luke 24:6–10 and 8:1–3, including the named Mary Magdalene and Joanna, implies these women's ongoing association with Jesus in the intervening material (see Karris, "Women"), this link is, unfortunately, considerably weaker than with Jesus's male disciples, who continue to be regularly featured in Jesus's remaining Galilean mission and long journey to Jerusalem. In turn, the Galilean women followers drop completely from view for almost sixteen chapters until resurfacing in 23:49 (the Martha and Mary snippet in 10:38–42 involves nontraveling Judean devotees of Jesus) (cf. Spencer, *Salty Wives*, 8–9, 111, and "Women," 1009–11).

172. Seim, "Gospel of Luke," 748–50.

... humbug."[173] The nearest related usage in Hellenistic Jewish literature comes from the lips of the Greek-Syrian tyrant Antiochus, attempting to shame the devout Jewish leader Eleazar into renouncing kosher law, on pain of torture and execution: "Come on [Eleazar]! Wake up from your silly philosophy, and get rid of your brainless [λῆρον, *lēron*] thinking!" (4 Macc 5:11 CEB). From the viewpoint of the apostles in Luke, we might suspect an added sexist component involving prejudgments of women's proclivities toward hysterical, "brainless" babbling.[174] At least Peter respects the women's report enough to dash to Jesus's tomb and check out the scene himself. But while confirming Jesus's missing body ("he saw the linen cloths by themselves"), he receives no interpretive word and is merely "amazed" at the situation, not (yet) with full understanding (24:12; cf. 24:24). Though the narrative focus begins to shift from the women to Peter as chief apostle (cf. 24:34), at this stage he still appears as a "pale variant," as Seim discerns, of the prescient women of Galilee.[175]

On the Road to Emmaus with Cleopas and Companion (24:13–35)

As the Galilean women upstage the Eleven in discovering the empty tomb and hearing about Jesus's resurrection, two otherwise unknown disciples, Cleopas and companion, precede the apostles in meeting the risen Christ in Luke. Once again, Simon Peter represents an exception of sorts: as he ran to the tomb to investigate the women's report (24:12), so he has some private experience with the living Jesus; but Luke relates this rendezvous only briefly and belatedly, almost as an afterthought, when the Emmaus couple returns to Jerusalem to relay their good news (24:33–35). Luke's Emmaus Road story constitutes the longest and liveliest postresurrection narrative in the Gospels, matched for sheer dramatic power only by John's account of Mary Magdalene's garden meeting (John 20:1–18).[176] The original apostles have no special claim on Jesus, who remains after his death, as he was before it, the accessible and embracive Lord of the least in society, including a group of women and a pair of ordinary travelers.

173. BDAG, 594.

174. On the Greco-Roman stereotype of the "hysterical woman," exploited by Celsus, for example, in his critique of early Christian origins stemming from a "fantastic tale" of resurrection promulgated by dubious female witnesses (Origen, *Cels.* 2.55), see Margaret MacDonald, *Early Christian Women*, 1–8, 104–9.

175. Seim, "Gospel of Luke," 751.

176. The Emmaus incident holds a prominent place in the history of interpretation, not least in vivid artistic renderings by Titian, Rembrandt, and Caravaggio; see Hornik and Parsons, *Illuminating*, 119–49; for other art related to this incident, see Vinson, 748–52.

Once again, knowledge breaks through a thicket of confused thoughts and mixed feelings. As with the women, the "aha" moment for the Emmaus duo culminates a complex deliberative-emotional process, rather than erupting out of the blue.[177] Moreover, their experience has a marked *comic* edge, both in the literary sense of a positive outcome to a tragic plot and in the mundane sense of a funny, almost farcical, turn of events. It is hard not to laugh at the hapless couple as they wax on about the devastating death of their beloved Jesus to this *very same Jesus*, whom they do not recognize, now alive and walking right beside them! They even blurt out in exasperation: "Are you the only stranger in Jerusalem who does not know the things that have taken place there in these days . . . the things about Jesus of Nazareth?" (24:18–19). It is a testimony to Jesus's self-control that he doesn't burst out laughing at this point! But he keeps playing the part—and playing with the two travelers—teasing out their state of heart and mind and teaching them what they need (what is "necessary") to know (24:26). In a more philosophical vein, humor functions to expose starkly incongruous aspects of life—like coming to grips with a *crucified Messiah*—and to manage them via mocking protest (satire, sarcasm) or therapeutic release (comic relief) en route to creative resolution.[178]

Irony, a close cousin of comedy, also emerges as Cleopas and companion proclaim key features of Jesus's identity in the midst of their doubt and despair. They declare more than they know at the time, unwittingly setting the stage for what they will soon know with assurance (solidity). The analysis below will track their perceptual pilgrimage from confusion to recognition and their christological proclamation from (1) stranger to (2) prophet to (3) host.[179]

Emmaus couple	**Risen Jesus**
Walking and talking with each other →	Introductory question: "What are you discussing?" (24:17)
Standing still, looking sad, mocking this *stranger's* (Jesus's) ignorance of recent events ("things") →	Clarifying question: "What things?"

177. Cf. Aristotle, *Rhet.* 2.5 (1383a): "Fear makes people inclined to deliberation, while no one deliberates about hopeless things" (trans. Kennedy).

178. On incongruity in humor/comedy, see Jackson, *Comedy*, 6–9, 35, 61–62, 68–69, 225–26, 231–33; Spencer, *Dancing Girls*, 26–28.

179. The arrows in the chart represent the direction of activity/response. Notice the middle shift in the flow of initiation from the travelers to Jesus.

Emmaus couple	**Risen Jesus**
Recounting *prophet* Jesus, who was "mighty in deed and word" (24:19), and his crucifixion and the women's report of the empty tomb →	Prophetic interpretation of "the things about himself in all the scriptures" (24:27)
Urging the stranger (Jesus) to stay at their house	← Walking ahead as if departing
Recognize Jesus as risen Lord	← Staying with them, but acting as *host*, breaking, blessing, and distributing bread at the table
Reflect on road encounter with Jesus and return to Jerusalem to report to the Eleven and companions	← Vanishes from their sight

Along their seven-mile trudge from Jerusalem to the village of Emmaus, the two disciples, likely among Jesus's "acquaintances" at the outer edges of Skull Place, discuss the terrible events surrounding his crucifixion and the implications for their lives.[180] Luke's use of present and imperfect verb forms casts their speech as a "sustained conversation," according to Carroll, perhaps even "a spirited exchange of differing opinions" concerning the tragedy of Jesus's death: they were "talking [ὡμίλουν, *hōmiloun* (imperfect)]," "talking [ὁμιλεῖν, *homilein*] and discussing [συζητεῖν, *syzētein* (present infinitives)]," and "you are discussing [ἀντιβάλλετε, *antiballete* (present)]" (24:14–15, 17).[181] The last two terms especially connote a more disputative dialogue than casual conversation: "debating, arguing" (συζητέω, *syzēteō* [cf. Luke 22:23; Acts 6:9; 9:29]); "throwing, tossing [ideas] back and forth" (ἀντιβάλλω, *antiballō* [used only here in the NT]). Grappling with the scandal of the crucified Messiah is no easy matter, no cushy fit within a nice little "homily" (derived from ὁμιλέω, *homileō*).

The promise, however, of a quick and happy resolution arises with a third traveler, whom we know to be the living "Jesus himself," sidling up alongside the couple (24:15). Although Jesus makes no dramatic entrance (he just seems to join the two travelers in "natural" fashion), we expect Cleopas and friend

180. The perfect participle in the phrase "all these things that had happened [συμβεβηκότων, *symbebēkotōn*]" (24:14) suggests discussion of the completed past events surrounding Jesus's death that held fast or stood pat in present memory.

181. Carroll, 483.

to notice him straightaway and hang on his every word. But stunningly, "their eyes were kept from recognizing [ἐπιγνῶναι, *epignōnai*] him" (24:16), and they bring him into their dispute about Jesus's identity and mission. Of course, this is not the first time that perception has been "hidden" from Jesus's disciples, specifically regarding his betrayal, death, and resurrection. In previous texts, passive verbs with no designated agent implied divine causation of the "hiding" effect (9:45; 18:34),[182] as the flip side of God's sight-giving revelation through Jesus and the Spirit (10:21–24). But in the present case, Luke uses a stronger verb, assessing the eyes of the Emmaus pair as "being seized up" or "forced shut" (ἐκρατοῦντο, *ekratounto*)—not simply "kept" (NRSV, NIV) or "prevented" (CEB, NAB)—"from recognizing [Jesus]" (24:16). A divine passive may not be apt here. The immediate context accentuates less God or Jesus's role in the two travelers' experience than their self-inflicted turmoil. Their own bitter distress over Jesus's horrific death has "seized" their senses, effectively rendering them incapable of more accurate, positive appraisals. Anyone who has suffered deep grief and depression will acknowledge the distortive, even blinding, effects of these negative thoughts and emotions.[183] The narrative attributes three muddled states of mind and "heart" to the Emmaus couple, the first (hopelessness) and last (heartburn) self-confessed, the middle one (heart-slowness) diagnosed by Jesus.

1. *Hopelessness*: "They stood still, looking sad. . . . 'But we had hoped that he was the one to redeem Israel'" (24:17, 21). The death of Jesus by crucifixion shattered Cleopas's and his companion's hopes and dreams, which they had pinned on Jesus as God's dynamic prophet and Messiah, for the salvation of God's people (24:19–20). The cross cast its dark, thick shadow across their consciousness, stripping Jesus of all his "mighty" force (24:19), reinforcing the corrupt authority of the priestly leaders who delivered him to death (24:20), and rendering the empty tomb of Jesus ("just as the women had said") a puzzling curiosity at best, a pernicious indignity at worst. Though the women also relayed the angelic announcement that Jesus was alive, "they did not see him" (nor did anyone else) (24:22–24). Unlike the women's troubled minds, which quickly opened up to divine revelation, those of the Emmaus couple remain closed and snared in the vortex of a depressive spiral.[184] Like the devastated

182. These texts use perfect participle forms of different verbs, both denoting "hide/conceal": παρακαλύπτομαι, *parakalyptomai* (9:45) and κρύπτω, *kryptō* (18:34). The latter also applies in 19:42 to the wider Jerusalem populace, from whom the significance of God's visitation in Jesus Messiah is "hidden."

183. For an insightful discussion of the five human senses in relation to life, not least "spiritual" life, see Moltmann, *Living God*, 157–75 (in relation to grief in particular, see 165–66).

184. The term for "looking sad" in 24:17 (σκυθρωπός, *skythrōpos*), used only here and in

house of Israel in Ezekiel's vision of dry bones ("our hope is lost; we are cut off completely" [Ezek 37:11]) or the passengers on the storm-wracked ship transporting the prisoner Paul to Rome ("all hope of our being saved was at last abandoned" [Acts 27:20]), the pair of Judean travelers are frozen in their tracks of despondency, unable to entertain any hopeful prospects of salvation. The irony, however, both tragic (in the present painful confusion) and comic (in the pending joyful resolution), in all these cases is that the Creator-Redeemer God of Israel remains firmly committed to rescuing—*resurrecting*—God's people from lethal fates. The desiccated bones of Israel *live again*, with vibrant flesh and breath infused by God's Spirit (Ezek 37:1–14); God assures the safety of Paul and all who sail with him through turbulent waters (Acts 27:22–25), in order that Paul may testify in Rome to the abiding "hope of Israel" (28:20), which he intimately ties to the *general resurrection of the dead*, spearheaded and guaranteed by the *particular resurrection of Jesus Messiah* (23:6–8; 24:15, 21; 26:6–8, 22–23); and this very risen Jesus lives and breathes, walks and talks, alongside the downcast couple toward Emmaus, though the light of recognition has not yet dawned on their hopeless minds.

This "principle of hope," propounded by the philosopher Ernst Bloch and modulated into a Christian key by Jürgen Moltmann, the prominent "theologian of hope," stands at the heart of Jewish-Christian faith. As Moltmann reflects on the origins of his monumental *Theology of Hope* (1964) fifty years later: "I asked myself: Why has Christian theology allowed this theme of hope to escape it? Are not God's promises and human hopes the scarlet thread running right through the prophets of the Old Testament and the apostles of the New? Aren't Jews and Christians the people of hope in this world? Doesn't everything in Christian theology draw toward the future of God—that is to say, eschatology?"[185] Of course, the central, most crucial, strand in this eschatological scarlet threat is the *resurrection of Christ*. As Paul so aptly puts it, "If for this life only we have hoped in Christ, we are of all people most to be pitied [most miserable, KJV]. But in fact Christ has been raised from the dead, the first fruits of those who have died" (1 Cor 15:19–20).

2. *Heart-slowness*: "Oh, how foolish you are, and how slow of heart to believe all that the prophets have declared!" (24:25). The pitiable/miserable mental and emotional state of the Emmaus couple is complicated by a heart condition, as Jesus diagnoses, specifically "bradycardia" (βραδεῖς τῇ καρδίᾳ, *bradeis tē kardia* [24:25]), or slow pulse, as opposed to the runaway beat of tachycardia.

Matt 6:16 in the NT, mixes the prospect of anger with grief: "of sad or angry countenance, sullen," "gloomy" (LSJ, s.v.).

185. Moltmann, *Living God*, 177.

Of course, this is not a physical cardiac condition, but rather a psychological phenomenon related to the heart as the seat of will, thought, and emotion. Ancient notions of the passions could closely associate with organic heart functions—such as fear with heart pounding or anger with blood boiling around the heart—but Aristotle, for example, also distinguished between physiological and more broadly philosophical analyses of psychic or "soulish" responses (see *De an.* 1.1.25–33 [403a]). Even today, though our neuroscience view pinpoints the brain, not the heart, as the primary locus of cognitive, affective, and volitional activity, metaphors of "heartfelt" experience remain alive and well.

In the present case, Jesus's exposure of Cleopas's and his associate's "slow" hearts closely entwines with their "foolish" minds, their nonunderstanding, thoughtless, "anoetic" (ἀνόητοι, *anoētoi*) disposition, especially with respect to "believing" (apprehending, affirming, trusting) "all that the prophets have declared"—including the prophet Jesus speaking to them now! (24:25). Jesus takes a direct cognitive-affective approach, challenging the couple to defang their misguided despair with a healthy dose of prophetic truth, of seeing and feeling things as they truly are from God's life-restoring perspective. Moreover, Jesus engages the troubled pair, not as an armchair professional or even a stump-standing prophet, but as a *fellow traveler*, on the road and in the trenches with them, not only sympathizing with their plight, but also agonizing over it to the point of frustration: "*Oh* [Ὦ, Ō], how foolish you are" carries more than a tinge of "*Oh, for goodness' sake!* How can you keep acting, thinking, and feeling this way?!"

The temporal image of "slowness" to reflect mental dysfunction or deficiency carries over in common English usage (a "slow" learner), though not in more recent psychological research. In *Thinking, Fast and Slow* the eminent psychologist Daniel Kahnemann tracks two main systems of thought: System 1, involving fast, intuitive, emotion-charged responses; and System 2, involving slower, more deliberative, logic-based assessments. While System 1 gut reactions can be perceptive, even life-saving (quick recoils from danger), they can also be deceptive and limited in scope (most serpentine objects on the ground are not snakes). Better decisions about complex matters usually result from careful, slower, System 2 cogitations, which check and balance first emotional impulses.[186]

The NT makes the same point in its only other uses of "slow" (βραδύς, *bradys*): "You must understand this, my beloved: let everyone be quick to listen, *slow* to speak, *slow* to anger" (Jas 1:19). With respect to the Emmaus disciples, then, we might say that their slowness to grasp the truth of Jesus's resurrected presence is because of an overreliance on *fast*, snap judgments clouded by exces-

186. Kahneman, *Thinking*, 19–105; Haidt, *Righteous Mind*, 27–51.

sive grief and despair; what they need—and what Jesus guides them through—is a *slower*, more deliberative, trek through the Scriptures, "beginning with Moses and all the prophets" (24:26). In other words, their "slowness" to believe relates to their not thinking *slowly enough* about the right things.[187]

3. *Heartburn:* "Were not our hearts burning within us while he was talking to us on the road, while he was opening the scriptures to us?" (24:32). This query constitutes a retrospective reflection on Jesus's walking Scripture seminar *after* the Emmaus couple finally recognizes—when Jesus breaks bread at their house—that he was traveling and talking with them all along. We may interpret these afterthoughts as a classic case of dealing with *cognitive dissonance*, a natural human proclivity labeled and investigated by Leon Festinger and colleagues.[188] In the face of exposed failures, people tend to reframe past attitudes and circumstances to mitigate their erroneous beliefs. "How could we have been so blind and hardhearted," Cleopas and companion may be musing, "to treat our Lord like a stranger while he was right there with us? But come to think of it, we weren't complete dullards, were we? Didn't we begin to feel some inner firing of recognition, some stirring of Christ's dynamic presence in our hearts?" Of course, considering the possible rationalizing elements of their reflections doesn't mean they experience no "real" heartburn along the road. They may simply fan into greater flame certain flickers of early perceptiveness.

In any event, what does the image of "burning" (καίω, *kaiō*) hearts signify? In biblical usage, the verb often signals God's authoritative and supportive presence among the people, as at Mount Sinai with Moses ("burning bush") and the Israelites (Exod 3:2; Deut 4:11; 5:23; 9:15) on the altar and lampstand of the tabernacle throughout the desert journey ("keep a light burning constantly" (Lev 24:2 CEB; cf. 6:12–13; 24:3–4; Exod 27:20–21). But such divine burning can scorch as well as sustain, expressing God's *anger* with Israel and/or her *enemies* (e.g., Isa 10:16–18; 30:27; 33:14; 50:11; Jer 7:20; 15:14; 21:12; 30:23). So a certain volatility and mix of feelings boils within a burning heart. With the Emmaus pair, this electric experience is wired to Jesus's *Scripture-saturated words* regarding Moses and the prophets, reminiscent of Jeremiah's lament:

> O Lord you have misled me, and I was misled;
> you got the upper hand and prevailed;
> I have become a laughingstock all day long;

187. Cf. Moltmann, *Living God*, 170: "The spirit must free itself from worries and expectations and must learn how to be still. . . . 'The discovery of slowness' and calm give back health and happiness to the tense and harassed life, as wisdom tells us."

188. Festinger, *Cognitive Dissonance*; Festinger, Riecken, and Schachter, *When Prophecy Fails*; cf. Tavris and Aronson, *Mistakes*, 13–51; Gilovich and Ross, *Wisest One*, 112–27, 172, 205–6.

I continued to be mocked,
because I will laugh with my bitter speech;
I will call upon faithlessness and wretchedness,
because the Lord's word has become for me
a reproach and a derision my whole day.
And I said, "I will not name the name of the Lord
and will no longer speak in his name."
And it became like a *burning* [καιόμενον, *kaiomenon*] *fire flaming* in my
bones,
and I became limp everywhere, and I cannot bear up.

(Jer 20:7–9 NETS)

Though dropped by the LXX (and NRSV), the MT speaks of the Lord's word burning in the prophet's "heart" (לב) as well as his bones: "But His word was like a *fire raging in my heart*, Shut up in my bones; I could not hold it in" (20:9 NJPS; cf. CEB, NAB, NASB, NIV).

Clearly this inner word-burning is not an altogether pleasant experience for Jeremiah, as it proves unbearable, uncontainable ("I am drained trying to contain it" [CEB]), and uncongenial ("The Lord's word has become for me a reproach and a derision my whole day" [NETS]). But the prophet also realizes that "the Lord is with me like a strong warrior," who vindicates his word and messenger in the face of persecution, "who tests what is right . . . who understands kidneys [νεφρούς, *nephrous* = passions][189] and hearts [καρδίας, *kardias*]" (20:11–12 [NETS]). Similarly, we might infer that Cleopas and companion recollect an incipient effect of Jesus's Scripture-based prophetic word as paradoxically destabilizing and solidifying, disorienting and reorienting, weakening and quickening—a complex stirring of hearts.

As already noted, the hermeneutical key to the Emmaus disciples' understanding of the living, saving Christ is *Jesus himself* mediated through the word of Scripture and the bread of Communion: "he interpreted [διερμήνευσεν, *diermēneusen*] to them the things about himself" (24:27). This christological principle keeps the sacraments of word and bread in proper perspective, clarifying their function as means *of* Christ's self-disclosing grace more than *to* Christ's discovery by seekers. Christ's roles as authoritative prophet-teacher *of* God's word (which testifies to Christ) and incarnate breaker-giver *of* God's bread (which is Christ's body) are indispensable, not optional, to God's redemptive

189. Or "emotions" as in NETS annotation; νεφρός, *nephros* ("kidney") functions similarly to σπλάγχνον, *splanchnon* ("bowel, intestine") as a metaphor for intense mental and emotional stirring of the "inner life" (see BDAG, 670; cf. Jer 11:20; 17:10).

plan. The two travelers are not in fact seeking the living Christ (any more than were the women at the tomb: "Why do you look for the living among the dead?" [24:5]), as they trudge away from Jerusalem to Emmaus, discussing their *loss* of Jesus. But he seeks them and reveals himself, though not immediately. He takes them as they are, where they are, leading them to knowing recognition slowly (matching their "slowness of heart"), but surely. Though in charge of the walking tutorial, Jesus does not impose himself on the distressed pair. He draws them out step by step, responding to their words about him and actions toward him. The Emmaus Road is not the Damascus Road. No blinding light or knock-down punch here.

Notice the couple's progressive perception of Jesus, under his guidance, from *stranger* to *prophet* to *host*.

First, they initially peg Jesus as a *stranger* or, literally, "one living away from home [παροικεῖς, *paroikeis*]," either as a resident immigrant or a visiting pilgrim. Moreover, in their almost farcical ignorance, they further marginalize this presumed interloper as a clueless dolt, "the only stranger in Jerusalem who *does not know* [οὐκ ἔγνως, *ouk egnōs*] the things that have taken place there in these days" (24:18). Amid the comedy, irony piles upon irony. Obviously, it is the Emmaus couple who don't know what really happened with Jesus's death in Jerusalem or what's going on now with his living presence right next to them. And, of course, no one is more "in the know" about these events than Jesus himself.

Nevertheless, as we have tracked, Luke's Jesus in fact *has intimately identified* with strangers, exiles, and other displaced homeless persons throughout his life: from his birth in a manger, since there was "no [other] place for them in the lodging site" (2:7 AT), through his drifter mission with "nowhere to lay his head" (9:58), his death on a Roman cross, and isolated burial in a nonfamilial tomb, which he left (empty) as soon as possible to hit the road again! As God's dynamic presence sustained Abraham, Moses, and their people throughout their long journeys and stints as "resident aliens [πάροικον, *paroikon*] in a country belonging to others" (Acts 7:6; cf. 7:29)—and since Israel's God is also the Creator and Sustainer of all peoples and abides "not far from each one of us" (Acts 17:27; cf. 17:24–31; 10:34–36)—so Jesus embodies God's saving presence with all beings, near and far (2:39), resident and itinerant, settled and exiled, Jew and Gentile (cf. Luke 2:30–32).

But Cleopas and companion are not yet ready to grasp this bigger picture. And Jesus does not immediately confront their rude mistaking him as a foreign fool with a counterrebuke or bombshell revelation. Instead, he continues his opening gambit of drawing them out. His initial query regarding their general topic of conversation ("What are you discussing?" [24:17]) now extends, after their mocking his ignorance, to more particular interest in their concerns: "What things [are bothering you]?" (24:19). He aims to hear from them, to know their story, before moving to correct and comfort them.

At this point, the travelers unload their confusing thoughts and feelings (examined above) about Jesus's dynamic ministry, tragic death, and enigmatic absence from the tomb (24:19–24). Here we focus on their headline description of "Jesus of Nazareth [as] a *prophet* mighty in deed and word before God and all the people" (24:19). This prophetic profile nicely encapsulates Jesus's vocation in Luke, consonant with his self-proclaimed agenda in Nazareth, linked with Isaiah, Elijah, and Elisha (4:16–30), and Peter's summary review: "You know the message . . . how God anointed Jesus of Nazareth with the Holy Spirit and with power; how he went about doing good and healing all who were oppressed by the devil, for God was with him" (Acts 10:36, 38). Picking up on the Emmaus couple's prophetic cue, Jesus shifts from exploratory to hortatory mode, challenging and instructing them in God's word.

We have already discussed the basic "burning" impact of Jesus's prophetic-scriptural exposition on Cleopas and partner. We now add two points of clarification. First, Luke offers no particular prooftexts or "fulfillment" references here, only the bare report that Jesus unfolds the scriptural plan concerning the Messiah's "necessary" passion: he "must suffer [ἔδει παθεῖν, *edei pathein*] these things and then enter into his glory" (24:26–27 AT). In fact, no prophetic text explicitly announces the Messiah's death and consequent glory, still less his crucifixion and resurrection. But christological biblical hermeneutics is less about compiling a catena of texts than discovering the panoramic vision of the whole Bible, "beginning with Moses and all the prophets" (24:27), disclosing God's purpose of salvation pulsing through rejected prophets, suffering servants, and persecuted righteous ones, preparing the way for God's consummate Messiah, the crucified-risen Jesus. The scandal of the cross begins to make sense only in light of postresurrection reviews of God's word illumined by the Spirit and tutored by Christ himself.

Second, the risen Jesus confirms his prophetic power (δυνατός, *dynatos*) with the two interlocutors primarily in "word" rather than "in deed" (24:19). Of course, returning from the dead is as dynamic a manifestation of God's might as one could hope for. But no divine voice or dove sign manifests itself on the Emmaus Road, unlike at Jesus's baptism in the Jordan River; his glorified body does not glow here, as on the transfiguration mount; and he performs no special feats for the two travelers. By his prophetic word, he guides them through the scriptural word, which provides a permanent, solid path to saving knowledge now and for all generations. Miracles are nice, but they tend to be sporadic and transitory; by contrast, "the word of our God will stand forever" (Isa 40:8; 1 Pet 1:25; cf. Luke 21:33—"Heaven and earth will pass away, but my words will not pass away").

The one act Jesus does perform at journey's end in Emmaus is notable for its *ordinariness*, its *mundane materiality*, infused with sacred significance. At table in Cleopas's home, Jesus shifts from stranger and prophet-guest to *host* without fanfare: he simply "took bread, blessed and broke it, and gave it to them" (24:30). No multiplying loaves and fishes for a spontaneous feast (9:10–17); no summoning manna (Exod 16) or raven-caterers (1 Kgs 17:6) from the heavens; no overflowing of flour jar and oil jug (1 Kgs 17:13–16). Just blessing and sharing the daily bread Cleopas and companion have on hand, communing with one another around common goods. Of course, this act evokes the mirror scene—accompanied by explanatory words—at Jesus's institution of the Eucharist on the eve of his crucifixion, memorializing Jesus's death "until the kingdom of God comes" (Luke 22:18). As God's right-making kingdom flourished in Jesus's pre-Easter earthly life (11:20; 17:20–21), so God's salvation "comes" afresh in the risen Jesus, mediated through the domestic realia of bread-breaking. God's gracious rule keeps breaking into earth, into earthiness, into earthly things. More personally, it finally breaks into the consciousness of the Emmaus couple. Now they remember. Now they "recognized [ἐπέγνωσαν, *epegnōsan*]" the living Jesus (24:31).

But no sooner do they discern his real identity than he "vanished from their sight [ἄφαντος ἐγένετο, *aphantos egeneto* (lit. became invisible)]" (24:31). Well, that certainly is a nice trick beyond Jesus's capability before his resurrection. But critically, it is *not* this "invisible man" routine that impresses the Emmaus disciples. In fact, it is completely irrelevant to them: they do not say a word about it. After scurrying back to Jerusalem to report to the apostles and others, they focus strictly on "[1] what had happened on the road, and [2] how he had been made known to them [ἐγνώσθη, *egnōsthē*] in the breaking of the bread [in their home]" (24:35). Jesus's bread-breaking and table-fellowship, not his disappearing act, are definitive and declarative for resurrection faith.

Though Jesus takes charge of matters when the traveling party reaches Emmaus, the two disciples initiate one final act. When the group approaches the village, the still unrecognized Jesus stretches ahead of the pair, "pretending to go much further away" (24:28b AT).[190] He continues his play acting, but with a purpose. In pretending to leave, he *intends* to stay but opens up space for the disciples to participate in the communion process. Far from leaving

190. Πορρώτερον (*porrōteron*), the comparative form of πόρρω (*porrō*), conveys the idea of considerable distance ("[much] further away") rather than simply "ahead" (NRSV); cf. 14:32 and the cognate πόρρωθεν (*porrōthen*), "from afar, at a distance," in 17:12.

them in limbo, he aims to stimulate their desire to learn more. And they do not disappoint, for "they urged him strongly" to lodge with them in Emmaus (24:29a),[191] precisely as the "open-hearted" Lydia presses Paul to stay at her home in Philippi (Acts 16:14–15).[192] As the risen Lord reveals himself through Scripture-exposition and bread-breaking, he also longs to be sought, to be invited to the table. Such mutual involvement provides the optimal environment for knowing God's way in Jesus Messiah.

Given Jesus's evident longing, however, to stay at Cleopas's home—similar to, though more subtly expressed than with Zacchaeus ("I must stay at your house today" [19:5])—why does he pop out so quickly, the very moment he's recognized? What purpose does this sudden getaway serve? On one level, it matches the Spirit-snatching and relocating of Elijah the prophet (1 Kgs 18:12; 2 Kgs 2:11) and of Philip the evangelist (Acts 8:39), accentuating the Spirit's sovereign guidance of God's emissaries.[193] Luke's Jesus soon pops *in* on the apostles and associates (including the Emmaus couple) in Jerusalem and from there leads the group to Bethany, from where he's "carried *up* into heaven" (24:36, 50–51). Jesus's sudden vanishing from the Emmaus table, then, portends his interim heavenly destiny. He has come back to life to solidify God's reign on earth, but not yet to complete it; he jump-starts God's kingdom but does not yet stay to charge it fully. His followers must carry on his work when he's carried away, as Jesus soon explains (24:47–49). He will remain with them in memory, in spirit, in word and bread shared in his corporate, ecclesial body, but not (for a while) in his corporeal, individual body. They must not hold on to him. Luke's Jesus scarcely gives the Emmaus couple any chance to touch him in their home. Though he invites them and others to "handle" (ψηλαφάω, *psēlaphaō*) him in Jerusalem (24:39), it is not clear that anyone takes up his offer (cf. John 20:17–18, 24–29). Jesus's followers must find their own feet, hands, and voices, as they learn to know, experience, and serve him through Bible- and table-sharing.

191. Luke accentuates the action of the minidrama in 24:28b–29a with an alliterative sequence of "p" and "r" sounds: προσεποιήσατο πορρώτερον πορεύεσθαι καὶ παρεβιάσαντο (*prosepoiēsato porrōteron poreuesthai kai parebiasanto*), which we might approximate as "[he] pretended to proceed past, and they pressed [him to stay]."

192. The hospitality invitations of the Emmaus couple in Luke 24:29 and Lydia in Acts 16:15 represent the only two uses of παραβιάζομαι, *parabiazomai* ("urge") in the NT, suggesting a forceful, pressured plea. Moreover, in both stories, the hosts who open their homes also find their eyes/hearts "opened" (from διανοίγω, *dianoigō*) to the Lord's word (Luke 24:31, 32; Acts 16:14).

193. For connections between the Emmaus Road incident in Luke, Philip's encounter with the Ethiopian eunuch in Acts, and the Elijah narratives, see Spencer, *Portrait*, 135–45.

In Jerusalem and Bethany with the Eleven Apostles and Companions (24:36–53)

The risen Jesus appears to his followers "while they were talking" about the strange events surrounding his death, resurrection, and appearances to Simon Peter and the two Emmaus disciples (24:36a; cf. 24:15). He thus interrupts their christological conversation, suggesting that they cannot simply talk their way to the truth about him but still require his tutelage. As with prior in-group discussions, they are liable to be led astray by self-interested preoccupations (cf. 9:46; 22:24); and of course, reports of Jesus's empty tomb and, now, two sightings, plunge the company into a whirlpool of perplexing thoughts and feelings. There is still much to sort out.

The present group numbers the eleven apostles, Cleopas and associate, and various unspecified "companions" with them (24:33), likely including the Galilean women. The group situates in Jerusalem, probably in the same large upstairs room where the apostles celebrated their last Passover with Jesus (22:12; cf. Acts 1:13). Unlike on the Emmaus Road, where Jesus unobtrusively "comes near" and engages the two travelers (24:15), here he materializes inside the room (24:36), just as suddenly as he vanished from Cleopas's home. Doors and walls seem no obstacle for Jesus's resurrected body. Although Luke doesn't overplay Jesus's supertransport capabilities (no "locked doors" as in John 20:19, 26), his pop-in appearance jolts the assembly and ramps up their already agitated and excited state. Again, the effects cut to the "hearts" (Luke 24:38) of the disciples, this time stirring up an inner maelstrom of fear and "doubts/questions/arguments [διαλογισμοί, *dialogismoi*]" (cf. Luke 2:35; 5:22; 6:8; 9:46–47), with strong undercurrents of joy and surprise (wonder/amazement [θαυμάζω, *thaumazō*; 24:41]).[194] In Kahnemann's terms, their System 1 impulses kick into overdrive. They scarcely know how to process this vision. Is it a true appearance or a mere apparition of Jesus? Is this the resurrected embodied Jesus or some metaphysical postmortem manifestation of Jesus's "spirit" (πνεῦμα, *pneuma* [24:37, 39])? Is this the "real" Jesus they followed or just his "ghost"—holy or not?!

Again Jesus responds to his disciples' confusion with some frustration, though not quite with the stinging rebuke he levied against the Emmaus travelers. Here he offers a gentler indicting query—"Why are you frightened, and why do doubts arise in your hearts?" (24:38)—still tinged, however, with an

194. The verb (ταράσσω, *tarassō*) which Jesus uses to describe the disciples' agitated condition in 24:38, rendered "frightened" in the NRSV, means "to cause movement, usually as the result of shaking or stirring . . . to 'stir up'" (Louw and Nida, *Greek-English Lexicon*, 1:212); cf. reference to an actual whirlpool in John 5:7, prompting my use of "maelstrom" and "undercurrents" language.

edge of personal disappointment: "Don't you recognize me? It is I, Jesus! I've come back alive to you, and you do not seem to know me!" But whatever his own feeling, Jesus aims to guide his befuddled disciples to greater understanding, particularly seeking to ground their continuing relationship with him in *peace* and *faith*.

He opens with a conventional "Peace be with you [εἰρήνη ὑμῖν, *eirēnē hymin*]" greeting, though with more intent than satisfying social protocol. Various levels of "peace" are in view: internal (within), relational (among), and universal (throughout).

- First and most immediately, Jesus tries to forestall the terror and anxiety *within* the disciples that his sudden appearance evokes. Their "startle" reaction, however, is primary (and primal) and not much eased by Jesus's "peace" salutation, which they can scarcely "hear" yet.[195]
- Second, Luke's Jesus doubtless seeks peace *among* the group and himself: not simply individual relief, but also interpersonal reconciliation. Jesus previously predicted the divisive household strife that his mission would foment (12:49–53), which has proven all too true in relation to his own "family" of followers plagued by betrayal, denial, distancing, and doubt. But such discord was never Jesus's goal. Recall that at the Last Supper, Jesus both predicted Peter's threefold denial and pledged his prayerful support for Peter's restoration and outreach to his beleaguered "brothers" (22:31–34). Now, the risen Jesus voices that prayer for peace for the wider body of disciples.
- Third, within the larger arc of Luke's Gospel, Jesus's greeting evokes God's grand purpose to bring peace *throughout* the world, to forge the "way of peace" (1:79) for all peoples on earth in reflection of the Creator's glory "in the highest heaven" (2:14). From birth (2:14) through life, death, and resurrection (24:36), Jesus inexorably works out God's cosmic purpose for perfected peace.

At the moment, however, Jesus's disciples are not able to hear Jesus's word of peace or to see the big theological picture of God's peaceable kingdom. Understanding requires some response of *faith* (πίστις *pistis*), which Jesus also

195. On the hard-wired "startle reflex" in most animals to various fear-inducing stimuli, see Panksepp and Biven, *Archaeology of Mind*, 184–86, 224–26. Note especially the preconditions of anxiety and visual perception (relevant to the disciples' present experience) that prime the pump for a startle reaction: "It is well-established that anxiety—sustained fearfulness—sensitizes this startle pathway. For instance, visual cues that predict shock make the startle response more intense" (224, 226; cf. 186 on this "potentiated startle" effect).

seeks to inspire.[196] Again we may consider various levels of faith, including cognitive belief, affective trust, and active loyalty.[197] Clearly sensing the disciples' failure to accept his overture of peace amid their fears and doubts, Jesus doesn't simply retort, "Why do think and feel this way?" (24:38 AT), and pop out again until they are in a better frame of mind. Rather, he tries to build their faith, to boost their confidence, by offering visible and tactile evidence of his risen body (24:39–40). By both showing them his hands and feet and inviting them to touch his body,[198] he desires to trigger their (re)cognition ("it is [really] I myself" [24:39]) and affection (physical and emotional feeling), to rekindle their belief and trust (reconciliation again). Until these first "stages of faith" happen, there is no point pressing the disciples into active duty or commanding them to do anything.[199] As opposed to blind faith or banal obedience, genuine faith leading to faithful action must be grounded in solid knowledge (cognitive belief) and experience (affective trust). But Jesus's "proof of identity" display doesn't completely do the trick. Though the disciples begin to feel stirrings of joy and amazement (24:41), they do not yet "feel" full-blown faith; and they do not, as far as we know, actually touch Jesus, as he urges. Still embroiled in fears and doubts, they remain "disbelieving" or "without faith" (ἀπιστούντων, *apistountōn* [24:41]).

For the most part unsuccessful in helping his distressed disciples by "passing the peace" and showing them his body, Luke's Jesus again resorts to the twin paths to knowledge—shared food and scriptural word, though with some variations. First, with respect to *food*, Jesus makes an incredibly ordinary request, given the high drama of the situation: "Have you anything here to eat?" The matter-of-factness of the scene continues as they "gave him a piece of broiled fish, and he took it and ate in their presence" (24:41b-43). Fine, a snack break may be useful before getting back to tense negotiations. But in Luke's scheme of things, this is no casual interlude; by now we know that nothing related to

196. See Anselm's *Proslogion*, 1: "I believe so that I may understand" (*credo ut intelligam*); and the alternative title to this work (see preface), disclosing his theological banner: "Faith Seeking Understanding" (*fides quaerens intellectum*); cf. Migliore, *Faith*, 4–7.

197. For helpful theological discussions of faith as belief and trust, see Tillich, *Dynamics*; Peters, *Sin*, 273–313; for in-depth historical analysis of the various dimensions of faith in Greco-Roman literature, including the LXX and NT, see Morgan, *Roman Faith*.

198. The Lukan Jesus's invitation for his disciples to see and touch his flesh-and-bone hands and feet, as proof of his identity and humanity, resonates with a similar offer in the Fourth Gospel; there, however, in order to satisfy Thomas, Jesus presents his nail-printed hands and sword-pierced side as evidence (John 20:24–27). Luke makes no mention of the nail marks or gashed side.

199. See Fowler's influential study (*Stages*), which tracks contemporary faith development through the life cycles. With respect to the disciples in Luke, I use "stages of faith" more loosely to indicate a broadly developmental process (journey, pilgrimage), but no set sequence.

food and eating is *merely* ordinary. Though Luke does not explicitly state that the apostolic company recognizes Jesus in table fellowship, as with the Emmaus couple (24:35), he clearly implies that they come to know the living Lord with assurance *in* his requesting, taking, and eating of the fish. For whereas just before this action, the narrator mentions the disciples' persisting disbelief (21:41a), thereafter he reports nothing more about their qualms. The story concludes on a series of high notes, as Jesus's confidants duly receive his teaching, follow him to Bethany, worship him after his ascension, and return to Jerusalem "with *great joy*" (24:44–53).

So why is this fish nosh so revealing? At first blush, it may not seem to carry the symbolic weight of Jesus's Eucharistic bread-and-wine ritual. There was no fish at the Last Supper, and Jesus functions more as guest than host in the present table scene. But his very first revelatory encounter with Peter, James, and John, was altogether enmeshed in a *fishing* expedition. After expounding the "word of God" to the crowd from Peter's shore-moored boat, Jesus directed him out into the lake for a fresh catch, even though the entire evening's work had yielded nothing (5:1–5). The ensuing huge haul of fish directly triggered Peter's initial recognition of Jesus's lordship (5:8), total renunciation (with James and John) of everything to follow Jesus (5:9, 11), and official commission by Jesus in fishermen's terms: "From now on you will be catching people" (5:10).

If this was the greatest fishing incident in Luke, the greatest feeding episode also involved fish, this time in tandem with bread. Again after teaching the crowd, Jesus functioned not only as the host who "blessed and broke" the comestibles, but also as the agent who *first* told the apostles, "*You* give them something to eat" (9:13). Then after they brought him the available five loaves and two fish, he sanctified, multiplied, and "gave them to the disciples to set before the crowd" (9:16). Jesus thus enlisted the Twelve (and the Seventy[-Two] soon thereafter) as fellow hosts and servants to multitudes of needy people, intimating their wider mission to come (9:1–6; 10:1–20).

These two major fishing scenes prove just as revealing of Jesus's identity and vocation as the Last Supper. Aptly, then, Jesus evokes these deep-seated memories in his farewell visit with his disciples. Just "a piece [μέρος *meros*] of broiled fish" given *to* and eaten *by* Jesus is all that is needed (24:42–43). No big splash of fish in nets or on the table this time (note again, lesser miraculous deeds give way to the consummate act of Jesus's resurrection)—just enough to activate the disciples' recognition of their Lord and their readiness to carry on his serving and saving work in his name.

Second, with respect to *word*, now having the disciples' full attention, Jesus again turns to the Bible, with the specific goal of opening "their minds [νοῦν, *noun*] to understand the scriptures" about his messianic vocation (24:45).

Given the tight mind-heart, cognitive-affective nexus, Jesus's calming of the disciples' troubled "hearts" has created more "open," less cluttered, space for contemplative reflection on God's word. As on the Emmaus Road, Jesus focuses on the overarching scriptural drama unveiling the Messiah's necessary passion and resurrection. Though still refraining from text citations, the risen Jesus fleshes out his biblical vision in notable ways.

Christological word. Jesus prefaces this Scripture seminar with an emphatic link to his prior teaching: "These are *my words* [οἱ λόγοι μου, *hoi logoi mou*] that I spoke to you while I was still with you—that everything written about me . . ." (24:44). This link recalls the messengers' announcement to the women at the tomb ("Remember how he told you, while he was still in Galilee" [24:6]). But apart from reminding the disciples that he had already covered this material (which they never quite learned), Jesus also ties a taut knot between *his words* and the words of Scripture about him. He speaks as God's ultimate authorized prophet and interpreter of holy writ.

Canonical word. To "Moses and all the prophets" in 24:27, Jesus now adds "the psalms" (24:44), hinting at the emerging tripartite Hebrew canon of Torah (Moses) + Nevi'im (Prophets) + Ketuvim (Writings, featuring the Psalms) = the *TaNaK* acronym (cf. the prologue to Sirach). God's central purpose of salvation through the suffering and rising Christ thus spans the whole horizon of Jewish Scripture, including its principal hymnbook. God's redemptive work through the suffering "Holy and Righteous" Jesus (Acts 3:14; 7:52), adumbrated in the Psalms, is worth singing about (cf. Ps 16:8–11/Acts 2:25–31; Ps 110:1/Luke 20:41–42; Acts 2:34–35; Ps 118:22/Luke 20:17; Acts 4:11; Ps 2:1–2/Acts 4:25–26).

Consummated word. Framing, confirming, and expanding his inaugural prophetic announcement in the Nazareth synagogue that "today this scripture [from Isaiah] *has been fulfilled* [πεπλήρωται, *peplērōtai*] in your hearing" (Luke 4:21), the risen Jesus now proclaims that "everything written about me in the law of Moses, the prophets, and the psalms *must be fulfilled* [δεῖ πληρωθῆναι, *dei plērōthēnai*]" (24:44). Without Matthew's catalog of specific "fulfillment" texts, Luke still shares the conviction that Jesus Messiah's life, death, and resurrection represent the climactic realization of God's saving plan unveiled across the canon. Also like Matthew, Luke envisions this fulfillment as a positive, consummative "filling full" of scriptural promise, not a negative, substitutive replacement (cf. Matt 5:17–20).

Commissioned word. In concert with Jesus's passion and resurrection, he adds the vital dimension of *proclamation*. Notice the triad of infinitive complements to what "is written" in Scripture: "Thus it is written, that the Messiah is [1] *to suffer* [παθεῖν, *pathein*] and [2] *to rise* [ἀναστῆναι, *anastēnai*] from the dead on the third day, and that [3] repentance and forgiveness of sins is *to be proclaimed* [κηρυχθῆναι, *kērychthēnai*] in his name to all nations [ἔθνη, *ethnē*]" (Luke 24:46–47). The good news of Christ's restorative, reconciling death and resurrection is not for private, elite, or ethnocentric consumption, but rather for the whole world. It is multinational or global in scope, as it *always has been* in the mind of the Creator-Redeemer God. And it is intentionally collaborative, co-missional, in active partnership with the living Lord, not accomplished by him alone. Accordingly, Christ commissions (co-missions) his followers to proclaim God's saving word throughout the world—the gospel word rooted not only in scriptural revelation, but also in *personal experience*, as Jesus adds: "You are *witnesses* of these things" (24:48). Jesus's ambassadors can speak with authority, authenticity, and compassion only concerning *what they know intellectually and experientially* from God's inscribed and incarnate word fulfilled in the suffering and living Christ (cf. Acts 4:19–20).

In laying out the global project of proclaiming God's restorative gospel throughout the earth, "beginning from Jerusalem" (Luke 24:47; cf. Acts 1:8), the risen Jesus retains an integral connection with the interests of heaven, where God's righteous rule already flourishes without hindrance. The eternal God inexorably drives toward the cosmic eschatological goal of reconciling all things in heaven and earth through Christ, "so that God may be all in all" (1 Cor 15:28). Accordingly, Luke's Jesus promises to equip his commissioned witnesses with "power [δύναμιν, *dynamin*] from on high [the heavenly sphere]." They have no hope of participating in God's mission apart from divine energy. Indeed, they must not begin bearing witness *until* (ἕως, *heōs*) they are Spirit-"clothed" (ἐνδύω, *endyō*) to do so, to bring heaven to earth, so to speak (Luke 24:49).

Of course, Jesus's own endowment with the power of *God's Spirit* has been evident from the beginning of his life and ministry (1:35; 3:22; 4:1, 18–19), and he already promised that the "heavenly Father" is "much more" than willing "to give the Holy Spirit to those who ask him" (11:13). Now the crucified and risen Jesus is about to take another monumental step, solidifying his command of all the resources of heaven to equip his witnesses on earth for their evangelical mission in his name. Nothing and no one stand still long in Luke's story; God's redemptive project moves persistently forward, outward—and upward. In his last acts in this Gospel, Jesus leads his followers *out* of town to nearby Bethany, from where he "is carried *up* into heaven." Both before and "while" Jesus ascends, he "blesses" his disciples with uplifted (not laid-on) hands,[200] prompting

200. Syntactically, "he withdrew/departed [διέστη, *diestē* (aorist passive indicative)]" in 24:51 is framed by contemporaneous, iterative actions of "blessing" (ἐν τῷ εὐλογεῖν, *en tō eulogein* [articular present infinitive]) and "carrying-up" (ἀνεφέρετο, *anephereto* [imperfect passive indicative]) *during* the departure. In the book of Acts, the early church shows solidarity with and support of commissioned agents through the laying on of hands (Acts 6:1–6; 13:1–3). But uplifted hands are

their worship of Jesus, return to Jerusalem, and perpetual "blessing [of] God in the temple" (note well the mutual flow of blessing [εὐλογέω, *eulogeō*] among Jesus, the disciples, and God [24:50–52]). Though Jesus "withdrew" or "departed" (διΐστημι, *diïstēmi*) from his followers (24:51), these dramatic actions attending his ascension certify a *continuing dynamic connection* between Lord and disciples, God and people, heaven and earth, rooted in practices of joyous worship and gracious blessing. And the stage is set for Jesus's *majestic session* at God's right hand, from where, as Luke picks up in his second volume, the Father will hand off, as it were, "the promise of the Holy Spirit" to the Lord Jesus Messiah, which he "poured out" on the believing assembly in Jerusalem (Acts 2:33).[201]

Luke ends his Gospel as a cliffhanger drama to be resumed and partly represented in the Acts sequel.[202] Note the following bridges between Luke and Acts:

- Jesus's revealed "proof of life" to his disciples through table fellowship (Luke 24:30–31, 35, 41–42; Acts 1:1–3; 10:40–41—"God . . . allowed him to appear . . . to us who were chosen as witnesses, and who *ate and drank with him after he rose from the dead*").
- Jesus's charge that the disciples bear witness to God's saving purpose (including repentance and forgiveness of sins) in Christ's suffering and resurrection to the whole earth, beginning in Jerusalem (Luke 24:46–48; Acts 1:8; 2:32, 38; 3:14–20; 10:39–43).
- Jesus's charge that the disciples wait in Jerusalem for the outpouring of divine power (Luke 24:49; Acts 1:4–5).
- Jesus's ascension into heaven (Luke 24:51–53; Acts 1:9–11; 2:33).
- The disciples' joyous worship of God in the temple (Luke 24:53; Acts 2:46–47; 3:1; 5:42).

The promises of God remain sure and enduring. The redemptive work of God in Christ proceeds "without hindrance," despite much opposition, ob-

---

also familiar signs of blessing and communing with God and God's people (see Exod 9:22; 1 Kgs 8:22, 54; Neh 8:6; Pss 28:2; 63:4; 134:2; 141:2; 1 Tim 2:8). Here the ascending Jesus's raised hands mark a closing benediction (as practiced in many churches), though by no means a final separation.

201. See the clear and careful exposition "The Ascension and Session of Jesus" in Bird, *Evangelical Theology*, 449–59.

202. See Skinner, *Intrusive God*, 4–5: "Acts does not pick up exactly where Luke left off. Jesus ascended to heaven at the end of Luke's Gospel after making a few brief appearances to his followers during the course of a single day. When we read about the ascension in Acts, the clock has been turned back. Acts first describes Jesus still physically present with his followers, interacting with them in Jerusalem over a protracted, forty-day period."

struction, and confusion (cf. Acts 28:31).[203] And it proceeds apace during Jesus's physical *absence* from earth through the Spirit-empowered mission of Jesus's followers. To be sure, Luke's second volume quickly adds to the ascension scene two white-clad messengers encouraging Jesus's disciples that he "will come in the same way as you saw him go into heaven" (Acts 1:11); and in the interim the living Jesus also makes a dramatic personal visit to Saul/Paul on behalf of his harassed witnesses, with whom he empathizes ("I am Jesus, whom you are persecuting" [9:5]).

But as we end our journey through Luke's Gospel, we pause a moment and "wait" with the disciples, trying to apprehend their expectation of God's guiding care, their disposition of "great joy," and their commitment to grateful worship *after* Jesus has left them. They have finally found their feet—and their faith—on solid ground and stand poised to carry on Jesus Messiah's gospel mission in his name.

203. The very last word in Luke's two-volume narrative is ἀκωλύτως, *akōlytōs* ("unhinderedly," "without obstruction" [Acts 28:31], reinforcing the breakdown of social, ethnic, and religious boundaries that "hinder/block" (κωλύω, *kōlyō* [Luke 6:29; 9:49–50; 11:52; 18:16; Acts 8:36; 10:47; 11:17]) the outreaching and embracive thrust of the gospel.

Integration: Theological Reflection on Luke

Reflecting on Luke Systematically

Referencing Luke's prologue, Kevin Vanhoozer avers that "a 'system' of theology must ultimately give 'an orderly account' concerning the things of which Scripture informs us (Luke 1:3–4)." Vanhoozer, of course, is not claiming that Luke—or even Paul, for that matter—was a systematic theologian in the traditional sense.[1] Luke was a historical storyteller,[2] not an academic philosopher or theologian. But he was an "orderly" plotter of a story conveying "solid" (ἀσφαλής, *asphalēs* [1:4]) beliefs, ideas, and perspectives about the protagonist, Jesus the Christ, the supreme divine-human agent of God's saving work in the world. Luke was thus a *narrative theologian*[3] in the dual sense that (1) his story serves as a dramatic vehicle for "know[ing] the truth" (1:4) about God's climactic work in Christ, and (2) this theological truth may be unpacked, as a

1. Vanhoozer, *Faith*: "The apostle Paul was neither academic theologian nor ethicist; instead, he was a pastor *and* theologian who speaks about the 'is' and the 'ought' in Christ at one and the same time" (31, emphasis original).

2. See Parsons, *Luke: Storyteller*, 13–50.

3. Vanhoozer would doubtless prefer labeling Luke a *dramaturgic theologian* or *theodramatist*, given Vanhoozer's preference for drama over narrative as a foundation biblical-theological genre. His suspicions of narrative, which he dubs tongue-in-cheek as "the generic darling of the canon" for postliberal interpreters (*Drama*, 273), have to do with narrative's supposed priority of "telling" the "word" over "showing" the "act" as drama does, on "story-telling" over "story-dwelling" (a lovely phrase stressing how biblical characters inhabit, and embody or live out, their parts *within* the drama of redemption) (*Faith*, 29; cf. *Drama*, 48–49). In another place, however, Vanhoozer impugns "the narrativist tendency to make action more important than thought" (*Faith*, 32). Though I recognize certain generic distinctions between narrative and drama, I also see considerable overlap and do not find word/act, act/thought, telling/showing binaries helpful or necessary. For a rich, multitextured narrative-critical reading of Luke's two-volume story, there's no better place to start than Tannehill's works *Narrative Unity* and *Shape*.

second-order operation, in an "orderly," systematic array of topics. I focus on the latter in this concluding section.

Since theological interpretation of Scripture is grounded in both general (universal, catholic) and particular (local, eccentric) ecclesial tradition, my approach has a certain Baptist flavor appropriate to my religious location. We Baptists lack the historic theological giants of other Protestant traditions (Luther, Calvin, Wesley), though we do not hesitate to poach their classic ideas (and those of Catholic thinkers, patristic, medieval, and modern) and also have our own cadre of favored theologians.[4] Furthermore, many Baptists remain staunchly committed to individual and local-church religious freedom,[5] concomitant with a certain wariness of ecumenical creeds ("no creed but Christ") and ecclesiastical authority. Such freedom by no means suggests a free-for-all smorgasbord of Christian beliefs and practices, but Baptists have generally been more comfortable with *confessional* than creedal language, that is, with voluntarily consented corporate confessions or statements of faith, supporting but in no way superseding or delimiting personal *professions* of faith.[6] In any case, Baptists above all have placed the highest premium on *biblical authority* interpreted "from below," by each believer ("priesthood of the believer"); whatever quibbles we might have with Luther and Lutherans and however suspicious we might be of Latin expressions, Baptists readily rally around the Protestant emphasis on *sola Scriptura* and back-to-the-Bible roots.

As it happens, in no area has Baptist commitment to biblical-theological exegesis been more evident in recent generations than in the study of Luke's Gospel. Major commentaries on Luke in recent decades have come from seasoned "moderate" Baptist scholars from the southern US, notably by Alan Culpepper (1996), Richard Vinson (2008), David Garland (2011), and Mikeal Parsons (2015).[7] I highly recommend all of these works. Though sharing a similar Baptist heritage, however, these scholars' interpretations of Luke have their own distinctive hues—appropriate to the freedom principle in Baptist thought (and the angle of the commentary series they write for). Along with consulting

4. I will engage with some of these below, particularly Walter Rauschenbusch, Paul Fiddes, and James McClendon.

5. See Shurden's treatment of "four fragile freedoms" (Bible, soul, church, and religious) in *Baptist Identity*.

6. See Lumpkin, *Baptist Confessions*.

7. "Moderate" is the broad, preferred label marking these Baptists off from the "fundamentalist" zealots who assumed control of the major Southern Baptist seminaries in the early 1990s. All four of the commentators had close ties to the flagship "former" Southern Baptist Theological Seminary in Louisville, KY. An older Baptist scholar, Charles Talbert, who pioneered fresh approaches to Lukan study, also merits high recognition.

theologians of different stripes, I engage with these Baptist NT colleagues at various points in this "Integration" section.

In order to provide a solid bridge from my interpretive journey through Luke's Gospel to this more integrative segment organized around various theological foci, I first reflect more systematically on the climactic material in Luke 24, especially pertaining to key matters of theological *knowing* (epistemology), which I have stressed throughout the commentary following Luke's opening cue (1:4).

Theological Knowing

Consider, in turn, a negative and a progressive schema. From a *negative* viewpoint, the dramatic revelation of the risen Jesus in word and deed runs diametrically counter to common gnostic perspectives.

Anti-gnostic Knowing

I do not claim that Luke mounts a direct polemic against any particular system of Gnosticism, like that advanced by Marcion or others in the second century.[8] But Luke's path to knowing God via the risen Christ affords no footing for alternative, proto-gnostic epistemologies.

Open Knowledge

Unlike the Gospel of Thomas, which contains 114 "secret sayings that the living Jesus spoke" and dictated to Didymos Judas for the exclusive enlightenment of Jesus's intimate followers (Gos. Thom. 1), the Gospel of Luke sets Jesus's teachings within an extended narrative of his life and ministry so that Theophilus and all fellow "God-lovers" "*may know* the matters about which you've been instructed with *solid assurance*" (Luke 1:4 AT). Although Luke's Jesus does engage in some private, "secret" talks with his disciples concerning God's realm (8:10; 9:43b–45; 10:23–24; 18:31–34), as often as not, insight remains temporarily "hidden" from them (9:45; 18:34). The ultimate goal, however, is full and final disclosure of God's saving will to the world, not just to a select few: "For nothing is hidden that will not be disclosed, nor is anything secret that will not become

8. Cf. Talbert, *Luke and the Gnostics*; Tyson, *Marcion*.

known and come to light" (8:17). Although both Thomas's and Luke's Jesus urge "seeking and finding" the truth (Gos. Thom. 3, 92, 94; Luke 11:9–10), the latter envisions a much wider network of seekers and lays major stress on *Jesus himself* as the seeking Savior of the lost, least, and last—down to the last "one" who has gone astray (15:3–32; 19:1–10).

The postresurrection scenes in Luke 24 reinforce the public (nonsecret) and populist (nonselect) thrust of knowing God through the living Christ. Though Jesus initially plays coy with the Emmaus couple to involve them in the learning process, his goal is *open, revealed knowledge* through means of *Scripture-study* and *bread-breaking*—means of revelation available to anyone, including this ordinary pair of travelers who see the light *before* the chosen (now eleven) apostles (24:13–35). Moreover, the risen Jesus's popping out on the Emmaus duo (24:31) and then in on the larger group, including the apostles (24:36), stresses that no one has exclusive, esoteric claims on him or his gospel. The dynamic, saving word of the crucified-and-risen Messiah is to be *proclaimed* "in his name to all nations" (24:47).

If any group deserves special recognition in Luke's closing chapter, it would be Mary Magdalene, Joanna, and the other women who first bore witness to the risen Christ before skeptical male apostles (24:1–11, 22–24). Though Luke then edges these women to the background of Jesus's postresurrection appearances, he confirms their testimony—against the apostles' dismissal (24:11) and the despair of Cleopas and his companion (24:22–24)—and never suggests their unfitness *as women* for full inclusion in God's realm. In sharp contrast to the final saying in Thomas, Luke's Peter, though dubious, never goes so far as to ban Mary and the other women from the community of the living Lord; and Luke's Jesus never suggests a sex-change operation as part of his restorative mission, as does his Thomas counterpart: "Simon Peter said to them, 'Make Mary [Magdalene] leave us, for females do not deserve life.' Jesus said, 'Look, I will guide her to make her male, so that she too may become a living spirit resembling you males. For every female who makes herself male will enter the domain of Heaven'" (Gos. Thom. 114).[9] As Luke's Jesus ascends into heaven (24:51), he opens the way for all people, "men and women," to enter into God's domain as they are (cf. Acts 1:14; 2:17–18; 6:1–7; 8:3; 9:2; 12:12–17; 13:50; 16:11–18, 40; 17:12; 18:1–3, 18–28).

9. Trans. from Robert J. Miller, *Complete Gospels*, 322.

Embodied Knowledge

Discussion of gendered bodies leads to broader reflection on somatic existence in relation to spiritual experience. Gnostic anthropology typically imagined a dualistic framework of a divine spark of good spirit/soul trapped in a diabolical cage of evil flesh/body. Accordingly, salvation required releasing the inner spirit from its bodily prison through special "spiritual" knowledge (gnosis). Obviously, this antibody perspective has no place for an *incarnate* Savior God, still less for One who brings salvation, liberation, and restoration *to embodied persons* created in God's image *through a suffering, crucified body* raised to new *embodied life*.

The portrait of the risen Jesus in Luke 24 has dimensions of an escape artist free from constraints of ordinary bodily experience: Jesus breaks the bounds of burial clothes, rock-hewn tomb, household doors, and ultimately earth's atmosphere, as he conquers death, defies gravity, and departs to heaven. But significantly, his transcending of bodily limits manifests as *extending* rather than shedding his embodied nature. The risen Christ is still the *incarnate* Jesus in a glorified *body*. Though he might look somewhat different to Cleopas and friend on the Emmaus Road (I suggested in the commentary, however, that their initial misrecognition owed more to their grief-skewed perspective), Jesus still walked and talked with them as an embodied person—with his feet on the ground and his voice in normal tone—not as an apparition. And he finally became known to them in "the breaking of bread" (24:35)—the staff of bodily life—along with the exposition of Scripture.

When he appears to the larger group, the risen Lord makes certain that they do not mistake him as a ghost or some disembodied or docetic (only *seeming* to have a body) spirit, but rather as one with real "flesh and bones," with hands and feet—*his* bodily parts available for touching and viewing and consuming food (broiled fish now), as they had felt, seen, and eaten with him before his death (24:37–43).[10] And speaking of his death, Jesus affirms that his crucifixion was no mirage or stage act, but rather real bodily death, as all human beings experience, though in his case with extraordinary pain and suffering, "necessary" to share in the depths of brokenness and emptiness as the way to

10. See the perceptive assessment of Luke's "touching" portrait of Jesus by the systematic theologian Willie James Jennings, *Acts*, 15: "Jesus gives himself (*paristemi*) to be viewed, touched, and even handled over many days. This giving of himself continues what began with Mary's touch of her child; through the crowds that pressed in to grasp hold of his healing body; to the brutal hands of a Roman military committed to practices of torture; to this moment when disciples, confused, fearful, unclear of the future, needed to hear the words of Jesus: here and now touch me (Luke 24:38–40). Jesus always presents himself to be touched."

restoration and fullness of life (24:25–27, 44–46). He lives as *Christus Victor* only because of his vocation as *Christus Dolor*.[11] The *Via Paradisus* runs on the same track as the *Via Dolorosa*. And only *human bodies* qualify for the race, led by the pacesetting incarnate Jesus Messiah.

Earthly Knowledge

In biblical theology, human bodies fashioned in God's image are inextricably linked with all material creation—with the dust and humus of earth out of which God first made "earthlings" (and to which they return in death)—and infused with God's breath to form a body-spirit unity. Furthermore, humans not merely survive, but thrive, by cultivating and consuming the fruit and grain that the *earth/land* produces (as living subject [see Gen 1:11–12, 20, 24; Luke 12:16]). Thus, far from separating God and God's Spirit from corrupt flesh, earth, and matter by a long chain of subordinate aeons (or demiurges), as Gnosticism demanded, Judaism happily celebrated God as "hands-on" Creator of a "very good" material world (Gen 1:31; 2:7–8), and the (proto-orthodox) Christian branch of Judaism confessed Jesus Messiah as the incarnate (enfleshed) Son of God and Adam (Son of Humankind) filled with God's Spirit.

Such a worldview Marcion of Sinope, who became an influential gnostic Christian in second-century Rome, could not stomach. Accordingly, he completely disavowed the Jewish Scriptures and the God revealed therein (as truly "old," outdated, even immoral) and accepted as canonical only a limited number of Paul's letters and a bowdlerized version of Luke's Gospel—with the birth narratives lopped off from the start (we can't have the Redeemer Jesus springing from a woman's messy, bloody womb).[12] Though some modern interpreters have, for various reasons, bracketed out Luke 1–2 as extraneous to the Third Gospel, few today question the overall thematic harmony of the birth stories with the larger narrative of Jesus's life, ministry, death, and resurrection.[13]

In the commentary, I highlighted several thematic links between the opening and closing chapters of Luke. Here I simply reprise the creational and sacramental elements of the risen Christ's words and deeds in Luke 24 antithetical to Marcionite ideology.

11. See Mouw and Sweeney, *Suffering*.

12. See the recent, wide-ranging studies of Lieu, *Marcion*; and BeDuhn, *First New Testament*.

13. See the sterling defense of the integral, stage-setting connection of Luke's birth narrative with the entire Luke-Acts corpus in Minear, "Luke's Use."

- Far from jettisoning the Jewish Scriptures, the risen Jesus accepts the entire corpus—including the foundational Genesis creation stories in the Torah of "Moses"—as authoritative, "necessary" prologue to his climactic messianic mission of suffering, death, and resurrection (24:25–27, 44–46).
- Sacramental food shared in table fellowship, in conjunction with scriptural word interpreted by Christ, constitutes primary means of participating in God's saving grace. Though blessed by Christ, such food is no magical, otherworldly fare, but rather the ordinary stuff of created life: bread from the land, fish from the sea (24:30–31, 41–42).
- The ascension, in which Luke's Jesus is "carried up into heaven" (24:51), is no desperate escape launch from a polluted earth. No "good riddance" from Jesus's lips. Though he knows full well how evil the earthly realm can be—earthly powers just crucified him!—he remains committed to its redemption and the restoration of all God's creation. The Creator of "the heavens and the earth" (Gen 1:1) is the Renewer of heaven and earth. God's kingdom is "among you" here and now (Luke 17:20–21), and as Jesus has inaugurated this fresh outburst of kingdom life, he will come again to complete the mission. In the meantime, he leaves his followers to spread the gospel in his name through the power of the Spirit, from Jerusalem to the "ends of the earth/land [γῆς, *gēs*]" (Acts 1:8; cf. Luke 24:47–49). Matter matters deeply to God. "The earth is the Lord's and all that is in it" (Ps 24:1).

Having considered key aspects of knowing the saving God through the risen Christ in sharp contrast to gnostic approaches, I turn to a more *positive* evaluation of epistemological processes in Luke 24.

Progressive Knowing

We may profitably track self-disclosures of the risen Lord and disciples' perceptions of him along a continuum of three levels of progressive knowledge sketched by the theologian Jürgen Moltmann.[14]

14. Moltmann, *Living God*, 185–87.

Dominating Knowledge: Directed toward Objects

The scientific method seeks knowledge by "objective" analysis of the world, by attempting to master (rule over) the world's "objects" through reason and manipulation. Much has been learned through this dominating approach; objects have little choice but to yield to the probes and prods of superior powers—to some extent. But Moltmann properly questions the adequacy of this top-down, "overpowering" knowledge, as it ignores the integrity of the object under investigation, failing to respect the object's own "voice" and deep "self"-understanding. Moltmann particularly cites Rome's imperial policy of "divide and conquer" (*divide et impera*) and Bacon's anthropology of "lordship over the earth" (*dominium terrae*) as examples of one-sided, domineering pursuits of world knowledge.[15]

As conqueror of death (on a Roman cross!), manipulator of the Emmaus travelers, and transporter through space, the risen Lord (*dominus*) dominates the scenes in Luke 24. He knows the spirit and character of Rome better than Rome knows him (they completely misjudged him); and he knows the thoughts, feelings, and movements of his followers. In one sense, the women at the tomb, couple on the road, and disciples in Jerusalem are treated as "objects" under Christ's control, pawns on his chessboard to play with as he wills and beyond their reciprocal grasp. All their first impressions miss the mark. It is hard to latch on to a "ghost"-like vanisher and intruder. Now you see him, now you don't. You will know only what he wants you to know about him and his Father (10:21–22). In fact, in his dominant divine position, you cannot control him and must humbly and gratefully receive what he chooses to reveal.

Participatory Knowledge: Related to Subjects

Fortunately, however, the risen Jesus ultimately chooses to be open (see above) and generous with his self-disclosure and primarily engages with his followers as *sensitive subjects* and *participating partners* in the divine-human, Lord-disciple relationship. The epistemological framework is communal, not imperial; expansive, not exploitative; mutual, not manipulative. As Moltmann defines it, "Participatory knowledge is a relational knowledge with empathy and receptivity"; and drawing on Augustine, "We know the other or others only insofar as we can love them and, in respect, can let them be themselves."[16]

15. Moltmann, *Living God*, 185; cf. Caputo, *Weakness*, throughout.
16. Moltman, *Living God*, 186.

Though in total control as risen Lord, Jesus does not lord himself over his subjects (subjugated ones = objects), as rulers commonly do (cf. 22:25), but rather nudges them to participate with him in intersubject perception and communion. The dazzling attendants at Jesus's empty tomb enjoin the bewildered women to "remember" what Jesus told them in Galilee, that is, to commemorate the communication they enjoyed with Jesus. When the women "remembered his words" (24:8), they promptly shared their knowledge of the risen Christ "with the eleven and . . . all the rest" (24:9), thus expanding the communal circle. With the traveling couple on the Emmaus road, Jesus draws them out of their abject despair and into participatory recognition through probing questions, challenging exposition of Scripture, and eye-opening sharing of bread "at table *with them*" (24:30–31)—again sparking their report to "the eleven and their companions" (24:33). When Jesus then appears to this larger group, he overcomes their doubts and fears with an invitation to touch and see his body, a request for them to *give him* something to eat, further scriptural exposition of Jesus's sympathetic suffering, and fresh exhortations to bear witness in his name throughout the world (24:36–49).

Throughout Luke 24 the relationship between the risen Jesus and his disciples clearly operates and develops in participatory interchange among thinking, feeling, and acting *subjects*. Moreover, the course is laid out for continuing growth in participatory knowledge by engaged subjects witnessing in Christ's name, worshiping in God's temple, and waiting on the power of God's Spirit (24:48–49, 52–53).

Transforming Knowledge: Committed to Projects

Though all three means of knowing have their place in Moltmann's scheme, he presents them in an escalating order of value and potential, as the following summary indicates: "Dominating knowledge establishes facts. Participatory knowledge leads to community with what already exists. The knowledge of possible change [transforming knowledge] perceives the future of things and communities, and evaluates their potentialities."[17] Full, dynamic knowledge of God progresses from "objective" information about God, to "subjective" participation in God's life (see more below on the Trinity), to "projective" transformation of selves, societies, and the entire world according to God's saving plan. Objects and subjects, however seemingly static and self-determinant, are inexorably caught up in the flow of history, which affects them for good and

17. Moltmann, *Living God*, 186.

ill. Fortunately, in theological terms, the influence tilts toward the good, as God's plan/project bends toward a future restoration of all creation. In Pauline eschatological terms, "We know that all things work together for good for those who love God, who are called according to his purpose [project]" (Rom 8:28). "I am confident of this, that the one who began a good work among you will bring it to completion by the day of Jesus Christ" (Phil 1:6).

Quite counter to the modern adage, "the more things change, the more they stay the same," reprising Qoheleth's pessimistic mantra "nothing new under the sun" (Eccl 1:9), this worldview boldly asserts God's commitment to a perfected future in an open universe brimming with flourishing potentiality. Such a courageous perspective is just as far, however, from the insipid platitude, "Every day in every way I am getting better and better." The changed future in God's cosmic project emerges out of terrible groaning conflict (cf. Rom 8:18–26) with suffering, which Jesus Messiah endures in all its excruciating pain as the "Crucified God" and emerges out of—though still bearing its torturous scars—as the risen Lord. Knowledge of *this* divine project of systemic change *through suffering* is "*the reason of hope*" (emphasis Moltmann's) in Christian faith and practice.[18] Epistemology joins eschatology in fueling active hope in God's ultimate plan of salvation in Christ. We might say that knowing *Christus Victor* (the dominating Lord of all) via *Christus Dolor* (the participating Son of Humankind in the depths of human suffering) propels dynamic confidence in *Christus Futurus* (the transforming Savior and Restorer of the world for God's glory).

The experience of such transformative knowledge should be obvious in the postresurrection episodes of Luke 24. All characters experience change, including the risen Jesus as he relates to his disciples in a new mode (transfigured from corpse to glorified body), and must overcome their initial lack of recognition, which had caused him no little frustration (24:25–26, 38). The disciples in turn undergo their own dramatic transformation from doubt to faith, despondence to joy, despair to hope, as they begin to see, feel, and know the open, optimistic future certified by the risen Christ. They whose hopes for redemption had been so brutally dashed on Jesus's cross (24:21) now find these hopes not merely rekindled but supercharged, as they come to grasp the reality of his empty tomb, eternal body, and enduring salvation project to which they will testify, energized by "power from on high" (24:49). No wonder we find them in the last words of Luke infused "with great joy and . . . continually in the temple blessing God" (24:53). They have glimpsed the life-giving future of God encompassing them and the entire world: cause for joyous thanksgiving indeed!

18. Moltmann, *Living God*, 186.

Trinitarian Theology

As we move to more systematic categories of understanding Luke's narrative theology of knowing God, we start appropriately with the doctrine of God—the prime object, subject, and project of all theological and theophilic knowing—grounded in Christian terms in the Trinity, not simply as a focus of intellectual study, but as a wholehearted engagement in *participatory* fellowship. As Vanhoozer constructs his doctrinal dramatic model, "Knowing God is a form of participatory theater and doctrine is the actors' aid. It is because knowing God means participating not just in any drama but in the *right* drama—the one whose climax is Jesus Christ—that the church moved from proclaiming the gospel to formulating the doctrines of the Trinity and incarnation."[19] Our knowing involvement in the "drama of redemption," while vital, is secondary and supportive (as in supporting roles, though not merely scene-filling "extras") to the Triune God's starring, interacting, role(s), without whom the play would be "no" thing. "To know God as Savior, then is to know the *Triune* God. Indeed, the drama *is* the *dramatis personae*: Father, Son, and Spirit. It is not that human actors play no part in the drama, only that the ordering, reconciling, and perfection of creation is a work of the Triune God, and salvation a matter of participating in the Triune economy."[20]

Likewise, though less dependent on a dramaturgic metaphor, the British Baptist theologian Paul Fiddes (Regent's Park College, Oxford) explicates his rich understanding of the Trinity around the core concept of *participating in God*, whereby we come to know God not simply by observation but by participation ("an epistemology of participation") in God's dynamic Triune "event of relationships" among the three persons of God's united self, in their loving interpersonal *movement* in and out, out and in, in mutual relation to each other and the world of God's beloved creation.[21] "Through our participation, we can identify three distinct movements of speech, emotion and action which are like relationships 'from father to son,' 'from son to father' and a movement of 'deepening relations.' They are mutual relations of ecstatic, outward-going love, giving and receiving. . . . A triune doctrine of God encourages us to *discover* our roles as we participate in a God who is always in the movement of sending."[22]

Contemporary discussions of the Trinity routinely evaluate three main models: (1) *immanent*—who God is internally, "psychologically," within God's

19. Vanhoozer, *Drama*, 81 (emphasis original).

20. Vanhoozer, *Drama*, 81 (emphasis original).

21. Fiddes, *Participating*, 36–38.

22. Fiddes, *Participating*, 38, 51 (emphasis original).

Triune self, God *in se*; (2) *economic*—how the Triune God works in the world for our salvation, God "for us" (*pro nobis*); and (3) *social*—how God lovingly interrelates within God's Triune self and invites humanity and all creation into free fellowship within the divine circle (the *perichoretic* God [see below]).[23] Though one model may be pitted against another in the heat of doctrinal debate in various eras, they are not mutually exclusive. Indeed, some consensus has emerged in contemporary theology regarding the dialectic value of all three models in ascertaining the ineffable mystery of the Triune God. The so-called Rahner's Rule (named after the German Catholic theologian Karl Rahner) stipulates, "The 'economic' Trinity is the 'immanent' Trinity, and the 'immanent' Trinity is the 'economic' Trinity."[24] Or more colloquially, "God does what God is"; God's external action in the world naturally grows out of who God *is*, internally and existentially, within God's Triune self.

The social, *perichoretic* (circumnavigating/interpenetrating)Trinity, rooted in the fourth-century Greek Eastern tradition of the Cappadocian fathers (i.e., Basil the Great, Gregory of Nyssa, and Gregory of Nazianzus), has enjoyed a renaissance in modern Western theology, owing in large measure to liberation theologians Leonardo Boff (Brazilian Catholic) and Jürgen Moltmann (German Reformed).[25] The *participatory* emphasis, stressed above, fits within this *perichoretic* framework, which also happily encompasses economic and immanent dimensions: what the Triune God does flows out of who God is in *dynamic interpersonal loving relations* within God's Triune self and among humanity and the entire world God made *for covenantal fellowship*.

So what does any of this highfaluting trinitarian language have to do with Luke, who uses none of the classic terminology in his narrative portrait of Jesus's life and work? Of course, all ecclesiastical formulations of the doctrine of the Trinity are post-NT ("Trinity" never appears in the Christian canon), which is not to deny, however, that the NT provides the vital seedbed for trinitarian faith. In Moltmann's key "presupposition": "The New Testament talks about God by proclaiming in narrative the relationships of the Father, the Son and the Spirit, which are relationships of fellowship and are open to the world."[26] Though Moltmann does not single out the Third Gospel, his statement perfectly applies to Luke's narrative. While Luke's entire story unfolds in a network of

23. See helpful surveys in Thiselton, *Systematic Theology*, 32–39; Migliore, *Faith*, 64–91; Gerrish, *Christian Faith*; 291–306; Elizabeth A. Johnson, *She Who Is*, 191–223, and *Quest*, 202–25; Grenz, *Theology*, 53–76.

24. Rahner, *Trinity*, 22; cf. Gerrish, *Christian Faith*, 302–3; Elizabeth A. Johnson, *She Who Is*, 199; LaCugna, *God for Us*, 211–13.

25. Boff, *Trinity*; Moltmann, *Trinity*; see Elizabeth A. Johnson, *She Who Is*, 207–9.

26. Moltmann, *Trinity*, 64; cf. Thiselton, *Systematic Theology*, 34.

intra- and interdivine, human, and creational "relationships of fellowship," the *prayer life* of Luke's Jesus marks particularly salient "trinitarian" moments.[27]

- *Baptismal prayer (3:21–22).* Only Luke among the Gospels stages Jesus's baptism as a *prayerful*, loving engagement not with John the Baptist (who exits the stage in 3:20), but exclusively with God the Father of the "beloved" Son and the Holy Spirit, who rests "upon him in bodily form like a dove." This formative experience presents the "open" traffic between heaven and earth and prepares for Jesus's outreach of God's realm to an oppressed world in the power of the Spirit (4:14–18). The loving, Triune God seeks out, releases, and draws into God's fellowship the bound, the blind, and the bereft.
- *Prayer of thanksgiving (10:21–22).* Though sharing with Matthew's Gospel the Son's praise to his Father, the Creator "Lord of heaven and earth," for their intimate mutual knowledge, graciously revealed to "infants" (the most vulnerable in society) enveloped in the divine household (Matt 11:25–27), only Luke features this prayer of thanksgiving as flowing out of Jesus's joyful experience "in the Holy Spirit" (10:21) between the event of the Seventy(-Two)'s gospel mission, bringing God's kingdom "near" (10:1–20), and the parable of the good Samaritan, promoting active, inclusive neighborly love (10:25–37). Triune divine love spills over into the world to grace the needy with peace and mercy.
- *Lord's Prayer (11:1–13).* Soon thereafter, Luke presents his distinctive version of the Lord's Prayer (cf. Matt 6:1–15) as an extension of Jesus's personal practice of prayer *shared with* his disciples (Luke 11:1–2). Remarkably, he invites them to pray with him, as he does, to *his Father as their Father*, regarding practical, mutual matters of divine-human household management (see more below) pertaining to daily bread provision, debt freedom, and hardship (trial) endurance (11:2–4). And all of this "economic" administration operates in the heavenly Father's bountiful gift of the *Holy Spirit* (11:13)—which is to say, the giving of God's very self—received in the fellowship of prayer exemplified by and embodied in Jesus the Son.
- *Last prayer (23:46).* In his loud, gut-wrenching, breath-gasping final utterance from the cross, the impassioned, incarnate Son "commend[s] his spirit" to his divine Father in hopeful affirmation of continuing fellowship with the life-giving God beyond the bounds of death and partnership in

27. On prayer as a key means of entering into God's trinitarian life, see Fiddes, *Participating*, 115–51; Coakley, *God*, 111–44; Thiselton, *Systematic Theology*, 37–38.

God's redemptive mission to the world. The echo with the lamenting, suffering psalmist strikes a more trustful tone of intimate communion from Ps 31:5 than the tragic note of agonistic separation from Ps 22:1 sounded in Mark 15:34//Matt 27:46 ("My God, my God, why have you forsaken me?").[28] Though the Psalm parallel suggests Jesus's focus on his human "spirit," in Luke's view Jesus's entire human being—body and spirit—is generated (conceived) by the Holy Spirit in Mary's womb (1:35) and "full" of the Holy Spirit throughout his ministry (4:1). We may thus say that the incarnate Jesus's spirit and God's Spirit interpenetrate in perfect dynamic communion.

Luke also casts interrelations between Father, Son, and Spirit in "sending" terms (ἀποστέλλω [*apostellō*] or πέμπω [*pempō*]), though not in a strict procession—the Father sends → the Son, who with the Father sends → the Spirit—as formulated in some patristic traditions.[29] Luke's Jesus refers:

1. *passively*, to "being sent": "For I was sent for this purpose" (4:43)—by God (implied);
2. *vaguely*, to "the one who sent me" (9:48; 10:16)—again, implying God, but not in "Father" terms;
3. *parabolically*, to the vineyard owner who sends "my beloved son" (20:13; cf. 3:22; 9:35);
4. *specifically*, to the "Spirit of the Lord" who "sent me to proclaim release" (4:18), and
5. *metonymically*, to the "Wisdom of God" who sends prophets and apostles (of which Jesus the Son is the supreme model) typically rejected by God's people (11:49); God's personified Spirit (πνεῦμα, *pneuma*) and Wisdom (σοφία, *sophia*) closely align in Hellenistic-Jewish thought (see Wis 7:22–27).

Jesus the Christ thus appears at the nexus of a dynamic outreach (sending) into the world by the Triune God imaged in terms that are more circular-mutual

28. Though see the discussion in the commentary on Luke 23:46 and below under "Passional Theology," stressing that such communion still carries elements of anxiety at this excruciating climax of the Son's suffering.

29. The schism between Eastern and Western churches was fueled in no small part by the *filioque* ("and the Son") clause, which Western-Augustinian theology added to the Nicene-Constantinopolitan Creed (381 CE) in order to clarify that the Holy Spirit "proceeds from the Father *and from the Son*." Eastern Orthodox theologians saw no need for the modification, which in their view tended to unduly limit the Spirit's divine role to being the handmaiden of the Son's saving work; see Grenz, *Theology*, 62–63, 69–71; Moltmann, *Trinity*, 178–87.

than linear-processional.[30] In turn, Jesus operates as the chief sender of associate apostles ("sent-ones"), prophets, and other gospel and kingdom emissaries (9:1–6; 10:1–12; 24:48–49).

This circulatory pattern brings us back to *perichōrēsis* (περιχώρησις) in Greek, *circuminsessio* in Latin, and the discussions of the social-relational Trinity. Fiddes relates the Latin concept to both "being" (immanent) and "doing" (economic) trinitarian models in medieval theology: (1) *being*: "one person [of the Trinity] is contained in another—literally 'seated' in another, filling the space of the other, present in the other" (advocated by Aquinas); and (2) *doing*: "the interpenetrating of one person in another; it captures the sense of a moving in and through the other" (promoted by Bonaventure).[31] Again, Luke's narrative fits comfortably with these trinitarian emphases, though strictly speaking, his "seated" ("session") language places the exalted Christ *at/beside* God's right hand rather than in/among the Father and Spirit's positional circle (22:69). But the distinction is slight, especially when we appreciate the divine "right hand" as an *extension* of God's person and power and as the *connection* through which Jesus receives the Father's promise of the Holy Spirit and delivers it to "all flesh" (Acts 2:17, 33; here, the traditional flow of procession applies).

Stressing the more active dimension of circulating trinitarian relations, various theologians have noted the happy word play in Greek between περιχωρέω (*perichōreō*, "*move* around") and περιχορεύω (*perichoreuō*, "*dance* around"). From there it is a short step to envisioning mutual, interactive trinitarian relations as a lively *circle dance* among Father, Son, and Spirit *choreographed* within and among them *as they go along*, interpreting the plan (script, score) of God in response to the free unfolding of human history. Eternal program and historical process thus work together in creative tension to propel the divine triadic tango.

Though Luke develops no trinitarian theology linked to these two verbs, he does use both ideas in ways we might imaginatively appropriate for understanding his presentation of God the Father, Christ, and Spirit in relation to the world. Multiple times the noun περίχωρος (*perichōros*) appears in its

30. Elizabeth A. Johnson (*She Who Is*) sagely observes that "processions, whether academic, liturgical, funeral, and so on, imply rank" (197). Accordingly, on biblical grounds overall and Lukan grounds in particular, she resists a strict hierarchical trinitarian structure with the despotic "sending/ordering" Father at the top: "When the totality of biblical witness is taken into account, it becomes apparent that theology has been highly selective in its focus on the Father-Son-Spirit pattern, for other options are also realizable. In a key Lukan passage, for example, it is not the Father but the Spirit who sends Jesus to bring good news to the poor and proclaim liberty to the oppressed (Lk 4:16–30)" (195).

31. Fiddes, *Participating*, 71–72.

basic geographic meaning of "surrounding area," typically the regions of Galilee and Judea in which reports circulate about the itinerant Jesus's amazing words and deeds. The saving gospel of God in Jesus Messiah thus begins to encompass and interpenetrate the land of Israel and people of God. The inaugural summary of Jesus's mission also features the Spirit's integral role in this pervasive outreach: "Then Jesus, filled with the power of the Spirit, returned to Galilee, and a report about him spread through all the surrounding country [περιχώρου, *perichōrou*]" (Luke 4:14; cf. 4:37; 7:17). As for "dance" moves, Luke 15:25 marks the only NT use of χορός (*choros*, "dancing), the noun from which the verb χορεύω (*choreuō*, "I dance") is derived (there are no examples of the verb with the prefix περι- [*peri*]). The setting is the famous parable's spontaneous party thrown by the loving father in celebration of his lost son's return, with sumptuous food and joyous "music and dancing [χορῶν, *chorōn*]" by the whole household (elder brother excepted, but invited). This outburst of choreographic delight, less staged than extemporaneous, among longing father, lost-and-found/dead-and-alive son, and attendant community offers a suggestive illustration of dynamic divine-human familial fellowship wide enough to embrace restored "sinners" in God's circle dance.

The household as the locus of God's loving rule among Son Jesus's communal "mother[s]" and "brothers [and sisters]" who follow God's way (8:19–21)—a major model of Luke's theology and ethics—combines "social" and "economic" conceptions of God's saving work in Christ through the Spirit, with particular stress on faithful "household/economic management" (οἰκονομία, *oikonomia* [16:2–4]). Concluding her magisterial study *God for Us: The Trinity and Christian Life*, Catherine LaCugna summarizes the "practical" import of the "economic" Trinity with a subtle nod to Luke's prodigal story: "God's economy, *oikonomia tou theou*, is the wellspring of trinitarian faith. We recall that *oikonomia* comes from *oikos nomos*, the law or management of the household. The economy is not an abstract idea, nor a theological principle, but *the life of God and creature existing together as one*. . . . God's economy is not the austere distribution of meager resources but lavish grace, a glorious inheritance, bestowed in *prodigal* good pleasure, foreordained to be consummated."[32] The "prodigal" reference hints at the *father's wasteful, embracive love*, discussed in the commentary section on the parable, toward sinful younger brother and stingy elder brother alike, as a poignant illustration of God's seeking and saving compassion.

A further bridging of familial/economic and social/perichoretic trinitarian images in Luke may cohere around χωρέω (*chōreō*), the practice of hos-

32. LaCugna, *God for Us*, 377 (all emphasis original except for "prodigal").

pitality or "having room for," one of the core meanings of the verb in the NT (Mark 2:2; John 2:6; 21:25).[33] As Daniel Migliore explains, "The God of the Bible establishes and maintains life in communion. . . . Since John of Damascus . . . this ineffable communion of the triune life has been expressed by the Greek word *perichoresis*, 'mutual indwelling' or 'being-in-one-another.' The three of the Trinity 'indwell' and pervade each other . . . or to use still another metaphor, they *'make room' for each other, are incomparably hospitable to each other*."[34] Out of this magnanimous, capacious divine hospitality, they naturally "make room" for God's children and the world. The Triune God's tent is as big as all creation. Though Luke never uses χωρέω (*chōreō*) in the "room-making" sense, he frequently enjoins the practice of hospitality by and to the "hosting" and "visiting" God, Christ, disciples—and sinners—as a prime practice of God's inclusive, redemptive love. Recall in particular Jesus's sympathetic fellowship with the homeless and displaced who have "no [secure] space in which to lodge" (Luke 2:7 AT) or sheltered "place to lay their head" (9:58 AT), as well as his servant-oriented lordship "among" sinners, seekers, and followers alike "as one who serves" (22:27).

LaCugna's insistence that "the doctrine of the Trinity is ultimately a practical doctrine with radical consequences for Christian life"[35] has received a hearty "Amen" from many contemporary theologians, against the dismissive swipe of Kant that "from the doctrine of the Trinity . . . nothing whatsoever can be gained for practical purposes,"[36] symptomatic of the "indignity" that the "'Trinity' has suffered among many," in Eugene Peterson's stinging judgment, "of being treated as a desiccated verbal artifact poked and probed by arthritic octogenarians of the sort skewered by Robert Browning as 'dead from the waist down.'"[37]

To state the obvious (though not commonly acknowledged), the "social" and "economic" models of the Trinity have profound *socioeconomic* implications for life in community.[38] As Migliore puts it, "Confession of the triune God, properly understood, radically calls in question all totalitarianisms that deny the freedom and rights of all people. . . . The doctrine of the Trinity seeks to describe God's 'being in love,' God's 'ecstatic,' outreaching, ingathering love . . .

33. BDAG, 1094.

34. Migliore, *Faith*, 79 (emphasis added).

35. LaCugna, *God for Us*, 1, 224, 377; cf. 377–417.

36. Cited (in critique) in Moltmann, *Trinity*, 6.

37. Peterson, *Christ Plays*, 7. Other theologians who argue for the Trinity's centrality to personal, practical, pastoral, and political issues include Moltmann, *Trinity*, xi–20; Elizabeth A. Johnson, *Quest*, 222–24; Fiddes, *Participating*, 11–61; Migliore, *Faith*, 79–82.

38. See Meeks, *God*, 70–73, 109–23, 132–34, 162–73.

beyond all sexism, racism, and classism."[39] Luke's emphasis on social leveling and reversal, manifest not least in economic liberation for the poor, flows out of Christ's passionate, self-emptying life and death in loving service of God and neighbor as oneself. This way of life naturally inspires the early church of the risen Lord in Acts, blessed by God and filled with the Spirit, to adopt a "community of goods" such that "there was not a needy person among them" (Acts 4:34; cf. 2:44–46). Their communitarian fellowship (κοινωνία, *koinōnia*) merges with and mirrors the trinitarian fellowship of God (see 5:3–4, 9).[40]

In concluding this discussion of the affinity of Luke's narrative with trinitarian thought, I focus on one prime generative event—the Annunciation—unique to Luke 1:26–38, which does not typically receive as much attention as the Synoptic accounts of Jesus's baptism, where the Father, Son, and Spirit make such dramatic, distinct-yet-convergent appearances. The theologian Eugene Rogers, however, redresses this relative neglect of the Annunciation, giving it due consideration (along with Jesus's baptism, transfiguration, and ascension) in the history of Christian theology and art as a banner event in the creative, cooperative interpenetration of Father, Son, and Spirit in/with Mary of Nazareth.[41] Though not exegeting Luke's text, Rogers aptly distills Luke's narrative theology of the Annunciation: "The angel comes from the Father, and the Spirit overshadows Mary in the conception of the Son, three Persons taking characteristic roles in the one indivisible *ops ad extra* [outward operation] of the incarnation."[42] He further interprets the Spirit's dynamic work in this trinitarian enterprise as acts of *brooding aviation* (resting upon waters) and *birthing dilation* (both delaying and opening).[43] "In the Annunciation the Spirit rests on the Son in the waters of the womb of Mary [as in the primeval waters of creation]. Her womb becomes the locus of excess, a happy opening, where consummation and contingency coincide. In the Annunciation it becomes manifest that the Spirit does this also elsewhere, both in the Trinity and therefore in the world. Paraphysically she accompanies, befriends, and exceeds the physical. The Spirit dilates: she opens, she takes time."[44]

39. Migliore, *Faith*, 80; supporting this point, Migliore recommends consulting Anthony Kelly, *Trinity*, 147–49, 157–59.

40. Ananias and Sapphira's financial deception is symptomatic of their bald-faced breaking covenant with God, Spirit, and community (Acts 5:1–11).

41. Rogers, *After the Spirit*, 11–16, 98–134.

42. Rogers, *After the Spirit*, 11–12.

43. Rogers, *After the Spirit*, 11: "Interactions among the Persons recorded in the NT give glimpses of the intratrinitarian life as it dilates—delays and opens up—to include human beings within it."

44. Rogers, *After the Spirit*, 98.

In the commentary, I accentuated the Spirit's "over"-arching, moving-upon (ἐπί, *epi*), interweaving of the incarnate Son in creative partnership with Mary as a mark of her extensive (deliberative, dilative) engagement with God's development in Jesus's Spirit-anointed life and work, though I pushed the "wild," churning, electric element of the Spirit's operation more than the "resting" dimension: "Mary is . . . caught up in the Spirit as whirling force (cf. Acts 2:2; 8:39; John 3:8)—no gentle breeze, to be sure, but still a generative rather than destructive exhalation of divine wind power [as at creation]. . . . Mysteriously, but materially, Mary's entire embodied being, not least her amniotic waters, [are] swept up and over in the dynamic crosswinds of trinitarian vitality."[45]

And what say my Baptist scholar-friends? Though none of the four recent commentators mention the Trinity in discussing the Annunciation or Magnificat that follows (just as Luke never uses the term), they all incorporate God-centered and God-loving insights in their exegetical and reflective segments. *Culpepper* focuses less on the agency of the Spirit and more on the unified purpose of God and Son in the "economy" of salvation: "The annunciation ultimately is an announcement of hope for humankind. . . . God has sent Jesus as our deliverer. There is another way, a commonwealth under Jesus's lordship."[46] And on Mary's Magnificat: "Verse 47 is theologically clear: God is our Savior. The title should never be limited to our confession of Jesus, as though it did not apply to God. All that Jesus does in the Gospel of Luke to effect salvation . . . he does according to God's purpose and intent."[47]

Likewise, *Garland* gives priority to God's saving operation in Christ over human participation (including Mary's), citing with approval Green's assessment of the Magnificat as a "celebration of God's action. Indeed, God's dramatic work is *against* those who would take power into their own hands."[48] Of course, both Garland and Green affirm the (secondary) importance of human receptivity to God's saving work in obedience and faith, as Mary exemplifies as God's servant (1:38, 48), the very antithesis of a manipulative power broker. Garland also accentuates the Spirit's "divinely active, creative function" manifest in the Annunciation, distinguishing this role from "the Spirit of prophecy that inspires speech" and directly linking it to the beginning of created life: "As God created the world out of nothing through the Spirit, so he will create this unique child."[49] Though I think that Luke envisions this divine Spirit hyperlink between world creation and Jesus's conception, I do not see Luke (or Genesis) endorsing

45. Reprised from my commentary on 1:26–38 (see pp. 39–40 above).

46. Culpepper, 53.

47. Culpepper, 56.

48. Garland, 99; Green, 100 (emphasis original).

49. Garland, 81.

a strictly *ex nihilo* operation.[50] God creates in and through messy material-hydraulic processes, not least the bloody waters of Mary's womb which *she* supplies in partnership with God, in whose image she is created—and creates.

The other two commentators branch out in sidebars and theological addenda to engage with artistic and spiritual interpretations of the Annunciation. *Vinson*, for example, interprets Henry O. Tanner's portrait (1898) of Mary's dubious facial response to the angel's announcement in line with my emphasis on her thoughtful, puzzled pushback, as if she's "thinking, 'You've got to be kidding—and this is going to start *when*?'"[51] On the more devout side, Vinson cites Hans Urs von Balthasar's assessment of Mary's "prototypical" participation in the divine project of incarnation as "the place of the real and bodily indwelling of the Word in the most intimate union of mother and child sharing the same flesh . . . a servant, in her entire person, body and soul."[52] Vinson also associates the Spirit's "overshadowing" (ἐπισκιάζω, *episkiazō*) Mary at the Annunciation (1:35) with the "cloud's" epiphany at Jesus's transfiguration (9:34 [same verb]) and "the way God is manifest in all believers" (cf. Acts 5:15).[53] Rogers teases out trinitarian developments in Orthodox reception history of Luke's transfiguration, with its explicit envelopment of Fatherly Word, Beloved Son, and human emissaries, past (Moses and Elijah) and present (Peter, James, and John) in the cloud.[54] The celestial "cloud" image, generated by the Spirit, may be linked, I suggest, with current cybernetic "cloud" concepts in conjunction with Rogers's exposition of the Spirit as divine channel of reception or communication within the Triune God and between God and humanity: "Mary's reception of the Son by the Spirit happens that way because it already does so in the Trinity: it is by the Spirit that the Trinity chooses and desires to *receive*. And as it is by the Spirit that the Trinity receives, so too it is by the Spirit that also the economy receives."[55] The Spirit, then, represents the dynamic *wireless interconnectivity* linking together in "the cloud" a *worldwide web* of spirited communication among God and all of God's people.

Parsons highlights the association in Jacopo Pontormo's painting of the Annunciation (ca. 1514–16) with Abraham's sacrifice of Isaac (depicted above the visitation scene)—more commonly connected, for obvious reasons, with Jesus's crucifixion than his conception.[56] But the link between "your only son

50. See Caputo, *Weakness*, 55–83 (esp. 75–82).

51. Vinson, 35 (emphasis original).

52. Vinson, 45 (citing Balthasar, *Prayer*, 22–23).

53. Vinson, 39.

54. Rogers, *After the Spirit*, 12, 172–99.

55. Rogers, *After the Spirit*, 117 (emphasis original).

56. Parsons, 42–43.

. . . whom you love" (Gen 22:2) and God's dealings with Abraham and Mary finds illuminating support in Luke's story via the pivotal theme of God's saving mercy (Luke 1:54–55; cf. 1:72–73), in Parsons's view, and the faithful "Here am I" response to God's call to sacrificial giving/bearing of the choice son (Gen 22:1–2; Luke 1:38), in Rogers's view.[57]

Spiritual Theology

"Spiritual theology" sounds about as tautological as "theological theology." As obvious as theology's involvement with God (*theos*) should be, so should its engagement with the Spirit and related "spiritual" things. An "unspiritual" theology would be an odd duck indeed! But just as the long history and industry of ecclesiastical and/or academic theology has sometimes forgotten God along the way—gotten too big for God, as strange as that sounds—so it needs some reminding from time to time of its true "spiritual" grounds and goals, roots and routes, along with some clear exposition of what "spirituality" does and does not *mean* and *matter* in the Christian life, not least its relationship to *material matters*, to which it is still too often *opposed* (spiritual *vs.* material) in gnostic-style dualism. And when it is not falsely defined, it is too often fuzzily described: "spiritual" and "spirituality" can pretty much mean anything and everything these days beyond an actual steel nut or bolt, though one might "spiritually" (mindfully, devotionally, passionately) screw a nut on a bolt, if one is so inclined.

So we need both inspired reclamation and incisive declamation of "spiritual theology." The recovery project has been in full swing for several years, as most seminary and theological college curricula now require courses in spirituality, spiritual formation, or some such rubric. Of course, such courses may differ considerably, ranging from academic studies of spiritual-mystical traditions throughout Christian history (or, more adventurously, with dashes of non-Christian, especially Eastern, thought) to practical skills training in spiritual techniques: "how to" pray, meditate, center one's life in Christ, live in the fullness of the Spirit, and so on. Or perhaps more often, various hybrids of these academic/practical approaches are offered. But there is no official curriculum in spiritual theology across ATS (Association of Theological Schools in the US and Canada) or any other ecumenical accreditation body.

A leading contemporary spiritual theologian, Eugene Peterson—who actually holds the title of professor emeritus of spiritual theology at Regent

57. Rogers, *After the Spirit*, 108–9.

College in Vancouver—has authored a monumental five-volume series "Conversations in Spiritual Theology" (2005–10). He opens his first volume with a helpful definition of sorts (by definition, "spiritual theology"—driven by the dynamic wind of the Spirit—defies definition): "Spiritual theology is the attention that we give to the details of living life on this way [the Jesus-revealed Way]. It is a protest against theology depersonalized into information about God; it is a protest against theology functionalized into a program of strategic planning for God."[58] Spiritual theology thus mounts a rather ornery "protest" against digitizing the knowledge of God into a set piece of programmatic beliefs and/or practices. Though we may affirm the venerable tradition of promoting "spiritual disciplines," the spiritual life animated by the Spirit of God retains a certain undisciplined character, an unpredictable streak, a "wild side" (see discussion on the Spirit's conception of Jesus in Mary's womb in the commentary on Luke 1:26–38). It carries a vibrant S/spirit of Christ-like "play" into "ten thousand places" and more, accentuating the "exuberance and freedom that mark life when it is lived beyond necessity, beyond mere survival."[59]

Yet, Christian spirituality is not a free-for-all, anything-goes playground or impromptu theater of the absurd. Like all Christian knowing and living, it runs best on well-oiled (by the Spirit!) train tracks within established (not encrusted) guardrails.[60] As Peterson states: "It seems preferable to use the term 'spiritual theology' to refer to the specially Christian attempt to address the lived experience revealed in our Holy Scriptures and the rich understandings and practices of our ancestors as we work this experience out in our contemporary world of diffused and unfocused 'hunger and thirst for righteousness.'" Though he cites Matthew's more "spiritualized" beatitude focused on yearnings for "righteousness" (Matt 5:6) rather than Luke's more "materialized" version concerned with physically "hungry" (Luke 6:21, 25), Peterson's view of spirituality is thoroughly rooted in quotidian existence "lived by ordinary men and women in their homes and workplaces."[61] This "spiritual" dimension keeps theology's feet on the ground and holds them to the fire; conversely, "'Theology' . . . [as] the effort we give to knowing God as revealed in the Holy Scriptures and in Jesus Christ . . . keeps 'spiritual' from becoming merely thinking and talking and writing about the feeling and thoughts one has about God."[62] In

58. Peterson, *Christ Plays*, 1.

59. Peterson, *Christ Plays*, 3 (drawing on Gerard Manley Hopkins's poem "As Kingfishers Catch Fire" [1877]).

60. I draw the hermeneutical "guardrail" image from Westphal ("Philosophical/Theological View," 78–79), who derives it from Derrida, *Of Grammatology*, 158.

61. Peterson, *Christ Plays*, 5.

62. Peterson, *Christ Plays*, 5.

sum, Scripture and Christ reveal a dynamic-yet-disciplined spirituality inspired by God's Spirit and incarnate in Jesus Messiah.

From this perspective it is a short step to further envisioning the spiritual life as a walk, a way, a wandering (though not aimlessly) mapped out in Scripture and modeled in the earthly life of Jesus. Or to change the alliteration, it is a jaunt, a jostling, a journey. The last term is perhaps the most pithy and the most popular. As philosopher and theologian John Caputo remarks, "Over the ages the spiritual masters have described spiritual life as a journey."[63] In the NT, no spiritual master makes more of a journey paradigm for the life of Christ and the early Christians than the author of Luke and Acts.[64] While actual journeys between Galilee (Nazareth) and Judea (Jerusalem) especially propel the plots of the Birth Narrative in Luke 1–2 and the extended Travel Narrative in 9:51–19:44, the entire Third Gospel may be tracked, as I endeavored to do in the commentary, as a spiritual journey (or pilgrimage) in coming to know God in Christ through the Spirit step after step in the steps of Jesus—*not* in a lock step-by-step formula—but in a more erratic stepping-stone fashion where the stones sometimes wiggle and wobble, slip and slide, and seekers (including Jesus's disciples) sometimes just flat out miss the step or shoot out on their own wayward courses. Even with Jesus himself, though he is the most surefooted of journeyers, indeed the authoritative Guide to follow, he too in our reading has to find his feet along the way with eyes wide open and vigilantly trained to keep on the narrow, solid "asphalt" (*asphaleia*) path. He too must learn and grow in wisdom on his developing messianic way (cf. 2:40, 52), ever alert to dangers and detours that threaten to derail him—as in the desert, where the Spirit *leads* him to confront the devil (4:1). And Luke's Jesus especially finds power and perspective for the journey in the *practice of prayer*—not simply as an exemplar for his followers (11:1–4), but as a necessity for his own spiritual growth and guidance (3:21; 4:42; 5:16; 6:12; 9:28; 10:21–22; 11:1–4; 22:39–45; 23:34, 46).

Though guided by the Holy Spirit and Scripture within the unfolding plan/purpose (βουλή, *boulē*) of God, a certain uncertainty or "spookiness," even, as Caputo suggests, marks the Jesus way—his and ours as we follow him—confronting the "radical contingency of our situation, individual and communal . . . the contingency of the network of steps, tracks, and traces within which we find ourselves."[65] Luke partly casts such a precarious-yet-promising situation

63. Caputo, *What Would Jesus Deconstruct?*, 38.

64. See Green (*Conversion*), with particular focus on the depiction of conversion in Luke-Acts: "Again and again, we will find ourselves pressed to conceptualize conversion as a journey, including emphases on the trajectory of one's life path, the practices that are integral to this journey, and the quality of one's traveling companions along the way" (16); cf. Spencer, *Journeying*.

65. Caputo, *What Would Jesus Deconstruct?*, 40.

in terms of *desert spirituality* (1:80; 3:2, 4; 4:1, 42; 5:16; 7:24; 8:29; 9:12; 15:4; Acts 7:30–44; 8:26), though more reminiscent of Israel's desert/wilderness trek than the early Christian hermits' (desert fathers') isolationism. Luke also, more than any other NT writer, casts the human condition in terms of *lostness*—a journey gone wild and wayward seeking direction, security, and founding (found-ation). Though not referencing Luke, Caputo aptly captures a critical angle on the third Evangelist's view of life:

> Are we not all a little "lost," like the people who crash-landed on that island in *Lost*, looking for clues about where they are and frightened by the mysterious things going on around them? Is that not a figure of our lives? Are we not like people following an obscure clue, on the tracks, on the trail, in the trace of something-we-are-not-sure-what? Are not those who write about spiritual journeys sometimes a little too assured about where they are going and how to get there? . . . If we were not lost, if we were just hardwired to a spiritual global positioning system, we would not need to be saved. We must appreciate that we are lost before being "found" or being "saved" makes any sense.[66]

This description of the lost, meandering (though "not wandering aimlessly") "hauntological principle" of spiritual life, as Caputo so evocatively dubs it, sounds as Lukan as it is Derridean.[67] Luke's Jesus expressly comes "to seek out and to save the lost" (19:10), which is not simply a grand, singular rescue operation ("once saved always saved") but a lifelong securing, shaping, saving project by diligent, compassionate shepherds, housekeepers, and fathers, as his stunning trio of lost-and-found parables at the heart of this Gospel showcases (15:3–32). In my commentary on the long final story, I especially focused on elements of prodigality, or "waste" (via Tillich and Haught), both negative (waste of self and joy) and positive (waste of love).

Again, Jesus's own spiritual quest to "find" himself and his mission as God's beloved and chosen Son-Messiah and the Son of Humankind should not be dismissed or downplayed. His only adolescent act in Luke (or any other canonical Gospel) features his running away from home or, rather, staying behind in what he senses is his true home, his Father's arena in Jerusalem, where he

66. Caputo, *What Would Jesus Deconstruct?*, 39, 41; cf. Caputo, *Weakness*, 283: "I am praying not to be lost, praying because I am already lost, praying not to get any more lost than I already am, praying that my prayer does not make things worse."

67. Caputo, *What Would Jesus Deconstruct?*, 40. Here and elsewhere (e.g., Caputo, *Insistence*, 5, 53, 62, 77, 101, 104, 114, 219, 256; *Prayers*, 118–22; *Folly*, 30, 33–36, 49–50, 57–58, 78, 106, 118), Caputo develops his view of "hauntology" derived from Derrida, *Specters*.

can devote himself to his true Father's "things," while his earthly family heads back to Nazareth (2:41–46). But for all his apparent "finding" where he truly belongs, his mother, who is no spiritual slouch, regards him as distressingly, even impudently, *lost*—certainly to her (she's been searching frantically for three days)—but perhaps to some extent even to himself and to God (2:48–49). She and Joseph "did not understand" his abandonment of them, even though it was to God's house among the temple teachers (2:50). And evidently this lack of understanding is not exclusively indicative of their spiritual dullness but has some merit; for the twelve-year-old Wunderkind promptly goes back to Nazareth with his parents and remains "obedient to them" for eighteen more years (2:51; cf. 3:23). *He* doesn't yet "understand" all there is to know; there's more to "find" out, more to learn and "grow" into (2:40, 52), before he's fully ready to seek out and save the lost, which he will be all the more determined and qualified to do after sorting out his own "lost" youthful experience.

In the course of his wandering, itinerant lost-seeking-and-saving mission, where he has "nowhere to lay his head" (9:58), no base of operations, no administrative staff, and no remunerative employment, Luke's Jesus and his associates must depend on others' material *generosity* and *hospitality*. Although Jesus grants a certain "right" to such support for his ministry ("the laborer deserves to be paid" [10:7]), he never demands it for himself (if a household or village wants nothing to do with him, he promptly moves on, shaking the dust from his feet [9:51–56; cf. 9:5; 10:11]), still less does he bask in it like some sort of pampered rock star. In fact, when and where he can, he turns the tables by *hosting* and *serving* others, as (1) in the "deserted place" near Bethsaida, where—after a long day of preaching-and-healing ministry to a large crowd—he insists on breaking what bread and fish are available and stretching this fare to feed the whole lot, rather than sending them away for dinner in their own homes (9:12–17); and (2) in a borrowed "upstairs guest room" in Jerusalem, where—on the brink of his betrayal and arrest—he breaks bread (again) and personally serves his disciples ("I am among you as one who serves" [22:27; see 22:7–30]).

Such reciprocal, give-and-receive, bless-and-thank hospitality is more than a practical survival strategy in a tough economy. In Luke's perspective, as in biblical theology across the board, it is part and parcel of loving neighbor as self, of being faithful to the gracious, hospitable God we serve—in short, of being *spiritual*. Hospitality and spirituality interpenetrate so thickly as to obliterate so-called material/spiritual, practical/theological dichotomies.

Women have always felt this material spirituality or spiritual materiality (partly, though not exclusively, because of their *maternity*) in their bones and acted it out in their lives more readily than men, caught up in their endless scrambles for power and authority. Luke's Jesus has a devil of a time convincing his male apostles that the greatest among them is the greatest *servant* to the last, least, and lost (see 9:46–48; 22:24–27). Women like Mary Magdalene, Joanna, Susanna, Martha, and Mary are way ahead of the diaconal/ministerial (διακονέω/διακονία, *diakoneō/diakonia*) curve—and not simply because they extend their servant places in the world. Mary Magdalene was a well-heeled businesswoman, Joanna a sociopolitical aristocrat, and Martha a household head (8:1–3; 10:38–42). Unfortunately, their "much ministry [πολλὴν διακονίαν, *pollēn diakonian*]" (10:40 AT) has often been ignored or downplayed by interpreters: for example, by making Mary Magdalene a whore, reducing Joanna to a wife, and branding Martha as a whiny nag and hassled homemaker frustrated by her "many tasks" (the NRSV's clunky rendering of "much ministry").

In the latter case, Martha has even routinely assumed the role of the spiritual antipode to her devout sister Mary: the antsy, active Martha represents the unspiritual complainer, while the silent, sitting Mary exhibits the paragon contemplative. Lord, save us from Martha and make us more like Mary. It is really quite amazing how influential the five-verse snippet in Luke 10:38–42 has been as a locus classicus in Christian spirituality, the subject of myriad commentaries, reflections, sermons, and devotionals up to the present day. As Giles Constable states:

> Every generation, almost since the beginning of Christianity, has tried to fit the story of Mary and Martha to its needs and to find in it a meaning suited to the Christian life of its time. Over the years its significance for the lives both of withdrawal and worldly activity and for this life and the next have changed, and the parts of Mary and Martha and the significance of Christ's words to Martha have been interpreted in different ways. The very variety and ambiguity of these interpretations is evidence for the richness of the text and the ingenuity of the interpreters.[68]

Overall, Mary has gotten the "better part" of the interpretive deal over Martha. For example, Luther predictably pounced on the sibling rivalry as a showcase of his works vs. faith, law vs. gospel agenda: "Martha, your work must be punished and counted as nought. . . . I will have no work but the work of Mary; that is the faith you have in the word."[69] Yet, there have been more complementary (and complimentary toward Martha) perspectives, allowing

68. Constable, "Interpretation," 141. I draw some of the material on reception history in this section from Spencer, *Salty Wives*, 173–84.

69. Cited in Moltmann-Wendel, *Women*, 17–18 (from Luther's festival sermon on the feast of the Assumption of Mary).

for both Martha- and Mary-style modes of serving Christ, operating in balance, for both men and women.[70] In the commentary on Luke 10:38–42, I cited Augustine's appreciation for both sister-disciples, "both laudable—two lives in the same house and just one fountain of life," and Calvin's endorsement of their joint modeling of "hearing and doing" the word of Christ. I add here the testimony of Teresa of Ávila, who, "while undergoing great sufferings . . . complain[s] of her soul as Martha did of Mary, reproaching it with enjoying solitary peace while leaving her so full of troubles and occupations that she could not keep it company." (St. Teresa sympathizes with Martha's apparent shadow state of soul, "though the soul is known to be undivided.") Ultimately, however, St. Teresa beautifully and forcefully affirms the spiritual service of both sisters: "Believe me, both Martha and Mary must entertain our Lord and keep Him as their Guest, nor must they be so inhospitable as to offer Him no food. How can Mary do this while she sits at His feet, if her sister does not help her?"[71] Note the interesting twist: Martha in fact *helps Mary*; without Martha's actions, Jesus and Mary's contemplative encounter would not have been possible.

Perhaps the most surprising twist on Luke's Martha/Mary story comes from the early-fourteenth-century Dominican mystic Meister Eckhart, who eschews balance in favor of preferring *Martha over Mary*, of "displac[ing] Mary and set[ting] Martha on the throne,"[72] of "turn[ing] the literal sense of Luke's Bethany story inside-out."[73] From Eckhart's viewpoint, active Martha exemplifies the more mature sister, in spiritual attainment as well as in age, anxious about the progress of naive Mary. Specifically, Martha worries about young Mary's motivation for listening to Jesus: "We harbor the suspicion that dear Mary was sitting there more for enjoyment than for spiritual profit. Therefore Martha said, 'Lord, tell her to get up,' because she feared that [Mary] might remain stuck in this pleasant feeling and would progress no further."[74] Martha knows by experience that faithful communion with Christ prompts loving ministry. Thus, as Constable summarizes Eckhart's view: "Mary was in the process of becoming what Martha already was. Mary was only at the beginning of the

70. See Allen, *Spiritual Theology*, 11: "The early church—and the Eastern Orthodox churches to this day—treated Mary and Martha . . . as symbols of two tendencies within one person's life rather than as symbols for different kinds of life. In other words, all Christians are to practice both aspects of the spiritual life to the degree suitable to their temperament and occupation" (cf. 99).

71. Teresa of Ávila, *Interior Castle* 7.1.14; 7.4.17; cf. Elizabeth Newman, *Attending Wounds*, 64.

72. Moltmann-Wendel, *Women*, 28.

73. Heffner, "Meister Eckhart," 179; see further on Eckhart's maverick interpretation (esp. Sermon 86), McGinn, *Mystical Thought*, 157–61; Constable, "Interpretation," 116–17; Gench, *Back to the Well*, 75.

74. Cited in Heffner, "Meister Eckhart," 179 (from Sermon 86).

mystic fulfillment which involved work, asceticism, and apostolic activity as well as contemplation, and Martha was closer to God."[75]

One of Eckhart's and Martha's biggest fans (the word is not too strong) happens to be John Caputo, whom we have already met in this section as a champion of contingent, itinerant spirituality seeking to find and guide lost wanderers in paths of flourishing life. One might think that Martha is the "lost" one in Luke's scene, lost (in her own home!) in a distracted frazzle, at a loss for what to do and how to get it all done, while Mary has "found" her place, her contemplative comfort zone, at Jesus's feet. But alas, though Mary has chosen a truly "good" part to play in this short vignette, it is far from sufficient to carry the whole spiritual drama and in fact is not even the spotlight role in the present scene, according to Luke's chief protagonist and spiritual director, Jesus. Affirming Eckhart's reading, Caputo states: "Martha chose the better part, for Jesus speaks Martha's name twice ['Martha, Martha' (10:41)], secretly signifying that Martha had two gifts to Mary's one. Martha lived *both* the contemplative and the active life while Mary languished at his feet in adoring love, as if her union with God were too fragile to withstand commerce with the actual world."[76] Though we might grant that this Mary is a tad "too good for this earth" (that is, she can't be bothered with it),[77] and we can certainly see how Martha embodies a more activist form of service, how does Martha herself, apart from Mary, blend in the contemplative ingredient? Here Caputo invokes Eckhart's mystical, monkish bent to profile Martha as a contemplative *via* (not vs.) her active demeanor: "Martha is preparing the house for the arrival of hospitality. Martha is preparing the house for the arrival of Jesus, which is a mystical figure for receiving God into the soul. The work that embodies the kingdom of God is a literal work of welcoming God into her house, her soul, her life. The religion of Martha is a religion of hospitality; it is not the means to attain the kingdom of God but its actualization."[78] In sum, "There is a marvelous materialism in Martha's mystical unity with Jesus. . . . There is no shrinking from Jesus's animal nature, his animal needs; her theology is a zoo-theology"—which we might gloss, without denying the "animal" part, as incarnational theology or life (ζωή, *zōē*)-theology.[79]

75. Constable, "Interpretation," 116.

76. Caputo, *Hoping*, 77 (emphasis original).

77. Adapting Abraham Lincoln's statement after the death of his eleven-year-old son Willie in 1862 ("He was too good for this earth").

78. Caputo, *Hoping*, 84.

79. Caputo, *Hoping*, 77; for further reflections on Martha and Mary, see Caputo, *Insistence*, 21–22, 36, 39–55, 63–67, 91, 118–19, 135, 150–51, 163, 167, 169–70, 174, 177–78, 189, 197, 205, 211, 231–32, 246–49, 251–52, 254, 261–62.

In the commentary I endeavored to rehabilitate Martha's tarnished spiritual image as a vocal, dynamic model of "much ministry" in tandem with, not "better than," quieter sister Mary. Luke's Martha is no simple, subordinate "handmaid" of the Lord,[80] any more than Mary of Nazareth is, but more of a partner with Jesus (as well as both Marys) in diaconal work. In her own ways, Martha is just as "good" (*agathē*) as sister Mary, and together they make the perfect spiritual team. I must say, however, that I am drawn to Eckhart and Caputo's material-mystical-Marthan spirituality—fully earthy, noisy, and "quotidian,"[81] and less ethereal, numinous, and quiescent than often touted in Christian interpretation.

And what say my Baptist colleagues on the spirituality of Martha and Mary? Before briefly surveying the four commentators, I must give more than honorable mention to E. Glenn Hinson, the esteemed Baptist church historian who, first at Southern Baptist Theological Seminary in Louisville, KY (1962–92), and then at Baptist Theological Seminary in Richmond, VA (1994–2000), played a seminal role in putting spirituality (back) on the radar of Baptists in America in recent decades. Influenced by Thomas Merton at the Abbey of Gethsemani (Trappist, KY), Hinson began to (re)discover the vital contemplative tradition in Christian history largely forgotten among the typically hyperactive evangelistic and "mission-minded" Baptist congregations of the American South. Amid the religious busyness and social turbulence of the 1960s and 1970s, Hinson "began to discern Merton's message for our day, the dire necessity of contemplation for a world of action, a world that no longer accorded time and made room to seek wisdom for its own sake, to seek God."[82] Although clearly tilting more toward contemplation as a corrective, centering measure *for* a world of volatile action careening out of control, Hinson also valued Merton's broader spiritual perspective that "contemplation could lead *to* more purposeful action."[83]

Not surprisingly, then, Hinson gravitates to Mary's side of the picture, though not without sympathy for dear Martha, whose diligent action Jesus does

80. Here I riff on both the KJV of Luke 1:38 ("Behold, the handmaid of the Lord"; see my commentary on this verse for a more robust interpretation of Mary's "servant" role) and Margaret Atwood's *Handmaid's Tale*, in which the "Marthas" represent the lowest level of household servants: infertile women cooking, cleaning, and babysitting for elite families headed by "Commanders" in a dystopian society.

81. See Caputo, "Quotidianism," ch. 8 in *Weakness*, 155–81; e.g., "Jesus did not take the daily, the day to day, the quotidian, to be a sphere of fallenness from God . . . but to be precisely a delicate sensor of God's rhythm, of the beat of God in time, the way that God gives time from day to day" (161).

82. Hinson, *Baptist Spirituality*, 71.

83. Hinson, *Baptist Spirituality*, 72 (emphasis added); cf. Merton, *Contemplation*.

not chide, only her petulant attitude. In Hinson's pastoral application, Martha reflects "precisely how you may feel when you see people sitting around while you work! Or in the case of many Protestants when they think of people claiming to devote themselves to prayer rather than 'doing something.'"[84] The crux of the matter comes down to Jesus's assessment that, as Hinson renders it, "Martha, Martha, you are worrying and upset about a lot of things, but there is need of one. For Mary has chosen the good part [*not* 'better' part] which will not be taken from her." Hinson particularly hones in on the ambiguity of the genitive ἑνός, *henos* ("of one"), which can be masculine (personal) or neuter. Accordingly, "The one thing, or just as likely, *the One* who was needful was there, and Martha's busyness was keeping her from realizing that moment of grace while Mary was lapping it up."[85] Training the true spotlight on Jesus captures his prominent role in the scene as *Lord*. But Martha fully acknowledges this role as much, if not more than, sister Mary—which is precisely why Martha devotes so much anxious attention to ministering *to him*, to *this One*, this most honored guest. Apart from Martha's frustration, which makes *her* miserable but which she feels keenly enough to express honestly to Jesus, her ministerial/diaconal spirituality is just as authentic, if not more so (remember Luke's Jesus says, "I am among you as *one who serves*"), as Mary's more contemplative approach.

Though acknowledging Jesus's preference of Mary's choice in the present scene, and thus not championing Martha *over* Mary, as Eckhardt and Caputo would have it, all four of my Baptist commentary friends take care not to drive too sharp a wedge between the two sisters' forms of attending to Jesus, generally following Hinson's approach (all four commentators have been Hinson's students and/or colleagues at Southern Seminary and influenced by him in varying degrees). All value the complementary "service" of both Martha and Mary, though not so much as an active-contemplative tandem, but more as exemplars of doing and hearing the word of God, stressing that, in Luke's terms, Mary's priority "hearing" must—and surely will—produce faithful "doing" (though the narrative offers no sequel to this effect). They also admirably set the Martha/Mary episode in its wider Lukan narrative, though emphasizing different cotexts or interpreting the connections in distinct ways.

Culpepper concentrates on the story's link with the immediately preceding parable of the Samaritan as illustrations of the double command to love neighbor (like the Samaritan) and love God (like Mary), set up by the Torah discussion between Jesus and the lawyer (10:25–29).[86] Their respective loving actions

84. Hinson, *Spiritual Preparation*, 85.

85. Hinson, *Spiritual Preparation*, 85.

86. Similar to Talbert, 120–26.

are marked by proper "seeing" of the needy neighbor (injured man) (10:33) and "hearing" of Jesus's instruction (10:39). In the latter case, "the story of Mary and Martha highlights the overriding importance of devotion to the Lord's Word as an expression of one's love for God."[87] By affirming both the Samaritan and Mary as "model disciples," Luke's Jesus breaks sharply with Jewish conventions that repudiate Samaritans as hostile "foreigners" and dissociate women from seminar sessions at (male) sages' feet. In Culpepper's view, Luke depicts "Mary's radical violation of Palestinian social roles" in her attending so raptly to Jesus's didactic discourse rather than to her expected domestic duties.[88]

To the extent that this story exemplifies spiritual practice, it promotes more of a word-centered (*lectio*) approach than a prayer-centered (*contemplativa*) or service-centered (*diakonia*) one. In this respect it coordinates, in Culpepper's view, with the parallel incident in Acts 6:1–6, where the apostles confront the widows' feeding crisis with a diaconal solution, but one *not* involving themselves: "It is *not right* that we should neglect the word of God to wait on tables" (Acts 6:2). Effectively, then, Luke's Jesus includes Mary in the apostolic circle.[89] That is great news for women in general and Mary in particular, though we must still confront the thorny counterpoint of Mary's silence (she has no word[s] herself) and the fact that, in wider Lukan terms, the apostles in Acts 6 are *not right* about what they claim to be "not right" concerning leaving their word-serving to engage in food-serving. These are not competing, but rather thoroughly complementary, ministries; there's no leaving one to do another, but rather cleaving them together as Jesus routinely does (though, oddly, *not* in the Mary/Martha scene). The male apostles struggle with this balanced approach to service, particularly when it comes to the more truly servant duties of feeding and caretaking (see Luke 9:10–17; 17:7–10; 22:24–30). They haven't yet fully learned their lesson in Acts 6, as they are feeling their authoritative oats and flexing their vocal cords more than their helping hands.[90]

Which brings us back to sister Martha's "much ministry," much deaconing. Culpepper values Martha's work and regards Jesus's double "Martha" address as a "mild rebuke or lament," correlating with the parable of the soils,

87. Culpepper, 231.

88. Culpepper, 232. Though Mary is not attending to the full range of hospitality duties normally expected of her in this society, I am not sure to what degree her sitting at Jesus's feet would have been perceived as radical. She still tends to her honored guest in her own way (she's not off in a corner somewhere in her own little world). Culpepper (231) cites m. 'Abot 1:4–5, enjoining male scholars to avoid excessive "talk with womankind" as evidence of Mary's shameful behavior. But if anyone violates this norm in the present scene, it is Jesus, not Mary. She doesn't talk at all.

89. Culpepper, 232.

90. See Spencer, "Neglected Widows."

where he warns against the potential of "anxious cares [μεριμνῶν, *merimnōn*]" to choke the divine word (8:14; 10:41). I also cited this parallel in my commentary, though I am not as comfortable with Culpepper's fuller application: not only like word-stifling thorns, but also "like demons, her cares about fulfilling her duties have thrown her life into disorder."[91] *Demonic* comparisons are always rather supercharged toward the negative; Martha's (understandable) fretting over ministry is problematic, but not chaotic. The devil may be in the details of "much ministry" (do not thankless administrative tasks always carry seeds of frustration in their nitty-gritty, but still necessary, functions?), but so is the Spirit: the hospitable Spirit, the quotidian Spirit, the mundane Spirit. I argue in my commentary that the more apt parallel between the parable and household scenes in Luke 10:25–42 focuses on the *hospitable actions and concerns* of the "good" Samaritan and the equally "good" Martha.

Garland adds to the Samaritan parable parallel a key link with God's pronouncement at Jesus's transfiguration in the previous chapter: "This is my Son, my Chosen; listen to him!" (9:35). Better than the bustling, building-planning Peter and the hustling, homemaking Martha, Mary "has chosen the best portion" (Garland's translation) of listening to Jesus's word.[92] Again, a logocentric spirituality takes precedence, though Garland also cites with approval Merton's reading of this scene that "the superiority of contemplation over action is explicitly stated there."[93] But in a thoughtful engagement with George Santayana's "Sonnet III"—which begins "O world, Thou choosest not the better part!" with clear reference to Jesus's rebuke of Martha—Garland resists the modern poet's further explication of that "better part" as following one's subjective "inward vision" or inner light. Rather, Garland follows Luke, who follows Jesus as "the better pathway . . . who shines the light ahead, and 'divine thought' is taught only by him. . . . Sadly, the world mostly chooses different guides and different paths, but those paths lead only to despair and destruction"[94] (thus Garland spins without suspending Santayana's anti-"world" perspective).

To be sure, Garland does not discount Martha's hospitable activity as much as her irritable attitude: Jesus "is not censuring Martha for paying attention to this important duty [hospitality]. She is scolded not for hustling

91. Culpepper, 232.

92. Garland, 450–52; Culpepper also indicates that "Mary . . . has chosen the 'Chosen One' (9:35)" (232).

93. Garland, 455, citing Merton, *Entering*, 2:347; Garland further appends in a footnote (455n14) Merton's partially qualifying statement downplaying any opposition "between contemplation and activity when they are properly ordered."

94. Garland, 455.

and bustling but for fretting and fussing."[95] Fair enough: but Garland drops in various comments that ramp up the level of Jesus's scolding, such as:

- Jesus's double "Martha" address "adds emphasis" to his "reproach" (rather than a persisting touch of sympathy, as I suggested, or Eckhart's reading of Martha's double-"giftedness").[96]
- Martha's "Lord" address is "ironic," since she aims to tell him what to do rather than attend to his word: "Instead of having a private word with Mary or giving her a meaningful look, Martha wipes her dishpan hands on her apron and complains directly to Jesus about her do-nothing sister."[97] (I argued for her genuine acknowledgment of his lordship over her home; otherwise, Martha would have simply ordered her sister directly [whether privately or publicly] to help her.)
- Martha runs the risk of "majoring in minors and passing over what is of chief importance," like the Pharisees whom Jesus chided for tithing minutiae while neglecting love and justice (11:42).[98]
- Martha is too emotional in this scene to respond "properly" to the (rational) word of God. Here Garland sees the Martha episode as providing a corrective to the popular *misunderstanding* of the good "Samaritan's actions [as] motivated by his feelings of compassion." He cites John Kilgallen for support: "Possibly the conclusion might be drawn that moral action is motivated by one's feelings. With this troublesome possibility in view, Luke followed the good Samaritan story with the proper motivation of all moral decision: the word of the Lord."[99]

My main quibble with Garland's portrait of Martha is tonal-emotional—a matter of interpretive "feel"—which is part of the art of hermeneutics. There is certainly room for hearing Jesus's double "Martha" on a scale from censorious to harmonious. But the pile-up of Martha's characterization as a bossy (not really accepting Jesus's lordship), nit-picking (like certain Pharisees), cantankerous cook-style (complete with "dishpan hands" and "apron"), histrionic hausfrau "feels" a bit like piling on to me and not a little antifeminist (though feminism can assume many forms). In this guise, Martha seems not simply to need a little spiritual guidance, but a complete overhaul—one *pulled away* (περιεσπᾶτο, *periespato*) from the domestic, diaconal ministries she's devoted to and desires

95. Garland, 455.
96. Garland, 453–54; 454n8.
97. Garland, 453.
98. Garland, 455.
99. Garland, 451; Kilgallen, "Martha and Mary," 560.

to pull her sister *to*.[100] No doubt without intending so, Garland's language leaves the door open to a nonquotidian, antimaterial, hyperrational/hypoemotional spirituality. Poor Martha lets her frenetic feminine feelings get the best of her and lead her astray. I take a more aggressive feminist and emotional (see on "Passional Theology" below) line on Luke's theology, but in so doing I may well be distracted by "many things" on the periphery rather than at the center of Luke's interests.

Combining intensive and imaginative reading of Luke's text, with the aid of artistic interpretations, *Vinson* treats Martha's emotional response more seriously and sympathetically. A staccato alliterative trio of short words beginning with μ (*m*) accentuates her deep sense of personal pain. Building on this insight from Vinson, we might render Martha's plea: "Lord, do you not care that this sister of *mine* has left *me marooned* to minister!" (10:40). The order of Greek words runs μου μόνην με (*mou monēn me*)—"my-alone/marooned-me" (note the centrality of her feeling of isolation).[101] Vinson also reflects upon the stunning portrait of *Christ in the House of Martha and Mary* by Diego Rodriguez de Silva y Velázquez (1599–1660), featuring the food-preparing Martha with the most pained expression on her face (Vinson describes her "staring into space, looking like she is about to burst into tears")—with an inset window of Jesus and Mary's tête-à-tête in the background—while an older woman hovers menacingly behind Martha with pointed, scolding finger urging her to "get her mind back on the cooking."[102] (Note: it is this added woman to the scene who chides Martha, *not* Jesus). Reminiscent of Hinson's perspective (see above), Vinson remarks: "Velázquez's painting captures the emotion we all have felt when it seems to us that our hard service is taken for granted."[103]

Vinson's reading of Martha's hospitality also includes a bit of delicious derring-do associated with her "welcoming/receiving" Jesus into her home (10:38). Of course, the usual (safe) interpretation is that Jesus sent word that he was coming to Martha's house or that he knocked on her door for a surprising, though altogether "welcome," house call on this pair of sisters he had somehow met and recruited before (though they are not mentioned by name among the women disciples in 8:2–3 and are not from Galilee). But Luke's introducing the hospitality of "a [certain] woman named Martha" right after reporting Jesus's entry into "a certain village" raises the possible scenario that "while he was preaching and healing and doing his kingdom of God thing, he met this woman

100. As Garland (453) notes, the verb for "distracted" in 10:40 carries the idea of "pulled away."

101. Vinson, 352.

102. Vinson, 344–45.

103. Vinson, 354.

named Martha, *who invited him home*. And he went with her."[104] The whiff of a tongue-wagging scandal drifts in the air, only to become more pungent (than any kitchen aromas) when the house in question includes another woman (Mary)—and no brother Lazarus, as in John 11–12 (it is *his* home according to 12:1), to tidy up the arrangement. Of course, neither Luke nor Vinson argues for any unseemly ménage à trois, and Vinson does not push the point beyond suggesting that gender differences matter less in the kingdom of God than the practice of hospitable fellowship, especially for traveling missionaries (cf. Luke 10:1–16).[105] But the rich history of Christian spirituality includes strands that do not blush at passionate, erotic-like communion with God and Christ. The current story does not go as far in that direction as Jesus's encounter with the loving anointing woman in 7:36–50, but it may tilt that way. Martha's "much ministry" represents a tangible, tactile, embodied, impassioned expression of "much love."

From the fruit of his expertise in Greco-Roman rhetoric, *Parsons* gives Martha due credit for her hospitality—a highly valued, honorable social virtue for men and women not only in Luke's narrative world but throughout ancient society—even as he acknowledges that, in the present case, Mary makes "the right choice" for this moment with Jesus.[106] Parsons bolsters his claim that "it is difficult to imagine that the authorial audience would understand Jesus's praise of Mary to be an implicit criticism of Martha's hospitality" with the observation that Jesus's doubling of Martha's name exemplifies the rhetorical move of "*conduplicatio* . . . to indicate compassion or pity" (*Rhet. Her.* 4.28.38).[107] Here *Jesus's* emotional engagement with Martha is properly educed.

More broadly, Parsons nicely clusters the Martha/Mary vignette with the preceding parable of the Samaritan and the succeeding parable of the midnight caller (10:25–11:13) as presenting a triad of virtuous practices: *philanthropy*, *hospitality*, and *friendship*—particularly associated in that respective order with the parable-story-parable hinge between Luke 10–11, but also overlapping all three scenes. Notice that Parsons doesn't play up Mary's contemplative connection with the prayer-related material in 11:1–13 (which wouldn't work, in any case, since Mary is listening to Jesus, not praying to him or to God in his name) but keeps the focus on *hospitality* (displayed by both sisters in their own ways), which goes hand in hand with the philanthropic Samaritan (who provides for the victim's lodging and sustenance) and the amicable friend at midnight (who

104. Vinson, 348 (emphasis added).
105. Vinson, 348–49.
106. Parsons, 182–83, 186–88; cf. Parsons, *Luke: Storyteller*, 54–61; Arterbury, *Entertaining*.
107. Parsons, 182–83.

eventually helps his neighbor *host* his surprise guest). Although this section may seem more relevant to Luke's "social ethic" than to his spiritual theology, our active-material emphasis on spirituality clearly intersects with social and ethical behavior. Though not using "spiritual" language as such, Parsons makes the point very effectively: "The ancient Christian virtues of philanthropy and especially hospitality demand that we engage and interact with the Other, whether we are guest or host, and Christian friendship obligates us to practices that are mutually beneficial to the whole community, even when we may not always be in complete agreement with our Christian friends. Philanthropy, hospitality, and friendship are three Christian virtues well worth our consideration and cultivation as we attempt to practice the 'one necessary thing.'"[108]

Creational Theology

I could have treated this theological topic first with good biblical warrant: "In the beginning God created" (Gen 1:1). All the rest is commentary, as Rabbi Hillel said about the foundational mandates to love God and love neighbor (b. Šabb. 31a). But of course there would be no selves or neighbors to love if God had not brought us into being in the first place. Organizing theological analysis into systematic categories inevitably involves some order of presentation, since we can't deal with everything at once. My foregoing discussions of trinitarian theology and of spiritual theology precede this "creational" focus more by arbitrary selection than intentional hierarchy, since these three categories inevitably interpenetrate in a kind of conceptual "trinity." The dynamic, interloving, perichoretic Triune God—Father, Son, and Spirit—most palpably manifests to us in, with, and through the totality of God's creation, over which God's inbreathing Spirit broods and in which God's incarnate Son dwells. And the mundane, material, Marthan spirituality we unpacked works itself out in the workaday world starting in Eden, set to rhythms of six beats practical, world-tending (and world-mending) activity, service, and ministry (Martha's "much ministry") and one beat Sabbath rest (restoration), though in fact the Sabbath "spirit" permeates the whole. In this systematic "Integration" section, it is vital not only to integrate broad theological topics with Luke's text, but also to integrate the topics themselves.

Throughout the commentary, I endeavored to highlight creational elements of Luke's narrative theology, from the Spirit's hovering over and conceiving within Mary's womb the embodied (fleshed and blooded) Son of God (1:35),

108. Parsons, 188.

to Jesus's prayer in the Spirit to the "Father, Lord of heaven and earth" (10:21), to Jesus's wisdom teaching about God's care for soil and grain, ravens and lilies (8:4–21; 12:16–18, 22–31; 13:6–9), and his own hen-like care for God's children (13:34), to multiple blessings and distributions of daily foodstuffs (bread, fish, wine—that hospitality business again) (9:10–17; 11:3–13; 22:7–23; 24:28–35, 41–42). The God who creates the seed- and fruit-yielding land, the fish of the sea, and the birds of the air is the God with whom we have to do, who continues to do, to make, to (re)create the world according to God's good purposes in Christ. Marcion needed to excise a lot more than the birth narratives from Luke to suit his purposes.

We may further integrate Luke's creational theology with two other para-categories dear to the hearts of Christian faith and practice, but sadly, too often divided in church history since the Reformation. Nothing has rent Protestants from Catholics more sharply than the supposed dichotomy between *word* and *sacrament*, *faith* and *works*, *inscribed-lettered* (scriptural) and *imaged-signified* (sacramental) revelation of Christ's presence and mediation of God's grace. Daniel Migliore contends that the Reformers, though abridging the number of sacraments to two primary acts (baptism and Lord's Supper), still maintained "the inseparability of Word and sacrament and . . . the importance in both Word and sacrament of the working of the Spirit and of the response of faith. These emphases countered every quasi-magical view of the nature and efficacy of the sacraments."[109] The more, however, one inveighs against "every quasi-magical view" of the sacraments—the more one insists on what they do *not* do and mean—the more one chips away at their sacred "mystery" (Latin *sacramentum* = Greek *mystērion*). Effectively, then, the sacraments sacrifice much of their "efficacy" to the preeminent Word (witness the centrality of the Protestant sermon vs. the Catholic Mass and, in many Protestant congregations, the tack-on of the Lord's Supper at the end of worship once a month [if you're lucky] or quarter).

Thankfully, recent ecumenical discussion has begun to heal some of these rifts toward the mutual enrichment, rather than entrenchment, of all sides of the issue (see more below). Migliore acknowledges that since Vatican II, Catholics and Protestants have found increasingly common ground rooted in the "inseparability of Word and sacraments" (again) within a dynamic trinitarian, Christ-centered, creational, and ethical framework. In particular, ecumenical congresses have made a concerted "effort to interpret the sacraments in a way that illuminates the 'sacramental' character of the whole of creation."[110] As for Luke, after lamenting that we got into this schismatic mess in the first place, he,

109. Migliore, *Faith*, 280.
110. Migliore, *Faith*, 282.

like other NT writers, would no doubt exhort us to go back to beginnings, back to biblical foundations—a good Protestant move, to be sure—but with strong creational roots as well, firmly anchored in the Catholic tradition.

Word and sacrament tightly inhere within creation from the start: God *speaks* into being the living world and all creatures therein (Gen 1:6, 9, 14, 20, 24, 26, 29), and everything God makes is suffused from the beginning with God's *good*, indeed *very good*, character (nature) (1:31)—which is to say, creation reflects the consummate goodness of God and assumes a *sacred* identity, a *sacramental* stamp of God's presence in the world. This is not to equate God with nature or matter,[111] but to engage nature and matter ("all things") as means of understanding and experiencing God's grace, as points of visible, tangible contact with the divine: "Ever since the creation of the world [God's] eternal power and divine nature, invisible though they are, have been understood and seen through the things [God] has made" (Rom 1:20). And even in a sin-marred world, God persists in "working together [synergizing (συνεργεῖ, *synergei*)] all things for good" (8:28 AT; cf. the creational horizon in 8:18–39).[112]

We learn and become solidly assured of these creational-theological fundaments through the written word of *Scripture* and the enacted drama of revelatory *sacraments* (baptism and Eucharist) mediating the dynamic presence of the incarnate Christ, the Living Word of God.[113] In the most ecumenical sense, to keep from ruffling too many ecclesiastical feathers, we might say, not as mere concession but with real conviction: the creational word and sacraments are authoritative, *substantial* paths to knowing God (leaving the various doctrine committees to hash out con-substantial, trans-substantial, or symbolic fine points, as they wish). Word and sacrament *matter*—and they matter *substantially, substantively*.

Though this "high" language of creational Christology has soared a tad above and further back than Luke, who never explicitly puts Jesus at the primordial Genesis event, as John, Paul, and the writer of Hebrews do (John 1:1–5, 14–18;

111. As Moltmann (*Sun*) succinctly observes, amid an otherwise robust creational theology: "If the world is understood as creation, it cannot be divine like its creator. . . . As the creation of a transcendent God, it issues from God's free will and is not a necessary expression of his being, although it corresponds to that being" (203).

112. See Horrell, Hunt, and Southgate, *Greening*, 63–86.

113. Peterson's perspective is worth quoting at length from his foreword to Boersma, *Sacramental Preaching*, viii: "The story that is Holy Scripture invites us into a world of God's creation and salvation and blessing, God in human form in action on the very ground on which we also live, an incarnational *story*, that is, a flesh and blood story, a story worked out in actual lives and places (not in abstract ideas or programs or inspirational uplifting anecdotes), but a Jesus *story* in which we recognize the action of God in the everydayness of a local history in our stories, a *sacramental* story" (emphasis original).

Col 1:15–20; Heb 1:1–4), Luke still casts Christ as the consummating restorer of God's creation through dynamic word and sacramental practice. Luke's Jesus not only speaks with definitive authority about God and God's realm, he speaks with performative, (re)creative power: releasing demon-possessed persons, two men and one boy (4:31–37; 8:26–33; 9:37–43); healing the infirm of fever, leprosy, and various physical disabilities (4:38–39; 5:12–26; 6:6–11; 13:10–17; 17:11–19; 18:35–43); resuscitating the dead (7:10–17; 8:49–56); and calming the chaotic storm (8:22–25)—all through some *vital-verbal* means. And two of these cases of restoration *pronounced* by Jesus—on behalf of a man with a withered hand (6:6–11) and a woman with a bent back (13:10–17)—occur on the *Sabbath*, amid opposition from some strict legal observers, but altogether fitting the Sabbath's climactic *creational* affirmation baked into the "very good" septimal routine of JST.

As Luke's Jesus mediates and incarnates God's generative word in the world, particularly operative on enfeebled human bodies, he also appropriates and incarnates God's documentary word in Israel's sacred Scriptures. And not just select portions or prooftexts here and there, but the *whole* of Scripture, as his final Gospel address to his disciples stresses: "These are my words that I spoke to you while I was still with you—that *everything written about me* in the law of Moses, the prophets, and the psalms must be fulfilled" (24:44). Of course, Law (Torah)-Prophets (Nevi'im)-Writings (Ketuvim)—the entire Tanak—includes the foundational creation narratives from Genesis. More often than not, Luke and Luke's Jesus focus on the *prophetic* Scriptures, again in comprehensive fashion ("*all* the prophets" [24:27; cf. 18:31; Acts 3:18, 24; 10:43]).[114] All Scripture, from beginning to end, sustains a prophetic pulse, proclaiming or bearing witness to God's redemptive, formative, and covenantal relationship with God's people past, present, and future (biblical prophecy is temporally panoramic, encompassing the whole of history, not only the future or final end). In Luke's theological vision, this prophetic heartbeat soars to its crescendo in the Christ event—the complex of Jesus's birth, life, ministry, death, resurrection, and ascension. Or in a word, Jesus *fulfills* Israel's Scriptures, which is *not* to supplant or replace them as obsolete, but to "fill them full," flesh them out, realize their full potential in Jesus's flesh-and-blood life and work.

Darrell Bock rightly discerns the richly textured and mutually interpretive conversation between Luke and Scripture within what he variously calls a "prophecy-fulfiliment," "promise-pattern fulfillment," or "typological-prophetic reading" approach: "It would be wrong to view promise and fulfillment as a unidirectional activity, where a repository of texts was simply lined up with

114. See Jervell, *Theology*, 62: "[When] Luke speaks of 'all the prophets' . . . he understands all the Scriptures of the Old Testament, Moses, the prophets, the psalms and 'the writings.'"

events. . . . The relationship between text and event is two-way."[115] This dual-lane perspective resonates with Richard Hays's intertextual or "figural" hermeneutic, though with tighter strictures. Hays's reading is rather too "free and haphazard" for Bock's tastes, who prefers to cast Luke's method in terms of a "very thought-through fundamental claim about Scripture considered from the perspective of a prioritized theology grounded in the Christ event."[116] I am not entirely sure where the lines deviate between "free-flowing" and "thought-through": can't one engage texts, including sacred texts, both freely (openly, allusively, critically) and thoughtfully (respectfully, literally, traditionally)? I think Hays's "figural" framework better accounts for Luke's dynamic, dialectical reading of Scripture than Bock's more "fundamental" one. Hays applies Erich Auerbach's vintage formulation of "figural interpretation" to the Gospel writers' (and Paul's) reading of the OT:

> Figural reading of the Bible need not presume that the Old Testament authors—or the characters they narrate—were conscious of predicting or anticipating Christ. Rather, the discernment of a figural correspondence is necessarily retrospective rather than prospective. (Another way to put this point is that figural reading is a form of intertextual interpretation that focuses on an intertextuality of *reception* rather than of *production.*) The act of retrospective recognition is the *intellectus spiritualis* ["spiritual act" (Auerbach)]. Because the two poles of a figure are within the "flowing stream" [Auerbach] of time, the correspondence can be discerned only after the second event has occurred and imparted a new pattern of significance to the first. But once the pattern of correspondence has been grasped, the semantic force of the figure flows both ways, as the second event receives deeper significance from the first.[117]

Luke is so steeped in scriptural story and language that imaginative allusions, for example, to Moses-exodus-wandering and Elijah/Elisha-kingdom-

115. Bock, *Theology*, 412–13 (cf. 273).

116. Bock, *Theology*, 409; cf. Jervell, *Theology*, 61: "[Luke] actually intends to omit nothing that Scripture offers. Everything in the Old Testament is Scripture, everything is important, everything is binding. Luke is the fundamentalist within the New Testament. There is in Luke-Acts no criticism whatsoever of Scripture, such as we find in Matthew and Mark, not to mention Paul." While I appreciate Jervell's insistence on the centrality and totality of Scripture for Luke's theology, I think his "fundamentalist" tag misses the mark somewhat, ignoring Luke's often creative and allusive use of biblical images and narratives; see Spencer, *Gospel of Luke*, 28–29.

117. Hays, *Reading Backwards*, 2–3 (emphasis original); see also Hays, *Echoes*. Hays's figural hermeneutic builds on the work of Frei (*Eclipse*), as well as Auerbach (*Mimesis*).

exile seep through his portrait of Christ as easily as direct citations from Isaiah or the Psalms. He is certainly "thinking through" (and thoroughly) the Christ event in light of Israel's Scriptures, but he has not shut down this thoroughfare; he has not closed the book on these sacred books. I take seriously that the living Christ (through God's Spirit) must continue to *open the Scriptures* for seeking disciples, as he does for the Emmaus couple on the road and the larger group inside a residence (Luke 24:32, 45). Note well that Luke offers a broad but mostly bare outline of the testimony to the "things about himself [Jesus Messiah] in all the scriptures," with the provocative tease, but *not* a fully "thought through" textual exegesis, of the "necessity" of the Messiah's suffering, death, and resurrection (24:26–27, 44–46).

As Luke's Jesus consummates his Gospel journey on the Emmaus Road and in Emmaus and Jerusalem residences by mapping his prophetic mission, "mighty in deed and word" and culminating in suffering and glory, back onto the whole scriptural pattern (24:19, 25–27, 44–47), so he inaugurates his ministry in the Nazareth synagogue on the Sabbath by appropriating more specific prophetic models from Isaiah and the Elijah/Elisha narratives. Though overstating the case, Jacob Jervell makes a key point concerning the congregational, liturgical setting of Scripture engagement in Luke's writings: "The place of Scripture is the synagogue, so that Scripture has its 'home' in the house of Israel. Scripture does not exist for private reading. It belongs to recitation and exposition in the synagogal worship of God" (Luke 4:16; Acts 13:14–15, 27; 17:1–2, 10–11).[118] While the synagogue (the "assembly," the "ecclesial" community) is certainly foundational for interpreting Scripture in Luke (it is no accident that Jesus starts here), it is not the only venue. The word of God in Scripture is equally "at home" in actual homes of ordinary folk and "on the road" from Emmaus to the ends of the earth. Have Scripture, will travel (cf. Acts 8:28–35), which again suggests the progressive "openness" and process of biblical interpretation.

Back to the programmatic prophetic texts in Luke 4:16–30. Jesus publicly makes the Isaiah and Elijah/Elisha prototypes his own: "Today this scripture has been fulfilled in your hearing" (4:21). The impression Luke gives us is not so much that Jesus has been poring over the Scriptures in intensive study for the past eighteen years (since age twelve), compiling a careful messianic profile to fit into. Rather, in the wake of dramatic encounters with his Father and the Spirit at his baptism and the devil during his testing ordeal (3:21–22; 4:1–13) and his initial ventures in Spirit-empowered teaching (4:14–15), Jesus now, "today," at this momentous moment, this eschatological watershed, reads himself back into Scripture and finds assurance and guidance there for the "anointed"

118. Jervell, *Theology*, 73 (cf. 63).

(messianic/christological) mission to which God has called him: "The Spirit of the Lord is upon me, because he has anointed/Christened me [ἔχρισέν με, *echrisen me*]" (4:18). Jesus finds himself filled full with this prophetic calling: Isaiah's "me" becomes Jesus's "I."

The particulars of Isaiah's messianic vision, focusing on Jubilary liberation from forces of oppression and enslavement (Isa 61:1–2; 58:6; cf. Lev 25; Deut 15:1–18) may appear to echo Exodus more than creation traditions. I will discuss Luke's "Social [Liberation] Theology" in the next section, but now I stress that separating Exodus from creation is a false dichotomy, not least from Isaiah's perspective that scans the biblical horizon backward and forward to envision a *new exodus* for God's exiled people in the pattern of a *new creation*. "The LORD, your Redeemer, the Holy One of Israel" is "the LORD, your Holy One, the Creator of Israel, your King" (Isa 43:14–15), poised to do a "new thing" (43:19) that both renews and outstrips the "old" in God's dynamic re-creative project:

> I am about to *create* new heavens
> and a new earth;
> the former things shall not be remembered
> or come to mind.
> But be glad and rejoice forever
> in what I am *creating*.
>
> (65:17–18; cf. 66:22–23)[119]

Redemption flows out of creation as the natural work of the one holy, mighty, and gracious Creator-Redeemer Lord. And sacred ("sacramental") rhythms like Sabbath and Jubilee reinforce the creation-Exodus link: the holy rest of Sabbath rests in God's perfect goodness worked into the fabric of creation (Gen 2:1–3; Exod 20:8–11) and redeems the dignity of human and animal labor as it resists the life-strangling oppression of slavery, like that under Egypt (Deut 5:12–15); and the fresh freedom of Jubilee provides not only release of slaves and remission of debt (which often led to slavery), but also restoration of land to original owners and respite *for the earth*, refraining from cultivation for a full year (a "sabbath of complete rest for the land" [Lev 25:4]), allowing it to breathe, reset, and settle back into a fertile creational tempo. Neither human nor animal nor land—all interdependent in God's good creation—should be worked to death![120]

119. On Luke's appropriation of Isaiah's "new exodus" pattern, see Pao, *Acts*; Green, *Conversion*, 51, 57–60, 65–69, 73.

120. For helpful biblical and theological ecologies, see Davis, *Scripture*, and Wirzba, *Paradise*.

Adding Jesus's Elijah/Elisha references to his Jubilee sermon, we have more emphasis on granular-material, earthly embodied ministry to all people—Gentile and Jew, female and male, lowborn and highbrowed (Luke 4:25–27)—starting with Elijah's *feeding* of the destitute widow at Sidonian Zarephath during a season of "severe famine over all the land" (4:25). Luke's Jesus's fleshes out (kneads, rolls out) this prophetic prototype of "bread for the world" (cf. meal-and-oil biscuits in 1 Kgs 17:11–14) in a desert feast for the masses (9:10–17), his model prayer for communal "daily bread" (11:3, 5–8), his personal identification with broken bread "given for you [all]" at the Last Supper (22:19), and his postresurrection revelation to the Emmaus couple "in the breaking of the bread" (24:35; cf. 24:30–31). Without doubt, the presence and efficacy of Christ are baked into "eucharistic" practice, and not only the formal, institutionalized Eucharist, as significant as that act is. Jesus says, "*Keep doing this* [τοῦτο ποεῖτε, *touto poiete* (present imperative)] in remembrance of me" (22:19 AT) as an emblematic part of a grateful/graceful (εὐχαριστέω, *eucharisteō*), dutiful life-habit of bread-baking, -breaking, and -sharing in Christ's name. Without John's dominical "I am" statement, Luke's Jesus is just as truly the "Bread of Life," manifestly *known* in breaking bread for others in various "daily" engagements, but especially in his broken body on the cross. "Breaking of bread" is an essential means of knowing, meeting, and sharing the incarnate Christ. Or better put perhaps, Christ himself is the ultimate sacrament in his sacrifice "remembered" in the staff of life.[121]

None of this sounds very Baptist, at least not in the Texas independent and Southern Baptist traditions I grew up in. The word "sacrament" was sacrilegious from the get-go, sure to cause us to break out in hives on the very thought of it, not that we thought very deeply about it; just knowing that it was "Catholic" was sufficient to reject it. We had *two ordinances* (not the seven or God knows how many sacraments the Catholics had)—*ordained* by Christ and Scripture: baptism and the Lord's Supper (or "communion," but never "Eucharist," another of those mumbo-jumbo ritual terms we distrusted, this time roping the Episcopalians into our censure). Of course, preaching the biblical word was central in our services, and baptism (it is in our name, for goodness' sake) also held a high place and would happily be done every Sunday we had candidates in the *first slot* of the service (it was a mark of honor for the baptized to soon join the audience with wet heads) from the lofty baptistery, the high

121. On Christ himself as the quintessential sacrament, see Boersma, "Anchored": "Scripture and tradition both participate sacramentally in Jesus Christ—himself the great revelatory sacrament of God" (31); see also Boersma, "Reconnecting": "All . . . talk about participation and about sacraments is ultimately talk about Christ" (36).

"altar" (higher than the pulpit!) in many Baptist churches. The Lord's Supper, however, was practiced infrequently (once a quarter, as I recall, in my home church), hurriedly, and always at the end of the service pushing the 12:00 limit for lunch (and, more important, the Dallas Cowboys game on TV). Moreover, the preacher seemed more obsessed with what this ordinance did *not* mean rather than its significance for our lives—it did *not* carry any "real," substantial value as the Catholics (again) claimed—which might make one wonder why be bothered with it at all. Well, Jesus said, "Do this," so we did it, but we did it with as little gusto as possible and certainly no presto change-o (and, it goes without saying, no alcoholic wine, which no prayer or blessing could ever make holy; a little watered down Welch's grape juice was all we could safely handle).

Creation, to the extent it was discussed, was also primarily a *via negativa*, a broadside polemic against the atheistic evolutionists, with no practical theological value. Philip Thompson aptly captures a prevailing "scorning of creation among Baptists": "Over the past two centuries, Baptists have devalued physical creation vis-à-vis the spiritual as the means by, through, and in which God works. . . . We see a growing opinion among Baptist theologians that physical matter is less worthy, even less capable of being used by God in the transaction of saving grace."[122] So much for any creational-sacramental appreciation.

But all this is changing, at least among some "other Baptists."[123] A number of Baptist scholars through the Baptist World Alliance (BWA) and other organizations have engaged in fruitful ecumenical dialogue with various Christian groups—including Roman Catholics.[124] Though debates continue to swirl around various desiderata (what do you expect among Baptists?), these ecumenical Baptists generally show greater appreciation for communal, unifying, signifying (not "mere symbol"), vivifying dimensions of Christian faith and practices. Some are even willing to adopt "Bapto-catholic" and "Baptist sacramentalist" labels, though I am less sanguine these will catch on: one "ist" (Baptist) is probably enough; and ecumenical discussion is as much about denominational *distinctives* in open dialogue with other groups as it is about flattening those on common ground.[125]

A particularly clear and clarion call for this "re-envisioned Baptist identity"—dubbed a Manifesto, no less—was sounded two decades ago (1997) by a group of Baptist scholars and ministers in North America (six drafters

122. Thompson, "Re-envisioning," 296.

123. The term coined by Curtis Freeman, *Contesting* (see subtitle).

124. See Fiddes, "Conversation," and entire Spring *ABQ* 31 (2012) issue, *Baptists and Catholics Together.*

125. See Cross and Thompson, *Baptist Sacramentalism*; Harmon, *Towards Baptist Catholicity*; Bullard, "James William McClendon"; Freeman, *Contesting*, 311–38.

and fifty-five signatories). Of the five main planks, two pertain to word and sacrament.[126]

1. *We affirm Bible Study in reading communities rather than relying on private interpretation or supposed "scientific" objectivity.* This communal, congregational context for biblical interpretation corresponds to the synagogal setting for reading and expositing Scripture in Luke and Acts, noted above. But the Manifesto explanation that follows assumes a rather "authoritarian" (even as it argues against it), dogmatic position:

- We reject all forms of authoritarian interpretation, whether they come from the ranks of the academy or the clergy.
- We deny that the Bible can be read as Scripture . . . apart from the gospel and the community in which the gospel is proclaimed.
- Scripture wisely forbids and we reject every form of private interpretation that makes Bible reading a practice which can be carried out according to the dictates of individual conscience (2 Pet 1:20–21).
- We therefore cannot commend Bible study that is insulated from the community of believers or that guarantees individual readers an unchecked privilege of interpretation.[127]

The welcome, positive affirmation of communal reading turns direly dark and denunciatory (notice the drumbeat of "reject," "deny," "forbids," "cannot") against individual "consciences." Certainly the caution against untested, seat-of-the pants, idiosyncratic proclamations of Scripture, whether in baptistic or in charismatic traditions (which, by the way, can occur as easily in public pulpit as private closet), is salutary. But is it really as necessary as this Manifesto makes out in its strident prohibitive tone? As leading Baptist historian Walter Shurden notes, the long-standing Baptist commitment to a robust concept of the priesthood of all believers respecting the integrity of each person's "conscience" has never endorsed solipsistic Christianity (*sola Scriptura*, yes; solo practice, no) or "theological anarchy": "the individual is always an 'individual in community' in Baptist life."[128] Nevertheless, the responsibility of each believer within the community to exercise *freely* his or her conscience in striving *faithfully* to understand God's word under the personal guidance of the Holy Spirit (by all means, the Holy Spirit speaking directly and critically to "my" mind as well

126. Freeman et al., "Re-envisioning," 303–10.

127. Freeman et al., "Re-envisioning," 305.

128. Shurden, "Baptist Identity," 328. Though writing a very serious article critiquing the Manifesto, Shurden can't help from quipping in his first response to this plank: "Are you serious, or are you just pulling our Baptist legs?" (326).

as "yours" and "ours") remains a vital countercheck on corrupt institutions, calcified traditions, and mass delusional contagions.[129]

As it happens, 2 Peter and Luke strike a useful balance between "private" and "communal" interpretation. The former actually advocates "a most reliable prophetic word" regarding Scripture uttered by individual prophets truly tutored by the Holy Spirit *against false prophets and teachers* who worm their way into the community. I cite from the CEB:

> We have a most reliable prophetic word, and you would do well to pay attention to it, just as you would to a lamp shining in a dark place, until the day dawns and the morning star arises in your hearts. Most important, you must know that no prophecy of Scripture represents the prophet's own understanding of things, because no prophecy ever came by human will. Instead, men and women led by the Holy Spirit spoke from God. But false prophets also arose among the people. In the same way, false teachers will come among you. They will introduce destructive opinions and deny the master who bought them, bringing quick destruction upon themselves. (2 Pet 1:19–2:1)

I take "prophecy of Scripture [προφητεία γραφῆς, *prophēteia graphēs*]" to refer both to the words *of* Scripture uttered by biblical prophets and to words *about* Scripture spoken by interpretive prophet-teachers in the church. In both cases, the authenticity of the message depends on the dynamic "leading" ("moving," "carrying" [φερόμενοι, *pheromenoi*]) of the *Holy Spirit* in and through the prophets, individually or communally. The social setting of the prophecy is secondary to the *Spirit source*. Indeed, in biblical history, it is often the lone, ostracized, individual Spirit-driven prophet who speaks God's inconvenient truth to a wayward people and their unjust rulers.

Luke's Jesus and John the Baptist (I am tempted, tongue-in-cheek, to underscore *Baptist*) precisely fit this maverick prophetic bill: "voice[s] of one[s] crying out in the wilderness" to reveal "the dawn from on high . . . to give light to those who sit in darkness," to shine the lamp of God's word on a solid stand so that truth may "come to light" (1:78–79; 3:4; 8:16–17—note the affinities with 2 Pet 1:19). And as mentioned above, this prophetic-scriptural word is as much at home on the road and in individual homes as it is in synagogues and the temple, as remarkably experienced by a couple of ordinary travelers not simply thinking their own private thoughts, but having those private thoughts

129. On the delusional susceptibilities of mass movements, religious and otherwise, see Hoffer, *True Believer*.

ignited and lit up ("Were not our hearts burning . . . while he was opening the scriptures to us?" [Luke 24:32]) by the living Jesus himself, first of all incognito to them, and then more clearly known in his breaking bread at their table. To be sure, they promptly share this radical testimony with the wider community of disciples, who confirm a similar postresurrection appearance to Simon (24:33–35). But it starts with "Scripture, Jesus, and me" (well, two of us, Cleopas and companion): a private showing, a select previewing, a grand "opening" of God's word involving just Jesus and an ordinary couple. The wider fellowship is vital, but I doubt, if the eleven apostles had kept mocking the notion of an empty tomb and risen Christ, as they first did in response to the women's witness (24:10–11), that Cleopas and friend would have backed down one iota.

2. *We affirm baptism, preaching, and the Lord's table as powerful signs that seal God's faithfulness in Christ and express our response of awed gratitude rather than as mechanical rituals or mere symbols.*[130] The language here regarding word (preaching), baptism, and Lord's Supper in fact steers clear of both the blander term "ordinances" and the bolder "sacraments," preferring to speak positively of "powerful signs" over against "mechanical rituals or mere symbols." Few nonfundamentalist Baptists would blanch too much, I think, at this formulation, particularly with the key qualifiers "powerful" and *not* "mechanical/mere." These are *sign*ificant acts, powerful practices, dynamic demonstrations, provided we do not get too mystical or metaphysical about their operation.

In the explanatory comments on this affirmation, the Manifesto does lament that "Baptist reflections on 'the sacraments' [note the scare quotes] have for too long been fixed on late medieval and early modern theories." It then resumes its polemical "rejection" tone, but in a much more balanced way than manifested in the first plank: "We reject all accounts of these practices that would limit the presence of the Risen Lord to the performance of the enacted signs as we also reject all accounts that deny the reality of his presence in their enactment. The Lord is present and active both in the performance of these remembering signs and with the community that performs them."[131] This carefully nuanced statement I, and many other Baptists worldwide, could happily sign on to.

I also strongly concur, in light of my foregoing discussion, with the creational underpinnings of the Manifesto's comments: "In and through these remembering practices, God's grace and Christian obedience converge in a visible sign of the new creation. By repeating these signs we learn to see the world as

130. This is actually the fourth of five affirmations listed in the "Manifesto."

131. Freeman et al., "Re-envisioning," 307–8.

created and redeemed by God."[132] That said, however, in this and other welcome contributions of Baptist thinkers to ecumenical faith and practice, I would push for greater engagement with creational-ecological elements alongside communal-ecclesiastical contexts. Though I can't claim to have read everything on the subject, my general impression is that the latter (church community) trumps the former (world creation) among "sacramental" Baptists.

With respect to the Lord's Supper, Curtis Freeman, a leading voice among "other Baptists" endorsing the Manifesto, unpacks the meaning of this significant liturgical practice in a rich three-ingredient dish with a classic Greek flavor:

- *Paradosis* ("tradition"): the Supper proclaims the macro-gospel-narrative running from God's calling of Israel to sending Jesus Messiah, "culminating in the cross and resurrection."[133] (Though Freeman does not go back to creation at this point, he soon briefly, though clearly, aligns his view against "an incipient Marcionism that separates the spheres of creation and redemption.")[134]
- *Anamnesis* ("commemoration"): The Supper is rooted in Jesus's practice and words of institution which we remember, reenact, reconstitute in fellowship with other believers ("Do this in remembrance of me" [Luke 22:19; 1 Cor 11:25]).
- *Paraclesis* (Spirit work as "Paraclete"): Drawing on Johannine language of the Holy Spirit's "called-alongside" administration of Christ's word and presence, Freeman stresses here the work of "the Holy Spirit to unite in mystery this practice with the sacrifice of Christ so God's people may by faith receive nourishment from the [Supper] table."[135]

I suggest putting a fourth item on the plate that goes well with the conceptual meaning of παράκλησις (*paraklēsis*) as "encouragement, exhortation,"[136] adding an *ethical* nutrient to the mix. For the sake of distinction, I use the different but related term *parenesis*,[137] commonly employed by NT scholars to refer to the practical-behavioral segments in Paul's and other letters.

- *Parenesis* ("instruction, exhortation"): The Supper is a ritual practice of worship that dramatizes the ethical practice of food-sharing in the work-

132. Freeman et al., "Re-envisioning," 306–7.

133. Freeman, *Contesting*, 329.

134. Freeman, *Contesting*, 330.

135. Freeman, *Contesting*, 329.

136. BDAG, 766.

137. Sometimes spelled "paraenesis" (Greek παραίνεσις, *parainesis*).

> aday world, exhorting believers to move from sanctuary to society, from bowed knees and receiving hands to blistered feet and giving hands to a hungry world, as Jesus did.

As the Baptist theologian James McClendon—the elder-dean of late twentieth-century Baptist ecumenical thought (and signatory to the 1997 Manifesto)[138]—avers (with acknowledged dependence on Mennonite ethicist John Howard Yoder): "Almost lost to sight in ecclesiastical struggles over what happens to bread and wine when certain words are said over them is that for New Testament disciples 'the *primary* meaning of the eucharistic gathering in the Gospels and Acts is economic' . . . [related to] *primeval socialism*, a commonwealth of possessions and their use. 'At the Lord's table, those who have bread bring it, and all are fed.'"[139] Of course, this perspective on the Supper as an "economic act"[140] especially accords with the bread-sharing practices of Luke's Jesus and the early believers in Acts.

I finally reinforce this more extensive engagement with Baptist theologians, historians, and ethicists with some interaction with my four fellow Baptist commentators on Luke 24:13–35, arguably the principal "sacramental" passage on "word and bread" not only in this Gospel, but in the entire NT.[141] Beyond what I've written on this text in the commentary and above in this "Integration" section, I simply want to underscore the *creational* foundation. Again, Jesus's appeal to "all the scriptures" includes the Torah with its Genesis beginnings, and the bread he breaks in Cleopas's house (and the fish he later requests and eats with the disciples [24:41–43]) is made possible because of God's primordial provision of productive land (and sea), which God's human creatures are to manage as responsible stewards of God's gracious bounty. In addition, however, we must not lose sight of the preeminent, climactic enacted word of Luke 24 regarding the life-giving God who raised the suffering, crucified Jesus Messiah from the dead (24:45–46). This risen Jesus—who embodies Scripture and bread-needing life—bears ultimate witness in his person, words, and works to the creative, restorative purpose of God. Any hope of "redeem[ing] Israel" (24:21)—which,

138. See Bullard, "James William McClendon."

139. McClendon, with Murphy, *Witness*, 379 (emphasis original); see Yoder, *Body*.

140. Yoder, *Body*, 21.

141. Risking excommunication from my Baptist fellowship, I prescind the ordinance/sacrament of baptism from the discussion in favor of the Lord's Supper. Though John's baptism is certainly foundational in Luke's Gospel, the early Christian practice of baptizing in Jesus's name comes to the fore in Acts. Somewhat curiously, the risen Jesus does not specifically commission his followers to baptize in his name at the end of Luke. In any case, this Gospel focuses much more on meal sharing and hospitality than baptism.

thankfully (eucharistically) remains a very live hope now—is predicated on God the Creator's resurrection of Jesus. Creation and redemption are inextricable.

Culpepper looks not so much to creation motifs for understanding the Emmaus narrative as to dramatic appearance accounts, in both the Bible and Greco-Roman literature, of angels, gods, and other supernatural beings to various figures, including travelers. It is not uncommon for these stories to feature suspenseful elements like incognito appearances ("entertaining angels unawares") followed by sudden moments of "recognition," as in the Emmaus episode.[142] Though such background greatly helps to illuminate Luke's story, it perhaps overaccents the "heavenly" aura of the narrative at the expense of the earthier elements. I also have a slight quibble with Culpepper's reflection on the "always elusive" nature of the divine presence in which "God's faithful perceive God's presence in fleeting moments, and then the mundane closes in again."[143] I prefer to read the Emmaus story as finding the "elusive" (from our perspective) Christ *in* the mundane, the worldly, the earthy, if we have eyes to see.

Even so, Culpepper does not hesitate also to highlight the "liturgical language" from the scene in Cleopas's home, signifying "that every meal [with Luke's Jesus] has the potential of being an event in which hospitality and table fellowship can become sacred occasions. The eucharistic language further implies that the church experiences the continuing presence of the risen Lord when it gathers at the Lord's table." Culpepper also affirms Christ's "opening" (διανοίγω, *dianoigō*) of the Scriptures to "interpret" (διερμηνεύω, *diermēneuō*) the saving significance of his entire mission as "the heart of Luke's hermeneutics" (24:27, 32).[144]

In addition to being an astute interpreter in his own right, *Garland* excels in mining others' studies for choice nuggets. Two of these stand out in the Emmaus story related to our interests. He cites Arnold Ehrhardt regarding the intense, "disputative" (συζητέω, *syzēteō* [24:15]) exchange between the two travelers over Jesus's death: "Cleopas and his companion were not walking meditatively, on an Easter outing . . . but passionately discussing the events of Good Friday"—particularly (now in Garland's words), "Where did things go wrong?"[145] What will soon become a profoundly sacramental (my language), revelatory experience through Jesus's breaking open word and bread occurs along a dusty road and within an ordinary home in the throes of impassioned *doubt and*

142. Culpepper, 475–79.

143. Culpepper, 482.

144. Culpepper, 480.

145. Garland, 950; Ehrhardt, "Disciples," 186.

debate, not sanctimonious and antiseptic pseudoliturgy (note implications for "Spiritual Theology" above and "Passional Theology" below).

Garland also clarifies the timing of the Emmaus incident, drawing on the work of Adelbert Denaux. Though the "almost evening" setting, glossed as "the day is now nearly over" (24:29), is commonly interpreted as on the brink of sundown, the term for "evening" (ἑσπέρα, *hespera*) in fact was associated in JST with the wider "period after noon, when the sun begins its decline and moves toward sunset." Hence, the traveling couple first encountered the risen Jesus at noontime, "the moment," as Denaux comments, "the sun is at its zenith, which would fit the biblical motif of God revealing his glory at this moment (cf. Gen 18; Acts 8,26–40; 22,1–21; 26,1–23; Jn 4,1–45)."[146] The meal, then, probably took place around 3:00 p.m., the time of the evening sacrifice in the temple (*Ant.* 14.65; cf. Luke 1:9), the death of Jesus (23:44), and the first restorative sign performed in the name of the risen Jesus (Acts 3:1).[147] Though Garland does not explicitly mention creational elements, the manifestation of Christ's sacred presence to the Emmaus pair clearly unfolds within the day-night, life-death rhythms of ordinary time (ORT) in the world.

Vinson (like Culpepper) interprets the Emmaus story in light of suspenseful "recognition" scenes in Greek literature, focusing particularly on the return home of the long lost Odysseus, first disguised as a beggar before revealing himself. He also makes effective use of parallels from the Hellenistic-Jewish writer Philo, concerning the Emmaus pair's reception of Jesus's scriptural word, and from Aristotle's *Poetics*, regarding the recognition of Jesus at table.[148] Though again eschewing "creational" and "sacramental" language (I do not aim to turn these into litmus-test words for any commentator or to assume some tendentious aim behind their absence), Vinson gets at the basic idea via the Greek intertexts. From Philo, he highlights the natural (creational) image of fire to illuminate the "burning heart" of the couple ignited by Jesus's scriptural exposition. But for Philo, the fiery voice of God, as at the burning bush, can sear as much as soothe: "Since the property of fire is partly to give light and partly to burn, those who think themselves fit to show themselves obedient to the sacred commands shall live for ever and ever as in a light which is never darkened. . . . But all those who are stubborn and disobedient are forever inflamed, and burnt, and consumed by their internal appetites, which, like flame, will destroy all the life of those who possess them" (*Decal.* 48–49).[149]

146. Garland, 954; Denaux, "Meaning," 87.

147. Garland, 954–55.

148. Vinson, 744–51.

149. Cited in a sidebar in Vinson, 751. (The numerous sidebars throughout this stellar commentary are worth the price of the volume.)

The climactic event of recognition in the common breaking of daily bread, which had characterized Jesus's ministry in Luke, resolves an intriguing narrative-poetic plot in real world terms: "Aristotle would approve: their recognition of Jesus came from the events themselves, from his repetition of a familiar act in a plausible setting, and the moment of recognition was also a reversal of their state of mind. They go from deep grief to joy, from confusion to understanding, and most importantly from disbelief to faith, and the crucial moment is the breaking of the bread. What a brilliant pastoral theologian!"[150]

Parsons completes the quartet of Baptist commentators who emphasize, in other terms, what I've called the creational-sacramental dimensions of the Emmaus story. One vivid "resonance" Parsons detects with the spiritual journey of all God's people is that "the Emmaus path to spiritual illumination and growth is a downward one. . . . The path to wholeness . . . is downward as we turn to embrace the loss and pray for transforming grace. The old Shaker hymn is surely right: ''Tis a gift to be simple, 'tis a gift to be free, 'tis a gift to *come down* where we *ought* to be.'"[151] The Emmaus couple discovers the hope of the living Lord right where they are, in the *depths* of their despair, or as we might gloss, *down* in the dirt where they trudge, *down* the road, as Jesus comes *down* to their level and drills *down* into the heart of Scripture. They may not see him clearly at first, because they are looking and feeling down, but the means of uplifting and rekindling their depressed spirits become available because the risen Jesus meets them where they walk, live, and hurt—on the road, in the home; in the unexpected scriptural insights of a stranger, in the unexceptional sharing of an ordinary meal. "One need not be in the religious center of Jerusalem (or anywhere else) for a religious revelation. One might experience the presence of the resurrected Christ in one's own home. So Luke encourages the audience, then and now, to take heart in that the resurrected Lord revealed himself through the faithful exposition of Scripture, in an obscure place, in a humble home, in a shared meal to little-known followers who had experienced devastating loss. He continues to come to us in Word and at Table. So goes the good news!"[152]

The final exclamatory assessments of Vinson and Parsons bear repeating as fitting banners over Luke's Emmaus narrative: "What a brilliant pastoral theologian!" (Vinson). "So goes the good news!" Amen and Amen.

150. Vinson, 751; cf. Aristotle, *Poet.* 11.20–30 (1452a); 17.15–20 (1455a).

151. Parsons, 356–57 (emphasis original). He cites with approval N. T. Wright, *Resurrection*, 657: the notion of "resonances which echo out . . . from the original event itself."

152. Parsons, 357.

Social Theology

From the somewhat tautological "Spiritual Theology" (what other kind is there?) to the audaciously cosmological "Creational Theology" (how can we pretend to take in everything?), I turn to what some might claim to be another odd category—"Social Theology"—this time potentially suffering from banality ("socializing"), on the one hand, and volatility ("socialism"), on the other. Are we talking about that lovely but limp tradition of "church socials" or some version of that radical agenda associated with Marxist/Communist politics? No, of course not! This is about something more substantial than dinner on the grounds, more "spiritual" (that slippery word again) than (godless) proletarian revolution, and more "practical" (utilitarian) than communitarian pooling of all property and goods (these goods are too limited, and self-interest is too hardwired into the human condition).

Yet Luke has a pesky tendency to commit and commend these various social faux pas:

- In a sense Jesus founds the grand "dinner on the grounds" tradition with his insistence on feeding the multitude to whom he has proclaimed God's kingdom and administered healing all day in the desert, even though his disciples want to send them home to fend for themselves (Luke 9:10–17). Enough socializing with the rabble already, they seem to think; time for some private "us time" with Jesus. But Jesus carries the commitment to shared fellowship (κοινωνία, *koinōnia*)[153] all the way through, from preaching to healing to feeding, all social—and spiritual and creational—events. No *mere* socializing, to be sure, but socializing all the same.
- Though no labor union organizer or workers' rights advocate, Luke's Jesus, embodying "one who is himself among the poor,"[154] manifests a patent "preference for the poor," as the liberation theologians would put it, whether working the land of exploitative landlords and their managers or displaced from land and home and forced to beg or rot in debtors'

153. Though this term does not appear in this feeding scene, the concept of shared fellowship of goods is central here and characterizes the earliest Christian community in Acts 2:42 (cf. 4:32). It also figures prominently in today's ecumenical exchange. Note the statement by Paul Fiddes ("Conversation") related to Baptist-Catholic dialogue: "Ecumenical conversations . . . begin by bringing together the three realities of God as the triune fellowship of love, Christ as the Word of God, and the church under the rule of Christ. The concept that unites these three is communion or *koinonia*" (9; see 9–15).

154. Luke Timothy Johnson, *Prophetic Jesus*, 97; cf. 96–99 for a helpful synopsis of the Lukan Jesus's practices of "prophetic embodiment" in solidarity with the poor.

prison. While the present worldly order is stacked toward the powerful and wealthy, the rule of God incarnated in Jesus protects, provides for, and prioritizes the poor: "yours is the kingdom of God" (6:20). Top spots at God's royal banquet table hosted by Jesus Messiah go to "the poor, the crippled, the lame, and the blind" (14:13, 21; cf. 7:22). Luke's Jesus does not call the poor, employed or unemployed, landed or homeless, to rise up themselves in revolution; but he declares God's realm of renewal and reversal already established on their behalf and demands that followers of God's way "lift up" the least, last, and lowly, which is to say, each other, through concrete charitable actions (cf. 1:52–53; 6:30–31; 12:32–33; 16:19–31; 18:22).

- While we can try to massage the impracticality and impossibility of Jesus's call for complete divestiture of private property and possessions—especially in light of the long haul of human history, two millennia and counting now, that Jesus might not have taken into full account—his stark mandate seems to brook no mitigation or finagling: "So therefore, none of you can become my disciple if you do not give up all your possessions" (14:33). "There is still one thing lacking. Sell all that you own and distribute the money to the poor, and you will have treasure in heaven; then come, follow me. . . . What is impossible for mortals is possible for God" (18:22, 27). And, by God's grace, possible for the early church in Acts in their voluntary "communistic" community (Acts 2:44–45; 4:32–37),[155] though not without glitches of some deceptive withholders (5:1–11) and some poor members slipping through the safety net (6:1–7). But utilitarian capitalists the early believers in Christ most definitely were not!

Labeling Luke or Luke's Jesus a socialist or a communist is no more useful than dubbing him a revolutionist or a feminist: all such tags are hopelessly anachronistic and tangled in a thicket of historical and cultural debates. But denying that Jesus's gospel has strong "social," "communal," "revolutionary," or "pro-women" dimensions—within its own contexts—won't work either. It is no accident that contemporary Christian socialists, Marxists, feminists, liberationists, deconstructionists, and political theologians of various stripes all find congenial—though not necessarily total—support for their views in critical engagement with the teaching and practice of Jesus, not least Luke's

155. Green (*Conversion*) rightly stresses this voluntary dimension of Christian communalism over against totalitarian sects and societies: "Selling what one has is customary within the community Luke depicts, but such giving is voluntary and oriented above all toward addressing the plight of the needy. . . . The voluntary character of the *koinōnia* Luke portrays is underscored" (129–30).

Jesus.[156] Do we read into Luke too much of our own politics and interests? No doubt. But many of us ideological readers are also careful readers of iconic texts, aiming to read out (exegete) what is there with the aid of the best critical tools we have. It is a delicate hermeneutical dance, but for Luke and Luke's Jesus, it is inevitably a "social" dance with profound "societal" implications.

Though "Social Theology" may seem like a fairly innocuous category (provided we do not add the "-ist" suffix), safer than the more freighted liberation, feminist (including womanist and mujerista), black, Marxist, or deconstructionist theologies—all with acute (some would say skewed) "social" perspectives—"social" itself becomes much more highly charged when fused with "gospel"—another "good," even great, word by itself—the "good news," the "evangel" (εὐαγγέλιον, *euangelion*), a Lukan favorite. But when the "social gospel" is invoked, sparks tend to fly, at least in American theological settings.

Even though a century or so has passed, "social gospel" still readily evokes the popular reform movement by this name from the late nineteenth and early twentieth centuries, spearheaded by Congregational ministers Washington Gladden and Charles Sheldon, Evangelical Alliance General Secretary Josiah Strong, economist and social theorist Richard Ely, and American Baptist pastor and theologian Walter Rauschenbusch.[157] Yet, such memories are not altogether positive, especially for many who proudly call themselves evangelicals today, that is, "Gospellers," avid advocates of the good news of Jesus Christ, but *not* an avowedly "social" one. In his recent, robust *Evangelical Theology*, biblical scholar Michael Bird, who proves himself an able systematic theologian as well, flatly calls the "social gospel" a "false" and "truncated" gospel.[158] That is strong stuff, but Bird thankfully doesn't leave it there: "This is not to say that pursuing justice and helping the poor is not an important task for God's people; it is part of our mission to be salt and light! God's concern for justice, helping the poor, and showing compassion lies at the heart of the Mosaic legislation, it permeates the prophets, and it is key in the Sermon on the Mount."[159] And Bird would no doubt add Luke's Sermon on the Plain and indeed Luke's entire Gospel, itself permeated by the social justice of Israel's Torah and Prophets.

156. I have ventured my own feminist-critical engagement with Luke in Spencer, *Dancing Girls*, 108–91; and *Salty Wives*. Though not specifically focused on Luke, Moltmann (a white, male, German, Reformed theologian) has sought with remarkable openness to integrate his views of Christ and Christian faith and practice with black theology, Latin American liberation theology, feminist theology, and Minjung theology; see chapters on each perspective in Moltmann, *Experiences*, 183–299.

157. See the new superb historical introduction by Christopher Evans, *Social Gospel*.

158. Bird, *Evangelical Theology*, 52–54.

159. Bird, *Evangelical Theology*, 53.

So are we just quibbling over semantics while still getting at the same point? Is Bird simply hyperallergic to "social" language applied to the gospel, because of the toxic residue of an early-twentieth-century American reform movement (Bird himself is Australian, not American), while basically affirming the gospel's (social) justice orientation? Not quite. Bird sees something more fundamental at stake:

> Social action and caring for the poor is not, however, the gospel; it is simply what Christians are expected to do alongside the gospel. Showing compassion and pursuing justice are implications of the gospel, implications of the fact that Christians belong to a kingdom, not simply share a final heavenly destination. . . . A truncated gospel that includes only social programs and economic policies as its contents strips the gospel of its powerful message of how sinful men and women can be reconciled to God through the cross of Jesus Christ. The gospel of old liberalism . . . is no gospel at all.[160]

Apart from the question of whether Bird fairly assesses the gospel message of "old liberals" like Rauschenbusch (was it really so tunneled and truncated? [see below]), the issue of what beats at the heart of the gospel versus what runs "alongside" it—what the gospel impels at its core versus what it implies around the edges—begs for further examination. Bird's entire theological project, owing in part to Vanhoozer's performative-dramatic scheme, advances the evangel's central (not peripheral) active-verb thrust conveyed in the neologism "gospelize," including but expanding beyond the popular revivalistic nuance of "evangelize": "Evangelical theology . . . is the drama of *gospelizing*. By 'gospelizing' I mean trying to become what the gospel intends believers to be: slaves of Christ, vessels of grace, agents of the kingdom, and a people worthy of God's name. . . . The purpose of gospelizing is to ensure that those who bear Christ's name walk in Christ's way."[161] And what is God's way (of life) and Christ's way if not Micah's way, which Bird cites as "summ[ing] up God's will for his people" in that classic text: "He has shown you, O mortal, what is good. And what does the LORD require of you? To act justly and to love mercy and to walk humbly with your God" (Mic 6:8).[162] Clearly, *social justice* is integral to gospel faith and practice for many evangelicals as well as liberals, to say nothing for Catho-

160. Bird, *Evangelical Theology*, 53–54.

161. Bird, *Evangelical Theology*, 30–31 (emphasis original).

162. Bird, *Evangelical Theology*, 53 (citing NIV).

lics in the vein of Edward McGlynn, Dorothy Day, Sister Simone Campbell, and Popes Leo XIII and Francis I.[163]

An easier ecumenical case is made these days for faithful, gospel-rooted commitment to "social justice" than to a "social gospel," though again we run the risk of a rather bland, nominal consensus: who doesn't claim to believe in social justice, except for bombastic tyrants and callous sociopaths? I have no particular axe to grind for "social gospel" as a banner, though I will try to set the historical record straighter below. But it seems to me that the gospel as proclaimed and performed by Luke's Jesus is social "all the way down" (to crib a phrase often used by John Caputo).

If Jesus's programmatic synagogue sermon in Luke 4:16–30 is symptomatic of his creational theology, as suggested above, it is also axiomatic of a socially engaged gospel by whatever name. Indeed, it is arguably the locus classicus, some would say "manifesto," for such a gospel project (program, platform, agenda—again, by whatever name). The Isaiah lection, wholly embraced by Jesus as his own commission, begins: "The Spirit of the Lord is upon me, because he has anointed me to bring good news to the poor [εὐαγγελίσασθαι πτωχοῖς, *euangelisasthai ptōchois*]"—or, to better reflect the Greek's two-word phrase: "to-gospelize the-poor" (Luke 4:18/Isa 61:1). The remainder of this core "script," which shapes Jesus's evangelical "role," stresses Jubilary liberation from all types of oppression—from destitution, disease, and debt, from enslavement and imprisonment to sinful institutions as well as inclinations—encapsulated in the pithy term ἄφεσις (*aphesis*), "release, redemption, forgiveness." To coin a phrase, social theology is "aphesian theology."

This Isaiah-rooted platform for the redemptive mission of Luke's Jesus has indeed inspired in manifesto-fashion much social-gospelizing in Jesus's name, such as that spearheaded by the Baptist pastor and theologian Walter Rauschenbusch a century ago. Before focusing on this influential figure, however, I briefly highlight the work of a contemporary minister-activist, Wendy McCaig, typical of countless lesser-known, but no less significant, promoters and practitioners of Jesus's Luke 4 vision in local hands-on, feet-on-the-ground contexts. McCaig founded and continues to serve as the executive director of Embrace Richmond, a faith-based nonprofit organization devoted to meeting the social-justice challenges of inner-city communities in Richmond, Virginia, especially the Highland Park neighborhood. Beginning with a small ecumenical home Bible study

163. For basic readings in Catholic social justice, see Windley-Daoust, *Primary Source Readings*; for a brief survey, see Christopher Evans, *Social Gospel*, 68–73; for an interesting case study of St. Malachy's Church in North Philadelphia, led by John McNamee, see his *Diary of a City Priest*, discussed at length in Caputo, *What Would Jesus Deconstruct?*, 118–31.

and prayer group comprising seven women (rather like Lydia and company in Acts 16:13–15, 40) dubbed the Yada Yadas—five Catholics, a Presbyterian, and "one confused nondenominational Methodist-Baptist-Lutheran mutt," as McCaig describes herself[164]—the ministry mushroomed into a multifaceted movement devoted, among other projects, to homeless settlement, furniture distribution, drug rehabilitation, and care for battered women. McCaig recounts this poignant missional journey, integrated with her MDiv studies at Baptist Theological Seminary of Richmond (she received her degree in 2007), in *From the Sanctuary to the Streets: How the Dreams of One City's Homeless Sparked a Faith Revolution That Transformed a Community* (2010). We can easily adapt the main title for Luke's Jesus to "From the Synagogue to the Side-Roads," particularly since in public talks McCaig regularly cites Jesus's Nazareth sermon as prime motivation for her ministry.[165]

McCaig has also been inspired by renewed, radical biblical and theological understandings of hospitality beyond petty pursuits of throwing nice parties toward an inclusive vision of social activism. McCaig cites the trenchant perspective of Christian ethicist Christine Pohl: "Christian hospitality has always had a subversive, countercultural dimension. 'Hospitality is resistance' . . . Especially when the larger society disregards certain persons, small acts of respect and welcome are potent far beyond themselves. They point to a different system of valuing and an alternate model of relationships."[166] Moreover and not surprisingly, McCaig's view of God's kingdom has expanded beyond popular preoccupations with heavenly destiny after death to redemptive realities "on earth as it is in heaven," here and now. Her holistic vision embraces that of World Vision president Richard Stearns, who seeks to fill the "hole in our gospel" with "whole gospel"—the whole socially embedded gospel. Notice the Lukan roots of this "revolutionary" vision, which McCaig quotes from Stearns:

> The kingdom of God, which Christ said is "within you" (Luke 17:21 NKJV), was intended to change and challenge everything in our fallen world in the here and now. It was not meant to be a way to leave the world but rather the means to actually redeem it. . . . Those words from the Lord's prayer, "your kingdom come, your will be done on earth, as it is in heaven" were and are

164. McCaig, *From Sanctuary*, 6.

165. McCaig cites Luke 4:19 in *From Sanctuary*, 155. She also makes frequent reference to Jesus's "least of these" parable in Matt 25:31–46 as foundational for her work.

166. Pohl, *Making Room*, 61 (with Luke 5:32 as the epigraph on the same page heading the chapter "Hospitality, Dignity, and the Power of Recognition"); cited in McCaig, *From Sanctuary*, 24–25.

> a clarion call to Jesus's followers not just to proclaim the good news but to *be* the good news, here and now. This gospel—the *whole* gospel—means much more than the personal salvation of individuals. It means a *social revolution.*[167]

Though in *The Hole in Our Gospel* or its sequel (*Unfinished: Filling the Hole in Our Gospel*) Stearns never mentions either Walter Rauschenbusch or the social gospel as such, his stress on the radical social implications of the gospel worked out in God's present kingdom beyond the experience of "personal salvation" fits Rauschenbusch's agenda to a tee (not to mention the agenda of Luke's Jesus [see more below]). But as already hinted above, while "social" and "gospel" may be acceptably used by evangelicals and others in the same sentence or paragraph, many insist that these terms should never kiss each other directly, lest they evoke that old toxic, liberal "social gospel" movement led by that German guy with the convoluted name (can anything truly good and "evangelical" come out of modern Germany?).

American church history has not been kind to Brother Rauschenbusch. Even among his Baptist brethren, especially those in the American South (he was a northerner, a New Yorker no less), he came to be widely dismissed and impugned, although he was not only the "prophetic soul" and "scholarly theologian of the [social gospel] movement," as later Baptist theologian and ethicist James McClendon (of southern and western American provenance) acknowledges, but also the object of "fierce opposition," not from McClendon and ecumenically minded Baptists (a minority), but from fundamentalist and other conservative Christians (including a majority of Baptists) throughout the balance of the twentieth century.[168] As William Ramsay sums up Rauschenbusch's notoriety, "It shocks many of us to see this good Baptist preacher preaching socialism. Advocate it he did, however, repeatedly."[169]

Yet for all his shocking views, Rauschenbusch still arguably stands as the most notable Baptist theologian of the modern era, one who "alone has attained cosmopolitan status."[170] As for wider influence on church and society, he would be surpassed only by Martin Luther King Jr., the iconic Baptist preacher,

167. Stearns, *Hole*, 17, 20 (emphasis original; cited in McCaig, *From Sanctuary*, 154). Elsewhere in this volume, Stearns focuses on Jesus's Nazareth sermon in Luke 4:18–19 as Jesus's "mission statement" and inauguration of a "social revolution with a vision for a changed world" (21–22, 53, 67–68).

168. McClendon, with Murphy, *Witness*, 93, 95.

169. Ramsay, *Four Modern Prophets*, 21; though offering some reasonable critique, Ramsay himself presents an overall sympathetic portrait of Rauschenbusch (9–28).

170. McClendon, *Ethics*, 21.

prophet, pastor, and civil rights activist and martyr.[171] And as it happens, King happily acknowledges his inspirational debt to Rauschenbusch: "I came early to Walter Rauschenbusch's *Christianity and the Social Crisis*, which left an indelible imprint on my thinking by giving me a theological basis for the social concern which had already grown up in me as a result of my early experiences. . . . Rauschenbusch had done a great service for the Christian Church by insisting that the gospel deals with the whole man—not only his soul, but his body; not only his spiritual well-being, but his material well-being."[172]

A person of his time, Rauschenbusch no doubt became too enamored with a particular political ideology percolating in the early twentieth century; his social gospel too easily elided into a *socialist* gospel with utopian ideals of transforming America through the Christian evangel into a socialist democracy (of course, the most prominent socialist/communist models of the century turned out to be not at all democratic or theistic or pacific). For all his appreciation of Rauschenbusch, King offers a trenchant critique from his social location in the 1960s after two world wars, the Korean conflict, and ongoing Cold War and Viet Nam crises: "Of course there were points at which I differed with Rauschenbusch. I felt that he had fallen victim to the nineteenth-century 'cult of inevitable progress' which led him to a superficial optimism concerning man's nature. Moreover, he came perilously close to identifying the Kingdom of God with a particular social and economic system—a tendency which should never befall the Church."[173]

For all his interest, however, in the intersection between Christian faith, society, and politics, Rauschenbusch was no social scientist or politician. He was first and foremost personally a man of faith and prayer[174] and professionally

171. To this modern Baptist Hall of Fame in America, one might well add former president Jimmy Carter, a quieter, steadier activist, now a nonagenarian and still going strong, a lifelong Baptist and still a regular Sunday School teacher at Maranatha Baptist Church in Plains, GA. In addition to his numerous nonsectarian national and international humanitarian efforts through the Carter Center, he has recently promoted the Baptist New Covenant as a religious means of combating racism and effecting racial reconciliation (see Emma Green, "Jimmy Carter"; and http://newbaptistcovenant.org/president-jimmy-carter). His advocacy of women's full equality in the face of religious sexist strictures, not least among Southern Baptists, is vigorously manifest in Carter, *Call to Action*.

172. King, *Autobiography*, 18; cf. King, *Strength*, 158–59.

173. King, *Autobiography*, 18.

174. See Rauschenbusch, *Prayers of Social Awakening* (1910), including an introductory chapter "The Social Meaning of the Lord's Prayer" (15–23); cf. Ramsay, *Four Modern Prophets*, 17. See also Rauschenbusch's *Social Principles*, written late in his career (1916), a widely popular and practical guide for college students, including daily Scripture readings and commentary. For a helpful summary and "reexamination" of this work, see Shields, "*Social Principles*."

a pastor and scholar-teacher. No ivory tower social theorist, Rauschenbusch's views on the social gospel were forged in the fiery crucible of New York City, bordering the Hell's Kitchen area of the Bowery district, where he pastored for eleven years (1886–97) Second German Baptist Church, whose members were poor working-class German immigrants living in squalid tenement conditions. Though a young man of twenty-four when he commenced this work, it took its toll on his own health, including a long illness in the brutal winter of 1888 that exacerbated his congenital hearing deficiency almost to the point of deafness.[175] Finally, he moved to the more congenial environment of his alma mater, Rochester Theological Seminary, where he eventually became professor of church history and greatly expanded his social-gospel vision through speaking and writing.

Though generally accepting the historical biblical criticism of the time (he had an early stint of study in Germany), Rauschenbusch firmly grounded his theology and practice in biblical soil, especially the social-justice commitments of the Hebrew prophets and Jesus of Nazareth.[176] Relevant to our focus on the Third Gospel, Rauschenbusch frankly tags Luke as "the socialist among the evangelists." Though a twentieth-century "socialist" boot ill fits Luke's first-century sandal, Rauschenbusch clarifies his understanding of Luke's portrait of Jesus as one that "gives a sharper social turn to sayings reported by the other gospels" (e.g., the Beatitudes for the poor and hungry simpliciter), alongside the unique presentation of parables denouncing the wealthy and favoring the destitute (rich fool, unjust steward, rich man and Lazarus).[177] Moreover, while granting the radical, revolutionary, reformative thrust of Jesus's teachings and practices, Rauschenbusch the historian flatly acknowledges that "Jesus was not a social reformer of the modern type. Sociology and political economy were just as far outside of his range of thought as organic chemistry or the geography of America."[178]

As for the "radical attitude toward wealth taken by Jesus according to Luke" and perpetuated by the sharing of property and possessions in the early Jerusalem church, Rauschenbusch insists on distinguishing such patterns of life as "revolutionary," but not "ascetic" in orientation. Rather than being rooted in certain Greek ideals of self-discipline and self-denial, the economic generosity and mutuality of Jesus and his early followers reflected "simply the strong

175. See Christopher Evans, *Kingdom*, 45–127.

176. See Rauschenbusch, *Christianity*, 1–31, 39–73; *Theology*, 133–34, 210–16; *Christianizing*, 48–58.

177. Rauschenbusch, *Christianity*, 64–66.

178. Rauschenbusch, *Christianity*, 41.

democratic and social feeling which pervaded later Judaism."[179] Such "social feeling," however, far from a cozy, sappy sentimentalism or a clubby, cliquish sectarianism, generates a dynamic, prophetic apocalypticism (the work of God's kingdom) that seeks to change the world root and branch, not end it or escape from it: "Ascetic Christianity called the world evil and left it. Humanity is waiting for a revolutionary Christianity which will call the world evil and change it."[180] After citing this statement, Moltmann comments: "Walter Rauschenbusch . . . was right, although doors for a 'revolutionary Christianity' are not open always and everywhere—not in America either. But then the true Christianity, which calls the world what it is in the light of the crucified Jesus, will become a resistance movement. . . . A Christianity which is completely 'in line' with the state of the world and rule of 'other lords' is a Christianity without the remembrance of 'Christ crucified,' and is therefore a Christianity without Christ."[181] Thus the great German Reformed political theologian of hope and the "crucified God" appropriates the great German-American Baptist advocate of the social gospel.

Back to the first-century church reported in Luke's second volume. Rauschenbusch is careful not to reify the liberal, loving, land-ceding fellowship into some strategic socioeconomic system optimal for all times and places or to idealize it into some romantic utopian community. The early believers in Jerusalem were no social theorists or managerial experts. They simply continued sharing the "common purse" mode of life they pursued with Jesus when they left their homes and jobs to follow him and in which they lacked "not a thing," as they affirm in Luke 22:35.[182] And though their resource pooling was thoroughly voluntary and initially salutary ("there was not a needy person among them" [Acts 4:34]), it was not without its problems, as Rauschenbusch acknowledges. In the short run, the "system" could be scammed and seeds of mistrust sown by deceptive members like Ananias and Sapphira (5:1–11); and in the longer run, the massive divestiture of estates and commodities possibly contributed

179. Rauschenbusch, *Christianity*, 65. For Rauschenbusch, "later Judaism" entails a "social radicalism," a "strong democratic and social feeling" (65) characteristic of the Ebionites (an early Jewish-Christian sect) and the NT book of James in particular. Conversely, throughout his writings, Rauschenbusch is highly critical of what he sees as traditional Judaism's tendency to legalistic, ritualistic religious performance divorced from sincere faith and loving action. In this critique he follows the polemic of the prophets and Jesus, but without their fuller appreciation for God's gift of Torah and the nexus between obedience and faith(fulness), law and love. Rauschenbusch's picture of ancient Judaism needs considerable updating in light of recent scholarship.

180. Rauschenbusch, *Christianity*, 72.

181. Moltmann, *Experiences*, 177.

182. This text is specifically cited in Rauschenbusch, *Christianity*, 101.

to the community's later economic poverty—a point Rauschenbusch concedes but that, he rightly assesses, is "pure inference," unsubstantiated by any explicit cause-and-effect statement.[183]

At any rate, the communistic practice of the fledgling Jerusalem church remains clear in the Acts record and should not be dismissed, as Rauschenbusch describes the typical stance of American preachers (as typical now as then), with "a sort of deprecatory admiration"—which I colloquially paraphrase, "Well ain't that nice and sweet, but wholly impractical as a policy for church or society"—and a one-off exceptionalist excuse that does *not* prove the rule. Most interpreters "seem more anxious to emphasize that it did not occur twice than to show that it did occur once." Moreover, the spirit of radical "generosity"—which Rauschenbusch insists is the correct term "and not communism in any proper sense"—while perhaps not manifesting in such extreme measures as practiced in Jerusalem, certainly carried on to some degree in churches outside Palestine, evident not least in the Pauline collection project among the Gentile congregations for their poor brothers and sisters in Jerusalem! In short, though "the church at Jerusalem was not quite as communistic as is usually supposed, on the other hand, the other churches were not as completely devoid of communistic features as is commonly assumed."[184]

While along with most Christians of whatever stripe we may politely applaud the charitable aims of Rauschenbusch and company in a churchly context,[185] we still haven't addressed the big theological bugbears of social-gospelism: its (supposed) softness on sin and secularization of salvation; or put another way, its downplaying, if not downright denial, of humanity's direst need for personal salvation from sin by God's grace through the redemptive death of Jesus Christ. The lost sinner-seeking and -saving Jesus of Luke's Gospel—one by one, as the triad of parables in Luke 15 accentuate—is lost in the shuffle of the social gospel.

Or is it? Though a common old chestnut thrown at the social gospel movement, the charge of not taking sin seriously simply doesn't stick, at least

183. Rauschenbusch, *Christianity*, 100–102.

184. The cited material in this paragraph comes from Rauschenbusch, *Christianity*, 100–102.

185. The fundamental ecclesial roots of the social gospel movement (most of its leaders were pastors of local congregations) should not be neglected. As McClendon, with Murphy (*Witness*), puts it: "It would certainly be misleading to treat the Social Gospel as primarily a political movement, a kind of socialism whose present-day counterpart might be left-wing Democratic politics. One can be a political party member without joining a church, but *churchlessness was never an option for sharers of the Social Gospel*. . . . Europe had various movements and parties designated both as socialist and Christian. . . . This was not true of the Social Gospelers, who consistently spoke to and through the churches they served" (89 [emphasis added]).

not to Walter Rauschenbusch, who devotes no fewer than four early chapters of his *Theology of the Social Gospel* (the most substantive theological defense of the movement) to *sin* ("The Consciousness of Sin," "The Fall of Man," "The Nature of Sin," and "The Transmission of Sin") and the next two to discussions of *evil* ("The Super-Personal Forces of Evil" and "The Kingdom of Evil").[186] To be sure, he *extends* the problem of sin and evil beyond the merely private, personal, and internal subject to the societal, structural, and institutional sphere, but such an expansive view *intensifies* (not nullifies) the dilemma and *implicates* (not exculpates) the individual in a heavier debt. Isaiah's "Woe is me! I am lost, for I am a man of unclean lips" is inextricable from "and I live among a people of unclean lips" (Isa 6:5). As Rauschenbusch explains regarding Isaiah, "His cleansing and the dedication which followed were his preparation for taking hold of the social situation of his nation."[187] This comment comes right after the fourfold analysis of sin and evil in the ensuing chapter entitled "The Social Gospel and Personal Salvation," which Rauschenbusch obviously does not ignore.

Far from ignoring personal conversion, Rauschenbusch positively insists upon it, while lamenting the often superficial and ephemeral effects of revivalist "decisions" for Christ. Without equivocation, Rauschenbusch affirms that "the salvation of the individual is . . . an essential part of salvation. . . . It is always a great and wonderful thing when a young spirit enters into voluntary obedience to God and feels the higher freedom with which Christ makes us free. It is one of the miracles of life. . . . The consciousness of wrongdoing, of imperfection, of a wasted life lies on many and they need forgiveness and strength for a new beginning."[188] Of course, we can scarcely find a more apt model for the redemption of "a wasted life" than that of the prodigal son in the classic Luke 15 parable. In his earlier *Christianity* volume, Rauschenbusch immediately clarifies his labeling of Luke as a "socialist" (see above) with typical evangelical language: "The socialist among the evangelists was also the one who has given us the richest expressions of the free grace of God to sinful men, without which our evangel would be immeasurably poorer."[189]

No cheap grace, mind you. In contrast to the knee-jerk, hand-raising, aisle-walking, card-signing invitations of popular mass evangelists, Rauschenbusch longs for a return to "some deep-soil ploughing," as he vividly puts it,[190] with not so subtle evocation of Jesus's parable of the soils, which admonishes

186. Rauschenbusch, *Theology*, 31–94; cf. Shriver, Introduction, xvi–xvii; Ramsay, *Four Modern Prophets*, 17–18.

187. Rauschenbusch, *Theology*, 106.

188. Rauschenbusch, *Theology*, 95–96.

189. Rauschenbusch, *Christianity*, 66.

190. Rauschenbusch, *Theology*, 97.

deep thinking, feeling, and fruit-bearing responses to the gospel word (Luke 8:4–15). As always, Rauschenbusch returns to biblical prophetic roots, particularly the social-justice "theology of the prophets [Moses, Samuel, Isaiah, Jeremiah, Jesus, Paul] . . . *based on their personal experiences*" with God[191]—profound, provocative, radically transformative experiences.

> These prophetic experiences were not superficial. There was soul-shaking emotion, a deep sense of sin, faith in God, longing for him, self-surrender, enduement with spiritual power. Yet they were not ascetic, not individualistic, not directed toward a future life [afterlife]. They were social, political, solidaristic.
>
> The religious experiences evoked by the social gospel belong to the same type. . . .
>
> Other things being equal a solidaristic religious experience is more distinctively Christian than an individualistic religious experience.[192]

Although never referencing Rauschenbusch or the social gospel, Joel Green's astute treatment of conversion in his *Conversion in Luke-Acts*, anchored in careful exegesis of Luke's narratives and informed by recent advances in cognitive science and neurobiology (beyond that known to William James, the preeminent American psychologist-scholar of Rauschenbusch's day, who had a deep interest in religious experience), resonates nicely with Rauschenbusch's emphasis on necessary (not ancillary) emotional, relational, communal, and behavioral concomitants of personal conversion. For Luke and all who follow his narrative pattern, "Conversion is embodied religious experience . . . that could never be consigned to the ethereal or the 'spiritual.' 'Spiritual conversion' is nothing less than human transformation . . . in its most integrated sense of personal and communal life. With conversion, people undergo relational reformation and full-bodied transformation of their most basic patterns of believing, thinking, feeling, and behaving."[193] Rauschenbusch puts less explicit emphasis than Green on somatic experience ("embodied/full-bodied"), but the former certainly knew the effects (and affects) of sinful and unjust practices on human bodies and the need to transform these in salutary social-relational action. The holistic meaning of "save/salvation" (σῴζω/σωτηρία, *sōzō*/*sōtēria*) as "making whole, restoring, healing" applies throughout Luke and Acts.

191. Rauschenbusch, *Theology*, 107 (emphasis added).
192. Rauschenbusch, *Theology*, 107–8.
193. Green, *Conversion*, 123–24.

Ultimately, conversion and all healthy, healing, whole-making religious experience engage the wider culture and creation. At the end of an illuminating chapter "Religion and Culture" that surveys the American historical experiment, including a key section on the social gospel, McClendon sums up the integrative vision with particular reference to Luke's "earthy" perspective (see "Creational Theology" above). "The proposal to treat religion as culture or vice versa was alarming if it denied the transcendent or holy nature of religion, regarded it as merely of the earth, earthly. No such reductionism was intended, for the true gospel appears on earth or not at all; even when sung by angels it proclaims not only glory to God in the highest, but also 'on earth, peace' (Luke 2:14). Gospel religion partakes of transcendence in order to announce God's immanence; it heralds faith *on earth* (cf. Luke 18:8). Religion and culture belong together indivisibly."[194] This allusion to Luke 18:8—"When the Son of Humankind comes, will he find faith on earth?"—caps off the parable of the persistent widow, who pleads for a callous judge to "grant her justice" (18:3, 5).

This parable and its frame in 18:1–8 thus provides an apt focal text for our brief Baptist commentary review. Beyond this passage's concern with social justice on earth as a natural bridge to social-gospel interests, it also features a female protagonist (some would even say a "feminist" paragon) and an eschatological horizon[195]—both of which (women's issues and future kingdom) Rauschenbusch addressed more lightly than other social problems (workers' rights, housing, healthcare, alcoholism, though of course these deeply touched women and children's lives as well as men's)[196] and the present action of God's kingdom (though "the kingdom is always, but [yet] coming").[197]

Although none of my esteemed Baptist commentator predecessors on Luke 18:1–8 pushes critical issues related to feminism and theodicy as far as I do, they all affirm Jesus's positive presentation of the persistent widow in the face of injustice and acknowledge the awkward juxtaposition of the parable's unjust judge, "who neither feared God nor had respect for people" (18:2, 4),

194. McClendon, with Murphy, *Witness*, 97 (emphasis original).

195. In addition to the commentary, see my extensive feminist-critical analysis of this parable and surrounding context in Spencer, *Salty Wives*, 264–314.

196. Though the women's suffrage movement and first-wave feminism was very active in Rauschenbusch's day, he showed scant interest in women's issues as such. See the thoughtful, generally appreciative, yet feminist-critical response to Rauschenbusch's opening chapter on the Hebrew prophets in *Christianity* (1–31) by a leading feminist biblical scholar, Phyllis Trible, in "Rhetorician of Righteousness," 33–37.

197. From the conclusion of Rauschenbusch, *Christianity*, 338: "At best there is always but an approximation to a perfect social order. The kingdom of God is always but coming. But every approximation to it is worthwhile." See also the chapter on eschatology in Rauschenbusch, *Theology*, 208–39.

with the just and merciful God in the parable's context of prayer (18:1, 7) and "faith" at the Son of Humankind's return (18:8). Also, though none alludes to the "social gospel" as such in their exposition of this passage (neither do I in the commentary section), all stress, from various angles, Jesus's commitment to social justice as a vital component of Christian, that is, Christ-like "faith."

Culpepper evinces a robust appreciation for the relentless widow as a model of active (activist) faith in the service of justice, which is to say, *faithfulness* to the just will of God on earth, with particular attention to the unfortunate and exploited: "The reader must be ready to profess a *faith* like that of the persistent widow who demands justice and the pious widow who prays night and day. . . . Many find it far easier to worry over the health of their prayer life than to be concerned for the well-being of widows. No expression of *faithfulness* to God is more deeply rooted than the duty to care for the widows, orphans, and strangers—the powerless and homeless in our midst."[198]

Garland views the parable and surrounding context as offering both a "consoling message" for those suffering from and pleading for justice in an unjust world and a "warning of judgment" for those who fail to persevere to the end in the interest of justice. However, following the prayerful focus of the verses immediately surrounding the parable, Garland interprets the active "faith" Jesus will look to find at his return as faithful praying "for God's final vindication of the elect," petitioning "for God to do something"—including the prospect of drawing oppressors to repentance.[199]

Parsons also connects God's dilatory patience in the face of desperate cries for justice with the long-suffering opportunity God affords unjust adversaries and judges "for repentance and restoration," while making clear that "the absence of God's judgment is a sign, not of God's approval, but of God's mercy."[200] Moreover, alongside challenges to faithful prayer and endurance, Parsons stresses "the relentless pursuit of justice as an important element of the story in its final form," demanding the "human obligation to act responsibly" as God's agents of justice in the entire interim period of suffering up to the Son of Humankind's climactic coming to finalize God's redemptive realm.[201]

Vinson follows suit in acknowledging that God's "tardiness" in delivering supplicants like the widow from their unjust plights owes to extended grace-time for the unjust *perpetrators* to change their nefarious ways. But he hastens to qualify, with appropriate candor and even protest, that "from where the

198. Culpepper, 339 (emphasis added).

199. Garland, 712.

200. Parsons, 271.

201. Parsons, 262, 271.

righteous sit," God's delayed judgment on the unjust "feels like callousness to them [the righteous victims]."[202] Moreover, while persistent, faithful prayer is good and necessary for God's beleaguered children, this is no substitute for faithful *action*, not simply by oppressed sufferers (the parable's widow is first and foremost a model of social-justice activism), but even more so, by "a *community* who will make certain that [the widow] is not crushed and forgotten. As we pray for justice and wait for Christ to come . . . we should also imitate the early Christian community of Acts who met the needs of the widows around them. If the poor, the orphans, the widows and the aliens are going to have their injustices rectified quickly, then it will be *by God acting through us*."[203]

Passional Theology

Rauschenbusch's appraisal of the biblical prophets' commitment to social justice rooted in intense religious experience of "soul-shaking emotion, a deep sense of sin, faith in God, longing for him, self-surrender, [and] enduement with spiritual power"[204] sounds downright revivalistic. One can hear Charles Finney and Billy Sunday shouting a hearty "Amen" (to the "spiritual" part at least, maybe not so much the "social" effects): "Preach it, Brother Walt!" But for soberer theologians and clergy, there's too much "shakin' goin' on" for comfort. A little soul warming (even "strangely" as with Wesley) is fine, provided it doesn't get too hot and bothered. Sound reason, not soft emotion, must primarily undergird and guide sound faith. Fickle feelings are ever the bane of firm faith.

But Rauschenbusch has a point. Without any psychoanalytic tweaking, an honest reading of the "former" prophets (such as Elijah, Elisha, Ahijah), as well as the "latter" prophets (such as Isaiah, Jeremiah, Ezekiel), readily reveals an impassioned company of men (and a few women) of God all in—body, soul, family, occupation—for God's sovereignty and justice, crazy in love with God, and willing to do whatever it takes, bordering on madness, to fulfill God's mission.[205] The prophets are not shy about shaking their people and the world as they have been shaken by God, whose presence shakes heaven and earth, even

202. Vinson, 565.

203. Vinson, 566 (emphasis added).

204. See n. 192 above in this chapter.

205. For a deconstructive twist on prophetic "madness," see Caputo, *What Would Jesus Deconstruct?*: "The voice of deconstruction is not far from the voice of the prophets, which call for justice to flow like water over the land" (65). "There is . . . something wonderfully 'mad' here—'deconstruction is mad about this kind of justice' [Derrida, "Force of Law," 25]—with a kind of divinely deconstructive madness, the way one is a mad fool for the kingdom of God" (67).

the foundations of God's temple-house (Isa 6:4). The Holy Spirit's shaking the place where the early Jesus believers gathered, further empowering them for bold, prophetic witness, follows suit (Acts 4:31; cf. 2:1–4, 17–18). Non-"shakers" need not apply for prophetic service. (See more on prophetic models below.)

But we can't really be expected to serve God in a perpetual stir, can we, especially a state of emotional upheaval? We can't all be prophetic types—hyped-up, eccentric, histrionic poets, protesters, dramatists, and even mimes (at times). Let's not forget the vital discipline of contemplative prayer. And everyone knows that passions, to use the most common ancient term, even if one doesn't go the extreme Stoic-Vulcan route of tamping them down altogether, are distractive, disorienting, destabilizing, and often flat-out dangerous to our well-being. Reason must rule for right to be realized—not least in matters of right religion. Such has been the party line for most of Christian history following the Greek hierarchy of *logos* over *pathos*. I mean, above all, Jesus is the Divine Logos of God, the Incarnate Word (John 1:1, 14)—*not* the Divine *Pathos* of God, whatever that might mean. God speaks, commands, charges, and instructs as King, Father, and Lawgiver. But does God feel, emote, sympathize, and suffer as Servant, Mother, and Caregiver, for example? Does Jesus, Luke's Jesus in particular?

For many Christian scholars and ministers (less so perhaps among the laity), the answer to these touchy-feely questions about the omni-sufficient and -potent God and Christ's emotions or passion*s* ("the passion" is another matter [see below]) is so patently negative as to hardly be worth discussion, certainly not as a major category of biblical-theological analysis, as I am offering here. As Elizabeth Johnson describes the traditional theological view (which she then proceeds to challenge): "Incapable of being affected by outside influences, the classical apathic God acts not out of need or compulsion but from serene self-sufficiency."[206] God is impassible and immutable, period, the very essence of serenity and sufficiency. If "social theology" is hard to swallow, "passional theology," as I am calling it, is beyond the pale.

But a notable strand of modern biblical and systematic theology interlaced with recent developments in biological and neuroscientific study has brought emotions (back) into the complex picture, indeed into the foreground, of human experience, religious and otherwise. I begin with a capsule of scientific views, followed by a sketch of biblical-theological perspectives.

Not surprisingly, scientific research into emotion is extremely complex and involves lively internal debates on key questions, including those on the most fundamental lexical and semantic levels: What is the best word for what

206. Elizabeth A. Johnson, *She Who Is*, 247.

we're studying: "emotion," "affect," "feeling," "passion," "sensation," or something else (and how might these terms be distinguished)? And most basically: What is an *emotion*, anyway?[207] So what's a poor biblical scholar to do who labors in the library, not the laboratory? The best one can, which is preferable to parochial, silo entrenchment and ignorance of important scientific knowledge. The field of interdisciplinary investigation of "the Bible and emotion" is a new and exciting project, with much room to grow.[208]

While "emotion" may seem to be a fairly straightforward term, Thomas Dixon, historian of psychology and medicine, calls it a "keyword in crisis,"[209] and research psychologist Carroll Izzard flatly states that the word, as currently used in both everyday and scientific discourse, "cannot be defined as a unitary concept."[210] Though acknowledging a rocky trail of twists and turns in emotion-related terminology and taxonomy, too complicated to track in a brief space, leading to the present "crisis," we may settle on "emotion" as the best available starter-term for discussion, allowing for the widest sense in both academy and society of having some idea of what we're talking about.[211] As Dixon proposes, after summarizing his meticulous plotting of the historical linguistic-conceptual shifts in passion/emotion language: "If the science of emotion is supposed to provide an explanation of a widely experienced kind of mental state, and in terms that can be communicated to the general public, then it might be better to stick with the complexity, fuzziness, and overinclusivity of 'emotion' than to retreat still further from the world of everyday concerns into new scientific jargons." To be fair, he does not leave the matter there, proceeding to commend some "subcategories," like Paul Griffith's "more primitive 'affect programs' and the 'higher cognitive emotions,'"[212] which immediately raises definitional issues of emotions in relation to mental (cognitive) and other human functional systems. Indeed, the study of emotion, by whatever name, throughout history has grappled with understanding emotional associations—conjunctive and disjunctive—among physical, psychological, cognitive, social, and environmental factors affecting human experience from within and without.

207. See the essays in Solomon, *What Is an Emotion?*, including a reprint of the classic article by William James "What Is an Emotion?," 66–76 (orig. 1884); and Kagan, *What Is Emotion?*

208. See the recent essay collection in Spencer, *Mixed Feelings*, including the introductory overview by Spencer, "Getting a Feel."

209. Dixon, "Emotion," 338–44. This article summarizes and updates Dixon's fuller argument in *From Passions*.

210. Izzard, "Many Meanings," 363.

211. See fuller discussion in Spencer, "Getting a Feel," 4–13, 19–30.

212. Dixon, "Emotion," 343; see Griffiths, *What Emotions*, 77–136.

Though considerable debate swirls around fine points of emotion theory, which is to be expected in any boom-phase of fresh interdisciplinary investigation,[213] broad support has emerged for three "properties" of emotion, as I call them.

First, the *associative property* stresses the inextricable interconnectivity of emotions, thoughts, actions, and social relations in a complex network or interlaced web. Emotions and thoughts *fire and wire* together in the circuits of the brain, both answering and affecting embodied human experience. With regard to decision-making, for example, leading neuroscientist Antonio Damasio has advanced the "somatic-marker hypothesis": "The emotional signal . . . covertly or overtly . . . focuses attention on certain aspects of the problem and thus enhances the quality of reasoning over it. . . . In brief, the signal *marks* options and outcomes with a positive or negative signal that narrows the decision-making space and increases the probability that the action will conform to past experience. Because the signals are, in one way or another, body-related, I began referring to this set of ideas as 'the somatic-marker hypothesis.'"[214]

Emotion-marked decisions are not merely private, internal negotiations with reason, but they carry into action, as Damasio indicates, related to other embodied beings. One decides to *do* something that *affects* (and is affected by) others. Dutch psychology scholar Nico Frijda identifies "action readiness" or "action tendency" as a basic "law of emotion": "All [emotion] states . . . involve some change in action readiness: (a) in readiness to go at it or away from it or to shift attention; (b) in sheer excitement, which can be understood as being ready for action but not knowing what actions; (c) in being stopped in one's tracks or in loss of interest."[215] And while the nature-nurture, universalist-constructionist debate continues apace regarding the degree to which emotions are innate biologically hardwired equipment and/or influenced social software applications, few dispute that cultural norms and social relations shape emotional experience in some fashion. It is widely acknowledged, for example, that contemporary Asian and American societies "think" and "feel" differently about themselves in relation to others, which is not to deny a common humanity or capacity for cross-cultural communication, but it is to highlight critical contextual factors of emotional engagement.[216] Of

213. See the comment in 2015 by historian Jan Plamper, *History of Emotions*: "I write during a boom in the history of emotions; there is gold rush fever in the air" (297).

214. Damasio, *Looking for Spinoza*, 147–48 (emphasis original); see two further works of Damasio: *Feeling*, 40–42, and *Descartes' Error*, 205–22.

215. Frijda, "Laws of Emotions," 351; cf. Frijda, *Laws of Emotion*, 3–46; Elster, "Emotion."

216. See Biehl, Matsumoto, Ekman et al., "Matsumoto"; Tsai, "Culture" and "Ideal Affect"; Nisbett, *Geography*, 59–61, 187–88.

course, social relations can resist as well as reinforce emotional norms within a culture as much as between cultures. On the American scene, just plop a Manhattan liberal in the middle of rural Alabama and watch the fur fly; or closer to home, eavesdrop on (most) any teenager's argument with parents about true love.

In short, this associative (integrative, holistic) property shatters long-standing reason/emotion, thought/feeling, mind/body, individual/collective, intention/action dichotomies in Western thought, with typical hierarchical preference for the first element in the duality.

Second, the *evaluative property* stresses that emotions do not simply provoke thoughts but in fact constitute *judgments* or *appraisals* in themselves.[217] They come, so to speak, prepackaged with perceptive-cognitive content, however preliminary and (often) unconscious. Surges of fear and anger, for example, do not simply incite us; they *instruct* us that something seems wrong and threatening and we should do something about it. Precisely what we should do requires more careful feeling-thinking attention (we can overreact and make things worse); but in any case, emotions ensure that we do not ignore the problem.

It turns out that Aristotle was rather prescient about these matters, describing emotions (πάθη, *pathē*) as "those things through which, by undergoing change, people come to differ in their judgments and which are accompanied by pain and pleasure, for example, anger, pity, fear, and other such things and their opposites. There is need to divide the discussion [further] . . . into three headings . . . for example, in speaking of anger, what is their *state of mind* when people are angry and against *whom* are they usually angry and for what sort of *reasons* (*Rhet.* 2.8–9 [1378a])."[218] In a word, emotions are *about* something and not arbitrary or abnormal impulses. This property further cements the mental-emotional, cognitive-affective nexus.

Finally, and logically, the *salience property* stresses that emotions, in conjunction with their associative and evaluative aspects, play a primary role in flagging what is most salient and highly valued (a corollary of the evaluative property) to an individual or community at a given time. Simply put, emotions tell us what matters most to us, what we are most *passionate* about, for good or ill. Philosophers of emotion have effectively argued this point. Martha Nussbaum, for example, regards emotions as

217. See various philosophical studies by Nussbaum: *On Emotions*; "Rational Judgments"; and *Upheavals*; and by Solomon: "Emotions"; *Passions*; and *True to Our Feelings*. For psychological appraisal theories, see Lazarus, *Emotions*; Oatley, Keltner, and Jenkins, *Understanding Emotions*, 166–80; Agnes Moors et al., "Appraisal."

218. Aristotle, *On Rhetoric*, trans. Kennedy (emphasis original).

> suffused with intelligence and discernment . . . part and parcel of the system of ethical reasoning. . . . Emotions involve judgments about important things, judgments in which, appraising an external object as salient for our own well-being, we acknowledge our own neediness and incompleteness before parts of the world that we do not fully control. . . . The object of the emotion is seen as *important for* some role it plays in the person's own life. I do not go about fearing any and every catastrophe anywhere in the world. . . . What inspires fear is the thought of damages impeding that cut to the heart of my own cherished relationships and projects. What inspires grief is the death of someone beloved, someone who has been an important part of one's life.[219]

Robert Roberts's philosophical analysis of emotions as "concern-based construals," which I referred to in the commentary, fits both the evaluative and salience properties.[220] The notion of "construal" entails an evaluative construct, a take or slant on some object, event, or person that emotions provide. One suddenly sees a thin crooked object along a hiking trail, which may be emotionally construed as a potential, fear-worthy poisonous snake. More refined assessment may relax the panic feeling (it is just a stick or a harmless grass snake), but the initial emotional construal of threat (the trail guide warned hikers to keep a wary eye out for rattlers) just might save one's life—a matter of prime *concern*. While one may later feel silly or superficial for jumping back at a serpentine-shaped stick, emotions do not trade in the trivial or petty (though they may be carried to ridiculous extremes): they signal what matters most to a person, "what the subject cares about, what is important to him or her," including matters of "moral importance," as well as physical survival (of course, preservation of life is a core moral issue).[221] What we feel passionately about betrays our moral values, not simply our personal tastes or preferences as in a buffet line. I should ask myself (one of these days) why I really like singing along to country radio and watching football on TV, but I am afraid of the answers. To deny that such gut-grabbing, emotion-stirring activities have conflicting moral implications (CW music: church with Mama on Sunday mornin'—after carousing all Saturday night! NFL: teamwork and discipline—for the aim of delivering maximal violence on the opponent!) just doesn't play.

219. Nussbaum, *Upheavals*, 1, 19, 30–31 (emphasis original).

220. See n. 29 above in "Introduction." For a thoughtful appropriation of Roberts's emotion theory by a theologian, see Vanhoozer, *Remythologizing*, 408–16.

221. Roberts, *Spiritual Emotions*, 11, 14.

Along with the obvious Christian affirmation of the moral dimension of emotional concern, which Roberts is not shy about registering, we may also note the relevance to pastoral care. We not only are emotionally concerned with and care about events, experiences, ideas, and things, but also, even especially, with/about *people* we love—or hate. Emotions like sympathy, passion, mercy—and their opposites—factor mightily in our construals of relations with family, neighbors, communities, and nations like and unlike us. In Roberts's view, the Christian gospel provides a clear motivation for compassionate (com-passionate) care and family feeling: "You are a child of God, destined along with many brothers and sisters to remain under his protection forever and to be transformed into something unspeakably lovely. Because these others are also his children, you are expected to treat them gently, to help them when they are in need, and in general to respect and love them as fellow heirs of your Father's kingdom. If a person doesn't feel a hunger for the righteousness and eternal life proclaimed and promised in the Christian message, then it is not surprising that the gospel falls on deaf ears."[222]

This brief "property" analysis of current emotion research demonstrates that emotion is a fundamental part of embodied human life—essential, not ancillary, integral not alien, symbiotic with reason, not subordinate to it. Holistic understanding of human life, including Christian life, must include careful consideration of emotional dimensions, especially since they specialize in matters of utmost importance to the individual and community. This is not to deny the potential of unruly emotions to overrun their value. Emotion regulation is vital to optimal flourishing, but regulation does not mean ascetic negation or extirpation in quest of a thoroughly undisturbed and unperturbed tranquil (tranquilized) state. Where's the fun in that? Where's the fire for life? Where's the concern, the care, the cause to live for?

Wesleyan theologian Samuel Powell captures a nice balance in his astute, scientifically informed assessment:

> Theologically . . . it is difficult to sustain the claims of extraordinary asceticism without also implying that the body's emotions are inherently and irredeemably corrupt. . . . Scientifically considered, emotions are an intrinsic element of human nature; they perform vital functions. Anger and jealousy and fear are the organism's way of perceiving threats or potential threat and preparing the body to act. Admittedly, sometimes the appraisal that launches the emotion is a misapprehension. . . . Further, there is no doubt that behavioral consequences of our emotional feelings can be out of

222. Roberts, *Spiritual Emotions*, 13.

> proportion to the actual threat. But neither of these considerations signifies that these emotions are inherently evil and inconsistent with the life of discipleship. Theological and scientific considerations thus yield diminished support for heroic asceticism.[223]

Powell further affirms the "epistemic dimension" and "hermeneutical phenomenon" of emotion as a prime—even "primordial"—avenue for "perceiving or experiencing the world" and for providing "an interpretation of our world."[224]

Epistemology and hermeneutics have constituted the beating heart of this commentary on Luke, focused not simply on the world, but more pointedly on *knowing* God and Jesus Messiah and on *interpreting* the text of Luke's Gospel in conversation with its scriptural intertexts. Does the general epistemological and hermeneutical function of emotion apply to the more specialized realms of God and God's holy word? We are back to the problem of God's passion, God's *passibility*: how can this be possible, given the long tradition avowing God's impassible, immutable nature? To be sure, Christ took on full human nature, emotions and all: the Word (*logos*) became flesh, including enfleshed feeling (*pathos*). But did Jesus not live the perfect human life, overcoming sin with its proclivities for misguided and often malevolent sentiments? And what happens in the trinitarian communion (yes, we circle back to the perichoretic Trinity) with the Son's human emotions? Does he ever get a tad "emotional" with the Father (and vice versa) and let emotions get the best of him? Or does he effectively check all his emotions at the trinitarian door?

Though scholars across the theological spectrum have little problem affirming God's loving, compassionate side—God *Is* Love (1 John 4:8, 16)—the superficiality of treating true love as (simply) a passionate eruption and the supposed special quality of divine "agapic" love beyond human comprehension gets God off the emotional hook, if one is inclined to do so, as most church fathers have been through the years. But over the last century or so, some countervoices have been raised in favor of God's *pathos*, particularly in relation to God's *pain and suffering*, the flip side of God's love, the anguish God *feels* and even the mixed feelings and churning changes God experiences when God's love for Israel and the world is spurned or betrayed or when disaster befalls God's beloved people and creation. Although the HB has no precise term for "emotion," and the Greek noun πάθος (*pathos*) appears only twice in the LXX rendering of the Hebrew (both in contexts of suffering [Job 30:31; Prov 25:20])

223. Samuel M. Powell, *Impassioned Life*, 362, 396.

224. Samuel M. Powell, *Impassioned Life*, 366–67. On the epistemic dimension of emotions, see also De Sousa, *Emotional Truth*, 153–70; Morton, "Epistemic Emotions."

and only three times in the NT (all related to illicit sexual lust [Rom 1:26; Col 3:5; 1 Thess 4:5]),[225] the cognate verb πάσχω/παθεῖν (infinitive) (*paschō/pathein*), though still sparse in the Greek OT, proliferates in the NT as the main term for "suffer," not least in connection with the suffering of Christ on the cross—his "passion" as we commonly call it. How much actual painful, passionate feeling or emotion (I loosely mix the terms at this point) should be packed into Jesus's passion remains debatable, but the fact of Jesus's suffering is secure.[226] Hence, my labeling of this section as "Passional Theology" ("Pathological Theology" would scarcely work today, and "Emotional Theology" smacks too much of emotionalism).

Terminology aside, the Bible wrestles throughout with the problem of pain and suffering in deeply poignant, emotionally engaged ways. Job speaks in stirring Hebrew poetry from the depths of his agony. The tortured man from Uz is no Oxbridge don propounding a philosophical essay like *The Problem of Pain* (apologies to C. S. Lewis, who provides a thoughtful analysis here and then later in life faces his own Joban loss with brutal honesty in *A Grief Observed*). But not only Job and Jesus endure unspeakable suffering. The Hebrew prophets experience more than their fair share and even, it seems, dare to implicate *God* in the process. HB/OT scholars have paved the way in unfolding the pathos/suffering of God in prophetic literature, which various theologians have followed in various directions.

Consider the work of biblical theologians across the volatile twentieth century, particularly attending to their treatments of Jeremiah, who arguably ranks as the Bible's most passionate prophet struggling in the throes of (before, during, and after) Babylon's brutal conquest of Jerusalem in the late sixth-century BCE. Despite the large time gap, Jeremiah proves remarkably relevant for both Jesus's first-century passion reported in Luke (as noted in the commentary) and for our own age.

225. In the LXX, the book of 4 Maccabees has by far the most occurrences of πάθος (*pathos*)—some sixty-two uses, virtually all in a negative sense of cowardly fear of suffering vs. courageous, rational, stoic submission to brutal martyrdom displayed by Eleazar and his family of Maccabean martyrs. See the discussion in Spencer, "Getting a Feel," 5–9.

226. In a carefully argued essay, Matthew Schlimm ("Different Perspectives") calls for biblical scholars to clarify emotion-related language. He is particularly concerned to distinguish God's sympathetic, intentional "pathos" from irrational, impulsive "passion" (676–78). Furthermore, "one should not make exegetical or theological claims about divine suffering without explaining what type of suffering is under discussion" (690). I survey the vexed issue of emotion terms and taxonomies in Spencer, "Getting a Feel," 4–13. Though I tend to mix "emotion" and "passion" as reasonable approximations of the Greek πάθος (*pathos*), I do not assume any of these terms, or the "emotional" experience to which they refer, as inherently irrational, irruptive, or antireason (see the "evaluative property" discussed above).

Toward the end, and in the wake, of World War I, the British Baptist OT scholar H. Wheeler Robinson penned a series of studies entitled *The Cross of Job* (1916; 2nd ed. 1937), *The Cross of Jeremiah* (1925), and *The Cross of the Servant* (1926), later collected in *The Cross of the Old Testament* (1955). These are no naive attempts to interject (retroject) a cross typology into the OT or to submit some flimsy "proofs from prophecy" for the death of Jesus Messiah, but rather a critical biblical-theological analysis of suffering. To be sure, Robinson perceives a close fellowship of suffering between Jeremiah of Anathoth and Jesus of Nazareth: "There is no life in the Old Testament which more closely resembles the life of our Lord [than Jeremiah's]." But the solidarity evident, for example, in weeping over Jerusalem (Jer 8:18–21; Luke 19:41–44) and denouncing the priestly leaders' deformation of the temple into a "den of robbers" (Jer 7:11/Luke 19:46) does not amount to mirror imaging of the two prophets. Jeremiah's "passion and cross," as Robinson references, flows out of his "deepest experience of God" manifest in three main expressions: his (1) prevailing "sense of loneliness"; (2) "intense sympathy" with the people God called him to condemn as well as comfort; and (3) "divided heart and the divine compulsion" that drove his mission and nearly drove him mad.[227] His "divided heart"—his mixed and vexed feelings—come to most volatile expression in his frustrated outburst:

> Yet you, O Lord, know
>   all their plotting to kill me.
> Do not forgive their iniquity,
>   do not blot out their sin from your sight.
> Let them be tripped up before you;
>   deal with them while you are angry.
>
> (Jer 18:23)

Obviously, this punitive plea is diametrically opposed to the "Father, forgive them" supplication uttered by Luke's Jesus on the cross (Luke 23:34).[228] But thankfully, it is also in marked tension with Jeremiah's own profound sense in other places of God's steadfast, loving commitment to forgive and restore God's wayward people, especially in Jer 31, where the prophet affirms God's faithful "everlasting love" for faraway Israel, evocative of Jesus's parable of the forgiving father, as Robinson dubs it (Jer 31:3; Luke 15:11–32), and God's promise of a "new covenant," alluded to at Jesus's Last Supper (Jer 31:31–34; Luke 22:20).[229]

227. Robinson, *Cross*, 153, 155

228. Robinson, *Cross*, 150–51.

229. Robinson, *Cross*, 187.

And what of the passion of God? Robinson speaks of "the sorrow of God," "the eternal cross in the heart of God," and "pain to Himself" when God punishes the people, and Robinson even goes so far as to entertain "the thought of God's failure" underlying Jeremiah's mediation of God's word to Baruch: "Thus says the LORD: I am going to break down what I have built, and pluck up what I have planted—that is, the whole land. . . . I am going to bring disaster upon all flesh" (Jer 45:4–5). Robinson may be overinterpreting God's depressed emotional state here, though God certainly takes no glee in bringing down and uprooting God's creation. In any case, Robinson does not stress God's changeable, passible nature: sympathetic suffering is part and parcel of God's "eternal" essence. God's primary emotional concern focuses on intimate probes of the inner lives of God's prophet and people as "the trier of heart and kidneys, that is, of the will and the emotions" (as Robinson reads Jer 11:20; 20:12).[230]

The next generation of biblical theologians was forced to grapple with a second devastating World War, compounded by Nazi atrocities in Europe and nuclear holocaust in Japan. A Jewish refugee from Poland, eventually settling in the US, became a rabbi, biblical scholar, theologian, and one of the most important Jewish thinkers of the century. In his most famous work, a magisterial two-volume study *The Prophets* (1962), Abraham Joshua Heschel reads the prophetic corpus as an unabashed witness to the *pathos of God*, a *theology of pathos*. Far from simply allowing God an occasional nod of sympathy with the human condition, always duly reserved and circumspect, Heschel regards the God of the prophets as thoroughly imbued with pathos in manifold expressions, personally and perpetually involved in and affected by the entire world God created. "New is the prophetic conception that [God's] mercy or anger are not sporadic reactions, but expressions of a constant care and concern. The divine pathos embraces all life, past, present, and future; all things and events have a reference to Him. It is a concern that has the attribute of eternity, transcending all history, as well as the attribute of universality, embracing all nations, encompassing animals as well as human beings."[231]

Notice the emphasis on God's pathos, in anger as much as mercy, an integral part of God's "constant care and concern," which dovetails nicely with the philosophical appraisal of emotion as "construal-based concern" noted above. Also note Heschel's unpacking of the "constant" dimension of God's passionate concern as "the attribute of eternity," a core characteristic of God's nature (similar to Robinson's view), a testimony to "God's aliveness."[232] But Heschel clar-

230. Robinson, *Cross*, 178–80.

231. Heschel, *Prophets*, 2:57.

232. Heschel, *Prophets*, 2:57; see also the stress on God's "overwhelming livingness and concern" (2:56).

ifies that the prophets did not equate eternality with inalterability, an absolute equanimity and sameness yesterday, today, and forever: "This was the central endeavor of the prophet: to set forth not only a divine law, but divine life; not only a covenant, but also a pathos; *not eternal immutability* of his Being, but the presence of His pathos in time; not only absolute Lordship, but also direct relatedness to man."[233] Even so, God's changeable emotions are not capricious; God remains fully in control of his passionate responses. Regarding divine anger in particular, Heschel stresses that "it is not an expression of irrational, sudden, and instinctive excitement, but a free and deliberate reaction of God's justice to what is wrong and evil. . . . It is never a spontaneous outburst, but rather a state which is occasioned and determined by man."[234]

Though Heschel tracks the relationship of the sympathetic, suffering God throughout the biblical prophets, Jeremiah naturally receives special attention, as one whose "whole being convulsed" with the divine pathos. Caught up in this passionate bond, "Jeremiah depicted the dramatic tension in the inner life of God," its "inner oscillation" and "inner wrestling" fueled by "God's pain and disappointment," by "God Who felt shunned, pained, and offended."[235] And without doubt, Jeremiah regularly responded in emotional kind—though sometimes too much so, in Heschel's estimation. While God had no desire to quench Jeremiah's passionate engagement with God and God's people, the prophet could get carried away in a "hypertrophy of sympathy for God," a bloated sense of affront demanding that God "bring down retribution for me on my persecutors" (15:15), as well as "not forgive [the people's] iniquity," mentioned above (18:23). Though some psalmists also lodged imprecatory prayers against their enemies (e.g., Pss 35, 69, 109), in Jeremiah's case God reins in the hot-blooded prophet for his "independent pathos" from God's righteous anger, which is always expressed in "nonfinality" with yearning for reconciliation and restoration. Indeed, God summons Jeremiah to "turn back" (שׁוּב, *šub*), to repent from his inordinate indignation and vengeful spirit and return to his true mission as God's grace-filled servant: "If you turn back, I will take you back, and you shall stand before me. If you utter what is precious, and not what is worthless, you shall serve as my mouth" (15:19).[236]

On the other side of the world, Japanese Lutheran pastor and scholar Kazoh Kitamori reflected deeply on God's pain in his book *Theology of the Pain of God* (1946, original Japanese version) in light of the unprecedented military

233. Heschel, *Prophets*, 2:57 (emphasis added).

234. Heschel, *Prophets*, 2:66, 77; see the careful, nuanced discussion of Heschel's theology of God's pathos in Schlimm, "Different Perspectives."

235. Heschel, *Prophets*, 1:118, 108–12

236. Heschel, *Prophets*, 1:126–27

tsunami unleashed on Hiroshima and Nagasaki. Though not an OT specialist as such, Kitamori's theology is first and foremost inspired by the prophet Jeremiah, that "most precise interpreter of the gospel, for he 'saw the heart of God most deeply.'"[237] And no divine utterance through Jeremiah more poignantly reveals God's heart than the aching paternal plea in 31:20: "Is Ephraim my dear son? Is he a pleasant child? For since I spake against him, I do earnestly remember him still: therefore my bowels are troubled for him; I will surely have mercy upon him, saith the Lord" (Jer 31:20 KJV). Here Jeremiah gets God's compassionate pathos exactly right, a pathos pulsing with love, but "beating wildly" not calmly, painfully not placidly. The best commentary on God's "troubled bowels" in 31:20 is Jeremiah's previous account of his own distressed "heart," using the same "trouble/pain" verb (המה, *hamah*) that Kitamori envisions as inducing severe tachycardia:

> My anguish, my anguish! I writhe in pain!
> Oh, the walls of my heart!
> My heart is beating wildly.
>
> (4:19)

Love-and-pain, pain-and-love are inextricable and "simultaneous" in Kitamori's theology rooted in Jeremiah and then sprouting to full fruition in Jesus's life and teaching, especially that presented in Luke.[238]

The picture of the loving divine Father painfully pining for the restoration of his wayward "dear" son Ephraim (Israel) finds its close match in the father's compassionate longing for his prodigal son in the Lukan parable and its ultimate satisfaction in the promised "new covenant" immediately following in Jer 31 and later reprised (renewed) by Jesus at the Last Supper (Kitamori joins Robinson in these intertextual echoes).[239] But if anthropomorphic analogies to the nature of God inevitably fall short of hitting their theological mark, are not anthropo*pathic* comparisons even more fraught? Can we fairly associate, even on a proximal level, the *feelings* of human fathers with those of the heavenly Father? (cf. Luke 11:11–13). Kitamori cites with approval Calvin's careful commentary on the "troubled bowels" text from Jer 31:20: "Here God attributes human feelings to himself; for our bowels are shaken and roar under extraordinary 'pain' (*dolor*), and we sigh and groan deeply under the pres-

237. Kitamori, *Theology*, 20. See the brief discussion of Kitamori's work in Fiddes, *Creative Suffering*, 20–22; for a broader survey of Japanese-Christian perspectives on suffering, see Mouw and Sweeney, *Suffering*, 1–4.

238. Kitamori, *Theology*, 152, 157.

239. Kitamori, *Theology*, 152–53, 160–62.

sure of great sorrow. God, therefore, expresses his feelings as an affectionate father. . . . Such a thing does not properly belong to God. God's nature is to feel this way, but he expresses himself *imperfectly* in terms of our human ignorance, knowing no other way to communicate the greatness of his love toward us."[240] Calvin walks a fine line here not only to protect the sacred uniqueness (otherness) of God, but also to promote God's genuine "feelings" of sympathy and sorrow, love and pain, however "imperfectly" we might understand them. In any event, Calvin clearly does not wish to paint God as some detached, apathetic, "unmoved" figure.[241]

But can we go further toward a more perfect union of divine and human feeling potential, toward a relationship of mutual sympathy and sharing in suffering that truly affects God in some fashion, even while granting God's infinitely greater capacity than that of flawed human beings for making the "right" emotional response, as Aristotle would put it?[242] Writing later in the twentieth century, with the horrific devastation of two World Wars still raw enough in historical memory and with heightened fears of nuclear annihilation fueling the current Cold War, Terence Fretheim probes deeper dimensions of the topic in his book *The Suffering of God: An Old Testament Perspective*, written in the ominous Orwellian year of 1984. Jeremiah again figures prominently in the discussion—but also more provocatively in Fretheim's account.

Building on the frequent blur of first- and third-person speech related to and running between God and prophet in Jeremiah's text, Fretheim dares to surmise that "the tension in God over what to do with the people whom he loves has its earthly counterpart in the prophet. As a member of the divine council he *incarnates* the story of God in his own tension-filled life." And with particular respect to the prophet's confession of his pained, pounding heart in Jer 4:19: "The speech expresses more than his own empathy with the destroyed people and land; the prophet is an *enfleshment of the emotions of God* over what is about to occur. God and prophet speak with one voice." Such reference to Jeremiah's "incarnation/enfleshment" of God's divine pathos is freighted theological rhetoric, and Fretheim knows it, even as he clarifies on the last page of

240. Kitamori, *Theology*, 154; citation from Calvin, *Commentaries*, 2:106–9 (emphasis original).

241. Fiddes (*Creative Suffering*) pushes the "imaginative" point further: "Indeed, the idea of a merely imaginative response of God to the suffering of this world hardly does justice to the religious experience of the Old Testament prophets, who believed that *they* were being called into sympathy with *God's* unique plan" (59 [emphasis original]).

242. Aristotle, *Eth. nic.* 4.5.32–33 (1125b): "Now we praise a man who feels anger on the right grounds and against the right persons, and also in the right manner and at the right moment and for the right length of time" (trans. Rackham, LCL).

his book that "the prophet's life as embodied Word of God is partial and broken" in comparison with the "culminating" incarnation in Christ.[243]

Moreover, such "tension-filled" affective intimacy with God is not simply a prophetic privilege (which Jeremiah in fact regards more as a terrible burden), but it characterizes God's relationship with all God's people. God engages human beings not only in intellectual and juridical terms, but "also at the emotional level. God shares feelings, not just thoughts. The people know not only what God thinks, but what God feels. Thus a holistic picture of God emerges. God relates at every level with the whole person of each individual."[244] And God cares enough on this emotional level to risk disappointment, frustration, anger, and intense suffering when God's people spurn God's love and go their own way. And out of these hurt feelings of abandonment and betrayal, God acts, reacts, and is *acted upon*, is *affected by* the emotional judgments God exacts upon God's wayward dear children: "God's judgment is not a detached decision. . . . God is caught up in the matter; and in some respects God will never be the same again. And so the judgment is a very personal decision, with all the mixed sorrow and anger that go into the making of decisions that affect the people whom one loves."[245] How can God not help but be *changed* by a genuine bond of love that must be allowed to bend, if it is a truly free relationship, and even break at times—and break God's heart!—precisely because God honors the covenant bond so strongly.

As God gets thoroughly, emotionally "caught up" in the lives of the people, however, God does not, in Fretheim's view, get carried away in a flood of rash, harmful, unreasonable emotion. Recall the evaluative property of emotion involving cognitive judgments, which, despite their potential to run amok, are not inherently irrational or irresponsible. If such emotional logic and discipline obtain on the human level, how much more on the divine: "God's suffering is not such that he is overwhelmed by the experience; his emotions do not get out of control or lead to incapacitation. Nor is God embittered in any way by what has occurred. God is able to 'be angry and sin not.' God is able to absorb all the arrows of outrageous fortune that pierce him through and, instead of becoming callous or removing himself from the line of fire, still seek to bring about a future which is good for those who inflict the wounds."[246]

243. Fretheim, *Suffering*, 159 (emphasis added), 160 (emphasis added; cf. 156), 166.

244. Fretheim, *Suffering*, 123.

245. Fretheim, *Suffering*, 112.

246. Fretheim, *Suffering*, 124. Schlimm ("Different Perspectives") rightly reads Fretheim as advocating God's *emotional* changeability without, however, "entail[ing] any sort of *ethical* mutability" (689 [emphasis added]).

This survey of OT theology on God's pathos, particularly God's suffering in the book and person of Jeremiah, repays our attention in setting the stage for both Luke's Scripture-saturated theology/Christology and contemporary systematic-theological reflection on God and Christ's impassibility. The Jewish Scriptures remain foundational for Christian thought. In this commentary, I have followed the pattern of many of my predecessors in unpacking numerous intertextual links, direct and allusive, with the Law, Prophets, and Writings throughout Luke's Gospel narrative. More than most, however, I have also examined the emotional tenor of the story and its characters at various points, including but not only in the passion narrative, where I have continued to advance a "passionate" portrayal of the suffering Jesus over against the majority position that views him as a cool, calm, collected stoic martyr, even amid his Jeremian weeping over Jerusalem and warning against exploiting the temple as a "den of robbers." Such displays of compassion and conviction, however intense, are commonly viewed as fully under Jesus's control and wholly consistent with his immutable divine nature.

While I agree that Luke's Jesus characteristically makes proper, considered emotional judgments supporting God's will and embodying love of God and neighbor, I do not see him as altogether unflappable and impassible, the epitome of equanimity, as if that were a consummate virtue. I take very seriously Luke's statements that Jesus *grows into* his messianic vocation in relation to his Father-God and people (2:40, 52); and in the focal scene these statements frame—featuring Jesus's interactions with the temple scholars and his parents at age twelve—I suggest that Jesus still evinces some emotional immaturity (what do you expect from a twelve-year-old?) in snapping back at his extremely anxious mother and stepfather. The simple fact that he returns home to Nazareth with his parents "and was obedient to them" for another eighteen years (2:51; 3:23) proves the point that he has more growing to do in all the ways human grow—physically, intellectually, socially, and emotionally (all of these intertwined). And after his christological mission goes public at age thirty, Jesus still from time to time shows not only amazing compassion for needy people, but also a range of other emotions, including *surprise* (at the centurion's "amazing" faith [7:9] and the bleeding woman's audacious touch [8:45]), *frustration* (with "you faithless and perverse generation" [9:41] and with his closest confidants at various junctures [e.g., 8:25; 22:38, 46, 51; 24:25]), and *maternal disappointment* (with stubborn-willed Jerusalem, like that of a hen with her wandering, wayward brood [13:34]) that palpably *affect him*, pull him up short, and reorient his life-course into greater alignment with God's purpose.

And what of *God the Father's* emotions entwined with those of Jesus the Son in dynamic trinitarian communion explored above? As Father and Son (and Spirit) share complete intimate *knowledge* of and with one another (Luke 10:21–22), such knowing, as all relational knowing, includes some common sympathy—"feeling with"—but to what extent? Are Jesus's passions, his passion in particular, God's passions? Does the Father *feel his way* with and through the Son in his embodied emotional development? Does God suffer with and through Jesus, as the OT scholars suggested that God did with and through Jeremiah, only to a greater extent, indeed to the fullest extent imaginable in the divine being—heart, "bowels," and mind?

Although Luke's narrative outpaces all the other Gospels in accentuating Jesus's prayerful fellowship with his Father, it does not disclose much content of this communication, certainly not to the degree reported between Jeremiah and God. And Luke provides even less reporting of *God's* passions/emotions in clear distinction from Jesus's. Yet early on, in the conclusion to Zechariah's prophetic hymn inspired by the Holy Spirit, the old priest and new father exults in the "bowels-mercies of our God" (lit. rendering of σπλάγχνα ἐλέους θεοῦ ἡμῶν, *splanchna eleous theou hēmōn*; cf. "our God's deep compassion" CEB [1:78]), because of which (διά, *dia*) Zechariah's prophetic son John will prepare the divine Lord's saving, peacemaking ways paved in Jesus Messiah (1:76–79).[247] This substantival identification of God's gut-level (com)passions finds a verbal match in σπλαγχνίζομαι (*splanchnizomai*)—"act/move with deep compassion" (AT)—in Jesus's ministry (7:13) and teaching about ministry in two major parables: one showcasing the Samaritan's active response to being "moved with pity/compassion" toward the beaten, "half dead" victim (10:30, 33), a model example of "one who showed [the victim] mercy [ἔλεος, *eleos*]" (10:37); the other featuring the father's dramatic demonstration of being "filled with compassion" (15:20) toward his wastrel, as-good-as-dead, returning son (15:20–32). Obviously, this second parable—the longest and most central in Luke's account—most directly depicts Jesus's understanding of *God the Father's* passionate love (as usual, Jesus himself is not the main subject of Jesus's parables, though they dramatically reveal his values and commitments), which is anything but passive and impassible: the story's father keeps his eyes peeled to the "far" horizon in search of his lost son and then runs, hugs, kisses, clothes, feeds, and celebrates his son's return almost before the prodigal can get a word in edgewise (15:20–23). And if there's any doubt of the ripping *pain* the father

247. Vanhoozer (*Remythologizing*) misstates that "according to Luke 1:78, Jesus is the *splanghna theou*: the 'compassion of God'" (435). Though Zechariah's prophecy, like his son John, prepares the way for Jesus's compassionate ministry, linguistically the present focus is on *God's* compassionate mercy. Jesus, who's not even born yet, is never named in Zechariah's hymn. The "Lord" reference in 1:76 again previews Jesus's mission, but in this context most immediately parallels "the Most High [God]."

suffered in the son's rebellious absence or the roiling *change* of emotions he experienced from despair to delight, we need only reprise the father's final appraisal: "But we had to celebrate and rejoice, because this brother of yours [this other son of mine] was dead and has come to life; he was lost and has been found" (15:32 [previewed in 15:24]). We are left with a strong sense that the father had virtually died and risen, drifted and returned, *with* his son.

In the parable of the loving father, Luke's Jesus expands on the theme of God's love for rebellious Ephraim/Israel in Jer 31:20 (see above), which Jesus also exemplifies in his dealing with "sinners" throughout the Gospel. But again, Jesus's parable is not autobiographical; while sympathetic with the story's father, Jesus is the opposite of the prodigal son. So we still find ourselves on the periphery of the emotional character of the Father-Son communion. To get closer to the heart of that matter, we must get to the heart of the passion, especially to the stations of the cross at Gethsemane and Golgotha, which Moltmann analogically marks as "Ground Zero" for the passionate, suffering Father and Son, primed by the weeping Jesus (only in Luke) over Jerusalem at the commencement of passion week.[248] Deeply moved by Heschel's monumental work[249] and by his own experiences of and reflections on suffering from his late teenage-soldier trauma of bombardment by Allied forces in his native Hamburg and eventual imprisonment in a British camp (1943), to the assassination of Martin Luther King (1968) while Moltmann attended an international "Theology of Hope" conference in America, to the horror of the 9/11 attacks, Moltmann has emerged as the most impassioned—and rigorously reasoned!—proponent of a theology of divine passion, which he dubs with purposeful redundancy "the passion of the passionate God."[250]

Against Aristotle's famed apathetic axiom of the Unmoved Mover—the unitary "eternal and immovable (ἀκίνητος, *akinētos* [a-kinetic]) . . . impartible and indivisible . . . impassive (ἀπαθές, *apathes*] and unalterable" metaphysical substance[251]—Moltmann follows the biblical revelation of God as unabashedly "pathetic," moved with fervent "passion" in the double sense of "overwhelming emotion and suffering"[252] and of "suffering and overwhelming feeling and ardor . . . for the life of his people and for justice on his earth."[253] The biblical God,

248. Moltmann, *"Crucified God,"* 72; cf. Moltmann, *Trinity*, 76, and *Living God*, 48.

249. See Jaeger, "Abraham Heschel."

250. Moltmann, *"Crucified God,"* 74 (see 69–73). On his sympathetic reading of Heschel (and other Jewish writers such as Gershom Scholem, Franz Rosenzweig, and Elie Wiesel), see Moltmann, *Crucified God*, 270–74, and *Trinity*, 25–30.

251. Aristotle, *Metaph.* 12.7 (1073a) (trans. Tredennick, LCL).

252. Moltmann, *Living God*, 40; see 37–40.

253. Moltmann, *"Crucified God,"* 74.

however, is not "movable" after the fashion of the moody, sulky, capricious gods of Greek lore, but rather responds voluntarily from the depths of God's constant covenantal love. Yet, such faithful, loving response is not a mechanical, preset program secured in some inviolable celestial vault, bringing us right back to the "unmoved" deity, which the God of Israel is anything but. God's personal, sympathetic rescue of the Israelites from slavery and leading them via the prophet Moses, pillars of light and fire, direct words of Torah, and the "tent of meeting" (tabernacle) bear unequivocal witness to God's attentive involvement with God's people, God's active *moving* with them through the wilderness, not only territorially, but also temperamentally, emotionally. This journey is as painful as it is joyous in fitful twists and turns for God, as surely as it is for God's people, who so often frustrate God.

The participatory, passionate, passible, pained God wholly engaged with God's people is, in Moltmann's view, not only the God of the Bible, but also the only God worthy of worship and fellowship. Put in negative terms: "A God who cannot suffer is poorer than any man. For a God who is incapable of suffering is a being who cannot be involved. Suffering and injustice do not affect him. And because he is so completely insensitive, he cannot be affected or shaken by anything. He cannot weep, for he has no tears. But the one who cannot suffer cannot love either. So he is also a loveless being."[254]

Jesus the Son incarnates God's emotive, suffering love both in his *Leiden* (passion) and in his *Leidenschaft* ("passionate devotion of his life to God's reign of righteousness").[255] His tears over Jerusalem are God's tears, his crucifixion the experience of "the crucified God." But as seriously as Moltmann argues for this theological crux, he takes pains to distinguish it from "the death of God," which became philosophically fashionable in the 1960s (channeling Nietzsche).[256] Here Moltmann's trinitarian perspective is crucial. The Son dies, truly and excruciatingly, and he appeals to his Father from the depths of his agony. Accordingly, it "kills" the Father to see and feel the Son go through this torture, as we might say of any human parent watching their beloved child die in this

254. Moltmann, *Crucified God*, 222.

255. Meeks, Introduction (to Moltmann, *Passion*), 16; see also 21–22.

256. Also distinguished from "patripassian" and "theopaschite" perspectives in earlier church history. Note the careful statement in Moltmann, *Crucified God*, 243: "The Father who abandons [the Son] and delivers him up suffers the death of the Son in the infinite grief of love. We cannot therefore say here in patripassian terms that the Father also suffered and died. The suffering and dying of the Son, forsaken by the Father, is a different kind of suffering from the suffering of the Father in the death of the Son. Nor can the death of Jesus be understood in theopaschite terms as the 'death of God'. To understand what happened between Jesus and his God and Father on the cross, it is necessary to talk in trinitarian terms."

(or any other) way. The Father acutely feels the Son's pain and demise so intimately *as if* it were the Father's own death, but the fact that it is not makes the suffering worse because the loss lingers postmortem, while the dead one finds rest. "Patri*com*passionism" (as Moltmann coins)—the Father's suffering *with* the Son, but also separately from him (as opposed to modalistic patripassionism, where the Father sacrifices *himself* in death)—tears God apart, having lost part of God's self.[257] The brutal death of the Son cuts the Father so raw and deep that he cannot bear this most vulnerable divine moment in which he seems helpless either to rescue the Son or to remain by his side, evoking the Son's unbearable, gut-wrenching cry of dereliction reported by Matthew and Mark in Aramaic and Greek, which chills the blood just as achingly in English: "My God, my God, why have you forsaken me?" (Matt 27:46//Mark 15:34). Though not signaling any *essential* (ontological) dismembering of God's trinitarian being (if anything, the death of the Son grafts him even more deeply into the Father's heart, if that were possible), the cross does mark an *existential* (emotional) crisis in the divine fellowship, a heart-breaking, intratrinitarian wound of knowledge and love for the healing of a broken world.[258]

But this is a commentary on Luke, not Matthew or Mark, and Luke's triple sayings of Jesus from the cross move in a different direction from the other Synoptics' singular cry. Or so it appears to many, including Moltmann. The double, more impersonal "My God" becomes a double, more intimate "*Father*, forgive them" (23:34) and "*Father*, I commend my spirit" (23:46)—both expressions of the Father's perpetuating love and care, love for sinners in the first case, care for the Son in the last. Yes, though that may not be all. The Father's forgiveness, *if* in fact granted (to be a strict constructionist, the text does not say that a pardon was issued at that moment), would hardly come cheaply or easily in this case. And the Son's final-breath "commending" or "entrusting" his dying life into his Father's hands cries out for a more considered, painstaking (and pain-sensitive) evaluation beyond that of a mellow farewell from a model martyr. To repeat part of my commentary: "We should not overplay the comforting, confident tone of his 'trustful' prayer to the exclusion of tense, even tortured, counterstrains. Recall that Jesus utters this last-gasp plea in a gut-wrenching, ear-splitting 'loud voice' consonant with the temple curtain's fabric-rending screech. Once again, though not knowing Jesus's precise emotional state, we should not deny his agonizing struggle with death. At the very least, his concluding prayer of en-

257. Moltmann, *Living God*, 40; cf. Moltmann, "*Crucified God*," 77–79, and *Crucified God*, 242–47.

258. I draw this imagery from two modern spiritual classics: Rowan Williams, *Wound of Knowledge*, and Henri Nouwen, *Wounded Healer*.

trustment to the Father does not simply sound a triumphal shout of victory, still less a gentle lullaby into that good night" (see above, p. 605).

The mention of Jesus's "agonizing struggle with death" immediately kicks us back one chapter and one evening to the Son's pleading on Mount Olivet (Luke's Gethsemane): "Father, if you are willing, remove this cup from me" (Luke 22:42). Though Moltmann again contends, with some justification, that Luke ("Father, if/since you are willing [εἰ βούλει, *ei boulei*], remove this cup from me") has sanded off the edges of Mark's rougher version ("Abba, Father, for you all things are possible; remove this cup from me" [Mark 14:36]), Luke in fact keeps the heat on and even ratchets it up with the comment directly after Jesus's apparent resignation ("yet, not my will but yours be done") and assistance from a heavenly minister (Luke 22:42b–43) that "in his anguish he prayed more earnestly," to the point of working up a blood-like flood of boiling sweat (22:44). Evidently the angel did not help enough to assuage Jesus's struggle with his and his Father's clashing *wills*. "Not my will but yours be done" signifies a capitulation to the Father's will that *is not Jesus's will*—and in the agony that follows, this capitulation is not a happy one.

The *will to life*, the *passion for life* pulses at the very heart of God's heart, not least the passion for *God's own life*. One who gives up on life has no capacity to inspire anyone else's life.[259] An indomitable will to life—God's own and that of all creation—drives God's passion and purpose, which is why God is so pained when people hurt and destroy each other and all other forms of created life. And this is why Gethsemane/Olivet represents such a critical test of trinitarian integrity, of divine "family" loyal love. Jesus the Son *wants to live*, not just as most humans would (in sad fact, some people wish to die by their own hand or the hand of others [martyrdom, euthanasia, and certain suicides conceived as "noble" actions]), but also as *God* desires, as the God-Human. Jesus is scarcely being selfish here in the sense we normally think of selfishness. Throughout his ministry, his barebones personal existence and his others-oriented benevolent service—"I am among you as one who serves [the serving one]" (22:27)—have been utterly self-giving. But not self-killing, not suicidal. How can a dead person, even the dead incarnate God, further serve to restore the lives of other incarnate beings? Paradoxes serve their purpose to push outside narrow conceptual boxes and stimulate creative thought, paradoxes like "those who want to save their life will lose it, and those who lose their life for my sake will save

259. See Moltmann, *Passion*, 22: "When the passionate devotion to life is missing, the powers to resist are paralyzed. Therefore if we want to live today, we must consciously *will* life. We must learn to love life with such a passion that we no longer become accustomed to the powers of destruction. We must overcome our own apathy and be seized by the passion for life" (emphasis original); cf. Spencer, "Why Did the 'Leper'?," 126–28.

it" (9:24). And by no means should we forget the hope of third-day resurrection appended to the first and last of Jesus's passion predictions (9:22; 18:33—but *not* 9:44). But Jesus does not take paradoxes as magic pills or hold the hope of resurrection as a blissful anesthetic to suffering, his own or anyone else's.

At crunch time in perspiring prayer to the Father on the eve of crucifixion, Jesus just can't bring himself to surrender his life without a fight, not with his arresters (of whom he heals a severed ear rashly lopped off by one of his followers) or with his attackers (for whom he prays): he wants his enemies to live! No, Jesus's beef is *with his Father*, who seems to be acting very un-Fatherly and stretching the trinitarian bond of love to the breaking point. Luke may not air Jesus's stark "My God, my God" cry from the cross, and he might even tone down a tad the Markan Jesus's plea for rescue ("cup"-removal) even if it takes an "impossible" move, since "Abba, Father, for you all things are possible" (Mark 14:36). But Luke's Jesus knows just as surely as Mark's that God specializes in what seems impossible to ordinary conception—indeed, the Lukan Jesus's very formation in Mary's womb by the Holy Spirit marks the banner case of God's inexhaustible life-giving God potentiality ("For nothing will be impossible with God" [Luke 1:37; cf. 18:27])—and that God has staked God's very reputation, engraved in the divine words of Torah, on holistic covenantal love with (and within) God and God's people for the thriving of *life* ("Do this, and you will live" [10:28]).

Why, then, in heaven's name, is the Father persisting at the eleventh hour in *willing the Son's death*? Or if this puts the matter too strongly (the Father certainly takes no willful *delight* in purposing Jesus's death), we must still struggle *with Jesus* in querying what, for God's sake, is God doing abandoning the Son at the end of his life and forcing him to plead, first, for release from death (Olivet) and, finally, for postmortem consideration (Golgotha). Why would Jesus need to pray at all in this intimate trinitarian communion, assuming that the Holy Spirit was already bombarding the Father's heart with unutterable guttural groaning (see Rom 8:26–27)?

In one of the most arresting passages I've encountered in Moltmann's writings, he exposes in haunting terms Jesus's theological Gethsemane crisis as *abject abandonment and aloneness*. As Jesus withdraws from his disciples ("about a stone's throw" in Luke 22:41) to plead privately with his Father, "the Father withdraws from the Son, leaving him alone. That is why the disciples fall into a deep sleep, out of grief [only in Luke 22:45]. It is only by contradicting his very self that Jesus clings to fellowship with the God who as Father withdraws from him: 'Not what I will, but what thou wilt.'"[260] Moreover:

260. Moltmann, *Trinity*, 76.

> This *unanswered prayer* is the beginning of Jesus's real passion—his agony at his forsakenness by the Father. Of course there is also quite simply fear of the horribly slow death ahead of him. It would be ridiculous to say—as Augustine did—that, as the Son of God, Jesus could not have experienced the fear of death, because his soul lived in unbroken enjoyment of divine bliss and power; and that he only suffered in the body. But it would be equally foolish to see him . . . overcome by self-pity at the prospect of the torments of death awaiting him. In the fear that laid hold of him and lacerated his soul, what he suffered from was God. Abandonment by God is the "cup" which does not pass from him. The appalling silence of the Father in response to the Son's prayer in Gethsemane is more than the silence of death. Martin Buber called it the eclipse of God. . . . The Father withdraws. God is silent. This is the experience of hell and judgment.[261]

In his passion predictions in Galilee and near Jericho (9:22; 18:31) and in his postresurrection reflections on the Emmaus road and in the Jerusalem (upper) room (24:26–27, 44–46), Luke's Jesus affirms the divine necessity (δεῖ, *dei*) of the Messiah's suffering (πάσχω, *paschō*) unfolded in Scripture, though as I stressed in the commentary, Luke only hints at a few traces of *particular* biblical texts that supposedly preview the suffering-crucified Messiah. *That* Jesus Messiah should die (and rise) is clear enough; *why* he should do so, apart from generally fulfilling Scripture, is not so clear. In any event, the bridge from confident passion prediction to postresurrection reflection must tunnel through the lonely, "lacerating" (Moltmann) thicket of the Mount of Olives, to say nothing of climbing the cruel peak of Skull Hill, *without* the Father's comfort and close companionship, *as if* the Father-Son bond had been broken and if not that, certainly broken-hearted. The Father and Son, each in his own way, goes through "hell and judgment," and neither will be the same again. Resurrection and ascension, for all their glorious vindication of God's purpose of life and salvation, cannot, *must not* erase the emotional scars of Olivet, compounded by the torturous physical effects (and affects) of Golgotha. The Son's broken body and drained blood must be forever *remembered* (22:19) mentally, liturgically—and *passionately*.

If this bold, provocative consideration of God's *passibility*—mutability, sufferability—bumps up against classic theological dogma, then perhaps the dogma needs recasting, reforming (*semper reformanda*). There seems to be ample biblical warrant across the Testaments for such a view. And along with a prophetic-scriptural foundation, Moltmann also lays down a *personal-pastoral* plank in a

261. Moltmann, *Trinity*, 76–77 (emphasis original).

remarkably candid letter responding to the eminent Catholic theologian Karl Rahner, who, in his last interview, denounced Moltmann's alleged patripassianism as being as futile as it is heretical: "What use would that [view] be to me in consolation in the truest sense of the word?" (Rahner). Of plenty use, Moltmann counters: "Of course God entered into our history of suffering in a different way, he was not subjected to it against his will. That God does not suffer as finite creatures do does not mean [however] that he is incapable of suffering in any way. God is capable of suffering because he is capable of love. . . . I cannot imagine an impassible God as a God who consoles in a personal sense." And then the coup de grâce of Moltmann's polemic: "With what right do we human beings say that God is 'incapable'? Do we not 'cement' God in with the negations of this negative theology? If that is the case, then a personal experience of being locked in and a divine image of a *Deus* go closely together. How can a God who is locked into his immobility and impassibility become a comfort for the person whose situation also seems to be like that?"[262] Elizabeth Johnson echoes this expansive view of God's *capability* of suffering from a feminist Sophia perspective (Sophialogy): "Interpreting the metaphysical notion of pure act through the relational lens of trinitarian life delivers a notion of Holy Wisdom *capax passionis*, capable of suffering, while as God she does not perish and can bring forth new life."[263]

Divine impassibility seems to be the most proper, passable way to refer to the supreme deity *only if* we forget that the true God, the God of Israel and the Bible, trades in the *impossible*, ever stretching the limits of possibility, including within God's own being permitting the possibility of passibility, of changing through suffering as the loving Father endures the Son's "learn[ing] obedience through what he suffered" (Heb 5:8), which the Father could have prevented, but opted not to. Divine love learns and groans with growing pains into ever more complete and sympathetic love. In a word: *compassion*.[264]

262. Moltmann, *"Crucified God,"* 80–82.

263. Elizabeth A. Johnson, *She Who Is*, 266. Her entire chapter "Suffering God: Compassion Poured Out" (246–72) repays careful study. For a contrasting position, see Vanhoozer (*Remythologizing*, 387–468), defending the traditional patristic understanding of God as impassible, that is: "(1) *incapable* of experiencing passion; (2) *incapable* of suffering; (3) *incapable* of being acted upon by an external force" (397 [emphasis on *incapable* added]). Vanhoozer by no means strips God of all emotional feeling, however; but instead of conceptualizing God's mutual-relational responsive interaction with humanity, Vanhoozer "focuses on communicative action and upon God's taking the communicative initiative via Word and Spirit (i.e., triune Authorship)" (391–92). God reaches out rather than reacts: "We can therefore think of God's emotions in terms of *theodramatic construals*. God's emotions proceed from his construals of the way in which human beings respond to his own words and deed—to the drama of redemption—especially as these come to a climactic focus in Jesus Christ" (413 [emphasis original]).

264. I have been stimulated to become more critically and vitally open to the "possibility

My passional reading of Luke's account of Jesus's prayer on the Mount of Olives just before his arrest pushes the emotional envelope beyond that of my Baptist commentary colleagues. Although they are split in tilting for (Garland, Parsons) and against (Culpepper, Vinson) the originality of the "agony" text in 22:43–44, they all make a point, to one degree or another, of Luke's sanding Mark's rawer emotional edge into a more stoic-martyr image. *Culpepper* claims that Luke views "Jesus as the model for the Christian martyr."[265] *Garland* perceives that Luke's "Jesus remains composed, fearless, and positive, able to perceive the divine will and obey it. He can therefore meet death nobly."[266] *Vinson* likewise profiles Luke's "Jesus as martyr-to-be, fully imagining what is about to happen, wrestling with it in prayer, and then rising from prayer, prepared to face his destiny."[267] *Parsons* demurs somewhat from this impassible portrait, though still contrasting Luke's more athletic Jesus with Mark's weaker image: "Jesus's 'agony' . . . in this context reflects more the strenuousness of his prayer than any sense of being distraught (as does Mark's reference to Jesus being 'sorrowful unto death'), though it does not suggest Jesus is totally devoid of any emotion."[268] This last concession by Parsons cracks the door to a more passional interpretation, which I open wider.

These commentators get caught in a common redaction-critical trap. Though all are skilled narrative critics with a strong commitment to primary literary contexts (indeed, Culpepper is a notable pioneer of this method in the study of John's Gospel), in this passage at least, Luke's supposed redaction of—in other words, his reaction to/against Mark—seems to drive the interpretation of Luke. Though Vinson, for example, vigorously insists that "to read Luke correctly, we must first put Mark out of our minds"—the anguished, agitated Markan Jesus in Gethsemane, that is—this powerful Markan image keeps serving as a foil for Vinson's reading of a "nonemotional Jesus" in Luke.[269] I wonder, if we simply didn't have Mark or any theory of Mark as one of Luke's sources (which, generally, I am happy to affirm)—if we just read Luke's narrative itself, would we be so inclined to anesthetize Jesus's prayer on Olivet and to lionize Jesus's virile (android?) approach to his impending death? Without question, whether we accept the lathered "agony" text and how we interpret it

---

of the impossible," to radical hospitality concerning a truly surprising, creative (inventive) future, by the writings of Caputo: e.g., *Hoping*, 55, 157–61, 184–97; *Weakness*, 102–12, 203–7; *Insistence*, 17–18, 50–52; *What Would Jesus Deconstruct?*, 71–73, 118–28, 134–35; *Prayers*, 20–26, 49–51, 160–73.

265. Culpepper, 433.

266. Garland, 884.

267. Vinson, 696–97.

268. Parsons, 320.

269. Vinson, 689–90.

(athletic, militant, angst-filled "sweat"?) is a critical factor—but not the only one. In my commentary, I endeavored to correlate emotions of *anguish*, *grief*, and *frustration* among Jesus and his disciples in the prayer-and-arrest scene as part of a developing "emotion episode" (emotions typically mix and vex as narrative human experiences unfold). This is crisis mode, crunch time, crux hour—with the cross looming large and dark. Even allowing for the fact that Gospel narratives are not psychological novels or memoirs, why should we not expect some emotional tenor to this stressful human event for a fully human (non-gnostic) Jesus?

An even more important crux is the wording of Jesus's plea: "Father, if you are willing, remove this cup from me; yet, not my will but yours be done" (22:42). Yes, the wording is less obviously desperate and plaintive than Mark's version, but it is hardly pro forma or blandly compliant. As a first-class conditional clause, "if you are willing [εἰ βούλει, *ei boulei*]," if not pushing as far as "since [I know] you are willing," at least grants the Father's willingness to change Jesus's death destiny for the sake of argument: God's will, God's plan (βουλή, *boulē*) of salvation is a *will to saving life* above all; accordingly, it is altogether *reasonable* for Jesus to assume his Father's *passionate* commitment to life and desire to *remove* cups of suffering and death from him, as well as others, if possible—and all things are possible with God (though not here—see explicitly Luke 1:37; 18:27).

Moreover, both Garland and Parsons refer to a lesser known textual variant, substituting an *infinitive* form of "take/remove" (παραφέρω, *parapherō*) for the imperative. But they read the import of the variant differently. *Garland* understands "if you wish *to take* this cup from me" leading into an awkward break (aposiopesis), in turn "impl[ying] that this is a preference, but it is not a direct request." Accordingly, the ensuing "yet" (πλήν, *plēn*) carries, according to Garland, a stronger sense of "nevertheless, however, in any case, only," which, granting that "Jesus is not itching to go through the suffering that looms ahead," clearly introduces Jesus's unequivocal "affirm[ation] that his own will does not enter into consideration. It is God's will alone that is to be done."[270] This is not so clear-cut in my judgment, however. Why even mention "my will" and intimate that the Father might entertain altering his will if true independent volition "does not enter into consideration"?

In an illuminating box entry, which I assume Parsons takes seriously and does not simply offer as an alternative view, he considers the infinitive verb with the aposiopsesis break as a rhetorical device that "reflects the speaker's 'passion' or 'anger' or 'anxiety' or 'scruple'" (Quintilian, *Inst.* 9.2.54). In the present case,

270. Garland, 881.

Parsons cites David Stanley's suggested gloss "If you decide to take away this cup . . . [I should prefer that!]," signaling "the intense quality of Jesus's experience" (Stanley) or "Jesus's struggle" (Parsons).[271] I discussed a similar use of such broken, emotionally tortured aposiopsesis in Jesus's weeping lament over Jerusalem in Luke 19:41–44. This approach better reflects, in my judgment, the fraught mood of the Olivet event and the clash of wills in the divine heart, as well as between Jesus and his depressed and impulsive disciples, on the one hand, and his treacherous arresters, on the other.

At the end of his introduction to Moltmann's *Passion for Life*, M. Douglas Meeks crisply summarizes Moltmann's vision for the contemporary church: "The congregation can and must become passionate, evangelical, diaconal, missional, ecumenical, charismatic, and esthetic [opposed to ascetic]."[272] As it happens, this may also serve as an apt capsule of Luke's sweeping theological vision for the people of God seeking to follow the path of Jesus Messiah in the power of the Holy Spirit.

271. Parsons, 319; Stanley, *Jesus*, 217.

272. Meeks, Introduction, 18.

Bibliography

Commentaries are cited by author's name only, all other works by author's name and short title.

Commentaries on Luke

Bock, Darrell L. *Luke*. 2 vols. BECNT 3. Grand Rapids: Baker Academic, 1994–96.

Bovon, François. *Luke*. 3 vols. Hermeneia. Minneapolis: Fortress, 2002.

Carroll, John T. *Luke: A Commentary*. NTL. Louisville: Westminster John Knox, 2012.

Culpepper, R. Alan. "The Gospel of Luke: Introduction, Commentary, and Reflections." In *NIB* 9, edited by Leander Keck, 1–490. Nashville: Abingdon, 1996.

Culy, Martin M., Mikeal C. Parsons, and Joshua J. Stigall. *Luke: A Handbook on the Greek Text*. Waco, TX: Baylor University Press, 2010.

Danker, Frederick W. *Jesus and the New Age: A Commentary on St. Luke's Gospel*. 2nd ed. Philadelphia: Fortress, 1988.

Edwards, James R. *The Gospel of Luke*. PNTC. Grand Rapids: Eerdmans, 2015.

Evans, C. F. *Saint Luke*. TPI New Testament Commentaries. Philadelphia: Trinity Press International, 1990.

Fitzmyer, Joseph A. *The Gospel according to Luke: Introduction, Translation, and Notes*. 2 vols. AB 28, 28A. New York: Doubleday, 1981–85.

Garland, David E. *Luke*. ZECNT. Grand Rapids: Zondervan, 2011.

González, Justo L. *Luke*. Belief: A Theological Commentary on the Bible. Louisville: Westminster John Knox, 2010.

Green, Joel B. *The Gospel of Luke*. NICNT. Grand Rapids: Eerdmans, 1997.

Jeffrey, David Lyle. *Luke*. Brazos Theological Commentary on the Bible. Grand Rapids: Brazos, 2012.

Johnson, Luke Timothy. *The Gospel of Luke*. SP 3. Collegeville, MN: Liturgical Press, 1991.

Just, Arthur A., Jr., ed. *Luke*. ACCS 3. Downers Grove, IL: IVP, 2003.

Marshall, I. Howard. *The Gospel of Luke: A Commentary on the Greek Text*. NIGTC. Grand Rapids: Eerdmans, 1978.

Nolland, John. *Luke*. 3 vols. WBC 35A–C. Waco, TX: Word, 1989–93.
Parsons, Mikeal C. *Luke*. PCNT. Grand Rapids: Baker Academic, 2015.
Talbert, Charles H. *Reading Luke: A Literary and Theological Commentary*. Rev. ed. Macon, GA: Smyth & Helwys, 2002.
Tannehill, Robert C. *Luke*. ANTC. Nashville: Abingdon, 1996.
Tiede, David L. *Luke*. ACNT. Minneapolis: Augsburg, 1988.
Vinson, Richard B. *Luke*. SHBC. Macon, GA: Smyth & Helwys, 2008.

Other Works

Abbott, E. A. *The Son of Man*. Cambridge: Cambridge University Press, 1910.
Achor, Shawn. *The Happiness Advantage: The Seven Principles of Positive Psychology That Fuel Success and Performance at Work*. New York: Crown Business, 2010.
Achtemeier, Paul J., Joel B. Green, and Marianne Meye Thompson. *Introduction to the New Testament: Its Literature and Theology*. Grand Rapids: Eerdmans, 2001.
Adam, A. K. A., Stephen E. Fowl, Kevin J. Vanhoozer, and Francis Watson. *Reading Scripture with the Church: Toward a Hermeneutic for Theological Interpretation*. Grand Rapids: Baker Academic, 2006.
Alexander, Loveday C. A. "Reading Luke-Acts Back to Front." In *Acts in Its Ancient Literary Context*, 207–29. LNTS 298. London: T&T Clark, 2005.
Allen, Diogenes. *Spiritual Theology: The Theology of Yesterday for Spiritual Help Today*. Lanham, MD: Cowley, 1997.
Allison, Dale C., Jr. "The Eye Is the Lamp of the Body (Matthew 6.22–23 = Luke 11.34–36)." *NTS* 33 (1987): 61–83.
———. *Jesus of Nazareth: Millenarian Prophet*. Minneapolis: Fortress, 1998.
Anderson, Gary A. *Charity: The Place of the Poor in the Biblical Tradition*. New Haven: Yale University Press, 2013.
———. *Sin: A History*. New Haven: Yale University Press, 2009.
Appiah, Kwame Anthony. *Cosmopolitanism: Ethics in a World of Strangers*. New York: Norton, 2006.
Arendt, Hannah. *Eichmann in Jerusalem: A Report on the Banality of Evil*. Rev. ed. London: Penguin, 2006 (orig. 1965).
———. *Love and Saint Augustine*. Edited by Joanna Vecchiarelli Scott and Judith Chelius Stark. Chicago: University of Chicago Press, 1996 (orig. 1929).
Aristotle. *Aristotle's "Nicomachean Ethics."* Translated by Robert C. Bartlett and Susan D. Collins. Chicago: University of Chicago Press, 2011.
———. *On Rhetoric: A Theory of Civic Discourse*. Translated by George A. Kennedy. 2nd ed. New York: Oxford University Press, 2007.
Arterbury, Andrew E. *Entertaining Angels: Early Christian Hospitality in Its Mediterranean Setting*. Sheffield: Sheffield Phoenix, 2005.
Ateek, Naim Stifan. *A Palestinian Christian Cry for Reconciliation*. Maryknoll, NY: Orbis Books, 2008.
Atwood, Margaret. *The Handmaid's Tale*. New York: Anchor Books, 1998 (orig. 1986).

Auerbach, Erich. *Mimesis: The Representation of Reality in Western Literature*. Translated by Willard R. Trask. Princeton: Princeton University Press, 2013 (orig. 1953).

Baarda, Tjitze. "Luke 17,21 in Ephraem's Diatessaron." *ZNW* 105 (2014): 289–93.

Baden, Joel S., and Candida R. Moss. "The Origin and Interpretation of *ṣāraʿat* in Leviticus 13–14." *JBL* 130 (2011): 643–62.

Bailey, Kenneth E. *The Good Shepherd: A Thousand-Year Journey from Psalm 23 to the New Testament*. Downers Grove, IL: IVP Academic, 2014.

———. *Jacob and the Prodigal: How Jesus Retold Israel's Story*. Downers Grove, IL: IVP Academic, 2003.

———. *Jesus through Middle Eastern Eyes: Cultural Studies in the Gospels*. Downers Grove, IL: IVP Academic, 2008.

———. *Poet and Peasant*. In *Poet and Peasant* and *Through Peasant Eyes: A Literary-Cultural Approach to the Parables in Luke*. Combined ed. Grand Rapids: Eerdmans, 1983.

———. *Through Peasant Eyes*. In *Poet and Peasant* and *Through Peasant Eyes: A Literary-Cultural Approach to the Parables in Luke*. Combined ed. Grand Rapids: Eerdmans, 1983.

Bakewell, Sarah. *How to Live; or, A Life of Montaigne in One Question and Twenty Attempts at an Answer*. New York: Other Press, 2010.

Bakhtin, Mikhail M. *The Dialogic Imagination: Four Essays*. Translated by Michael Holquist. Edited by Caryl Emerson and Michael Holquist. Austin: University of Texas Press, 1981.

Balentine, Samuel E. *Leviticus*. Interpretation. Louisville: John Knox, 2002.

Balthasar, Hans Urs von. *Prayer*. Translated by A. V. Littleton. New York: Paulist, 1961.

Barrett, Lisa Feldman. *How Emotions Are Made: The Secret Life of the Brain*. New York: Houghton, Mifflin, Harcourt, 2017.

Bartholomew, Craig G., and Heath A. Thomas, eds. *A Manifesto for Theological Interpretation*. Grand Rapids: Baker Academic, 2016.

Bauckham, Richard. *Gospel Women: Studies of the Named Women in the Gospels*. Grand Rapids: Eerdmans, 2002.

Baumeister, Roy F., and John Tierney. *Willpower: Rediscovering the Greatest Human Strength*. London: Penguin, 2011.

Beauvoir, Simone de. *The Second Sex*. Translated by Constance Border and Sheila Malovany-Chevallier. New York: Knopf, 2010.

Beavis, Mary Ann. "From the Margin to the Way: A Feminist Reading of the Story of Bartimaeus." *JFSR* 14 (1998): 19–39.

———. *Mark*. PCNT. Grand Rapids: Baker Academic, 2011.

Beck, Aaron T. *Prisoners of Hate: The Cognitive Basis of Anger, Hostility, and Violence*. New York: HarperCollins, 1995.

Beck, Richard. *Unclean: Meditations on Purity, Hospitality, and Mortality*. Eugene, OR: Cascade, 2011.

Becker, Ernest. *The Denial of Death*. New York: Free Press, 1973.

Becker, Gavin de. *The Gift of Fear: Survival Signals That Protect Us from Violence*. New York: Dell, 1997.

BeDuhn, Jason D. *The First New Testament: Marcion's Scriptural Canon*. Salem, OR: Polebridge, 2013.

Bertschmann, Dorothea H. "Hosting Jesus: Revisiting Luke's 'Sinful Woman' (Luke 7.36–50) as a Tale of Two Hosts." *JSNT* 40 (2017): 30–50.

Betz, Hans Dieter. "Matt vi.22f. and Ancient Greek Theories of Vision." In *Text and Interpretation: Studies in the New Testament Presented to Matthew Black*. Edited by Ernest Best and Robert McL. Wilson, 43–56. Cambridge: Cambridge University Press, 1979.

Biddle, Mark E. *Missing the Mark: Sin and Its Consequences in Biblical Theology*. Nashville: Abingdon, 2005.

———. "Sin." *DSE*, 730–33.

Biehl, Michael, David Masumoto, Paul Ekman, et al. "Matsumoto and Ekman's Japanese and Caucasian Facial Expressions of Emotion (JACFEE): Reliability Data and Cross-National Differences." *Journal of Nonverbal Behavior* 21 (1997): 3–21.

Billings, Bradly S. "'At the Age of Twelve': The Boy Jesus in the Temple (Luke 2:41–52), the Emperor Augustus, and the Social Setting of the Third Gospel." *JTS* 60 (2009): 70–89.

Billings, J. Todd. *The Word of God for the People of God: An Entryway to the Theological Interpretation of Scripture*. Grand Rapids: Eerdmans, 2010.

Bird, Michael F. *Evangelical Theology: A Biblical and Systematic Introduction*. Grand Rapids: Zondervan, 2013.

Bishop, E. F. F. "The Parable of the Lost or Wandering Sheep (Matthew 18.1–14; Luke 15:3–7)." *ATR* 44 (1962): 44–57.

Blomberg, Craig L. "Midrash, Chiasmus, and the Outline of Luke's Central Section." In *Studies in Midrash and Historiography*. Edited by R. T. France and David Wenham, 217–62. Sheffield: JSOT, 1983.

Bloom, Paul. "Against Empathy." *Boston Review*, September 10, 2014. https://bostonreview.net/forum/paul-bloom-against-empathy.

———. *Against Empathy: The Case for Rational Compassion*. New York: Ecco, 2016.

———. *Just Babies: The Origins of Good and Evil*. New York: Crown, 2013.

Bock, Darrell L. *A Theology of Luke and Acts: God's Promised Program Realized for All Nations*. Grand Rapids: Zondervan, 2012.

Boehm, Christopher. *Moral Origins: The Evolution of Virtue, Altruism, and Shame*. New York: Basic Books, 2012.

Boersma, Hans. "Anchored in Christ." *Christian Century*, February 8, 2011, 26–31.

———. "Reconnecting the Threads: Theology as Sacramental Tapestry." *Crux* 47 (2011): 29–37.

———. *Sacramental Preaching: Sermons on the Hidden Presence of Christ*. Grand Rapids: Baker Academic, 2016.

Boff, Leonardo. *Trinity and Society*. Translated by Paul Burns. Maryknoll, NY: Orbis Books, 1988.

Bok, Derek. *The Politics of Happiness: What Government Can Learn from the New Research on Well-Being*. Princeton: Princeton University Press, 2010.

Bok, Sissela. *Exploring Happiness: From Aristotle to Brain Science*. New Haven: Yale University Press, 2011.

Bond, Helen K. "Barabbas Remembered." In *Jesus and Paul: Global Perspectives in Honor of James D. G. Dunn for His Seventieth Birthday*. Edited by B. J. Oropeza, C. K. Robertson, and Douglas C. Mohrman, 59–71. London: T&T Clark, 2009.

Bonhoeffer, Dietrich. *The Cost of Discipleship*. Translated by R. H. Fuller. Rev. ed. New York: Macmillan, 1963 (orig. 1937).

Borg, Marcus J. *Conflict, Holiness, and Politics in the Teachings of Jesus*. 2nd ed. Harrisburg, PA: Trinity Press International, 1998.

———. *The Heart of Christianity: Rediscovering a Life of Faith*. New York: HarperSanFrancisco, 2003.

Boring, M. Eugene. *Mark: A Commentary*. NTL. Louisville: Westminster John Knox, 2006.

Bovon, François. "The Soul's Comeback: Immortality and Resurrection in Early Christianity." *HTR* 103 (2010): 387–406.

Braun, Willi. *Feasting and Social Rhetoric in Luke 14*. SNTSMS 85. Cambridge: Cambridge University Press, 1995.

Brawley, Robert L. *Luke-Acts and the Jews: Conflict, Apology, and Conciliatio*. SBLMS 33. Atlanta: Scholars Press, 1987.

Brink, Laurie. *Soldiers in Luke-Acts; Engaging, Contradicting, and Transcending the Stereotypes*. WUNT 2/362. Tübingen: Mohr Siebeck, 2014.

Brodd, Jeffrey, and Jonathan L. Reed, eds. *Rome and Religion: A Cross-Disciplinary Dialogue on the Imperial Cult*. Atlanta: SBL, 2011.

Brodie, Thomas L. *The Crucial Bridge: The Elijah-Elisha Narrative as an Interpretive Synthesis of Genesis–Kings and a Literary Model for the Gospels*. Collegeville, MN: Liturgical Press, 2000.

———. "The Departure for Jerusalem (Luke 9:51–56) as a Rhetorical Imitation of Elijah's Departure for the Jordan (2 Kgs 1:1–2:6)." *Bib* 70 (1989): 96–109.

———. "Luke-Acts as an Imitation and Emulation of the Elijah-Elisha Narrative." In *New Views on Luke and Acts*. Edited by Earl Richard, 78–85. Collegeville, MN: Liturgical Press, 1990.

———. "Towards Unravelling Luke's Use of the Old Testament: Luke 7:11–17 as an Imitatio of 1 Kings 17:17–24." *NTS* 32 (1986): 247–67.

Brookins, Timothy A. "Dispute with Stoicism in the Parable of the Rich Man and Lazarus." *JGRChJ* 8 (2011–12): 34–50.

———. "Luke's Use of Mark as παράφρασις in the 'Healing of Blind Bartimaeus' Pericope (Mark 10.46–52/Luke 18.35–43)." *JSNT* 34 (2011): 70–89.

Brown, Raymond E. *The Birth of the Messiah: A Commentary on the Infancy Narratives in the Gospels of Matthew and Luke*. 2nd ed. ABRL. New Haven: Yale University Press, 1993.

———. *The Death of the Messiah from Gethsemane to the Grave: A Commentary on the Passion Narratives in the Four Gospels*. 2 vols. ABRL. New York: Doubleday, 1994.

Brueggemann, Walter. *Israel's Praise: Doxology against Idolatry and Ideology*. Philadelphia: Fortress, 1988.

———. *Reality, Grief, Hope: Three Urgent Prophetic Tasks*. Grand Rapids: Eerdmans, 2014.

———. *Theology of the Old Testament: Testimony, Dispute, Advocacy*. Minneapolis: Fortress, 1997.

———. *An Unsettling God: The Heart of the Hebrew Bible*. Minneapolis: Fortress, 2009.

Buber, Martin. *I and Thou*. Translated by Walter Kaufmann. New York: Scribner's Sons, 1970.

Bullard, Scott W. "James McClendon Jr., the New Baptist Sacramentalists, and the Unitive Function of the Eucharist." *PRSt* 38 (2011): 267–88.

Bunyan, John. *A Treatise of the Fear of God*. Legacy Publications, 2011 (orig. 1679).

Burridge, Richard A. *Four Gospels, One Jesus: A Symbolic Reading*. 3rd ed. Grand Rapids: Eerdmans, 2014.

———. *Imitating Jesus: An Inclusive Approach to New Testament Ethics*. Grand Rapids: Eerdmans, 2007.

———. *What Are the Gospels? A Comparison with Graeco-Roman Biography*. 2nd ed. Biblical Resources. Grand Rapids: Eerdmans, 2004.

Byrne, Brendan J. *The Hospitality of God: A Reading of Luke's Gospel*. Collegeville, MN: Liturgical Press, 2000.

Cadbury, Henry J. "Four Features of Lucan Style." In *Studies in Luke-Acts*. Edited by Leander E. Keck and J. Louis Martyn, 87–102. London: SPCK, 1966.

———. *The Making of Luke-Acts*. 2nd ed. London: SPCK, 1958.

———. *The Style and Literary Method of Luke*. HTS 6. Cambridge, MA: Harvard University Press, 1920.

Calvin, John. *Commentaries on the Book of the Prophet Jeremiah and the Lamentations*. 5 vols. Edited and translated by John Owen. Edinburgh: Calvin Translation Society, 1854.

———. *A Harmony of the Gospels: Matthew, Mark, and Luke*. Vol. 2. Translated by T. H. L. Parker. Edited by David W. Torrance and Thomas F. Torrance. Grand Rapids: Eerdmans, 1979.

Caputo, John D. *The Folly of God: A Theology of the Unconditional*. Salem, OR: Polebridge, 2016.

———. *Hoping against Hope: Confessions of a Postmodern Pilgrim*. Minneapolis: Fortress, 2015.

———. *The Insistence of God: A Theology of Perhaps*. Bloomington: Indiana University Press, 2013.

———. *The Prayers and Tears of Jacques Derrida: Religion without Religion*. Bloomington: Indiana University Press, 1997.

———. *The Weakness of God: A Theology of the Event*. Bloomington: Indiana University Press, 2006.

———. *What Would Jesus Deconstruct? The Good News of Postmodernism for the Church*. Grand Rapids: Baker Academic, 2007.

Cardenal, Ernesto. *The Gospel in Solentiname*. Translated by Donald D. Walsh. Rev. ed. Maryknoll, NY: Orbis Books, 2010.

Carey, Greg. "The Book of Revelation as Counter-Imperial Script." In *In the Shadow of Empire: Reclaiming the Bible as a History of Faithful Resistance*. Edited by Richard A. Horsley, 157–76. Minneapolis: Fortress, 2008.

———. *Sinners: Jesus and His Earliest Followers*. Waco, TX: Baylor University Press, 2009.

Carlson, Stephen C. "The Accommodations of Joseph and Mary in Bethlehem: Κατάλυμα in Luke 2.7." *NTS* 56 (2010): 326–42.

Carras, George P. "A Pentateuchal Echo in Jesus's Prayer on the Cross: Intertextuality between Numbers 15,22–31 and Luke 23,34a." In *The Scriptures in the Gospels*. Edited by Christopher M. Tuckett, 605–16. BETL 131. Leuven: Leuven University Press, 1997.

Carroll, John T. *Response to the End of History: Eschatology and Situation in Luke-Acts*. SBLDS 92. Atlanta: Scholars Press, 1988.

Carter, Jimmy. *A Call to Action: Women, Religion, Violence, and Power*. New York: Simon & Schuster, 2014.

Carter, Warren. "Are There Imperial Texts in the Class? Intertextual Eagles and Matthean Eschatology as 'Lights Out' Time for Imperial Rome (Matt 24:27–31)." *JBL* 122 (2003): 467–87.

———. *Matthew and Empire: Initial Explorations*. Harrisburg, PA: Trinity Press International, 2001.

———. *Matthew and the Margins: A Sociopolitical and Religious Reading*. Maryknoll, NY: Orbis Books, 2000.

———. *Pontius Pilate: Portraits of a Roman Governor*. Interfaces. Collegeville, MN: Liturgical Press, 2003.

———. *The Roman Empire and the New Testament: An Essential Guide*. Nashville: Abingdon, 2006.

———. *Seven Events That Shaped the New Testament World*. Grand Rapids: Baker Academic, 2013.

Charlesworth, James H. "Paradise." *ABD* 5:154–55.

Charry, Ellen T. *By the Renewing of Your Minds: The Pastoral Function of Christian Doctrine*. Oxford: Oxford University Press, 1997.

———. *God and the Art of Happiness*. Grand Rapids: Eerdmans, 2010.

———. "The Necessity of Divine Happiness: A Response from Systematic Theology." In *The Bible and the Pursuit of Happiness: What the Old and New Testaments Teach Us about the Good Life*. Edited by Brent A. Strawn, 229–47. Oxford: Oxford University Press, 2012.

Chilton, Bruce. *Rabbi Jesus: An Intimate Biography*. New York: Doubleday, 2000.

Clivaz, Claire. "The Angel and the 'Sweat like Drops of Blood' (Lk 22:43–44): P69 and *f*13." *HTR* 98 (2005): 419–40.

Coakley, Sarah. *God, Sexuality, and the Self: An Essay "On the Trinity."* Cambridge: Cambridge University Press. 2013.

Cohn-Sherbok, Dan M. "An Analysis of Jesus's Arguments concerning the Plucking of Grain on the Sabbath." *JSNT* 2 (1979): 31–41.

Collins, Adela Yarbro, and John J. Collins. *King and Messiah as Son of God: Divine, Human, and Angelic Figures in Biblical and Related Literature*. Grand Rapids: Eerdmans, 2008.

Constable, Giles. "The Interpretation of Mary and Martha." In *Three Studies in Medieval and Religious Thought*, 1–141. Cambridge: Cambridge University Press, 1995.

Conzelmann, Hans. *The Theology of St. Luke*. Translated by Geoffrey Buswell. London: SCM, 1960.

Corley, Kathleen E. *Private Women, Public Meals: Social Conflict in the Synoptic Tradition*. Peabody, MA: Hendrickson, 1993.

Cosgrove, Charles H. "The Divine *Dei* in Luke-Acts: Investigations into the Lukan Understanding of God's Providence." *NovT* 26 (1984): 168–90.

Costandi, Moheb. *Neuroplasticity*. Cambridge, MA: MIT Press, 2016.

Cotter, Wendy J. "Children Sitting in the Agora." *Forum* 5, no. 2 (1989): 63–82.

———. "The Parable of the Children in the Market-Place, Q (Lk) 7:31–35: An Examination of the Parable's Image and Significance." *NovT* 29 (1987): 289–304.

———. "The Parable of the Feisty Widow and the Threatened Judge (Luke 18.1–8)." *NTS* 51 (2005): 328–43.

Croatto, J. Severino. "Jesus, Prophet like Elijah, and Prophet-Teacher like Moses in Luke-Acts." *JBL* 124 (2005): 451–65.

Crockett, Larrimore C. "Luke 4:25–27 and Jewish-Gentile Relations in Luke-Acts." *JBL* 88 (1969): 177–83.

Cross, Anthony R., and Philip E. Thompson, eds. *Baptist Sacramentalism. Studies in Baptist History and Thought*. Carlisle: Paternoster, 2003.

Crossan, John Dominic. *God and Empire: Jesus against Rome, Then and Now*. New York: HarperCollins, 2007.

———. *The Greatest Prayer: Rediscovering the Revolutionary Message of the Lord's Prayer*. New York: Harper One, 2010.

———. *The Historical Jesus: The Life of a Mediterranean Jewish Peasant*. New York: HarperSanFrancisco, 1991.

———. *Jesus: A Revolutionary Biography*. New York: HarperCollins, 1994.

———. *Who Killed Jesus? Exposing the Roots of Anti-Semitism in the Gospel Story of the Death of Jesus*. New York: HarperSanFrancisco, 1995.

Crossan, John Dominic, and Jonathan L. Reed. *Excavating Jesus: Beneath the Stones, behind the Texts*. New York: HarperSanFrancisco, 2001.

Culpepper, R. Alan. "Seeing the Kingdom: The Metaphor of Sight in the Gospel of Luke." *CurTM* 21 (1994): 434–43.

Cunningham, Conor. *Darwin's Pious Idea: Why the Ultra-Darwinists and Creationists Both Get It Wrong*. Grand Rapids: Eerdmans, 2010.

Curkpatrick, Stephen. "A Parable Frame-up and Its Audacious Reframing." *NTS* 48 (2003): 22–38.

Damasio, Antonio. *Descartes' Error: Emotion, Reason, and the Human Mind*. New York: Penguin, 1994.

———. *The Feeling of What Happens: Body and Emotion in the Making of Consciousness*. Orlando, FL: Harcourt, 1999.

———. *Looking for Spinoza: Joy, Sorrow, and the Feeling Brain*. Orlando, FL: Harcourt, 2003.

———. *Self Comes to Mind: Constructing the Conscious Brain*. New York: Pantheon, 2010.

Danby, Herbert. *The Mishnah*. London: Oxford University Press, 1933.

D'Angelo, Mary Rose. "Reconstructing 'Real' Women from Gospel Literature: The Case of Mary Magdalene." In *Women and Christian Origins*. Edited by Ross Shepard Kraemer and Mary Rose D'Angelo, 105–28. New York: Oxford University Press, 1999.

Danker, Frederick W. *Benefactor: Epigraphic Study of a Graeco-Roman and New Testament Semantic Field*. St. Louis: Clayton, 1982.

———. *Luke*. Proclamation Commentaries. Philadelphia: Fortress, 1976.

———. "Luke 16:16. An Opposition Logion." *JBL* 77 (1958): 231–43.

Darley, John M., and C. Daniel Batson. "From Jerusalem to Jericho: A Study of Situational and Dispositional Variables in Helping Behavior." *Journal of Personality and Social Psychology* 27 (1973): 100–119.

Darr, John A. *Herod the Fox: Audience Criticism and Lukan Characterization*. JSNTSup 163. Sheffield: Sheffield Academic, 1998.

———. *On Character Building: The Reader and the Rhetoric of Characterization in Luke-Acts*. Literary Currents in Biblical Interpretation. Louisville: Westminster John Knox, 1992.

Darwin, Charles. *The Expression of the Emotions in Man and Animals*. Edited by Paul Ekman. 4th ed. Oxford: Oxford University Press, 2009 (orig. 1872).

Daube, David. "Shame Culture in Luke." In *Paul and Paulinism: Essays in Honour of C. K. Barrett*. Edited by Morna D. Hooker and Stephen G. Wilson, 355–72. London: SPCK, 1982.

Davis, Ellen F. *Proverbs, Ecclesiastes, and the Song of Songs*. Westminster Bible Companion. Louisville: Westminster John Knox, 2000.

———. *Scripture, Culture, and Agriculture: An Agrarian Reading of the Bible*. Cambridge: Cambridge University Press, 2009.

Davis, Ellen F., and Richard B. Hays, eds. *The Art of Reading Scripture*. Grand Rapids: Eerdmans, 2003.

Dawn, Marva J. *Keeping the Sabbath Wholly: Ceasing, Embracing, Resting, Feasting*. Grand Rapids: Eerdmans, 1989.

Deigh, John. *Emotions, Values, and the Law*. New York: Oxford University Press, 2008.

Denaux, Adelbert. "The Meaning of the Double Expression of Time in Luke 24,29." In *Miracles and Imagery in Luke and John: Festschrift Ulrich Busse*. Edited by J. Verheyden, G. Van Belle, and J. G. Van der Watt, 67–88. Leuven: Peeters, 2008.

———. "The Parable of the King-Judge (Luke 19,12–28) and Its Relation to the Entry Story (19,28–44)." *ZNW* 93 (2002): 35–57.

Derrett, J. Duncan M. "Contributions to the Study of the Gerasene Demoniac." *JSNT* 3 (1979): 2–17.

———. "The Evil Eye in the New Testament." In *Modelling Early Christianity: Social-Scientific Studies of the New Testament in Its Context*. Edited by Philip F. Esler, 65–72. London: Routledge, 1995.

Derrida, Jacques. "Force of Law: The 'Mystical Foundations of Authority.'" Translated by Mary Quantaince. In *Deconstruction and the Possibility of Justice*. Edited by Drucilla Cornell, 3–67. New York: Routledge, 1992.

———. *Of Grammatology*. Translated by Gayatri Chaktravorty Spivak. Baltimore: Johns Hopkins University Press, 1976.

———. *Specters of Marx: The State of the Debt, the Work of Mourning, and the New International*. Translated by Peggy Kamuf. London: Routledge, 1994.

deSilva, David A. *Honor, Patronage, Kinship, and Purity: Unlocking New Testament Culture*. Downers Grove, IL: IVP, 2000.

———. *The Hope of Glory: Honor Discourse and New Testament Interpretation*. Collegeville, MN: Liturgical Press, 1999.

De Sousa, Ronald. *Emotional Truth*. Oxford: Oxford University Press, 2011.

DeSteno, David. *The Truth about Trust: How It Determines Success in Life, Love, Learning, and More*. New York: Hudson Street, 2014.

Dicken, Frank E. *Herod as a Composite Character in Luke-Acts*. WUNT 2/375. Tübingen: Mohr Siebeck, 2014.

———. "Herod as Jesus's Executioner: Possibilities in Lukan Reception and *Wirkungsgeschichte*." In *Characters and Characterization in Luke-Acts*. Edited by Frank E. Dicken and Julia A. Snyder, 199–211. LNTS 548. London: Bloomsbury T&T Clark, 2016.

Dinkler, Michal Beth. "Reflexity and Emotion in Narratological Perspective: Reading Joy in the Lukan Narrative." In Spencer, *Mixed Feelings and Vexed Passions*, 265–86.

———. *Silent Statements: Narrative Representations of Speech and Silence in the Gospel of Luke*. BZNW 191. Berlin: de Gruyter, 2013.

———. "'The Thoughts of Many Hearts Shall Be Revealed': Listening In on the Lukan Interior Monologues." *JBL* 134 (2015): 373–99.

Dixon, Thomas. "'Emotion': The History of a Key Word in Crisis." *Emotion Review* 4 (2012): 338–44.

———. *From Passions to Emotions: The Creation of a Secular Psychological Category*. Cambridge: Cambridge University Press, 2003.

Dodd, C. H. *The Parables of the Kingdom*. Rev. ed. New York: Scribner, 1961.

Doidge, Norman. *The Brain's Way of Healing: Remarkable Discoveries and Recoveries from the Frontiers of Neuroplacticity*. New York: Penguin, 2015.

———. *The Brain That Changes Itself: Stories of Personal Triumph from the Frontiers of Brain Science*. New York: Penguin, 2007.

Donaldson, Terence L. *Jesus on the Mountain: A Study in Matthean Theology*. JSNTSup 8. Sheffield: JSOT, 1985.

Doran, Robert, "The Pharisee and the Tax Collector: An Agonistic Story." *CBQ* 69 (2007): 259–70.

Douglas, Mary. *Thinking in Circles: An Essay on Ring Composition*. New Haven: Yale University Press, 2007.

Douglass, Frederick. *Narrative of the Life of Frederick Douglass: An American Slave, Written by Himself*. Edited by John W. Blassingame, John R. McKivigan, and Peter P. Hinks. New Haven: Yale University Press, 2001.

Downing, F. Gerald. "Dale Martin's Swords for Jesus: Shaky Evidence?" *JSNT* 37 (2015): 326–33.

Drury, John. *Tradition and Design in Luke's Gospel: A Study in Early Christian Historiography*. London: Darton, Longman & Todd, 1976.

Dumoulin, Pierre. "La Parabole de la Veuve de Ben Sira 35,11–24 à Luc 18,1–8." In *Treasures of Wisdom: Studies in Ben Sira and the Book of Wisdom*. Edited by N. Calduch-Benages and J. Vermeylen, 169–79. Leuven: Leuven University Press, 1999.

Dunn, James D. G. "Pharisees, Sinners, and Jesus." In *Jesus, Paul, and the Law: Studies in Mark and Galatians*, 61–88. Louisville: Westminster John Knox, 1990.

Durber, Susan, "The Female Reader of the Parables of the Lost." *JSNT* 45 (1992): 69–78.

Ehrhardt, Arnold. "The Disciples of Emmaus." *NTS* 10 (1963–64): 182–201.

Ehrman, Bart D. *Misquoting Jesus: The Story Behind Who Changed the Bible and Why*. New York: HarperSanFrancisco, 2005.

Eisenstadt, S. N., and Luis Roniger. *Patrons, Clients, and Friends: Interpersonal Relations and the Structure of Trust in Society*. Cambridge: Cambridge University Press, 1984.

Ekman, Paul, ed. *Darwin and Facial Expression: A Century of Research in Review*. Los Altos, CA: Malor Books, 2006.

———, ed. *Emotion in the Human Face*. 2nd ed. Cambridge: Cambridge University Press, 1982.

———. *Emotions Revealed: Recognizing Faces and Feelings to Improve Communication and Emotional Life*. Rev. ed. New York: St. Martin's Griffin, 2003.

Ekman, Paul, and Erica Rosenberg, eds. *What the Face Reveals: Basic and Applied Studies of Spontaneous Expression Using the Facial Action Coding System (FACS)*. 2nd ed. Oxford: Oxford University Press, 2005.

Elliott, John H. "Paul, Galatians, and the Evil Eye." In *The Social World of the New Testament: Insights and Models*. Edited by Jerome H. Neyrey and Eric C. Stewart, 223–34. Peabody, MA: Hendrickson, 2008.

———. "Temple versus Household in Luke-Acts: A Contrast in Social Institutions." In *The Social World of Luke-Acts: Models for Interpretation*. Edited by Jerome H. Neyrey, 211-40. Peabody, MA: Hendrickson, 1991.

Elster, Jon. "Emotion and Action." In *Thinking with Feeling: Contemporary Philosophers on*

Emotion. Edited by Robert C. Solomon, 151–62. Oxford: Oxford University Press, 2004.

Elvey, Anne. "Storing Up Death, Storing Up Life: An Earth Story in Luke 12.13–34." In *The Earth Story in the New Testament*. Edited by Norman C. Habel and Vicky Balabanski, 95–107. London: Sheffield Academic, 2002.

Emmons, Robert A. *Thanks! How Practicing Gratitude Can Make You Happier*. Boston: Houghton Mifflin, 2007.

Emmons, Robert A., and Michael E. McCollough, eds. *The Psychology of Gratitude*. Series in Affective Science. New York: Oxford University Press, 2004.

Engster, Daniel. "Rethinking Care Theory: The Practice of Caring and the Obligation to Care." *Hypatia* 20 (2005): 50–74.

Etcoff, Nancy L. *Survival of the Prettiest: The Science of Beauty*. New York: Doubleday, 1999.

Evans, C. F. "The Central Section of St. Luke's Gospel." In *Studies in the Gospels: Essays in Memory of R. H. Lightfoot*. Edited by Dennis E. Nineham, 37–53. Oxford: Blackwell, 1955.

Evans, Christopher H. *The Kingdom Is Always but Coming: A Life of Walter Rauschenbusch*. Grand Rapids: Eerdmans, 2004.

———. *The Social Gospel in American Religion*. New York: New York University Press, 2017.

Evans, Craig A. "The Function of the Elijah/Elisha Narratives in Luke's Ethic of Election." In Evans and Sanders, *Luke and Scripture*, 70–83.

———. "'He Set His Face': On the Meaning of Luke 9:51." In Evans and Sanders, *Luke and Scripture*, 93–105.

———. *Jesus and His World: The Archaeological Evidence*. Louisville: Westminster John Knox, 2012.

———. "Luke 16:1–18 and the Deuteronomy Hypothesis." In Evans and Sanders, *Luke and Scripture*, 121–39.

——— "Luke's Good Samaritan and the Chronicler's Good Samaritans." In *Biblical Interpretation in Early Christian Gospels*. Vol. 3: *The Gospel of Luke*. Edited by Thomas R. Hatina, 32–42. LNTS 376. London: T&T Clark, 2010.

Evans, Craig A., and James A. Sanders. *Luke and Scripture: The Function of Sacred Scripture in Luke-Acts*. Eugene, OR: Wipf & Stock, 2001.

Farris, Michael. "A Tale of Two Taxations (Luke 18:10–14b): The Parable of the Pharisee and Tax Collector." In *Jesus and His Parables: Interpreting the Parables of Jesus Today*. Edited by V. George Shillington, 23–33. Edinburgh: T&T Clark, 1997.

Fee, Gordon D. "'One Thing Is Needful'?: Luke 10:42." In *New Testament Textual Criticism: Its Significance for Exegesis; Essays in Honour of Bruce M. Metzger*. Edited by Eldon Jay Epp and Gordon D. Fee, 61–75. Oxford: Clarendon, 1981.

Feldman, Louis. *Jew and Gentile in the Ancient World*. Princeton: Princeton University Press, 1993.

Festinger, Leon. *A Theory of Cognitive Dissonance*. Stanford, CA: Stanford University Press, 1957.

Festinger, Leon, Henry W. Riecken, and Stanley Schachter. *When Prophecy Fails: A Social and Psychological Study of a Modern Group That Predicted the Destruction of the World*. Minneapolis: University of Minnesota Press, 1956.

Fiddes, Paul S. "A Conversation in Context: An Introduction to the Report *The Word of God in the Life of the Church*." *ABQ* 31 (2012): 7–27.

———. *The Creative Suffering of God*. Oxford: Clarendon, 1988.
———. *Participating in God: A Pastoral Doctrine of the Trinity*. Louisville: Westminster John Knox, 2000.
———. *Seeing the World and Knowing God: Hebrew Wisdom and Christian Doctrine in Late-Modern Context*. Oxford: Oxford University Press, 2013.
Fiensy, David A., and Ralph K. Hawkins, eds. *The Galilean Economy in the Time of Jesus*. SBLECL 11. Atlanta: SBL, 2013.
Fisher, Philip. *The Vehement Passions*. Princeton: Princeton University Press, 2002.
Fisk, Bruce N. "See My Tears: A Lament for Jerusalem (Luke 13:31–35; 19:41–44)." In *The Word Leaps the Gap: Essays on Scripture and Theology in Honor of Richard B. Hays*. Edited by J. Ross Wagner, C. Kavin Rowe, and A. Katherine Grieb, 147–78. Grand Rapids: Eerdmans, 2008.
Foster, George M. "Peasant Society and the Image of Limited Good." *American Anthropologist* 67 (1965): 293–315.
Fowl, Stephen E. *Theological Interpretation of Scripture*. Cascade Companions. Eugene, OR: Cascade, 2009.
Fowler, James W. *Stages of Faith: The Psychology of Human Development and the Quest for Meaning*. New York: HarperCollins, 1981.
Fox, Michael V. *Proverbs 1–9: A New Translation with Introduction and Commentary*. AYBC. New Haven: Yale University Press, 2000.
Frank, Robert H. *Success and Luck: Good Fortune and the Myth of Meritocracy*. Princeton: Princeton University Press, 2016.
Frazzetto, Giovanni. *Joy, Guilt, Anger, Love: What Neuroscience Can—and Can't—Tell Us about How We Feel*. New York: Penguin, 2013.
Fredrickson, David E. *Eros and the Christ: Longing and Envy in Paul's Christology*. Minneapolis: Fortress, 2013.
Fredriksen, Paula. "Arms and the Man: A Response to Dale Martin's 'Jesus in Jerusalem: Armed and Not Dangerous.'" *JSNT* 37 (2015): 312–25.
Freeman, Curtis W. "Can Baptist Theology Be Revisioned?" *PRSt* 24 (1997): 273–310.
———. *Contesting Catholicity: Theology for Other Baptists*. Waco, TX: Baylor University Press, 2014.
———. "A New Perspective on Baptist Identity." *PRSt* 26 (1999): 59–65.
Freeman, Curtis W., et al. "Re-envisioning Baptist Identity: A Manifesto for Baptist Communities in North America." Appendix to Freeman, "Can Baptist Theology Be Revisioned?" *PRSt* 24 (1997): 303–10.
Frei, Hans W. *The Eclipse of Biblical Narrative: A Study in Eighteenth and Nineteenth Century Biblical Hermeneutics*. New Haven: Yale University Press, 1974.
Freitheim, Terence E. *The Suffering of God: An Old Testament Perspective*. OBT. Philadelphia: Fortress, 1984.
Freyne, Sean. "Herodian Economics in Galilee: Searching for a Suitable Model." In *Modeling Early Christianity: Social-Scientific Studies of the New Testament in Its Context*. Edited by Philip F. Esler, 23–46. London: Routledge, 1995.
———. "Jesus the Wine-Drinker: A Friend of Women." In *Transformative Encounters: Jesus and Women Re-viewed*. Edited by Ingrid Rosa Kitzberger, 162–80. Leiden: Brill, 2000.
Friedrichsen, Timothy A. "The Temple, a Pharisee, a Tax Collector, and the Kingdom of God: Rereading a Jesus Parable (Luke 18:10–14a)." *JBL* 124 (2005): 89–119.

Frijda, Nico H. "The Laws of Emotion." *American Psychologist* 43 (1988): 349–58.

———. *The Laws of Emotion*. New York: Routledge, 2013.

Gaiser, Frederick J. *Healing in the Bible: Theological Insight for Christian Ministry*. Grand Rapids: Baker Academic, 2010.

Galinsky, Karl. "The Cult of the Roman Emperor: Uniter or Divider?" In *Rome and Religion: A Cross-Disciplinary Dialogue on the Imperial Cult*. Edited by Jeffrey Brodd and Jonathan L. Reed, 1–21. Atlanta: SBL, 2011.

Garrett, Susan R. *The Demise of the Devil*. Minneapolis: Fortress, 1969.

Gaventa, Beverly Roberts. *Acts*. ANTC. Nashville: Abingdon, 2003.

———. "'All Generations Will Call Me Blessed': Mary in Biblical and Ecumenical Perspective." In *A Feminist Companion to Mariology*. Edited by Amy-Jill Levine with Marianne Mayo Robbins, 121–29. Cleveland: Pilgrim, 2005.

———. *Mary: Glimpses of the Mother of Jesus*. Columbia: University of South Carolina Press, 1995.

Gench, Frances Taylor. *Back to the Well: Women's Encounters with Jesus in the Gospels*. Louisville: Westminster John Knox, 2004.

Gerrish, B. A. *Christian Faith: Dogmatics in Outline*. Louisville: Westminster John Knox Press, 2015.

Gilbert, Daniel T. *Stumbling on Happiness*. New York: Vintage, 2006.

Gilbert, Daniel T., and Timothy D. Wilson. "Prospection: Experiencing the Future." *Science* 317 (2007): 1351–54.

Gilligan, Carol. *Joining the Resistance*. Cambridge: Polity, 2011.

Gilovich, Thomas, and Lee Ross. *The Wisest One in the Room: How You Can Benefit from Social Psychology's Most Powerful Insights*. New York: Free Press, 2015.

Goldingay, John. *Do We Need the New Testament? Letting the Old Testament Speak for Itself*. Downers Grove, IL: IVP Academic, 2015.

Gomes, Peter J. *The Good Book: Reading the Bible with Mind and Heart*. New York: Morrow, 1996.

Goodrich, John K. "Voluntary Debt Remission and the Parable of the Unjust Steward (Luke 16:1–13). *JBL* 131 (2012): 547–66.

Goulder, Michael D. *The Evangelists' Calendar: A Lectionary Explanation of the Development of Scripture*. London: SPCK, 1978.

Gowler, David B. "The Enthymematic Nature of Parables: A Dialogic Reading of the Parable of the Rich Fool." *RevExp* 109 (2012): 199–217.

———. *Host, Guest, Enemy, and Friend: Portraits of the Pharisees in Luke and Acts*. Emory Studies in Early Christianity 2. New York: Peter Lang, 1991.

———. *What Are They Saying about the Parables?* Mahwah, NJ: Paulist, 2000.

Graham, Carol. *The Pursuit of Happiness: An Economy of Well-Being*. Washington, DC: Brookings Institution, 2011.

Graver, Margaret R. *Stoicism and Emotion*. Chicago: University of Chicago Press, 2009.

Gray, Rebecca. *Prophetic Figures in Late Second Temple Jewish Palestine: The Evidence from Josephus*. New York: Oxford University Press, 1993.

Grayston, Kenneth. "The Significance of the Word *Hand* in the New Testament." In *Mélanges bibliques en homage au R. P. Béda Rigaux*. Edited by Albert Descamps and R. P. André de Halleux, 479–87. Paris: Duculot, 1970.

Green, Emma. "Jimmy Carter Makes One Final Push to End Racism." *Atlantic*, May 31, 2016. https://

www.theatlantic.com/politics/archive/2016/05/jimmy-carter-makes-one-final-push-to-end-racism/484859/

Green, Joel B. *Body, Soul, and Human Life: The Nature of Humanity in the Bible*. STI. Grand Rapids: Baker Academic, 2008.

———. "A Cognitive Narratological Approach to the Characterization(s) of Zacchaeus." In *Characters and Characterization in Luke-Acts*. Edited by Frank E. Dicken and Julia A. Snyder, 109–20. LNTS 548. London: Bloomsbury T&T Clark, 2016.

———. *Conversion in Luke-Acts: Divine Action, Human Cognition, and the People of God*. Grand Rapids: Baker Academic, 2015.

———. *1 Peter*. THNTC. Grand Rapids: Eerdmans, 2007.

———. "Healthcare Systems in Scripture." *DSE*, 358–60.

———. "Jesus on the Mount of Olives (Luke 22:39–46): Tradition and Theology." *JSNT* 26 (1986): 29–48.

———. "Luke-Acts or Luke and Acts? A Reaffirmation of Unity." In *Reading Acts Today: Essays in Honour of Loveday C. A. Alexander*. Edited by Steve Walton et al, 101–19. LNTS 427. London: T&T Clark, 2011.

———. *Practicing Theological Interpretation: Engaging Biblical Texts for Faith and Formation*. Grand Rapids: Baker Academic, 2011.

———. *Seized by Truth: Reading the Bible as Scripture*. Nashville: Abingdon, 2007.

———. "The Social Status of Mary in Luke 1,5–2,52: A Plea for Methodological Integration." *Bib* 73 (1992): 457–72.

———. "'Was It Not Necessary for the Messiah to Suffer These Things and Enter into His Glory?': The Significance of Jesus's Death for Luke's Soteriology." In *The Spirit and Christ in the New Testament and Christian Theology: Essays in Honor of Max Turner*. Edited by I. Howard Marshall and Cornelis Bennema, 71–85. Grand Rapids: Eerdmans, 2012.

———. "'We Had to Celebrate and Rejoice!' Happiness in the Topsy-Turvy World of Luke-Acts." In *The Bible and the Pursuit of Happiness: What the Old and New Testaments Teach Us about the Good Life*. Edited by Brent A. Strawn, 169–83. Oxford: Oxford University Press, 2012.

Green, Joel B., and Max Turner, eds. *Between Two Horizons: Spanning New Testament Studies and Systematic Theology*. Grand Rapids: Eerdmans, 2000.

Greenblatt, Stephen. *The Swerve: How the World Became Modern*. New York: Norton, 2011.

Grenz, Stanley J. *Theology for the Community of God*. Grand Rapids: Eerdmans, 2000.

Griffiths, Paul. *What Emotions Really Are: The Problem of Psychological Categories*. Chicago: University of Chicago Press, 1997.

Gupta, Nijay K. "Fasting." *DJG*, 269–70.

Hahn, Robert A. *Sickness and Healing: An Anthropological Perspective*. New Haven: Yale University Press, 1995.

Haidt, Jonathan. *The Happiness Hypothesis: Finding Modern Truth in Ancient Wisdom*. New York: Basic Books, 2006.

———. *The Righteous Mind: Why Good People Are Divided by Politics and Religion*. New York: Vintage, 2012.

Hamm, Dennis. "The Freeing of the Bent Woman and the Restoration of Israel: Luke 13.10–17 as Narrative Theology." *JSNT* 31 (1987): 23–44.

———. "Luke 19:8 Once Again: Does Zacchaeus Defend or Resolve?" *JBL* 107 (1988): 431–37.

———. "Sight to the Blind: Vision as Metaphor in Luke." *Bib* 67 (1986): 457–77.

———. "The Tamid Service in Luke-Acts: The Cultic Background behind Luke's Theology of Worship (Luke 1:5–25; 18:9–14; 24:50–53; Acts 3:1; 10:3, 30)." *CBQ* 65 (2003): 215–31.

———. "What the Samaritan Leper Sees: The Narrative Christology of Luke 17:11–17." *CBQ* 56 (1994): 273–87.

———. "Zacchaeus Revisited Once More: A Story of Vindication or Conversion?" *Bib* 72 (1991): 248–52.

Hanson, K. C. "The Galilean Fishing Economy and the Jesus Tradition." *BTB* 27 (1997): 99–111.

Hanson, K. C., and Douglas E. Oakman. *Palestine in the Time of Jesus: Social Structures and Social Conflicts*. Minneapolis: Fortress, 1998.

Harmon, Steven R. *Towards Baptist Catholicity: Essays on Tradition and the Baptist Vision*. Studies in Baptist History and Thought 27. Milton Keynes: Paternoster, 2006.

Harrill, J. Albert. "The Dramatic Function of the Running Slave Rhoda (Acts 12:13–16): A Piece of Greco-Roman Comedy." *NTS* 46 (2000): 150–57.

Harris, Sam. *The Moral Landscape: How Science Can Determine Human Values*. New York: Free Press, 2010.

Harris, William V. *Restraining Rage: The Ideology of Anger Control in Classical Antiquity*. Cambridge, MA: Harvard University Press, 2001.

Hartsock, J. Chad. "The Healing of the Man with Dropsy (Luke 14:1–6) and the Lukan Landscape. *BibInt* 21 (2013): 341–54.

———. *Sight and Blindness in Luke-Acts: The Use of Physical Features in Characterization*. Biblical Interpretation 94. Leiden: Brill: 2008.

Haruf, Kent. *Benediction*. New York: Knopf, 2013.

Hatcher, Karen M. "In Gold We Trust: The Parable of the Rich Man and Lazarus (Luke 16:19–31)." *RevExp* 109 (2012): 277–83.

Haught, John F. *Making Sense of Evolution: Darwin, God, and the Drama of Life*. Louisville: Westminster John Knox, 2010.

Hays, Richard B. *Echoes of Scripture in the Gospels*. Waco, TX: Baylor University Press, 2016.

———. *The Moral Vision of the New Testament: Community, Cross, New Creation; A Contemporary Introduction to New Testament Ethics*. New York: HarperCollins, 1996.

———. *Reading Backwards: Figural Christology and the Fourfold Gospel Witness*. Waco, TX: Baylor University Press, 2014.

Hazony, Yoram. *The Philosophy of Hebrew Scripture*. Cambridge: Cambridge University Press, 2012.

Hecht, Jennifer Michael. *The Happiness Myth: Why What We Think Is Right Is Wrong*. New York: HarperSanFrancisco, 2007

Heffner, Blake R. "Meister Eckhart and a Millennium with Mary and Martha." *LQ* 5 (1991): 171–85.

Heil, John Paul. *The Transfiguration of Jesus: Narrative Meaning and Function of Mark 9:2–8, Matt 17:1–8, and Luke 9:28–36*. AnBib 144. Rome: Pontifical Biblical Institute, 2000.

Held, Virginia. *The Ethics of Care: Personal, Political, and Global*. Oxford: Oxford University Press, 2006.

Herzog, William R., II. "Dissembling, a Weapon of the Weak: The Case of Christ and Caesar in Mark 12:13–17 and Rom 13:1–7." *PRSt* 21 (1994): 339–60.

———. *Parables as Subversive Speech: Jesus as Pedagogue of the Oppressed*. Louisville: Westminster John Knox, 1994.

———. "Sowing Discord: The Parable of the Sower (Mark 4:1–9)." *RevExp* 109 (2012): 187–98.

Heschel, Abraham Joshua. *The Prophets*. 2 vols. in 1. Peabody, MA: Hendrickson, 2009 (orig. 1962).

Hill, Craig C. *In God's Time: The Bible and the Future*. Grand Rapids: Eerdmans, 2002.

Hinson, E. Glenn. *Baptist Spirituality: A Call for Renewed Attentiveness to God*. Macon, GA: Nurturing Faith, 2013.

———. *Spiritual Preparation for Christian Leadership*. Nashville: Upper Room, 1999.

Hock, Ronald F. *The Infancy Gospels of James and Thomas, with Introduction, Notes, and Original Text*. SB 2. Santa Rosa, CA: Polebridge, 1995.

Hoffer, Eric. *The True Believer: Thoughts on the Nature of Mass Movements*. New York: Harper & Row, 1951.

Holmgren, Frederick C. "The Pharisee and the Tax Collector: Luke 18:9–14 and Deuteronomy 26:1–15." *Int* 48 (1994): 252–61.

Hornik, Heidi J., and Mikeal C. Parsons. *Illuminating Luke*. Vol. 3: *The Passion and Resurrection Narratives in Italian and Baroque Paintings*. London: Bloomsbury, 2008.

Horrell, David G., Cherryl Hunt, and Christopher Southgate. *Greening Paul: Rereading the Apostle in a Time of Ecological Crisis*. Waco, TX: Baylor University Press, 2010.

Horsley, Richard A. *Covenant Economics: A Biblical Vision of Justice for All*. Louisville: Westminster John Knox, 2009.

———. *Hearing the Whole Story: The Politics of Plot in Mark's Gospel*. Louisville: Westminster John Knox, 2001.

———. *Jesus and Empire: The Kingdom of God and the New World Disorder*. Minneapolis: Fortress, 2003.

———. *Jesus and the Spiral of Violence: Popular Jewish Resistance in Roman Palestine*. San Francisco: Harper & Row, 1987.

Horsley, Richard A., and John S. Hanson. *Bandits, Prophets, and Messiahs: Popular Movements at the Time of Jesus*. NVBS. New York: Harper & Row, 1985.

Hultgren, Arland J. "The Bread Petition of the Lord's Prayer." *ATR* 72 (1990): 41–54.

——— *The Parables of Jesus: A Commentary*. Grand Rapids: Eerdmans, 2000.

Ilan, Tal. "The Attraction of Aristocratic Women to Pharisaism in Second Temple Judaism." *HTR* 88 (1995): 1–33.

———. *Integrating Women into Second Temple History*. Peabody, MA: Hendrickson, 1999.

———. "Notes on the Distribution of Women's Names in Palestine in the Second Temple and Mishnaic Period." *JJS* 40 (1989): 186–200.

Isasi-Díaz, Ada María. "Communication as Communion: Elements in a Hermeneutic of *Lo Cotidiano*." In *Engaging the Bible in a Gendered World: An Introduction to Feminist Biblical Interpretation in Honor of Katharine Doob Sakenfeld*. Edited by Linda Day and Carolyn Pressler, 27–36. Louisville: Westminster John Knox, 2006.

———. *La Lucha Continues: Mujerista Theology*. Maryknoll, NY: Orbis Books, 2004.

Izzard, Carroll E. "The Many Meanings/Aspects of Emotion: Definitions, Functions, Activation, and Regulation." *Emotion Review* 2 (2010): 363–70.

Jackson, Melissa A. *Comedy and Feminist Interpretation of the Hebrew Bible: A Subversive Collaboration*. Oxford Theological Monographs. Oxford: Oxford University Press, 2012.

Jaeger, John. "Abraham Heschel and the Theology of Jürgen Moltmann." *PRSt* 24 (1997): 167–79.

Jeeves, Malcolm. *Minds, Brains, Souls, and Gods: A Conversation on Faith, Psychology, and Neuroscience.* Downers Grove, IL: IVP Academic, 2013.

Jennings, Willie James. *Acts.* Belief: A Theological Commentary on the Bible. Louisville: Westminster John Knox, 2017.

Jeremias, Joachim. *Jerusalem in the Time of Jesus.* Translated by F. H. Cave, C. H. Cave, and M. E. Dahl. Philadelphia: Fortress, 1969.

———. *The Parables of Jesus.* Translated by S. H. Hooke. 2nd ed. New York: Scribner's Sons, 1972.

Jervell, Jacob. "The Divided People of God: The Restoration of Israel and Salvation for the Gentiles." In *Luke and the People of God: A New Look at Luke-Acts*, 41–74. Minneapolis: Augsburg, 1972.

———. *The Theology of the Acts of the Apostles.* Cambridge: Cambridge University Press, 1996.

Johnson, Adam J. *Atonement: A Guide for the Perplexed.* London: Bloomsbury, 2015.

Johnson, Elizabeth A. *Ask the Beasts: Darwin and the God of Love.* London: Bloomsbury, 2014.

———. *Friends of God and Prophets: A Feminist Theological Reading of the Communion of Saints.* New York: Continuum, 1998.

———. *Quest for the Living God: Mapping Frontiers in the Theology of God.* New York: Continuum, 2008.

———. *She Who Is: The Mystery of God in Feminist Theological Discourse.* New York: Crossroad, 1993.

Johnson, Luke Timothy. "The Lukan Kingship Parable (Lk. 19:11–27)." *NovT* 24 (1982): 139–59.

———. *Prophetic Jesus, Prophetic Church: The Challenge of Luke-Acts to Contemporary Christians.* Grand Rapids: Eerdmans, 2011.

———. *The Writings of the New Testament: An Interpretation.* 3rd ed. Minneapolis: Fortress, 2010.

Johnson-Debaufre, Melanie. "Bridging the Gap to 'This Generation': A Feminist-Critical Reading of the Rhetoric of Q 7:31–35." In *Walk in the Ways of Wisdom: Essays in Honor of Elisabeth Schüssler Fiorenza.* Edited by Shelly Matthews, Cynthia Briggs Kittredge, and Melanie Johnson-DeBaufre, 214–33. Harrisburg, PA: Trinity Press International, 2003.

Jones, Serene. *Trauma and Grace: Theology in a Ruptured World.* Louisville: Westminster John Knox, 2009.

Josephus, Flavius. *The New Complete Works of Josephus.* Translated by William Whiston. Commentary by Paul L. Maier. Grand Rapids: Kregel, 1999.

Kagan, Jerome. *What Is Emotion? History, Measures, and Meanings.* New Haven: Yale University Press, 2007.

Kahl, Brigitt. "Reading Luke against Luke: Non-uniformity of Text, Hermeneutics of Conspiracy, and the 'Scriptural Principle' in Luke 1." In *A Feminist Companion to Luke.* Edited by Amy-Jill Levine with Marianne Blickenstaff, 70–88. London: Sheffield Academic, 2002.

Kahneman, Daniel. *Thinking, Fast and Slow.* New York: Farrar, Straus & Giroux, 2011.

Kaiser, Walter C., Jr. "The Book of Leviticus: Introduction, Commentary, and Reflections." In *NIB* 1. Edited by Leander Keck, 985–1191. Nashville: Abingdon, 1994.

Karris, Robert J. *Eating Your Way through Luke's Gospel*. Collegeville, MN: Liturgical Press, 2006.

———. *Luke: Artist and Theologian; Luke's Passion Account as Literature*. New York: Paulist, 1985.

———. "Women and Discipleship in Luke." In *A Feminist Companion to Luke*. Edited by Amy-Jill Levine with Marianne Blickenstaff, 23–43. London: Sheffield Academic, 2002 (orig. *CBQ* 56 [1994]: 1–20]).

Kawashima, Robert S. "The Jubilee Year and the Return of Cosmic Purity." *CBQ* 65 (2003): 370–89.

Kazen, Thomas. *Emotions in Biblical Law: A Cognitive Science Approach*. Hebrew Bible Monographs. Sheffield: Sheffield Phoenix, 2011.

Kee, Howard Clark. "Jesus: A Glutton and a Drunkard." *NTS* 42 (1996): 374–93.

Kelly, Anthony. *The Trinity of Love: A Theology of the Christian God*. Wilmington, DE: Glazier, 1989.

Kierkegaard, Søren. *Fear and Trembling*. Translated by Alistair Hannay. London: Penguin, 1985 (orig. 1843).

Kilgallen, John J. "Martha and Mary: Why at Luke 10:38–42?" *Bib* 84 (2003): 554–61.

King, Martin Luther, Jr. *The Autobiography of Martin Luther King, Jr.* Edited by Clayborne Carson. New York: Intellectual Property Management, in association with Warner Books, 1998.

———. *Strength to Love*. Minneapolis: Fortress, 2010 (orig. 1963).

Kirkpatrick, Frank G. *The Mystery and Agency of God: Divine Being and Action in the World*. Minneapolis: Fortress, 2014.

Kitamori, Kazoh. *Theology of the Pain of God*. 5th ed. Richmond: John Knox, 1965 (orig. Japanese, 1946).

Klassen, William. "'A Child of Peace' (Luke 10:6) in First Century Context." *NTS* 27 (1981): 484–506.

Kloppenborg, John S., and Joseph Verheyden, ed. *The Elijah-Elisha Narrative in the Composition of Luke*. LNTS 493. London: Bloomsbury Academic, 2014.

Knight, Douglas A., and Amy-Jill Levine. *The Meaning of the Bible: What the Jewish Scriptures and Christian Old Testament Can Teach Us*. New York: HarperCollins, 2011.

Koch, L. W. "Brassica nigra." In *Plants of the Bible*. By Harold N. Moldenke and Alma L. Moldenke, 59–62. New York: Dover, 1986 (orig. 1952).

Koenig, John. *New Testament Hospitality: Partnership with Strangers as Promise and Mission*. OBT 17. Philadelphia: Fortress, 1985.

Konstan, David. *Before Forgiveness: The Origins of a Moral Idea*. Cambridge: Cambridge University Press, 2010.

———. *The Emotions of the Ancient Greeks: Studies in Aristotle and Classical Literature*. Toronto: University of Toronto Press, 2006.

———. *Friendship in the Classical World*. Key Themes in Ancient History. Cambridge: Cambridge University Press, 1997.

———. *Pity Transformed*. Classical Inter/Faces. London: Duckworth, 2001.

Koosed, Jennifer L., and Stephen D. Moore. "Introduction: From Affect to Exegesis." *BibInt* 22 (2014): 381–87.

Kotrosits, Maia. *Rethinking Early Christian Identity: Affect, Violence, and Belonging*. Minneapolis: Fortress, 2015.

Krückemeier, Nils. "Der zwölfjährige Jesus im Tempel (Lk. 2.40–52) und die biographische Literatur der hellenistichen Antike." *NTS* 50 (2004): 307–19.

Kübler-Ross, Elisabeth. *On Death and Dying: What the Dying Have to Teach Doctors, Nurses, Clergy, and Their Own Families*. New York: Scribner, 1969.

Kuhn, Karl Allen. *The Heart of Biblical Narrative: Rediscovering Biblical Appeal to the Emotions*. Minneapolis: Fortress, 2009.

LaCugna, Catherine Mowry. *God for Us: The Trinity and Christian Life*. New York: HarperSanFrancisco, 2006.

LaHurd, Carol Schersten. "Re-viewing Luke 15 with Arab Christian Women." In *A Feminist Companion to Luke*. Edited by Amy-Jill Levine with Marianne Blickenstaff, 246–57. London: Sheffield Academic, 2002.

Lambert, David A. *How Repentance Became Biblical: Judaism, Christianity, and the Interpretation of Scripture*. New York: Oxford University Press, 2016.

———. "Mourning over Sin/Affliction and the Problem of 'Emotion' as a Category in the Hebrew Bible." In Spencer, *Mixed Feelings and Vexed Passions*, 139–60.

Lang, T. J. "'Where the Body Is, There Also the Eagles Will Be Gathered': Luke 17:37 and the Arrest of Jesus." *BibInt* 21 (2013): 320–40.

Langer, Ellen J. *Mindfulness*. 2nd ed. Philadelphia: Da Capo, 2004.

Layard, Richard. *Happiness: Lessons from a New Science*. 2nd ed. London: Penguin, 2011.

Lazarus, Richard S. *Emotion and Adaptation*. Oxford: Oxford University Press, 1991.

Lecky, William E. H. *History of European Morals from Augustine to Charlemagne*. 2 vols. New York: Appleton, 1870.

LeDoux, Joseph. *The Emotional Brain: The Mysterious Underpinnings of Emotional Life*. New York: Simon & Schuster, 1996.

Levenson, Jon D. *Inheriting Abraham: The Legacy of the Patriarch in Judaism, Christianity, and Islam*. Princeton: Princeton University Press, 2012.

———. *Resurrection and the Restoration of Israel: The Ultimate Victory of the God of Life*. New Haven: Yale University Press, 2006.

Levine, Amy-Jill. "Bearing False Witness: Common Errors Made about Early Judaism." In *The Jewish Annotated New Testament: New Revised Standard Bible Translation*. Edited by Amy-Jill Levine and Marc Zvi Brettler, 501–4. Oxford: Oxford University Press, 2011.

———. "Discharging Responsibility: Matthean Jesus, Biblical Law, and Hemorrhaging Woman." In *Treasures New and Old: Contributions to Matthean Studies*. Edited by David R. Bauer and Mark Allan Powell, 379–97. SBLSymS 1. Atlanta: Scholars Press, 1996.

———. "Matthew, Mark, and Luke: Good News or Bad?" In *Jesus, Judaism, and Christian Anti-Judaism: Reading the New Testament after the Holocaust*. Edited by Paula Fredriksen and Adele Reinhartz, 77–98. Louisville: Westminster John Knox, 2002.

———. *The Misunderstood Jew: The Scandal of the Jewish Jesus*. New York: HarperSanFrancisco, 2006.

———. *Short Stories by Jesus: The Enigmatic Parables of a Controversial Rabbi*. New York: HarperOne, 2014.

Lewis, C. S. *A Grief Observed*. New York: HarperCollins, 1994 (orig. 1961).

———. *The Problem of Pain*. New York: HarperCollins, 1996 (orig. 1940).

Liddell, Henry George, Robert Scott, Henry Stuart Jones, and Roderick McKenzie. *Greek-English Lexicon*. 9th ed. Oxford: Clarendon, 1940.

Lieu, Judith. *Marcion and the Making of a Heretic God and Scripture in the Second Century*. Cambridge: Cambridge University Press, 2014.

Liew, Tat-Siong Benny. "Postcolonial Criticism: Echoes of a Subaltern's Contribution and Exclusion." In *Mark and Method: New Approaches in Biblical Studies*. Edited by Janice Capel Anderson and Stephen D. Moore, 211–31. 2nd ed. Minneapolis: Fortress, 2008.

Lischer, Richard. *Reading the Parables*. Louisville: Westminster John Knox, 2014.

Longenecker, Bruce W. "A Humorous Jesus? Orality, Structure, and Characterisation in Luke 14:15–24, and Beyond." *BibInt* 16 (2008): 179–204.

———. *Hearing the Silence: Jesus on the Edge and God in the Gap—Luke 4 in Narrative Perspective*. Eugene, OR: Cascade, 2012.

Louw, Johannes P., and Eugene A. Nida. *Greek-English Lexicon of the New Testament Based on Semantic Domains*. 2 vols. 2nd ed. New York: United Bible Societies, 1988–89.

Lucretius. *The Nature of Things*. Translated by A. E. Stallings. London: Penguin, 2007.

Lumpkin, William L. *Baptist Confessions of Faith*. Edited by Bill J. Leonard. 2nd ed. Valley Forge, PA: Judson, 2011.

Luskin, Frederic. *Forgive for Good: A Proven Prescription for Health and Happiness*. New York: HarperCollins, 2002.

Lyons, William John. *Joseph of Arimathea: A Study in Reception History*. Biblical Refigurations. Oxford: Oxford University Press, 2014.

MacDonald, Dennis R. "Toward an Intertextual Commentary on Luke 7." In Kloppenborg and Verheyden, *The Elijah-Elisha Narrative*, 130–52.

MacDonald, Margaret Y. *Early Christian Women and Pagan Opinion: The Power of the Hysterical Woman*. Cambridge: Cambridge University Press, 1996.

Madigan, Kevin J. "Ancient and High-Medieval Interpretations of Jesus in Gethsemane: Some Reflections on Tradition and Continuity in Christian Thought." *HTR* 88 (1995): 157–73.

Madigan, Kevin J., and Jon D. Levenson. *Resurrection: The Power of God for Christians and Jews*. New Haven: Yale University Press, 2008.

Mainardi, Pat. "The Politics of Housework." In *Dear Sisters: Dispatches from the Women's Liberation Movement*. Edited by Rosalyn Baxendall and Linda Gordon, 255–57. New York: Basic Books, 2000 [orig. article, 1968].

Malherbe, Abraham J. "The Christianization of a *Topos* (Luke 12:13–24)." *NovT* 38 (1996): 123–35.

Malina, Bruce J. *Christian Origins and Cultural Anthropology: Practical Models for Biblical Interpretation*. Atlanta: John Knox, 1986.

———. "Early Christian Groups: Using Small Group Formation Theory to Explain Christian Organizations." In *Modelling Early Christianity: Social-Scientific Studies of the New Testament in Its Context*. Edited by Philip F. Esler, 96–113. New York: Routledge, 1995.

———. *The New Testament World: Insights from Cultural Anthropology*. 3rd ed. Louisville: Westminster John Knox, 2001.

———. *Windows on the World of Jesus: Time Travel to Ancient Judea*. Louisville: Westminster John Knox, 1993.

Malina, Bruce J., and Jerome H. Neyrey. "First-Century Personality: Dyadic, Not Individual." In *The Social World of Luke-Acts: Models for Interpretation*. Edited by Jerome H. Neyrey, 67–96. Peabody, MA: Hendrickson, 1991.

———. "Honor and Shame in Luke-Acts." In *The Social World of Luke-Acts: Models for Interpretation*. Edited by Jerome H. Neyrey, 25–65. Peabody, MA: Hendrickson, 1991.

Malina, Bruce J., and Richard L. Rohrbaugh. *Social-Science Commentary on the Synoptic Gospels*. Minneapolis: Fortress, 1992.

Maloney, Linda. "'Swept under the Rug': Feminist Homiletical Reflections on the Parable of the Lost Coin (Lk. 15:8–9)." In *The Lost Coin: Parables of Women, Work, and Wisdom*. Edited by Mary Ann Beavis, 34–38. London: Sheffield Academic, 2002.

Marshall, Christopher D. *Compassionate Justice: An Interdisciplinary Dialogue with Two Gospel Parables on Law, Crime, and Restorative Justice*. Theopolitical Visions 15. Eugene, OR: Cascade, 2012.

Martin, Dale B. "Jesus in Jerusalem: Armed and Not Dangerous." *JSNT* 37 (2014): 3–24.

———. "Response to Fredriksen and Downing." *JSNT* 37 (2015): 334–45.

———. *Sex and the Single Savior: Gender and Sexuality in Biblical Interpretation*. Louisville: Westminster John Knox, 2006.

Martin, Troy. "Time and Money in Translation: A Comparison of the Revised Standard Version and the New Revised Standard Version." *BR* 38 (1993): 55–73.

Matson, David L. *Household Conversion Narratives in Acts: Pattern and Interpretation*. JSNTSup 123. Sheffield: Sheffield Academic, 1996.

———. "Pacifist Jesus? The (Mis)Translation of ἐᾶτε ἕως τούτου in Luke 22:51." *JBL* 134 (2015): 157–76.

Matthews, Shelly. "The Weeping Jesus and the Daughters of Jerusalem: Gender and Conquest in Lukan Lament." In *Doing Gender—Doing Religion: Fallstudien zur Intersectionalität im frühen Judentum, Christentum und Islam*. Edited by Ute E. Eisen, Christine Gerber, and Angela Standhartinger, 381–403. WUNT 2/302.Tübingen: Mohr Siebeck, 2013.

Mayo, Maria. *The Limits of Forgiveness: Case Studies in the Distortion of a Biblical Ideal*. Minneapolis: Fortress, 2015.

McCaig, Wendy. *From the Sanctuary to the Streets: How the Dreams of One City's Homeless Sparked a Faith Revolution That Transformed a Community*. Eugene, OR: Cascade, 2010.

McCane, Byron R. "'Let the Dead Bury Their Own Dead': Secondary Burial and Matt 8:21–22." *HTR* 83 (1990): 31–43.

———. *Roll Back the Stone: Death and Burial in the World of Jesus*. Harrisburg, PA: Trinity Press International, 2003.

McClendon, James William, Jr. *Doctrine*. Vol. 2 of *Systematic Theology*. Nashville: Abingdon, 1994.

———. *Ethics*. Vol. 1 of *Systematic Theology*. Nashville: Abingdon, 1986.

McClendon, James William, Jr., with Nancy Murphy. *Witness*. Vol. 3 of *Systematic Theology*. Nashville: Abingdon, 2000.

McGinn, Bernard. *The Mystical Thought of Meister Eckhart: The Man from Whom God Hid Nothing*. New York: Herder & Herder, 2001.

McGonigal, Kelly. *The Willpower Instinct: How Self-Control Works, Why It Matters, and What You Can Do to Get More of It*. New York: Penguin, 2012.

McLean, Kalbryn A. "Calvin and the Personal Politics of Providence." In *Feminist and Wom-*

anist Essays in Reformed Dogmatics. Edited by Amy Plantinga Pauw and Serene Jones, 107–24. Louisville: Westminster John Knox, 2006.

McNamara, Martin. *Targum and Testament Revisited: Aramaic Paraphrases of the Hebrew Bible*. 2nd ed. Grand Rapids: Eerdmans, 2010.

McNamee, John P. *Diary of a City Priest*. Lanham, MD: Sheed & Ward, 1995.

Meacham, Jon. *American Gospel: God, the Founding Fathers, and the Making of a Nation*. New York: Random House, 2006.

Meeks, M. Douglas. *God the Economist: The Doctrine of God and Political Economy*. Minneapolis: Fortress, 1989.

———. Introduction to *The Passion for Life: A Messianic Lifestyle*, by Jürgen Moltmann. Philadelphia: Fortress, 1978.

Meier, John P. *The Marginal Jew: Rethinking the Historical Jesus*. Vol. 2: *Mentor, Message, and Miracles*. ABRL. New York: Doubleday, 1994.

Menken, M. J. J. "The Position of ΣΠΛΑΓΧΝΙΖΕΣΘΑΙ and ΣΠΛΑΓΧΝΑ in the Gospel of Luke." *NovT* 30 (1988): 107–14.

Merritt, Robert L. "Jesus Barabbas and the Paschal Pardon." *JBL* 104 (1985): 57–68.

Merton, Thomas. *Contemplation in a World of Action*. Garden City, NY: Doubleday, 1971.

———. *Entering the Silence: The Journals of Thomas Merton*. Vol. 2: *1941–52*. Edited by Jonathan Montaldo. San Francisco: Harper, 1996.

Metzger, Bruce M. *A Textual Commentary on the Greek New Testament*. 2nd ed. Stuttgart: Deutsche Bibelgesellschaft, 1994.

Metzger, James A. "God as F(r)iend? Reading Luke 11:5–13 and 18:1–8 with a Hermeneutic of Suffering. *HBT* 32 (2010): 33–57.

Meyers, Eric M. "Synagogue." *ABD* 6:251–60.

Michaels, J. Ramsey. "Almsgiving and the Kingdom Within: Tertullian on Luke 17:21." *CBQ* 60 (1998): 475–83.

Migliore, Daniel L. *Faith Seeking Understanding: An Introduction to Christian Theology*. 2nd ed. Grand Rapids: Eerdmans, 2004.

Milgrom, Jacob. "Leviticus." In *The HarperCollins Study Bible*. Edited by Harold W. Attridge, 150–93. New York: HarperCollins, 2006.

Miller, David M. "Seeing the Glory, Hearing the Son: The Function of the Wilderness Theophany Narrative in Luke 9:28–36." *CBQ* 72 (2010): 498–517.

Miller, Robert J., ed. *The Complete Gospels: Annotated Scholars Version*. Rev. ed. Sonoma, CA: Polebridge, 1994.

Minear, Paul S. "Luke's Use of the Birth Stories." In *Studies in Luke-Acts: Essays Presented in Honor of Paul Schubert*. Edited by Leander E. Keck and J. Louis Martyn, 111–30. London: SPCK, 1966.

———. "A Note on Luke 17:7–10." *JBL* 93 (1974): 82–87.

Mirguet, Françoise, and Dominika A. Kurek-Chomycz. "Emotions in Ancient Jewish Literature." *BibInt* 24 (2016): 435–41.

Mitchell, Alan C. "The Use of συκοφαντεῖν in Luke 19,8: Further Evidence for Zacchaeus's Defense." *Bib* 72 (1991): 546–47.

———. "Zacchaeus Revisited: Luke 19,8 as a Defense." *Bib* 71 (1990): 153–76.

Mithen, Steven. *The Singing Neanderthals: The Origins of Music, Language, Mind, and Body*. Cambridge, MA: Harvard University Press, 2006.

Moessner, David P. *Lord of the Banquet: The Literary and Theological Significance of the Lukan Travel Narrative*. Harrisburg, PA: Trinity Press International, 1989.

———. "Luke 9:1–50: Luke's Preview of the Journey of the Prophet Like Moses in Deuteronomy." *JBL* 102 (1983): 575–605.

———. "Luke as Tradent and Hermeneut: 'As one who has a thoroughly informed familiarity with all the events from the top' (παρηκολουθηκότι ἄνωθεν πᾶσιν ἀκριβῶς, Luke 1:3)." *NovT* 58 (2016): 259–300.

Moldenke, Harold N., and Alma L. Moldenke. *Plants of the Bible*. New York: Dover, 1986 (orig. 1952).

Moll, Jorge, Ricardo de Oliveira-Souza, and Roland Zahn. "The Neural Basis of Moral Cognition: Sentiments, Concepts, and Values." *Annals of the New York Academy of Sciences* 1124 (2008): 161–80.

Moltmann, Jürgen. *A Broad Place: An Autobiography*. Translated by Margaret Kohl. Minneapolis: Fortress, 2009.

———. *The Coming of God: Christian Eschatology*. Translated by Margaret Kohl. Minneapolis: Fortress, 1996.

———. *The Crucified God: The Cross of Christ as the Foundation of Christian Theology*. Translated by R. A. Wilson, John Bowden, and Margaret Kohl. Minneapolis: Fortress, 1993.

———. "*The Crucified God* Yesterday and Today: 1972–2002." Translated by Margaret Kohl. In Jürgen Moltmann and Elisabeth Moltmann-Wendel, *Passion for God: Theology in Two Voices*, 69–85. Louisville: Westminster John Knox, 2003.

———. *Ethics of Hope*. Translated by Margaret Kohl. Minneapolis: Fortress, 2012.

———. *Experiences in Theology: Ways and Forms of Christian Theology*. Translated by Margaret Kohl. Minneapolis: Fortress, 2000.

———. *God in Creation: A New Theology of Creation and the Spirit of God*. Translated by Margaret Kohl. Minneapolis: Fortress, 1993.

———. *In the End—the Beginning: The Life of Hope*. Translated by Margaret Kohl. Minneapolis: Fortress, 2004.

———. *The Living God and the Fullness of Life*. Translated by Margaret Kohl. Louisville: Westminster John Knox, 2015.

———. *The Passion for Life: A Messianic Lifestyle*. Translated by M. Douglas Meeks. Philadelphia: Fortress, 1978.

———. *Sun of Righteousness, Arise! God's Future for Humanity and the Earth*. Translated by Margaret Kohl. Minneapolis: Fortress, 2010.

———. *Theology of Hope: On the Ground and the Implications of a Christian Eschatology*. Translated by James W. Leitch. Minneapolis: Fortress, 1993.

———. *The Trinity and the Kingdom: The Doctrine of God*. Translated by Margaret Kohl. Minneapolis: Fortress, 1993.

Moltmann-Wendel, Elisabeth. "Self-Love and Self-Acceptance." In *Love: The Foundation of Hope: The Theology of Jürgen Moltmann and Elisabeth Moltmann-Wendel*. Edited by Frederick B. Burnham, Charles S. McCoy, and M. Douglas Meeks, 23–38. San Francisco: Harper & Row, 1988.

———. *The Women around Jesus*. Translated by John Bowden. New York: Crossroad, 1997.

Moore, Stephen D. *Poststructuralism and the New Testament: Derrida and Foucault at the Foot of the Cross*. Minneapolis: Fortress, 1994.

———. "The Song of Songs in the History of Sexuality." *CH* 69 (2000): 328–49.

Moore, Stephen D., and Janice Capel Anderson. "Taking It like a Man: Masculinity in 4 Maccabees." *JBL* 117 (1998): 249–73.

Moors, Agnes, et al. "Appraisal Theories of Emotion: State of the Art and Future Development." *Emotion Review* 5 (2013): 119–24.

Morgan, Teresa. *Roman Faith and Christian Faith:* Pistis *and* Fides *in the Early Roman Empire and Early Churches*. Oxford: Oxford University Press, 2015.

Morton, Adam. "Epistemic Emotions." In *The Oxford Handbook of Philosophy of Emotion*. ed. Peter Goldie, 385–400. Oxford: Oxford University Press, 2010.

Moule, C. F. D. *Idioms of the New Testament*. 2nd ed. Cambridge: Cambridge University Press, 1959.

Mouw, Richard J., and Douglas A. Sweeney. *The Suffering and Victorious Christ: Toward a More Compassionate Christology*. Grand Rapids: Baker Academic, 2013.

Moxnes, Halvor. *The Economy of the Kingdom: Social Conflict and Economic Relations in Luke's Gospel*. Eugene, OR: Wipf & Stock, 2004 (orig. 1988).

———. "Honor and Shame." *BTB* 23 (1993): 167–76.

———. "Patron-Client Relations and the New Community in Luke-Acts." In *The Social World of Luke-Acts: Models for Interpretation*. Edited by Jerome H. Neyrey, 241–68. Peabody, MA: Hendrickson, 1991.

Muddiman, John. "Fast, Fasting." *ABD* 2:773–76.

Murphy, Frederick J. *Early Judaism: The Exile to the Time of Jesus*. Peabody, MA: Hendrickson, 2002.

Myers, Ched. *Binding the Strong Man: A Political Reading of Mark's Story of Jesus*. Maryknoll, NY: Orbis Books, 1988.

Myers, David G. *The Pursuit of Happiness: Who Is Happy—and Why*. New York: William Morrow, 1992.

Nave, Guy D., Jr. *The Role and Function of Repentance in Luke-Acts*. AcBib 4. Atlanta: SBL, 2004.

Neusner, Jacob. *From Politics to Piety: The Emergence of Pharasaic Judaism*. Eugene, OR: Wipf & Stock, 2003 (orig. New York: Ktav, 1973).

———. *Judaism in the Beginning of Christianity*. Philadelphia: Fortress, 1984.

Newberg, Andrew, Eugene D'Aquill, and Vince Rause. *Why God Won't Go Away: Brain Science and the Biology of Belief*. New York: Ballentine, 2001.

Newberg, Andrew, and Mark Robert Waldman. *How Enlightenment Changes Your Brain: The New Science of Transformation*. New York: Avery, 2016.

———. *How God Changes Your Brain: Breakthrough Findings from a Leading Neuroscientist*. New York: Ballentine, 2009.

Newell, John Philip. *The Rebirthing of God: Christianity's Struggle for New Beginnings*. Nashville: SkyLight Paths, 2016.

Newman, Barclay M. *A Concise Greek-English Dictionary of the New Testament*. Rev. ed. Stuttgart: Deutsche Bibelgesellschaft, 2010.

Newman, Elizabeth. *Attending the Wounds on Christ's Body: Teresa's Spiritual Vision*. Eugene, OR: Wipf & Stock, 2012.

Neyrey, Jerome H. "The Absence of Jesus's Emotions—the Lucan Redaction of Lk 22,39–46." *Bib* 61 (1980): 153–71.

———. "Ceremonies in Luke-Acts: The Cases of Meals and Table-Fellowship. In *The Social World of Luke-Acts: Models for Interpretation*. Edited by Jerome H. Neyrey, 360–87. Peabody, MA: Hendrickson, 1991.

———. *The Passion according to Luke: A Redactional Study of Luke's Soteriology*. New York: Paulist, 1985.

Nicholson, William. *Shadowlands: A Play*. New York: Plume, 1991.

Nickelsburg, George W. E., and James C. VanderKam. *1 Enoch: A New Translation Based on the Hermeneia Commentary*. Minneapolis: Fortress, 2004.

Nisbett, Richard E. *The Geography of Thought: How Asians and Westerners Think Differently. . . and Why*. New York: Free Press, 2003.

———. *Mindware: Tools for Smart Thinking*. New York: Farrar, Straus & Giroux, 2015.

Noble, Joshua A. "'Rich toward God': Making Sense of Luke 12:21." *CBQ* 78 (2016): 302–20.

Noddings, Nel. *Caring: A Feminine Approach to Ethics and Moral Education*. 2nd ed. Berkeley: University of California Press, 2003.

Nolland, John. "Classical and Rabbinic Parallels to 'Physician, Heal Yourself' (Lk. IV 23)." *NovT* 21 (1979): 193–209.

———. "Luke's Use of χάρις." *NTS* 32 (1986): 614–20.

Noorda, S. J. "'Cure Yourself, Doctor!' (Luke 4,23): Classical Parallels to an Alleged Saying of Jesus." In *Logia: Les paroles de Jésus—The Sayings of Jesus; Mémorial Joseph Coppens*. Edited by Joël Belobel, 459–67. BETL 59. Leuven: Leuven University Press, 1982.

Nouwen, Henri J. M. *The Return of the Prodigal Son: A Story of Homecoming*. New York: Image Books, 1994.

———. *Wounded Healer: Ministry in Contemporary Society*. New York: Doubleday, 1972.

Nussbaum, Martha C. *Anger and Forgiveness: Resentment, Generosity, Justice*. New York: Oxford University Press, 2016.

———. *Creating Capabilities: The Human Development Approach*. Cambridge, MA: Harvard University Press, 2011.

———. *Cultivating Humanity: A Classical Defense of Reform in Liberal Education*. Cambridge, MA: Harvard University Press, 1997.

———. *From Disgust to Humanity: Sexual Orientation and Constitutional Law*. Inalienable Rights. Oxford: Oxford University Press, 2010.

———. *Frontiers of Justice: Disability, Nationality, and Species Membership*. Tanner Lectures on Human Values 8. Cambridge, MA: Harvard University Press, 2007.

———. *Hiding from Humanity: Disgust, Shame, and the Law*. Princeton: Princeton University Press, 2006.

———. *On Emotions: Philosophical Essays*. Oxford: Oxford University Press, 2013.

———. "Patriotism and Cosmopolitanism." In *For Love of Country?* Edited by Joshua Cohen, 2–17. New Democracy Forum. Boston: Beacon, 2002.

———. *Political Emotions: Why Love Matters for Justice*. Cambridge, MA: Harvard University Press, 2013.

———. "Rational Judgments." In Nussbaum, *Poetic Justice: The Literary Imagination and Public Life*, 53–78. Boston: Beacon, 1995.

———. *The Therapy of Desire: Theory and Practice in Hellenistic Ethics*. Princeton: Princeton University Press, 1994.

———. *Upheavals of Thought: The Intelligence of Emotions*. Cambridge: Cambridge University Press, 2001.

———. *Women and Human Development: The Capabilities Approach*. Cambridge: Cambridge University Press, 2000.

Nussbaum, Martha C., et al. *For Love of Country?* New Democracy Forum. Edited by Joshua Cohen. Boston: Beacon, 2002.

Oakman, Douglas E. "The Buying Power of Two Denarii (Luke 10:35)." In *Jesus and the Peasants*, 40–45. Matrix: The Bible in Mediterranean Context 4. Eugene, OR: Cascade, 2008.

———. "Execrating? Or Execrable Peasants!" In *The Galilean Economy in the Time of Jesus*. Edited by David A. Fiensy and Ralph K. Hawkins, 139–64. ECL 11. Atlanta: SBL, 2013.

———. "Jesus and Agrarian Palestine: The Factor of Debt." In *The Social World of the New Testament: Insights and Models*. Edited by Jerome H. Neyrey and Eric C. Stewart, 65–82. Peabody, MA: Hendrickson, 2008.

———. *Jesus and the Peasants*. Matrix: The Bible in Mediterranean Context 4. Eugene, OR: Cascade, 2008.

———. *The Political Aims of Jesus*. Minneapolis: Fortress, 2012.

———. "Was Jesus a Peasant? Implications for Reading the Samaritan Story (Luke 10:30–35)." In *The Social World of the New Testament: Insights and Models*. Edited by Jerome H. Neyrey and Eric C. Stewart, 125–40. Peabody, MA: Hendrickson, 2008.

Oatley, Keith, Dacher Keltner, and Jennifer M. Jenkins. *Understanding Emotions*. 2nd ed. Malden: Blackwell, 2006.

O'Connell, Maureen H. *Compassion: Loving Our Neighbor in an Age of Globalization*. Maryknoll, NY: Orbis Books, 2009.

O'Day, Gail. "Singing Woman's Song: A Hermeneutic of Liberation." *CurTM* 12 (1985): 203–10.

O'Kane, Martin. "'The Bosom of Abraham' (Luke 16:22): Father Abraham in the Visual Imagination." *BibInt* 15 (2007): 485–518.

Okin, Susan Moller. *Justice, Gender, and the Family*. New York: Basic Books, 1989.

Olson, Dennis. "Emotion, Repentance, and the Question of the 'Inner Life' of Biblical Israelites: A Case Study of Hosea 6:1–3." In Spencer, *Mixed Feelings and Vexed Passions*, 161–76.

Omanson, Roger L. *A Textual Guide to the Greek New Testament*. Stuttgart: Deutsche Bibelgesellschaft, 2006.

Oster, Richard E. "'Show Me a Denarius': Symbolism of Roman Coinage and Christian Beliefs." *ResQ* 28 (1985/86): 107–15.

O'Toole, Robert F. "Some Exegetical Reflections on Luke 13,10–17." *Bib* 73 (1992): 84–107.

Paffenroth, Kim. *Judas: Images of the Lost Disciple*. Louisville: Westminster John Knox, 2002.

Panksepp, Jaak, and Lucy Biven, *The Archaeology of Mind: Neuroevolutionary Origins of Human Emotions*. New York: Norton, 2012.

Pao, David W. *Acts and the Isaianic New Exodus*. Biblical Studies Library. Grand Rapids: Baker, 2002.

———. "Family and Table-Fellowship in the Writings of Luke." In *This Side of Heaven: Race, Ethnicity, and Christian Faith*. Edited by Robert J. Priest and Alvaro L. Nieves, 181–94. Oxford: Oxford University Press, 2007.

Parsons, Mikeal C. *Body and Character in Luke and Acts: The Subversion of Physiognomy in Early Christianity*. Grand Rapids: Baker Academic, 2006.

———. *Luke: Storyteller, Interpreter, Evangelist.* Peabody, MA: Hendrickson, 2007.

Parsons, Mikeal C., and Richard I. Pervo. *Rethinking the Unity of Luke and Acts*. Minneapolis: Fortress, 1993.

Peppard, Michael. *The Son of God in the Roman World: Divine Sonship in Its Social and Political Context.* New York: Oxford University Press, 2012.

Pervo, Richard I. *Dating Acts: Between the Evangelists and the Apologists*. Santa Rosa, CA: Polebridge, 2006.

Peters, Ted. *Sin Boldly: Justifying Faith for Fragile and Broken Souls.* Minneapolis: Fortress, 2015.

Peterson, Eugene H. *Christ Plays in Ten Thousand Places: A Conversation in Spiritual Theology*. Grand Rapids: Eerdmans, 2005.

———. "Foreword: Sacramental Theology" to *Sacramental Preaching: Sermons on the Hidden Presence of Christ*, by Hans Boersma, vii–xii. Grand Rapids: Baker Academic, 2016.

———. *Tell It Slant: A Conversation on the Language of Jesus in His Stories and Prayers.* Grand Rapids: Eerdmans, 2008.

Phillips, Thomas E. "Why Did Mary Wrap the Newborn Jesus in 'Swaddling Clothes'? Luke 2.7 and 2.12 in the Context of Luke-Acts." In *Reading Acts Today: Essays in Honour of Loveday C. A. Alexander*. Edited by Steve Walton et al., 59–80. LNTS 427. London: T&T Clark, 2011.

Pilch, John J. "Biblical Leprosy and Body Symbolism." *BTB* 11 (1981): 108–13.

———. "Sickness and Healing in Luke-Acts." In *The Social World of Luke-Acts: Models for Interpretation*. Edited by Jerome H. Neyrey, 181–209. Peabody, MA: Hendrickson, 1991.

Pitre, Brant J. "Blessing the Barren and Warning the Fecund: Jesus's Message for Women concerning Pregnancy and Childbirth." *JSNT* 81 (2001): 59–80.

Plamper, Jan. *The History of Emotions: An Introduction*. Translated by Keith Tribe. Emotions in History. Oxford: Oxford University Press, 2015.

Pohl, Christine D. *Making Room: Recovering Hospitality as a Christian Tradition*. Grand Rapids: Eerdmans, 1999.

Pokorný, Petr. *Theologie der lukanischen Schriften*. FRLANT 174. Göttingen: Vandenhoeck & Ruprecht, 1998.

Pols, Edward. *Meditation on a Prisoner: Towards Understanding Action and Mind.* Carbondale: Southern Illinois University Press, 1975.

Poon, Wilson C. K. "Superabundant Table Fellowship in the Kingdom: The Feeding of the Five Thousand and the Meal Motif in Luke." *ExpT* 114 (2003): 224–30.

Pope, Michael. "The Downward Motion of Jesus's Sweat and the Authenticity of Luke 22:43–44." *CBQ* 79 (2017): 261–81.

Porter, Stanley E. *Idioms of the Greek New Testament*. 2nd ed. Sheffield: Sheffield Academic, 1994.

———. "'In the Vicinity of Jericho': Luke 18:35 in the Light of Its Synoptic Parallels." *BBR* 2 (1992): 91–104.

———. "The Parable of the Unjust Steward (Luke 16:1–13): Irony Is the Key." In *The Bible in Three Dimensions: Essays in Celebration of Forty Years of Biblical Study at the University of Sheffield*. Edited by David J. A. Clines, Stephen E. Fowl, and Stanley E. Porter, 127–53. JSOTSup 87. Sheffield: JSOT, 1990.

Powell, Mark Allan. *What Do They Hear? Bridging the Gap between Pulpit and Pew*. Nashville: Abingdon, 2007.

Powell, Samuel M. *The Impassioned Life: Reason and Emotion in the Christian Tradition*. Minneapolis: Fortress, 2016.

Price, Carolyn. *Emotion*. Cambridge: Polity, 2015.

Pummer, Reinhard. *The Samaritans: A Profile*. Grand Rapids: Eerdmans, 2016.

Purvis, James D. "The Samaritans and Judaism." In *Early Judaism and Its Modern Interpreters*. Edited by Robert A. Kraft and George W. E. Nickelsburg, 81–98. Phildelphia: Fortress, 1986.

Rahner, Karl. *The Trinity*. Translated by Joseph Donceel. New York: Herder & Herder, 1970.

Ramsay, William M. *Four Modern Prophets*. Louisville: John Knox, 1986.

Rauschenbusch, Walter. *Christianity and the Social Crisis in the Twenty-First Century: The Classic That Woke the Church Up*. Edited by Paul Rauschenbusch. New York: HarperCollins, 2007 (orig. 1907).

———. *Christianizing the Social Order*. New York: Macmillan, 1912.

———. *Prayers of the Social Awakening*. Boston: Pilgrim, 1910.

———. *The Social Principles of Jesus*. New York: Association Press, 1916.

———. *A Theology for the Social Gospel*. LTE. Louisville: Westminster/John Knox, 1997 (orig. 1917).

Rawls, John. *Justice as Fairness: A Restatement*. Edited by Erin Kelly. 2nd ed. Cambridge, MA: Harvard University Press, 2001.

———. *Political Liberalism*. 2nd ed. New York: Columbia University Press, 1996.

———. *A Theory of Justice*. Cambridge, MA: Harvard University Press, 1971.

Reid, Barbara E. "Beyond Petty Pursuits and Wearisome Widows: Three Lukan Parables." *Int* 53 (2002): 284–94.

———. *Choosing the Best Part? Women in the Gospel of Luke*. Collegeville, MN: Liturgical Press, 1996.

———. "'Do You See This Woman?' Luke 7:36–50 as a Paradigm for Feminist Hermeneutics." *BR* 40 (1995): 37–49.

———. *Taking Up the Cross: New Testament Interpretations through Latina and Feminist Eyes*. Minneapolis: Fortress, 2007.

———. *The Transfiguration: A Source- and Redaction-Critical Study of Luke 9:28–36*. CahRb 32. Paris: Gabalda & Cie, 1993.

———. "Voices and Angels: What Were They Talking about at the Transfiguration? A Redaction-Critical Study of Luke 9:28–36." *BR* 34 (1989): 19–31.

Reid, Jonathan L. *Archaeology and the Galilean Jesus*. Harrisburg, PA: Trinity Press International, 2000.

Rindge, Matthew S. *Jesus' Parable of the Rich Fool: Luke 12:13–34 among Ancient Conversations on Death and Possessions*. SBLECL 6. Leiden: Brill, 2012.

———. "Mortality and Enjoyment: The Interplay of Death and Possessions in Qoheleth." *CBQ* 73 (2011): 265–80.

Ringe, Sharon H. *Jesus, Liberation, and the Biblical Jubilee: Images for Ethics and Christology*. OBT. Philadelphia: Fortress, 1985.

Ritmeyer, Leen. "Herod's Temple Mount—Stone by Stone." *BAR* 15 (1989): 23–53.

Roberts, Robert C. "Emotions and the Canons of Evaluation." In *The Oxford Handbook of*

Philosophy of Emotion. Edited by Peter Goldie, 561–83. Oxford: Oxford University Press, 2010.

———. *Emotions: An Essay in Aid of Moral Psychology*. Cambridge: Cambridge University Press, 2003.

———. *Spiritual Emotions: A Psychology of Christian Virtues*. Grand Rapids: Eerdmans, 2004.

Robertson, A. T. *A Grammar of the Greek New Testament in Light of Historical Research*. London: Hodder & Stoughton, 1923.

Robin, Corey. *Fear: The History of a Political Idea*. Oxford: Oxford University Press, 2004.

Robinson, H. Wheeler. *The Cross in the Old Testament*. London: SCM, 1955.

Rogers, Eugene F. *After the Spirit: A Constructive Pneumatology from Resources outside the Modern West*. London: SCM Press, 2006.

Rohr, Richard. *Eager to Love: The Alternative Way of Francis of Assisi*. Cincinnati: Franciscan Media, 2014.

Rohrbaugh, Richard L. "A Peasant Reading of the Parable of the Talents/Pounds: A Text of Terror?" *BTB* 23 (1993): 32–39.

———. "The Pre-industrial City in Luke-Acts: Urban Social Relations." In *The Social World of Luke-Acts: Models for Interpretation*. Edited by Jerome H. Neyrey, 125–49. Peabody, MA: Hendrickson, 1991.

Rorty, Amelie. "A Plea for Ambivalence." In *The Oxford Handbook of Philosophy of Emotion*. Edited by Peter Goldie, 425–44. New York: Oxford University Press, 2010.

Rossing, Barbara R. *The Rapture Exposed: The Message of Hope in the Book of Revelation*. New York: Basic Books, 2004.

Rousseau, John J., and Rami Arav. *Jesus and His World: An Archaeological and Cultural Dictionary*. Minneapolis: Fortress, 1995.

Rowe, C. Kavin. *Early Narrative Christology: The Lord in the Gospel of Luke*. Grand Rapids: Baker Academic, 2009.

Rozin, Paul, Jonathan Haidt, and Clark R. McCauley. "Disgust." In *Handbook of Emotions*. Edited by Michael Lewis, Jeannette M., Haviland-Jones, and Lisa Freeman Barrett, 757–76. 3rd ed. New York: Guilford, 2008.

Rozin, Paul, Laura Lowery, Sumio Imada, and Jonathan Haidt. "The CAD Triad Hypothesis: A Mapping between Three Moral Emotions (Contempt, Anger, Disgust) and Three Moral Codes (Community, Autonomy, Divinity." *Journal of Personality and Social Psychology* 76 (1999): 574–86.

Ryan, Jordan J. "Jesus and Synagogue Disputes: Recovering the Institutional Context of Luke 13:10–17." *CBQ* 79 (2017): 41–59.

Sacks, Jonathan. *To Heal a Fractured World: The Ethics of Responsibility*. New York: Schocken, 2005.

Saldarini, Anthony J. *Pharisees, Scribes, and Sadducees in Palestinian Society: A Sociological Approach*. Biblical Resources Series. Grand Rapids: Eerdmans, 2001 (orig. 1988).

———. "Sanhedrin." *ABD* 5:975–80.

Saller, Richard P. *Personal Patronage under the Early Empire*. Cambridge: Cambridge University Press, 1982.

Salmon, Marilyn J. *Preaching without Contempt: Overcoming Unintended Anti-Judaism*. Minneapolis: Fortress, 2006.

Sanders, E. P. *The Historical Figure of Jesus*. London: Penguin, 1993.

———. *Jesus and Judaism*. London: SCM, 1985.

———. *Judaism: Practice and Belief (63 BCE–66 CE)*. London: SCM, 1992.

Sanders, Jack T. *The Jews in Luke-Acts*. London: SCM, 1987.

Sanders, James A. "The Ethic of Election in Luke's Great Banquet Parable." In Evans and Sanders, *Luke and Scripture*, 106–20.

———. "Isaiah in Luke." In Evans and Sanders, *Luke and Scripture*, 14–25.

Sapolsky, Robert. *Behave: The Biology of Humans at Our Best and Worst*. New York: Penguin, 2017.

———. *Why Zebras Don't Get Ulcers*. 3rd ed. New York: Owl, 2004.

Sawicki, Marianne. *Crossing Galilee: Architectures of Contact in the Occupied Land of Jesus*. Harrisburg, PA: Trinity Press International, 2000.

———. "Magdalenes and Tiberiennes: City Women in the Entourage of Jesus." In *Transformative Encounters: Jesus and Women Re-viewed*. Edited by Ingrid R. Kitzberger, 181–202. Biblical Interpretation 43. Boston: Brill, 1999.

Schaberg, Jane. "Luke." In *Women's Bible Commentary*. Edited by Carol A. Newsom and Sharon H. Ringe, 363–80. 2nd ed. Louisville: Westminster John Knox, 1998.

Scheffler, Eben. "The Assaulted (Man) on the Jerusalem-Jericho Road: Luke's Creative Interpretation of 2 Chronicles 28:15." *HvTSt* 69 (2010): 1–8 (doi:10.4102/hts.v69i1.2010).

Schellenberg, Ryan S. "Which Master? Whose Steward? Metalepsis and Lordship in the Parable of the Prudent Steward (Lk. 16.1–13)." *JSNT* 30 (2008): 263–88.

Schifferdecker, Kathryn. "Creation Theology." In *Dictionary of the Old Testament: Wisdom, Poetry, and Writings*. Edited by Tremper Longman III and Peter Enns, 63–71. Downers Grove, IL: IVP Academic, 2008.

Schlimm, Matthew R. "Different Perspectives on Divine Pathos: An Examination of Hermeneutics in Biblical Theology." *CBQ* 69 (2007): 673–94.

———. *From Fratricide to Forgiveness: The Language and Ethics of Anger in Genesis*. Siphrut 7. Winona Lake: Eisenbrauns, 2011.

Schmidt, Daryl D. "Anti-Judaism and the Gospel of Luke." In *Anti-Judaism and the Gospels*. Edited by William R. Farmer, 63–96. Harrisburg, PA: Trinity Press International, 1999.

———. "The Sabbath Day: To Heal or Not to Heal." *Di* 7 (1994): 124–47.

Schottroff, Luise. *Lydia's Impatient Sisters: A Feminist Social History of Early Christianity*. London: SCM Press, 1995.

———. *The Parables of Jesus*. Translated by Linda M. Maloney. Minneapolis: Fortress, 2006.

Schultz, Brian. "Jesus as Archelaus in the Parable of the Pounds (Luke 19:11–27)." *NovT* 49 (2007): 105–27.

Schumacher, R. Daniel. "Saving like a Fool and Spending like It Isn't Yours: Reading the Parable of the Unjust Steward (Luke 16:1–8a) in Light of the Parable of the Rich Fool (Luke 12:16–20)." *RevExp* 109 (2012): 269–76.

Schüssler Fiorenza, Elisabeth. *But She Said: Feminist Practices of Biblical Interpretation*. Boston: Beacon, 1992.

———. *In Memory of Her: A Feminist Theological Reconstruction of Christian Origins*. 2nd ed. New York: Crossroad, 1993.

———. "Introduction to the Tenth Anniversary Edition." In *In Memory of Her: A Feminist Theological Reconstruction of Christian Origins*, xii–xlii. New York: Crossroad, 1993.

———. *Jesus: Miriam's Child, Sophia's Prophet; Critical Issues in Feminist Christology*. New York: Continuum, 1994.

Scott, Bernard Brandon. *Hear Then the Parable: A Commentary on the Parables of Jesus.* Minneapolis: Fortress, 1989.

Scott, James C. *Domination and the Arts of Resistance: Hidden Transcripts.* New Haven: Yale University Press, 1990.

Seigworth, Gregory J., and Melissa Gregg, "An Inventory of Shimmers." In *The Affect Theory Reader.* Edited by Melissa Seigworth and Gregory J. Seigworth, 1–25. Durham, NC: Duke University Press, 2010.

Seim, Turid Karlsen. "Children of the Resurrection: Perspectives on Angelic Asceticism in Luke-Acts." In *Asceticism and the New Testament.* Edited by Leif E. Vaage and Vincent L. Wimbush, 115–25. New York: Routledge, 1999.

———. *The Double Message: Patterns of Gender in Luke and Acts.* Nashville: Abingdon, 1994.

———. "Feminist Criticism." In *Methods for Luke.* Edited by Joel B. Green, 42–73. Cambridge: Cambridge University Press, 2010.

———. "The Gospel of Luke." In *Searching the Scriptures.* Vol 2: *A Feminist Commentary.* Edited by Elisabeth Schlüssler Fiorenza, 728–62. New York: Crossroad, 1994.

Seligman, Martin P. *Authentic Happiness: Using the New Positive Psychology to Realize Your Potential for Lasting Fulfillment.* New York: Free Press, 2002.

Sellew, Philip. "Interior Monologue as a Narrative Device in the Parables of Luke." *JBL* 111 (1992): 239–53.

Sen, Amartya. *The Idea of Justice.* Cambridge: Belknap Press of Harvard University Press, 2009.

———. *Identity and Violence: The Illusion of Destiny.* New York: Norton, 2006.

Seppälä, Emma. *The Happiness Track: How to Apply the Science of Happiness to Accelerate Your Success.* New York: HarperOne, 2016.

Shaw, Brent D. "Bandits and the Roman Empire." *Past and Present* 105 (1984): 3–52.

———. "Tyrants, Bandits, and Kings: Personal Power in Josephus." *JJS* 44 (1993): 176–204.

Shelton, John. "The Healing of Naaman (2 Kgs 5:1–19) as a Central Component for the Healing of the Centurion's Slave (Luke 7:1–10)." In Kloppenborg and Verheyden, *The Elijah-Elisha Narrative*, 65–87.

Shields, James Mark. "*The Social Principles of Jesus:* A Reexamination of Walter Rauschenbusch's 1916 Social Gospel Text." *Journal of Liberal Religion* 8 (2008): 1–8.

Shrenk, Gottlob. "εὐδοκέω, εὐδοκία." *TDNT* 2:738–51.

Shriver, Donald W., Jr. "Introduction" to *A Theology for the Social Gospel*, by Walter Rauschenbusch. LTE. Louisville: Westminster John Knox, 1997.

Shurden, Walter B. "The Baptist Identity and the Baptist *Manifesto. PRSt* 25 (1998): 321–40.

———. *The Baptist Identity: Four Fragile Freedoms.* Macon, GA: Smyth & Helwys, 1993.

Siegel, Daniel J. *Mind: A Journey to the Heart of Being Human.* New York: Norton, 2017.

Sigal, Phillip. *The Halakhah of Jesus of Nazareth according to the Gospel of Matthew.* SBLStBL 18. Atlanta: SBL, 2007.

Singer, Peter, *The Expanding Circle: Ethics, Evolution, and Moral Progress.* Princeton: Princeton University Press, 2011.

Skinner, Matthew L. *Intrusive God, Disruptive Gospel: Encountering the Divine in the Book of Acts.* Grand Rapids: Brazos, 2015.

Smith, Abraham. "Cultural Studies: Making Mark." In *Mark and Method: New Approaches in Biblical Study.* Edited by Janice Capel Anderson and Stephen D. Moore, 181–209. 2nd ed. Minneapolis: Fortress, 2008.

Smith, Dennis E. *From Symposium to Eucharist: The Banquet in the Early Christian World.* Minneapolis: Fortress, 2003.

———. "Table Fellowship as a Literary Motif in the Gospel of Luke." *JBL* 106 (1987): 613–38.

Smith, James K. A. *Desiring the Kingdom: Worship, Worldview, and Culture Formation.* Grand Rapids: Baker Academic, 2009.

———. *You Are What You Love: The Spiritual Power of Habit.* Grand Rapids: Baker Academic, 2016.

Smith, Mark S. *How Human Is God? Seven Questions about God and Humanity in the Bible.* Collegeville, MN: Liturgical Press, 2014.

Smith, Mitzi J. *The Literary Construction of the Other in the Acts of the Apostles: Charismatics, the Jews, and Women.* Cambridge: James Clarke, 2012.

Snodgrass, Klyne R. "*ANAIDEIA* and the Friend at Midnight." *JBL* 116 (1997): 505–13.

———. *Stories with Intent: A Comprehensive Guide to the Parables of Jesus.* Grand Rapids: Eerdmans, 2008.

Sobrino, Jon. *The Principle of Mercy: Taking the Crucified People from the Cross.* Maryknoll, NY: Orbis Books, 1994.

Solomon, Robert C. "Emotions, Thoughts, and Feelings: Emotions as Engagements with the World." In *Thinking about Feeling: Contemporary Philosophers on Emotions.* Edited by Robert C. Solomon, 76–88. Oxford: Oxford University Press, 2004.

———. *The Passions: Emotions and the Meaning of Life.* 2nd ed. Indianapolis: Hackett, 1993.

———. *True to Our Feelings: What Our Emotions Are Really Telling Us.* New York: Oxford University Press, 2007.

———, ed. *What Is an Emotion? Classic and Contemporary Readings.* 2nd ed. Oxford: Oxford University Press, 2003.

Solomon, Robert C., and Fernando Flores. *Building Trust in Business, Politics, Relationships, and Life.* Oxford: Oxford University Press, 2001.

Sorabji, Richard. *Animal Minds and Human Morals: The Origins of the Western Debate.* Cornell Studies in Classical Philology. Ithaca, NY: Cornell University Press, 1993.

———. *Emotion and Peace of Mind: From Stoic Agitation to Christian Imagination.* Oxford: Oxford University Press, 2000.

Spencer, Althea Miller. "Lucy Bailey Meets the Feminists." In *Feminist New Testament Studies: Global and Future Perspectives.* Edited by Kathleen O'Brien Wicker, Althea Miller Spencer, and Musa W. Dube, 209–44. New York: Palgrave Macmillan, 2005.

Spencer, F. Scott. *Dancing Girls, "Loose" Ladies, and Women of "the Cloth": Women in Jesus' Life.* London: Continuum, 2004.

———. "Feminist Criticism." In *Hearing the New Testament: Strategies for Interpretation.* Edited by Joel B. Green, 289–325. 2nd ed. Grand Rapids: Eerdmans, 2010.

———. "'Follow Me': The Imperious Call of Jesus in the Synoptic Gospels." *Int* 59 (2005): 142–53.

———. "Forgiveness of Sins." *DJG*, 284–88.

———. "Getting a Feel for the 'Mixed' and 'Vexed' Study of Emotions in Biblical Literature." In Spencer, *Mixed Feelings and Vexed Passions*, 1–41.

———. *The Gospel of Luke and Acts of the Apostles.* IBT. Nashville: Abingdon, 2008.

———. *Journeying through Acts: A Literary-Cultural Reading.* Peabody, MA: Hendrickson, 2004.

———. "Jubilee." *DSE*, 428–29.

———, ed. *Mixed Feelings and Vexed Passions: Exploring Emotions in Biblical Literature*. RBS 90. Atlanta: SBL, 2017.

———. "The Narrative of Luke-Acts: Getting to Know the Savior God." In *Issues in Luke-Acts: Selected Essays*. Edited by Sean A. Adams and Michael Pahl, 121–45. Piscataway, NJ: Gorgias, 2012.

———. "Neglected Widows in Acts 6:1–7." *CBQ* 56 (1994): 714–33.

———. "Paul's Odyssey in Acts: Status Struggles and Island Adventures." *BTB* 28 (1998): 150–59.

———. *The Portrait of Philip in Acts: A Study of Roles and Relations*. JSNTSup 67. Sheffield: Sheffield Academic, 1992.

———. "Preparing the Way of the Lord: Introducing and Interpreting Luke's Narrative; A Response to David Wenham." In *Reading Luke: Interpretation, Reflection, Formation*. Edited by Craig G. Bartholomew, Joel B. Green, and Anthony C. Thiselton, 104–24. Grand Rapids: Zondervan, 2005.

———. Review of John T. Carroll, *Luke: A Commentary*. *Int* 67 (2013): 423–27.

———. Review of Richard I. Pervo (*Dating Acts*) and Joseph B. Tyson (*Marcion and Luke-Acts*). *Int* 62 (2008): 190–93.

———. Review of Jack T. Sanders, *The Jews in Luke-Acts*. *WTJ* 49 (1987): 427–30.

———. *Salty Wives, Spirited Mothers, and Savvy Widows: Capable Women of Purpose and Persistence in Luke's Gospel*. Grand Rapids: Eerdmans, 2012.

———. "Scared to Death: The Rhetoric of Fear in the 'Tragedy' of Ananias and Sapphira." In *Reading Acts Today: Essays in Honour of Loveday C. A. Alexander*. Edited by Steve Walton et al., 63–80. LNTS 427. London: T&T Clark, 2011.

———. "Scripture, Hermeneutics, and Matthew's Jesus." *Int* 64 (2010): 368–78.

———. "2 Chronicles 28:5–15 and the Parable of the Good Samaritan." *WTJ* 46 (1984): 317–49.

———. *Song of Songs*. Wisdom Commentary 25. Collegeville, MN: Liturgical Press, 2017.

———. "Son of God." In *The Oxford Encyclopedia of Bible and Theology*. Vol. 2. Edited by Samuel E. Balentine, 308–16. Oxford: Oxford University Press, 2015.

———. "To Fear and Not to Fear the Creator God: A Theological and Therapeutic Interpretation of Luke 12:1–34." *JTI* 8 (2014): 75–96.

———. *What Did Jesus Do? Gospel Profiles of Jesus's Personal Conduct*. Harrisburg, PA: Trinity Press International, 2003.

———. "Why Did the 'Leper' Get under Jesus' Skin? Emotion Theory and Angry Reaction in Mark 1:40–45." *HBT* 36 (2014): 107–28.

———. "A Woman's Touch: Manual and Emotional Dynamics of Female Characters in Luke's Gospel." In *Characters and Characterization in Luke-Acts*. Edited by Frank E. Dicken and Julia A. Snyder, 73–94. LNTS 548. London: Bloomsbury T&T Clark, 2016.

———. "Women." *DJG*, 1004–13.

———. "'Your Faith Has Made You Well' (Mark 5:34; 10:52): Emotional Dynamics of Trustful Engagement with Jesus in Mark's Gospel." In Spencer, *Mixed Feelings and Vexed Passions*, 73–94.

Spinoza, Benedict de. *Ethics*. Translated by Edwin Curley. London: Penguin, 1996 (orig. 1677).

Squires, John T. *The Plan of God in Luke-Acts*. SNTSMS 76. Cambridge: Cambridge University Press, 1993.

Stanley, David M. *Jesus in Gethsemane*. New York: Paulist, 1980.

Stanton, Graham. *The Gospels and Jesus*. 2nd ed. Oxford Bible Series. Oxford: Oxford University Press, 2002.

Stearns, Richard E. *The Hole in Our Gospel: What Does God Expect of Us?* Nashville: Nelson, 2009.

———. *Unfinished: Filling the Hole in Our Gospel*. Nashville: Nelson, 2014.

Steele, E. Springs. "Luke 11:37–54: A Modified Hellenistic Symposium?" *JBL* 103 (1984): 379–94.

Stegner, William Richard. "The Temptation Narrative: A Study in the Use of Scripture by Early Jewish Christians." *BR* 35 (1990): 5–17.

Stein, Bradley L. "Who the Devil Is Beelzebul?" *BRev* 13 (1997): 43–45, 48.

Strahan, Joshua Marshall. "Jesus Teaches Theological Interpretation of the Law: The Parable of the Good Samaritan in Its Literary Context." *JTI* 10 (2016): 71–86.

———. *The Limits of a Text: Luke 23:34a as a Test Case in Theological Interpretation*. JTISup 8. Winona Lake, IN: Eisenbrauns, 2013.

Strange, W. A. *Children in the Early Church: Children in the Ancient World, the New Testament, and the Early Church*. Bletchley: Paternoster, 1996.

Strawn, Brent A., ed. *The Bible and the Pursuit of Happiness: What the Old and New Testaments Teach Us about the Good Life*. Oxford: Oxford University Press, 2012.

Stump, Eleonore. "The Non-Aristotelian Character of Aquinas's Ethics: Aquinas on the Passions." In *Faith, Rationality, and the Passions*. Edited by Sarah Coakley, 91–106. Directions in Modern Theology. Malden, MA: Wiley-Blackwell, 2012.

Swartley, Willard M. *Covenant of Peace: This Missing Peace in New Theology and Ethics*. Grand Rapids: Eerdmans, 2006.

———. "Sabbath." *DSE*, 695–96.

Sylva, Dennis D. "The Cryptic Clause *en tois tou patros mou dei einai me*." *ZNW* 78 (1987): 132–40.

Talbert, Charles H. *Luke and the Gnostics: An Examination of the Lucan Purpose*. Nashville: Abingdon, 1966.

Tallis, Raymond. *The Hand: A Philosophical Inquiry into Human Being*. Edinburgh: Edinburgh University Press, 2003.

Tannehill, Robert C. "Israel in Luke-Acts: A Tragic Story." In Tannehill, *The Shape of Luke's Story*, 105–24. Eugene, OR: Cascade, 2005.

———. "The Mission of Jesus according to Luke 4:16–30." In Tannehill, *The Shape of Luke's Story*, 3–30.

———. *The Narrative Unity of Luke-Acts: A Literary Interpretation*. Vol. 1: *The Gospel according to Luke*. Philadelphia: Fortress, 1986.

———. *The Narrative Unity of Luke-Acts: A Literary Interpretation*. Vol. 2: *The Acts of the Apostles*. Minneapolis: Fortress, 1990.

———. *The Shape of Luke's Story: Essays on Luke-Acts*. Eugene, OR: Cascade, 2005.

Tavris, Carol, and Elliot Aronson. *Mistakes Were Made (but Not by Me): Why We Justify Foolish Beliefs, Bad Decisions, and Hurtful Acts*. Rev. ed. New York: Houghton Mifflin Harcourt, 2015.

Taylor, Joan E. *The Immerser: John the Baptist within Second Temple Judaism*. Grand Rapids: Eerdmans, 1997.

Taylor, Shelley E. *The Tending Instinct: How Nurturing Is Essential to Who We Are and How We Live*. New York: Times Books, 2002.

Teresa of Ávila, *The Interior Castle*. 3rd ed. Edited by Benedict Zimmerman. London: Thomas Baker, 1921 (orig. 1577).

Thayer, Joseph Henry. *Greek-English Lexicon of the New Testament*. New York: Harper & Brothers, 1886.

Theissen, Gerd. *Sociology of Early Palestinian Christianity*. Philadelphia: Fortress, 1978.

Thiselton, Anthony C. *Systematic Theology*. Grand Rapids: Eerdmans, 2017.

Thomas, Heath A. "The Telos (Goal) of Theological Interpretation." In Bartholomew and Thomas, *A Manifesto for Theological Interpretation*, 197–217.

Thompson, Philip E. "Re-envisioning Baptist Identity: Historical, Theological, and Liturgical Analysis." *PRSt* 27 (2000): 287–302.

Throckmorton, Burton H. *Gospel Parallels: A Comparison of the Synoptic Gospels*. Nashville: Nelson, 1992.

Tiede, David L. *Prophecy and History in Luke-Acts*. Philadelphia: Fortress, 1980.

Tiede, David L., and Christopher R. Matthews. "The Gospel according to Luke." In *The HarperCollins Study Bible*. Edited by Harold W. Attridge, 1759–1813. New York: HarperCollins, 2006.

Tillich, Paul. *The Courage to Be*. 2nd ed. New Haven: Yale University Press, 2000 (orig. 1957).

———. *Dynamics of Faith*. New York: Harper & Row, 1957.

———. *The New Being*. Lincoln: University of Nebraska Press, 2005 (orig. 1955).

Treier, Daniel J. *Introducing Theological Interpretation of Scripture: Recovering a Christian Practice*. Grand Rapids: Baker Academic, 2008.

Trible, Phyllis. "A Rhetorician of Righteousness." In Rauschenbusch, *Christianity and the Social Crisis in the Twenty-First Century*, 33–37. New York: HarperCollins, 2007.

Trudinger, Paul. "Ire or Irony? The Enigmatic Character of the Parable of the Dishonest Steward (Luke 16:1–13)." *DRev* 116 (1998): 85–102.

Tsai, Jeanne L. "Culture and Emotion." In *Noba Textbook Series: Psychology*. Edited by R. Biswas-Diener and E. Diener. Champaign, IL: DEF publishers, 2017 (doi: nobaproject .com).

———. "Ideal Affect: Cultural Causes and Behavioral Consequences." *Perspectives on Psychological Science* 2 (2007): 242–59.

Tuckett, Christopher M. "Luke 22,43–44: The 'Agony' in the Garden and Luke's Gospel." In *New Testament Textual Criticism and Exegesis*. Edited by Adelbert Denaux, 131–44. BETL 161. Leuven: Leuven University Press, 2002.

———. *Q and History of Early Christianity: Studies on Q*. Peabody, MA: Hendrickson, 1996.

Tutu, Desmond. *No Future without Forgiveness*. New York: Image, 1999.

Tyson, Joseph B. *Images of Judaism in Luke-Acts*. Columbia: University of South Carolina Press, 1992.

———, ed. *Luke-Acts and the Jewish People: Eight Critical Perspectives*. Minneapolis: Augsburg, 1988.

———. *Marcion and Luke-Acts: A Defining Struggle*. Columbia: University of South Carolina Press, 2006.

Ukpong, Justin S. "The Parable of the Shrewd Manager (Luke 16:1–13): An Essay in Inculturation Biblical Hermeneutic." *Semeia* 73 (1996): 189–210.

Van den Hengel, John. "Miriam of Nazareth: Between Symbol and History." In *A Feminist Companion to Mariology*. Edited by Amy-Jill Levine with Marianne Mayo Robbins, 130–46. Cleveland: Pilgrim, 2005.

Van der Horst, Peter. "Abraham's Bosom, the Place Where He Belonged: A Short Note on ἀπενεχθῆναι in Luke 16:22." *NTS* 52 (2006): 142–44.

VanderKam, James C. *An Introduction to Early Judaism*. Grand Rapids: Eerdmans, 2001.

Van Eck, Ernest. "Social Memory and Identity: Luke 19:12b-24 and 27." *BTB* 41 (2011): 201–12.

Van Elderen, Bastiaan. "Another Look at the Parable of the Good Samaritan." In *Saved by Hope*. Edited by J. I. Cook, 109–19. Grand Rapids: Eerdmans, 1978.

Vanhoozer, Kevin J. *The Drama of Doctrine: A Canonical-Linguistic Approach to Christian Theology*. Louisville: Westminster John Knox, 2005.

———. *Faith Speaking Understanding: Performing the Drama of Doctrine*. Louisville: Westminster John Knox, 2014.

———. *Remythologizing Theology: Divine Action, Passion, and Authorship*. Cambridge: Cambridge University Press, 2012.

———. "Word of God." *DTIB*, 850–53.

Van Unnik, W. C. "Die Rechte Bedeutung des Wortes Treffen, Lukas II 19." In *Sparsa Collecta: The Collected Essays of W. C. van Unnik*. Part 1: *Evangelia, Paulina, Acta*, 75–91. Leiden: Brill, 1973.

Varki, Ajit, and Danny Brower. *Denial: Self-Deception, False Beliefs, and the Origins of the Human Mind*. New York: Twelve, 2013.

Verhey, Allen. *The Great Reversal: Ethics and the New Testament*. Grand Rapids: Eerdmans, 1984.

———. *Remembering Jesus: Christian Community, Scripture, and the Moral Life*. Grand Rapids: Eerdmans, 2002.

Verheyden, Joseph. "By Way of Epilogue: Looking Back at the Healing of Naaman and the Healing of the Centurion's Slave—in Response to John Shelton." In Kloppenborg and Verheyden, *The Elijah-Elisha Narrative*, 153–60.

Vermes, Geza. *The Complete Dead Sea Scrolls in English*. 4th ed. London: Penguin, 1995.

Vinson, Richard B. "The Minas Touch: Anti-kingship Rhetoric in the Gospel of Luke." *PRSt* 35 (2008): 69–86.

Volf, Miroslav. *Exclusion and Embrace: A Theological Exploration of Identity, Otherness, and Reconciliation*. Nashville: Abingdon, 1996.

———. *Free of Charge: Giving and Forgiving in a Culture Stripped of Grace*. Grand Rapids: Zondervan, 2005.

———. *A Public Faith: How Followers of Christ Should Serve the Common Good*. Grand Rapids: Brazos, 2011.

Von Drehle, David, Jay Newton-Small, and Maya Rhodan. "Murder, Race, and Mercy: Stories from Charleston." *Time*, November 23, 2015, 42–68.

Voorwinde, Stephen. *Jesus' Emotions in the Gospels*. New York: T&T Clark, 2011.

Waetjen, Herman C. "The Subversion of 'World' by the Parable of the Friend at Midnight." *JBL* 120 (2001): 703–21.

Wailes, Steven L. *Medieval Allegories of Jesus's Parables: An Introduction*. Center for Medieval and Renaissance Studies, UCLA 23. Berkeley: University of California Press, 1987.

Waldron, Jeremy. *The Harm in Hate Speech*. Oliver Wendell Holmes Lectures 10. Cambridge, MA: Harvard University Press, 2012.

Waldron, Samuel E., and Richard C. Barcellos. *A Reformed Baptist Manifesto: The New Covenant Constitution of the Church*. Palmdale, CA: Reformed Baptist Academic Press, 2004.

Wall, Robert W. "'The Finger of God': Deuteronomy 9.10 and Luke 11.20." *NTS* 33 (1987): 144–50.

Wallace, Daniel B. *Greek Grammar beyond the Basics: An Exegetical Syntax of the New Testament*. Grand Rapids: Zondervan, 1996.

Walzer, Michael. *Thick and Thin: Moral Argument at Home and Abroad*. Notre Dame: University of Notre Dame Press, 1994.

Webster, John. *Holy Scripture: A Dogmatic Sketch*. Current Issues in Theology. Cambridge: Cambridge University Press, 2003.

Westphal, Merold. "The Philosophical/Theological View." In *Biblical Hermeneutics: Five Views*. Edited by Stanley E. Porter and Beth M. Stovell, 70–88. Downers Grove, IL: IVP Academic, 2012.

White, Ronald C., Jr. *Lincoln's Greatest Speech: The Second Inaugural*. New York: Simon & Schuster, 2002.

Whitehead, Jason C. *Redeeming Fear: A Constructive Theology for Living into Hope*. Minneapolis: Fortress, 2013.

Wilcox, Max. "Mammon." *ABD* 4:490.

Wilkins, Michael J. "Barabbas." *ABD* 1:607.

Williams, Clifford. *Existential Reasons for Belief in God: A Defense of Desires and Emotions for Faith*. Downers Grove, IL: IVP Academic, 2011.

Williams, Rowan. *The Wound of Knowledge: Christian Spirituality from the New Testament to St. John of the Cross*. 2nd ed. London: Darton, Longman & Todd, 1990.

Wilson, Brittany E. "Sight and Spectacle: 'Seeing' Paul in the Book of Acts." In *Characters and Characterization in Luke-Acts*. Edited by Frank Dicken and Julia Snyder, 141–53. LNTS 548. London: Bloomsbury T&T Clark, 2016.

———. *Unmanly Men: Refigurations of Masculinity in Luke-Acts*. Oxford: Oxford University Press, 2015.

Wilson, E. O. *The Social Conquest of Earth*. New York: Liveright, 2012.

Wilson, Timothy D. *Strangers to Ourselves: Discovering the Adaptive Unconscious*. Cambridge, MA: Harvard University Press, 2002.

Windley-Daoust, Jerry. *Primary Source Readings in Catholic Social Justice*. Winona, IN: St. Mary's, 2007.

Wink, Walter. *The Human Being: Jesus and the Enigma of the Son of Man*. Minneapolis: Fortress, 2002.

———. *When the Powers Fall: Reconciliation in the Healing of Nations*. Minneapolis: Fortress, 1998.

Winston, David. *The Wisdom of Solomon: A New Translation, with Introduction and Commentary*. AB 43. Garden City, NY: Doubleday, 1979.

Winston, David, and Thomas H. Tobin. "Wisdom of Solomon." In *The HarperCollins Study Bible*. Edited by Harold W. Attridge, 1348–77. New York: HarperCollins, 2006.

Winter, Bruce W. *Seek the Welfare of the City: Christians as Benefactors and Citizens*. Grand Rapids: Eerdmans, 1994.

Wirzba, Norman. *The Paradise of God: Renewing Religion in an Ecological Age*. Oxford: Oxford University Press, 2003.

Witherington, Ben, III. *New Testament Rhetoric: An Introductory Guide to the Art of Persuasion in and of the New Testament*. Eugene, OR: Cascade, 2009.

Wolterstorff, Nicholas. *Justice in Love*. Grand Rapids: Eerdmans, 2011.

———. *Justice: Rights and Wrongs*. Princeton: Princeton University Press, 2008.

Wright, Addison G. "The Widow's Mites: Praise or Lament?—a Matter of Context." *CBQ* 45 (1982): 32–43.

Wright, N. T. *Jesus and the Victory of God*. Vol. 2 of *Christian Origins and the Question of God*. Minneapolis: Fortress, 1996.

———. *Justification: God's Plan and Paul's Vision*. Downers Grove, IL: IVP Academic, 2009.

———. *The Resurrection of the Son of God*. Vol. 3 of *Christian Origins and the Question of God*. Minneapolis: Fortress, 2003.

———. *Simply Jesus: A New Vision of Who He Was, What He Did, and Why He Matters*. New York: HarperOne, 2011.

———. *Surprised by Hope: Rethinking Heaven, Resurrection, and the Mission of the Church*. New York: HarperOne, 2008.

Yee, Gale A. "'I Have Perfumed My Bed with Myrrh': The Foreign Woman (*'iššâ zārâ*) in Proverbs 1–9." *JSOT* 43 (1989): 53–68.

———. *Poor Banished Children of Eve: Woman as Evil in the Hebrew Bible*. Minneapolis: Fortress, 2003.

Yoder, John H. *Body Politics: Five Practices of the Christian Community before the Watching World*. Scottdale: Herald Press, 2001 (orig. 1992).

———. *The Politics of Jesus*. 2nd ed. Grand Rapids: Eerdmans, 1994.

Young, Brad H. *The Parables: Jewish Tradition and Christian Interpretation*. Grand Rapids: Baker Academic, 2012 (orig. 1998).

Young, Iris Marion. *Responsibility for Justice*. Oxford: Oxford University Press, 2011.

Zack, Naomi. *Inclusive Feminism: A Third Wave Theory of Women's Commonality*. Lanham, MD: Rowman & Littlefield, 2005.

Index of Authors

Index of Subjects

Index of Scripture and Other Ancient Writings